OOSTERHOFF ON TRUSTS:
TEXT, COMMENTARY AND MATERIALS

Sixth Edition
by

A.H. OOSTERHOFF
B.A., LL.B., LL.M.
of the Ontario Bar
Professor, Faculty of Law
The University of Western Ontario

ROBERT CHAMBERS
B.Ed., LL.B., D.Phil. (Oxon.)
of the Alberta Bar
Professor, Faculty of Law
University of Alberta

MITCHELL MCINNES
B.A., LL.B., LL.M., Ph.D. (Cantab.)
of the Alberta Bar
Professor, Faculty of Law
The University of Western Ontario

LIONEL SMITH
B.Sc., LL.B., LL.M. (Cantab.),
D.Phil, M.A. (Oxon.)
of the Alberta Bar
James McGill Professor of Law
Faculty of Law
McGill University

Madame Justice Eileen E. Gillese co-authored the
3rd through 5th editions of this book.

THOMSON
™
CARSWELL

Library and Archives Canada Cataloguing in Publication

Oosterhoff on trusts : text, commentary and cases on trusts / Robert Chambers ... [et al.].—6th ed.

First-2nd eds. published under title: Cases and materials on the law of trusts; 3rd-4th: A.H. Oosterhoff : text, commentary and cases on trusts; 5th ed.: Oosterhoff & Gillese : text, commentary and cases on trusts.

Includes bibliographical references and index.

ISBN 0-459-24142-7 (bound).—ISBN 0-459-24141-9 (pbk.)

1. Trusts and trustees—Canada—Cases. I. Chambers, Robert, 1957-
II. Oosterhoff, A.H. Oosterhoff & Gillese.

KE787.A7O68 2004   346.7105'9   C2004-903067-1
KF729.O68 2004

Composition: Computer Composition of Canada Inc.

THOMSON
CARSWELL

One Corporate Plaza
2075 Kennedy Road
Toronto, Ontario
M1T 3V4

Customer Service:
Toronto 1-416-609-3800
Elsewhere in Canada/U.S. 1-800-387-5164
Fax 1-416-298-5082

PREFACE

It has been six years since the last edition of this book and there have been significant changes in the law of trusts since that time, particularly in the law of remedial trusts. Further, one co-author was appointed to the bench and was unable to continue to contribute to this work. It is appropriate that I wish Madam Justice Gillese well in her new position and to thank her for her contributions to the previous three editions.

It is also appropriate and a pleasure for me to welcome Professors Robert Chambers, Mitchell McInnes, and Lionel Smith as new co-authors. They have written widely on the law of Trusts. Their addition to the authorial board has been and will continue to be of great benefit to the book. I am very grateful for their willingness to take on this position. It has been a pleasure to work with them on this edition and I look forward to working with them in the future.

My colleagues and I have taken the opportunity to rewrite large parts of the book and, in the process, have further edited down quite a number of the cases reproduced. We have also reorganized the book by placing the part on Purpose Trusts after the part on Express Trusts, believing that this is a more logical place for the former. The major changes occurred in the chapters on Non-charitable Purposes, Remedial Trusts, and Breach of Trust. We have completely reorganized and rewritten these chapters and replaced older cases with important new ones. These cases include *Twinsectra Ltd. v. Yardley* in chapter 8; *Schmidt v. Air Products of Canada Ltd.*; *Air Jamaica Ltd. v. Charlton*; *Re Wilson (Attorney of)*; *McLear v. McLear Estate*; and *Clark, Drummie & Co. v. Ryan* in chapter 9; *Chase Manhattan Bank N.A. v. Israel-British Bank (London) Ltd.* in chapter 11; and *Foskett v. McKeown*; and *Law Society of Upper Canada v. Toronto-Dominion Bank* in chapter 15.

In chapter 4 we replaced the unsatisfactory case, *Re Romaniuk Estate* with *Hunter v. Moss*. In chapter 7 on Charitable Trusts we have made reference to important recent cases, including *Christian Brothers of Ireland in Canada*; *Vancouver Society of Immigrant and Visible Minority Women v. M.N.R.*; and others. In chapter 13 on Duties of Trustees, we replaced *Re Londonderry's Settlement* with the important new Privy Council case, *Schmidt v. Rosewood Trust Ltd.* In chapter 14 on the Powers and Rights of Trustees, we added a new section on Judicial Interference with the Trustees' Discretion and replaced *Re Atkinson* with *Laing Estate v. Hines*. We believe that all of these changes will enhance the use of the book as a teaching tool in law schools and as a reference by bench and bar.

This edition continues the practice of including comprehensive references to legislation in all the common law provinces and territories whenever statutory materials are reproduced. It was not possible to include such references for the new Territory of Nunavut, which came into existence on April 1, 1999. Section 29 of the *Nunavut Act*, S.C. 1993, c. 28, am. S.C. 1998, c. 15, s. 4, provides that the laws in force in the Northwest Territories continue in force for Nunavut until repealed, amended, or rendered inoperable in respect of Nunavut. Pursuant to the Act and to accommodate modifications of Northwest Territories laws that were required to be in force when the new Territory came into being, the Northwest Territories did enact certain statutes on behalf of Nunavut. Further, the Nunavut legislature has since enacted a number of statutes. However, none of these appear to affect the law of trusts. The Nunavut statutes are available online and include Northwest Territories statutes that affect trusts.[1]

My colleagues and I wish to record our indebtedness to our research assistants, Cathleen Herrera, Linda Smits, and Roxana Tavana. Without their careful research, this edition would not have been possible. We also wish to thank the Faculty of Law, The University of Western Ontario, the Ontario Law Foundation, and the Social Sciences and Humanities Research Council of Canada for making the necessary research money available.

A.H. Oosterhoff
Faculty of Law
The University of Western Ontario
London, Ontario
March, 2004

---

1 See, *e.g.* http://www.canlii.org/nu/sta/cons/index.html.

ACKNOWLEDGMENTS

The authors are grateful to the following persons and organizations for permission to reproduce the materials or excerpts from the sources indicated.

Chapter 1, Part 4

Excerpt from Underhill and Hayton, *Law Relating to Trusts and Trustees*, 14th ed. by David J. Hayton (Butterworth & Co. (Publishers) Ltd., 1987).

Excerpt from *Lewin on Trusts*, 16th ed. by W.J. Mowbray (Sweet & Maxwell Ltd.).

Chapter 1, Part 7(b)

Excerpt from F.W. Maitland, *Equity: A Course of Lectures*, rev. ed. by John Brunyate (Cambridge University Press, 1936).

SUMMARY OF CHAPTERS

For a detailed Table of Contents see page ix

CONTENTS

NOTE: The cases reproduced in this book have been taken from the reports given in the Table of Contents. Alternative citations are given in the text.

PART I
INTRODUCTION

PART III
PURPOSE TRUSTS

PART IV
REMEDIAL TRUSTS

PART V
THE ADMINISTRATION OF TRUSTS

TABLE OF CASES

PART I

INTRODUCTION

1

THE HISTORY AND NATURE OF TRUSTS

1. SCOPE

In this chapter we shall consider the history of trusts first. While the trust is a creature of equity, many aspects of the common law also impinge upon the subject. Hence, we shall also briefly explore the relationship between law and equity.

Second, we shall define the trust (insofar as that is possible) and briefly consider how trusts are classified. Third, we shall explore certain problems unique to the law of trusts, including the nature of the trust beneficiary's interest, the treatment of trusts in conflict of laws and the trust in civil law. Finally, we shall explore the use of the trust in aboriginal land claims.

2. HISTORICAL BACKGROUND

(a) Introduction

The trust is peculiar to the common law; there is nothing comparable in other legal systems. It is true that the civil law has other devices which are used for purposes similar to the trust. Thus, Roman Law recognized the *usus*, *usufructus*, *fidei commissum* and *bonorum possessio*, and civil law jurisdictions today have their modern equivalents,[1] but the common law trust remains unique. At one time it was thought that the trust had its origin in the civil law because it was supposed that the early English chancellors applied the civil law concept of the *fidei commissum* to English circumstances. In modern times it has been shown, however, notably by Mr. Justice Holmes,[2] that the origin of the trust is to be found in the

---

1 The use of the trust in the civil law is discussed below.
2 O.W. Holmes, "Early English Equity" (1885), 1 L.Q. Rev. 162.

Germanic Salman or Treuhand. The Salman or Treuhand was a person to whom property was transferred for purposes to be carried out during the life or after the death of the transferor.

Nevertheless, the use and its successor, the trust, are English products, and they evolved because of the English judicial system which maintained separate courts of equity and courts of law.

Professor Maitland considered that "[o]f all the exploits of Equity the largest and the most important is the invention and development of the trust."[3] The trust is unique because it is such a flexible tool for making dispositions of property. It is not limited to specific situations such as bailment or agency, but can be created for any purpose that is not illegal or contrary to public policy. Some of these purposes are enumerated later in this chapter.

The key to the trust and its direct ancestor, the use, is that they are creatures of equity. That is, they were enforced in the courts of Chancery on the basis of conscience.

Courts with solely equitable jurisdiction no longer exist in England or Canada. The old common law and chancery courts were fused by the Supreme Court of Judicature Acts in England in 1875[4] and in Ontario by the *Ontario Judicature Act* in 1881.[5] The resulting fused court[6] has concurrent jurisdiction in equity and common law,[7] subject to the following proviso:[8]

Where a rule of equity conflicts with a rule of common law, the rule of equity prevails.

To understand the development of the trust, we must make a brief excursion into the history of the courts of equity. By the 13th century, the courts of common law — King's Bench, Common Pleas and Exchequer — were well established. Originally, these courts exercised powers similar to the equity jurisdiction of the later chancery courts. In time, however, the common law courts became rigid in their application of established rules. In order to find justice, petitioners then began to seek the aid of the King's Council on the theory that a residuum of

---

3 F.W. Maitland, *Equity: A Course of Lectures*, rev. ed. by John Brunyate (Cambridge: Cambridge University Press, 1936), p. 23 ("Maitland").

4 *Supreme Court of Judicature Act 1873*, (36 & 37 Vict.), c. 66 (U.K.); *Supreme Court of Judicature (Commencement) Act 1874*, (37 & 38 Vict.), c. 83 (U.K.); *Supreme Court of Judicature Act 1875*, (38 & 39 Vict.), c. 77 (U.K.).

5 S.O. 1881, c. 5. Similar legislation was enacted in other Canadian common law jurisdictions.

6 In England the Supreme Court of Judicature and in the Canadian common law provinces the superior court of each province. Other courts may have similar jurisdiction. See, *e.g.*, *Courts of Justice Act*, R.S.O. 1990, c. C. 43, s. 96(3) (am. by S.O. 1996, c. 25, s. 9(17), which provides that only the Court of Appeal, and the Superior Court of Justice, exclusive of the Small Claims Court may grant equitable relief, unless otherwise provided.

7 *Ibid.*, s. 96(1).

8 *Ibid.*, subs. (2). See also *Judicature Act*, R.S.A. 2000, c. J-2, s. 15; R.S.N.B. 1973, c. J-2, s. 39; R.S.N.L. 1990, c. J-4, s. 107; R.S.N.S. 1989, c. 240, s. 43(11); R.S.N.W.T. 1988, c. J-1, s. 45; R.S.Y. 2002, c. 128, s. 29; *Supreme Court Act*, R.S.P.E.I. 1988, c. S-10, s. 29(2); *Law and Equity Act*, R.S.B.C. 1996, c. 253, s. 44; *The Court of Queen's Bench Act*, S.M. 1988-89, c. 4, s. 33(4); *The Queen's Bench Act, 1998*, S.S. 1998, c. Q-1.01, s. 52(2).

justice resided in the King, not all having been conferred by him upon the common law courts.

In practice, the early petitions to the *Curia Regis* were dealt with by the Chancellor, often the only learned member of the Council and usually an ecclesiastic. Later, they were made directly to the Chancellor. The petitions or bills would complain that the petitioner, although entitled, could not get a remedy in the common law courts, and asked the Chancellor to provide a remedy "for the love of God and in the way of Charity."[9] A common reason was that the complainant was poor and his or her opponent rich and influential.

The Chancellor would consider the bill and then subpoena the alleged wrongdoer to come before him to answer the complaint. A wrongdoer who failed to appear would forfeit a sum of money. The wrongdoer would be examined under oath before the Chancellor and had to answer the plaintiff's bill. If, in fact, a wrong had been committed which the law courts could not redress because of their strict procedures, the Chancellor could and did demand that the wrong be remedied. The Chancellor assumed jurisdiction over matters of conscience. If a wrong was done, then in conscience the wrongdoer would be obliged to right it.

The method of enforcement was simple. The wrongdoer was enjoined from doing what he or she proposed to do and what, under the strict rules of the common law, he or she may have had a right to do. For instance, the wrongdoer might have obtained a judgment in the common law courts. The Chancellor, if he found that a wrong had been committed, would simply enjoin the wrongdoer from enforcing that judgment on pain of being sent to prison.

You should note that there is an important distinction between legal and equitable procedures. A judgment obtained in the common law courts gives the plaintiff the right to do certain things. The judgment declares those rights. But a decree in equity imposes obligations on the defendant. Equity does not declare rights. It acts *in personam*. That is, it demands that a person refrain from exercising certain rights for reasons personal to himself or herself which make it inequitable to enforce those rights.

Understandably, the common law bench was disturbed by what they considered to be interference by the Chancellors in their rightful jurisdiction. The quarrel between common law and equity came to a head during the reign of James I. Lord Coke, the Chief Justice, and Lord Ellesmere, the Lord Chancellor, argued the matter before the King. Lord Coke maintained that a petitioner who obtained an injunction in equity was guilty of the offence of calling into question the judgments of the King's courts and other courts contrary to the *Statute of Praemunire*.[10] King James, however, decreed in favour of Chancery and it has had the upper hand ever since.[11]

The court of Chancery did not assert its superiority over the courts of law. It merely prevented plaintiffs from going to those courts or from exercising rights

---

9 Maitland, at 4.
10 16 Ric. 2, c. 5 (1351). This statute was directed against interference by the Papal curia in the judicial affairs of England.
11 Maitland, at 9-10.

obtained there. But a judgment obtained in a court of law was not annulled. The Chancellor simply required that it not be enforced in certain circumstances. Equity, therefore, did not conflict with the common law. Indeed, it could not supplant the common law, for equity was but a gloss on the law. It was not a self-sufficient system, whereas the common law was. Equity presupposed the existence of common law and added to it. It was and is appendicular to the law.

The common law recognized ownership of property, that is, legal ownership. Situations arose, however, in which a person held the legal title to property — a title recognized by law — but which the title holder had agreed to hold for the benefit of some other person — an obligation not recognized at law. If the owner of the legal title refused to carry out the undertaking to the other person, Chancery could compel the title holder to exercise his or her legal rights for the benefit of the other person in accordance with the dictates of conscience. More important, in due course the Chancellor would not only compel the legal owner to act in accordance with the dictates of conscience, but would also come to recognize and enforce those rights against purchasers who took with notice of the equitable interest and against gratuitous purchasers.[12] In effect, the person for whose benefit the property was held, acquired ownership in the eyes of equity. The result was a kind of dual ownership, or two recognizable interests in property. This dual ownership is still recognized in the law of mortgages in some jurisdictions. The mortgagee is granted the legal title to the lands. The "owner" or mortgagor retains the right is to redeem his or her title in accordance with the terms of the mortgage and this legal right is enhanced by equity. Hence, the mortgagor holds the "equity of redemption" — an equitable interest.[13]

(b) Uses

As stated above, the modern trust developed from the old use. The word "use" derives from the Latin *opus*. In vulgar Latin, the term *ad opus* was used for a long time to mean "on behalf of," or "for the benefit of" another, who is called a beneficiary. The old term for beneficiary, "*cestui que use*," still used occasionally, is an abbreviation of the legal French, "*cestui a que use le feoffment fuit fait*."

The first period in the development of uses probably began very soon after the Norman conquest. Maitland suggests that uses were first employed in relation to land during the 13th century.[14] At that time the Franciscan friars were coming to England. The rules of their order required them to maintain perfect poverty. In order to make provision for them, the wealthy faithful adopted the device of conveying land to a town or city, or to individuals for the use of friars.

---

12 The word "purchaser" in this context means a person who acquires title otherwise than by descent. Hence, it includes someone who takes title by gift.

13 In many jurisdictions a mortgage is now simply a charge, that is, a security interest in the land, which does not involve the conveyance of the fee. The parties' rights, obligations and remedies in that situation do not differ materially from the situation in which the mortgage operates as a conveyance, however.

14 Maitland, at 25.

In the next century the use was employed also for the following purposes:

1. To evade the feudal burdens of wardship and marriage.
2. To evade the law of forfeiture for treason and escheat by felony.
3. To evade the statutes of mortmain.[15]
4. To defeat one's creditors.
5. To acquire a kind of testamentary power with respect to land.

How was this done? By conveying to a number of feoffees who were joint tenants. Thus X might enfeoff lands to his or her friends, A, B and C, *ad opus suum*, that is, to his or her own use (or to the use of the friars). The friends would agree to let X (or the friars) enjoy the profits of the land, while they were the legal owners.

1. Feudal burdens could, of course, be exacted by the lord from A, B or C, since they were the lord's tenants. However, when one of them died, his or her interest devolved upon those remaining by survivorship and another person would be appointed as a replacement. The more important of the feudal burdens could be evaded in this way. For example, if the feoffor died, leaving an infant heir, the lord could not claim wardship because the land did not devolve upon the heir.
2. If the feoffor committed treason or felony, the land, which was no longer his or hers in law, could not be forfeited.
3. The Statutes of Mortmain prohibited the conveyance to a religious corporation in perpetuity. But if the legal owner were an individual, then the fact that he or she permitted the religious order to enjoy the profits did not breach the statutes.
4. A creditor who obtained a judgment against a person and attempted to execute it against the debtor's lands would not succeed if the debtor had disposed of the land to uses. The debtor was no longer the legal owner.
5. By means of a use a landowner could, in effect, make a testamentary gift of land by requiring the feoffees to carry out instructions respecting the disposition of the land after his or her death. Thus X might enfeoff A, B and C to the use of himself or herself for life and thereafter to hold the land for the benefit of his or her children. The use was employed for this purpose because at common law it was not possible to dispose of one's land by will.

The common law had no forms or concepts to deal with the use. It recognized only the legal estate of the feoffees to uses and disregarded the obligations the feoffees owed to the *cestuis que use*, that is, the persons for whom they had agreed to hold the land. If the common law had then recognized the relationships created

---

15 These were a series of statutes which prohibited the conveyance of land to religious houses, and later to corporations generally, in perpetuity. The first was contained in *Magna Carta* 1217 (25 Edw. 1), cc. 39, 43. See A.H. Oosterhoff, "The Law of Mortmain: An Historical and Comparative Review" (1977), 27 U. of T.L.J. 257.

by agency or contract, the common law courts might have enforced the use. If they had enforced the use, there would have been no need for the Chancellors to intervene and the feudal incidents would have attached to the interests of the *cestuis que use* as a matter of course.

During this period uses were only obligations of conscience in the feoffees. They were not enforceable by the *cestui que use*.

The second period in the development of uses began around 1400 when the Chancellor started to enforce uses, and ended with the enactment of the *Statute of Uses* in 1535.[16] The Chancellor was forced to take cognizance of the use because of the many complaints against faithless feoffees brought before him, and because the courts of law would not enforce the obligations undertaken by the feoffees. The Chancellor, therefore, began to demand that feoffees honour their obligations in conscience. This greatly reduced the risk of employing the use, namely, the risk that feoffees would refuse to perform their obligations. Also, it laid the foundation for the distinction between equitable and legal estates in land, for the Chancellors treated the use as an estate (an equitable estate) in land and applied the legal rules relating to estates by analogy. Thus, for example, it was held that if the *cestui que use* died, his or her interest descended in the same way as a legal interest in land and the equitable interest was held to be assignable just like an estate in land.

Nevertheless, equity disregarded many of the technical rules of law concerning the creation of estates, which were based on old feudal theories and were strictly followed in courts of law. For example, at common law there could not be an abeyance of seisin. However, equity did not worry about abeyance of seisin, because it was always in the feoffee to uses. Thus, by the simple addition of the words "to the use of," equity got around the common law remainder rules, which made springing, shifting, and resulting uses possible. In other words, interests were allowed to spring up and to shift to other persons in the future, and to result to the feoffor in ways not permitted under a common law grant.[17]

The third period in the history of uses began with the enactment of the *Statute of Uses* and lasted for about 100 years thereafter.

The long preamble to the Act lists the many evils which the use supposedly encouraged, the most important of which undoubtedly was the King's loss of his feudal rights and aids. The King had nothing to lose and everything to gain by the abolition of uses and it seems that he forced the Act through an unwilling Parliament, whose members employed the use to evade their obligations.

The language of the Statute is arcane, but this is its substance:[18]

---

16 1535 (27 Hen. 8), c. 10.

17 It was presumed that a use would result to the feoffor if the interests were not completely disposed of. To circumvent the presumption of a resulting use one of the following had to exist: (1) a close blood relationship between the feoffee and feoffor; (2) a declaration that the feoffment was made to the use of the feoffee and his or her heirs; or (3) consideration for the enfeoffment.

18 The full text of the Act is set out in R.S.O. 1980, App. A. It is still in force in the Canadian common law jurisdictions.

Where any person stands . . . seized of . . . lands . . . to the use . . . of any other person, or . . . body politic . . . such person and body politic . . . shall from henceforth stand . . . seized . . . in lawful seizin . . . of . . . the same lands . . . in such like estates as they had . . . in use . . . in the same.

The effect of the statute was not to abolish the use, but to give the legal title to the property to the *cestui que use*. If the *cestui que use* formerly had an equitable estate for life, he or she now acquired a legal life estate. It was said that the statute executed the use because it removed the feoffee from the scene and directed that the *cestui que use* step into the feoffee's place. In the result, the use became a legal interest enforceable in courts of law.

The fourth period in the history of uses commenced when astute conveyancers realized that ways could be found around the *Statute of Uses*. The following list enumerates the situations in which it was held that the Statute does not execute the use:

1. When the feoffee to uses does not stand seised of the land. This will happen if the use is imposed on a chattel real or on other personal property.
2. When the use is an active one, that is, one in which the feoffee has an active duty to perform, such as collecting the rents and profits and paying them over to the *cestui que use*. Even before the Statute the feoffee had two active duties, namely to convey the land at the direction of the *cestui que use* and to defend the land against third persons, and a passive one of permitting the *cestui que use* to enjoy the rents and profits. But the two active duties by themselves were held to be insufficient to make the trust an active one.[19]
3. When a corporation is seised to uses, that is, when the corporation is the feoffee. This exception arose because the Statute refers only to a person or persons who stand seised to uses, whereas, by contrast, it specifically refers to a person or persons *or body politic* as *cestui que use*.
4. When a person is seised to his or her own use, as in a conveyance "To A to the use of A." This exception arose because the feoffee must stand seised to the use of another before the Statute operates.
5. A use upon a use, as in a conveyance, "To X and his heirs to the use of A and his heirs to the use of B and her heirs." The Statute would execute only the first use, so that A got the legal estate. *Tyrrel's Case*[20] held that B's interest was repugnant to the grant, both in law and in equity, and was therefore void.

---

19 It is interesting to note that in Illinois, where the so-called Illinois Land Trust has been used for a long time as a vehicle for land development and real estate syndication, the duty of the trustee to sell the property at the end of a stipulated period is sufficient to prevent the trust from being treated as a passive or dry trust, even though the Land Trust is in reality a passive device in which the trustee has no active duty to perform and the real power lies with the investors. The device has also spread to other states. See George G. Bogert and George T. Bogert, *The Law of Trusts and Trustees*, rev. ed. (St. Paul: West Publishing Co., 1978), §249 ("Bogert").

20 (1557), 2 Dyer 115a, 73 E.R. 336.

(c) The Development of Trusts

Tyrrel's Case was a decision of the common law courts, but its reasons were adopted in equity. However, only 77 years after *Tyrrel* the Chancellor changed his mind and began to enforce the second use.[21]

Thus, in a grant, "To X and his heirs to the use of A and his heirs to the use of B and her heirs," X dropped out and A held the legal estate by the operation of the Statute. The second use was not executed because it was a use upon a use, but equity now enforced it, so that A now held to the use of B.

It is apparent that this is exactly the situation that existed before the Statute; thus, equitable estates were revived despite the attempt of the *Statute of Uses* to eliminate them. The only difference was that one now had to put in one more use, which caused Lord Hardwicke to exclaim:[22]

> . . . a statute made upon great consideration, introduced in a solemn and pompous manner, by this strict construction, has had no other effect than to add at most, three words to a conveyance.

Nevertheless, the strict construction opened the way for the modern trust.

After equity began to enforce the second use, it came to be called a trust and the words "in trust for" became common instead of the phrase "to the use of" in the second use. But there is no legal distinction between the two phrases. You should remember that it is the second use that creates the trust, whether the conveyance says "to the use of" or "in trust for." Thus, a conveyance of the fee simple "to A and his heirs in trust for B and her heirs," does not create a trust, since there is only one use and it is executed.

(d) The Statute of Wills

You will remember that the device of the use before the *Statute of Uses*[23] permitted a person to overcome the common law prohibition against devises of real property. The Statute was extremely unpopular because it was thought that this practice was now forbidden.[24] Landowners presented their grievances to the king in 1536 in what became known as the Pilgrimage of Grace.[25] It provided the impetus for the enactment of the *Statute of Wills* in 1540.[26] This statute permitted

---

21 See *Sambach v. Dalston* (1634), Toth. 188, 21 E.R. 164.

22 *Hopkins v. Hopkins* (1738), 1 Atk. 581 at 591, 26 E.R. 365.

23 1535 (27 Hen. VIII), c. 10.

24 In fact, although conveyancers did not realize it at the time, the Statute, as later construed, permitted persons to use similar devices to achieve a measure of testation, with the additional advantage that the estates created thereunder were thereafter legal, rather than equitable.

25 See Sir William Holdsworth, *A History of English Law* (London: Methuen and Co. Ltd. and Sweet and Maxwell Ltd., 1903-1972), vol. 4, at 465-466.

26 1540 (32 Hen. VIII), c. 1.

a person to devise all land held by him in socage tenure and two-thirds of land held by him in knight's service "at his free will and pleasure."[27]

(e) Trusts of Personalty

Originally, trusts were used for estates in land only. Ownership of chattels was not an important concept in feudal times, although possession was. It was common to hold chattels to the use of another from early times, but that did not create equitable interests or estates, for the parties' rights were not enforced in equity, but at law. There are two reasons for this:

1. In those early times, the wealth of the nation consisted of real estate, not of personalty, so that trusts of chattels were not important.
2. The common law had remedies to deal with the delivery of chattels to the use of another, such as debt, detinue, bailment and the action of account.

However, the common law remedies became inadequate when the nation's wealth shifted from realty to personalty, however. At that stage, which was in comparatively modern times, equity took over the enforcement of trusts of personal property. The principles which pertain to trusts of real property also apply to trusts of personal property. However, since seisin is irrelevant in the context of personal property, it is not necessary to employ a use upon a use, or rely upon any of the other exceptions to the statute in order to create a trust of personal property.

Further Reading

Sir William Holdsworth, *A History of English Law* (London: Methuen and Company Limited and Sweet and Maxwell Limited, 1903-1972), vols. 3 and 7.

3. THE RELATIONSHIP BETWEEN LAW AND EQUITY TODAY

Equity assumed jurisdiction over trusts (as well as many other matters) because the common law could not accommodate the concept of the trust and because the forms of action at common law had become ossified. Equity provided remedies to aggrieved litigants where none existed, or where the legal remedies were inadequate or too lengthy and cumbersome.

Regrettably, the ready availability of remedies in equity did not continue. In time, the court of Chancery became as fustian and its procedures as complex and

---

27 *Ibid.*, ss. 1, 2. Tenure denotes the basis upon which a person holds land from his or her feudal lord. The obligations owed to the lord varied with the type of tenure. Socage tenure was a free tenure which required the tenant to perform services of an agricultural nature. Knight's service was a free tenure which required the tenant to provide a specified number of knights to the king for 40 days per year for his army.

as lengthy as those in the common law courts.[28] One only has to read Charles Dickens' *Bleak House* to learn about the problems in Chancery in the 18th and early 19th centuries.

As a result of reform movements in England in the 19th century, various changes were introduced, both at common law and equity. In this respect the Common Law Procedure Acts of 1852[29] and 1854,[30] which abolished the old forms of action, and the *Chancery Appeals Act* of 1851,[31] which restructured the court of Chancery, deserve mention. These and other reforms led to the enactment of the *Supreme Court of Judicature Act* in 1873.[32] The Act created a single, fused court, albeit composed of separate divisions, to administer both law and equity. These various reforms were followed or became received law in the Canadian common law jurisdictions, although the division of the superior court into separate divisions was either not adopted or was later abolished.

Despite the fusion of the courts of common law and equity, the orthodox view has always been that the two systems of law, that is, common law and equity, were not fused. Thus, Ashburner said of the two systems of law,[33]

> ... the two streams of jurisdiction, though they run in the same channel, run side by side, and do not mingle their waters.

In other words, although they are administered in the same courts, the two systems of law have not been fused. Nevertheless, in *United Scientific Holdings Ltd. v. Burnley Borough Council*[34] Lord Diplock, in reference to the above quotation from Ashburner, said:[35]

> By 1977, this metaphor has in my view become most mischievous and deceptive. The innate conservatism of English lawyers may have made them slow to recognize that by the *Supreme Court of Judicature Act 1873* the two systems of substantive and adjectival law formerly administered by courts of law and Courts of Chancery (as well as those administered by courts of admiralty, probate and matrimonial causes), were fused.

Lord Diplock's view was quoted with approval by the Ontario Court of Appeal in *LeMesurier v. Andrus*.[36] Neither of these cases was concerned with

---

28 Indeed, in some cases they could be as long, as appears from *Godfrey v. Saunders* (1770), 3 Wils. K.B. 73, 95 E.R. 940. In that case the plaintiff's proceeding for an account in Chancery had been dragging on for 12 years. Hoping to have better luck in the King's Bench, he commenced an action for an account at common law in 1756, only to find that he had to wait 14 years for a result there.

29 1852 (15 & 16 Vict.), c. 76 (U.K.).

30 1854 (17 & 18 Vict.), c. 125 (U.K.).

31 1851 (14 & 15 Vict.), c. 83 (U.K.).

32 1873 (36 & 37 Vict.), c. 66 (U.K.).

33 W. Ashburner, *Principles of Equity*, 2nd ed. by Denis Browne (London: Butterworth and Co. Limited, 1933), at 18.

34 [1978] A.C. 904, [1977] 2 W.L.R. 806 (H.L.).

35 *Ibid.*, at 925.

36 (1986), 54 O.R. (2d) 1 at 9, 25 D.L.R. (4th) 424, 38 R.P.R. 183, 12 O.A.C. 299 (C.A.), leave to appeal to S.C.C. refused 74 N.R. 239 (note), 21 O.A.C. 239 (note), 63 O.R. (2d) x (note), [1986] 2 S.C.R. v (note).

trusts. The Supreme Court of Canada followed both cases in *Canson Enterprises Ltd. v. Boughton & Co.*[37]

It is true that law and equity have grown closer together over the years and have influenced each other. However, they are not (yet) fused. This is particularly evident in the law of trusts, which presupposes a distinction between legal and equitable ownership and rights.

Further Reading

Paul M. Perell, *The Fusion of Law and Equity* (Toronto: Butterworths, 1990).

Paul M. Perrell and Jeff G. Cowan, "In Defence of Chippewas of Sarnia Band v. Canada (Attorney General)" (2002), 81 Can. Bar Rev. 727.

D.W.M. Waters, "The Reception of Equity in the Supreme Court of Canada (1875-2000)" (2001), 80 Can. Bar Rev. (1 & 2) 620-698.

4. DEFINITIONS

It is an unenviable task to define the trust. In order to be complete, the definition would have to be so comprehensive as to be unintelligible and, therefore, useless; whereas a short definition might express the principal elements of the trust and, thus, be clear but fail to speak of the institution's many and different facets. Most definitions of the trust, therefore, attempt to define only the express private trust. Sometimes they try to encompass purpose trusts as well, but resulting and constructive trusts are not usually part of the definition. With these qualifications in mind, the following two definitions may suffice.

Underhill's definition is as follows:[38]

A trust is an equitable obligation, binding a person (who is called a trustee) to deal with property over which he has control (which is called the trust property), for the benefit of persons (who are called the beneficiaries or *cestuis que trust*), of whom he may himself be one and any one of whom may enforce the obligation. Any act or neglect on the part of the trustee which is not authorized or excused by the terms of the trust instrument, or by law, is called a breach of trust.

Lewin defines a trust as:[39]

. . . the duty or aggregate accumulation of obligations that rest upon a person described as a trustee. The responsibilities are in relation to property held by him, or under his control. That property he will be compelled by a court in its equitable jurisdiction to administer in the manner lawfully prescribed by the trust instrument, or where there be no specific provision written or oral, or to the extent that such provision is invalid or lacking, in accordance with equitable principles. As a consequence the administration will be in such a manner that the consequential benefits and advantages accrue, not to the trustee, but to the persons called *cestuis que trust*, or beneficiaries,

---

37 (1991), 85 D.L.R. (4th) 129 (S.C.C.).

38 Underhill and Hayton, *Law Relating to Trusts and Trustees*, 15th ed. by David J. Hayton (London: Butterworth & Co. (Publishers) Ltd. 1995), at 3 ("Underhill").

39 *Lewin on Trusts*, 17th ed. by W.J. Mowbray (London: Sweet & Maxwell Limited, 2000), at 4 ("Lewin").

if there be any; if not, for some purpose which the law will recognize and enforce. A trustee may be a beneficiary, in which case advantages will accrue in his favour to the extent of his beneficial interest.

The trust is, therefore, a fiduciary relationship imposing certain obligations on the person who holds title to the property. The relationship is fiduciary, because, while the trustees have substantial control over the trust property, they are bound to act in strict confidentiality, with honesty and candour, and entirely in the interests of the *cestuis que trust*.

The courts often use the term "trust" to describe other fiduciary relationships such as bailment, agency, directorship, guardianship and executorship, as well as the obligations of confidential relationships, such as those between priest and penitent, doctor and patient, lawyer and client, *etc.* However, the term "trust" applies only to that fiduciary relationship which evolved out of the use.[40] Nevertheless, many other fiduciary relationships partake of the characteristics of the trust.

The following terms require definition:

The *settlor*: This is the person who creates the trust. If the trust is testamentary, this person is called the *testator* (fem., *testatrix*, pl., *testatrices*). The settlor or testator of an express trust intended to create the trust. In those trusts which arise by operation of law, *viz.*, resulting and constructive trusts, however, there is no settlor in the sense of a person intentionally wishing to create a trust.

The *trustee*: This is the person who holds the title to the trust property for the benefit of the beneficiaries. There may be one trustee or more than one. The settlor and trustee may be one and the same person, as where the settlor declares himself or herself to be a trustee of property for the benefit of others.

The *beneficiary* or *cestui que trust* (pl., *cestuis que trust*): This is the person for whose benefit the trustee holds the trust property. There may be one beneficiary or more than one. The trustee may be one of several beneficiaries, but not the sole beneficiary.

The *trust property, trust res, corpus*, or *subject matter of the trust*: This is the property which the trustee holds for the benefit of the beneficiaries. A trustee may hold either a legal or equitable title to the trust property depending upon the nature of the property as it comes into the trust or as it is subsequently dealt with.

The *trust instrument*: In most situations a trust is created by a document called a trust instrument, which vests the trust property in the trustee and describes the rights and obligations of the parties to the trust. Those rights and obligations are called the terms of the trust. Typically, a trust instrument is either a deed or a will. However, not all trusts are created by an instrument, nor do they always have to be so created. The law in many jurisdictions requires that some trusts, such as trusts involving land, be evidenced by writing, while other trusts may be created orally.

The *bare trust*: A trust exists whenever title to property is vested in one person to be held for the benefit of another. The trustee is subjected to various duties,

---

40 Described above.

some imposed by equity, such as the obligation to make the property productive and to exercise reasonable care over it; other duties are imposed by the creator of the trust (such as a direction to apply the income for the maintenance of minors); yet others may be imposed by statute. When the trustee no longer has active duties to perform (that is, duties imposed by the creator of the trust), except to convey the trust property to the beneficiaries upon demand, the trust is said to be a *bare*, *naked*, *simple* or *dry trust*. At that point the duties imposed upon the trustee by equity are regarded as passive duties.[41]

Unless a statute provides otherwise,[42] beneficiaries are entitled to call for a conveyance of the trust property when they are *sui juris*[43] and solely entitled to the property.[44] Thus, for example, if S transfers property to T in trust for A and directs that the property be transferred to A at age 25, A is entitled to call for a transfer upon reaching the age of majority. Regardless of whether A does call for a conveyance at that time, it is arguable that the trust becomes a bare trust when he or she attains the age of majority.

A *fixed trust*: This is a trust in which each beneficiary's interest is fixed, either by amount or as a proportion of the total.

A *discretionary trust*: This is a trust in which the trustees are given a power to decide how income, capital, or both, should be distributed to a class of beneficiaries. The trustees are under a duty to appoint, that is, to pay or distribute, but they have a discretion about the amount any beneficiary will receive, or about the choice of beneficiaries, or both. While the class of beneficiaries as a whole may be said to have a proprietary interest in the trust property, no individual member of the class has such an interest because the trustee may not appoint to him or her.[45]

A discretionary trust is sometimes called a trust power, but we recommend that you avoid using that term since it invites confusion.[46]

A *power*: A power is an authority to deal with someone else's property. It may exist outside a trust, such as a power of attorney and a mortgagee's power of sale, or in a trust, such as the discretionary trust.

Powers contained in a trust can take a variety of forms. For example, we can distinguish between administrative and dispositive powers. The former are powers conferred upon the trustees by the trust instrument, or by law, which permit them to manage the trust property. Administrative powers include powers to sell, mortgage and invest. Dispositive powers are powers to pay or transfer trust

---

41 See D.W.M. Waters, *Law of Trusts in Canada*, 2nd ed. (Toronto: Carswell, 1984), at 27-29 ("Waters"). See also *De Mond v. R.*, 29 E.T.R. (2d) 226, 1999 CarswellNat 1397, [1999] 4 C.T.C. 2007, 99 D.T.C. 893, 1 R.F.L. (5th) 359 (T.C.C. [General Procedure]).

42 As to which see the chapter on revocation, termination and variation of trusts.

43 *I.e.*, not under a legal disability, such as minority or lack of mental capacity.

44 This is the rule in *Saunders v. Vautier* (1841), 4 Beav. 115, 49 E.R. 282, affirmed (1841), 1 Cr. & Ph. 240, 41 E.R. 482, [1835-42] All E.R. Rep. 58.

45 See Shannon Lindsay and Peter Ziegler, "Trust of an Interest in a Discretionary Trust — Is it Possible?" (1986), 60 Austr. L.J. 387.

46 *Cf.* Waters, at 76, who defines a trust power as a duty to make a one-time distribution, and a discretionary trust as a duty to distribute over a period of time, both duties being coupled with a power of selection.

property to beneficiaries. They include the *powers of appointment, maintenance, advancement* and *encroachment*. All of them permit distribution of property among a specified class of persons. A dispositive power may be given to a trustee or to a beneficiary. If it is held by a trustee, it is sometimes called a *fiduciary power*.

The person who creates the power is called the *donor* of the power, while the recipient is the *donee* of the power. The persons to whom the property may be appointed are the potential beneficiaries or, when property is transferred to them, the *appointees*.

While a discretionary trust contains a power, it is a power coupled with a duty to distribute the entire subject matter of the power. Hence, it is really a trust. If a power of appointment is not coupled with a duty to appoint, that is, if the donee has a discretion to appoint or not, the power is often called a *mere power* to distinguish it from a discretionary trust.

A power of appointment may be *general, special* or *hybrid*. A general power enables the donee to appoint to anyone, including himself or herself. Hence, it is usually treated as being the equivalent of ownership. A special power enables the donee to appoint to anyone among a named class of persons. A hybrid power enables the donee to appoint to anyone, save a named class of persons.

5. CLASSIFICATION OF TRUSTS

(a) Introduction

There are various ways to classify trusts. Most writers agree on the standard divisions, but there are different opinions about some types of trust, as will appear below. The following is the generally accepted taxonomy.

(b) Express Trusts

An express trust is one in which the person creating it has expressed his or her intention to have property held by one or more persons for the benefit of another or others. The intention may be expressed orally, by deed, or by will. Moreover, the creator of the trust may intend him- or herself to be the trustee of property he or she owns, or the creator may intend another person to be the trustee. In the latter situation it is necessary to transfer the property which is to form the subject matter of the trust to the trustee.

Express trusts may be subdivided into a number of different types. First, there is the distinction between *trusts for persons* and *trusts for purposes*. The former, sometimes called private trusts, are trusts for the benefit of individuals or corporate persons, whereas the latter do not have persons as beneficiaries, but rather defined purposes. The main type of purpose trust is the *charitable trust*, sometimes called a public trust. Examples of charitable trusts are trusts for the advancement of education, such as the establishment of scholarships and the provision of funds to construct a building at a university. Charitable trusts enjoy a number of advantages in law, chiefly exemption from taxation and from the perpetuity rules.[47]

There are other purpose trusts which are not charitable and which are usually called *non-charitable purpose trusts*. They are not charitable because the law does not regard their objects to be of sufficient benefit to the public to be accorded the advantages of charitable trusts. An example of such a trust is a trust to promote fox hunting.[48]

Under the heading of express trusts, we can distinguish further between *executed* and *executory trusts*. Of the two, executed trusts are more common. Executed trusts are those in which the settlor has completely set out the beneficial interests. The word "executed" does not mean that the trust is fully administered or completed, since the trustees still have active duties to perform.

An executory trust is one in which the settlor has expressed only a general intention about who shall have the property, while final disposition is left to a later time or to other persons, such as the trustees. This trust is common in marriage settlements under which the issue of the marriage must later be provided for, in trusts with powers of appointment, and in discretionary trusts.

The distinction is important and is relevant to the interpretion of the trust. If the trust is executed, the courts will interpret the document strictly, that is, according to the strict legal meaning of the language used. In an executory trust the court will look at the whole instrument to discover, and carry out, the real intention of the settlor.

Executed and executory trusts should not be confused with *completely* and *incompletely constituted trusts*. A completely constituted trust is simply one in which the settlor has properly transferred to and vested the property in the trustees and has declared the trusts that govern such property. Until that is done the trust is incomplete and, hence, unenforceable. If the settlor has declared an intention to create a trust, but has not transferred the property that is to form its subject matter to the trustees, there is no trust. In such a situation, the intended beneficiaries, if volunteers,[49] have no remedy, either against the trustees or the settlor. It is, however, possible in certain limited and defined circumstances to raise a trust in this situation. This matter is explored later.[50]

(c) Trusts Arising by Operation of Law

Certain kinds of trust are said to arise by operation of law because they are imposed by law regardless of the expressed intention of the parties. Three such trusts have been recognized, namely, the resulting trust, the constructive trust and the implied trust.

---

47 The rule against remoteness of vesting does apply to charitable trusts in part. See the chapter on charitable trusts.

48 See the chapter on non-charitable purpose trusts.

49 A volunteer is a person who has not paid valuable consideration for the transfer of the beneficial interest. Someone who has paid valuable consideration has contractual remedies.

50 See the chapter on the creation of express trusts.

The *resulting trust* is imposed in certain defined situations to return property to the person who gave it and is entitled to it beneficially, from someone else who has title to it. Thus, the property "results" to the true owner. Resulting trusts are of two kinds: (a) those in which an express trust fails in whole or in part for any reason; and (b) those in which a person makes a voluntary transfer of property to another or others or purchases property and directs that title be taken in the name of another or others.

The first kind arises when the beneficial interest is not exhausted, as when A transfers property "to B in trust for C for life" and leaves the remainder interest undisposed of, so that it results to A. It also arises when a trust fails for illegality or contravention of a rule of law.

Such resulting trusts have nothing to do with the settlor's or testator's intention, because it is unlikely that he or she considered what should happen to the property if the trust should fail. For this reason they have been called "automatic resulting trusts."[51] In fact, some analyses of this kind of resulting trust state that they arise because of the implied intention of the creator of the express trust that if the trust should fail, the property should result. It is submitted that it is better not to regard these trusts as based upon intention, but simply upon the application of a prophylactic rule of law. The law rejects a hiatus in ownership of property. Hence, in the circumstances described the property can only revert to the creator of the trust, since the beneficial interest is not effectively disposed of, and the trustee is not intended to have the beneficial interest.

The second kind of resulting trust, namely voluntary transfer and purchase money resulting trusts, only arise in *inter vivos* transactions. They are based upon the idea that when a person transfers property to, or purchases property but directs title to be taken in the name of, another and the latter pays no consideration, it must be presumed that the grantor or purchaser did not intend to give the grantee the beneficial interest but rather to retain it. The machinery to recover title is the resulting trust. However, since the law raises a presumption in these situations, it is open to the recipient to rebut the presumption by appropriate evidence and show that a gift was intended. These resulting trusts have, thus, been called "presumed resulting trusts."[52]

If the transfer is made to, or the purchase is made in the name of, the transferor's spouse or child, a presumption of advancement, rather than a presumption of resulting trust, is raised.[53] In other words, it is presumed that a gift was intended. However, the presumption of advancement in favour of a spouse

---

51 *Re Vandervell's Trusts (No. 2), White v. Vandervell Trustees Ltd.*, [1974] Ch. 269 at 294, [1974] 1 All E.R. 47, *per* Megarry J., reversed on other grounds [1974] Ch. 269, [1974] 3 All E.R. 205 (C.A.).

52 *Ibid.*

53 Traditionally, the presumption was only raised when a husband transferred property to his wife or a father transferred property to his child. However, modern law applies the presumption also when a wife transfers property to her husband and when a mother transfers property to her child.

has been abolished and replaced with the presumption of resulting trust by matrimonial property law reform legislation in some Canadian jurisdictions.[54]

While it is possible to argue that voluntary transfer and purchase money resulting trusts are based upon intention, it is submitted that it is unnecessary to do so and is apt to lead to confusion. Again, the presumption is but a prophylactic rule designed to return property to the person who is most likely entitled to it. If you use the intention analysis, you must remember that it is not an intention expressed by the "creator" of the trust, but rather an intention implied from what he or she has done.

It is clear that the *constructive trust* has nothing whatsoever to do with intention, but is imposed by law to prevent injustice. The constructive trust is a device imposed to prevent unjust enrichment.[55]

Constructive trusts most often arise from a fiduciary relationship, such as trustee and beneficiary, solicitor and client, agent and principal, company director or officer and corporation, and real estate broker and vendor or purchaser. A constructive trust may be imposed to strip the fiduciary of a gain made from the relationship and which in conscience belongs to the beneficiary. However, a fiduciary relationship is not required before such a trust can be imposed. Thus, for example, it can be imposed for misuse of confidential information obtained from a person with whom the constructive trustee has an "arm's-length" relationship, upon a vendor of property under a specifically enforceable agreement of purchase and sale, and upon a person who has title to property to the acquisition, maintenance, or improvement of which another has contributed in money's worth.

The term "constructive" does not, therefore, mean that the court construes a trust from certain documents or from the intention of the parties, but rather from a certain factual situation. That is to say, the word "constructive" in this sense does not imply "as interpreted," but "established" or "declared," quite apart from the parties' intention, and it is related to redressing a wrong or preventing unjust enrichment.

It remains now to describe the *implied trust*. This is a concept that does not have a definite meaning. Formerly, implied trusts were sometimes regarded as being those where the words imposing the trust relationship are not clearly expressed, but where the court nevertheless finds an intention to create a trust. This may happen where precatory language[56] is used, where the settlor or testator employs what appears to be a condition rather than a trust, or where there is what appears to be a mere power. This approach is now deprecated, however. Such

---

54 See, *e.g., Family Law Act*, R.S.O. 1990, c. F.3, s. 14; R.S.N. 1990, c. F-2, s. 31; S.P.E.I. 1995, c. 12, s. 14; *Matrimonial Property Act*, R.S.A. 2000 c. M-8, s. 36(1); R.S.N.S. 1989, c. 275, s. 21; *The Matrimonial Property Act, 1997*, S.S. 1997, c. M-6.11, s. 50; *Marital Property Act*, S.N.B. 1980, c. M-1.1, s. 15; *Family Property and Support Act*, R.S.Y. 2002, c. 83, s. 7(2).

55 *Pettkus v. Becker*, [1980] 2 S.C.R. 834, 19 R.F.L. (2d) 165, 8 E.T.R. 143, 117 D.L.R. (3d) 257, 36 N.R. 384.

56 That is, language expressing a wish, hope, desire or expectation, rather than mandatory or directory language.

trusts are in fact express trusts, although the expression of trust is imperfectly stated and only becomes apparent after interpretation.[57]

The term "implied trust" is sometimes used in the cases in the string, "implied, resulting and constructive trusts,"[58] rather with the suggestion that it is a trust arising by operation of law, but without explanation of its distinguishing features. By contrast, sometimes the term "implied trust" is used to encompass all trusts arising by operation of law, or to refer only to resulting trusts.[59] Underhill appears to take the former view, calling trusts arising "by implication of a court of equity" implied trusts, which are then further subdivided into resulting and constructive trusts.[60]

It would be convenient if all could agree on the proper meaning of the term "implied" trust. However, it is apparent that there is no such agreement. Moreover, it often seems that users of the term do not know what it means, but use it for fear they may otherwise leave out something important, or simply because it has become customary to let the triad "implied, resulting and constructive trusts" roll off the tongue.[61] It is submitted that the term adds nothing to a discussion of the classification of trusts and should, therefore, not be used.

(d) Statutory Trusts

Trusts have also been utilized in legislation. A well-known example of a statutory trust is that arising under the *Estates Administration Act*,[62] which provides that all real and personal property of a deceased person, other than joint interests, vests in his or her personal representative in trust to pay the deceased's debts and to distribute the remainder among the persons beneficially entitled thereto under the deceased's will or on his or her intestacy. Other types of statutory trusts will be referred to below.

(e) Deemed Trusts

One type of statutory trust which is now quite common is the "deemed trust." It is imposed by legislation to ensure that employers do not avoid various revenue and social obligations. Thus, for example, the amounts that employers are required to deduct for vacation pay and income tax are subject to such deemed trusts.

Deemed trusts are necessary when at least one of the three certainties of a trust is missing. The deeming legislation, often provides two of the certainties: the intention to create a trust and the objects. For example, under common

---

57 See Lewin, at 8.

58 See, *e.g.*, *Gissing v. Gissing* (1970), [1971] A.C. 886, [1970] 2 All E.R. 780 at 789-790, *per* Lord Diplock (H.L.).

59 See, *e.g.*, *Rupar v. Rupar* (1964), 49 W.W.R. 226, 46 D.L.R. (2d) 553 at 561 (B.C. S.C.).

60 Underhill, art. 3.

61 A typical failing of lawyers, who often use two or three words when one will do, such as "last will and testament," "all and singular that certain parcel or tract of land and premises," "nominate, constitute and appoint," *etc.*

62 R.S.O. 1990, c. E.22, s. 2.

provisions in provincial sales tax legislation, the vendor is designated a trustee for the Crown. However, the lack of certainty of subject matter in deemed trusts is sometimes problematic.

Deemed trust legislation generally provides either that the funds collected are deemed to be held separate and apart, or that the funds are subject to a lien in favour of the Crown, or both.[63] Deemed trusts avoid the complexities of the tracing remedy when a trustee has commingled trust funds with other funds and the beneficiary is claiming a breach of trust.[64]

There are, however, problems with deemed trusts. These arise principally when the trustee becomes bankrupt. A discussion of these problems is beyond the scope of this chapter.[65]

---

63 For example, see s. 40 of the *Employment Standards Act*, S.O. 2000, c. 41 and s. 57(1) and (5) of the *Pension Benefits Act*, R.S.O. 1990, c. P.8.

64 The tracing remedies are discussed in the chapter on breach of trust.

65 Section 67(1)(a) of the *Bankruptcy and Insolvency Act*, R.S.C. 1985, c. B-3, as am., provides that assets held in trust are not included in the estate of the bankrupt or considered property of the bankrupt. Trusts referred to in s. 67(1)(a) are express trusts which satisfy the three certainties. Deemed trusts fall under s. 67(2) and (3). Section 67(2) renders all federal or provincial statutory deemed trusts invalid in a bankruptcy except those mentioned in s. 67(3). Section 67(3) provides that deemed trusts created under the *Income Tax Act*, R.S.C. 1985, c. 1 (5th Supp.), the *Employment Insurance Act*, S.C. 1996, c. 23, s. 155, and the *Canada Pension Plan*, R.S.C. 1985, c. C-8, are considered trusts for the purposes of s. 67(1). Therefore, these deemed trusts enjoy priority, except as against a creditor who holds a prior security interest in the bankrupt's property: *Royal Bank of Canada v. Sparrow Electric Corp.*, [1997] 1 S.C.R. 411, 143 D.L.R. (4th) 385, [1997] 2 W.W.R. 457, 193 A.R. 321, 135 W.A.C. 321, 46 Alta. L.R. (3d) 87, 44 C.B.R. (3d) 1, 208 N.R. 161, (sub nom. *R. v. Royal Bank of Canada*) 97 D.T.C. 5089, 1997 CarswellAlta 112, 1997 CarswellAlta 113, 12 P.P.S.A.C. (2d) 68.

The status of a deemed trust created by provincial statute was dealt with in *British Columbia v. Henfrey-Samson Belair Ltd.*, [1989] 2 S.C.R. 24, 59 D.L.R. (4th) 726, 38 B.C.L.R. (2d) 145, [1989] 5 W.W.R. 577. It severely restricted the ability of a province to create a deemed trust for the purpose of gaining priority in a bankruptcy. McLachlin J., writing for the majority, held that a province is entitled to take advantage of the priority accorded trusts under the *Bankruptcy and Insolvency Act*, so long as the trust complies with the requirements of a true trust. Therefore, a deemed trust will only benefit from s. 67(1) if the trust property is held separate and apart, so as to be identifiable and traceable. In *Henfrey-Samson Belair*, the debtor was a deemed trustee of provincial sales tax collected pursuant to the British Columbia *Social Service Tax Act*, R.S.B.C. 1979, c. 388, s. 18(1). The deemed trust was ineffective because the deemed trustee commingled tax funds with its other funds. It was, therefore, not a true trust since the trust property was no longer identifiable and traceable. *Husky Oil Operations Ltd. v. Minister of National Revenue* (1995), 128 D.L.R. (4th) 1, [1995] 10 W.W.R. 161, 35 C.B.R. (3d) 1, 188 N.R. 1, 24 C.L.R. (2d) 131, 137 Sask. R. 81, 107 W.A.C. 81, [1995] 3 S.C.R. 453, is to the same effect. So also is *Continental Casualty Co. v. Macleod-Stedman Inc.* (1996), 141 D.L.R. (4th) 36, 43 C.B.R. (3d) 211, [1997] 2 W.W.R. 516, 113 Man. R. (2d) 212 (C.A.), which involved a deemed trust of a bankrupt employer's pension contributions.

Apart from bankruptcy, s. 30(7) of Ontario's *Personal Property Security Act*, R.S.O. 1990, c. P.10, accords limited priority to a deemed trust arising under the Ontario *Employment Standards Act, 2000*, S.O. 2000, c. 41 or the Ontario *Pension Benefits Act*, R.S.O. 1990, c. P.8. Section 30(7) states that a security interest in an account or inventory and its proceeds is subordinate to the interest of a person who is the beneficiary of a deemed trust arising under the *Employment Standards Act* or the *Pension Benefits Act*. It codifies the policy underlying the decision in

(f) Trusts in the Higher and Lower Sense

The word "trust" can have different meanings depending upon the context in which it is used. It is sometimes used in the context of government or Crown obligations. The question whether such a trust is justiciable arose in *Tito v. Waddell (No. 2)*.[66] The case involved a phosphate mining operation on Ocean Island, a small island in the Pacific, which was carried on by the British Phosphate Commissioners. Royalties were paid to the inhabitants, who called themselves Banabans, but they sought increased payments. The Banabans claimed that, as the relevant documents used the word "trust," the Crown stood in a fiduciary relationship towards them and, being in breach of trust, was liable to the islanders. Vice Chancellor Megarry held that the documents imposed only a governmental obligation or "trust in the higher sense," which is not justiciable, but is enforceable only in the political arena. This type of trust is, thus, distinguishable from the "trust in the lower sense," that is, the fiduciary obligation described earlier in this chapter, which is justiciable.

The same issue arose in *Guerin v. R.*[67] That case involved a proposal by officials of the Indian Affairs Branch to an Indian band in Vancouver that part of the band's reserve be leased to a golf club. On the basis of information supplied by the officials of the Branch, the band voted to surrender part of the reserve to the Crown "in trust to lease the same to such person or persons, and upon such terms as the Government of Canada may deem most conducive to our Welfare and that of our people." In fact, the Indian Affairs Branch negotiated a lease upon terms substantially less favourable to the band than its officials had originally disclosed to the band. The band's action for damages for breach of trust was successful at trial,[68] but that decision was reversed on appeal, the Federal Court of Appeal holding that the surrender only created a trust in the higher sense.[69] A further appeal to the Supreme Court of Canada was successful. This case is discussed at greater length later in this chapter.

Armstrong v. Cdn. Admiral Corp. (Receiver of) (1987), 8 P.P.S.A.C. 7 (Ont. C.A.), which subordinated a security interest created under s. 178 of the *Bank Act*, S.C. 1991, c. 46 [unofficial Chapter: B-1.01], to the beneficiary of a deemed trust arising under the Ontario *Employment Standards Act*. There are no equivalent provisions in other provincial personal property security statutes. Arguably, however, the reasoning in *Armstrong* also applies in other provinces. See further Andrew J. Roman and M. Jasmine Sweatman, "The Conflict between Canadian Provincial Personal Property Security Acts and the Federal Bankruptcy Act: The War is Over" (1992), 71 Can. Bar Rev. 77.

66 [1977] Ch. 106, [1977] 3 All E.R. 129.
67 (1984), [1984] 6 W.W.R. 481, 13 D.L.R. (4th) 321, 20 E.T.R. 6, 55 N.R. 161, [1985] 1 C.N.L.R. 120, [1984] 2 S.C.R. 335, (sub nom. *Guerin v. Canada*) 36 R.P.R. 1.
68 *Guerin v. R.*, [1982] 2 F.C. 385, 10 E.T.R. 61, [1982] 2 C.N.L.R. 83 (T.D.), supplementary reasons [1982] 2 F.C. 445, 127 D.L.R. (3d) 170 (T.D.).
69 *Guerin v. R.*, [1983] 2 W.W.R. 686, 13 E.T.R. 245, 143 D.L.R. (3d) 416, [1983] 1 C.N.L.R. 20, [1983] 2 F.C. 656, (sub nom. Guerin v. Canada) 45 N.R. 181 (C.A.).

Notes and Questions

1. In *Green v. R.*[70] the plaintiff argued that the Crown in right of the Province of Ontario was in breach of the statutory trust established under the *Provincial Parks Act*,[71] which dedicates provincial parks to the people of the province and requires that parks be maintained for the benefit of future generations. The court held that the statute did not, in fact, create a trust. However, the court did not base its decision on the distinction between trusts in the higher and lower sense, although it might have done so, but on the fact that there was no certainty of objects.

Further Reading

George P. Costigan Jr., "The Classification of Trusts as Express, Resulting and Constructive" (1913-14), 27 Harv. L. Rev. 437.

6. MODERN USES OF THE TRUST

The trust was originally a conveyancing and estate planning tool. Now it is used for a much wider variety of purposes. This is because the trust is a unique tool in the management and disposition of property. If properly drafted, it can give its creator a desirable level of control while at the same time it can confer on the trustees flexibility to react to changes in circumstances, thus enabling them to protect the trust property and to ensure that it is used in the most efficient and least costly manner.

It is impossible to give a comprehensive list of the many uses to which the trust has been put and for which it is being used, but the following will give some idea of its versatility:

1. *Estate Planning. Inter vivos* and testamentary trusts are used to permit a person to provide for his or her dependants in ways deemed most appropriate. Some of the things one may wish to do are:
   (a) To enable property to be held for persons under a disability. Thus, a minor cannot hold land, having no power to dispose of it, but land can be vested in trustees for the benefit of the child.
   (b) To benefit persons in succession. Instead of giving property to A absolutely in the hope that some will be left to go to A's children on her death, a trustee, X, can be appointed to hold the property in trust to pay the income from the property to A for life, and on her death, to pay the capital to her children.

---

70 [1973] 2 O.R. 396, 34 D.L.R. (3d) 20 (H.C.). *Cf.* Constance D. Hunt, "The Public Trust Doctrine in Canada," in John Swaigen, ed., *Environmental Rights in Canada* (Toronto: Butterworths, 1981), at 151.

71 R.S.O. 1970, c. 371, s. 2 (now R.S.O. 1990, c. P.34, s. 2). *Cf. The Provincial Parks and Consequential Amendments Act*, S.M. 1993, c. 39, s. 4; *Parks Act*, S.N.B. 1982, c. P-2.1, s. 2; S.S. 1986, c. P-1.1, s. 3.

(c) To ensure that the next generation will not waste the property by placing it in a protective trust. For example, instead of giving money outright to a wastrel son, a parent could give it to trustees in trust to pay a certain amount of income to the son and provide that if the son becomes insolvent, there will be a gift over to other persons, or a discretionary trust in favour of the son and other persons.

(d) To provide for persons without publicity. For example, suppose that a person has offspring born outside marriage and wants to provide for them without letting everyone know. The person could, of course, make outright gifts to the children, but this would be difficult if they were young. If they were provided for by will, the object of secrecy would be defeated. The parent may instead execute a deed of trust transferring money or property to trustees who are to hold it for the benefit of the children, pay them income, and so on. Alternatively, the money could be given by will to a friend and a secret trust arrangement made with the friend to pay the money over to the intended beneficiaries.

There are innumerable other purposes to which a trust can be put for private purposes. And the settlor or testator can impose such conditions or stipulations as desired, so long as they are not illegal or contrary to public policy.

2. *Tax Planning.* One of the most important uses of the trust in modern times is to minimize the incidence of income tax and death taxes. This has become a highly specialized field which will be dealt with only incidentally in this book.

3. *Public Trusts.* The trust can be used not only for private, but also for public purposes. For example, it can be used to provide for various charitable purposes such as the advancement of education and religion, and the relief of poverty.

4. *Business Applications.* The trust has been used with great effectiveness in business. The following are examples:

(a) *The business* or *Massachusetts trust.* This device can be used in place of incorporation. Here commercial property is simply transferred to trustees (often a trust company) to manage the property on behalf and for the benefit of, investors who supply the money to buy the property and take "trust units," (which are comparable to corporate shares) in return, as evidence of their beneficial ownership. This form of organization has been used especially in large real estate transactions, where there are too many persons involved — because of the size of the investment — to permit holding the property as tenants-in-common, because it is desirable that title be held by one person or company as trustee for all, and to avoid the burdens of management. By this method office buildings, subdivisions, apartment buildings, shopping centres, *etc.*, have been financed or syndicated.

When creating a business trust, the drafter must make sure that the vehicle being used is, indeed, a trust, that is a device in which the trustee acts as principal. If the trustee's role is essentially that of agent for the beneficiaries, only an agency relationship will have been created.[72]

---

72 See, *e.g.*, *Trident Holdings Ltd. v. Danand Investments Ltd.* (1988), 30 E.T.R. 67 (Ont. C.A.).

(b) *The investment trust*. This is similar to the business trust but is used primarily for investment in securities of various kinds. A mutual fund is a typical example, although it can also be organized as a corporation. The great advantage of the investment trust is that the investor, who in effect buys shares or trust certificates in a trust, is able to minimize the risks, since the fund is usually diversified by investment in a large number and type of securities. Besides, the trust offers management and financial expertise, because it has access to experts in those areas. The real estate investment trust is used for similar reasons and to obtain tax advantages.

(c) *Insurance trusts*. These involve transfers to, or purchases by, trustees of contracts of insurance on the life of the settlor under a trust agreement. The purpose may be to provide for the settlor's dependants, or to protect a business against the death of one of the proprietors, managers, *etc*. In the latter case, contracts of insurance may be taken out on the lives of each of the partners and made payable to trustees to secure a fund to enable the trustees to buy the interest of a deceased partner. In this way, cash is readily available to buy such a business interest, the business can be continued without interruption, and the estate of the deceased has the advantage of a quick sale at a fair price.

(d) *Liquidation trusts*. These can be used when a business is insolvent and cannot pay its creditors. Rather than sacrificing the business, the creditors may enter into an agreement whereby trustees continue to operate the business in the hope of getting the debts paid over a number of years.

(e) *The voting trust*. This is an instrument for securing the management of a corporation in a desired manner. Several shareholders will transfer their shares to a trustee under an agreement that the trustee will vote the shares in a particular way for a predetermined period. It is used, for example, to ensure that certain directors will continue to be elected, so that control of the company remains in the hands of the beneficiaries of the trust.

(f) *Trusts to secure creditors*. A corporation wishing to float a large loan, that is, to issue bonds, debentures, or notes for sale to the public, enters into a trust agreement, called a trust indenture, with a trustee, usually a trust company. Under the trust indenture the issue and sale of the securities to be issued is regulated and security, such as land, shares and inventory, may

---

For an application of the *Trident* test, see *Advanced Glazing Systems Ltd. v. Frydenlund*, [2000] B.C.J. No. 1075, 2000 CarswellBC 1165, 2000 BCSC 804, 32 R.P.R. (3d) 162, 2 C.L.R. (3d) 241 (S.C.); *642947 Ontario Ltd. v. Fleischer* (2001), 209 D.L.R. (4th) 182, 2001 CarswellOnt 4296, 152 O.A.C. 313, 56 O.R. (3d) 417, 47 R.P.R. (3d) 191, 16 C.P.C. (5th) 1 (C.A.). See also A.I. Ogus, "The Trust as Governance Structure" (1986), 36 U. of T.L.J. 188; Robert D. Flannigan, "The Nature and Duration of the Business Trust" (1982-84), 6 E. & T.Q. 181; "Beneficiary Liability in Business Trusts" (1982-84), 6 E. & T.Q. 278; "Business Trusts — Past and Present" (1982-84), 6 E. & T.Q. 375; "The Control Test of Principal Status Applied to the Business Trust" (1986), 8 E. & T.Q. 37 and 97; Maurice C. Cullity, "Liability and Beneficiaries — A Rejoinder" (1985), 7 E. & T.Q. 35; "Liability of Beneficiaries — A Further Rejoinder" (1986), 8 E. & T.Q. 130.

be called for. The trustee issues and (often) transfers the securities and acts on behalf of the creditors to protect their interests.

(g) *Pension trusts.* This is a method to provide pensions for retired employees by means of registered plans under the *Income Tax Act*[73] and provincial legislation. These are usually created under a scheme whereby the employer enters into a trust agreement with a trust company as trustee to hold and administer the funds paid in and to pay out the pensions.

5. *Statutory Trusts.* Parliament and the Legislatures have also recognized the utility of the trust device and use it for a variety of purposes, including the following:

(a) The office of the personal representative as regards the property that must be administered.[74]

(b) The trust established under construction lien statutes of moneys paid in respect of a construction project for the protection of those who work on the project and those who supply materials to it.[75]

(c) Solicitors in respect of their trust accounts.[76]

(d) Employers in respect of vacation pay accruing due to their employees.[77]

(e) Employers in respect of income tax deducted or required to be deducted from their employees' earnings.[78]

(f) The office of the Public Trustee.[79]

Statutory trusts involving deemed trusts have already been discussed above.

---

73 R.S.C. 1985, c. 1 (5th Supp.).

74 *Estates Administration Act*, R.S.O. 1990, c. E.22, s. 2; *Devolution of Real Property Act*, R.S.A. 2000, c. D-12, ss. 2-4; R.S.N.W.T. 1988, c. D-5, ss. 3, 4; R.S.S. 1978, c. D-27, s. 4; R.S.Y. 2002, c. 57, ss. 2, 3; *Estate Administration Act*, R.S.B.C. 1996, c. 122, Part 9, s. 78; *Devolution of Estates Act*, R.S.N.B. 1973, c. D-9, ss. 3-6; *The Trustee Act*, R.S.M. 1987, c. T160, ss. 42-44; *Chattels Real Act*, R.S.N.L. 1990, c. C-11, s. 2.

75 *Construction Lien Act*, R.S.O. 1990, c. C.30, ss. 7, 8; *Builders Lien Act*, S.B.C. 1997, c. 45, s. 10; *Builders' Lien Act*, R.S.M. 1987, c. B91, ss. 4, 5; S.S. 1984-85-86, c. B-7.1, s. 6; *Mechanics' Lien Act*, R.S.N.B. 1973, c. M-6, s. 3 [am. 1981, c. 40, s. 1; 1981, c. 80, s. 30; 1990, c. 61, s. 77; 1994, c. 70, s. 4].

76 *Law Society Act*, R.S.O. 1990, c. L.8; R.R.O. 1990, Reg. 708, s. 14; *Law Society Act, 1990*, S.N. 1999, c. L-9.1, s. 68; *Legal Profession Act*, R.S.A. 2000, c. 8, s. 126; S.B.C. 1998, c. 9, s. 63; S.M. 2002, c. 44, s. 49(1); *The Legal Profession Act, 1990*, S.S. 1990-91, c. L-10.1, s. 78; *Legal Profession Act*, R.S.P.E.I. 1988, c. L-6.1, s. 44 [am. S.P.E.I. 1999, c. 33, s. 5]. *Barristers and Solicitors Act*, R.S.N.S. 1989, c. 30, s. 57; *Legal Profession Act*, 1992, c. 39.

77 *Employment Standards Act, 2000*, S.O. 2000, c. 41, s. 40; *Labour Standards Code*, R.S.N.S. 1989, c. 246, s. 36.

78 *Income Tax Act*, R.S.C. 1985, c. 1 (5th Supp.), s. 227(4) [am. by 1994, c. 21, s. 104(1); 1998 c. 19, s. 226(1)].

79 Actually the Public Trustee is a corporation sole, but the incumbent's duties are those of a trustee. See *Public Guardian and Trustee Act*, R.S.O. 1990, c. P.51, s. 1(2) [re-en. 1992, c. 32, s. 25(1)], s. 7(1) (am. 1992, c. 32, s. 25(2); re-en. 1996, c. 2, s. 75(2)]; R.S.B.C. 1996, c. 383, s. 2; S.S. 1983, c. P-36.3, s. 3 [am. 2001, c. 33, ss. 7, 23(1) (Sched.); *Public Trustee Act*, R.S.A. 2000, c. P-44, s. 2; R.S.M. 1987, c. P275, s. 1 [am. 1992, c. 29, s. 2]; R.S.N.L. 1990, c. P-46, s. 3 [not yet in force] [am. 2001, c. N-31, s. 2]; R.S.N.S. 1989, c. 379, s. 3; R.S.N.W.T. 1988, c. P-19, s. 2.

7. NATURE OF THE TRUST BENEFICIARY'S INTEREST

(a) Introduction

Having considered the nature and kind of trusts in some detail, it is also convenient to discuss the nature of the interest that a trust beneficiary holds. We will do so by paying particular attention to the beneficiary's rights and remedies, and by contrasting the trust beneficiary's interest with the interest of a beneficiary under an unadministered estate.

(b) The Trust Beneficiary

Much has been written about the nature of the trust beneficiary's interest. There are essentially two views of the beneficiary's rights, which were thus compendiously summarized by Maitland:[80]

> (1) *Cestui que trust* has rights enforceable against any person who has undertaken the trust, against all who claim through or under him as volunteers (heirs, devisees, personal representatives, donees) against his creditors, and against those who acquire the thing with notice actual or constructive of the trust.
>
> Or (2) *Cestui que trust* has rights enforceable against all save a *bona fide* purchaser ("purchaser" in this context always includes a mortgagee) who for value has obtained a legal right in the thing without notice of the trust express or constructive.

While these two approaches say essentially the same thing, Maitland preferred the first because it stresses the fact that the beneficiary's right is to compel the trustee to properly administer the trust. Hence, the right is personal as against the trustee. Maitland took issue with Austin's distinction between rights *in rem* and rights *in personam*.[81] He thought this distinction mischievous and productive of confusion,[82] and required one to adopt the second view which stresses the proprietary nature of the beneficiary's interest or his rights *in rem*. Maitland was, thus, of opinion that the owner of the legal estate has rights *in rem*, but that the owner of the equitable interest only has rights *in personam*.

Unfortunately the Latin terms have tended more often to confuse than to illuminate the issue. In fact, a trust beneficiary has both a proprietary and a personal right and it would seem that one or the other may be emphasized depending upon the factual situation in which the issue arises, or upon a statute which impinges on the issue.

If we consider first the personal aspect of the beneficiary's right, it will be apparent that, since the management and control of the trust property is vested in the trustee, the beneficiary only has a personal right against the trustee if the issue is whether the trustee has improperly administered the estate, or whether the

---

80 Maitland, at 115.

81 John Austin, *Lectures on Jurisprudence*, 4th ed. by Robert Campbell (London: John Murray, 1873), vol. 1, at 388.

82 Maitland, at 106ff.

beneficiary has direct access to the property. This is illustrated by *Schalit v. Joseph Nadler Ltd.*[83] in which the trustee had properly leased some commercial properties, which he held in trust for the beneficiary. The latter sought to obtain the rents and profits directly. However, the court held that he was not entitled to them but only to an accounting from the trustee of the profits received, less costs of administration.[84]

Similarly, the beneficiaries are not entitled to direct the trustee. For example, the beneficiaries cannot require the trustee to resign and appoint another person as a replacement.[85] As against the trustee, the beneficiary's right is, thus, usually personal.

The proprietary aspect of the beneficiary's right may, however, predominate. Thus, for example, if the beneficiary is *sui juris* and solely entitled to the trust property in the sense that no one else has a beneficial interest in it, vested or contingent, he or she is entitled to terminate the trust and call upon the trustee to convey the property under the rule in *Saunders v. Vautier.*[86] Indeed, if there is more than one beneficiary and they are all *sui juris* and are together entitled to the entire beneficial interest, they can terminate the trust, provided they can agree to do so and to divide the property among themselves.[87]

The beneficiary's right against the trustee is proprietary in nature if the trustee has misapplied the trust property but retains it in its original or converted form. In these circumstances, the beneficiary is allowed to trace the trust property into its product. The beneficiary has a similar right against anyone to whom the trustee has transferred the property, provided the transferee was a volunteer, or took with notice of the trust.[88]

The proprietary aspect of the trust beneficiary's interest is stressed particularly in the context of taxing statutes. In that context, the beneficiary is not asserting a right against the trustee but the right to, or enjoyment of, the beneficial interest. Hence, its taxability is in issue. Whether the interest is taxable depends upon the language of the particular statute.

The leading case in this context is *Baker v. Archer-Shee.*[89] Alfred Pell, a citizen of the United States, left the residue of his estate by his will upon trust (in the events which happened) to apply "the whole of the . . . income and profits . . .

---

83 [1933] 2 K.B. 79 (U.K. K.B.).

84 In certain situations the trust instrument may direct that the beneficiary be put in possession of specific property, in which case he or she would have access to the property directly. This might happen when the beneficiary is a life tenant of residential property. A situation similar to that in *Schalit* occurred in *Parker-Tweedale v. Dunbar Bank plc (No. 1)*, [1990] 2 All E.R. 577 (C.A.). The beneficiary of a trust of mortgaged property sued the mortgagee for breaching its duty in selling the property under its power of sale. The court held that the mortgagee owed such a duty only to the mortgagor-trustee.

85 See *Re Brockbank*, [1948] Ch. 206, [1948], All E.R. 287. The beneficiaries can apply to the court to have the trustee removed for breach of trust. This topic will be discussed later.

86 (1841), 4 Beav. 115, 49 E.R. 282, affirmed (1841), 1 Cr. & Ph. 240, 41 E.R. 482, [1835-42] All E.R. Rep. 58.

87 See *Re Smith*, [1928] 1 Ch. 915.

88 Tracing is discussed in the chapter on remedies for breach of trust.

89 [1927] A.C. 844 (H.L.).

to the use of my daughter Frances . . . during her life," with remainder over. The trust was situate in New York and the trustee was a New York trust company. The trust property consisted entirely of non-British securities. Frances was married to the respondent, Sir Martin Archer-Shee, in 1923 and he was assessed under the British *Income Tax Act, 1918*[90] for the income paid to Frances' use from the trust since the marriage. None of this income had ever been remitted to her in England, but had been paid by the trustee (less any sums required for American income tax and the trustee's fees and expenses) to her order at a New York bank.

Under the Act, a person resident in the United Kingdom was liable for tax on all "possessions out of the United Kingdom [including] stocks, shares, or rents in any place out of the United Kingdom" on which the taxpayer was entitled to receive and did receive the interest and dividends, but with respect to "possessions out of the United Kingdom other than stocks, shares, or rents" the tax liability extended only to "the full amounts of the actual sums annually received in the United Kingdom."[91]

The House of Lords assumed that the New York law of trusts (which governed under the rules of conflict of laws) was the same as English law. They held,[92] in effect rejecting Maitland's view, that Lady Archer-Shee was the beneficial owner of the securities themselves and Sir Martin was, thus, assessable on the income from them.

Lord Wrenbury said:[93]

> I have to read the will and see what is Lady Archer-Shee's right of property in certain ascertained securities, stocks and shares now held by the Trust Company "to the use of my said daughter." It is, I think, if the law of America is the same as our law, an equitable right in possession to receive during her life the proceeds of the shares and stocks of which she is tenant for life. Her right is not to a balance sum, but to the dividends subject to deductions as above mentioned. Her right under the will is "property" from which income is derived.

Lord Carson said:[94]

> [i]n my opinion upon the construction of the will of Alfred Pell once the residue had become specifically ascertained, the respondent's wife was sole beneficial owner of the interest and dividends of all the securities, stocks and shares forming part of the trust fund therein settled and was entitled to receive and did receive such interest and dividends. This, I think, follows from the decision of this House in *Williams v. Singer*,[95] and in my opinion the Master of the Rolls correctly stated the law when he said,[96]
>
> > . . . that in considering sums which are placed in the hands of trustees for the purpose of paying income to beneficiaries, for the purposes of the Income Tax Acts, you may eliminate

---

90 1918 (8 & 9 Geo. V), c. 40 (U.K.). Under s. 16 of the Act the income of a married woman living with her husband was deemed to be his and was assessed to him.
91 *Ibid.*, s. 1, Sched. D, Case V.
92 Viscount Sumner dissented.
93 *Supra*, note 89, at 866.
94 *Ibid.*, at 870.
95 [1927] 1 K.B. 109, at 123 (C.A.).
96 *Ibid.*

the trustees. The income is the income of the beneficiaries; the income does not belong to the trustees.

His Lordship said further:[97]

> [m]y Lords, I am unable to understand why or how the character of the sum paid to the respondent's wife ever became changed or, as the Master of the Rolls graphically says, "was no longer clothed in the form in which it was originally received, having no trace of its ancestry," simply because the deductions due by law have been made and because it has been mixed up with other trust moneys by the trustees. It is, in my view, in the same position as if the trustees had arranged to have the interest and dividends paid direct to the respondent's wife and she had discharged the necessary outgoings in accordance with the law. Whether the necessary outgoings according to law were discharged by the trustees or by the *cestui que trust* cannot, in my opinion, make any difference.

Baker v. Archer-Shee was decided on the assumption that the New York law of trusts was the same as English law. When Sir Martin was assessed again in a subsequent year for his wife's income from the New York trust, he appealed and Professor Powell gave expert evidence on his behalf to the effect that under New York law Maitland's view of the rights of a trust beneficiary prevailed, so that Lady Archer-Shee had only a right in equity to compel the trustee to fulfil its trusts and not a right to call for immediate payment of the income. Upon that evidence the House of Lords upheld the appeal and set aside the assessment.[98] It has been doubted that Professor Powell stated the law of New York correctly.[99]

Further Reading

Austin Wakeman Scott, "The Nature of the Rights of the *Cestui que Trust*" (1917), 17 Col. L. Rev. 269.

Harlan F. Stone, "The Nature of the Rights of the *Cestui que Trust*" (1917), 17 Col. L. Rev. 467.

D.W.M. Waters, "The Nature of the Trust Beneficiary's Interest" (1967), 45 Can. Bar Rev. 219.

M.A. Springham, "Trust Property and Execution against a Trust Beneficiary's Interest: Does the Writ Bind?" (1986), 19 E.T.R. 227.

Notes and Questions

1. The Supreme Court of Canada applied the foregoing principles in *Minister of National Revenue v. Trans-Canada Investment Corp. Ltd.*[100] The respondent company carried on business in British Columbia as the administrator of an investment trust. Pursuant to the trust agreement the respondent purchased common shares in selected Canadian corporations from time to time to constitute a "trust unit" and endorsed the share

---

97 *Supra*, note 89, at 871.

98 See *Archer-Shee v. Garland*, [1931] A.C. 212 (H.L.).

99 See Austin Wakeman Scott and William Franklin Fratcher, *The Law of Trusts*, 4th ed. (Boston: Little, Brown and Company, 1987-89), vol. 2, §130, at 414-415 ("Scott").

100 (1955), [1956] S.C.R. 49, [1955] 5 D.L.R. 576, [1955] C.T.C. 275.

certificates in favour of and delivered them to the trustee, which registered the shares in its name. The trustee would then issue certificates representing 1,000 undivided one-thousands' interests in the trust unit in denominations requested by the respondent and would deliver them to the respondent. The latter would deliver them to the purchasers of the certificates who were beneficiaries of the trust. The trustee, being the registered owner of the shares in the "underlying companies," received the semi-annual dividend payments and, after deducting the respondent's fee and its own fee and taxes, paid the net dividends out to the beneficiaries in proportion to the certificates held by them. The trust agreement permitted the beneficial owner of certificates representing 200 shares or multiples thereof to surrender his or her certificates to the trustee and demand a sale of shares in the underlying companies representing one-fifth of the trust unit or multiples thereof and payment of the proceeds, or a transfer of those shares. The respondent itself also held a certificate for 1,000 shares and in 1950 received net dividends thereon in the amount of $737.26 from the trustee. The respondent reported this amount as income in its tax return as dividends received from corporations resident in Canada, but claimed a deduction in like amount under section 27(1)(a) of *The Income Tax Act*,[101] a section designed to prevent double taxation by permitting a deduction of dividends paid by such corporations (which, of course, had already paid tax on their income). The Minister disallowed the deduction on the ground that it was not a dividend received from a corporation resident in Canada. The Income Tax Appeal Board disallowed the respondent's appeal, but its appeal to the Exchequer Court was allowed.[102]

Cameron J. held, first, that the payment to the respondent company was a *dividend* from a Canadian corporation not exempt from taxation. In that context his Lordship said:[103]

> From these facts, and particularly because he could at any time demand that the Trustee deliver to him his proper proportion of the shares in the "underlying companies," it seems to me that the holder of the [share] certificate was, in fact, the beneficial owner of the basic shares represented thereby. While he was not the registered owner, and although the administrator had the right to vote the said shares at any meeting of the "underlying companies," no one other than the holder of [the] certificates had any beneficial interest in such shares. The number of shares to which he was entitled in each company was fixed at the time he purchased the certificates, remained the same throughout, and he was entitled to physical possession thereof upon demand.
>
> Under these circumstances I do not think that the amounts which the appellant received were other than dividends from the "underlying companies." The majority decision of the House of Lords in *Archer-Shee v. Baker*[104] strongly supports that view.

Cameron J. further held that the moneys paid to the respondent were a dividend from a Canadian corporation. Having regard to the purpose of the legislation, (namely to prevent double taxation) the interposition of the trustee made no difference, for a direct payment by the corporation to the owner of the shares was not necessary.

The Supreme Court of Canada dismissed the Minister's appeal.

---

101 S.C. 1948, c. 52.

102 (Sub nom. *Trans-Canada Investment Corp. Ltd. v. Minister of National Revenue*), [1953] Ex. C.R. 292.

103 *Ibid.*, at 296-297.

104 [1927] A.C. 844 (H.L.).

It is clear from the *Trans-Canada Investment* case that the rights of the trust beneficiary under the trust depended in large part upon the interpretation of a statute which was
extraneous to that relationship.[105] Is this appropriate?

2. A testatrix left all her estate to her husband as trustee for her two children and
others and empowered him to carry on her business. The trustee did carry on the business
and allocated the net income therefrom to the two children who were entitled to it under
the will. The two children were assessed for investment income surtax on the net income
under section 32(3) of the *Income Tax Act*[106] which imposed such a tax. Subsection (4)
defined "investment income" for this purpose as the income of a taxpayer "for the taxation
year less the aggregate of the earned income for the year. . . ." Subsection (5)(b) defined
"earned income" as "income from carrying on of a business either alone or as a partner
actively engaged in the business."

Were the two children liable for the surtax?[107]

3. So far we have assumed that a trust beneficiary has both a right against the trustee
to ensure due administration, which is an equitable chose in action, and a proprietary
interest in the trust property. However, only one or the other is likely to be relevant in any
particular case. Further, it is not always true that a trust beneficiary has a proprietary
interest. Thus, a beneficiary under a discretionary trust has no interest in the *corpus* unless
and until the trustee appoints property to him or her.[108] It follows that such a beneficiary
does not have an interest to assign. At most the beneficiary has a *spes successionis*. The
beneficiary can, however, release his or her rights.[109]

On the other hand, a beneficiary under a discretionary trust would seem to have
standing to trace trust property in the hands of third persons who are not *bona fide*
purchasers for value without notice and, thus, probably has a quasi-property interest.
However, the property is recovered for the trust, not for the beneficiary personally.[110]

4. A trust beneficiary's proprietary right is emphasized where the beneficiary seeks
to enforce his or her rights against the trustees and the property is situate in one jurisdiction
while the trustees are in another. In that situation the action may be brought where the
property is situate if the beneficiary's rights are closely associated with the property. This
would be the case if the beneficiary is entitled in remainder to certain real property under
the trust. If his or her rights are not property-specific, however, the action must be brought
where the trustee is.[111]

5. The problem about the *locus* of the proprietary interest is that it must rest some-
where, for the law abhors a vacuum. It cannot reside in the trustee, unless that person is
also a beneficiary. In a fixed trust, the property interest resides in the beneficiaries. In a
discretionary trust the matter is more problematic, but the interest can be said to reside in

---

105 See also *Pan American Trust Company v. Minister of National Revenue*, [1949-50] 49 D.T.C.
     672 (Ex. Ct.).

106 R.S.C. 1952, c. 148.

107 See *Quinn v. M.N.R.; Shortt v. M.N.R.*, [1960] Ex. C.R. 414, [1960] C.T.C. 78.

108 See, *e.g.*, *Ontario (Ministry of Community & Social Services) v. Henson* (1989), 36 E.T.R. 192
     (Ont. C.A.).

109 *Re Gulbenkian's Settlements (No. 2)*, [1970] Ch. 408.

110 See H.A.J. Ford and W.A. Lee, assisted by Peter M. McDermott, *Principles of the Law of
     Trusts*, 3rd ed. (Sydney: L.B.C. Information Services, 1996), §1790 ("Ford and Lee"), who
     state this proposition by analogy to the right of the beneficiary of an unadministered estate to
     recover estate assets. Such a beneficiary asserts "the estate's right of property" according to
     Commissioner of Stamp Duties v. Livingston, [1965] A.C. 694 at 714, [1964] 3 All E.R. 692
     (P.C.).

111 Ford and Lee, §1800.

all the beneficiaries on the ground that they can enforce due administration, can trace property for the trust and can, if they are all *sui juris* and solely entitled, together end the trust. In the case of a mere power, that is, one which the trustee does not have to exercise, the property interest resides either in the settlor under a resulting trust, or else in persons to whom the settlor has given the property expressly or impliedly in default of appointment.[112]

6. A testator owned property in the United States and in Hong Kong. He made two wills. One disposed of his Hong Kong property, the other disposed of his American property. He appointed X his American trustee and Y his Hong Kong trustee. The testator directed that if he owned a house in Hong Kong on his death and either or both his sister and brother survived him, X would have no duty with respect to the house until he received the proceeds of sale from Y, or until the death of the survivor of the brother and sister. By a trust for sale with a power to postpone sale, the testator directed Y to sell the house and transfer the proceeds to X. When the testator died, his brother and sister were living in his Hong Kong house rent free and continued to do so after his death. The testator's sons were the beneficiaries under his American will. They instructed Y to sell the Hong Kong house and pay the proceeds to X. X countermanded the order out of regard for the testator's elderly brother and sister. Subsequently, the value of the house dropped.

Could the testator's sons direct Y to sell the house? Are either or both X and Y liable to the testator's sons for the decrease in value of the asset?[113]

7. Another situation in which the nature of the trust beneficiary's interest may arise is in proceedings to equalize net family properties or with proceedings to divide family assets. The issue arose in *Brinkos v. Brinkos.*[114] Mrs. Brinkos had settled moneys received from her parents, before and after her marriage, in a trust under which she was entitled to an inalienable life interest in the net income. Mrs. Brinkos brought proceedings for divorce and related relief. The court had to decide whether the entitlement to the future income from the trust was "property" under the *Family Law Act.*[115] Section 4(1) of the Act defines "property" as "any interest, present or future, vested or contingent, in real or personal property. . . ." The court followed *Archer-Shee* in concluding that Mrs. Brinkos' beneficial interest was indeed property. As a result, she had to bring a portion of the capitalized present value of the income stream into her net family property.

(c) The Estate Beneficiary

The position of the trust beneficiary must be distinguished from the beneficiary under an unadministered estate. Such a beneficiary appears to have only a personal right against the personal representatives of the deceased until administration of the estate is complete.

---

112 *Ibid*, §150. See also D.W. Maclean, *Trusts and Powers* (Sydney: The Law Book Company Limited, 1989), pp. 25ff.

113 See *Hayim v. Citibank N.A.*, [1987] A.C. 730 (P.C.).

114 (1989), 60 D.L.R. (4th) 556, 20 R.F.L. (3d) 445, 69 O.R. (2d) 225 (C.A.), additional reasons at (1989), 69 O.R. (2d) 798, 61 D.L.R. (4th) 766 (C.A.), further additional reasons at (1989), 69 O.R. (2d) 798 at 800, 61 D.L.R. (4th) 766 at 768 (C.A.). For an application of the principles established in *Brinkos*, see *Clarke v. Read Estate* (2000), 2000 CarswellOnt 3028, [2000] O.J. No. 4155, 12 R.F.L. (5th) 305, 37 E.T.R. (2d) 13 (S.C.J.), additional reasons at (2001), 2001 CarswellOnt 597 (S.C.J.).

115 R.S.O. 1990, c. F.3.

The leading case on this issue is *Commissioner of Stamp Duties (Queensland) v. Livingston*.[116] A testator, D.H. Livingston, died domiciled in New South Wales owning real and personal property in that state and in Queensland. By the residuary clause in his will, he left his real estate and the residue of his personal estate to his executors upon trust as to one-third for his widow. She was remarried to a Mr. Coulson and died intestate shortly thereafter, domiciled in New South Wales. At the time of her death, her first husband's estate had not yet been fully administered. The appellant Commissioner claimed that the respondent, Livingston, Mrs. Coulson's administrator and one of her next of kin, was liable to pay succession duty and administration duty on Mrs. Coulson's share of the testator's Queensland assets. To be liable, Mrs. Coulson would have to have had a "beneficial interest" in the property on her death under the applicable statutes. No letters of administration for Mrs. Coulson's estate were granted or resealed in Queensland because she had no assets there other than those, if any, to which she was entitled under her first husband's will.

The Privy Council concluded that Mrs. Coulson did not have a beneficial interest in the Queensland property and was, thus, not liable to pay the duties claimed. Viscount Radcliffe, who delivered the Board's opinion, said:[117]

[w]hen Mrs. Coulson died she had the interest of a residuary legatee in the testator's unadministered estate. The nature of that interest has been conclusively defined by decisions of long-established authority, and its definition no doubt depends upon the peculiar status which the law accorded to an executor for the purposes of carrying out his duties of administration. There were special rules which long prevailed about the devolution of freehold land and its liability for the debts of a deceased, but subject to the working of these rules whatever property came to the executor virtute officii came to him in full ownership, without distinction between legal and equitable interests. The whole property was his. He held it for the purpose of carrying out the functions and duties of administration, not for his own benefit; and these duties would be enforced upon him by the Court of Chancery, if application had to be made for that purpose by a creditor or beneficiary interested in the estate. Certainly, therefore, he was in a fiduciary position with regard to the assets that came to him in the right of his office, and for certain purposes and in some aspects he was treated by the court as a trustee. "An executor," said Kay J. in *In re Marsden*,[118] "is personally liable in equity for all breaches of the ordinary trusts which in Courts of Equity are considered to arise from his office." He is a trustee "in this sense."

It may not be possible to state exhaustively what those trusts are at any one moment. Essentially, they are trusts to preserve the assets, to deal properly with them, and to apply them in a due course of administration for the benefit of those interested according to that course, creditors, the death duty authorities, legatees of various sorts, and the residuary beneficiaries. They might just as well have been termed "duties in respect of the assets" as trusts. What equity did not do was to recognise or create for residuary legatees a beneficial interest in the assets in the executor's hands during the course of administration. Conceivably, this could have been done, in the sense that the assets, whatever they might be from time to time, could have been treated as a present, though fluctuating, trust fund held for the benefit of all those interested in the estate according to the measure of their respective interests. But it never was done. It would have been a clumsy and unsatisfactory device from a practical point of view; and, indeed, it would have been in plain conflict with the basic conception of equity that to impose the fetters of a trust upon property, with the resulting creation of equitable interests in that property, there had to be specific

---

116 [1965] A.C. 694, [1964] 3 All E.R. 692 (P.C.).
117 *Ibid.*, at A.C. 707-708.
118 (1884), 26 Ch. D. 783 at 789.

subjects identifiable as the trust fund. An unadministered estate was incapable of satisfying this requirement. The assets as a whole were in the hands of the executor, his property; and until administration was complete no one was in a position to say what items of property would need to be realised for the purposes of that administration or of what the residue, when ascertained, would consist or what its value would be. Even in modern economies, when the ready marketability of many forms of property can almost be assumed, valuation and realisation are very far from being interchangeable terms.

At the date of Mrs. Coulson's death, therefore, there was no trust fund consisting of Mr. Livingston's residuary estate in which she could be said to have any beneficial interest, because no trust had as yet come into existence to affect the assets of his estate. The relation of her estate to his was . . . that . . . Mr. Livingston's property in Queensland, real or personal, was vested in his executors in full right, and no beneficial property interest in any item of it belonged to Mrs. Coulson at the date of her death.

His Lordship then dealt with the argument that the residuary legatee must have the beneficial interest since it cannot reside in the personal representative. On this point he said:[119]

[w]here, it is asked, is the beneficial interest in those assets during the period of administration? It is not, ex hypothesi, in the executor: where else can it be but in the residuary legatee? This dilemma is founded on a fallacy, for it assumes mistakenly that for all purposes and at every moment of time the law requires the separate existence of two different kinds of estate or interest in property, the legal and the equitable. There is no need to make this assumption. When the whole right of property is in a person, as it is in an executor, there is no need to distinguish between the legal and equitable interest in that property, any more than there is for the property of a full beneficial owner. What matters is that the court will control the executor in the use of his rights over assets that come to him in that capacity; but it will do it by the enforcement of remedies which do not involve the admission or recognition of equitable rights of property in those assets. Equity in fact calls into existence and protects equitable rights and interests in property only where their recognition has been found to be required in order to give effect to its doctrines.

. . .

Therefore, while it may well be said in a general way that a residuary legatee has an interest in the totality of the assets (though that proposition in itself raises the question what is the local situation of the "totality"), it is in their Lordships' opinion inadmissible to proceed from that to the statement that such a person has an equitable interest in any particular one of those assets. . .

And:[120]

It is not enough for this purpose to speak of an "interest" in a general or popular sense.

. . .

[T]heir Lordships regard it as clearly established that Mrs. Coulson was not entitled to any beneficial interest in any property in Queensland at the date of her death. What she was entitled to in respect of her rights under her deceased husband's will was a chose in action, capable of being invoked for any purpose connected with the proper administration of his estate; and the local situation of this asset, as much under Queensland law as any other law, was in New South Wales, where the testator had been domiciled and his executors resided and which constituted the proper forum of administration of his estate.

---

119 *Supra*, note 116, at A.C. 712-713.
120 *Ibid.*, at A.C. 716-717.

The implications of the *Livingston* case and of the distinction between the rights of a beneficiary under a trust and the rights of a person in an unadministered estate will be explored further in the Notes and Questions below.

Notes and Questions

1. The opinion of the Privy Council in *Commissioner of Stamp Duties v. Livingston*[121] on the position of the beneficiary of an unadministered estate was foreshadowed in *Sudeley v. Attorney-General*,[122] which was followed in *Fitzgerald v. Minister of National Revenue*.[123] The latter case involved the following facts.

Adolphus Williams died domiciled in British Columbia in 1921. His estate consisted mostly of real property situate in British Columbia. By his will he left one-half of his estate or $150,000, whichever was larger, to his widow, Katherine. She died domiciled in British Columbia in 1924, having received income, but no capital, from her husband's estate. By her will all her property went to her sister, Bonnie Steed, who died domiciled in California in 1941. Bonnie left all her property by will to her husband, George. He died domiciled in California in 1944, leaving all his property by will to his nephew, James Raeburn. The latter died shortly after his uncle and left his property by will to members of his family. The executor of Adolphus Williams finally sold the real property in 1945 and realized $250,000 from the sale. Fitzgerald was Bonnie Steed's administrator. Walsh was the ancillary administrator of that estate in British Columbia and the sole surviving executor of the Adolphus and Katherine Williams' estates.

The Minister of National Revenue assessed duties on the succession from George Steed to James Raeburn and on the succession from the latter to his family under *The Dominion Succession Duty Act*.[124] The Act came into force shortly after Bonnie Steed's death in 1941. Section 6(b) of the Act levied duty on "the succession to all property situated in Canada" where the deceased was domiciled in Canada. "Property" was defined by s. 2(k) as including:

> . . . property, real or personal, movable or immovable, of every description, and every estate and interest therein or income therefrom capable of being devised or bequeathed by will or of passing on the death, and any right or benefit mentioned in section 3 of this Act.

The Supreme Court held that there was no "property situated in Canada" because neither George Steed nor James Raeburn had the interest in property required for that purpose by s. 2(b). All that passed on their deaths was a right to have Bonnie Steed's estate administered. That right was a chose in action enforceable in her domicile, that is, California, and not in British Columbia.[125]

2. It is clear from *Steed*[126] and *Livingston*[127] that equity regards the personal representatives to an unadministered estate as having the whole, unfragmented title to a deceased's

---

121 *Supra*, note 116.
122 [1897] A.C. 11 (P.C.).
123 [1949] S.C.R. 453.
124 S.C. 1940-41, c. 14.
125 See also *Conetta v. Conetta*, [1990] O.J. No. 1112 (Ont. Dist. Ct.); *Re Gareau Estate* (1990), 9 E.T.R. (2d) 25 (Ont. Gen. Div.), additional reasons at (1996), 13 E.T.R. (2d) 316 (Ont. Gen. Div.).
126 *Supra*, note 123.
127 *Supra*, note 116.

assets. The beneficiaries do not have an equitable interest. Is this a good approach? Why can one not say that the beneficiaries have an equitable interest since it is clear that the personal representatives do not have title for their own benefit?

In the two cases mentioned, this approach worked to the advantage of the beneficiary. But it can also work to his or her disadvantage. *Eastbourne Mutual Building Society v. Hastings (Borough)*[128] is an example. A person owned a house and died intestate. Her husband continued to live in the house. The property was then expropriated and under the applicable expropriation statute[129] the expropriating authority only had to pay for the value of the land and not for the value of the house on it unless it was occupied by a member of the owner's family who was entitled to an interest in it. The court held that the husband, although he was the sole heir of his deceased wife, did not have an interest in the house because he was a beneficiary under an unadministered estate.

Lall v. Lall[130] is another example. The defendant claimed that her son, the plaintiff, held the house in which she was living in trust for his father's estate. If that were true, she would be entitled to it as beneficiary of her husband's estate. However, the court held that she had no standing to contest the son's proceedings for possession since she had no equitable interest in the property.[131]

3. The beneficiary of an unadministered estate does not have an equitable property interest but does have an interest sufficient to be able to transmit it to another on death.[132] This is implicit in the *Steed* case,[133] but the point was dealt with expressly in *Re Leigh's Will Trusts, Handyside v. Durbridge*.[134]

Mr. Leigh owned a controlling interest in a company. The company also owed him a certain sum of money on a loan. He died intestate and his widow was his sole administratrix and beneficiary. By her will she left all the shares and any other interest she had in the company to X. When she died her husband's estate was not yet fully administered. The court held that she transmitted the chose in action that she held to her executor. In other words, she transmitted to her executor the right to require the administrator of her husband's estate to administer the estate appropriately, consistent with the rights of others. Further, she effectively directed her executor to procure the shares and the debt when and if possible.

Some cases regard the beneficiary's equitable right to compel an executor properly to administer the estate as an asset of the estate.[135]

4. Although the *Leigh* case was mentioned, *Livingston* was followed instead in *Farrell v. Farrell*.[136] Mr. Farrell conveyed a parcel of land to his son Gerald. Then he made his will by which he gave the remainder of his real property equally to his two other sons, Philip and Joseph, and he gave the residue to Joseph. Gerald then died intestate and his father was his sole beneficiary. When Mr. Farrell died, Gerald's estate was not yet admin-

---

128 [1965] 1 All E.R. 779, [1965] 1 W.L.R. 861 (Ch. Div.).

129 *Housing Act, 1957*, (5 & 6 Eliz. 1), c. 56, s. 61 (U.K.).

130 [1965] 3 All E.R. 330.

131 See also *Barclay v. Barclay*, [1970] 2 Q.B. 677, [1970] 2 All E.R. 676 (C.A.).

132 Thus, the estate beneficiary's position differs from that of a beneficiary under a discretionary trust, discussed above.

133 *Supra*, note 123.

134 [1970] Ch. 277, [1969] 3 All E.R. 432.

135 See *R. v. Eide*, [1974] C.T.C. 353, 74 D.T.C. 6286 (Fed. Ct.); *Covert v. Nova Scotia (Minister of Finance)*, [1980] 2 S.C.R. 774; *Christie v. Minister of National Revenue*, [1968] 2 Ex. C.R. 544, [1968] C.T.C. 371, 68 D.T.C. 5240 (Ex. Ct.). See also *Earnshaw v. Hartley*, [2000] Ch. 15, with respect to the application of the *Statute of Limitations* to the beneficiary's interest.

136 (1983), 16 E.T.R. 310, 44 Nfld. & P.E.I.R. 251, 130 A.P.R. 251 (Nfld. T.D.).

istered and the question arose whether Philip and Joseph took Gerald's parcel of land equally or whether it went solely to Joseph. The court held that Gerald's land had not vested in Mr. Farrell when the latter died. All he and, consequently, his executor had, was a right against Gerald's personal representative to the due administration of Gerald's estate. Gerald's personal representative had title to it and when Gerald's estate was administered, title would pass to the father's estate and go out under the residuary clause to Joseph.

Which approach is correct, that of *Leigh* or that of *Farrell*? If the former, can *Farrell* be justified on the basis that the testator only meant to give Philip and Joseph whatever real property he had left when he made his will?

In *Quinan v. MacKinnon*,[137] the court followed *Farrell* in holding that land does not become part of the assets of the heir unless it has been conveyed to the heir by a duly appointed administrator.

5. The issue also arose in *Ogilvie-Five Roses Sales Ltd. v. Hawkins*.[138] A father, I, died intestate years ago, survived by his widow, W, and five children. I owned a farm and W continued to live on it and to farm it for several years, until her two eldest sons, A and B, took over the farming. The children who, with W, were I's heirs intended to assign their interests to their mother, but no formal assignments in her favour were registered until much later, when title was transmitted to (that is, registered in the name of) W. Prior to the registration of the transmission, O Ltd. had filed two caveats against the title. O Ltd. was a creditor of A and the caveats sought to attach A's interest in the land. Under the applicable recording statute, an execution creditor was permitted to file a caveat against the title of lands in which the debtor "is interested beneficially." The court held that, because A was a residuary beneficiary of an unadministered estate, he had no proprietary interest in any asset to which the caveats could attach.

6. *Mugford v. Mugford*[139] is to the same effect. The plaintiff sought a declaration that he enjoyed a legal interest in certain lands that made up part of his grandfather's estate. The estate had never been fully administered. The plaintiff had previously acquired whatever interest his father had in the disputed land. The court held that the plaintiff had no legal interest in the land and, therefore, no standing to bring the action. The interest which his father Mugford had and the only interest he could pass on to his son or to anyone else was an interest in the estate of his father, the plaintiff's grandfather. That interest was a chose in action; a right to have the estate administered according to law and to receive a distributive portion of the estate when the debts and other costs of the estate had been discharged.

See also *Petten v. Petten*,[140] in which the court followed *Mugford* and held that an individual with an interest in an unadministered estate did not have standing to bring an action with respect to a dispute arising over property.

7. The Federal Court of Appeal took a different view in *Boger Estate v. Minister of National Revenue*.[141] The testator's children claimed a "farm roll over" of farm land and equipment bequeathed by their father. Section 70(9) of the *Income Tax Act*[142] permits land

---

137 [2001] P.E.I.J. No. 15, 2001 CarswellPEI 16, 2001 PESCTD 14 (T.D.).

138 (1979), 9 Alta. L.R. 271, 8 R.P.R. 244, 4 E.T.R. 163 (T.D.).

139 (1992), 49 E.T.R. 229, 103 Nfld. & P.E.I.R. 136, 326 A.P.R. 136 (Nfld. C.A.).

140 (1999), [1999] N.J. No. 117, 1999 CarswellNfld 104, 177 Nfld. & P.E.I.R. 1, 543 A.P.R. 1 (T.D.).

141 (1993), 50 E.T.R. 1, 155 N.R. 303, 65 F.T.R. 160 (note), [1993] 2 C.T.C. 81, (sub nom. *R. v. Boger Estate*) 93 D.T.C. 5276 (Fed. C.A.).

142 R.S.C. 1985, c. 1 (5th Supp.).

and depreciable property used in the business of farming to be transferred or distributed to a child of the taxpayer within 15 months of the death of the taxpayer without attracting liability for income tax. The court had to decide whether the property had been "transferred or distributed" to the children within the meaning of the Act. Revenue Canada argued that the reasoning in *Livingston* should apply; there had been no transfer or distribution to the beneficiaries until the administration of the estate had been completed and title had been conveyed to the beneficiaries. Since the estate had not been fully administered at the time the rollover was claimed, it should be disallowed. The court rejected this argument and held that, in the province of Alberta, beneficial entitlement arose on death, in spite of jurisprudence to the contrary in other jurisdictions. The decision was based on the court's interpretation of s. 3 of the *Devolution of Real Property Act*[143] read in conjunction with ss. 9 and 10(1) of that Act.[144]

Is the case correct?[145]

8. H and W were married. Then H's mother died, naming him executor and trustee. The mother left H and his brother shares in the residue of the estate which included a home. H and W moved into the house and used it as their matrimonial home for three years, when they separated. Shortly thereafter, H obtained letters probate of the will and transferred title to the house to himself and his brother. W brought equalization proceedings under the *Family Law Act*.[146] Does H have to include the value of the house in his net family property?[147]

9. The cases on the rights of a beneficiary under an unadministered estate are all concerned with residuary beneficiaries. The view that such beneficiaries have no beneficial interest in the estate assets until administration is complete has some merit. This is because, until the personal representative has paid the debts and expenses, transferred specific bequests and devises, paid general legacies and established trusts as directed by the will, it is not known whether there will be any residue.

Can the same be said of specific legatees? A specific legatee is entitled to the specific item of property bequeathed or devised and, hence, it might be possible to say that the legatee has an equitable interest in it. The *Livingston* case[148] and *Re Leigh*[149] only spoke of residuary beneficiaries when enunciating the rules for which those cases stand. By

---

143 R.S.A. 2000, c. D-12.

144 Section 3 provides:

> 3. . . . the personal representative of a deceased person holds the real property as trustee for the persons ... beneficially entitled to it...

> Sections 9 and 10(1) of the Act read as follows:

> 9. The personal representative may sell the real property for the purpose not only of paying debts, but also of distributing the estate among the persons beneficially entitled to it, whether there are or are not debts, and it is not necessary for the persons beneficially entitled to concur in any sale except when it is made for the purpose of distribution only.

> 10. (1) Subject to this Act, no sale of real property for the purpose of distribution only is valid as respects any person beneficially interested, unless that person, or that person's trustee pursuant to the *Dependent Adults Act*, concurs in the sale.

145 For the traditional view, see *Re Curlett Estate* (1995), 36 Alta. L. R. (3d) 196, 11 E.T.R. (2d) 18, [1996] 3 W.W.R. 545 (Surr. Ct.).

146 R.S.O. 1990, c. F.3.

147 See *Gennaro v. Gennaro* (1994), 2 R.F.L. (4th) 179, 111 D.L.R. (4th) 379 (Ont. U.F.C.); A. H. Oosterhoff, Case Comment, *ibid.*, at 184.

148 [1965] A.C. 694, [1964] 3 All E.R. 692 (P.C.).

149 [1970] Ch. 277, [1969] 3 All E.R. 432.

contrast, in *Re Hayes' Will Trusts*[150] Ungoed-Thomas J. noted in *dictum* that no beneficiary of an estate has a beneficial interest in the assets under administration. The point also came up in *Kavanagh v. Best*[151] but did not have to be decided. However, Gibson J. stated that a specific legatee knows from the outset what asset he or she is entitled to and need not wait until administration is complete for that purpose. While this is so, specific bequests and devises are available for the payment of debts, albeit after residuary and general legacies. Hence, at least until the debts are paid the beneficiary will not know whether he or she will actually get the property.

10. Once an estate has been fully administered and the residue ascertained, the personal representative holds the residue in trust for the residuary beneficiary.[152] It follows that, if the residuary beneficiary dies after that date but before distribution, his or her interest is a proprietary interest in the property, sufficient to attract estate tax on death.[153]

8. THE TRUST IN CIVIL LAW

(a) Generally

We noted at the beginning of this chapter that the trust is an institution peculiar to the common law. This is because the rules of equity permit ownership to be split between the trustees and the beneficiaries, so that the trustees hold title to certain property for the benefit of the beneficiaries. The latter have title in equity but for most purposes their rights are protected because they can force the trustees to administer the trust properly. Because the trust was received into most former British colonies and because it is widely used throughout the world for many different purposes, including commercial ones, civil law jurisdictions have had to take cognizance of the trust and, in some cases, to adopt it.

The difficulties of incorporating the trust into a civil law system will be explored in this part; the problem respecting inter-jurisdictional uses of the trust will be dealt with below.

One of the main reasons why the trust works is because the common law permits fragmentation of title or ownership by the theory of estates. In particular, it recognizes the titles of both trustees and beneficiaries. The civil law, on the other hand, only knows absolute ownership of property. It follows that in civil law only one person[154] can be owner and have all the rights of ownership. In the context of trusts, the civil law would say that this person would have to be the beneficiary since the trustees do not have title for their own benefit.

This does not mean that the civil law does not recognize the position of a fiduciary; it does, but the term denotes something entirely different from that understood in the common law. Thus, the civil law recognizes representative offices, such as executorship, tutorship and curatorship. The civil law also recognizes a limited number of "real rights" which include the usufruct. The latter

---

150 [1971] 1 W.L.R. 758 at 765, [1971] 2 All E.R. 341.
151 [1971] N.I. 89.
152 *Dr. Barnardo's Homes v. Special Income Tax Commissioners*, [1921] 2 A.C. 1 (H.L.).
153 *R. v. Myre* (1974), 46 D.L.R. (3d) 298 (Fed. T.D.).
154 This statement is somewhat simplistic, for the civil law recognizes the concept of co-ownership.

is similar to the common law life estate. Yet in all these situations, there is but the one owner and it is not the "fiduciary," but rather the person who has the "beneficial interest" in the property. It may be that the latter has to admit of rights with respect to his or her property held by others, such as the usufructuary's right to enjoy the property which is owned absolutely by the "successors," but that does not diminish the latter's ownership.[155]

There has been substantial interaction between the common and the civil law in a number of jurisdictions. This is because (1) the jurisdiction had originally adopted the civil law and certain aspects of the common law were superimposed upon it consequent upon the conquest of the jurisdiction by Great Britain; (2) the jurisdiction is surrounded by common law jurisdictions and strongly influenced by the common law; or (3) trade or tax implications make the adoption of certain common law concepts desirable.[156]

South Africa and Sri Lanka fall into the first category. The law of both jurisdictions is Roman-Dutch law, but the English trust has found ready acceptance.[157] The law of trusts has been incorporated in a statute in Sri Lanka.[158]

To some extent, the Philippines are in a similar position. Its law is civil, being Spanish in origin. However, because of American influence, the trust has made substantial inroads into its law.[159]

Quebec and Louisiana fall into the second category. The law in both jurisdictions is civil, being French in origin, and is comprehended in civil codes which are derived from the Napoleonic Code. Because of the interaction between the legal systems of Quebec and the other Canadian jurisdictions, the reception of the trust in the former will be considered in more detail below.

In Louisiana the trust was first introduced by statute in 1920. The concept was broadened by a more comprehensive statute in 1938, and the subject was incorporated into the *Louisiana Trust Code*[160] in 1964.[161] The adoption of trusts

---

155 Pierre Lepaulle, "Civil Law Substitutes for Trusts" (1927), 36 Yale L.J. 1126; V. Bolgar, "Why No Trusts in the Civil Law?" (1953), 2 Am. J. Comp. L. 204; Jaro Mayda, "'Trusts' and 'Living Law' in Europe" (1955), 103 U. of Pa. L. Rev. 1041; W.A. Wilson, ed., *Trusts and Trust-Like Devices* (London: Chameleon Press, 1981).

156 See Sir Maurice Amos, "The Common Law and the Civil Law in the British Commonwealth" (1937), 50 Harv. L. Rev. 1249; George Keeton and L.A. Sheridan, "The Comparative Law of Trusts in the Commonwealth and the Irish Republic" (Chichester: Barry Rose, 1976).

157 See Tanbyah Madaraja, *The Roman-Dutch Law as Applied in Ceylon and South Africa* (Colombo: Associated Newspapers of Ceylon, 1949); B. Beinart, "Trusts in Roman-Dutch Law" (1980), 1 J. Leg. Hist. 6; A.M. Honoré, "The South African Law of Trusts," [1969] Cam. L.J. 301; L.S.M. Cooray, *The Reception in Ceylon of the English Trust* (Colombo: Lake House Printers and Publishers, 1971); H.R. Hahlo, "The Trust in South African Law" (1961), 78 S.A.L.J. 195.

158 Ceylon Ord. 1917, No. 9; Ceylon, Legislative Enactments, 1956, c. 87.

159 See Scott, §1.9, fn. 1.

160 La. Rev. Stats, §§9:1721-9:2252.

161 Scott, §1.10.

into a civil law system is not without its problems as the Louisiana experience shows.[162]

Jersey and some Latin American countries fall into the third category. Jersey is a civil law jurisdiction but it is subject to the British Crown. It has become a tax haven for wealthy British and their trusts. For that reason it enacted a comprehensive trust statute in 1984.[163] The statute is based largely upon the English law of trusts and does not purport to be a codification.[164]

The trust has also made some inroads into Mexico and other Latin American countries — all civil law jurisdictions — because of trade connections with the United States.[165]

The difficulty with the recognition and application of the trust concept in a civilian jurisdiction is that it is foreign to a civilian's training and does not fit within the framework of the civil law. Civil lawyers, therefore, usually attempt to fit the trust into some civil law construct in order to understand it. It has been suggested that it is also necessary for a lawyer from the common law world to do this when called upon to support the validity of a trust in a civil law jurisdiction.[166] While this is not ideal, it may be the best solution until the trust is generally recognized for conflict of laws purposes as a *sui generis* institution. In any event, the incorporation of trusts legislation into a civil law system remains fraught with difficulties and is regarded warily by civilians who fear the implications upon the rest of their laws.[167]

Further Reading

D.M.W. Waters, *Law of Trusts in Canada*, 2nd ed. (Toronto: Carswell, 1984), at 14-16, 1089-96.

Donovan W.M. Waters, "The Institution of the Trust in Civil and Common Law", in Hague Academy of International Law, *Recueil des Cours 1995*, 113.

---

162 See, *e.g.*, John Minor Wisdom, "A Trusts Code in the Civil Law, Based on the Restatement and Uniform Acts: The Louisiana Trust Estates Act" (1938), 13 Tulane L. Rev. 70; Leon O'Quinn, "Our Trust Estates and Their Limitations" (1948), 22 Tulane L. Rev. 585; Leonard Oppenheim, "A New Trust Code for Louisiana" (1965), 39 Tulane L. Rev. 187. See also Jose R. Cortina, "The Jus Emphyteuticarum and Trust: A Byzantine Solution for an Acadian Problem" (1982), 8 So. Univ. L. Rev. 85; Gerald Le Van, "Louisiana Counterparts to Legal and Equitable Title" (1981), 41 La. L. Rev. 1977; Thomas B. Lemann, "Conditional Substitutions in Trusts" (1976), 50 Tulane L. Rev. 346.

163 *Trusts (Jersey) Law, 1984*, Jersey Laws 1984, No. 11.

164 *Ibid.*, art. 1(5).

165 Ruford G. Patton, "Future of Trusts Legislation in Latin America" (1946), 20 Tulane L. Rev. 542; R. Batiza, "Trust Business in Mexico" (1958), 97 Trusts and Estates 69.

166 See J.A. Schoenblum, *Multistate and Multinational Estate Planning* (Boston: Little, Brown and Company, 1982), vol. 1, at 722. See also D.W.M. Waters, "The Common Law Trust in the Modern World" (1984), Forum Internationale, No. 5.

167 The introduction of the trust into civil law has been likened to the cuckoo which lays its egg in another bird's nest and then abandons it. When the egg hatches, the cuckoo chick has the nasty habit of ousting the other chicks. Having done so, it is then nurtured by its foster parents. See Amos, *op. cit.*, at 50 Harv. L. Rev. 1263.

Austin Wakeman Scott and William Franklin Fratcher, *The Law of Trusts*, 4th ed. (Boston: Little, Brown and Company, 1987-89), §§1.9, 1.10.

(b) Quebec

(i) *History*

Quebec adopted a statutory version of the trust in 1879[168] and this version was incorporated into the *Civil Code of Lower Canada* in 1888.[169] While this trust code has been superseded, as related below, not all the problems associated with it have been overcome. It is, therefore, useful to consider briefly the terms and the various interpretations of the "old trust."

Articles 981a to 981n, which contained the old trust code, did not, by any means, adopt the common law trust and have generally been construed strictly. Moreover, they attempted to mould the trust into civil law concepts.

Article 981a provided that persons could convey property to trustees by gift or will for the benefit of other persons. Article 981b stated that trustees were seized as depositaries and administrators for the benefit of the donees or legatees, could claim possession of the property and could sue and be sued in respect of it. These two articles were the most important ones. The others made provision for the replacement, removal, duties and powers of trustees. Article 981f illustrated a difference from the common law trust in that it permitted the majority of several trustees to act unless the trust instrument provided otherwise. Further, art. 981i provided that trustees were not personally liable to third parties with whom they contracted.

Much has been written on the nature of the old Quebec trust and the interpretation of articles 981a to 981n.[170] A synopsis of the various views with reference to the leading cases follows.

One of the main difficulties with the old Quebec trust was that the articles were so brief and unclear. Since they were part of the *Civil Code*, they had to be interpreted in its context. While the Supreme Court of Canada has said that reference could be had to English law to assist in interpreting the articles, this was only allowed if that law was compatible with the articles.[171] The English law of trusts was adopted only to a limited extent, namely as expressed in articles 981a-981n.[172]

---

168 By *An Act Concerning the Trust*, S.Q. 1879, c. 29.

169 See R.S.Q. 1888, art. 5803. The *Civil Code of Lower Canada* is hereafter referred to as "CCLC."

170 See *e.g.*, R.H. Mankiewicz, "La Fiducie Québécoise et le Trust de Common Law" (1952), 12 R. du. B. 16; D.N. Mattarlin, "The Quebec Trust and the Civil Law" (1975), 21 McGill L.J. 175; Y. Caron, "The Trust in Quebec" (1980), 25 McGill L.J. 421; A.J. McClean, "The Common Law and the Quebec Trusts — Some Comparisons" (1967), U.B.C.L.R. Centennial ed. 333; *ibid.*, "The Quebec Trust: Role Rich and Principle Poor?" (1984), 29 McGill L.J. 312. For a more complete bibliography, see Waters, *Trusts*, ch. 28.

171 *Royal Trust Co. v. Tucker*, [1982] 1 S.C.R. 250 at 261, 12 E.T.R. 257, *per* Beetz J.

172 *Laverdure v. Du Tremblay*, [1937] A.C. 666 at 682 (P.C.).

Another main problem with the old trust derives from the civil law's idea of property. The civil law does not recognize the fragmentation of ownership among several persons. Rather, the civil law views ownership of property as single and indivisible. Thus, the bifurcation of ownership between trustee and beneficiary in the common law is an unacceptable concept in civil law. This poses problems when deciding who should hold title. The old trust did not deal with this issue.

As distinct from the common law trust, the *Code* did not appear to vest title in the trustees and since the trustees were not made personally liable to third parties they appeared to be more like agents for the beneficiaries. It is likely that absolute ownership was, therefore, vested in the latter. In a landmark decision, *Royal Trust Co. v. Tucker*,[173] however, the Supreme Court of Canada held that the property vested in the trustees for the duration of the trust. Beetz J. said on this point:[174]

> . . . ownership cannot remain in suspense. . . . The grantor is no longer the owner of property conveyed in trust: if it is a testamentary trust, he is dead, and if it is a trust created by way of gift *inter vivos*, it is essential to its validity that the grantor has actually and irrevocably divested himself of the property conveyed in trust. Property cannot be both given and retained. Ownership is not vested in the beneficiary of the income, who is only a creditor of the trustee. It also is not vested during the trust in the beneficiary of the capital — in a great many cases he ranks second or third and has not even been born or conceived. When the property held in trust is finally conveyed to him, as art. 981*l* expressly provides, the trust has terminated. That leaves only the trustee in whom ownership of the trust property can be vested. Clearly the right of ownership is not the traditional one, since, for example, it is temporary and includes no *fructus*. It is a *sui generis* property right, which the legislator implicitly but necessarily intended to create when he introduced the trust into the civil law.

That the old Quebec trust was quite different from the common law trust is clear from articles 981a-981n and from a number of cases. The articles only permitted trusts for the making of testamentary and *inter vivos* gifts. They did not contemplate commercial uses of the trust. Thus, for example, they did not permit voting trusts between shareholders[175] nor real estate investment trusts.[176] Debenture trusts were permitted, but only by virtue of special legislation.[177]

The courts have also held that the *Code* did not permit a person to transfer property to himself or herself as trustee.[178] Hence, the creation of a trust by declaration was impossible. On the other hand, trusts in favour of unborn persons were valid.[179]

There were ways in which gifts could be made to persons in succession under the *Code* other than by trust. Thus, art. 443 provided for the usufruct, a concept similar to the life estate, but in which the absolute owner is the successor, being

---

173 *Supra*, note 171.
174 *Ibid.*, at S.C.R. 272-273.
175 See *Birks v. Birks* (1983), 15 E.T.R. 208 (Que. C.A.). See Martin Boodman, "Royal Trust v. Tucker: The Status of the Trust in the Law of Quebec" (1983), 43 R. du B. 801.
176 *Crown Trust Co. v. Higher*, [1977] 1 S.C.R. 418, 69 D.L.R. (3d) 404.
177 *An Act Respecting the Special Powers of Legal Persons*, R.S.Q., c. P-16.
178 *O'Meara v. Bennett*, [1922] 1 A.C. 80 (P.C.).
179 *Royal Trust Co. v. Tucker, supra*, note 171.

entitled "in remainder," while the usufructuary or "life tenant" has the right to enjoy the property, but is required to preserve the corpus for the proprietor.

The substitution could be used to benefit unborn persons.[180] In essence, a substitution confers absolute property upon one person, coupled with a requirement that ownership will pass to another when the first owner dies, or upon another specified event. Under art. 964, moreover, it was possible to appoint either a fiduciary legatee or a legatee who is an institute. The former is obliged to administer the property and pass it on to the intended recipient. The latter is both a beneficiary and a fiduciary and a substitution occurs on his or her death or other stipulated event. Finally, under art. 869, legatees could be appointed fiduciaries for charitable and other lawful purposes. The relationship of these articles to the trust was not entirely clear.[181]

A complete revision of the *Civil Code* was begun in 1955. One part of the new *Code* was enacted in 1980.[182] Other parts, including the new trusts provisions, were enacted in 1987.[183] However, these enactments were superseded in 1991 by new legislation entitled the *Civil Code of Quebec*.[184] The trust provisions in this Bill are articles 1260 to 1297.

(ii) *The Present Law*

Article 1260 of the new *Civil Code of Quebec* provides that a trust is established when a settlor transfers property from his or her patrimony to another patrimony which he or she constitutes and appropriates to a particular purpose, and article 1261 says that the trust patrimony consists of the property transferred in trust.[185] Articles 1264 and 1265 provide that the trust is created when the trustees accept the trust, and that their acceptance divests the settlor of the property, requires the trustees to appropriate the property and administer the trust, and confers certain rights on the beneficiaries. This is not, except in detail and method, much different from the common law trust, but the nature of the new trust differs markedly from the common law trust. Article 1261 states that the trust patrimony consists of the property transferred in trust and constitutes a patrimony by appro-

---

180 CCLC, arts. 925-981.

181 See Waters, at 1113-1115.

182 Book Two, "The Family," was enacted by S.Q. 1980, c. 39.

183 By *An Act to Add the Reformed Law of Persons, Succession and Property to the Civil Code of Quebec*, S.Q. 1987, c. 18. The Act adopts Book One, "Persons," Book Three, "Successions," and Book Four, "Property." The trust provisions are contained in Book Four, Title Six, "Certain Patrimonies by Appropriation," Chapter II, "The Trust."

184 S.Q. 1991, c. 64. It came into force on January 1, 1994: see Décret 712-93 (Gaz. 2/6/93, p. 2805). Hereafter referred to as "CCQ."

185 A "patrimony" is "[t]he whole of the rights and obligations of a person having an economic or pecuniary value." *S.v.*, *Private Law Dictionary and Bilingual Lexicons*, 2nd ed., rev. and enl. (Cowansville: Quebec Research Centre of Private Law (Les Éditions Yvon Blais Inc.), 1991. It is, therefore, a "juridical or legal universality consisting of property and liabilities, which are considered as forming a whole. Hence the property is liable for the debts." *Ibid.*, *s.v.*, "legal personality." In the context of the trust, the trust patrimony may be regarded as similar to the common law concept of the trust estate.

priation, autonomous and distinct from that of the settlor, trustee or beneficiary and in which none of them has any real right. Thus, neither the trustee nor the beneficiary has title to the trust property. It might appear that art. 1278 resolves this problem. It provides:

> A trustee has the control and the exclusive administration of the trust patrimony, and the titles relating to the property of which it is composed are drawn up in his name; he has the exercise of all the rights pertaining to the patrimony and may take any proper measure to secure its appropriation.
>
> A trustee acts as the administrator of the property of others charged with full administration.

This section does give the trustee a title, but its purpose is not to make him or her the effective owner, but rather to confer upon the trustee the powers necessary to permit the proper administration of the trust. Whether this will be sufficient to overcome the failure of the old trust to deal with the *locus* of the title remains to be seen.

The new trust has overcome another defect of the old trust. The new trust may be established by contract, whether by onerous title or gratuitously, by will, or by operation of law.[186] Thus, for example, a trust for a commercial purpose is now possible. Further, the *Code* now recognizes three kinds of trusts: those created for personal, private and social purposes.[187] The personal trust is the equivalent of the common law family trust. The private trust includes non-charitable purpose trusts and trusts for commercial and semi-public purposes, such as investment and pension trusts. The social trust is the equivalent of the common law charitable trust.

Other articles of the new *Code* make provision for the appointment and supervision of trustees, the rights of beneficiaries, and the variation and termination of trusts. These provisions are unexceptional from the point of view of the common law.

The new provisions only allow for express trusts; remedial trusts are precluded. It remains to be seen how the courts will interpret these provisions and how well the new Quebec trust can be integrated into the mainstream common law trust of North America.

Further Reading

D.M.W. Waters, *Law of Trusts in Canada*, 2nd ed. (Toronto: Carswell, 1984), Chapter 28.

A.H. Oosterhoff, "The New Quebec Trust" (1991), 10 E. & T.J. 322.

Guy Fortin, "How the Province of Quebec Absorbs the Concept of Trust" (1999), 18 E.T. & P.J. 285.

William E. Stavert, "The Quebec Law of Trust" (2002), 21 E.T. & P.J. 130.

---

186 CCQ, art. 1262.
187 See CCQ, art. 1266.

9. THE TRUST IN CONFLICT OF LAWS

In view of the mobility of the population and the use of trusts for trans-border estate planning, tax planning and commercial purposes, a brief introduction to the treatment of trusts in the conflict of laws is desirable. There is not much Canadian law on the topic.

Conflicts issues may arise in a number of situations. For example, an Ontario court may be faced with a trust created in Florida by Florida domiciliaries respecting American property, but which is administered by Ontario trustees for the benefit of beneficiaries domiciled in Ontario. The question may arise whether the interests of the beneficiaries are taxable in Ontario.[188] Alternatively, some beneficiaries may propose a variation of the trust. Whether or not Florida has variation of trusts legislation, does the Ontario court have jurisdiction to entertain the application. If it does, should Ontario's or Florida's law be applied? Again, suppose that the trust is void for perpetuities or accumulation under Ontario law, but valid under Florida law, how should an Ontario court deal with the question of validity? Would it matter that the trust property consists of land situate in Florida or Texas, or that it consists of shares traded on American stock exchanges as well as the Toronto Stock Exchange?

When faced with a conflicts situation you should first characterize the issues. For example, you may distinguish between the validity of a trust and its administration. Validity is concerned with a trust's formal validity, its creator's capacity and its essential validity. Formal validity and capacity concern such things as the observance of the formalities necessary to create the trust. The proper law governing formal validity and capacity is normally the law of the creator's domicile, or last domicile in the case of a testamentary trust. Essential validity is concerned with whether the substantive provisions of the trust are valid. The proper law in this case is the creator's domicile, or last domicile in respect of a testamentary trust, as regards movables, and the *lex situs* in respect of immovables.

Administration is concerned with the management of the trust over time and encompasses such matters as the appointment and retirement of trustees, investment powers, breach of trust and the court's power to advise the trustees. The proper law in this case appears to be the law of the place where the trustees reside and are administering the trust.

There are certain issues which may partake of essential validity and of administration and it may be difficult to determine under which heading they should be classified. Policy rules, such as the rule against perpetuities, and the right of a trust beneficiary to assign his or her interest, which may be restricted in one jurisdiction and not restricted in another, are examples. It is arguable that these are largely matters of policy and, therefore, should be governed by the law of the place where the trust is administered.[189] Modern English cases suggest that the courts are willing to apply the latter law in such cases. Thus, in *Re Ker's Settlement*

---

188 An issue which was particularly relevant when several provinces levied succession duty.
189 See Waters, at 1125.

Trusts[190] and *Re Paget's Settlement*[191] the courts held that they had power to vary trusts governed by foreign law under English variation of trusts legislation, unless the foreign elements were substantial.[192]

Tax assessments are usually made on the basis that the beneficiary has an interest in the trust property, rather than merely a chose in action against the trustee to enforce due administration. On that basis, the issue is the *situs* of the trust property.[193] On the other hand, the *situs* of the trust, that is, where it is being administered, is the relevant issue if it is argued that the beneficiary only has a chose in action against the trustee.[194] The failure to agree upon the correct approach can lead to double taxation. For example, if a testator dies domiciled in the Bahamas and establishes a trust in favour of his or her issue, the property of which trust is situate in Quebec, but which is administered in Nova Scotia, it is possible that both Nova Scotia and Quebec might levy tax.[195]

For trusts of immovable, the general rule is that the *lex situs* of the property is the proper law, but American decisions take a more realistic view. They hold that the *situs*, while important, is not the only criterion. It seems that in the United States the law of the jurisdiction with which the creator of an *inter vivos* trust had the greatest contact at relevant times is the proper law.[196]

On the other hand, if there is evidence in the trust that the settlor intends the law of another jurisdiction to govern, his or her intention will be honoured. Thus, in *Norton v. Bridges*[197] the settlor was domiciled in Illinois, but the trust was made and registered in Wisconsin, and the settlor had given a Wisconsin court power to appoint successor trustees. It was held that the trust should be administered in Wisconsin.

These issues are largely resolved in those jurisdictions which adhere to the Convention on the Law Applicable to Trusts and on their Recognition. This convention is discussed in the Notes and Questions below.

Further Reading

J.-G. Castel, *Canadian Conflict of Laws* (Butterworth and Co. (Canada) Ltd., 2000), vol. 2, at 505-517.

Lester Hoar, "Some Aspects of Trusts in the Conflict of Laws" (1948), 26 Can. Bar Rev. 1415.

David F. Cavers, "Trusts *Inter Vivos* and the Conflict of Laws" (1930-31), 44 Harv. L. Rev. 161.

---

190 [1963] Ch. 553, [1963] 1 All E.R. 801.

191 [1965] 1 W.L.R. 1046, [1965] 1 All E.R. 58.

192 *Ibid.*, at W.L.R. 1050.

193 See, *e.g.*, *Royal Trust Co. v. R.*, [1949] S.C.R. 329, [1949] 2 D.L.R. 153, [1949] C.T.C. 59; *A.-G. Ont. v. Fasken*, [1935] O.R. 288, [1935] 3 D.L.R. 100 (C.A.).

194 See, *e.g.*, *A.-G. N.S. v. Davis*, [1937] 3 D.L.R. 673 (N.S. C.A.).

195 The facts are those of the *Davis* case, *ibid.*

196 See, *e.g.*, *Rudow v. Fogel* (1981), 426 N.E. 2d 155 (Mass. Apps. Ct.), *inter vivos* trust of real property in Massachusetts, but all relevant parties domiciled in New York; held that New York law governs.

197 (1983), 712 F. 2d 1156.

Robert D.M. Flannigan, "Trust Obligations and Residence" (1985), 7 E. & T.Q. 83.

Alfred E. von Overback, "Trusts in Civil Law Countries: the Hague Convention and the Law Applicable to Trusts and their Recognition," Cambridge Lectures 1989 Frank E. McArdle, ed. (Montreal: Edition Y. Blais, 1990), at 167-185.

Stephen W. Bowman, "Sophisticated Estate — Planning Techniques: Cross Border Dimensions" (1993), Can. Tax Found., 38:1-38:45.

Notes and Questions

1. What should a court do if the law of its jurisdiction governs the essential validity of the trust and holds it to be void, whereas the law where the trust is administered would hold the trust to be valid? This issue arose in an important Canadian case, *Re Schechter, Jewish National Fund (Keren Kayemeth Le Israel) Inc. v. Royal Trust Co. and Richter.*[198]

The testator, Frank Schechter, died domiciled in British Columbia in 1961, having made a will and appointed Royal Trust Company as his executor. He directed that the residue of his estate be sold and converted into money and the proceeds paid to the Jewish National Fund, a corporation based in New York City. The trustees of that fund were to use the moneys as a continuing and separate trust to purchase lands in Palestine, the United States of America or any British Dominion, and to establish Jewish colonies on the lands. These purposes were compatible with the purposes of the Jewish National Fund. The purposes of the corporation were regarded as charitable under the laws of New York.

The executor applied to the court to determine whether the gift was valid. The court upheld the gift at first instance,[199] but it was declared invalid on appeal.[200] The Court of Appeal held that the gift to the Jewish National Fund was not an absolute gift, but a trust; and that the trust was not exclusively charitable and was, therefore, void as offending the rule against perpetuities.[201] The Court of Appeal followed the decision of the House of Lords in *Keren Kayemeth Le Jisroel Ltd. v. Commissioners of Inland Revenue,*[202] in which the English counterpart of the Jewish National Fund was held not to be charitable on the ground that is was not for the advancement of religion, for relief of poverty, or for other purposes beneficial to the community and, in any event, there was no identifiable community being benefited.

The Jewish National Fund appealed to the Supreme Court of Canada and argued the following additional grounds: (i) that the rule against perpetuities is based on considerations of internal policy and does not invalidate a trust of movables created by a British Columbia domiciliary which is to be administered elsewhere; (ii) that the trust was to be administered in New York; (iii) that the issue should therefore be determined by the law of that state; and (iv) that the trust was a valid charitable trust under New York law.

Cartwright J., speaking for the majority, dismissed the appeal. He agreed with the Court of Appeal that the gift was a trust and was not exclusively charitable. Hence, it was void for perpetuity under the law of British Columbia. His Lordship applied the rule that the essential validity of a gift of movables is to be determined by the law of the testator's domicile. He noted that the testator did not direct his executor to pay the residue to the Fund to purchase land in New York. Had he done so, the trust might have been valid.

---

198 [1965] S.C.R. 784, 53 D.L.R. (2d) 577.

199 (Sub nom. *Re Schechter*) (1963), 41 W.W.R. 392, 37 D.L.R. (2d) 433 (B.C. S.C.).

200 (Sub nom. *Royal Trust Co. and Jewish National Fund v. Schechter*)(1964), 46 W.W.R. 577, (sub nom. *Re Schechter*) 43 D.L.R. (2d) 417 (B.C. C.A.).

201 That is, the rule against perpetual duration or perpetual trusts.

202 [1932] A.C. 650 (H.L.).

However, the testator gave the Fund the choice of purchasing land in a number of different jurisdictions. The law in one of those jurisdictions, British Columbia, the testator's domicile, regarded the trust as invalid and, absent proof to the contrary, the presumption that the law in the other potential jurisdictions was the same should be applied. Further, His Lordship held that the place of administration of the trust would be the jurisdiction in which the land was purchased, so that the place of residence of the trustees would be irrelevant.

Judson J., for the minority, would have allowed the appeal. He noted that the executor's only function was to pay the money to the New York based Fund. It had no function in the administration of the trust in or outside British Columbia. He said:[203]

> The residue is to be turned over to New York trustees upon clearly defined trusts which are recognized as valid by the law of that state. At that moment it becomes a New York trust to be administered there according to the law of the state. What difficulties of administration, if any, may be encountered outside the boundaries of that state are of no further concern to the court of the domicile. The testator has directed the delivery of the residue to trustees in a foreign jurisdiction where the trust is valid. The administration of the trust from then on is controlled by the laws of a jurisdiction which recognizes its validity.

Which opinion offers the better approach in the *Jewish National Fund* case, that of the majority or that of the minority? Why?

2. Two related issues arose in *Branco v. Veira*.[204] The testator, a resident of St. Vincent, left a $15 million estate to be split amongst his beneficiaries. The testator's wife and daughter, both residents of St. Vincent, were the trustees of the estate and two of its beneficiaries. A second beneficiary, a daughter residing in Ontario, applied for an order to collapse the trust and to vest the corpus of it in her absolutely. She also sought an order to remove the trustees. One of the questions the court had to answer was whether the proper law governing the existence of the alleged trust was the law of Ontario or the law of St. Vincent. Carnwath J. concluded that when the validity of a trust has been called into question and when the settlor and the trustees reside in the same jurisdiction, the proper law is the law of that jurisdiction. Generally, the express intention of the settlor will govern the validity of a trust. Failing such express intention, a court will attempt to determine the implied intention of the settlor.[205]

The second issue examined by the court was the jurisdiction that should govern the administration of the alleged trust. The court once again held that the law of St. Vincent governed, despite the fact that the trust assets and its custodians were located in Ontario. The residence of the trustees was found to be the most important factor in determining the choice of law for the administration of the trust. Another important factor was the residence of the person who gave the final instructions with regard to the investment of trust assets.

---

203 *Supra*, note 198, at 588-589.

204 (1995), 8 E.T.R. (2d) 49 (Ont. Gen. Div.).

205 As was explained by Lester G. Hoar in "Some Aspects of Trusts in the Conflict of Laws" (1948), 26 Can. Bar Rev. 1415 at 1426:

> Implied intent appears to have at least three connotations: (1) intent, as it comes into play in the interpretation of a document; (2) intent arising through a presumption that the creator of a trust intended that the trust should be governed by the law of the state that would uphold the trust provisions; and (3) intent arising by implication from the fact of a preponderance of operative factors within a particular jurisdiction, and through a deduction that the grouping of these factors was a conscious effort on the part of the creator.

In *Branco*, the trustees made these decisions, but the court noted that there may be situations in which the *de facto* decision maker is someone other than the trustee.

3. Recent Canadian cases have held that a trust which would be regarded as charitable in Canada does not lose its charitable character merely because its activities are carried on in a foreign state.[206]

4. The rule that a testamentary trust is to be interpreted in accordance with the law of the testator's domicile at death is not a rule of law, but a rule of interpretation. Thus, in *Re Wilkison*,[207] a testatrix, domiciled in Switzerland but a British subject, made a will in Ontario while visiting there with respect to personal property situate in Ontario. It was held that if there is "any reason from the nature of the will *or otherwise*" to depart from the general rule, the court should do so. The court concluded that, in the circumstances, the testatrix wrote her will with reference to the law of Ontario and that it should, therefore, be interpreted in accordance with that law.

5. Wills statutes typically contain conflict of laws rules which also govern testamentary trusts but perhaps only as regards their initial validity.[208]

6. The *Trusts (Jersey) Law, 1984*,[209] a statute incorporating the law of trusts in a civil law jurisdiction, contains specific conflicts provisions. Article 4 provides that the proper law of a trust is the law of the jurisdiction defined by the trust, or intended by the settlor, or with which the trust at the time it was created had the closest connection.[210] Article 5 confers jurisdiction upon the court where a trust is a Jersey trust, the trustee of a foreign trust is resident in Jersey, any property of a foreign trust is situate in Jersey, or administration of any trust property of a foreign trust is carried on in Jersey.

The statute gives the court powers in the administration of Jersey and foreign trusts.[211] Moreover, a foreign trust is declared to be unenforceable in Jersey if it does or authorizes any action that is contrary to Jersey law, if it applies directly to immovable property situate in Jersey, and to the extent the court declares the trust to be immoral or contrary to public policy.[212]

7. Would provisions like those in the Jersey legislation and those in wills statutes be desirable in trusts statutes?

8. The Hague Convention of July 1, 1984[213] on the law applicable to trusts unified the conflict of laws rules of the signatory states.[214] Article VI of the Convention sets out

---

206 See, *e.g.*, *Re Levy Estate* (1989), 58 D.L.R. (4th) 375, 68 O.R. (2d) 385, 33 E.T.R. 1 (C.A.); *Re Gray* (sub nom. *Gray Estate v. Yule*) (1990), 73 D.L.R. (4th) 161, 75 O.R. (2d) 55, 39 E.T.R. 102 (Gen. Div.).

207 [1934] O.R. 6 (H.C.).

208 See *Wills Act*, R.S.A. 2000, c. W-12, Part 2; R.S.B.C. 1996, c. 489, Part 3; R.S.M. 1988, c. W150, Part II; R.S.N.B. 1973, c. W-9, Part II; R.S.N.L. 1990, c. W-10, Part II; *The Wills Act, 1996*, S.S. 1996, c. W-14.1, ss. 4, 5 [am. S.S. 2001, c. 51, s. 10(2)], 6; *Wills Act*, R.S.Y. 2002, c. 230, ss. 24-26; *Succession Law Reform Act*, R.S.O. 1990, c. S.26, ss. 34-41. See also to the same effect, the *New York Estates, Powers and Trusts Law* (enacted by N.Y. Laws 1966, c. 952), s. 3-5.1.

209 Jersey Laws 1984, No. 11.

210 Article 37, *ibid.*, states that a Jersey trust may provide for the proper law of the trust to be changed from the law of Jersey to the law of another jurisdiction.

211 *Ibid.*, arts. 47-49.

212 *Ibid.*, art. 45. For similar legislation see the *Trusts Ordinance 1990*, Ord. Turks and Caicos Islands, 1990, No. 25, especially ss. 4 and 5.

213 *Convention on the Law Applicable to Trusts and their Recognition*, Final Act, XVth Sess.,

the rules dealing with the governance of the trust. A trust is to be governed by the law chosen by the settlor. The choice may be express or implied. Article VII states that when no applicable law has been chosen, a trust shall be governed by the law with which it most closely connected. In ascertaining the law with which a trust is most closely connected, particular reference should be made to the place of administration of the trust designated by the settlor; the *situs* of the assets of the trust; the place of residence or business of the trustee; and the place of residence of the objects of the trust. The law specified by Article VI or VII governs the validity of the trust, its construction, its effects, and the administration of the trust.

The Convention also makes provision for the recognition of trusts created in accordance with the law so determined. Canada has ratified this convention[215] and it has been extended by legislation to several provinces.[216]

9. A similar conflict of laws problem arises as between the several provinces. Some provinces have enacted legislation which introduces choice of law rules governing the validity of extra-provincial trusts and makes provision for their recognition.[217] These rules and provisions are similar to those contained in the convention referred to in the preceding Note and Question.

10. Under the *Income Tax Act*[218] a trust is taxed as a person and persons are taxed on the basis of residence, not domicile.[219]

10. THE TRUST AND ABORIGINAL LAND CLAIMS

In recent years, the trust or, more precisely, the fiduciary concept, has also been applied to aboriginal land claims. The leading case is *Guerin v. R.*[220]

In 1957, an Indian Band surrendered a portion of its reserve, located in Vancouver, to the Crown "in trust to lease the same to such person or persons, and upon such terms as the Government of Canada may deem most conducive to our Welfare and that of our people." The lands surrendered were some of the most valuable in the city. The band voted in favour of the surrender based on

---

Hague Conference on Private International Law. See also (1984), 23 *International Legal Materials*, at 1388.

214 The Convention has been signed by Canada, the United States, Italy, Luxembourg, the Netherlands, and the United Kingdom, among other countries.

215 On October 11, 1988.

216 See *International Conventions Implementation Act*, R.S.A. 2000, c. I-6; *International Trusts Act*, R.S.B.C. 1996, c. 237; R.S.P.E.I. 1988, c. I-7; R.S.N.L. 1990, c. I-17. The statutes are based on the *Uniform International Trusts Act*, promulgated by the Uniform Law Conference of Canada, *Proceedings of the Sixty-Ninth Annual Meeting* (1987), App. E., amended *Proceedings of the Seventieth Annual Meeting* (1988), at 30, 156.

217 See *Conflict of Laws Rules for Trusts Act*, R.S.B.C. 1996, c. 65; S.N.B. 1988, c. C-16.2. This legislation is based on the *Uniform Conflict of Laws Rules for Trusts Act*, promulgated by the Uniform Law Conference of Canada, *Proceedings of the Sixty-Ninth Annual Meeting* (1987), App. J; amended *Proceedings of the Seventieth Annual Meeting* (1988), at 32.

218 R.S.C. 1985, c. 1 (5th Supp.), s. 104(2).

219 See further R.A. Green, "The Residence of Trusts for Income Tax Purposes" (1973), 21 Can. Tax J. 217; Gordon Cooper, "Canadian Resident Inter Vivos Trusts with Non-Resident Beneficiaries" (1982), 30 Can. Tax J. 422; *Thibodeau Family Trust v. R.* (1978), 78 D.T.C. 6376 (sub nom. *Dill v. R.*), 3 E.T.R. 168 (Fed. T.D.).

220 *Guerin v. R.*, [1984] 2 S.C.R. 335, 20 E.T.R. 6, 55 N.R. 161, 13 D.L.R. (4th) 321.

information supplied by an official of the Indian Affairs Branch. That information was incomplete, incorrect, and misleading. The lease that was actually entered into between the Department of Indian Affairs and the golf club provided for: (1) a 75-year lease of five 15-year terms; (2) rent of $29,000 per annum for the first 15 years; (3) a 15% maximum rent increase during the second 15-year term; and (4) the removal of any improvements made by the golf club upon termination. These terms were significantly different from those the band had assented to at its surrender meeting. The band did not receive a copy of the lease until 12 years later. It sued the Crown for damages and was successful at trial,[221] but lost on appeal to the Federal Court of Appeal.[222] The Supreme Court of Canada restored the trial judgment.

Dickson J., speaking for the majority,[223] discussed the existence and nature of aboriginal title. He said:[224]

> Indians have a legal right to occupy and possess certain lands, the ultimate title to which is in the Crown. While their interest does not, strictly speaking, amount to beneficial ownership, neither is its nature completely exhausted by the concept of a personal right. It is true that the *sui generis* interest which the Indians have in the land is personal in the sense that it cannot be transferred to a grantee, but it is also true, as will presently appear, that the interest gives rise upon surrender to a distinctive fiduciary obligation on the part of the Crown to deal with the land for the benefit of the surrendering Indians. These two aspects of Indian title go together, since the Crown's original purpose in declaring the Indian's interest to be inalienable otherwise than to the Crown was to facilitate the Crown's ability to represent the Indians in dealings with third parties. The nature of the Indians' interest is therefore best characterized by its general inalienability, coupled with the fact that the Crown is under an obligation to deal with the land on the Indians' behalf when the interest is surrendered. Any description of Indian title which goes beyond these two features is both unnecessary and potentially misleading.

His Lordship then held that, since the *Royal Proclamation* of 1763,[225] the Crown has had a fiduciary obligation towards Indians, because it assumed a responsibility to act on behalf of Indians to protect their interests in transactions with third parties. That obligation is now codified in the s. 18(1) of the *Indian Act*.[226] The obligation arises out of the Crown's discretion, conferred by that provision, to decide what is in the best interests of the Indians. His Lordship stated that the obligation does not give rise to a trust in the strict common law sense of that term, saying:[227]

> The issue of the Crown's liability was dealt with in the courts below on the basis of the existence or non-existence of a trust. In dealing with the different consequences of a "true" trust, as opposed to a "political" trust, Le Dain J. noted that the Crown could be liable only if it were subject to an "equitable obligation enforceable in a court of law." I have some doubt as to the cogency of the terminology of "higher" and "lower" trusts, but I do agree that the existence of an

221 [1982] 2 F.C. 385, 10 E.T.R. 61, [1982] 2 C.N.L.R. 83 (Fed. T.D.).
222 [1983] 2 F.C. 656, 13 E.T.R. 245, 143 D.L.R. (3d) 416, [1983] 2 W.W.R. 686.
223 Estey and Wilson JJ., wrote concurring opinions.
224 *Supra*, note 220, at D.L.R. 339.
225 R.S.C. 1970, App. II, No. 1.
226 R.S.C. 1985, c. I-5.
227 *Supra*, note 220, at D.L.R. 334-335.

equitable obligation is the *sine qua non* for liability. Such an obligation is not, however, limited to relationships which can be strictly defined as "trusts." As will presently appear, it is my view that the Crown's obligations *vis-à-vis* the Indians cannot be defined as a trust. That does not, however, mean that the Crown owes no enforceable duty to the Indians in the way in which it deals with Indian land.

In my view, the nature of Indian title and the framework of the statutory scheme established for disposing of Indian land places upon the Crown an equitable obligation, enforceable by the Court, to deal with the land for the benefit of the Indians. This obligation does not amount to a trust in the private law sense. It is rather a fiduciary duty. If, however, the Crown breaches this fiduciary duty, it will be liable to the Indians in the same way and to the same extent as if such a trust were in effect. The fiduciary relationship between the Crown and the Indians has its roots in the concept of aboriginal, native, or Indian title. The fact that Indian bands have a certain interest in lands does not, however, in itself give rise to a fiduciary relationship between the Indians and the Crown. The conclusion that the Crown is a fiduciary depends upon the further proposition that the Indian interest in the land is inalienable except upon surrender to the Crown.

His Lordship discussed the reason for the existence of a fiduciary relationship in the circumstances in the following terms:[228]

The concept of fiduciary obligation originated long ago in the notion of breach of confidence, one of the original heads of jurisdiction in Chancery. In the present appeal its relevance is based on the requirement of a "surrender" before Indian land can be alienated.

The *Royal Proclamation* of 1763 provided that no private person could purchase from the Indians any lands that the Proclamation had reserved to them, and provided further that all purchases had to be by and in the name of the Crown, in a public assembly of the Indians held by the governor or commander-in-chief of the colony in which the lands in question lay. As Lord Watson pointed out in *St. Catherine's Milling*,[229] this policy with respect to the sale or transfer of the Indian's interest in land has been continuously maintained by the British Crown, by the governments of the colonies when they became responsible for the administration of Indian affairs, and, after 1867, by the federal government of Canada. Successive federal statutes, predecessors to the present *Indian Act*, have all provided for the general inalienability of Indian reserve land except upon surrender to the Crown, the relevant provisions in the present Act being ss. 37-41.

The purpose of this surrender requirement is clearly to interpose the Crown between the Indians and prospective purchasers or lessees of their land, so as to prevent the Indians from being exploited. . . . Through the confirmation in the *Indian Act* of the historic responsibility which the Crown has undertaken, to act on behalf of the Indians so as to protect their interests in transactions with third parties, Parliament has conferred upon the Crown a discretion to decide for itself where the Indians' best interests really lie. This is the effect of s. 18(1) of the Act.

This discretion on the part of the Crown, far from ousting, as the Crown contends, the jurisdiction of the Courts to regulate the relationship between the Crown and the Indians, has the effect of transforming the Crown's obligation into a fiduciary one. Professor Ernest Weinrib maintains in his article "The Fiduciary Obligation"[230] that "the hallmark of a fiduciary relation is that the relative legal positions are such that one party is at the mercy of the other's discretion." Earlier,[231] he puts the point in the following way:

[Where there is a fiduciary obligation] there is a relation in which the principal's interests can be affected by, and are therefore dependent on, the manner in which the fiduciary uses the

---

228 *Ibid.*, at D.L.R. 339-341.
229 *St. Catherine's Milling & Lumber Co. v. R.* (1888), 14 App. Cas. 46 at 54 (P.C.).
230 (1975), 25 U.T.L.J. 1 at 7.
231 *Ibid.*, at 4.

discretion which has been delegated to him. The fiduciary obligation is the law's blunt tool for the control of this discretion.

I make no comment upon whether this description is broad enough to embrace all fiduciary obligations. I do agree, however, that where by statute, agreement, or perhaps by unilateral undertaking, one party has an obligation to act for the benefit of another, and that obligation carries with it a discretionary power, the party thus empowered becomes a fiduciary. Equity will then supervise the relationship by holding him to the fiduciary's strict standard of conduct.

It is sometimes said that the nature of fiduciary relationships is both established and exhausted by the standard categories of agent, trustee, partner, director, and the like. I do not agree. It is the nature of the relationship, not the specific category of actor involved that gives rise to the fiduciary duty. The categories of fiduciary, like those of negligence, should not be considered closed.[232]

It should be noted that fiduciary duties generally arise only with regard to obligations originating in private law context. Public law duties, the performance of which requires the exercise of discretion, do not typically give rise to a fiduciary relationship. As the "political trust" cases indicate, the Crown is not normally viewed as a fiduciary in the exercise of its legislative or administrative function. The mere fact, however, that it is the Crown which is obligated to act on the Indian's behalf does not of itself remove the Crown's obligation from the scope of the fiduciary principle. As was pointed out earlier, the Indians' interest in land is an independent legal interest. It is not a creation of either the legislative or executive branches of government. The Crown's obligation to the Indians with respect to that interest is therefore not a public law duty. While it is not a private law duty in the strict sense either, it is nonetheless in the nature of a private law duty. Therefore, in this *sui generis* relationship, it is not improper to regard the Crown as a fiduciary.

Section 18(1) of the *Indian Act* confers upon the Crown a broad discretion in dealing with surrendered land. In the present case, the document of surrender, set out in part earlier in these reasons, by which the Musqueam band surrendered the land at issue, confirms this discretion in the clause conveying the land to the Crown "in trust to lease . . . upon such terms as the Government of Canada may deem most conducive to our Welfare and that of our people". When, as here, an Indian band surrenders its interest to the Crown, a fiduciary obligation takes hold to regulate the manner in which the Crown exercises its discretion in dealing with the land on the Indians' behalf.

His Lordship held that the Crown breached its fiduciary duty when it ignored the oral terms the band agreed to, failed to inform the band of terms the golf club insisted upon and to obtain new instructions from the band, and leased the land upon the terms the golf club imposed. The Crown was, therefore, liable for the resulting loss to the band.

The issue has been raised in a number of cases since *Guerin*. One of them is *Blueberry River Indian Band v. Canada*,[233] reproduced below.

BLUEBERRY RIVER INDIAN BAND v. CANADA

[1995] 4 S.C.R. 344, 130 D.L.R. (4th) 193, 190 N.R. 89
Supreme Court of Canada

The Crown in right of the Dominion established a reserve for an Indian Band

---

232 See, e.g., *Laskin v. Bache & Co.*, [1972] 1 O.R. 465, 23 D.L.R. (3d) 385 at 392 (CA); *Goldex Mines Ltd. v. Revill* (1974), 7 O.R. (2d) 216 at 224, 54 D.L.R. (3d) 672 (C.A.).
233 [1995] 4 S.C.R. 344, 130 D.L.R. (4th) 193, 190 N.R. 89.

in British Columbia in 1916. In 1940 the band surrendered the mineral rights in the reserve to the Crown "in trust to lease the same." In 1945 the band agreed to surrender the reserve to the Crown in furtherance of the federal government's desire to provide farm land for veterans returned from the Second World War and of the band's wish to have a reserve closer to its members' trap lines. The surrender was in favour of the Crown "in trust to . . . sell or lease . . . the same." In 1950 the Crown did establish a new reserve for the band closer to its trap lines, using the proceeds of sale of the old reserve to purchase the new one. Later the band was split into two. The bands did not fare well economically.

In 1948 the Department of Indian Affairs ("DIA") sold the land to the Director, *The Veterans' Land Act, 1942*[234] ("DVLA") for $70,000. Contrary to its usual practice, the DIA did not reserve the mineral rights; that is, it did not except those rights from the sale. Consequently, those rights passed to the DVLA. The DVLA sold the land (including the mineral rights) to veterans over a period of time. Also in 1948, gas was discovered in land near the reserve and eventually also on former reserve lands. In 1978 the bands sued the Crown for damages. They alleged that the Crown breached its duties to the band in a number of ways, including permitting the band to make an improvident surrender, disposing of the land at an undervalue, and permitting the disposition of the mineral rights.

Addy J., at trial,[235] held that the lands were sold at an undervalue, but otherwise dismissed the action and the Federal Court of Appeal dismissed the bands' appeal and the Crown's cross-appeal.[236] The bands appealed to the Supreme Court of Canada and the Crown cross-appealed.

There were two judgments in the Supreme Court of Canada, as there was a difference of opinion on the combined effect of the 1940 and 1945 surrenders and the nature of the breach of the fiduciary duty the Crown owed the band. The former is not critical to the issue under consideration, but will be summarized below; the latter is a difference in approach and excerpts from the two judgments will be reproduced below on this issue.

GONTHIER J.:

> [His Lordship was of opinion that the 1945 surrender included the mineral rights. He emphasized the importance of deciding the issue not on the basis of technical land transfer requirements, but on the basis of the band members' intention. On that basis, he regarded the 1945 surrender as a variation of a "trust" in Indian land,[237] in that the 1945 surrender subsumed the 1940 surrender. In consequence, the Crown held both the surface and mineral rights in trust to "sell or lease." His Lordship then addressed the Crown's fiduciary duty in the following terms:]

---

234 S.C. 1942-43, c. 33.
235 (1987), [1988] 3 F.C. 20, 14 F.T.R. 161, [1988] 1 C.N.L.R. 73 (Fed. T.D.).
236 [1993] 3 F.C. 28, 100 D.L.R. (4th) 504, 151 N.R. 241.
237 His Lordship noted that this "trust" could not be equated to the common law trust.

III

BREACH OF FIDUCIARY DUTY BY THE DIA SUBSEQUENT TO THE 1945 SURRENDER

[16] The terms of the 1945 surrender transferred I.R. 172 to the Crown "in trust to sell or lease the same to such person or persons, and upon such terms as the Government of the Dominion of Canada may deem most conducive to our welfare and that of our people." By taking on the obligations of a trustee in relation to I.R. 172, the DIA was under a fiduciary duty to deal with the land in the best interests of the members of the Beaver band. This duty extended to both the surface rights and the mineral rights.

[17] In my view, it is critical to the outcome of this case that the 1945 agreement was a surrender in trust, *to sell or lease*. The terms of the trust agreement provided the DIA with the discretion to sell or lease, and since the DIA was under a fiduciary duty *vis-à-vis* the band, it was required to exercise this discretion in the Band's best interests. Of equal importance is the fact that the 1945 surrender gave the DIA a virtual carte blanche to determine the terms upon which I.R. 172 would be sold or leased. The only limitation was that these terms had to be "conducive" to the "welfare" of the Band. Because of the scope of the discretion granted to the DIA, it would have been open to the DIA to sell the surface rights in I.R. 172 to the [DVLA], while continuing to lease the mineral rights for the benefit of the Band, as per the 1940 surrender agreement.

[18] Why this option was not chosen is a mystery. As my colleague McLachlin J. observes, the DIA had a long-standing policy, predating the 1945 surrender, to reserve out mineral rights for the benefit of the aboriginal peoples when surrendered Indian lands were sold off. This policy was adopted precisely because reserving mineral rights was thought to be "conducive to the welfare" of aboriginal peoples in all cases. The existence and rationale of this policy (the wisdom of which, though obvious, is evidenced by the facts of this case) justifies the conclusion that the DIA was under a fiduciary duty to reserve, for the benefit of the Beaver Band, the mineral rights in I.R. 172 when it sold the surface rights to the DVLA in March, 1948. In other words, the DIA should have continued to lease the mineral rights for the benefit of the Band as it had been doing since 1940. Its failure to do so can only be explained as "inadvertence."

[19] The DIA's failure to continue the leasing arrangement could be excused if the department had received a clear mandate from the Band to sell the mineral rights. As I stated above, the Band's intention leads me to the conclusion that both the surface and mineral rights in I.R. 172 were included in the 1945 surrender. However, the 1945 surrender was "to sell or lease". At no time during the negotiations leading to the 1945 agreement was the sale of the mineral rights discussed specifically. The authorization given encompassed leasing as well as selling. There was therefore no clear authorization from the Band which justified the DIA in departing from its long-standing policy of reserving mineral rights for the benefit of the aboriginals when surface rights were sold. This underscores the critical distinction between the Band's intention to include the mineral rights in

the 1945 surrender, and an intention of the Band that the mineral rights must be sold and not leased by the Crown. Given these circumstances, the DIA was under a fiduciary duty to continue the leasing arrangement which had been established in the 1940 surrender. It was a violation of the fiduciary duty to sell the mineral rights to the DVLA in 1948.

[Gonthier J. agreed with McLachlin J. that the action was not statute-barred and that, therefore, the Bands were able to recover the damages claimed.]

McLACHLIN J.:

II

ANALYSIS

(1) *Pre-surrender duties and breaches*

[32] The Bands argue that the Crown was under a fiduciary obligation prior to the 1945 surrender of the land to ensure that the Band did not enter into the surrender improvidently. This raises the issue of the nature of the duty owed by the Crown when a band wishes to surrender its reserve. The Bands admit that in 1945 they wished to surrender the Fort St. John reserve in order to obtain other lands closer to its trap lines, and the remaining cash lump sum. They contend that the Crown should not have allowed them to make this surrender since, viewed in the long term, surrender was not in their best interest.

(a) *Whether the Indian Act imposed a duty on the Crown to prevent the surrender of the reserve*

[33] The first issue is whether the *Indian Act* imposed a duty on the Crown to refuse the Band's surrender of its reserve. The answer to this question is found in *Guerin v. R.*,[238] where the majority of this court, *per* Dickson J. (as he then was), held that the duty on the Crown with respect to surrender of Indian lands was founded on preventing exploitative bargains.

[34] The Bands contend that the *Indian Act*[239] imposed a duty on the Crown to refuse to allow the band to surrender its lands in light of its interest in the land and the paternalistic scheme of the *Indian Act*. When a reserve is granted to a band, as was done here in 1916, title does not pass to the band. Rather the Crown holds the fee simple title. The Crown thus possesses power with respect to those lands and must, it is argued, exercise that power as a fiduciary on behalf of the Band. This is reinforced by the paternalistic tone of the *Indian Act*, which it is argued imposes a duty upon the Crown to protect the Indians from themselves and prevent them from making foolish decisions with respect to their land. This

---

238 [1984] 2 S.C.R. 335, 13 D.L.R. (4th) 321, 20 E.T.R. 6.
239 R.S.C. 1927, c. 98.

is why, it is submitted, title remains in the Crown. The Crown, on the other hand, paints the Band as an independent agent with respect to the surrender of its lands.

[35] My view is that the *Indian Act*'s provisions for surrender of band reserves strikes a balance between the two extremes of autonomy and protection. The band's consent was required to surrender its reserve. Without that consent the reserve could not be sold. But the Crown, through the Governor in Council, was also required to consent to the surrender. The purpose of the requirement of Crown consent was not to substitute the Crown's decision for that of the band, but to prevent exploitation. As Dickson J. characterized it in *Guerin*:[240]

> The purpose of this surrender requirement is clearly to interpose the Crown between the Indians and prospective purchasers or lessees of their land, so as to prevent the Indians from being exploited.

It follows that under the *Indian Act*, the Band had the right to decide whether to surrender the reserve, and its decision was to be respected. At the same time, if the Band's decision was foolish or improvident — a decision that constituted exploitation — the Crown could refuse to consent. In short, the Crown's obligation was limited to preventing exploitative bargains.

[36] Subject to the issue of the value of the reserve and the matter of mineral rights, which I deal with later, the evidence does not support the view that the surrender of the Fort St. John reserve was foolish, improvident, or amounted to exploitation. In fact, viewed from the perspective of the Band at the time, it made good sense. The measure of control which the Act permitted the Band to exercise over the surrender of the reserve negates the contention that absent exploitation, the Act imposed a fiduciary obligation on the Crown with respect to the surrender of the reserve.

(b) *Whether the circumstances of the case gave rise to a fiduciary duty on the Crown with respect to the surrender*

[37] If the *Indian Act* did not impose a duty on the Crown to block the surrender of the reserve, the further question arises of whether on the particular facts of this case a fiduciary relationship was superimposed on the regime for alienation of Indian lands contemplated by the *Indian Act*.

[38] Generally speaking, a fiduciary obligation arises where one person possesses unilateral power or discretion on a matter affecting a second "peculiarly vulnerable" person.[241] The vulnerable party is in the power of the party possessing the power or discretion, who is in turn obligated to exercise that power or discretion solely for the benefit of the vulnerable party. A person cedes (or more often

---

240 *Supra*, note 238, at D.L.R. 340.

241 See *Frame v. Smith*, [1987] 2 S.C.R. 99, 42 D.L.R. (4th) 81, 42 C.C.L.T. 1, 78 N.R. 40, 9 R.F.L. (3d) 225; *Norberg v. Wynrib*, [1992] 2 S.C.R. 226, 92 D.L.R. (4th) 449, 12 C.C.L.T. (2d) 1, additional reasons at [1992] 2 S.C.R. 318, [1992] 6 W.W.R. 673, 74 B.C.L.R. (2d) 2; and *Hodgkinson v. Simms*, [1994] 3 S.C.R. 377, 117 D.L.R. (4th) 161, 57 C.P.R. (3d) 1, [1994] 9 W.W.R. 609.

finds himself in the situation where someone else has ceded for him) his power over a matter to another person. The person who has ceded power *trusts* the person to whom power is ceded to exercise the power with loyalty and care. This is the notion at the heart of the fiduciary obligation.

[39] The evidence supports the view that the Band trusted the Crown to provide it with information as to its options and their foreseeable consequences, in relation to the surrender of the Fort St. John reserve and the acquisition of new reserves which would better suit its life of trapping and hunting. It does not support the contention that the Band abnegated or entrusted its power of decision over the surrender of the reserve to the Crown. . . .

[40] I conclude that the evidence does not support the existence of a fiduciary duty on the Crown prior to the surrender of the reserve by the Band.

> [Her Ladyship then considered whether the surrender was invalid for failure to comply with certain technical statutory requirements and held that it was valid. She continued:]

(2) *Post-surrender duties and breaches regarding surface rights*

[45] The 1945 surrender conveyed the Band's lands to the Crown "in trust to sell or lease the same to such person or persons, and upon such terms as the Government of the Dominion of Canada may deem *most conducive to our welfare and that of our people*" (emphasis added). The Crown concedes that this surrender imposed a fiduciary duty on the Crown with respect to the subsequent sale or lease of the lands.[242] The only issue is whether the Crown breached that duty when in 1948 it sold the lands to the DVLA for $70,000.

[46] The duty imposed upon the Crown by the terms of surrender (converted to a statutory duty by s. 54 of the Act) was broad. It extended not only to the monetary aspects of the transaction, but to whether the arrangement would be conducive to the welfare of the Indians in the broader sense. The Bands argue that the Crown breached this duty by: (a) failing to consider leasing rather than selling the land; (b) selling the land undervalue; and (c) not restoring the reserve to the Band after surrender in view of its impoverished situation. I will consider each allegation in turn.

(a) *Failure to consider leasing rather than sale of the surface rights*

[47] The trial judge held that the Crown considered the best interests of the band in disposing of the land and that, viewed from the perspective of the time, the sale of the land to the Department of Veterans' Affairs was in fact in the best interests of the Band. He held that the band was interested in obtaining reserves nearer to its hunting and trapping grounds. If the surface rights had been leased rather than sold, the Band might not have had enough money up front to purchase replacement lands.

---

242 *Guerin, supra,* note 238.

[48] Against this, the Bands point to policy statements of the DIA in the early 1940s which suggest that the DIA would have preferred to lease unused Indian interests rather than sell them, so that the land would be available for use by the Indians and their descendants in the future. The Bands claim that the DIA failed to follow its own policy. The Bands also rely on the fact that the Director of Indian Affairs, Dr. McGill, wrote to the Deputy Minister in August 1944, strongly advising against the sale of the lands and suggesting that the annoyance of seeing good agricultural land unused could be assuaged by leasing it to suitable tenants, if available.

[49] The evidence is clear that the government's general policy was against selling Indian lands. The evidence is also clear that a debate took place over whether the Fort St. John reserve, which the Crown now held upon trust for the Indians, should be sold. In the end, the initial inclination of the DIA not to sell the reserve was outweighed by two factors: the desire of the Band to get money for the purchase of substitute lands nearer their trap lines; coupled with political pressure for release of the lands for agricultural purposes. Dr. McGill pointed out that although the Band did not use the reserve for agriculture, it might be compelled to use it in the future due to dwindling fur supplies. The Deputy Minister responded that he agreed that any suggestion to dispose of Indian lands "should be most carefully considered before any final decision is reached," and wrote to the Canadian Legion (interested in acquiring the land for veterans) suggesting an alternative plan in which only a portion of the reserve would be sold. A non-surrender lease, pursuant to s. 93(3) of the 1927 *Indian Act*, was also considered by the Superintendent of Reserves and Trusts in 1945. Throughout this time, the DIA took the view that it should bring no pressure to bear on the Band to promote the sale.

[50] Armed with these instructions, the local agent, Grew, visited the Band. He reported back that the Band was willing to surrender the land for sale or lease provided that they would be supplied with other lands nearer their trap lines. He also suggested that it was unlikely that the Band would ever make use of the reserve for farming, as they were trappers. The Director of Indian affairs (then a Mr. Hoey) wrote back that in addition to political pressure to open the lands for "ordinary settlement," the cash received as a result of the sale would be "for many years of more practical value to the Indians" than the land of the reserve. Once Dr. McGill left office, the general policy of maintaining the Fort St. John reserve for the Band appears to have succumbed to political demands for farm land. This, coupled with the apparent desire of the band to exchange their more southern reserve for other lands nearer their trap lines, resulted in the sale of the land to the DVLA.

[51] In the face of this evidence, it cannot be said that Addy J. erred in concluding that the sale of the land to the DVLA was not in breach of the Crown's fiduciary duty. A number of options — lease, partial sale, and outright sale — were considered. The interests and wishes of the Band were given utmost consideration throughout. The choice that was made — to sell the land — possessed the advantage of allowing the Band to get other lands nearer its trap lines. At the time, that was a defensible choice. Indeed, it can be argued that the sale of the

surface rights was the only alternative that met the Band's apparent need to obtain land nearer its trap lines. In retrospect, with the decline of trapping and the discovery of oil and gas, the decision may be argued to have been unfortunate. But at the time, it may be defended as a reasonable solution to the problems the Band faced.

(b) *Sale at undervalue*

[52] The DIA received an appraisal of the land which placed its value at approximately $93,160. The DVLA's appraisals suggested a lower value. Ultimately, the DIA sold the land to the DVLA *en bloc* for $70,000. The trial judge accepted the Bands' contention that the Crown breached its fiduciary duty by selling the land undervalue, since it sold at less than value suggested by its appraisers. He stated:[243]

> The defendant had a duty to convince the Court that it could not reasonably have been expected to obtain a better price. There was no evidence as to what other offers were sought and what efforts were made to obtain a better price elsewhere. Since the onus of establishing that a full and fair price was in fact obtained in March 1948 has not been discharged by the defendant, I find that the latter was guilty of a breach of its fiduciary duty towards the plaintiffs in that regard.

The Crown appeals this finding, arguing first that the onus was on the Bands to show that the sale was undervalue and, second, that the price of $70,000 was unreasonable.

[53] The trial judge was correct in finding that a fiduciary involved in self-dealing, *i.e.*, in a conflict of interest, bears the onus of demonstrating that its personal interest did not benefit from its fiduciary powers.[244] The Crown, facing conflicting political pressures in favour of preserving the land for the Band on the one hand, and making it available for distribution to veterans on the other, may be argued to have been in a position of conflict of interest.

[54] More problematic is the trial judge's conclusion that the Crown failed to discharge the onus of showing the price of $70,000 to be reasonable. While the DIA received a higher appraisal, there were also appraisals giving lower value to the land. In fact, there appears to have been no alternate market for the land at the time, which might be expected to make accurate appraisal difficult. The evidence reveals the price was arrived at after a course of negotiations conducted at arm's length between the DIA and the DVLA.

[55] This evidence does not appear to support the trial judge's conclusion that the Crown was in breach of its fiduciary obligation to sell the land at a fair value. In finding a breach despite this evidence, the trial judge misconstrued the effect of the onus on the Crown. The Crown adduced evidence showing that the sale price lay within a range established by the appraisals. This raised a *prima*

---

243 At F.C. 76.

244 J.C. Shepherd, *The Law of Fiduciaries* (Toronto: Carswell, 1981), at 157-159; and A.H. Oosterhoff and E.E. Gillese, *Text, Cases and Commentary on the Law of Trusts*, 4th ed. (Toronto: Carswell, 1992).

facie case that the sale price was reasonable. The onus then shifted to the Bands to show it was unreasonable. The Bands did not adduce such evidence. On this state of the record, a presumption of breach of the Crown's fiduciary duty to exact a fair price cannot be based on a failure to discharge the onus upon it. I note that the trial judge made no finding as to the true value of the property, nor any finding that it was significantly greater than $70,000, deferring this to the stage of assessment of damages.

[56] I conclude that the trial judge erred in concluding that the Crown breached its fiduciary duty to the Band by selling the land for $70,000.

(c) *Failure to restore the surface rights to the band after the 1945 surrender*

[57] The Bands argue that they should have been given their reserve back because of their apparent impoverishment between 1945 and 1961. The Crown, in the Bands' submission, should have realized that the surrender had been a mistake. Instead of confirming the mistake by selling the land to the DVLA, it should have cancelled the surrender and transferred the land back to the Band.

[58] There can be no doubt that the Band lived in abject poverty and ill health between 1945 and 1961. The problem the Bands' argument faces is that their condition appears to have been unrelated to possession of the Fort St. John reserve. In fact, the Band did not make significant use of the reserve from 1916 to 1945, one of the primary reasons behind the move to surrender it and purchase more suitable property. Nor did the Band make much use of the land from 1945 to 1950 when alternative lands were purchased, despite the fact that it was entitled to use the land during this period. Finally, the purchase of new lands in 1950 did not, by the Bands' own admission, alleviate the situation.

[59] Accepting that the Band was living in poverty, one cannot infer that the solution was to cancel the 1945 surrender or refuse to sell the Fort St. John reserve land. The Crown cannot be said to have breached the fiduciary duty it owed the Band after surrender of the Fort St. John reserve by failing to restore the land to the Indians.

(d) *Conclusions on post-surrender duty and breach with respect to surface rights*

[60] I conclude that the Bands have not established breach of fiduciary duty with respect to the sale of the surface rights.

(3) *Post-surrender duties and breaches regarding mineral rights*

[Her Ladyship next considered the combined effect of the 1940 and 1945 surrenders. She concluded that the 1945 surrender had no effect on the mineral rights, since those had already been surrendered in 1940. The 1940 surrender made the Crown a fiduciary with respect to the mineral rights for the benefit of the band and the terms of the surrender were that the Crown could only lease, not sell, the mineral rights. She continued:]

(c) *Did the transfer of the mineral rights in 1948 constitute a breach of fiduciary duty?*

[93] Until 1948 the DIA held the surface rights and the mineral rights in trust for the Indians, pursuant to the surrenders of 1945 and 1940 respectively. In 1948, after concluding negotiations for the reserve, it assigned the land to the DVLA. The assignment did not reserve out mineral rights despite the fact that the Crown had no right to sell them under the terms of the 1940 surrender and s. 54 of the Act,[245] and despite the fact that they had not been mentioned in the negotiations leading to the sale and appear to have played no role in determining the price paid. Since the transfer to the DVLA did not reserve out the mineral rights, and since the DIA had always held legal title to both the mineral rights and the surface rights, the transfer must be taken to have legally passed the mineral rights as well as the surface rights.[246] So the DVLA, without ever having sought them, found itself in possession of the mineral rights. The DVLA in turn passed the mineral rights on to the veterans as they met the terms of their agreements for sale, in the form of original Crown grants, pursuant to s. 5(2) of the *Veterans' Land Act*.

[94] Years later, wonderment persisted as to why the mineral rights had been passed to the DVLA. The wonderment was understandable given the well-known policy of the DIA to reserve out mineral rights and the fact that the only interest of the DVLA was to obtain land for agricultural purposes, not to enrich veterans through procuring mineral rights for them. The best explanation of how the mineral rights came to be transferred to the DVLA appears to lie in simple inadvertence. . . .

[Her Ladyship quoted from the evidence and continued:]

[95] There exist two grounds for arguing that transfer of the minerals to the DVLA in 1948 constituted a breach of fiduciary duty by the Crown. The first argument is that the transfer breached the 1940 surrender of the minerals, which restricted the DIA to *leasing* them for the benefit of the Band. A fiduciary is at very least bound to adhere to the terms of the instrument which bestows his powers and creates the trust.

[96] In any event, even if one were to accept for the sake of the argument that the 1945 surrender revoked the 1940 surrender of mineral rights, the 1945 surrender still imposed an obligation on the Crown to lease or sell *in the best interests of the Band*. This would leave for consideration the argument that the Crown breached its fiduciary obligations by transferring the mineral rights to the DVLA in 1948, because transfer rather than reservation for future leasing was contrary to the best interests of the Indians.

---

245 Section 54 codified the principle that the Crown had to hold surrendered lands for the purpose specified in the surrender.

246 *Attorney-General of British Columbia v. Attorney-General of Canada* (1889), 14 App. Cas. 295 (P.C.).

[97] The trial judge rejected this argument on the ground that it was not foreseeable in 1948 that the mineral rights could have any value. . . .

[98] The finding of the trial judge that the Crown could not have known in 1948 that the mineral rights might possess value flies in the face of the evidence on record. Accordingly, this is one of those rare cases where departure from a trial judge's finding may be warranted.

> [Her Ladyship noted that the federal and provincial Crowns had both, for many years, routinely reserved mineral rights from grants they made because they recognized the value of those rights. She also noted that in 1948 the Crown knew or could have known the potential value of those rights because of exploration in the vicinity of the reserve. She continued:]

[102] Secondly, the trial judge's inference from low value of the absence of a duty to reserve the mineral from the 1948 transfer is suspect. If indeed the mineral rights had minimal sale value in 1948, it does not follow that a prudent person would give them away. It is more logical to argue that since nothing could be obtained for them at the time, and since it would cost nothing to keep them, they should be kept against the chance, however remote, that they might acquire some value in the future. The wisdom of the latter course is demonstrated by the Crown's policy with respect to its own mineral rights; it reserved them to itself, regardless of actual value. It lies ill in the mouth of the Crown to argue that it should have done less with the property entrusted to it as fiduciary to lease for the welfare of the Band.

[103] The trial judge's emphasis on the apparent low value of the mineral rights suggests an underlying concern with the injustice of conferring an unexpected windfall on the Indians at the Crown's expense. This concern is misplaced. It amounts to bringing foreseeability into the fiduciary analysis through the back door. This constitutes an error of law. The beneficiary of a fiduciary duty is entitled to have his or her property restored or value in its place, even if the value of the property turns out to be much greater than could have been foreseen at the time of the breach.[247]

[104] The matter comes down to this. The duty on the Crown as fiduciary was "that of a man of ordinary prudence in managing his own affairs."[248] A reasonable person does not inadvertently give away a potentially valuable asset which has already demonstrated earning potential. Nor does a reasonable person give away for no consideration what it will cost him nothing to keep and which may one day possess value, however remote the possibility. The Crown managing its own affairs reserved out its minerals. It should have done the same for the Band.

---

247 *Hodgkinson v. Simms*, [1994] 3 S.C.R. 377, [1994] 9 W.W.R. 609, 117 D.L.R. (4th) 161 at 199, *per* La Forest J.

248 *Fales v. Canada Permanent Trust Co.* (1976), 70 D.L.R. (3d) 257 at 267, [1977] 2 S.C.R. 302, [1976] 6 W.W.R. 10.

(d) *Conclusions on post-surrender duty and breach with respect to mineral rights*

[105] I conclude that the 1940 surrender of the mineral rights imposed a fiduciary duty to the Band with respect to the mineral rights under the terms of the 1940 surrender, and that the DIA breached this duty by conveying the mineral rights to the DVLA.

> [Her Ladyship then went on to consider the defence of limitation of actions and held that the bands' claim was not statute-barred, since the Crown was under a continuing duty to revoke the erroneous transfer of the mineral rights.
>
> The court allowed the appeal and the cross-appeal.
>
> La Forest, L'Heureux-Dubé and Sopinka JJ., agreed with Gonthier J., while Cory and Major JJ. agreed with McLachlin J.]

Notes and Questions

1. Based on *Guerin* and *Blueberry*, state the obligation that the Crown has towards Indian bands with respect to reserve lands, whether surrendered or unsurrendered.

2. In *Chief Chipeewayan Band v. R.*,[249] the Federal Court of Canada held that the Crown's fiduciary duty regarding the surrender of tribal lands included the determination of whether a band was still in existence. The Crown's failure to ensure that the band ceased to exist before relinquishing the land comprising the reserve therefore constituted a violation of its fiduciary duty to the band.

3. In *Osoyoos Indian Band v. Oliver (Town)*[250] the Supreme Court of Canada held that the Crown also stands in a fiduciary relationship towards a band when all or part of the reserve is being expropriated under the provisions of s. 35 of the *Indian Act*[251] by a federal or provincial authority.[252]

---

249 [2001] F.C.J. No. 1229, 2001 CarswellNat 1678, 2001 FCT 858, 209 F.T.R. 211 (T.D.), affirmed 2002 CarswellNat 1210, [2002] F.C.J. No. 831, 2002 FCA 221, 291 N.R. 314, [2003] 1 C.N.L.R. 54, 226 F.T.R. 94 (note) (C.A.), affirmed (2003), 2003 CarswellNat 278, 2003 CarswellNat 279, 307 N.R. 400 (note) (S.C.C.).

250 (2001), 206 D.L.R. (4th) 385, 2001 CarswellBC 2703, 2001 CarswellBC 2704, [2001] S.C.J. No. 82, 2001 SCC 85, 95 B.C.L.R. (3d) 22, [2002] 1 W.W.R. 23, 45 R.P.R. (3d) 1, 278 N.R. 201, 75 L.C.R. 1, [2002] 1 C.N.L.R. 271, 160 B.C.A.C. 171, 261 W.A.C. 171, [2001] 3 S.C.R. 746; followed in *BC Tel v. Seabird Island Indian Band (Assessor of)* (2002), 216 D.L.R. (4th) 70, 2002 CarswellNat 1697, 2002 CarswellNat 4555, 231 F.T.R. 159 (note), 2002 FCA 288, 292 N.R. 120, [2002] 4 C.N.L.R. 1, [2003] 1 F.C. 475 (C.A.).

251 R.S.C. 1985, c. I-5.

252 See also *Kruger v. R.* (1985), [1986] 1 F.C. 3, 17 D.L.R. (4th) 591, 1985 CarswellNat 97, 1985 CarswellNat 55F, 58 N.R. 241, [1985] 3 C.N.L.R. 15, 32 L.C.R. 65 (C.A.), leave to appeal refused (1985), 33 L.C.R. 192n, 62 N.R. 103n (S.C.C.). The action for damages for breach of trust in that case failed because it was statute barred.

4. In *R. v. Sparrow,*[253] the Supreme Court of Canada characterized the relationship between the Crown and aboriginals as a "special trust relationship" by virtue of the *sui generis* nature of the Indian title and the historic powers and responsibility assumed by the Crown in respect of Indian lands. It is from this relationship that the Crown's fiduciary duty, to deal with the lands in the best interest of the bands, flows. The test developed in *Sparrow* relating to the special trust relationship between the Crown and aboriginals has been applied in other cases.[254]

5. In his decision in *Canadian Pacific v. Paul,*[255] Dickson J. considered whether Indian title should be characterized as a beneficial interest in land or a personal usufructuary right. He concluded that neither of these characterizations is quite accurate. Indians have a legal right to occupy and possess certain lands, the ultimate title to which lies in the Crown. The interest does not amount to beneficial ownership nor is its nature completely exhausted by the concept of a personal right. The *sui generis* interest which Indians have in the land is personal in the sense that it cannot be transferred to a grantee, but the interest also gives rise upon surrender to a distinctive fiduciary obligation on the part of the Crown to deal with the land for the benefit of the surrendering Indians.

6. In *Samson Indian Band and Nation v. Canada,*[256] certain Indian bands were seeking an order requiring production of documents for which the Crown claimed privilege. The Federal Court of Appeal agreed that the Crown was in a "trust type" relationship with the Indian Bands. However, the court ruled that the rules and practices developed with respect to private trusts do not automatically flow to Crown trusts.

7. The concept of pre- and post-surrender fiduciary duties, discussed in *Blueberry*, was picked up in *Semiahmoo Indian Band v. Canada.*[257] The Crown had accepted the absolute surrender of a portion of an Indian band in 1951 for the purpose of a federal work. It never proceeded with the work and did not use most of the land, but retained title to it. The band sued to recover the land and was successful. The court held that the Crown breached its pre-surrender fiduciary duty to the band by accepting an absolute surrender rather than a surrender conditional on the land being used. While the band's claim based on that duty was statute-barred, the court also recognized a post-surrender fiduciary duty which required the Crown to correct any breach of the pre-surrender fiduciary duty if the Crown retained the land. The claim based on that duty was not barred. The court held that the appropriate remedy was a constructive trust with compensation. The personal remedy of an account of profits in lieu of compensation was inappropriate since the Crown had not used the land.

8. When a portion of a reserve is taken for a specific purpose and that purpose comes to an end, the land reverts to the Crown, which then holds title upon resulting trust for the

---

253 [1990] 1 S.C.R. 1075, 70 D.L.R. (4th) 385, [1990] 4 W.W.R. 410, 46 B.C.L.R. (2d) 1.
254 See *R. v. Badger*, [1996] 1 S.C.R. 771, [1996] S.C.J. No. 39, 1996 CarswellAlta 365F, 1996 CarswellAlta 587, [1996] 4 W.W.R. 457, 37 Alta. L.R. (3d) 153, 195 N.R. 1, 105 C.C.C. (3d) 289, 133 D.L.R. (4th) 324, [1996] 2 C.N.L.R. 77, 181 A.R. 321, 116 W.A.C. 321; *R. v. Nikal*, [1996] 1 S.C.R. 1013, 1996 CarswellBC 950, 1996 CarswellBC 950F, [1996] 5 W.W.R. 305, 19 B.C.L.R. (3d) 201, 105 C.C.C. (3d) 481, 196 N.R. 1, 133 D.L.R. (4th) 658, 74 B.C.A.C. 161, 121 W.A.C. 161, 35 C.R.R. (2d) 189, [1996] 3 C.N.L.R. 178.
255 [1988] 2 S.C.R. 654, 53 D.L.R. (4th) 487, 1 R.P.R. (2d) 105, 89 N.R. 325.
256 (sub nom. *Buffalo v. Canada*) (1995), 125 D.L.R. (4th) 294, 184 N.R. 139, 96 F.T.R. 239.
257 (1997), 148 D.L.R. (4th) 523, 215 N.R. 241, 131 F.T.R. 319 (note) (C.A.).

benefit of the Indian band. Can it be said that the reserve is revived in those circumstances?[258]

9. In *Guerin*, Dickson J. noted[259] that it does not matter whether a claim arises out of reserve lands or with respect to traditional tribal lands that were never set aside as a reserve. The Indian interest in the land is the same in both cases.[260]

The Crown's obligation towards Indians with respect to their traditional tribal lands was an issue in *Delgamuukw v. British Columbia*.[261] Although the question of the Crown's fiduciary obligation was not directly relevant in that case, it is useful to give a brief outline of the facts. Fifty-one hereditary chiefs representing subgroups of two aboriginal peoples claimed ownership of and jurisdiction over a large area of northern British Columbia. They based their claim on occupation and use, the *Royal Proclamation* of 1763, and s. 35(1) of the *Constitution Act, 1982*. The trial judge dismissed most of the claim, holding that all aboriginal rights had been extinguished by colonial enactments. However, he declared that the Indians were entitled, based on the Crown's fiduciary obligation, to use vacant Crown land for aboriginal purposes. On appeal, the majority of the British Columbia Court of Appeal varied the judgment of the trial judge by holding that not all of the Indians' aboriginal rights had been extinguished, but that they held non-exclusive rights protected at common law and s. 35(1). On further appeal, the Supreme Court of Canada reversed and directed a new trial. There were defects in the pleadings and in the procedure in the lower courts which prevented the court from considering the merits of the appeal.

The court discussed at length the nature of the aboriginal title, how it is protected at common law and under s. 35(1) of the *Constitution Act, 1982*, and how it can be proved. The court held that the plaintiffs' oral histories on which they based their claims were to be considered and were as valid as written records. It also held that governments have a moral duty to negotiate aboriginal land claims in good faith. Further, the court held that the province did not have the power to extinguish aboriginal title after it entered the union.

Since the issue of the Crown's fiduciary obligations was not directly relevant, a discussion of the details of the case is beyond the scope of this book.

Problems

1. Theodore died domiciled and resident in Ontario. By his will he left all his property to his trustees in trust to pay his debts and then to transfer his oil patch in Alberta to his son, John, and his 10,000 shares in Shell Oil Ltd. to his daughter, Mary. He directed his trustees to transfer the residue of his estate to his wife, Fern, for life, with remainder to his two children. The residue comprised a ranch in Alberta and substantial real and personal property in Ontario.

John was short of cash, so he agreed to sell his interest in the oil patch to Petro Canada. Then he died intestate. His mother is his closest relation. Mary made a will by which she left the 10,000 shares to her husband, Bill, and all her other property

---

258 See *Canada (Attorney General) v. Canadian Pacific Ltd.*, 217 D.L.R. (4th) 83, 2002 CarswellBC 1983, 2002 BCCA 478, 2 R.P.R. (4th) 249, [2002] 4 C.N.L.R. 32, 172 B.C.A.C. 188, 282 W.A.C. 188 (C.A.), additional reasons at 2003 CarswellBC 1128, 2003 BCCA 283, 226 D.L.R. (4th) 681, 182 B.C.A.C. 259, 300 W.A.C. 259 (C.A.).

259 [1984] 2 S.C.R. 335, 13 D.L.R. (4th) 321 at 336-337, [1984] 6 W.W.R. 481, 20 E.T.R. 6.

260 See *A.-G. Que. v. A.-G. Can.*, [1921] 1 A.C. 401 at 410-411, 56 D.L.R. 373 (P.C.).

261 (1997), 153 D.L.R. (4th) 193 (S.C.C.), reversing [1993] 5 W.W.R. 97, 104 D.L.R. (4th) 470 (B.C. C.A.).

to her children equally. Then she died. Fern died not long after her children. Theodore's estate is not yet fully administered. There are substantial debts, but the assets should easily offset them.

What are the rights of Petro Canada, Bill, and Mary's children to the several assets?

2. Tom died domiciled and resident in Alberta two years ago. Three years ago, he established an *inter vivos* trust, naming Canada Trust as his trustee and transferring various stocks, traded on the Montreal and Toronto stock exchanges, as well as a number of interests in oil wells located in Alberta to the trustee. The trust instrument required that the trust be administered by Canada Trust's head office in London, Ontario. It directed the trustee to retain the original assets and to pay the income to the settlor's wife, Lola, for life, and then to accumulate the income for a period of 60 years. At the end of that time the accumulated income and capital was to be paid to Tom's issue then living in Manitoba. Tom and Lola's only child, Carita, lives in Manitoba with her husband. They have several children, all minors. Lola died last year, domiciled in Alberta. Canada Trust has offices in all three provinces.

Ontario has accumulations legislation and both Ontario and Alberta have perpetuities statutes. Manitoba had neither and Alberta did not have accumulations legislation at the relevant times. The accumulation is excessive in Ontario and the trust is likely to be void in part for perpetuities in Ontario and Alberta.[262]

What law governs the trust?

---

262 See the chapter on limitations on the creation of trusts.

2

A COMPARISON BETWEEN TRUSTS AND OTHER RELATIONSHIPS

1. SCOPE

Thus far, we have focused primarily on providing an overview of the concept of a trust. In this chapter, we will attempt to broaden your basic appreciation for the role and function of a trust. To begin with, we will consider the trust from the vantage point of the trustee. Because trustees are one kind of fiduciary, the first part will be devoted to an examination of trustee *qua* fiduciary.

Thereafter, we will compare the trust with other legal relationships with which you are already familiar. These legal relationships are: agency, contract, debt, bailment, the office of personal representative, conditions, charges, and personal obligations. In each part, we will focus upon the similarities and differences between the trust and these various concepts; how the courts determine which relationship exists; and the consequences of such a determination.

2. TRUST AND THE FIDUCIARY RELATIONSHIP

In this part, we consider the trust not in contrast to, but as an example of, a fiduciary relationship. Historically, fiduciary relationships were thought to be confined to certain well-recognized categories such as that of an agent and principal, solicitor and client, director and company, and trustee and beneficiary. This compartmentalized view of fiduciary relationships was, however, put to rest by the Supreme Court of Canada in a series of cases beginning with *Canadian Aero Services v. O'Malley.*[1] Rather than relying on the historical categories, the courts now take a fact-driven approach, looking for the characteristics that signify the existence of a fiduciary relationship. A court will determine whether a relationship existed between the two parties in which one party reasonably placed his or her trust or confidence in the other or was dependent on the other in some significant way. The key factual components of a fiduciary relationship are:

---

1 [1974] S.C.R. 592.

a. discretionary power in one person;
b. the ability to exercise that power to affect the other's interest;
c. vulnerability on the part of the second person; and
d. reasonable reliance by the second on the first.

Thus, a fiduciary relationship involves an imbalance of power that must not be exploited by the fiduciary for his or her own benefit. A trustee qualifies as a fiduciary under either the historical, compartmentalized view or the modern, fact-driven approach.

The law imposes a general duty of loyalty upon all fiduciaries. The duty of loyalty subsumes the following: an obligation to act honestly, prudently, diligently, even-handedly, candidly, and strictly in the best interests of the other person. A fiduciary is precluded from making unauthorized profits, from delegating its responsibilities, and from placing itself in a conflict of interest. In short, a fiduciary cannot act in a self-interested fashion.

Trustees, although a type of fiduciary, are unique in two ways. First, there can be no trust absent trust property. Clearly, there can be fiduciary relationships in which no specific property is involved. Second, the trust relationship is the most intense of the fiduciary relationships because the trustee has the greatest scope to exercise independent authority over the trust property. As a result, the trustee is held to the most stringent fiduciary standards.

Hodgkinson v. Simms[2] illustrates the modern approach to the question of whether a fiduciary relationship exists. This approach to the determination of a fiduciary relationship can be traced to the reasoning in Wilson J.'s dissent in *Frame v. Smith,*[3] which was subsequently adopted in *LAC Minerals Ltd. v. International Corona Resources Ltd.*[4]

Further Reading

Scott, "The Fiduciary Principle," (1949), 37 Cal. L. Rev. 539.
T.G. Youdan, ed., *Equity, Fiduciaries and Trusts* (Toronto: Carswell, 1989), at 1.
John D. McCamus, "The Recent Expansion of Fiduciary Obligation: Common themes and Future Developments" 23 E.T.R. 301.

HODGKINSON v. SIMMS

[1994] 3 S.C.R. 377, [1994] 9 W.W.R. 609, 117 D.L.R. (4th) 161
Supreme Court of Canada

The plaintiff retained the investment counselling services of the defendant.

---

2 [1994] 3 S.C.R. 377, 117 D.L.R. (4th) 161, [1994] 9 W.W.R. 609, reversing 1992 CarswellBC 73, 6 C.P.C. (3d) 141, 5 B.L.R. (2d) 236, 45 E.T.R. 270, 11 B.C.A.C. 248, 22 W.A.C. 248, 65 B.C.L.R. (2d) 264, [1992] 4 W.W.R. 330 (C.A.).
3 [1987] 2 S.C.R. 99, 42 D.L.R. (4th) 81, 42 C.C.L.T. 1, 78 N.R. 40, 9 R.F.L. (3d) 225.
4 [1989] 2 S.C.R. 574, 6 R.P.R. (2d) 1, 61 D.L.R. (4th) 14, 101 N.R. 239, 26 C.P.R. 97.

The plaintiff told the defendant that his primary objectives were to minimize taxes and acquire stable, long-term investments. The plaintiff invested significant sums of money in multi-unit residential buildings ("MURBs") recommended by the defendant. The plaintiff's confidence in the defendant was such that he did not ask many questions regarding proposed investments. During the time he was advising the plaintiff, the defendant was also acting for the developers of the MURBs and received, as part of his compensation, a commission for each MURB unit purchased by one of his clients. When the real estate market crashed in 1981, the investments lost virtually all of their value. The plaintiff claimed that he would not have invested in the project had he known the true nature of the defendant's relationship with the developers.

The plaintiff brought an action for breach of fiduciary duty, breach of contract and negligence, claiming damages totalling all of his losses on the investments. The trial judge allowed the plaintiff's action for breach of fiduciary duty and awarded him damages in the amount of $350,507.62. The British Columbia Court of Appeal upheld the trial judge on the breach of contract issue, but reversed on the issue of fiduciary duties. The Court of Appeal also varied the damages award, setting it at an amount equal to the fees received by the defendant from the developers, pro-rated as between all of the investors in the MURBs. On further appeal to the Supreme Court of Canada, the appeal was allowed and the trial judgment restored.

La Forest J.:

. . .

While the legal concept of a fiduciary duty reaches back to the famous English case of *Keech v. Sandford*,[5] until recently the fiduciary duty could be described as a legal obligation in search of a principle.

. . .

[O]ver the past 10 years or so this court has had occasion to consider and enforce fiduciary obligations in a wide variety of contexts, and this has led to the development of a "fiduciary principle" which can be defined and applied with some measure of precision. One may begin with the following words of Dickson J. (as he then was) in *Guerin v. R.*:[6]

> . . . where by statute, agreement, or perhaps by unilateral undertaking, *one party has an obligation to act for the benefit of another*, and that obligation carries with it a discretionary power, the party thus empowered becomes a fiduciary.
>
> It is sometimes said that the nature of the fiduciary relationships is both established and exhausted by the standard categories of agent, trustee, partner, director and the like. I do not agree. *It is the nature of the relationship, not the specific category of actor involved that gives rise to*

---

5 (1726), Sel. Cas. t. King 61, 25 E.R. 223.
6 [1984] 2 S.C.R. 335, 13 D.L.R. (4th) 321 at 341, 20 E.T.R. 6, [1984] 6 W.W.R. 481, emphasis added.

the fiduciary duty. The categories of fiduciary, like those of negligence, should not be considered closed.

This conceptual approach to fiduciary duties was given analytical structure in the dissenting reasons of Wilson J. in *Frame v. Smith*,[7] who there proposed a three-step analysis to guide the courts in identifying new fiduciary relationships. She stated that relationships in which a fiduciary obligation has been imposed are marked by the following three characteristics: (1) scope for the exercise of some discretion or power; (2) that power or discretion can be exercised unilaterally so as to effect the beneficiary's legal or practical interests; and (3) a peculiar vulnerability to the exercise of that discretion or power. Although the majority held on the facts that there was no fiduciary obligation, Wilson J.'s mode of analysis has been followed as a "rough and ready guide" in identifying new categories of fiduciary relationships.[8] Wilson J.'s guidelines constitute *indicia* that help recognize a fiduciary relationship rather than ingredients that define it.

In *LAC Minerals* I elaborated further on the approach proposed by Wilson J. in *Frame v. Smith*.[9] I there identified three uses of the term fiduciary, only two of which I thought were truly fiduciary. The first is in describing certain relationships that have as their essence discretion, influence over interests, and an *inherent* vulnerability. In these types of relationships, there is a rebuttable presumption, arising out of the inherent purpose of the relationship, that one party has a duty to act in the best interests of the other party. Two obvious examples of this type of fiduciary relationship are trustee-beneficiary and agent-principal. In seeking to determine whether new classes of relationships are *per se* fiduciary, Wilson J.'s three-step analysis is a useful guide.

As I noted in *LAC Minerals*, however, the three-step analysis proposed by Wilson J. encounters difficulties in identifying relationships described by a slightly different use of the term "fiduciary," *viz.*, situations in which fiduciary obligations, though not innate to a given relationship, arise as a matter of fact out of the specific circumstances of that particular relationship.[10] In these cases, the question to ask is whether, given all the surrounding circumstances, one party could reasonably have expected that the other party would act in the former's best interests with respect to the subject-matter at issue. Discretion, influence, vulnerability, and trust were mentioned as non-exhaustive examples of evidential factors to be considered in making this determination.

Thus, outside the established categories, what is required is evidence of a mutual understanding that one party has relinquished its own self-interest and agreed to act solely on behalf of the other party. This idea was well-stated in the

---

7 *Supra*, note 3, at 99.
8 See *LAC Minerals, supra*, note 4, *per* Sopinka J., at 62-63 and *per* La Forest J., at 27 [D.L.R.]; *Canson Enterprises Ltd. v. Boughton & Co.*, [1991] 3 S.C.R. 534, 85 D.L.R. (4th) 129 at 155, 39 C.P.R. (3d) 449, [1992] 1 W.W.R. 245; *M. (K.) v. M. (H.)* (1992), 96 D.L.R. (4th) 289 at 325.
9 *Supra*, note 3.
10 See *LAC Minerals, supra*, note 4, at 29.

American case of *Dolton v. Capitol Federal Sav. and Loan Ass'n*,[11] in the banker-customer context, to be a state of affairs,

> . . . which impels or induces one party "to relax the care and vigilance it would and should have ordinarily exercised in dealing with a stranger." . . . [and] . . . has been found to exist where there is a repose of trust by the customer along with an acceptance or invitation of such trust on the part of the lending institution.

In relation to the advisory context, then, there must be something more than a simple undertaking by one party to provide information and execute orders for the other for a relationship to be enforced as fiduciary. For example, most everyday transactions between a bank customer and banker are conducted on a creditor-debtor basis.[12] Similarly, the relationship of an investor to his or her discount broker will not likely give rise to a fiduciary duty, where the broker is simply a conduit of information and an order taker. There are, however, other advisory relationships where, because of the presence of elements such as trust, confidentiality, and the complexity and importance of the subject-matter, it may be reasonable for the advisee to expect that the advisor is in fact exercising his or her special skills in that other party's best interests, unless the contrary is disclosed. Professor Finn describes these kinds of relationships in the following terms in "The Fiduciary Principle":[13]

> . . . fiduciary responsibilities will be exacted where the function the advisor represents himself as performing, and for which he is consulted, is that of counselling an advised party as to how his interests will or might best be served in a matter considered to be of importance to his personal or financial well-being, and in which the adviser would be expected both to be disinterested, save for his remuneration, and to be free of adverse responsibilities unless the contrary is disclosed at the outset. *It does seem to be the case, here, that our ready acceptance of a fiduciary expectation is coloured both by our assumption that credence is likely to be given to any advice given and by our perception of the social importance of the advisory function itself.*

More generally, relationships characterized by a unilateral discretion, such as the trustee-beneficiary relationship, are properly understood as simply a species of a broader family of relationships that may be termed "power-dependency" relationships. I employed this notion, developed in an article by Professor Coleman, to capture the dynamic of abuse in *Norberg v. Wynrib*.[14] *Norberg* concerned an aging physician who extorted sexual favours from a young female patient in exchange for feeding an addiction she had previously developed to the pain-killer Fiorinal. The difficulty in *Norberg* was that the sexual contact between the doctor

---

11 642 P.2d 21 (Colo. App. 1982), at 23-24.

12 See *Canadian Pioneer Management Ltd. v. Labour Relations Board of Saskatchewan*, [1980] 1 S.C.R. 433, 107 D.L.R. (3d) 1, [1980] 3 W.W.R. 214; *Thermo King Corp. v. Provincial Bank of Canada* (1981), 130 D.L.R. (3d) 256, 34 O.R. (2d) 369 (C.A.), leave to appeal refused (1982), 130 D.L.R. (3d) 256n, 42 N.R. 352n.

13 In T.G. Youdan, ed., *Equity, Fiduciaries and Trusts* (Toronto: Carswell, 1989) at 50-51, emphasis added.

14 [1992] 2 S.C.R. 226, 92 D.L.R. (4th) 449 at 463, 12 C.C.L.T. (2d) 1, additional reasons at [1992] 2 S.C.R. 318, [1992] 6 W.W.R. 673, 74 B.C.L.R. (2d) 2.

and patient had the appearance of consent. However, when the pernicious effects of the situational power imbalance were considered, it was clear that true consent was absent. While the concept of a "power-dependency" relationship was there applied to an instance of sexual assault, in my view, the concept accurately describes any situation where one party, by statute, agreement, a particular course of conduct, or by unilateral undertaking, gains a position of overriding power or influence over another party. Because of the particular context in which the relationship between the plaintiff and the doctor arose in that case, I found it preferable to deal with the case without regard to whether or not a fiduciary relationship arose. However, my colleague Justice McLachlin did dispose of the claim on the basis of the fiduciary duty, and whatever may be said of the peculiar situation in *Norberg*, I have no doubt that had the situation there arisen in the ordinary doctor-patient relationship, it would have given rise to fiduciary obligations: see, for example, *McInerney v. MacDonald*.[15]

As is evident from the different approaches taken in *Norberg*, the law's response to the plight of vulnerable people in power-dependency relationships gives rise to a variety of often overlapping duties. Concepts such as the fiduciary duty, undue influence, unconscionability, unjust enrichment, and even the duty of care are all responsive to abuses of vulnerable people in transactions with others. The existence of a fiduciary duty in a given case will depend upon the reasonable expectations of the parties, and these in turn depend on factors such as trust, confidence, complexity of subject matter, and community or industry standards. For instance in *Norberg*, the Hippocratic Oath was evidence that the sexual relationship diverged significantly from the standards reasonably expected from physicians by the community. This inference was confirmed by expert evidence to the effect that any reasonable practitioner in the defendant's position would have taken steps to help the addicted patient, in stark contrast to the deplorable exploitation which in fact took place.[16]

In seeking to identify the various civil duties that flow from a particular power-dependency relationship, it is simply wrong to focus only on the degree to which a power or discretion to harm another is somehow "unilateral". In my view, this concept has neither descriptive nor analytical relevance to many fact-based fiduciary relationships. *Ipso facto*, persons in a "power-dependency relationship" are vulnerable to harm. Further, the relative "degree of vulnerability", if it can be put that way, does not depend on some hypothetical ability to protect one's self from harm, but rather on the nature of the parties' reasonable expectations. Obviously, a party who expects the other party to a relationship to act in the former's best interests is more vulnerable to an abuse of power than a party who should be expected to know that he or she should take protective measures. J.C. Shepherd puts the matter in the following way:[17]

---

15 [1992] 2 S.C.R. 138, 93 D.L.R. (4th) 415, 12 C.C.L.T. (2d) 225, 137 N.R. 35, 7 C.P.C. (3d) 269.

16 See also *Harry v. Kreutziger* (1978), 95 D.L.R. (3d) 231 at 241, 9 B.C.L.R. 166 (C.A.) *per* Lambert J.A.

17 *The Law of Fiduciary Duties* (Toronto: Carswell, 1981), at 102, emphasis in original.

> Where a weaker or reliant party trusts the stronger party not to use his power and influence against the weaker party, and the stronger party, if acting *reasonably*, would have known or ought to have known of this reliance, we can say that the stronger party had notice of the encumbrance, and therefore in using the power has accepted the duty.

Thus in *LAC Minerals*,[18] I felt it perverse to fault Corona for failing to negotiate a confidentiality agreement with LAC in a situation where the well-established practice in the mining industry was such that Corona would have had no reasonable expectation that LAC would use the information to its detriment. To imply that one is not vulnerable to an abuse of power because one could have protected, but did not protect oneself is to focus on one narrow class of "power-dependency relationship" at the expense of the general principle that transcends it. I recognize, of course, that the majority holding in that case was that "the evidence does not establish in this case the existence of a fiduciary relationship."[19] But as I will indicate presently, there is a basic difference between the type of situation that arises here and that which arose in *LAC Minerals*.

In summary, the precise legal or equitable duties the law will enforce in any given relationship are tailored to the legal and practical incidents of a particular relationship. To repeat a phrase used by Lord Scarman, "[t]here is no substitute in this branch of the law for a meticulous examination of the facts."[20]

The authorities

The Court of Appeal relied heavily on this court's reasons in *LAC Minerals* and, more particularly, on the reasons of Justice Sopinka. In my view the Court of Appeal erred in importing the analysis in the *LAC Minerals* case to professional advisory relationships. Commercial interactions between parties at arm's length normally derive their social utility from the pursuit of self-interest, and the courts are rightly circumspect when asked to enforce a duty (*i.e.*, the fiduciary duty) that vindicates the very antithesis of self-interest.[21] The requirement of vulnerability was addressed in *LAC Minerals* in a context where the parties were engaged in negotiations with a view to entering into a joint mining venture. While I viewed the facts differently, I quite understand the reluctance on the part of some of my colleagues to extend the fiduciary principle to what they perceived to be an arm's length commercial relationship. Similarly, the *Hospital Products* case,[22] which was central to Sopinka J.'s analysis of vulnerability in *LAC Minerals*, was a case about two commercial actors dealing at arm's length, there in the context of an exclusive distributorship agreement. No doubt it will be a rare occasion where parties, in all other respects independent, are justified in surrendering their self-

---

18 *Supra*, note 4.

19 *Ibid., per* Lamer C.J., at [D.L.R.] 15-16.

20 See *National Westminster Bank plc v. Morgan*, [1985] 1 All E.R. 821 at 831, [1985] A.C. 686 (H.L.).

21 See *Jirna Ltd. v. Mister Donut of Canada Ltd.* (1971), 22 D.L.R. (3d) 639, 3 C.P.R. (2d) 40, [1972] 1 O.R. 251 (C.A.), affirmed 40 D.L.R. (3d) 303, 12 C.P.R. (2d) 1, [1975] 1 S.C.R. 2; *Midcon Oil & Gas Ltd. v. New British Dominion Oil Co.*, 12 D.L.R. (2d) 705, [1958] S.C.R. 314.

22 *Hospital Products Ltd. v. United States Surgical Corp.* (1984), 55 A.L.R. 417 (Aust. H.C.).

interest such as to invoke the fiduciary principle. Put another way, the law does not object to one party taking advantage of another *per se*, so long as the particular form of advantage-taking is not otherwise objectionable. In *LAC Minerals*, for instance, the majority viewed the particular form of advantage-taking as not unfair. This was primarily owing to their view that International Corona could have protected, but did not protect itself from harm by contract. On the other hand, it was my view that the particular form of advantage-taking was in fact objectionable, given the expectations of the parties generated, *inter alia*, by industry practice concerning the treatment of confidential information between parties negotiating towards a joint venture.[23] The situation here is quite different from that which arose in *LAC Minerals*. In the professional advisor context, the situation here, it would be surprising indeed to expect an advisee to protect himself or herself from the abuse of power by his or her independent professional advisor when the very basis of the advisory contract is that the advisor will use his or her special skills on behalf of the advisee. The difficulty with this proposition was forcefully expressed by MacFarlane J.A. in *Burns v. Kelly Peters & Associates Ltd.*:[24]

> . . . I do not think that an investor must inquire whether his trusted and paid adviser is joined with the developer in making secret profits at his expense, and in concealing facts material to his financial well-being.

Similarly, in *Nocton v. Lord Ashburton*,[25] another case of non-disclosure, the House of Lords summarily dismissed the defendant's submission that the client had the means to correct the false impression made on him by his solicitor's misleading statement.

In sharp contrast to arm's length commercial relationships, which are characterized by self-interest, the essence of professional advisory relationships is precisely trust, confidence, and independence. Thus, the concern expressed by Wilson J. in *Frame*,[26] and echoed by Sopinka J. in *LAC Minerals*,[27] about the dangers of extending the fiduciary principle in the context of an arm's length commercial relationship is simply not transferable to professional advisory relationships.

I note in passing that the dissenting reasons of Lambert J.A. in *Kelly Peters*, upon which the Court of Appeal relied in the present case, turned, at least in part, on the absence of fees between the parties. The plaintiffs in *Kelly Peters* were clients of Kelly Peters & Associates Ltd. (K.P.A.) (the defendant), a financial planning and counselling concern. K.P.A. had been retained by the various plaintiffs to set up a "base plan" on their behalf. This included such services as drawing up a will, making arrangements for life insurance, RRSPs, and so on. K.P.A. also

---

23 R. E. Hawkins, "LAC and the Emerging Obligation to Bargain in Good Faith" (1990), 15 Queen's L. Rev. 65.

24 [1987] 6 W.W.R. 1, 41 D.L.R. (4th) 577 at 620, 16 B.C.L.R. (2d) 1 (C.A.).

25 [1914] A.C. 932, [1914-15] All E.R. Rep. 45 (H.L.).

26 *Supra*, note 3.

27 *Supra*, note 4.

offered an "investment plan" whereby clients received counselling regarding the purchase of real estate for investment and tax purposes. As it turned out, the defendants advised the plaintiffs on the purchase of certain Hawaiian MURBs without disclosing that they (the defendants) were receiving a substantial commission on each sale. At the time the plaintiffs were being advised to purchase the Hawaiian MURBs the adviser was not asking for any fee for the advice or making any arrangements to secure payment of a fee. This fact led Lambert J.A. to infer that the plaintiffs must have known that the advice was not independent, but rather that it was tainted by self-interest. He stated:[28]

> The plaintiffs must have known that commissions were being paid to someone, and they must have known that KPA Ltd., William Kelly, John Peters, Maureen Kelly, and the associates obtained commission income from transactions. There is no evidence that if the plaintiffs had asked about commissions they would not have been told the precise situation.

I would add, however, that while Lambert J.A. was willing to infer from the absence of fees an understanding on the part of the plaintiffs that the advice of K.P.A. was tainted, the majority was unwilling to draw such an inference. Having said this, I note that the facts in the present case are much stronger than those in *Kelly Peters* with respect to this crucial point. The appellant adduced uncontradicted evidence to the effect that the respondent went out of his way to represent himself as independent, and this factor was of critical importance to the appellant. In fact, the respondent made a conscious decision not to disclose his fee arrangement with the developers to his investor clients for fear it would interfere with his lucrative practice. At a meeting of July 21, 1980, attended by the respondent, the Olma brothers, and the Olmas' attorney, it was explained that any fees and moneys paid to the respondent must be disclosed to the investors, otherwise such fees could be construed as a secret commission or bribe under the *Criminal Code*. The discussion then turned to other ways in which the respondent could earn income from the Olmas without having to make disclosure to the investors. By that point the respondent had already billed the Olma brothers in the amount of $24,500.

The finding of a fiduciary relationship in the independent professional advisory context simply does not represent any addition to the law. Courts exercising equitable jurisdiction have repeatedly affirmed that clients in a professional advisory relationship have a right to expect that their professional advisors will act in their best interests, to the exclusion of all other interests, unless the contrary is disclosed. J.C. Shepherd states the following in his treatise, *The Law of Fiduciary Duties*:[29]

> It appears to be settled that any person can, by offering to give advice in a particular manner to another, create in himself fiduciary obligations stemming from the confidential nature of the relationship created, which obligations limit the adviser's dealings with the advisee.

---

28 *Kelly Peters, supra*, note 24, at 604.
29 (Toronto: Carswell, 1981) at 28.

Indeed, nobody would argue against the enforcement of fiduciary duties in policing the advisory aspect of solicitor-client relationships.[30] Similar rules apply in the fields of real estate and insurance counselling.[31]

More importantly for present purposes, courts have consistently shown a willingness to enforce a fiduciary duty in the investment advice aspect of many kinds of financial service relationships.[32] In all of these cases, as here, the ultimate discretion or power in the disposition of funds remained with the beneficiary. In addition, where reliance on the investment advice is found, a fiduciary duty has been affirmed without regard to the level of sophistication of the client, or the client's ultimate discretion to accept or reject the professional's advice.[33] Rather, the common thread that unites this body of law is the measure of the confidential and trust-like nature of the particular advisory relationship, and the ability of the plaintiff to establish reliance in fact.

Much of this case law was recently canvassed by Keenan J., in *Varcoe v. Sterling*,[34] in an effort to demarcate the boundaries of the fiduciary principle in the broker-client relationship. Keenan J. stated:[35]

> The relationship of broker and client is not *per se* a fiduciary relationship. . . . Where the elements of trust and confidence and reliance on skill and knowledge and advice are present, the relationship is fiduciary and the obligations that attach are fiduciary. On the other hand, if those elements are not present, the fiduciary relationship does not exist. . . . The circumstances can cover the whole spectrum from total reliance to total independence. An example of total reliance is found in the case of *Ryder v. Osler, Wills, Bickle Ltd.*[36] A \$400,000 trust for the benefit of an

---

30 See *Nocton v. Lord Ashburton, supra*, note 35; *Jacks v. Davis* (1982), 141 D.L.R. (3d) 355, [1983] 1 W.W.R. 327, 39 B.C.L.R. 353 (C.A.).

31 See *Henderson v. Thompson* (1909), 41 S.C.R. 445 (real estate agents); *Fine's Flowers Ltd. v. General Accident Assurance Co. of Canada* (1977), 81 D.L.R. (3d) 139, 2 B.L.R. 257, 17 O.R. (2d) 529 (C.A.); *Fletcher v. Manitoba Public Insurance Co.*, [1990] 3 S.C.R. 191, 74 D.L.R. (4th) 636, 1 C.C.L.I. (2d) 1, 116 N.R. 1 (insurance agents); J.G. Edmond, "Fiduciary Duties Owed by Insurance, Real Estate and Other Agents" in *The 1993 Isaac Pitblado Lectures: Fiduciary Duties/Conflicts of Interest* (Winnipeg: Law Society of Manitoba, 1993) at 75-86.

32 See *582872 Saskatchewan Ltd. v. Thurgood*, [1992] 5 W.W.R. 193, 93 D.L.R. (4th) 694, 46 E.T.R. 28, 100 Sask. R. 214 (C.A.); *Kelly Peters, supra*, note 24; *Elderkin v. Merrill Lynch, Royal Securities Ltd.* (1977), 80 D.L.R. (3d) 313, 22 N.S.R. (2d) 218, 31 A.P.R. 218 (C.A.) (investment counsellor-client); *Glennie v. McDougall & Cowans Holdings Ltd.*, [1935] 2 D.L.R. 561, [1935] S.C.R. 257; *Burke v. Cory*, 19 D.L.R. (2d) 252, [1959] O.W.N. 129 (C.A.); *Maghun v. Richardson Securities of Canada Ltd.* (1986), 34 D.L.R. (4th) 524, 58 O.R. (2d) 1, 18 O.A.C. 141 (C.A.) (stockbroker-client); *Lloyds Bank Ltd. v. Bundy*, [1975] Q.B. 326, [1974] 3 All E.R. 757 (U.K. C.A.); *Standard Investments Ltd. v. Canadian Imperial Bank of Commerce* (1985), 22 D.L.R. (4th) 410, 52 O.R. (2d) 473, 11 O.A.C. 318 (C.A.), leave to appeal refused, 53 O.R. (2d) 663n, 15 O.A.C. 237 (note) (banker-client); *Wakeford v. Yada Tompkins Huntingford & Humphries* (August 1, 1985), Doc. Van. Reg. C826216 (B.C.S.C.), affirmed (1986), 28 D.L.R. (4th) 481, 4 B.C.L.R. (2d) 306 (C.A.) (accountant-client); see, generally, Mark Ellis, "Financial Advisors" (cc. 7 and 8) in *Fiduciary Duties in Canada* (Don Mills: R. DeBoo, 1988, looseleaf).

33 See *Elderkin, ibid.*; *Laskin v. Bache & Co. Inc.* (1971), 23 D.L.R. (3d) 385, [1972] 1 O.R. 465 (C.A.); *Wakeford, ibid.*, at 8.

34 (1992), 7 O.R. (3d) 204 (Gen. Div.), affirmed (1992), 10 O.R. (3d) 574 (C.A.), leave to appeal to S.C.C. refused (1992), 10 O.R. (3d) xv (note), 145 N.R. 390 (note), 60 O.A.C. 74 (note).

35 *Ibid.*, at 234-236.

36 (1985), 49 O.R. (2d) 609, 16 D.L.R. (4th) 80 (H.C.).

elderly widow was deposited with the broker. An investment plan was prepared and approved and authority given to operate a discretionary account. . . . At the other end of the spectrum is the unreported case of *Merit Investment Corp. v. Mogil*,[37] in which the client used the brokerage firm for processing orders. He referred to the account executive as an "order-taker," whose advice was not sought and whose warnings were ignored.

. . .

The relationship of the broker and client is elevated to a fiduciary level when the client reposes trust and confidence in the broker and relies on the broker's advice in making business decisions. When the broker seeks or accepts the client's trust and confidence and undertakes to advise, the broker must do so fully, honestly and in good faith. . . . It is the trust and reliance placed by the client which gives to the broker the power and in some cases, discretion, to make a business decision for the client. Because the client has reposed that trust and confidence and has given over that power to the broker, the law imposes a duty on the broker to honour that trust and respond accordingly.

In my view, this passage represents an accurate statement of fiduciary law in the context of independent professional advisory relationships, whether the advisers be accountants, stockbrokers, bankers, or investment counsellors. Moreover, it states a principled and workable doctrinal approach. Thus, where a fiduciary duty is claimed in the context of a financial advisory relationship, it is at all events a question of fact as to whether the parties' relationship was such as to give rise to a fiduciary duty on the part of the advisor.

. . .

Application to the case at bar

. . .

The Court of Appeal was of the opinion that the parties' relationship lacked the level of vulnerability required by this court in *LAC Minerals*. The court stated[38] that *LAC Minerals* represented a "substantial development in the law on the scope of fiduciary duty and it is unfortunate that the learned trial judge did not have the benefit of that judgment." Later, the court continued:[39] "Until *LAC Minerals* the line between reliance and vulnerability to the extent required for the creation of a fiduciary duty seems to have been blurred and any degree of dependency was often sufficient to establish a fiduciary obligation."

Two points must be made about this statement. First, as discussed earlier, the Court of Appeal failed to recognize a basic difference between the factual context of *LAC Minerals* and that of this case. I see nothing in *LAC Minerals* that purports to create a new, higher legal standard for the finding of a fiduciary duty. Rather, in *LAC Minerals* this court grappled with a difficult fact situation and the result was, perhaps not surprisingly, differing views among the various justices. Second, the trial judge examined the dynamic underlying the parties' relationship and, in doing so, examined the *indicia* of vulnerability in the way it was set out in *Hospital*

---

37 (March 23, 1989), Anderson J. (Ont. H.C.), [summarized at 14 A.C.W.S. (3d) 378].
38 *Hodgkinson, supra*, note 2, at 242 [B.L.R.] (C.A.).
39 *Ibid.*, at 247.

Products,[40] which is the very test used by Sopinka J. in *LAC Minerals*.[41] Moreover, she quoted[42] the definition of vulnerability set out by Lambert J.A. (dissenting) in *Kelly Peters*[43] which definition the Court of Appeal itself stated, "more closely accord[s] with the judgment [of Sopinka J.] in *LAC Minerals*."[44]

In short, I simply cannot agree that the trial judge applied the wrong legal test, or that the test she applied was eclipsed by *LAC Minerals*. On the contrary, her analysis of the facts was on the whole consistent with the relevant authorities and does not disclose an error of law. The trial judge carefully considered the parties' relationship and found it to have all the characteristics of those relationships the law labels as fiduciary. In the end, she had little difficulty concluding that the appellant relied on the respondent's recommendations in deciding to make the four impugned investments, and that the respondent was aware of this reliance.

. . .

Conclusion on fiduciary duty issue

To conclude, I am of the view that the trial judge did not err in finding that a fiduciary obligation existed between the parties, and that this duty was breached by the respondent's decision not to disclose pecuniary interest with the developers.

Damages

The trial judge assessed damages flowing from both breach of fiduciary duty and breach of contract. She found the quantum of damages to be the same under either claim; namely, the return of capital (adjusted to take into consideration the tax benefits received as a result of the investments), plus all consequential losses, including legal and accounting fees. As I stated at the outset, I cannot find fault with the trial judge's disposition of the damages question.

It is useful to review some key findings of fact that bear on the issue of damages. The trial judge found the appellant paid fair market price for each of the four investments. However, she found that throughout the period during which the appellant was induced by the respondent's recommendations into making the investments, the respondent was in a financial relationship with the developers of the projects. In short, the trial judge found the respondent stood to gain financially if the appellant invested according to his recommendations. She further found that if the appellant had known of the true relationship between the respondent and the developers, he would not have invested. She also found that had the parties turned their minds to the potential consequences of the respondent's relationship with the developers it would have been reasonably foreseeable that

---

40   *Supra,* note 22.
41   *Supra*, note 4, at 63.
42   At 164.
43   *Supra*, note 24.
44   *Hodgkinson, supra*, note 2, at 243 (C.A.).

the appellant would not have invested. I turn now to the principles that bear on the calculation of damages in this case. It is well-established that the proper approach to damages for breach of a fiduciary duty is restitutionary. On this approach, the appellant is entitled to be put in as good a position as he would have been in had the breach not occurred. On the facts here, this means that the appellant is entitled to be restored to the position he was in before the transaction. The trial judge adopted this restitutionary approach and fixed damages at an amount equal to the return of capital, as well as all consequential losses, minus the amount the appellant saved on income tax due to the investments.

The respondent advanced two arguments against the trial judge's assessment of damages for breach of fiduciary duty. Both raise the issue of causation, and I will address these submissions as they were argued.

. . .

The Court of Appeal's approach to contractual damages is puzzling in that it seemed to accept the finding that if the contractual duty had not been breached the investments would not have been made, yet it proceeded to award damages in proportion to the amounts paid by the developer to the defendant. It is clear, however, that there would have been no such fees had the investments not been made. In short, I am unable to follow the Court of Appeal's reasoning on the issue of damages for breach of contract, and I would restore the award of damages made by the trial judge.

Disposition

I would allow the appeal, set aside the order of the British Columbia Court of Appeal and restore the order of the trial judge with costs throughout, including letter of credit costs to avoid a stay and allow recovery on the trial judgment pending appeal to the Court of Appeal.

[L'Heureux-Dubé and Gonthier JJ. concurred with La Forest J.

Iacobucci concurred in the result.

Sopinka and McLachlin JJ. wrote a joint dissenting judgment in which Major J. concurred.]

Notes and Questions

1. What were the practical effects of the defendant being found in a fiduciary position *vis-à-vis* the plaintiff?

2. In the principal case the court used the reasonable expectation test to determine whether the facts gave rise to a fiduciary obligation. In *Apsassin v. Canada (Department of Indian Affairs & Northern Development)*[45] the Supreme Court of Canada applied the

---

45 (1995), (sub nom. *Blueberry River Indian Band v. Canada (Department of Indian Affairs &*

ceding of power-vulnerability test. Are these tests identical? If not, ought they to be amalgamated into a unified test?[46]

3. There is a fiduciary relationship between parent and child. In *M. (K.) v. M. (H.)*[47] the Supreme Court of Canada held that a parent's fiduciary duty includes refraining from incestuous assaults on a child. Wilson J. extended fiduciary law to the protection of non-economic interests of a child, such as human and personal interests.

4. Can a fiduciary relationship exist between spouses? If so, what results follow from such a determination? *Gregoric v. Gregoric*[48] held that a husband was a fiduciary *vis-à-vis* his wife during settlement negotiations after their marriage broke down. The husband controlled a business in which his wife had an interest. However, this case may be restricted to situations in which one spouse controls an asset registered in the name of another spouse.[49] In general courts have held that upon marriage breakdown spouses are not in a fiduciary relationship.[50] Indeed, the nature of the relationship at that stage is such that a fiduciary relationship is not well possible or workable.[51]

5. The Supreme Court of Canada also applied the modern approach to the characterization of a fiduciary relationship in *LAC Minerals Ltd. v. International Corona Resources Ltd.*[52] During joint venture discussions, International Corona disclosed to LAC Minerals confidential geological reports regarding a certain site. The parties did not enter into a confidentiality agreement and LAC Minerals subsequently acquired the property. International Corona claimed liability under three heads: breach of contract, breach of confidence, and breach of fiduciary duty. The court held that LAC Minerals did not owe International Corona a fiduciary duty, but did engage in a breach of confidence. Do you think the hallmarks of a fiduciary relationship, reasonable reliance and vulnerability, were present in the case? Note that both parties were sophisticated and could afford good advisors.

Northern Development)) [1995] 4 S.C.R. 344, 1995 CarswellNat 1279, 1995 CarswellNat 1278, 130 D.L.R. (4th) 193, [1996] 2 C.N.L.R. 25, 190 N.R. 89, 102 F.T.R. 160 (note).

46 See *Chippewas of Nawash First Nation v. Canada (Minister of Fisheries & Oceans)* (2000), 196 F.T.R. 249, 2000 CarswellNat 2775, [2000] F.C.J. No. 1833, 79 C.R.R. (2d) 46, 37 C.E.L.R. (N.S.) 44, [2001] 1 C.N.L.R. 20 (T.D.), appeal dismissed on other grounds 2002 FCA 22, 2002 CarswellNat 291, 2002 CarswellNat 1421, 2002 CAF 22 (C.A.), affirmed (2002), 2002 CarswellNat 3552, 2002 CarswellNat 4180, 2002 FCA 485, 2002 CAF 485, 298 N.R. 305, [2003] 2 C.N.L.R. 78, [2003] 3 F.C. 233 (C.A.), leave to appeal refused 2003 CarswellNat 2776, 2003 CarswellNat 2777, [2003] 4 C.N.L.R. iv (note) (S.C.C.). The court found that the facts did not give rise to a fiduciary duty by applying the reasonable expectation test and the ceding power - vulnerability test separately.

47 (sub nom. *M. c. M.*) [1992] 3 S.C.R. 6, 1992 CarswellOnt 841, 1992 CarswellOnt 998, [1992] S.C.J. No. 85, 142 N.R. 321, 96 D.L.R. (4th) 289, 57 O.A.C. 321, 14 C.C.L.T. (2d) 1. See also *Hodgkinson, supra,* note 2, at 408. And see Ian M. Hull, "A New Twist on Breach of Fiduciary Duty in Estate Litigation" (1998), 25 E.T.R. (2d) 153.

48 (1990), 4 O.R. (3d) 588, [1990] O.J. No. 1692, 1990 CarswellOnt 296, 28 R.F.L. (3d) 419, 39 E.T.R. 63 (Gen. Div.), additional reasons at (1991), 1991 CarswellOnt 3151, 4 O.R. (3d) 604 (Gen. Div.).

49 See *Leopold v. Leopold* (2000), 51 O.R. (3d) 275, 2000 CarswellOnt 4707, [2000] O.J. No. 4604, 12 R.F.L. (5th) 118, 195 D.L.R. (4th) 717 (S.C.J.).

50 See *Murray v. Murray* (1994), 157 A.R. 224, 119 D.L.R. (4th) 46, 1994 CarswellAlta 361, [1994] A.J. No. 762, 77 W.A.C. 224, 10 R.F.L. (4th) 60 (C.A.); *Fleming v. Fleming* (2001), 19 R.F.L. (5th) 274, 2001 CarswellOnt 974, [2001] O.J. No. 1052, 6 C.C.L.T. (3d) 271 (S.C.J.).

51 See J.G. McLeod, "Annotation" (1995), 15 R.F.L. (4th) 216.

52 *Supra*, note 4.

6. What level of vulnerability is required to warrant a finding of a fiduciary relationship? In *Zraik v. Levesque Securities Inc.*[53] the Ontario Court of Appeal used the modern approach to determine the existence of a fiduciary relationship. The court held that the investment advisor was negligent in failing to supervise his client's commodities account properly, but that he did not owe the client a fiduciary duty. The determinative factor was the level of experience and sophistication the client possessed in commodities trading. Having found that Zraik was an intelligent business man and a sophisticated and frequent commodities trader who analysed trades independently, the court held that Zraik was not sufficiently vulnerable or reliant upon his investment advisor to support a fiduciary relationship.

7. Even if all the hallmarks of a fiduciary relationship are present, carelessness by the fiduciary does not amount to a breach of fiduciary duty.[54] What is the practical significance of a finding of negligence instead of a breach of fiduciary duty?

8. What degree of power must the defendant possess to be found a fiduciary? It has been held that the defendant will not be regarded as a fiduciary if the defendant's discretionary power over the plaintiff was not exercised unilaterally.[55] Similarly, in *Secord v. Global Securities Corp.*[56] the court found that there was an agency relationship between a stockbroker and a client, but not a fiduciary relationship. Although the stockbroker was more than a mere order taker since it provided the client with investment advice, the broker did not have unilateral discretion over the trading of the client's accounts.

9. Can a fiduciary relationship be imposed by statute absent the traditional hallmarks? Is so, under what circumstances? Note that some duties imposed by statute may not be fiduciary even if the duty arises in the context of a fiduciary relationship, because they do not derive from the fiduciary character of the relationship.[57]

---

53 (2001), 153 O.A.C. 186, 2001 CarswellOnt 4468, [2001] O.J. No. 5083 (C.A.), additional reasons at (2002), 2002 CarswellOnt 363 (C.A.). See also *Kent v. May* (2001), 2001 CarswellAlta 721, 298 A.R. 71 (Q.B.), affirmed 2002 CarswellAlta 1311, 2002 ABCA 252, 317 A.R. 381, 284 W.A.C. 381 (C.A.), additional reasons at 2002 CarswellAlta 1626, 2002 ABCA 306 (Alta. C.A.), in which the court considered the client's investment knowledge and experience, as well as other factors, such as whether the stock account was discretionary and the level and frequency of client contact, to determine whether the client was sufficiently vulnerable to his investment dealer.

54 See *Pryce v. Vuckovich* (1999), 90 O.T.C. 283, 1999 CarswellOnt 27, [1999] O.J. No. 20 (Gen. Div.), affirmed (2000), 144 O.A.C. 256, 2000 CarswellOnt 3251 (C.A.), leave to appeal refused (2001), 271 N.R. 393 (note), 150 O.A.C. 198 (note), 2001 CarswellOnt 5608, 2001 CarswellOnt 5609 (S.C.C.). The defendant accountant stood in a fiduciary relationship towards his client and provided investment advice to the client that he believed to be sound. The court held that the defendant was negligent, but did not breach his fiduciary obligations to his client.

55 *Stoney Tribal Council v. PanCanadian Petroleum Ltd.* (1998), 65 Alta. L.R. (3d) 353, [1999] 1 W.W.R. 41, 1998 CarswellAlta 310, [1998] A.J. No. 381, 218 A.R. 201, 39 B.L.R. (2d) 203, [1999] 1 C.N.L.R. 219 (Q.B.), varied on other grounds (2000), 86 Alta. L.R. (3d) 147, [2001] 2 W.W.R. 442, 2000 CarswellAlta 760, [2000] A.J. No. 870, 2000 ABCA 209, 261 A.R. 289, 225 W.A.C. 289, 12 B.L.R. (3d) 228, [2001] 3 C.N.L.R. 347 (C.A.).

56 81 B.C.L.R. (3d) 235, 8 B.L.R. (3d) 238, [2000] B.C.J. No. 2096, 2000 CarswellBC 2141, 2000 BCSC 1544 (S.C.), reversed 2003 CarswellBC 332, 2003 BCCA 85, [2003] 3 W.W.R. 612, 11 B.C.L.R. (4th) 62, 179 B.C.A.C. 12, 295 W.A.C. 12 (C.A.). *Cf. Fogo v. F.C.G. Securities Corp.* (1998), 172 N.S.R. (2d) 266, 1998 CarswellNS 378, [1998] N.S.J. No. 455, 524 A.P.R. 266 (S.C.), in which the broker was only an order taker.

57 See *Terra Energy Ltd. v. Kilborn Engineering Alberta Ltd.*, 232 A.R. 101, 170 D.L.R. (4th) 405, 1999 CarswellAlta 141, [1999] A.J. No. 221, 43 C.L.R. (2d) 190, 195 W.A.C. 101, [1999] 6 W.W.R. 483, 45 B.L.R. (2d) 170 (C.A.), reconsideration refused (1999), 1999 CarswellAlta 348, [1999] A.J. No. 444, 232 A.R. 297, 195 W.A.C. 297 (C.A.), leave to appeal refused (2000), 255

10. The British Columbia Court of Appeal applied the modern approach in finding that a fiduciary relationship existed between a real estate agent and vendor in *Baillie v. Chairman*.[58] What is interesting about the case is that the court held that a real estate agent-vendor relationship is not *per se* fiduciary, but that such a relationship can be found to exist in certain circumstances. Tory J.A. held that the agent put himself in a fiduciary relationship when he wrote a letter to the vendor advising the vendor to accept an offer that was $29,000 lower than the recently lowered list price and the vendor acted on that advice. Before the transaction closed, the purchaser decided he did not want the property. The agent substituted a company controlled by him as purchaser and did so without disclosing his interest to the vendor, thereby breaching his fiduciary duty. The agent then re-sold the property within weeks of the initial sale and earned a net profit in excess of $30,000.

What is the correct measure of damages? Did the selling agent's fiduciary duty extend past the completion of the contract?[59]

11. Modern statutes in Canada now permit trustees to receive reasonable remuneration, a right not recognized in equity.[60]

12. Parties to a joint venture stand in a fiduciary relationship.[61] Do fiduciary obligations under a joint venture agreement survive the termination of the agreement?[62]

13. Do partners owe fiduciary duties to their partners or to the partnership?[63] Are intending partners and joint venturers presumed to be fiduciaries?[64]

14. In addition to fiduciary relationships there are also confidential relationships. These may arise in situations of reliance such as between priest and penitent, when the parties have entered into a confidentiality agreement, and when the circumstances give

---

A.R. 399 (note), [1999] S.C.C.A. No. 316, 253 N.R. 193 (note), 220 W.A.C. 399 (note), in which the court found that a statute can only create a fiduciary relationship if it confers power on one party that enables that party to appropriate or misuse the other party's property. The court held that the Code of Ethics governing a professional engineering firm did not create a fiduciary relationship.

58 (1992), 94 D.L.R. (4th) 403, [1993] 1 W.W.R. 232, 70 B.C.L.R. (2d) 388 (C.A.), additional reasons at (1993), 107 D.L.R. (4th) 577, 86 B.C.L.R. (2d) 83, 51 C.P.R. (3d) 437 (C.A.).

59 *Cf. Kaczmarczyk v. Vogelsberg* (1995), 50 R.P.R. (2d) 233, 1995 CarswellOnt 1196, [1995] O.J. No. 904 (Gen. Div.), varied (1998), 1998 CarswellOnt 1367 (C.A.), in which the fiduciary duty between a real estate agent and a vendor was held to extend beyond the contractual relationship of the parties.

60 See the *Trustee Act*, R.S.O. 1990, c. T.23 and comparable legislation listed in part 6, *infra*.

61 *Wonsch Construction Co. v. National Bank of Canada* (1990), (sub nom. *Wonsch Construction Co. v. Danzig Enterprises Ltd.*) 1 O.R. (3d) 382, 75 D.L.R. (4th) 732, 1990 CarswellOnt 135, 42 O.A.C. 195, 50 B.L.R. 258 (C.A.), additional reasons at (1994), 1994 CarswellOnt 2442 (C.A.).

62 See *Visagie v. TVX Gold Inc.* (2000), 49 O.R. (3d) 198, 187 D.L.R. (4th) 193, 2000 CarswellOnt 1888, 6 B.L.R. (3d) 1, 132 O.A.C. 231 (C.A.).

63 See *Rochwerg v. Truster* (2002), [2002] O.J. No. 1230, 2002 CarswellOnt 990, 23 B.L.R. (3d) 107, 158 O.A.C. 41, 58 O.R. (3d) 687 (C.A.), additional reasons at (2002), 2002 CarswellOnt 1456, 212 D.L.R. (4th) 498 (C.A.); *Molchan v. Omega Oil & Gas Ltd.*, [1988] 1 S.C.R. 348, 1988 CarswellAlta 17, 1988 CarswellAlta 549, [1988] 3 W.W.R. 1, 57 Alta. L.R. (2d) 193, 83 N.R. 25, 87 A.R. 81, 47 D.L.R. (4th) 481, reconsideration refused (1988), 49 D.L.R. (4th) vii (S.C.C.).

64 See *Western Delta Lands Partnership v. 3557537 Canada Inc.*, 44 C.P.C. (4th) 382, 2000 CarswellBC 55, [2000] B.C.J. No. 56, 2000 BCSC 54 (S.C. [In Chambers]).

rise to a duty of confidence.[65] Confidential relationships are not fiduciary in nature and no duty of loyalty exists in them *per se*. The Ontario Superior Court recently outlined the test for determining whether a duty of confidence has been breached and provided a comparison between breach of confidence and breach of fiduciary duty.[66] What are some of the key differences?

15. S, the trustee of a lease, was unable to obtain a renewal of the lease for the trust beneficiary. He was able, however, to renew the lease in his own name and did so. S claims to be entitled to the lease beneficially. What result?[67] Is it relevant whether the fiduciary gains were derived innocently or fraudulently?

16. Company directors, officers and banking institutions are all fiduciaries. Although they are not held to the same high standard as trustees, they do have some fiduciary obligations. For instance, they must disclose any conflicts of interest between their personal dealings and those of their office.[68] Do the directors owe their fiduciary duty solely to the corporation, or also to other directors and to the shareholders?[69] Do the directors have a fiduciary duty towards the corporation's creditors? If so, in what circumstances?[70]

17. For a recent Australian case which explores the boundaries of fiduciary law in that country, see *Pilmer v. Duke Group Ltd. (In Liquidation.)*.[71]

3. TRUST AND AGENCY

The trustee's obligations bear some resemblance to those of an agent. There are, however, critical distinctions between the two offices with important legal consequences.

The similarity which exists between the role of the trustee and that of the agent stems from the fact that both are fiduciaries, although their fiduciary duties differ in degree.[72] Both are under a duty not to permit their personal interests to conflict with the responsibilities of their office; not to make unauthorized profits; not to delegate their responsibilities; to act strictly for the benefit of the beneficiaries or principal respectively; and to keep proper accounts.[73]

---

65 See *Cadbury Schweppes Inc. v. FBI Foods Ltd.* (1999), [1999] 1 S.C.R. 142, 1999 CarswellBC 77, 1999 CarswellBC 78, [1999] S.C.J. No. 6, 167 D.L.R. (4th) 577, 83 C.P.R. (3d) 289, 235 N.R. 30, 42 B.L.R. (2d) 159, 117 B.C.A.C. 161, 191 W.A.C. 161, 59 B.C.L.R. (3d) 1, [1999] 5 W.W.R. 751, [2000] F.S.R. 491; and *Visagie, supra*, note 62.

66 In *Rodaro v. Royal Bank* (2002), [2002] O.J. No. 1365, 2002 CarswellOnt 1047, 22 B.L.R. (3d) 274, 157 O.A.C. 203, 49 R.P.R. (3d) 227, 59 O.R. (3d) 74 (C.A.). See also Chapter 9, part 2(d), below.

67 See *Keech v. Sandford, supra*, note 5; *Plus Group Ltd. v. Pyke*, [2002] E.W.C.A. Civ. 370, [2002] E.W.J. No. 1392 (C.A.).

68 See, for example, *Boardman v. Phipps* (1966), [1967] 2 A.C. 46, [1966] 3 All E.R. 721 (H.L.).

69 See *Sports Villas Resort Inc., Re*, 185 Nfld. & P.E.I.R. 281, 2000 CarswellNfld 49, 2000 NFCA 11, 562 A.P.R. 281 (C.A.).

70 See Andrew Keay, "The Director's Duty to Take into Account the Interests of Company Creditors: When is it Triggered?" (2001), 25 Melb. U.L. Rev. 315.

71 [2001] H.C.A. 31, 207 C.L.R. 165 (Australia H.C.).

72 See part 2, *supra*, and see also Scott, "The Fiduciary Principle" (1949), 37 Cal. L. Rev. 539.

73 *Ibid.*

Because of these similarities in responsibilities, it is often difficult to determine whether a person is acting as a trustee or an agent. *Lister & Co. v. Stubbs*,[74]
below, shows the often fine distinction between a trust and an agency relationship.

There are seven significant differences between the office of trustee and that
of agent. First, the agency relationship is a personal one as between principal and
agent, while the trust relationship is proprietary in nature.[75]

Second, the agent and principal relationship is normally construed as one of
debtor and creditor while the trustee and beneficiary relationship is construed in
trust terms. As discussed below,[76] this distinction and the first become critical
when an agent is insolvent.

Third, an agent does not normally hold title to the subject property, whereas
the trustee always has title, either legal or equitable, vested in him- or herself.

Fourth, an agent acts on behalf of, and subject to the control of, his principal.
In contrast, a trustee is not subject to direction or control by the beneficiaries,
beyond his obligation to deal with the trust property in accordance with his trust
duties.[77] This distinction holds even where all the beneficiaries are *sui juris* and
unanimous in their desire to replace the current trustee with a trustee of their
choosing; no beneficiary can interfere with the exercise of the trustee's fiduciary
powers in the administration of the trust.[78] The beneficiaries may, in certain
circumstances, band together and end the trust,[79] or sue to compel the due performance by the trustee of his duties, but that is the extent to which they can
control the trustee.

Fifth, agency is based on agreement between the parties, and the relationship
may be modified by further agreement. A trust, on the other hand, may be created
without agreement between the trustee and the beneficiaries or the trustee and the
settlor. In addition, once a trust is constituted it may not be varied by the settlor
unless he or she has reserved an express power of revocation.[80]

Sixth, an agent can subject his or her principal to liabilities with third parties,[81]
whereas a trustee cannot so involve a trust beneficiary or settlor.[82]

Seventh, an agency relationship is normally terminated by the death, or at
the wish, of either party, while a trust is not terminated by the death or wish of
the trustee, beneficiaries, or settlor.

The consequences of finding an agency relationship rather than a trust can
be critical. The most important consequence arises when the agent is insolvent
because, unless the agent has agreed to keep the subject property separate from
his own, the principal is entitled only to an accounting by the agent and cannot

---

74 (1886), 45 Ch. D. 1, [1886-90] All E.R. Rep. 797 (U.K. C.A.).
75 See Chapter 1, part 7, *supra*.
76 See part 5, *infra*.
77 See *Re Brockbank*, [1948] Ch. 206, [1948] 1 All E.R. 287.
78 *Ibid*.
79 See Chapter 6, part 3, *infra*.
80 See Chapter 6, part 2(c), *infra*.
81 *Investors Syndicate Ltd. v. Versatile Investments Inc.* (1983), 42 O.R. (2d) 397, 149 D.L.R. (3d)
    46, 1983 CarswellOnt 1270, 73 C.P.R. (2d) 107 (C.A.).
82 Keeton & Sheridan, *Law of Trusts*, 11th ed. (Barry Rose Publishers Ltd., 1983), at 16.

claim any special right to the specific property or its proceeds. The result is that the principal will rank as a general creditor.[83] In contrast, a trust beneficiary has a proprietary right to the trust assets or the proceeds from the trust assets and the profits thereon, which right ranks above all creditors.[84]

A separate but related issue arises in the case of bribes. In *Lister & Co. v. Stubbs*,[85] Cotton L.J. held that when money is acquired from a third party as a result of a corrupt bargain, such money is aquired by way of agency and while the principal is entitled to an accounting for the money received, the agent does not hold the money on trust for the principal. However, if the person improperly uses money belonging to the principal, the money will be seen to be held by the person as trustee. Thus, *Lister & Co. v. Stubbs* established that the relationship between an agent and principal was one of debtor and creditor when the agent did not use the principal's money or property to secure the bribe, and that the agent would be liable only to account for the bribe. As an accounting is a personal remedy, the principal would not take priority over other unsecured creditors; whereas, if a trust had been created, the principal would have a priority claim.

In *A.-G. for Hong Kong v. Reid*,[86] the court presents a different approach to bribes. The court extended the established principle that when an agent uses the principal's money to acquire property, then that property will be held on trust for the principal. In *Reid*, the court held that bribes were considered in equity to be legitimate payments to the principal. This decision is not reconcilable with *Lister & Co. v. Stubbs*. It is not clear which view will dominate in Canada.

Further Reading

M.C. Cullity, "Liability of Beneficiaries — A Rejoinder" (1985), 7 E. & T. Q. 35.

M.C. Cullity, "Liability of Beneficiaries — A Further Rejoinder to Mr. Flannigan" (1986), 8 E. & T. Q. 130.

Flannigan, "Beneficiary Liability in Business Trusts" (1984), 6 E. & T. Q. 278.

Flannigan, "The Control Test of Principal Status Applied to Business Trusts" (1986), 8 E. & T. Q. 37.

A.-G. FOR HONG KONG v. REID

[1994] 1 All E.R. 1
Privy Council

Reid, a solicitor, joined the Hong Kong government service and held a number of positions, the last of which was Acting Director of Public Prosecutions. In the course of his career, in breach of his fiduciary duty as a servant of the Crown, he accepted bribes to obstruct the prosecution of certain criminals. He was arrested, pleaded guilty and was ordered to pay the Crown the sum of $HK 12.4m which

---

83 See *Lister & Co. v. Stubbs, supra*, note 74.

84 *Ibid.*

85 Excerpted in *A.-G. For Hong Kong v. Reid, infra.*

86 (1993), [1994] 1 All E.R. 1, [1994] 1 A.C. 324 (New Zealand P.C.).

was the value of assets held by Reid, determined to be solely derived from the bribes. Among those assets were three properties in New Zealand. The Hong Kong government claimed a proprietary interest in these properties as beneficiaries by way of constructive trust. However, the Supreme Court of New Zealand and the Court of Appeal of New Zealand refused to extend previously granted caveats on the properties registered by the Hong Kong government as they held that Reid did not hold the property as trustee. Applying *Lister & Co. v. Stubbs*, they held that the relationship was one of debtor and creditor. Reid did not pay any part of the money. The Attorney General then appealed to the Privy Council.

TEMPLEMAN L.J. delivered the judgment of the court:

. . .

The trial judge's finding that the Attorney General for Hong Kong had established an arguable case that each of the three properties was acquired with moneys received by Mr. Reid as bribes has not been challenged.

. . .

A bribe is a gift accepted by a fiduciary as an inducement to him to betray his trust. A secret benefit, which may or may not constitute a bribe, is a benefit which the fiduciary derives from trust property or obtains from knowledge which he acquires in the course of acting as a fiduciary. A fiduciary is not always accountable for a secret benefit, but he is undoubtedly accountable for a secret benefit which consists of a bribe. In addition a person who provides the bribe and the fiduciary who accepts the bribe may each be guilty of a criminal offence. In the present case Mr. Reid was clearly guilty of a criminal offence.

. . .

When a bribe is offered and accepted in money or in kind, the money or property constituting the bribe belongs in law to the recipient. Money paid to the false fiduciary belongs to him. The legal estate in freehold property conveyed to the false fiduciary by way of bribe vests in him. Equity, however, which acts *in personam* insists that it is unconscionable for a fiduciary to obtain and retain a benefit in breach of duty. The provider of a bribe cannot recover it because he committed a criminal offence when he paid the bribe. The false fiduciary who received the bribe in breach of duty must pay and account for the bribe to the person to whom that duty was owed. In the present case, as soon as Mr. Reid received a bribe in breach of the duties he owed to the government of Hong Kong, he became a debtor in equity to the Crown for the amount of that bribe. So much is admitted. But, if the bribe consists of property which increases in value or if a cash bribe is invested advantageously, the false fiduciary will receive a benefit from his breach of duty unless he is accountable not only for the original amount or value of the bribe but also for the increased value of the property representing the bribe. As soon as the bribe was received it should have been paid or transferred instantly to the person who suffered from the breach of duty. Equity considers as done that which ought to have been done. As soon as the bribe was received, whether in cash or in kind, the false fiduciary held the bribe on a constructive trust for the person injured. Two objections have been raised to this analysis. First it is said that, if the fiduciary is in equity a debtor to the person injured, he cannot also be a trustee of the bribe. But there is no reason why equity should not provide two remedies, so long as they do not result in double recovery. If the property representing the bribe exceeds the original bribe in value, the fiduciary cannot retain the benefit of the increase in value which he obtained solely as a result of his breach of duty. Secondly, it is said that if the false fiduciary holds property representing the bribe in trust for the person injured and if the false fiduciary is or becomes insolvent, the unsecured creditors of the false fiduciary will be deprived of their right to share in the proceeds of that property. But the unsecured creditors cannot be in a better position than their debtor. The authorities show that property acquired by a trustee innocently but in breach of trust and the property from time to time representing the same belong in equity to the *cestui que* trust and not to the trustee personally whether he is solvent or insolvent. Property acquired by a trustee as a result of a criminal breach of trust and the property from time to time representing the same must also belong in equity to his *cestui que* trust and not to the trustee whether he is solvent or insolvent.

When a bribe is accepted by a fiduciary in breach of his duty then he holds that bribe in trust for the person to whom the duty was owed. If the property representing the bribe decreases in value the fiduciary must pay the difference between that value and the initial amount of the bribe because he should not have accepted the bribe or incurred the risk of loss. If the property increases in value, the fiduciary is not entitled to any surplus in excess of the initial value of the bribe because he is not allowed by any means to make a profit out of a breach of duty.

The courts of New Zealand were constrained by a number of precedents of the New Zealand, English and other common law courts which established a settled principle of law inconsistent with the foregoing analysis. That settled principle is open to review by the Board in the light of the foregoing analysis of the consequences in equity of the receipt of a bribe by a fiduciary.

In *Keech v. Sandford*[87] a landlord refused to renew a lease to a trustee for the benefit of an infant. The trustee then took a new lease for his own benefit. The new lease had not formed part of the original trust property, the infant could not have acquired the new lease from the landlord and the trustee acted innocently, believing that he committed no breach of trust and that the new lease did not belong in equity to his *cestui que* trust. Lord King LC held nevertheless that "the trustee is the only person of all mankind who might not have the lease";[88] the trustee was obliged to assign the new lease to the infant and account for the profits he had received. The rule must be that property which a trustee obtains by use of knowledge acquired as trustee becomes trust property. The rule must, *a fortiori*, apply to a bribe accepted by a trustee for a guilty criminal purpose which injures

---

87 *Supra,* note 5.
88 *Ibid.,* at 62.

the *cestui que* trust. The trustee is only one example of a fiduciary and the same rule applies to all other fiduciaries who accept bribes.

. . .

In *Sugden v. Crossland*[89] a trustee was paid £75 for agreeing to retire from the trust and to appoint in his place the person who had paid the £75. Stuart V.-C. said:[90]

> It has been further asked that the sum of £75. may be treated as a part of the trust fund, and as such may be directed to be paid by Horsfield to the trustee for the benefit of the *cestui que trusts* under the will. It is a well-settled principle that if a trustee makes a profit of his trusteeship, it shall enure to the benefit of his *cestui que trusts*. Though there is some peculiarity in the case, there does not seem to be any difference in principle whether the trustee derived the profit by means of the trust property, or from the office itself.

This case is of importance because it disposes succinctly of the argument which appears in later cases and which was put forward by counsel in the present case that there is a distinction between a profit which a trustee takes out of a trust and a profit such as a bribe which a trustee receives from a third party. If in law a trustee who in breach of trust invests trust moneys in his own name holds the investment as trust property, it is difficult to see why a trustee who in breach of trust receives and invests a bribe in his own name does not hold those investments also as trust property.

[His Lordship reviewed a number of earlier cases and continued:]

It has always been assumed and asserted that the law on the subject of bribes was definitively settled by the decision of the Court of Appeal in *Lister & Co. v. Stubbs.*[91]

In that case the plaintiffs, Lister & Co., employed the defendant, Stubbs, as their servant to purchase goods for the firm. Stubbs, on behalf of the firm, bought goods from Varley & Co. and received from Varley & Co. bribes amounting to £5,541. The bribes were invested by Stubbs in freehold properties and investments. His masters, the firm Lister & Co., sought and failed to obtain an interlocutory injunction restraining Stubbs from disposing of these assets pending the trial of the action in which they sought, *inter alia*, £5,541 and damages. In the Court of Appeal the first judgment was given by Cotton L.J., who had been party to the decision in *Metropolitan Bank v. Heiron.*[92] He was powerfully supported by the judgment of Lindley L.J. and by the equally powerful concurrence of Bowen L.J. Cotton L.J. said that the bribe could not be said to be the money of the plaintiffs.[93] He seemed to be reluctant to grant an interlocutory judgment

---

89 (1856) 3 Sm. & 8 G 192, 65 E.R. 620.
90 *Ibid.*, at 194.
91 *Supra*, note 74.
92 (1880), 5 Ex. D. 319 (U.K. C.A.).
93 *Lister, supra,* note 74, at 12.

which would provide security for a debt before that debt had been established. Lindley L.J. said that the relationship between the plaintiffs, Lister & Co., as masters and the defendant, Stubbs, as servant who had betrayed his trust and received a bribe:

> is that of debtor and creditor; it is not that of trustee and *cestui que* trust. We are asked to hold that it is — which would involve consequences which, I confess, startle me. One consequence, of course, would be that, if *Stubbs* were to become bankrupt, this property acquired by him with the money paid to him by Messrs. *Varley* would be withdrawn from the mass of his creditors and be handed over bodily to *Lister & Co.* Can that be right? Another consequence would be that, if the Appellants are right, *Lister & Co.* could compel *Stubbs* to account to them, not only for the money with interest, but for all the profit which he might have made by embarking in trade with it. Can that be right?[94]

For the reasons which have already been advanced, their Lordships would respectfully answer both these questions in the affirmative. If a trustee mistakenly invests moneys which he ought to pay over to his *cestui que* trust and then becomes bankrupt, the moneys together with any profit which has accrued from the investment are withdrawn from the unsecured creditors as soon as the mistake is discovered. *A fortiori*, if a trustee commits a crime by accepting a bribe which he ought to pay over to his *cestui que* trust, the bribe and any profit made therefrom should be withdrawn from the unsecured creditors as soon as the crime is discovered.

The decision in *Lister & Co. v. Stubbs* is not consistent with the principles that a fiduciary must not be allowed to benefit from his own breach of duty, that the fiduciary should account for the bribe as soon as he receives it and that equity regards as done that which ought to be done. From these principles it would appear to follow that the bribe and the property from time to time representing the bribe are held on a constructive trust for the person injured. A fiduciary remains personally liable for the amount of the bribe if, in the event, the value of the property then recovered by the injured person proved to be less than that amount.

The decisions of the Court of Appeal in *Metropolitan Bank v. Heiron* and *Lister v. Stubbs* are inconsistent with earlier authorities which were not cited. Although over 100 years has passed since *Lister & Co. v. Stubbs*, no one can be allowed to say that he has ordered his affairs in reliance on the two decisions of the Court of Appeal now in question. Thus no harm can result if those decisions are not followed.

. . .

The authorities which followed *Lister & Co. v. Stubbs* do not cast any new light on that decision. Their Lordships are more impressed with the decision of Lai Kew Chai J. in *Sumitomo Bank Ltd. v. Kartika Ratna Thahir*.[95] In that case General Thahir, who was at one time general assistant to the president director of the Indonesian state enterprise named Pertamina, opened 17 bank accounts in

---

94 *Ibid.*, at 15.
95 [1993] 1 S.L.R. 735.

Singapore and deposited DM54m in those accounts. The money was said to be bribes paid by two German contractors tendering for the construction of steel works in West Java. General Thahir having died, the moneys were claimed by his widow, by the estate of the deceased general, and by Pertamina. After considering in detail all the relevant authorities the judge determined robustly that *Lister & Co. v. Stubbs* was wrong and that its "undesirable and unjust consequences should not be imported and perpetuated as part of the law of Singapore."[96] Their Lordships are also much indebted for the fruits of research and the careful discussion of the present topic in the address entitled "Bribes and secret commissions"[97] delivered by Sir Peter Millett to a meeting of the Society of Public Teachers of Law at Oxford in 1993. The following passage elegantly sums up the views of Sir Peter Millett:[98]

> [The fiduciary] must not place himself in a position where his interest may conflict with his duty. If he has done so, equity insists on treating him as having acted in accordance with his duty; he will not be allowed to say that he preferred his own interest to that of his principal. He must not obtain a profit for himself out of his fiduciary position. If he has done so, equity insists on treating him as having obtained it for his principal; he will not be allowed to say that he obtained it for himself. He must not accept a bribe. If he has done so, equity insists on treating it as a legitimate payment intended for the benefit of the principal; he will not be allowed to say that it was a bribe.

The conclusions reached by Lai Kew Chai J. in *Sumitomo Bank Ltd. v. Kartilca Ratna Thahir* and the views expressed by Sir Peter Millett were influenced by the decision of the House of Lords in *Boardman v. Phipps*,[99] which demonstrates the strictness with which equity regards the conduct of a fiduciary and the extent to which equity is willing to impose a constructive trust on property obtained by a fiduciary by virtue of his office. In that case a solicitor acting for trustees rescued the interests of the trust in a private company by negotiating for a take-over bid in which he himself took an interest. He acted in good faith throughout and the information which the solicitor obtained about the company in the take-over bid could never have been used by the trustees. Nevertheless, the solicitor was held to be a constructive trustee by a majority in the House of Lords because the solicitor obtained the information which satisfied him that the purchase of the shares in the take-over company would be a good investment and the opportunity of acquiring the shares as a result of acting for certain purposes on behalf of the trustees: see per Lord Cohen.[100] If a fiduciary acting honestly and in good faith and making a profit which his principal could not make for himself becomes a constructive trustee of that profit, then it seems to their Lordships that a fiduciary acting dishonestly and criminally who accepts a bribe and thereby causes loss and damage to his principal must also be a constructive trustee and must not be allowed by any means to make any profit from his wrongdoing.

---

96 *Ibid.*, at 810.
97 [1993] R.L.R. 7.
98 *Ibid.*, at 20.
99 *Supra*, note 68.
100 *Ibid.*, at 743.

. . .

Their Lordships will therefore humbly advise Her Majesty that this appeal should be allowed. Since an unfulfilled order has been made against Mr. Reid in the courts of Hong Kong to pay $HK12.4m, his purpose in opposing the relief sought by the Crown in New Zealand must reflect the hope that the properties, in the absence of a caveat, can be sold and the proceeds whisked away to some Shangri-La which hides bribes and other corrupt moneys in numbered bank accounts. In these circumstances Mr. and Mrs. Reid must pay the costs of the Attorney General before the Board and in the lower courts.

Notes and Questions

1. Is it possible for an agent to become a trustee? Is the reverse possible?[101]

2. In many real estate transactions, there are two agents involved: the listing agent and the selling agent. Each earns a portion of the commission. The commission is generally paid to the listing agent by the purchaser. There is conflicting case law on the issue whether the listing agent holds the portion of the commission due to the selling agent in trust. *Re/ Max West Realty Inc. v. Homelife/Tri-Corp Realty Ltd. (Trustee of)*[102] held that the monies were held in trust thereby protecting the selling agent's interest in the bankrupt's estate; *Courtesy Transfer & Recycling Inc. v. Re/Max Renown Ltd.*[103] held that no trust was created in favour of the selling agent.[104]

3. A man died shortly after instructing an agent to purchase an annuity for him to benefit a third party.

(a) What is the result given the agency relationship between the deceased and his agent?

(b) Had this been a trust relationship, would the third party have taken?[105]

4. Trustees are not agents of the settlor or the beneficiaries.[106] Rather, they are officers of the court in that they perform a task which would otherwise be that of the court. For this reason a trustee may apply to the court for instruction as to how the trust should be administered.

---

101 See *Secord v. Costello* (1870), 17 Gr. 328 (Ont. H.C.); *Maguire v. Maguire and Toronto Gen. Trusts Corp.* (1921), 50 O.L.R. 162, 64 D.L.R. 204 (H.C.); *Re Preston* (1906), 13 O.L.R. 110 (Div. Ct.); *Trident Holdings Ltd. v. Danand Investments Ltd.* (1988), 64 O.R. (2d) 65, 49 D.L.R. (4th) 1, 1988 CarswellOnt 112, 25 O.A.C. 378, 30 E.T.R. 67, 39 B.L.R. 296 (C.A.).

102 (1992), 9 O.R. (3d) 762, 45 E.T.R. 317, 12 C.B.R. (3d) 209, 92 D.L.R. (4th) 251 (Gen. Div.).

103 (1993), 49 E.T.R. 171 (Ont. Gen Div.).

104 To the same effect, see *Ontario (Director, Business Practices Division, Ministry of Consumer & Commercial Relations) v. Safeguard Real Estate Ltd.* (1994), 114 D.L.R. (4th) 546, 27 C.B.R. (3d) 103, 1994 CarswellOnt 292 (Gen. Div. [Commercial List]); *Ontario (Director, Real Estate & Business Brokers Act) v. NRS Mississauga Inc.* (2000), 194 D.L.R. (4th) 527, 2000 CarswellOnt 4216 (S.C.J.), reversed (2003), 2003 CarswellOnt 1239, 40 C.B.R. (4th) 127, 49 E.T.R. (2d) 256, 8 R.P.R. (4th) 13, 170 O.A.C. 259, 64 O.R. (3d) 97, 226 D.L.R. (4th) 361 (C.A.), additional reasons at (2003), 2003 CarswellOnt 1888, 42 C.B.R. (4th) 280, 1 E.T.R. (3d) 220 (C.A.), leave to appeal refused (2003), 2003 CarswellOnt 5191, 2003 CarswellOnt 5192 (S.C.C.).

105 *McIntyre v. Royal Trust Co.*, [1946] 1 D.L.R. 655, [1946] 1 W.W.R. 210, 53 Man. R. 353 (C.A.).

106 See D.W.M. Waters, *Law of Trusts in Canada*, 2d ed. (Toronto: Carswell, 1984), at 43.

5. Limitation periods run for actions between principals and agents. No limitation period runs for actions by a beneficiary against and express trustee in respect of fraud, fraudulent breach of trust, or the recovery of trust property or its proceeds.[107]

6. A was the exclusive sales representative for B Corp. to sell its products. Under the sales representation agreement, B Corp. was required to pay commissions to A on sales to customers with whom B Corp had contracts at the time of termination. Two years ago, A secured a contract to sell B Corp. products to C Corp. However, A failed to disclose to B Corp. that he held a 25% equity interest in C Corp. B Corp. learned of that fact this year and terminated the sales representation agreement with A. Is A entitled to commissions for the next two years?[108]

4. TRUST AND CONTRACT

Trusts and contracts sometimes exhibit a superficial similarity because both can exist in the same transaction. For instance, there can be a contract to create a trust or a trust may arise by operation of law to support a contract.[109] Then, too, contractual rights may be the subject-matter of a trust. A gift to an unincorporated association, as will be seen later,[110] is yet another example of where either or both contract and trust law may apply.

Apart from the possible overlap between trust and contract, however, the two are quite different. *Re Schebsman*,[111] below, illustrates the test used to determine whether a trust or a contract exists, and the consequences of such a finding.

There are six significant differences between trusts and contracts. First, a contract results from mutual agreement and contains reciprocal obligations, while a trust can be created without agreement between the parties, and it normally results in obligations being placed only upon the trustee.

Second, consideration is an essential element of a contract, whereas a trust may be established voluntarily, for consideration or by law.[112]

Third, the transfer of property to the trustee — be it realty or personalty — is essential to the creation of a trust, whereas a contract need not involve the transfer of property.[113]

Fourth, contracts arise at common law and create personal rights between the parties. The trust, however, is a creature of equity and creates proprietary rights in the beneficiary.[114] Because contracts are associated with obligations and trusts with the transfer of property, the terms of a contract can be varied only by those who were party to the original agreement and no outside person can object or interfere. With a constituted trust, however, the property has been dedicated and the beneficiaries have obtained proprietary rights. Accordingly, unless the settlor

---

107 See Chapter 15. See also G.H.L. Fridman's *Law of Agency* (7th ed., 1996), at 26-7.

108 See *McBride Metal Fabricating Corp. v. H & W Sales Co.* (2002), 59 O.R. (3d) 97, 2002 CarswellOnt 1200, 158 O.A.C. 214, 19 C.P.R. (4th) 440 (C.A.).

109 Keeton & Sheridan, *Law of Trusts*, (11th ed., 1983) (Barry Rose Publishers Ltd.), at 5.

110 See Chapter 8, part 4, *supra*.

111 [1944] Ch. 83, [1943] 2 All E.R. 768 (C.A.).

112 See *Haigh v. Kaye* (1872), L.R. Ch. 469.

113 See Chapter 4, part 7, *infra*.

114 See Chapter 1, part 6, *supra*.

reserves a power of revocation, no variation of the trust can occur, unless all the trust beneficiaries are *sui juris* and consent or the court so orders.[115]

Fifth, the common law privity of contract rule prevents any person who is not a party to the contract from suing to enforce it. Equity enables the trust beneficiary to sue to enforce the trust regardless of whether the beneficiary is a party to the trust agreement. To avoid the enforceability problem in contract situations, a trust relationship must exist. That is, one party to the contract must be found to have acted as a trustee for the third person benefited by the contract. This gives the third person the status of a trust beneficiary and the right to enforce the obligations in equity. *Re Schebsman*, below, also illustrates the modern judicial attitude against finding a trust in a contract setting in order simply to preserve the benefit to a third person.

Sixth, different limitation periods apply to actions for breach of trust and breach of contract.[116]

Further Reading

S.M. Waddams, "Comments on Legislation and Judicial Decisions" (1981), 50 Can. Bar Rev. 549.

Glanville Williams, "Contracts for the Benefit of Third Parties" (1943), 7 Mod. L. Rev. 123.

RE SCHEBSMAN

[1944] Ch. 83, [1943] 2 All E.R. 768
Court of Appeal

Schebsman's employer agreed to pay certain sums of money to him during his lifetime and after his death, to his wife and daughter. In exchange, Schebsman agreed to retire. Within two years of the agreement Schebsman became bankrupt and died. The employer was willing to pay the balance of the moneys to the wife and daughter, but Schebsman's trustee in bankruptcy claimed that they formed part of the bankrupt's estate.

LORD GREENE M.R.:

. . .

The first question which arises is whether or not the debtor was a trustee for his wife and daughter of the benefit of the undertaking given by the English company in their favour. An examination of the decided cases does, it is true, show that the courts have on occasions adopted what may be called a liberal view on questions of this character, but in the present case I cannot find in the contract anything to justify the conclusion that a trust was intended. It is not legitimate to

---

115 See Chapter 6, parts 3 and 4, *infra*.
116 See Waters, *supra*, note 106, at 1014-1025.

import into the contract the idea of a trust when the parties have given no indication that such was their intention. To interpret this contract as creating a trust would, in my judgment, be to disregard the dividing line between the case of a trust and the simple case of a contract made between two persons for the benefit of a third. That dividing line exists, although it may not always be easy to determine where it is to be drawn. In the present case I find no difficulty.

I will now turn to the other questions which arise. At the outset of his address Mr. Roxburgh suggested that the trustee in bankruptcy as claiming through the debtor could claim all sums paid by the English company to Mrs. Schebsman or her daughter as money had and received to his use. As the discussion proceeded, this argument was abandoned by Mr. Roxburgh and rightly so. It was also conceded that at common law the English company is bound, as between itself and the trustee, to make payments to Mrs. Schebsman or her daughter in accordance with the contract, and that the trustee, as claiming through the debtor, has no right at common law to require the company to pay these sums to himself. The contract was tripartite and its terms could only be varied by the consent of all three parties. Mrs. Schebsman and her daughter have, of course, no right to demand payment from the English company since they are not parties to the contract. When the company makes a payment to one of them it is, as between the company and the payee, a gratuitous payment made with the intention of passing the property in the money paid, and this is sufficient to give to the payee at common law a good title to the money against the whole world. The question of what damages could be recovered by the representative of the debtor if the company were to break its contract has no bearing on anything that we have to decide. Mr. Roxburgh's argument, as he developed it, rests entirely on equitable principles. It may be summarized as follows: The debtor provided the whole of the consideration for the English company's undertaking to make the payments to his widow and daughter. These payments must, therefore, be regarded in the same light as voluntary gifts. In the case of a completed transfer of property by a man to his wife or daughter a presumption of advancement arises, but in the present case the transfer was not completed since Mrs. Schebsman and her daughter have no title to demand payment to themselves. It was, therefore, possible for the debtor in his lifetime, and for the trustee, as his representative, to intervene at any time and to assert as against Mrs. Schebsman and her daughter that any payments thereafter made to either of them would be held by the payee on behalf of the debtor's estate. The effect of such an intervention, it was said, makes it impossible to treat any money in fact received thereafter by Mrs. Schebsman or her daughter as an advancement. If, notwithstanding the intervention, the company makes a payment to either of them, there will be a resulting trust for the trustee as representing the debtor. As a corollary to this it was said that in properly constituted proceedings the English company can be compelled to make the covenanted payments direct to the trustee. The case, it was said, is analogous to that of an uncompleted gift or that of an imperfectly constituted trust. Mrs. Schebsman and her daughter are mere volunteers and equity will do nothing to assist them.

This argument is attractive but, in my opinion, fallacious. It is important to bear in mind at the outset that, as between himself and the English company, the debtor had no right to intervene and direct the company to make the payments to someone other than Mrs. Schebsman or her daughter. As between the three parties to the contract, its terms were that the payments should be made to Mrs. Schebsman and her daughter and made to them, clearly, for their own benefit. If, therefore, the debtor in his lifetime had directed the company to make these payments to his executors, the company would have been entitled to ignore the direction. The proposition that in properly constituted proceedings the trustee could obtain direct payment to himself depends for its validity on the truth of the proposition that, as between himself and Mrs. Schebsman and her daughter, the trustee is entitled to claim the money as his own. The former proposition cannot, therefore, be relied on to establish the latter proposition which must be made good, if at all, on its own merits. Indeed, the former proposition relates to procedure only and means nothing more than that, if A is proposing to pay money to B which, as between B and C, belongs in equity to C, C can join A as a defendant in his action against B and thus procure payment by A directly to himself. It throws no light on the question which, for our purposes, is the relevant one; namely, as between B and C, does the money belong in equity to C?

We must, therefore, consider the position as between the debtor and his wife and daughter. I do not think that any help is obtained by considering the cases of uncompleted gifts or imperfectly constituted trusts. Indeed, these analogies seem to me to be misleading. If A instructs an agent to carry a present to B, the agent's authority is in its nature revocable and A can revoke his instructions at any time before the present is delivered. Similarly, if A is minded to create a trust in favour of B, a volunteer, and fails properly to constitute the trust, B has no remedy, but the present case is quite different. When he made the contract the debtor did not constitute the English company his mandatory to transfer property of his own to his wife and daughter. Not only was the money in question never his property but, once having made the contract, he had, as I have already pointed out, no right to call on the company to make the payment to his estate. In making the contract he set in motion a piece of machinery which he had no power to stop on his own unilateral action save by releasing the company from the contract. Its operation would inevitably result in money reaching the hands of his widow and daughter, assuming, as we must assume, that the English company would perform its contract. This, therefore, was no revocable mandate, nor was there any lack of completeness in the constitution of the machinery devised for securing these benefits of the widow and daughter. When he made the contract, the debtor intended that his widow should receive those benefits for herself. It was part of the bargain between himself and the two companies that she should receive them, and he reserved to himself no right to call for payment to himself. The trustee could, presumably, release the company from its undertaking, but this would do no more than deprive the trustee of the right to sue for damages for its breach. The fact that such a release can be effected is no argument for saying that the trustee can claim the moneys as his own.

The question, therefore, is not: "Will equity help the widow and daughter to retain the sums which will inevitably be paid to them?" but "Will equity help the trustee in bankruptcy to recover them from the payees?" I can find no principle which calls for an affirmative answer to this question. If it were otherwise, the result would be a curious one. The debtor makes a contract intended to secure benefits for his wife and daughter after his death. It is true that they obtain no right to call for those benefits but the debtor with good reason trusts the company to make them. The company cannot avoid making them unless it is prepared to break its contract. In this confidence, let me assume, the debtor makes his testamentary dispositions and dies with the satisfaction of knowing that the contract makes provision for his widow and daughter. It is said that his representative can abrogate his intention and call on his widow and daughter to pay over to his estate any sums they may receive and that equity will compel them to do so. In my opinion, no principle of equity requires this to be done.

It is, of course, true that the debtor provided part of the consideration for which the English company gave its undertaking to make the payments, but he did so with the intention that the money paid should belong to the recipients beneficially, and in this sense the provision secured by the contract for the widow and daughter may perhaps be regarded as being an advancement of them. This was clearly his intention at the date of the contract. It is true that at that date and down to the date of his death all that Mrs. Schebsman and her daughter had was an expectancy. They had no legal rights whatever, but it was an expectancy that would necessarily mature into actual payment, subject always to the possibility that the three parties to the contract or their representatives might put an end to the contract by mutual consent and the possibility that the debtor or his successors in title might release the company from its obligation. This being so, the advancement must, in my opinion, be regarded as completed when the contract was made, since it was not in the power of the debtor to change his mind and prevent it from becoming effective unless he could secure the agreement of both the other two parties to the contract or was prepared to release the company. I do not see how there can arise a resulting trust for the debtor of money that was never his, the receipt of which by the payees he had no power by himself to prevent save by a release.

To say that there can be no effective advancement unless and until either the subject-matter reaches the hands of the person to be advanced or that person acquires a legal title to claim it, appears to me to be too narrow a proposition. I see no reason why in principle an advancement should not be regarded as complete and effective where the person desiring to make it sets in train for that purpose a process which it is out of his power to control by his own action. If the process is one which he can by his own action control as, for example, where he uses a mandatory to deliver the subject-matter of the advancement to the person whom he desires to benefit, the case is, of course, different, but where a person has done everything which the nature of the subject-matter permits to ensure that it will reach the object of his bounty, and the nature of the transaction precludes the possibility of any subsequent intervention or change of mind on his part, the advancement must, in my opinion, be regarded as complete. In the present case the special nature of the transaction satisfies these tests. The circumstances that the three parties to the contract could put an end to it by mutual consent and that the company could be released are immaterial. They mean no more than that limited powers of revocation are provided. If, and only if, one or other of those powers is exercised, can the intended advancement be prevented from taking effect. Cases of advancement made by such methods as these may be rare, but that is no reason for refusing to give effect to them when they occur.

There appears to me to be an additional reason why equity should not interfere. It is a fair inference from the form and substance of the contract that the two companies had themselves an interest in seeing that the widow and daughter of their employee should be provided for. The manner in which compensation should be provided for the loss by the debtor of his employment was agreed between the three parties to the contract. The contract on its face could only mean that the sums payable to Mrs. Schebsman and her daughter are to be paid to them for their own benefit. How can the debtor claim them for himself without breaking his contract? I do not see how he can, and, if this view be correct, it cannot be that as between himself and the payees the debtor can be heard to assert in a court of equity a claim the enforcement of which involves a breach of contract even when that contract is one to which Mrs. Schebsman and her daughter were not parties.

. . .

The other argument on behalf of the trustee was based on s. 42 of the *Bankruptcy Act, 1914*. I agree with the decision of Uthwatt J. on this point and adopt his reasons as my own. The sums in question were never property of the debtor. He never had any right to them, either at law or in equity, and I cannot see how he can be said to have settled them on his wife and daughter. True it is that the effect of the contract, assuming that the company performed it, was to bring these sums into the hands of the widow and daughter and that the machinery provided has resulted in a benefit to them, but this does not mean that they were the debtor's property or that the contract was a settlement within the meaning of the section. The section clearly deals with property which, but for the settlement, would have been available to pay the debts of the settlor. These sums never would have been available for that purpose. The appeal is dismissed with costs.

Notes and Questions

1. (a) In *Re Schebsman*, what factors did the court consider in determining whether a contract or a trust existed?

(b) What consequences would follow a finding of a trust in the above case?

(c) Do you agree with the court's reluctance to find a trust?

2. Contrast the *Schebsman* case with *Re Garbett*.[117] Under his employer's superannuation scheme, Garbett exercised an option to surrender part of his pension in consideration of the employer paying a pension to his widow after his death. After Garbett's retirement, the widow's pension was no longer subject to forfeiture and became irrevocable. Because of that fact it was concluded that Garbett did not intend to keep alive his rights to change the terms of the agreement in concert with his employer because he knew that he could not do so. Accordingly, once Garbett retired, a trust arose under which his wife had an immediate and vested right as a beneficiary.

---

117 [1963] N.Z.L.R. 348.

3. In *Beswick v. Beswick*,[118] the House of Lords modified the privity of contract rule slightly, by permitting a widow to sue to enforce her rights under a contract to which she was not a party. She was able to do so in her capacity as administratrix of her husband's estate.[119]

Is this exception to the privity of contract rule more sensible than the finding of a trust?

4. In *Gasparini v. Gasparini*[120] the widow of a contracting party, suing in her capacity as executrix and trustee, was allowed to enforce a contract to which she was a third party beneficiary. The court held that the contract between shareholders of a corporation was enforceable even though the corporation was not a party to the contract.[121]

In *Blake v. Fireman's Fund Ins. Co. of Can.*[122] the estate of the deceased was permitted to sue for specific performance of an insurance policy in favour of the beneficiaries when the latter, being infants, failed to sue.

It is clear, however, that the *Beswick* case does not really open up another avenue of escape from the contract rule except in the particular circumstances of that case. The Ontario Court of Appeal attempted to extend *Beswick* in *Sears v. Tanenbaun*[123] but that case was reversed by the Supreme Court of Canada.[124]

Nevertheless, in some recent cases there have been extensions of the *Beswick* principle that go beyond the ratio of that case. Thus, in *Waugh v. Slavik*[125] the court held that specific performance of a contract may be ordered where the persons between whom consideration passed are parties to the action, even though the decree will benefit other parties to the contract who gave no consideration.

5. A recent case which further modified the privity of contract rule is *Jackson v. Horizon Holiday Tours Ltd.*[126] The court awarded damages for breach of contract to the plaintiff in respect of a lost holiday for himself, his wife, and two children. The court held that a person who has entered into a contract for the benefit of himself and others who are not parties to the contract, and for whom he is not a trustee, can nevertheless sue on the contract for the loss suffered by himself and the others.

(a) Is this exception to the privity of contract rule more sensible than finding a trust?

(b) If so, what is left of the privity of contract doctrine?

---

118 [1966] 3 All E.R. 1, [1966] Ch. 538 (C.A.), affirmed [1967] 2 All E.R. 1197, [1968] A.C. 58 (H.L.).

119 See also *London Drugs Ltd. v. Kuehne & Nagel International Ltd.* (1992), [1992] 3 S.C.R. 299, 97 D.L.R. (4th) 261, 1992 CarswellBC 913, 1992 CarswellBC 315, [1993] 1 W.W.R. 1, (sub nom. *London Drugs Ltd. v. Brassart*) 143 N.R. 1, 73 B.C.L.R. (2d) 1, 43 C.C.E.L. 1, 13 C.C.L.T. (2d) 1, 18 B.C.A.C. 1, 31 W.A.C. 1; *Fraser River Pile & Dredge Ltd. v. Can-Dive Services Ltd.* (1999), [1999] 3 S.C.R. 108, 1999 CarswellBC 1927, 1999 CarswellBC 1928, [1999] S.C.J. No. 48, [1999] 9 W.W.R. 380, 11 C.C.L.I. (3d) 1, 176 D.L.R. (4th) 257, 245 N.R. 88, [1999] I.L.R. I-3717, 67 B.C.L.R. (3d) 213, 47 C.C.L.T. (2d) 1, 127 B.C.A.C. 287, 207 W.A.C. 287, 50 B.L.R. (2d) 169, [2000] 1 Lloyd's Rep. 199; *Tony & Jim's Holdings Ltd. v. Silva*, 43 O.R. (3d) 633, 170 D.L.R. (4th) 193, 23 R.P.R. (3d) 1, 1999 CarswellOnt 660, [1999] O.J. No. 705, [1999] I.L.R. I-3669, 118 O.A.C. 236, 11 C.C.L.I. (3d) 117 (C.A.).

120 (1978), 20 O.R. (2d) 113, 87 D.L.R. (3d) 282 (C.A.).

121 Contrast *O'Brien v. O'Brien Estate* (1999), 180 Sask. R. 33, 27 E.T.R. (2d) 117, 1999 CarswellSask 358, 205 W.A.C. 33 (C.A.).

122 (1980), 110 D.L.R. (3d) 44 (Alta. Q.B.).

123 [1970] 1 O.R. 743, 9 D.L.R. (3d) 425 (C.A.).

124 [1972] S.C.R. 67, 18 D.L.R. (3d) 709.

125 [1976] 1 W.W.R. 273, 62 D.L.R. (3d) 577 (B.C. S.C.).

126 [1975] 1 W.L.R. 1468, [1975] 3 All E.R. 92 (U.K. C.A.).

6. The court disapproved of *Jackson* in *Woodar Investment Development Ltd. v. Wimpey Construction.*[127] *Woodar* held that vendors under a contract for the sale of land which requires the purchaser to pay part of the purchase price to a third party cannot recover damages for non-payment of that amount unless they can show that they themselves have suffered a loss or were agents or trustees for the third party.

7. The problem of third party beneficiaries suing on a contract also arises under performance bonds entered into for the protection of suppliers of labour and material on construction projects. In these cases the rule that such third parties cannot succeed in the absence of a trust in their favour is maintained.[128]

However, in *Johns-Manville Canada Inc. v. John Carlo Ltd.*[129] a labour and material bond entitled a claimant to sue on it "as a beneficiary of the trust herein provided for." The court held that this showed a sufficient intention to create a trust in favour of unpaid claimants.

Similarly, in *Truro v. McCulloch*[130] the third party was successful under a construction performance bond because the owner had expressly contracted with the surety as a trustee. This judgment was reversed by the Nova Scotia Court of Appeal[131] but reinstated by the Supreme Court of Canada.[132]

8. In *Re Miller's Agreement; Uniacke v. A.-G.*[133] the court held that, in the absence of a trust, an annuitant has no right to sue a party to a contract who has undertaken to pay him periodic annuities.

9. X sold his share in a partnership to his two partners, who covenanted to pay X's daughter an annuity each year after X's death. X died and the partners refused to pay. The daughter sued. What is her cause of action? Will she succeed?

10. Z made a gift of $10,000 to the Society for the Prevention of Cruelty to Cats. Does the Society get the funds in trust or as an accretion to its existing funds and subject to the contractual obligations of its members?[134]

11. The third party beneficiary rule has been abolished in New Brunswick.[135]

5. TRUST AND DEBT

It is often difficult to determine whether a trust or a debt exists in any given situation, but once again they differ conceptually and the consequences of finding one or the other are significant. The test to determine whether a trust or debt was created is simply: what did the parties intend? *Air Canada v. M & L Travel*,[136] below, illustrates the difficulties in applying this test.

---

127 [1980] 1 W.L.R. 277, [1980] 1 All E.R. 571 (H.L.).

128 See *R. v. Canadian Indemnity* (1963), 43 W.W.R. 641, 5 C.B.R. (N.S.) 293, 41 D.L.R. (2d) 617 (Man. Q.B.) and *Tobin Tractor (1957) Ltd. v. Western Surety Co.* (1963), 42 W.W.R. 532, 40 D.L.R. (2d) 231 (Sask. Q.B.).

129 (1980), 29 O.R. (2d) 592, 12 B.L.R. 80, 113 D.L.R. (3d) 686 (H.C.).

130 (1971), 4 N.S.R. (2d) 480, 22 D.L.R. (3d) 293, [1972] I.L.R. 1 457 (S.C.).

131 (1973), 4 N.S.R. (2d) 459, 30 D.L.R. (2d) 242, [1973] I.L.R. 1-522 (C.A.).

132 (sub nom. *Truro v. Toronto Gen. Ins. Co.*), [1974] S.C.R. 1129, 6 N.S.R. (2d) 163, 38 D.L.R. (3d) 1, [1973] I.L.R. 1-556.

133 [1947] Ch. 615, [1947] 2 All E.R. 78.

134 A full discussion of the ways in which unincorporated associations are treated in law as having received funds is undertaken in Chapter 15, part 4, *infra*.

135 See *Law Reform Act*, S.N.B. 1993, c. L-1.2, s. 4 (proclaimed and in force on June 1, 1994).

136 [1993] 3 S.C.R. 787, 108 D.L.R. (4th) 592, 50 E.T.R. 225, 159 N.R. 1.

There are five major distinctions between the role of a debtor and that of a trustee. First, the debtor is not a fiduciary whereas the trustee is a fiduciary in the highest sense.

Second, a creditor has no interest, legal or equitable, in the property of the debtor. There is simply a personal obligation upon the debtor to repay the debt when it is due. The trust beneficiary, on the other hand, has a beneficial proprietary interest in the trust property.

Third, a debt is created by agreement and the parties may compromise, alter, or extinguish the debt by further agreement. In contrast, there need be no agreement to create a trust. Further, there can be no bargaining between the trustee and the beneficiaries as the trustee must act strictly in the interest of the beneficiaries and not permit his or her own interest to conflict.

Fourth, the debtor always remains liable to the creditor until the debt is paid. The trustee, however, is not personally obligated to compensate the beneficiaries if the trust property is lost other than through the trustee's own fault.[137]

Fifth, the debtor has no duty to invest or deal with the subject property in any particular manner, while the trustee must administer the trust property in accordance with his or her trust duties, which ordinarily include a duty to invest.

The consequences that follow a finding of debt or a trust can be critical in cases of lost or stolen property and in cases of insolvency. If the subject property is lost or stolen, a debtor remains liable to the creditor until the debt is paid, even if the property is lost through no fault of the debtor's own. The trustee, however, does not bear the loss of the trust property unless he or she is at fault.

If the debtor is insolvent, the creditor has no special interest in the subject property and will rank as a general creditor. The trust beneficiary, however, has a proprietary right to the trust property which entitles him or her to rank above all creditors *vis-à-vis* the trust property. It is, therefore, an advantage to be a trust beneficiary rather than a creditor in cases of insolvency.

AIR CANADA v. M & L TRAVEL LTD.

[1993] 3 S.C.R. 787, 108 D.L.R. (4th) 592, 50 E.T.R. 225, 159 N.R. 1
Supreme Court of Canada

M & L Travel Ltd. and Air Canada entered into an agreement providing that all moneys, less commissions, collected by the travel agency on the sale of the airline's travel tickets would be held in trust for the airline. The agency set up trust accounts but never used them. It deposited sale proceeds into its general operating account. When the agency failed to repay a demand loan due to its bank, the bank withdrew the amount outstanding from the agency's general operating account. The airline sued the agency and its two directors personally for breach of trust, claiming as damages the amount it was owed for ticket sales.

---

137 *Ontario Hydro-Electric Power Commission of Ontario v. Brown* (1959), 21 D.L.R. (2d) 551, [1960] O.R. 91 (C.A.).

The trial judge awarded judgment against the agency but not against the two directors. The Ontario Court of Appeal upheld the agency's liability and also imposed personal liability on the directors. An appeal to the Supreme Court of Canada was unsuccessful.

IACOBUCCI J.:

. . .

1. The nature of the relationship between M & L and Air Canada

In this court, the appellant initially argued that the relationship between M & L and the respondent airline was one of debtor and creditor, rather than one of trust. However, at the hearing, the appellant properly conceded that the relationship was one of trust. Given this concession, I will consider this question only briefly.

The appellant relied on the fact that the agreement between the airline and M & L did not require it to keep the proceeds of Air Canada tickets in a separate account or trust fund, or to remit the funds forthwith. Rather, M & L was permitted to keep such funds for a period of up to 15 days, and then for a further seven-day grace period. Furthermore, M & L was liable for the total sale price of all tickets sold, less its commission, regardless of whether it had actually collected the full amount from its customers. That is, M & L was free to sell Air Canada tickets on credit to its customers. Prior to his concession on this point, the appellant submitted that, in these circumstances, M & L was not a trustee of the sale proceeds of the Air Canada tickets.

In concluding that the relationship between M & L and the airline was one of trust, the Court of Appeal relied on *Canadian Pacific Air Lines Ltd. v. Canadian Imperial Bank of Commerce.*[138] Although the Court of Appeal's decision in that case[139] was brief, the reasons of the trial judge went into greater depth:[140]

> In order to constitute a trust, an arrangement must have three characteristics, known as the three certainties: certainty of intent, of subject-matter and of object. The agreement . . . is certain in its intent to create a trust. The subject-matter is to be the funds collected for ticket sales. The object, or beneficiary, of the trust is also clear; it is to be the airline. The necessary elements for the creation of a trust relationship are all present. I find that such a relationship did exist between CP and the two travel agencies.

This analysis is clearly applicable to the facts of the present case. That the intent of the agreement is to create a trust is evident from the following wording:

> All moneys, less applicable commissions to which the agent is entitled hereunder, collected by the agent for air passenger transportation (and for which the Agent has issued tickets or exchange

---

138 (1987), 42 D.L.R. (4th) 375, 71 C.B.R. (N.S.) 40, 61 O.R. (2d) 233, 27 E.T.R. 281 (H.C.), affirmed (1990), 71 O.R. (2d) 63, 37 E.T.R. 1, 4 C.B.R. (3d) 196 (C.A.).

139 *Ibid.*, (C.A.).

140 *Ibid.*, at 379 (H.C.).

orders) shall be the property of the Airline, and shall be held in trust by the agent until satisfactorily accounted for to the airline.

The object of the trust is the respondent airline, and its subject-matter is the funds collected for ticket sales.

While the presence or absence of a prohibition on the co-mingling of funds is a factor to be considered in favour of a debt relationship, it is not necessarily determinative.[141] In *Lowden*[142] McGillivray C.J.A. stated as follows:[143]

> Undoubtedly a direction that moneys are to be kept separate and apart is a strong indication of a trust relationship being created. It does not appear to me, however, that the converse is necessarily so. In the case of a travel agent, how he handled the funds handed to him for the purchase of a ticket would, as far as the public is concerned, be something that they would not have reason to think about. It would be a matter of internal management. The fact that there is no specific discussion about moneys being kept separate and apart from other moneys does not detract from the fact that the money is paid for a particular purpose; namely, the obtaining of tickets for specific flights or reservations at named accommodation for a particular period.

The appellant relied on the decision of this court in *M.A. Hanna Co. v. Provincial Bank of Canada*.[144] In that case, the court dealt with the relationship between a supplier of coal and its sales agent. The court concluded that the relationship was one of debtor-creditor, citing the fact that the parties had specifically cancelled a portion of their agreement requiring the separation of the funds collected by the sales agent. The sales agent paid the supplier by cheques drawn on its general account. The supplier's acquiescence to this practice and the fact that the agent had use of the funds before payment came due indicated to this court that the parties viewed their relationship as one of debtor-creditor. The court relied on the following passage from *Henry v. Hammond*:[145]

> It is clear that if the terms upon which the person receives the money are that he is bound to keep it separate, either in a bank or elsewhere, and to hand that money so kept as a separate fund to the person entitled to it, then he is a trustee of that money and must hand it over to the person who is his *cestui que* trust. If on the other hand he is not bound to keep the money separate, but is entitled to mix it with his own money and deal with it as he pleases, and when called upon to hand over an equivalent sum of money, then, in my opinion, he is not a trustee of the money, but merely a debtor.

---

141 See *R. v. Lowden* (1981), 59 C.C.C. (2d) 1 at 9-10, 27 A.R. 91, 15 Alta. L.R. (2d) 250 (C.A.); *Bank of Nova Scotia v. Société General (Canada)* (1988), 68 C.B.R. (N.S.) 1 at 7, [1988] 4 W.W.R. 232, 87 A.R. 133, 58 Alta. L.R. (2d) 193 (C.A.); *McEachren v. Royal Bank of Canada* (1990), 2 C.B.R. (3d) 29 at 53, [1991] 2 W.W.R. 702, 78 Alta. L.R. (2d) 158, 111 A.R. 188 (Q.B.); *Stephens Travel Service International Pty. Ltd. v. Qantas Airways Ltd.* (1988), 13 N.S.W.L.R. 331 at 341 (C.A.).

142 *Ibid.*

143 *Lowden, ibid.*, at 9-10.

144 [1935] 1 D.L.R. 545, [1935] S.C.R. 144.

145 [1913] 2 K.B. 515 at 521 (U.K. K.B.).

This decision was distinguished in *Qantas*[146] by Hope J.A. dealing with facts similar to the present case:

> As it seems to me . . . the decision . . . has no relevance to the circumstances of the present case where, on the proper construction of the agreement, a trust was expressly created, and where the distinction between an express and a constructive trustee does not affect the resolution of the rights of the parties.

Since there was clear language in the agreement that the funds were to be held in trust, Hope J.A. remarked that there would have to be extremely strong indications to alter the plain meaning of those words. On the question of the commingling of funds, Hope J.A. stated[147] that, "I do not understand why the absence of an express separate account provision should cut down the effect of the express provision of a trust. . ." This holding is consistent with the Canadian authorities.[148]

The majority of U.S. cases have concluded that relationships similar to the one in the present case are trust relationships.[149]

However, a contrary finding was made in *Re Morales Travel Agency*,[150] in which the court held that the terms of the IATA agreement between the airline and the travel agency were inadequate to give rise to a trust upon the proceeds from tickets sold by the agency to its customers:

> To be sure, Resolution 820(a) recited, in general terms, that the agent was to hold whatever moneys it collected in trust for the carrier until accounted for, and that these moneys were the carrier's property until settlement occurred. However, talismanic language could not throw a protective mantle over these receipts in the absence of a genuine trust mechanism. Here the relationship remained in practical fact that of debtor-creditor. The contract nowhere required Morales to keep the proceeds of Eastern's ticket sales separate from any other funds, whether Morales' own funds or the proceeds of other airlines' ticket sales. Nor was any specific restriction placed upon Morales' use of the supposed trust funds. Morales was left free to use what it received for its own benefit rather than Eastern's and to transform the receipts into assets with no apparent encumbrance upon which potential creditors might rely. The use of the word "trust" and the designation of the airline as title-holder, in a contract which is not publicly filed, would not save potential creditors from relying on such assets as office equipment, accounts receivable, and a bank account solely in the name of the agency. In the absence of any provision requiring Morales to hold the funds in trust by keeping them separate and otherwise restricting their use, the label "trust" could in these circumstances and for present purposes have no legal effect.[151]

---

146 *Qantas, supra*, note 141, at 348.

147 *Ibid.*, at 341.

148 See *Lowden, supra*, note 141, at 9-10; *Bank of Nova Scotia supra*, note 141, at 7; *McEachren supra*, note 141, at 53.

149 *Air Traffic Conference of America v. Downtown Travel Center, Inc.*, 14 Avi. 17,172 (N.Y. 1976); *Air Traffic Conference of America v. Worldmark Travel, Inc.*, 15 Avi. 18,483 (N.Y. 1980); *Myrta Forastieri v. Eastern Air Lines, Inc.*, 18 Avi. 17,145 (D.P.R. 1983).

150 667 F.2d 1069 (1st Cir. 1981), at 1071-1072.

151 See *In re Penn. Central Transportation Co.*, 328 F. Supp. 1278 (E.D.Pa., 1971); *Scott on Trusts*, 12.2 (3d ed.).

The *Morales* court relied on the District Court decision of *Re Penn. Central Transportation Co.*[152] This decision was subsequently reviewed by the U.S. Court of Appeals, 3rd Circuit, which concluded that a relationship of trust did exist, and that the commingling of funds was only one indication of a debtor-creditor relationship and was not necessarily conclusive.[153] Rosenn J. held at p. 325 that the "[c]ommingling of moneys has minimal significance in the extraordinary operations of interline railroads. . . . Normal operation conditions with innumerable daily collections of various categories preclude practically and economically any effective daily segregation [of funds]." The *Morales* decision and those which purport to follow it are therefore of questionable persuasion and contrary to other decisions.

In conclusion, it is well-established that the nature of the relationship between the parties is a matter of intention. In the present case, the relationship of trust is further evidenced by the express prohibition restricting the use of the funds and the supervision and control of the carrier over the financial dealings of M & L. Since there is clear evidence of intention to create a trust in the agreement between M & L and the respondent airline, the absence of a prohibition on the commingling of funds is not determinative, although it may be a factor to be taken into account by the trial judge, as it was here. Moreover, in the present case, M & L acted in accordance with that intention and set up trust accounts which, although never used, confirm that the relationship was viewed by the directors as a trust relationship. Finally, it must be noted that the nature of the relationship is consistent with trust as the IATA agreement allowed M & L to affect Air Canada's legal responsibilities.

[La Forest, Sopinka, Gonthier, Corier and Major JJ. concurred with Iacobucci J.

McLachlin concurred in the result.

The court dismissed the appeal.]

Notes and Questions

1. The test established in the principal case was recently restated and applied by the Supreme Court of Canada.[154]

---

152 *Penn, ibid.*

153 486 F.2d 519 (1973).

154 See *Citadel General Assurance Co. v. Lloyds Bank Canada* (1997), [1997] 3 S.C.R. 805, 152 D.L.R. (4th) 411, 19 E.T.R. (2d) 93, 1997 CarswellAlta 823, 1997 CarswellAlta 824, [1997] S.C.J. No. 92, (sub nom. *Citadel General Life Assurance Co. v. Lloyds Bank Canada*) 206 A.R. 321, 156 W.A.C. 321, 35 B.L.R. (2d) 153, 47 C.C.L.I. (2d) 153, 219 N.R. 323, [1999] 4 W.W.R. 135, 66 Alta. L.R. (3d) 241; *Gold v. Rosenberg*, [1997] 3 S.C.R. 767, 152 D.L.R. (4th) 385, 19 E.T.R. (2d) 1, 1997 CarswellOnt 3273, 1997 CarswellOnt 3274, [1997] S.C.J. No. 93, 219 N.R. 93, 35 O.R. (3d) 736, 104 O.A.C. 1, 35 B.L.R. (2d) 212. See also *Sorrel 1985 Ltd. Partnership v. Sorrel Resources Ltd.* (2000), 85 Alta. L.R. (3d) 27, 10 B.L.R. (3d) 61, 2000 CarswellAlta

2. *Ontario Hydro-Electric Power Commission v. Brown* illustrates the difference between trust and debt very well.[155] Brown was appointed by the plaintiff to collect payments on its behalf. Brown was paid a commission for making the collections. He received specific written instructions on how to make collections and remittances to the company, but he was never instructed on how or where to keep the collected funds before their remittance. Funds collected on the plaintiff's behalf were stolen from Brown's premises, where they had been stored separately from his own funds. The plaintiff sued Brown for the amount collected less his commission. Brown argued that he exercised due care in safeguarding the funds. Was Brown liable? On what basis? What is the relevance of Brown's due care argument?

3. A managing agent, that is, one who collects money and holds it on deposit for his principal, is normally regarded as a trustee. See *Brown v. I.R.C.*[156] which held that a solicitor is not entitled to retain interest on trust money deposited with him, but that this interest belongs to the client. As a result of that case, solicitors' general trust accounts in Canada became non-interest bearing. As a result of an amendment to the Ontario *Law Society Act*,[157] however, such accounts may again earn interest. The interest is transmitted to the Ontario Law Foundation which disburses it for Legal Aid and legal research purposes. There is similar legislation in the other provinces.

4. A mail-order company was in financial difficulty. In an attempt to protect its customers who paid in advance for goods, the company opened a separate bank account called "Customer's Trust Deposit Account" into which the purchase moneys were paid. The company then became bankrupt. How will the funds in the "Customer's Trust Deposit Account" be applied?[158]

5. Four real estate agents worked as independent contractors under a written agreement with FDR, a real estate broker. FDR signed a letter of intent to sell its assets to another real estate broker, RR. Although the transaction was never completed and the agents did not sign any agreement with RR, the agents acted as independent agents with RR. During this time they put money into RR's trust account for payments due to the broker, the corporation's own sales agents, and themselves. RR made an assignment in bankruptcy and the agents claimed commissions payable to them for sales that closed after the date of bankruptcy. The trustee in bankruptcy disallowed the claims on the basis that no trust was established between the agents and RR, as there was no agreement between RR and the agents and RR had never adopted the agreements between FDR and the agents. The registrar dismissed their appeal for the same reasons. The Ontario Court (Gen. Div.) allowed the appeal, holding that the ordinary practice of RR demonstrated that it had met the standard of certainty of intention to hold the commissions in trust for the agents.[159]

1023, 2000 ABCA 256, [2001] 1 W.W.R. 93, 277 A.R. 1, 242 W.A.C. 1 (C.A.); *Commercial Union Life Assurance Co. of Canada v. John Ingle Insurance Group Inc.* (2002), 217 D.L.R. (4th) 178, 61 O.R. (3d) 296, 2002 CarswellOnt 2707, [2002] O.J. No. 3200, 162 O.A.C. 203, 50 C.C.L.I. (3d) 6 (C.A.), additional reasons at (2002), 2002 CarswellOnt 2928 (C.A.).

155 *Supra*, note 137.

156 *Supra*, note 137.

157 R.S.O. 1990, c. L.8, s. 57.

158 See *Re Kayford Ltd.*, [1975] 1 W.L.R. 279, [1975] 1 All E.R. 604 (Ch. Div.).

159 *Eu v. Rosedale Realty Corp. (Trustee of)* (1997), 33 O.R. (3d) 666, 47 C.B.R. (3d) 218, 18 E.T.R. (2d) 288, 1997 CarswellOnt 2519 (Gen. Div.).

In contrast, the Manitoba Court of Appeal has held that a real estate broker held commissions as a debtor for its real estate agents and not as a trustee.[160] Although the parties had bargained specifically for the creation of a separate trust account to hold the agents' commissions, the court held that this contravened the regulations governing brokers. Hence, the court treated the separate trust account as a general expense account.

6. A corporation carried on the business of refining and storing precious metals. Metals received from its suppliers were treated to remove impurities and then mixed together with metals supplied by others during the refinement process. Price fluctuations in the market for precious metals drove the corporation into bankruptcy. The trustee recovered gold and silver bars worth over $500,000. Some of the corporation's suppliers claimed a proprietary interest in the bars. They argued that they had delivered the metal to the corporation for refining under a bailment relationship. In your view, what was created — a trust, bailment or debtor-creditor relationship?[161]

7. Can you explain why the question whether a trust or debtor-creditor relationship exists arises frequently in cases involving travel agents?

The prevailing view appears to be that reflected in *Canadian Pacific Air Lines Ltd. v. Canadian Imperial Bank of Commerce*[162] which held that travel agents become trustees of proceeds of ticket sales for the airlines. The court that the bank with which the travel agent had accounts was on notice that the proceeds of sale were impressed with a trust and, as a result, the bank could not apply money in the accounts against overdrafts.

Ontario Hydro-Electric Power Commission v. Brown[163] was questioned by McGillivray C.J.A., in *R. v. Lowden*.[164] Lowden operated a travel agency. He accepted cheques from customers for air fares and hotel reservations. At the time he was in financial difficulties and much of the money was never paid to the airlines and hotels but was applied to Lowden's own debts. Did Lowden stand in a debtor-creditor or a trust relationship towards his customers? What consequences flow from this determination? McGillivray C.J.A. held that the agent was a trustee for the moneys he collected less his commission, because the moneys, when collected, were the property of the principal. He rejected the proposition that because Brown was not contractually bound to keep the money separate and apart, he and the plaintiff were merely in a debtor-creditor relationship, not a trust relationship. He held that while the direction to keep money separate and apart is a strong indication of the existence of a trust relationship, the fact that there is no specific direction does not preclude the creation of a trust, nor does it lessen the significance of the fact that money may have been paid for a particular purpose.

See also on this point *Re H.B. Haina & Associates Inc.*,[165] which held that the mere fact that a travel agent keeps advance payments from its customers in a separate "Trust account" does not make him a trustee of those moneys.

8. *Barclay's Bank Ltd. v. Quistclose Investments Ltd.* also illustrates the difference between trust and debt. Q agreed to lend R a sum of[166] money to be used exclusively to pay a dividend. R agreed to this condition and arranged to have the money paid into a

---

160 *Arnal v. Land Exchange Ltd. Partnership* (2001), (sub nom. *Arnal v. Land Exchange*) 160 Man. R. (2d) 302, 46 R.P.R. (3d) 172, 2001 CarswellMan 611, 2001 MBCA 196, [2002] 3 W.W.R. 591, 262 W.A.C. 302 (C.A.).

161 See *Re Delta Smelting & Refining Co.* [1988] B.C.J. No. 2532 (B.C. S.C.).

162 *Supra*, note 138.

163 *Supra*, note 137.

164 *Supra*, note 141.

165 (1978), 28 C.B.R. (N.S.) 113, 86 D.L.R. (2d) 262 (B.C. S.C.).

166 [1970] A.C. 567, [1968] 3 All E.R. 651 (H.L.).

separate account. R's bank was informed of the condition on the loan. The dividend was never paid, and R went into liquidation. R's bank then applied the moneys to other debts of R. Q sued for the return of its money. The House of Lords found that a trust relationship existed with respect to the loan funds and that the bank was aware of the trust and bound by it. Q was, therefore, entitled to the return of the money. What kind of trust is this?

The Ontario Court of Appeal discussed the requirements of a Quistclose trust in *Del Grande v. McCleery*.[167]

9. A plaintiff gave a defendant $40 to be held for the plaintiff's use. The money was then stolen. Did the defendant hold the money as a trustee or a debtor? What consequences follow either determination?[168]

10. A person maintained two RRSPs with a bank. He decided to collapse the plans and reinvest the proceeds in self-directed RRSPs. The bank followed his instructions, received a notice from Revenue Canada that it had to pay withholding tax on the moneys, and complied with the notice. The customer sued to recover the moneys paid by the bank to Revenue Canada. What result?[169]

11. F maintained a savings account with B Trust Co. He also assigned a mortgage to the trust company for collection and payment into his account. The savings account paid 5% interest. B Trust Co. was entitled to invest the account money as it saw fit but had to pay F on demand. B Trust Co. collected some of the mortgage money but then became bankrupt. What is F's position *vis-à-vis* the general creditors of the trust company?[170]

12. CSP Ltd. was incorporated to carry on the business of issuing investment contracts to the public for money deposited with the company. The company invested the money and the investor was entitled in due course to receive the amount paid in plus interest. CSP Ltd. went into receivership and the receiver and manager continued to receive payments from investors. Being uncertain of the financial situation of the company, he kept these moneys separate and apart so that in due course they might be applied to the benefit of the persons best entitled thereto. CSP Ltd. then went bankrupt. Do the investors have a proprietary interest in the moneys paid during the receivership under a trust? It should be noted that in most cases they were not advised that these moneys would be kept separate and apart, or in trust.[171]

13. A New Brunswick company, FM, sought a large loan from a Bahamian bank, MB. The latter had liquidity problems but was anxious to make the loan, since it feared that an associated company of FM would otherwise withdraw its substantial deposits with MB. Accordingly, MB arranged through its American parent, which owned a substantial interest in a Luxembourg bank, CE, to borrow the amount of the loan from CE. These arrangements were concluded. There were substantial differences between the two loans and CE was not aware of MB's liquidity problems; nor did CE seek an assignment of the FM loan as security for its loan. There was no obligation on MB to keep CE's money separate and apart. MB subsequently became insolvent and went into liquidation. Its liquidators claimed that the moneys payable by FM were owed to MB. However, CE claimed that the moneys were owed to it. FM interpleaded. Assuming that the laws of

---

167 (2000), 31 E.T.R. (2d) 50, 2000 CarswellOnt 57, 127 O.A.C. 394 (C.A.).

168 See *Shoemaker v. Hinze* (1881), 10 N.W. 86.

169 *Bateman v. Toronto Dominion Bank* (1991), 86 D.L.R. (4th) 354, 64 B.C.L.R. (2d) 27, 44 E.T.R. 254 (S.C.).

170 See *Re Bergethaler-Waisenamt* (1946), 28 C.B.R. 1, [1947] 1 W.W.R. 132, 54 Man. R. 484, [1947] 2 D.L.R. 234 (K.B.).

171 See *Re Commonwealth Savings Plan Ltd.* (1970), 17 D.L.R. (3d) 34, 14 C.B.R. (N.S.) 260 (B.C. S.C.).

New Brunswick apply, what was the relationship between MB and CE, trust or loan? Alternatively, could CE claim an equitable charge because of MB's agreement to repay CE out of the FM loan?[172]

6. TRUST AND BAILMENT

There is a superficial similarity between trusts and bailment which has led some courts incorrectly to describe bailment in trust terms. More importantly, however, there are fundamental differences between the two situations which result in noteworthy consequences.

In both bailment and trusts, the owner of property gives control of it to another for a limited purpose. In both there is a close relationship of confidence which requires loyal performance in favour of the bailor or beneficiaries respectively with respect to the property involved. Because of these two similarities, the problem of distinguishing between trusts and bailment becomes difficult. The general rule is that if mere possession passes, the transferee is a bailee but if title passes a trust is created. However, if title is transferred in order to facilitate a particular purpose, it may be difficult to determine whether there is a bailment or a trust.

If the title is transferred simply to assist in the custodianship, then it is a bailment. But, if the title passes in order to allow a range of duties to be discharged by the transferee, then a trust is created.

There are five significant distinctions between bailments and trusts. First, the bailee is not a fiduciary, whereas the trustee is the highest example of a fiduciary.

Second, only personalty can be the subject-matter of bailment, while the trust can extend to all types of property.

Third, bailment is a legal relationship, whereas the trust is a creature of equity. Thus, in bailment there is only one owner recognized at law, while with a trust, ownership is divided between the legal and equitable owners.

Fourth, the bailee generally obtains only possession of the property and title remains in the bailor. With a trust, on the other hand, the trustee acquires the legal title to the trustee and the beneficiaries obtain beneficial title.

Fifth, the bailor can lose title only in a manner by which any legal owner can be deprived,[173] whereas a trust beneficiary can be defeated by transfer of legal title to a *bona fide* purchaser for value without notice of the trust.

As a consequence of the manner in which title is held, an unauthorized sale by a bailee will not vest good title in the purchaser as against the bailor, whereas a trustee can confer valid title upon a *bona fide* purchaser for value without notice of the trust to the exclusion of both settlor and beneficiary.

Elgin Loan and Savings Co. v. National Trust Co.,[174] below, illustrates the courts' approach to deciding whether a trust or a bailment exists.

---

172 See *Mercantile Bank & Trust Co. v. Crédit européen SA* (1981) 36 N.B.R. (2d) 339, 94 A.P.R. 339, 10 E.T.R. 165 (C.A.), affirmed (1980), 32 N.B.R. (2d) 239, 78 A.P.R. 239, 9 E.T.R. 195, leave to appeal refused (1981), 38 N.B.R. (2d) 540n, 100 A.P.R. 540n (S.C.C.).

173 Keeton & Sheridan, *Law of Trusts*, 11th ed. (Barry Rose Publishers Ltd., 1983), at 12.

174 (1903), 7 O.L.R. 1, 24 C.L.T. 55 (H.C.), affirmed 10 O.L.R. 41 (C.A.).

ELGIN LOAN AND SAVINGS CO. v. NATIONAL TRUST CO.

(1904), 7 O.L.R. 1, 24 C.L.T. 55
High Court of Justice

The plaintiff loan company became a holder of certain stock. Some of the stock was acquired under the terms of an agreement that the plaintiff loan company had with a second loan company.

The plaintiff loan company deposited the share certificates with the defendant trust company for safekeeping. The defendant agreed, for compensation, to hold the certificates and any dividends that accrued for the plaintiff loan company and to redeliver the assets upon demand. The plaintiff loan company transferred title to certificates to the defendant for this purpose. Shortly thereafter the plaintiff loan company and the second loan company were ordered wound up. The defendant was appointed liquidator of the second loan company and the plaintiff trust company was appointed liquidator of the plaintiff loan company.

The plaintiff trust company demanded the return of the share certificates from the defendant, but it refused to deliver them up. The plaintiff trust company then brought an action for damages for their unlawful retention. The issue was whether the defendant held the certificates as trustee or as bailee. The defendant claimed that it held as trustee and argued that, as the breach was technical in nature, it ought to be excused under the *Act respecting Liability of Trustees.*[175]

BOYD J.:

. . .

Now, one main line of defence is, that the defendants are as trustees to be protected under the provisions of the Act already referred to. And the case of *In re Tillsonburg, Lake Erie, and Pacific R.W. Co.*[176] is relied on to show that the relation between the Elgin Company and the defendants was that of trusteeship. That was a clear case of property being held in trust for the benefit of another upon certain conditions being complied with. There existed the three conditions usually to be found in trust transactions, *i.e.*, the creator of the trust, the trustee of the property, and the *cestui que trust* to be benefited by the creation of the trust. Here there is no *cestui que trust* in the ordinary sense, unless that term can be applied to the bailor of the scrip certificates. There were no duties to be performed by the defendants except to collect the dividends and transmit the money to Elgin Company and to hold safely the scrip till its return was demanded. All rested on the terms of the contract and not upon equitable obligations of fiduciary import.

---

175 (62 Vict. 2), c. 15, s. 1(O). The current equivalent legislation is *Trustee Act*, R.S.O. 1990, c. T.23, s. 35.

176 (1897), 24 A.C. 378.

The chief instrument between the parties was for the sole benefit of the Elgin Company as bailors, and the National Trust Company came in as a paid depositary to take custody and care of the securities for the owners.

Though the word "trust" is used in some of the letters, the word "agent" used in others is more pertinent. As said by Lord O'Hagan in *Kinloch v. Secretary of State for India*[177] there is no magic in the word "trust" and, except in the name of the defendants, the word is not used in the "Receipt and Guarantee" which manifests the transaction. Regard must be had to the nature of the transaction and the terms of the instrument relating thereto in order to determine whether the grantor, donor, settlor, or bailor intends to create a trust for the benefit of another (*cestui que trust*) or merely to arrange for the disposal of property to suit his own convenience by giving some revocable direction to the transferee of the property. In the one case the instrument is one of trust properly speaking, one in which we find the three parties, the owner — the maker of the instrument — transferring property to a trustee for the advantage of the beneficiaries; in the other case the owner gives directions to an agent for his own convenience with express or implied power at any time to countermand the instructions and recall the property: *New, Prance and Garrard's Trustee v. Hunting*;[178] *Johns v. James*;[179] *Alexander v. Wellington.*[180]

Even if a trust proper has been created, yet where the property is in the hands of the trustee merely for the benefit of the settlor himself, he can at any time revoke such trust, and call upon the trustee for a reconveyance to himself: Strong J. in *Poirier v. Brulé.*[181]

I have a strong impression that this bailment for the sole advantage of the bailor is not such a trust as is contemplated by the statute of 1899. And this view is strengthened when the property deposited has been recalled by the bailor and the depositary withholds in wrongful detention that which he should at once transmit to the owner from whom he received it. The relation of trust, if it existed, had been revoked, and the depositary, acting in plain violation of the terms of the contract, cannot invoke the aid of the Act relating to trustees. The law has already provided for a case of this kind, where a claim is made upon the property or an adverse interest alleged to exist therein, by permitting the bailee to interplead: *Biddle v. Bond.*[182] It would seem undesirable to extend the law of trusteeship to these dealings of commercial and financial import, where the law has settled into definite lines of responsibility and relief.

. . .

---

177 (1882), 7 App. Cas. 619 at 630 (H.L.).
178 [1897] 2 Q.B. 19 (C.A.).
179 [1878] 8 Ch. D. 744.
180 (1831), 2 R. & M. 35, 39 E.R. 308.
181 (1891), 20 S.C.R. 97.
182 (1865), 6 B. & S. 225, 122 E.R. 1179 (K.B.).

Notes and Questions

   1. The Ontario Court of Appeal affirmed the decision of Boyd J.[183] in *Elgin*.
   2. (a) How did the court in *Elgin* determine whether the relationship was one of trust or bailment?
   (b) What difference would it make to the defendant to be a trustee or a bailee?
   (c) What difference would it make to the plaintiff?
   3. X gave Y the possession of his car for the purpose of storage and maintenance. X transferred the ownership to Y to further the above purpose. Y then sold the car to Z without X's permission.
   (a) How did Y hold X's car? As bailee, trustee, or in some other way?
   (b) Who has the best legal right to the car?
   4. A manufacturer regularly supplied travel bags to a retailer on terms which extended a 45 day period of credit to the retailer. It was a condition of sale that ownership in the goods would not pass to the retailer until it had paid the total purchase price. The retailer sold the bags in the ordinary course of business and paid the proceeds into its general bank account, where they were mixed with other moneys. The retailer became bankrupt, still owing the purchase price of some of the bags. Is the retailer a bailee, an ordinary debtor, or a trustee with a duty to account for the proceeds of sale?[184]

7. TRUST AND THE OFFICE OF PERSONAL REPRESENTATIVE

   To a large extent the roles of trustee and personal representative have become blurred by statutes which assimilate the functions of the two,[185] and by the modern practice of appointing the same person to both positions. It is, however, an error to equate the office of trustee with that of personal representative as significant distinctions and consequences follow a finding of one or the other.
   The similarities which exist between the functions of the trustee and those of the personal representative are considerable. Both are fiduciaries, the trustee having duties *vis-à-vis* the trust beneficiaries and the personal representative having duties toward the estate as a whole. Both hold title on behalf of someone else. Finally, through a variety of statutory provisions, both now have overlapping functions. The significant portions of two such statutes, the *Trustee Act*[186] and the *Estates Administration Act*[187] are set out below.
   The function of the personal representative ceases once his or her duties are completed. If any trusts are created, the trustee takes over. When these two offices are performed by the same person, the court must determine when the transformation takes place. *Attenborough v. Solomon*,[188] below, illustrates how to distin-

---

183 *Supra*, note 174.
184 See *Re Andrabell Ltd.*, [1984] 3 All E.R. 407 at 413-4.
185 See, for example, *Trustee Act*, R.S.O. 1990, c. T.23, s. 1 and *Estates Administration Act*, R.S.O. 1990, c. E.22, s. 2.
186 R.S.O. 1990, c. T.23, s. 1.
187 R.S.O. 1990, c. E.22, s. 2.
188 [1913] A.C. 76 (H.L.).

guish between a personal representative and a trustee, and how to determine when the transformation from the former to the latter is complete.

There are eight important distinctions between the functions of a personal representative and those of a trustee. First, the duty of a personal representative is to administer the estate by collecting the assets, paying the liabilities and distributing the property to those entitled. A trustee's duty, on the other hand, is to manage the trust and this duty lasts for as long as the trust continues, subject only to retirement, removal, or death of the trustee.

Second, the beneficiary under a will has no property interest in the assets of the estate until administration is complete, whereas the trust beneficiary has a proprietary interest in the trust property.

Third, the power of personal representatives to dispose of personalty is several; that of trustees is joint.[189] There is no distinction with regard to the disposition of real property; it must be done jointly in both cases.

Fourth, different limitation periods apply to the two offices.

Fifth, the origins of the relationships are quite different. The office of personal representative originated with the ecclesiastical courts while the trustee is a creation of the chancery courts.

Sixth, a personal representative has no power to replace him- or herself, while a trustee may appoint his or her successor. When an executor dies without completing his or her obligations, the office devolves upon his or her executor.

Seventh, a personal representative retains the office for life, unless the grant is otherwise limited or the court releases the personal representative. His or her duties are concluded with the administration of the estate but the liabilities continue. The trustee, however, holds office only while the trusts are in existence.

Eighth, a personal representative who has accepted the office and taken steps to administer the estate cannot resign. A trustee, however, is permitted to retire.

As a consequence of the distinction in powers of disposition of personalty, a personal representative can bind the estate, whereas a trustee acting without the consent of his or her fellow trustees cannot. *Attenborough v. Solomon*, below, also illustrates this issue.

TRUSTEE ACT

R.S.O. 1990, c. T.23

1. In this Act,

. . .

"personal representative" means an executor, an administrator, and an administrator with the will annexed;

. . .

"trust" does not mean the duties incident to an estate conveyed by way of mortgage

---

189 *Ibid.*

but, with this exception, includes implied and constructive trusts and cases where the trustee has some beneficial estate or interest in the subject of the trust, and extends to and includes the duties incident to the office of personal representative of a deceased person, and "trustee" has a corresponding meaning and includes a trustee however appointed and several joint trustees;

. . .

Comparable Legislation

Trustee Act, R.S.B.C. 1996, c. 464, s. 1; R.S.M. 1987, c. T160, s. 1; R.S.N.L. 1990, c. T-10, s. 2; R.S.N.S. 1989, c. 479, s. 2; R.S.P.E.I. 1988, c. T-8, s. 1; *Trustees Act*, R.S.N.B. 1973, c. T-15, s. 1 as amended S.N.B. 1979, c. 41, s. 123(1).

ESTATES ADMINISTRATION ACT

R.S.O. 1990, c. E.22

2.(1) All real and personal property that is vested in a person without a right in any other person to take by survivorship, on the person's death, whether testate or intestate and despite any testamentary disposition, devolves to and becomes vested in his or her personal representative from time to time as trustee for the persons by law beneficially entitled thereto, and, subject to the payment of the person's debts and so far as such property is not disposed of by deed, will, contract or other effectual disposition, it shall be administered, dealt with and distributed as if it were personal property not so disposed of.

Comparable Legislation

Chattels Real Act, R.S.N.L. 1990, c. C-11, s. 2; *Devolution of Estates Act*, R.S.N.B. 1973, c. D-9, s. 3; *Devolution of Real Property Act*, R.S.A. 2000, c. D-12, s. 2; R.S.S. 1978, c. D-27, ss. 4, 5; R.S.N.W.T. 1988, c. D-5, s. 2, as amended S.N.W.T. 2003, c. 5, s. 3 (Sched. C, item 1); R.S.Y. 2002, c. 57, s. 3; *Estate Administration Act*, R.S.B.C. 1996, c. 122, Part 9, s. 77; *Intestate Succession Act*, S.M. 1989-90, c. 43, s. 17.3; *Real Property Act*, R.S.N.S. 1989, c. 385, s. 7(1); *Probate Act*, R.S.P.E.I. 1988, c. P-21, s. 103.

ATTENBOROUGH v. SOLOMON

[1913] A.C. 76
House of Lords

The testator gave the residue of his estate to his executors and trustees, A.S. and J.S., upon trust for sale and distribution. Within one year of the testator's death, the debts and legacies were paid and the executors passed the residuary accounts. However, the residue was not completely distributed. Some 14 years after the testator's death, A.S., without J.S.'s knowledge, improperly pledged some silver plate to the appellant pawnbrokers, who took without notice that A.S. was an executor and trustee. When A.S. died, J.S. and a new executor sought to recover the plate from the appellants. They were successful in the Court of Appeal and in the House of Lords.

VISCOUNT HALDANE L.C.:

. . .

Now, my Lords, the meaning of a residuary account must of course be construed with reference to its purpose. It is not a document which is intended to have the operation of a declaration of trust; but it may be looked at as against the executor as evidence of what he regarded as being the position of the estate. I think it is plain from that document that Mr. J.D. Solomon regarded the debts as having been all paid and the estates ready to be held upon the trusts of the will which affected it in the hands of the trustees.

. . .

The general principles of law which govern this case are not doubtful. The position of an executor is a peculiar one. He is appointed by the will, but then, by virtue of his office, by the operation of law and not under the bequest in the will, he takes a title to the personal property of the testator, which vests him with the plenum dominum over the testator's chattels. He takes that, I say, by virtue of his office. The will becomes operative so far as its dispositions of personalty are concerned only if and when the executor assents to those dispositions. It is true that by virtue of his office he has a general power to sell or pledge for the purpose of paying debts and getting in the money value of the estate. He is executor and he remains executor for an indefinite time. Authorities were cited to us by Mr. Hughes to the effect that an executor can sell at a period long after the death of the testator, and that where it is a question of conveyancing, as for instance in the case of the sale of leaseholds by the executor, the purchaser is not entitled to make requisitions as to whether debts remain unpaid because the executor's office remains intact and he may exercise his functions at any time. That is true as a general principle, and I have no comment to make upon it except that it is qualified by another principle, which is this: The office of executor remains, with its power attached, but the property which he had originally in the chattels that devolved upon him, and over which these powers extended, does not necessarily remain. So soon as he has assented, and this he may do informally and the assent may be inferred from his conduct, the dispositions of the will become operative, and then the beneficiaries have vested in them the property in those chattels. The transfer is made not by the mere force of the assent of the executor, but by virtue of the dispositions of the will which have become operative because of this assent.

Now, my lords, in view of the residuary account passed as it was and in the form it was, in view of the evidence of Mr. J.D. Solomon, and in view of the 14 years which had passed since the testator died before the time when Mr. A.A. Solomon made the pledge to the appellants in 1892, I am of the opinion that the true inference to be drawn from the facts is that the executors considered that they had done all that was due from them as executors by 1879 and were content when the residuary account was passed that the dispositions of the will should take effect. That is the inference I draw from the form of the residuary account; and the inference is strengthened when I consider the lapse of time since then, and that in the interval nothing was done by them purporting to be an exercise of power as executors. My Lords, if this be so, this appeal must be disposed of on the footing that in point of fact the executors assented at a very early date to the dispositions of the will taking effect. It follows that under these dispositions the residuary estate, including the chattels in question, became vested in the trustees as trustees. That they were the same persons as the executors does not affect the point, or in my opinion present the least obstacle to the inference. But if that was so, then the title to the silver plate of A.A. Solomon as executor had ceased to exist before he made the pledge of 1892. What then was the position of the appellants? By the law of England the property in a chattel must always be in one person or body of persons. When the person who owns the chattel makes a pledge of it to a pawnbroker he is not purporting to part with the full property or giving any thing which is in the nature of a title to that property to the pawnee, excepting to a limited extent. The expression has been used that the pawnee in such a case has got a special property in the chattel. My Lords, that is true in this sense, that the pawnbroker, is entitled to hold the chattel upon the terms that when the possession has been lawfully given to him it is not to be taken away from him, and that if default is made in the redemption of the pledge, or it may be in the payment of interest, he may go further and by virtue of his contract, assuming it to be valid, sell the chattel. But the contract of pawn . . . rests upon this foundation, that the property remains in the bailor, and that the bailee, whether it be a bailment by way of pawn or in any other form, simply takes at the outside a right to the possession dependent on the validity of the title of the bailor with the other rights possibly superadded to which I have referred. If that be true, upon no hypothesis did the appellants get a legal title to the property in the plate. When A.A. Solomon handed over these articles of silver to Messrs. Attenborough he had no property to pass as executor; and they got no contractual rights which could prevail against the trustees. The latter were the true owners and they are now in a position to maintain an action, which under the old forms would have been an action of trover or detinue, to recover possession of the chattels free from the restrictions or the right to reclaim possession which were sought to be imposed by the contract between A.A. Solomon and the appellants. My Lords, the property, if I am right in the inference which I draw from the circumstances of the case, was vested not in A.A. Solomon but in A.A. Solomon and his co-trustee jointly in 1892, when the attempted pledge was made; and I see no answer to the case made for the respondents that the present trustees, in whom that property is now vested, are entitled to recover it.

A great deal of authority has been cited to us in the course of this case. Mr. Hughes has said, and with truth so far as the bare proposition goes, that persons dealing with the executors have not got to inquire whether the debts are paid, and must assume that their powers are operative. Two of the learned judges in the Court of Appeal appear to have felt some concern over the question of the relevancy of that proposition. But the question which goes to the root of this case is one which renders such a proposition wholly beside the point. If I am right, there is no question here of an executor acting in the execution of his powers, so far as this residue is concerned. The executors had long ago lost their vested right of property as executors and become, so far as the title to it was concerned trustees under the will. Executors they remained, but they were executors who had become divested, by their assent to the dispositions of the will, of the property which was their *virtute officii*; and their right *in rem*, their title of property, had been transformed into a right *in personam*, a right to get the property, back by proper proceedings against those in whom the property should be vested if it turned out that they required it for payment of debts for which they had made no provision. My Lords, that right always remains to the executors and they can always exercise it, but it is a right to bring an action, not a right of property, and not such a right as would enable such pledge as this to be validly made. I have therefore arrived at the clear conclusion that at the time when the pledge to Messrs. Attenborough was attempted A.A. Solomon had no title in virtue of which he could make it; and that the respondents are therefore entitled to succeed in their action. I move that the appeal be dismissed with costs.

[Lords Atkinson and Shaw concurred.]

Notes and Questions

1. (a) How did the court in *Attenborough* distinguish between the duties and powers of a personal representative and those of a trustee?

(b) At what point did the transformation from personal representative to trustee occur?

2. See also *Booty v. Hutton*,[190] which applied *Attenborough v. Solomon* and outlined the duties of personal representatives; and *Singer v. Singer Estate*,[191] which held that the passing of accounts by the personal representatives was not of itself indicative of a change in roles from personal representative to trustee, but that the circumstances surrounding the passing of accounts must be considered.

3. *Harvell v. Foster*[192] also illustrates when the change from personal representative to trustee takes place. The testator left his estate to his daughter who was a minor when it was administered. The estate funds were given to the daughter's husband who signed an administration bond in which the defendant solicitors joined as sureties. The husband then absconded with the money and the solicitors were held responsible for the due administration of the estate by the husband and accountable for the default.

4. Originally, assents applied only to personal property. They did not apply to real property, because it devolved directly upon the devisee or heir-at-law. Real property now devolves upon the personal representative in most jurisdictions. It is debatable whether a

---

190 (1999), 140 Man. R. (2d) 186, 30 E.T.R. 159, [1999] M.J. No. 410, 1999 CarswellMan 447, [2000] 1 W.W.R. 81 (Q.B.).

191 (2000), 280 A.R. 127, 90 Alta. L.R. (3d) 387, [2001] 6 W.W.R. 192, 2000 CarswellAlta 1580, 2000 ABQB 944 (Surr. Ct.), affirmed (2002), 2002 CarswellAlta 1600, 2002 ABCA 294, [2003] 3 W.W.R. 31, 9 Alta. L.R. (4th) 10, 320 A.R. 143, 288 W.A.C. 143 (C.A.).

192 [1954] 2 Q.B. 367, [1954] 2 All E.R. 736 (C.A.).

written assent or deed from the personal representative to him- or herself is required since transfers of land must be in writing. The English *Administration of Estates Act*[193] requires a written assent in such circumstances. For a case dealing with this provision, see *Re King's Will Trusts*.[194] There appears to be no similar legislation in the Canadian provinces, except the British Columbia *Estate Administration Act*,[195] which refers to an assent by personal representatives, but only in the sense of their giving their assent, by instrument attested and proved, to a devise contained in the deceased's will.[196]

5. Unlike the trust beneficiary, a beneficiary under a will does not have a proprietary interest in the property until the administration of the will is complete.

6. In *Re Cockburn's Will Trusts*,[197] the court held that once the estate administrators have completed their administration duties, they become trustees with the ability to appoint new trustees in their place and thus to retire.

8. TRUSTS AND CONDITIONS, CHARGES AND PERSONAL OBLIGATIONS

A gift to one person which requires him or her to hold, pay, or transfer it to another may be construed in various ways. The gift may be interpreted as a trust in favour of a third party, as subject to a condition, as creating a charge on the property, or as a personal obligation on the donee.

Each of the latter three constructions has similarities to the trust. Each is also different and bears different legal consequences, thus, each will be examined in turn.

Further Reading

T.C. Thomas, "Conditions in Favour of Third Parties" (1952), 11 Camb. L.J. 240.

(a) Conditions

A gift may be made subject to a condition precedent or a condition subsequent. Those gifts made subject to the occurrence of a certain event are subject to a condition precedent. Those conditional upon the happening of an event which will cause the property to be transferred to another or revert to the donor are subject to a condition subsequent. *Re Frame*,[198] below, illustrates how the court determines if a condition exists and the effect of such a determination.

---

193 1925 (15 & 16 Geo. 5), c. 23, s. 36(4).

194 [1964] Ch. 542, [1964] 1 All E.R. 833.

195 R.S.B.C. 1996, c. 122, s. 78.

196 On the matter of assents, see also the following Canadian cases: *Ewart v. Gordon* (1867), 13 Gr. 40, 1867 CarswellOnt 4 (U.C. Ch.); *Cumming v. Landed Banking & Loan Co.* (1893), 22 S.C.R. 246, 1893 CarswellOnt 16; *Dover v. Denne* (1902), 3 O.L.R. 664 (C.A.), *per* MacLennan J.A.; *Baty, Re* (1958), [1959] O.R. 13, 16 D.L.R. (2d) 164, 1958 CarswellOnt 131 (C.A.); and *Cassidy, Re*, [1931] O.R. 259, [1931] 3 D.L.R. 392 (S.C.).

197 [1957] Ch. 438, [1957] 2 All E.R. 522.

198 [1939] Ch. 700, [1939] 2 All E.R. 865.

RE FRAME

[1939] Ch. 700, [1939] 2 All E.R. 865
Chancery Division

The testator appointed the defendant, Mrs. Taylor, his housekeeper, to be his executrix and gave her all his money and insurance policies on condition that she adopt his daughter, Alma Edwards, and also gave £5 to each of the testator's son and two daughters. Mrs. Taylor attempted to adopt Alma Edwards, but her application was dismissed. An application was then made to the court to determine whether the defendant was absolutely entitled to the bequest.

SIMONDS J.:

. . .

I have listened to an able and interesting argument on these questions: Whether the condition is a condition subsequent or a condition precedent; whether, if it be a condition precedent, the condition has become impossible of performance, and whether, if so, the gift fails; whether, if it be a condition subsequent, the donee has failed, through no fault of her own, to comply with the condition, and whether, in that event, the gift has failed. As I listened to that argument it impressed itself more and more on me that, after all, this was not a condition at all, for, in my view, on the true construction of this clause, the word "condition" is not used in its strict legal sense. It is a gift to Mrs. Taylor on condition, in the sense of on the terms or on the trust that she does certain things, and that, I think, becomes clearer when it is realized that the condition relates not only to the adoption of one daughter, but to the payment of certain sums to other daughters. A devise, or bequest, on condition that the devisee or legatee makes certain payments does not import a condition in the strict sense of the word, but a trust, so that, though the devisee or legatee dies before the testator and the gift does not take effect, yet the payments must be made; for it is a trust, and no trust fails for want of trustees. When I come to look at the condition, it seems clear that what the testator intended was that Mrs. Taylor should receive certain moneys on the terms that she performed certain acts. Much argument has been directed to what is involved in condition that "she adopts my daughter." It seems clear that whether or not an adoption under the authority of an order made under the *Adoption of Children Act, 1926*, is necessary, what is intended is not any single formal act, but a series of acts to establish as between Mrs. Taylor and the testator's daughter the relationship of parent and child — in a word, Mrs. Taylor was to treat the child as if she were her daughter, because that is what adoption means. Is that a trust which the court can enforce? It includes not only the parental duties of care, advice, and affection, but also the duty of maintenance. This court cannot compel, so far as adoption involves the giving of care, advice and affection, that such things be given. But, seeing that it involves the duty of maintenance, that is a trust which the court can enforce directing, if necessary, an inquiry in that regard. It will not allow the whole trust to fail because in part it cannot be enforced.

Therefore, I come to the conclusion that the gift to Mrs. Taylor of all the money and insurance policies — what that means will have to be considered — on condition "that she adopts my daughter" involves that she receives those things, whatever they may be, on trust to make proper provision for the maintenance of the child as her adopted daughter. That is a trust which can be enforced, and, if necessary, an inquiry can be directed in regard to it.

Notes and Questions

1. How did the court in *Re Frame* construe the words "on condition that"?[199]

2. *Attorney-General v. The Cordwainer's Co.*[200] illustrates the point further. The testator devised an inn to the Cordwainer's Company "for the interest, use, and performance of this my last will and testament . . ." The Company was required to pay £6 a year to the testator's brother and after his death to his widow. There was a gift over to the testator's brother in fee simple if the Company failed to pay the money. The Company carried out the terms of the will and the question then arose whether it was entitled to the surplus after payment of the £6 annually or whether it held the surplus on trust. The court held that the devise was made on a condition which, if performed, entitled the Company to keep the surplus beneficially. The reason for this conclusion was that the property was given absolutely to the Company, not upon trust, but for the use, interest, and performance of the testator's will.

3. In *Re Frame* the donee was to hold any excess moneys after the performance of the condition on resulting trust, while in *A.-G. v. The Cordwainers Company*, the donee was permitted to keep any excess moneys after the condition was performed.

How is the difference in result explained?

(b) Charges

When a gift is construed as creating a charge on property, the donee takes beneficially subject to the charge. A charge is enforceable in equity by the third party in whose favour the charge applies.

A charge on property is security for the payment of an obligation. It encumbers the property and is not a personal obligation on the donee. Once the debt or obligation is satisfied, the charge is extinguished. The person who holds property subject to a charge is not a trustee or fiduciary. He or she is entitled to rents and profits and has an interest in the whole of the property subject to the charge.

A charge is similar to a trust in two respects. First, neither the trustee nor the person who takes the property subject to a charge is under a personal obligation to make up a deficiency in the assets not caused by their fault.[201]

---

199 See also *Associated Alloys Pty. Ltd. v. ANC 001452 106 Pty. Ltd.* (2000), 202 C.L.R. 588 (Australia H.C.) in which the court interpreted a clause containing the words "trust" and "charge" to determine which of these devices was intended.

200 (1833) 3 My. & K. 534, 40 E.R. 203.

201 See *Re Oliver* (1890), 62 L.T. 533 (Ch. Div.).

Second, both a trust and a charge create equitable interests which may be defeated by the *bona fide* purchase for value of the legal estate without notice of the equitable interest.[202]

A charge differs from a trust in two respects. First, once the obligation supporting the charge is fulfilled, the donee receives the balance of the property absolutely, while the trustee always holds the surplus property on a resulting trust.[203]

Second, a trustee who occupies trust property must account for rents and profits, whereas a person holding property subject to a charge need not do so.

Re Oliver,[204] below, illustrates the test applied by the courts to determine whether a charge or a trust exists, and the consequences which follow such a determination.

RE OLIVER

(1890), 62 L.T. 533
Chancery Division

The testator gave an annuity to his sister charged upon some real property. Then he devised the real property to his nephew, John Beckitt, "he also paying thereout the following legacies . . ." The testator directed that these legacies were to be paid six months after the death of his sister and he referred to these legacies as "charged on" his real property. The legatees argued that Beckitt was a trustee and therefore accountable for the rents and profits he made on the realty in the six months after the testator's death but before payment of the legacies.

CHITTY J.:

. . .

This question relates to the testator's real estate at North Collingham and South Collingham, and the question is this: Is the testator's nephew, John Beckitt, liable to account for the rents and profits of that estate which he received between the date of the testator's death and the completion of the sale of the property under an order of the court. That question depends upon whether, on the true construction of the testator's will, John Beckitt is a trustee of the property for the legatees, or whether he is the owner of the property subject to a charge in respect of the legacies. In the latter case the legatees would not be entitled to call upon John Beckitt to account for the back rents and profits received by him. On behalf of the legatees it is contended that the testator's nephew is a trustee for them, and that everything he received he must account for.

---

202 Nathan & Marshall, *Cases and Commentary on The Law of Trusts*, 7th ed. (Stevens & Sons, 1980), 44. This point is not carried forward to later editions.
203 *Re Oliver supra*, note 201 and *Re West, George v. Grose*, [1900] 1 Ch. 84, 69 L.J. Ch. 71.
204 *Ibid.*

. . .

The words "he paying thereout the following legacies" are *prima facie* words of condition, and in this case the condition is a condition subsequent. That is shown by the direction that the legacies shall be paid at the end of six calendar months after the death of the annuitant, the testator's sister, Mary Glew. Consequently, John Beckitt, who is immediately entitled to the benefit of the devise, does not have to pay the legacies until six months after the death of the testator's sister. Therefore he would enter into receipt of the rents and profits of the property for six months before he would be bound to pay the legacies. Now, there is a well-known rule of construction that a devise upon condition that the devisee makes certain payments within a given time will, as a general rule, be construed as a trust and not as a condition, because, if construed as a condition, the only person who takes advantage of the condition being unperformed, when the devise is by will, is the testator's own heir.

> The right of entry for breach of a condition subsequent could not be reserved in favour of a stranger, but only of the grantor or his heirs; and the effect of entry by him, or them, after breach; was to defeat altogether the estate which had before passed to the grantee; so that the grantor or his heirs were in as of their former seisin.

That is a passage of familiar law which is to be found in Stephen's Commentaries.[205] If it was held that the devise must be construed as importing a condition and nothing else, the person entitled to receive the payments would lose the payments, because, if the payments were not made within a given time, the heir of the testator would enter and take the estate and take it free. It was to get over that objection that it has been said that generally the right construction is to hold that the devise creates a trust and not a condition. It has been termed a trust without any particular regard to the language, a legal effect being given so as to enable the person entitled to get the payments. It is upon that class of cases, to which I have referred only in general terms, that the argument has been based that here the devise is not a condition and is therefore a trust. But it is equally plain, for ordinary purposes, that the effect of the devise is to create a charge and not a trust. Now, I proceed to consider whether it is a trust or a charge. On the face of the will, when the testator intends to create a trust, he knows how to do it.

[His Lordship discussed the provisions of the will and continued:]

The testator imposes a trust upon one of the persons who takes beneficially, and if the matter stood there I should find some difficulty in deciding that this was a charge and not a trust. But the testator is entitled to explain his own meaning, and he says in so many words, in a subsequent part of his will, that the trustees shall stand possessed of the £1000 which he has "charged on My Collingham estate." I see no reason to say that the testator does not know the meaning of his

---

205 9th ed., vol. 1, at 299.

own will. On the contrary, I think that the testator has shown that he is well-acquainted with what he has done before. Therefore, upon the true construction of this will, I think that the legacies constitute a charge and only a charge. Unquestionably a difficulty arises on the part of the will where the testator says, "he is also paying thereout the following legacies." But there are the subsequent words by which he explains that they are a charge. Those words "he paying thereout" are only words upon which it turns whether there is a charge or a trust. But the testator has given, in respect of those words, a "dictionary" explaining their effect. These legacies are consequently simply a charge on the North and South Collingham estate, as I am satisfied looking at the will as a whole. I hold, therefore, that the devisee is not liable to account for the back rents and profits.

Notes and Questions

1. What is the difference between holding property subject to a charge and holding property as a trustee?

(a) Can the holder in either case keep the rents and profits from the property?

(b) Can either keep the property left after the charge or the trust respectively are satisfied?

2. Historically, an executor was beneficially entitled to the residue of an estate unless it was expressly disposed of. This rule was, however, reversed by statute. See the *Succession Law Reform Act*,[206] which provides that the executor is deemed to be a trustee of the residue for the persons entitled on an intestacy. Where, however, there is an express gift of the residue to the executors, the section does not apply and in that case the court must determine as a matter of construction whether the executors are intended to have the residue beneficially.[207]

3. T died, leaving all his effects to his sister on the condition that she pay his wife an annuity. The bequest was far larger than the amount needed to pay the annuity. The sister applied to the court to find out what was to be done with the surplus. What is the result?[208]

(c) Personal Obligations

When a gift is given subject to, or in consideration of, a payment to a third party, the court may construe the gift as creating a personal obligation on the donee of the gift. In that case, the third party has no right against the subject property, but only against the donee of the gift personally. The third party has equitable rights but not such as those created under a trust or a charge.

Because the obligation is personal against the donee, the third party normally loses his or her funds if the donee becomes insolvent. On the other hand, the

---

206 R.S.O. 1990, c. S.26, s. 33.

207 See *Re Gracey* (1928), 63 O.L.R. 218, [1929] 1 D.L.R. 260 (C.A.) and compare *Re Melvin*, [1972] 3 W.W.R. 55, 24 D.L.R. (3d) 240 (B.C. S.C.).

208 See *Re West, supra*, note 203; *Re Foord*, [1922] 2 Ch. 519; and *Moffit v. Moffit*, [1954] 2 D L.R. 841, 13 W.W.R. (N.S.) 145 (B.C. S.C.).

donee may be liable to such a third person for an amount greater than the value of the property received.[209]

It can be very difficult to distinguish between a personal obligation and a trust, a condition, or a charge. *Re Lester*,[210] below, reviews how the courts determine when a personal obligation exists and the consequences which follow such a determination.

RE LESTER

[1942] Ch. 324
Chancery Division

The testator bequeathed certain shares in two companies to his son "subject . . . to the payment by him" of certain annuities. The son made this application to determine whether the shares were charged with the annuities. He admitted that, having assented to the legacy, he was under a personal obligation to pay the annuities.

SIMONDS J.:

Various authorities have been cited to me and the result of them is, in my judgment, that it must be a question of construction in each case whether an obligation or a charge is created or whether both are created. I find it difficult to construe such words as those in this case as creating both a personal obligation and a charge. There may be words which create both, as in *Welby v. Rockcliffe*[211] and *Wright v. Wilkin*[212] where the language does not admit fairly of any other conclusion than that there was both a personal obligation and a charge. In *Rees v. Engelback*[213] the language was such as to create a personal obligation and there are two Irish cases, *In Re M'Mahon*[214] and *Duffy v. Duffy*,[215] where language was used which was apt to impose a personal obligation but not to create a charge. In *Rees v. Engelback* the testator had devised his business to his trustees on trust to allow his son to carry it on "upon the terms and conditions following" — *i.e.*, that he should pay certain annuities, and the only question was whether his son, having accepted the legacy, had incurred a personal liability; and the Vice-Chancellor said:[216]

---

209 Nathan & Marshall, *Cases and Commentary on The Law of Trusts*, 7th ed. (Stevens & Sons, 1980), 47. This point is not carried forward in later editions.
210 [1942] Ch. 324.
211 (1830), 1 Russ. & My. 571.
212 (1860), 7 Jur. N.S. 441.
213 (1871), L.R. 12 Eq. 225.
214 [1901] 1 I.R. 489.
215 [1920] 1 I.R. 122.
216 *Supra*, note 213, at 237.

Now, upon the authority of the case of *Messenger v. Andrews*[217] and even without the authority of that case, upon very plain principles of justice and law, the defendant, who admits that he has enjoyed the benefit given to him by a will upon the conditions expressed in it, is under a personal liability, which can be enforced in this court, of fulfilling those conditions.

It is true that in the bill the plaintiff had claimed a declaration that the annuities were by the will charged on the business, but that question was not ventilated. In *In re Hodge*[218] a testatrix devised to her husband, who was her executor and sole residuary legatee, certain freehold property in consideration of his paying her sister £2 a week for life. There it will be observed that a condition was introduced by the words "in consideration of," and the judge came to the conclusion that there was a personal obligation on the husband, if he accepted the devise. I think there is very little difference between a bequest "in consideration of" and a bequest "subject to" the payment by the legatee of certain sums. In either case the words are apt to create a personal obligation. On the other hand, where there is no reference to the legatee as the person by whom the payment is to be made, but the property is merely given subject to the payment of a certain sum, it may well be that the effect is to create a charge on the property but not to impose a personal obligation on the legatee. The distinction is a fine but, I think, a real one. Here where it is rightly, in my view, conceded that a personal obligation is imposed on the legatee to make the payment, I see no ground for saying that in addition a charge is created.

I must refer to two other cases that were cited to me. In *In Re Cowley*[219] a testator gave all his interest in certain leasehold premises to his son, subject to payment of all his debts, funeral and testamentary expenses. The son accepted the bequest and it was held that he must be deemed to have accepted it, but was not personally liable to pay the debts, funeral or testamentary expenses. In his judgment Kay J. says:

> In the absence of authority, I am not prepared to say that the gift of specific legacies contained in the present will, subject to payment of his debts, funeral and testamentary expenses, means anything but that the testator gives this property and the other property subject to payment of his debts, funeral, and testamentary expenses. It does not seem to me at all intended that, whether or not the property is enough, the legatee is to pay the debts.

From the passage that follows it is clear that the learned judge is assuming that the words under consideration were apt to create a charge on the property of the debts, funeral, and testamentary expenses. He goes on:

> It is commonly expressed in very different terms — he paying the debts. Here I take the words only as amounting to a charge by the testator between that property and the other property. I think that the testator's son must be deemed to have elected to accept the legacies, subject to payment of the debts, funeral, or testamentary expenses, or any part thereof.

---

217 (1828), 4 Russ. 478.
218 [1940] Ch. 260.
219 (1885), 53 L.T. 494.

The opening word "It" in the passage last cited means "the intention that, whether or not the property is enough, the legatee is to pay the debts." The learned judge does not in so many words say that in that case a charge would not be created, but he is clearly contrasting the two cases of charge and personal liability. The other case is *In re Oliver*.[220] There the testator gave his real estate at North and South Collingham and his residuary estate to his nephew "he also paying thereout the following legacies . . ." but later referred to the legacies as "charged on my Collingham estate." Chitty J. held that the words "he also paying thereout the following legacies . . ." would by themselves have been apt to create a trust (he does not use the words "personal obligation"), but as the testator had referred to the legacies as "charged" on the Collingham estate, he was constrained to hold that a charge only, not a trust, was created. He was, I think, clearly of opinion that such an expression could not carry the double burden of creating a charge and imposing a personal obligation. So also in the present case, since it is clear that a personal obligation is imposed on the legatee on his assenting to the legacy. I should not be justified in saying that the words in question also create a charge on the subject-matter of the legacy.

. . .

Notes and Questions

1. T died leaving the following bequests:
(a) all my bonds to my trustees for distribution amongst my children as they see fit;
(b) all my shares to A for the benefit of maintaining B, and after the death of B, to C;
(c) the residue of my estate to X subject to the payment of $1,000 to P.
Advise the trustees, A and X.

2. Is it preferable to hold property as
(a) a trustee rather than subject to a condition?
(b) a trustee rather than subject to a charge?
(c) a trustee rather than subject to a personal obligation? Give reasons for your answers.

Problems

1. John works for Fred. A couple of weeks ago John handed Fred $200 and asked him to look after it for him since he was afraid that otherwise his wife would spend it on alcohol. Fred, after some hesitation, accepted the money and in John's presence put the bills in his wallet together with his own money. The understanding was that Fred would give John the money back as soon as John's wife finished a "cure" which she was about to start.

The same night Fred met some friends of his and lost $50 to them in a friendly card game. He paid the $50 out of the money in his wallet. An hour later he won $20 on a bet which he put back into the wallet. When he came home Fred discovered that the wallet was stolen during the evening.

---

220 *Supra*, note 201.

John now claims the $200 which Fred refuses to pay. The evidence indicates that Fred had about $40 in his wallet when John gave him the $200.

What is the result?

2. A operates a travel agency. He accepts cheques from customers for air fares and hotel accommodations. The moneys, less his commission, are paid into his "trust account." However, they were not paid to him "in trust" or upon similar terms. Nor did A tell his customers that he would pay the moneys into a trust account. A continued to accept such moneys after he encountered financial difficulties. Since that time, the moneys remain in the trust account and have not been paid to the appropriate airlines and hotels. B was appointed receiver and manager of the business and seeks payment of the moneys to him for the benefit of A's creditors. Is he entitled to the moneys? Give reasons.

3. A testatrix bequeathed $15,000 to her trustees in trust to provide a university education for her grandson, Aquarius Dropout, and directed them to pay the balance of the fund to Aquarius when he completed his education. Aquarius, who is now 30, never went to university. Recently he became heavily indebted to L. Shark, Esq., having bought diving equipment, a new Harley Davidson, and a complete new sound system for his apartment. To settle the debts he assigned his interest under the trust to Shark. Shark now sues the trustees to recover the amount owing him — most of the $15,000 and the interest that has accumulated thereon. Is he entitled to succeed?

4. Joe deposited money in a savings account with the Commercial Royalty Bank under a written agreement between him and the bank that the bank would hold the deposits in trust and would pay the principal and accrued interest to him or to such persons as he might in writing direct and, on his death, would pay the principal and accrued interest to his sister, Doe. Apart from these special terms the account was of the standard type; namely, that the bank had to pay interest at the rate that it might from time to time set on the moneys. The bank paid the interest as stipulated. It commingled the money with other moneys received on deposit from other customers. Some time later Joe married Roe and then died. Roe is his executrix and claims the money. So does Doe. Who is entitled and why?

5. Some years ago, Speedy engaged the services of Muffler, a solicitor, to act on the sale of some real property for him. When the transaction was concluded, Muffler was paid for his legal services and Speedy endorsed the purchaser's cheque for $50,000 made payable to him, over to Muffler and requested Muffler to hold the proceeds for him and to pay moneys out to him or to such other persons as he might direct on demand. Muffler, on the assumption that the arrangement was to be a temporary one, deposited the cheque in his general non-interest bearing trust account in which trust funds for other clients were kept as well. (Such an account was permitted by the Law Society.) It became apparent that Speedy, for reasons known only to himself, found the arrangement convenient and so, after about a year, Muffler transferred the balance of the moneys to a separate trust account which was interest-bearing (as permitted by the Rules of the Law Society). Muffler paid moneys out to Speedy and to third parties at Speedy's request.

Speedy recently died. Speedy's widow, Queenie, has now threatened to sue Muffler for damages and an accounting alleging that he should have invested the moneys instead of placing them in the bank at only nominal interest.

Muffler never charged for his services in connection with the moneys after the original real estate transaction, except for normal bank charges that were deducted at source.

You are articled to Muffler and are asked to write him a memorandum about his possible liability.

3

TRUSTS AND POWERS

1. SCOPE

There are major differences between trusts and powers and, in a carefully drafted document, it is clear whether a trust or a power has been created. However, not all documents are skilfully drawn and therein lies the problem. In order to properly draft or interpret a document, it is imperative that you clearly understand what powers are and how they differ from trusts. Chapters 1 and 2 were devoted to familiarising you with the concept of a trust; this chapter begins with a discussion of what powers are and, in particular, what a power of appointment is. The balance of the chapter is devoted to an examination of the differences between powers of appointment and discretionary trusts: both vehicles are in common use but they are fundamentally different.

Thereafter, we examine the three major consequences that follow from classifying a provision as a discretionary trust or a power of appointment. First, the obligations of the person in the "middle," that is, the trustee or the donee of the power are different. Second, the rights of a trust beneficiary are more extensive than those of a potential appointee under a power. Third, the requirements of certainty of objects may differ. We explore each of these differences in the balance of the chapter.

Further Reading

J.D. Davis, *Trusts*, [1970] A.S.C.L. 187.

K.G. Clarkson, "Powers of Appointment: Retaining Flexibility in an Effective Estate Plan," (1985), 21 Willamette L. Rev. 813.

M.C. Cullity, "Fiduciary Powers," (1976), 54 Can. B. Rev. 229.

Y.F.R. Grbich, "Certainty of Objects: The Rule That Never Was," (1974), 37 Mod. L. Rev. 643.

O.R. Marshall, "Trusts and Powers," [1957], 35 Can. B. Rev. 1060.

M.C. Cullity, "Trustees' Duties, Powers and Discretion - Exercise of Discretionary Powers," (1980), *Special Lectures of the Law Society of Upper Canada: Recent Developments in Estate Planning and Administration* 13.

M.C. Cullity, "Judicial Control of Trustees' Discretions," (1975), 25 *University of Toronto Law Journal* 99.

John Mowbray, "Choosing Among the Beneficiaries of Discretionary Trusts," (1998), 5 *Priv. Client Bus.* 239.

Richard T. Oerton, "The Scope of Special Powers of Appointment, Powers of Advancements and Similar Powers: Part I," (1994), 5 *Priv. Client Bus.* 317.

2. POWERS

(a) Defined

In its simplest terms, a power is authority vested in a person to deal with property that he or she does not own. The word "authority" is important because it focuses attention on the fact that a power enables its holder to deal with property; it does not impose an obligation on the holder of the power to do anything.

The source of a power may be an express grant or legislation. Where the source is an express grant, the person who owns the property and grants the authorization is called the donor of the power and the person in whom the power is vested is called the donee of the power.

A settlor or testator can create a variety of powers. They are of two general types: administrative and dispositive. Administrative powers are those which enable the donee to manage property. They include the power to sell, mortgage, and invest property. Dispositive powers give the donee the power to pay income or transfer property. They are often called powers of appointment.

One well-known example of a power is the power of attorney. Under a power of attorney, one person, called the attorney, is empowered to represent another person or to act in his or her stead, for certain purposes. However, numerous other powers exist because, without them, few agency relationships could function. For example, a stockbroker has the power of alienation (*i.e.*, the power to sell), the power to invest funds and to enter into certain kinds of contracts, and the power to buy stocks, to name but a few.

Modern trustees have, by grant and from statute, a wide variety of powers including powers to invest, use agents, lease, advance, hold assets *in specie*, and various powers of appointment.

(b) Powers Of Appointment

This chapter focuses primarily on the power of appointment because it is the type of power most easily confused with the discretionary trust and because many discretionary trusts are coupled with powers of appointment.

A power of appointment is the authority conferred by one person upon another to appoint (select) the person or persons who are to receive property. The donee of a power of appointment is, thus, also known as the appointor and the person who the appointor selects to receive property is called the appointee.

In diagrammatical form, the parties are:

DONOR OF POWER	DONEE OF POWER	APPOINTEE
(Owner of Property)	(Appointor of Property)	(Recipient of Property)

Depending upon the terms of the power established by the donor powers of appointment are exercisable by deed or will. There are three kinds of powers of appointment: general, special, and hybrid or intermediate. Under a general power of appointment, the donee may appoint to anyone in the world. The donee may even appoint to him or herself unless the power is exercisable only by will.

Under a special power of appointment, the choice of appointees is restricted by the donor of the power to a particular class such as the donor's issue or a list of individuals.

A hybrid or intermediate power of appointment enables the appointor to appoint to anyone except certain individuals designated by the donor.

(c) The Holders Of Powers Of Appointment

A donee of a power of appointment may be given the power in his or her personal capacity or as a fiduciary. The nature of the power does not change depending upon how it is held — it is still merely an authorization and not an obligation to perform. If the donee holds the power in his or her personal capacity, he or she may ignore the power with impunity. The donee need not exercise it nor even consider its exercise.

However, a fiduciary who holds a power is in a different position. By virtue of being a fiduciary, the donee must consider whether the power should be exercised, the range of possible objects, and appointees who put themselves forward for consideration.[1] It must be emphasized that the fiduciary's obligations flow from his or her status as a fiduciary and not from the power.

A fiduciary cannot release a power, once it is conferred, unless the release is expressly authorized.[2] In contrast, a donee holding in his or her personal capacity can release a power at will.

A further difference exists in relation to who can exercise the power. The general rule is that only the donee of a power may exercise it.[3] So, for example, if the donee of a power created by will predeceases the testator, the power lapses. However, if the donee is a fiduciary, then the power is normally construed as being given to the fiduciary *virtute officii* and whomever holds the office may exercise the power. You will find a fuller discussion of the obligations of a fiduciary holding a power of appointment later in this chapter.

---

1 See *Re Gulbenkian's Settlement* (sub nom. *Whishaw v. Stephens*), [1970] A.C. 508, [1968] 3 All E.R. 785 (H.L.).

2 *Re Will's Trust Deeds*, [1964] Ch. 219, [1963] 1 All E.R. 390. Even if the donees are referred to by name, if they were selected because of their positions as fiduciaries, the powers cannot be released absent express authorization.

3 *Re Harding*, [1923] 1 Ch. 182.

Donees of a power, whether they hold the power in a personal or fiduciary capacity, need not exercise the power, but if they do exercise it, they must do so honestly and in accordance with the terms of the power. Any exercise in favour of non-objects is void.

Notes and Questions

1. How is a general power of appointment different from an outright gift?

2. Under a will, the residue of an estate was to be held in trust with the income going to the life tenant. Upon her death, the residue was to be disposed of as the life tenant wished by deed or will. Can the life-tenant exercise the power in her own favour?[4]

Assume that the residue was to be disposed of as the life tenant wished by will only. Can the life tenant exercise the power of appointment in her own favour during her lifetime?[5]

3. What happens if a power is not exercised? Is your answer different when the donee of the power holds in his or her personal capacity rather than as a fiduciary?

4. In *Re MacIvor*,[6] the deceased was the holder of a general power of appointment. At the time, legislation provided that any property held by the deceased at the time of death was subject to succession duties, except any power exercisable in a fiduciary capacity not created by the deceased. Was the power exercisable personally or as a fiduciary? Bear in mind the following facts: in the document, the deceased was designated by name in relation to the power and as trustee in relation to the trust; the deceased could appoint her own executors; and the power was to operate after the deceased's death.

5. A donee decides to exercise a power of appointment. Part of the appointment is good but part bad because it goes to non-objects. What is the result?[7]

In *Knight v. Dick*,[8] the holder of a power could only exercise the power in favour of members of her family. She appointed her sister, intending and confident that her sister would use the funds for the benefit of a non-object. The Court of Appeal held that the exercise of the power was invalid because there was a fraud on the power.

Would the exercise of the power still be considered fraudulent, if:

  (i) the appointee of the power was unaware of the appointor's fraudulent intent? or,

 (ii) the appointee of the power did not secure any benefit in favour of a non-object?

6. Under modern perpetuities legislation, only general and special powers are recognized, all powers being treated as special except those that are exercisable by a single donee at any time in favour of him- or herself without the consent of any other person.[9]

---

4 See *Re Mewburn Estate*, [1939] S.C.R. 75.

5 See *Berwick v. Canada Trust Co.*, [1948] S.C.R. 151, [1948] 3 D.L.R. 81, 1948 CarswellSask 79. See also *Law of Trusts in Canada*, 2nd ed. by D.W.M. Waters (Toronto: Carswell, 1984), at 971-2 for a review of English and Canadian authorities on this point.

6 [1966] 1 O.R. 307 (H.C.).

7 See *Hanbury and Maudsley: Modern Equity*, 15th ed. by Jill E. Martin (London: Sweet & Maxwell, 1997), at 177-178.

8 *Knight v. Dick*, [1953] Ch. 343 (Eng. C.A.). See also *Vatcher v. Paull* (1914), [1915] A.C. 372, [1914-15] All E.R. Rep. 609, 112 L.T. 737, 84 L.J.P.C. 86 (H.L.), in which the principles of fraud governing the exercise of powers of appointment are discussed.

9 See, e.g., *Perpetuities Act*, R.S.O. 1990, c. P.9, s. 11.

7. In *Re Manisty's Settlement, Manisty v. Manisty*,[10] the court upheld a power conferred upon the trustees which enabled them to add to the class of stated beneficiaries. The power to give to anyone in the world other than members of an excepted class was held to be very wide in ambit but did not make the power uncertain.

A discretionary trust in which the trustees invariably have a power to add additional persons or objects to the class of beneficiaries has been termed a "black hole" trust. What are some of the advantages and disadvantages of such a trust?[11]

3. POWERS OF APPOINTMENT AND DISCRETIONARY TRUSTS

There are a number of practical differences between trusts and powers, most of which flow from the fundamental difference between the two: a trust is imperative, whereas a power is discretionary. That is, a trustee must perform the terms of a trust whereas the donee of a power need not exercise the power. If a trustee fails to perform, the court will order equal division among beneficiaries or in such proportions as is appropriate in the circumstances.[12] Failure to perform the trust renders the trustee liable for breach of trust. Failure to exercise a power is not, and cannot be, a breach because the essence of the power is that its holder has a discretion whether to exercise the power. This fundamental distinction has important consequences not only for the trustee/donee but also for the beneficiaries/appointees. Potential appointees under a power of appointment have no proprietary interest in the subject matter of the power unless and until the donee exercises it in their favour. The beneficiaries of a trust, on the other hand, have a proprietary interest in the trust property. In the following parts of this chapter, these consequences will be explored more fully.

In order to appreciate fully the similarities and differences between a discretionary trust and a power of appointment, it is useful to visualize powers and trusts as being on a spectrum.

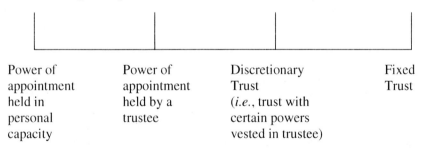

| Power of appointment held in personal capacity | Power of appointment held by a trustee | Discretionary Trust (*i.e.*, trust with certain powers vested in trustee) | Fixed Trust |

---

10 [1974] 1 Ch. 17, [1973] 2 All E.R. 1203.
11 See Paul Matthews, "The Black Hole Trust- Uses, Abuses and Possible Reforms: Part I," (2002), 1 *Priv. Client Bus.* 42.
12 *MacPhail v. Doulton*, [1971] A.C. 424, [1970] 2 All E.R. 228 (H.L.).

At one end of the spectrum is the power of appointment held by the donee in his or her personal capacity. This is frequently termed a "bare power of appointment."[13] The donee who holds a power of appointment in his or her personal capacity has only one right and that is to select persons to enjoy property that belongs to another person. Such a donee has only two obligations, namely to act honestly and, if he or she decides to exercise the power, to appoint to members of the class designated by the donor.

At the other end of the spectrum is the fixed trust. A trustee of a fixed trust must perform the trust and has no discretion, that is, the trustee has no power to decide who will take or in what proportions. The trustee's rights under a fixed trust are extremely limited and his or her obligations are onerous.

The dividing line between the two categories in the centre of the spectrum is often unclear. A power held by a trustee is still discretionary in that the trustee need not perform although he or she must, as discussed above, consider the exercise of his or her discretion. The discretionary trust, on the other hand, still has as its fundamental characteristic the fact that the trustee must perform the trust. But, in a discretionary trust, the trustee may have many powers such as the power to decide who will take or in what proportions or both. To describe such powers as powers of appointment is misleading because the use of that term suggests that the holder has the power to decide whether to perform. It is more accurate to describe such powers as powers of selection attached to a trust; such a description makes it clear that a trust exists which obliges the trustee to perform. In short, a trustee (or other fiduciary) holding a power of appointment has the right to decide *whether* to exercise the power, whereas in a discretionary trust, a trustee has only the right to decide *how* to exercise the powers given to him or her.

The concepts and distinctions posed in this area are often difficult. They are made even more difficult by the use of imprecise terminology. A power of appointment is discretionary. If it is held by a trustee or other fiduciary, then say so and recognize the additional obligations that ensue, but try not to use terms such as "fiduciary powers" or "powers in the nature of a trust." Such terms are bandied about in the context of powers and discretionary trusts and cause much confusion. Similarly, if the underlying nature of a provision is obligatory then the provision is a trust, either discretionary or fixed. Such a provision should be called either a discretionary trust or a fixed trust as those terms have clear meanings. Again, to use other phrases such as "trust powers" is only confusing.

While this chapter focuses on a comparison of discretionary trusts and powers of appointment, you should note that many instruments are capable of a third interpretation, namely, an outright gift. To determine whether a trust, power, or gift has been created, the courts construe the document in question in order to ascertain the intention of the transferor. The use of the word trust, power, or gift is not conclusive of what was intended. However, if there is a gift over in default

---

13 Unfortunately, the term "bare power of appointment" has also been used to describe a power of appointment by way of contrast with a discretionary trust.

of appointment, it is clear that a power of appointment was intended.[14] A gift over in default of appointment arises when the creator of the power stipulates who should receive the property if the donee fails to act. For example, a transfer "to A for life, remainder to such of her children as she may appoint, failing which to B" creates a power of appointment in A and a gift over in favour of B. While we term the transfer to B a "gift over," it is, in fact, a gift to B that is vested subject to divestment in favour of the children, if and when the power is exercised.

A gift over in default of appointment is not to be confused with the creation of successive interests such as a transfer "to A for life, remainder to B" nor with the disposition of the residue of an estate which is a gift of an interest and not the stipulation of who is to receive the property if the donee fails to act.

In the absence of a gift over in default of appointment, the deed may be treated as having created a trust, power, or gift. While all three constructions are often possible on the same facts, it is the power of appointment and discretionary trust which are the most difficult to distinguish, especially when the power of appointment is held by a fiduciary such as a trustee.

For example, in *Burrough v. Philcox*[15] a testator gave property to his two children for life with remainder to their issue. If the children died without issue, the remainder was to go as the survivor appointed, by will, among the testator's nephews and nieces or their children. There was no gift over in default and the children both died without issue and without exercising the power of appointment. The court held that what was intended was not a mere power of appointment, but a trust in favour of the nephews and nieces equally, subject only to a power of selection in the surviving child of the testator. Lord Cottenham enunciated the test to be applied in such cases as follows:[16]

> [W]hen there appears a general intention in favour of a class, and a particular intention in favour of individuals of a class to be selected by another person, and the particular intention fails, from that selection not being made, the Court will carry into effect the general intention in favour of the class. When such an intention appears, the case arises . . . of the power being so given as to make it the duty of the donee to execute it; and, in such case, the Court will not permit the objects of the power to suffer by the negligence or conduct of the donee, but fastens upon the property a trust for their benefit.

Nevertheless, in each case it depends upon the testator's or settlor's intention as is evident from *Re Lloyd*,[17] reproduced below, and the cases referred to in it. *Re Lloyd* shows, as well, that the greater the degree of specificity used in describing the objects, the more likely it is that the courts will find the imperative flavour of a trust.

---

14 See *Re Llewellyn's Settlement*, [1921] 2 Ch. 281.
15 (1840), 5 My & Cr. 71, 41 E.R. 299.
16 *Ibid.*
17 [1938] O.R. 32, [1938] 1 D.L.R. 450 (H.C.).

RE LLOYD

[1938] O.R. 32, [1938] 1 D.L.R. 450
Supreme Court of Ontario
[High Court of Justice]

A testatrix died leaving her estate to her husband for his life. She gave her husband "the power to appoint" the remainder of her estate among three named sisters and a niece. The will did not contain a gift over in default of appointment nor a disposition of the residue.

The testatrix's husband predeceased her. All of the testatrix's sisters also predeceased her. In order to determine who became entitled to the remainder, it was necessary to determine whether the husband had been given a power of appointment or whether the testatrix had created a discretionary trust in favour of the three named sisters and the niece. If, on construction, it was determined that the testatrix had intended to create a power of appointment, an intestacy would result. If, on construction, a discretionary trust was found, the niece would take as sole survivor.

Rose C.J.H.C.:

. . .

The testatrix made her will in July, 1922. She died on June 5, 1937. She was a daughter of Dr. John J. Dickinson, who had ten children, four sons and six daughters. One of the sons died in infancy; the other three sons and all of the daughters were living when Mrs. Lloyd made her will — or so the affidavit of Dr. Charles James Hamilton seems to show, although there is some vagueness as to the dates of the deaths of some of the members of the family; and there were also living two nephews and a niece of the testatrix — Charles Reginald Hamilton (a son of the testatrix's sister, Harriet Sara Hamilton), Eric Dickinson (a son of the testatrix's brother Salter), and Dorothy, now Mrs. Crowley (a daughter of the testatrix's sister Rose Marion Barry).

By her will the testatrix left all her estate, real and personal, to her husband for his life, and she gave to him a power of appointment expressed as follows:

> I give to my husband Sandford McVillie Lloyd power to devise, bequeath and appoint all my estate among my three sisters, Eva Margaret Jackson, Rose Marion Barry and Florence Lucy Salscheider, and my niece Dorothy, daughter of my sister Rose Marion Barry in such amounts and in such manner as my husband shall in his discretion see fit and deem prudent and advisable.

She made neither a gift over in default of appointment nor any disposition of residue.

The testatrix's husband died in 1929; and all of the testatrix's brothers and sisters predeceased her. Three of them left issue, the two nephews and the niece who have been mentioned and who appear to be the next of kin to whom the estate descends if in the circumstances there is an intestacy. The question is whether there is such an intestacy or whether there was in effect a gift of the remainder after the life-estate to the objects of the power; in which case Mrs. Crowley, as the sole survivor of those objects, will take the whole.

In the third edition of Farwell on Powers,[18] it is stated that:

> if there is a power to appoint among certain objects, but no gift to those objects, and no gift over in default of appointment, the Court implies a trust for or a gift to those objects equally, if the power be not exercised.

And,[19] there is a discussion of the holding by Romer J. in *In re Weekes's Settlement*,[20] that, in such case the court is not bound, without more, to imply a gift to the class; and there is a submission that the decision is inconsistent with the authorities and cannot be supported. But this criticism of the judgment in *In re Weekes's Settlement* is not carried into the article on Powers in Halsbury's *Law of England*[21] contributed by the very learned editor of the 3rd edition of Farwell on Powers and Mr. V.M.C. Pennington. The statement in Halsbury is:[22]

> If the power to appoint among certain objects, but no gift to those objects and no gift over in default of appointment, the court may imply a trust for or a gift to those objects equally if the power is not exercised . . . but for the rule to apply there must be a clear intention that the donor intended the power to be in the nature of a trust, and any contrary intention defeats an implied trust.

This statement accords with the opinion that had been expressed by Tomlin J. in *In Re Combe*.[23] Tomlin J. came to the conclusion, after a consideration of *In re Weekes' Settlement*, that he was not to approach the will which he had under consideration governed by an inflexible and artificial rule of construction to the effect that where there is found a power of appointment of a class not followed by any gift in default of appointment, the court is bound to imply a gift to that class in default of the exercise of the power. On the contrary, he thought that the will ought to be approached for the purpose of construction in the same spirit as any other will is approached, and that the court ought to endeavour to construe the will and arrive at the testator's meaning by examining the words expressly used, and ought to imply only those things that are necessarily and reasonably to be implied.

Proceeding in the manner in which Tomlin J. proceeded, examining the words expressly used and implying only those things that are necessarily and reasonably to be implied, I have come to the conclusion that in Mrs. Lloyd's will there is a gift to the objects of the power. The objects are a "class" only in the sense that they are such objects. It is not the case that is found so frequently in which the testator makes his children or his family or his descendants or his brothers and

---

18   (3rd ed., 1916), at 528.
19   *Ibid.*, at 529.
20   [1897] 1 Ch. 289 (Ch. Div.).
21   (2nd ed., 1937).
22   *Ibid.*, at 596.
23   [1925] Ch. 210 (Ch. Div.).

sisters the objects of the power. On the contrary, the testatrix selected, no doubt for reasons which seemed to her to be sufficient, three of her five sisters and the daughter of one of the three and excluded the other two sisters and the son of one of them as well as her three brothers and a son of one of them; and it appears to me that in selecting and naming three of her sisters and her niece, she did clearly signify her intention that the power should be in the nature of a trust. Certainly there is no indication of a contrary intention; and I do not read either *In re Weekes' Settlement* or *In re Combe* as authority for saying that when the intention to benefit the objects of the power seems, as it does in the case seems to me, to be evidenced by the words of the will, effect shall not be given to that intention unless there are found in the will some direct words of gift to the objects and the power itself is a mere power of selection of some or one of them or a mere power of apportionment amongst them. In this latter case — when there are direct words of gift to the objects of the power — there is no need for the court to draw any inference: the testator had made the gift, and all that remains to be settled is the question of the distribution of the property among the donees. The case in which the necessity for drawing an inference arises is the case in which the testator has not made a direct gift; and upon the authorities it is clear that in a proper case the inference may be drawn.

In *In re Combe* there was in the will, if not an indication of a contrary intention, at least something which raised a very grave doubt as to whether the testator really meant his relations of the whole blood to benefit in any fund: see the judgment;[24] and *In Re Weekes' Settlement* was not the simple case that is presented in respect of Mrs. Lloyd's will.

[His Lordship went on to discuss the *Weekes* case, set out in part 5, below.]

Notes and Questions

1. What is the test for determining whether a testator or testatrix intended to create a trust or a power?

2. Did the court construe the provision in question in *Lloyd* as a power or a trust? What factors led to its conclusion?

In *Perowne, Re,*[25] the testatrix left her estate to her husband, adding, "knowing that he will make arrangements for the disposal of my estate, according to my wishes, for the benefit of my family." There was no express gift over in default of appointment and the court refused to infer one because the class was large and indefinite. The court concluded that the testatrix had only intended to create a power of appointment and not a trust. Her words did not indicate that she intended the class or some members of the class to take, but only that she intended to give her husband a power of selection. The court was also reluctant to infer a trust because the beneficiaries of the trust would not have constituted the same class of people as the objects of the power of selection.

---

24 *Ibid.*, at 218.
25 [1951] Ch. 785, 2 All E.R. 201 (Ch. Div.).

In *Ferguson Estate v. MacLean*,[26] the court interpreted a will to determine that a particular clause did not create a power of appointment, but rather a trust. Another clause in the will stated that before the trustees could distribute to themselves, they could seek independent advice. The court found that had the will created a power of appointment, the trustees would have been free to distribute to themselves and the clause regarding independent advice would have been unnecessary. Note that the trust failed because of uncertainty of objects.

Compare the *Lloyd* case with *Manning, Re*.[27] In *Manning*, the testator gave the beneficiaries of his will the power to appoint to a class. There was no gift over in default of appointment. The testator did not give the donees the power to select specific members amongst the class, nor did he make a gift to the class. The Ontario Court of Appeal held that a mere power was created and, since the power was not exercised, there was an intestacy. The case applied *Re Weekes's Settlement*. It distinguished *Lloyd* and *Official Solicitor v. Evans*.

Assume that T gave his wife, the life tenant, a special power to appoint the residue to her "friends and family" by will. There was no gift over in default of appointment. Is this a bare power or a trust?[28]

3. Why is a gift over in default of appointment held to show conclusively that the creator intended a power?[29] What happens if the gift over is void for some reason?[30]

4. Assume the intention to create a trust is found in certain documents, but that those same documents state that the uses and purposes of the trust property are to be determined in the sole discretion of the trustees. Does the conferral of absolute discretion on a trustee negative the inference of the intention to create a trust?[31]

5. It is possible to create a power of appointment with a discretionary trust in default of appointment if the donees of the power and objects of the trust are the same people. Where should this be placed on the spectrum drawn above? How is this different than a discretionary trust? Should the exercise of such a power be controlled in the same way as a discretionary trust? Consider this question again after reading the next part.

6. The distinction between discretionary trusts and powers of appointment is even further blurred in the cases of non-exhaustive trusts. A non-exhaustive trust is one in which the trustees are empowered to decide not to distribute any income at all, but rather, to accumulate it.

(i) Describe in your own words the differences between a discretionary trust and a non-exhaustive discretionary trust focusing on the different powers that the trustees hold.

(ii) Where on the spectrum would you place non-exhaustive discretionary trusts?

---

26 198 N.S.R. (2d) 55, [2001] N.S.J. No. 441, 2001 CarswellNS 384, 2001 NSSC 154, 621 A.P.R. 55 (S.C.).

27 (1978), 19 O.R. (2d) 257, 2 E.T.R. 195, 84 D.L.R. (3d) 715, 1978 CarswellOnt 518 (C.A.).

28 See *Dowsley, Re* (1958), 15 D.L.R. (2d) 560 (Ont. H.C.).

29 See *Official Solicitor v. Evans*, [1921] 2 Ch. 281.

30 See *Sprague, Re* (1880), 43 L.T. 236 and *Sayer, Re*, [1957] Ch. 423.

31 See *Lewis v. Union of B.C. Performers*, 18 B.C.L.R. (3d) 382, 11 E.T.R. (2d) 137, [1996] 6 W.W.R. 588, 1996 CarswellBC 160, 70 B.C.A.C. 99, 115 W.A.C. 99 (C.A.).

4. DONEE OBLIGATIONS

You have seen that the essence of a trust is that an obligation is placed on a trustee to perform the trust according to its terms. A trustee who refuses to perform the trust can be replaced or the court can act in the trustee's stead.

A power, on the other hand, is discretionary. Despite a power's discretionary nature, when the holder of a power is a fiduciary, certain obligations are imposed upon the holder. It is not the power that imposes obligations but the office of fiduciary. Of course, just because the holder is a fiduciary does not mean that he or she must exercise the power, as that would be contrary to the nature of a power. The duties imposed by the fiduciary relationship between the donor and donee of the power are to consider the exercise of the power, survey the range of possible objects, consider any application made to the donee of the power by a person within the ambit of the power, and ensure the appropriateness of any particular appointment. If the fiduciary does exercise the power, he or she must do so honestly, in accordance with the terms of the power, refrain from acting capriciously.

In *Turner v. Turner*,[32] below, the duties of a fiduciary holding a power of appointment are examined, as are the effects of an invalid exercise of such a power.

TURNER v. TURNER

[1984] Ch. 100
[Chancery Division]

A settlor established an *inter vivos* trust for the benefit of his wife, children, remoter issue and any spouse of such issue. He appointed his father, his sister-in-law, and her husband to be the trustees. None of the trustees had any experience or understanding of trusts.

The trust document conferred powers of appointment on the trustees. The trustees let the settlor make all the decisions about the trust. The settlor instructed the trustees to make three appointments, one in 1967, the next in 1971, and a final one in 1976. The trustees complied with the settlor's instructions and made the appointments.

An application was made to the court to determine whether any of the three appointments had been a valid exercise of the trustees' power of appointment.

MERVYN DAVIES J.:

. . .

It is this question about the trustees' understanding of their rights, powers, and duties that gives rise to question 1 in the originating summons. Question 1 asks, as respects (i) the 1967 appointment, (ii) the 1971 appointment, and (iii) the

---

32 [1984] 1 Ch. 100 (Ch. Div.).

1976 conveyance, whether or not the trustees effectively exercised their powers of appointment. In effect the question is whether or not the trustees so far failed to direct their minds to the matter of their discretionary powers of appointment that the deeds of appointment ought not to be regarded as an exercise of the powers of appointment. To see such a question asked is at first sight surprising but the evidence given in this case shows good reason for it.

. . .

One is naturally reluctant to contemplate that documents admittedly executed by persons of intelligence may be ineffective by reason of the fact that the persons executing did not address their minds to the documents signed. To do so makes for uncertainty, confusion, and dishonesty. On the other hand here there are two considerations which may justify that course in the particular circumstances of this case. First there is the consideration that all the persons involved in the administration of the trusts have been perfectly frank and are plainly to be believed. There has been no rancour or dispute. No one other than the Turner family and the Nutlands are concerned in the immediate difficulties that have arisen. There has been on all sides a straightforward assertion of misunderstanding and a desire to set right anything that is wrong. The second consideration is that it is not any ordinary document that is being examined but, in the case of all three documents under consideration, a document whereby a discretionary power appears to have been exercised. When a discretionary power is given to trustees they come under certain fiduciary duties. In a context removed from the present case Sir Robert Megarry V.-C. said in *In Re Hay's Settlement Trusts*:[33]

a trustee to whom, as such, a power is given is bound by the duties of his office in exercising that power to do so in a responsible manner according to its purpose.

The Vice-Chancellor said:[34]

If I am right in these views, the duties of a trustee which are specific to a mere power seem to be threefold. Apart from the obvious duty of obeying the trust instrument, and in particular of making no appointment that is not authorised by it, the trustee must, first, consider periodically whether or not he should exercise the power; second, consider the range of objects of the power; and third, consider the appropriateness of individual appointments. I do not assert that this list is exhaustive; but as the authorities stand it seems to me to include the essentials, so far as relevant to the case before me.

Accordingly the trustees exercising a power come under a duty to consider. It is plain on the evidence that here the trustees did not in any way "consider" in the course of signing the three deeds in question. They did not know they had any discretion during the settlor's lifetime, they did not read or understand the effect of the documents they were signing and what they were doing was not preceded by any decision. They merely signed when requested. The trustees therefore made

33 [1982] 1 W.L.R. 202 at 209c.
34 *Ibid.*, at 210.

the appointments in breach of their duty in that it was their duty to "consider" before appointing and this they did not do.

It is accordingly necessary to consider what is the effect of a deed of appointment, on the face of it effective, but executed by the appointors in breach of their duty, in so far as they have signed, in all good faith, without ever having given any attention to the contents of the deed. *In re Pilkington's Will Trusts*[35] was concerned with the exercise of a power of advancement conferred by section 32 of the *Trustee Act, 1925.* In that case the trustees asked the court whether a proposed advance by way of sub-settlement could be made. So the case differs from this case where one is concerned with an appointment not an advancement and with an appointment "made" and not "to be made." However that may be, some observations of Upjohn L.J. in the same case in the Court of Appeal seem to bear on the present situation. Upjohn L.J.'s words in the Court of Appeal were approved by Viscount Radcliffe.[36] Upjohn L.J. said:[37]

> The effect, therefore, of the rule against perpetuities upon the proposed settlement is basic; it entirely alters the settlement, and that seems to me to be fatal to this case, for the trustees have never been asked to express any opinion as to whether they would think the proposed settlement, modified by reason of the rule against perpetuities in the manner I have mentioned, is for the benefit of Penelope. That is a matter to which they have never addressed in their minds, and, therefore, it cannot possibly be justified under section 32, for it has not been shown that the trustees think that the settlement, as so modified, is for the advancement or benefit of Penelope. On that ground too, therefore, I would think that the transfer to the trustees on this new settlement is entirely beyond the powers of the trustees.

Those words suggest that when trustees, in the course of exercising a power in a way that they suppose will effect a sub-settlement, fail to appreciate what they are doing in some important respect (in the *Pilkington* case the impact of the perpetuity rule), then the sub-settlement will be void.

In re Abrahams' Will Trusts[38] is an instance of the court declaring a settlement wholly void when made in exercise of a power of advancement. The exercise of the power had been made without a due regard to the rule against perpetuities so that the trustees had not had a right appreciation of their discretion. This case must now be treated as limited in its application: see *In re Hastings-Bass, decd.*[39] However that may be, the words of Cross J. in *In re Abrahams' Will Trusts*[40] show that when the facts fit the exercise of a power may be set aside:

> But here there is no doubt that the effect of the operation of the rule is wholly to alter the character of the settlement. In my judgment the result of that must be that there never was a valid exercise by the trustees of the power of advancement.

---

35 [1964] A.C. 612 (H.L.).
36 *Ibid.*, at 641-642.
37 [1961] Ch. 466 at 489 (C.A.).
38 [1969] 1 Ch. 463, [1967] 2 All E.R. 1175.
39 [1975] Ch. 25 at 41, [1974] 2 All E.R. 193 (C.A.).
40 *Supra*, note 38.

The authorities I have mentioned, including *In re Hastings-Bass, decd.*, permit the inference that, in a clear case on the facts, the court can put aside the purported exercise of a fiduciary power, if satisfied that the trustees never applied their minds at all to the exercise of the discretion entrusted to them. If appointers fail altogether to exercise the duties of consideration referred to by Sir Robert Megarry V.-C., then there is no exercise of the power and the purported appointment is a nullity. Applying those principles to this case I am satisfied on the evidence that all three purported appointments ought to be set aside. It was urged that the 1976 conveyance stood on a footing apart from the 1967 and 1971 appointments; in that in the case of the 1976 conveyance the trustees knew that their signature would transfer Camel Hill Farm to John Gregory Turner and, moreover, that the trustees thought at the time that it was a "good idea" to make a transfer to John Gregory Turner, whereas in the case of the earlier appointment they did not know at all what was being done. In my view the 1976 conveyance as an instrument of appointment fails as well as the earlier appointments. At the time of the execution of the 1976 conveyance there was a total failure on the part of the trustees to consider whether or not in their discretion Camel Hill Farm ought to go to John Gregory Turner. They did not appreciate that they had a discretion to exercise.

The 1976 conveyance is of course effective as a conveyance of the legal estate and nothing I say affects the rights of the mortgagees. The 1976 conveyance is set aside insofar as it purports to operate as an exercise of the trustee's powers of appointment under the 1967 settlement. Subject to the mortgagee's rights John Gregory will hold the legal estate on trust for the trustees of the 1967 settlement.

The three appointments are set aside with effect from the dates that they bear. In the circumstances of this case I would have liked to set aside the 1976 conveyance (considered as an appointment) with effect from today. But since I regard the 1976 appointment as wholly void I do not think that that course is open to me.

Notes and Questions

1. List the duties of a fiduciary holding a power.

2. How many possible objects must a fiduciary survey? Consider?

3. What will the courts do if a fiduciary fails to consider the exercise of a power?

4. Describe the differences in how the court set aside the first two conveyances from how it set aside the third conveyance. Do you understand why the court made the order it did? Do you see that it took cognizance of intervening third party rights?

5. A most instructive article in this area is *Recent Cases: Powers, Trusts and Classes of Objects*, by Andrew Gubb.[41]

6. The principle of *In re Hastings-Bass*,[42] discussed in the principal case, has been broadened more recently. In *Mettoy Pension Trustees Ltd. v. Evans*,[43] the rule, rendering

---

41 [1982] *The Conveyancer and Property Lawyer*, 432.

42 *Supra*, note 39.

43 [1991] 2 All E.R. 513 (Ch. Div.). See, *Green v. Cobham* (2000), 1 W.T.L.R. 1101 (Eng. Ch. Div.) and *Abacus Trust Company (Isle of Man) Ltd. v. National Society for the Prevention of Cruelty to Children*, [2001] S.T.C. 1344 (Eng. Ch. Div.) in which the principles *In re Hastings-*

an exercise of power ineffective where trustees fail to take into account matters which they ought to have, was extended to situations in which the matters were overlooked by the trustees' legal advisors.[44]

7. In *Breadner v. Granville-Grossman*,[45] the settlor created a discretionary trust in 1973 in favour of a class of beneficiaries, including J, and J's three cousins. In 1976, the trustees made an appointment creating trusts in which J and the three cousins each had a quarter interest. Those trusts would stay in force unless the trustees exercised the 1976 power of appointment before August 2nd 1989. The settlor informed one of the trustees that he wished the trust to be held for J alone. The other trustee was not told of the requested appointment until August 2nd 1989. A deed appointing the entire trust capital to J was executed on this date. Is the 1989 deed effective? The trustees were under a duty to consider the exercise of the 1976 power of appointment. Will equity save the deed because the trustees failed to consider the exercise of their power before the expiration date?

8. Courts will generally intervene in the exercise of a discretionary power given to a trustee if there is *mala fides* on the part of the trustee.[46]

Intervention is justified to ensure that the purpose of the trust has not been defeated by the trustee. In *Schipper v. Guaranty Trust Co. of Canada*,[47] the trustee refused the wife's request to encroach on the capital. The Court of Appeal intervened and ordered the encroachment notwithstanding the fact that the trustee had acted *bona fide*. The court found that the testator's main purpose in creating the trust was not to preserve the capital, but to provide care for his wife. The trustee was attempting to achieve a purpose not intended by the terms of the trust.[48] Courts may also intervene when the trustee has acted contrary to public policy.[49]

Bass were applied. See also Ian Dawson, "The Effect of an Unthinking Trustees' Action," [2002] *The Conveyancer and Property Lawyer*, 67; and David Hayton, "Some Major Developments in Trust Law," (2001), 6 *Priv. Client Bus.* 361.

44 See also *Barr's Settlement Trusts, Re*, [2003] 1 All E.R. 763 (Ch. Div.).

45 [2000] 4 All E.R. 705 (Ch. Div.).

46 *Gisborne v. Gisborne* (1877), 2 App. Cas. 300 (U.K. H.L.), recently applied in *Martin v. Banting* (2000), 37 E.T.R. (2d) 270, 2001 CarswellOnt 405 (S.C.J.), affirmed (2002), [2002] O.J. 381, 2002 CarswellOnt 318, 46 E.T.R. (2d) 93 (C.A.). See also *Edell v. Sitzer* (2001), 55 O.R. (3d) 198, 40 E.T.R. (2d) 10, [2001] O.J. No. 2909, 2001 CarswellOnt 5020 (S.C.J.) and *McGoey v. Wedd* (1999), 45 O.R. (3d) 300, 28 E.T.R. (2d) 236, 1999 CarswellOnt 2777 (S.C.J.) in which the court refused to intervene since there was no evidence that the trustees had exercised their discretionary powers improperly.

47 (1989), 69 O.R. (2d) 386, 33 E.T.R. 149, 1989 CarswellOnt 525, 35 O.A.C. 238 (C.A.).

48 See also *Edge v. Pension Ombudsman* (1997), [1998] 2 All E.R. 547, [1998] Ch. 512, [1998] 3 W.L.R. 466 (Ch. Div.), affirmed (1999), [2000] 3 W.L.R. 79, [1999] 4 All E.R. 546, [2000] I.C.R. 748, [2000] Ch. 602 (C.A.) in which the Court of Appeal upheld the lower court's decision not to intervene in the trustees' exercise of their discretionary power to choose among different beneficiaries. The trustees exercised their power *bona fide*, considered all relevant matters and did not consider any irrelevant or irrational matters and exercised the power in accordance with the purpose for which the trust had been created.

49 See *Fox v. Fox Estate* (1996), 28 O.R. (3d) 496, 88 O.A.C. 201, 10 E.T.R. (2d) 229, 1996 CarswellOnt 317 (C.A.), leave to appeal refused (1996), 207 N.R. 80 (note), 97 O.A.C. 320 (note) (S.C.C.). The court found that it was contrary to public policy to allow a trustee to deprive a residual beneficiary of income because the latter intended to marry outside the executor's religion. The court also discussed the doctrine of *mala fides*.

5. APPOINTEE RIGHTS

Beneficiaries under a trust are the equitable owners of the trust property: the trustees are under a duty to hold the trust property for the benefit of the beneficiaries. Objects of a power, on the other hand, own nothing unless and until the donee appoints in their favour. They merely have a hope that the power will be exercised in their favour. Until a power is exercised, those who will take in default of an appointment are the equitable owners, their interest being subject to defeasance on the exercise of the power.

Recall the spectrum diagram in part 3 above. The only right of an object of a power of appointment held by a donee in his or her personal capacity is this: if the donee attempts to exercise the power incorrectly, the object of the power may go to court and complain. At the other end of the spectrum are the beneficiaries under a fixed trust who are the equitable owners of the trust property. They have full equitable proprietary rights. So far the distinction between an appointee's rights and those of a beneficiary are clear.

But what rights do beneficiaries under a discretionary trust have?[50] You will recall that under a discretionary trust, a trustee has a discretion to select beneficiaries from a specified class, or to determine the shares in which the beneficiaries are to take, or both. Unlike the beneficiary of a fixed trust, the beneficiaries of a discretionary trust are not entitled to any specific part of the trust assets until the trustee exercises his or her discretion in their favour. In that respect, their position is very similar to that of an object of a power. However, if all of the beneficiaries of a discretionary trust are *sui juris*, they may join together, terminate the trust, and obtain the trust property.[51] And, if a trustee of a discretionary trust fails to exercise his or her discretion, the class of beneficiaries will take.[52] *In Re Weekes' Settlement*,[53] below, illustrates the differences between the rights of objects of a power and the rights of beneficiaries of a discretionary trust.

---

50 See *Vestey v. Inland Revenue Commissioners (No. 2)*, [1979] Ch. 198 (Ch. Div.), affirmed (1979), [1980] A.C. 1148, [1979] 3 All E.R. 976, [1984] T.C. 503, [1980] S.T.C. 10, [1979] T.R. 381 (H.L.), at 206 [Ch.].

51 The rule in *Saunders v. Vautier* (1841), 4 Beav. 115, 49 E.R. 282, affirmed (1841), 1 Cr. & Ph. 240, 41 E.R. 482, [1835-42] All E.R. Rep. 58. See *Campeau Family Trust, Re* (1984), 44 O.R. (2d) 549, 4 D.L.R. (4th) 667, 1984 CarswellOnt 552, 16 E.T.R. 97 (Ont. H.C.), affirmed (1984), 50 O.R. (2d) 296, 8 D.L.R. (4th) 159, 1984 CarswellOnt 563, 17 E.T.R. 297 (C.A.) in which the court considered the application of the rule in *Saunders v. Vautier*.

52 See *Burrough v. Philcox*, discussed in part 3, *supra*, note 15.

53 [1897] 1 Ch. 289.

IN RE WEEKES' SETTLEMENT

[1897] 1 Ch. 289
Chancery Division

A testatrix bequeathed to her husband a life interest in certain real property and gave him "power to dispose of all such property by will amongst the children." The will contained no gift over in default of appointment. There were children but the husband died without having exercised the power of appointment. The question arose whether the children were entitled to the property.

ROMER J.:

Now, apart from the authorities, I should gather from the terms of the will that it was a mere power that was conferred on the husband and not one coupled with a trust that he was bound to exercise. I see no words in the will to justify me in holding that the testatrix intended that the children should take if her husband did not execute the power.

This is not a case of a gift to the children with power to the husband to select, or to such of the children as the husband should select by exercising the power.

If in this case the testatrix really intended to give a life interest to her husband and a mere power to appoint if he chose, and intended if he did not think fit to appoint that the property should go as in default of appointment according to the settlement, why should she be bound to say more than she has said in this will?

I come to the conclusion on the words of this will that the testatrix only intended to give a life interest and a power to her husband — certainly she has not said more than that.

Am I then bound by the authorities to hold otherwise? I think I am not. The authorities do not show, in my opinion, that there is a hard and fast rule that a gift to A for life with a power to A to appoint among a class and nothing more must, if there is no gift over in the will, be held a gift by implication to the class in default of the power being exercised. In my opinion the cases show (though there may be found here and there certain remarks of a few learned judges which, if not interpreted by the facts of the particular case before them, might seem to have a more extended operation) that you must find in the will an indication that the testatrix did intend the class or some of the class to take — intended in fact that the power should be regarded in the nature of a trust — only a power of selection being given, as, for example, a gift to A for life with a gift over to such of a class as A shall appoint.

. . .

Notes and Questions

1. In *In Re Weekes Settlement*, Mr. Justice Romer held that the husband was given a life interest and a mere power to appoint. What was the effect of this holding on the rights of the children? What result would have followed a finding that the testatrix intended to create a trust? Do you agree with the result *In Re Weekes*?

2. Compare the result in *Re Weekes* with that in *Lloyds* in part 3, above. Can the two cases be reconciled?

3. The distinction between a discretionary trust and a power becomes even more difficult when the trust is non-exhaustive. Why?[54]

6.   CERTAINTY OF OBJECTS OF A POWER OF APPOINTMENT

Whereas trusts must comply with a great many legal requirements to be valid,[55] powers need only comply with two,[56] in addition to any imposed by the terms of the power itself. First, special and hybrid (intermediate) powers must pass the certainty of objects test.[57] Second, a power may be void if it is capricious; that is, if "it negatives a sensible consideration by the trustees of the exercise of the power."[58] Thus, a power to appoint in favour of the residents of Greater London could be void for being capricious.[59]

Certainty of objects means that the description of the class of possible appointees must be sufficiently clear that the donee can properly perform the power, if he or she so chooses. The test for certainty of objects of a power of appointment, as set out in *Re Gulbenkian's Settlements Trusts*[60] below, is that there may be no conceptual uncertainty about "whether any given individual is or is not a member of the class." However, ". . . you do not have to be able to ascertain every member of the class."[61]

RE GULBENKIAN'S SETTLEMENT TRUSTS

[1970] A.C. 508, [1968] 3 All E.R. 785
House of Lords

A settlement was created to run for the duration of Nubar Gulbenkian's lifetime. The trustees of the settlement were empowered, in their absolute discretion, to pay all or any part of the income from the fund for the benefit of all or

---

54 Non-exhaustive trusts are considered in note 6 in part 2, *supra*.

55 See Chapter 4, parts 2 through 9.

56 Unless the appointment relates to land in which case it must comply with the writing requirements of the various provincial statutes.

57 *Re Manisty's Settlement, Manisty v. Manisty, supra*, note 10.

58 *Ibid*.

59 *Ibid*.

60 *Supra*, note 1.

61 *Ibid*., at 525.

any number of the following persons: Nubar Gulbenkian, his wife, his children, or remoter issue; and "any person in whose house or in whose company, or under whose care, or by or with whom Nubar Gulbenkian might, from time to time, be employed or residing." There were further trusts created in default of appointment. An application was brought to determine whether the settlement was void for uncertainty of objects.

LORD UPJOHN:

My Lords, on May 31, 1929, the late Mr. Calouste Sarkis Gulbenkian made a settlement expressed to be in consideration of his natural love and affection for his son Nubar Sarkis Gulbenkian, one of the respondents, who, however, has taken no part in the argument, for he has assigned away his rights, if any, to income during his life; I shall call him "the son."

The first operative clause of the settlement was clause 2(i) in these terms:

> 2.(i) The trustees shall during the life of the said Nubar Sarkis Gulbenkian at their absolute discretion pay all or any part of the income of the property hereby settled and the investments for the time being representing the same (hereinafter called the trust fund) to or apply the same for the maintenance and personal support or benefit of all or any one or more to the exclusion of the other or others of the following persons namely the said Nubar Sarkis Gulbenkian and any wife and his children or remoter issue for the time being in existence whether minors or adults and any person or persons in whose house or apartments or in whose company or under whose care or control by or with whom the said Nubar Sarkis Gulbenkian may from time to time be employed or residing and the other persons or person other than the settlor for the time being entitled or interested whether absolutely contingently or otherwise to or in the trust fund under the trusts herein contained to take effect after the death of the said Nubar Sarkis Gulbenkian in such proportions and manner as the trustees shall in their absolute discretion at any time or times think proper.
>
> (ii) Subject to the discretionary trust or power herein before contained the trustees shall during the life of the said Nubar Sarkis Gulbenkian hold the said income or so much thereof as shall not be paid or applied under such discretionary trust or power upon the trusts and for the purposes for which the said income would for the time being be held as if the said Nubar Sarkis Gulbenkian were then dead.

After the death of the son the capital and future income of the trust fund was to be held upon terms with which your Lordships are not concerned.

On July 18, 1938, the father made another settlement by way of further provision for the son. During the lifetime of the son the income was to be held upon trusts similar to those set out above, save that the words "or in whose company or under whose care or control" are omitted, but counsel on neither side has sought to differentiate between the two settlements on this ground and I shall therefore refer only to clause 2(1) of the 1929 settlement.

The whole question before your Lordships is whether that clause is void for uncertainty or whether the clause is valid so that the son is an object of the discretion. If so, certain subsidiary questions are raised by the originating summonses which have been issued, but these questions are not before your Lordships.

My Lords, upon the main arguments presented to your Lordships the decision upon this matter lies in a very small compass though, in view of the secondary argument of the respondents with which the majority of the Court of Appeal agreed, I shall have later to deal with the issues rather more generally.

It is agreed between the parties that the discretion to the trustees in clause 2(i) to pay all or any part of the income of the trust fund at their absolute discretion to one or more of the persons therein mentioned to the exclusion of the other or others or to apply it for their maintenance, support, or benefit is a mere or bare power or a power collateral, as it is sometimes called. It is not a trust power: the trustees have no duty to exercise it in the sense that the court has any power to compel the trustees to exercise it or to exercise it itself if the trustees refuse or neglect to do so. Insofar as the power is not exercised by the trustees or if it is void for uncertainty, the income falls to be held upon the trusts declared by clause 2(ii).

It is curious that there is no long line of decided cases as to what is the proper test to apply when considering the validity of a mere power when the class of possible appointees is or may be incapable of ascertainment, but there is a body of recent authority to the effect that the rule is, that provided there is a valid gift over or trust in default of appointment which was fundamental to the decision of Clauson J. in *In re Park*,[62] a mere or bare power of appointment among a class is valid if you can with certainty say whether any given individual is or is not a member of the class; you do not have to be able to ascertain every member of the class.

This was stated by Harman J. in *In re Gestetner Settlement*[63] followed by Roxburgh J. in *Re Coates*[64] and by me in *In re Sayer*.[65] Its reasoning was, I think, approved in the Court of Appeal in *Inland Revenue Commissioners v. Broadway Cottages Trust*;[66] I say that because it is a little difficult to know whether Jenkins was doing more than setting out the Crown's argument. I note that Danckwerts L.J.[67] (probably rightly) treated it in the court below as part of the judgment of the learned Lord Justice.

And the rule was in general terms approved by Lord Evershed M.R. in *In re Hain's Settlement*.[68] Counsel for the appellants submits that the foregoing authorities correctly state the law and on his first line of argument counsel for the respondents agrees.

Let me assume, then, for the present that that is the right test. Does clause 2(i) satisfy that test or is it too uncertain? A very similar clause came before Harman J. in *In re Gresham's Settlement*[69] and he held it void for uncertainty even after construing it, as he described it, "benevolently."

Counsel for the appellants argued that you must give the words used their literal meaning and then apply the test to see whether you can predicate with

---

62 [1932] 1 Ch. 580.
63 [1953] Ch. 672, [1953] 1 All E.R. 1150.
64 [1955] Ch. 495.
65 *Supra,* note 30.
66 [1955] Ch. 20.
67 [1968] Ch. 126.
68 [1961] 1 W.L.R. 440.
69 [1956] 1 W.L.R. 573.

certainty whether a given individual is or is not within the class and no modification of the literal language is permissible to make sense of it. This argument is
based on a fallacy.

There is no doubt that the first task is to try to ascertain the settlor's intention,
so to speak, without regard to the consequences, and then, having construed the
document, apply the test. The court, whose task it is to discover that intention,
starts by applying the usual canons of construction; words must be given their
usual meaning, the clause should be read literally and in accordance with the
ordinary rules of grammar. But very frequently, whether it be in wills, settlements,
or commercial agreements, the application of such fundamental canons leads
nowhere, the draftsman has used words wrongly, his sentences border on the
illiterate, and his grammar may be appalling. It is then the duty of the court by
the exercise of its judicial knowledge and experience in the relevant matter, innate
common sense and desire to make sense of the settlor's or parties' expressed
intentions, however obscure and ambiguous the language that may have been
used, to give a reasonable meaning to that language if it can do so without doing
complete violence to it. The fact that the court has to see whether the clause is
"certain" for a particular purpose does not disentitle the court from doing otherwise than, in the first place, try to make sense of it.

My Lords, I do not think the late Mr. Wither's language (if indeed he was
responsible for the draftsmanship) is open to very serious criticism; the clause, it
is true, ran together too many possible situations and did so rather ungrammati-
cally, but its general object was clear; it was a "spendthrift" clause and must be
read in the light of that general intention and construed with the object to giving
effect to it if it is possible to do so.

I adopt the construction propounded by Harman J. in *Gresham* with amendments. I do not regard his construction as benevolent in the least degree but as
the proper construction of the settlor's imperfectly expressed language; indeed, I
do not regard my own interpretation of his language as perfect; it is merely
sufficient for the decision of this case.

So I would read the relevant words in this way:

After the words —

> the said Nubar Sarkis Gulbenkian and any wife and his children or remoter issue for the time
> being in existence whether minors or adults, I would paraphrase the words of the clause thus:
>
> > any person or persons by whom the son may from time to time be employed and any person
> > or persons with whom the son from time to time is residing whether in the house or apartment of
> > such person or persons or whether in the company or under the care or control of such person or
> > persons.

Is such a clause too vague and indefinite to satisfy the test, namely, whether a
given person is within or without the class? Even adopting this construction
counsel for the appellants argued that it was uncertain and Harman J. thought so
because of the difficulty of the interpretation of the word "residing."

In a very careful argument counsel for the appellants advanced a number of
points which he submitted showed there were 14 cases where the trustees would
have an impossible task to execute, but these alleged impossibilities can be

classified I think under four headings; uncertainty upon the meaning of (1) "residing," (2) persons "with whom" the son is residing, (3) persons "in whose company" the son is residing, (4) persons "under whose care or control" the son is residing. My Lords, upon this matter I agree entirely with the Court of Appeal. Many difficult and borderline cases may occur in any one of these situations. But mere difficulty is nothing to the point. If the trustees feel difficulty or even doubt upon the point the Court of Chancery is available to solve it for them. It solves many such problems every year. I cannot for myself see any insuperable difficulty arising in the solution of any given state of affairs which would make it necessary to hold that the relevant clause as I have construed it fails to comply with the test. Of course I have not overlooked *Sifton v. Sifton*[70] but that was an entirely different case of a divesting clause. In my opinion, this clause is not void for uncertainty, and the Court of Appeal was quite right to overrule the decision of Harman J. in *In re Gresham*[71] where he held a similar clause was void on that ground.

My Lords, that is sufficient to dispose of the appeal, but, as I have mentioned earlier, the reasons of two members of the Court of Appeal went further and have been supported by counsel for the respondents with much force and so must be examined.

The Master of the Rolls[72] propounded a test in the case of powers collateral; namely, that if you can say of one particular person meaning thereby, apparently, any one person only that he is clearly within the category the whole power is good though it may be difficult to say in other cases whether a person is or is not within the category; and he supported that view by reference to authority. Winn L.J.[73] said that where there was not a complete failure by reason of ambiguity and uncertainty the court would give effect to the power as valid rather than hold it defeated since it will not have wholly failed, which put — though more broadly — the view expressed by the Master of the Rolls. Counsel for the respondents in his second line or argument relied upon these observations as a matter of principle but he candidly admitted that he could not rely upon any authority. Moreover, the Master of the Rolls[74] expressed the view that the different doctrine with regard to trust powers should be brought into line with the rule with regard to conditions precedent and powers collateral.

So I propose to make some general observations upon this matter.

If a donor (be he a settlor or testator) directs trustees to make some specified provision for "John Smith," then to give legal effect to that provision it must be possible to identify "John Smith." If the donor knows three John Smiths then by the most elementary principles of law neither the trustees nor the court in their place can give effect to that provision; neither the trustees nor the court can guess at it. It must fail for uncertainty unless of course admissible evidence is available to point to a particular John Smith as the object of the donor's bounty.

---

70 [1938] A.C. 656, [1938] 2 W.W.R. 465, [1938] 3 All E.R. 435, [1938] O.R. 529 (P.C.).
71 *Supra*, note 69.
72 [1968] Ch. 126 at 134E.
73 *Ibid.*, at 138E.
74 *Ibid.*, at 133B.

Then, taking it one stage further, suppose the donor directs that a fund or the income of a fund should be equally divided between members of a class. That class must be as defined as the individual; the court cannot guess at it. Suppose the donor directs that a fund be divided equally between "my old friends," then unless there is some admissible evidence that the donor has given some special "dictionary" meaning to that phrase which enables the trustees to identify the class with sufficient certainty, it is plainly bad as being too uncertain. Suppose that there appeared before the trustees (or the court) two or three individuals who plainly satisfied the test of being "my old friends," the trustee could not consistently with the donor's intentions accept them as claiming the whole or any defined part of the fund. They cannot claim the whole fund for they can show no title to it unless they prove they are the only members of the class, which of course they cannot do and so, too, by parity of reasoning they cannot claim any defined part of the fund and there is no authority in the trustees or the court to make any distribution among a smaller class than that pointed out by the donor. The principle is, in my opinion, that the donor must make his intentions sufficiently plain as to the objects of his trust and the court cannot give effect to it by misinterpreting his intentions by dividing the fund merely among those present. Secondly, and perhaps it is the more hallowed principle, the Court of Chancery, which acts in default of trustees, must know with sufficient certainty the objects of the beneficence of the donor so as to execute the trust. Then, suppose the donor does not direct an equal division of his property among the class but gives a power of selection to his trustees among the class; exactly the same principles must apply. The trustees have a duty to select the donees of the donor's bounty from among the class designated by the donor; he has not entrusted them with any power to select the donees merely from among known claimants who are within the class, for that is constituting a narrower class and the donor has given them no power to do this.

So if the class is insufficiently defined the donor's intentions must in such cases fail for uncertainty. Perhaps I should mention here that it is clear that the question of uncertainty must be determined as of the date of the document declaring the donor's intention (in the case of a will, his death). Normally the question of certainty will arise because of the ambiguity of definition of the class by reason of the language employed by the donor, but occasionally owing to some of the curious settlements executed in recent years it may be quite impossible to construct even with all the available evidence anything like a class capable of definition (*In re Sayer*[75]) though the difficulty in doing so will not defeat the donor's intentions (*In re Hains' Settlement*).[76] But I should add this: If the class is sufficiently defined by the donor the fact that it may be difficult to ascertain the whereabouts or continued existence of some of its members at the relevant time matters not. The trustees can apply to the court for directions or pay a share into court.

---

75 *Supra*, note 30.
76 [1961] 1 W.L.R. 440.

But when mere or bare powers are conferred upon donees of the power (whether trustees or others) the matter is quite different. As I have already pointed out, the trustees have no duty to exercise it in the sense that they cannot be controlled in any way. If they fail to exercise it then those entitled in default of its exercise are entitled to the fund. Perhaps the contrast may be put forcibly in this way: in the first case, it is a mere power to distribute with a gift over in default; in the second case, it is a trust to distribute among the class defined by the donor with merely a power of selection within that class. The result is in the first case even if the class of appointees among whom the donees of the power may appoint is clear and ascertained and they are all of full age and *sui juris*, nevertheless they cannot compel the donees of the power to exercise it in their collective favour. If, however, it is a trust power, then those entitled are entitled (if they are all of full age and *sui juris*) to compel the trustees to pay the fund over to them, unless the fund is income and the trustees have power to accumulate for the future.

Again the basic difference between a mere power and a trust power is that in the first case trustees owe no duty to exercise it and the relevant fund or income falls to be dealt with in accordance with the trusts in default of its exercise, whereas in the second case the trustee *must* exercise the power and in default the court will. It is briefly summarised in *Halsbury's Laws of England*:[77]

> The court will not exercise or compel trustees to exercise a purely discretionary power given to them; but the court will restrain the trustee from exercising the power improperly, and, if it is coupled with a duty, the court can compel the trustees to perform their duty.

It is a matter of construction whether the power is a mere power or a trust power and the use of inappropriate language is not decisive: *Wilson v. Turner*.[78]

So, with all respect to the contrary view, I cannot myself see how, consistently with principle, it is possible to apply to the execution of a trust power the principles applicable to the permissible exercise by the donees (even if trustees) of mere powers; that would defeat the intention of donors completely.

But with respect to mere powers, while the court cannot compel the trustees to exercise their powers, yet those entitled to the fund in default must clearly be entitled to restrain the trustees from exercising it save among those within the power. So the trustees or the court must be able to say with certainty who is within and who is without the power. It is for this reason that I find myself unable to accept the broader proposition advanced by Lord Denning M.R. and Winn L.J. mentioned earlier, and agree with the proposition as enunciated in *In re Gestetner's Settlement*[79] and the later cases.

My Lords, I would dismiss these appeals.

[Lords Reid, Hodson, Guest, and Donovan agreed that the appeals should be dismissed. After the validity of the trusts was determined by the House of

---

77 3rd ed., vol. 30, (1959), at para. 445.
78 (1883), 22 Ch. D. 521 at 525 (U.K. C.A.).
79 *Supra*, note 63.

Lords, the summonses originally taken out by the trustees to test the validity of the trusts were restored to the Chancery Division for directions as to the exercise of their discretion with respect to the payment of accumulated and future income under the trusts. That case is reported as *Re Gulbenkian's Settlements Trusts (No. 2)*.][80]

Notes and Questions

1. As will be seen, the test for certainty of objects of a discretionary trust has been assimilated to that for certainty of objects of a power. A discussion of the ambiguities inherent in the test is postponed until the next chapter.[81]

2. Will the certainty of objects test be met if the instrument creating the power, expressly or by implication, provides criteria sufficient to enable the court to "police" those exercising the power? Should extrinsic evidence be admissible to provide such criteria?

3. Should a power vested in a person *in his or her personal capacity* have to meet the certainty of objects test at all? Why or why not?[82]

4. Why did Lord Upjohn hold that a power and not a trust was created in *Re Gulbenkian*?

5. *Re Gulbenkian* is an example of what type of power of appointment?

6. At what date is a power tested for certainty of objects?[83]

7. Is a power in favour of "my old friends" valid? Why or why not? Can a distinction be drawn between that power and one for "such persons as my trustees know to be my old friends"?[84]

8. An older test for certainty of objects of a power was "whether any given postulant is a member of the specified class."[86] How does this test differ from that in *Re Gulbenkian*?

9. Describe the difference between conceptual and evidential uncertainty.[86] Which type of uncertainty invalidates a power of appointment and why? Is the uncertainty surrounding the words "persons with whom [my son] is residing" in *Re Gulbenkian* conceptual or evidentiary?

10. If you can say that one particular person is within the class of objects, is the class certain?[87]

Problems

1. A testator bequeathed certain property to his executors and trustees "for distribution among such of my friends and relatives" as the trustees should select. Any property not so distributed was to be sold and disposed of as part of the residue of the estate.

---

80 [1970] Ch. 408, [1969] 2 All E.R. 1173.

81 See Chapter 4, part 6, below.

82 See *Blausten v. I.R.C.*, [1972] 1 All E.R. 41, [1972] Ch. 256, [1972] 2 W.L.R. 376 (C.A.) and *Re Manisty's Settlement supra*, note 10.

83 See Lord Upjohn's judgment in *Re Gulbenkian's Settlement Trusts, supra*, note 1.

84 See *Re Tuck's Settlement Trusts*, [1978] Ch. 49, [1978] 1 All E.R. 1047 (C.A.).

85 *Gestetner's, supra*, note 63.

86 A description of the two types of uncertainty can be found in Chapter 4, part 6, below.

87 See *McPhail v. Doulton* (1970), [1971] A.C. 424, [1970] 2 All E.R. 228 (H.L.). The approach in the *McPhail* case was adopted by the Supreme Court of Canada in *Jones v. T. Eaton Co.*, [1973] S.C.R. 635, 1973 CarswellOnt 227, 1973 CarswellOnt 227F, 35 D.L.R. (3d) 97.

(a) Was a trust or a power created?

(b) Is the provision valid? Why or why not?

(c) Would it make any difference if the will had said "in case of doubt my trustees shall have the power to designate who my relatives and friends are"?

(d) What would be the result if the will had directed the trustees to distribute the articles "among such of A, B, C, and D as my trustees see fit"?

(e) What would be the result if the will had directed the trustees to distribute to "A, B, C, and D equally"?

2. T made a will in which he gave his wife a life estate with a power to encroach on the corpus. The will then continued "since my wife will know which of my children will be most deserving and in need, I give her power to appoint the capital of my estate by her will among such of my children as she shall deem fit." T's wife died after T did, but intestate, without exercising her power of appointment.

(a) How will the capital of T's estate be distributed?

(b) Would it make any difference if T's wife had predeceased him?

3. An *inter vivos* trust was created by H. The trustees held the fund "for such persons or purposes as the trustees shall within 21 years from the date hereof appoint." The trustees were prohibited from appointing to the settlor, her husband, or any past or present trustee.

(a) Does this provision create a trust or a power?

(b) If a power, what type?

(c) What are the objects of the provision?

(d) Would this provision be held valid? Why or why not?

4. A testamentary trust was created to benefit one or more of the testator's children. The testator's sister, the named trustee, was given the power to select the child or children that she felt showed "a special ability and desire to maintain the family fortune." In default of appointment, the trust property was to go to the trustee absolutely.

(a) Does the provision create a power or a trust?

(b) Can the testator's sister be released from making the appointment?

(c) What rights would B, the testator's son, who has "a special ability and desire to maintain the family fortune" have?

5. Anne was a mentally handicapped person residing in a group home and receiving an allowance as a single disabled person. When her father died, he left a will in which he named her as beneficiary of a "discretionary trust." The will gave the trustees to the estate an "absolute and unfettered discretion" to make payments of income or capital from the trust for her benefit. While the testator made it clear that he wished the trustees to "take such steps as will maximize the benefits" for his daughter, he also stated that this wish was, in no way, to bind the trustees.

Anne's government assistance was cancelled on the basis that her liquid assets exceeded the cut-off point for receiving benefits. Liquid assets, under the regulations to the *Family Benefits Act*, include "a beneficial interest in assets held in trust and available to be used for maintenance."

Is the vehicle created by the will a power of appointment or a discretionary trust? Does Anne have a "beneficial interest" in the funds? If it creates a discretionary trust, was the government correct to cut off government assistance? Does Anne's interest in the fund fall within the meaning of the definition of "liquid assets"?[88]

---

88 See *Ontario (Ministry of Community & Social Services) v. Henson* (1988), 28 E.T.R. 121, 26 O.A.C. 332 (Div. Ct.), affirmed (1989), 36 E.T.R. 192, 1989 CarswellOnt 542 (Ont. C.A.). See also, Ellen B. Zweibel, "Private and Public Assistance: Discretionary Trusts for the Disabled Social Assistance Recipient," 32 E.T.R. 261 in which she considers the *Henson* case and the interpretation of "liquid assets."

PART II

EXPRESS TRUSTS

4

THE CREATION OF EXPRESS TRUSTS

1. SCOPE

An express trust is one that is intentionally created by its maker. It is to be contrasted with resulting and constructive trusts, which are created by operation of law.

There are four requirements that all valid express private trusts must meet.[1] First, all of the parties to the trust must be capacitated. Second, there must be certainty of intention to create a trust, certainty of subject-matter and certainty of objects. Third, the trust must be constituted in the sense that the trust property must be transferred to the trustees. And, fourth, all the requisite formalities must be met. We will explore each of these requirements in this chapter.

2. CAPACITY

(a) Introduction

The rules that apply to capacity in the trust setting are essentially the same as those that apply to the holding and transfer of property generally. However, it is worth considering what, if any, specific incapacities exist for the creator of the trust, the trustee and the beneficiary.

---

1 Because charitable trusts are express but not private, the requirements that they must meet to be valid are different from those for express, private trusts. For example, the requirement of certainty of objects is relaxed for charitable trusts.

(b) The Creator of the Trust

There are three potential incapacities for the creator of a trust: minority, mental incompetency, and bankruptcy. Each of these will be considered in turn.

In the Canadian common law jurisdictions, minors may not make valid wills unless they fall within a statutory exception. Such statutory exceptions can be seen in Ontario's *Succession Law Reform Act*,[2] which enables a minor to make a valid will if, at the time of making it, the minor is or has been married, is contemplating marriage and the marriage subsequently occurs, is a member of the Canadian Forces, or is a sailor at sea or in the course of a voyage. Most other provinces have similar enabling legislation.[3] Obviously, a minor who cannot make a valid will cannot create a valid testamentary trust. Further, any *inter vivos* settlement made by a minor is voidable at his or her option. In most Canadian jurisdictions, however, minors are permitted to enter into marriage settlements with the court's approval.[4]

A person found to be mentally incompetent[5] cannot make a valid will or *inter vivos* settlement except as permitted by statute. In Ontario, a mentally incompetent person, through his or her committee or the Public Trustee, may enter into a domestic settlement subject to the court's approval.[6] Most other Canadian provinces have similar statutory provisions.[7]

Finally, bankrupt persons are subject to a number of statutory controls on their ability to alienate their assets.[8] A bankrupt, accordingly, cannot make a valid *inter vivos* settlement.

(c) The Trustee

Anyone capable of holding property in his or her own right is capable of holding property as a trustee. Thus, any capacitated individual or limited company can be a trustee. Because unincorporated associations have no separate legal

---

2   See, for example, the *Succession Law Reform Act*, R.S.O. 1990, c. S.26, s. 8.

3   For similar legislation see *Wills Act*, R.S.A. 2000, c. W-12, s. 9 (am. S.A. 2002, c. A-4.5, s. 80(3); R.S.B.C. 1996, c. 489, s. 7; R.S.M. 1988, c. W150, s. 8; R.S.N.L. 1990, c. W-10, s. 3; R.S.N.B. 1973, c. W-9, s. 8; R.S.N.S. 1989, c. 505, s. 4; *The Wills Act, 1996*, S.S. 1996, c. W-14.1, ss. 4-6 (s. 5 am. S.S. 2001, c. 51, s. 10(2)); *Probate Act*, R.S.P.E.I. 1988, c. P-21, s. 62(2); *Wills Act*, R.S.N.W.T. 1988, c. W-5, s. 4; R.S.Y. 2002, c. 230, s. 4.

4   See *Family Law Act*, R.S.N.L. 1990, c. F-2, s. 65(2); R.S.O. 1990, c. F.3, s. 55(2); S.P.E.I. 1995, c. 12, s. 54(2); *Family Relations Act*, R.S.B.C. 1996, c. 128, s. 61(5); *Marital Property Act*, S.N.B. 1980, c. M-1.1, s. 37(3); *Matrimonial Property Act*, R.S.N.S. 1989, c. 275, s. 25.

5   See Note and Question 2, below, for a discussion of when "mental incompetency" is of a sufficient degree to render a person unable to make a valid will or gift *inter vivos*.

6   See the *Family Law Act*, R.S.O. 1990, c. F.3, s. 55(3) (am. by S.O. 1992, c. 32, s. 12).

7   See *Family Law Act*, R.S.N.L. 1990, c. F-2, s. 65(3) (am. by S.N.L. 2000, c. 29, s. 10(1)); S.P.E.I. 1995, c. 12, s. 54(3) (am. by S.P.E.I. 2002, c. 7, s. 11(a)); *Marital Property Act*, S.N.B. 1980, c. M-1.1, s. 37(3).

8   See D.W.M. Waters, *Law of Trusts in Canada*, 2nd ed. (Toronto: Carswell, 1984), at 91 ("Waters") for a fuller discussion of this point.

personality, they are incapable of holding title to property and thus are incapable of acting as trustees.

It is unwise to appoint a minor as trustee because a minor is incapable of making a valid conveyance of the trust property.[9] Canadian common law courts have the authority, under various provincial statutes, to replace trustees who are minors.[10]

The courts also have the power to deal with situations in which a mentally incapable person has been appointed trustee.[11] In Ontario, for example, the court may empower a committee to fulfil the duties of the office of trustee.[12] Further, the court has the power to appoint a new trustee when it is for the benefit of the incapable person or is otherwise expedient.[13]

(d) The Beneficiary

All persons including minors, mentally incapable persons, bankrupts and corporations can be the beneficiaries of a trust. A trust may even benefit unborn or unascertained persons. In such cases, a representative is appointed to protect their potential interests. Incapable beneficiaries are usually represented by an official, such as the Public Guardian and Trustee, the Official Guardian, or the Guardian of Minors.[14]

Again, because unincorporated associations have no separate legal personality, they are incapable of being beneficiaries of a trust. It is possible, however, to transfer property to trustees of an unincorporated association who may then hold on trust for the individual members of the association.

Trust beneficiaries may be persons or purposes. When the object of a trust is a purpose, the purpose may be charitable or non-charitable. Both charitable and non-charitable purpose trusts are dealt with elsewhere in the text. In this chapter, the discussion is limited to objects who are persons.

Notes and Questions

1. The Ontario *Trustee Act*[15] gives the Ontario Superior Court of Justice power to make vesting orders when an appointed trustee is a minor, out of the province, or cannot be found. Section 10 of the Act applies when the trust property is land, and section 13 applies where the property is stock, the right to receive dividends, or a chose in action.

---

9   See Waters, at 95-96.
10 The *Trustee Act*, R.S.A. 2000, c. T-8, s. 16 (am. by R.S.A. 2000, c. 16 (Supp.), s. 59(c)); R.S.B.C. 1996, c. 464, s. 31; R.S.M. 1987, c. T160, s. 9(1)(a) (am. by S.M. 1993, c. 29, s. 206(4)); R.S.N.L. 1990, c. T-10, s. 33; R.S.N.S. 1989, c. 479, s. 31; R.S.O. 1990, c. T.23, s. 5 (am. by S.O. 2000, c. 26, Sched. A, s. 15(2) (item 1)); R.S.P.E.I. 1988, c. T-8, s. 4(a); R.S.S. 1978, c. T-23, s. 14(1); *Trustees Act*, R.S.N.B. 1973, c. T-15, s. 29(1).
11 *Ibid.*
12 *Trustee Act*, R.S.O. 1990, T.23, s. 5 (am. S.O. 2000, c. 26, Sched. A, s. 15(2) (item 1)).
13 *Ibid.*
14 See Waters, at 97ff., for a description of the office of the Public Guardian and Trustee.
15 R.S.O. 1990, c. T.23, ss. 10 (am. S.O. 2000, c. 26, Sched. A, s. 15(2) (item 2)), 13 (am. S.O. 2000, c. 26, Sched. A, s. 15(2) (item 5)).

The Ontario Law Reform Commission[16] has recommended that these two sections be amalgamated and a new section be created which would empower the court to make vesting orders in relation to any kind of trust property. Further, the Commission recommends that the court be empowered to act, not just in certain specific circumstances, but if "the best interests of the trust" so require.

2. What degree of incapacity must exist to render a person incapable of dealing with his or her own property? In *Royal Trust Co. v. Diamant*,[17] Whittaker J. provided the following test:

> In order to render a transaction *inter vivos* invalid such a degree of incapacity [must be shown] as would interfere with the capacity to understand substantially the nature and effect of the transaction.

In *Ouderkirk v. Ouderkirk*,[18] Kerwin J. provided the following test for a testamentary trust:

> The testator has not only to understand the nature and effect of making a will, but the soundness of his mind must be such that he understands the extent of the property of which he is disposing, and comprehends and appreciates the claims to which he ought to give effect.

Finally, in *Re Beaney*,[19] the court described the test for both *inter vivos* and testamentary trusts as:

> The degree or extent of understanding required in respect of any instrument is relative to the particular transaction which it is to effect. In the case of a will the degree is always high. In the case of . . . a gift *inter vivos*, whether by deed or otherwise, the degree required varies with the circumstances of the transaction.

3. A person suffers from manic-depression and immature personality. Is the person capable of entering into an *inter vivos* trust? A testamentary one?[20]

3. AN INTRODUCTION TO THE THREE CERTAINTIES

The creation of a trust is premised upon the existence of the three certainties: (i) *certainty of intention* — the settlor must have intended to create a trust, (ii) *certainty of subject matter* — the trust property must be sufficiently ascertained or ascertainable, and it must be sufficiently certain as to how that property will be divided amongst the beneficiaries, and (iii) *certainty of objects* — the beneficiaries of the trust must be sufficiently identified.

Each of these three requirements is considered separately below but it is important to realize that they are inter-related and reflexive. *Knight v. Knight*,[21]

---

16 See Ontario Law Reform Commission, *Report on the Law of Trusts* (Toronto: Ministry of the Attorney General, 1984), at 133-163 ("O.L.R.C. Report").

17 [1953] 3 D.L.R. 102 (B.C. S.C.).

18 [1936] S.C.R. 619, [1936] 2 D.L.R. 417.

19 [1978] 1 W.L.R. 770 at 774, [1978] 2 All E.R. 595 (H.C.).

20 See *Goodman Estate v. Geffen*, [1991] 2 S.C.R. 353, 80 Alta. L.R. (2d) 293, [1991] 5 W.W.R. 389, 81 D.L.R.(4th) 211.

21 (1840), 3 Beav. 148, 49 E.R. 58 (Ch.).

the seminal English case in this area that has been followed in Canada on numerous occasions, describes this inter-relationship among the three certainties in the following way:

> On the other hand, if the giver accompanies his expression of wish, or request by other words, from which it is to be collected, that he did not intend the wish to be imperative; or if it appears from the context that the first taker was intended to have a discretionary power to withdraw any part of the subject from the object of the wish or request; or if the objects are not such as may be ascertained with sufficient certainty, it has been held that no trust is created. Thus the words "free and unfettered," accompanying the strongest expression of request, were held to prevent the words of the request being imperative. Any words by which it is expressed or from which it may be implied, that the first taker may apply any part of the subject to his own use, are held to prevent the subject of the gift from being considered certain; and a vague description of the object, that is, a description by which the giver neither clearly defined the object himself nor names a distinct class out of which the first taker is to select, or which leaves it doubtful what interest the object or class of objects is to take, will prevent the objects from being certain within the meaning of the rule; and in such cases we are told that the question:[22]

> > never turns upon the grammatical import of words — they may be imperative, but not necessarily so; the subject-matter, the situation of the parties, and the probable intent must be considered.

A classic example of the reflexive nature of the certainties can be found in cases in which one person, A, gives property to another person, B, and in the same instrument attempts to give a portion of the property to yet another person, C. The issue arises whether B takes the property absolutely, as a gift subject to a condition or personal obligation, or as a life estate subject to a trust in favour of C. If, on construction, the court is inclined to find that a trust in favour of C was intended, it must go on to determine the subject-matter of the trust. As you can see, there is no clear answer to that issue (*i.e.*, there is apparent uncertainty of subject-matter). This uncertainty, in turn, casts doubt on whether the intention to create a trust truly exists. *Re Walker*,[23] below, illustrates the foregoing and, in so doing, shows the inter-related nature of the three certainties.

RE WALKER

(1925), 56 O.L.R. 517
Court of Appeal

Except for some specific legacies, the testator gave his wife all his real and personal property and directed that "should any portion of my estate still remain in the hands of my said wife at the time of her decease undisposed of by her such remainder shall be divided" among certain persons in named proportions.

The executors applied to the court for an interpretation of this provision. Riddell J. held that the will contemplated that the wife could dispose of the estate

---

22 2 Ves. Jun. 632 at 633.
23 (1925), 56 O.L.R. 517 (C.A.).

as she wished during her lifetime but at her death what was left was to be distributed in accordance with the testator's instructions. The executors appealed to the Ontario Court of Appeal.

MIDDLETON J.A.:

. . .

From the earliest times the attempt has been made to accomplish the impossible, to give and yet to withhold, to confer an absolute estate upon the donee, and yet in certain events to resume ownership and to control the destiny of the thing given. By conveyance this is impossible. Where there is absolute ownership, that ownership confers upon the owner the rights of an owner and restrains an alienation; and similar attempts to mould and control the law are void.[24]

When a testator gives property to one, intending him to have all the rights incident to ownership, and adds to this a gift over of that which remains *in specie* at his death or at the death of that person, he is endeavouring to do that which is impossible. His intention is plain but it cannot be given effect to. The court has then to endeavour to give such effect to the wishes of the testator as is legally possible, by ascertaining which part of the testamentary intention predominates and by giving effect to it, rejecting the subordinate intention as being repugnant to the dominant intention.

So the cases fall into two classes: the first, in which the gift to the person first named prevails and the gift over fails as repugnant; the second, in which the first named takes a life-estate only, and so the gift over prevails. Subject to an apparent exception to be mentioned, there is no middle course, and in each case the inquiry resolves itself into an endeavour to apply this rule to the words of the will in question. The sheep are separated from the goats; and, while in most instances there is not much doubt, in some instances the classification is by no means easy.

. . .

Turning now to the will before the court. I agree with the judgment in review that the words "undisposed of" do not refer to a testamentary disposition by the widow but refer to a disposal by her during her lifetime. I am, however, unable to agree with the construction placed upon the will otherwise. It appears to be plain that there is here an attempt to deal with that which remains undisposed of by the widow, in a manner repugnant to the gift to her. I think the gift to her must prevail and the attempted gift over must be declared to be repugnant and void.

I would therefore allow the appeal and declare the construction of the will accordingly. Costs may well come out of the wife's estate.

---

24 *In Re Rosher* (1884), 26 Ch. D. 801.

Notes and Questions

1. The statement in *Walker* that suggests that only two interpretations are possible, namely, a life estate followed by a trust or, an absolute gift, is misleading. In cases like *Walker*, it is possible, as well, to interpret the language as creating a gift subject to a condition or personal obligation.

2. *Re Walker* may be contrasted with *Re Shamas*.[25] The latter case concerned a testator who made a will with the following provisions:

> I give all I belong [*sic*; have] to my wife. I want her to pay my debts — raise the family. All will belong to my wife until the last one comes to the age of 21 years old. If my wife marries again she should have her share like the other children, if not, she will keep the whole thing and see that every child gets his share when she dies.

The court held that the estate vested in the children in equal shares, subject to a life interest in the widow which would be divested on her remarriage. The widow was held, as well, to have a power of encroachment upon capital for the support and maintenance of herself and the children until the youngest reached the age of 21.

3. *Sprange v. Barnard*[26] is another example. A testatrix left £300 in annuities to her husband for his sole use and, at his death, whatever he did not use was to be divided equally among three named persons. The High Court of Chancery held that the testatrix had made an absolute gift of the annuities to the husband and that he was free to deal with them as he wished. Can you think of any other possible constructions of the bequest? If the court had found that the testatrix had intended to create a trust, what would its subject-matter be?

4. A testator gave all his property to his wife "trusting" that she would use it for the spiritual and temporal good of herself and her children, remembering always the church and the poor. What interest did the wife receive in the property?[27]

5. For a discussion of the "what remains" cases, see G.D. Kennedy, "Gift by Will to W: At Her Death 'What Remains' to the Children,"[28] and L.A. Sheridan, "Gifts over with Floating Subject-Matter: Estates, Powers, Repugnancy (and the Intention of the Testator)."[29]

4. CERTAINTY OF INTENTION TO CREATE A TRUST

To satisfy the certainty of intention requirement, the court must find an intention that the trustee is placed under an imperative obligation to hold property on trust for the benefit of another and ultimately to distribute the property to the other. Certainty of intention is a question of construction; the intention is inferred from the nature and manner of the disposition considered as a whole. The language employed must convey more than a moral obligation or mere wish as to what is to be done with certain property.[30] The language used need not be technical so

---

25 [1967] 2 O.R. 275, 63 D.L.R. (2d) 300 (C.A.).

26 (1789), 2 Bro. C.C. 585, 29 E.R. 320 (U.K. Ct. of Chan.).

27 See *Curtis v. Rippon* (1820), 5 Madd. 434.

28 (1950), 28 Can. Bar Rev. 839.

29 (1977), 7 Man. L.Q. 249.

30 *Knight v. Knight, supra,* note 21.

long as the intention to create a trust can be found or inferred with certainty.[31] You must be careful to consider not only the words of request but the entire document as a whole when determining whether the requisite intention exists. A consideration of *LeBlanc Estate v. Belliveau*,[32] should highlight this point. A testator directed that his executor "may hold [certain] Bonds to maturity, and keep in trust thereafter, in order to help some bright young boys and girls through college." The court found that, although the language did not initially appear to be imperative, when the will was considered as a whole the language was sufficient to meet the certainty of intention requirement.

What is the result if, on construction, it is found that no certainty of intention exists? To answer this question, it is necessary to determine what was intended. If the intention was that the "trustee" receive an outright gift, then the "trustee" will take absolutely; the rules determining ownership in this situation are those that govern gifts, not trust law. If it was intended that the holder of the property was to have a power of appointment over it, then the persons entitled in default of exercise of the power will take equitable title subject to divestment. In this situation, the rules that are relevant are those related to powers, not trusts.

Johnson v. Farney,[33] below, illustrates the manner in which the courts construe a document to determine whether a wish has been described in sufficiently mandatory terms that an intention to create a trust is held to exist.

JOHNSON v. FARNEY

(1913), 29 O.L.R. 223, 9 D.L.R. 782
Ontario Supreme Court

A man died, leaving a will which began with the words "I leave all my real and personal property to my dear wife." Towards the end of the will, it said: "I also wish if you (my wife) die soon after me that you will leave all you are possessed of, to my people and your people equally divided between them, that is to say your mother and my mother's families."

In a codicil, the testator referred to real estate purchased after the date of the will, and said: "Property known as the William McGuire property to go to my wife to do as she sees fit with it . . . If she my wife dies intestate divide what is left of it equally among my brothers and sisters . . ."

After her husband's death, the widow spoke of the provisions in his will as being just and fair and said that she wanted it carried out. In her will, however, the wife left all her property to her own family.

The issue arose whether the wife was free to dispose of the property as she saw fit or whether a trust in favour of her and her husband's family had been imposed by his will.

---

31 *Royal Bank of Canada v. Eastern Trust Co.* (1951), 32 C.B.R. 111, 3 D.L.R. 828 (P.E.I. T.D.).
32 (1986), 68 N.B.R. (2d) 145, 175 A.P.R. 145 (N.B. Q.B.).
33 (1913), 29 O.L.R. 223, 9 D.L.R. 782 (S.C.).

BOYD C.:

. . .

I think that she had the power and the right to do this, and that no trust is imposed upon the property devised to her by the husband. The codicil implies that she had testamentary power over what came from her husband, and his direction was only if she died intestate; and what would have happened had she died intestate need not be discussed. But in the will the expression used is that of a wish, not a direction; and, according to the present lines of decision, the language is insufficient to create an obligation, *i.e.*, a legal obligation enforceable in the courts.

As said in one of the later cases, the husband may have thought that the influence of an express wish would be sufficient to induce the wife to apply the property in the way suggested; but it was not put upon her as a duty, a mandate, or a legal obligation. He did not mean this second stage of the transfer to be under his will, but to be bestowed under the influence of his express wish and by the testamentary act of the wife. His words, taken literally, would cover all the possessions of the wife, however acquired, and this shows that he did not seek to control her free action, but only to give advice, as he does in so many parts of the will and codicil, which need not be quoted.

The earlier cases on precatory trusts have been departed from, and a stricter rule now applies, which may be thus expressed: an absolute gift is not to be cut down to a life interest merely by an expression of the testator's wish that the donee shall, by will or otherwise, dispose of the property in favour of individuals or families indicated by the testator.

A wish or desire so expressed is no more than a suggestion, to be accepted or not by the donee, but not amounting to a mandate or an obligatory trust. This is the result of *Re Hamilton*.[34] The modern view, as thus expounded, is recognised and acted on by Joyce J., in a recent case, *Re Conolly*.[35]

The parting of the ways is marked in our court by the case decided by the Chancery Division in 1889, *Bank of Montreal v. Bowers*.[36] The whole situation is fully discussed and the cases collected in *Re Atkinson*.[37]

I therefore declare that there is no trust attaching to the provisions of the husband's will and that the wife held the property absolutely as her own.

. . .

[The plaintiff appealed upon the question of the construction of the will only. The Ontario Court of Appeal affirmed the trial judgment.]

---

34 [1895] 1 Ch. 373, affirmed [1895] 2 Ch. 370 (C.A.).
35 [1910] 1 Ch. 219 (Ch. Div.).
36 (1889), 18 O.R. 226 (Ch.).
37 (1911), 80 L.J. Ch. 370 (C.A.).

Notes and Questions

1. *Johnson v. Farney* can be contrasted with *Daniels v. Daniels Estate*.[38] A testator executed a will which included the following residuary clause: "All the residue of my estate not hereinbefore disposed of I devise and bequeath unto my executors to distribute as they see fit." The issue was whether the testator intended to create a trust, confer a general power of appointment on his executors, or make a gift of the residue to them personally. The court held that the testator intended to create a trust but, as the objects were uncertain, it failed.

Are the two cases reconcilable? Do you agree with the result in both cases? If not, with which do you agree and why?

2. What factors led the court in the *LeBlanc* case, referred to in the textual portion of this heading, to a conclusion that a trust was created? What factors suggested otherwise?

3. Do you agree with the court in the *LeBlanc* case that a valid trust was created? Reconsider your answer after completing part 6, *infra*.

4. Is the test of certainty of intention objective or subjective? What if a person went through the motions of creating a trust, but secretly did not want to effect such a disposition?

5. There is no magic in words. A trust does not exist merely because the parties referred to a disposition as a "trust." *Howitt v. Howden Group Canada Ltd.*[39] is illustrative. A company established a pension plan in 1958. Funding was provided through the vehicle of contract. The company contributed approximately 70% and the employees contributed approximately 30%. In 1995, the plan was wound up. At that point, it contained a surplus of $3.8 million. The company argued that the money should be split in proportion to the original contributions; the employees argued that they were entitled to the whole. The correct answer depended upon whether or not the plan consisted of a trust. Although various documents used to create and operate the pension fund referred to "the trust," the court held that, having regard to all of the circumstances, that the phrase had not been used in its technical sense and that the parties had not intended to create a trust.

That decision can be contrasted with *Dalhousie Staff Assn. Contingency Fund (Trustee of), Re*.[40] In 1979, the Dalhousie Staff Association began to collect money from its members for use in emergencies. The fund grew considerably over the years until 1996, when members voted to terminate it. The proper disposition of the money at that point depended upon whether or not the fund was held in trust. Hamilton J. reviewed the evidence and found that a trust did exist. "While the use or failure to use the word 'trust' is not determinative of whether a trust has been created, here the use of the word trust goes some way to indicate the intention of the members of the DSA to create a trust at the time the Fund was created, since the name was the subject of considerable discussion which included consideration of other names for the Fund such as Strike Fund or Investment Building Fund." Why was use of the word "trust" important here, but not in *Howitt v. Howden Group Canada Ltd.*?

---

38 (1991), 85 D.L.R. (4th) 116, 84 Alta. L.R. (2d) 356, 120 A.R. 17, [1992] 2 W.W.R. 697 (C.A.), leave to appeal to S.C.C. refused [1992] 4 W.W.R. ixix (note), 2 Alta. L.R. (3d) xlvii (note), 90 D.L.R. (4th) viii (note).

39 (1999), 170 D.L.R. (4th) 423, 1999 CarswellOnt 659, 26 E.T.R. (2d) 1, C.E.B. & P.G.R. 8356 (headnote only), 20 C.C.P.B. 250 (Ont. C.A.).

40 (1999), 27 E.T.R. (2d) 310, 1999 CarswellNS 23, 175 N.S.R. (2d) 102, 534 A.P.R. 102 (N.S. S.C.). See also *Creaghan v. Hazen* (1999), 32 E.T.R. (2d) 180, 1999 CarswellNB 603, 215 N.B.R. (2d) 240, 551 A.P.R. 240 (N.B. Q.B.).

6. A disposition will be effective as intended or not at all. A court will not re-construe the would-be donor's intention simply because the intended disposition fails.

> I have a son called Thomas. I wrote a letter to him saying, "I give you my Blackacre estate, my leasehold in the High Street, the sum of £1000 consuls standing in my name, the wine in my cellar." This is ineffectual — I have given nothing — a letter will not convey freehold or leasehold land, it will not transfer Government stock, it will not pass the ownership in good. . . . It would be an imperfect gift, and being an imperfect gift the Court will not regard it as the declaration of a trust. I have made quite clear that I do not intend to make myself a trustee, I meant to give. The two intentions are very different — the giver means to get rid of his rights, the man who is intending to make himself a trustee intends to retain his rights but to come under an onerous obligation. The latter intention is far rarer than the former.[41]

5. CERTAINTY OF SUBJECT-MATTER

(a) Introduction

The certainty of subject-matter requirement has two components. First, a trust must have property which can clearly be identified as its subject-matter. Second, the terms of the trust must either define the portion which each beneficiary is to receive or vest the discretion to so decide in the trustees.

(b) When the Subject-Matter of the Trust Is Uncertain

Even if the language used in the trust instrument illustrates a clear intention to create a trust, no trust exists unless the subject-matter of the trust is ascertained or ascertainable.

Any type of property is capable of being the subject matter of a trust. The word "property" includes all equitable and legal interests in realty or personalty. Consequently, for example, an equitable interest under a trust is property and is capable of forming the subject matter of a further trust. So, too, the benefit of a contract is a property right capable of forming the subject matter of a trust.[42]

Whatever type of property is involved, however, it must be ascertained or ascertainable. The subject-matter is ascertained when it is a fixed amount or specified piece of property; it is ascertainable when a method by which the subject-matter can be identified is available from the terms of the trust or otherwise. For example, the "residue" of an estate is ascertainable because it has been legally defined as the estate's assets minus debts and legacies. *Id certum est quod potest redid certum.*[43]

---

41 F.W. Maitland, *Equity* rev'd edn. (Cambridge, 1936) at 71-72.
42 *Maclellan v. Wimbush* (1985), 20 E.T.R. 300, 1985 CarswellOnt 705 (Ont. Dist. Ct.).
43 "That is certain which can readily be made certain."

HUNTER v. MOSS

[1994] 1 W.L.R. 452, [1994] 3 All E.R. 215
Court of Appeal

A company, MEL, had issued 1000 shares. The defendant, Moss, held 950. He declared himself to be a trustee of a 5 per cent interest in the company (*i.e.* 50 shares) for the benefit of the plaintiff, Hunter. The defendant did not, however, identify any specific shares for the purposes of that disposition. A dispute later arose regarding the existence of a trust. The trial judge held that the defendant held 50 of his 950 shares on trust for the plaintiff. The defendant appealed on the ground that there was not sufficient certainty of subject matter. The critical question was whether or not a trust could be created even though the defendant had not actually separated out 50 shares.

DILLON L.J.:

. . .

I pass then to the second point of uncertainty. It is well established that for the creation of a trust there must be the three certainties referred to by Lord Langdale in his judgment in *Knight v. Knight*.[44] One of those is, of course, that there must be certainty of subject matter. All these shares were identical in one class: 5% was fifty shares and Mr Moss held personally more than fifty shares. It is well known that a trust of personalty can be created orally. . . .

In the present case there was no question of an imperfect transfer. What is relied on is an oral declaration of trust. Again, it would not be good enough for a settlor to say, "I declare that I hold fifty of my shares on trust for B," without indicating the company he had in mind of the various companies in which he held shares. There would be no sufficient certainty as to the subject matter of the trust. But here the discussion is solely about the shares of one class in the one company.

It is plain that a bequest by Mr Moss to Mr Hunter of fifty of his ordinary shares in MEL would be a valid bequest on Mr Moss's death which his executors or administrators would be bound to carry into effect. Mr Hartman sought to dispute that and to say that if, for instance, a shareholder had two-hundred ordinary shares in ICI and he wanted to give them to A, B, C and D equally he could do it by giving two-hundred shares to A, B, C and D as Tenants in Common, but he could not validly do it by giving fifty shares to A, fifty shares to B, fifty shares to C and fifty shares to D because he has not indicated which of the identical shares A is to have and which B is to have. I do not accept that. That such a testamentary bequest is valid, appears sufficiently from the cases of *In re Clifford*[45] and *In re Cheadle*.[46] It seems to me, again, that if a person holds, say, two-hundred

---

44 *Supra,* note 21.
45 [1912] 1 Ch. 29.
46 [1900] 2 Ch. 620.

ordinary shares in ICI and he executes a transfer of fifty ordinary shares in ICI either to an individual donee or to trustees, and hands over the certificate for his two-hundred shares and the transfer to the transferees or to brokers to give effect to the transfer, there is a valid gift to the individual or trustees/transferees of the fifty shares without any further identification of their numbers. It would be a completed gift without waiting for registration of the transfer. (See *In re Rose*[47]). In the ordinary way a new certificate would be issued for the fifty shares to the transferee and the transferor would receive a balance certificate in respect of the rest of his holding. I see no uncertainty at all in those circumstances.

Mr Hartman, however, relied on two authorities in particular. One is a decision of Oliver J. (as he then was) in the case of *Re London Wine Company Shippers Limited*[48] which was decided in 1975. That was a case in which the business of the company was that of dealers in wine and over a period it had acquired stocks of wine which were deposited in various warehouses in England. Quantities were then sold to customers (but in many instances the wine remained at the warehouse) by the company. There was no appropriation — on the ground, as it were — from bulk, of any wine, to answer particular contracts. But the customer received from the company a certificate of title for wine for which he had paid which described him as the sole and beneficial owner of such-and-such wine of such-and-such a vintage. The customer was charged for storage and insurance, but specific cases were not segregated or identified.

Subsequently, at a stage when large stocks of wine were held in various warehouses to the order of the company and its customers, a receiver was appointed by a debenture holder. The question that arose was whether the customers who had received these certificates of title had a good title to the quantity of wine referred to in the certificate as against the receiver appointed under a floating charge. The learned judge held that it could not be said that the legal title to the wine had passed to individual customers and the description of the wine did not adequately link it with any given consignment or warehouse. And, furthermore, it appeared that there was a lack of comparison at the time the certificates were issued in that, in some cases, the certificates were issued before the wine which had been ordered by the company had actually been received by the company. It seems to me that that case is a long way from the present. It is concerned with the appropriation of chattels and when the property in chattels passes. We are concerned with a declaration of trust, accepting that the legal title remained in Mr Moss and was not intended, at the time the trust was declared, to pass immediately to Mr Hunter. Mr Moss was to retain the shares as trustee for Mr Hunter.

Mr Hartman also referred to a case of *Mac-Jordon Construction Limited v. Brookmount Erostin Limited*,[49] a decision of this court. The position there was that Mac-Jordon were sub-contractors for Brookmount as main contractors. There was retention money kept back by Brookmount which, on the documents, was to be held on a trust for the sub-contractors, but it had not been set aside as a separate

---

47 [1952] 1 Ch. 499.
48 [1986] P.C.C. 121.
49 (1991), 56 B.L.R. 1.

fund when a receiver was appointed by the main contractor, Brookmount's, bank. It was, consequently, held that Mac-Jordon was not entitled to payment in full of the retention moneys in priority to the receiver and the secured creditor. It was common ground in that case that, prior to the appointment of the receivers, there were no identifiable assets of Brookmount impressed with the trust applicable to the retention fund. At best, there was merely a general bank account.

In reliance on that case Mr Hartman submits that no fiduciary relationship can attach to an unappropriated portion of a mixed fund. The only remedy is that of a floating charge. He refers to a passage in the judgment of Lord Greene MR *In re Diplock*[50] where he said:

> The narrowness of the limits within which the common law operated may be linked with the limited nature of the remedies available to it ... In particular, the device of a declaration of charge was unknown to the common law and it was the availability of that device which enabled equity to give effect to its wider conception of equitable rights.

So Mr Hartman submits that the most that Mr Hunter could claim is to have an equitable charge on a blended fund. He mentions the decision of Chitty J in *In re Earl of Lucan*[51] which points out that, where there was merely an equitable charge which did not grant perfect and complete rights to the chargee and it was given by way of gift to a volunteer, there could be no specific performance in favour of the volunteer who would have no priority over the creditors of the grantor. As I see it, however, we are not concerned in this case with a mere equitable charge over a mixed fund. Just as a person can give, by will, a specified number of his shares of a certain class in a certain company, so equally, in my judgment, he can declare himself trustee of fifty of his ordinary shares in MEL or whatever the company may be and that is effective to give a beneficial proprietary interest to the beneficiary under the trust. No question of a blended fund thereafter arises and we are not in the field of equitable charge.

Therefore, I agree with the learned Deputy Judge on the conclusion of the uncertainty point which he dealt with in his November judgment.

Notes and Questions

1. *Hunter v. Moss* is a controversial case. Before passing judgment, however, it is necessary to know why the law requires certainty of subject matter. What are the reasons for that rule? Is the Court of Appeal's decision consistent with those reasons?

2. How did the Court of Appeal distinguish the facts before them from those in *Re London Wine Company Shippers Limited*? Is Dillon L.J.'s analysis convincing? Is there a material difference between wine and shares?

3. Shortly after *Hunter v. Moss* was decided, the Privy Council delivered its advice in *Re Goldcorp*.[52] The defendant, a bullion dealer, sold gold to customers. Under the terms of the sale contracts, the customers did not take immediate possession of any property. Rather, they were issued certificates and were entitled, on seven days' notice, to take

---

50 [1948] 1 Ch. 465 at 519.
51 (1890), 45 Ch. 470.
52 [1995] 1 A.C. 74 (P.C.).

physical possession of the appropriate amount of gold. The company also promised that it would always retain sufficient amounts of gold to meet all of its obligations. Unfortunately, the company later collapsed and a dispute arose as to the ownership of the bullion in the defendant's possession. A bank claimed to be entitled as a result of holding a floating charge over all of the defendant's assets. The purchasers also claimed to be entitled to the gold on the ground that the defendant held it on trust for them.

There were several categories of customers. One category consisted of people who had purchased distinct pieces of gold that the defendant kept separate from its general holdings. Because of that separation, title and risk passed to the individual customers. When the defendant collapsed, those customers were able to take possession of the appropriate amounts of gold. The outcome was less favourable for another category of customers, known as "non-allocated claimants." Under their purchase contracts, the defendant was not required to physically separate out and set aside pieces of gold on a case-by-case basis. Instead, the purchasers merely were entitled, under normal circumstances, to draw from an undifferentiated mass. The Privy Council held that since individual allotments had never been ascertained, property never passed. The purchasers consequently had no legal or equitable interest in the remaining gold. Is that decision consistent with *Hunter v. Moss*?

4. Suppose that, after declaring the trust in *Hunter v. Moss*, the defendant physically gave 475 shares to X, and the other 475 shares to Y, as gifts. Would the trust in favour of the plaintiff continue to exist? If so, who currently is holding the relevant shares: X or Y? Would your analysis be any different if instead of shares (each of which bears a distinct registration number), the property involved was 950 silver dollars (which are indistinguishable)?

Likewise, what if the defendant, after declaring himself to be trustee of 50 shares, sold 50 shares to a *bona fide* purchaser for value without notice? Has he committed a breach of trust by selling property to which the plaintiff is beneficially entitled?

5. In *Hunter v. Moss*, Dillon L.J. drew an analogy to cases in which the courts allow a testamentary disposition of a specific number of unascertained shares from an undifferentiated mass. Is the analogy sound? Is there a significant difference between the obligations performed by an executor and those performed by a trustee?[53]

6. A husband and wife entered into a separation agreement. The husband purported to settle property in favour of his wife for life or until remarriage, remainder to his two children. The subject matter of the settlement was to consist of three-fifths of the settlor's net estate on his death.[54] Was the subject matter of the trust void for uncertainty? What if the husband intended to create an *inter vivos* trust that was created immediately, but that was intended to take effect upon his death? What if he intended to create a testamentary trust?

7. A testatrix, after making several specific bequests, gave her residuary estate to A for his own use, as she had full confidence in him that, if he should die without lawful issue, he would, after providing for his widow during her life, leave "the bulk of" her residuary estate to B, C, D and E equally. What does A take? Does he take personally or as a trustee? If he takes as the latter and the trust fails, can he then take personally?[55]

---

53 See M. Ockelton, "Share and Share Alike?" (1994), 53 Cambridge L.J. 451; D. Hayton, "Uncertainty of Subject-Matter of Trusts" (1994), 110 L.Q. Rev. 335.

54 *Beardmore Trusts, Re* (1951), [1952] 1 D.L.R. 41, [1951] O.W.N. 728, 1951 CarswellOnt 304 (Ont. H.C.).

55 *Palmer v. Simmonds* (1854), 2 Drew. 221, 61 E.R. 704 (Eng. Ch. Div.).

8. See also *Green v. Ontario*,[56] which involved an action by Pollution Probe to preserve Sandbanks Provincial Park. One of the claims made by the plaintiff was that the Ontario government and Lake Ontario Cement Ltd., both defendants, were in breach of a statutory trust established under the *Provincial Parks Act*[57] which provides that:

> All provincial parks are dedicated to the people of the Province of Ontario and others who may use them for their healthful enjoyment and education, and the provincial parks shall be maintained for the benefit of future generations in accordance with this Act....

The court held that no trust had been created. There was no certainty of subject matter since s. 3(2) of the Act empowered the government to increase, decrease or delimit the physical size of any park.

9. Several provincial statutes create "deemed trusts".[58] They say that moneys meant to be set aside for such things as taxes collected or deducted are deemed to be subject to a trust in favour of the Crown. As discussed in Chapter 1, however, deemed trusts raise a number of issues, including the extent to which they confer priority in the event of bankruptcy.

(c) Uncertainty in the Quantum of the Beneficiaries' Interest

A trust will fail and the property will result to the creator's estate if the quantum of the beneficial shares is uncertain. However, the requirement of certainty of quantum of the beneficiaries' interest is unusual in that the courts have accepted that this kind of uncertainty can be cured. The first "cure" occurs when the creator gives the trustees the discretion to decide quantum. Note that this must be done expressly as the courts will not imply such a discretion. Second, in appropriate circumstances, the court will rely on the equitable maxim "equity is equality" to cure uncertainty of quantum. A third possible cure for uncertainty in the quantum of a beneficiary's interest was set down in *Re Golay's Will Trusts*,[59] below.

RE GOLAY'S WILL TRUSTS

[1965] 1 W.L.R. 969, [1965] 2 All E.R. 660
Chancery Division

A testator provided in his will:

> I direct my executors to let Tossy — Mrs. F. Bridgewater — enjoy one of my flats during her lifetime and to receive a reasonable income from my other properties; she is, if she so wishes, to wear any of my jewellery, car, etc., until her death. Nothing to be distracted, given, or loaned to any of her relations or friends, money or goods.

---

56 (1972), [1973] 2 O.R. 396, 34 D.L.R. (3d) 20, 1972 CarswellOnt 438 (Ont. H.C.).
57 R.S.O. 1970, c. 371, s. 2.
58 See, for example, *Employment Standards Act*, R.S.O. 1990, c. E.14 and *Pension Benefits Act*, R.S.O. 1990, c. P.8.
59 [1965] 1 W.L.R. 969, [1965] 2 All E.R. 660 (Ch. Div.).

The executor made application to the court to determine whether the direction to permit Mrs. Bridgewater to receive a "reasonable income" from the testator's properties was void for uncertainty.

UNGOED-THOMAS J.:

. . .

Another question that arises is whether this gift of reasonable income fails for uncertainty.

There are two classes of cases with which I am concerned in interpreting this particular provision in the will: the first is where a discretion is given to specified persons to quantify the amount; the other class of case is where no such discretion is expressly conferred upon any specified person.

It is common ground that in this case the trustees are not given a discretion so that if "reasonable income" does not fail for uncertainty then it would be open to a beneficiary to go to court to ascertain whether any amount quantified by the trustees was a "reasonable" amount in accordance with the provisions of the will.

Does this gift of a "reasonable income" without specifying any person to quantify it fail for uncertainty?

The principal case referred to on this question was *Jackson v. Hamilton*,[60] an Irish case, where the testator:

> did devise, and by his will request that his said trustees should from time to time retain in their hands any reasonable sum or sums of money which should be sufficient to renumerate them for the trouble they should have in carrying the trusts of his will into execution.

It seems from the report that no objection on the ground of uncertainty was taken against the quantum. It was also argued before me that in that case a discretion was in the first place given to the trustees to decide what the amount should be and that the master quantified the amount, so that the court would merely have been exercising the discretion which the will had given to the trustees and had been surrendered to the court. But the master, when the matter came before him, had no difficulty in quantifying what was "reasonable" remuneration and Sir Edward Burtenshaw Sugden L.C. confirmed the course which the master had taken. Indeed, it is conceded in this case — and I think rightly conceded — that the court would have no difficulty in quantifying "reasonable income."

It is, however, submitted that what the court is concerned with in the interpretation of this will is not to ascertain what is "reasonable income" in the opinion of the court but to ascertain the testator's intention in using the words "reasonable income."

The question therefore comes to this: Whether the testator by the words "reasonable income" has given a sufficient indication of his intention to provide

---

60 (1846), 3 J. & Lat. 702, 705.

an effective determinant of what he intends so that the court in applying that determinant can give effect to the testator's intention.

Whether the yardstick of "reasonable income" were applied by trustees under a discretion given to them by a testator or applied by a court in the course of interpreting and applying the words "reasonable income" in a will, the yardstick sought to be applied by the trustees in the one case and the court in the other case would be identical. The trustee might be other than the original trustees named by the testator and the trustees could even surrender their discretion to the court. It would seem to me to be drawing too fine a distinction to conclude that an objective yardstick which different persons sought to apply would be too uncertain, not because of uncertainty in the yardstick but as between those who seek to apply it.

In this case, however, the yardstick indicated by the testator is not what he or some other specified person subjectively considers to be reasonable but what he identifies objectively as "reasonable income." The court is constantly involved in making such objective assessments of what is reasonable and it is not to be deterred from doing so because subjective influences can never be wholly excluded. In my view the testator intended by "reasonable income" the yardstick which the court could and would apply in quantifying the amount so that the direction in the will is not in my view defeated by uncertainty.

Notes and Questions

1. Do you agree with the decision in *Re Golay* that the words "reasonable income" can be determined objectively? If so, describe how that can be done.

2. Is the trust in *Re Golay* fixed or discretionary? If discretionary, what discretion is in the trustees? Can "reasonable income" have more than one possible quantification? If so, is it possible to implicitly vest a discretion in the courts to decide quantum?

3. Why is uncertainty of quantum "curable" when uncertainty of object and intention are not?

4. Can the *Saunders v. Vautier*[61] principle be invoked to cure an uncertainty in the quantum of beneficial interest? Give reasons for your answer.

5. T left, among other things, three houses to his trustees in trust for his wife for life, then in trust to convey one house to his daughter M, as she should select, and the other two houses to his daughter C. All parties mentioned in the will, except C, predeceased the testator. What interest does C have in the estate?[62] Is it acceptable to give the power of selection to a beneficiary? Should it be?

6. Does constitution cure uncertainty of subject-matter? If so, how? Refer back to this question after completing the heading on constitution, below.

---

61 (1841), 4 Beav. 115, 49 E.R. 282, affirmed (1841), 1 Cr. & Ph. 240, 41 E.R. 482.
62 See *Boyce v. Boyce* (1849), 16 Sim. 476, 60 E.R. 959.

6. CERTAINTY OF OBJECTS

(a) Introduction

The third requirement that all trusts must meet in order to be valid is that the objects must be described with sufficient certainty. The phrase "certainty of objects" is used to describe two very different concepts. First, it sometimes is used to indicate that a trust must be in favour of persons, not non-charitable purposes. More often, however, it is used to indicate that the class of beneficiaries must be described with sufficient certainty as to facilitate the performance of the trust. This section deals with that second conception of "certainty of objects."

Certainty of objects is required because, unless the objects are clearly specified at the time of distribution, the trustee cannot be sure that they are performing properly. The requirement of certainty of objects is also important to the creator of the trust and the beneficiaries. The creator must be assured that the trustees will carry out his or her intention. If the creator has not defined the class to be benefited in sufficiently clear terms, there can be no assurance that the intended class will take. The beneficiaries have an obvious interest in the requirement. If the class of objects is not sufficiently well-defined, no one can know whether he or she is a member of the class and therefore entitled to a proprietary interest in the subject-matter of the trust. The beneficiaries will be unable to join together and terminate the trust once all are *sui juris* and absolutely entitled. Indeed, the court itself has an interest in having the class adequately defined for, if the trustees fail to distribute, the court must be able to step in and perform. A trust that fails to pass the certainty of objects test will fail and the property will result to the settlor or testator's estate.

The test for certainty of objects is different for a fixed trust than for a discretionary trust. As will be seen in the following sections, the former is subject to the "class ascertainability" test whereas the latter must comply with the "individual ascertainability" test. The individual ascertainability test is rife with ambiguities as the final section in this heading illustrates.

Further Reading

J.W. Harris, "Trust, Power and Duty" (1971), 87 L.Q. Rev. 31.

J. Hopkins, "Certain Uncertainties of Trusts and Powers," [1971] C.L.J. 68.

Y.F.R. Grbich, "Certainty of Objects: The Rule That Never Was" (1973), 5 N.Z.U.L. Rev. 348.

G.E. Palmer, "Private Trusts for Indefinite Beneficiaries" (1972), 71 Mich L. Rev. 359.

L. McKay, "Re Baden and the Criterion of Validity" (1974), 7 V.U.W.L. Rev. 258.

M.C. Cullity, "Fiduciary Powers" (1976), 54 Can. Bar Rev. 229.

R. Burgess, "The Certainty Problem" (1979), 30 N.I.L.Q. 24.

(b) Test for Certainty of Objects of a Fixed Trust: Class Ascertainability

In the case of a fixed trust, it must be possible to ascertain each and every object so that the trustees can make a complete list of all beneficiaries. This is known as the class ascertainability test.

A moment's reflection on the nature of a fixed trust will illustrate why this requirement is necessary. A fixed trust is one in which the trustees have no discretion to decide who the beneficiaries are nor in what proportions they are to take; the shares or interests of the beneficiaries are specified in the trust instrument or are ascertainable and to perform the trustees must know the identity of each and every beneficiary. For example, a trust of $10,000 "to the members of my family in equal shares" is a fixed trust. Unless the trustees know who all the family members are, they cannot distribute equally.

Notes and Questions

1. Explain why the example given in the text to this heading — "$10,000 to be held in trust for the members of my family in equal shares" — is a fixed trust. Does it pass the certainty of objects test for a fixed trust? Why or why not?

2. Is the class ascertainability test concerned with conceptual or evidential uncertainty?

3. A testatrix left $10,000 in trust in equal shares for her aged housekeepers. She had four housekeepers whose ages, at the time of her death, were 21, 45, 87 and 89.

(i) Is the trust fixed or discretionary?

(ii) Does the description "aged housekeepers" pass the certainty of objects test? Should it?

(iii) Reconsider your answer to question 2 above.

(c) Test for Certainty of Objects of a Discretionary Trust: Individual Ascertainability

(i) *McPhail v. Doulton*

Until the House of Lords' decision in *McPhail v. Doulton*,[63] below, the courts drew a sharp distinction between the certainty requirement for objects of a power of appointment and that for a discretionary trust. Until the *McPhail* case, all trusts, whether fixed or discretionary, were subject to the class ascertainability test set out above.

The test for certainty of objects of a power of appointment, on the other hand, was that of individual ascertainability. That test asks: can it be said with certainty "that any given individual is or is not a member of the class?" *McPhail v. Doulton* held that the test for certainty of objects for a discretionary trust should be essentially the same as the certainty of objects test for a power of appointment.[64]

---

63 [1971] A.C. 424, [1970] 2 All E.R. 228 (H.L.).

64 See the judgment of Lord Upjohn in *Re Gulbenkian's Settlement Trusts*, [1968] 3 All E.R. 785, [1970] A.C. 508 (H.L.).

Thus, there is now no need to be able to ascertain every member of the class of objects of a discretionary trust.

Note that the two tests are now "assimilated"; they are not identical. The differences that exist arise from the caveat that Lord Wilberforce added in his judgment in *McPhail v. Doulton* when assimilating the tests. He said that discretionary trusts which pass the individual ascertainability test may fail if "the definition of beneficiaries is so hopelessly wide as not to form 'anything like a class' so that the trust is administratively unworkable."

The reasons for the assimilation of the two tests are set out in Lord Wilberforce's judgment in *McPhail v. Doulton*, below. They are that: discretionary trusts and powers of appointment held by trustees are very similar in nature; a trustee's obligations under a discretionary trust are similar to those of a trustee holding a power of appointment; and a trustee need not distribute the subject-matter of a discretionary trust in equal shares.

McPHAIL v. DOULTON

[1971] A.C. 424, [1970] 2 All E.R. 228
House of Lords

Mr. Baden established a trust the subject-matter of which was shares in Mathew Hall & Co. Ltd. The fund was intended to benefit the officers and employees, both past and present, of the company and their relatives or dependants. The trustees were given absolute discretion to apply the net income of the fund among the class of beneficiaries but no person was to have an interest in the fund other than pursuant to the exercise of this discretion.

Mr. Baden died in 1960. The executors of his estate claimed that clause 9 of the trust was invalid for reasons of uncertainty and any assets that had been transferred to the trustees should revert to the estate.

Clause 9 provided that:

9.(a) The trustees shall apply the net income of the fund in making at their absolute discretion grants to or for the benefit of any of the officers and employees or ex-officers or ex-employees of the company or to any relatives or dependants of any such persons in such amounts at such times and on such conditions (if any) as they think fit and any such grant may at their discretion be made by payment to the beneficiary or to any institution or person to be applied for his or her benefit and in the latter case the trustees shall be under no obligation to see to the application of the money.

At first instance, the Chancery Division held that clause 9 created a power and that it was valid. On appeal, the majority of the Court of Appeal sustained the holding as to the existence of a power but ordered the matter back to the Chancery Division for a further hearing to determine whether the provision was valid. The executors then appealed to the House of Lords on the question whether the provision was a power of appointment or a trust and whether the provision was sufficiently certain.

LORD WILBERFORCE:

. . .

The present proceedings were started in 1963 by an originating summons taken out in the Chancery Division by the trustees of the deed seeking the decision of the court upon various questions, including that of the validity or otherwise of the trusts of the deed. It came before Goff J. in 1967. He first decided that the references in clauses 9 and 12 to employees of the company were not limited to the "staff" but comprised all the officers and employees of the company. There was no appeal against this.

On the main question of validity, the learned judge was, it seems, invited first to decide whether the provisions of clause 9(a) constitute a trust or a power. This was on the basis that certain decided cases (which I shall examine) established a different test of invalidity for trusts on the one hand and powers on the other. He decided in favour of a power, and further that on this footing clause 9(a) was valid. On appeal, the Court of Appeal by a majority upheld the decision in favour of a power, but held also that the learned judge had applied the wrong text for the validity of powers, the correct test being that stated (subsequent to the hearing before Goff J.) by this House in *Re Gulbenkian's Settlement*.[65] The Court of Appeal therefore remitted the case to the Chancery Division to reconsider the validity of clause 9(a) as a power.

In this House, the appellants contend, and this is the first question for consideration, that the provisions of clause 9(a) constitute a trust and not a power. If that is held to be the correct result, both sides agree that the case must return to the Chancery Division for consideration, on this footing, whether this trust is valid. But here comes a complication. In the present state of authority, the decision as to validity would turn on the question whether a complete list (or on another view a list complete for practical purposes) can be drawn up of all possible beneficiaries. This follows from the Court of Appeal's decision in *Inland Revenue Commissioners v. Broadway Cottages Trust*[66] as applied in later cases by which, unless this House decides otherwise, the Court of Chancery would be bound. The respondents invite your Lordships to review this decision and challenge its correctness. So the second issue which arises, if clause 9(a) amounts to a trust, is whether the existing test for its validity is right in law and, if not, what the test ought to be.

Before dealing with these two questions some general observations, or reflections, may be permissible. It is striking how narrow and in a sense artificial is the distinction, in cases such as the present, between trusts or as the particular type of trust is called, trust powers. It is only necessary to read the learned judgments in the Court of Appeal to see that what to one mind may appear as a power of distribution coupled with a trust to dispose of the undistributed surplus, by accumulation or otherwise, may to another appear as a trust for distribution

---

65 *Ibid.*
66 [1955] Ch. 20, [1954] 3 All E.R. 120 (C.A.).

coupled with a power to withhold a portion and accumulate or otherwise dispose of it. A layman and, I suspect, also a logician would find it hard to understand what difference there is.

It does not seem satisfactory that the entire validity of a disposition should depend on such delicate shading. And if one considers how in practice reasonable and competent trustees would act, and ought to act, in the two cases, surely a matter very relevant to the question of validity, the distinction appears even less significant. To say that there is no obligation to exercise a mere power and that no court will intervene to compel it, whereas a trust is mandatory and its execution may be compelled, may be legally correct enough but the proposition does not contain an exhaustive comparison of the duties or persons who are trustees in the two cases. A trustee of an employee's benefit fund, whether given a power or a trust power, is still a trustee and he would surely consider in either case that he has a fiduciary duty: he is most likely to have been selected as a suitable person to administer it from his knowledge and experience, and would consider he has a responsibility to do so according to its purpose. It would be a complete misdescription of his position to say that, if what he has is a power unaccompanied by an imperative trust to distribute, he cannot be controlled by the court if he exercised it capriciously, or outside the field permitted by the trust.[67] Any trustee would surely make it his duty to know what is the permissible area of selection and then consider responsibly, in individual cases, whether a contemplated beneficiary was within the power and whether, in relation to other possible claimants, a particular grant was appropriate.

Correspondingly a trustee with a duty to distribute, particularly among a potentially very large class, would surely never require the preparation of a complete list of names, which anyhow would tell him little that he needs to know. He would examine the field, by class and category; might indeed make diligent and careful inquiries, depending on how much money he had to give away and the means at his disposal, as to the composition and needs of particular categories and of individuals within them; decide upon certain priorities or proportions, and then select individuals according to their needs or qualifications. If he acts in this manner, can it really be said that he is not carrying out the trust?

Differences there certainly are between trusts (trust powers) and powers, but as regards validity, should they be so great as that in one case complete, or practically complete ascertainment is needed, but not in the other? Such distinction as there is would seem to lie in the extent of the survey which the trustee is required to carry out: if he has to distribute the whole of a fund's income, he must necessarily make a wider and more systematic survey than if his duty is expressed in terms of a power to make grants. But just as, in the case of a power, it is possible to underestimate the fiduciary obligation of the trustee to whom it is given, so, in the case of a trust (trust power), the danger lies in overstating what the trustee requires to know or to inquire into before he can properly execute his trust. The difference may be one of degree rather than of principle: in the well-known words

---

67 *Farwell on Powers*, 3rd ed., (1916), at 524.

of Sir George Farwell,[68] trusts and powers are often blended, and the mixture may vary in its ingredients.

With this background I now consider whether the provisions of clause 9(a) constitute a trust or a power. I do so briefly because this is not a matter on which I or, I understand, any of your Lordships have any doubt. Indeed, a reading of the judgments of Goff J. and of the majority in the Court of Appeal leave the strong impression that, if it had not been for their leaning in favour of possible validity and the state of the authorities, these learned judges would have found in favour of a trust. Naturally read, the intention of the deed seems to me clear: clause 9(a), whose language is mandatory ("shall"), creates, together with a power of selection, a trust for distribution of the income, the strictness of which is qualified by clause 9(b), which allows the income of any one year to be held up and (under clause 6(a)) either placed, for the time, with a bank, or, if thought fit, invested. Whether there is, in any technical sense, an accumulation seems to me in the present context a jejune enquiry; what is relevant is that clause 9(c) marks the difference between accumulations of income and the capital of the fund: the former can be distributed by a majority of the trustees, the latter cannot. As to clause 10, I do not find in it any decisive indication. If anything, it seems to point in favour of a trust, but both this and other points of detail are insignificant in the face of the clearly expressed scheme of clause 9. I therefore agree with Russell L.J. and would to that extent allow the appeal, declare that the provisions of clause 9(a) constitute a trust and remit the case to the Chancery Division for determination whether on this basic clause 9 is (subject to the effects of section 164 of the *Law of Property Act, 1925*) valid or void for uncertainty.

This makes it necessary to consider whether, in so doing, the court should proceed on the basis that the relevant test is that laid down in *Inland Revenue Commissioners v. Broadway Cottages Trust* or some other test.

That decision gave the authority of the Court of Appeal to the distinction between cases where trustees are given a power of selection and those where they are bound by a trust for selection. In the former case the position, as decided by this House, is that the power is valid if it can be said with certainty whether any given individual is or is not a member of the class and does not fail simply because it is impossible to ascertain every member of the class. But in the latter case it is said to be necessary, for the trust to be valid, that the whole range of objects (I use the language of the Court of Appeal) should be ascertained or capable of ascertainment.

The respondents invited your Lordships to assimilate the validity test for trusts to that which applies to powers. Alternatively they contended that in any event the test laid down in the *Broadway Cottages* case was too rigid, and that a trust should be upheld if there is sufficient practical certainty in its definition for it to be carried out, if necessary with the administrative assistance of the court, according to the expressed intention of the settlor. I would agree with this, but this does not dispense from examination of the wider argument. The basis for the *Broadway Cottages* principle is stated to be that a trust cannot be valid unless, if

---

68 *Ibid.*, at 10.

need be, it can be executed by the court, and (though it is not quite clear from the judgment where argument ends and decision begins) that the court can only execute it by ordering an equal distribution in which every beneficiary shares. So it is necessary to examine the authority and reason for this supposed rules as to the execution of trust by the court.

Assuming, as I am prepared to do for present purposes, that the test of validity is whether the trust can be executed by the court, it does not follow that execution is impossible unless there can be equal division.

As a matter of reason, to hold that a principle of equal division applies to trusts such as the present is certainly paradoxical. Equal division is surely the last thing the settlor ever intended: equal division among all may, probably would, produce a result beneficial to none. Why suppose that the court would lend itself to a whimsical execution? And as regards authority, I do not find that the nature of the trust, and of the court's powers over trusts, calls for any such rigid rule. Equal division may be sensible and has been decreed, in cases of family trusts for a limited class, here there is life in the maxim "equality is equity," but the cases provide numerous examples where this has not been so, and a different type of execution has been ordered, appropriate to the circumstances.

. . .

In the time of Lord Eldon, the Court of Chancery adopted a less flexible practice: in *Kemp v. Kemp*,[69] Sir Richard Arden M.R., commenting on *Warburton v. Warburton*,[70] ("a very extraordinary" case), said that the court now disclaims the right to execute a power (*i.e.*, a trust power) and gives the fund equally. But I do not think that this change of attitude, or practice, affects the principle that a discretionary trust can, in a suitable case, be executed according to its merits and otherwise than by equal division. I prefer not to suppose that the great masters of equity, if faced with the modern trust for employees, would have failed to adapt their creation to its practical and commercial character. Lord Eldon himself, in *Morice v. Bishop of Durham*[71] laid down clearly enough that a trust fails if the object is insufficiently described or it cannot be carried out, but these principles may be fully applied to trust powers without requiring a complete ascertainment of all possible objects. His earlier judgment in the leading, and much litigated, case of *Brown v. Higgs*,[72] shows that he was far from fastening any rigid test of validity upon trust powers. After stating the distinction, which has ever since been followed, between powers, which the court will not require the donee to execute, and powers in the nature of a trust, or trust powers, he says of the latter that if the trustee does not discharge it, the court will, *to a certain extent*, discharge the duty in his room and place. To support this, he cites *Harding v. Glyn*,[73] an early case

---

69 (1795), 5 Ves. Jr. 849.
70 4 Bro. P.C. 1.
71 (1805), 10 Ves. Jun. 522, 32 E.R. 947 (Ch.).
72 (1803), 8 Ves. Jun. 561, 32 E.R. 473 (Ch.).
73 (1739), 1 Atk. 469.

where the court executed a discretionary trust for "relations" by distributing to the next-of-kin.

I dwell for a moment upon this point because, not only was *Harding v. Glyn* described by Lord Eldon[74] as having been treated as a clear authority in his experience for a long period, but the principle of it was adopted in several 19th century authorities. When the *Broadway Cottages Trust*[75] case came to be decided in 1955, these cases were put aside as anomalous, but I think they illustrate the flexible manner in which the court, if called on, executes trust powers for a class. At least they seem to prove that the supposed rule as to equal division does not rest on any principle inherent in the nature of a trust. They prompt me to ask why a practice, or rule, which has been long followed and found useful in "relations" cases should not also serve in regard to "employees," or "employees and their relatives," and whether a decision which says the contrary is acceptable.

I now consider the modern English authorities, particularly those relied on to show that complete ascertainment of the class must be possible before it can be said that a discretionary trust is valid.

Re H.J. Ogden[76] is not a case which I find of great assistance. The argument seems to have turned mainly on the question whether the trust was a purpose trust or a trust for ascertained objects. The latter was held to be the case and the court then held that all the objects of the discretionary gift could be ascertained. It is weak authority for the requirement of complete ascertainment.

The modern shape of the rule derives from *Re Gestetner Settlement*,[77] where the judgment of Harman J., to his later regret, established the distinction between discretionary powers and discretionary trusts. The focus of this case was upon powers. The judgment first establishes a distinction between, on the one hand, a power collateral, or appurtenant, or other powers "which do not impose a trust on the conscience of the donee"[78] and on the other hand a trust imposing a duty to distribute. As to the first, the learned judge said:[79] "I do not think it can be the law that it is necessary to know of all the objects in order to appoint to one of them." As to the latter he uses these words:[80] "It seems to me there is much to be said for the view that he must be able to review the whole field in order to exercise his judgment properly." He then considers authority on the validity of powers, the main stumbling-block in the way of his own view being some words used by Fry J. in *Blight v. Hartnoll*,[81] which had been adversely commented on in *Farwell on Powers*,[82] and I think it worth while quoting the words of his conclusion. He says:[83]

---

74 *Supra*, note 72, at 570.
75 *Supra*, note 66.
76 [1933] 1 Ch. 678 (Ch. Div.).
77 [1953] Ch. 672 (Ch. Div.).
78 *Ibid.*, at 684.
79 *Ibid.*
80 *Ibid.*, at 685.
81 (1881), 19 Ch. D. 294 at 301 (Ch. Div.).
82 3rd ed., (1916) at 168, 169.
83 *Supra*, note 77, at 688 (Ch. Div.).

The settlor had good reason, I have no doubt, to trust the persons whom he appointed trustees; but I cannot see here that there is such a duty as makes it essential for these trustees, before parting with any income or capital, to survey the whole field, and to consider whether A is more deserving of the bounty then B. That is a task which was and which must have been known to the settlor to be impossible, having regard to the ramifications of the persons who might become members of this class. If, therefore, there be no duty to distribute, but only a duty to consider, it does not seem to me that there is any authority binding on me to say that this whole trust is bad. In fact, there is no difficulty, as has been admitted, in ascertaining whether any given postulant is a member of the specified class. Of course, if that could not be ascertained the matter would be quite different, but of John Doe or Richard Doe it can be postulated easily enough whether he is or is not eligible to receive the settlor's bounty. There being no uncertainty in that sense, I am reluctant to introduce a notion of uncertainty in the other sense, by saying that the trustees must worry their heads to survey the world from China to Peru, when there are perfectly good objects of the class in England.

Subject to one point which was cleared up in this House in *Re Gulbenkian's Settlement*, all of this, if I may say so, seems impeccably good sense, and I do not understand the learned judge to have later repented of it. If the judgment was in any way the cause of future difficulties, it was in the indication given — not by way of decision, for the point did not arise — that there was a distinction between the kind of certainty required for powers and that required for trusts. There is a difference perhaps but the difference is a narrow one, and if one is looking to reality one could hardly find better words than those I have just quoted to describe what trustees, in either case, ought to know. A second look at this case, while fully justifying the decision, suggests to me that it does not discourage the application of a similar test for the validity of trusts.

So I come to *Inland Revenue Commissioners v. Broadway Cottages Trust*. This was certainly a case of trust, and it proceeded on the basis of an admission, in the words of the judgment, "that the class of 'beneficiaries' is incapable of ascertainment." In addition to the discretionary trust of income, there was a trust of capital for all the beneficiaries living or existing at the terminal date. This necessarily involved equal division and it seems to have been accepted that it was void for uncertainty since there cannot be equal division among a class unless all the members of the class are known. The Court of Appeal applied this proposition to the discretionary trust of income, on the basis that execution by the court was only possible on the same basis of equal division. They rejected the argument that the trust could be executed by changing the trusteeship, and found the relations case of no assistance as being in a class by themselves. The court could not create an arbitrarily restricted trust to take effect in default of distribution by the trustees. Finally they rejected the submission that the trust could take effect as a power: a valid power could not be spelt out of an invalid trust.

My Lords, it will have become apparent that there is much in this which I find out of line with principle and authority but before I come to a conclusion on it, I must examine the decision of this House in *Re Gulbenkian's Settlement* on which the appellants placed much reliance as amounting to an endorsement of the *Broadway Cottages* case. But is this really so? That case was concerned with a power of appointment coupled with a gift over in default of appointment. The possible objects of the power were numerous and were defined in such wide terms that it could certainly be said that the class was unascertainable. The decision of this House was that the power was valid if it could be said with certainty whether any given individual was or was not a member of the class, and did not fail simply because it was impossible to ascertain every member of the class. In so deciding, their Lordships rejected an alternative submission, to which countenance had been given in the Court of Appeal, that it was enough that one person should certainly be within the class. So, as a matter of decision, the question now before us did not arise or nearly arise. However, the opinions given were relied on, and strongly, as amounting to an endorsement of the "complete ascertainment" test as laid down in the *Broadway Cottages* case.

[His Lordship reviewed the *Gulbenkian* case and concluded that it did not endorse the *Broadway Cottages* case.]

So I think that we are free to review the *Broadway Cottages* case. The conclusion which I would reach, implicit in the previous discussion, is that the wide distinction between the validity test for powers and that for trust powers is unfortunate and wrong, that the rule recently fastened upon the courts by *Inland Revenue Commissioners v. Broadway Cottages Trust* ought to be discarded, and the test for the validity of trust powers ought to be similar to that accepted by this House in *Re Gulbenkian's Settlement* for powers, namely, that the trust is valid if it can be said with certainty that any given individual is or is not a member of the class.

I am interested, and encouraged, to find that the conclusion I had reached by the end of the argument is supported by distinguished American authority, Professor Scott in his well-known book on trusts[84] discusses the suggested distinction as regards a validity between trusts and powers and expresses the opinion that this would be "highly technical." Later in the second *Restatement of Trusts*[85] (which *Restatement* aims at stating the better modern view and which annotates the *Broadway Cottages* case), a common test of invalidity is taken, whether trustees are "authorized" or "directed": this is that the class must not be so indefinite that it cannot be ascertained whether any person falls within it. The reporter is Professor Austin Scott. In his abridgment published in 1960[86] Professor Scott maintains the same position:

It would seem that if a power of appointment among the members of an indefinite class is valid, the mere fact that the testator intended not merely to confer a power but to impose a duty to make such an appointment should not preclude the making of such an appointment. It would seem to be the height of technicality that if a testator *authorises* a legatee to divide the property among such of the testator's friends as he might select, he can properly do so, but that if he *directs* him to make such a selection, he will not be permitted to do so.

Assimilation of the validity test does not involve the complete assimilation of trust powers with powers. As to powers, I agree with my noble and learned

---

84 *Scott on Trusts*, (1939), at 613.
85 (1959), at 122.
86 *Scott's Abridgement of the Laws of Trusts*, at 239.

friend Lord Upjohn in *Re Gulbenkian's Settlement* that although the trustees may, and normally will, be under a fiduciary duty to consider whether or in what way they should exercise their power, the court will not normally compel its exercise. It will intervene if the trustees exceed their powers, and possibly if they are proved to have exercised it capriciously. But in the case of a trust power, if the trustees do not exercise it, the court will: I respectfully adopt as to this the statement in Lord Upjohn's opinion[87] I would venture to amplify this by saying that the court, if called upon to execute the trust power, will do so in the manner best calculated to give effect to the settlor's or testator's intentions. It may do so by appointing new trustees, or by authorising or directing representative persons of the classes of beneficiaries to prepare a scheme of distribution, or even, should the proper basis for distribution appear by itself directing the trustees so to distribute.The books give many instances where this has been done, and I see no reason in principle why they should not do so in the modern field of discretionary trusts (see *Bruden v. Woolredge*,[88] *Supple v. Lowson*,[89] *Liley v. Hey*,[90] and *Lewin on Trusts*).[91] Then, as to the trustee's duty of inquiry or ascertainment, in each case the trustees ought to make such a survey of the range of objects or possible beneficiaries as will enable them to carry out their fiduciary duty. A wider and more comprehensive range of inquiry is called for in the case of trust powers than in the case of powers.

Two final points: first, as to the question of certainty. I desire to emphasise the distinction clearly made and explained by Lord Upjohn[92] between linguistic or semantic uncertainty which, if unresolved by the court, renders the gift void, and the difficulty of ascertaining the existence or whereabouts of members of the class, a matter with which the court can appropriately deal on an application for directions. There may be a third case where the meaning of the words used is clear but the definition of beneficiaries is so hopelessly wide as not to form "anything like a class" so that the trust is administratively unworkable or in Lord Eldon's words one that cannot be executed (*Morice v. Bishop of Durham*).[93] I hesitate to give examples for they may prejudice future cases, but perhaps "all the residents of Greater London" will serve. I do not think that a discretionary trust for "relatives" even of a living person falls within this category.

I would allow the appeal and make the order suggested earlier in this opinion. The costs of the appellants of this appeal taxed on a common fund basis should be paid out of so much of the trust fund subject to the trust deed of July 17, 1941, as was derived from Bertram Baden deceased.

---

87 *Supra*, note 64, at 793 [All E.R.].
88 (1765), 1 Amb. 507.
89 (1773), 2 Amb. 729.
90 (1842), 1 Hare 580.
91 16th ed., (1964), at 630.
92 *Supra*, note 64, at 793 [All E.R.].
93 *Supra*, note 71, at 527.

. . .

[Lord Reid and Viscount Dilhorne agreed with Lord Wilberforce. Lord Guest agreed with Lord Hodson.]

Notes and Questions

1. In *McPhail*, why was clause 9(a) held to be a discretionary trust and not a power of appointment?

2. Is the caveat that Lord Wilberforce adds to the certainty of objects test for discretionary trusts concerned with conceptual or evidentiary difficulties?

3. Of what effect is Lord Wilberforce's caveat prohibiting a class from being "administratively unworkable"?

4. What are the duties of a trustee under a discretionary trust? How do they differ, if at all, from a trustee holding a power of appointment?

5. Why did Lord Wilberforce reject the view that, in the absence of specified proportions, trust property should be distributed in equal shares?

6. Since trustees under a discretionary trust have a duty to make a comprehensive inquiry as to the beneficiaries, what is their liability when the class of beneficiaries is so large that they cannot possibly consider every possible claimant? Should they take out insurance for this purpose? Should the trustees invariably make application to the court to protect themselves?

7. Lord Wilberforce suggests in *McPhail v. Doulton* that a trust for "all the residents of Greater London" would be void. Would a power of appointment for the benefit of such a class also be void? If so, why? Would such a trust be void if the trust instrument contained criteria for choosing which residents were to benefit and in what degree?

8. The Supreme Court of Canada drew upon *McPhail v. Doulton* in *Jones v. T. Eaton Co.*[94] That case involved a charitable purpose trust for the benefit of the "Toronto members of the Eaton Quarter Century Club." That club was made up of people who had worked for the T. Eaton Company for twenty-five years or more. Spence J. said that it was "a matter of some little difficulty to determine the meaning of the words 'Toronto members'." Nevertheless, he read those words in the context of the settlor's entire will, applied Lord Wilberforce's test and found that there was sufficient certainty.

> The testator would mean those members who were employed by the company in Toronto at the time when they became members. If they were members when the testator was a member and when he was still employed by the company, it is almost inevitable that he would have a degree of acquaintance with persons with such seniority in the service of the company. . . . I do not think the testator would have been concerned with whether those who worked in the Toronto store when they became members of the Quarter Century Club lived within the strict environs of Toronto or close by. They might well have lived in a suburban area. After their retirement, they might continue to live in that area or in some more salubrious climate. What influenced the testator in his choice of the words "Toronto members" was his thinking of those who had spent twenty-five years working, as he had, for the T. Eaton Company right in Toronto.

Because *Jones* involved a charitable purpose trust, rather than a personal trust, certainty of objects was not necessary for the *validity* of the disposition; it was relevant, instead, to

---

94 [1973] S.C.R. 635, 35 D.L.R. (3d) 97, 1973 CarswellOnt 227, 1973 CarswellOnt 227F (S.C.C.).

the actual *distribution* of the property. Charitable purpose trusts are examined elsewhere in this book.

The Supreme Court of Canada has not yet approved of *McPhail v. Doulton* in the context of a personal trust. Should it do so when the opportunity arises?

(ii) *Ambiguities in the Individual Ascertainability Test*

After *McPhail v. Doulton* was decided, the case was remitted to the Chancery Division to determine whether the class of objects including "dependants" and "relatives" was certain. The ambiguities inherent in the test for certainty of objects of a discretionary trust became obvious when all three judges in the Court of Appeal in *Re Baden's Deed Trusts (No. 2)*,[95] below, differed in their interpretations of the test.

There are at least five ambiguities inherent in the test.

First, how does one distinguish between that which is conceptually certain and that which is conceptually uncertain?

Second, what happens if there are several categories of potential beneficiaries, some of which pass the certainty test and others which do not?

Third, must a beneficiary show that he or she is included in the class or is it sufficient to show that he or she is not excluded?

Fourth, do the words "given individual" exclude hypothetical applicants?

Fifth, when have a sufficient number of objects qualified for inclusion so that the trustees may conclude that the class is certain and they may distribute?

RE BADEN'S DEED TRUSTS (No. 2)

(1972), [1973] Ch. 9, [1972] 2 All E.R. 1304
Court of Appeal

A settlor established a trust to benefit the officers and employees or ex-officers or ex-employees of a company, or any relatives or dependants of such persons.[96] The trustees were given full discretion to decide what amounts, if any, were to go to such persons. The House of Lords held that the settlement created a discretionary trust and not a power. It applied the individual ascertainability test to determine whether the class of objects was described with sufficient certainty. The House of Lords then remitted the case to the Chancery Division to determine whether, on the new test, the trust was valid. The Chancery Division held that the words "dependants" and "relatives" were sufficiently certain to enable the court to come to a conclusion in any given case whether a particular person was within the class. The executors appealed the decision.

SACHS L.J.:

---

95 (1972), [1973] Ch. 9, [1972] 2 All E.R. 1304 (C.A.).

96 See *McPhail v. Doulton supra*, note 63, reproduced, in part, above.

. . .

It is submitted on behalf of the defendant executors that each of the words "relatives" and "dependants" imports such an uncertainty that the trusts as a whole are void.

The test to be applied to each of these words is: "can it be said with certainty that any given individual is or is not a member of the class?" per Lord Wilberforce,[97] words which reflect those of Lord Reid and Lord Upjohn in *Re Gulbenkian's Settlement Trusts*.[98] Being in general agreement, as already indicated, with everything that Brightman J.[99] has said as regards the two relevant words, it is sufficient first to make some observations as to the approach to be adopted to the questions raised before us and then in the light of those observations to deal comparatively compactly with the effect of the use of the two relevant words.

It is first to be noted that the deed must be looked at through the eyes of a businessman seeking to advance the welfare of the employees of his firm and of those so connected with the employees that a benevolent employer would wish to help them. He would not necessarily be looking at the words he uses with the same eyes as those of a man making a will. Accordingly, whether a court is considering the concept implicit in relevant words, or whether it is exercising the function of a court of construction, it should adopt that same practical and common sense approach which was enjoined by Upjohn J. in *Re Sayer Trust*[100] and by Lord Wilberforce in the present case[101] and which would be used by an employer setting up such a fund.

The next point as regards approach that requires consideration is the contention, strongly pressed by counsel for the defendant executors, that the court must always be able to say whether any given postulant is not within the relevant class as well as being able to say whether he is within it. In construing the words already cited from the speech of Lord Wilberforce in the present case (as well as those of Lord Reid and Lord Upjohn in the *Gulbenkian* case),[102] it is essential to bear in mind the difference between conceptual uncertainty and evidential difficulties. That distinction is explicitly referred to by Lord Wilberforce when he said:[103]

> . . . as to the question of certainty, I desire to emphasise the distinction clearly made and explained by Lord Upjohn, between linguistic or semantic uncertainty which, if unresolved by the court, renders the gift void, and the difficulty of ascertaining the existence of the whereabouts of members of the class, a matter with which the court can appropriately deal on an application for directions.

As counsel for the defendant executors himself rightly observed, "the court is never defeated by evidential uncertainty," and it is in my judgment clear that it is

---

97 *Ibid.*, at 450.
98 *Supra*, note 64, at 518, 521, 525.
99 [1971] 3 All E.R. 985 (H.L.).
100 [1957] Ch. 423 at 436, [1956] 3 All E.R. 600.
101 *Supra*, note 63, at 452.
102 *Supra*, note 64, at 518, 521, 525.
103 *Supra*, note 63, at 457.

conceptual certainty to which reference was made when the "is or is not a member of the class" test was enunciated. (Conceptual uncertainty was in the course of argument conveniently exemplified, rightly or wrongly matters not, by the phrase "someone under a moral obligation" and contrasted with the certainty of the words "first cousins.") Once the class of persons to be benefited is conceptually certain it then becomes a question of fact to be determined on evidence whether any postulant has on enquiry been proved to be within it; if he is not so proved then he is not in it. That position remains the same whether the class to be benefited happens to be small (such as "first cousins") or large (such as "members of the X Trade Union" or "those who have served in the Royal Navy"). The suggestion that such trusts could be invalid because it might be impossible to prove of a given individual that he was not in the relevant class is wholly fallacious — and only the persuasiveness of counsel for the defendant executors has prevented me from saying that the contention is almost unarguable.

. . .

Turning now to the word "dependants" — a word used over several generations in comparable trust deeds — I confess that the suggestion that it is uncertain seems no longer arguable. In *Simmons v. White Brothers*[104] Collins L.J., albeit when considering that word when used in the *Workmen's Compensation Act, 1897*, quoted with approval the following passage from the then current work dealing with that subject:

> It would be hopeless to attempt to lay down any rule of guidance, because every case would probably differ in some material circumstance from almost every other. Dependent probably means dependent for the ordinary necessaries of life for a person of that class and position in life. Thus the financial and social position of the recipient of compensation would have to be taken into account. That which would make one person dependent upon another would in another case merely cause the one to receive benefit from the other. Each case must stand on its own merits and be decided as a question of fact . . .

It is true that the court was then dealing with a specific Act, but the good sense of the above quotation has, in relation to the meaning of "dependant," a general application and has frequently been cited with approval. It demonstrates, incidentally, that such difficulties as may arise in determining whether an individual is a dependant are evidential and raise questions of fact and not of law. Indeed the whole stream of authority runs counter to the contentions put forward on behalf of the defendant executors — save only the first instance decision in *Re Ball*,[105] a will case which would probably be decided differently today. In agreement with the practical approach of Brightman J.,[106] I consider that the trustees, or if necessary the court, are quite capable of coming to a conclusion in any given case whether or not a particular candidate could properly be described

---

104 [1899] 1 Q.B. 1005 at 1007 (C.A.).
105 [1947] Ch. 228, [1947] 1 All E.R. 458.
106 *Supra*, note 99, at 994.

as a dependant — a word that, as the learned judge said, "conjures up a sufficiently distinct picture." I agree, too, that any one wholly or partly dependent on the means of another is a "dependant." There is thus no conceptual uncertainty inherent in that word and the defendant executors' contentions as to the effect of its use fail.

As regards "relatives" Brightman J.,[107] after stating "It is not in dispute that a person is a relative of an . . . employee . . . if both trace legal descent from a common ancestor," a little later said:[108] "In practice the use of the expression 'relatives' cannot cause the slightest difficulty." With that view I agree for the reasons he gave when he correctly set out the evidential position.

As regards the suggested uncertain numerative range of that concept of the word "relative" (a matter which strictly would only be relevant to the abandoned "administratively unworkable" point) and also when considering the practical side of the functions of the trustees, it is germane to note that in *Re Scarisbrick's Will Trusts*[109] Sir Raymond Evershed M.R. observed with regard to a class of "relations": "That class is, in theory, capable of almost infinite expansion, but proof of relationship soon becomes extremely difficult in fact." That factor automatically narrows the field within which the trustees select. Further, a settlor using the word "relatives" in the context of this deed (which is not the same context as that of a will) would assume that the trustees would in the exercise of their discretion make their selection in a sensible way from the field, however wide. Thus in practice they would presumably select those whom a reasonable and honest employee or ex-employee would introduce as "relative," rather than as a "kinsman" or as a "distant relative." Indeed, on a construction summons some such definition might emerge for the word "relative" — but that is not relevant to the present appeal as the widest meaning that has been suggested for that word does not in my judgment produce uncertainty.

As a footnote to this conclusion it is interesting to observe that no case was cited to us in which a court has actually decided that a trust was invalid on account of the use of that word, whatever may have been said *obiter*. If this is due to a tendency to construe deeds and wills so as to give effect to them rather than to invalidate trusts, that is an approach which is certainly in accord with modern thought. I would accordingly dismiss this appeal.

MEGAW L.J.:

If this trust were to be held void for uncertainty because of the inclusion of the word "dependants" in clause 9 (a), I think that few trusts would stand. I do not find any greater uncertainty in it than is inherent in, or can by ingenuity be conjured up in relation to, any ordinary, well-understood word. It would be odd indeed, and wholly regrettable, if a word which was regarded as sufficiently certain to be used, without further explanation or definition, for the purposes of

---

107 *Ibid.*, at 995 (H.L.).
108 *Ibid.*
109 [1951] Ch. 622 at 632, [1951] 1 All E.R. 822.

an Act of Parliament[110] had nevertheless to be condemned by the courts as being so uncertain as to involve the validity of a trust deed.

Then it is said that the deed is invalid because of the inclusion of the word "relatives." Brightman J.[111] approached that question on the basis that:

> It is not in dispute that a person is a relative of an officer or employee or ex-officer or ex-employee, if both trace legal descent from a common ancestor.

He held that the executors' argument on this issue also failed. I agree, for the reasons given by the learned judge. But out of deference to the clear and forceful submission addressed to us by counsel for the defendant executors, I shall state in my own words why in my judgment that submission is wrong.

First, lest there should be any suggestion that the inclusion of "relatives" makes this trust so wide as to be administratively unworkable, I would respectfully agree with Lord Wilberforce's words — *obiter dicta*, it is true — when the present case was earlier considered by the House of Lords:[112] "I do not think that a discretionary trust for 'relatives' even of a living person falls within the category." Lord Wilberforce's *dictum* was, I have no doubt, directed towards the terms of this particular trust deed. I do not think it was intended to be confined, or ought to be confined, to a provision specifying one single living person. It is apt as regards relatives of employees in the plural. Such a trust is not administratively unworkable.

The main argument of counsel for the defendant executors was founded on a strict and literal interpretation of the words in which the decision of the House of Lords in *Re Gulbenkian's Settlement Trusts* was expressed. That decision laid down the test for the validity of powers of selection. It is relevant for the present case, because in the previous excursion of this case to the House of Lords it was held that there is no relevant difference in the test of validity, whether the trustees are given a power of selection or, as was held by their Lordships to be the case in this trust deed, a trust for selection. The test in either case is what may be called the *Gulbenkian* test. The *Gulbenkian* test, as expressed by Lord Wilberforce[113] (and again in almost identical words in a later passage) is this:

> . . . whether any given individual is or is not a member of the class and does not fail simply because it is impossible to ascertain every member of the class.

The executors' argument concentrates on the words "or is not" in the first of the two limbs of the sentence quoted above: "if it can be said with certainty whether any given individual is or is not a member of the class." It is said that those words have been used deliberately, and have only one possible meaning; and that, however startling or drastic or unsatisfactory the result may be — and

---

110 See, for example, s. 46(i),(vi) of *The Administration of Estates Act*, 1925 (15 & 16 Geo. 5), c. 23.

111 *Supra*, note 99, at 995.

112 *Supra*, note 63, at 457.

113 *Ibid.*, at 450.

counsel for the defendant executors does not shrink from saying that the consequence is drastic — this court is bound to give effect to the words used in the
House of Lords' definition of the test. It would be quite impracticable for the
trustees to ascertain in many cases whether a particular person was not a relative
of an employee. The most that could be said is: There is no proof that he is a
relative. But there would still be no "certainty" that such a person was not a
relative. Hence, so it is said, the test laid down by the House of Lords is not
satisfied, and the trust is void. For it cannot be said with certainty, in relation to
any individual, that he is not a relative.

I do not think it was contemplated that the words "or is not" would produce
that result. It would, as I see it, involve an inconsistency with the latter part of the
same sentence: "does not fail simply because it is impossible to ascertain every
member of the class." The executors' contention, in substance and reality, is that
it does fail "simply because it is impossible to ascertain every member of the
class."

The same verbal difficulty, as I see it, emerges also when one considers the
words of the suggested test which the House of Lords expressly rejected. That is
set out by Lord Wilberforce in a passage[114] immediately following the sentence
which I have already quoted. The rejected test was in these terms: ". . . it is said
to be necessary . . . that the whole range of objects . . . shall be ascertained or
capable of ascertainment." Since that test was rejected, the resulting affirmative
proposition, which by implication must have been accepted by their Lordships,
is this: a trust for selection will not fail simply because the whole range of objects
cannot be ascertained. In the present case, the trustees could ascertain, by investigation and evidence, many of the objects; as to many other theoretically possible
claimants, they could not be certain. Is it to be said that the trust fails because it
cannot be said with certainty that such persons are not members of the class? If
so, is that not the application of the rejected test; the trust failing because "the
whole range of objects cannot be ascertained?"

In my judgment, much too great emphasis is placed in the executors' argument
on the words "or is not." To my mind, the test is satisfied if, as regards at least a
substantial number of objects, it can be said with certainty that they fall within
the trust; even though, as regards a substantial number of other persons, if they
ever for some fanciful reason fell to be considered, the answer would have to be,
not "they are outside the trust," but "it is not proven whether they are in or out."
What is a "substantial number" may well be a question of common sense and of
degree in relation to the particular trust: particularly where, as here, it would be
fantasy, to use a mild word, to suggest that any practical difficulty would arise in
the fair, proper and sensible administration of this trust in respect of relatives and
dependants.

I do not think that this involves, as counsel for the defendant executors
suggested, a return by this court to its former view which was rejected by the
House of Lords in the *Gulbenkian* case. If I did so think, I should, however
reluctantly, accept his argument and its consequences. But as I read it, the criticism

114 *Ibid.*

in the House of Lords of the decision of this court in that case related to this court's acceptance of the view that it would be sufficient if it could be shown that one single person fell within the scope of the power or trust. The essence of the decision of the House of Lords in the *Gulbenkian* case, as I see it, is not that it must be possible to show with certainty that any given person is or is not within the trust; but that it is not, or may not be, sufficient to be able to show that one individual person is within it. If it does not mean that, I do not know where the line is supposed to be drawn, having regard to the clarity and emphasis with which the House of Lords has laid down that the trust does not fail because the whole range of objects cannot be ascertained. I would dismiss the appeal.

STAMP L.J.:

   . . .

On the footing that a reference to the "relatives" of a given person is *prima facie* a reference to all who are descended from a common ancestor, it must in my judgment follow that unless a gloss be put on that word that the trust here would if the law laid down in *Inland Revenue Comrs. v. Broadway Cottages Trust*[115] was still good law, be void for uncertainty.

In this case the House of Lords[116] was invited to consider the test of validity laid down in *Inland Revenue Comrs. v. Broadway Cottages Trust* and Lord Wilberforce, after expressing the opinion that it ought to be declared that the provisions of clause 9(a) constituted a trust and that the case should be remitted to the Chancery Division for determination whether on this basis the clause was valid or void for uncertainty, remarked that this made it necessary to consider whether in so doing the court should proceed on the basis that the relevant test was that laid down in that case.

That Lord Wilberforce, whose opinion was that of the majority, rejected the *Broadway Cottages Trust* test is not in doubt, and he rejected the reasoning on which it was founded. In his view it did not follow that because the test of validity of a trust is whether the trust can be executed by the court, execution is impossible unless there can be equal division. He pointed to cases up to the time of Lord Eldon L.C. from which he deduced the principle that a discretionary trust "can in a suitable case, be executed according to its merits and otherwise than by equal division," and remarked that he preferred not to suppose that the great masters of equity, if faced with the modern trust for employees, would have failed to adopt their creation to its practical and commercial character. Lord Wilberforce examined what had been said in the House of Lords in the *Gulbenkian* case regarding the *Broadway Cottages Trust* test, and more particularly the speech of Lord Upjohn, and having done so concluded that the House was free to review the *Broadway Cottages Trust* case and that the test for validity of "trust powers" (the expression "trust powers" connoting, I think, a trust for division coupled or

---

115 *Supra*, note 66.
116 *Supra*, note 63.

combined with a power of selection or, as it is now more commonly referred to, a "discretionary trust") ought to be similar to that accepted by the House of Lords in the *Gulbenkian* case for powers, namely — and here I quote the words of Lord Wilberforce:[117]

> that the trust is valid if it can be said with certainty that any given individual is or is not a member of the class.

Counsel for the defendant executors, fastening on those words, "if it can be said with certainty that any given individual is or is not a member of the class," submitted in this court that a trust for distribution among officers and employees or ex-officers or ex-employees or any of their relatives or dependants does not satisfy the test. You may say with certainty that any given individual is or is not an officer, employee, ex-officer or ex-employee. You may say with certainty that a very large number of given individuals are relatives of one of them; but, so the argument runs, you will never be able to say with certainty of many given individuals that they are not. I am bound to say that I had thought at one stage of counsel's able argument that this was no more than an exercise in semantics and that the phrase on which he relies indicated no more than that the trust was valid if there was such certainty in the definition of membership of the class that you could say with certainty that some individuals were members of it; that it was sufficient that you should be satisfied that a given individual presenting himself has or has not passed the test and that it matters not that having failed to establish his membership — here his relationship — you may, perhaps wrongly, reject him. There are, however, in my judgment serious difficulties in the way of a rejection of counsel's submission.

The first difficulty, as I see it, is that the rejection of counsel's submission involves holding that the trust is good if there are individuals — or even one — of whom you can say with certainty that he is a member of the class. That was the test adopted by and the decision of the Court of Appeal in the *Gulbenkian* case where what was under consideration was a power of distribution among a class conferred on trustees as distinct from a trust for distribution: but when the *Gulbenkian* case came before the House of Lords that test was decisively rejected and the more stringent test on which counsel for the defendant executors insists was adopted. Clearly Lord Wilberforce in expressing the view that the test of validity of a discretionary trust ought to be similar to that accepted by the House of Lords in the *Gulbenkian* case did not take the view that it was sufficient that you could find individuals who were clearly members of the class; for he himself remarked, towards the end of his speech as to the trustee's duty of enquiring or ascertaining, that in each case the trustees ought to make such a survey of the range of objects or possible beneficiaries as will enable them to carry out their fiduciary duty. It is not enough that trustees should do nothing but distribute the fund among those objects of the trust who happen to be at hand or present themselves. Lord Wilberforce, after citing that passage which I have already

---

117 *Ibid.*, at 456.

quoted from the speech of Lord Upjohn in the *Gulbenkian* case, put it more succinctly by remarking that what this did say (and he agreed) was that the trustees must select from the class, but that passage did not mean (as had been contended) that they must be able to get a complete list of all possible objects. I have already called attention to Lord Wilberforce's opinion that the trustee ought to make such a survey of the range of objects or possible beneficiaries as will enable them to carry out their fiduciary duty, and I ought perhaps to add that he indicated that a wider and more comprehensive range of enquiry is called for in the case of what I have called discretionary trusts than in the case of fiduciary powers. But, as I understand it, having made the appropriate survey, it matters not that it is not complete or fails to yield a result enabling you to lay out a list or particulars of every single beneficiary. Having done the best they can, the trustees may proceed on the basis similar to that adopted by the court where all the beneficiaries cannot be ascertained and distribute on the footing that they have been: see, for example, *Re Benjamin*.[118] What was referred to as "the complete ascertainment test" laid down by this court in the *Broadway Cottages* case is rejected. So also is the test laid down by this court in the *Gulbenkian* case. Validity or invalidity is to depend on whether you can say of any individual — and the accent must be on that word "any," for it is not simply the individual whose claim you are considering who is spoken of — that he "is or is not a member of the class," for only thus can you make a survey of the range of objects or possible beneficiaries.

If the matter rested there, it would in my judgment follow that, treating the word "relatives" as meaning descendants from a common ancestor, a trust for distribution such as is here in question would not be valid. Any "survey of the range of the objects or possible beneficiaries" would certainly be incomplete, and I am able to discern no principle on which such a survey could be conducted or where it should start or finish. The most you could do, so far as regards relatives, would be to find individuals who are clearly members of the class — the test which was accepted in the Court of Appeal, but rejected in the House of Lords, in the *Gulbenkian* case.

The matter does not, however, rest there, and I must return to examine more closely Lord Wilberforce's reasons for rejecting the *Broadway Cottages* test. Lord Wilberfore in his speech referred to *Kemp v. Kemp*,[119] where Sir Richard Arden M.R. had held that the court disclaimed the right to execute a power (*i.e.,* a trust power) and gave the fund equally. It was on this basis that this court in the *Broadway Cottages* case held that a discretionary trust is not valid unless all the beneficiaries are ascertainable; for otherwise the court being called on to execute the trust cannot divide the fund in equal shares. But, as I have already said, accepting that the test of validity is whether the trust can be executed by the court, Lord Wilberforce did not think it followed that execution is impossible unless there can be equal division. He cited cases where prior to the time of Sir Richard Arden M.R. a discretionary trust had been executed otherwise than by equal

---

118 [1902] 1 Ch. 723 (Ch. Div.).
119 (1801), 5 Ves. 849.

division. *Harding v. Glyn*,[120] he said, was an early case where the court executed a discretionary trust for "relations" — and it is a discretionary trust for relations that I am considering — by distributing to the next-of-kin in equal shares.

[He then quoted from Lord Wilberforce's judgment.]

I have referred to this part of Lord Wilberforce's speech because what he said regarding *Harding v. Glyn* was, as I read the speech, part of the foundation on which he built his conclusion, first that the court can execute a discretionary trust otherwise than by directing an equal division, and secondly, and consequently, that the *ratio decidendi* of the *Broadway Cottages* case was wrong and that that case was wrongly decided. *Harding v. Glyn* accordingly cannot be regarded simply as a case where in default of appointment a gift to the next-of-kin is to be implied as a matter of construction, but as authority endorsed by the decision of the House of Lords[121] that a discretionary trust for "relations" was a valid trust to be executed by the court by distribution to the next-of-kin. The class of beneficiaries thus becomes a clearly defined class and there is no difficulty in determining whether a given individual is within it or without it.

Does it then make a difference that here the discretionary trust for relations was a reference not to the relations of a deceased person but of one who was living? I think not. The next-of-kin of a living person are as readily ascertainable at any given time as the next-of-kin of one who is dead. A trust for the next-of-kin of a person, without more, was not a trust for the next-of-kin according to the statutes which would regulate the distribution of the personal property of a deceased person had he died intestate, but a trust for his nearest blood relations: see *Re Gray's Settlement*.[122] To execute a discretionary trust for the relations or relatives of a living person by distribution among his nearest blood relations appears to me a satisfactory method of so doing; and, if it were necessary to give a construction to the word "relatives" in relating to a living person in an *inter vivos* settlement, to construe it as a reference to his nearest blood relations would be far more likely to give effect to the intention than a construction which embraced all who were descended from one of his ancestors. Putting aside the doctrine *ut res magis valeat quam pereat*, which would if necessary have persuaded me that the word "relatives" in this settlement should be construed to mean nearest blood relations, nothing could be more improbable than that Mr. Baden should have intended the trustees to be at liberty to make grants to a relative of an employee of whose very existence that employee might be ignorant. "Nearest blood relations or dependants" makes more sense. In *Eagles v. Le Breton*,[123] which was expressly approved by this court in *Re Gansloser's Will Trusts*[124] and see *Re Kilvert*,[125] gift by will "to my relations in America" was held to be a gift to the next-of-kin of the testatrix in America; and, if it were necessary to do so, I

---

120 *Supra*, note 73.
121 *Supra*, note 96.
122 [1896] 2 Ch. 802.
123 (1873), L.R. 15 Eq. 148.
124 [1952] Ch. 30, [1951] 2 All E.R. 936 (C.A.).
125 [1957] Ch. 388, [1957] 2 All E.R. 196.

would have thought an *inter vivos* trust for the relatives of a living person could properly be similarly construed. And if there were no authority constraining me to adopt a different view, I can for myself see no good reason for construing the class of relatives to take under a trust for division among relatives in such shares as trustees think fit differently from the class to take under a trust for division among relatives in equal shares.

In coming to these conclusions I remain haunted by a remark towards the end of Lord Wilberforce's speech when, in considering the possible unworkability of a trust, he speaks of "relations" as if it were a very wide class; for I confess that I find a difficulty in treating a discretionary trust as one which may be executed by the trustees among a wider class than would be contemplated if the court were required to execute it. It may be, however, that such cases as *Re Scarisbrick's Will Trusts*[126] can only be reconciled with the views of the House of Lords in the instant case on the footing that I am wrong in this regard, and since we are only concerned with the question whether the trust here is valid, I resist the plaintiff trustees' invitation to go outside that question.

The only other challenge to the validity of the trust is directed against the use of the word "dependants" which it is said introduces a linguistic or semantic uncertainty. That in the context the word connotes financial dependence I do not doubt, and although in a given case there may be doubt whether there be a sufficient degree of dependence to satisfy the qualification of being a "dependant," that is a question which can be determined by the court and does not introduce linguistic uncertainty. On this part of the case I would follow *Re Hooper's 1949 Settlement*[127] and *Re Sayer Trust*.[128] As was held by Lord Upjohn in the *Gulbenkian* case,[129] the strict test of certainty required in a divesting clause[130] is not the test for the validity of a trust.

I agree that the appeal should be dismissed.

Notes and Questions

1. Five ambiguities in the test for certainty of object of discretionary trusts were set out at the beginning of this section. Are any of them resolved by *Baden No. 2*? Can you resolve them?

2. Reread question 7 in the Notes and Questions following the previous section. Does your answer to the question change after reading *Baden No. 2*?

3. A case predating *McPhail v. Doulton, Re Connor*,[131] dealt with the validity of a bequest by a testatrix that the residue of her estate be held in trust to be divided "among my close friends in such a way and at such time as my trustee in her discretion should determine." The executrix applied to the court for direction as to the validity of the residuary clause. The Court of Appeal held that the class of beneficiaries — "my close friends" — was too uncertain to be ascertained. The test applied by the majority was as

---

126 *Supra*, note 109.

127 (1955), 34 A.T.C. 3.

128 *Supra*, note 100.

129 *Supra*, note 64.

130 *Sifton v. Sifton*, [1938] A.C. 656, [1938] 3 All E.R. 435, [1938] 2 W.W.R. 465, [1938] O.R. 529 (P.C.).

131 (1970), 72 W.W.R. 388, 10 D.L.R. (2d) 5 (Alta. C.A.).

follows: "To make the gift valid the trustee must be able to ascertain the whole class of 'close friends.'"

(a) Which ascertainability test did the majority apply in *Connor*?

(b) Is the *Connor* case still good law after *McPhail v. Doulton*?

(c) Is the description "close friends" conceptually certain?

(d) Can one draw a distinction between a trust for "my close friends" and a trust for "such persons as my executor knows to be my old friends"?

(e) Is the class description "close friends" sufficiently certain on the interpretation of the test by any of Lords Justices Sachs, Megaw or Stamp?

4. Kane J.A. dissented in *Re Connor*. In his view, the fact that the testatrix had lived in a small town for most of her life made it possible to ascertain "without too great difficulty" who her close friends were.

What approach did Kane J.A. take to the question of certainty of objects? Is it preferable to that of the majority in the case? Why or why not?

5. In *Dickson v. Richardson*,[132] the Ontario Court of Appeal applied the *Baden* test. In that case, mining shares were held in trust for two classes of beneficiaries, namely "cash investors" and "administrative shareholders" in a mining venture. The settlor did not allocate the shares between the two classes. The court held that the trust did not fail simply because it was difficult to determine all the beneficiaries of the trust. It held, adopting *McPhail*, that where there is a gift to a class it must be possible to say with certainty whether any given individual is a member of the class, but it is only conceptual uncertainty and not evidential difficulties, which would cause a trust to fail.

7. CONSTITUTION OF TRUSTS

(a) Introduction

As previously noted, a valid express private trust must: (i) comply with the three certainties requirement, (ii) be constituted, and (iii) satisfy the requisite formalities. The focus of this part of the chapter is on the second requirement: constitution. Constitution of a trust occurs when there has been a declaration of the trust plus conveyance of the property to the trustee. Suppose that A declares that he will transfer Blackacre to B in trust for C. A trust does not exist. All three certainties are satisfied: there is a clear declaration of intention, the subject-matter is ascertained (Blackacre) and the object or beneficiary is identified (C). Nevertheless, A may with impunity refuse to transfer the land to B. Since title to Blackacre is not yet vested in B, there is no constitution and without constitution there is no trust. As discussed below, however, if C had given consideration for the promise or if A had made his promise under seal, A could be forced either to constitute the trust or to pay damages.[133]

Constitution may occur in one of three ways: (i) direct transfer of the property by the trust's creator to trustees, (ii) transfer of the property to the trustees by a third party, (iii) or declaration of self as trustee. Once constitution takes place, in the absence of a power of revocation, the creator of the trust cannot revoke even if the beneficiary is a volunteer.

---

132 (1981), 9 E.T.R. 66, 121 D.L.R. (3d) 206, 32 O.R. (2d) 158 (C.A.).

133 Contractual principles, not equity or trusts, would come to C's aid.

The case of *Paul v. Paul*[134] is a clear example of the effect of constitution. Under a marriage settlement, the wife's property was settled upon the husband and wife successively for life with the remainder to go to the children of the marriage. In default of children, the remainder was to go to the wife if she survived her husband or as she might appoint by will if she predeceased her husband. In default of appointment, the remainder was to go to the wife's next-of-kin excluding the husband.

After the husband and wife separated, the wife wanted to encroach upon the trust property. The husband consented. Counsel for the wife argued that, as there were no children of the marriage, the only persons who had any interest in the capital (*i.e.* the next of kin) were volunteers and that equity should not assist volunteers.

The Court of Appeal held that the trust could not be broken. Since constitution had occurred, the next of kin enjoyed full status as beneficiaries. It was irrelevant that they had acquired that position as volunteers.

Further Reading

C.E.F. Rickett, "The Constitution of Trusts: Contracts to Create Trusts" (1979), 32 Curr. L. Prob. 1.

C.E.F. Rickett, "Two propositions in the Constitution of Trusts" (1981), 34 Curr. L. Prob. 189.

Notes and Questions

1. What interest did the next-of-kin have in the trust property in *Paul v. Paul*? Do you agree with the result in the case? Why or why not?

2. Why is the creator of a trust precluded from revoking once the trust is constituted?

3. In *Re Bowden*,[135] the plaintiff by voluntary settlement purported to assign to trustees such property as she should become entitled to under the will of her father, who was then still alive. Upon the death of her father, the property to which she became entitled was transferred to the trustees of the settlement. Many years later she claimed to be entitled to the property absolutely.

(i) What result should follow?

(ii) When the plaintiff executed the settlement, was the subject-matter of the trust certain?

4. Does constitution of a trust cure uncertainty of intention, subject-matter or objects? Give reasons for your answers.

(b) Transferring Property to Another

There are three ways to transfer property to another. (i) The first is an outright transfer by way of gift, sale, or assignment. This method of transfer is beyond the scope of this text.[136] (ii) The second method is by transferring property to trustees

---

134 (1882), 20 Ch. 742.
135 [1936] Ch. 71 (Ch. Div.).
136 See, for example, B. Ziff, *Principles of Property Law*, 3rd ed. (Carswell, Scarborough, 2000).

for beneficiaries. (iii) The third is by declaring oneself to be trustee of property for another. The second and third methods are explored in the following sections. Before dealing with them, however, it is prudent to grasp the lesson of *Carson v. Wilson*,[137] below. A court will not complete an imperfect gift, nor will it re-characterize the method of transfer in order to see that the intention of the giver is carried out.

CARSON v. WILSON

[1961] O.R. 113, 26 D.L.R. (2d) 307
Supreme Court of Ontario
Court of Appeal

The deceased, Wilson, owned various parcels of land and mortgages on other lands. In his lifetime he executed valid deeds and assignments of these assets to certain named persons. He gave the deeds and assignments to his solicitor who was instructed to deliver them to the named persons only after Wilson's death.

Until his death, Wilson managed and controlled the assets, collecting rents, interest and principal. He could have demanded the deeds and assignments back from his solicitor at any time.

While the documentation was in proper form, it did not comply with the formalities required for wills. The solicitor warned Wilson that a gift of the documents would be ineffective without delivery.

When Wilson died, the grantees and assignees brought actions against Wilson's executors claiming delivery of the documents. The trial judge found in their favour. The executors appealed.

SCHROEDER J.A. (for the court):

. . .

It is not easy to discern the principle upon which the judgments in appeal are founded, but it would be a fair inference from the learned judge's reasons that he held the grants and assignments made by the deceased to be good and valid gifts *inter vivos*. This would follow from his conclusion that the deceased had delivered the instruments of grant and assignment to his solicitor "as completed gifts to hold for him and, I presume, for the grantees too." That raises the question as to when the grantees' interests should be brought into being, for, manifestly, if the deeds were delivered to the solicitor to hold for the grantor, there was in law and in fact no delivery at all.

[His Lordship reviewed the law on this question and concluded:]

---

137 [1961] O.R. 113, 26 D.L.R. (2d) 307 (C.A.).

It is my conclusion on this branch of the argument that the purported gifts fail as *inter vivos* since the execution of the deeds of grant or assignment was defective for want of delivery and cannot take effect as the grantor's deed. Nor, for the reasons stated are they capable of taking effect as escrows.

I turn now to a consideration of the alternative submission made on behalf of the respondents, that if the deeds of grant or assignment were inoperative as such, they should be construed as declarations of trust for the various grantees or assignees. If it be the correct view that the purported gifts to the plaintiffs, although expressed in the form of deeds of transfer, were in character and essence testamentary documents since they were only to become operative on the death of the grantor, then they cannot be given effect as trusts unless created by a duly executed will or codicil.[138]

But I think that this contention fails on another ground, namely, that the respondents are asking the court to perfect by indirection an imperfect gift, something to which the equitable jurisdiction of the court does not now and never did extend, as stated in judgments of commanding authority. The contention that an instrument executed as a present assignment but not operative as such ought to be held to be equivalent to a declaration by the donor that he holds the property in trust for the purported donee, is doubtless an enticing one, but it has been repudiated by the substantial weight of authority. To establish that a trust has been created, it is essential to prove an intention to create the trust. Here the donor purported to make a gift by deed of transfer or assignment to the supposed *cestuis que trustent*. This is wholly incompatible with the view that he intended to declare himself a trustee, for that is a character which assumed that he was to retain the property himself and not to part with it.

[The court quoted from *Milroy v. Lord*[139] and other cases and continued:]

I refer also to *Richards v. Delbridge*.[140] There the owner of leasehold business premises and stock in trade shortly before his death purported to make a voluntary gift in favour of his grandson, who was an infant and who had assisted in the operation of the business, by the following memorandum signed and endorsed on the lease: "This deed and all thereto belonging I give to E from this time forth, with all the stock-in-trade." The lease was then delivered to the mother of E on his behalf. Holding that there had been no valid declaration of trust of property in favour of the grandson. Sir G. Jessel M.R., stated:[141]

The principle is a very simple one. A man may transfer his property, without valuable consideration, in one of two ways: he may either do such acts as amount in law to a conveyance or assignment of the property, and thus completely divest himself of the legal ownership, in which case the person who by those acts acquires the property takes it beneficially, or on trust, as the

---

138 *Re Boyes, Boyes v. Carritt* (1884), 26 Ch. D. 531 (Ch. Div.), followed in *Re Hawksley's Settlement, Black v. Tidy*, [1934] Ch. 384.
139 (1862), 4 De G.F. & J. 264, 45 E.R. 1185.
140 (1874), L.R. 18 Eq. 11.
141 *Ibid.*, at 14.

case may be; or the legal owner of the property may, by one or other of the modes recognized as amounting to a valid declaration of trust, constitute himself a trustee, and, without an actual transfer of the legal title, may so deal with the property as to deprive himself of its beneficial ownership, and declare that he will hold it from that time forward on trust for the other person. It is true he needs not use the words, "I declare myself a trustee," but he must do something which is equivalent to it, and use expressions which have that meaning; for, however anxious the court may be to carry out a man's intention, it is not at liberty to construe words otherwise than according to their proper meaning.

The Master of the Rolls approved the law as laid down by Lord Justice Turner in *Milroy v. Lord*, and he quoted[142] the following extract from the judgment of Lord Justice Turner in that case:

The cases, I think, go further, to this extent, that if the settlement is intended to be effectuated by one of the modes to which I have referred, the court will not give effect to it by applying another of those modes. If it is intended to take effect by transfer, the court will not hold the intended transfer to operate as a declaration of trust, for then every imperfect instrument would be made effectual by being converted into a perfect trust.

The law laid down in these cases disposes decisively of the alternative contentions advanced on behalf of the respondents, and the gifts cannot be supported on the theory that a valid and effectual trust has been created in their favour. . . .

Notes and Questions

1. In *Carson v. Wilson*, why was the solicitor held to be an agent and not a trustee? Could the solicitor have been found to be a trustee? Why did that option not appeal to Wilson?

2. In *Jones v. Lock*,[143] Mr. Jones, having returned home from a business trip without a gift for his infant son, made out a cheque in his own name for £900 and declared before his wife and a nurse "I give this to baby." He placed the cheque in the baby's hand but then took it back and put it away. He did not endorse the cheque over to the infant. Further evidence indicated that Mr. Jones intended to see his solicitor to make provision for his child but he died before he could do so.

This case has been said to be the classic case where an intention to make a gift fails because the gift was not completed. Moreover, the court refused to find a trust to complete the intended, but uncompleted, gift.

(a) Why did the court hold that there was no valid gift?

(b) Why was the father not viewed as holding the cheque in trust for his son?

3. In *Anderson v. Patton*,[144] the estate of Mr. Costello sued for the return of $5,000 delivered to the defendant by Mr. Costello. At the time that the money was received, the defendant signed the following receipt:

Received from Francis C. Costello the sum of $5,000 which I am to hold in trust for the said Francis C. Costello, and which I am to pay as instructed to Mary Gertrude Patton and Mrs. R.L.

---

142 *Ibid.*, at 15.
143 (1865) L.R. 1 Ch. App. 25.
144 [1948] 1 W.W.R. 461, [1948] 2 D.L.R. 202 (Alta. C.A.).

Keiver, if anything should happen to the said Francis C. Costello. The money will be returned if the said Francis C. Costello should demand it.

The Alberta Court of Appeal held that the $5,000 was held in trust for Mr. Costello for life, then in trust for the two named beneficiaries. The trusteeship was held to be effective upon transfer and was not dependent on the settlor's death for its vigour and effect. The power of revocation was held not to be inconsistent with the creation of a trust.

Parlee J.A., in dissent, found that no trust on behalf of the two named persons had been created. He found that the defendant was a mere custodian of the money and that Costello could re-claim ownership of the funds at any time.

Do you agree with the majority of the Court of Appeal or with the dissenting judge?

(c) Transfer of Property to Trustees

(i) *By the Settlor*

Title to the trust property will not be vested in the trustees unless the settlor effects a valid transfer. Different procedures must be used with respect to different forms of property. It therefore is necessary to determine whether the property is legal or equitable, and whether it is, for example, realty, a chose in possession or a chose in action. Suppose, for instance, that a settlor wants to place corporate shares into trust. It will be necessary to execute the appropriate share transfer, and to then deliver the shares and the transfer to the trustees. If there are any special corporate rules regarding share transfers, they must be satisfied as well. This may include approval by company directors or entry of the transfer in the corporate share registry. Once the requisite formalities are met, title to the shares will be vested in the trustees.

A problem may arise, however, if the settlor cannot guarantee that the corporation will approve the transfer (if that is required) or ensure that the transfer will be registered. Does this preclude the settlor from establishing a trust of the shares? What happens when the settlor has done everything that is within his or her power to effect the transfer? These questions were posed in the leading English case, *Milroy v. Lord*.[145]

In *Milroy v. Lord*, the settlor by deed purported to transfer company shares to the defendant, Lord, as trustee. The company regulations provided that shares could only be transferred in the corporate books if they complied with certain formalities which the deed did not meet as the settlor had not signed the share certificates. He merely gave Lord a power of attorney to enable Lord to transfer the shares to himself or otherwise deal with them. Lord never transferred the shares to himself. Upon the settlor's death, the beneficiary under the trust claimed to be entitled to the shares. The Court of Appeal rejected this claim, stating that the gift was incomplete. Turner L.J. made the following comment on the question of what must be done to transfer the assets effectively.

---

145 *Supra*, note 139.

I take the law of this court to be well-settled, that, in order to render a voluntary settlement valid and effectual, the settlor must have done everything which, according to the nature of the property comprised in the settlement, was necessary to be done in order to transfer the property and render the settlement binding upon him. He may of course do this by actually transferring the property to those persons for whom he intends to provide . . . and it will be equally effectual if he transfers the property to a trustee for the purposes of settlement, or declares that he himself holds it in trust for those purposes; . . . one or other of these modes must be resorted to, for there is no equity in this court to perfect an imperfect gift.

Re Rose,[146] reproduced below, explains and applies the test laid down in *Milroy v. Lord*.

RE ROSE

[1952] Ch. 499, [1952] 1 All E.R. 1217
Court of Appeal

On March 30, 1943, the deceased transferred 10,000 shares in a company to his wife. He transferred a further 10,000 shares in the same company to his wife and the company's secretary as trustees for his wife and son under a voluntary settlement of the same date. The transfers were in the form required by the company and were properly executed. The transfers were delivered to the wife and the trustees by or before April 10, 1943. They were not, however, registered on the books of the company until June 30, 1943. The articles of association of the company provided that all transfers were to be registered only with the approval of the directors, who might refuse to register without reason.

The deceased died on February 16, 1947 and the Inland Revenue Commissioners claimed estate duty on both transfers under legislation which brought *inter vivos* transfers back into the estate if they were made within a certain period before death which, for the purposes of this case, began April 10, 1943.

To determine whether the duty was payable, the court had to decide whether the settlor was divested of the shares on March 30 or June 30, 1943.

EVERSHED M.R.:

. . .

It is the claim of the Crown in both the present cases that the property, namely, the shares which were the subject of the two transfers were not property comprehended within the language of section 38(2)(a) of the *Customs and Inland Revenue Act, 1881*, and of section 11(1) of the *Customs and Inland Revenue Act, 1889*, so as to be freed from liability thereunder. The Crown's argument may be put on alternative grounds: (1) That the shares were not taken under a voluntary disposition made by a person purporting to operate as an immediate gift; or, alternatively, if they were, (2) that *bona fide* possession and enjoyment was not assumed

---

146 [1952] Ch. 499, [1952] 1 All E.R. 1217 (C.A.).

on the date of the transfers by the donee immediately upon the gift and thenceforward retained to the entire exclusion of the donor. The Crown says that until the transfers were registered in the books of the Leweston Estates Company on June 30, 1943, either there was no effective transfer of the shares to the donee or, alternatively, there was not until that date an entire exclusion of the donor from all benefit in respect of the shares.

By way of illustration, the matter has been put thus for the purposes of the argument: that the result of these transfers was such that if, between their date, March 30, and the date of registration, June 30, the company had declared and paid a dividend in respect of its shares, that dividend must have been paid to the deceased, and could have been retained by him for his own benefit, and, indeed, that the respective donees could have had against him no claim whatever to have the amount of the dividend handed over to her or to them respectively.

That is the problem; and Roxburgh J. decided the question which arose in both cases adversely to the Crown. From those decisions the Crown has appealed. It will be sufficient and convenient for me now to confine myself to one of the appeals, and I take the first, which relates to the transfer from the deceased to his wife, Mrs. Rose. A decision on that matter will necessarily involve a similar decision on the other.

[His Lordship read the transfer and continued:]

There are certain observations which may be made upon that document. The first is this: It was in form in exact correspondence with the requirements of the company's regulations; for in article 29, dealing with the transfer of shares, it is provided that: "Shares in the company shall be transferred in the following form, or as near thereto as circumstances will permit." The form which followed was that which the deceased adopted. On its execution the deed of transfer was, beyond question, delivered to the transferee, together with the certificate relative to those shares. It follows, therefore, that so far as lay in his power, the deceased did all that he could — he followed carefully and precisely the obligations imposed on a proposing transferor by the article — to divest himself then and there in favour of his wife of all his interest, legal and equitable, in the 10,000 shares.

The next thing to notice (and it is, I think, not without significance) is this: The company was unlimited, and this form of transfer differed, therefore, in one respect from the forms of transfer sometimes found in the case of limited companies, in that it contained what was, in effect (because it was under seal) a covenant by Mrs. Rose to accept and take the shares subject to the conditions — that is, the conditions imposed on shareholders by the regulations of the company — and it was executed not only by the transferor but also by the transferee.

There is a third matter to which I think some relevance also attaches in considering the validity of the Crown's claim. On April 12, 1943, the transfer was presented for adjudication to the stamping authority, and it bears on it an *ad valorem* stamp. The impressing of that stamp is justified by section 74 of the *Finance (1909-1910) Act, 1910*, on the ground that "Any conveyance or transfer operating as a voluntary disposition *inter vivos* shall be chargeable with the like stamp duty as if it were a conveyance or transfer on sale" subject as thereinafter provided. Approaching the matter then as one of common sense, or one from which the application of common sense is not excluded, and having regard to the terms of the transfer, I should have thought it was exceedingly difficult to contend successfully that on the date of the transfer, March 30, 1943, the deceased did not, within the terms of section 38(2)(a) of the Act of 1881, make, and Mrs. Rose did not take under a voluntary disposition purporting to operate as an immediate gift. That is not conclusive, for there still remains, on any view, the question whether, during the period up to June 30, 1943, the transferor did not, by virtue of the peculiar characteristics attaching to shares in companies, and particularly in this company, retain an interest which interest did not cease until June 30, a date too late for the plaintiffs.

The burden of the case presented by the Crown may be briefly put as it was formulated in reply by Mr. Pennycuick. This document, he said, on the face of it, was intended to operate and operated, if it operated at all, as a transfer. If for any reason it was at its date incapable of so operating, it is not legitimate, either by reference to the expressed intention in the document or on a well-established principle of law, to extract from it a wholly different transaction — that is, to make it take effect not as a transfer but as a declaration of trust. Now I agree that on the face of the document it was obviously intended (if you take the words used) to operate and operate immediately as a transfer — "I do hereby transfer to the transferee" these shares "to hold unto the said transferee, subject to the several conditions on which I held the same at the time of the execution hereof." It plainly was intended to operate immediately as a transfer of rights. To some extent at least, it is said, it could not possibly do so. To revert to the illustration which has throughout been taken, if the company had declared a dividend during this interim, it is not open to question that the company must have paid that dividend to the deceased. So that *vis-a-vis* the company, this document did not, and could not, operate to transfer to Mrs. Rose the right against the company to claim and receive that dividend. Shares, Mr. Pennycuick says, are property of a peculiar character consisting, as it is sometimes put, of a bundle of rights — that is, rights against or in the company. It has followed from his argument that if such a dividend had been paid, the deceased could, consistently with the document to which he has set his hand and seal, have retained that dividend, and, if he had handed it over to his wife, it would have been an independent gift. I think myself that such a conclusion is startling. Indeed, I venture to doubt whether to anybody but a lawyer such a conclusion would even be comprehensible — at least without a considerable amount of explanation. That again is not conclusive; but I confess that I approach a matter of this kind with a pre-conceived notion that a conclusion that offends common sense, so much as this would *prima facie* do, ought not to be the right conclusion.

Jenkins L.J. carried the illustration a stage further. He said: Suppose, on the Crown's view, the deceased, retaining, pending registration, full rights over these shares (for Mr. Pennycuick argued that this document not only did not transfer the legal estate but that it transferred no interest or estate whatever), repented of his generosity and told the company not to register the transfer. Supposing Mrs.

Rose went to the company and the directors of the company had nevertheless said that they were willing to register the transfer. Let it be then further supposed that the deceased proceeded to take action to restrain the company by injunction from registering the transfer. If the deceased in truth retained at that time a proprietary interest, the court would be bound to protect it by granting an injunction. That, indeed, was perhaps too startling for Mr. Pennycuick, for he said that he thought the court would not grant an injunction and that, the document having at least operated as a gift of a piece of paper, namely, the share certificate, the deceased could not be heard to claim the court's assistance so as to restrain the company from doing that which possession, as upon gift, of the certificate and of this transfer, enabled the donee to require the company to do.

I do not pursue these examples; but it seems to follow from testing this matter by such extreme cases, that the assertion that nothing whatever passed under this deed except the right to possess, as articles, as physical things, two pieces of paper, is not right. I will now go to the case of *Milroy v. Lord*,[147] which is in truth the foundation of the Crown's argument; since it is on that case that depends the proposition that, if this document was intended to operate as a transfer, effect cannot be given to what may be thought to have been the intention behind it by treating it as operating as a declaration of trust.

[His Lordship stated the facts of this case, discussed the quotation from *Milroy v. Lord* reproduced in the introduction to this case and continued:]

Those last few sentences form the gist of the Crown's argument and on it is founded the broad, general proposition that if a document is expressed as, and on the face of it intended to operate as, a transfer, it cannot in any respect take effect by way of trust — so far I understand the argument to go. In my judgment, that statement is too broad and involves too great a simplification of the problem; and is not warranted by authority. I agree that if a man purporting to transfer property executes documents which are not apt to effect that purpose, the court cannot then extract from those documents some quite different transaction and say that they were intended merely to operate as a declaration of trust, which *ex facie* they were not; but if a document is apt and proper to transfer the property — is in truth the appropriate way in which the property must be transferred — then it does not seem to me to follow from the statement of Turner L.J. that, as a result, either during some limited period or otherwise, a trust may not arise, for the purpose of giving effect to the transfer. The simplest case will, perhaps, provide an illustration. If a man executes a document transferring all his equitable interest, say, in shares, that document, operating, and intended to operate, as a transfer, will give rise to and take effect as a trust; for the assignor will then be a trustee of the legal estate in the shares for the person in whose favour he has made an assignment of his beneficial interest. And, for my part, I do not think that the case of *Milroy v. Lord* is an authority which compels this court to hold that in this case — where, in the terms of Turner L.J.'s judgment, the settlor did everything which, according

---

147 *Supra*, note 139.

to the nature of the property comprised in the settlement, was necessary to be done by him in order to transfer the property — the result necessarily negatives the conclusion that, pending registration, the settlor was a trustee of the legal interest for the transferee.

. . .

[I]t seems to me that it cannot be asserted on the authority of *Milroy v. Lord*, and I venture to think it also cannot be asserted as a matter of logic and good sense or principle, that because, by the regulations of the company, there had to be a gap before Mrs. Rose could, as between herself and the company, claim the rights which the shares gave her *vis-a-vis* the company, the deceased was not in the meantime a trustee for her of all his rights and benefits under the shares. That he intended to pass all those rights, as I have said, seems to me too plain for argument. I think the matter might be put perhaps in a somewhat different fashion, though it reaches the same end. Whatever might be the position during the period between the execution of this document and the registration of the shares, the transfers were on June 30, 1943, registered. After registration, the title of Mrs. Rose was beyond the doubt complete in every respect; and if the deceased had received a dividend between execution and registration and Mrs. Rose had claimed to have that dividend handed to her, what would have been the deceased's answer? It could no longer be that the purported gift was imperfect: it had been made perfect. I am not suggesting that the perfection was retroactive. But what else could he say? How could he, in the fact of his own statement under seal, deny the proposition that he had, on March 30, 1943, transferred the shares to his wife? — and by the phrase "transfer the shares" surely must be meant transfer to her "the shares and all my right title and interest thereunder." Nothing else could sensibly have been meant. Nor can he, I think, make much of the fact that this was a voluntary settlement on his part. Being a case of an unlimited company, as I have said, Mrs. Rose had herself to undertake by covenant to accept the shares subject to their burdens — in other words, to relieve the deceased of his liability as a corporator. I find it unnecessary to pursue the question of consideration, but it is, I think, another feature which would make it exceedingly difficult and, sensibly impossible, the assertion on the deceased's part of any right to retain any such dividend. Nor is the Crown's argument made any easier by the circumstance that another emanation of the Crown has adjudicated that stamp duty *ad valorem* under section 74 of the Act of 1910 was payable upon this transfer as a disposition of the subject-matter transferred.

For the reasons I have stated, I do not think that *Milroy v. Lord* covers the case and I agree with Roxburgh J. in his conclusion to that effect. I also think that upon principle the statement upon which Mr. Pennycuick has made the foundation of his argument, if it covers this case, is too widely stated. If, as I have said, the phrase "transfer the shares" is taken to be and to mean a transfer of all rights and interests in them, then I can see nothing contrary to the law in a man saying that so long as, pending registration, the legal estate remains in the donor, he was, by the necessary effect of his own deed, a trustee of that legal estate. Nor do I think that that is an unjustifiable addition to or gloss upon the words used in the transfer. Indeed, for my part, I find that a less difficult matter in the way of interpretation than to say that this was, upon its terms, merely a conditional gift, merely a transfer as a gift to Mrs. Rose of a particular right, namely, the right to get herself registered and thenceforward, but not before, to enjoy the benefits which the donor previously had in these shares. That is nothing like what the deed set out to do I have said that I reject the proposition that the distinction between a case such as this and a case such as *Milroy v. Lord* is, as Mr. Pennycuick urged, indefensible. I think it is sensible and real; and for these reasons I would dismiss the appeals.

[Jenkins L.J. delivered a concurring opinion. Morris L.J. agreed with both judgments.]

Notes and Questions

1. *Re Rose* is often thought to be inconsistent with *Milroy v. Lord*. In fact, it is not. In *Milroy v. Lord*, the testator had not done everything "necessary to be done by him in order to transfer the property" as he had failed to endorse the share certificates. Mr. Rose, in contrast, had done everything necessary to effect the transfer.

2. Explain the trust that operated in the period before the share transfer was registered on June 30, 1943. Was it an express trust? If so, is it realistic to say that it reflected the settlor's intention?

3. Some commentators suggest that there were two trusts in *Re Rose*. The intended express trust took effect only after the share transfer was registered. Prior to that time, the settlor held the shares on constructive trust. That constructive trust arose by operation of law, rather than in response to the settlor's intention. It was imposed by equity in order "to perfect the donor's intention to benefit another."[148] That explanation is discussed further in the chapter on constructive trusts. In *Pennington v. Waine*, however, the English Court of Appeal suggested that the trust in question arose from the settlor's intention and hence was express.[149] Could that possibly be correct?

4. A testatrix appointed a trust company as her executor and directed that the income from the residue of her estate be paid to her son for life with the capital thereafter to go to a charity. During her lifetime she deposited fifteen $1,000 bonds in four separate envelopes in her safety deposit box at the trust company. The bonds were fully registered in her name. On her death the envelopes were found endorsed as follows: "The contents of the envelopes are to be used solely for the benefit of my . . . son . . . by the [trust company]." Was a valid trust of the bonds constituted in favour of the son?[150]

5. In *Re Amland Estate*,[151] the New Brunswick Supreme Court held that a transfer of a share certificate signed in blank by the owner and handed to the donee completed the gift.

---

148 See R. Chambers, "Constructive Trusts in Canada" (1999), 37 Alberta L. Rev. 173 at 196-197.
149 [2002] 1 W.L.R. 2075 (Eng. C.A.). See also A. Doggett, "Explaining *Re Rose*: The Search Goes On?" (2003), 62 Cambridge L.J. 263.
150 See *Re Mellen Estate*, [1933] O.W.N. 118 (H.C.), 246n (C.A.); noted at (1933), 11 Can. Bar. Rev. 569. See also *Re Shirley* (1965), 49 D.L.R. (2d) 474 (Sask. Q.B.); and *Re Parke* (1965), 49 D.L.R. (2d) 568 (B.C. S.C.).
151 (1975), 10 N.B.R. (2d) 285 (Q.B.).

(ii) *By a Third Party*

A trust may be constituted by a transfer of title to the trustees from someone other than the trust's creator. *Re Ralli's*,[152] below, illustrates that if title to the property is vested in the trustee through a third party the trust may still be held to be constituted and beyond revocation.[153]

RE RALLI'S WILL TRUSTS

CALVOCORESSI v. RODOCANCACHI

[1964] 1 Ch. 288, [1964] 2 W.L.R. 1144, [1963] 3 All E.R. 940
Chancery Division

The testator gave the residue of his estate, subject to a life interest to his widow, absolutely to his two daughters, Irene and Helen. Thereafter, Helen made a marriage settlement, clause 7 of which provided that:

[t]he said Helen Ralli doth hereby for herself her heirs executors administrators and assigns covenant with the trustees that if the said Helen Ralli now is or shall become . . . possessed of . . . property . . . the said Helen Ralli . . . shall . . . convey assign and assure the said . . . property to or otherwise cause the same to be vested in the trustees . . . upon the trusts and with and subject to the powers and provisions hereinbefore declared . . .

Clause 8 declared that it was the intention of the parties that:

all the property comprised within the terms of such covenants shall become subject in equity to the settlement hereby covenanted to be made therefor and that . . . Helen Ralli . . . and [her] respective representatives shall be liable to be sued by virtue thereof but that the trustees . . . shall not be bound to [enforce the covenants] or any of them (except so far as they shall be required so to do by . . . any person interested in the property which may be subject to any of such covenants) nor shall the trustee be obliged to inquire whether any property has actually become subject to any of such covenants . . .

Helen never transferred her share of her father's estate to the trustees of the settlement. She died in 1956 and the testator's widow died in 1961.

The plaintiff, Irene's husband, was the sole surviving trustee of Helen's marriage settlement and of the testator's estate. He made application to the court to determine whether Helen's interest in the residue of the testator's estate should be paid to the beneficiaries under the settlement or to Helen's estate. Helen died without issue and the substitutionary beneficiaries under the settlement were Irene's children.

BUCKLEY J.:

---

152 [1964] 1 Ch. 288, [1963] 3 All E.R. 940.

153 Unless the settlor has reserved a power of revocation.

In this case I have to consider whether certain investments which are now standing in the plaintiff's name, representing one-half of the residuary estate of the late Ambrose Pandia Ralli (whom I will call "the testator"), form in the events which have happened part of the estate of the testator's daughter Helen Petroco-chino (whom I will call "Helen") are held upon the trusts of Helen's marriage settlement.

[His Lordship stated the facts and referred to the submissions on the construc-tion of the terms of the marriage settlement. He rejected the plaintiff's first submission that clause 7 operated as an assignment of the settlor's vested share of the residue, but accepted his second submission that clause 8 was an express declaration that the settlor held her share of residue on the trust of the settlement pending the transfer of that interest in accordance with the covenant in clause 7. Unlike the executory obligation in *Re Anstis*,[154] said his Lordship, this was a distinct separate declaration which bound the settlor and her personal representatives and was enforceable by the beneficiaries even if they were mere volunteers outside the marriage consideration. His Lordship continued:]

If this view is right, this disposes of the case, but I think I should go on to state what would be my view, if I were mistaken in the view I have expressed. The investments representing the share of residue in question, which I shall call "the fund," stand in the name of the plaintiff. This is because he is now the sole surviving trustee of the testator's will. Therefore, say the defendants, he holds the fund primarily on the trusts of the will, that is to say, in trust for them as part of Helen's estate. The plaintiff is, however, also the sole surviving covenantee under clause 7 of the settlement as well as the sole surviving trustee of that settlement. This, however, affords him no answer, say the defendants, to their claim under the will unless the plaintiff, having transferred the fund to them in pursuance of the trusts of the will, could compel them to return it in pursuance of their obligation under the covenant, and this, they say, he could not do. In support of this last contention they rely on *Re Plumptre's Marriage Settlement*,[155] *Re Pryce*[156] and *Re Kay's Settlement*.[157]

The plaintiff, on the other hand, contends that, as he already holds the fund, no question of his having to enforce the covenant arises. The fund, having come without impropriety into his hands, is now, he says, impressed in his hands with the trust upon which he ought to hold it under the settlement; and because of the covenant it does not lie in the mouth of the defendants to say that he should hold the fund in trust for Helen's estate. He relies on *Re Bowden*[158] in which a lady by a voluntary settlement purported to assign to trustees, *inter alia*, such property as

---

154 (1886), 31 Ch. D. 596 (C.A.).
155 [1910] 1 Ch. 609.
156 [1917] 1 Ch. 234.
157 [1939] Ch. 329, [1939] 1 All E.R. 245.
158 [1936] Ch. 71.

she should become entitled to under the will of her father, who was still alive, and authorised the trustees to receive the property and give receipts for it. In due course her father died and the property to which the lady became entitled under his will was transferred to the trustees of the settlement. Many years later the lady claimed that the property belonged to her absolutely. Bennett J., holding that she was not entitled to the property, said:[159] "Counsel for the settlor submitted that the question should be answered in the affirmative and that the property the subject of the trusts of the settlement should be transferred to her. He based his argument on the authority of *Meek v. Kettlewell*[160] and *Re Ellenborough*[161] and contended that the settlement, being a voluntary settlement, was void and altogether unenforceable. Neither of these authorities supports either of his propositions. All that was decided in *Meek v. Kettlewell* was that where the assistance of the court of equity is needed to enable the trustees of a voluntary settlement to obtain possession of property subjected to the trusts of the voluntary settlement, the property not having been vested in the trustees, a court of equity will render no assistance to the plaintiff. But here nobody is seeking the assistance of the court of equity to enforce the voluntary settlement. Under a valid authority, unrevoked, the persons appointed trustees under the settlement received the settlor's interest under her father's will, and, immediately after it had been received by them, as a result of her own act and her own declaration, contained in the voluntary settlement, it became impressed with the trusts contained in the settlement."

The plaintiff also relies on *Re Adlard*,[162] where Vaisey J. followed *Re Bowden*, and on the observations of Upjohn J. in *Re Burton's Settlements*.[163]

Mr. Goff, for the defendants, says that *In re Bowden* and *In re Adlard* are distinguishable from the present case because in each of those cases the fund had reached the hands of the trustees of the relevant settlement and was held by them in that capacity, whereas in the present case the fund is, as he maintains, in the hands of the plaintiff in the capacity of trustee of the will and not in the capacity of trustee of the settlement. He says that *Re Burton's Settlements*, the complicated facts of which I forbear to set out here, should be distinguished on the ground that, when the settlement there in question was made, the trustee of that settlement under which the settlor had expectation was the same, so that the settlor by her settlement gave directions to the trustee of the settlement under which she had expectations, who then already held the relevant fund.

Sir Milner Holland, for the plaintiff, says that the capacity in which the trustee has become possessed of the fund is irrelevant. Thus in *Strong v. Bird*[164] an imperfect gift was held to be completed by the donee obtaining probate of the donor's will of which he was executor, notwithstanding that the donor died intestate as to her residue and that the donee was not a person entitled as on her

159 *Ibid.*, at 75.
160 (1842), 1 Hare 464.
161 [1903] 1 Ch. 697.
162 [1954] Ch. 29.
163 [1955] Ch. 82, [1954] 3 All E.R. 193.
164 (1874), L.R. 18 Eq. 315.

intestacy. Similarly in *Re James*[165] a grant of administration to two administrators was held to perfect an imperfect gift by the intestate to one of them, who had no beneficial interest in the intestate's estate.

In my judgment the circumstances that the plaintiff holds the funds because he was appointed a trustee of the will is irrelevant. He is at law the owner of the fund, and the means by which he became so have no effect upon the quality of his legal ownership. The question is: For whom, if anyone, does he hold the fund in equity? In other words, who can successfully assert an equity against him disentitling him to stand upon his legal right? It seems to me to be indisputable that Helen, if she were alive, could not do so, for she has solemnly covenanted under seal to assign the fund to the plaintiff, and the defendants can stand in no better position. It is, of course, true that the object of the covenant was not that the plaintiff should retain the property for his own benefit, but that he should hold it on the trusts of the settlement. It is also true that, if it were necessary to enforce performance of the covenant, equity would not assist the beneficiaries under the settlement, because they are mere volunteers; and that for the same reason the plaintiff, as trustee of the settlement, would not be bound to enforce the covenant and would not be constrained by the court to do so, and indeed, it seems, might be constrained by the court not to do so. As matters stand, however, there is no occasion to invoke the assistance of equity to enforce the performance of the covenant. It is for the defendants to invoke the assistance of equity to make good their claim to the fund. To do so successfully they must show that the plaintiff cannot conscientiously withhold it from them. When they seek to do this, he can point to the covenant which, in my judgment, relieves him from any fiduciary obligation he would otherwise owe to the defendants as Helen's representatives. In so doing the plaintiff is not seeking to enforce an equitable remedy against the defendants on behalf of persons who could not enforce such a remedy themselves: he is relying upon the combined effect of his legal ownership of the fund and his rights under the covenant. That no action on the covenant might be statute-barred is irrelevant, for there is no occasion for such an action.

Had someone other than the plaintiff been the trustee of the will and held the fund, the result of this part of the case would, in my judgment, have been different; and it may seem strange that the rights of the parties should depend upon the appointment of the plaintiff as a trustee of the will in 1946, which for present purposes may have been a quite fortuitous event. The result, however, in my judgment, flows — and flows, I think, quite rationally — from the consideration that the rules of equity derive from the tenderness of a court of equity for the consciences of the parties. There would have been nothing unconscientious in Helen or her personal representatives' asserting her equitable interests under the trusts of the will against a trustee who was not a covenantee under clause 7 of the settlement, and it would have been unconscientious for such a trustee to disregard those interests. Having obtained a transfer of the fund, it would not have been unconscientious in Helen to refuse to honour her covenant, because the beneficiaries under her settlement are mere volunteers: nor, seemingly, would the court

---

165 [1935] Ch. 449.

have regarded it as unconscientious in the plaintiff to have abstained from enforcing the covenant either specifically or in damages, for the reason, apparently,
that she would have been under no obligation to obtain for the volunteers indirectly
what they could not obtain directly. In such circumstances Helen or her personal
representatives could have got and retained the fund. In the circumstances of the
present case, on the other hand, it is not unconscientious in the plaintiff to withhold
from Helen's estate the fund which Helen covenanted that he should receive: on
the contrary, it would have been unconscientious in Helen to seek to deprive the
plaintiff of that fund, and her personal representatives can be in no better position.
The inadequacy of the volunteers' equity against Helen and her estate consequently is irrelevant, for that equity does not come into play but they have a good
equity as against the plaintiff, because it would be unconscientious in him to
retain as against them any property which he holds in consequence of the provisions of the settlement.

For these reasons I am of opinion that in the events which have happened the
plaintiff now holds the fund in question on the trusts of the marriage settlement,
and I will so declare.

Notes and Questions

1. The court offered two reasons as to why the disputed property was constituted into
the settlement trust. Distinguish and explain those reasons.

2. What is the logic behind the principle in *Re Ralli*? How was that principle defined?
Would that principle have worked if the trustee had acquired possession of the disputed
property, but had not been the recipient of Helen's covenant?

3. Is *Re Ralli* a case on future property? Would the result have been different if it
were? Reconsider your answer to this question after completing Part 8, *infra*.

4. A father, while his two sons were infants, purchased shares in a limited company
and had the certificates issued to himself "as trustee for" each of his sons. The certificates
were signed by the father "as trustee for" the sons. They were approved by the company
and the shareholders' list reflected the father holding as trustee. The father continued to
collect the dividends but never accounted to his sons or informed them of the trust. The
company share register showed only the father as owner of the shares.

(a) Are the shares part of the father's estate?

(b) Was a trust created in favour of the sons? If so, how?[166]

(c) Could the father have revoked the trust?

(d) Declaration of Self as Trustee

The preceding section focused on the requirement that title to the subject-
matter of the trust must be vested properly in the trustee. In this section, that
aspect of constitution is not a problem because title is already vested in the owner.
The difficulty in the area of declaration of self as trustee lies in proving that the
creator of the trust actually intended to become trustee of the property.

---

166 See *Glynn v. Commissioner of Taxation* (1964), 111 C.L.R. 189 (Aust. H.C.).

Paul v. Constance,[167] below, demonstrates that there be a manifestation of the intention to become a trustee for another person. It also shows that no technical words need be used. Finally, it reiterates the point that the court will not "discover" a trust if the facts show that what was intended was a gift: the intention to make a gift is not equivalent to declaring oneself to be a trustee for another.

PAUL v. CONSTANCE

[1977] 1 W.L.R. 527, [1977] 1 All E.R. 195
Court of Appeal

The deceased received £950 from his employers as damages for injuries sustained. The deceased and the plaintiff, a woman with whom he had lived since 1967, resolved to deposit the money in the bank. After discussions with the bank manager, who was informed that the deceased and the plaintiff were not married, they decided to open an account in the deceased's name only. The deceased told the plaintiff on many occasions, both before the money was deposited and after, that it was as much hers as his and that the plaintiff could draw on the account. Further moneys were deposited into the account from time to time and there was one withdrawal from it, which was shared between the deceased and the plaintiff. The deceased died in 1974 and his wife, the defendant, from whom he separated in 1965, took out letters of administration and closed the bank account. The plaintiff then brought this action and alleged that the money in the account had been held by the deceased on an express trust for himself and the plaintiff jointly. The plaintiff was successful at trial and the defendant appealed.

SCARMAN L.J.:

. . .

A number of issues were canvassed at the trial, but the only point taken by the defendant on her appeal to this court goes to the question whether or not there was, in the circumstances of this case, an express declaration of trust. It is conceded that if there was a trust it would be enforceable. The one question is whether there was an express declaration of trust.

The case has been argued with great skill and ability by counsel on both sides, and I should like to express my appreciation for the way in which counsel for the defendant opened the appeal and the way in which counsel for the plaintiff, very shortly and vigorously, put his contentions.

Counsel for the defendant drew the attention of the court to the so-called three certainties that have to be established before the court can infer the creation of a trust. He referred us to Snell's Principles of Equity[168] in which the three

---

167 [1977] 1 W.L.R. 527, [1977] 1 All E.R. 195 (C.A.).
168 27th ed., (1973) at 111.

certainties are set out. We are concerned only with one of the three certainties, and it is this:

> The words [that is the words of the declaration relied on] must be so used that on the whole they ought to be construed as imperative. [A little later on the learned author says:] No particular form of expression is necessary for the creation of a trust, if on the whole it can be gathered that a trust was intended. "A trust may well be created, although there may be an absence of an expression in terms imposing confidence." A trust may thus be created without using the word "trust," for what the court regards is the substance and effect of the words used.

Counsel for the defendant has taken the court through the detailed evidence and submits that one cannot find anywhere in the history of events a declaration of trust in the sense of finding the deceased man, Mr. Constance, saying: "I am now disposing of my interest in this fund so that you, Mrs. Paul, now have a beneficial interest in it." Of course, the words which I have just used are stilted lawyers' language, counsel for the plaintiff was right to remind the court that we are dealing with simple people, unaware of the subtleties of equity, but understanding very well indeed their own domestic situation. It is right that one should consider the various things that were said and done by the plaintiff and Mr. Constance during their time together against their own background and in their own circumstances.

Counsel for the defendant drew our attention to two cases, both of them well enough known (at any rate in Lincoln's Inn, since they have been in the law reports for over 100 years), and he relies on them as showing that, though a man may say in clear and unmistakable terms that he intends to make a gift to some other person, for instance his child or some other member of his family, yet that does not necessarily disclose a declaration of trust; and, indeed, in the two cases to which we have been referred the court held that, though there was a plain intention to make a gift, it was not right to infer any intention to create a trust.

The first of the two cases is *Jones v. Lock*.[169] In that case Mr. Jones, returning home from a business trip to Birmingham, was scolded for not having brought back anything for his baby son. He went upstairs and came down with a cheque made out in his own name for £900 and said, in the presence of his wife and nurse: "Look you here, I give this to baby," and he then placed the cheque in the baby's hand. It was obvious that he was intending to make a gift of the cheque to his baby son but it was clear, as Lord Cranworth L.C. held, that there was no effective gift then and there made of the cheque; it was in his name and had not been endorsed over to the baby. Other evidence showed that he had in mind to go and see his solicitor, Mr. Lock, to make proper provision for the baby boy, but unfortunately he died before he could do so. *Jones v. Lock* was a classic case where the intention to make a gift failed because the gift was imperfect. So an attempt was made to say: "Well, since the gift was imperfect, nevertheless, one can infer the evidence of a trust." But Lord Cranworth L.C. would have none of it.

---

169 (1865), 1 Ch. App. 25.

In the other case to which counsel for the defendant referred us, *Richards v. Delbridge*,[170] the facts were that a Mr. Richards, who employed a member of his family in his business, was minded to give the business to the young man. He evidenced his intention to make this gift by endorsing on the lease of the business premises a short memorandum to the effect that:[171]

> This deed [*i.e.*, the deed of leasehold] and all thereto belonging I give to Edward . . . [*i.e.*, the boy] from this time forth with all the stock-in-trade.

Jessel M.R., who decided the case, said that there was in that case the intention to make a gift, but the gift failed because it was imperfect; and he refused from the circumstances of the imperfect gift to draw the inference of the existence of a declaration of trust or his intention to create one. The *ratio decidendi* appears clearly from the report. It is a short passage, and because of its importance I quote it:

> In *Milroy v. Lord*[172] Lord Justice Turner, after referring to the two modes of making a voluntary settlement valid and effectual, adds these words: "The cases, I think, go further, to this extent, that if the settlement is intended to be effectuated by one of the modes to which I have referred, the court will not give effect to it by applying another of those modes. If it is intended to take effect by transfer, the court will not hold the intended transfer to operate as a declaration of trust, for then every imperfect instrument would be made effectual by being converted into a perfect trust." It appears to me that that sentence contains the whole law on the subject.

There is no suggestion of a gift by transfer in this case. The facts of those cases do not, therefore, very much help the submission of counsel for the defendant, but he was able to extract from them this principle: that there must be a clear declaration of trust, and that means there must be clear evidence from what is said or done of an intention to create a trust or, as counsel for the defendant put it, "an intention to dispose of a property or fund so that somebody else to the exclusion of the disponent acquires the beneficial interest in it." He submitted that there was no such evidence.

When one looks to the detailed evidence to see whether it goes as far as that — and I think that the evidence does have to go as far as that — one finds that from the time that Mr. Constance received his damages right up to his death he was saying, on occasions, that the money was as much the plaintiff's as his. When they discussed the damages, how to invest them or what to do with them, when they discussed the bank account, he would say to her: "The money is as much yours as mine." The judge, rightly treating the basic problem in the case as a question of fact, reached this conclusion. He said:

> I have read through my notes, and I am quite satisfied that it was the intention of [the plaintiff] and Mr. Constance to create a trust in which both of them were interested.

---

170 (1874), L.R. 18 Eq. 11.
171 *Ibid.*, at 15.
172 *Supra*, note 139, at 274.

In this court the issue becomes: was there sufficient evidence to justify the judge reaching that conclusion of fact? In submitting that there was, counsel for the plaintiff draws attention first and foremost to the words used. When one bears in mind the unsophisticated character of Mr. Constance and his relationship with the plaintiff during the last few years of his life, counsel for the plaintiff submits that the words that he did use on more than one occasion namely "This money is as much yours as mine," convey clearly a present declaration that the existing fund was as much the plaintiff's as his own. The judge accepted that conclusion. I think he was well justified in doing so and, indeed, I think he was right to do so. There are, as counsel for the plaintiff reminded us, other features in the history of the relationship between the plaintiff and Mr. Constance which support the interpretation of those words as an express declaration of trust. I have already described the interview with the bank manager when the account was opened. I have mentioned also the putting of the "bingo" winnings into the account, and the one withdrawal for the benefit of both of them.

It might, however, be thought that this was a borderline case, since it is not easy to pinpoint a specific moment of declaration, and one must exclude from one's mind any case built in the existence of an implied or constructive trust; for this case was put forward at the trial and is now argued by the plaintiff as one of express declaration of trust. It was so pleaded, and it is only as such that it may be considered in this court. The question, therefore, is whether in all the circumstances the use of those words on numerous occasions as between Mr. Constance and the plaintiff constituted an express declaration of trust. The judge found that they did. For myself, I think he was right so to find. I therefore would dismiss the appeal.

[Bridge and Cairns L.JJ. concurred.]

Notes and Questions

1. Upon what factors did the court rely in *Paul v. Constance* to find that the deceased had effectively declared himself to be trustee for himself and the plaintiff?

2. Should the courts be reluctant to find trusts in which the settlor declares him- or herself trustee? If so, why?

3. What elements are required for effective constitution of a trust?

4. At what time must constitution take place?

5. Re-read note 4 in part (c) above. Do your answers change in light of the material in this section?

6. A testator executed a voluntary settlement several years before his death in which he covenanted with named trustees that his executors should, within one year of his death, pay to the trustees the sum of £60,000 upon trust for his son, the plaintiff, at age 21. The testator retained the deed of settlement in his possession and it was discovered some years after his death. He had not communicated its contents to the trustees nor to the plaintiff. When the plaintiff turned 21 he claimed the £60,000 plus interest. What is the result?[173]

---

173 See *Fletcher v. Fletcher* (1844), 4 Hare 67, 67 E.R. 564.

7. Shortly before his death, a settlor decided to make provision for a recently adopted grandchild. He owned shares in a mutual fund and he wrote to the company telling them that he wished to create a trust of the shares in favour of the grandchild with her mother as trustee. The settlor asked the company to send or draft any necessary documentation requiring his signature. The company did not reply. Shortly before his death the settlor gave a copy of the letter to his daughter. The daughter was appointed executrix of the estate. What is the result?[174]

8. COVENANTS IN FAVOUR OF A VOLUNTEER

(a) Introduction

Once a trust is constituted, the settlor cannot revoke it unless there is a power of revocation.[175] In the eyes of equity, the property belongs to the beneficiaries, and equity will permit no one, not even the settlor, to interfere with their vested rights.

What if the settlor has promised to constitute a trust, but has not actually done so? Is the promise enforceable? The answer largely lies in the law of contract.

There is an equitable maxim that says, "equity will not assist a volunteer."[176] The law is to similar effect. Consequently, as a general rule, a promise is not enforceable in either jurisdiction unless it is supported by consideration.

Consideration at common law consists of money or money's worth. That definition extends, under the peppercorn theory, to nominal consideration. Common law courts also give effect to promises which, while not supported by consideration, are contained in covenants — that is, documents that are under seal.

Although equity's conception of consideration generally mirrors the common law's, it is slightly narrower in some respects and slightly wider in others. Since equity is concerned with substance, rather than form, it does not recognize a seal. It does, however, give generous effect to marriage settlements. Indeed, it has been said that marriage is "the most valuable consideration imaginable."[177] A marriage settlement is a trust created by a man and a woman in contemplation of marriage. (The concept does not extend to a trust that is created by people who are already married to each other.) They once were very common among the upper classes and recently have begun to reappear, especially in connection with second or subsequent marriages. At common law, a woman's property became her husband's upon marriage. That rule, and the obvious risks that it entailed, could be circumvented by means of a settlement. Prior to marriage, property would be transferred to trustees, who would then deal with it according to the terms of the trust. For present purposes, the interesting effect of a marriage settlement is that equity regards the husband, the wife and the issue of the marriage as having given

---

174 See *Re Halley Estate* (1959), 43 M.R.R. 79 (Nfld. S.C.).

175 See *Paul v. Paul, supra*, note 134. The rules regarding revocation are discussed in a later chapter.

176 Significantly, however, once a trust is constituted, equity will fully protect the beneficiaries, even if they obtained their positions voluntarily.

177 *Attorney General v. Jacobs-Smith*, [1895] 2 Q.B. 341 (C.A.).

valuable consideration for any promises contained within it. That is true even though the issue obviously did not exist at the time that the settlement was created.

Pullan v. Koe[178] is illustrative. Under a marriage settlement, property was settled on trust for a husband and wife for life and, after the death of the survivor, for prospective children. As often happened, it contained a covenant by the wife to settle any after-acquired property in excess of £100. She later received £285, part of which she used and part of which she invested in bonds in her husband's name. When she died, the trustees were allowed to recover the bonds from the husband on the ground that they belonged to the trust beneficiaries, not him. It was clearly stated by the court that the children could have taken the action had the trustees failed to act. It should be noted, however, that such a covenant is not enforceable by, or in favour of, next of kin who become entitled in default of children of the marriage, since they are volunteers.[179]

A distinction must also be drawn between common law and equity in terms of remedies. At law, the courts will award monetary damages, but not specific performance. In contrast, the courts of equity will award specific performance or, where that remedy is inadequate or impossible, damages in lieu.

As a result of the fusion in the late 19th century of the courts of common law and equity, Canadian judges now apply both law and equity. The traditional rules nevertheless continue to operate. It therefore remains necessary to draw the preceding distinctions.

As the following cases demonstrate, the application of the governing rules in the present context is often highly complex. In each instance, you should address a number of questions. To whom was the promise made (*e.g.* beneficiary or trustee)? By whom was the action commenced? What type of relief was claimed (*e.g.* monetary damages or specific performance)? Was the consideration requirement satisfied in law or in equity or in both? To which type of property did the promise pertain (*e.g.* a chose in possession, a chose in action or future property)?

Further Reading

D.W. Elliott, "The Power of Trustees to Enforce Covenants in Favour of Volunteers" (1970), 76 L.Q. Rev. 100.

J.L. Barton, "Trusts and Covenants" (1975), 91 L.Q. Rev. 236.

R.P. Meagher and J.R.F. Lehane, "Trusts of Voluntary Covenants" (1976), 92 L.Q. Rev. 427.

Notes and Questions

1. Which of the following are included as being within the marriage settlement consideration? Which ought to be?
   (a) grandchildren
   (b) illegitimate children
   (c) children by a former marriage

---

178 (1912), [1913] 1 Ch. 9 (Eng. Ch. Div.).
179 See *Plumptre's Marriage Settlement, Re*, [1910] 1 Ch. 609.

(d) children to whom the party stands *in loco parentis*?[180]

2. Is the material covered in this heading applicable to testamentary trusts? If not, why not?

(b) Mechanisms to Circumvent the Constitution Requirement

(i) *The Beneficiary is Party to the Covenant*

CANNON v. HARTLEY

[1949] 1 Ch. 213, [1949] 1 All E.R. 50
Chancery Division

By a deed of separation made in 1941, between the defendant of the first part, his wife of the second part and the plaintiff, their daughter, of the third part, the defendant covenanted,

> If and whenever during the lifetime of the wife or the daughter the husband shall become entitled ... under the will or codicil ... of either of his parents ... to any money or property exceeding in net amount or value of £1,000 he will forthwith at his own expense ... settle one-half of such money or property upon trust for himself for life and for the wife for life after his death and subject thereto in trust for the daughter absolutely ...

In 1944 the defendant became entitled, subject to a prior life interest in favour of his mother, to a quarter share of a fund of approximately £50,000. The defendant's wife died in 1946. The defendant refused to execute a settlement in accordance with his covenant. The plaintiff brought an action for damages for breach of the covenant.

ROMER J.:

The question with which I have now to deal follows on my finding that the reversionary interest to which the defendant became entitled under his father's will was caught by clause 7 of the deed of separation. It has been argued on behalf of the defendant that the plaintiff, not having given any consideration for this covenant by her father, is not only unable to apply to a Court of Equity for the enforcement of the covenant by way of specific performance, but that she is also disqualified from suing at common law for damages for breach of the covenant.

It is, of course, well established that in such a case as this a volunteer cannot come to court of equity and ask for relief which is peculiar to the jurisdiction of equity, *viz.*: specific performance; but for my part I thought it was reasonably clear that, the document being under seal, the covenantee's claim for damages would be entertained, and that is still my belief.

---

180 Hanbury & Martin, *Modern Equity*, 14th ed. by Jill E. Martin (London, Sweet & Maxwell, 1993), Chapter 4.

The matter has, I think, been a little confused by reference to cases where volunteers who are not parties to (for example) a marriage settlement have sought to obtain an indirect benefit through the medium of trustees, which they themselves could not legally obtain. It has, however, been recognized that the court (and by that I mean a court of equity) will in some cases assist persons who are not parties to a settlement, and persons who by the nature of things could not have been parties to such a settlement (for example, the children of a marriage) in an attempt to enforce the provisions of the settlement and the covenants therein contained. That was well established and recognized by the time of *Re D'Angibau*.[181]

. . .

Now it appears to me that neither *Re Pryce*[182] nor *Re Kay's Settlement*[183] is any authority for the proposition which has been submitted to me on behalf of the defendant. In neither case were the claimants parties to the settlement in question, nor were they within the consideration of the deed. When volunteers were referred to *Re Pryce* it seems to me that what Eve J. intended to say was that they were not within the class of non-parties, if I may use that expression, to whom Cotton L.J. recognized in *Re D'Angibau* that the court would afford assistance. In the present case the plaintiff, although a volunteer, is not only a party to the deed of separation but is also a direct covenantee under the very covenant upon which she is suing. She does not require the assistance of the court to enforce the covenant for she has a legal right herself to enforce it. She is not asking for equitable relief but for damages at common law for breach of covenant.

For my part, I am quite unable to regard *Re Pryce*, which was a different case dealing with totally different circumstances, or anything which Eve J. said therein, as amounting to an authority negativing the plaintiff's right to sue in the present case. I think that what Eve J. was pointing out in *Re Pryce* was that the next-of-kin who were seeking to get an indirect benefit had no right to come to a court of equity because they were not parties to the deed and were not within the consideration of the deed and, similarly, they would have no right to proceed at common law by an action for damages, as the court of common law would not entertain a suit at the instance of volunteers who were not parties to the deed which was sought to be enforced, any more than the court of equity would entertain such a suit.

It was suggested to me in argument that in such a case as the present, where the covenant is to bring in after-acquired property, an action for damages for breach of that covenant is in effect the same as a suit for specific performance of a covenant to settle. I myself think that the short answer to that is that the two things are not the same at all. The plaintiff here is invoking no equitable relief; she is merely asking for monetary compensation for a breach of covenant.

---

181 (1880) 15 Ch. D. 228 at 242 (Ch. Div.).
182 [1917] 1 Ch. 234.
183 *Supra*, note 157.

It was next said that, in relation to the claim for damages, having regard to the fact that clause 7 of the settlement contemplates that certain terms of the settlement upon which after-acquired property should be settled are in default of agreement to be decided by arbitration, an element of uncertainty is introduced into the clause which is such that the court would not, or should not, entertain a claim for damages for its breach. In my judgment, that argument is unsound, for this reason, that the beneficial interests contemplated to arise in relation to this after-acquired property are perfectly clearly set out and the only thing which had to be agreed, and in default of agreement would have to be arbitrated, was pure machinery for carrying out the beneficial interest so defined.

Finally, it was suggested to me that, inasmuch as this action is an action for damages by a daughter against her father, and as the quantum of damages must be related to the father's expectation of life, a question arises which, from reason, as I understand it, of delicacy the court would decline to entertain. I can only describe that proposition as novel and I reject it without further comment.

I shall accordingly direct an inquiry as to the damages sustained by the plaintiff for breach by the defendant of the covenant with the plaintiff contained in clause 7 of the deed of separation and the plaintiff will have her costs of the action, the costs of the inquiry to be reserved.

Notes and Questions

1. Describe the disputed promise. To whom was it given? Was the consideration requirement satisfied in law or in equity?

2. By whom was the action brought? Was the action brought in law or in equity?

3. What relief did the court award? Did that remedy arise in law or in equity?

4. Did a trust ever arise, either initially or as a result of the court's order?

5. Was there any difficulty regarding "future property," as that concept is explained below?

(ii) *The Trustee is Party to the Covenant*

What happens if a covenant is made with a trustee (or would-be trustee), but the beneficiaries (or would-be beneficiaries) are not parties to the promise and have not given consideration? Will the common law rely upon the presence of a seal and allow the trustee to sue for substantial damages? Unfortunately, the cases do not provide a clear answer to this question. *Re Kay's Settlement*,[184] below, holds that the trustee should be instructed not to pursue the common law remedies, but other cases variously suggest that a trustee should be given the discretion to sue, compelled to sue, or forbidden to sue.[185]

An additional question arises: even if the trustee is permitted to sue, what relief is available? Damages are the usual remedy at common law, but the trustee

---

184 *Ibid.*

185 See, for example, *Pryce, Re*, [1917] 1 Ch. 234, and *Cook's Settlement Trusts, Re*, [1965] Ch. 902. See also the extract from *Fletcher v. Fletcher* (1844), 4 Hare 67, 67 E.R. 564, reproduced below, in which the trustees were instructed to sue.

has not personally suffered any compensable loss. Moreover, while the intended beneficiaries have suffered a loss as a result of the broken promise, the common law generally will not allow one party to recover damages with respect to a loss suffered by someone else.

One possible way around that problem is for a common law court to return to its roots by refusing to recognize equitable interests. In other words, a judge could look at the covenantee not as a potential trustee (because the law does not recognize trusts), but rather as the personal recipient of the covenantor's enforceable promise to convey a benefit. If that approach was followed, the same court would then be required to determine, in the exercise of its equitable jurisdiction, whether or not the covenantee's receipt of damages amounts to constitution of the trust that the parties initially contemplated. That question is complicated by the fact that an affirmative answer arguably would violate the maxim that "equity will not assist a volunteer," and by the fact that a negative answer would allow the covenantee to retain a benefit that he or she knew was never intended for him or her personally.

Another possible way around that problem is to argue that the measure of damages for breach of a covenant to pay a certain amount must be that sum certain.[186] *Cavendish – Browne's Settlement Trusts, Re*[187] supports this argument. The settlor covenanted with trustees that she would transfer all property to which she was entitled under certain wills. When the settlor died, part of the real property in Canada to which she was entitled under the wills had not been transferred by her to the trustees. The settlor's personal representatives applied for a determination as to whether or not they ought to pay the value of the real estate to the trustees. The court held that the trustees were entitled to recover damages for breach of the covenant and that the measure of the damages was the value of the property.

Nevertheless, given the paucity of cases in this area, it is more likely that, because the trustee suffers minimal or no loss, only nominal damages will be awarded in such situations.

RE KAY'S SETTLEMENT

BROADBENT v. MACNAB

[1939] 1 Ch. 329, [1939] 1 All E.R. 245
Chancery Division

An unmarried woman executed a voluntary settlement that contained a covenant to settle all of her after-acquired property with certain exceptions. Subsequently, the settlor married and had three children. When she later became entitled under a will to certain property which fell within the terms of the covenant, the

---

186 D.W. Elliot, "The Power of Trustees to Enforce Covenants in Favour of Volunteers" (1960), 76 L.Q. Rev. 100 at 112.

187 [1916] W.N. 341.

trustees claimed the property but the settlor refused to transfer it to them. The trustees then applied for the court's direction whether they ought to take action to compel the settlor to perform.

SIMONDS J.:

. . .

The argument before me has been, on behalf of the children of the marriage, beneficiaries under the settlement, that, although it is conceded that the trustees could not successfully take proceedings for specific performance of the agreements contained in the settlement, yet they could successfully, and ought to be directed to, take proceedings at law to recover damages for the non-observance of the agreements contained in the settlement, first, the covenant for further assurance of the appointed share of the first-mentioned £20,000 and, secondly, the covenant with regard to after-acquired property. In the circumstances I must say that I felt considerable sympathy for the argument which was put before me by Mr. Winterbotham on behalf of the children, that there was, at any rate, on the evidence before the court today, no reason why the trustees should not be directed to take proceedings to recover what damages might be recoverable at law for breach of the agreements entered into by the settlor in her settlement. But on a consideration of *Re Pryce*[188] it seemed to me that so far as this court was concerned the matter was concluded and that I ought not to give any directions to the trustees to take the suggested proceedings.

In *Re Pryce* the circumstances appear to me to have been in no way different from those which obtain in the case which I have to consider. In that case there was a marriage settlement made in 1887. It contained a covenant to settle the wife's after-acquired property. In 1904 there was a deed of gift under which certain interests in reversion belonging to the husband were assured by him absolutely to his wife. The husband was also entitled to a one-third share in certain sums appointed to him by the will of his father in exercise of special power of appointment contained in a deed of family arrangement. The share of the £9000 fell into possession in 1891 on the death of his father, and was paid to him, unknown to the trustees of his marriage settlement, and spent. The interests given by the husband to the wife and his share of the £4700 came into possession in 1916 on the death of the husband's mother, and were outstanding in the trustees of his parent's settlement and of the deed of family arrangement respectively. The husband died in 1907, and there was no issue of the marriage. Subject to his widow's life interest in both funds, the ultimate residue of the wife's fund was held in trust for her statutory next-of-kin, and the husband's fund was held in trust for him absolutely. The widow was also tenant for life under her husband's will. The trustees of the marriage settlement in that case took out a summons "to have it determined whether these interests and funds were caught by the provisions of the settlement, and, if so, whether they should take proceedings to enforce

---

188 *Supra*, note 182.

them." In those proceedings, apparently, the plaintiffs were the trustees of the marriage settlement, and the only defendant appears to have been the widow of the settlor; that is to say, there were no other parties to the proceedings to whose beneficial interest it was to argue in favour of the enforceability and enforcement of the covenant, but the trustees no doubt argued in favour of their interests, as it was their duty to do.

Eve J., in a considered judgment, held that although the interests to which I have referred were caught by the covenant of the wife and the agreement by the husband respectively, yet the trustees ought not to take any steps to recover any of them. In the case of the wife's fund he said that her next-of-kin were volunteers, who could neither maintain an action to enforce the covenant nor for damages for breach of it, and that the court would not give them by indirect means what they could not obtain by direct procedure; therefore he declined to direct the trustee to take proceedings either to have the covenant specifically enforced or to recover damages at law. The learned judge, as I have said, took time to consider his judgment. Many of the cases which have been cited to me, though not all of them apparently, were cited to him, and after deciding that no steps should be taken to enforce specific performance of the covenant he used these words:[189]

> The position of the wife's fund is somewhat different, in that her next-of-kin would be entitled to it on her death; but they are volunteers, and although the court would probably compel fulfilment of the contract to settle at the instance of any persons within the marriage consideration[190] and in their favour will treat the outstanding property as subjected to an enforceable trust[191] "volunteers have no right whatever to obtain specific performance of a mere covenant which has remained as a covenant and has never been performed."[192] Nor could damages be awarded either in this court, or, I apprehend, at law, where since the *Judicature Act, 1873*, the same defences would be available to the defendant as would be raised in an action brought in this court for specific performance or damages.

That is the exact point which has been urged on me with great insistence by Mr. Winterbotham. Whatever sympathy I might feel for his argument, I am not justified in departing in any way from this decision, which is now 21 years old. The learned judge went on:

> In these circumstances, seeing that the next-of-kin could neither maintain an action to enforce the covenant nor for damages for breach of it, and that the settlement is not a declaration of trust constituting the relationship of trustee and *cestui que trust* between the defendant and the next-of-kin, in which case effect could be given to the trusts even in favour of volunteers, but is a mere voluntary contract to create a trust, ought the court now for the sole benefit of these volunteers to direct the trustees to take proceedings to enforce the defendant's covenant? I think it ought not; to do so would be to give the next-of-kin by indirect means relief they cannot obtain by any direct procedure, and would in effect by enforcing the settlement as against the defendant's legal right to payment and transfer from the trustees of the parents' marriage settlement.

---

189 *Ibid.*, at 241.
190 See *per* Cotton L.J. in *Re D'Angibau* (1880), 15 Ch. D. 228 (C.A.).
191 *Pullan v. Koe*, [1913] 1 Ch. 9.
192 See per James L.J. in *Re D'Angibau, supra*, note 190.

It is true that in those last words the learned judge does not specifically refer to an action for damages, but it is clear that he has in mind directions both with regard to an action for specific performance and an action to recover damages at law — or, now, in this court.

In those circumstances it appears to me that I must follow the learned judge's decision and I must direct the trustees not to take any steps either to compel performance of the covenant or to recover damages through her failure to implement it. I have been dealing so far expressly with the covenant for the settlement of after-acquired property. Exactly the same considerations arise with regard to the appointed sum under the parent's marriage settlement, for there it is conceded that the settlement, if it operated at all, operated by virtue of the implied covenant for further assurance and, since it rests in covenant, it stands on exactly the same footing as the property which would be caught by the covenant for settlement of after-acquired property. Accordingly, the summons being amended, I will answer that question specifically in that way. I direct that the trustees are not to take any steps or proceedings. The costs of all parties will be paid as between solicitor and client out of the capital of the settled fund.

Notes and Questions

1. Explain the circumstances surrounding the promise. Who was the promisor? Who was the promisee? Who were the intended beneficiaries of the promise? Was the consideration requirement satisfied in law or in equity? Was the promise given as part of a marriage settlement? What relief was sought?

2. State the result and explain the court's reasons. Do you agree with the decision in *Re Kay*? Is it fair? As a matter of practice, how could the problem have been averted at the outset?

(iii) *Recharacterization of the Subject-Matter of the Trust*

A final mechanism for allowing a volunteer beneficiary to enforce a promise requires a recharacterization of the subject matter of the intended trust. The key to this possibility is the fact that any form of property may be the subject matter of a trust. That rule obviously includes physical things, such as land and paintings. But it also includes intangible things — choses in action — such as covenants and contractual promises.

Take a simple situation. The (would-be) settlor covenants with the (would-be) trustee to settle Blackacre on trust for the (would-be) beneficiaries. No trust exists at the outset. Moreover, *Re Kay* suggests that the covenant is, from a practical perspective, unenforceable. The trustee theoretically has a right to sue at law, but has not suffered any compensable loss. The beneficiaries have suffered a compensable loss, but do not have a right of action in either law or equity.

Now take a slight variation on the facts. The settlor covenants with the trustee to settle Blackacre on trust for the beneficiaries. The settlor and the trustee also agree that the trustee immediately holds the covenant itself (a chose in action) on trust for the beneficiaries. In that situation, there is a fully constituted trust at the outset, with the covenant as the subject matter. And as the equitable owners of that covenant, the beneficiaries arguably can call for its enforcement.

That analysis was suggested in *Fletcher v. Fletcher*,[193] but has gained little acceptance since. The testator executed a voluntary deed several years before his death in which he covenanted with named trustees that his executors should, within one year after his death, pay to the trustees the sum of £60,000 in trust for his natural son at age 21. The testator retained the deed in his possession and it was discovered some years after his death. He had not communicated its contents to the trustees or his son. When his son attained age 21, he brought an action claiming the £60,000 and interest from the estate. With the following words, the court declared the deed to constitute a debt upon the estate and ordered its payment.[194]

> The rule against relief to volunteers cannot, I conceive, in a case like that before me, be stated higher than this, that a Court of Equity will not, in favour of a volunteer, give to a deed any effect beyond what the law will give to it. But if the author of the deed has subjected himself to a liability at law, and the legal liability comes regularly to be enforced in equity, as in the cases before referred to, the observation that the claimant is a volunteer is of no value in favour of those who represent the author of the deed. If, therefore, the Plaintiff himself were the covenantee, so that he could bring the action in his own name, it follows, from what I have said, that in my opinion he might enforce payment out of the assets of the covenantor in this case. Then, does the interposition of the trustee of this covenant make any difference? I think it does not. Upon this part of the case I have asked myself the question, proposed by Vice-Chancellor Knight Bruce, in *Davenport v. Bishopp*[195] whether, if the surviving trustee chose to sue , there would be any equity on the part of the estate to restrain him from so doing; or, which is the same question, in principle, whether in a case in which the author of the deed has conferred no discretion on the trustees (upon which supposition the estate is liable at law) the right of the Plaintiff is to depend upon the caprice of the trustee, and to be kept in suspense until the *Statute of Limitations* might become a bar to an action by the Trustee? Or, in the case of new trustees being appointed (perhaps by the Plaintiff himself, there being a power to appoint new trustees), supposing his own nominees to be willing to sue, the other trustees might refuse to sue? I think the answer to these and like questions must be in the negative. The testator has bound himself absolutely. There is a debt created and existing. I give no assistance against the testator. I only deal with him as he has dealt by himself, and, if in such a case the trustee will not sue without the sanction of the Court, I think it is right to allow the *cestui que trust* to sue for himself, in the name of the trustee, either at law or in this Court, as the case may require. The rights of the parties cannot depend upon mere accident and caprice.

The problem with this approach is that it is rarely clear that the settlor intended to settle a promise, as opposed to the anticipated product of the promise (*e.g.* money or land), on trust. That intention was somewhat difficult to find in the situation contemplated in *Fletcher*. It was impossible to establish in *Cook's Settlement Trust, Re*,[196] below. In that case, Buckley J. insisted that the requisite intention must be manifest. A court generally will assume that the settlor merely intended to create a trust of the subject matter of the covenant — not of the covenant itself. And in that situation, there is only a promise to constitute the trust

---

193 (1844), 4 Hare 67, 67 E.R. 564.
194 *Ibid.*, at 568.
195 2 Y. & C.C.C. 451.
196 (1964), [1965] Ch. 902, [1964] 3 All E.R. 898.

at some future date — a promise that the beneficiary, as a volunteer, cannot enforce.

RE COOK'S SETTLEMENT TRUSTS

[1965] Ch. 902, [1964] 3 All E.R. 898
Chancery Division

Sir Herbert Cook and his son, Sir Francis, resettled the family fortune. Sir Francis received consideration from his father for the resettlement. The resettlement gave a life interest to Sir Francis with remainder over to his children in default of appointment by him among them. Certain paintings were not included in the settlement but Sir Francis covenanted that he would not, during his lifetime, sell any of them without previous notice in writing to the trustees and that, if any of such paintings were sold during the lifetime of the settlor, the net proceeds of sale would be paid into the settlement. Sir Francis gave one of these paintings, Rembrandt's "Titus," to his third wife and she wanted to sell it. Sir Francis had two children by his first two wives. The trustees sought the direction of the court as to their duties with respect to this covenant.

BUCKLEY J.:

Mr. Goff, appearing for Sir Francis, has submitted first that, as a matter of law, the covenant contained in clause 6 of the settlement is not enforceable against him by the trustees of the settlement; and, secondly, that upon the true construction of the settlement it is and has always been open to Sir Francis to make a valid gift of any of the Part II works of art and that the covenant is not applicable to a sale by a donee. Upon the first of these contentions Mr. Goff submits that the covenant was a voluntary and executory contract to make a settlement in a future event and was not a settlement of a covenant to pay a sum of money to the trustees. He further submits that as regards the covenant all the beneficiaries under the settlement are volunteers, with the consequence that not only should the court not direct the trustees to take proceedings on the covenant but it should positively direct them not to take proceedings. He relies upon *Re Pryce*[197] and *Re Kay's Settlement.*[198]

Counsel for the second and third defendants have contended that on the true view of the facts there was an immediate settlement of the obligation created by the covenant, and not merely a covenant to settle something in the future. It was said, as Mr. Monckton put it, that by the agreement Sir Herbert bought the rights arising under the covenant for the benefit of the *cestui que trustent* under the settlement and that, the covenant being made in favour of the trustees, these rights became assets of the trust. He relied on *Fletcher v. Fletcher;*[199] *Williamson v.*

---

197 [1917] 1 Ch. 234.
198 [1939] Ch. 329, 1 All E.R. 245.
199 *Supra*, note 173.

Codrington[200] and *Re Cavendish Browne's Settlement Trusts*.[201] I am not able to accept this argument. The covenant with which I am concerned did not, in my opinion, create a debt enforceable at law, that is to say, a property right, which, although to bear fruit only in the future and upon a contingency, was capable of being made the subject of an immediate trust, as was held to be the case in *Fletcher v. Fletcher*. Nor is this covenant associated with property which was the subject of an immediate trust as in *Williamson v. Codrington*. Nor did the covenant relate to property which then belonged to the covenantor, as in *Re Cavendish Browne's Settlement Trusts*. In contrast to all these cases, this covenant upon its true construction is, in my opinion, an executory contract to settle a particular fund or particular funds of money which at the date of the covenant did not exist and which might never come into existence. It is analogous to a covenant to settle an expectation or to settle after-acquired property. The case, in my judgment, involves the law of contract, not the law of trusts.

As an alternative argument, Mr. Brightman formulated this proposition, which he admitted not to be directly supported by any authority, but he claimed to conflict with none: that where a covenantor has for consideration moving from a third party covenanted with trustees to make a settlement of property, the court will assist an intended beneficiary who is a volunteer to enforce the covenant if he is specially an object of the intended trust or (which Mr. Brightman says is the same thing) is within the consideration of the deed. In formulating this proposition Mr. Brightman bases himself on language used by Cotton L.J. in *Re D'Angibau*[202] and by Romer J. in *Cannon v. Hartley*.[203] As an example of a case to which the proposition would apply, Mr. Brightman supposes a father having two sons who enters into an agreement with his elder son absolutely in consideration of the son covenanting with his father and the trustees, or with the trustees alone, to settle an expectation on trusts for the benefit of the younger son. The younger son is a stranger to the transaction, but he is also the primary (and special) beneficiary of the intended settlement. A Court of Equity should, and would, Mr. Brightman contends, assist the younger son to enforce his brother's covenant and should not permit the elder son to frustrate the purposes of the agreement by refusing to implement his covenant although he has secured the valuable consideration given for it. This submission is not without attraction, for it is not to be denied that, generally speaking, the conduct of a man who, having pledged his word for valuable consideration, takes the benefits he has so obtained and then fails to do his part, commands no admiration. I have, therefore, given careful consideration to this part of the argument to see whether the state of the law is such as might justify me (subject to the construction point) in dealing with the case on some such grounds.

There was no consideration for Sir Francis's covenant moving from the trustees; nor, of course, was there any consideration moving from Sir Francis's

---

200 (1750), 1 Ves. Sen. 511.
201 [1916] W.N. 341.
202 *Supra*, note 190.
203 [1949] Ch. 213 at 223, [1949] 1 All E.R. 50.

children. Mr. Goff has submitted that there was no consideration for the covenant moving from Sir Herbert, for he says in effect that Sir Francis's reversionary interest in the settled part of the collection valued at £177,407 and the property of an aggregate value of £177,407 which Sir Francis was to receive under the agreement cancelled one another out leaving no consideration moving from Sir Herbert in respect of the covenant. I cannot accept this. The agreement must be considered as a whole. There is no ground for severing it and treating it as comprising two distinct transactions. It contains promises by Sir Herbert and promises by Sir Francis, I am not at liberty to appropriate a particular promise on the one side as consideration for a particular promise on the other, nor to balance the consideration given by one party against that given by the other. Except as a basis for inferring fraud (which is not suggested here) the court never assumes the burden of weighting consideration. It is the existence of consideration, not its value, that is significant. Sir Francis's covenant was, in my judgment, clearly given for valuable consideration moving from his father.

It is an elementary general rule of law that a contract affects only the parties to it and their successors in title and that no one but a party or the successor in title to a party can sue or be sued upon it. There are, however, exceptions to this rule, some legal, some equitable and some statutory. If there is any such exception as Mr. Brightman contends, it must be equitable.

It has long since been recognised that if marriage articles or a marriage settlement contain an executory agreement to settle property, equity will assist an intended beneficiary who is issue of the marriage to enforce the agreement. Such a beneficiary is described as being within the marriage consideration. Perhaps the neatest statement of what is meant by this expression is that of Kay L.J. in *Attorney-General v. Jacobs Smith*,[204] where he says:

> Now, what in the ordinary course of things the marriage consideration covers has been decided again and again. It covers *prima facie* the husband and the wife and the issue of that marriage, and any limitation in favour of any one of those persons comes within the marriage consideration. That is to say they are all treated for every purpose of the settlement as though a consideration moved from each one of them.

In *Hill v. Gomme*,[205] Lord Cottenham L.C. described the children of the marriage as quasi-parties to the contract. This fiction by which a child of the marriage is treated as if he were a party to and as having given consideration for his parents' marriage settlement is no doubt associated with his intimate connection with the marriage which was in fact the consideration for it, and it is, as I understand the law, because he is treated as a party who has given consideration that equity will assist him to enforce any contract to settle property which that settlement may contain. This conception is at least as old as the days of Lord Hardwicke, who in *Harvey v. Ashley*,[206] speaks of the children of the marriage as equally purchasers under both father and mother. He is here, I think, speaking of them as purchasers

---

204 [1895] 2 Q.B. 341 (C.A.).
205 (1841), 5 M. & C. 250.
206 (1748), 3 Alk. 607.

for value not as purchasers in the technical sense used by conveyancers. On the other hand, an intended beneficiary who is not issue of the marriage is not within the marriage consideration, is not treated as though any consideration moved from him, and will not be assisted to enforce a contract to make a settlement. Thus the next-of-kin of the covenantor who are intended to take the property which is to be brought into settlement in the event of a failure of issue cannot enforce a covenant to settle,[207] nor can the children by a previous marriage of one of the parties, unless maybe, their interests are interwoven with those of children of the marriage;[208] nor can the children of the marriage, if the settlement is a post-nuptial one, for in such a case, though there may be consideration as between the husband and the wife, that consideration would not be their marriage but consideration of some other kind to which their children would be strangers.[209]

These authorities show that there is an equitable exception to the general rule of law which I have mentioned where the contract is made in consideration of marriage and the intended beneficiary who seeks to have the contract enforced is within the marriage consideration. They do not support the existence of any wider exception save perhaps in the case of a beneficiary who is not within the marriage consideration but whose interests under the intended trusts are closely interwoven with interests of others who are within that consideration. They do not support the view that any such exception exists in favour of a person who was not a party to the contract and is not to be treated as though he had been and who was given no consideration and is not to be treated as if he had given consideration. Where the obligation to settle property has been assumed voluntarily it is clear that no object of the intended trusts can enforce the obligation. Thus in *Re Kay's Settlement*, a spinster made a voluntary settlement in favour of herself and her issue which contained a covenant to settle after-acquired property. She later married and had children who, as volunteers, were held to have no right to enforce the covenant. Mr. Brightman distinguishes that case from the present on the ground that in *Re Kay's Settlement* the settlement and covenant were entirely voluntary, whereas Sir Francis received consideration from Sir Herbert; but Sir Francis received no consideration from his own children. Why, it may be asked, should they be accorded an indulgence in a Court of Equity which they would not have been accorded had Sir Herbert given no consideration? As regards them the covenant must, in my judgment, be regarded as having been given voluntarily. A plaintiff is not entitled to claim equitable relief against another merely because the latter's conduct is unmeritorious. Conduct by A which is unconscientious in relation to B so as to entitle B to equitable relief may not be unconscientious in relation to C so that C will have no standing to claim relief notwithstanding that the conduct in question may affect C. The father in Mr. Brightman's fictitious illustration could after performing his part of the contract release his elder son from the latter's covenant with him to make settlement on the younger son, and the younger son could, I think, not complain. Only the covenant with the trustees

207 *Re D'Angibau, supra*, note 190.
208 See *Attorney-General v. Jacobs Smith, supra*, note 204.
209 *Green v. Paterson* (1886), 32 Ch. D. 95.

would then remain, but this covenant would be a voluntary one, the trustees having given no consideration. I can see no reason why in these circumstances the court should assist the younger son to enforce the covenant with the trustees. But the right of the younger son to require the trustees to enforce their covenant could not, I think, depend on whether the father had or had not released his covenant. Therefore, as it seems to me, on principle the younger son would not in any event have an equitable right to require the trustees to enforce their covenant. In other words, the arrangement between the father and his elder son would not have conferred any equitable right or interest upon his younger son.

I reach the conclusion that Mr. Brightman's proposition is not well-founded. There is no authority to support it and *Green v. Paterson* is, I think, authority the other way. Accordingly, the second and third defendants are not, in my judgment, entitled to require the trustees to take proceedings to enforce the covenant even if it is capable of being construed in a manner favourable to them.

[His Lordship then held that the words "in case any of such pictures shall be sold" in clause 6 of the settlement following the covenant that Sir Francis would not during his lifetime sell without previous notice in writing to the trustees, only referred to a sale by Sir Francis and did not preclude a disposition of any of the pictures in any other way, *e.g.*, by gift.

The judgment was appealed, but the case was settled before the appeal was heard.]

Notes and Questions

1. By whom was the action brought? Would the result have been any different if Sir Herbert had claimed relief, either in law or in equity?

2. Why were the beneficiaries of the settlement trust unable to enforce the covenant?

3. Should a court be eager to employ the recharacterization analysis, so as to enable voluntary beneficiaries to enforce a promise to place property in trust? Why or why not?

4. Buckley J. said, "The covenant with which I am concerned did not, in my opinion, create a debt enforceable at law, that is to say, a property right, which, although to bear fruit only in the future and upon a contingency, was capable of being made the subject of an immediate trust, as was held to be the case in *Fletcher v. Fletcher*." Is that statement correct as a matter of law?[210]

(c) Future Property

A final complication in the area of constitution involves future property. Suppose that S expects to inherit Blackacre from his father, who is still alive. S purports to immediately transfer his interest in that land to T on trust for B. There

---

210 *Lloyd's v. Harper* (1880), 16 Ch. D. 290 (C.A.).

is, in fact, no trust at all. Equity does not recognize a mere expectation as a form of property. And without property, there cannot be a trust.[211]

That is not, however, necessarily the end of the matter. Although equity does not recognize a mere expectation as a form of property, it does recognize a contractual right as such. That is significant because future property may form the subject matter of a contract.

Suppose that S enters into a contract with T. In exchange for valuable consideration, S promises that, if and when he inherits Blackacre from his father, he will settle it on trust for B. As before, there cannot be an immediate trust of S's expectation of receiving Blackacre. There can, however, be an immediate trust of the contractual right that was created between S and T with respect to the future property. In other words, the recharacterization analysis that was examined in the previous section may be used once again. Assuming that the parties' actual intentions are supportive, the court may find that T received S's contractual promise on trust for B, and that as the beneficial owner of that promise, B enjoys a right of enforcement.

For obvious reasons, that sort of analysis seldom applies in practice. Cases involving future property tend instead to look like *Ellenborough, Re*.[212]

RE ELLENBOROUGH

TOWRY LAW v. BURNE

[1903] 1 Ch. 697
Chancery Division

Miss E.J. Towry Law, the settlor, executed a voluntary settlement that purported to grant to trustees any property that she might receive, by will or intestacy, from her brother or sister. When her sister died, the settlor gave the trustees the property that she received from the estate. When her brother died the settlor became entitled to all his property. She did not wish to transfer this property to the trustees, and she brought an application to determine whether she could refuse to do so.

BUCKLEY J.:

On December 22, 1893, there were living Lord Charles Ellenborough and Gertrude Edith Towry Law, brother and sister of the applicant upon this summons. They were entitled respectively to certain property absolutely. In their property the applicant had no property or interest of any kind. She had an expectation

---

211 *Ernst & Young Inc. v. Central Guaranty Trust Co.* (2001), 36 E.T.R. (2d) 200, 2001 CarswellAlta 151, [2001] A.J. No. 148, 2001 ABQB 92, 12 B.L.R. (3d) 72, 283 A.R. 325 (Alta. Q.B.), additional reasons at (2002), 2002 CarswellAlta 1124, 304 A.R. 1, 29 B.L.R. (3d) 222 (Alta. Q.B.).

212 [1903] 1 Ch. 697.

arising from the fact that, owing to the relationship between them and herself and to their state of health, she might be (as was subsequently the case) the survivor, and might under their respective wills or intestacies become entitled to their property. She had neither a future interest nor a possibility coupled with an interest capable of being disposed of under section 6 of (8 & 9 Vict.), c. 106. She had only a *spes successionis*, and that is not a title to property by English law.[213] In that state of facts the applicant, on December 22, 1893, executed a voluntary settlement by deed by which she granted to the trustees, who are the respondents of this summons, the real estate, and assigned the personal estate to which the applicant, in the event of the death of her brother and sister respectively in her lifetime, might become entitled under their respective wills or intestacies. That deed could not operate by way of grant, but could in a Court of Equity operate as an agreement on the part of the applicant to grant and assign that which in fact could not by the deed be granted or assigned. The brother and sister are now dead, intestate, and the applicant has become entitled by devolution. The property coming to the applicant from her sister has been handed over to the trustees, and the applicant does not say that she can get it back. The property of the brother has not so been handed over, and the applicant does not desire to hand it over unless she is compelled to do so. The question to be determined upon this summons is whether she can be called upon by the trustees to assign and hand over to them that which has come to her by devolution from the late Lord Ellenborough, or whether she can refuse to do anything further to perfect that which was a mere voluntary deed. In order to raise the question in proper form a writ has been, or will be, issued by the trustees against the applicant seeking to recover the funds, and the order will be drawn up on this summons and in that action. The deed was purely voluntary. The question is whether a volunteer can enforce a contract made by deed to dispose of an expectancy. It cannot be and is not disputed that if the deed had been for value the trustees could have enforced it. If value be given, it is immaterial what is the form of assurance by which the disposition is made, or whether the subject of the disposition is capable of being thereby disposed of or not. An assignment for value binds the conscience of the assignor. A Court of Equity as against him will compel him to do that which *ex hypothesi* he has not yet effectually done. Future property, possibilities, and expectancies are all assignable in equity for value.[214] But when the assurance is not for value, a Court of Equity will not assist a volunteer. In *Meek v. Kettlewell*,[215] affirmed by Lord Lyndhurst,[216] the exact point arose which I have here to decide, and it was held that a voluntary assignment of an expectancy, even though under seal, would not be enforced by a Court of Equity. "The assignment of an expectancy," says Lord Lyndhurst,[217] "such as this is, cannot be supported unless made for a valuable consideration." It is however suggested that that decision was overruled or af-

---

213 *Re Parsons* (1890), 45 Ch. D. 51.
214 *Tailby v. Official Receiver* (1888), 13 App. Cas. 523 (H.L.).
215 (1842), 1 Hare 464, 66 E.R. 1114.
216 (1843), 1 Ph. 342.
217 *Ibid.*, at 347.

fected by the decision of the Court of Appeal in *Kekewich v. Manning*,[218] and a passage in White and Tudor's Leading Cases in Equity,[219] was referred to upon the point. In my opinion *Kekewich v. Manning* has no bearing upon that which was decided in *Meek v. Kettlewell*. The assignment in *Kekewich v. Manning* was not of an expectancy, but of property. "It is on legal and equitable principles," said Knight Bruce L.J., "we apprehend, clear that a person *sui juris*, acting freely, fairly, and with sufficient knowledge, ought to have and has it in his power to make, in a binding and effectual manner, a voluntary gift of any part of his property, whether capable or incapable of manual delivery, whether in possession or reversionary, and howsoever circumstanced." The important words there are "of his property." The point of *Meek v. Kettlewell* and of the case before me is that the assignment was not of property, but of a mere expectancy. On December 22, 1893, that with which the grantor was dealing was not her property in any sense. She had nothing more than an expectancy. In *Re Tilt*[220] there was again a voluntary assignment of an expectancy, and the point was not regarded as arguable. "It was rightly admitted" said Chitty J., "that as, when this plaintiff executed the deed of 1880, she had no interest whatever in the fund in question, which was a mere expectancy, the deed was wholly inoperative both at law and in equity, being entirely voluntary." By "wholly inoperative" there the learned judge of course did not mean that if the voluntary settlor had handed over the funds the trustees would not have held them upon the trusts, but that the grantees under the deed could not enforce it as against the settlor in a Court of Equity or elsewhere. In my judgment the interest of the plaintiff as sole heiress-at-law and next-of-kin of the late Lord Ellenborough was not effectually assigned to the trustees by the deed, and the trustees cannot call upon her to grant, assign, transfer, or pay over to them his residuary real and personal estate.

Notes and Questions

1. Why was Miss Towry Law not required to transfer the property she inherited from her brother to the voluntary trust she had covenanted to create?

2. Why did the court conclude that the property that Miss Towry Law inherited from her sister was held on trust?

3. Would the result in *Re Ellenborough* have been different if the "future property" had been characterized as a chose in action? Why or why not?

4. Formulate an argument that would support the view that the "future property" was a chose in action.

5. Is after-acquired property future property? Are settlements of after-acquired property valid trusts? If so, how can you reconcile that with the fact that future property is not property in the eyes of equity?

---

218 (1851), 1 D. M. & G. 176, 42 E.R. 519.
219 7th ed., Vol. ii, at 851.
220 (1896), 74 L.T. 163.

(d) Exceptions to the Rule that Equity Will Not Assist a Volunteer

The rule that equity will not assist a volunteer is subject to a number of exceptions. These exceptions include the doctrine of part performance, equitable estoppel, gifts *mortis causa* and the rule in *Strong v. Bird*.[221] The rule in *Strong v. Bird* can be stated as follows: when an incomplete gift is made during the donor's lifetime and the donor appoints the would-be recipient as executor,[222] the vesting of the property in the donee as executor may be treated as completion of the gift. The rule in *Strong v. Bird* is considered in *Re Gonin*, below. The other exceptions are examined in the standard texts on contract and property.[223]

RE GONIN

[1977] 2 All E.R. 720
Chancery Division

In 1944 the plaintiff's parents persuaded her to return home to look after them. She did so, but alleged that in consideration of her so doing, they promised to make a gift of the house which they owned and its contents, which were owned by the mother, to her. She stayed with her parents until they died. The mother, being the survivor, died intestate. The mother was under the impression that she could not make a valid will in favour of the plaintiff and the defendants, her two sisters, because they were born outside marriage. For this reason she wished to do something for the plaintiff during her lifetime. In 1962, she made a cheque for £33,000 in favour of the plaintiff which the plaintiff was to receive when her mother died and, over the years, made specific gifts of items of furniture to the plaintiff. Later the mother sold part of the house and also three building lots which adjoined the house. She offered part of the proceeds to the plaintiff as a gift but the plaintiff declined. After the mother died, the plaintiff was granted letters of administration of her mother's estate and subsequently she brought two actions. In the second action the plaintiff sought a declaration that, as administratrix of her mother's estate, she became entitled to the house and the contents absolutely, either on the basis of an oral contract between herself and her parents, whereby the latter gave the property to her in consideration of her promise to look after them for the rest of their lives, or under the rule in *Strong v. Bird*.[224]

---

221 *Supra*, note 164. *Strong v. Bird* involved a testator who intended during his life, and up to the time of death, to forgive a particular debt and who appointed the debtor to be his executor. That reasoning was later extended from the forgiveness of a debt to the completion of a gift: *Stewart v. McLaughlin*, (sub nom. Stewart, Re) [1908] 2 Ch. 251, 77 L.J. Ch. 525, 99 L.T. 106, 24 T.L.R. 679 (Eng. Ch. Div.).

222 Or, in cases of intestacy, where the would-be recipient is appointed administrator.

223 See, for example, G.L.H. Fridman, *The Law of Contracts in Canada*, 2nd ed., (Carswell: Toronto, 1986) and *Oosterhoff on Wills and Successions*, 5th ed., (Carswell: Toronto, 2001) ("Oosterhoff, *Wills*").

224 *Supra*, note 164.

The court held that there was no memorandum in writing of the alleged contract and thus no compliance with the statutory requirements. The plaintiff could not rely on the doctrine of part performance either because she could not show any acts of part performance that were referable solely to the contract with respect to the real property.

The court then dealt with the question of the application of the rule in *Strong v. Bird.*

WALTON J.:

. . .

I now turn to the second way in which Miss Gonin's case is put, namely reliance on the doctrine in *Strong v. Bird.* It was accepted by both counsel before me, following the decision of Farwell J. in *Re James, James v. James*[225] that the doctrine applied to administrators as well as to executors. I shall accordingly proceed on that agreed view of the law but I feel that before I do so I must express my own difficulties in accepting this position, leaving it to a higher court to determine what, if any, validity they have.

I start from the simple proposition that if the defendant in *Strong v. Bird* itself had been an administrator instead of an executor the case would have been decided the other way, since it distinctly proceeded on the basis that at law the appointment of the person as an executor effected a release of any debt due from the executor to the testator, a doctrine which was never applied to an administrator.[226]

One can see why this should be so: By appointing the executor, the testator has by his own act made it impossible for the debtor to sue himself. And, indeed, so far the rule has been taken that although it will no longer apply if the person appointed executor has renounced probate, yet it will still apply if power to prove has been reserved to him.[227]

The appointment of an administrator, on the other hand, is not the act of the deceased but of the law. It is often a matter of pure chance which of many persons equally entitled to a grant of letters of administration finally takes them out. Why, then, should any special tenderness be shown to a person so selected by law and not the will of the testator, and often indifferently selected among many with an equal claim? It would seem an astonishing doctrine of equity that if the person who wishes to take the benefit of the rule in *Strong v. Bird* manages to be the person to obtain a grant then he will be able to do so, but if a person equally entitled manages to obtain a prior grant, then he will not be able to do so. This appears to me to treat what ought to be a simple rule of equity, namely that if the legal title to a gift is perfected by the appointment by the intending donor of the intended donee as the executor, and the latter proves his will, then the coincidence

---

225 [1935] Ch. 449.
226 See *Nedham's Case* (1610), 8 Co. Rep. 135a; *Wankford v. Wankford* (1704), 1 Salk. 299, 89 E.R. 390 (K.B.); *Seagram v. Knight* (1867), 2 Ch. App. 628.
227 *Re Applebee, Leveson v. Beales*, [1891] 3 Ch. 422.

of the donor's having intended the gift and having vested the legal estate in the intended donee should coalesce into absolute ownership, as something in the nature of a lottery. I cannot think that equity is so undiscriminating. I am of course aware that *Re James, James v. James* was cited with no dissent by Buckley J. (as he then was) in *Re Ralli's Will Trusts,*[228] though I think the matters there in issue were fundamentally different from those which arose under the rule in *Strong v. Bird* and as I read his judgment. *Re James* was only used as an illustration. However, in spite of these doubts I shall follow, as I have said, *Re James* leaving it for another court to consider at some appropriate time whether there is or is not any solid foundation for these misgivings.

In order for the rule in *Strong v. Bird* to apply at all I have to find a continuing intention on the part of the deceased that Miss Gonin should immediately take both the land and the furniture. In my judgment, so far as the land is concerned no such continuing intention can be found. I think the manner in which the deceased dealt with the sale of the two portions of the gardens of The Gables, retaining the proceeds of sale of the first without any discussion whatsoever with Miss Gonin, and, it is true, offering the proceeds of the sale of the second to Miss Gonin, not as owner, but as recompense for her hard work without remuneration, points most clearly away from the deceased ever having had any such intention by 1963 anyway, whatever her earlier intentions may have been. If there had been a previous intention to give the property then I think that that intention changed by the latest by 1962 when the deceased drew the cheque in favour of her daughter. I find it impossible to think that from then on what she really had in her mind was anything other than that Miss Gonin would inherit the cheque on the deceased's death — no immediate gift, and no gift of land. And also there is no other memorandum of any description speaking of any other arrangement.

As regards the furniture, however, I think it is possible for me to take a more liberal view of the position. Mrs. Webb's evidence is very clear about this, and she drew a very careful distinction indeed between the furniture, which the deceased had already given, in her view, to Miss Gonin, and the property, which Miss Gonin was ultimately going to inherit by means of a cheque in her favour representing its value. I think she meant what she said. For what it is worth her evidence is corroborated in one small particular by Mr. Collins, the person who lived in the house in return for doing odd jobs about it. Furthermore Miss Gonin told me, and, as I say, she is in general a truthful witness though by no means an accurate one, that from time to time at birthdays and Christmas she was further actually given various easily portable pieces of the furniture as Christmas and birthday presents. While this might, I suppose, be interpreted as the deceased going back on the gift she had already made, I think it is permissible to treat this as being in the circumstances in confirmation rather than in derogation of the general gift.

Accordingly, at the end of the day, I have come to the conclusion that Miss Gonin succeeds as to the furniture with the trifling exception of the furniture in her mother's room, but fails as to The Gables itself. A houseful of furniture is not

---

228 [1964] Ch. 288, [1963] 3 All E.R. 940.

much reward for a lifetime's devoted service to one's parents. I should have been glad to have been able to come, consistently with the evidence, to a conclusion more favourable to her, I much regret I am unable to do so.

Notes and Questions

1. What are the exceptions to the rule that equity will not assist a volunteer?

2. Is the rule in *Strong v. Bird* generally defensible? How often does a testator truly intend to perfect an otherwise imperfect gift by naming the donee as executor? Is the operation of the rule simply fortuitous?

3. Is *Re Gonin* a strict application of the rule in *Strong v. Bird*? If not, how does it alter the rule in *Strong v. Bird*?

4. The settlor had two sons and a daughter. She attempted to create a trust, with her two sons as trustees, that gave her a life estate, with the remainder to her daughter and the daughter's children. The subject matter fell into two groups. The Group A assets were already registered in the names of the settlor and her two sons, although the settlor was the sole beneficiary. The Group B assets were registered in the settlor's name alone. The settlor subsequently made a series of wills over a period of several years. Some of those wills presumed the existence of the purported trust, but the last one did not. When the settlor died, her daughter and two sons became personal representatives of her estate.

(a) Was a trust created? If so, what was its subject matter? When was the subject matter constituted into the trust?

(b) If a trust was created, was it constituted with assets in Group A or Group B or both?[229]

9. FORMAL REQUIREMENTS

(a) Generally

Historically, a trust could be created orally or in writing regardless of whether the subject-matter of the trust was land or personal property. It was, therefore, relatively easy for someone to manufacture evidence after the fact and to present a perjured claim to an interest under an alleged trust. To reduce this problem, the *Statute of Frauds*[230] was enacted in England in 1677. The Act imposed minimal formal requirements for the creation and transfer of interests in land, contracts respecting interests in land, the creation of trusts, the transfer of equitable interests, and the making of wills. Over the years, the scope of the statute has been reduced because several of these areas were transferred to other statutes. For example, the creation of interests in land is now covered in property statutes[231] and the formalities governing wills were transferred, with amendments, to the English *Wills Act, 1837*.[232] The latter was adopted, with various changes, in all the Canadian common law jurisdictions.

---

229 See *Wale, Re,* [1956] 1 W.L.R. 1346, [1956] 3 All E.R. 280.

230 1676 (29 Car. 2), c. 3.

231 Such as the *Conveyancing and Law of Property Act,* R.S.O. 1990, c. C.34.

232 1837 (7 Will. 4 & 1 Vict.), c. 26, s. 9. The *Statute of Wills,* 1540 (32 Hen. 8), c. 1, s. 1, did require a will of real property to be in writing but imposed no other formalities.

Certain sections of the *Statute of Frauds* nevertheless remain in effect, in particular those pertaining to *inter vivos* trusts. Since the statute was enacted before the colonization of Canada, it became part of the received English law in all the Canadian common law jurisdictions. It has been re-enacted in some of those jurisdictions with amendments. The relevant sections have also been re-enacted in England in a slightly different form.[233]

One important reason for the enactment of the *Statute of Frauds* in 1677 was that the law of evidence had not yet developed sufficiently to provide protection against tainted or unreliable evidence. For example, a jury traditionally was allowed to rely not only upon the evidence presented in court, but also upon its own knowledge of the dispute. There were other problems regarding the receipt of evidence. For instance, it was difficult to obtain an order for a new trial because of a perverse verdict, and persons interested in the outcome of the dispute, including the parties and their spouses, were precluded from testifying.[234]

It may be questioned whether the statute still serves a useful purpose. The problems mentioned in the last paragraph are now addressed by the modern law of evidence. Moreover, the statute can be avoided under the doctrine of part performance and under the principle that prevents the legislation from being used as an instrument of fraud.[235] Finally, the statute continues to be a source of frequent litigation.

Nevertheless, the statute remains in force for now. Its effect upon contracts to create trusts, the creation of trusts, and the transfer of equitable interests under trusts therefore needs to be examined.

Further Reading

G.H.L. Fridman, "The Necessity for Writing in Contracts within the Statute of Frauds" (1985), 35 U. of T. L.J. 43.

M.G. Bridge, "The Statute of Frauds and Sale of Land Contracts" (1986), 64 Can. Bar. Rev. 58.

(b) Inter Vivos Formalities

(i) *Statutory Provisions*

The formal requirements governing contracts to create *inter vivos* trusts, the creation of *inter vivos* trusts and the transfer of equitable interests under trusts are contained in the *Statute of Frauds*.[236] The relevant sections of the Ontario version are reproduced below. The original English Act[237] is in force in Alberta, Saskatch-

---

233 *Law of Property Act, 1925*, (15 & 16 Geo. 5), c. 20, s. 53.
234 See Theodore F.T. Plucknett, *A Concise History of the Common Law*, 5th ed. (London: Butterworth & Co. Ltd., 1956), pp. 55-7; Sir William Holdsworth, *A History of English Law* (London: Methuen & Co. Ltd. and Sweet & Maxwell Ltd., 1903-1972), vol. 6, at 379-97.
235 This principle is discussed in detail in the chapter on constructive trusts.
236 R.S.O. 1990, c. S.19.
237 *Statute of Frauds*, 1677 (29 Cha. 2), c. 3.

ewan, Newfoundland, the Northwest Territories, and Yukon Territory, as received English law.[238] This Act was also in force in Manitoba but has been repealed in that province[239] and in British Columbia.[240] The *Statute of Frauds* of Prince Edward Island[241] does not contain any similar provisions.

STATUTE OF FRAUDS

R.S.O. 1990, c. S.19

4. No action shall be brought . . . to charge any person upon any contract or sale of lands, tenements or hereditaments, or any interest in or concerning them, unless the agreement upon which the action is brought, or some memorandum or note thereof is in writing and signed by the party to be charged therewith or some person thereunto lawfully authorized by the party.

. . .

9. Subject to section 10, all declarations or creations of trusts or confidences of any lands, tenements or hereditaments shall be manifested and proved by a writing signed by the party who is by law enabled to declare such trust, or by his or her last will in writing, or else they are void and of no effect.

10. Where a conveyance is made of lands or tenements by which a trust or confidence arises or results by implication or construction of law, or is transferred or extinguished by act or operation of law, then and in every such case the trust or confidence is of the like force and effect as it would have been if this Act had not been passed.

11. All grants and assignments of a trust or confidence shall be in writing signed by the party granting or assigning the same, or by his or her last will or devise, or else are void and of no effect.

Comparable Legislation

Statute of Frauds, 1677 (29 Cha. 2), c. 3, ss. 4, 7-9; R.S.N.B. 1973, c. S-14, ss. 1, 8-10; R.S.N.S. 1989, c. 442, ss. 3-7.

---

238 J.E. Côté, "The Introduction of English Law into Alberta" (1964), 3 Alta. L. Rev. 262; *ibid.*, "The Reception of English Law" (1977), 15 Alta. L. Rev. 29; *Balaberda v. Mucha* (1960), 25 D.L.R. (2d) 76 (Sask. C.A.).

239 By *The Statute of Frauds Repeal Act*, S.M. 1982-83-84, c. 34.

240 *Statute of Frauds*, R.S.B.C. 1979, c. 393, first specifically enacted by R.S.B.C. 1948, c. 130 and substantially revised by S.B.C. 1958, c. 18. Repealed by the *Law Reform Amendment Act, 1985*, S.B.C. 1985, c. 10, s. 8.

241 R.S.P.E.I. 1988, c. S-6.

(ii) *Contracts to Create a Trust*

Section 4 of the *Statute of Frauds*[242] does not, at first blush, appear to have much to do with trusts. It is concerned with contracts. However, a closer reading of section 4 will show that it governs contracts for the sale of land, or any interest therein — including contracts to create trusts of lands or interests therein.

The courts have interpreted that section in such a way as to minimize its application. It has been held that the section does not apply "unless by the terms of the contract a sale of land or some interest in land or concerning land is dealt with as part of the contract."[243] Several situations should be distinguished.

- If A agrees to sell land to B if B will hold the land in trust for B and C, the contract is within the statute. But it has been held that if A also agrees at the outset to resell the property on B and C's behalf after a stated period of time, the second part of the contract is outside the statute. It is not a contract for the sale of land, but rather a contract to sell, that is, an ongoing agreement.[244]
- An agreement under which A purchases Blackacre on behalf of B and herself and agrees to resell a one-half interest to B is outside the statute. In this situation, the agreement between A and B is not one concerning land, but rather the land is the subject matter of trust.[245]
- An agreement to establish a trust with the proceeds of the sale of lands is outside the statute.[246]

When a contract to create a trust is breached, various remedies may be available, depending upon the circumstances. As usual, the party in breach may be liable for compensatory damages or nominal damages. An example was seen in *Cannon v. Hartley, supra*. Alternatively, if the agreement is enforceable in equity, the court may order specific performance of the disputed obligation. In other words, the promisor may be required to fulfill an undertaking to put certain property into trust. Of course, all of those options presume that the claimant has cleared the obstacles discussed in the preceding section.

Remedies are available, however, only if the requirements of section 4 have been met. What, then, does that section require? Note that the agreement itself need not be in writing. There only has to be a written note or memorandum which contains the essential terms of the agreement and which is signed by the defen-

---

242 R.S.O. 1990, c. S.19.
243 *Leslie v. Stevenson* (1915), 34 O.L.R. 473, 24 D.L.R. 544 (Ont. C.A.) at 483 [O.L.R.].
244 *Canadian General Securities Co. v. George* (1918), 42 O.L.R. 560, 43 D.L.R. 20 (Ont. C.A.), reversed on other grounds (1919), 59 S.C.R. 641, 1919 CarswellOnt 23, 52 D.L.R. 679 (S.C.C.). See also *Standard Realty Co. v. Nicholson* (1911), 24 O.L.R. 46, [1911] O.J. No. 49 (Ont. H.C.); *McIlvride v. Mills* (1906), 16 Man. R. 276 (Man. C.A.).
245 *Morris v. Whiting* (1913), 24 Man. R. 56, 5 W.W.R. 936, 15 D.L.R. 254, 1913 CarswellMan 327 (Man. K.B.).
246 *Harris v. Lindeborg* (1930), [1931] S.C.R. 235, [1931] 1 D.L.R. 945, 1930 CarswellBC 127 (S.C.C.). But see *contra Cooper v. Critchley*, [1955] Ch. 431, [1955] 1 All E.R. 520 (Eng. C.A.) at 439 [Ch.], *per* Jenkins L.J.

dant.[247] Indeed, the note or memorandum may consist of several documents incorporated together to form a sufficient memorandum[248] and the signature may be that of the defendant's agent.[249] Moreover, the note or memorandum does not have to be made contemporaneously with the oral agreement, so long as it is in existence when the action is commenced.[250]

In the event of non-compliance, the effect of the section is not to render contracts which do not meet its requirements void, but merely unenforceable.[251] This means, among other things, that the defendant must specifically plead the statute in order to succeed.[252]

The section sometimes may be avoided through the doctrine of part performance. This doctrine prevents a defendant from relying upon the statute if the plaintiff has changed position in reliance upon the contract by performing part of it. In those circumstances, the plaintiff is permitted to prove the contract. Significantly, however, the doctrine is applicable only if the acts of part performance are unequivocally referable to the alleged contract.[253] Mere payment of money under the alleged contract is insufficient.[254]

English courts have taken a more liberal approach to the doctrine of part performance. In *Steadman v. Steadman*,[255] a majority of the House of Lords held that if the alleged acts of part performance tend to show, on the balance of probabilities, that there was some underlying contract between the parties, and if those acts are consistent with the alleged agreement, then the contract may be proved.[256] The *Steadman* case has been cited with approval in Canada, but does

---

247 See *Ackerman v. Thomson* (1974), 47 D.L.R. (3d) 524, 1974 CarswellOnt 815, 4 O.R. (2d) 240 (Ont. C.A.); *Ward v. Coffin* (1972), 27 D.L.R. (3d) 58, 1972 CarswellNB 44, 4 N.B.R. (2d) 481 (N.B. C.A.).

248 *Harvie v. Gibbons* (1980), 109 D.L.R. (3d) 559, 1980 CarswellAlta 20, 12 Alta. L.R. (2d) 72, 16 R.P.R. 174 (Alta. C.A.).

249 *Leeman v. Stocks*, [1951] Ch. 941, [1951] 1 All E.R. 1043 (Eng. Ch. Div.).

250 *MacIntyre v. Spierenburg* (1979), 41 N.S.R. (2d) 584, 1979 CarswellNS 331, 76 A.P.R. 584 (N.S. T.D.).

251 *McMillan v. Barton* (1890), 19 O.A.R. 602, affirmed (1892), 20 S.C.R. 404, 1892 CarswellOnt 19 (S.C.C.) at 616 [O.A.R.]; *Maloughney v. Crowe* (1912), 26 O.L.R. 579, 6 D.L.R. 471 at 473 [D.L.R.], *per* Middleton J.

252 *Beemer v. Brownridge*, [1934] 1 W.W.R. 545, 1934 CarswellSask 9 (Sask. C.A.) at 549 [W.W.R.], *per* Turgeon J.A.

253 *McNeil v. Corbett* (1907), 39 S.C.R. 608, 1907 CarswellNS 180 (S.C.C.) at 611 [S.C.R.], *per* Duff J.; *Deglman v. Guaranty Trust Co. of Canada*, [1954] S.C.R. 725, [1954] 3 D.L.R. 785, 1954 CarswellOnt 140 (S.C.C.); *Thompson v. Guaranty Trust Co.* (1973), [1973] 6 W.W.R. 746, 39 D.L.R. (3d) 408, 1973 CarswellSask 106, 1973 CarswellSask 143, [1974] S.C.R. 1023 (S.C.C.). These cases followed the English Case, *Alderson v. Maddison* (1883), 8 App. Cas. 467, [1881-85] All E.R. Rep. 742, 52 L.J.Q.B. 737 (U.K. H.L.) at 479 [A.C.], *per* Lord Selborne L.C..

254 *McNeil v. Corbett, ibid.*

255 (1974), [1976] A.C. 536, 29 P. & C.R. 46, [1974] 3 W.L.R. 56, [1974] 2 All E.R. 977 (U.K. H.L.) at 560 [A.C.].

256 See, however, *Gonin, Re*, [1979] 1 Ch. 16, which construes the *Steadman* case restrictively.

not yet appear to have been followed.[257] Finally, even if the section renders a contract unenforceable, relief may be imposed on the basis of the action in unjust enrichment. Restitution may be available if one party conferred a benefit upon another.[258]

Notes and Questions

1. X and Y are entitled to the life interest and remainder, respectively, in Blackacre. Y agrees to sell her interest to X, so that the life interest and the remainder will merge. Moreover, X and Y agree that X will declare a trust of Blackacre for the benefit of Z.

(a) Does the *Statute of Frauds* apply to this arrangement?

(b) Assume instead that X disclaims her life interest when it is created, thereby accelerating Y's fee simple interest[259] and they agree that Y will declare a trust of Blackacre for the benefit of Z. Does the *Statute of Frauds* apply to this arrangement?

(c) Would the statute apply if X and Y agreed to sell Blackacre and to settle the proceeds of sale upon Z?

2. In view of the court's construction of section 4 and its circumvention in many cases, is there much continuing utility in the section?

(iii) *Creation of Inter Vivos Trusts*

Sections 9 and 10 of the *Statute of Frauds*[260] are concerned with the formalities required to create an *inter vivos* trust of land. Several things must be noted about these sections. First, trusts of personalty are not covered by section 9. Second, section 10 provides that resulting and constructive trusts are outside the ambit of the statute.[261] Third, section 9 applies both to a transfer of land to a trustee and to a declaration by the owner of land that it is to be held in trust.

Interesting questions arise when, in an existing trust for B, B states that he or she will thereafter hold the equitable interest in trust for C, or when B informs the trustee, T, that T is thenceforth to hold the equitable interest in trust for D. Has B created a trust? Declared a trust?

Somewhat surprisingly the requirements of section 9 have been construed in much the same fashion as those of section 4. Accordingly, the trust need not be in writing itself,[262] so long as it is evidenced by some writing signed by the person entitled to create the trust (that is, the person who owns the interest in the land in

---

257 See *Shillabeer v. Diebel* (1979), 100 D.L.R. (3d) 279, 1979 CarswellAlta 118, 9 Alta. L.R. (2d) 112, 18 A.R. 173, 5 E.T.R. 30 (Alta. T.D.); *Colberg v. Braunberger* (1978), 8 Alta. L.R. (2d) 73, 1978 CarswellAlta 155, 12 A.R. 183 (Alta. C.A.). See generally Oosterhoff, *Wills*, ch. 4, part 3.

258 See *Deglman v. Guaranty Trust Co. of Canada*, [1954] S.C.R. 725, [1954] 3 D.L.R. 785, 1954 CarswellOnt 140 (S.C.C.).

259 On the effects of disclaimer see Oosterhoff, *Wills*, Chapter 11, part 10.

260 R.S.O. 1990, c. S.19.

261 See, *e.g.*, *Bannister v. Bannister*, [1948] 2 All E.R. 133 (C.A.); *Vaselenak v. Vaselenak* (1921), 57 D.L.R. 370, 16 Alta. L.R. 256, [1921] 1 W.W.R. 889 (C.A.); *Homeplan Realty Ltd. v. Rasmussen (No. 2)*, [1978] 3 W.W.R. 304 (B.C. S.C.).

262 The New Brunswick and Nova Scotia statutes require that the trust itself be in writing and not merely evidenced by some writing.

respect of which the trust is created, whether the interest is legal or equitable.)[263] Notice that section 9 differs slightly from section 4 in that respect, insofar as the latter may be satisfied by a signature of the relevant person's agent. The writing must sufficiently state the terms of the trust,[264] although it has been held that a conveyance of land to a grantee "in trust" complies with the section.[265] Although the writing may predate the creation of the trust,[266] the reference in section 9 to the creator's last will suggests that the creation of the trust may be evidenced by his or her will. In the original statute[267] this reference probably meant that the section also applied to testamentary trusts.[268]

Although the section states that trusts which fail to comply with its requirements are void, the cases hold that this simply means that they are unenforceable, since the statute is a procedural or evidentiary statute and does not affect the substance.[269] As in the case of section 4, this suggests that the statute must be specifically pleaded in order to sustain a defence based on it.

(iv) *Transfers of Equitable Interests*

Section 11 of the *Statute of Frauds*[270] may be construed to include the transfer by beneficiaries of beneficial interests under trusts. If so, such transfers must be in writing in order to be valid.

The most significant difference between the provisions of section 9 (creation of trusts of land) and those of section 11 (the disposition of beneficial interests) is that section 9 applies only to interests in land, whereas section 11 applies to all property interests, both realty and personalty. The collocation of the sections in the *Statute of Frauds* suggests that the disposition of an equitable interest under a resulting or constructive trust is caught by section 11, although its creation is not caught by section 9.

Section 11 appears to apply in the simple situation in which T holds property in trust for A for life with remainder to B and B assigns his or her interest to C. The assignment appears to be caught by the legislation. It is not so easy to determine whether the legislation applies if A disclaims, thus accelerating B's interest; if B surrenders his or her interest to A, so that the two interests merge; if A and B direct T thenceforth to hold in trust for D; if B assigns his or her interest to U to hold in trust for E; if A and B, being together the absolute beneficial owners and able to terminate the trust, direct T to convey the legal title to F; and if B agrees for value to assign his or her interest to G.

---

263 *Tierney v. Wood* (1854), 19 Beav. 330, 52 E.R. 377.
264 *Rochefoucauld v. Boustead* (1986), [1897] 1 Ch. 196 (C.A.).
265 *Melnychuck v. Susko*, [1953] O.R. 127, [1953] 1 D.L.R. 761 (H.C.), affirmed [1954] O.R. 173, [1954] 2 D.L.R. 218 (C.A.).
266 *Wilde v. Wilde* (1873), 20 Gr. 521 at 531 (Ont. C.A.).
267 *Statute of Frauds*, 1677 (29 Cha. 2), c. 3, s. 9.
268 However, s. 5 of that statute specifically required devises of land to be in writing. The formalities of testamentary trusts are now covered by wills statutes.
269 *Leroux v. Brown* (1852), 12 C.B. 801, 138 E.R. 1119.
270 R.S.O. 1990, c. S.19.

There is almost no Canadian case law on these problems,[271] but there are a few cases in England. Since the two statutes are similar, this has implications for Canada. Regrettably, the law in this area is not particularly clear. The English cases are mostly concerned with situations in which a taxpayer is seeking to avoid a tax.[272]

Further Reading

G. Battersby, "Some Thoughts on the Statute of Frauds in Relation to Trusts" (1975), 7 Ottawa L. Rev. 483.

G. Battersby, "Formalities for the Disposition of Equitable Interests under Trusts" [1979] Conv. 17.

Notes and Questions

1. Would the statute be applicable if there was a trust of personalty in favour of A for life with remainder to B, and A disclaimed, thereby accelerating B's interest? Would A's disclaimer amount to a grant or assignment under the Ontario Act?[273]

2. T holds stocks and bonds worth $100,000 on trust for A for life, with remainder to B for life. What is the effect of the following:

(a) A declares himself trustee of his interest for C on terms that A will invest the income and pay the income thereon to C, less her fees as trustee. A then retires and appoints D in his stead.

(b) B agrees to give his remainder interest to F, in return for F's yacht. F gives B her yacht pursuant to the agreement.

(c) S, the settlor, accepts T's declaration that the reversion will thenceforth be held on trust for all of S's children equally.

3. A and B hold property on trust for C. Discuss the formalities that are required in the following circumstances both if the property is land or personalty and if the property is held upon express or resulting trust.

(a) C assigns her equitable interest to D.

(b) C assigns her equitable interest to X and Y in trust for D.

(c) C directs A and B to hold the property on trust for D.

(d) C contracts with D to transfer her equitable interest to D.

(e) C declares herself to be a trustee of her interest for D.

---

271 The only Canadian case, *Transco Mills Ltd. v. Louie* (1975), 59 D.L.R. (3d) 665 (B.C. S.C.), held that the expression "evidenced in writing" in section 2 of the now repealed British Columbia statute meant that the terms of the agreement should be set out in detail in the document evidencing it.

272 See *Grey v. Inland Revenue Commissioners* (1959), [1960] A.C. 1, [1959] 3 All E.R. 603 (H.L.); *Oughtred v. Inland Revenue Commissioners* (1959), [1960] A.C. 206, [1959] 3 All E.R. 623 (H.L.); *Vandervell v. I.R.C.* (1996), [1967] 2 A.C. 291, [1967] 1 All E.R. 1 (H.L.); *Re Vandervell's Trusts (No. 2)*, [1974] 1 Ch. 269, [1974] 3 All E.R. 205 (C.A.); *Re Holt's Settlement* (1968), [1969] 1 Ch. 100, [1968] 1 All E.R. 470.

273 See *Re Paradise Motor Co. Ltd.*, [1968] 1 W.L.R. 1125, [1968] 2 All E.R. 625 (C.A.); *Law of Property Act, 1925*, (15 & 16 Geo. 5), c. 20, s. 205(1)(ii). See also *Re Stratton's Disclaimer*, [1958] Ch. 42 (C.A.); *Re Jacques* (1985), 49 O.R. (2d) 623, 18 E.T.R. 65, 16 D.L.R. (4th) 472 (H.C.). And see Oosterhoff, *Wills*, Chapter 11, part 11.

(v) *Circumvention of the Statute*

A person may convey land to another in a manner that appears to give the transferee absolute title. However, at the time of the conveyance, the parties may have reached an understanding, or oral agreement, that the transferee would hold the property for the benefit of the transferor. If the transferee subsequently denies the trust and the transferor brings action to enforce it, he or she will be met with the defence that the trust was not in writing. If the defence were to succeed, a fraud would be perpetrated. The law will not permit this. In those circumstances the plaintiff is permitted to prove and enforce the oral trust. The defendant cannot use the *Statute of Frauds* as an instrument of fraud.

While there remains debate about the nature of the oral trust in such circumstances, it most likely is a constructive trust and therefore is discussed elsewhere in this book.

(c) Testamentary Formalities

(i) *Statutory Provisions*

The formalities for testamentary trusts are those required of wills. As we saw, these were at one time contained in the *Statute of Frauds*,[274] but they have long since been transferred, with amendments, to legislation governing wills. The Ontario requirements are contained in the *Succession Law Reform Act*,[275] reproduced below.

SUCCESSION LAW REFORM ACT

R.S.O. 1990, c. S.26

. . .

3. A will is valid only when it is in writing.

4. (1) Subject to sections 5 and 6, a will is not valid unless,

(*a*) at its end it is signed by the testator or by some other person in his or her presence and by his or her direction;

(*b*) the testator makes or acknowledges the signature in the presence of two or more attesting witnesses present at the same time; and

(*c*) two or more of the attesting witnesses subscribe the will in the presence of the testator.

(2) Where witnesses are required by this section, no form of attestation is necessary.

---

274 1677 (29 Car. 2), c. 3.
275 R.S.O. 1990, c. S.26.

. . .

6. A testator may make a valid will wholly by his or her own handwriting and signature, without formality, and without the presence, attestation or signature of a witness.

7. (1) In so far as the position of the signature is concerned, a will, whether holograph or not, is valid if the signature of the testator made either by him or her or the person signing for him or her is placed at, after, following, under or beside or opposite to the end of the will so that it is apparent on the face of the will that the testator intended to give effect by the signature to the writing signed as his or her will.

[Section 7 goes on to provide that minor variations in the form prescribed by subsection (1) do not render the will invalid. However, dispositions or directions underneath or following the signature, or which are inserted after the signature was made are not effective.]

Comparable Legislation

Wills Act, R.S.A. 2000, c. W-12, ss. 4-8; R.S.B.C. 1996, c. 489, ss. 3-6; R.S.M. 1988, c. W150, ss. 3, 4, 6, 7; R.S.N.B. 1973, c. W-9, ss. 3-7; R.S.N.L. 1990, c. W-10, s. 2; R.S.N.S. 1989, c. 505, ss. 6, 7; R.S.N.W.T. 1988, c. W-5, ss. 5-7; *The Wills Act, 1996*, S.S. 1996, c. W-14.1, ss. 6-8; *Probate Act*, R.S.P.E.I. 1988, c. P-21, s. 60; *Wills Act*, R.S.Y. 2002, c. 230, s. 5.

Notes and Questions

1. The various statutes generally impose the same formal requirements.[276] There are, however, occasional differences. For instance, some do not permit holograph wills,[277] while others make provision for internationally valid wills.[278]

2. The statutes contain special provisions for privileged wills, that is, wills made by sailors at sea or in the course of a voyage and members of the Canadian Forces placed on active duty.[279]

(ii) *Circumvention of the Legislation*

Testators sometimes leave property by will to a person upon the latter's undertaking that he or she will hold the property upon trust for specified objects. Such secret trusts are apt to circumvent the statutory writing requirements.

Suppose, for example, that when drafting a will, a testatrix wants to make provision for A and B. However, she does not want that fact to become public

---

276 For further details and differences, see Oosterhoff, *Wills*, Chapter 6.
277 *Ibid.*
278 *Ibid.*
279 See, *e.g., Succession Law Reform Act*, R.S.O. 1990, c. S.26, ss. 5 and 8. And see Oosterhoff, *Wills*, Chapter 6, part 4.

knowledge. She therefore tells her friend, X, that she is leaving him $20,000 by will if X will agree to hold it upon trust for A for life, with remainder to B. If X agrees to do so before the testatrix dies, the obligation is binding upon him. This is a fully-secret trust. If the testatrix prefers to have some record of the trust, she can give the $20,000 to X "upon trust," or "for such purpose as I have communicated to him." Provided that X agreed to undertake the trust before the will was made, he is bound to do so. This is a semi-secret trust.

Secret trusts circumvent the statute because they involve testamentary trusts which are oral. They are permitted because otherwise the statute could be used by the legatee to perpetrate a fraud.

There is a continuing debate about the nature of secret trusts. In this book they are treated as constructive trusts and therefore are discussed elsewhere in this book.

Problems

1. In 1978, John orally agreed with Bill that he (John) would purchase Blackacre, owned by X, and that he would resell it to Bill. John used his own money to buy Blackacre and then refused to resell it to Bill.

(a) Is Bill's estate entitled to Blackacre upon payment of the purchase price?

(b) Would it make any difference if John had agreed to buy Blackacre for Bill (that is, in Bill's name) and John used his own money but took title in his own name?

2. A testator left his wife the residue of his estate indicating that it was his wish "that my wife should leave any property remaining on her death equally to our children."

What interest does the wife have in the residue?

3. By her will a testatrix left her house to a friend for life and to a charity thereafter. The friend was also to receive a "reasonable income" until his death. Is this provision valid? Give reasons for your answer.

5

LIMITATIONS ON THE CREATION OF TRUSTS

1. SCOPE

This chapter is concerned with the various ways in which a trust or dispositions thereunder may be held void. This may happen because the objects of the trust are illegal or because the trust imposes conditions which the law does not countenance or will not enforce. Such conditions include those which are uncertain, impossible of performance, or contrary to public policy. The latter include conditions which interfere with marital relations and parental duties and those which restrain alienation. We shall discuss the device of the protective trust in the context of restraints on alienation.

The chapter concludes with three other reasons why a trust may be set aside in whole or in part, namely, infringement of the perpetuity rules, fraud on creditors and deprivation of family support.

2. TRUSTS FOR ILLEGAL OBJECTS

(a) Generally

It may happen occasionally that the purposes of a trust are illegal. Such a trust is unenforceable. A clear example is a trust to establish a school for prostitutes or pickpockets.[1] Trusts whose purposes are illegal are contrary to public policy and that was the basis upon which a testamentary trust for convicted poachers was held to be void in *Thrupp v. Callett*.[2] Other examples might be given. Typically, they would involve purposes which involve or foster criminal acts or civil wrongs, or which are contrary to statute or public policy generally.

The illegality of trusts is not often a litigated issue. This is because many trusts for illegal purposes are trusts for non-charitable purposes and they are struck

---

1 An example given by Harman L.J. in *Re Pinion*, [1965] Ch. 85, [1964] 1 All E.R. 890 (C.A.).
2 (1858), 26 Beav. 125, 53 E.R. 844.

down under the rules pertaining to such trusts. Those rules are considered elsewhere in this book.

It is important to distinguish between a trust the purposes of which are illegal and a trust that would be valid of itself but the trustee of which is not entitled by law to act as a trustee. This distinction was discussed in *Parkland Mortgage Corp. Ltd. v. Therevan Development Corp. Ltd.*[3] Certain investors placed money with the plaintiff corporation with the intention that it be lent to the defendant corporation upon the security of a mortgage to the plaintiff. The plaintiff was to, and did, hold the mortgage in trust for the investors. The principals of the plaintiff were involved in a number of improprieties. When the defendant defaulted, the investors brought an action in the plaintiff's name on the mortgage. In the course of the proceedings a dispute over priorities between the investors and two execution creditors of the plaintiff arose. The creditors argued that the trust was illegal, because the plaintiff lacked power to carry on the business of a trust company.[4]

The court held that the plaintiff was merely exercising a limited form of trusteeship that was not *ultra vires*. Moreover, Feehan J. opined that even if the plaintiff were prohibited from acting as a trustee, the statute did not render the purposes of the trust illegal. Hence, the investors would have been able to succeed under a resulting trust.

Trusts, the purposes of which are *contra bonos mores,* are also void, even though they do not foster criminal or civil wrongs. For example, trusts providing for *future* illegitimate children were formerly regarded as void on the ground that they tended to encourage immorality.[5] Beginning in the second quarter of the 20th century, legislation has gradually enabled children born outside of marriage to inherit in prescribed circumstances on the mother's intestacy. Later statutes provide that an illegitimate person shall be treated as though it were legitimate for the purpose of intestacy and in some respects for the purpose of testate succession.[6] Even if a trust for illegitimate persons does not fall within the statutes, it is likely that a modern court would hold that the statutes evince a change in public policy sufficient to validate the trust.[7]

---

3 (1981), 11 E.T.R. 8, 130 D.L.R. (3d) 682, 17 Alta. L.R. (2d) 44, [1982] 1 W.W.R. 587 (Q.B.).

4 Section 13(1)(d) of the *Companies Act*, R.S.A. 1970, c. 60 (now R.S.A. 2000, c. C-21), precluded the incorporation of a company under the Act with power to act as an executor, trustee, etc. Such powers were conferred only by the *Trust Companies Act*, R.S.A. 1970, c. 372 (R.S.A. 1980, c. T-9, repealed by *Loan and Trust Corporations Act*, S.A. 1991, c. L.26.5, s. 336(2)).

5 *Occleston v. Fullalove* (1874), L.R. 9 Ch. App. 147. *Cf. dicta in Re Millar,* [1937] 3 D.L.R. 234, [1937] O.R. 362 at 391, *per* Rowell C.J.O., 403, *per* Riddell J.A. (C.A.), affirmed [1938] S.C.R. 1, [1938] 1 D.L.R. 65.

6 The statutory provisions are collected and discussed in *Oosterhoff on Wills and Succession: Text, Commentary and Cases*, 5th ed. (Toronto: Carswell, 2001), Chapter 9, part 2 (hereafter referred to as "Oosterhoff, *Wills*"). And see M.A. Shore, "The Withering Status of Illegitimacy in Canada Today" (1977-78) 1 E.T.R. 181.

7 See, *e.g., Re Hervey* (1961), 38 W.W.R. 12, 30 D.L.R. (2d) 615 (B.C. S.C.); *Re Stephenson* (1966), 66 D.L.R. (2d) 717 (B.C. S.C.). See *contra Belanger v. Pester* (1979), 6 E.T.R. 21, 108 D.L.R. (3d) 84, [1980] 2 W.W.R. 155, 2 Man. R. (2d) 283 (Q.B.); *Re Herlichka,* [1969] 1 O.R. 724, 3 D.L.R. (3d) 700. *Cf. Re Wright Estate* (1988), 30 E.T.R. 181, 65 O.R. (2d) 257 (H.C.).

The issue is academic in jurisdictions that have abolished the status of illegitimacy.[8] Trusts in favour of named or existing illegitimate persons or illegitimate persons *en ventre sa mère* are valid in any event.[9]

A trust for a fraudulent purpose is also void. A trust whose object is to transfer assets from the settlor to another in order to defeat the settlor's creditors falls into this category. In such a case, as with illegal trusts generally, the courts apply the maxim *ex turpi causa non oritur actio*.[10] It follows that the beneficiary cannot sue upon it.

(b) Consequences of Illegality

A question that has been much litigated is whether the settlor of an illegal trust can recover the trust property. Generally, if an express trust fails, the property results to the settlor. If, however, the trust is illegal or fraudulent, is it proper for the court to allow recovery? The modern approach appears to be that if the illegal or fraudulent purpose has not been carried out, the settlor can recover under a resulting trust.[11] The leading case on this point is *Symes v. Hughes*.[12] The plaintiff made an assignment of certain leases while he was insolvent, but he retained the title deeds. The assignment was a fraud on his creditors. The defendant, a subsequent assignee of the leases, sued at law to recover the title deeds, but the plaintiff brought proceedings in equity for a declaration that the defendant held the leases in trust for him. The plaintiff subsequently covenanted with his creditors

---

See also W. Holland, "Gifts to Children by Will: The Effect of Illegitimacy" (1980), 3 E.T.R. 21. It was held in *Surette v. Harris Estate* (1989), 34 E.T.R. 67, 91 N.S.R. (2d) 418, 233 A.P.R. 418, 43 C.R.R. 22 (T.D.) that s. 15 of the *Intestate Succession Act*, R.S.N.S. 1967, c. 153 (now 1989, c. 236, s. 16), which permitted illegitimate children to inherit from their mother but not their father, violated s. 15(1) of the *Canadian Charter of Rights and Freedoms* and was not justified under s. 1 of the *Charter*. In *Tighe (Guardian ad litem of) v. McGillivray Estate* (1994), 127 N.S.R. (2d) 313, 2 E.T.R. (2d) 45, 112 D.L.R. (4th) 201, 1994 CarswellNS 109, 20 C.R.R. (2d) 54, 355 A.P.R. 313 (C.A.) the Court of Appeal similarly found that s. 16 of the *Intestate Succession Act*, R.S.N.S. 1989, c. 236 violated the *Charter*. Since there were no legislative changes to the section after the *Surette* decision, the court in the *Tighe* case decided to extend the benefits of the legislation to the disadvantaged class of illegitimate children by reading in the words "or father" after the word "mother" into the text of s. 16. In 1999, the Nova Scotia legislature amended s. 16 of the *Intestate Succession Act*, R.S.N.S. 1989, c. 236 (am. S.N.S. 1999, c. 8 (2nd Sess.), s. 7) to reflect the *Tighe* decision.

8 *Family Services Act*, S.N.B. 1980, c. F-2.2, ss. 96, 97 (am. 1997, c. 2, s. 15); *Children's Act*, R.S.Y. 2002, c. 31, s. 5; *Children's Law Act*, S.N.W.T. 1997, c. 14, ss. 2 (am. 1998, c. 17, s. 6(2)), 3, 2002; *The Children's Law Act, 1997*, S.S. 1997, c. C-8.2, ss. 40-44; *Child Status Act*, R.S.P.E.I. 1988, c. C-6, ss. 1, 2; *Children's Law Reform Act*, R.S.O. 1990, c. C.12, ss. 1, 2; *The Family Maintenance Act*, R.S.M. 1987, c. F20, Part II, ss. 17, 18. *Cf. Family Law Reform Act* 1987, c. 42 (U.K.), ss. 1, 18.

9 *Occleston v. Fullalove, supra*, note 5.

10 That is, a disgraceful matter cannot be the basis of an action.

11 See, *e.g., Symes v. Hughes* (1870), L.R. 9 Eq. 475; *Petherpermal Chetty v. Muniandi Servai* (1980), 24 T.L.R. 462 (P.C.); *Chettiar v. Chettiar*, [1962] A.C. 294; *Tribe v. Tribe* (1995), [1996] Ch. 107, [1995] 3 W.L.R. 913, [1995] 4 All E.R. 236 (C.A.). *Cf. Tinsley v. Milligan* (1993), [1994] 1 A.C. 340, [1993] W.L.R. 126, [1993] 3 All E.R. 65 (H.L.).

12 *Ibid.*

to proceed with the action against the defendant. In those circumstances the fraudulent purpose had not been carried out, and the court held that the plaintiff was entitled to succeed.

To be allowed to recover, however, the settlor must undergo a timely repentance. If the illegal purpose has been carried out, or if the fraud has served its purpose, even though it was not relied on by others, the repentance comes too late and the settlor cannot recover. *Re Great Berlin Steamboat Company*[13] affords an example. The appellant paid money to the credit of a company with the object of deluding certain bankers about its financial picture. The company was trying to place company shares with the bankers. The bankers never inquired into the company's financial state. In due course the company was ordered to be wound up and the appellant then claimed the moneys back under a resulting trust. The court held that he "repented" too late.

The issue of recovering property transferred for an illegal purpose has been dealt with many times in the Canadian courts in the context of voluntary transfers of property by husbands to their wives to avoid actual or anticipated creditors. When the transferors then attempted to recover the property (this invariably occurred after a marriage breakdown) they were met with the presumption of advancement, that is, of gift.[14] To overcome the presumption they had to rely on evidence of their illegal intention and almost always lost. The issue of timely repentance has not really been addressed in this context.[15]

Further Reading

J.K. Grodecki, "In Pari Delicto Potior Est Conditio Defendentis" (1955), 71 L.Q. Rev. 254.

Notes and Questions

1. A number of persons held an illegal raffle to raise money for a personal trip. The prize was tickets in a foreign lottery. The organizers of the raffle did not know that the raffle was illegal, but withheld the prize when they learned of the illegality. The winner of the raffle brings action to recover the prize. What is the result?[16]

2. In a land development scheme, "client-developers" contributed money to A Ltd., which held the land in trust for them. A termination clause in the agreement between the client-developers and A Ltd. provided that A Ltd. could end the agreement should it become unable to fulfil its obligations and should the funds be tied up in the land and therefore unavailable for distribution to the client-developers. Upon termination of the agreement, the land would vest in A Ltd. and the client-developers would obtain a promise of repayment. A Ltd. became bankrupt and the land was subsequently sold under court

---

13 (1884), 26 Ch. D. 616 (C.A.). See also *Barclay v. Pearson*, [1893] 2 Ch. 154 (Eng. Ch. Div.) in which the court held that money paid for an illegal purpose, which has been partially performed, cannot be recovered.

14 The presumption, as between spouses, has been abolished in a number of Canadian provinces. See Chapter 9 on resulting trusts.

15 This matter is discussed in detail in Chapter 9 on resulting trusts.

16 See *Smith v. Williams* (1983), 698 F.2d 611.

order. The trustee in bankruptcy, representing the interests of A Ltd., argued that the trust was illegal because A Ltd. lacked the capacity to carry on the business that of a trust business.[17] Should the proceeds from the sale of the land be paid to the estate of the bankrupt or to the client-developers on the basis that A Ltd. held the land in trust for them?[18]

3. TRUSTS IMPOSING INVALID CONDITIONS

(a) Introduction

Dispositions under trusts are often made subject to conditions. For example, a testator may establish a trust for his or her children, but state that they only become entitled if they are members of a particular church. Alternatively, the testator may give the equitable interest to the children, but provide that they may not dispose of it outside the family, or to named persons.

Many such conditions are void for public policy. They include conditions that tend to restrain marriage, interfere with the discharge of parental duties, or require the beneficiary to do an illegal act. Other conditions are merely voidable.

In this connection it is important to distinguish between conditions precedent and subsequent. A condition precedent operates to prevent vesting of the property in the beneficiary unless the condition is satisfied, while a condition subsequent allows the property to vest, but causes it to divest if the event specified by the condition happens.

The general rule is that a condition precedent, which is void for public policy, uncertainty, repugnancy to a prior gift, or illegality, renders the gift void. If the condition is precedent, annexed to a gift of personal property, and is illegal, the English rule, applied in some Canadian provinces, is that the gift is void only if the condition is *malum in se*; whereas, if the condition is *malum prohibitum* the gift is free of the condition.[19] A condition subsequent which is void, however, makes the gift absolute and free of the condition,[20] whether the property is realty or personalty.

If the condition is only voidable and is avoided by the beneficiary, is repugnant to the gift, is *in terrorem*,[21] or does not happen, the gift is absolute and free of the condition, whether it is precedent or subsequent.[22]

---

17 Section 21(2)(d) of the *Company Act*, R.S.B.C. 1979, c. 59 (see now *Financial Institutions Act*, R.S.B.C. 1996, c. 141, s. 70 prohibited a company from carrying on a business that is a trust business as defined in Schedule A of the *Trust Company Act*, R.S.B.C. 1979, c. 412 (as repealed by *Financial Institutions Act*, R.S.B.C. 1989, c. 47, s. 406). The definition of the business of a trust company included accepting and executing trusts of every description.

18 See *Thorne Riddell Inc. v. Rolfe*, 47 B.C.L.R. 196, 149 D.L.R. (3d) 622, [1983] 6 W.W.R. 97, 1983 CarswellBC 561, 49 C.B.R. (N.S.) 161, B.C. Corps. L.G. 78,217 (C.A.).

19 These terms are explained below.

20 *Wilkinson, Re*, [1926] Ch. 842; *Croxon, Re*, [1904] 1 Ch. 252; *McColgan, Re*, [1969] 2 O.R. 152, 4 D.L.R. (3d) 572, 1969 CarswellOnt 151 (H.C.).

21 This term is explained below.

22 See *Williams' Law Relating to Wills*, 6th ed. by C.H. Sherrin, R.F.D. Barlow and R.A. Wallington (London: Butterworth and Co. (Publishers) Ltd., 1987), vol. 1, at 335.

Because the law favours vested gifts and disfavours the divesting of gifts, the courts prefer a construction that will permit a gift to take effect. Hence, traditionally the courts will attempt to construe a condition as subsequent and, if it is subsequent, will readily strike down the condition for one of the above-mentioned reasons.

If the gift does not create a condition, but rather a determinable limitation as in a gift "to A so long as she lives apart from her husband," and the determining event is void for any of the reasons given above, the entire gift will fail.[23]

Since you will have encountered these principles in other contexts, the following is merely a synopsis.

(b) Conditions Contrary to Public Policy

Conditions contrary to public policy include conditions in restraint of marriage, *in terrorem* conditions, conditions *malum prohibitum* and *malum in se*, conditions that interfere with the discharge of parental duties, and discriminatory conditions. These will now be considered.

Conditions in restraint of marriage are relatively common and, if intended to prohibit marriage, are normally invalid.[24]

A general restraint on marriage for a gift of real property is *prima facie* void as being contrary to public policy, whether the condition be precedent or subsequent.[25] If, however, the will shows that the testator did not intend to promote celibacy, but to provide for the person while single, or for some other lawful reason, the condition will be regarded as valid.[26]

Partial restraints on marriage annexed to a gift of real property, such as a condition against remarriage,[27] against marriage to a named person,[28] or against marriage without consent[29] are valid, if reasonable in the circumstances. *MacDonald v. Brown Estate*[30] was such a case. A testator gave one-twentieth of his estate to his niece subject to her becoming "widowed or divorced from her present husband." The court considered the question of whether the testator's purpose, aim, object or motive was pure inducement to divorce or whether it was protective as determinative in assessing whether the restraint on marriage was void as against

---

23 *Re Moore, Trafford v. Maconochie* (1888), 39 Ch. D. 116; *Moore v. Royal Trust Co.* (sub nom. *Re Moore Estate*), [1954] 3 D.L.R. 407, 13 W.W.R. (N.S.) 113 (B.C. S.C.), reversed [1955] 4 D.L.R. 313, 16 W.W.R. 204 (B.C. C.A.), varied [1956] S.C.R. 880, 5 D.L.R. (2d) 152.

24 The law on the validity of conditions in restraint on marriage differs for gifts of real property and gifts of personal property. See generally *Modern Law of Real Property*, 16th ed. by E.H. Burn (London: Butterworths, 2000), pp. 370-371.

25 *Re Cutter* (1961), 37 O.L.R. 42, 31 D.L.R. 382 (H.C.).

26 *Re McBain* (1915), 8 O.W.N. 330 (H.C.).

27 *Re Deller* (1903), 6 O.L.R. 711 (H.C.); *Cowan v. Allen* (1896), 26 S.C.R. 292 at 313. But see *Re Tucker* (1910), 16 W.L.R. 172, 3 Sask. L.R. 473 (S.C.); *Re Muirhead*, [1919] 2 W.W.R. 454, 12 Sask. L.R. 123 (K.B.).

28 *Re Bathe, Bathe v. Public Trustee*, [1925] Ch. 377.

29 *Re Whiting's Settlement, Whiting v. De Rutzen*, [1905] 1 Ch. 96 (C.A.).

30 (1995), 139 N.S.R. (2d) 252, 6 E.T.R. (2d) 160, 1995 CarswellNS 22, 397 A.P.R. 252 (S.C.). See also *Goodwin, Re* (1969), 3 D.L.R. (3d) 281, 1969 CarswellAlta 114 (T.D.).

public policy. It was held that the testator's intentions were protective and supportive, that is, it was intended to provide for the beneficiary while she was a widow. Consequently, the condition was not objectionable. The court also held that each case must be decided with regard to its circumstances, the nature of the provision, the extent to which the provision would actually induce divorce or separation and the motives of the settlor.

Generally, a condition imposed on a gift of personalty in total restraint of marriage is void, while a partial restraint may be valid if it does not contravene public policy[31] and there is a gift over to another person in the event the condition is not complied with.[32] In the absence of such a gift over, the condition is considered as imposed *in terrorem*.[33] An *in terrorem* is a mere threat to induce the beneficiary to comply with it. The rules respecting these conditions derive from the civil law formerly administered by the ecclesiastical courts and, since those courts only had jurisdiction over testaments of personal property, they apply even now only to gifts of personal property,[34] and to gifts made out of a mixed fund of real property and personal property.[35]

The *in terrorem* doctrine strikes down conditions, both precedent and subsequent, in partial restraint of marriage[36] and conditions prohibiting a beneficiary from disputing the will. The doctrine is normally avoided if there is a gift over, or a direction that the gift is to fall into residue on failure to fulfil the condition, since this indicates that the testator did not merely threaten the beneficiary, but wanted to make a different disposition if the condition should not be complied with.[37] A provision for the beneficiary whether the condition is complied with or not also avoids the doctrine.[38]

Re Kent[39] affords an example. A testator left his estate in trust, after an intervening life estate, for his two children for life with remainder over. He provided that if they should litigate the will, other than for the purpose of interpretation or directions, their interests would be revoked and fall into residue. The children made application to determine whether an application for support out of

---

31 *Lanyon, Re*, [1927] 2 Ch. 264 (Eng. Ch. Div.).

32 *Whiting's Settlement, Re*, [1905] 1 Ch. 96. *Cf. Leong v. Lim Beng Chye*, [1955] A.C. 648, [1955] 2 All E.R. 903, [1955] 3 W.L.R. 303 (P.C.), in which there was no gift over on breach of the condition subsequent in restraint of marriage. The gift was therefore *in terrorem* and the condition ineffective.

33 *Ibid.*

34 *Bellairs v. Bellairs* (1874), L.R. 18 Eq. 510 at 515-516; *Reynish v. Martin* (1746), 3 Atk. 330, 26 E.R. 991.

35 *Re Hamilton* (1901), 1 O.L.R. 10 (H.C.); *Re Schmidt*, [1949] 2 W.W.R. 513, 57 Man. R. 316 (K.B.).

36 *Reynish v. Martin, supra*, note 34.

37 *Re Pashak*, [1923] 1 W.W.R. 873, [1923] 1 D.L.R. 1130 (Alta. T.D.), actually a case involving a determinable interest *Cf. Leong v. Lim Beng Chye, supra*, note 32, in which the Judicial Committee of the Privy Council held that in the absence of a gift over the court will apply the *in terrorem* rule without regard to the testator's intention. The Privy Council distinguished the case of *Jones v. Jones* (1876), 1 Q.B.D. 279, in which the court had considered the intention of the testator, because in that case there was a gift over.

38 *Re Nourse, Hampton v. Nourse*, [1899] 1 Ch. 63 at 71.

39 [1982] 6 W.W.R. 165, 38 B.C.L.R. 216, 13 E.T.R. 53, 139 D.L.R. (3d) 318 (S.C.).

the estate under the *Wills Variation Act*[40] would offend the prohibition against litigation. The court held that the condition was not *in terrorem* because of the gift over. However, it held the gift to be contrary to public policy, as expressed in the statute, in that it would prevent an application for support. Hence, it was struck down for that reason and the gift became absolute.

The distinction between conditions which are *malum in se* and those which are *malum prohibitum* also derives from the civil law and, therefore, also applies only to personalty and to a mixed fund of realty and personalty.[41] Unfortunately, the distinction between these two types of condition has never been clearly defined. The cases usually refer back to *Sheppard's Touchstone* which defines these terms as follows:[42]

> . . . anything which in its nature, is *malum in se*, as to kill a man, or the like; or *malum prohibitum*, being a thing forbidden of any statute or the like.

Thus, *malum in se* is conduct which is wrong in itself, or is against the law of nature or God, while *malum prohibitum* is conduct which offends human rules, such as a statute or a rule of law.

The English rule is that a condition precedent *malum prohibitum* annexed to a gift of personal property is void, but the gift is valid, while a condition precedent *malum in se* annexed to a gift of personal property renders both the condition and the gift void.[43] With respect to real property, the English rule is that a void condition renders the gift void also. The Ontario Court of Appeal appears to have rejected the English rule regarding personal property, albeit in *dicta*, and applied the English rule regarding real property instead.[44] The English rule regarding personal property was, however, resurrected at first instance in *McBride, Re*.[45] The testator left personal property to certain charities if his son should be married to a named person, but to his son if he was not. The court held that the condition precedent was void for public policy, but as it was only *malum prohibitum*, the gift itself was good. The English rule has been followed in British Columbia.[46]

---

40 R.S.B.C. 1979, c. 435. (See now R.S.B.C. 1996, c. 490).

41 *Bellairs v. Bellairs, supra*, note 34; *Reynish v. Martin, supra*, note 34; *Re Hamilton, supra*, note 35; *Re Schmidt, supra*, note 35.

42 *Sheppard's Touchstone of Common Assurances*, 8th ed. by E.G. Atherley (London: Butterworth and Company, 1826), vol. 1, at 123.

43 Thomas Jarman, *A Treatise on Wills*, 8th ed. by Raymond Jennings, assisted by John C. Harper (London: Sweet and Maxwell Limited, 1951), vol. 2, at 1457-8. See *In Re Elliott, Lloyds Bank LD. v. Burton-on-Trent Hospital Management Committee*, [1952] Ch. 217, [1952] 1 All E.R. 145.

44 *Gross, Re*, [1937] O.W.N. 88, 1937 CarswellOnt 124 (C.A.). And see *Going, Re* (1950), [1951] O.R. 147, [1951] 2 D.L.R. 136, 1950 CarswellOnt 92 (C.A.), which disregarded the rule. The approach in *Gross, Re* and *Going, Re* was applied in *Mercer, Re* (1953), [1954] 1 D.L.R. 295 (H.C.).

45 (1980), 27 O.R. (2d) 513, 6 E.T.R. 181, 107 D.L.R. (3d) 233, 1980 CarswellOnt 523 (H.C.). See further A.H. Oosterhoff, Comment (1980), 5 E. & T.Q. 97.

46 *Re Fairfoull* (1973), 41 D.L.R. (3d) 152 (B.C. S.C.), further proceedings (sub nom. *Re Fairfoull (No. 2)*) (1974), 44 D.L.R. (3d) 765 (B.C. Co. Ct.), and [1974] 6 W.W.R. 471, 18 R.F.L. 165 (B.C. S.C.).

A condition that interferes with the marital relationship is void. If it is subsequent, it will be struck down and the gift will become absolute.[47]

Conditions which purport to interfere with the discharge of parental duties are also void. Thus, if a gift to a minor is subject to forfeiture should the donee reside with his or her parents, the condition, being subsequent, will be struck down and the gift becomes absolute.[48] If the condition is precedent, however, the gift itself is also void, whether the property is realty or personalty.[49]

Conditions which purport to require the beneficiary to adhere to a particular religion are not regarded as contrary to public policy.[50]

There used not to be much Canadian law on conditions that are discriminatory. In *Re Drummond Wren*[51] Mackay J. held a covenant in a deed prohibiting sale to "Jews or persons of objectionable nationality" void for public policy.[52] Similarly, when a testator made a gift to his daughter provided she was not married to a Jew, the court struck down the condition precedent as *malum prohibitum*, since it interfered with marital relations (the daughter being married to a Jew).[53] However, in *dictum* McInnes J. noted that racially restrictive covenants were void in any event.[54]

Whether discriminatory conditions are void by reason of the equality provisions in the *Charter*[55] or human rights legislation[56] is a moot point. In *Canada Trust Co. v. Ontario (Human Rights Commission)*,[57] the Ontario Court of Appeal held a trust, which set eligibility requirements based on race, religion, ethnic origin and sex, void as against contemporary public policy.[58] In an opinion con-

---

47 *Re Nurse* (1921), 20 O.W.N. 428 (H.C.); *Re Blanchard Estate* (1963), 48 M.P.R. 134, (sub nom. *Eastern Trust Co. v. McTague*), 39 D.L.R. (2d) 743 (P.E.I. C.A.).

48 *Clarke v. Darraugh* (1884), 5 O.R. 190 (Ch.); *Re Thorne* (1922), 22 O.W.N. 28 (H.C.).

49 As regards personalty, this is the rule in Ontario: *Re Gross, supra*, note 44.

50 *Re Curran*, [1939] O.W.N. 191 (H.C.); *Re Going, supra*, note 44; *Blathwait v. Baron Cawley*, [1976] A.C. 397, [1975] 3 All E.R. 625 (H.L.). And see *Re Tuck's Settlement Trusts*, [1978] Ch. 49, [1978] 1 All E.R. 1047 (C.A.).

51 [1945] O.R. 778, [1945] 4 D.L.R. 674 (H.C.).

52 In *Noble v. Wolf and Alley*, [1951] S.C.R. 64, [1951] 1 D.L.R. 321, the Supreme Court of Canada declined to deal with the issue of public policy in respect of a similar covenant, but held it to be, not a restrictive covenant, but a restraint on alienation which was uncertain and, therefore, void. Covenants of this type are now prohibited by legislation: *Conveyancing and Law of Property Act*, R.S.O. 1990, c. C.34, s. 22; *The Law of Property Act*, R.S.M. 1987, c. L90, s. 7 (am. S.M. 2002, c. 24, s. 35); *Land Title Act*, R.S.B.C. 1996, c. 250, s. 220.

53 *Re Hurshman* (1956), 6 D.L.R. (2d) 615 (B.C. S.C.).

54 *Ibid.*, at 619. See also *Kirk v. Distacom Ventures Inc.* (1996), 81 B.C.A.C. 5, 4 R.P.R. (3d) 240, [1996] B.C.J. No. 1879, 1996 CarswellBC 1878, 132 W.A.C. 5 (C.A.) in which the Court of Appeal affirmed the principle that restrictive covenants are strictly construed and that any ambiguity is resolved in favour of non-enforcement of the covenant.

55 *Canadian Charter of Rights and Freedoms* (being Part I of the *Constitution Act, 1982*), s. 15, as en. by *Canada Act 1982*, c. 11 (U.K.).

56 Such as the *Human Rights Code*, R.S.O. 1990, c. H.19.

57 (1990), 69 D.L.R. (4th) 321 (Ont. C.A.).

58 *Cf. University of Victoria Foundation v. British Columbia (Attorney General)*, 73 B.C.L.R. (3d) 375, 185 D.L.R. (4th) 182, 32 E.T.R. (2d) 98, 2000 CarswellBC 529, 2000 BCSC 445, 37 C.H.R.R. D/200 (S.C. [In Chambers]), in which the court upheld a scholarship trust that restricted recipients to members of a particular religious faith. The court held that although the trust was

curring in the result, Tarnopolsky J.A., opined that the public policy against discrimination was reflected in anti-discrimination laws, constitutional guarantees of equality and international agreements subscribed by Canada.

A repugnant condition is one that interferes with or restricts the enjoyment of the property. Gifts which offend the rule in *Saunders v. Vautier*,[59] that is, which postpone enjoyment to a time after the person or persons solely entitled to the property become *sui juris*, fall into this category.[60] So do conditions which attempt to interfere with the legal course of devolution. *Re Gee*[61] was such a case. A testator left a gift to a son, but provided that if the son died before his discharge from a mental institution, the property would pass to two grandsons. Thus, the gift was absolute, but the testator tried to control where the property would go on his son's death. The condition was struck down as repugnant to the absolute gift to the son because it interfered with the devolution of the property on the death intestate (a probable event) of the son.[62]

Conditions which restrict alienation are also repugnant. Thus, a devise of real property provided that it shall not be sold out of the family, is a restraint on alienation and void.[63] Restraints on alienation are not objectionable if they are relatively minor, however, and they are valid if cast in the form of a determinable life estate. This matter is considered below.[64]

(c) Conditions Impossible of Performance

A condition annexed to a gift of personal property, which is based on an assumption of the existence of a state of facts which does not and which cannot exist[65] has no effect and the beneficiary will take free of the condition. However, if the testator clearly intended that the condition should operate in any event, the condition is impossible to perform. If the condition is precedent and if it was impossible at the date of the will or becomes so by act of God or through

---

discriminatory, it was reasonably justified and did not violate the *Human Rights Code* because the interest of upholding freedom of testamentary disposition outweighed the interest of avoiding a relatively inoffensive breach of the *Human Rights Code*. The court also found that the provision was not offensive enough to contravene public policy.

59 (1841), Cr. & Ph. 240, 41 E.R. 482, [1835-42] All E.R. Rep. 58.

60 The rule is discussed in the next chapter.

61 (1973), 41 D.L.R. (3d) 317 (B.C. Co. Ct.).

62 *Cf. Parsons Estate, Re* (1993), 107 Nfld. & P.E.I.R. 338, 1993 CarswellNfld 157, 336 A.P.R. 338 (T.D.) in which the court found that one of the provisions in the will reflected the testator's intention to give the donee an absolute interest, while another provision tried to limit the donee's interest. The court held that the gift over was not repugnant to the absolute interest created because the limitation upon the interest, the attainment of a particular age, was something that the law recognized as beyond the control of the donee. The provisions created a vested interest in the donee subject to divestment.

63 *Re Collier* (1966), 52 M.P.R. 211, 60 D.L.R. (2d) 70 (Nfld. T.D.).

64 In part 4, *infra*.

65 Such as a requirement that the trustees build a house and there are insufficient funds for the purpose: *Re Jones*, [1948] Ch. 67, [1947] 2 All E.R. 716.

circumstances beyond the control of the testator or the beneficiary, the gift fails.[66] By contrast, if the condition is subsequent, the gift becomes absolute and the condition is struck down.[67]

The above rules derive from the civil law formerly administered by the ecclesiastical courts and apply only to gifts of personalty. If a condition precedent annexed to a devise of real property is impossible of performance, the devise will fail.[68] However, the same rules apply to real property as to personal property in respect of conditions subsequent.

These rules were applied in *Re MacDonald*.[69] A testator gave part of the residue of his estate in trust to maintain an historic house provided that the municipality agreed not to move the house. The condition precedent was incapable of performance when the testator drew his will. The testator knew this to be so, since the municipality did not own the house. The condition was, therefore, struck down and the gift failed.

In *Unger v. Gossen*,[70] however, a gift upon condition precedent that was impossible of performance by operation of law was upheld as valid. The testator provided that his estate was to be equally divided among the beneficiaries, but he incorporated a condition that the beneficiaries had to become Canadian residents within fifteen years after his death to receive their shares. It was unclear whether the testator knew that the condition was impossible of performance at the time of the creation of the will. The court concluded that the test was whether the primary intention of the testator was the performance of the condition or the gift itself. If the testator's dominant consideration was the condition then the gift would fail, but if it was the gift then the court should give effect to that intention and uphold the gift. Although the condition of residency was impossible to fulfil by operation of law, the gift was upheld because the testator's intention to distribute the estate among the beneficiaries was clearly his main concern.

(d) Uncertain Conditions

If a condition is uncertain in its meaning or operation, it is void[71] and, if it is a condition precedent, the gift fails,[72] whereas, if it is a condition subsequent, the condition is struck down and the gift becomes absolute.[73] Because the law prefers a gift to take effect, the test for certainty is less strict for a condition precedent than for a condition subsequent. If the condition annexed to a gift is precedent, a

---

66 *Yates v. University College, London* (1873), 8 Ch. App. 454 at 461, affirmed (1875), L.R. 7 H.L. 438.

67 *Egerton v. Earl Brownlow* (1853), 4 H.L. Cas. 1 at 120, 10 E.R. 359 (H.L.).

68 *Re Croxon, Croxon v. Ferrers*, [1904] 1 Ch. 252.

69 [1971] 2 O.R. 577, 18 D.L.R. (3d) 521 (H.C.).

70 (1996), 13 E.T.R. (2d) 194, [1996] B.C.J. No. 1211, 1996 CarswellBC 1248 (S.C.).

71 *Lysiak, Re* (1975), 7 O.R. (2d) 317, 55 D.L.R. (3d) 161, 1975 CarswellOnt 358 (H.C.).

72 Thomas Jarman, *A Treatise on Wills*, 8th ed. by Raymond Jennings, assisted by John C. Harper (London: Sweet and Maxwell Limited, 1951), vol. 2, p. 1457.

73 *Re Down*, [1968] 2 O.R. 16, 68 D.L.R. (2d) 30 (C.A.), affirmed [1969] S.C.R. v. See, *e.g.*, *Czykalenko, Re* (1983), 42 O.R. (2d) 631, 150 D.L.R. (3d) 68, 15 E.T.R. 3, 1983 CarswellOnt 614 (H.C.).

beneficiary who claims the gift merely has to satisfy the court that he or she complies with the condition and not that it must be certain with respect to all possible claimants.[74] Hence, a condition precedent is struck down for uncertainty only if it is devoid of all meaning, or is internally inconsistent or repugnant.[75]

By contrast, for a condition subsequent the court must be able to determine "from the beginning, precisely and distinctly, upon the happening of what event it was that the preceding vested estate was to determine."[76]

These rules were applied in *Re Tuck's Settlement Trusts*.[77] The settlor, a baronet, gave moneys in trust to his successors if they should be of the Jewish faith and married to and living with "an approved wife." The latter term was defined as a person of Jewish blood by one or both of her parents and brought up in and practising the Jewish faith. In cases of doubt the decision of the chief rabbi was to be conclusive. The court treated the condition as precedent and held it to be certain. Lord Denning, however criticized the principle that a condition might be void for uncertainty if it was a condition subsequent, but valid if it was a condition precedent.

4. TRUSTS WHICH RESTRAIN ALIENATION: THE PROTECTIVE TRUST

We have made brief reference to the principle that general restraints on alienation are contrary to public policy, although some partial restraints are valid.[78] This rule presents problems for settlors or testators who wish to protect wastrel heirs from their own folly. They wish to make provision for their heirs, but they do not want their bounty to fall into the hands of the heirs' creditors. The protective trust is a device designed to accomplish their purpose.[79]

The protective trust is based upon the distinction in the doctrine of estates between conveyances upon determinable limitation and upon conditions subsequent. The latter purport to convey an absolute interest which is cut short by a

---

74 *Re Lowry's Will Trusts, Barclays Bank Ltd. v. United Newcastle-upon-Tyne Board of Governors*, [1967] Ch. 638, [1966] 3 All E.R. 955.

75 *Re Allen, Faith v. Allen*, [1953] Ch. 810, [1953] 2 All E.R. 898 at 900-901; *Re Mercer*, [1953] O.W.N. 765 (H.C.).

76 *Clavering v. Ellison* (1859), 7 H.L. Cas. 707 at 725, 11 E.R. 282, *per* Lord Cranworth, quoted by Laskin J.A. in *Re Down, supra*, note 73, at 23. See also *Sifton v. Sifton*, [1938] A.C. 656, [1938] 2 W.W.R. 465, (sub nom. *Re Sifton*), [1939] O.R. 529, [1938] 3 D.L.R. 577, [1938] 3 All E.R. 435 (P.C.). As in *Sifton v. Sifton*, in *Clayton* the House of Lords applied the test for uncertainty of a condition subsequent laid out in *Clavering v. Ellison*. In *Clayton*, the House of Lords also held that if one part of the condition is void, the entire condition is void. The condition in the will was a prohibition of marriage with a person "not of Jewish parentage and of the Jewish faith." Having found that the first part of the condition, "not of Jewish parentage," was void for uncertainty, the House of Lords found it unnecessary to apply the test for uncertainty to the second part of the condition, "of the Jewish faith."

77 [1978] Ch. 49, [1978] 2 W.L.R. 411, [1978] 1 All E.R. 1047 (C.A.).

78 In part 3(b), *supra*.

79 See Ontario Law Reform Commission, *Report on the Law of Trusts* (Toronto: Ministry of the Attorney General, 1984), at 355ff ("O.L.R.C. Report").

condition subsequent; the former convey a qualified estate which is, or may be, shorter in duration than the full estate. The difference in wording between the two can be slight; estates upon condition subsequent typically incorporate words of condition, while determinable limitations incorporate words of duration. The consequences of the distinction are significant, however. This caused one jurist to call the distinction and its consequences "little short of disgraceful to our jurisprudence."[80]

Brandon v. Robinson[81] is a leading case. A testator left part of his estate upon trust for his son, Thomas, for life. The trustees were directed to pay the income to him, but Thomas was not permitted to assign future payments. Upon Thomas's death the principal was to be paid to his statutory next of kin. When Thomas became bankrupt, his assignee in bankruptcy claimed the life interest. Lord Eldon held that the assignee was entitled to it. The testator had given his son an absolute life interest and then purported to cut it down by an unlawful condition subsequent, that is, a restraint on alienation. However, his Lordship noted that the testator could have achieved his purpose if he had made Thomas's interest determinable upon bankruptcy.

In *Rochford v. Hackman*[82] the court applied Lord Eldon's *dictum* to a situation in which a life interest was given to the testator's son determinable upon his bankruptcy.

Thus, a person may give property to trustees upon trust for a "primary beneficiary" for life so long as he or she does not alienate it, or become bankrupt or insolvent. Furthermore, the donor may then provide that upon the happening of a determining event the property shall go over to others. Indeed, provided the interest is equitable, it is also possible to create a fee simple, or an equivalent interest in personalty, determinable upon alienation or bankruptcy.[83] As a general rule, the party alleging that the principal beneficiary's interest has ended has the onus of proving that the terminating event has occurred.[84]

Originally it was common to give the interest over to other members of the primary beneficiary's family once a determining event occurred. Subsequently, however, it became common to provide that when a determining event occurred, the trustees held the property upon a discretionary trust in favour of a class of persons that included the primary beneficiary. Thereafter, the primary beneficiary could assign any income actually received by him or her, but could not count on receiving any amount.

The device of a determinable life interest with a gift over upon discretionary trust is the classic type of protective trust. It has been put into statutory form in

---

80 *Re King's Trusts* (1892), 29 L.R. Ir. 401 at 410, per Porter M.R. See Gerald McCormack, *Proprietary Claims and Insolvency* (London: Sweet & Maxwell, 1997) at 18.

81 (1811), 18 Ves. Jun. 429, 34 E.R. 379.

82 (1852), 9 Hare 475, 68 E.R. 597. And see *In re Scientific Investment Pension Plan Trusts*, [1999] Ch. 53.

83 *Re Leach*, [1912] 2 Ch. 422.

84 *Baring's Settlement Trusts, Re*, [1940] Ch. 737.

England,[85] some Australian states and New Zealand.[86] The legislation renders it unnecessary to set out the trusts in detail in the trust instrument. Instead, the statutory form may simply be incorporated by giving the beneficial interest to a named person "upon protective trusts."[87] It is not necessary to incorporate the statute by reference.

There is no comparable legislation in Canada. Hence, it is necessary to set out the trusts in detail. *Re Williams*,[88] reproduced below, is an example of a Canadian protective trust.

There are other ways to prevent a beneficiary from wasting the testator's bounty. One variation of the classic protective trust is to direct accumulation of the income after a determining event occurs, rather than to give the income upon a discretionary trust. The beneficiaries entitled to the capital and accumulated income must be named and care must be taken to avoid the rule in *Saunders v. Vautier*.[89] It would apply if the original life tenant were the sole beneficiary of the capital interest and would entitle the beneficiary to terminate the trust upon becoming *sui juris*.[90]

Instead of creating a protective trust, a settlor or testator can simply create a discretionary trust under which the trustees have a discretion to pay or not to pay the wastrel beneficiary any income. Indeed, such a discretionary trust can incorporate a protective element by excluding the wastrel from the class of beneficiaries after he or she becomes insolvent. Alternatively, the trustees may be given a mere power to pay the wastrel.

The same objective can also be achieved with payments of capital. Thus, for example, the trustees may be directed to pay a specific sum to a beneficiary provided he or she is not insolvent. Such a trust would require a gift over to prevent the application of the rule in *Saunders v. Vautier*.[91]

---

85 *Trustee Act, 1925*, (15 & 16 Geo. 5), c. 19, s. 33(1) (U.K.), amended by *Family Law Reform Act*, 1987, c. 42, s. 19, Sched. 3, para. 9.

86 As regards Australia and New Zealand, see H.A.J. Ford and W.A. Lee, assisted by Peter M. McDermott, *Principles of the Law of Trusts*, 3rd ed. (Sydney: L.B.C. Information Services, 1996), §7200.

87 *Re Wittke*, [1944] Ch. 166. But see *In re Trafford's Settlement, Moore v. Inland Revenue Commissioners*, [1985] Ch. 32 in which the settlor directed his trustees to hold funds on protective trust and in the same clause he gave his trustees immediate and absolute discretion over the trust funds during his life. Despite the settlor's reference to a protective trust, the court opined that the settlement only created an immediate discretionary trust during the life of the settlor. The intent to create an immediate discretionary trust cannot exist concurrently with an intent to create a determinable life interest. Effectively, the settlor skipped the first part of the protective trust, the determinable life interest, and moved immediately to the second part, the discretionary trust.

88 [1947] O.R. 11, [1947] 1 D.L.R. 882 (C.A.). See also *Driscoll, Re* (1983), 40 O.R. (2d) 744, 1983 CarswellOnt 616, 15 E.T.R. 34 (H.C.) in which the court refused to uphold a protective trust.

89 (1841), Cr. & Ph. 240, 41 E.R. 482.

90 See *Re Hamilton* (1912), 27 O.L.R. 445, 8 D.L.R. 529 (H.C.), affirmed (1913), 28 O.L.R. 534, 12 D.L.R. 861 (C.A.).

91 *Supra*, note 59.

It is clear from *Brandon v. Robinson*[92] that while a provision for termination of the interest on alienation or bankruptcy is valid, a provision which purports to prevent a beneficiary from alienating his or her interest, whether voluntarily or involuntarily, as in bankruptcy, is void as a restraint on alienation. Only a provision for termination on such events is valid. In contrast, American law permits this type of restraint on alienation. A trust which contains such a restraint is called a "spendthrift trust." Spendthrift trusts are permitted under case law in some states and under statute in others. There is substantial variation between the laws of the several states in this matter. Some permit virtually unrestricted spendthrift trusts, while others allow certain types of creditors to attach the spendthrift's interest.[93]

Further Reading

Erwin N. Griswold, *Spendthrift Trusts*, 2nd ed. (Albany and New York: Mathew Bender and Company, Inc. and Prentice-Hall, Inc, 1947).

James Rossiter, "The Case for Protective Trusts: A Response to the Recommendations of the Ontario Law Reform Commission" (1986), 7 E. & T.Q. 229.

Gregory S. Alexander, "The Dead Hand and the Law of Trusts in the Nineteenth Century" (1985), 37 Stanford L. Rev. 1189.

RE WILLIAMS

[1947] O.R. 11, [1947] 1 D.L.R. 882
Supreme Court of Ontario
[Court of Appeal]

By her will, Harriet Madeline Williams left the residue of her estate, subject to a small annuity, in trust to pay the income to her daughter, Helen Madeline Peck, for life, subject to the following provisions:

THIRD: I hereby direct and declare that in the case of my said daughter Helen Madeline Peck, the said income payable to her shall be paid to her as aforesaid unless or until she shall become bankrupt or shall assign, charge or encumber the said income or do or suffer something whereby the said income or some part thereof would through her act or default or by operation or process of law if belonging to her absolutely become vested in or become payable to some other person or persons, or in the event that my Trustees in their sole discretion are of the opinion that my said daughter is reckless or improvident in the use of the said income, and upon the occurring of any such event and so long as the effect and operation thereof shall continue and so long as my said Trustees shall deem advisable, her right to receive such income shall cease and the said income shall be no longer payable to her and so until the cause of the said income ceasing to be payable to her shall have ceased to exist or to be effectual or operate and then her right to receive such income shall revive and the said income shall thereafter be payable to her as aforesaid unless or until the like event or any such event as aforesaid shall happen again whereby the said income, or some part thereof, would, if belonging absolutely to her, become vested in or payable to some other person or persons or my said daughter is making improvident use of such income

---

92 *Supra*, note 81.

93 See generally Austin Wakeman Scott and William Franklin Fratcher, *The Law of Trusts*, 4th ed. (Boston: Little, Brown and Company, 1987-89), §151ff.

whereupon her right to receive it shall again cease and it shall no longer be payable to her until the cause for the said income ceasing to be payable to her shall have ceased to exist or to be effectual or operate in the manner or to the like effect as above mentioned and then her right to receive the said income shall immediately revive and the said income shall be payable to her as aforesaid and so from time to time if and whenever any of such events shall occur and the effect and operation thereof continue or discontinue as aforesaid. If any such event occurs above mentioned in consequence of it the said income shall not be payable to my said daughter then so long as the right of my said daughter to receive it shall have ceased and be not existing the Trustees herein may in their uncontrolled absolute discretion;

(1) expend such part of the said income, if any, as they shall deem advisable in the maintenance of my said daughter, or

(2) pay the said income or any part thereof to any person or persons for and on behalf of my said daughter for her maintenance or general welfare on such terms and conditions as my Trustees may have power to prescribe, or

(3) retain the said income or any part thereof and add it to the capital of the trust fund or

(4) pay and dispose of the said income in partially one manner and partially the other or others.

The testatrix left the capital to two charities.

Upon an application by the executors for advice and directions, Barlow J. held, *inter alia*, that the provisions of cl. 3 of the will were valid and were not void for uncertainty.[94] Helen Madeline Peck appealed.

LAIDLAW J.A. delivered the judgment of the court:

. . .

When all the relevant provisions are given full and proper consideration, it is not difficult in this case to find, from the language of the will, what the testatrix had in her mind at the time she made it in regard to her daughter Helen Madeline Peck. She thought that a bequest of money to her daughter might not be used with care and prudence. She wanted to guard against waste and dissipation of any of her money in the hands of her daughter, but, at the same time, wanted her daughter to have the enjoyment of it in a proper way during her lifetime. She intended that there should be a supervision and control exercisable at any and all times as to the manner of spending the money to be provided in her will for her daughter. It was logical and reasonable that the responsibility for seeing to the proper use of that money should be placed upon the trustees of her estate. Therefore, her plan and intention was to give her trustees power to deprive her daughter of the income if, in their opinion, it was being used by her in a reckless and improvident manner. The vesting of such a power in trustees of an estate is not unusual. It may be found in reported cases, and nowhere, so far as I know, has such a provision been rejected by the courts. In *In re Coe's Trusts*[95] it was the testator's wish that his son should have the whole benefit of certain moneys if he should conduct himself "steadily and to the satisfaction of his trustees." It was held that this was in effect

94 [1946] O.W.N. 805 (H.C.).
95 (1858), 4 K. & J. 199, 70 E.R. 83.

a trust for the son with the power to the trustees to deprive him of the fund if he should not conduct himself steadily and to their satisfaction. Vice-Chancellor Sir W. Page Wood says:[96]

> The trustees had clearly a discretionary power of *depriving* the son of the principal moneys in question. . . .
> In *Re Fox*[97] it appears that the following provision in a will was in question:
> If at any time during the period of five years after my death it appears to my executors . . . that my said son . . . does not remain sober, I give them power to sell and dispose of the said property. . . .

That provision was held to be valid.

The only question arising after the intention of the testatrix has been discovered is whether there is any rule or principle of law which prevents the carrying out of that intention. It is said in argument by counsel for the beneficiary that the provision in question is so uncertain as to have no effect in law. In my opinion this argument is founded upon a misapprehension of the condition annexed to the bequest. The condition which operates to deprive the beneficiary of the income is the exercise of the discretion of the trustees. When that discretion has been exercised, the event which brings about a cessation of the right to receive the income is an established fact, with no element whatever of uncertainty. It is a happening as certain as any of the other events named or described in the third clause of the will and causing the same result. It is certain both in expression and in operation, and counsel was not able to refer the court to any case in which such a provision, giving to the trustees a discretion in the manner and with the object operating in this will, has been held void. The words of Boyd C. in *Re Fox*[98] are most pertinent in this case. He said:

> It would be unfortunate if the court was obliged to interpose difficulties in giving effect to the intentions of testators so obviously framed for the well-being, and well-doing, of the objects of their bounty, and especially so when these objects are their own children.

. . .

[The court dismissed the appeal.]

Notes and Questions

1. In *Re Williams* the court declined to give advice to the trustees concerning the kind of reckless or improvident conduct on the part of the daughter that would permit the trustees to interrupt the payment of income. The court held that this was a matter for the judgment of the trustees only and their discretion would not be interfered with if they acted in good faith.

Should a court decline to give such advice?

---

96 *Ibid.*, at K. & J. 203.
97 (1885), 8 O.R. 489 (Ch.).
98 *Ibid.*, at 492.

2. Forfeiture may occur for reasons other than bankruptcy. *Re Balfour's Settlement*[99] is illustrative. The provision for termination encompassed assignment and bankruptcy, as well as any act or default of the primary beneficiary, and termination by operation or process of law or otherwise whereby the income should become payable to another person. The trustee impounded the income in order to remedy a breach of trust by a previous trustee. The court held that the beneficiary's interest had been determined by the trustee's action.[100]

3. A court order may also effect forfeiture. *Re Richardson's Will Trusts*[101] is an example. A court order imposed a lien on the income interest under a trust to secure maintenance for the principal beneficiary's divorced wife. It was held that he thereby forfeited the interest. Is this correct?[102]

4. A court order effecting forfeiture of a determinable life interest may also effect the forfeiture of the gift over upon discretionary trust. *Re Allsopp's Marriage Settlement Trusts, Public Trustee v. Cherry*[103] illustrates this point. A divorce settlement had created a determinable life interest for H with a discretionary trust in favour of issue of marriage after the determination of H's life interest. A Divorce Court order was held to have forfeited H's determinable life interest. The issue before the Chancery Division was whether the discretionary trust was similarly extinguished by the order. The court opined that the discretionary trust and the determinable life interest could have no separate existence since the former had been engrafted on the latter. The Divorce Court order therefore extinguished all of H's interests under the marriage settlement as if "he died in the lifetime of the petitioner."

5. It is clear that you cannot settle property upon yourself until bankruptcy. Such a disposition is regarded as a fraud on the creditors.[104] This issue arose in *Re Knechtel Furniture Ltd.*[105] A company had established a pension plan for its employees pursuant to a trust agreement. Both the employer and the employees contributed to the plan. The plan provided that on dissolution of the plan any surplus funds were to be paid to the company, but that if the company was then bankrupt or insolvent, the surplus should be allocated to provide increases in benefits to the employee beneficiaries. The company made an assignment in bankruptcy and the court held that the provision to pay the surplus to the beneficiaries on the company's bankruptcy was void as against the trustee in bankruptcy insofar as it concerned contributions to the plan by the company.

The court distinguished *Knechtel* in *Re Tomlin Estate*[106] on the ground that in the latter case the donor and beneficiary were different persons. A testatrix set up a trust for a nephew. He was to receive the interest on the principal for 15 years, after which the principal was to be paid to him. However, if he sold, assigned, or otherwise dealt with the interest or principal during the 15 years, the principal was to be paid to a charity. The nephew made a voluntary assignment in bankruptcy during the 15 years. The court held that his trustee in bankruptcy had no claim to the money. The assignment made the bequest

---

99 [1938] Ch. 928.

100 To the same effect is *Re Baring's Settlement Trusts*, [1940] Ch. 737, in which the court made a sequestration order against the property of a mother for failure to return her children to the jurisdiction. The order effected a forfeiture.

101 [1958] Ch. 504, [1958] 1 All E.R. 538.

102 See *General Accident Fire and Life Assurance Corp. Ltd. v. I.R.C.*, [1963] 1 W.L.R. 1207, [1963] 3 All E.R. 259 (C.A.), which came to a different conclusion.

103 [1959] Ch. 81.

104 *Re Burroughs-Fowler*, [1916] 2 Ch. 251.

105 (1985), 56 C.B.R. (N.S.) 258, 20 E.T.R. 217, 8 C.C.E.L. 193 (Ont. S.C. (in Bktcy.)).

106 (1996), 15 E.T.R. (2d) 179, 41 C.B.R. (3d) 107, 9 O.T.C. 220 (Gen. Div.).

void. Further, the condition ensured that the gift was not absolute and could, therefore, not be interpreted as a forfeiture clause which would be void.

6. On the other hand, English law appears to permit forfeiture for reasons other than bankruptcy. *Re Detmold*[107] illustrates this. A settlor settled property upon protective trusts for himself for life, with remainder to his wife for life. A court order was made appointing a judgment creditor as the receiver of the income. The settlor subsequently became bankrupt, but the court held that the receiver order forfeited the settlor's interest, so that the income shifted to his wife.

If the settlor in *Detmold* was insolvent when he made the settlement, it is likely that the settlement could have been set aside at the instance of his creditors.[108]

7. You can make a gift, such as a testamentary gift, to a person conditional on that person not being bankrupt at the time of vesting or receipt. That is a gift upon condition precedent and the condition renders the gift void if not satisfied at the relevant time.[109]

8. The Ontario Law Reform Commission declined to recommend the incorporation of a statutory protective trust in its proposed trusts legislation.[110] The Commission believed that protective trusts are not widely used in Ontario and it regarded the protective trust as incompatible with the rule which invalidates restraints on the alienability of a legal fee simple.

The Commission, nevertheless, declined to recommend the abolition of this type of restraint.[111] However, it proposed to empower the court to order payment of a claim by a creditor out of the income payable to a protected beneficiary, or out of the capital.[112] The proposal would thus achieve indirectly what the Commission refused to do directly.

Is the Commission's approach convincing?[113]

5. TRUSTS WHICH CONTRAVENE PERPETUITIES

Dispositions under trusts which contravene a perpetuity rule are void. These rules are not discussed in detail in this book, since the student will have studied them elsewhere.

There are two main perpetuity rules: the rule against remoteness of vesting and the rule against indefinite duration or perpetual trusts. The common law rule against remoteness of vesting (commonly called "the rule against perpetuities") avoids an interest which may by possibility vest beyond a period of a life or lives in being at the creation of the interest plus 21 years. Some jurisdictions have enacted legislation to modify this rule.[114] The statutes remedy some of the obvious traps which existed at common law and modify the common law rule by replacing the possibility principle with the wait and see principle. The latter allows one to

---

107 (1888), 40 Ch. D. 585 (Ch. Div.).
108 This is discussed further below.
109 See *Cox v. Fonblanque* (1868), L.R. 6 Eq. 482.
110 O.L.R.C. Report, at 362ff.
111 It intends to address the matter in its pending report on Basic Principles of Land Law: *ibid.*, at 363, fn. 249.
112 "An Act to revise the *Trustee Act*," *ibid.*, at 479, s. 52.
113 See further James Rossiter, "The Case for Protective Trusts: A Response to the Recommendations of the Ontario Law Reform Commission" (1986), 7 E. & T.Q. 229.
114 *Perpetuities Act*, R.S.A. 2000, c. P-5; R.S.O. 1990, c. P.9; R.S.N.W.T. 1988, c. P-3; R.S.Y. 2002, c. 168; *Perpetuity Act* R.S.B.C. 1996, c. 358.

wait and see whether an interest will in fact offend the rule. If it does, the interest is void; if it does not, it is valid.[115]

The rule against remoteness of vesting has been abolished in Manitoba.[116]

The rule against indefinite duration avoids non-charitable purpose trusts which last, or may last, beyond the perpetuity period. It will be discussed further in connection with that topic later in this book. The rule has been modified in some jurisdictions and has been abolished in Manitoba.[117]

In addition to the perpetuity rules, there are statutory restrictions on the accumulation of income in some provinces. These derive from the English *Thellusson Act*.[118] The latter was received English law in Manitoba, Alberta and Saskatchewan, and probably also in British Columbia, the Northwest Territories, Nunavut, Yukon and Newfoundland. It was re-enacted in British Columbia, New Brunswick,[119] and Ontario.[120] However, accumulation restrictions have since been abolished in Alberta,[121] British Columbia,[122] and Manitoba,[123] and New Brunswick.[124]

The legislation (where it remains in force) avoids accumulations of income beyond certain specified periods. The period that applies to a particular disposition depends upon the intention of the creator of the trust and the nature of the disposition. Common periods for *inter vivos* settlements are 21 years from the making of the settlement and 21 years from the settlor's death. A common period for a testamentary trust is 21 years from the testator's death.

Further Reading

A.H. Oosterhoff, *Text, Commentary and Cases on Wills*, 4th ed. (Toronto: Carswell, 1995), Chapter 15.

Anger and Honsberger, *Law of Real Property*, 2nd ed. by A.H. Oosterhoff and W.B. Rayner (Aurora: Canada Law Book Inc., 1985), Chapter 11.

6. TRUSTS WHICH DEFRAUD CREDITORS

A person in financial difficulties who settles property upon others to avoid his or her creditors, acts fraudulently and the creditors will be able to reach the

---

115 *The Perpetuities Act*, R.S.P.E.I. 1988, c. P-3, merely varies the perpetuity period to a life in being plus 60 years.

116 By *The Perpetuities and Accumulations Act*, R.S.M. 1987, c. P33, s. 3. See Jane Matthews Glenn, "Perpetuities to Purefoy: Reform by Abolition in Manitoba" (1984), 62 Can. Bar Rev. 618, reprinted (1986), 7 E. & T.Q. 307.

117 By *The Perpetuities and Accumulations Act* (Man.), *ibid.*

118 *Accumulations Act*, 1800, (39 & 40 Geo. 3), c. 98 (U.K.). Now *Law of Property Act*, 1925, (15 & 16 Geo. 5), c. 20, s. 164, am. by *Perpetuities and Accumulations Act*, 1964, c. 55, s. 13.

119 *Property Act*, R.S.N.B. 1973, c. P-19, ss. 1, 2.

120 *Accumulations Act*, R.S.O. 1990, c. A.5.

121 *Perpetuities Act*, R.S.A. 2000, c. P-5, s. 24.

122 *Perpetuity Act* (B.C.), *supra*, note 114, s. 25.

123 *The Perpetuities and Accumulations Act* (Man.), *supra*, note 116, s. 2.

124 By S.N.B. 1997, c. 9, ss. 1, 2.

property. There are two main statutes which assist the creditor in this respect, the *Bankruptcy Act*[125] and the fraudulent conveyances statutes. The latter derive from an English statute[126] which was received law in all common law jurisdictions of Canada and which has been re-enacted in some, as indicated below. The relevant sections of these statutes are reproduced below. In addition, the fraudulent preferences statutes[127] are sometimes used to recover property transferred by a debtor to one or more creditors in preference to others.

The effect of the several statutes is discussed in *Re Kreutzweiser*,[128] reproduced below.

Parliament enacted the *Bankruptcy Act* in 1919 and the question whether the provincial legislation was thereafter *ultra vires* remained unsettled for some time. In *Robinson v. Countrywide Factors Ltd.*[129] the Supreme Court of Canada held that the Saskatchewan *Fraudulent Preferences Act*[130] was not in conflict with the federal statute, although insofar as the provincial statutes permit assignments for the benefit of creditors, they are unconstitutional. The court further opined in *dicta* that the fraudulent conveyances statutes were also not in conflict with the federal legislation. The federal and provincial statutes overlap to some extent, but in other respects the provincial statutes are wider in scope and complement the federal statute.

BANKRUPTCY AND INSOLVENCY ACT

R.S.C. 1985, c. B-3 (am. S.C. 1992, c. 27, s. 2)

. . .

---

125 R.S.C. 1985, c. B-3 (renamed *Bankruptcy and Insolvency Act* by S.C. 1992, c. 27, s.2).

126 *Fraudulent Conveyances Act*, 1571, (13 Eliz. 1), c. 5 (Eng.), (now the *Law of Property Act*, 1925, (15 & 16 Geo. 5, c. 20, s. 207, Sch. 7 was later repealed by the *Statute Law Revision Act 1950*).

127 *Fraudulent Preferences Act*, R.S.A. 2000, c. F-24; *The Fraudulent Preferences Act*, R.S.S. 1978, c. F-21; *Fraudulent Preference Act*, R.S.B.C. 1996, c. 164; *Assignments and Preferences Acts*, R.S.N.B. 1973, c. A-16; R.S.N.S. 1989, c. 25, as am. by S.N.S. 1995-96, c. 13, s. 77; R.S.O. 1990, c. A.33, as am. by S.O. 1993, c. 27, s. 3 (Sched.), and by S.O. 2001, c. 9, Sched. D, s. 14; *Frauds on Creditors Act*, R.S.P.E.I. 1988, c. F-15; *Fraudulent Preferences and Conveyances Act*, R.S.Y. 2002, c. 95. Newfoundland and the Northwest Territories do not appear to have similar legislation.

128 (1965), 8 C.B.R. (N.S.) 225 (Ont. S.C. (in Bktcy.)).

129 [1978] 1 S.C.R. 753, 72 D.L.R. (3d) 500. In *Giffen, Re*, [1998] 1 S.C.R. 91, 155 D.L.R. (4th) 332, 1998 CarswellBC 147, 1998 CarswellBC 148, [1998] S.C.J. No. 11, 45 B.C.L.R. (3d) 1, 222 N.R. 29, 101 B.C.A.C. 161, 164 W.A.C. 161, 1 C.B.R. (4th) 115, [1998] 7 W.W.R. 1, 13 P.P.S.A.C. (2d) 255, the Supreme Court of Canada held that although bankruptcy is a federal matter, the *Bankruptcy and Insolvency Act*, *supra* is dependant on provincial property and civil rights legislation to inform the terms of the *Bankruptcy and Insolvency Act* and the rights of the parties in the bankruptcy.

130 *Supra*, note 127.

Settlements and Preferences

2. (1) . . .

"settlement" includes a contract, covenant, transfer, gift and designation of beneficiary in an insurance contract, to the extent that the contract, covenant, transfer, gift or designation is gratuitous or made for merely nominal consideration;

. . .

91. (1) Any settlement of property made within the period beginning on the day that is one year before the date of the initial bankruptcy event in respect of the settlor and ending on the date that the settlor became bankrupt, both dates included, is void against the trustee.

(2) Any settlement of property made within the period beginning on the day that is five years before the date of the initial bankruptcy event in respect of the settlor and ending on the date that the settlor became bankrupt, both dates included, is void against the trustee if the trustee can prove that the settlor was, at the time of making the settlement, unable to pay all the settlor's debts without the aid of the property comprised in the settlement or that the interest of the settlor in the property did not pass on the execution thereof.

(3) This section does not extend to any settlement made in favour of a purchaser or incumbrancer in good faith and for valuable consideration.

92. [Repealed 2000, c. 12, s. 12.]

93. [Repealed 2000, c. 12, s. 12.]

FRAUDULENT CONVEYANCES ACT

R.S.O. 1990, c. F.29

1. In this Act,

"conveyance" includes gift, grant, alienation, bargain, charge, encumbrance, limitation of use or uses of, in, to or out of real property or personal property by writing or otherwise;

"personal property" includes goods, chattels, effects, bills, bonds, notes and securities, and shares, dividends, premiums and bonuses in a bank, company or corporation, and any interest therein;

"real property" includes lands, tenements, hereditaments and any estate or interest therein.

2. Every conveyance of real property or personal property and every bond, suit, judgment and execution heretofore or hereafter made with intent to defeat, hinder, delay or defraud creditors or others of their just and lawful actions, suits, debts, accounts, damages, penalties or forfeitures are void as against such persons and their assigns.

3. Section 2 does not apply to an estate or interest in real property or personal property conveyed upon good consideration and in good faith to a person not having at the time of the conveyance to the person notice or knowledge of the intent set forth in that section.

4. Section 2 applies to every conveyance executed with the intent set forth in that section despite the fact that it was executed upon a valuable consideration and with the intention, as between the parties to it, of actually transferring to and for the benefit of the transferee the interest expressed to be thereby transferred, unless it is protected under section 3 by reason of good faith and want of notice or knowledge on the part of the purchaser.

. . .

[Sections 5-8 are concerned with conveyances made to defraud purchasers. They derive from another English statute[131] and are not relevant to the issue now under consideration.]

Comparable Legislation

Fraudulent Conveyances Act, 1571, c. 5 (Eng.), (now *Law of Property Act,* 1925, 15 & 16 Geo. 5, c. 20, s. 207, Sch. 7. Sch. 7 was later repealed by the *Statute Law Revision Act 1950)*; R.S.N. 1990, c. F-24; *The Fraudulent Conveyances Act,* R.S.M. 1987, c. F160; *Fraudulent Conveyance Act,* R.S.B.C. 1996, c. 163; *Fraudulent Preferences and Conveyances Act,* R.S.Y. 2002, c. 95, ss. 2-12.

Further Reading

Ronald C. Cuming, "Section 91 (Settlements) of the Bankruptcy and Insolvency Act: A Mutated Monster" (1995), 25 Can. Bus. L.J. 235.

VASEY v. KREUTZWEISER

(1965) 8 C.B.R. (N.S.) 225
Supreme Court of Ontario
[In Bankruptcy]

Reginald James Kreutzweiser, conveyed his house to his wife, the defendant, in 1961 for one dollar and natural love and affection. She assumed the existing mortgage. At that time he was unable to meet his debts as they became due and was unable to pay all his debts without the aid of the property so conveyed.

In 1963 Kreutzweiser became bankrupt. The plaintiff trustee in bankruptcy attacked the transfer on the ground that it was void under the *Bankruptcy Act,*[132]

---

131 *Fraudulent Conveyances Act,* 1584-85, (27 Eliz. 1), c. 4 (Eng.), (*Law of Property Act,* 1925, (15 & 16 Geo. 5), c. 20, s. 207, Sch. 7, consolidated under *Land Charges Act,* 1972, c. 61).

132 R.S.C. 1952, c. 14, s. 60. See now *Bankruptcy and Insolvency Act,* R.S.C. 1985, c. B-3, s. 91, *supra.*

the *Fraudulent Conveyances Act*,[133] and the *Assignments and Preferences Act*.[134] A trial of the issue was directed.

Mrs. Kreutzweiser testified that she agreed with her husband to pay the mortgage and that she would sell the house, pay off the mortgage and retain the proceeds. The property was worth approximately $18,000 and the principal owing on the mortgage was about $6,700.

BENNETT LOCAL MASTER:

. . .

I shall deal first with question (a) above, whether the conveyance . . . is fraudulent and void as against the trustee pursuant to the provisions of s. 60 of the *Bankruptcy Act*.

. . .

The onus is on the plaintiff under s. 60(2) to prove that:

1. A settlement was made within five years prior to the date of bankruptcy and

2. At the time of making the settlement, the bankrupt was unable to pay all his debts without the aid of the property comprised in the settlement or that the interest of the settlor in the property did not pass on the execution thereof.

I find that the conveyance dated the 31st December 1961 from Reginald James Kreutzweiser to Margaret Kreutzweiser was a settlement contemplated by s. 60(2) of the *Bankruptcy Act* and a settlement made within the five year period. In *Re Bozanich*,[135] Duff C.J. stated:

> "Settlement" implies an intention that the property shall be retained or preserved for the benefit of the donee in such a form that it can be traced.

In *Traders Trust Co. v. Cohen*,[136] Curran J. of the Court of King's Bench of Manitoba quoted from *Re Plummer*,[137] a decision of the Court of Appeal of England:

> "Settlement" in sec. 47 of *The Bankruptcy Act, 1883*,[138] means such a conveyance or transfer by the donor as contemplates the retention of the property by the donee either in its original form or in such a form that it can be traded and does not extend to a conveyance or transfer of property which cannot be traced, as, for instance, where there is a gift of money to be employed in a business or in the purchase of a business and the money is so employed or spent, the business itself not being settled.

---

133 R.S.O. 1960, c. 154, ss. 2, 4. See now R.S.O. 1990, c. F.29.
134 R.S.O. 1960, c. 25, s. 4. See now R.S.O. 1990, c. A.33, *supra*.
135 [1942] S.C.R. 130 at 135, 23 C.B.R. 234, [1942] 2 D.L.R. 145.
136 8 C.B.R. 513 at 524, [1927] 3 W.W.R. 473 (Man. K.B.).
137 [1900] 2 K.B. 790.
138 (46 & 47 Vict.), c. 52 (U.K.).

The evidence showed that Mrs. Kreutzweiser did not intend to spend the money from the sale of the house in an indifferent manner but planned to retain the proceeds for the benefit of herself or for herself and her husband. The property here could be traced. Counsel for the defendant conceded, "It is admitted that the evidence probably indicates that this transaction was a settlement." As to the five year period, the conveyance as stated was made in December 1961 and the trustee of the estate of Reginald James Kreutzweiser pursuant to the *Bankruptcy Act* was appointed on 6th June 1963.

I also find that Reginald James Kreutzweiser was during the year and in particular in the month of December 1961 unable to pay all his debts without the aid of the property comprised in the settlement.

In *Re Mitchell*,[139] the Registrar in Bankruptcy at Toronto discusses[140] the inability of a debtor to pay debts. The learned Registrar points out that, "inability to pay debts without the aid of the settled property" means that he is not meeting his obligations generally as they become due whether or not on a formal winding-up of his affairs his assets might equal his liabilities. A number of cases are cited by the Registrar, including *London and Counties Assets Company, Limited v. Brighton Grand Convert Hall and Picture Palace, Limited*,[141] in which Buckley L.J. . . . said:[142]

> There are decisions as to the meaning of the word "insolvent". They all state that "insolvency" means commercial insolvency, that is to say, inability to pay debts as they become due. The bankrupt was not meeting his obligations as they became due in December 1961.

[The learned Master reviewed the evidence and continued:]

Having found that the conveyance in December 1961 was a settlement of property by Kreutzweiser within five years of his bankruptcy and that Kreutzweiser was at the time of making the settlement unable to pay all his debts without the aid of the property settled, the next question to be decided is whether Mrs. Kreutzweiser was a purchaser in good faith and for valuable consideration under s. 60(3) of the *Bankruptcy Act*.

On the question of whether there was valuable consideration for the conveyance from the bankrupt to his wife, . . . Mrs. Kreutzweiser obtained for her one dollar, value in the neighbourhood of $5,500 (1/2 of $18,000 less mortgage of say $7,000). I conclude therefore that there was no valuable consideration for the conveyance from the bankrupt to his wife in December 1961. It is also my opinion for the same reasons that Mrs. Kreutzweiser was not a "purchaser" within the meaning of s. 60(3)(*b*) but was merely a beneficiary under a settlement.

I turn now to the question of good faith. On her examination for discovery . . . . Mrs. Kreutzweiser stated she persuaded her husband to execute the conveyance so that he could not mortgage the house to pay debts at the store which Mrs.

---

139 (1955), 35 C.B.R. 174, 1 D.L.R. (2d) 166.
140 *Ibid.*, at C.B.R. 180.
141 [1915] 2 K.B. 493 (C.A.).
142 *Ibid.*, at 501.

Kreutzweiser said he had done a short time before. At the trial, Mrs. Kreutzweiser gave as the sole reason for the transfer, the drinking problem of her husband and her fear that the property would be lost as a result of a claim arising out of an automobile accident caused by the negligence of her husband when he was impaired or drunk. Even if this evidence at the trial were accepted as the sole reason for the conveyance, I would find that the conveyance in December 1961 to Mrs. Kreutzweiser was not made in good faith because it was a conveyance made in contemplation of a debt arising in the future.[143] However I am satisfied that one of the substantial reasons, if not the main reason for the conveyance, was to place the house beyond the control of her husband so that it could not be mortgaged or be made available to her husband's creditors. . . . I am satisfied that Mrs. Kreutzweiser was well aware that her husband owed substantial sums of money in December 1961 which he could not pay if he stayed in business without resorting to the residential property. I conclude therefore that the conveyance in December 1961 was not a transaction carried out in good faith but one to place the property beyond the reach of the creditors, present and future.

Having found therefore that:

(a) Kreutzweiser made a settlement upon his wife within five years of his bankruptcy;

(b) Kreutzweiser was at the time of making the settlement unable to pay all his debts without the aid of the property settled; and

(c) the conveyance to Mrs. Kreutzweiser was not for valuable consideration and not a transaction in which Mrs. Kreutzweiser was acting in good faith,

I find that the said conveyance dated the 31st December 1961 from the said Reginald James Kreutzweiser to Margaret Kreutzweiser is void pursuant to the provisions of s. 60 of the *Bankruptcy Act*.

[The court reproduced section 2 of the *Fraudulent Conveyances Act* and continued:]

I find that the conveyance in question was made with the intent to defeat and defraud creditors. In *Traders Trust Co. v. Cohen*[144] Curran J. in the Supreme Court of Manitoba, interpreting the statute of Elizabeth (*Fraudulent Conveyances Act*)[145] states that when a conveyance is voluntary, the intent or purpose of the donor only in making the gift is the deciding factor whether or not the recipient of the gift participated in this intention. . . . His Lordship said this:[146]

It is not necessary therefore, in such circumstances to bring actual proof that the debtor had in his mind an intention to defeat, delay or defraud his creditors; for if it appears from all the facts of

---

143 See *The Bank of British North America v. Rattenbury* (1859), 7 Gr. 383 (U.C. Ch.), not a bankruptcy case, but where this principle was applied.

144 *Supra*, note 136.

145 1571 (13 Eliz.), c. 5 (Eng.).

146 *Supra*, note 136, at 519 [C.B.R.].

the case that the effect might be expected to be and has in fact been, to do so, the court will attribute the fraudulent intention to the settlor.

In the instant circumstances, the settlor and the person receiving the settlement both were well aware that the settlor was not meeting his obligations, in fact owed a great deal of money, that the creditors were pressing and that the conveyance was not made for any good consideration. I draw the inference from all the evidence that the debtor had the guilty intent to place the property beyond the reach of his creditors for the benefit of his wife or for their joint benefit.

[The court reproduced section 3 of the Act and continued:]

Section 3 does not assist the defendant because:

(1) There was no good consideration. As stated, the market value of the property was in the neighbourhood of $18,000 and the mortgage stood at between $6,000 and $7,000. It was Mrs. Kreutzweiser's intention to sell the property to obtain the net proceeds. The payment of $1 was not good consideration; and

(2) For reasons already given, the conveyance was not a *bona fide* one to a person not having at the time of the conveyance notice or knowledge of the guilty intent.

Moreover, section 4 of the *Fraudulent Conveyances Act* stipulates that section 2 applies to a conveyance executed with the intent set forth in that section notwithstanding that it was executed upon a valuable consideration and with the intention, as between the parties to it, of actually transferring to and for the benefit of the transferee the interest expressed to be thereby transferred, unless it is protected under section 3 by reason of *bona fides* and want of notice or knowledge on the part of the purchaser. Here, there was no *bona fides* and no want of knowledge on the part of the grantee.

I therefore find that the said conveyance is fraudulent and void as against the trustee pursuant to the provisions [of] sections 2 and 4 of the *Fraudulent Conveyances Act.*

I turn now to the *Assignments and Preferences Act.* Section 4(1) of the Act reads:

> Subject to section 5, every gift, conveyance, assignment or transfer, delivery over or payment of goods, chattels or effects, or of bills, bonds, notes or securities, or of shares, dividends, premiums or bonus in any bank, company or corporation, or of any other property, real or personal, made by a person when insolvent or unable to pay the person's debts in full or when the person knows that he, she or it is on the eve of insolvency, with intent to defeat, hinder, delay or prejudice creditors, or any one or more of them, is void as against the creditor or creditors injured, delayed or prejudiced.

Mr. Kreutzweiser was unable to pay his debts in full and the conveyance in December 1961 was made with an intent to defeat creditors. The defendant to avoid the provision of s. 4(1) must bring herself within s. 5(1) which provides that s. 4 does not apply to any *bona fide* conveyance that is made in consideration of "a present actual *bona fide* payment in money . . . when the money paid or the goods or other properties sold or delivered bear a fair and reasonable relative value to the consideration thereof." The money paid here ($1) did not bear a fair and reasonable relative value to the property conveyed. There was not a *bona fide* conveyance made in consideration of a present actual *bona fide* payment in money.

I find therefore that the conveyance in question is void pursuant to the provisions of the *Assignments and Preferences Act*.

I therefore:

Find that the conveyance, dated the 31st December 1961 from Reginald James Kreutzweiser to the defendant and registered in the registry office for the township of Derby on the 14th December 1961 as No. 72571 is fraudulent and void as against the trustee.

. . .

[McDermott J. affirmed the order on November 30, 1965.][147]

Notes and Questions

1. Subsections 91(1) and 91(2), as well as section 92, of the *Bankruptcy and Insolvency Act* were replaced in 1997.[148] Subsection 91(3) was replaced in 2000.[149] Finally, sections 92 and 93 were repealed in 2000.[150]

Section 92 provided that any covenant or contract by the settlor for the future payment of money for the benefit of the settlor's spouse or children, or for the future settlement of money on or for the settlor's spouse or children, of property in which the settlor had no interest at the date of the marriage and not being in the right of the settlor's spouse or children, was void against the trustee if the settlor becomes bankrupt and the covenant or contract had not been executed at the date of the bankruptcy. The covenant or contract was not void against the trustee if it enabled the persons entitled under it to claim for dividends in the settlor's bankruptcy proceedings under or in respect of it. The claim of such dividends was to be postponed until the claims of all creditors were first satisfied.[151]

Section 93(1) provided that any payment of money, which was not a payment of premiums of a life insurance policy in favour of the settlor's spouse or children, or any transfer of property made by the settlor pursuant to a covenant or contract mentioned in s. 70, was void against the trustee. Section 93(1) included three exceptions to this rule. Section 93(2) provided that where any payment or transfer mentioned in subsection (1) was declared void, any persons to whom the payment or transfer of property was made were entitled to claim for dividends under or in respect of the covenant or contract as if it had not been executed at the date of bankruptcy.[152]

2. Although both the *Bankruptcy and Insolvency Act* and the *Fraudulent Conveyances Act* speak of a settlement or conveyance in fraud on creditors as being void, in fact,

---

147 *Supra*, note 136, at 225 [C.B.R.].
148 By S.C. 1997, c. 12, s. 75.
149 By S.C. 2000, c. 12, s. 11.
150 *Ibid.*, s. 12.
151 R.S.C. 1985, c. B-3 as amended by R.S.C. 1997, c. 12, s. 76.
152 *Ibid.*, as amended by s. 77.

the courts have construed the statutes as making the settlement or conveyance voidable only at the instance of the trustee in bankruptcy or a creditor.[153]

3. The *Fraudulent Conveyances Act* applies to "creditors and others." It has been held that a wife who claims alimony from her husband is his creditor.[154] It is probable that a spouse who claims to be entitled to a resulting or constructive trust in property owned by the other spouse, while not a creditor, would fall within the meaning of the phrase "and others."[155]

4. In *Bozanich, Re*[156] the Supreme Court of Canada imported the common law qualification of the statutory definition of "settlement" into Canadian bankruptcy law. The court held that if it is the intention of the donor that the property transferred is retained or preserved for the benefit of the donee in such a form that it can be traced, the transfer is a "settlement," within the meaning of s. 91 of the *Bankruptcy and Insolvency Act*, but not otherwise.[157] Thus, for example, when a person rolls over RRSP funds into an annuity for him- or herself, or for others, the rollover is a settlement if made within one or five years of bankruptcy.[158]

In *Royal Bank v. Whalley*[159] the Ontario Court of Appeal held that the recent statutory changes to the *Bankruptcy and Insolvency Act* did not affect the common law qualification of the meaning of "settlement" as established by *Bozanich, Re* because the legislative changes failed to address it directly. Catzman J.A. opined that the transaction in question did not constitute a "settlement" within the meaning of s. 91 of the *Bankruptcy and Insolvency Act*. Although the transaction was a gratuitous transfer of property, it did not satisfy the additional requirement set out by *Bozanich, Re*.

5. A settlement may be void as against the trustee but not be available to the creditors. This issue was raised in *Ramgotra (Trustee of) v. North American Life Assurance Co.*[160] A husband transferred funds from registered retirement savings plans (RRSPs) into a registered retirement income fund (RRIF) within five years of his bankruptcy. He designated his wife as beneficiary. The RRIF was exempt from the claims of creditors under s. 158 of *The Saskatchewan Insurance Act*, R.S.S. 1978, c. S-26, and that exemption is carried forward into the federal legislation. Section 67(1)(b) of the *Bankruptcy and Insolvency Act*[161] provides that the property of a bankrupt divisible among the creditors shall

---

153 See, *e.g.*, *Donohoe v. Hull Bros. & Co.* (1895), 24 S.C.R. 683, 1895 CarswellNWT 34.

154 *Shephard v. Shephard*, 56 O.L.R. 555, [1925] 2 D.L.R. 897 (C.A.).

155 *Prytula v. Prytula* (1980), 30 O.R. (2d) 324, 116 D.L.R. (3d) 474, 1980 CarswellOnt 311, 19 R.F.L. (2d) 440 (H.C.).

156 [1942] S.C.R. 130, 23 C.B.R. 234, [1942] 2 D.L.R. 145, 1942 CarswellOnt 76.

157 *Ibid.*

158 *Alberta Treasury Branches v. Guimond* (1987), 53 Alta. L.R. (2d) 39, 1987 CarswellAlta 334, 27 C.C.L.I. 90, (sub nom. *Guimond (Bankrupt), Re*) 83 A.R. 392, 70 C.B.R. (N.S.) 125 (Q.B.); *Wozniuk, Re* (1987), 76 A.R. 42, 1987 CarswellAlta 396 (Q.B.).

159 (2002), 59 O.R. (3d) 529, 213 D.L.R. (4th) 106, 34 C.B.R. (4th) 277, 2002 CarswellOnt 1746, 160 O.A.C. 366 (C.A.). See also *Dowswell, Re* (1999), 124 O.A.C. 281, 11 C.B.R. (4th) 23, 178 D.L.R. (4th) 193, [1999] O.J. No. 3239, 1999 CarswellOnt 2765 (C.A.); *Toronto Dominion Bank v. Amex Bank of Canada*, 196 A.R. 307, 50 Alta. L.R. (3d) 310, 146 D.L.R. (4th) 55, 1997 CarswellAlta 345, 141 W.A.C. 307, [1997] 6 W.W.R. 530, 46 C.B.R. (3d) 304 (C.A.). *Cf. Grandview Ford Lincoln Sales Ltd., Re* (2000), 21 C.B.R. (4th) 51, [2000] O.J. No. 3280, 2000 CarswellOnt 3087 (Bktcy.), additional reasons at (2000), 2000 CarswellOnt 4090 (Bktcy.).

160 (sub nom. *Royal Bank v. North American Life Assurance Co.*) [1996] 1 S.C.R. 325, 132 D.L.R. (4th) 193, 13 E.T.R. (2d) 1, 1996 CarswellSask 212F, 1996 CarswellSask 418, [1996] S.C.J. No. 17, [1996] 3 W.W.R. 457, 37 C.B.R. (3d) 141, 10 C.C.P.B. 113, [1996] 1 C.T.C. 356, (sub nom. *Ramgotra (Bankrupt), Re*) 193 N.R. 186, 141 Sask. R. 81, 96 D.T.C. 6157.

161 R.S.C. 1985, c. B-3 (as amended), *supra*.

not comprise any property that is exempt under provincial law. Although the designation of the wife was a settlement that was void as against the trustee under s. 91, therefore, the trustee could not distribute the RRIF among the creditors.

6. In *Wilson v. Gill*[162] the British Columbia Court of Appeal considered the meaning of "settlement" in the context of s. 91 of the *Bankruptcy and Insolvency Act*. The court held that "settlement" does not include an ordinary business transaction between a debtor and a creditor. Thus, a transfer of property in discharge of an existing debt is not a "settlement." G had transferred land to his brother prior to becoming bankrupt. There was no consideration for the transfer of land. W, one of G's creditors, sued to have the land transferred to him. W alleged that G transferred the land to his brother to avoid his creditors and, therefore, the transfer violated the *Bankruptcy and Insolvency Act* and the *Fraudulent Conveyances Act*. The primary issue before the Court of Appeal was whether the transfer was in discharge of an existing indebtedness. The court found that G's transfer of title to his brother created a trust for G's benefit. G did not intend for his brother to have the beneficial interest in the land, but rather for his brother to hold the land in trust for him. The court concluded that a transfer from G to B, B to hold the lands in trust for G, is a "settlement" in the context of s. 91 of the *Bankruptcy and Insolvency Act*. The transfer was therefore void.

7. In *Whetstone, Re*[163] the court addressed the issue of the meaning of the term "settlement" and related matters. A husband conveyed his half interest in the matrimonial home to his wife. The deed was dated December 2, 1981 and was registered December 10, 1981. He continued to occupy the house with his wife thereafter. The husband had given personal guarantees on his company's obligations to a number of creditors. He was unable to meet those obligations and the creditors petitioned him into bankruptcy on December 8, 1982. The creditors then applied under s. 69(1) of the *Bankruptcy Act* [now s. 91(1) of the *Bankruptcy and Insolvency Act*] and s. 2 of the *Fraudulent Conveyances Act* to have the deed avoided. In the alternative, they asserted a claim under s. 69(2) of the *Bankruptcy Act* [now s. 91(3) of the *Bankruptcy and Insolvency Act*]. The court held that the conveyance was a settlement. However, it held that since the deed had been signed more than a year, albeit registered less than a year before the date of the bankruptcy, s. 69(1) [now s. 91(1)] did not apply to avoid it.

On the other hand, s. 2 of the *Fraudulent Conveyances Act* did apply, for the beneficiary of a guarantee is included in the term "others" referred to in s. 2. The court found that the husband made the conveyance in order to place the property beyond the reach of his creditors at a time when he knew his company was in financial difficulties.

The court held further that the deed was void under s. 69(2) of the *Bankruptcy Act* [now s. 91(3) of the *Bankruptcy and Insolvency Act*, which has since been repealed], under which intent is not relevant. The court opined that a contingent liability under a guarantee is not necessarily always a "debt," but that it was in this case, since the husband had virtually no assets to satisfy the guarantees after he executed the deed.

8. In *Bank of Montreal v. Bray*[164] the Ontario Court of Appeal affirmed that s. 2 of the *Fraudulent Conveyances Act* renders transactions made with the intent to defraud creditors void as against those creditors. In 1978, Mr. B signed a guarantee of indebtedness

---

162 (1998), 49 B.C.L.R. (3d) 137, 105 B.C.A.C. 225, 6 C.B.R. (4th) 121, 1998 CarswellBC 584, 171 W.A.C. 225 (C.A.).

163 (1984), 47 O.R. (2d) 719, 52 C.B.R. (N.S.) 280, 1984 CarswellOnt 157, 12 D.L.R. (4th) 249 (Bktcy.).

164 36 O.R. (3d) 99, 1997 CarswellOnt 3903, [1997] O.J. No. 4277, 153 D.L.R. (4th) 490, 50 C.B.R. (3d) 1, 104 O.A.C. 351, 33 R.F.L. (4th) 335, 14 R.P.R. (3d) 139 (C.A.).

of a corporation in favour of the plaintiff bank, which provided a line of credit to the corporation. In 1986, Mr. B acknowledged the continuing validity of the guarantee. Mrs. B was unaware of her husband's guarantee. Mr. and Mrs. B held title to their matrimonial home as joint tenants. In 1990, Mr. B conveyed his interest in the home to Mrs. B for one dollar. Since Mr. B intended to defraud his creditors, including the plaintiff bank, the 1990 conveyance was a fraudulent conveyance and was therefore void as against the bank. Since there is nothing in s. 2 of the *Fraudulent Conveyances Act* that renders the transaction void as against the parties to the transaction, the fraudulent conveyance to Mrs. B in 1990 effectively severed the joint tenancy. The court held that the creditor was entitled to relief under s. 2 even though the status quo ante could not be restored, that is, the conveyance could not be set aside.

9. The court addressed the issue of the onus of proof in *Fancy, Re.*[165] A bankrupt conveyed his interest in the matrimonial home to his wife within one year of his bankruptcy and continued to live in the house. Since the conveyance was a settlement that occurred in the year before the settlor became bankrupt, the court declared it void pursuant to section 91(1) of the *Bankruptcy and Insolvency Act*. The court was also willing to declare the transaction void based on section 2 of the *Fraudulent Conveyances Act*. Anderson J. remarked that although the primary burden of proof on a balance of probabilities remains with the plaintiff, the existence of one or more of the "badges of fraud" may give rise to an inference of intent to defraud in the absence of an explanation from the defendant. In such circumstances there is an onus on the defendant to adduce evidence showing an absence of fraudulent intent. The defendant was unable to produce such evidence.

10. In *Bank of Nova Scotia v. Simpson*,[166] the plaintiff satisfied the requisite intent to defeat, hinder, delay, or prejudice creditors under section 4(1) of the Nova Scotia *Assignments and Preferences Act*.[167] The court held that the burden may be met by showing the actual or expected effect of the transfer. Mr. Simpson, who was in financial difficulties and was being pressed by creditors, conveyed property to his son but continued to occupy the property as a residence and the son did not charge any rent, effect any repairs, or pay taxes. About two years later, the property was conveyed to the father's solicitor's wife upon the direction of the father and without any of the proceeds of sale going to the son. Instead, the proceeds were used to pay the debts of the father. The consideration was one third of the value of the property. The father retained the right to live in the house for a rent equal to the purchaser's mortgage payment. The solicitor's wife knew little of the transactions, but rather was a purchaser in name only for her husband, who had full knowledge of his client's financial circumstances and the claims against him.

11. B controlled F Ltd. and P Ltd. The business of F Ltd. was sold and the proceeds paid to P Ltd. P Ltd. paid all of the outstanding accounts of F Ltd., except that owing to E Ltd. E Ltd. obtained judgment against F Ltd. and then obtained a receiving order, placing F Ltd. into bankruptcy.

---

165 (1984), 46 O.R. (2d) 153, 8 D.L.R. (4th) 418, 51 C.B.R. (N.S.) 29, 1984 CarswellOnt 137 (Bktcy.). See also *Kostiuk, Re* (1999), 14 C.B.R. (4th) 101, 1999 CarswellBC 2528 (S.C.), additional reasons at 27 C.B.R. (4th) 67, 2001 CarswellBC 1604, 2001 BCSC 1002 (S.C. [In Chambers]), additional reasons at 27 C.B.R. (4th) 249, 2001 CarswellBC 1699, 2001 BCSC 1134 (S.C.), affirmed [2002] B.C.J. No. 1475, 2002 CarswellBC 1529, 2002 BCCA 410, 2 B.C.L.R. (4th) 284, [2002] 8 W.W.R. 457, 35 C.B.R. (4th) 123, 215 D.L.R. (4th) 78, 170 B.C.A.C. 215, 279 W.A.C. 215 (C.A.).

166 (1984), 64 N.S.R. (2d) 383, 52 C.B.R. (N.S.) 183, 1984 CarswellNS 22, 143 A.P.R. 383 (T.D.).

167 R.S.N.S. 1989, c. 25, am. 1995-96, c. 13, s. 77.

Can the trustee in bankruptcy recover from P Ltd. or F Ltd.? If so, on what basis?[168]

12. A transfer of the matrimonial home to one's former spouse, pursuant to minutes of settlement in the divorce action, is not a "settlement" within the meaning of s. 69 of the *Bankruptcy Act* [now s. 91 of the *Bankruptcy and Insolvency Act*].[169]

13. A judgment by a court is not a settlement under the *Bankruptcy and Insolvency Act*. A settlement involves an action specified in s. 91 by the settlor. A judgment is a decision of a court and not of the settlor.[170]

14. When the evidence clearly establishes that a spouse has had a half interest in the matrimonial home for many years under a resulting or constructive trust, the interest will survive the bankruptcy of the titled spouse. Further, a conveyance by the titled spouse within a year of bankruptcy to the other spouse cannot be set aside to the extent of the half interest.[171]

7. TRUSTS WHICH ARE DETRIMENTAL TO THE SETTLOR'S FAMILY

In recent years the courts have acquired statutory power to set aside or vary dispositions, including trusts, which have the effect of depriving the settlor's spouse or dependants of property or support. In addition, the court may vary a property division between spouses for those reasons. While this topic is beyond the scope of this book, the following may be mentioned.

1. The court, in enforcing a spouse's rights, may award more to one spouse than he or she is *prima facie* entitled to, because of dispositions made by the other spouse.[172] The court may also direct that property be settled upon a spouse,[173] and restrain the depletion of a spouse's property.[174]

2. The court may set aside a disposition of the matrimonial home made in contravention of the legislation.[175]

3. The court may set aside a provision for support or a waiver of the right for support in a domestic contract (including a settlement) if, *inter alia*, the provision

---

168 See *Profile United Industries Ltd. v. Coopers & Lybrand Ltd.* (1987), 79 N.B.R. (2d) 62, 64 C.B.R. (N.S.) 242, 38 D.L.R. (4th) 600, 1987 CarswellNB 27, 201 A.P.R. 62 (C.A.), leave to appeal refused (1987), 83 N.B.R. (2d) 90, 212 A.P.R. 90n, 86 N.R. 237n (S.C.C.).

169 *Canadian Imperial Bank of Commerce v. Shapiro* (1985), 49 O.R. (2d) 333, 44 R.F.L. (2d) 47, 1985 CarswellOnt 157, 54 C.B.R. (N.S.) 134 (H.C.).

170 *Bank of Montreal v. Coopers Lybrand Inc.*, 144 Sask. R. 207, 40 C.B.R. (3d) 161, 137 D.L.R. (4th) 441, 1996 CarswellSask 386, [1996] S.J. No. 387, [1996] 8 W.W.R. 153, 124 W.A.C. 207, 23 R.F.L. (4th) 415 (C.A.).

171 *Croteau, Re* (1985), 50 O.R. (2d) 629, 47 R.F.L. (2d) 45, 1985 CarswellOnt 294 (H.C.). See also *Lee, Re* (September 28, 1995), Doc. 35-045697, [1995] O.J. No. 3065 (Gen. Div.).

172 See, *e.g.*, *Family Law Act*, R.S.O. 1990, c. F.3, s. 5(6)(d), (h). For similar legislation see *Family Law Act*, R.S.N.L. 1990, c. F-2; S.N.W.T. 1997, c. 18, s. 71; *Matrimonial Property Act*, R.S.A. 2000, c. M-8; R.S.N.S. 1989, c. 275; S.S. 1997, c. M-6.11; *Family Relations Act*, R.S.B.C. 1996, c. 128; *Marital Property Act*, R.S.M. 1987, c. M45; S.N.B. 1980, c. M-1.1; *Family Law Act*, S.P.E.I. 1995, c. 12; *Married Women's Property Act*, R.S.Y. 2002, c. 147. See also *The Family Maintenance Act*, R.S.M. 1987, c. F20.

173 *Family Law Act, ibid.*, s. 9(1)(d)(i).

174 *Ibid.*, s. 12(a).

175 *Ibid.*, ss. 21(2), 23(d).

of support or the waiver results in unconscionable circumstances.[176] The court may also direct that moneys or property be held or property transferred in trust for the support of a dependant,[177] and it may restrain the depletion of a spouse's property if the depletion would defeat a claim for support.[178]

4. The court may disregard any provision in a domestic contract regarding the support, education, moral training, or the custody of or access to a child, where it would be in the best interests of the child.[179] It may also do so when the provision is unreasonable with respect to the child support guidelines or any other provision in the contract relating to support of the child.[180]

5. The court may set aside all or part of a domestic contract for failure to disclose significant assets or liabilities, failure of the other party to understand the nature and consequences of the contract, or other contractual reason.[181]

6. A separation agreement or settlement may be set aside in whole or in part if the removal by one spouse of barriers that would prevent the other spouse's remarriage within that spouse's faith was a consideration in the making of the agreement or settlement.[182]

7. In respect of support of dependants out of a deceased person's estate, the court may order that moneys be held or property transferred in trust for a dependant.[183] In addition, property devised under a contract to devise property by will, to the extent the contract was not made for valuable consideration, remains liable to an order for support.[184] Furthermore, the capital value of property settled by the deceased upon *inter vivos* trust for any person is included in the deceased's estate for the purpose of the support provision if the deceased retained the power to revoke the trust or to consume the capital.[185]

---

176 *Ibid.*, s. 33(4)(a).

177 *Ibid., s. 34(1)(b), (c).*

178 *Ibid.*, s. 40, as am. by S.O. 1999, c. 6, s. 25(18).

179 *Ibid.*, s. 56(1), as am. by S.O. 1997, c. 20, s. 10(1).

180 *Ibid.*, s. 56(1.1), added by S.O. 1997, c. 20, s. 10(2).

181 *Ibid.*, s. 56(4).

182 *Ibid.*, s. 56(5).

183 *Succession Law Reform Act*, R.S.O. 1990, c. S.26, s. 63(2)(b). For similar legislation see *Dependants of a Deceased Person Relief Act*, R.S.P.E.I. 1988, c. D-7; *The Dependants' Relief Act, 1996*, S.S. 1996, c. D-25.01, am. 2001, c. 34; 2001, c. 51; *Dependants Relief Act*, S.M. 1989-90, c. 42, s. 4; *Dependants Relief Act*, R.S.N.W.T. 1988, c. D-4; R.S.Y. 2002, c. 56; *Dependants Relief Act*, R.S.A. 2000, c. D-10.5; *Family Relief Act*, R.S.N.L. 1990, c. F-3; *Provision for Dependants Act*, R.S.N.B. 1973, c. P-22.3, as am. by S.N.B. 1991, c. 62, s. 3; *Testators' Family Maintenance Act*, R.S.N.S. 1989, c. 465; *Wills Variation Act*, R.S.B.C. 1996, c. 490.

184 *Succession Law Reform Act, ibid.*, s. 71.

185 *Ibid.*, s. 72, as am. by S.O. 1999, c.12, Sched. B, s.17

Problems

1. Mary and Esther were twin sisters. When they were married, they each made settlements. Mary's settlement was in favour of herself for life, then to her husband for life and then to their children, if any. The settlement contained a clause whereunder her own and her husband's interests were protected under a typical protective trust. The clause purported to terminate their respective life interests if they should voluntarily or involuntarily alienate their interests, or if their interests should fail for any other reason. Before Mary died, her husband became bankrupt.

Esther's settlement was *mutatis mutandis* to the same effect as Mary's. However, at the time she made her settlement Esther was unable to meet her liabilities as they became due. She became bankrupt some years later. Both sisters had children.

Discuss the effect of the two settlements and the rights of the beneficiaries and creditors.

6

THE ALTERATION AND TERMINATION OF TRUSTS

1. SCOPE

Normally, a trust ends when the trustees distribute the trust property to the beneficiaries in accordance with the terms of the trust. It may happen, however, that the settlor wishes to revoke[1] the trust, in whole or in part; the beneficiaries want to call for the property earlier than the trust allows; or, in very exceptional cases, the court may set the trust aside. In each of these situations, the trust would end prematurely.

This chapter explores each of these topics — revocation, setting aside and termination — to determine when and how each can occur. The related topic of variation of trusts is considered thereafter because there are occasions when the desired result is to keep the trust afoot, but with modifications. You need to understand the constraints governing an application to vary a trust in order to determine how to structure the application. As well, you need to appreciate the interrelationship between the common law right of termination and the variation of trusts legislation.

2. REVOCATION BY THE SETTLOR

(a) Generally

After constitution, settlors cannot revoke trusts, either completely or in part, unless they retain a power of revocation when creating the trust. This is because when a settlor establishes a trust he or she disposes of the property and no longer has control over it, save by express provision.[2] Before constitution, however, unless the declaration of trust is made for valuable consideration, the creator of a

---

1 A power of revocation enables the settlor to intervene and set the trust aside after its creation. The power of revocation is discussed more fully in part 2(c), *infra*.
2 See, for example, D.W.M. Waters, *Law of Trusts in Canada*, 2nd ed., (Toronto: Carswell, 1984), at 292. ("Waters")

trust is free to revoke because there is no trust without constitution.[3] Recent case law confirms that unrestricted powers of amendment or modification do not include the power to revoke.[4]

Because testamentary trusts are constituted on the testator's death, the issue of revocation is relevant only to *inter vivos* trusts. Before death, the testator can revoke the will containing the trust at any time. After the testator's death, there is no one with the power to revoke, so the issue does not arise. The testator may, however, make provision in the trust for its termination and typically does so. Thus, for example, a trust for the benefit of children will normally be scheduled to end when the children reach the age of majority and the capital is paid out to them, if the trust so provides.

(b) Exceptions to the Rule Against Revocation

If a debtor transfers money to a third party to hold for the purpose of paying his or her general creditors, the debtor may revoke unless the creditors joined as parties to the instrument transferring the funds or, having had notice of the transfer, they forbear from suing. Because of this power to revoke, it has been said that a debtor may revoke a trust made for creditors.

Subject to the exceptions noted in the preceding paragraph, it is correct to say that a debtor may call for the return of the property. However, it is not a true exception to the rule against revocation of trusts. The debtor is free to revoke because no trust in favour of creditors was ever created.[5] The courts have held that the necessary intention to create a trust is lacking because the debtor never intended that equitable title pass to the creditors. Rather, the courts have found that such arrangements are intended to benefit the debtors themselves. In the absence of the requisite certainty of intention no trust is created, the creditors never acquire an interest in the property and there is, therefore, no reason why the debtor may not revoke.[6]

An alternative explanation for the debtor's right to revoke is that the trust was created with the debtor as beneficiary. The trustee is to pay third parties for the benefit of the debtor. On this analysis, the debtor can wind up the trust and obtain the trust property under the rule in *Saunders v. Vautier* because the debtor is the sole capacitated beneficiary.[7]

---

3 Constitution occurs when trust property is vested in the trustee. See Chapter 4, *supra*, for a further discussion of constitution and the effect of consideration, or a seal, on a declaration of trust.

4 *Schmidt v. Air Products of Canada Ltd.*, [1994] 2 S.C.R. 611, [1994] 8 W.W.R. 305, 155 A.R. 81, 3 E.T.R. (2d) 1, 115 D.L.R. (4th) 631. And see *Buschau v. Rogers Cablesystems Inc.*, 83 B.C.L.R. (3d) 261, 195 D.L.R. (4th) 257, 2001 CarswellBC 40, 2001 BCCA 16, [2001] 3 W.W.R. 56, 26 C.C.P.B. 47, 36 E.T.R. (2d) 10, 10 B.L.R. (3d) 13, 148 B.C.A.C. 263, 243 W.A.C. 263, C.E.B. & P.G.R. 8378 (note) (C.A.), leave to appeal refused (2001), 2001 CarswellBC 1694, 2001 CarswellBC 1695, [2001] S.C.C.A. No. 107, 275 N.R. 389 (note), 160 B.C.A.C. 320, 261 W.A.C. 320.

5 *Bill v. Cureton* (1835), 2 My & K. 505, 39 E.R. 1036.

6 *Ibid.*

7 Waters, at 293-294.

If creditors join as parties to the conveyance, then the debtor is precluded from recovering the funds because the requisite certainty of intention exists. Similarly, the creditors have notice of the trust and forbear from suing, the debtor cannot get the property back. In that situation the parties have, in effect, given consideration for the transfer of the property.

If a trust is set up for the benefit of named creditors, the settlor cannot revoke because the creditors become beneficiaries at the time of the creation of the trust. No communication is necessary as the particular creditors' rights arise in the normal way.[8]

(c) Power of Revocation

Just as a valid gift can be made subject to a condition subsequent permitting revocation, a valid *inter vivos* trust may be created despite the settlor retaining an express power of revocation. For many years, academic debated the question whether a trust could be valid if a power of revocation was reserved by the settlor. That debate has ended; reservation of an express power of revocation does not render a trust invalid.[9] It is instructive to note that the use of such powers in the United States is extensive. However, creating a trust with an express power of revocation can lead to the following three types of problems.

(i) *Intention Problems*

When a settlor retains a power of revocation, it is sometimes difficult to know whether a trust has been created. The transfer of property to the trustee may be held to show an intention that an equitable interest pass to a beneficiary until such later time as the settlor decides to revoke. If so, a valid trust with a power of revocation has been created. Such a trust is like a gift made subject to a condition subsequent. However, the power of revocation may suggest that the settlor never intended equitable title to pass. If he or she did not, then the trustee merely holds the funds as agent for the settlor and no trust arises.[10] To carry through the analogy to a gift, this is equivalent to cases in which the courts have held that no gift was made because the necessary intention to give was lacking.

(ii) *A Testamentary Implication*

A second problem arises when the settlor retains a power of revocation that can be exercised until death. At the time of death, the power of revocation also "dies" as there is no one who can exercise it thereafter. The question arises: is there an *inter vivos* trust which takes immediate effect but, because of the power

---

8 See *Thomson v. Merchants Bank of Canada*, 58 S.C.R. 287, [1919] 1 W.W.R. 855, 45 D.L.R. 616 for a discussion of the distinctions between trusts for creditors generally and those for particular creditors.

9 *Schmidt, supra*, note 4.

10 *Carson v. Wilson*, [1961] O.R. 113, 26 D.L.R. (2d) 307 (C.A.).

of revocation, will not be performed until after the death of the settlor? Or, is the trust testamentary, since it is dependent upon the settlor's death for its effect? It is important to note that a testamentary trust must comply with the formalities required of wills.[11] *Inter vivos* trusts are not subject to the same formality requirements; for that reason alone it is important to know from the outset whether a trust is *inter vivos* or testamentary.

To determine whether a trust is *inter vivos* or testamentary, you must determine whether the trust is dependent upon the settlor's death for "its vigour and effect."[12] Two factors are crucial in deciding whether the trust takes its "vigour and effect" from the death of the settlor.[13] The first is the intention of the settlor, and the second is the time at which the trust property vests in the trustee. Although the intention of the settlor will normally determine which of the two constructions will prevail, the time at which the trust property vests in the trustee can dictate the answer to the question. This may happen when a settlor, although intending to create an *inter vivos* trust, retains title to the trust property until the time of his or her death, at which time title to the property vests in the trustee. The trust is testamentary as it is not constituted until the settlor's death. If, however, the trust property vests in the trustee at the time of declaration of trust, both constructions are possible. The determining factor will then be the settlor's intention. Two cases help illustrate these principles.

The first *Anderson v. Patton.*[14] The settlor transferred money to Patton to be held in trust for himself and, "if anything should happen to" the settlor, for two friends. He reserved the right to call for the return of the money at any time. A majority of the Alberta Court of Appeal declared this to be a fully constituted *inter vivos* trust. The right to call for the return of the funds was held to constitute a power of revocation and not a stipulation about when the trust was to take effect. Because the trust was a valid *inter vivos* one, it was not struck down for failing to comply with the formalities requirements of wills. The minority thought that the right to recall the money meant that the settlor retained full control of the property.

Re Beardmore Trusts[15] is an example of a case where the trust was held to be testamentary. There the settlor agreed to transfer "three-fifths of my net estate" upon trusts which contemplated payments to his ex-wife during her life or until remarriage and then for the benefit of their children. "Net estate" was defined as the estate left after payment of debts, funeral expenses and the like. The trust

---

11 In brief, this means that they must be in writing and witnessed but see Chapter 4, part 9, *supra*, for a fuller discussion of such formalities.

12 *Cock v. Cooke* (1866), L.R. 1 P.&D. 240.

13 *Goodman Estate v. Geffen*, 81 D.L.R. (4th) 211, [1991] 5 W.W.R. 389, 80 Alta. L.R. (2d) 293, 42 E.T.R. 97, [1991] 2 S.C.R. 353; *Fiorentino, Re*, 25 Alta. L.R. (2d) 296, 33 R.F.L. (2d) 259, 46 A.R. 37, 1983 CarswellAlta 63, [1983] 4 W.W.R. 213 (Q.B.).

14 [1948] 1 W.W.R. 461, [1948] 2 D.L.R. 202 (Alta. C.A.). See also *Hutton v. Lapka Estate* (1991), 5 B.C.A.C. 222, 62 B.C.L.R. (2d) 371, 44 E.T.R. 231, 1991 CarswellBC 327, 11 W.A.C. 222 (C.A.), leave to appeal refused (1992), 68 B.C.L.R. (2d) xxxi (S.C.C.); *Wonnacott v. Loewen* (1990), 44 B.C.L.R. (2d) 23, 37 E.T.R. 244, 1990 CarswellBC 46 (C.A.).

15 [1951] O.W.N. 728, [1952] 1 D.L.R. 41 (Ont. H.C.).

stipulated that the trust property was to be transferred to the trustees only upon the husband's death. The court accordingly held the trust to be testamentary and void for failure to comply with the necessary testamentary formalities.[16]

If we use the approach of the recent case law,[17] we note that in *Anderson v. Patton*,[18] title to the property was transferred to the trustee at the time of declaration. Therefore, either an *inter vivos* or a testamentary construction was possible.[19] In *Re Beardmore*,[20] however, as title to the property was not transferred to the trustee until the settlor's death, the trust had to be testamentary in nature.

(iii) *Tax Problems*

A final problem that arises from placing a power of revocation in a trust document is that, for tax purposes, the settlor is treated as having not alienated the property so that the income and capital remain the settlor's;[21] any income arising in the trust may be deemed to accrue to the settlor.[22] The settlor who wants a voice in the administration of the trust but no tax ramifications may wish to become a trustee instead of retaining a power of revocation.[23]

Notes and Questions

1. Do you agree with the majority decision in *Anderson v. Patton* or the dissent? Give reasons for your answer.

2. Is the general rule prohibiting revocation after constitution sensible? Why or why not?

3. Does a settlor who is sole trustee have a power of revocation? Why or why not?

4. Can a debtor revoke a trust created with the clear intention that it be held for creditors generally? Will notice to the creditors change the situation? If so, how?[24]

5. M executed a trust deed, a term of which was that she would leave money in her will to the trust. M later executed a will, a term of which purported to cancel the trust. Can she, in effect, revoke the trust by her will?

---

16 The trust failed as well because of uncertainty of subject-matter at the time the trust was created. This aspect of the case is discussed in Chapter 4, part 5, *supra*. See also *Ernst & Young Inc. v. Central Guaranty Trust Co.*, 283 A.R. 325, 36 E.T.R. (2d) 200, 2001 CarswellAlta 151, [2001] A.J. No. 148, 2001 ABQB 92, 12 B.L.R. (3d) 72 (Q.B.), additional reasons at (2002), 2002 CarswellAlta 1124, 304 A.R. 1, 29 B.L.R. (3d) 222 (Q.B.).

17 *Goodman Estate; Fiorentino Estate, supra*, note 13.

18 *Anderson, supra*, note 14.

19 See Waters, at 157-161 for additional discussion of this point.

20 *Supra*, note 15.

21 *Income Tax Act*, R.S.C. 1985, c.1 (5th Supp.) s. 75(2), as amended. See also Interpretation Bulletin IT-369R dated March 12, 1990.

22 *Re Vandervell's Trusts (No. 2)*, [1974] Ch. 269, [1974] 3 All E.R. 205 (noted (1975), 38 Mod. L.R. 557; (1975), 2 Est. & Tr. Q. 7).

23 See Waters, at 646, for a further discussion of this point.

24 See *Thomson v. Merchants Bank of Canada*, 58 S.C.R. 289, [1919] 1 W.W.R. 855 and Waters, at 293-294.

6. Is the original trust deed in question five, above, *inter vivos* or testamentary? Would it make any difference to your answer if the original trust document contained a power of revocation? With what formalities, if any, must it comply?

7. Does a disposition of property occur when a trust with a power of revocation is created?

8. R borrowed money from Q on condition that the money be used to pay a dividend. R went into voluntary liquidation before paying the dividend. R's general creditors claim the money as does Q. Which of the two is entitled and why?[25]

9. M borrowed money from B specifically to fund the security costs of his appeal against C. M paid the money into court as security for costs in accordance with the purpose for which he borrowed the money from B. The court ordered that M's appeal be withdrawn. Is C entitled to the money in satisfaction of its costs, or is B entitled to the money as the lender of the money to M?[26]

3. SETTING THE TRUST ASIDE

A settlor may apply to the court to have a trust set aside, even after constitution, if the trust was made because of fraud, undue influence,[27] duress, misrepresentation or mistake.[28]

4. TERMINATION BY THE BENEFICIARY

(a) The Rule in Saunders v. Vautier[29]

A settlor or testator who is minded to make a gift often wants to ensure that the recipient will be able to manage the property wisely. This is not impossible, especially if the recipient is a minor. It is also possible if the recipient has reached the age of majority. However, attempts to postpone receipt in the latter case can cause problems unless the document is drafted carefully. The reason is the Rule in *Saunders v. Vautier*.[30] It provides that a beneficiary who is *sui juris* and whose interest is vested absolutely, is entitled to immediate distribution of the trust property and, thus, to terminate the trust prematurely. The facts of the case are as follows. In 1832, a man died leaving £2,500 worth of stock in trust for his great-nephew. By the terms of the will, the great-nephew was to take when he attained the age of twenty-five. When the great-nephew turned 21 (the age of majority at

---

25 See *Barclay's Bank Ltd. v. Quistclose Investments Ltd.*, [1968] 3 W.L.R. 1097, [1970] A.C. 567, [1968] 3 All E.R. 651 (H.L.).

26 See *Mealing-McCleod v. Common Professional Examination Board* (2000), [2000] E.W.J. NO. 2217 (C.A.).

27 See *Goodman Estate v. Geffen*, 81 D.L.R. (4th) 211, [1991] 5 W.W.R. 389, 80 Alta. L.R. (2d) 293, 42 E.T.R. 97, [1991] 2 S.C.R. 353, in which the Supreme Court of Canada had occasion to explore the doctrine of undue influence.

28 See Waters, at 294-296 for examples of situations in which the trust may be set aside on these grounds. *Horvath, Re*, 32 E.T.R. (2d) 81, 2000 CarswellBC 171, 2000 BCSC 117 (S.C.) is an example of a case in which trust deeds were set aside for fundamental mistake.

29 (1814), 4 Beav. 115, 49 E.R. 282, affirmed (1841), 1 Cr. & Ph. 240, 41 E.R. 482, [1935-42] All E.R. Rep. 58.

30 *Ibid.*

that time), he successfully applied to the court to have the stock plus accrued interest and dividends paid to him.

The right to require the premature distribution of the trust property is based on the view that, as equitable ownership of the property resides in the beneficiaries, they have the right to decide what is to be done with it. The principle has been extended to trusts for more than one beneficiary, whether entitled successively or concurrently, so long as, together, the beneficiaries account for the full beneficial interest. Even when the principle is used in this extended sense, it is referred to as the Rule in *Saunders v. Vautier*.

Note that, in contrast to variations of trust which require court approval, the *Saunders v. Vautier* principle enables a beneficiary to terminate without court assistance except in jurisdictions that have modified the rule.[31] A second point to note is that the trust can be terminated prematurely contrary to the wishes of the creator of the trust. A final point is that when a trust is terminated under the rule in *Saunders v. Vautier*, the beneficiaries can compel the trustees to convey the property to whom they, the beneficiaries, direct.[32] The beneficiaries cannot, however, control the trustees: they must choose between terminating the trust or abiding by its terms, but they cannot direct the trustees to exercise their powers in a particular way, nor interfere with the trustees' exercise of powers.[33]

There are two parts to the *Saunders v. Vautier* rule, both of which must be met in order for it to apply. First, the beneficiary (or beneficiaries) must be *sui juris*, that is, adult and of full mental capacity. Second, the beneficiary (or beneficiaries) must be absolutely entitled to the trust property. To be absolutely entitled, all the beneficiaries must be ascertained and, together, their interests must account for all the interests in the trust property. If some beneficiaries are not *sui juris*, the court cannot consent on their behalf or waive consent.[34]

Trusts which postpone enjoyment of the trust property to a particular age or a future date are easily recognizable as potential *Saunders v. Vautier* situations. Beware of the following situations which may also trigger the rule: trusts which give a beneficiary the income from capital until a certain age, at which time the beneficiary is to take the capital;[35] trusts which settle property on a spouse for life with the remainder to children, if and when they attain a particular age; trusts which provide for instalment payments; and, discretionary trusts. In all these situations, once the beneficiary or beneficiaries are of age, so long as they are mentally competent, they can join together and call for the trust property under the rule in *Saunders v. Vautier*.

How does one prevent the rule in *Saunders v. Vautier* from applying? The short answer is through careful drafting. Where there is a sole beneficiary, draft

---

31 *Re Chardon*, [1928] Ch. 464; *Re Smith*, [1928] Ch. 915; *Re A.E.G. Unit Trust*, [1957] Ch. 415.

32 *Re Brockbank*, [1948] Ch. 206, [1948] 1 All E.R. 287.

33 *Ibid.*

34 *Buschau v. Rogers Cablesystems Inc.*, 2004 BCCA 80 (2004-02-20); related case: 2004 BCCA 142 (2004-03-12).

35 See, *e.g.*, *Grieg v. National Trust Co.* (1998), 47 B.C.L.R. (3d) 42, 20 E.T.R. (2d) 309, 1998 CarswellBC 71 (S.C.).

the beneficiary's interest so that it is either vested, but subject to divestiture, or contingent.

It is often a question of construction whether an equitable interest created under a trust is vested or contingent. You will recall that in *Saunders v. Vautier*, the great-nephew was to take when he attained the age of 25. It could be argued that the great-nephew merely had a contingent interest until he reached 25. Alternatively, it could be argued that the interest vested upon the testator's death and all that was postponed was actual enjoyment of the funds. When both interpretations are possible, the law prefers the latter construction because it favours early vesting.[36] It was the latter construction that was accepted in *Saunders v. Vautier* and is the reason that the great-nephew could call for the trust property before he reached 25.

Inserting a gift-over will ensure, as well, that the beneficiary alone cannot call for the trust property prematurely. For example, had the testator stipulated that if the great-nephew failed to attain 25, the funds were to go to the testator's great-niece, the great-nephew would not have met the second part of the rule in *Saunders v. Vautier* that requires absolute entitlement and he could not have invoked the *Saunders v. Vautier* principle when he turned 21.[37] Note, however, that in such a situation, the great-nephew and great-niece, once both were *sui juris*, could have banded together and called for the trust property under the *Saunders v. Vautier* principle.

Where there is more than one beneficiary, to avoid the rule in *Saunders v. Vautier*, choose beneficiaries who are unascertained or minors. To continue with the example above, assume that the great-niece is a very young infant. It is unlikely that she would reach the age of majority before the great-nephew attained 25 so it is unlikely that *Saunders v. Vautier* could be invoked to end the trust prematurely. In making gifts to minors or unascertained beneficiaries be careful not to infringe the rules against perpetuity.[38]

Notes and Questions

1. If some beneficiaries are not of the age of majority, can those of age call for their aliquot shares?[39]

2. The age of majority is 18 in Alberta, Manitoba, Saskatchewan, Ontario, and Prince Edward Island. It is 19 in British Columbia, New Brunswick, Newfoundland, Nova Scotia, the Northwest Territories, and Yukon.[40]

---

36 See *Oosterhoff on Wills and Succession, Text, Commentary and Materials*, 5th ed., (Toronto: Carswell, 2001), chapter 14 ("Oosterhoff: *Wills*").

37 For another example illustrating the effect of a gift over, see *Little v. Salterio* (sub nom. *Re Salterio*) (1981), 130 D.L.R. (3d) 341, 14 Sask. R. 18, 11 E.T.R. 174 (C.A.).

38 See standard texts on perpetuities such as R.H. Maudsley, *The Modern Law of Perpetuities*, (London: Butterworths, 1979). See also Oosterhoff: *Wills*, chapter 15.

39 See Maudsley & Burn, *Trusts & Trustees Cases & Materials*, 5th ed. (London: Butterworths, 1996), at 655.

40 *Age of Majority Act*, R.S.A. 2000, c. A-6; R.S.B.C. 1996, c. 7; R.S.M. 1987, c. A7; R.S.N.B. 1973, c. A-4; S.N.L. 1995, c. A-4.2; R.S.N.S. 1989, c. 4; R.S.N.W.T. 1988, c. A-2; R.S.P.E.I.

3. If it is clear that the rule in *Saunders v. Vautier* can be invoked, are the trustees under an obligation to inform the beneficiaries about the rule?

4. The principle in *Barford v. Street*[41] also enables a beneficiary to call for trust property contrary to the intention of the creator of the trust. *Barford v. Street* operates when A is given a life interest in property and a general power of appointment over the capital, exercisable by deed or will, with a gift over, in default of appointment, to third parties.

Under the rule in *Saunders v. Vautier* it is clear that A and the third parties (so long as all are ascertained, capable and adult) can join together and terminate the trust. *Barford v. Street* enables A *alone* to terminate the trust by either exercising the power in his or her own favour or applying to the court for an order to terminate.

5. The principle in *Barford v. Street* applies even when the general power to appoint is by will alone.[42]

6. An order of settlement established a trust in which G was to receive income starting at age 19 and ending at age 25. Upon turning 25, G was to be paid one half of the capital and the remainder was to be invested until she turned 30 years old, at which time she would receive the balance of the capital. G held a power of appointment whereby she could appoint the remaining capital to whom she chose if she died before reaching age 30. She exercised the power of appointment in favour of her estate. At age 21, she applied to have the trust terminated in her favour based on the rule in *Saunders v. Vautier*.

Did the fact that the trust was established by court order preclude the application of the rule in *Saunders v. Vautier*?[43] Assuming it did not, would G's application be granted if instead of exercising the power of appointment in favour of her estate, she exercised it in favour of a third party?

7. Trusts which contain powers of encroachment may be terminated in another fashion. Thus, if a trust gives B a life interest and a power to the trustees to encroach on capital for B's benefit, the trustees may be able to transfer all of the capital to B.[44] However, they can do so only if the power is sufficiently wide. If it is merely to provide support and maintenance for the life tenant, they are precluded from advancing all of the capital to B.[45] Significant tax repercussions can attach to retaining extensive control over the trust property.[46]

8. A final solution is the one adopted by the legislatures in Alberta[47] and Manitoba[48] which have abolished the rule in *Saunders v. Vautier* and replaced it with a judicial discretion to terminate or vary trusts which would otherwise attract the rule.[49]

1988, c. A-8; R.S.S. 1978, c. A-6; R.S.Y. 2002, c. 2; *Age of Majority and Accountability Act*, R.S.O. 1990, c. A.7.

41 (1809), 16 Ves. 135, 33 E.R. 935 (Ch. Div.).

42 *Re Johnston* (1964), 48 D.L.R. (2d) 573 (B.C. S.C.). But see also Waters, at 971ff. at note 44.

43 See *Grieg v. National Trust Co.* (1998), 47 B.C.L.R. (3d) 42, 20 E.T.R. (2d) 309, 1998 CarswellBC 71 (S.C.).

44 See, for example, *Re Powles*, [1954] 1 W.L.R. 336, [1954] 1 All E.R. 516.

45 *Re Rutherford and Rutherford*, [1961] O.R. 108 (H.C.). But see *Saunders v. Halom* (1986), 8 B.C.L.R. (2d) 117, [1987] 1 W.W.R. 557, 1986 CarswellBC 359, 32 D.L.R. (4th) 503, 25 E.T.R. 186 (C.A.) in which T gave W, who was both the trustee and the life tenant of the estate, power to encroach on the capital to provide proper care and maintenance for the life tenant. W advanced all of the capital to herself. The court refused to intervene in the exercise of W's discretion because it opined that T had given her a sufficiently wide power.

46 See, for example, *Chapman v. Chapman*, [1954] A.C. 429, [1954] 1 ALL E.R. 798 (H.L.).

47 *Trustee Act*, R.S.A. 2000, c. T-80, s. 42.

48 *The Trustee Act*, R.S.M. 1987, c. T160, s. 59(2).

9. The Ontario Law Reform Commission has recommended that Ontario reform its law to follow Alberta and Manitoba's lead.[50]

10. The rule in *Saunders v. Vautier* also applies to charitable trusts.[51]

11. A charity that directs the trust funds to be paid to a different charity cannot rely on the rule in *Saunders v. Vautier* to terminate the trust because such a direction effectively signifies a variation of the trust, not its termination. The charity is not seeking to eliminate a restraint on the ability of the beneficiaries to enter upon the absolute enjoyment of the property, but is instead seeking to divert the funds from the specific charity named in the trust instrument.[52]

12. An unlimited, unrestricted gift of income to an individual carries the right to the capital.[53]

13. An unlimited gift of income to charity does not necessarily give the charity the right to call for the capital because a gift to charity can be enjoyed in perpetuity. If the creator intended an endowment (*i.e.*, a gift of income alone to the charitable purpose to continue indefinitely) that intention will prevail.[54] Thus, when a gift of income, not capital, is given to a charity under a perpetual trust, the rule in *Saunders v. Vautier* does not apply to terminate the trust. To allow the beneficiary to take the corpus of the trust would be a variation, not a termination, of the trust. The reason given for preventing the charity from taking the capital is that the creator's intention ought not to be interfered with. The intention to create a perpetual trust is inconsistent with the intention to extinguish it and hand the corpus over to the beneficiary. Do the courts accord the creator's intention the same respect in *Saunders v. Vautier* situations? Should they?

14. A mother left her daughter cash and other items in her will. The will stated that the cash gift should be given to the daughter "if and only if" she reached the age of 30.

---

49 But see "A Case of Mistaken Identity: The Rule in *Saunders v. Vautier* and Section 61 of the *Trustee Act* of Manitoba" (1986), 15 Man. L.J. 135 where Ronald B. Cantlie argues that the Manitoba legislation does not have such an effect.

50 See the O.L.R.C. Report, *Report on the Law of Trusts* (Toronto: Ministry of the Attorney General, 1984), at 389 ("O.L.R.C. Report"). And see William S. Bernstein, "The Rule in Saunders v. Vautier and Its Proposed Repeal" (1986), 7 E.& T.Q. 251.

51 *Wharton v. Masterman*, [1895] A.C. 186 (H.L.). See also *Beresford Estate, Re* (1966), 57 D.L.R. (2d) 380, 56 W.W.R. 248, 1966 CarswellBC 61 (S.C.).

52 *Baker, Re* (1984), 17 E.T.R. 168, 1984 CarswellOnt 560, 47 O.R. (2d) 415, 11 D.L.R. (4th) 430 (H.C.). Since the court denied the application to vary the trust based on the rule in *Saunders v. Vautier*, the court considered whether it had the inherent jurisdiction to vary the trust as defined in *Chapman v. Chapman*, [1954] A.C. 429, [1954] 1 All E.R. 798 (H.L.). (See Part 5, *infra*, for a discussion of the court's inherent jurisdiction to vary trusts). The court also considered whether it had the special jurisdiction to vary a trust, which dealt with charitable matters, as outlined in *Royal Society's Charitable Trusts, Re* (1955), [1956] 1 Ch. 87 (Eng. Ch. Div.). The court in *Baker* concluded that, in the circumstances, it lacked both special and inherent jurisdiction to vary the trust.

53 *Re Coward* (1889), 60 L.T. 1 (H.L.).

54 *Halifax School for the Blind v. Chipman*, [1937] S.C.R. 196. But see *Re Johnston; Brown v. National Victoria & Grey Trust Co.* (1985), 35 Man. R. (2d) 300, 20 E.T.R. 209 (Q.B.), in which the Manitoba Court of Queens Bench varied a charitable trust although in the words of Monnin J. "it does change the testator's will, but does not do so with a flagrant disregard for his ultimate wishes." And see *Knox United Church v. Royal Trust Corp. of Canada* (1996), 12 E.T.R. (2d) 40, 1996 CarswellMan 96, 110 Man. R. (2d) 81, 118 W.A.C. 81 (C.A.), reversing (1995), 11 E.T.R. (2d) 57, 1995 CarswellMan 348, 106 Man. R. (2d) 130 (Q.B.), in which the Court of Appeal held that the lower court had placed too much emphasis on conforming the proposed variation of the trust to the testator's intentions.

There was no gift over of the cash. The daughter, who was of legal age, applied for an order that she be paid her cash gift now, rather than at age 30. Will her application be granted?[55]

15. C named his wife, O, and his daughter, H, as the only beneficiaries in his will. He left one half of the residue of his estate to H, but provided that H's portion would remain in trust for her until she reached the age of 25. At age 21, H applied for an order terminating the trust in her favour and directing that the assets be distributed to her for her own use absolutely based on the rule in *Saunders v. Vautier*. Why are the following questions relevant to the success of her application to terminate the trust?[56] (a) Was H's interest subject to divestment if she should not reach the age of 25? Or, (b) did she acquire a vested interest, the enjoyment of which was postponed until she reached the age of 25?

C provided for a second trust encompassing the remaining half of his estate in which O held the life interest. There was a gift over to H upon O's death. Relying on the rule in *Saunders v. Vautier*, O applied to have the trust terminated in her favour and the assets held in trust to be distributed in accordance with an agreement made between her and H. Will O's application succeed, assuming H supports it?[57]

16. By his will, T created a trust in favour of his grandson, W. By the terms of the trust, W, who was 19, was not to receive the capital of the trust until W's daughter, who was alive at the time of T's death, attained age 21. In the meantime, W was to receive most of the income from the funds and eventually any accumulated income. There was no gift over in the event W died before his daughter reached the required age of 21. In Ontario, when can W call for the capital of the fund?[58]

17. By trust deed, R.E. established a trust for the benefit of his children alive on the 29th day of August, 1965. On that date his four children were alive. By the terms of the trust, each child was to take his or her share upon reaching age 35. Can J, one of the children who is 30 years of age, call for her share?[59]

18. Z by his will, left the residue of his estate to his two children in equal shares to be paid only on the death of their mother or when they got married. Both children are of the age of majority, their mother is still living, and neither child has married. Can the two children call for the trust property?[60]

(b) Application of the Rule in *Saunders v. Vautier*

RE McCROSSAN

(1961), 36 W.W.R. 209, 28 D.L.R. (2d) 461
British Columbia Supreme Court

---

55 See *Re Monroe Estate*, 135 Sask. R. 155, 9 E.T.R. (2d) 174, [1995] 9 W.W.R. 372 (Q.B.).

56 See *Coman Estate, Re* (2000), 35 E.T.R. (2d) 195, 2000 CarswellNun 5 (Nun. C.J.). *Cf. Yeoman v. Yeoman Estate* (1986), 23 E.T.R. 136, 1986 CarswellOnt 663, [1986] O.J. No. 2669 (H.C.).

57 *Ibid.*

58 See *Whitman v. Hudgins* (1984), 19 E.T.R. 316, 65 N.S.R. (2d) 64, 1984 CarswellNS 88, 147 A.P.R. 64 (C.A.).

59 *Re Campeau Family Trust* (1984), 17 E.T.R. 297, 50 O.R. (2d) 296, 8 D.L.R. (4th) 159 (C.A.). And see D. Paciocco and V. Krishna, *Re Campeau Family Trust: Two Wrongs Make a Right* (1986), 7 E. & T.Q. 65.

60 *Re Better* (1983), 14 E.T.R. 189 (Ont. H.C.). *Newman v. Verrette Estate* (1966), (sub nom. *Verrette Estate, Re*) 16 O.T.C. 136, 14 E.T.R. (2d) 256, 1996 CarswellOnt 4139 (Gen. Div.).

The settlor made a voluntary settlement in favour of her husband for life, then in favour of herself for life with remainder as she should appoint by will. After her husband's death, she sought an order terminating the trust. She had not exercised the power of appointment.

VERCHERE J.:

. . .

In support of her application the settlor has stated that she has not exercised her power of appointment and that it is in her best interests to have possession of the securities representing the trust funds for investment by her in California where she has lived for many years. I was informed by her counsel that her children have agreed to the trust being terminated but no such consents have been filed. However, as the power of appointment is not limited I do not consider that it is necessary that the settlor's children or other next-of-kin be represented on this application.

It seems clearly established by the weight of authority that where a person creates a trust of which he is sole beneficiary he can at any time terminate the trust and have a reconveyance to him of the trust property even though the purposes of the trust have not been fully accomplished. In *Poirer v. Brule*[61] where the judgment of this court sitting *en banc* was affirmed, Strong J. said:[62]

> It is equally clear that when property is in the hands of a trustee merely for the benefit of the settlor himself he can at any time revoke such trusts and call upon the trustee to reconvey to him.

The difficulty, however, in many cases as here, is to determine whether the settlor is the sole beneficiary or whether there are contingent interests created under the trust in favour of others.

The effect of words of appointment such as those used here have been considered in a number of authorities. In *Re Bartlett Trust*,[63] where, by a deed of settlement declared to be irrevocable, the income from the settlement was made payable to the settlor for life and on her death the *corpus* was to be disposed of as "she shall by her will direct," Donovan J. pointed out that as there was no will and no one with a power of appointment or a right to compel the making of a will, there was no one with more than a potential interest in the deed or the moneys, and held that the settlor had the right to determine the settlement. In *Re Campbell Trusts*[64] where the trust instrument provided that the trustee was to receive the income from the trust property for the grantor, who had the right to demand half the capital at the end of 20 years, and the balance in the trustee's hands was to be subject to her will or the operation of the law as to intestate

---

61 (1891), 20 S.C.R. 97.
62 *Ibid.*, at 102.
63 [1939] 2 D.L.R. 759, 47 Man. R. 113 (K.B.).
64 (1919), 17 O.W.N. 23 (H.C.).

succession, Middleton J. held that it was the duty of the trustee to hand over the whole of the estate, and he said:[65]

> No one has any claim to this property save Mrs. Campbell and those who must claim under her, either under her appointment or as her representative; and so she may demand it. Had there been a gift over to a third person in default of appointment in the manner pointed out, the case would be very different, for an appointment by will cannot be made by an instrument to take effect in the testator's lifetime.

. . .

It is to be noted that in the trust deed the settlor, as in the *Bartlett* and *Luton*[66] cases, expressly revoked her right to demand from the trustee an assignment of the shares, and added, "the intention being that the said shares shall remain in my trustees during my lifetime." Although the shares were converted into money which was paid over by the original trustees to the present trustee it was with the settlor's consent, so the trust fund in the trustee's hands became subject to all the terms to which the shares were subject. In the *Bartlett* and *Luton* cases an expressed intention of irrevocability was held not to be a bar, presumably on the ground that the trust was executory. Here the trust is executed and in the *Knechtel*[67] case Manson J. following *Goodwin v. Royal Trust Co.*,[68] held that an executed trust in which there has been no power reserved to revoke cannot be revoked. But if the settlor is also the sole beneficiary and thereby absolutely entitled to the trust fund, as here, the settlor in her capacity as beneficiary may terminate the trust and demand the moneys. This seems to be the meaning of the words of Strong J., quoted from *Poirer v. Brule*, and consequently the expression of an intention by the settlor not to revoke the trust becomes inconsequential and beside the point.

In my opinion, therefore, the settlor is entitled to the relief requested and there will be an order that upon the release by her of her power of appointment under the trust deed and upon the release and discharge by her of the trustee in form satisfactory to it that the trustee is empowered to hand over the trust estate to the settlor. The trustee is entitled to its costs on a solicitor and client basis out of the estate, having properly appeared to make its position clear. Finally, I must add that I am indebted to Mr. Catliff for his very able and comprehensive review of the authorities which was most helpful.

. . .

65 *Ibid.*, at 24.
66 *Re Luton*, [1939] 3 D.L.R. 787, [1939] O.W.N. 404 (H.C.).
67 *Re Knechtel*, [1952] 4 D.L.R. 763, 7 W.W.R. (N.S.) 368 (B.C.S.C.).
68 [1928] 1 D.L.R. 309, 39 B.C.R. 113 (B.C.C.A.).

Notes and Questions

1. Is *McCrossan* decided on the basis of revocation or termination? What difference does it make?

2. Why was the settlor in *McCrossan* held to be the sole beneficiary and absolutely entitled?

3. How could the settlor regain the funds in light of her express intention not to revoke?

4. Why did the settlor have to release the power of appointment?

5. A testator left one-quarter of his residuary estate in trust for A for life. After A's death, the trust corpus was to be divided equally among those of her children who attained age 21 or, if female, reached age 21 or married. The trustees were given the power to decide what part of the annual income was to go to A but were directed to pay the balance to A's children.

A had three children. They all reached the age of 21, but one is now dead. A, her two surviving children and the personal representative of the deceased child, together mortgaged the whole interest. The mortgagee directed the trustees to pay all moneys owing under the trust to him. Advise the trustees. In doing so, consider the following points.

a) An equitable interest in a trust is property. Like any other chose in action, it can be assigned, sold, mortgaged, charged, and the like.

b) Did the actions of A, her children, and the personal representative have the effect of terminating the trust? Why or why not?

c) If A adopted a child, what rights would the child have? How will the trustee's actions affect that child's rights?[69]

6. Is *McCrossan* a true application of the rule in *Saunders v. Vautier*? In answering this question, recall the principle in *Barford v. Street* that was set out in Note and Question 4 in the previous part.

5. VARIATION OF THE TRUST

(a) At Common Law

The previous part illustrates that beneficiaries can, in certain circumstances, terminate a trust prematurely. In this part, you will see that the terms of a trust can be varied while leaving the original trust in place.

At common law, as illustrated by the leading case of *Chapman v. Chapman*,[70] the court's ability to vary terms of a trust was extremely limited. Sir Robert and Lady Chapman were wealthy individuals who did not like paying tax. During their lives they created various trusts for the benefit of the children of their son, Robert. Each trust provided that the capital could be encroached upon for the maintenance, education or other benefit of any of Robert's children. The Chapmans were advised that, because of the encroachment clauses, on the death of

---

69 This problem is based on *In Re Smith*, [1928] 1 Ch. 915. In considering an adopted child's rights, consider the effects of legislation such as the *Child and Family Services Act*, R.S.O. 1990, c. C.11, s. 158.

70 [1954] A.C. 429, [1954] 1 All E.R. 798 (H.L.).

both Sir and Lady Chapman liability for estate duty would be approximately £30,000.

To avoid that result, the Chapman family approached the courts with an arrangement to transfer the trust funds into a new settlement, identical to the existing trusts but without the encroachment clauses. This, they understood, would avoid the estate duty. The lower courts granted the variation, but the House of Lords reversed. The House of Lords held that the courts do not have an inherent jurisdiction to vary the terms of a trust. This inability exists even when beneficiaries who are *sui juris* agree to the variation and the variation would clearly benefit the remaining minor or unascertained beneficiaries. Indeed, that was the situation in *Chapman* itself, in which all parties were in agreement and a variation would have prevented the imposition of estate duty on the death of the settlors — an obvious benefit to the beneficiaries.

The House stated that the courts can only vary trusts in conversion, compromise, emergency, and maintenance situations. Each situation warrants a word of explanation.

First, the court has jurisdiction to convert a minor's property from realty to personalty and *vice versa*. The applicant must demonstrate that the conversion is for the minor's benefit.

Second, the court may approve settlements to disputes but only in cases of true compromise.[71] A true compromise arises when an actual lawsuit requires settlement. A true compromise arises when an actual law suit requires settlement. The court's compromise jurisdiction is now governed by the rules of court.[72]

Third, the court may approve variations in emergencies. Emergencies are situations unforeseen by the settlor, not provided for and which threaten the existence of the trust.

Finally, the court can direct that the terms of a trust be varied so that income, which the settlor directed be accumulated or used to pay debts, be used for the benefit of beneficiaries who need the money but who are not immediately entitled to it.

The conversion and compromise powers of the courts also exist in areas other than variation of trusts.[73]

(b) By the Trustee

In *Hunter Estate v. Holton*,[74] the court allowed the trustees to vary the trust as an exercise of the trustee's discretionary power. The testator established a trust fund to be paid to his issue upon a certain event. The trustees applied to the court to determine whether it was within their power to divide the trust for the benefit of the testator's two children. The court held that the trustees did have the power

---

71 Before the *Chapman* case, the courts used this head to consent to variations without requiring proof of a genuine dispute. After *Chapman*, such an approach was unacceptable.

72 See, for example, the Ontario Rules of Civil Procedure, rule 14.05(1)(f).

73 See generally, Waters, at 1060-1065 and Oosterhoff, *Wills*, at 688ff.

74 (1992), 46 E.T.R. 178, 7 O.R. (3d) 372 (Gen. Div.).

to alter the trust as the testator had expressly provided that the trustees "pay to or for the benefit" of the beneficiaries as they "in their sole discretion may from time to time determine."[75] The proposed change to the trust did not deviate from the testator's intentions and thus the arrangement was not an inappropriate exercise of the trustee's discretion.

It was an essential aspect of the court's decision that the testator had made an express provision that the trustee be given broad discretion to administer the trust. To what extent such variations will be permitted is not clear, but it appears that changes will be acceptable if they are within the trustee's prescribed powers and are not "alien to the testator's intentions."[76]

Notes and Questions

1. The extent to which a court is willing to accept a trustee's exercise of the power to vary a trust depends on whether the court applies a narrow or broad interpretation to the trustee's discretion. The court's choice of interpretation hinges largely on the degree to which the variation conforms with the intentions of the testator.

Fox v. Fox Estate[77] illustrates the point. The testator gave both M and W a life interest in his estate. If M survived W, he was to receive the residue. W, as sole trustee, had been granted a wide discretionary power to encroach on the capital for the benefit of M's children. W disapproved of M's remarriage and, therefore, used her discretion to transfer all of the residue to M's children. The result of W's transfer was to deprive M of any interest in the residue and of any income from it. The transfer therefore ran contrary to the testator's intentions to benefit M. For this reason, the Ontario Court of Appeal did not approve of W's exercise of her power. Consequently, the court narrowly interpreted the discretionary power granted to W.[78]

2. *Edell v. Sitzer*[79] is another example. G created two separate trusts in favour of her children, M and J, in her will. G named her husband, P, as the trustee for both. The trusts conferred on the trustee a broad discretionary power to distribute the capital. P exercised his power of encroachment by transferring shares from the J trust to M. J objected to the transfer and argued that it was an invalid exercise of P's power because, as a matter of interpretation, the power to encroach only authorized payments of money. The court determined that the testator's intent in creating the power was to provide the trustee with sufficient flexibility to permit dispositions of capital to be overridden if he considered it to be for the benefit of any one or more of the objects of power. Having found that the variation conformed with G's intentions, the court broadly interpreted the wide discretionary power conferred on P.[80] It therefore approved of the variation of the trust because it was within the exercise of the trustee's discretionary power.[81]

---

75 *Ibid.*, at E.T.R. 180.

76 *Ibid.*, at E.T.R. 186.

77 (1996), 28 O.R. (3d) 496, 10 E.T.R. (2d) 229, 1996 CarswellOnt 317, 88 O.A.C. 201 (C.A.), leave to appeal to S.C.C. refused (1996), [1996] S.C.C.A. No. 241, 207 N.R. 80 (note), 97 O.A.C. 320 (note).

78 The court also rejected the transfer because W's decision was made *mala fide*.

79 (2001), 55 O.R. (3d) 198, [2001] O.J. No. 2909, 2001 CarswellOnt 5020, 40 E.T.R. (2d) 10 (S.C.J.).

80 The court also held that the circumstances in which powers may be exercised and their potential

(c) Under Statute

Because of the common law restrictions on the court's ability to vary trusts, most Canadian jurisdictions have passed remedial legislation giving the court wider powers of variation. The Ontario *Variation of Trusts Act*, first passed in 1959, is reproduced below, together with the corresponding provisions of the Alberta *Trustee Act*. The former is representative of all other provincial legislation except Manitoba's. The Alberta legislation, which Manitoba followed, is markedly different.

Trustees have the right to bring an application for advice and directions in the administration of the trust.[82] An application to vary a trust differs from an application by trustees for advice and directions. The court does not have jurisdiction to vary a trust on an application for advice and directions.

Further Reading

A.J. McClean, "Variation of Trusts in England and Canada" (1965), 43 Can. Bar Rev. 181;

J.W. Harris, "Ten Years of Variation of Trusts" (1969), 33 Conv. (N.S.) 113;

Wilson A. McTavish and Ronald A. Anger, "Variation of Trusts: The Official Guardian's View" (1989), 9 E. & T.J. 132.

VARIATION OF TRUSTS ACT

R.S.O. 1990, c. V.1

1. (1) Where any property is held on trusts arising under any will, settlement or other disposition, the Ontario Court (General Division) may, if it thinks fit, by order approve on behalf of,

(a) any person having, directly or indirectly, an interest, whether vested or contingent, under the trusts who by reason of infancy or other incapacity is incapable of assenting;

(b) any person, whether ascertained or not, who may become entitled, directly or indirectly, to an interest under the trusts as being at a future date or on the happening of a future event a person of any specified description or a member of any specified class of persons;

(c) any person unborn; or

(d) any person in respect of any interest of the person that may arise by reason of any discretionary power given to anyone on the failure or determination of any existing interest that has not failed or determined,

---

effects on other dispositive powers are relevant factors that bear directly on the propriety of a trustee's exercise of the power to vary a trust.

81 The court also found that the variation was not motivated by *mala fides* on the part of the trustee.

82 See, for example, s. 60 of the *Trustee Act*, R.S.O. 1990, c. T.23, as am. by S.O. 2000, c. 26, Sched. A, s. 15(2) (item 14).

any arrangement, by whomsoever proposed and whether or not there is any other person beneficially interested who is capable of assenting thereto, varying or revoking all or any of the trusts or enlarging the powers of the trustees of managing or administering any of the property subject to the trusts.

(2) The court shall not approve an arrangement on behalf of any person coming within clause (1) (*a*),(*b*), or (*c*) unless the carrying out thereof appears to be for the benefit of that person.

Comparable Legislation

Trust and Settlement Variation Act, R.S.B.C. 1996, c. 463; *Trustees Act*, R.S.N.B. 1973, c. T-15, s. 26; *Variation of Trusts Act*, R.S.N.S. 1989, c. 486; R.S.P.E.I. 1988, c. V-1; R.S.S. 1978, c. V-1; R.S.N.W.T. 1988, c. V-1; R.S.Y. 2002, c. 224.

TRUSTEE ACT

R.S.A. 2000, c. T-8

42. (1) In this section, "beneficiary," "beneficiaries," "person," or "persons" includes charitable purposes and charitable institutions.

(2) Subject to any trust terms reserving a power to any person or persons to revoke or in any way vary the trust or trusts, a trust arising before or after the commencement of this section, whatever the nature of the property involved and whether arising by will, deed, or other disposition, shall not be varied or terminated before the expiration of the period of its natural duration as determined by the terms of the trust, except with the approval of the Court of Queen's Bench.

(3) Without limiting the generality of subsection (2), the prohibition contained in subsection (2) applies to

   (a) any interest under a trust where under the transfer or payment of the capital or of the income, including rents and profits
      (i) is postponed to the attainment by the beneficiary or beneficiaries of a stated age or stated ages,
      (ii) is postponed to the occurrence of a stated date or time or the passage of a stated period of time,
      (iii) is to be made by instalments, or
      (iv) is subject to a discretion to be exercised during any period by executors and trustees, or by trustees, as to the person or persons who may be paid or may receive the capital or income, including rents and profits, or as to the time or times at which or the manner in which payments or transfers of capital or income may be made,
      and
   (b) any variation or termination of the trust or trusts
      (i) by merger, however occurring;
      (ii) by consent of all the beneficiaries;

(iii) by any beneficiary's renunciation of interest so as to cause an acceleration of the beneficiary's remainder or reversionary interests.

(4) The approval of the Court under subsection (2) of a proposed arrangement shall be by means of an order approving

(a) the variation or revocation of the whole or any part of the trust or trusts,
(b) the resettling of any interest under a trust, or
(c) the enlargement of the powers of the trustees to manage or administer any of the property subject to the trusts.

(5) In approving any proposed arrangement, the Court may consent to the arrangement on behalf of

(a) any person who has, directly or indirectly, an interest, whether vested or contingent, under the trust and who by reason of minority or other incapacity is incapable of consenting,
(b) any person, whether ascertained or not, who may become entitled directly or indirectly to an interest under the trusts as being, at a future date or on the happening of a future event, a person of any specified description or a member of any specified class of persons,
(c) any person who is a missing person as defined in the *Public Trustee Act*[83] or who is unborn, or
(d) any person in respect of any interest of the person's that may arise by reason of any discretionary power given to anyone on the failure or determination of any existing interest that has not failed or determined.

(6) Before a proposed arrangement is submitted to the Court for approval it must have the consent in writing of all other persons who are beneficially interested under the trust and who are capable of consenting to it.

(7) The Court shall not approve an arrangement unless it is satisfied that the carrying out of it appears to be for the benefit of each person on behalf of whom the Court may consent under subsection (5), and that in all the circumstances at the time of the application to the Court the arrangement appears otherwise to be of a justifiable character.

(8) When an instrument creates a general power of appointment exercisable by deed, the donee of the power may not appoint to himself or herself unless the instrument shows an intention that he or she may so appoint.

(9) When a will or other testamentary instrument contains no trust, but the Court is satisfied that, having regard to the circumstances and the terms of the gift or devise, it would be for the benefit of a minor or other incapacitated beneficiary that the Court approve an arrangement whereby the property or interest taken by that beneficiary under the will or testamentary instrument is held

---

83 R.S.A. 2000, c. P-44, s. 1(f).

on trusts during the period of incapacity, the Court has jurisdiction under this section to approve that arrangement.

Comparable Legislation

The Trustee Act, R.S.M. 1987, c. T160, s. 59.

Notes and Questions

1. As previously noted,[84] the Alberta and Manitoba statutes reverse the rule in *Saunders v. Vautier*[85] by substituting a judicial discretion for the termination of trusts which would otherwise attract the rule. In addition, they incorporate variation of trusts provisions similar to those of the other provinces. Note, however, that the Alberta and Manitoba legislation apply specifically to charitable trusts whereas the legislation in the other provinces does not.

2. What other differences are there between the Ontario, and the Alberta[86] and Manitoba legislation?[87] Which statute is preferable?

3. Does either statute extend to discretionary trusts of the type found in *McPhail v. Doulton*?[88] If not, should they?

4. Does a variation satisfy *Statute of Frauds*[89] requirements? Must it? Does it comply with any formalities?

5. Is it possible to terminate a trust under either the Ontario or Alberta legislation?[90]

6. When does an approved variation take effect? Must the variation be implemented? Are the trustees liable if they do not implement the variation? *In Re Hambledon's Will Trusts*[91] held that the court order effectively varied the trust. However, in *Re Holt's Settlement*[92] Megarry J. held that it was the arrangement to which the adult capacitated

---

84 See part 4, *supra*.

85 (1841), 4 Beav. 115, 49 E.R. 282, affirmed (1841), 1 Cr. & Ph. 240, 41 E.R. 482.

86 See *Salt v. Alberta (Public Trustee)* (1986), 45 Alta. L.R. (2d) 331, 1986 CarswellAlta 127, [1986] A.J. No. 543, 71 A.R. 161, 23 E.T.R. 225 (Q.B.); *Samoil v. Buob Estate* (1999), (sub nom. *Buob Estate, Re*) 253 A.R. 44, 86 Alta. L.R. (3d) 250, [2001] 2 W.W.R. 280, 1999 CarswellAlta 928 (Q.B.), which holds that the Alberta legislation requires evidence that the arrangement is not only beneficial but also of a justifiable character. See also *Falkenberg v. Falkenberg Estate*, 188 A.R. 15, 39 Alta. L.R. (3d) 268, [1996] 7 W.W.R. 285, 1996 CarswellAlta 463 (Surr. Ct.) in which the testator's intentions were considered in deciding whether a proposed change was of a justifiable character as required by s. 42(7) of the *Trustee Act*, R.S.A. 2000, c. T-8.

87 See *Knox United Church v. Royal Trust Corp. of Canada* (1996), 12 E.T.R. (2d) 40, 1996 CarswellMan 96, 110 Man. R. (2d) 81, 118 W.A.C. 81 (C.A.), reversing (1995), 11 E.T.R. (2d) 57, 1995 CarswellMan 348, 106 Man. R. (2d) 130 (Q.B.), in which the court considered the relevance of the testator's wishes in determining whether a proposed variation was of a justifiable character as required by s. 59(7) of the *Trustee Act*, R.S.M. 1987, c. T-160.

88 [1971] A.C. 424, [1970] 2 All E.R. 228 (H.L.)

89 R.S.O. 1990, c. S.19.

90 According to *Re Johnston; Brown v. National Victoria & Grey Trust Co.* (1985), 35 Man. R. (2d) 300, 20 E.T.R. 209 (Q.B.) termination is permissible. See also *Re Assie Estate* (1985), 45 Sask. R. 124 (Q.B.).

91 [1960] 1 W.L.R. 82, [1960] 1 All E.R. 353.

92 [1969] 1 Ch. 100, [1968] 1 All E.R. 470.

beneficiaries consented and for which the court supplied the approval on behalf of infants, that varied the trust.[93] This latter view could lead to difficulties with implementation.

7. The arrangement plus the court order is an instrument in respect of which new perpetuity and accumulations periods are applicable.[94]

8. Apart from the *Variation of Trusts Act*, the court in Ontario has power under the *Settled Estates Act*,[95] to vary the terms of a settlement of land. Thus, in Ontario, if the trust involves land, the application to vary is brought under the *Variation of Trusts Act*[96] and the *Settled Estates Act*.[97]

9. The principal use of the variation of trust legislation has been to obtain variations to avoid tax and to widen investment powers.[98] Note, however, that suitably drafted powers should enable a trustee to alter investments and, indeed, vary beneficial entitlement.

10. The Ontario Act cannot be used to vary a trust in favour of a charity.[99] To change the application of funds held in trust for charity the *cy-près* doctrine must be used.[100] If the trust contains gifts to persons as well as gifts to charity, the Act can be used to vary the trust in favour of the persons named.

(d) Application of the Statute

(i) *Persons on Whose Behalf the Court Grants Approval*

An arrangement under variation of trusts legislation can be put forward by anyone.[101] The court's role is to determine whether to approve the arrangement on behalf of persons interested in the trust who are not *sui juris*. Section 1(1)(a)-(d) of the *Variation of Trusts Act* describes these persons as minors, those under an incapacity, unascertained members of a class or description, the unborn or those persons contingently entitled upon determination of a prior estate.

It is submitted that the courts (except in Alberta and Manitoba) cannot approve arrangements on behalf of adult capacitated beneficiaries; such beneficiaries must consent to the arrangements themselves.[102] It has been the prevailing view that if any adult, capacitated beneficiary refuses to consent, the arrangement cannot be implemented. In this way, the variation of trusts legislation is seen to be complementary to the rule in *Saunders v. Vautier*. This view was endorsed by the British Columbia Court of Appeal in *Buschau v. Rogers Communications Inc.*,[103] in which the court held that it cannot consent on behalf of beneficiaries who are missing

---

93 See also the *dicta* of Lords Reid and Wilberforce in *Re Holmden's Settlement*, [1968] A.C. 685, [1968] 1 All E.R. 148 (H.L.) at 701-702 and 710-713 to the same effect.

94 See *Re Holt's Settlement*, *supra*, note 92.

95 R.S.O. 1990, c. S.7, s. 13(1)(b).

96 R.S.O. 1990, c. V.1.

97 R.S.O. 1990, c. S.7.

98 See, *e.g.*, *Re Kiely*, [1972] O.R. 845, 24 D.L.R. (3d) 390 (H.C.).

99 See *Baker, Re* (1984), 47 O.R. (2d) 415, 17 E.T.R. 168, 1984 CarswellOnt 560, 11 D.L.R. (4th) 430 (H.C.).

100 This doctrine is discussed in the next chapter.

101 See the O.L.R.C. Report, at 390.

102 *Ibid.*, at 390; also see *Re Suffert's Settlement*, [1961] Ch. 1, [1960] 3 All E.R. 561.

103 2004 BCCA 80 (2004-02-20); related case: 2004 BCCA 142 (2004-03-12).

but who have capacity. In the process the court overruled earlier cases which held otherwise.[104]

Notes and Questions

1. Should the courts require unanimous consent of capacitated beneficiaries before approving a proposed variation? Why or why not?

2. Under the proposed changes to the Ontario legislation, the court would be able to give additional administrative powers to the trustees without the consent of all beneficiaries who are *sui juris*.[105]

3. Is there a difference between the situation in which a beneficiary refuses to consent and one in which it is unknown whether a beneficiary consents? In your opinion, is it acceptable for the courts to approve variation applications in the latter situation?

4. Can a variation be approved by the court if it is disadvantageous to some beneficiaries? If so, which ones?[106]

5. Who should make a variation application? Is it appropriate for a trustee to make such an application given the obligation to act impartially among beneficiaries?[107]

6. Applications to vary trusts to provide for surplus distribution in pension schemes frequently proceed under variation legislation. Can you describe the class of persons on whose behalf the court grants approval?[108]

(ii) *Arrangement*

The Act requires an "arrangement" to be presented to the courts. It is the arrangement as a whole that must be approved and not just the effects on those persons whose behalf the court is asked to consent. That aside, other questions arise. What is an arrangement? Is any variation an arrangement? What is the difference between an arrangement and a resettlement? Is the creator's intention

---

104 *Versatile Pacific Shipyards v. Royal Trust Corporation of Canada* (1991), 84 D.L.R. (4th) 761 (B.C.S.C.); *Bentall Corp. v. Canada Trust Co.* (1996), 26 B.C.L.R. (3d) 181 (B.C.S.C.); *Re Sandwell & Co. Ltd. and Royal Trust Corp. of Canada* (1985), 17 D.L.R. (4th) 337 (B.C. C.A.). See also *Continental Lime Ltd. v. Canada Trust Co.* (1998), 25 E.T.R. (2d) 128 (B.C. S.C.) to the same effect. Compare *Re Dalhousie Staff Assn. Contingency Fund (Trustee of)* (1999), 175 N.S.R. (2d) 102, 27 E.T.R. (2d) 310 (S.C.) in which one of the court's reasons for refusing to vary the pension trust was because the present members were far from unamimous in supporting the proposal.

105 O.L.R.C. Report at 424-427.

106 See *Sandwell & Co. v. Royal Trust Corp. of Canada* (1985), 17 D.L.R. (4th) 337, 1985 CarswellBC 683, [1985] B.C.J. No. 2093 (C.A.); *Continental Lime Ltd. v. Canada Trust Co.* (1998), 25 E.T.R. (2d) 128, 1998 CarswellBC 2757, 19 C.C.P.B. 160, 44 C.C.E.L. (2d) 158 (S.C.). But see *Wood Estate, Re*, 2001 ABQB 619, 40 E.T.R. (2d) 144, 2001 CarswellAlta 921 (Surr. Ct.); *Forsythe Estate, Re*, 192 N.S.R. (2d) 283, 2001 CarswellNS 98, 2001 NSSC 37, 599 A.P.R. 283 (S.C.); *Finnell v. Schumacher Estate* (1990), 74 O.R. (2d) 583, 1990 CarswellOnt 479, 37 E.T.R. 170, 38 O.A.C. 258 (C.A.); *Farrington v. Rogers* (1980), 6 E.T.R. 156, 1980 CarswellBC 62, 19 B.C.L.R. 373 (S.C.).

107 See *Re Druce's Settlement Trusts*, [1962] 1 W.L.R. 363, [1962] 1 All E.R. 563 (Ch. Div.) which states that, except in certain circumstances, the trustee ought not to make such applications. See also Waters, at 1069 and O.L.R.C. Report, at 391.

108 See *Sandwell & Co. Ltd. v. Royal Trust Corp. of Canada* (1985), 17 D.L.R. (4th) 337 (B.C. C.A.).

relevant? Recent decisions have held that the courts need not consider the intention of the settlor in evaluating the arrangement put before them.[109] The Act does not place any obligation on them to preserve the interests of the settlor. Furthermore, it would limit the ability of the court to approve settlements which would otherwise be of great benefit to the beneficiaries.

The following case explores further answers to the questions.

RE IRVING

(1975), 11 O.R. (2d) 443, 66 D.L.R. (3d) 387
Supreme Court of Ontario
[High Court of Justice]

Eliza Irving and her husband, David Irving, each created trusts which provided that their only daughter, Edith Shillington, would receive the income from the funds during her lifetime. Under her mother's trust, Edith could appoint the remainder by will. If Edith failed to do so, the remainder would pass equally *per stirpes* to her surviving issue.

Any child of Edith's who became entitled to share the fund on Edith's death, was not to receive the capital of his or her share until age 35. Prior to age 35, however, the income on such portion was to be paid to the child annually. There was a gift over to the issue of any child of Edith's who died after Edith but before attaining age 35. There was a further gift over to Eliza Irving's next of kin if Edith died without issue.

The David Irving trust was virtually identical except that Edith was not given a power of appointment.

At the time of the court application, Edith, aged 59, had two children, both of age. Each of Edith's children had one infant child. Edith and the two children made this application to the court to vary both trusts on the basis of two alternative arrangements. Shortly before the application was made the Eliza Irving trust had a value of $331,230; the David Irving trust a value of $488,910.

PENNELL J.:

. . .

This section confers on the court no more than a power of giving effective approval to a proposed arrangement on behalf of certain classes of people and gives no power of actually making or directing any variations. It will be observed that the classes of people affected are as follows:

---

109 See, *e.g.*, *Russ v. British Columbia (Public Trustee)* (1994), 89 B.C.L.R. (2d) 35, 3 E.T.R. (2d) 170 (C.A.), leave to appeal to S.C.C. refused (1994), 5 E.T.R. (2d) 147 (note), 97 B.C.L.R. (2d) xxvi (note). And see *Lafortune v. Lafortune Estate* (1990), 40 E.T.R. 299, 1990 CarswellOnt 507 (H.C.), in which the court afforded limited importance to the testator's intent. But see *Forsythe Estate, Re, supra*, note 106, in which it was held that courts should be reluctant to approve a variation of a trust if it would alter the intentions of the testator.

(1) Infants now alive who may ultimately take under the trust;
(2) those unborn who may be born and ultimately take under the trust;
(3) any person who may in future become persons of a particular description or specified class entitled to an interest in the trust, and
(4) persons who may benefit by reason of a discretionary power given to anyone and exercisable after an existing interest terminates.

All of the aforementioned classes can be said to exist in the instant applications.

The form of words used in s. 1 of the Act makes it clear that the court's power is an extremely broad one. It has the power to "vary or revoke all or any trusts or enlarge the powers of the trustee." It may do this for "any arrangement by whomsoever proposed and whether or not there is any other person beneficially interested." The court is to be governed throughout by "what it thinks fit" and its only other direction is that it "shall not approve an arrangement . . . unless the carrying out thereof appears to be for the benefit of that person." The thrust of s-s. (2) seems to be that the *status quo* should be upheld under any trust unless positive factors are shown to be in favour of the variation or revocation of the trust on a rather general principle of it being for the benefit of the person on whose behalf the court is approving the variation.

What is or is not included in the expression "for the benefit of the person"? Few precedents under the Ontario Act have been fitted to these words. On the other hand, decisions are manifold in England and sister Provinces under legislation not dissimilar. These judgments have been brought together for my guidance through the industry of counsel. The search in all these cases was to find the intention of the founder of the trust and then to decide whether the proposed arrangement remains within the ambit of the intention. The right of a testator to deal with his own property as he sees fit is a concept of so long standing and so deeply entrenched in our law, that it can neither be ignored nor flouted arbitrarily. It can never be pretended that the court has the power to make a new will in the guise of approving an arrangement under the *Variation of Trusts Act*.

I adopt the words of Wilberforce J. in *Re Towler's Settlement Trusts*:[110]

It is obviously not possible to define exactly the point at which the jurisdiction of the court under the *Variation of Trusts Act, 1958*, stops or should not be exercised. Moreover, I have no desire to cut down the very useful jurisdiction which this Act has conferred on the court, but I am satisfied that the proposal as originally made to me falls outside it. Though presented as a variation it is in truth a complete new re-settlement. The former trust funds were to be got in from the former trustees and held on totally new trusts such as might be made by an absolute owner of the funds. I do not think that the court can approve this. Alternatively, if it can, I think that it should not do so, because to do so represents a departure from well and soundly established principles.

I find in the opinion of Megarry J., in *Re Ball's Settlement*,[111] the same conception of a duty to refrain from drafting a new will or trust:

---

110 [1963] 3 All E.R. 759 at 761-762.
111 [1968] 2 All E.R. 438 at 442.

If an arrangement changes the whole substratum of the trusts, then it may well be that it cannot be regarded merely as varying that trust. But if an arrangement, while leaving the substratum, effectuates the purpose of the original trust by other means, it may still be possible to regard that arrangement as merely varying the original trusts, even though the means employed are wholly different and even though the form is completely changed.

The distinction between a complete reconstruction of a trust so as to thwart the intention of the testator and an arrangement that merely through a different scheme gives substantial effect to the intention may be indeed close.

Conjointly with an appraisal of intention, the court is directed to look steadfastly to the benefit to be gained by the parties, being those very persons whom the testator intended to benefit in the first instance. The economy is largely an uncharted sea. Changes may often work to the detriment or frustration of the testator's intention at a time when he is no longer able to modify the methods of the carrying out of his intention. The hope behind the Act is to provide protection against these problems. In my view this is the framework within which the court must approach the question of what is of benefit to the parties for whom the court is charged to exercise its jurisdiction.

A survey of the cases shows that the expression "for the benefit of the person" has been interpreted with flexibility of meaning. In *Re Remnant's Settlement Trusts*,[112] Pennycuick J. said that the court "is entitled and bound to consider not merely financial benefit but benefit of any other kind." And in *Re Zekelman*,[113] Osler J. said:

> However, there is ample authority in the English cases which consider legislation identical to ours for the proposition that the word "benefit" is to be liberally interpreted and is not confined to financial benefit.

From the foregoing the conclusion is inevitable, that in giving or withholding its consent to a proposed arrangement the function of the court is to protect the interests of those who cannot protect themselves; and so long as they are adequately protected, the court will as a rule give its consent. It becomes a matter of the court exercising the same degree of care and prudence that men prompted by self-interest generally exercise in their own affairs. In this regard, the headnote in *Re Cohen's Will Trusts*,[114] expresses the reason of Danckwerts J. neatly in these words:

> . . . the proposed arrangement would be approved on behalf of the infants, the risk being one which an adult would be prepared to take and which the court was accordingly prepared to take on behalf of infants.

In *Re Druce's Settlement Trusts*,[115] Russell J. uses the following language:

---

112 [1970] 2 All E.R. 554 at 559, [1970] 1 Ch. 560.
113 [1971] 3 O.R. 156 at 158, 19 D.L.R. (3d) 652 (H.C.).
114 [1959] 3 All E.R. 523.
115 [1962] 1 All E.R. 563 at 565, [1962] 1 W.L.R. 363 (Ch. Div.).

> Any arrangement is capable of being regarded as beneficial under the *Variation of Trusts Act, 1958*, if it can, on balancing probabilities, be regarded as a good bargain, and the fact that in improbable circumstances, no benefit, or even some loss is possible, does not necessarily deprive the arrangement of that quality. Viewing the financial proposals as affecting the reversion as a whole, I regard those proposals as beneficial to the reversion.

Further precedents are not lacking for this method of approach in approving a departure from the precise terms of a trust declared by a testator. It was applied for the purpose of freeing capital of the trust to members of the family so as to allow them to have possession of the capital during a time in their lives when it was advantageous to them[116] for the purpose of avoidance of the incidence of unnecessary taxation which in the rearranged circumstances would not arise[117] and for an arrangement where a sum certain was set aside for the persons on whose behalf the court was exercising its jurisdiction, and the proposed settlement was greater in amount than the reasonable value of their contingent interests.[118]

In each of these cases, the court was able to regard the particular variation as being for the benefit of the persons for whom the court interposed its discretion. In saying this, I am not unmindful that each must be viewed in its own setting. The decisive feature in each instance was duty of the court to consider the proposal from the view point of each of those persons on whose behalf the court was required to approve the arrangement.

The court is concerned whether the arrangement as a whole, in all the circumstances, is such that it is proper to approve it. By way of a brief prefatory summation then, and further to the powers conferred under s. 1 of the *Variation of Trusts Act*, approval is to be measured, *inter alia*, by reference to these considerations: First, does it keep alive the basic intention of the testator? Second, is there a benefit to be obtained on behalf of infants and of all persons who are or may become interested under the trusts of the will? And, third, is the benefit to be obtained on behalf of those for whom the court is acting such that a prudent adult motivated by intelligent self-interest and sustained consideration of the expectancies and risks and the proposal made, would be likely to accept?

The arrangements proposed in the two cases at hand are exhibited to the applicant's notice of motion. Their broad effect is that the capitalized value of Edith Caroline Shillington's life interest be paid to her and the balance of the capital be distributed in equal shares to David Gordon Shillington and Carol Devon Murray provided, however, that prior to the distribution one of two alternative means (hereafter referred to as "Alternative One" and "Alternative Two" respectively) is to be adopted to protect the possible beneficiaries of the trusts other than the applicants.

I propose, in the first instance, to take note of Alternative One with respect to the Eliza Irving Trust. By actuarial calculations, the approximate present value of the interest in the trust of the issue of Edith Caroline Shillington, other than the applicants, is $2,139. The approximate present value of the interest of the next

---

116 *Duchess of Westminister v. Royal Trust Co.* (1972), 32 D.L.R. (3d) 631 (N.S. Chambers).
117 *Windeatt's Will Trust*, [1969] 2 All E.R. 324.
118 *Re Berry's Settlement*, [1966] 1 W.L.R. 1515, [1966] 3 All E.R. 431.

of kin of Edith Caroline Shillington other than the issue is $ .10. These calculations assume no exercise of the power of appointment.

Alternative One in the proposed deed of arrangement would create a fund (Issue's Fund) in the amount of $10,000 to benefit the issue of Edith Caroline Shillington other than her co-applicants, her two children. This fund would go to such issue on Edith Caroline Shillington's death, in accordance with the terms of the will, as if her two children had predeceased her.

In addition, a second fund (Next of Kin's Fund) in the amount of $1,000 would be created to benefit the next of kin of Edith Caroline Shillington other than her children and issue. This fund would be distributed on the death of Edith Caroline Shillington in accordance with the terms of the will, as if her children and issue had predeceased her.

The income of the Issue's Fund and the Next of Kin's Fund would accumulate so long as the law permits, and be distributed in the same manner as capital.

Alternative One is intended to provide a benefit to the grandchildren and other issue and next of kin of Edith Caroline Shillington by setting aside for each group a sum certain greater in value than the present value of that group's contingent interest or possibilities.

. . .

[Alternative One in respect of the David Irving trust was identical to this except that the values of the proposed funds were slightly higher.]

Such is the proposed arrangement. It has evoked challenges and resistance. Mr. Beatty, counsel for the Official Guardian, advises that the applicants' proposal is an arrangement wholly novel in this Province.

The position of the Official Guardian must be considered from several distinct standpoints. Mr. Beatty's first line of attack is a submission that the proposed arrangements thwart the testators' intention. If that were their effect, the court would feel constrained to withhold approval. For the ascertainment of the testator's intentions, regard must be had to the language used and the context in which it is used:[119]

> . . . in considering what is the true construction of the will, it is open to the court to ascertain if there be a paramount intention expressed in the will, and if so, to consider whether particular directions are properly to be read as subordinate to such paramount intention, or are to be treated as independent positive provisions.

A mere reading of the Eliza Irving Trust will show that the ends that were uppermost in the thoughts of the testatrix were to provide, firstly, for her only child, the daughter Edith Caroline Shillington, and, secondly, her issue. To this end, a power of appointment was given to her daughter and a direction that in the event Edith Caroline Shillington failed upon her death to exercise this power of

---

119 *Re Walker*, [1901] 1 Ch. 879 at 885 (Ch. Div.).

appointment, it would pass to her issue *per stirpes*. This is the dominant motive, never relaxed and unmistakably expressed.

The David Irving Trust in its dominant purpose and effect is one, I think, to benefit his daughter, Edith Caroline Shillington, and his grandchildren, that is, the present life tenant and her two children. The infant beneficiaries on whose behalf the court's approval is now sought were, of course, not alive at the time of the death of either testator.

Impressive words of counsel for the Official Guardian remind me of my duty to maintain the *substratum* of the trusts. The submission is not ignored that the proposed arrangements would take away the managerial and administrative skills of the corporate trustee which has admittedly discharged its duty with constant and unqualified fidelity. But it is not the sole custodian of the fiduciary duties under the will of David Irving. Here Edith Caroline Shillington is also appointed a trustee, and some significance belongs to the fact that she was given a power of appointment, as we have seen, under the will of Eliza Irving. This provision permits the inference of a signal from the testatrix that she reposed trust in the sense and judgment of her daughter.

Edith Caroline Shillington claims to be domiciled and ordinarily resident in the Bahamas. On the basis of the actuarial evidence, the effect of the arrangements which I am asked to approve would be a substantial savings of Ontario succession duties. It appears that there would be an immediate potential savings of $30,605 and if Edith Caroline Shillington survives for a period of five years, the savings would be $64,259.

A detailed account of the complex principles on which the actuaries calculated the potential income tax savings is not perhaps important. The material facts and figures deposed to by them are all to be found in the documents which were duly made evidence in these applications. It is sufficient to say that if the proposed arrangements are approved, there will be an approximate potential savings of $5,000 a year. From the figures available, it is difficult for the actuaries to estimate the actual tax liability which may arise under the deemed disposition rule of the *Income Tax Act*.[120] Nevertheless, I am satisfied that the figures provide a real guide to the prospective savings.

One other circumstance or group of circumstances is the subject of much emphasis in the arguments of counsel for the applicants. If the deeds of arrangements are approved, Gordon David Shillington and Carol Devon Murray will have use of money during that period of their lives when it will be of greatest assistance to them. This carries consequences along with it (it is said) that would be beneficial to their infant children, as they would be able to provide better care and education for them. One might ask, with reason, what is the extent of the assets of the two children at this time. A persuasive answer might be that they are of age and the court is not asked to give any approval on their behalf. But the answer to this question is squarely in the record before me.

David Gordon Shillington was born March 7, 1947, so that he is now 28 years old. He was graduated from Queen's University in 1970 with the degree of

---

120 R.S.C. 1952, c. 148 [am. 1970-71-72, c. 63].

Bachelor of Engineering. Since 1970, he has been employed in Ottawa as a civil engineer by a well-established engineering firm. He and his wife possess assets, apart from personal effects, worth approximately $55,000. These consist of a building lot valued at approximately $40,000, together with mutual funds and savings bonds worth approximately $15,000.

Carol Devon Murray was born in the year 1948; she is therefore today in her 27th year. She married a graduate of the Royal Military College who now holds the rank of captain in the Canadian Armed Forces. Her husband has been accepted into the Master of Business Administration course at both Queen's University and the University of Western Ontario. He proposes to leave the Canadian Armed Forces in order to pursue eventually a business career, probably as a chartered accountant. Aside from personal effects, the combined net worth of the co-applicant Carol Devon Murrary and her husband is approximately $44,000.

Edith Caroline Shillington and her co-applicants assert that they intend to leave any funds that they may receive as a result of these applications, with the Royal Trust Company or a comparable trust company, so that they can receive continuous professional advice relating to investment of funds. Eventually, the two children intend to build or buy their own houses in which case they would take advantage of some of the funds.

Viewing the question now before me in the background of the financial summary of the two children, a "benefit" for the grandchildren may be inferred from the proposed arrangement. Yet I hesitate to lay emphasis upon this form of "benefit" in the circumstances of these particular applications.

Here another circumstance must be noted. The two trusts provide, in effect, that no grandchild — in the events which happened, that would be David Gordon Shillington and Carol Devon Murray — should take until attaining the age of thirty-five (35) years. An argument is made on behalf of the Official Guardian that the proposed arrangement is in contravention of the testators' intentions. I do not underrate its force. The argument may be conceded and the *substratum* of the trusts suffer no impairment.

I said a while ago that each proposed arrangement must be viewed in the setting of its own facts. Of the facts considered, the age of the children and their circumstances as shown forth in the pages of this record are significant. The proposed arrangement is helped by the fact that they are now in their twenty-eighth (28th) and twenty-seventh (27th) years and are parties to the deeds of arrangement. The court is not asked to give any approval on their behalf. That is not to say that there is no need to scrutinize the proposed arrangements as a whole in the light of the purpose of the trusts as shown by the wills and any relevant evidence. "It is the arrangement which has to be approved, not just the limited interest of the person on whose behalf the court's duty is to consider it."[121] But to hold that in no instance should the court override the age at which the beneficiary takes in accordance with the terms of a will, would be forgetful of the purpose and true significance of the Act. The spirit of the Act, as I read it, permits pruning of the trust in order to promote fruitfulness, but the root is to be preserved.

---

121 *Re Steed's Will Trusts*, [1960] 1 All E.R. 487 at 493, *per* Lord Evershed M.R.

It becomes necessary now to weigh the benefits contained in the proposed arrangements to those on whose behalf the court is asked to approve. . . .

. . .

It is all a question of fair judgment. Is this a bargain which a prudent adult would be expected to negotiate for himself? It is difficult, to say the least, to assess the future likelihood of people's lives on the basis of actuarial formulae. Nevertheless, in the instant case, the specific facts are pronounced enough so as to make actuarial evidence a plausible avenue to follow. I think, having regard to all the circumstances, that the two "Next-of-Kin's Funds" totalling $2,000 are a good bargain to be entered into on behalf of the relatives other than the issue of the life tenant, and can be regarded as a benefit within the meaning of the Act. In this connection, I recall that the power of appointment, as it has been exercised under the will of Eliza Irving, forecloses all possible benefit to this class of possible beneficiaries.

To my mind, the really significant question is whether the two "Issue's Funds" totalling $25,000 provide sufficiently for the issue of the life tenant other than her two children. This means that the issue *per stirpes* of the life tenant, other than her two children, will, on her death, share the capital of two trusts, the present value of which is $25,000. An able argument has been made by Mr. Beatty that the court should look to the alternative. If the trusts are not varied what might occur? If either of the children of Edith Caroline Shillington predecease their mother, the issue of that child might then become entitled to a share of an estate valued at about $400,000. This, of course, far exceeds $12,500, the value of their share in the funds proposed.

The argument is made that the chance of an untimely death is not lightly to be waived aside. Against this, two considerations come to mind. First, the son and daughter of Edith Caroline Shillington are both very young, being 28 and 27 years respectively. Mrs. Shillington is 59 years of age. The chance element involved in adopting a course of wait and see for the infant is very high due to the relevant ages of the parties involved. Secondly, as regards the Eliza Irving Trust, if one of her children predeceased her, Edith Caroline Shillington may see fit to vary her will so as not to appoint to the issue of that child such a large portion of the estate. These considerations, I think, tend to give support to the adequacy of the proposed arrangements but standing alone are insufficient for the purposes of the Act.

A final argument is made that because of the obvious and significant benefits which the adult children will receive in having the capital of the trust provided to them now instead of upon the death of the life tenant, it is highly reasonable to say that the grandchildren are in good bargaining positions vis-à-vis their parents. I confess that I am attracted to this argument.

I recall at this point that the court should look to see if, on balancing probabilities, the proposal can be regarded as a good bargain. I think for the reason given that a fund in the amount of $25,000 is too small an amount to constitute a benefit within the spirit of the Act.

To hold that the proposed "Issue's Fund" is insufficient is a long way from holding that the organic plan of the deeds of arrangement are not generally in accord with the principle of the Act. In my mind, the proposed arrangements are not new dispositions of the assets of the testators by changing the substance of the dispositions that they have made as between the actual and potential beneficiaries and are, therefore, not resettlements. They continue to exhibit broadly the map of the testators' minds as reflected in their respective wills. But this does not lead us to forget that an essential term of a deed of arrangement is a benefit for those on whose behalf the court is asked to give approval. For this problem, as for most, there are distinctions of degree. In the circumstances of these two applications, I am unable to satisfy myself that a total fund of $25,000 constitutes a benefit within the meaning of the Act.

I am of opinion that it is not the province of the court to modify the proposed deeds of arrangement by substituting for the total "Issue's Fund" of $25,000 an amount that might be deemed a benefit. As I have said already: This section confers on the court no more than a power of giving effective approval to a proposed arrangement on behalf of certain classes of people and gives no power of actually making or directing a variation. In any event, I would want to have the benefit of the views of the Official Guardian before passing upon a substituted amount, if any, I leave the door open to an amended application.

It remains to consider Alternative Two. This scheme is based on insurance so that in the event any of the contingencies occur which would entitle anyone other than the applicants to an interest in the estates, the proceeds of the insurance would pay an amount corresponding to the amount of the trust. Thus, the two children of the life tenant would each be insured in an amount to exceed one-half of the capital of the trusts. If either child predeceases the life tenant, the insurance will be payable and will then be held in trust until the death of the life tenant. At that time, the proceeds of the policy will be distributed to the issue of the deceased child *per stirpes*. The advantage to the insurance scheme is that it is designed to pay in the same way that the trust is designed to pay.

The applicants stipulate to the court that the premium for such insurance would be in the area of $100,000. From the applicants' point of view, they prefer Alternative One to Alternative Two (the insurance alternative because of what they submit is the high cost of the insurance).

In my view, benefits can be created by arrangements in the nature of Alternative One or Alternative Two in such a way as to justify approval by the court under the powers conferred by the Act.

Several matters of comment arise upon that observation. It appears that there are no details as to the insurance policies proposed. Furthermore, if these policies are to be held by the Royal Trust Company as trustee, there is no provision in the deeds of arrangements for the compensation of the trustee. There, for the moment, these applications must be left to await further representations, if any, of the parties concerned. I am prepared to restore the matter to the list at counsel's convenience.

For the reasons which I have given, I feel constrained to adjourn the motion *sine die* to be brought on a seven (7) days' notice. Costs may be spoken to.

Notes and Questions

1. The Ontario legislation empowers the court to vary a trust; it does not entitle it to resettle the property.[122] Note, however, that the Alberta legislation does contain a power to resettle. What is the difference between varying and resettling a trust? Is a power of resettlement desirable?

2. An arrangement which involves the replacement of trustees appears to be permissible.[123]

(iii) *Benefit*

The court may not approve an arrangement on behalf of any person mentioned in section 1(1)(a)-(c) of the Ontario Act unless it appears to be for the benefit of that person. The following case illustrates how the courts have recently interpreted the word "benefit." The case concerns an application to terminate a trust, since in Manitoba *The Trustee Act*[124] governs both termination and variation of a trust so that the test enunciated for benefit appears to be applicable to variation of trusts as well.

Previous case law[125] suggested that the test to be used by the courts on the question of benefit was whether "the benefit to be obtained on behalf of those for whom the court is acting such that a prudent adult motivated by intelligent self-interest and sustained consideration of the expectancies and risks and the proposal made, would be likely to accept."[126] Compare this test for "benefit" to that of Huband J.A. in *Teichman v. Teichman Estate*[127], who said, "[a]s long as the affected parties know what they are doing, and the proposed arrangement does not appear to give any beneficiary an advantage over any other beneficiary, the approbation of the court should not be withheld."[128] It appears that the Manitoba Court of Appeal has thereby lowered the threshold for demonstrating benefit.

TEICHMAN v. TEICHMAN ESTATE

(1996), 134 D.L.R. (4th) 155
Manitoba Court of Appeal

The testator left his estate equally to his son, Daniel, and daughter, Evelyn. Daniel was to take his one-half share immediately, whereas Evelyn's share was to be held in trust for a period of ten years from the date of the testator's death. If

---

122 *Re Holt's Settlement*, [1969] 1 Ch. 100, [1968] 1 All E.R. 470 (Ch. Div.); *Re Ball's Settlement* [1968] 1 W.L.R. 899, [1968] 2 All E.R. 438; *Re Harris* (1974), 47 D.L.R. (3d) 142, [1974] 6 W.W.R. 97 (B.C. S.C.).

123 *Re Heintzman* (1981), 31 O.R. (2d) 724, 120 D.L.R. (3d) 295, 9 E.T.R. 12 (H.C.).

124 R.S.M. 1987, c. T160, s. 59(5).

125 See *Farrington v. Rogers (Nanson)* (1980), 6 E.T.R. 156 (B.C. S.C.); *Re Irving* (1975), 66 D.L.R. (3d) 387, 11 O.R. (2d) 443 (H.C.).

126 *Re Irving, ibid.*, at 394.

127 (1996), 134 D.L.R. (4th) 155, 110 Man. R. (2d) 114, 118 W.A.C. 114 (C.A.).

128 *Ibid.*, at 157.

she were dead at the end of the ten-year period, her interest was to go to her issue, if any, or to her brother's issue, if none. A weekly income was to be paid to Evelyn out of the interest generated by the assets. The likely reason for establishing the trust for Evelyn was that she had suffered from depression. However, evidence presented by a psychiatrist demonstrated that Evelyn was fully capable of managing her affairs. Evelyn brought an application to have the trust terminated. Her brother, Daniel, consented to the proposed arrangements, as did the Public Trustee on behalf of the contingent minor beneficiaries.

HUBAND J.A.:

. . .

The application came before DeGraves J. who refused to grant the order on the ground that, while the trust conditions "may appear to be unfair to the applicant, this is not sufficient for me to overturn or subvert the testator's directions and instructions plainly and unambiguously expressed in his will." Evelyn Teichman appealed.

The appeal first came before this court on February 19, 1996, at which time the court expressed its general willingness to allow the variation, subject to certain conditions.

Section 59 of *The Trustee Act*, which was introduced as an amendment on October 1, 1983, now requires that a variation or termination of a trust must have the approval of the court. Under s-s. (5), the amendment empowered the court to consent to a variation or termination on behalf of a person who lacks capacity by reason of age or otherwise, and to consent on behalf of a potential beneficiary as yet unborn.

Subsection (7) establishes the criteria to be used by the court in determining whether an arrangement to vary or terminate a trust should be approved:

> Criteria for approval.
> 59. (7) The court shall not approve a proposed arrangement in respect of a trust unless it is satisfied
>
> (a) that the carrying out of the arrangement appears to be for the benefit of each person on whose behalf the court may consent under subsection (5); and
> (b) that in all the circumstances at the time of the application to the court, the arrangement appears otherwise to be of a justifiable character.

Prior to the enactment of s. 59, an individual who was of full age and of sound mind, and who was the sole beneficiary of a trust, could vary or terminate that trust. Similarly, two or more individuals, all of whom are of full age and of sound mind, and who constitute the only beneficiaries of a trust, could agree among themselves to vary or terminate the trust. The right of a beneficiary or beneficiaries to vary or terminate became known as the rule in *Saunders v.*

Vautier,[129] in which the rule found expression. Unanimity was required, except that the court could consent on behalf of beneficiaries who were minors or otherwise lacked capacity or who were as yet unborn, so long as the arrangement was for the benefit of those beneficiaries.

The 1983 amendments made a fundamental change. Even where there is unanimity among beneficiaries, and no contingent interests, the variation or termination will be permitted only when the court finds the arrangement to be of a justifiable character.

The fact that the application runs contrary to the express wishes of the testator does not, in and of itself, adversely affect the character of the arrangement. It is axiomatic that an application to vary or terminate will be contrary to the express wishes of the testator. But in *Brown v. National Victoria & Grey Trust Co.*,[130] and again in *Knox United Church v. MacDougall Estate*,[131] this court has stated that the rule in *Saunders v. Vautier* still makes considerable sense. As long as the affected parties know what they are doing, and the proposed arrangement does not appear to give any beneficiary an advantage over any other beneficiary, the approbation of the court should not be withheld. The intention of s. 59 was not to discourage such applications.

In the present case, however, two concerns emerged from the hearing on February 16th. Firstly, the affidavit evidence identified the probable reason for the ten-year delay before the gift to Evelyn Teichman would become absolute. From time to time Evelyn Teichman has been treated for a condition of depression which may have caused her late father to have concerns about her mental health. The court requested further evidence as to Evelyn Teichman's condition. Secondly, remote as it may be, there are possible contingent interests. If Evelyn Teichman should not live to February, 2005, the trust property would go to either her issue or her brother's issue. The court requested the involvement of the Public Trustee to represent those contingent interests.

As to the first matter, we have now been supplied with evidence by an associate professor of psychiatry who conducted an evaluation of Evelyn Teichman in 1995. His opinion is that she was fully capable of managing her own affairs.

As to the second concern, Evelyn Teichman has agreed to pay to the Public Trustee the sum of $40,000 which will be held in trust. If Evelyn Teichman has surviving issue as of February 6, 2005, the $40,000, plus accrued interest, will be held in trust for her issue payable to them in equal shares as they attain the age of majority. In the event of her death prior to February 6, 2005, without issue, then the trust funds will be paid to the issue of Daniel Teichman. And if Evelyn Teichman should live to February 6, 2005, with no living issue, then the $40,000, together with accrued interest, will be returned to her.

---

129 (1841), 4 Beav. 115, 49 E.R. 282, affirmed (1841), 41 E.R. 482, 1 Cr. & Ph. 240, [1835-42] All E.R. Rep. 58.
130 Unreported, November 12, 1985 [summarized at 61 A.C.W.S. (3d) 424].
131 Unreported, February 19, 1996.

The Public Trustee agrees to these arrangements on behalf of the contingent infant beneficiaries.

It should be noted that Daniel Teichman has also consented to all these arrangements.

This court finds the arrangements to be for the benefit of the contingent beneficiaries and of a justifiable character and the application of Evelyn Teichman is therefore allowed, subject to her undertaking to place funds in trust with the Public Trustee.

Notes and Questions

1. It must be remembered that the court has to apply the test of benefit only from the perspective of those for whom it is asked to approve and not from the perspective of the group as a whole.

For two cases in which the courts seem to have mistakenly applied the benefit test to the arrangement as a whole, rather than from the perspective of the interests it was there to protect, see *Re Kovish*,[132] and *Re Riddals*.[133] In both cases, the courts approved arrangements which effectively eliminated any benefit to the remote contingent beneficiaries under the trust.

2. Are the mechanisms for variation and termination of trusts satisfactory?

3. Will the court sanction an arrangement which involves a risk to minor or unborn beneficiaries if the risk is one which an adult might be prepared to take?[134]

4. When drafting an *inter vivos* trust, you must pay strict attention to the taxation implications associated with the provisions.

The income on an *inter vivos* trust, created since June 18, 1971 is taxable at a flat rate of approximately 56.0% in Ontario. It varies provincially between 45.5% in Alberta to 69.0% in Newfoundland. This income can be attributed to the settlor, along with any losses, taxable capital gains and allowable capital losses, if the settlor retains too much control over the trust property.

If powers of variation or revocation are reserved by the settlor, or if powers to direct the fund's distribution or veto dispositions are retained, the *Income Tax Act*[135] may permit the trust to be completely ignored for taxation purposes.[136]

5. For an example of how a variation may inadvertently affect one's tax liability see *Murphy v. M.N.R.*[137] The taxpayer was entitled to one-half of the income of a testamentary trust. The trust was varied so as to add several income beneficiaries, including the taxpayer's wife, and the taxpayer's income from the trust was reduced to one quarter. The court held that the taxpayer's consent to the arrangement meant that he had transferred a

---

132 (1985), 18 E.T.R. 133 (B.C. S.C.).

133 (1983), 14 E.T.R. 157 (Sask. Q.B.).

134 See *Re Irving* (1975), 66 D.L.R. (3d) 387, 11 O.R. (2d) 443 (H.C.). See Note and Question 4 in Part 5(d)(I) for relevant case law on the degree to which a proposed variation should benefit potential and contingent beneficiaries.

135 R.S.C. 1985, c. 1 (5th Supp.) and amendments thereto.

136 For a further discussion of the tax consequences following variations to a trust, see W. Innes and J.T. Cuperfain, "*Variation of Trusts: An Analysis of the Effects of Variations of Trusts Under the Provisions of the Income Tax Act*" (1995), 43 Can. Tax J. 16.

137 (1980), 80 D.T.C. 6314, [1980] C.T.C. 386 (Fed. T.D.).

benefit to his wife under a trust and, therefore, the income paid to her should be reported by him under the attribution rules contained in the *Income Tax Act*.[138]

6. Does a variation create a new *inter vivos* trust so as to attract the 50% rate under the *Income Tax Act?*[139]

Does a variation amount to a disposition of capital assets so as to attract capital gains tax?

7. In *Re Weston's Settlements*,[140] a settlor of a trust in favour of his sons wished to avoid taxation by relocating from England to Jersey, a tax haven. The settlor and beneficiaries applied to the court to permit the discharge of the English settlement and the creation of an identical Jersey settlement. The Court of Appeal would not permit such a replacement indicating that factors other than taxation benefits alone would be reviewed before the court would approve any variation.

For a contrasting result see *Re Windeatt's Will Trusts*[141] where the court approved a similar request to that found in the Weston case.

8. Can the court take into account collateral matters — such as the provision of insurance to cover risks — when deciding whether to approve an arrangement? Ought it to?[142]

Problems

1. A pension plan is established for the employees of ABC Ltd. The plan contained broad powers of amendment. A trust fund was established to hold both employee and employer contributions, which were made regularly in order to fund the benefits.

An actuarial valuation reveals that surplus funds have been built up in the trust. In other words, the corpus of the fund is greater than necessary to pay the accrued pension liabilities. Is it possible to amend the trust to provide that surplus funds will revert to the employer? Would such an amendment amount to a partial revocation?[143]

2. B has just died leaving the following testamentary trusts:

(i) the money in my bank account to M when she attains 30, the interest therefrom meanwhile to be held in trust;

(ii) my two seaside cottages to C for life, remainder to C's daughter D;

(iii) a $5,000 bond to E if she lives to see the sunrise on her 21st birthday, otherwise to X.

M, who is 25, wishes to receive her money now to launch a singing career; D, who is 50, requests that one of the cottages be transferred to her immediately; and E, who is 20, also wants a portion of her money so that she can attend university. Advise the trustee.

---

138 R.S.C. 1952, c. 148, s. 74(1), as rep. by S.C. 1986, c. 6, s. 37(1).
139 *Ibid.*, s. 122(10).
140 [1969] 1 Ch. 223, [1968] 3 All E.R. 338 (C.A.).
141 [1969] 1 W.L.R. 692, [1969] 2 All E.R. 324.
142 See *Farrington v. Rogers (Nanson)*, *supra*, note 108.
143 See *Hockin v. Bank of British Columbia* (1990), 46 B.C.L.R. (2d) 382, 38 E.T.R. 275, 71 D.L.R. (4th) 11 (C.A.), leave to appeal to S.C.C. refused (1991), 51 B.C.L.R. (2d) xxv (note), 74 D.L.R. (4th) viii (note), 130 N.R. 318 (note); *Maurer v. McMaster University* (1991), 4 O.R. (3d) 139, 82 D.L.R. (4th) 6 (Gen. Div.), reversed in part (1995), 23 O.R. (3d) 577, 125 D.L.R. (4th) 45 (C.A.); *Otis Canada Inc. v. (Superintendent of Pensions) Ontario* (1991), 40 E.T.R. 233, 34 C.C.E.L. 341, 2 O.R. (3d) 737 (Gen. Div.); *Schmidt v. Air Products of Canada Ltd.*, 115 D.L.R. (4th) 631, [1994] 2 S.C.R. 611, [1994] 8 W.W.R. 305, 3 E.T.R. (2d) 1.

3. R wishes to set up a trust in favour of X so that X will receive income until the age of 35 when he is to receive the balance. Once set up, R does not wish the trust to be altered in any manner. Advise R.

4. A testatrix left the residue of her estate equally between two charities with the provision that they receive the income from their respective shares plus the sum of $500 each from the capital per annum, the money to be used for building maintenance and new equipment. The evidence shows that the capital will thus be exhausted in about 75 years.[144] Can the charities terminate the trust? Alternatively, can they apply to vary it or ask the court to apply the moneys *cy-près*?

5. A testator, S, instructed his trustees to hold the residue of his estate and give the income generated therefrom to his three children. When the youngest child attained age 25, the residue was to be divided into three equal shares and each child was to receive one-third of his or her share. The trustees were to invest the balance and pay the net income to each child for life. Each child, however, was given the power to appoint his or her life estate in favour of another. This power could only be exercised by will.

After the youngest child attained age 25, the children agreed among themselves that they would each make an irrevocable will exercising the powers of appointment in favour of the other two. The children then duly amended their wills.

Can the children call for a termination of the trust and thereby obtain the balance held by the trustees? Why or why not?[145]

6. R designated his wife the beneficiary of his RRSP. Later, R and his wife were divorced. He then executed a will that revoked all former testamentary dispositions and left his whole estate to his three children.

R has died and his executors have come to you for advice as to who is entitled to the proceeds of the RRSP. Advise.

---

144 *Re Bell* (1980), 29 O.R. 278, 112 D.L.R. (3d) 573, 7 E.T.R. 129 (H.C.).

145 See *Saracini v. National Trust Co. Ltd.* (1989), 37 E.T.R. 311, 69 O.R. (2d) 640 (C.A.), affirming (1987), 59 O.R. (2d) 673, 27 E.T.R. 70, 39 D.L.R. (4th) 436 (H.C.).

PART III

PURPOSE TRUSTS

Chapter 7

CHARITABLE TRUSTS

1. SCOPE

This part of the book is concerned with purpose trusts, that is, trusts for purposes, rather than persons. Purpose trusts are either charitable or non-charitable. The former are discussed in this chapter; the latter in the next.

In the next part of this chapter we consider the advantages of charity. Then we discuss the legal meaning of charity and distinguish charitable trusts from other purpose trusts. Next, we discuss the traditional four heads of charity: the relief of poverty, the advancement of religion, the advancement of education, and other purposes beneficial to the community.

Then, we consider imperfect trusts provisions, that is, trusts which are not exclusively charitable. We follow this with a discussion of the application of the rule against perpetuities to charities. Then we consider the *cy-près* doctrine. The last part of the chapter is concerned with the regulation of charities.

You will appreciate that the concept, "charity," is wider than the subject, "charitable trusts." The term "charity" in its legal sense includes charitable organizations, whether incorporated or not, as well as trusts for charitable purposes. While this chapter is concerned primarily with charitable trusts, that topic cannot be understood without reference to "charity" generally. Hence, we shall also discuss the wider concept of "charity" as necessary.

You should also note that the term "registered charity" does not mean the same as "charity," or "charitable trust." A "registered charity" is a charity that is registered under the *Income Tax Act*.[1] We shall explore the meaning of this term below.

Further Reading

Michael Chesterman, *Charities, Trusts and Social Welfare* (London: Weidenfeld and Nicolson, 1979).

---

1 R.S.C. 1985 (5th Supp.), c. 1, as am.

Jeffrey Hackney, "The Politics of Chancery" (1981), 34 Curr. L. Prob. 113.

Keeton and Sheridan, *The Modern Law of Charities*, 4th ed. by L.A. Sheridan (Chichester: Barry Rose, 1992).

Gareth Jones, *History of the Law of Charity: 1532-1827* (Cambridge: Cambridge University Press, 1969).

Jean Washburton, "Charitable Companies," [1984] Conv. 112.

Public Trustee for Ontario, "Submissions to the Ontario Law Reform Commission: Project on the Law of Charities" (1990-91), 10 E. & T.J. 272.

Donald L. Bourgeois, *The Law of Charitable and Non-Profit Organizations*, 2nd ed. (Markham, Ont.: Butterworths, 1995).

Ontario Law Reform Commission, *Report on the Law of Charities* (Toronto: Minister of the Attorney General, 1996).

Law Reform Commission of British Columbia, *Report on Non-Charitable Purpose Trusts*, L.R.C. 128 (November 1992).

2. THE ADVANTAGES OF CHARITY

The law accords a number of advantages to charity that are not conferred upon trusts for persons or for non-charitable purposes. The following is a brief outline of these advantages.

Perpetuity. The rule against remoteness of vesting applies to charitable trusts, but not with the same strictness as to trusts for persons.

The rule against indefinite duration, which prevents a purpose trust from lasting beyond the perpetuity period, applies to non-charitable purpose trusts, but not to charitable trusts.

These matters are discussed in more detail below.

Certainty. Trusts for persons must comply with the requirement of certainty of objects. If the objects, that is, the beneficiaries, are uncertain, the trust fails.

Charitable trusts, however, do not have to satisfy this requirement. The cases sometimes speak of "uncertainty" of objects in the context of charity, but this merely means that the court cannot, as a matter of construction, determine whether the creator of the trust intended to give the property exclusively for charitable purposes.[2] In other words, the description of the purposes is too vague to permit the court to make that determination. As we shall see, if a trust is for the benefit of charitable and non-charitable purposes, it is, subject to some exceptions, void in its entirety.

However, if on construction the court determines that the creator of the trust intended to devote the property exclusively to charitable purposes, it does not matter that the purposes are not further, or are poorly defined. The court is then faced with deciding who should benefit from the trust. It does so by directing the making of a scheme, or by ordering a scheme itself. The scheme will list the purposes that should benefit from the trust and, if need be, provide the machinery

---

2 See, *e.g.*, *Cameron v. Church of Christ Scientist* (1918), 57 S.C.R. 298, 43 D.L.R. 668, leave to appeal to P.C. refused (1919), 57 S.C.R. vii (S.C.C.). See also *Jones v. The T. Eaton Co.*, [1973] S.C.R. 635, 35 D.L.R. (3d) 97, reproduced later in this chapter.

for administering the trust. The court's scheme-making power is inherent in its jurisdiction.

It is sometimes said that the court favours charity, so that it will give a benign construction to charitable bequests.[3] Thus, if a trust is capable of two interpretations, one of which will render it void and the other valid, the court will adopt the latter construction.[4] We shall see, however, that this principle is more often observed in the breach than in the observance, particularly in times when, for whatever reason, charity is in disfavour.

Cy-près. The court's scheme-making power must be distinguished from another inherent jurisdiction, namely the *cy-près* power.[5] The *cy-près* jurisdiction allows the court to order a scheme when the charitable purposes intended by the creator of the trust are impossible to carry out or are impracticable. The scheme carries out the intention of the creator of the trust by selecting objects as near as possible to those named.

Taxation. One of the main advantages accorded to charity is tax concessions. These consist principally of two kinds: (1) concessions for income tax purposes and (2) concessions for municipal tax purposes.[6]

The determination whether an organization or purpose is charitable for income tax purposes lies within the jurisdiction of Parliament. In practice, the Department of National Revenue generally follows the traditional definition of charity, a matter of provincial law, but this is merely a matter of comity and is not required.

The *Income Tax Act*[7] provides for the registration of charities. A "registered charity" is defined as a "charitable organization, private foundation or public foundation . . . resident in Canada . . . or a branch [thereof] . . . that receives donations on its own behalf" and that is registered by the Minister of National Revenue.[8] A "charitable organization" is an operating charity which applies all its resources to charitable activities carried on by itself. Public and private foundations are registered charities whose objects are to disburse funds to operating charities.[9] A charitable organization may be a trust, a corporation, or an unincorporated association. A foundation must be either a trust or a corporation.[10] The Act contains detailed provisions designed to ensure that moneys given for charitable purposes are devoted exclusively for that purpose and are not used for private purposes or to benefit donors or other persons for the purpose of tax evasion.[11] The registration of a charity may be revoked if the charity fails to

---

3   See, *e.g.*, *Weir v. Crum-Brown*, [1908] A.C. 162 at 167 (H.L.), *per* Lord Loreburn.

4   See, *e.g.*, *Housten v. Burns*, [1918] A.C. 337 at 342 (H.L.); *Dolan v. Macdermot* (1868), L.R. 3 Ch. 676 at 678, *per* Lord Cairns L.C.

5   D.W.M. Waters, *Law of Trusts in Canada*, 2nd ed. (Toronto: Carswell, 1984) at 514 ("Waters").

6   See, *e.g.*, *Family Service Assn. of Metropolitan Toronto v. Ontario Regional Assessment Commissioner, Region No. 9* (1995), 23 O.R. (3d) 382 (Gen. Div.). There are also concessions to charities under federal and provincial sales tax statutes, which we have not considered here.

7   R.S.C. 1985 (5th Supp.), c. 1, as am.

8   *Ibid.*, s. 248(1).

9   *Ibid.*, s. 149.1(1).

10   *Ibid.*, s. 149.1(1).

11   *Ibid.*, s. 149.1(1) (*a*), (*b*); and see Information Circular 80-10R (Dec. 17, 1985).

comply with the Act.[12] If a charity is registered, it is not subject to income tax or capital gains tax.[13]

An individual taxpayer who makes a gift to a registered charity is entitled to a tax credit against income in the year in which the gift was made up to a maximum of 20% of the taxpayer's net income,[14] provided the gift is supported by a valid receipt.[15]

Charities also enjoy exemptions from municipal taxation. These exemptions are within the legislative jurisdiction of the provinces. Hence, they vary from province to province. The exemptions are not based upon the traditional meaning of charity, but rather upon express statutory exemptions for certain types of charity. An example may illustrate the point. A statute exempts land from municipal assessment and taxation if the land is owned by an incorporated charity organized for the relief of the poor. An incorporated charity owns land on which it operates a home for mentally retarded children.[16] The organization and its purposes are clearly charitable, but do not fit within the statutory exemption, since the children it benefits are not necessarily poor. Hence, the organization would be subject to municipal assessment and taxation.[17]

The Ontario *Assessment Act*[18] includes the following exemptions: places of worship, churchyards, and burying grounds actually being used for the interment of the dead or any ancillary purpose prescribed by the Minister, and not including any portion of the land used for any other purpose; universities, high schools, and public and separate schools; seminaries of learning maintained for philanthropic or religious purposes; seminaries maintained for educational purposes; public hospitals; incorporated charitable institutions organized for the relief of the poor; The Canadian Red Cross Society; St. John's Ambulance Association, and similar incorporated institutions conducted for philanthropic purposes; public libraries and other public literary and scientific institutions; and agricultural or horticultural societies.[19]

Charities are not usually exempted from local improvement charges, that is, charges imposed on owners whose land fronts a street which is being improved

---

12 *Income Tax Act, ibid.*, s. 149.1(2)-(4). See *Briarpatch Inc. v. R.* (sub nom. *Briarpatch Inc. v. Minister of National Revenue*), [1996] 2 C.T.C. 94, 96 D.T.C. 6294, 197 N.R. 229 (C.A.).

13 *Ibid.*, s. 149(1)(*f*).

14 *Ibid.*, s. 118.1(1), (3). The taxpayer may carry forward any excess over 20% for five years. Gifts to charities by corporate taxpayers are treated as deductions from income.

15 *Ibid.*, s. 118.1(2). The tax credit amounts to 17% of total gifts up to $250 and 29% of total gifts in excess of $250.

16 A term used by the court.

17 See *LDARC v. London (City)* (1985), 50 O.R. (2d) 677, 10 O.A.C. 340, 29 M.P.L.R. 9 (Div. Ct.).

18 R.S.O. 1990, c. A.31, s. 3, paras. 3, 4, 5, 6, 12, 13 (Children's Aid Societies) and 14 (am. by S.O. 2002, c. 33, s. 141(2), not yet in force).

19 For similar legislation see *Assessment Act*, R.S.N.B. 1973, c. A-14, s. 4; R.S.N.S. 1989, c. 23, s. 5; *Assessment and Taxation Act*, R.S.Y. 2002, c. 13, s. 49; *Local Government Act*, R.S.B.C. 1996, c. 323, s. 339 (repealed by S.B.C. 2003, c. 52, s. 256; *The Municipal Assessment Act*, S.M. 1989-90, c. 24, s. 22(1); *Municipal Taxation Act*, R.S.Q., c. F-2.1, s. 204; *Municipal Government Act*, R.S.A. 2000, c. M-26, s. 362; *Real Property Tax Act*, R.S.P.E.I. 1988, c. R-5, s. 3; *The Rural Municipality Act, 1989*, S.S. 1989, c. R-26.1, s. 331; *Property Assessment and Taxation Act*, R.S.N.W.T. 1988, c. P-10, ss. 73, 74.

and the cost of which is not borne by the municipality as a whole because it is of particular benefit to the abutting owners.[20]

Further Reading

Rod Watson, "Charity and the Canadian Income Tax: An Erratic History" (1985), 5 Philanthrop. No. 1, 3.

Joseph R. Brown, "Sales and Property Tax Exemptions for Charities" (1984), 4 Philanthrop. No. 3, 34.

John D. Gregory, "Charities Respond to the Minister of Revenue" (1991), 10 Philanthrop. No. 2, 20.

Christina H. Medland, "Limitations on Charities under the Income Tax Act" (1990), 44 E.T.R. 111.

Law Reform Commission of British Columbia, *Report on Informal Public Appeals* (Vancouver: Minister of the Attorney General, 1993).

Ontario Law Reform Commission, *Report on the Law of Charities* (Toronto: Minister of the Attorney General, 1996).

Peter Broder, "The Legal Definition of Charity and Canada Customs and Revenue Agency's Charitable Registration Procedure" (2002), 17 Philanthrop., No. 2, 3.

James M. Parks, "Registered Charities: A Primer" (2002), 17 Philanthrop., No. 4, 4.

Robert B. Hayhoe, "Canada Customs and Revenue Agency Charity Audits" (2002), 17 Philanthrop., No. 4, 38.

Notes and Questions

1. Is a charity immune from tort claims brought against it? This issue was raised in *Christian Brothers of Ireland in Canada, Re*.[21] This case was one of the legal proceedings brought in the sorry saga of the Christian Brothers, a Roman Catholic lay order, members of which had physically and sexually abused boys in Mount Cashel Orphanage in Newfoundland. The perpetrators were charged and convicted. The victims then brought tort claims for damages against the secular arm of the order, Christian Brothers of Ireland in Canada Ltd. ("CBIC"), a charitable corporation formed to hold title to and administer the assets of the order.

The order decided voluntarily to liquidate CBIC in order to pay the victims. The liquidation proceeded in Ontario, where the head office of CBIC was located. It quickly became apparent that the assets would be insufficient to pay the victims' claims without resort to the assets of two incorporated schools in Vancouver which were operated by the order. The shares in the schools were held by members of the order in trust for the order.

The liquidator argued that the shares were the property of CBIC and, thus, available, together with the valuable land the schools occupied, to pay the claims of the victims. The schools argued that the shares were held upon special purpose charitable trusts and were, thus, not assets of CBIC that could be realized in the liquidation.

---

20 See, *e.g.*, *Local Improvement Act*, R.S.O. 1990, c. L.26, repealed 2001, c. 25, s. 484, effective Jan. 1, 2003.

21 (2000), 47 O.R. (3d) 674, 33 E.T.R. (2d) 32, 184 D.L.R. (4th) 445, 2000 CarswellOnt 1143, 17 C.B.R. (4th) 168, 6 B.L.R. (3d) 151, 132 O.A.C. 271 (C.A.), leave to appeal refused (2000), 265 N.R. 200 (note), 191 D.L.R. (4th) vi, 2000 CarswellOnt 4333, 2000 CarswellOnt 4334, [2000] S.C.C.A. No. 277, 146 O.A.C. 200 (note), reconsideration refused (2002), 2002 CarswellOnt 1770, 2002 CarswellOnt 1771 (S.C.C.).

On an application to the Ontario Court (General Division),[22] Blair J. granted the schools leave to apply to the British Columbia courts to have the question whether the shares were held upon a special purpose charitable trust decided there. Those courts ultimately decided that each school was held upon a special purpose charitable trust, but that the real trustee in each case was CBIC and not the individual brothers who held the shares in trust.[23] Meanwhile, in the Ontario proceedings, Blair J. held that while the general assets of CBIC were not immune from the claims of the victims, assets held upon a special purpose charitable trust were immune, unless the wrongs in question were committed in the context of the special purpose trust.

The Ontario Court of Appeal agreed with Blair J. that there is no principle of charitable immunity. In other words, a charity is just as much liable for its actions and the actions of its employees and agents, as an organization carried on for profit. Thus, it is liable for tort claims brought against it. However, the Court of Appeal, relying on *B. (P.A.) v. Curry*[24] disagreed with Blair J. on the issue of the exigibility of assets held upon a special purpose charitable trust. The court held that those assets are just as exigible as the general assets of CBIC.

The first holding, that there is no principle of charitable immunity, is not contentious. While there was nineteenth century English law that suggested such an immunity, the suggestion was discredited and no Canadian cases adopted the idea. Further, as a matter of logic and policy, there ought not be a principle of charitable immunity. An organization, whether charitable or not, ought to be liable for wrongs committed by it or under its auspices.

However, the second holding, that assets held by a charity upon a special purpose charitable trust are exigible, is contentious and is, with respect, wrong. The court failed to discuss, and thus disregarded, trust law, which regards assets held upon trust as separate from the assets of the trustee. Thus, in trust law, the creditors of the trustee are unable to reach assets held by the trustee in trust, but only the trustee's own assets. The court attempted to limit its decision to the special circumstances of the case, namely, the existence of tort claims against a charity in circumstances in which the charity has insufficient general assets, and when the charity is in liquidation. However, the exact extent of these limits has yet to be determined. They could potentially be applied to trust law generally with far-reaching consequences.[25]

---

22 (1998), 37 O.R. (3d) 367, 21 E.T.R. (2d) 93, 1998 CarswellOnt 815, 38 B.L.R. (2d) 286 (Gen. Div. [Commercial List]).

23 *Rowland v. Vancouver College Ltd.*, 34 E.T.R. (2d) 60, 2000 CarswellBC 1667, 2000 BCSC 1221, 78 B.C.L.R. (3d) 87, [2000] 8 W.W.R. 85 (S.C.), affirmed 41 E.T.R. (2d) 77, 205 D.L.R. (4th) 193, 2001 CarswellBC 2243, 2001 BCCA 527, 94 B.C.L.R. (3d) 249, [2001] 11 W.W.R. 416, (sub nom. *Rowland v. Christian Brothers of Ireland in Canada (Liquidation)*) 159 B.C.A.C. 177, 259 W.A.C. 177 (C.A.), leave to appeal refused (2002), 211 D.L.R. (4th) vi, 2002 CarswellBC 1207, 2002 CarswellBC 1208, 300 N.R. 196 (note), 179 B.C.A.C. 320 (note), 295 W.A.C. 320 (note) (S.C.C.).

24 [1999] 2 S.C.R. 534, 174 D.L.R. (4th) 45, 1999 CarswellBC 1264, 1999 CarswellBC 1265, [1999] S.C.J. No. 35, (sub nom. *B. v. Curry*) 99 C.L.L.C. 210-033, 43 C.C.E.L. (2d) 1, 62 B.C.L.R. (3d) 173, (sub nom. *P.A.B. v. Children's Foundation*) 124 B.C.A.C. 119, 203 W.A.C. 119, 241 N.R. 266, [1999] 8 W.W.R. 197, [1999] L.V.I. 3046-1, 46 C.C.L.T. (2d) 1, in which the Supreme Court of Canada held a charitable organization liable for the torts of its employee.

25 For discussions of the case, see Terence Carter, "Case Comment: *Christian Brothers* Decision Exposes Charitable Trust Assets to Tort Creditors" (2000), 16 Philanthrop., No. 1, 28; James Phillips, "Legal Developments" (2000), 16 Philanthrop., No. 1, 49; Kevin E. Davis, "Vicarious Liability, Judgment Proofing and Non-Profits" (2000), 50 U.T.L.J. 407; David R. Wingfield,

After all this, the two schools reached a settlement with the liquidator under which they agreed to pay $19 million.[26]

2. The Committee on the Modernization of the Trustee Act in British Columbia has recommended that the *Christian Brothers* case be reversed in that province by legislation.[27]

3. THE MEANING OF CHARITY

(a) Introduction

A charitable trust is a trust created by a settlor or testator for a purpose that is generally perceived as being for the public good, such as the relief of poverty.[28] What matters is that the trust's principal purposes are recognized as charitable. It does not matter that the trust may also have ancillary purposes that, by themselves, may not be charitable.[29] Those will not render the trust non-charitable. It is sometimes said that not only must a trust's purposes be charitable, a trust's activities must also be charitable.[30] This appears to be incorrect. A trust is charitable or not depending upon its purposes. If its activities are outside the bounds of charity, that does not make the trust non-charitable. It merely means that the trust is operating illegally.[31]

As distinguished from trusts for persons, charitable and other purpose trusts do not benefit persons directly, but the public or a segment of the public does derive a benefit from the trust indirectly. However, the law does not regard purpose trusts which are not charitable as conferring a benefit upon the public of a kind that merits special treatment. Indeed, non-charitable purpose trusts have in the past, save for some minor exceptions, been regarded as void for a variety of reasons. Modern legislation validates some non-charitable purpose trusts in part. This is discussed in the next chapter.

You know that a trust for persons confers upon the beneficiaries a right against the trustee to have the trust enforced. Since a purpose trust does not benefit persons directly, the question who has the right to enforce a purpose trust naturally arises. That right is held by the Crown.

"The Non-immunity of Charitable Trust Property" (2003), 119 L.Q.R. 44; David R. Wingfield, "The Short Life and Long After Life of Charitable Immunity in the Common Law" (2003), 82 Can. Bar Rev. 315; Donovan Waters, "Special Purpose Trusts and a Corporate Trustee in Liquidation: "The Story of Vancouver College and St. Thomas More Collegiate" (2003), 22 E.T. & P.J. 199.

26 Richard Foot, "Schools to pay $19M for abuse", National Post, Friday, July 26, 2002, at A5.

27 Committee on the Modernization of the Trustee Act, a Project Committee of the British Columbia Law Institute, *Report on Creditor Access to the Assets of a Purpose Trust*, BCLI Report No. 24 (March 2003), reprinted (2003), 22 E.T. & P.J. 214.

28 Ontario Law Reform Commission, *Report on the Law of Charities* (Toronto: Minister of the Attorney General, 1996), 147ff. ("O.L.R.C. *Report on Charities*").

29 See *Re Laidlaw Foundation* (1984), 48 O.R. (2d) 549, 18 E.T.R. 77, 13 D.L.R. (4th) 491, 6 O.A.C. 181 (Div. Ct.), additional reasons at (1983), 48 O.R. (2d) 549, 18 E.T.R. 77 (Surr. Ct.).

30 See, *e.g.*, O.L.R.C. *Report on Charities*, 226.

31 See Maurice C. Cullity, "The Myth of Charitable Activities" (1990-91), 10 E. & T.J. 7.

Charitable trusts are under the supervision of, and are enforceable by, the Crown in the exercise of its *parens patriae* jurisdiction. This is understandable, since a charitable trust benefits the public, and the state therefore has an interest in seeing that the trust is administered agreeably to its purposes.

This function of the Crown was recognized as long ago as the *Statute of Charitable Uses*,[32] the first important statute designed to regulate the administration of charity, *inter alia*, through the use of commissions of inquiry into abuses in the administration of charitable trusts. It was also recognized in *Morice v. Bishop of Durham*,[33] a leading case, to be discussed presently.

The supervisory function of the Crown over charities falls within the duties of the provincial attorneys-general, but it is usually delegated to an appointed officer, such as the Public Guardian and Trustee.[34]

Non-charitable purpose trusts do not have anyone who can require the trustee to administer the trust in accordance with the stated purposes. This is one of the reasons why such trusts have been held to fail. However, the problem has been overcome in a variety of ways for some non-charitable purpose trusts, as we shall see in the next chapter.

It is, thus, important to distinguish between trusts which are charitable and those which are not. The distinction is best understood by reference to the history of charity. We shall, therefore, consider that topic next.

(b) Historical Background

The concept of charity is part of the Judaeo-Christian tradition which was incorporated into the common law.[35] In that tradition, which is based on divine command, it has always been regarded as appropriate that persons who are able to do so help the less fortunate of society by acts of charity. To practice acts of charity gives expression to one's love for one's neighbour in accordance with Biblical precepts[26] and is an application of the golden rule.[37]

The early common law was not overly concerned with the concept of charity, for charity was given expression through the machinery of the universal church. The church and its institutions, such as convents and monasteries, administered the money given by the faithful for the relief of poverty, education, and other

---

32 1601, (43 Eliz. 1), c. 4.

33 (1805), 10 Ves. Jun. 522 at 541, 32 E.R. 947 (Ch.), *per* Lord Eldon L.C. affirming (1804), 9 Ves. Jun. 399, 32 E.R. 656 (Ch.). See also *National Anti-Vivisection Society v. Inland Revenue Commissioners* (1947), [1948] A.C. 31 at 62, [1947] 2 All E.R. 217 (H.L.), *per* Lord Simonds.

34 See *Official Trustee Act*, R.S.P.E.I. 1988, c. O-4 repealed by S.P.E.I. 1994, c. 52, s. 80 effective July 14, 1994; *Public Trustee Act*, R.S.B.C. 1996, c. 390 (repealed by *Supplement to the Public Trustee Act*, R.S.B.C. 1996 (Supp.), c. 390, s. 2 (B.C. Reg. 12/2000, see R.S.B.C. 1996 (Supp.), *Public Trustees Act*, c. 383, ss. 1-14, 16-26, 27(1) to (3) and (6) (repealed by 2002, c. 63, s. 21), 28-30 of *Public Guardian and Trustee Act* in force)); R.S.A. 2000, c. P-44; R.S.M. 1987, c. P275; R.S.N.L. 1990, c. P-46; R.S.N.S. 1989, c. 379; R.S.N.W.T. 1988, c. P-10; *Public Guardian and Trustee Act*, R.S.O. 1990, c. P.51 [am. 1992, c. 32, s. 25; 1996, c. 2, s. 75].

35 Which, of course, is not to say that there are no similar traditions in other religions.

36 See, *e.g.*, Lev. 19.18, Mt. 22.39, Rom. 13.9.

37 See Mt 7:12; Lk 6:31.

good works. Secular law only interfered in this process to protect the common weal. A prime example of such interference is the statutes of mortmain, which were designed to prevent the accumulation of lands in the hands of perpetual "corporations", such as convents and monasteries.[38] Although there were abuses in the system, it worked reasonably well.

The situation changed drastically after the English Reformation. When Henry VIII dissolved the religious houses,[39] charity ceased to be the preserve of the church and largely became a secular matter. Initially, charitable giving was encouraged, as several legislative enactments designed to promote education and the relief of the poor, sick, and aged attest.[40] It did not take long for abuses to occur, however, and to correct them Parliament enacted the *Statute of Charitable Uses*.[41] The statute, commonly referred to as "the Statute of Elizabeth" was designed to regulate the administration of charitable trusts and to define, albeit incompletely, the concept of "charity."

The preamble to the statute listed the abuses which were endemic in the administration of charities at the time and in that context listed the types of charities for which lands and other property had theretofore been given. The preamble read as follows:[42]

> WHEREAS lands, tenements, rents, annuities, profits, hereditaments, goods, chattels, money and stocks of money have been heretofore given, limited, appointed and assigned, as well by the Queen's most excellent majesty, and her most noble progenitors, as by sundry other well-disposed persons; some for relief of aged, impotent and poor people, some for maintenance of sick and maimed soldiers and mariners, schools of learning, free schools, and scholars in universities, some for repair of bridges, ports, havens, causeways, churches, sea-banks and highways, some for education and preferment of orphans, some for or towards relief, stock or maintenance for houses of correction, some for marriages of poor maids, some for supportation, aid and help of young tradesmen, handicraftsmen and persons decayed, and others for relief or redemption of prisoners or captives, and for aid or ease of any poor inhabitants concerning payments of fifteens, setting out of soldiers and other taxes; which lands, tenements, rents, annuities, profits, hereditaments, goods, chattels, money and stocks of money, nevertheless have not been employed according to the charitable intent of the givers and founders thereof, by reason of frauds, breaches of trust, and negligence in those that should pay, deliver and employ the same. . . .[43]

---

38 The first enactment against mortmain was in *Magna Carta*, 1217 (2 Hen. 3), cc. 32, 36. It was followed by numerous other statutes directed at the same problem. See generally, A.H. Oosterhoff, "The Law of Mortmain: An Historical and Comparative Review" (1977), 27 U. of T.L.J. 257.

39 By 1535 (27 Hen. 8), c. 28 (1535).

40 See Keeton and Sheridan, *The Modern Law of Charities*, 4th ed. by L.A. Sheridan (Chichester: Barry Rose, 1992) at 4-5 ("Keeton and Sheridan"); Gareth Jones, *History of the Law of Charity: 1532-1827* (Cambridge: Cambridge University Press, 1969) at 20 ("Jones").

41 1601 (43 Eliz. 1), c. 4.

42 Rendered in modern orthography.

43 It has been pointed out that the list of charitable purposes contained in the preamble bears a striking resemblance to the charities in William Langland's 14th century poem, the *Vision of . . . Piers Plowman* (F.W. Skeat, ed., L. 1906) at 80: W.K. Jordan, *Philanthropy in England 1480-1660* (London: George Allen & Unwin Ltd., 1959) at 112. This suggests that there was general agreement upon the meaning of charity at the time.

You should note that the list of charitable purposes contained in the preamble was not exhaustive and it was not intended to be. One obvious lacuna is the advancement of religion. The preamble does not mention any charitable purposes under this head, save the repair of churches. There was good reason for this. In 1601 the only recognized church was the Church of England. There was no doubt that gifts to it were charitable, but all other religions were illegal and thus not charitable.[44]

Although the preamble was not exhaustive, nonetheless, it is the *fons et origo* of the common law of charity.[45] But this did not happen immediately. For the first 200 years after the statute it appears that the concept of charity was well understood, so that little reference to the preamble was required.[46] However, in the first half of the eighteenth century the anti-clerical movement led to the enactment of the *Mortmain Act, 1736.*[47] The Act avoided testamentary dispositions of land and interests in land to charitable uses, as well as certain types of *inter vivos* dispositions to charity. Paradoxically, the Act had the effect of promoting a fairly liberal definition of charity. This was because, if dispositions could be held to be charitable, they were void.[48]

The Act did not extend to gifts of pure personalty. However, it seems to have affected the law's approach to the concept of charity in that all charitable giving was regarded with suspicion. Hence, if a gift of pure personalty was made to charity, it was construed strictly.[49] This is evident in the leading case, *Morice v. Bishop of Durham.*[50] A testatrix bequeathed the residue of her personal estate to the Bishop of Durham, her executor, to be disposed of by him in his discretion for "objects of benevolence and liberality." The case is significant for two reasons: (1) it held that if a trust is not wholly charitable it fails;[51] and (2) it declared that the preamble was the source of the definition of charity.

Before *Morice v. Bishop of Durham,* it was generally thought that a purpose trust was charitable if it benefited the public.[52] On that basis, virtually all purpose trusts would be charitable. However, the case rejected that view and held that "charity" has a restricted meaning derived from the preamble. Thus, the Master of the Rolls, Sir William Grant, held:[53]

> ... its signification is derived chiefly from the *Statute of Elizabeth.*[54] Those purposes are considered charitable, which that Statute enumerates, or which by analogies are deemed within its spirit and intendment ...

---

44 Keeton and Sheridan, at 3.
45 Jones, at 122.
46 *Ibid.*, at 120-121.
47 1736 (9 Geo. 2), c. 36.
48 Jones, *op. cit.*, at 132.
49 *Ibid.*
50 *Supra*, note 33.
51 The court held that the trust failed because, while "benevolence" might be equated with charity, "liberality" could not. This is discussed further below.
52 Jones, at 122.
53 *Supra*, note 50, at 9 Ves. Jun. 405.
54 *Supra*, note 41.

On appeal, Lord Eldon agreed, stating that "charity" means "either such purposes as are expressed in the Statute . . ., or . . . purposes analogous to those."[55]

Morice v. Bishop of Durham may, therefore, be regarded as the origin of the distinction between charitable and non-charitable purpose trusts. After that case, the courts have generally referred to the preamble to determine whether a particular purpose was listed in it or was within its spirit and intendment, or, as it is sometimes said, within "the equity" of the statute.[56] The courts have, thus, used the preamble as a "sort of index or chart" to determine whether a purpose is charitable.[57]

This does not mean that a purpose must be *ejusdem generis* with the purposes recited in the preamble: it must be "charitable in the same sense" as one of those purposes.[58] For example, a trust to establish a scholarship in a university, while not specifically mentioned in the preamble, is charitable in the same way as the enumerated purposes, "maintenance of schools of learning, free schools, and scholars in universities," are.

The list contained in the preamble is, however, not readily understood today. Moreover, as the cases on the meaning of charity multiplied, so did the desire to classify the list to make it more understandable. An early classification is that of Mr. Samuel Romilly,[59] presented in argument in *Morice v. Bishop of Durham*:[60]

> There are four objects, within which all charity, to be administered in this court, must fall: 1st, relief of the indigent; in various ways: money: provisions: education: medical assistance; &c.: 2dly, the advancement of learning: 3dly, the advancement of religion; and, 4thly which is the most difficult, the advancement of objects of general public utility.

This classification was adopted in amended form without attribution by Lord Macnaghten in *Commissioners for Special Purposes of the Income Tax v. Pemsel*,[61] where his Lordship said:

> "Charity" in its legal sense comprises four principal divisions: trusts for the relief of poverty; trusts for the advancement of education; trusts for the advancement of religion; and trusts for other purposes beneficial to the community, not falling under any of the preceding heads.

His Lordship added:[62]

---

55 *Supra*, note 50, at 10 Ves. Jun. 541.
56 *Inc. Council of Law Reporting for England & Wales v. A.-G.*, [1972] Ch. 73 at 88, [1971] 3 All E.R. 1029 (C.A.), *per* Russell L.J. And see *Tudor on Charities*, 8th ed. by Jean Warburton assisted by Debra Morris (London: Sweet and Maxwell Limited, 1995) at 82 ("Tudor").
57 *Commissioners for Special Purposes of the Income Tax v. Pemsel*, [1891] A.C. 531 at 581, [1891-94] All E.R. Rep. 28, *per* Lord Macnaghten (H.L.).
58 *Re Strakosch*, [1949] 1 Ch. 529 at 538, [1949] 2 All E.R. 6 (C.A.), *per* Lord Greene M.R.
59 Later Sir Samuel Romilly M.R.
60 *Supra*, note 33, at 10 Ves. Jun. 532.
61 *Supra*, note 57, at 583.
62 *Ibid*.

> The trusts last referred to are not the less charitable in the eye of the law, because incidentally they benefit the rich as well as the poor, as indeed, every charity that deserves the name must do either directly or indirectly.

You should note, however, that these were mere attempts at classification of the list in the preamble. Thus, neither Mr. Romilly nor Lord Macnaghten intended to include all trusts which are of benefit to the public under the fourth head. The fourth head merely refers to those purposes listed in the preamble, or which by analogy come within its spirit or intention, and which do not fall under the first three. It would seem, therefore, that the classifications did not really advance the definition of charity: you still had to refer back to the preamble and the cases decided thereunder to determine whether a given purpose was charitable.

In England the *Statute of Charitable Uses*[63] was repealed by the *Mortmain and Charitable Uses Act, 1888*.[64] However, section 13(2) of the Act recited the preamble of the Statute of Elizabeth and noted that enactments and documents have made reference to "charities within the meaning, purview, and interpretation of the said Act." Therefore it provided that:

> ... references to such charities shall be construed as references to charities within the meaning, purview, and interpretation of the said preamble.

Again, this enactment did not change the law, but was merely declarative of what the law and practice were.

The Act of 1888 was itself repealed by the *Charities Act, 1960*.[65] However, section 38(4) of that Act provided:

> Any reference in any enactment or document to a charity within the meaning, purview and interpretation of the *Charitable Uses Act, 1601*, or of the preamble to it, shall be construed as a reference to a charity within the meaning which the word bears as a legal term according to the law of England and Wales.

Further, section 46 of the Act defined "charitable purposes" as "purposes which are exclusively charitable according to the law of England and Wales." Section 97(1) of the *Charities Act 1993*,[66] which replaced the 1960 statute, is identical. A singularly unhelpful definition, indeed! The law of England and Wales defines "charity" by reference to the preamble and the cases decided thereunder. Hence, it remains necessary to refer to the preamble in England.

The Nathan Committee had earlier considered the question and had recommended that Lord Macnaghten's classification be used as a statutory definition

---

63 1601 (43 Eliz. 1), c. 4.

64 1888 (51 & 52 Vict.), c. 42, s. 13(1), Sched. The Act consolidated the old Statutes of Mortmain, referred to above, and the *Mortmain Act, 1736*, also referred to above. It was amended by the *Mortmain and Charitable Uses Act, 1891*, (54 & 55 Vict.), c. 73.

65 1960 (8 & 9 Eliz. 2), c. 58, ss. 38(1), 48, Sched. VII, Part II.

66 1993, c. 10 (U.K.). The 1993 Act consolidated most of the Act of 1960 and Part I of the *Charities Act 1992*, 1992, c. 41 (U.K.).

for lack of a better.[67] However, Parliament rejected the inclusion of any definition in the Act.[68]

In Canada the situation is not much better. Ontario appears to be the only province that has grappled with the question. By the *Mortmain and Charitable Uses Act* of 1902[69] it adopted the *English Act of 1888*[70] and repealed[71] the Statute of Elizabeth.[72] However, section 6 of the Ontario Act deemed a list of purposes which, in substance, were those contained in the Statute of Elizabeth ". . . and any other purposes similar to those hereintofore mentioned" to be valid charitable uses.

This flirtation with the preamble was short-lived, however. The *Mortmain and Charitable Uses Act* of 1909[73] repealed the 1902 statute and substituted another definition which deemed what were, in effect, Lord Macnaghten's four heads of charity to be charitable uses within the meaning of the Act.[74] This "definition" remained in the *Mortmain and Charitable Uses Act*[75] until it was repealed.[76] However it was moved in amended form to the *Charities Accounting Act*.[77] Section 7 of the current revision provides in part:

"charitable purpose" means,

    (a) the relief of poverty,
    (b) education,
    (c) the advancement of religion, and
    (d) any purpose beneficial to the community, not falling under clause (a), (b) or (c) . . .

Because this definition is a mere classification of the preamble, one would have thought that it did not alter the law. However, in *Re Orr*[78] Meredith C.J.O. held that this definition, in particular the fourth head, was enacted in Ontario in 1909 to prevent the adoption of the English doctrine that only those objects which have public utility and which fall within the purview of the preamble are charitable. In his Lordship's opinion, the 1909 statute directed the Ontario courts to

67 *Report of the Committee on the Law and Practice Relating to Charitable Trusts*, Cmd 8710 (1952), para. 140 ("Nathan Committee").
68 Keeton and Sheridan, at 56.
69 S.O. 1902, c. 2 (consolidated as R.S.O. 1897, c. 333).
70 *Supra*, note 64.
71 By s. 14 and Sched.
72 *Supra*, note 41.
73 S.O. 1909, c. 58. The Act consolidated the 1902 Act and the *Mortmain and Charitable Uses Act*, R.S.O. 1897, c. 112. The latter was first enacted as S.O. 1892, c. 20, and was a copy (with amendments) of the English Act of 1891, *supra*, note 64. The 1909 Act, s. 17, repealed both of the earlier Ontario Acts.
74 S. 2(2).
75 Last consolidated as R.S.O. 1980, c. 297.
76 By S.O. 1982, c. 12, s. 1(1).
77 By S.O. 1982, c. 11, s. 1, 1983, c. 61, s. 1. See now R.S.O. 1990, c. C.10.
78 (1917), 40 O.L.R. 567 at 595-597 (C.A.), reversed on other grounds (sub nom. *Cameron v. Church of Christ Scientist*) (1918), 57 S.C.R. 298, 43 D.L.R. 668, leave to appeal refused (1919), 57 S.C.R. vii.

have regard to the more liberal definition contained in it. This view was adopted by the Divisional Court in *Re Laidlaw Foundation*[79] and confirmed by the Ontario Court of Appeal in *Re Levy Estate*.[80]

If this view is correct, the meaning of charity, in particular the fourth head of charity, in Ontario is different from the rest of the Canadian provinces, England and other Commonwealth common law jurisdictions. In effect, this view means that a purpose, other than those for the relief of poverty, and the advancement of education or religion, is charitable if it is for the benefit of the public. Hence, the class of purposes falling under the fourth head is potentially much larger than was previously supposed. You will recall that this view was decisively rejected in *Morice v. Bishop of Durham*.[81] We shall discuss this issue in greater detail later in this chapter.

You will appreciate, however, that the meaning of charity may change with time: *tempora mutantur, et nos mutamur in illis*.[82] This is evident from the history of the meaning of "charity." *Morice v. Bishop of Durham* interpreted the term restrictively. But later cases tended to take a relatively lenient approach to charity. However, the English courts began taking a stricter approach to charity in the 1940s, and this approach was followed in Canada. The stricter approach resulted in the striking down of large numbers of meritorious purposes. The reasons for this are not readily apparent, but they include a strict constructionist tradition inherited from the 19th century and the state's need for increased tax revenue.

The strict constructionist approach is one in which the court, when interpreting a will, has regard only to the actual words used by the testator except in very limited circumstances. Hence, there can be no reference to extrinsic evidence tending to show the testator's actual intention. The state's need for increased tax revenue arose out of the prosecution of World War II and the establishment of the welfare state in England after that war. Cases from the 1940s and 1950s must be read in that light.[83]

---

79 *Supra*, note 29. This case is reproduced later in this chapter.
80 (1989), 58 D.L.R. (4th) 375, 68 O.R. (2d) 385, 33 E.T.R. 1, 33 O.A.C. 99 (C.A.).
81 *Supra*, note 50, at 10 Ves. Jun. 522.
82 *I.e.*, times change and we must change with them.
83 Cases such as *Oppenheim v. Tobacco Securities Trust Co.* (1950), [1951] A.C. 297, [1951] 1 All E.R. 31 (H.L.); *Gilmour v. Coat*, [1949] A.C. 426, [1949] 1 All E.R. 848 (H.L.); *National Anti-Vivisection Society v. Inland Revenue Commissioners*, *supra*, note 33; *Inland Revenue Commissioners v. Baddeley*, [1955] A.C. 572, [1955] 1 All E.R. 525 (H.L.); *Williams Trustees v. Inland Revenue Commissioners*, [1947] A.C. 447, [1947] 1 All E.R. 513 (H.L.); and *Chichester Diocesan Fund & Board of Finance Inc. v. Simpsons*, [1944] A.C. 341, [1944] 2 All E.R. 60 (H.L.), are examples of the strict approach.
   Whether, and to what extent, these decisions were influenced by the introduction of Lord Beveridge's Utopia in England in 1945 must await historical examination. However, the Nathan Committee appointed by the Attlee (Labour) government to investigate the law of charity was certainly influenced by it. The Committee referred, *inter alia*, to Lord Beveridge's *Voluntary Action: A Report on the Methods of Social Advance* (1948) at 10; Nathan Committee *Report*, at 1, para. 8. Nonetheless, the Committee considered that voluntary action, that is, private as distinct from state charity, should continue to exist in, and is essential to, the proper functioning of the democratic state: *Report, ibid.*, paras. 55, 57. It is apparent that the Committee viewed charity,

Since then, a more lenient approach to charity can be discerned. Thus, for example, more recently the House of Lords stated that the courts should construe trusts in favour of charity benignly.[84] Similarly, in the area of relief of poverty the English case *Dingle v. Turner*[85] and the Canadian case *Jones v. T. Eaton Co.*[86] evidence a more lenient attitude. Such an attitude is also apparent in *Re Laidlaw Foundation*, referred to above.

(c) The Necessity of Public Benefit

(i) *Generally*

A purpose is not charitable unless it is for the benefit of the public. Before *Morice v. Bishop of Durham*,[87] it seems that a purpose was regarded as *ipso facto* charitable if it benefited the public.[88] As we have seen, that case held that a trust which is merely for the benefit of the public is not charitable. To be charitable the trust must not only be for the public benefit, but also fall within the preamble of its spirit and intendment. As we have noted, the Ontario position seems to be that, as regards the fourth head, the qualification that the purpose must fall within the purview of the preamble is no longer valid.

What, then, does "public benefit" mean? It is important to note that the phrase "public benefit" comprises two elements, namely, that the *public* must benefit from the trust, and that, in fact, there be *benefit*. We shall see that there is a progression from a very limited requirement of public benefit of trusts for the relief of poverty, to a greater requirement of trusts for the advancement of religion, a still greater requirement of trusts for the advancement of education, and the most stringent requirement of trusts for other purposes beneficial to the community. This progression exists both as regards the public element and as regards the benefit element.

Most cases fail to recognize that there are two elements to the public benefit test and, indeed, the distinction is not always significant. This is because benefit is assumed to exist in many situations so long as the trust extends to the public and is not merely for the private benefit of some persons.

For example, a trust for the relief of the poor in a specific city satisfies the "public" requirement and it is assumed that the relief of poverty is then beneficial. Benefit is also normally assumed in the context of the advancement of religion. However, we shall see that the benefit element may be lacking in that context if the public aspect disappears. This occurs if the trust is for devotions which are conducted in private. The two elements, therefore, are interrelated.

---

even if conducted by religious organizations, to be divorced from piety and concerned essentially with secular, humanist ideals.

84 *Inland Revenue Commissioners v. McMullen* (1980), [1981] A.C. 1 at 18, [1980] 2 W.L.R. 416, [1980] 1 All E.R. 884, *per* Lord Hailsham L.C.

85 [1972] A.C. 601, [1972] 1 All E.R. 878 (H.L.).

86 *Supra*, note 2. This case is reproduced later in this chapter.

87 *Supra*, note 33.

88 Jones, at 121-122, 133.

On the other hand, the public element may exist, but the benefit element may not. This occurs, for example, if the trust is directed towards the education of the public generally, but the educational element is so negligible that the law is not prepared to enforce the trust. Similarly, in the context of a purpose that would otherwise fall under the fourth head in that it is designed to improve morals and ethics, such as a trust to promote anti-vivisection of animals, the trust may not be charitable because the disadvantages of the purpose outweigh its advantages. Indeed, the lack of benefit, or at least benefit that can be judged by the courts, is also the reason why trusts for political purposes under any of the four heads fail.

It is axiomatic that although an organization may be charitable, a payment to it will not attract the benefits generally accorded gifts to charity if the donor made the payment in return for consideration or a future benefit. The issue arose in *R. v. Burns*.[89] The defendant made payments to the Canadian Ski Association, a registered Canadian charitable organization. His daughter was a member of a division of the association and, while there was no contractual obligation to support the association, there were strong expectations that parents of members and participants would give financial support to the association. The court concluded that the defendant did not make true gifts, but received consideration in the form of ski training for his daughter.

The *Burns* case may be contrasted with *Brooks v. Richardson*.[90] The constitution of a hospital, a registered charity, provided that persons who gave beyond a minimum level automatically became governors of the hospital and entitled to participate in the running of its affairs. When the majority of the governors sought to sell the hospital as a going concern, one donor-governor sought an injunction to restrain them. The court held that the charity was not a private club, that the applicant did not receive consideration for his gift, and that he had no contractual rights to give him standing to contest the proposed sale.

Generally, however, the public element is the one that is stressed. The public element exists if a trust is for the benefit of the public or some sizeable or important segment of the community. A trust for a purpose which would otherwise be charitable fails (save for certain exceptions to be mentioned below) if it is for the benefit of private individuals.

This issue has arisen a number of times in the context of education. A leading case is *Re Compton, Power v. Compton*.[91] The testatrix had directed the establishment of a trust "for the education of Compton and Powell and Montague children . . . to be used to fit the children to be servants of God serving the nation. . . ." She defined the beneficiaries as "the lawful descendants" of three named persons. The Court of Appeal held that the gift was not charitable because the

---

89 [1988] 1 C.T.C. 201, 19 F.T.R. 275, (sub nom. *Burns v. Minister of National Revenue*) D.T.C. 6101 (T.D.), affirmed [1990] 1 C.T.C. 350, 35 F.T.R. 121 (note), 90 D.T.C. 6335, 107 N.R. 81 (C.A.). See also *Woolner v. R.* (1997), [1997] T.C.J. No. 1395, 1997 CarswellNat 2995, [1999] 4 C.T.C. 2512, 2000 D.T.C. 1956 (T.C.C. [Informal Procedure]), affirmed (1999), 1999 CarswellNat 1948, (sub nom. *Woolner v. Attorney General of Canada*) 99 D.T.C. 5722, [2000] 1 C.T.C. 35, 249 N.R. 129 (C.A.).

90 [1986] 1 All E.R. 952 (Ch. Div.).

91 [1945] Ch. 123, [1945] 1 All E.R. 198 (C.A.).

beneficiaries were not a section of the community; rather, they were a group of private individuals related to each other through a common ancestor. In this connection Lord Greene M.R. said that the public benefit will exist if the relationship between the beneficiaries is an impersonal one. Thus, if the gift is to relieve the poor in a certain parish, the beneficiaries take, not in their character as individuals, but because they are members of a class whose common quality is that they reside in the parish.[92] Of trusts which identify the beneficiaries by some personal nexus, his Lordship said:[93]

> . . . a gift under which the beneficiaries are defined by reference to a purely personal relationship to a named propositus cannot on principle be a valid charitable gift. And this, I think, must be the case whether the relationship be near or distant, whether it is limited to one generation or is extended to two or three or in perpetuity. The inherent vice of the personal element is present however long the chain and the claimant cannot avoid basing his claim on it.

The principle enunciated in *Re Compton*, that the public element is wanting if the beneficiaries are connected by a personal relationship, was followed in *Oppenheim v. Tobacco Securities Trust Co.*[94] That case concerned a settlement which directed that the income from the trust property be used to provide or help in providing for the education of children of employees or former employees of a named company and its subsidiaries and allied companies. The employees in those companies numbered in excess of 110,000. You might, therefore, think that their children would form a sufficient section of the public. However, the House of Lords held otherwise, because the children were connected by a personal relationship, namely the companies. In this context Lord Simonds said:[95]

> Then the question is whether that class of persons can be regarded as such a "section of the community" as to satisfy the test of public benefit. These words "section of the community" have no special sanctity, but they conveniently indicate first, that the possible (I emphasize the word "possible") beneficiaries must not be numerically negligible, and secondly, that the quality which distinguishes them from other members of the community, so that they form by themselves a section of it, must be a quality which does not depend on their relationship to a particular individual. It is for this reason that a trust for the education of members of a family or, as in *Re Compton*, of a number of families cannot be regarded as charitable. A group of persons may be numerous but, if the nexus between them is their personal relationship to a single propositus or to several propositi, they are neither the community nor a section of the community for charitable purposes.

You will see, however, that the public element requirement varies with the head of charity under which a particular purpose belongs. Thus, it is almost non-existent for relief of poverty, it is perhaps slightly stronger for advancement of religion, stronger still for advancement of education, and especially strong for purposes falling under the fourth head. Even under the fourth head, however, the public element requirement varies, at least in the sense that the number of people who benefit directly do not always have to be numerically large.

---

92 *Ibid.*, at 129-130.
93 *Ibid.*, at 131.
94 (1950), [1951] A.C. 297, [1951] 1 All E.R. 31 (H.L.).
95 *Ibid.*, at 306.

Whether the public element test as enunciated in *Compton*[96] and *Oppenheim* is too strict is a matter of debate. In recent years a movement away from the strict application of such rules is discernible. This is evident from certain *dicta* in the speech of Lord Cross of Chelsea in *Dingle v. Turner*.[97] His Lordship stated that he was dissatisfied with the distinction between personal and impersonal relationships. Further, he regarded the requirement that the class of persons to benefit must be a "section of the public," or a "fluctuating body of private individuals," as too vague to be of much assistance. He concluded:[98]

> In truth the question whether or not the potential beneficiaries of a trust can fairly be said to constitute a section of the public is a question of degree and cannot be by itself decisive of the question whether the trust is a charity. Much must depend on the purpose of the trust. It may well be that, on the one hand, a trust to promote some purpose, *prima facie* charitable, will constitute a charity even though the class of potential beneficiaries might fairly be called a private class and that, on the other hand, a trust to promote another purpose, also *prima facie* charitable, will not constitute a charity even though the class of potential beneficiaries might seem to some people fairly describable as a section of the public.[99]

(ii) *Extra-territorial Trusts*

Normally, trusts which are intended to effect a purpose outside the jurisdiction, but which are charitable within the jurisdiction, will be upheld as charitable. Thus, for example, a gift by an English testator to the German government for the benefit of disabled World War I German soldiers was upheld,[100] as was a trust for foreign educational objects.[101] It is not difficult to appreciate that such objects as the relief of poverty and the advancement of education in all parts of the world are likely to be regarded as charitable, particularly since international relief organizations perform work toward the same ends. Moreover, foreign mission work has always been regarded as charitable.[102]

It is arguable that such purposes are, in any event, of public benefit in the trust's jurisdiction. However, some *dicta* suggest that it is a requirement, particularly of purposes falling under the fourth head, that the purpose benefit the local

---

96 *Supra*, note 91.

97 *Supra*, note 85, at 623-4. See *Hobourn Aero Components Ltd. Air Raid Distress Fund, Re*, [1946] 1 All E.R. 501, [1946] 1 Ch. 194 (C.A.) in which funds that were intended to provide benefits for employees of a corporation were held non-charitable because the Court found they constituted a private trust for the benefit only of subscribers.

98 *Ibid.*, at 624.

99 For Canadian treatment of the public benefit tests enunciated above see *Baker v. National Trust Co., Cox, Re* (1952), [1953] 1 S.C.R. 94, 1952 CarswellOnt 119, [1953] 1 D.L.R. 577, affirmed [1955] A.C. 627, 1955 CarswellOnt 103, 16 W.W.R. 49, [1955] 2 All E.R. 550, [1955] 3 D.L.R. 497, [1955] 3 W.L.R. 42, 99 S.J. 383 (Ontario P.C.) and *L.I.U.N.A., Local 527 Members' Training Trust Fund v. R.*, 47 E.T.R. 29, 1992 CarswellNat 398, 92 D.T.C. 2365, (sub nom. *L.I.U.N.A. Local 527 Members' Training Trust Fund v. Canada)* [1992] 2 C.T.C. 2410 (T.C.C.). The Canadian cases tend to follow the English trends in this respect.

100 *Re Robinson*, [1931] 2 Ch. 122.

101 *Re Vaughan*, [1905] W.N. 179.

102 *Re Long* (1930), 37 O.W.N. 351 (H.C.).

public.[103] Further, it seems that there must in fact be a benefit to the host country's public. Thus, a trust which sought to promote the abolition of torture and inhuman punishment throughout the world was held not to be charitable, because the local court would be unable to judge whether the effects of the trust would be beneficial to the public of a particular country.[104]

By contrast, an Ontario trust which directed the payment of money to trustees in the United States upon trust "to promote, aid and protect citizens of the United States, of African descent, in the enjoyment of their civil rights," was held to be charitable.[105]

The issue has now largely been laid to rest by the Ontario Court of Appeal in *Re Levy Estate*.[106] The testator gave the residue of his estate to the state of Israel for charitable purposes only. The charities were to be decided upon by his trustees and be in the form of a dedication honouring and recognizing the testator. The trustee had tentatively selected several charities in Israel. If they existed in Ontario, they would have been regarded as charitable under the fourth head of charity. The court held that a trust which falls under the fourth head of charity is not void merely because the charity exists only in a foreign country and is carried on only for the benefit of that country and not for the benefit of Canada. In any event, the trustee's discretion was circumscribed: he had to select charities in Israel that were charitable in Ontario. Further, any purpose that would be contrary to the public policy of Canada would not, *ipso facto*, be charitable. Hence, no organizations could be selected whose purposes would offend Canadian public policy.

The *Levy* case may be contrasted with *Canadian Magen David Adom for Israel / Magen David Adom Canadien pour Israël v. Minister of National Revenue*[107] The taxpayer was incorporated to donate emergency medical supplies and ambulances to the people of Israel. It was registered as a charitable organization under the *Income Tax Act*.[108] The Minister issued a notice proposing to revoke the taxpayer's registration on the ground that it was not charitable. The court dismissed the taxpayer's appeal. In order for the taxpayer to retain its registered status, it would have to engage an Israeli organization as its agent. Further, it would have to monitor the use of the ambulances and supplies by the Israeli organization to show that its use of the goods amounted to the carrying on by the taxpayer of its charitable activities. Consequently, it seems that the extra-territorial

---

103 See, *e.g.*, *Camille and Henry Dreyfus Foundation Inc. v. I.R.C.*, [1954] 1 Ch. 672 at 684, [1954] 2 All E.R. 466 (C.A.).

104 *McGovern v. A.-G.*, [1982] Ch. 321, [1981] 3 All E.R. 493 (Ch.).

105 *Lewis v. Doerle* (1898), 25 O.A.R. 206 (C.A.).

106 (1989), 58 D.L.R. (4th) 375, 68 O.R. (2d) 385, 33 E.T.R. 1, 33 O.A.C. 99 (C.A.). See also, *Gray Estate v. Yule* (1990), 75 O.R. (2d) 55, 1990 CarswellOnt 500, 73 D.L.R. (4th) 161, 39 E.T.R. 102 (Gen. Div.) which followed the approach of the Ontario Court of Appeal in the *Levy* case with respect to extra-territorial trusts.

107 218 D.L.R. (4th) 718, 2002 CarswellNat 2354, 2002 CarswellNat 3154, 2002 FCA 323, 2002 D.T.C. 7353, [2002] 4 C.T.C. 422, 2002 CAF 323, 293 N.R. 144 (C.A.).

108 R.S.C. 1985, c. 1 (5th Supp.).

activities must be charitable under Canadian law. Otherwise, the organization will not be regarded as charitable.[109]

(iii) *Political Purposes*

A trust for political purposes is not charitable. This is because the courts cannot determine whether a proposed change in the law will be of benefit to the public. A case that is often cited for this proposition is *Bowman v. Secular Society Ltd.*[110] The testator left the residue of his estate upon trust for the Secular Society Ltd. The purposes of that incorporated body included the promotion of the secularization of the state and the repeal of all Sabbatarian laws. The House of Lords held that the gift was not to the Society in trust for its objects, but was an absolute gift and, as such, was unobjectionable. However, Lord Parker of Waddington stated in *dicta* that if the gift had been in trust for the Society's purposes, it would not have been charitable because its purposes were political:[111]

> The abolition of religious tests, the disestablishment of the Church, the secularization of education, the alteration of the law touching religion or marriage, or the observation of the Sabbath, are purely political objects. Equity has always refused to recognize such objects as charitable. It is true that a gift to an association formed for their attainment may, if the association be unincorporated, be upheld as an absolute gift to its members, or, if the association be incorporated, as an absolute gift to the corporate body; but a trust for the attainment of political objects has always been held invalid, not because it is illegal, for every one is at liberty to advocate or promote by any lawful means a change in the law, but because the court has no means of judging whether a proposed change in the law will or will not be for the public benefit, and therefore cannot say that a gift to secure the change is a charitable gift. . . . If, therefore, there be a trust in the present case it is clearly invalid. The fact, if it be the fact, that one or other of the objects specified in the society's memorandum is charitable would make no difference. There would be no means of discriminating what portion of the gift was intended for a charitable and what portion for a political purpose, and the uncertainty in this respect would be fatal.

More recently, however, the Humanist Association of Toronto was granted charitable status by the Canada Customs and Revenue Agency. Among other purposes, this organization holds lectures, provides public speakers, and performs weddings, "name-giving" ceremonies, and funerals "free of supernatural implications". It also provides information about public issues such as stem-cell research and abortion. The Association had applied for charitable status, but had been turned down on the ground that it fell under none of the four heads of charity. It appealed to the Federal Court of Appeal, arguing that the Agency's decision had violated its constitutional guarantees of equality and freedom of religion. In an out-of-court settlement, the Agency granted charitable status to the Association on the

---

109 The organization subsequently reached a settlement with the CCRA, which meant that it retained its charitable status. See Robert B. Hayhoe, "Canada Customs and Revenue Agency Charity Audits" (2002), 17 Philanthrop., No. 4, 38 at 53.

110 [1917] A.C. 406 (H.L.).

111 *Ibid.*, at 442.

ground that it was an organization "beneficial to the community as a whole", that is, that it fell under the fourth head of charity.[112]

National Anti-Vivisection Society v. Inland Revenue Commissioners is another example. A trust was created for the purposes of the society. The society's purposes included the promotion of legislation prohibiting vivisection of animals for medical and other research. Lord Simonds said on this point:[113]

> The same question may be looked at from a slightly different angle. One of the tests, and a crucial test, whether a trust is charitable, lies in the competence of the court to control and reform it. I would remind your Lordships that it is the King as *parens patriae* who is the guardian of charity and that it is the right and duty of his Attorney-General to intervene and inform the court, if the trustees of a charitable trust fall short of their duty. So too it is his duty to assist the court, if need be, in the formulation of a scheme for the execution of a charitable trust. But, my Lords, is it for a moment to be supposed that it is the function of the Attorney-General on behalf of the Crown to intervene and demand that a trust shall be established and administered by the court, the object of which is to alter the law in a manner highly prejudicial, as he and His Majesty's Government may think, to the welfare of the state? This very case would serve as an example, if upon the footing that is was a charitable trust it became the duty of the Attorney-General on account of its maladministration to intervene.

The trust, therefore, failed.[114] Similarly, organizations which promote the sanctity of human life, or oppose abortion and seek to persuade others to that view have been held not to be charitable because their purposes are political.[115] Thus, trusts which seek to influence Parliament to change the law to conform with the views of the members of particular organizations are void.[116]

Most trusts for political purposes appear to fall under the fourth head. However, they have also occurred in the context of education. In that context, trusts to promote the doctrines of political movements or parties have been held to be political and, thus, non-charitable.[117]

---

112 Tom Blackwell, "Humanists Win Victory over Status: Standing up for 'Godless Masses'". National Post, 14 February, 2004. The article does not indicate whether the Association engages in political purposes.

113 *Supra*, note 33.

114 The trust also failed because it lacked public benefit.

115 See, *e.g.*, *Human Life International In Canada Inc. v. Minister of National Revenue*, (sub nom. *Human Life International in Canada Inc. v. M.N.R.)* [1998] 3 F.C. 202, 1998 CarswellNat 366, 1998 CarswellNat 1646, 98 D.T.C. 6196, [1998] 3 C.T.C. 126, 232 N.R. 174 (C.A.); *Alliance for Life v. Minister of National Revenue*, 27 E.T.R. (2d) 1, 174 D.L.R. (4th) 442, 1999 CarswellNat 625, 1999 CarswellNat 2489, 99 D.T.C. 5228, [1999] 3 C.T.C. 1, 242 N.R. 106, [1999] 3 F.C. 504 (C.A.).

116 See *Patriotic Acre Fund, Re*, 1 W.W.R. (N.S.) 417, [1951] 2 D.L.R. 624, 1951 CarswellSask 6 (C.A.). See also *Toronto Volgograd Committee v. Minister of National Revenue*, [1988] 3 F.C. 251, 1988 CarswellNat 706, 1988 CarswellNat 287, 88 D.T.C. 6192, 83 N.R. 241, [1988] 1 C.T.C. 365, 29 E.T.R. 159 (C.A.) and *Co-operative College of Canada v. Saskatchewan (Human Rights Commission)* (1975), 64 D.L.R. (3d) 531, 1975 CarswellSask 85, [1976] 2 W.W.R. 84 (C.A.).

117 See, *e.g.*, *Bonar Law Memorial Trust v. I.R.C.* (1933), 49 T.L.R. 220, 17 Tax Cas. 508, a trust promoting education on conservative principles; *Re Hopkinson*, [1949] 1 All E.R. 346, a similar trust, but with a socialist bent; *Re Loney* (1953), 9 W.W.R. (N.S.) 366 (Man. Q.B.), to the same effect.

You should note that only trusts for the purposes of such organizations are invalid. Absolute gifts to them are valid.[118] However, if the organization is unincorporated and the gift is construed as being for the present and future members, it will fail for perpetuity.[118]

These cases may be contrasted with *Farewell v. Farewell*,[120] which involved a trust to promote the adoption by Parliament of legislation prohibiting the sale of liquor. Boyd C. held the gift to be charitable. His Lordship analogized political trusts to religious trusts. In the latter the courts assume that the trust is for the public benefit because they have no means of judging otherwise.[121] His Lordship concluded that political trusts ought to be treated in the same way.

The issue of political purposes arises regularly, both when determining whether a charity should be granted tax exempt status and when deciding whether an organization is charitable. The former was in issue in *N.D.G. Neighbourhood Association v. M.N.R.*[122] The taxpayer was a tenants' association, which sought registration as a charitable organization. The association purported to carry on educational activities and said it helped alleviate poverty, since it worked mainly among low-income groups. However, it was principally an activist organization which defended tenants' rights and conducted campaigns and lobbying activities on the political level. For that reason, the court held that its purposes were not charitable under the fourth head of charity.

To the same effect is *Positive Action Against Pornography v. M.N.R.*[123] The appellant purported to educate the public about the evils of pornography, but the court found that its main purpose was political in that it advocated legislative reform and greater governmental control of pornography. Accordingly, it was denied registration.

Yet another example is *Toronto Volgograd Committee v. M.N.R.*[124] The committee sought to promote understanding between the Canadian and Soviet societies, and help the two societies look for peaceful ways to live together. The court regarded these objects as political and, hence, non-charitable.

The question whether an organization failed to meet the criterion of charitableness because of its political activities was also in issue in *Ontario (Public Trustee) v. Toronto Humane Society*.[125] The Society was an incorporated charity. Its object was to "promote and develop humane public sentiment, and to secure the enactment and enforcement of suitable laws for the prevention of cruelty." An "animal rights" group got control of the society and began to solicit funds for

---

118 See, *e.g.*, *Re Ogden*, [1933] Ch. 678, a gift to the Liberal Party and its affiliates; *Van Kerkworde v. Hedley* (1917), 17 S.R. (N.S.W.) 265, a similar gift to the Socialist Party.

119 See *Bacon v. Pianta* (1966), 114 C.L.R. 634, a gift to the Communist Party. Today, a more benign construction of such gifts is likely upon principles discussed in the next chapter.

120 (1892), 22 O.R. 573 (H.C.).

121 Subject to the proviso that the devotions must be public.

122 30 E.T.R. 99, 85 N.R. 73, 88 D.T.C. 6279, [1988] 2 C.T.C. 14 (C.A.).

123 29 E.T.R. 92, [1988] 2 F.C. 340, 49 D.L.R. (4th) 74, 83 N.R. 214, [1988] 1 C.T.C. 232, 88 D.T.C. 6186 (C.A.).

124 *Supra*, note 116.

125 (1987), 60 O.R. (2d) 236, 27 E.T.R. 40, 40 D.L.R. (4th) 111 (H.C.).

and devote the society's funds to an organization whose purpose was to lobby for the abolition of legislation which permitted impounded animals to be used for research. The court appears to have regarded the second part of the society's purpose as ancillary to the first and, hence, not objectionable. This issue is dealt with in the next subheading and later in this chapter. The court applied a proportionality test to determine what portion of the charity's activities was legitimate and what was political. It regarded the society's support of the non-charitable organization with suspicion, but did not think the society had yet reached the stage where its non-charitable activities determined its objects and made it into a non-charitable organization. As we shall see, the activities of a charity are not what matter for this purpose, only the organization's objects are. A charity whose activities are questionable may, however, be subject to investigation and its officers may be removed and be liable to reimburse the charity.

(iv) *Exclusivity*[126]

A charitable trust must be devoted exclusively to charitable purposes. This is discussed in detail below, but requires brief mention at this point. If a trust permits the trustees to use the trust property for the benefit of charitable or non-charitable purposes, and if the trust does not allocate a proportion of the funds to charitable and to non-charitable purposes, the trustee can, in effect, use it exclusively for the latter. Since the latter have no recognized meaning in law and since the court cannot administer a non-charitable purpose trust, the entire trust will be invalid.

(d) Conclusion

It is apparent from the foregoing that the law does not define "charity." At most the law affords a means of identifying charitable purposes.[127] Indeed, it would be difficult to draft an intelligible and comprehensive definition. For this reason the Ontario Law Reform Commission did not recommend that the Legislature enact a statutory definition of "charity," but that the courts should continue to rely upon and develop the common law understanding of the term.[128] However, the Commission did adopt a working definition of "charity," namely,

> . . . a charitable act is an act whose form, effect and motive are the provision of the means of pursuing a common good — life, knowledge, play, religion, work, friendship, aesthetic experience, and practical reasonableness — to persons who are remote in affection and to whom no moral or legal obligation is owed.

---

126 See generally, *Native Communications Society of British Columbia v. Minister of National Revenue*, [1986] 3 F.C. 471, 1986 CarswellNat 361, 1986 CarswellNat 694, 86 D.T.C. 6353, 67 N.R. 146, [1986] 4 C.N.L.R. 79, [1986] 2 C.T.C. 170, 23 E.T.R. 210 (C.A.) and Ellen B. Zweibel, "A Truly Canadian Definition of Charity and a Lesson in Drafting Charitable Purposes: A Comment on Native Communications Society of BC v. MNR" (1987), 26 E.T.R. 41.

127 O.L.R.C. *Report on Charities*, at 174.

128 *Ibid.*, Chapter 7, and at 628, rec. 21.

While not perfect, this definition is a helpful statement of what charity is about. It is, therefore, useful to keep the definition in mind in considering the materials in this chapter.

Further Reading

Nigel P. Gravells, "Charitable Trusts and Ancillary Purposes" (1978), 42 Conv. 92.

Thomas Glyn Watkin, "Charity: The Purport of Purpose" (1978), 42 Conv. 277.

Harvey Cohen, "Charities — A Utilitarian Perspective" (1983), 36 Curr. Leg. Prob. 241.

Caroline J. Forder, "Too Political to be Charitable," [1984] Conv. 263.

Susan Bright, "Charity and Trusts for Public Benefit – Time for a Re-Think?", [1989] Conv. 28

Maurice C. Cullity, Q.C., "The Myth of Charitable Activities" (1990-91), 10 E. & T.J. 7.

E. Blake Bromley, "Contemporary Philanthropy — Is the Legal Concept of 'Charity' Any Longer Adequate?" in Donovan W.M. Waters, ed., *Equity, Fiduciaries and Trusts*, (Toronto: Carswell, 1993) at 59.

Blake Bromley, "Answering the Broadbent Question: The Case for a Common Law Definition of Charity" (1999), 19 E.T. & P.J. 21.

David G. Amy, "Foreign Activities by Canadian Charities" (2000), 15 Philantrop., No. 3, 41.

Richard Bridge, "The Law of Advocacy by Charitable Organizations: The Case for Change" (2002), 21 E.T. & P.J. 92, 17 Philanthrop., No. 2, 2.

4. THE HEADS OF CHARITY[129]

(a) Relief of Poverty

Relief of poverty is represented in the preamble to the *Statute of Charitable Uses*[130] by the reference to the relief of poor people. That reference is contained in the phrase "relief of aged, impotent and poor people." It might seem, therefore, that the relief of the aged and the impotent, that is, the incapacitated and handicapped, is also comprehended under this head. That is not so. Relief of the aged and impotent falls under the fourth head.

The triad is, thus, construed disjunctively, with the result that a trust for the aged is charitable even though the aged are not necessarily poor. For example, a trust for the benefit of old women of the working classes is charitable as being for the relief of the aged.[131]

In many cases, however, the intended beneficiaries are poor as well as old or impotent and the courts often do not bother to determine which head of charity the trust falls under. Indeed, it could fall under both the first and the fourth heads.

---

129 See further, O.L.R.C. *Report on Charities*, Chapter 8.

130 1601 (43 Eliz. 1), c. 4.

131 *Re Glyn's Will Trusts*, [1950] 2 All E.R. 1150n; *Re Robinson* (1950), [1951] Ch. 198, [1950] 2 All E.R. 1148; *Re Angell Estate*, (1955), 63 Man. R. 401, 1955 CarswellMan 44, 16 W.W.R. 342 (Q.B.).

Usually it does not matter that the classification is not made, but there may be situations in which it is significant. This is because, as we shall see, the requirement of public benefit is much less for the first head than for the fourth.[132] The same problem exists with some trusts for children. Normally these would fall under the fourth head, but can fall under the first if one of their objects is to benefit poor children.

Further, merely because an organization helps the poor in the sense that it provides services to the poor for free, it is not necessarily charitable. It will not be if its object is not the relief of poverty *per se*, but some other purpose. A family planning organization was held not to be charitable for municipal tax purposes on this ground.[133]

"Poverty" is a relative term. It does not just connote destitution in law, but can also describe limited means.[134] The word merely implies that in regard to a person's station in life, he or she is in straitened circumstances.[135] The terms "needy," "indigent" and "destitute" are synonyms of the word "poor." Thus, for example, a home for indigent bachelors and widowers of 55 years of age and over,[136] a residence for ladies of limited means,[137] a trust for the relief of "distressed gentlefolk,"[138] and a trust for ladies in reduced circumstances having an income

---

132 Waters, at 552.

133 *Re Planned Parenthood of Toronto and City of Toronto* (1980), 29 O.R. (2d) 289, 113 D.L.R. (3d) 218 (C.A.). The court applied the "controlling purpose" test by narrowing the meaning of "relief of the poor" by emphasizing the need for evidence of economic deprivation. See *Canadian Centre for Torture Victims (Toronto) Inc. v. Ontario Regional Assessment Commissioner, Region No. 9* (1998), 36 O.R. (3d) 743, 1998 CarswellOnt 406 (Gen. Div.), which cited *Re Planned Parenthood* as a case in which there was no evidence that those who benefited from the services of the organization were poor. The *Canadian Center* case involved an institution incorporated to care for persons who had been tortured. The center provided its clients with basic tools and skills to enable them to become financially self-sufficient as well as mentally and physically able to care for themselves and their families. The court found that this institution was organized for the relief of the poor because the modern approach to relieving the poor is a multidimensional one which seeks to provide something part from the basic necessaries of life such as food, shelter and clothing. The institution therefore qualified for the taxation exemption. See also *Family Service Assn. of Metropolitan Toronto v. Ontario Regional Assessment Commissioner, Region No. 9* (1995), [1995] O.J. No. 2133, 1995 CarswellOnt 850, 23 O.R. (3d) 382 (Gen. Div.). This organization also qualified for the taxation exemption because it was organized for "relief of the poor." Contrast *Canadian Mental Health Assn. v. Ontario Property Assessment Corp.*, [2002] O.J. No. 2199, 2002 CarswellOnt 2568, 31 M.P.L.R. (3d) 79 (S.C.J.) in which the property of the association, which was incorporated as a charitable institution, did not fall under the exemption from taxation because its primary purpose was to improve the treatment and rehabilitation services for the mentally ill. Access to the association's services was based on mental illness, not financial status (*i.e.*, poverty).

134 *Jones v. T. Eaton Co.* (sub nom. Re Bethel), [1971] 2 O.R. 316 at 330, 17 D.L.R. (3d) 652 (C.A.), affirmed, [1973] S.C.R. 635, 35 D.L.R. (3d) 97.

135 *Re Coulthurst's Will Trusts*, [1951] Ch. 661 at 665, [1951] 1 All E.R. 774 (C.A.), *per* Sir Raymond Evershed M.R.

136 *Weir v. Crum-Brown*, [1908] A.C. 162 (H.L.).

137 *Re Gordon*, [1914] 1 Ch. 662 (C.A.).

138 *Re Young* (1950), [1951] Ch. 344, [1950] 2 All E.R. 1245.

between £25 and £50 a year[139] have been held to be charitable. Even a trust to provide "luxuries" to the inmates of a poor house has been held charitable.[140] By contrast, a trust to provide a holiday fund for workers at a textile firm was held not charitable, even though the workers earned very small wages.[141] It seems, therefore, that if a person is employed, he or she is by definition not poor.[142]

In order to be charitable a trust for the relief of poverty must meet the public benefit requirement. Under this head the benefit element is satisfied virtually automatically, but the public element must be established. Thus, for example, a private gift to a poor person is not "charitable" in the legal sense; nor is a trust for named poor persons.[143] In those situations the public aspect is lacking, although the benefit element clearly exists. To be valid, a trust for the relief of poverty must benefit a section of the community.

Under relief of poverty, however, there is an important exception to the principle that there be public benefit. This exception derives from the "poor relations" cases. These cases hold that a charitable trust for one's poor relations is charitable despite the beneficiaries' personal nexus to the donor. An important case in this respect is *Re Scarisbrick, Cockshutt v. Public Trustee*.[144] A testatrix left (in events which happened) one-half of the residue of her estate upon trust "for such relations" of her son and two daughters as in the opinion of the survivor of the son and daughters "shall be in needy circumstances" and as the survivor should appoint. The court held that the word "relations" was not restricted to the statutory next-of-kin of the son and daughters, but extended to relations in any degree. This was significant, for a class comprising only the next-of-kin would be the equivalent of a gift to the members of the class *nominatim* and, thus, lack the public element. However, as construed by the court, the class was sufficiently wide to avoid that problem.

A further problem had to be resolved then. Before the case reached the courts, the "poor relations" cases had all involved perpetual trusts. This one was for immediate distribution. That made it effectively a gift to ascertainable persons, it was argued, and therefore the public element was missing. Jenkins L.J. held otherwise. He said:[145]

> If a gift or trust on its true construction does extend to those in need amongst relations in every degree, even though it provides for immediate distribution, then, inasmuch as the class of potential beneficiaries becomes so wide as to be incapable of exhaustive ascertainment, the impersonal quality, if I may so describe it, supplied in continuing gifts by the element of perpetuity, is equally present.

---

139 *Trustees of Mary Clark House v. Anderson*, [1904] 2 K.B. 645. See also *Re De Carteret*, [1933] Ch. 103, a maximum income of £120 per annum.
140 *Brown v. Brown* (1900), 32 O.R. 323 (H.C.).
141 *Re Drummond*, [1914] 2 Ch. 90.
142 *Re Saunders' Will Trusts*, [1954] Ch. 265.
143 *Re Scarisbrick, Cockshutt v. Public Trustee*, [1951] Ch. 622 at 650-651, [1951] 1 All E.R. 822 (C.A.), *per* Jenkins L.J.
144 *Ibid.*
145 *Ibid.*, at 655.

In *Keshen v. Ferguson*,[146] the Nova Scotia Supreme Court followed *Re Scarisbrick*. The testatrix gave the income of the residue of her estate in trust "for the support and maintenance, and assistance of my poor and needy relatives" for a period of 20 years. The court held the gift charitable since it was a trust to be executed over a period of time among a class of persons which was not restricted to the testatrix's next-of-kin. The court did seem to suggest in *dicta* that a trust for immediate distribution among a testator's relations would be confined to his or her next-of-kin. We submit that this is not correct. *Scarisbrick* makes it clear that it is a matter of construction; only if the testator intended to restrict the class to her or his next-of-kin, which is admittedly the *prima facie* construction, would the gift not be charitable.

More recently the "poor relations" exception has been extended to "poor employees," that is, to trusts in favour of needy employees of a company. Such a trust was upheld by the English Court of Appeal in *Gibson v. South American Stores (Gath & Chaves) Ltd.*[147] Similarly, in *Re Massey Estate*[148] Wells J. held that a trust for the benefit of employees of Massey-Harris Co. Ltd. was charitable. The trust was intended to provide financial relief for employees, retired employees, and their dependants.[149] This position was subsequently adopted by the House of Lords in *Dingle v. Turner*[150] and by the Supreme Court of Canada in *Jones v. T. Eaton Co.*[151] The latter is reproduced below.

JONES v. T. EATON CO.

[1973] S.C.R. 635, 35 D.L.R. (3d) 97
Supreme Court of Canada

The testator, Francis Bethel, made his will during the depression in the 1930s. He directed his executors to pay the following legacy:

> To the Executive Officers of The T. Eaton Company Limited, Toronto, to be used by them as a trust fund for any needy or deserving Toronto members of the Eaton Quarter Century Club as the said Executive Officers in their absolute discretion may decide, the sum of Fifty thousand dollars.

---

146 (*Sub. nom. Re Cohen Estate*) [1952] 3 D.L.R. 833 (N.S. T.D.).

147 (1950), [1950] Ch. 177, [1949] 2 All E.R. 985 (C.A.). The question whether the anomalous exception of "poor relations" should be upheld and whether their extension to "poor employees" was valid, was raised in *Oppenheim v. Tobacco Securities Trust Co.* (1950), [1951] A.C. 297 at 309, [1951] 1 All E.R. 31 (H.L.), but did not have to be decided in that case. *Oppenheim* involved a trust for the education of employees.

148 [1959] O.R. 608, [1959] O.W.N. 373, 21 D.L.R. (2d) 477 (H.C.).

149 See also *Re Cox*, [1950] O.R. 137, [1950] 2 D.L.R. 449 (H.C.), reversed [1951] O.R. 205, [1951] 2 D.L.R. 326 (C.A.), the Court of Appeal holding that the exception did not extend to "poor employees," affirmed [1953] 1 S.C.R. 94, [1953] 1 D.L.R. 577, affirmed [1955] A.C. 627, [1955] 2 All E.R. 550, 16 W.W.R. 49, [1955] 3 D.L.R. 497 (P.C.), the Privy Council holding that the trust was not restricted to relief of poverty, so that the common employment nexus caused the trust to fail.

150 *Supra*, note 85.

151 *Supra*, note 2.

The Timothy Eaton Quarter Century Club was an unincorporated association of persons. Employees of The T. Eaton Co. Ltd. became members of the Club after 25 years of service with the company. The Club's main function was to present certificates and watches to employees when they became members. Many members no longer resided in Toronto, but had been transferred or moved elsewhere. Approximately 3,500 persons who had worked for the company for 25 years until they retired were still living. Another 3,500, more or less, who had worked for the company for 25 years, were still employed by the company. The number of persons who were members of the Club but left the company prior to their retirement was unknown.

The executors brought an application to interpret the will. Grant J. held the bequest to be non-charitable.[152] A majority of the Ontario Court of Appeal reversed.[153] A further appeal was then brought.

SPENCE J. delivered the judgment of the court:

> [The first issue was whether the trust was exclusively charitable. "Needy" is charitable but, it was argued, "deserving" is not. Since the trustees could give all the money to deserving persons, the entire trust should fail. His Lordship disagreed:]

In my opinion, I need not deal with the first argument because I am ready to hold that this particular testator making this will on the date and under the circumstances that he did make it was expressing a charitable intent when he used the word "deserving." It is true that the word "deserving" [can be interpreted as having no meaning because it is too vague].

However, it is perfectly proper to interpret the words of a will in the context of that will and when the words are ambiguous it is proper to consider the factual situation in which the testator wrote those words. . . .

. . .

The testator executed his will in 1934 when the economic depression was far from its termination and died in 1936 when there still was a very considerable degree of economic depression. Even at that time, the number of employees of the T. Eaton Company Limited who had served the company for 25 years must have been very large. It would be inevitable that some of those members, particularly the ones who had retired from service with the company, might well become "needy or deserving." Even if such members were not so poverty stricken as being properly describable as "needy," illness of the member himself or of some member of his family, financial misfortune, or family tragedy might well justify in describing his condition as "deserving."

---

152 (Sub nom. *Re Bethel*), [1970] 3 O.R. 745, 14 D.L.R. (3d) 129 (H.C.).
153 (Sub nom. *Re Bethel Estate*), [1971] 2 O.R. 316, 17 D.L.R. (3d) 652 (C.A.). Gale C.J.O. dissented.

The testator's will was very carefully drafted with a most specific series of testamentary trust clauses.

. . .

Therefore, I think that a view attributing to the word "deserving," one of the non-charitable meanings which have been suggested throughout the argument here and below, would fail to do justice under these circumstances to the testator's very evident ability and intent. It has been well said that a rational meaning should be given to every word in the testator's will if it is possible and that capricious or whimsical intent should be avoided unless the words require it.[154]

. . .

It has been suggested that a member of the Timothy Eaton Quarter Century Club may be considered as deserving because of merit, industry, intelligence, imagination, honesty, sobriety and even punctuality, or loyalty, but it must be remembered that the testator was not directing a distribution of the funds of the T. Eaton Company Limited which might well have been interested in the exhibition by its employees of any of those virtues but was directing the disposal of his own estate and I find it hard to believe that he would consider any retired members of the T. Eaton Quarter Century Club to be "deserving" because he had been punctual or loyal. I am of the opinion that the only proper interpretation of the words "or deserving" following the word "needy" and as used by this testator at the time he did use it means a person who although not actually poverty stricken was nevertheless in a state of financial depression, perhaps as I said due to a sudden emergency and that his purpose is sufficient to qualify as a charitable trust.[155]

I have therefore, with respect, come to the conclusion as expressed by Jessup J.A. in his majority reasons for the Court of Appeal for Ontario:[156]

> In my opinion, therefore, the intention of the testator, by his use of the word "deserving," must be taken to benefit not only the necessitous whom he designated by the word "needy" but also those of moderate means who might require financial assistance in the exigencies from time to time arising.

Having come to the conclusion that the provision in the will constitutes a trust for the relief of poverty, I have now to determine whether it is valid in view of the fact that the possible beneficiaries do not include every member of the public but only the Toronto members of the Timothy Eaton Quarter Century Club. As I have pointed out, that limitation is far from confining as according to the evidence of the secretary-treasurer of the Timothy Eaton Company Limited it

---

154 Halsbury's Laws of England, 3rd ed., vol. 39 at 973ff. and 986-987.
155 *Re Clark*, [1901] 2 Ch. 110; *Re Coulthurst's Will Trusts*, [1951] Ch. 661 at 665-666, [1951] 1 All E.R. 774, *per* Evershed M.R.
156 *Supra*, note 153, at 330.

would include at least 7,000 persons and so might be considered to apply to a significant portion of the general public. I need not however rest my view as to the validity of the trust upon that ground for I am of the opinion that when a trust is not only charitable in the sense outlined by Lord Macnaghten in *Commissioners for Special Purposes of Income Tax v. Pemsel*,[157] but is a trust for one of those four purposes, *i.e.*, for the relief of poverty, then the courts have not required the element of public benefit in order to declare in favour of the validity of the trust.

[His Lordship considered a number of the cases we referred to above and continued:]

Finally, the House of Lords have dealt with this matter in *Dingle v. Turner*.[158] There the testator had made a disposition of his estate by the direction to the trustees to invest a sum of money and hold it in the name of certain pension fund trustees upon a trust to apply the income in paying pensions to poor employees of E. Dingle & Company Limited, who were of the age of 60 years at least or being of the age of 45 at least and were incapacitated from earning their living by reason of some physical or mental infirmity. The House of Lords affirming the judgment of Megarry J. held that the trust was a charitable trust. Lord Cross, giving the main opinion, referred *inter alia*[159] to the decision of the Judicial Committee in *Re Cox*,[160] and expressed the same view of it that I have expressed heretofore. . . . Lord Cross said:[161]

> But the "poor members" and "poor employees" decisions were a natural development of the "poor relations" decisions and to draw distinction between different sorts of "poverty" trusts would be quite illogical and could certainly not be said to be introducing "greater harmony" into the law of charity. Moreover, although not as old, the "poor relations" trust and "poor employee" trusts have been recognized as charities for many years; there are now a large number of such trusts in existence; and assuming, as one must, that they are properly administered in the sense that benefits under them are only given to people who are fairly to be said to be, according to current standards, "poor persons" to treat such trusts as charities is not open to any practical objection. So it seems to me that it must be accepted that wherever else it may hold sway, the *Compton*[162] rule has no application in the field of a trust for the relief of poverty and that there the dividing line between a charitable trust and a private trust lies where the Court of Appeal drew it in *Re Scarisbrick*.[163]

I have therefore come to the conclusion that this court should not find the trust in the will under consideration in this court invalid as a charitable trust for the relief of poverty simply on the ground that the public generally is not benefited.

I, therefore, am of the view that the bequest was a valid charitable bequest.

---

157 [1891] A.C. 531, 3 Tax Cas. 53, [1891-94] All E.R. Rep. 28 (H.L.).
158 *Supra*, note 85.
159 *Ibid.*, at 887.
160 *Supra*, note 149.
161 *Supra*, note 85, at 888.
162 *Re Compton*, [1945] Ch. 123, [1945] 1 All E.R. 198 (C.A.). The *Compton* rule was described above.
163 [1951] Ch. 623, [1951] 1 All E.R. 822 (C.A.).

. . .

It is . . . a matter of some little difficulty to determine the meaning of the words "Toronto members." I am of the opinion that the words must be interpreted in the light of the test as cited by Lord Wilberforce in *McPhail v. Doulton*,[164] that the trust is valid if it can be said with certainty that any given individual is or is not a member of a class.

[His Lordship thought that the expression "Toronto members" referred to the members of the club employed by the company in Toronto when they became members. It did not matter that they actually lived in Toronto, or continued to live there.

The court dismissed the appeal.]

Notes and Questions

1. In the *Jones* case Spence J. applied the certainty of objects test enunciated by the House of Lords in *McPhail v. Doulton*,[165] discussed elsewhere.[166] Is that test relevant in the context of a charitable trust?

2. A testatrix devised certain property to trustees to establish a retirement home and provided an endowment for the home. The home was intended to "provide board, lodging, and medical aid" for Protestant residents of Canada who were "in reduced circumstances and in need of and . . . most deserving" of the home in the opinion of the trustees. Residents were to pay for their accommodation according to their ability. In fact, the rent was fixed according to size and facilities and no means test was applied for admission. Most residents had some private financial resources. The home's operating costs were paid partly from the endowment and partly from the rents paid by the residents. The rents were comparable to those charged by similar institutions. Virtually all residents were 65 years of age or older.
Is the institution for the relief of poverty? If not, is it otherwise charitable?[167]

3. A testator left the residue of his estate on trust for "such Protestant homes or institutions for the care and welfare of children [as] my trustee . . . shall select."
Is it arguable that this trust is for the relief of poverty, considering that it does not, in terms, refer to poverty?[168]

4. Is a trust for the relief of impoverished members of The Law Society of Upper Canada valid?[169]

5. In *Dingle v. Turner*,[170] followed in the *Jones* case, Lord Cross argued that the state might wish to accord some of the benefits which charities enjoy, such as indefinite duration

---

164 (1970), [1971] A.C. 424 at 456, [1970] 2 All E.R. 228 (H.L.).
165 *Ibid.*
166 In the chapter on the creation of express trusts.
167 See *Maria F. Ganong Old Folks Home v. New Brunswick (Minister of Municipal Affairs)* (1981), 12 E.T.R 69, 129 D.L.R. (3d) 655, 37 N.B.R. (2d) 225, 97 A.P.R. 225 (C.A.).
168 See *Re Ryan*, [1972] 4 W.W.R. 593, (sub nom. Canada Permanent Trust Co. v. MacFarlane) 27 D.L.R. (3d) 480 (B.C. C.A.).
169 See *Re Denison Estate* (1974), 2 O.R. (2d) 308, 42 D.L.R. (3d) 652 (H.C.).
170 *Supra*, note 85, at 604.

and the relaxed certainty requirement, upon certain charities, while denying them other benefits, such as tax relief. This is, at least potentially, already the case in Canada because of the divided jurisdiction over property and civil rights and income taxation. Provincial law defines "charity" and confers various benefits upon charities, while Parliament confers tax relief upon charities. It generally follows the provincial definition, but need not do so. Is this kind of distinction desirable?

(b) Advancement of Religion

The only item in the preamble to the *Statute of Charitable Uses*[171] which concerns the advancement of religion is "the repair of churches." We have seen that this was because, at that time, the Church of England was the only recognized religion, all others being illegal. The limited reference to religion in the preamble did not mean, however, that only gifts to repair churches were charitable. The term "charity" was based in religion and it was well-understood that most matters concerning religion (at least of the established religion) were charitable.

The law, therefore, regards as charitable, not only gifts to repair or improve the fabric of churches, such as a memorial window[172] or a church bell,[173] but also burial grounds operated by churches.[174] Further, gifts to support ministers of religion are charitable,[175] as are missions conducted by churches.[176]

Sometimes gifts are made to religious advisors or religious corporations. If the gift is to a person by name, it is likely to be regarded as an absolute, private gift and, hence, not charitable. The gift may, however, be made to a person or corporation *virtute officii*. In that event the gift will be a valid charitable gift, provided that the person's duties or corporation's objects are exclusively charitable. We shall consider this issue later.

Religious toleration became official in England in the nineteenth century. In practice it happened earlier in Canada. Since religious toleration, trusts in favour of religions other than the established religion and the mainline churches have been charitable. Hence, the concept of religion is now quite wide; it embraces many faiths and sects, including non-Christian religions. In view of that, it is important to determine the meaning and scope of "religion."

It has been held in England that in order for a trust to be charitable under the head "advancement of religion," it must promote some form of "monotheistic theism."[177] Hence, polytheistic religions, or those that encourage ancestor worship, are not charitable. It followed in *Yeap Cheah Neo v. Ong Cheng Neo*[178] that a trust which directed that a house be erected by the testatrix's executors and

---

171 1601 (43 Eliz. 1), c. 4.
172 *Weatherby v. Weatherby* (1927), 53 N.B.R. 403 (K.B.).
173 *Re McConville Estate* (1926), 29 O.W.N. 347 (H.C.).
174 *Re Welton Estate*, [1950] 2 D.L.R. 280 (N.S. T.D.).
175 *Re Mountain Estate* (1912), 26 O.L.R. 163, 4 D.L.R. 737 (C.A.).
176 *Re Long Estate* (1930), 37 O.W.N. 351 (H.C.).
177 *Bowman v. Secular Society Ltd.*, [1917] A.C. 406 at 449 (H.L.), *per* Lord Parker of Waddington.
178 (1875), L.R. 6 P.C. 381 (P.C.).

dedicated for the performance of religious ceremonies to her late husband and herself was not charitable.

The Shorter Oxford English Dictionary defines "religion" as:

> . . . a particular system of faith and worship which involves the recognition on the part of man or some higher unseen power as having control of his destiny which is entitled to reverence and worship.

And in *United Grand Lodge of Ancient Free & Accepted Masons of England v. Holborn Borough Council*[179] Donovan J. said of "advancement of religion":[180]

> To advance religion means to promote it, to spread its message ever wider among mankind; to take some positive steps to sustain and increase religious beliefs; and these things are done in a variety of ways which may be comprehensively described as pastoral and missionary.

The Lodge did not meet that test; it promoted a system of ethics and encouraged a high standard of behaviour, but those objects did not constitute advancement of religion.

It may be supposed that Western society's predominant modern "religion," humanism, would also fail the test, since it is primarily a philosophy. This is evident from *Re South Place Ethical Society*.[181] That case involved an organization, whose members were agnostics, but not atheists, and which had as its objects "the study and dissemination of ethical principles and the cultivation of a rational religious sentiment." Dillon J. held that the organization did not advance religion and was, thus, not charitable under that head of charity.

In the course of his judgment he said:[182]

> Religion, as I see it, is concerned with man's relations with God, and ethics are concerned with man's relations with man. The two are not the same, and are not made the same by sincere inquiry into the question: what is God? If reason leads people not to accept Christianity or any known religion, but they do believe in the excellence of qualities such as truth, beauty and love, or believe in the platonic concept of the ideal, their beliefs may be to them the equivalent of a religion, but viewed objectively they are not religion.

and:[183]

> It seems to me that two of the essential attributes of religion are faith and worship; faith in a god and worship of that god.

---

179 [1957] 1 W.L.R. 1080, [1957] 3 All E.R. 281 (C.A.).

180 *Ibid.*, at 1090.

181 [1980] 1 W.L.R. 1565, [1980] 3 All E.R. 918.

182 *Ibid.*, at 1571.

183 *Ibid.*, at 1572. The Canada Customs and Revenue Agency recently denied charitable status to the Humanist Association of Toronto for similar reasons, holding that it did not qualify as a religion because its members did not "pray to a deity or supreme being". However, in an out-of-court settlement the agency subsequently granted charitable status to the Association under the fourth head of charity, holding that it was an organization "beneficial to the community as a whole." See Tom Blackwell, "Humanists Win Victory over Status: Standing up for 'Godless Masses'". National Post, 14 February, 2004.

However, he held the purposes of the Society to be charitable either under the head of education, or the fourth head of charity.

It is doubtful that these strictures are accepted to the same extent on the North American continent. Although the Church of England was the established church in a number of jurisdictions, voluntarism prevailed at an early date. Moreover, the Church of Rome was well-established in other jurisdictions, particularly in Quebec. At the time of the disestablishment of the Church of England in Upper Canada,[184] a statute was passed which recognized the principle of voluntarism and assured the free exercise of religious worship. This Act was first passed in 1852[185] and was last consolidated in 1897.[186] Part of the Act was subsequently re-enacted as the *Religious Freedom Act*[187] and it is reproduced below.

Nonetheless, it will continue to be difficult to decide in a particular situation whether a new sect is charitable. Such issues arise with amazing regularity. They may concern Jones's Peoples Temple (which resulted in the mass murder and suicide of some 900 adherents in the jungles of Guyana), a self-styled guru who establishes a sect in the wilds of Oregon (where he leads an extravagant life style and is forced to flee when investigated for tax evasion), a "Church of Bacchus" (which is to all intents and purposes a restaurant located in an area of a city where churches are allowed, but restaurants not permitted), or organizations which allegedly use brainwashing techniques to the higher glory of their "gods" while appropriating their disciples' assets. On the other hand, they may involve legitimate sects whose tenets are out of tune with those of the majority.

The nadir of the acceptance of cults as charitable was surely reached when an English court held the works of Joanna Southcote to be charitable. In *Thornton v. Howe*[188] a testatrix bequeathed the residue of her estate upon trust for the printing, publishing, and propagation of the works of Joanna Southcote. The latter believed that she was with child by the Holy Ghost at an advanced age in life, that a second Shilo or Messiah would be born of her and that she was selected by the Holy Ghost to pass divine revelations on to mankind. One would not have thought that her works were Christian, although the court seemed to think so. Sir John Romilly M.R. noted that the law does not make any distinction between one sect and another and opined that, since the purpose of the trust was to propagate a religion, the trust was charitable.[189]

---

184 Whether this church was indeed ever the established church in Upper Canada has been a matter of debate among historians. The point is discussed in A.H. Oosterhoff, "The Law of Mortmain: An Historical and Comparative Review" (1977), 27 U. of T.L.J. 257 at 305-306.

185 S.C. 1852, c. 175.

186 R.S.O. 1897, c. 306.

187 R.S.O. 1990, c. R.22.

188 (1862), 31 Beav. 14, 54 E.R. 1042. See similarly *Knight, Re*, [1937] O.R. 462, 1937 CarswellOnt 22, [1937] 2 D.L.R. 285 (H.C.); *Cameron v. Church of Christ, Scientist, supra*, note 78.

189 The trust in fact failed, because the property included realty and was, thus, void under the *Statute of Mortmain, 1736*, (9 Geo. 2), c. 36. G.K. Chesterton's reputed aphorism seems particularly apt here: "When people cease to believe in God it is commonly supposed that they believe in nothing. But the truth is much more sinister. They believe in anything." See Elizabeth M. Knowles, ed., *The Oxford Dictionary of Twentieth Century Quotations* (Oxford University Press, 1998), 67. And see Ro 1:21.

Regarding the public benefit requirement, it appears that, in general, the law presumes public benefit once it is shown that the trust satisfies the "religion" test. The courts can hardly do otherwise. Religion is a matter of faith, something the efficacy or validity of which cannot be measured in a court of law. Moreover, it would seem that the requirement under the fourth head of charity that the beneficiaries must not be negligible in number is not so important under the third head: a relatively small number of persons may form a church and it will be held charitable.

The public element is, thus, presumed, since it is assumed, unless otherwise shown, that all religions are open to a sufficiently broad segment of society. Generally, the benefit element is also presumed, but the opposite may be proved. This is illustrated by *Gilmour v. Coats*,[190] reproduced below.

Further Reading

Hubert Picarda, "New Religions and Charities" (1981), 131 New L.J. 436.

J.P. Moore, "Piercing the Religious Veil of the So-Called Cults" (1979-80), 7 Pepperdine L.R. 665.

Kathryn Bromley, "The Advancement of Religion in the Age of Fundamental Human Rights" (2000), 16 Philanthrop., No, 2, 74, (2001), 16 Philanthrop., No. 3, 193.

Carl Juneau, "Is Religion Passé as a Charity?" (2002), 17 Philanthrop., No. 2, 34.

RELIGIOUS FREEDOM ACT

R.S.O. 1990, c. R.22

WHEREAS the recognition of legal equality among all religious denominations is an admitted principle of Provincial legislation; And whereas, in the state and condition of this Province, to which such principle is peculiarly applicable, it is desirable that the same should receive the sanction of direct legislative authority, recognizing and declaring the same as a fundamental principle of the civil policy of this Province:

Therefore, Her Majesty, by and with the advice and consent of the Legislative Assembly of the Province of Ontario, enacts as follows:

1. The free exercise and enjoyment of religious profession and worship, without discrimination or preference, provided the same be not made an excuse for acts of licentiousness, or a justification of practices inconsistent with the peace and safety of the Province, is by the constitution and laws of this Province assured to all Her Majesty's subjects within the same.

---

190 [1949] A.C. 426, [1949] 1 All E.R. 848 (H.L.).

GILMOUR v. COATS

[1949] A.C. 426, [1949] 1 All E.R. 848
House of Lords

The respondent, Evelyn Coats, made a settlement in 1946 whereby she gave £500 to trustees upon trust for a Roman Catholic priory if its purposes were charitable, and upon trust for an alternative beneficiary if they were not.

The priory, a discalced Carmelite convent, was a purely contemplative order. The nuns in the priory devoted their lives to prayer, contemplation, and penance. They did not engage in works outside the walls of the priory.

The trustees took out an originating summons to determine whether the purposes of the Carmelite Priory were charitable. The real issue was whether these purposes involved a public benefit.

Evidence was submitted to the court, by means of affidavits of the prioress of the community and a cardinal, respecting the doctrine of the Roman Catholic Church. In summary, this doctrine is that those who follow the contemplative life obtain the benefit of sanctification for themselves. Further, by their intercessory prayers and the example of self denial they set in their lives (the purpose of which is to attain greater love of God and union with him), they also benefit members of the public both within and outside the church in bringing about their spiritual improvement.

At first instance, Jenkins J. held that the purposes were not charitable. His decision was affirmed by the Court of Appeal.[191] Ethel Gilmour, the prioress, appealed to the House of Lords.

LORD REID:

. . .

Mr. Russell for the appellant submitted three grounds on each of which he argued that the appellant is entitled to succeed: if none of these three grounds is valid the appeal must fail. His main argument was that a court is entitled to accept the belief of Roman Catholics that spiritual benefit to mankind flows from intercessory prayer as sufficient to establish the necessary element of public benefit. It was not suggested that the effect of prayer is capable of legal proof by evidence. No temporal court of law can determine the truth of any religious belief: it is not competent to investigate any such matter and it ought not to attempt to do so. How then does the law deal with a question like that now in issue?

The leading authority cited by Mr. Russell was *O'Hanlon v. Logue*.[192] In that case it was held, on a reconsideration of the older Irish authorities, that the celebration of Mass in private was a charitable purpose.

---

191 (Sub nom. *Re Coats' Trust, Coats v. Gilmour*), [1948] Ch. 340.
192 [1906] 1 I.R. 247.

[His Lordship refused to follow this case and rejected the arguments presented and accepted in it, namely, (1) a gift is charitable if the donor believes it to be for the advancement of religion; (2) gifts for the saying of masses in private was charitable before the Reformation and resumed that character when religious toleration became law in 1793; (3) divine service is, by virtue of spiritual efficacy, a charitable act, whether conducted in public or in private; and (4) the law holds that public benefit flows from divine worship because it accepts as true the beliefs of the worshippers.]

The law of England has always shown favour to gifts for religious purposes. It does not now in this matter prefer one religion to another. It assumes that it is good for man to have and to practise a religion but where a particular belief is accepted by one religion and rejected by another the law can neither accept nor reject it. The law must accept the position that it is right that different religions should each be supported irrespective of whether or not all its beliefs are true. A religion can be regarded as beneficial without it being necessary to assume that all its beliefs are true, and a religious service can be regarded as beneficial to all those who attend it without it being necessary to determine the spiritual efficacy of that service or to accept any particular belief about it. Admittedly public benefit in the present case can only be established if the court is entitled to accept and act on the beliefs of the Roman Catholic Church. This would, in my view, now be something new.

In *Cocks v. Manners*,[193] there was a gift to a community which belonged to a contemplative order of the Roman Catholic Church and in that case that gift was held not to be a charitable gift because it lacked the necessary element of public benefit. The only difference between that case and the present case is that in that case there was no evidence of the teaching of the Roman Catholic Church about the efficacy of intercessory prayer or of the special place which these orders occupy in that church. . . .

. . .

Before passing to the second argument I should notice the case of *Re Caus*.[194] In that case Luxmoore J. held following *O'Hanlon v. Logue* that a bequest for private Masses was a good charitable gift. There are grounds on which it can be argued that such a gift is charitable which do not apply to the present case. I express no opinion whether this decision can be supported on these grounds. But in my view it cannot be supported on the ground that a court is entitled to accept the beliefs of Roman Catholics or the teaching of the Roman Catholic Church regarding the Mass as sufficient to establish the necessary element of public benefit.

Mr. Russell's second argument . . . must be considered on the footing that it has already been decided that the necessary element of public benefit cannot be

---

193 (1871), L.R. 12 Eq. 574.
194 [1934] Ch. 162.

directly established under the first argument — otherwise the appellant would succeed without this argument. Mr. Russell relies on a passage in the judgment of Wickens V.-C. in *Cocks v. Manners*:[195]

> It is said, in some of the cases, that religious purposes are charitable, but that can only be true as to religious services tending directly or indirectly towards the instruction or the edification of the public.

He says that it is proved by evidence that the public or at least a sufficient section of the public are edified. I doubt whether Wickens V.-C. meant to use the word edification in this sense. But whether he did or not there must be some limit to the kind of indirect instruction or edification which will constitute a public benefit. It is hard to imagine any form of religious activity by an organized religious body which does not have some effect of this kind, and if the words were applied literally the requirement of public benefit would virtually disappear. Mr. Russell admitted that it must be a question of degree whether or not in any case the public benefit is too remote. In this case I think it is too remote. Moreover, I do not think that, when a decision has stood for three-quarters of a century as *Cocks v. Manners* has, it ought to be reversed on a question of degree of this kind. No broad principle is here involved. . . .

The third argument submitted by Mr. Russell is of a different character. It was not submitted to the Court of Appeal. It is that the existence of this community enables some 20 women to practise religion in a way which would otherwise be impossible for them; and that, if the law recognizes the practice of religion as beneficial, it must regard any gift to enable religion to be practised more fully as a gift for a beneficial purpose. On this argument the necessary element of public benefit is found in the fact that the 20 persons benefited are not drawn from any limited class but from the whole body of Roman Catholic women who have a vocation for a contemplative life. I am prepared to assume that, if the law can regard the purposes of this community as beneficial, the necessary element of public benefit could be so found. But this argument, like the last, can only be reached after the appellant has failed on the first argument and it has therefore been decided that the law is disabled from recognizing any public benefit resulting from the existence of the community. Mr. Russell when asked was unable to cite any authority to the effect that it can be a valid charitable purpose to assist persons to do something which cannot be shown to have any public utility. In the absence of authority I can see no reason why this should be regarded as a valid charitable purpose and therefore I think that this argument fails.

[Lord Simonds and Lord du Parq delivered concurring speeches. Lord Norman and Lord Morton of Henryton concurred.

In the course of his speech, Lord Simonds said:[196]

---

195 *Supra*, note 193, at 585.
196 *Supra*, note 190, at 446.

My Lords, I would speak with all respect and reverence of those who spend their lives in cloistered piety, and in this House of Lords Spiritual and Temporal, which daily commences its proceedings with intercessory prayers, how can I deny that the Divine Being may in His wisdom think fit to answer them? But, my Lords, whether I affirm or deny, whether I believe or disbelieve, what has that to do with the proof which the court demands that a particular purpose satisfies the test of benefit to the community? Here is something which is manifestly not susceptible of proof. But, then it is said, this is a matter not of proof but of belief: for the value of intercessory prayer is a tenet of the Catholic faith, therefore in such prayer there is benefit to the community. But it is just at this "therefore" that I must pause. It is, no doubt, true that the advancement of religion is, generally speaking, one of the heads of charity. But it does not follow from this that the court must accept as proved whatever a particular church believes. The faithful must embrace their faith believing where they cannot prove: the court can act only on proof. A gift to two or ten or a hundred cloistered nuns in the belief that their prayers will benefit the world at large does not from that belief alone derive validity any more than does the belief of any other donor for any other purpose. The importance of this case leads me to state my opinion in my own words but, having read again the judgment of the learned Master of the Rolls, I will add that I am in full agreement with what he says on this part of the case.

The House dismissed the appeal.]

Notes and Questions

1. In *Gilmour v. Coats* Lord Reid noted that the Irish cases were not *ad idem* on the question whether a gift to a contemplative religious order was charitable. Legislation in the Irish Republic may have settled the issue. The Irish *Charities Act*[197] provides[198] that it shall be conclusively presumed that a gift made for the advancement of religion "includes and will occasion public benefit." Moreover, the Act provides[199] that a gift for the advancement of religion is to be construed "in accordance with the laws, canons, ordinances and tenets of the religion concerned." Hence, the legislation replaces the objective test in *Gilmour* with a subjective one.[200]

Would such legislation be suitable for a pluriform society such as exists in Canada? Would it be desirable?

2. In *Gilmour v. Coats* it was pointed out that the House of Lords held in *Bourne v. Keane*[201] that the saying of masses are no longer regarded in law as superstitious. Hence, a gift to a church for that purpose is valid. A Canadian case had earlier come to the same

---

197 Stats. Ireland 1961, No. 17.
198 *Ibid.*, s. 45(1).
199 *Ibid.*, s. 45(2).
200 See Keeton and Sheridan, at 91-92.
201 [1919] A.C. 815 (H.L.).

conclusion.[202] However, those cases involved absolute gifts. In *Re Hallisy*[203] the Ontario Court of Appeal assumed that a trust to say masses for the repose of the souls of the testator, his wife and children, in perpetuity, was, therefore, charitable. That, of course, does not necessarily follow. If such masses are said in private, the trust would not be charitable if *Gilmour v. Coats* is correct and followed in Canada.

Is it relevant in deciding whether such a trust is charitable that a large proportion of the population belongs to the church in question?[204]

3. *Re Hetherington (deceased); Gibbs v. McDonnell*[205] is an English case on point. A testatrix left a bequest to a Roman Catholic bishop for saying masses for the repose of the souls of herself and her relations. The court held that a gift for the saying of masses is *prima facie* charitable because it is for a religious purpose. It accepted evidence that such masses would be celebrated in public (at least in the sense that the public would be free to attend). Hence, the necessary public element was present.

4. The English Charity Commissioners followed *Gilmour v. Coats* in denying registration to the Church of Scientology. In their view, the practices of this organization did not fall under the heading of religion, since it did not carry on worship. Rather, its practices were conducted largely in private and were similar to counselling and were paid for by the adherents.[206]

5. A testator bequeathed the residue of his estate "to St. Bartholemew's Anglican Church, Fiddler's Green Road, London, Ontario, to be added to the endowment fund." In fact the Church had no endowment fund.

Is this gift charitable? If there had been an endowment fund, would you want to know its purposes before you can determine whether or not the gift is charitable?[207]

6. A testator made a gift to "the Baha'i Temple at Chicago, Illinois." Affidavit evidence established that the faith is "founded on the purest principles of piety and virtue and it is based on a belief in God and the universal brotherhood of man and makes its appeal to all men regardless of their colour, race, or creed." Is this gift charitable?[208]

7. T, who was a prisoner in a penitentiary, founded the "Church of the New Song." Most of the parishioners were fellow prisoners. They held various meetings at which the curtailment of their rights was discussed in a raucous manner. They also sought to hold a paschal feast for which they requested steak and wine from the prison authorities, but were refused. Can T's "church" be held to be charitable and, hence, the refusal a denial of his right to the free exercise of his religion?[209]

8. A similar argument was made by the self-styled Grand Druid of the Edmonton Grove of the Church of Reformed Druids. Police raided the "church" and found people drinking and playing darts in what appeared to be an after-hours drinking club. The Grand Druid claimed that the drinks were "Druid fluid," which was used in a religious sacrament

---

202 *Elmsley v. Madden* (1871), 18 Gr. 536 (Ont. Ch.).

203 [1932] O.R. 486, [1932] 4 D.L.R. 516 (C.A.), overruling *Re Zeagman* (1916), 38 O.L.R. 536 (H.C.).

204 *Re Hallisy, ibid.*, was followed without a discussion of the issues in *Re Samson* (1966), 59 D.L.R. (2d) 132 (N.S. S.C.). See further on this issue, Robert Ombres O.P., "Charitable Trusts in The Catholic Church in English Law," [1995] Law and Justice: The Christian Law Rev. 72.

205 [1989] 2 All E.R. 129 (Ch. Div.).

206 The decision is discussed by James Phillips in "Legal Developments" (2000), 16 Philanthrop., No. 1, 49 at 51.

207 See *St. Andrews-Wesley Church v. Toronto General Trusts Corp.*, [1948] S.C.R. 500, [1948] 4 D.L.R. 241 and 875.

208 See *Re Grand Estate* (1945), [1945] O.W.N. 782, [1946] 1 D.L.R. 204 (H.C.J.).

209 See *Theriault v. Silber* (1975), 391 Fed. Supp. 578.

and that the money paid by the drinkers was not the list price but an offering. The police laid charges of contravention of the liquor licence laws.[210]

9. The *Religious Organizations' Lands Act*[211] empowers certain enumerated religions to hold land in the name of trustees in perpetual succession for their religious purposes. The Act defines[212] "religious organization" as including:

> . . . an association of persons that is charitable according to the law of Ontario and that is organized for the advancement of and for the conduct of worship, services or rites of the Buddhist, Christian, Hindu, Islamic, Jewish, Baha'i, Longhouse Indian, Sikh, Unitarian or Zoroastrian faith, or a subdivision or denomination thereof.

Does this definition give the Province's imprimatur to the religions listed as being charitable?[213] There is similar legislation in other provinces, but none which gives a list of religions.[214]

(c) Advancement of Education

(i) *The Meaning of Education*

The head of charity, "advancement of education," comprises several items in the preamble to the *Statute of Charitable Uses*,[215] namely, "schools of learning, free schools, and scholars in universities; and education . . . of orphans."[216]

It is clear that the promotion of education as understood in the traditional sense of teacher instructing pupil in a formal classroom environment will be charitable, whether the school benefits the rich or the poor.[217] So also, any purpose which tends to promote or foster that type of instruction, such as the provision of a scholarship[218] or prize,[219] is charitable.

---

210 *The London Free Press*, Wednesday, November 2, 1994, at A7.

211 R.S.O. 1990, c. R.23.

212 *Ibid.*, s. 1(1).

213 It has been said that Buddhism is not charitable because it does not depend upon a belief in a supreme being: *R. v. Registrar General*, [1970] 2 Q.B. 697 at 707, [1970] 3 All E.R. 886 (C.A.), *per* Lord Denning M.R.

214 *Religious Congregations and Societies Act*, R.S.N.S. 1989, c. 395; *An Act Respecting Lands of Religious Congregations*, R.S.Q., c. T-7; *Religious Societies' Land Act*, R.S.A. 2000, c. R-15; *The Religious Societies Land Act Religious Societies' Lands Act*, R.S.M. 1987, c. R70; *The Religious Societies Land Act*, R.S.S. 1978, c. R-19; *Religious Societies Land Act*, R.S.N.W.T. 1988, c. R-4; *Trustee (Church Property) Act*, R.S.B.C. 1996, c. 465. See further A.H. Oosterhoff, "Religious Institutions and the Law in Ontario: An Historical Study of the Laws Enabling Religious Organizations to Hold Land" (1981), 13 Ottawa L. Rev. 441.

215 1601 (43 Eliz. 1), c. 4.

216 The preamble speaks of the "education and preferment of orphans." Preferment in this context means to advance orphans in life. It falls under the fourth head.

217 *Re Hedgman* (1870), 8 Ch. D. 156 (C.A.), a school for poor people; *A.-G. v. Lonsdale* (1827), 1 Sim. 105, 57 E.R. 518, school for gentlemen's sons.

218 *Re Spencer Estate* (1928), 34 O.W.N. 29 (H.C.).

219 *Re Fitzgibbon Estate* (1916), 11 O.W.N. 71 (H.C.).

Further, places where persons are instructed in their ancestral language and customs are charitable,[220] as are places which engage in vocational training.[221] However, in the context of vocational training, there must in fact be advancement of education and not simply a private benefit to members of a particular group.[222]

A gift for education which fails to specify the method to be used is charitable.[223] The court will direct a scheme to carry out such a trust.

While schools generally are charitable, even if they charge tuition (provided they are not operated for profit),[224] tuition fees paid by parents to private schools for their children's education are not charitable gifts. Hence, they are not, except to the extent that they are attributable to religious instruction, deductible from income, or a credit against income tax.[225] Instead, the payments are treated as consideration for the education received and as paid pursuant to contract.[226]

Education is not restricted to traditional classroom instruction and the promotion thereof,[227] however. The following enumeration of activities shows that "education" has a much wider ambit.[228]

---

220 *Societa Unita v. Gravenhurst (Town)* (1977), 16 O.R. (2d) 785, 3 M.P.L.R. 24, 79 D.L.R. (3d) 281 (H.C.), affirmed (1978), 6 M.P.L.R. 172 (Div. Ct.). See *Associated Gospel Churches v. Ontario Assessment Commissioner, Region No. 13* (1979), 8 M.P.L.R. 37, 1979 CarswellOnt 564 (H.C.), affirmed (1979), 9 M.P.L.R. 287, 1979 CarswellOnt 626, 12 R.P.R. 241 (Div. Ct.).

221 *Seafarers Training Institute v. Williamsburg* (1982), 39 O.R. (2d) 370, 19 M.P.L.R. 183, 138 D.L.R. (3d) 407 (H.C.).

222 *Co-op. College of Canada v. Saskatchewan (Human Rights Commission)*, [1976] 2 W.W.R. 84, 64 D.L.R. (3d) 531 (Sask. C.A.).

223 *Whicker v. Hume* (1858), 7 H.L.R. 124, 11 E.R. 50 (H.L.), a trust "for the benefit, and advancement, and propagation of education and learning in every part of the world."

224 *Abbey Malvern Wells Ltd. v. Ministry of Local Government & Planning*, [1951] Ch. 728, [1951] 2 All E.R. 154.

225 *R. v. McBurney*, [1985] 2 C.T.C. 214, 85 D.T.C. 5433, 20 E.T.R. 283 (Fed. C.A.), leave to appeal refused (1986), 65 N.R. 320n (sub nom. *McBurney v. Minister of National Revenue*) (S.C.C.). In *Adler v. Ontario* (1996), 140 D.L.R. (4th) 385, 30 O.R. (3d) 642 (headnote only), 204 N.R. 81, [1996] 3 S.C.R. 609, 95 O.A.C. 1, 40 C.R.R. (2d) 1, the Supreme Court of Canada held that the absence of public funding for private religious schools does not violate the rights of the parents who send their children to such schools to freedom of religion and equality under the *Canadian Charter of Rights and Freedoms*.

226 Department of National Revenue, Information Circular No. 75-23 (September 29, 1975).

227 For example, cultural activities not associated with formal education were considered charitable under the heading of "education" in *Royal Choral Society v. Commissioners of Inland Revenue*, [1943] 2 All E.R. 101 (C.A). The determining factor was that the activities of the society were directed towards raising the artistic sensibility of society as a whole. For the Canadian view see *Shapiro, Re* (1979), 27 O.R. (2d) 517, 1979 CarswellOnt 607, 6 E.T.R. 276, 107 D.L.R. (3d) 133 (H.C.); *Senecal v. R.* (1983), 3 D.L.R. (4th) 684, 1983 CarswellNat 52, 1983 CarswellNat 52F, [1984] 1 F.C. 169 (T.D.). Compare *Quinn, Re* (1984), 52 B.C.L.R. 273, 1984 CarswellBC 82, 16 E.T.R. 257 (C.A.).

228 For the definition of education, see also, *L.I.U.N.A., Local 506 Training Fund (Trustees of) v. Ontario Regional Assessment Commissioner, Region No. 14* (1993), 1993 CarswellOnt 2926 (Gen. Div.), reversed (1994), 1994 CarswellOnt 2198, 70 O.A.C. 389 (Div. Ct.); *Windsor Flying Club v. Ontario Regional Assessment Commissioner, Region No. 27* (2000), 12 M.P.L.R. (3d) 285, 2000 CarswellOnt 2130 (S.C.J.), affirmed (2001), 2001 CarswellOnt 1842, 20 M.P.L.R. (3d) 296, 147 O.A.C. 294 (Div. Ct.); *Vancouver Society of Immigrant & Visible Minority Women v. Minister of National Revenue*, 169 D.L.R. (4th) 34, 1999 CarswellNat 18, 1999

Sports. The promotion of sports *per se* has traditionally not been regarded as charitable, even if the sports were amateur in nature.[229] In Canada it is now accepted, however, that amateur sports are charitable under the fourth head.[230] But if a trust is in favour of a school and its object is to provide sporting or athletic facilities at the school, it will be charitable.[231]

An important decision in this regard is *Inland Revenue Commissioners v. McMullen*.[232] The English Football[233] Association established a trust to provide facilities enabling students at schools and universities

> . . . to play Association Football or other games or sports and thereby to assist in ensuring that due attention is given to the physical education and development of [students] as well as to the development and occupation of their minds. . . .

It seemed clear that the Football Association was interested in providing a training ground for prospective soccer players. The lower courts therefore held that the trust was not charitable; it was principally for the Association's private benefit.[234] However, the House of Lords upheld the trust. It construed the trust as meaning that the Association's real purpose was to promote students' physical education, not just football, to supplement their mental education.[235] Further, the House upheld the *mens sane in corpore sane* principle, holding that education includes spiritual, moral, mental and physical elements and that it does not preclude pleasure in the exercise of a skill. Since the trust was restricted to students at schools and universities, the trust was, therefore, clearly charitable.

Lord Hailsham said:[236]

> I do not share the view . . . that the words "education" and "educational" bear, or can bear, for the purposes of the law of charity, meanings different from those current in present-day educated English speech. I do not believe that there is such a difference. What has to be remembered, however, is that . . . both the legal conception of charity, and within it the educated man's ideas about education, are not static, but moving and changing. Both change with changes in ideas about social values. Both have evolved with the years.

And:[237]

CarswellNat 19, 99 D.T.C. 5034, 234 N.R. 249, 59 C.R.R. (2d) 1, [1999] 2 C.T.C. 1, [1999] 1 S.C.R. 10.

229 *Re Nottage*, [1895] 2 Ch. 649 (Ch. Div.).

230 *Re Laidlaw Foundation*, *supra*, note 29, reproduced later in this chapter.

231 *Re Mariette*, [1915] 2 Ch. 284, [1914-15] All E.R. Rep. 794 (Ch. Div.).

232 [1981] A.C. 1, [1980] 2 W.L.R. 416, [1980] 1 All E.R. 884 (H.L.).

233 *I.e.*, soccer.

234 [1978] 1 W.L.R. 664, [1978] 1 All E.R. 230, affirmed [1979] 1 W.L.R. 130, [1979] 1 All E.R. 588 (C.A.).

235 On the matter of construing trust deeds, including deeds purporting to establish charitable trust, Lord Hailsham of St. Marylebone L.C. stated in a *dictum* that, in case of ambiguity, the court should give the deed a benignant construction if possible: *McMullen*, *supra*, note 232, at 14. *Cf. Bruce v. Deer Presbytery* (1867), L.R. 1 Sc. & Div. 96 at 97 (H.L.), *per* Lord Chelmsford L.C.

236 *Ibid.*, *McMullen*, at 15.

237 *Ibid.*, at 16-17.

... I would be very reluctant to confine the meaning of education to formal instruction in the classroom or even the playground, and I consider it sufficiently wide to cover all the activities envisaged by the settlor in the present case. One of the affidavits filed on the part of the respondent referred to the practices of ancient Sparta. I am not sure that this particular precedent is an entirely happy one, but from a careful perusal of *Plato's Republic* I doubt whether its author would have agreed . . . in regarding "physical education and development" as an elusive phrase, or as other than an educational charity, at least when used in association with the formal education of the young during the period when they are pupils of schools or in statu pupillari at universities. . . .

And:[238]

It is important to remember that in the instant appeal we are dealing with the concept of physical education and development of the young deliberately associated by the settlor with the status of pupilage in schools or universities. . . . It is the picture of a balanced and systematic process of instruction, training and practice containing . . . both spiritual, moral, mental and physical elements, the totality of which in any given case may vary with, for instance, the availability of teachers and facilities, and the potentialities, limitations and individual preferences of the pupils. But the totality of the process consists as much in the balance between each of the elements as in the enumeration of the things learned or the places in which the activities are carried on. I reject any idea which would cramp the education of the young within the school or university syllabus, confine it within the school or university campus, limit it to formal instruction, or render it devoid of pleasure in the exercise of skill.

Research. Research, the object of which is to increase and disseminate knowledge, is also charitable. This issue arose in *Re Hopkins' Will Trusts, Naish v. Francis Bacon Society Inc.*[239] A testatrix gave part of the residue of her estate in trust for the Francis Bacon Society, to be used

... towards finding the Bacon-Shakespeare manuscripts and in the event of the same having been discovered by the date of my death then for the general purposes of the work and propaganda of the society.

The objects of the society, of which the testatrix was a member, were to encourage the study of the works of Francis Bacon and "the general study of the evidence in favour of Francis Bacon's authorship of the plays commonly ascribed to Shakespeare . . ." The court held the trust charitable. Wilberforce J. said:[240]

... it would seem to me that a bequest for the purpose of search, or research, for the original manuscripts of England's greatest dramatist (whoever he was) would be well within the law's conception of charitable purposes. The discovery of such manuscripts, or of one such manuscript, would be of the highest value to history and to literature. It is objected, against this, that as we already have the text of the plays, from an almost contemporary date, the discovery of a manuscript

---

238 *Ibid.*, at 18.

239 (1964), [1965] Ch. 669, [1964] 3 All E.R. 46 (Ch. Div.). See *Wood v. R.*, 9 A.R. 427, 1977 CarswellAlta 240, [1977] 6 W.W.R. 273, 1 E.T.R. 285 (T.D.); *Alliance for Life v. Minister of National Revenue*, 27 E.T.R. (2d) 1, 174 D.L.R. (4th) 442, 1999 CarswellNat 625, 1999 CarswellNat 2489, 99 D.T.C. 5228, [1999] 3 C.T.C. 1, 242 N.R. 106, [1999] 3 F.C. 504 (C.A.); *Vancouver Society of Immigrant & Visible Minority Women v. Minister of National Revenue*, *supra*, note 228.

240 *Ibid.*, at 679-681.

would add nothing worth while. This I utterly decline to accept. Without any undue exercise of the imagination, it would surely be a reasonable expectation that the revelation of a manuscript would contribute, probably decisively, to a solution of the authorship problem, and this alone is benefit enough. It might also lead to improvements in the text. It might lead to more accurate dating.

. . .

I think . . . that the word "education" must be used in a wide sense, certainly extending beyond teaching, and that the requirement is that, in order to be charitable, research must either be of educational value to the researcher or must be so directed as to lead to something which will pass into the store of educational material, or so as to improve the sum of communicable knowledge in an area which education may cover — education in this last context extending to the formation of literary taste and appreciation.

. . .

I accept that research of a private character, for the benefit only of the members of a society, would not normally be educational — or otherwise charitable — . . . but I do not think that the research in the present case can be said to be of a private character, for it is inherently inevitable, and manifestly intended, that the result of any discovery should be published to the world.

By contrast, trusts which, while educational in some respects, are in fact political in purpose, will not be upheld. Thus, a gift to the Simplified Spelling Society for the simplification or improvement of English spelling or the English language failed for this reason.[241] So also did a trust in George Bernard Shaw's will.[242] Shaw left part of his estate upon trust to conduct research leading to the development of a larger alphabet of at least 40 letters. Harman J. held that the trust failed as being political, since the terms of the trust required advertisement, propaganda and research on a controversial matter. His Lordship also said: "if the object be merely the increase of knowledge, that is not in itself a charitable object unless it be combined with teaching and education."[243] The action was settled and compromised on appeal.[244]

Education in the Arts.[245] Trusts which support the arts are also charitable and fall under advancement of education. *Royal Choral Society v. Commissioners of Inland Revenue*[246] is an important case on this point. The Society was an unincorporated organization whose objects were to provide choral concerts in the Royal Albert Hall and to encourage and advance choral singing in London. Its performances were usually conducted at a loss, but when the Society made a profit, the Inland Revenue sought to tax it. The court held, however, that the purposes of the Society were educational and, hence, exempt from taxation.

---

241 *Trustees of the Sir G.B. Baker (1922) "C" Trust v. Inland Revenue Commissioners* (1929), 25 T.L.R. 344.

242 *Re Shaw* (sub som. Public Trustee v. Day), [1957] 1 W.L.R. 729, [1957] 1 All E.R. 745 (C.A.).

243 *Ibid.*, at W.L.R. 737.

244 (1957), [1958] 1 All E.R. 245n.

245 See Kevin A. Janus, "Artistic Endeavours in Charity Law" (1999), 15 Philanthrop., No. 1, 5.

246 [1943] 2 All E.R. 101 (C.A.).

The argument that, in the domain of art the only thing that can be education is the education of the performers, was rejected. So was the argument that the sole purpose of the Society was to entertain.

In the course of his judgment Lord Greene M.R. said:[247]

> Very few people can become executants, or at any rate executants who can give pleasure either to themselves or to others; but a very large number of people can become instructed listeners with a trained and cultivated taste. In my opinion, a body of persons established for the purpose of raising the artistic taste of the country and established by an appropriate document which confines them to that purpose, is established for educational purposes, because the education of artistic taste is one of the most important things in the development of a civilised human being.
>
> In the case of artistic taste, one of the best ways of training it is by presenting works of high class and gradually training people to like them in preference to works of an inferior class. The people who undergo this process go no doubt with the idea of being amused or entertained; but it is not the state of mind of the people who go to the performance which matters for the present purposes, it is the purpose of the people who provide it which is important. If the people who are providing the performance are really genuinely confining their objects to the promotion of aesthetic education by presenting works of a particular kind, or up to a particular standard, it seems to me that that is just as much education (and, in fact, having regard to the subject-matter the best available method of education) as lecturing or teaching in a class, or anything of that kind.

His Lordship was, thus, of the opinion that a purpose can be pleasurable as well as educational.

Professional Education. Trusts which further education of the learned professions have always been regarded as charitable. Thus, a gift to an inn of court is charitable, it being a school of learning.[248] Similarly, trusts to promote and encourage the study and practice of surgery[249] and to promote the general advancement of the study of mechanical engineering,[250] have been held to be charitable. By contrast, gifts to professional bodies are not charitable, since their purpose is to benefit the members of those bodies.[251]

Education for the professions also extends beyond the traditional concept of education. This is apparent from *Incorporated Council of Law Reporting for England & Wales v. A.-G.*,[252] reproduced below.

INCORPORATED COUNCIL OF LAW REPORTING FOR ENGLAND & WALES v. ATTORNEY-GENERAL

[1972] Ch. 73, [1971] 3 All E.R. 1029
Court of Appeal

The Incorporated Council of Law Reporting for England and Wales was

---

247 *Ibid.*, at 105.
248 *Re Kerr*, [1902] 1 Ch. 774.
249 *Royal College of Surgeons of England v. National Provincial Bank Ltd.*, [1952] A.C. 631 (H.L.).
250 *Institution of Civil Engineers v. Commissioners of Inland Revenue*, [1932] 1 K.B. 149.
251 *General Nursing Council for England and Wales v. St. Marylebone Borough Council*, [1959] A.C. 540.
252 (1972), [1972] Ch. 73, [1971] 3 All E.R. 1029 (C.A.).

incorporated in 1870. It had 20 members, all members of the legal professions. Its primary purpose was to publish "at a moderate price, and under gratuitous professional control," reports of judgments of the superior and appellate courts in England. The council had certain ancillary objects as well, which included the publishing of statutes. The income and property of the Council were to be applied solely for the promotion of its objects and no portion thereof could be paid in any manner by way of profit to the members. Remuneration of officers, editors, reporters, and other employees was permitted.

In 1966 the Council applied to be registered as a charity, but the Charity Commissioners refused to register it. The Council appealed, joining the Commissioners of Inland Revenue and the Attorney-General as parties. The appeal was allowed by Foster J.,[253] who held that the Council's purposes fell under the fourth head of charity. The Commissioners of Inland Revenue appealed to the Court of Appeal.

SACHS L.J.:

> [His Lordship held, first, that, in determining whether the Council was charitable, the court was not restricted to a consideration of the Council's objects, but could look at its historical background and the sphere in which it operates. He continued:]

The kernel of the matter is the vital function of judge-made law in relation not only to the common law and to equity, but to declaring the meaning of statutory law. No one — layman or lawyer — can have reasonably full knowledge of how the law affects what he or his neighbours are doing without recourse to reports of judicial decisions as well as to the statutes of the realm.

What in that state of affairs is the purpose of law reports? There is in substance only one purpose. To provide essential material for the study of the law — in the sense of acquiring knowledge of what the law is, how it is developing, and how it applies to the enormous range of human activities which it affects.

At this juncture it is apposite to recall that the profession of the law is a learned profession. It was one of the earliest to be recognised as such — well before the *Statute of Elizabeth I*:[254] to establish that point there is no need to have recourse to examples of this recognition such as the traditional House of Commons appellation "honourable and *learned*" to members of the profession. Similarly it is plainly correct to speak of law as a science and of its study as a study of science in the same way as one speaks of the study of medicine or chemistry. . . . It may at this point be of relevance to note that Lord Macnaghten's phrase "advancement of education" has consistently been taken to be an *enlargement* of the phrase "advancement of learning" used by Sir Samuel Romilly for his second division of charities in *Morice v. Bishop of Durham*:[255] in other words, there can be no

---

253 [1971] Ch. 626.
254 1601 (43 Eliz. 1), c. 4.
255 *Supra*, note 33, at 531.

question but that the latter is included in the former, as is illustrated by the authorities.

Against that background I turn to the question whether the council's purposes are educational. It would be odd indeed and contrary to the trend of judicial decisions if the institution and maintenance of a library for the study of a learned subject or of something rightly called a science did not at least *prima facie* fall within the phrase "advancement of education," whatever be the age of those frequenting it. The same reasoning must apply to the provision of books forming the raw material for that study, whether they relate to chemical data or to case histories in hospitals: and I can find no good reason for excluding case law as developed in the courts. If that is the correct approach, then when the institution is one whose individual members make no financial gain from the provision of that material and is one which itself can make no use of its profits except to provide further and better material, why is the purpose not charitable?

On behalf of the Attorney-General the only point taken against this conclusion was that the citation of the reports in court cannot be educational — in part, at any rate, because of the theory that the judges are deemed to have complete knowledge of the law. For the Commissioners of Inland Revenue the main contention was that the use by the legal profession of the reports was in general (not merely when in court) a use the purpose of which was to earn professional remuneration — a use for personal profit: and that it followed that the purpose of the council was not charitable.

Taking the latter point first, it is, of course, the fact that one of the main, if not the main, uses to which law reports are put is by members of the legal profession who study their contents so as to advise clients and plead on their behalf. Those reports are as essential to them in their profession as the statutes: without them they would be ill-equipped to earn professional fees. Does it follow, as submitted by Mr. Francis, that a main purpose of the reports is the advancement of professional interests and thus not charitable? The argument put thus is attractive, not least to those who, like myself, are anxious not to favour or to seem to favour their one-time profession. But the doctor must study medical research papers to enable him to treat his patients and earn his fees; and it would be difficult indeed to say that because doctors thus earn their emoluments the printing and sale of such papers by a non-profit making institution could not be held to be for the advancement of education in medicine.

Where the purpose of producing a book is to enable a specified subject, and a learned subject at that, to be studied, it is, in my judgment, published for the advancement of education, as this, of course, includes as regards the Statute of Elizabeth I the advancement of learning. That remains its purpose despite the fact that professional men — be they lawyers, doctors, or chemists — use the knowledge acquired to earn their living. One must not confuse the results flowing from the achievement of a purpose with the purpose itself, any more than one should have regard to the motives of those who set that purpose in motion.

As to the point that the citation of reports to the judiciary is fatal to the council's claim, this, if independent of the contention concerning professional user to earn fees, seems to turn on the suggestion that as the judges are supposed to know the law, the citations cannot be educative. That, however, is an unrealistic approach. It ignores the fact that citation of authority by the bar is simply a means by which there is brought to the attention of the judge the material he has to study to decide the matter in hand: in this country he relies on competent counsel to quote the extracts relevant to any necessary study of law on the points in issue, instead of having to embark on the time consuming process of making the necessary researches himself. Indeed, it verges on the absurd to suggest that the courteous facade embodied in the traditional phrase "as, of course, your Lordship knows" can be used to attempt to conceal the fact that no judge can possibly be aware of all the contents of all The Law Reports that show the continuing development of our ever changing laws. . . .

For these reasons I reject the contentions that the user of The Law Reports by the legal profession for earning fees of itself results in the purposes of the council not being charitable and thus return to the question whether they are charitable on the footing that their substantially exclusive purpose is to further the study of the law in the way already discussed. Such a purpose must be charitable unless the submission that the advancement of learning is not an advancement of education within the spirit and intendment of the preamble is upheld: but for the reasons already given that submission plainly fails. Accordingly, having regard to the fact that the members of the council cannot themselves gain from its activities, its purposes in my judgment fall within the second of Lord Macnaghten's divisions.

[His Lordship went on to hold in the alternative that the purposes of the Council were also valid under the fourth head of charity.]

BUCKLEY L.J.:

. . .

What then does the evidence establish about the need for reliable law reports and the reasons for publishing them? As the uncontradicted evidence of Professor Goodhart makes clear, in a legal system such as ours, in which judges' decisions are governed by precedents, reported decisions are the means by which legal principles (other than those laid down by statutes) are developed, established and made known, and by which the application of those legal principles to particular kinds of facts are illustrated and explained. Reported decisions may be said to be the tissue of the body of our non-statutory law. Whoever, therefore, would carry out any anatomical researches upon our non-statutory corpus juris must do so by research amongst, and study of, reported cases.

Professor Goodhart recalls that Sir Frederick Pollock in his paper entitled *The Science of Case Law* published in 1882 pointed out that the study of law is a science in the same sense as physics or chemistry are sciences, and that the material with which it is concerned consists of individual cases which must be analysed and measured as carefully as is the material in the other sciences. At about the same time the "case system" of teaching law was introduced at the Harvard Law

School, which has since become generally adopted. Accurate and authoritative law reports are thus seen to be essential both for the advancement of legal education and the proper administration of justice. As Professor Goodhart says: "Accuracy in The Law Reports is, therefore, as important for the science of law as is the accuracy of instruments in the physical sciences."

The legal profession has from times long past been termed a learned profession, and rightly so, for no man can properly practise or apply the law who is not learned in that field of law with which he is concerned. He must have more than an aptitude and more than a skill. He must be learned in a sense importing true scholarship. In a system of law such as we have in this country this scholarship can only be acquired and maintained by a continual study of case law.

I agree with Foster J. in thinking that, when counsel in court cites a case to a judge, counsel is not in any real sense "educating" the judge, counsel performing the role of a teacher and the judge filling the role of a pupil; but I do not agree with him that the process should not be regarded as falling under the charitable head of "the advancement of education."

In a number of cases learned societies have been held to be charitable. Sometimes the case has been classified under Lord Macnaghten's fourth head, sometimes under the second. It does not really matter under which head such a case is placed, but for my own part I prefer to treat the present case as falling within the class of purposes for the advancement of education rather than within the final class of other purposes for the benefit of the community. For the present purpose the second head should be regarded as extending to the improvement of a useful branch of human knowledge and its public dissemination.

. . .

The council was established for the purpose of recording in a reliably accurate manner the development and application of judge-made law and of disseminating the knowledge of that law, its development and judicial application, in a way which is essential to the study of the law. The primary object of the council is, I think, confined to this purpose exclusively and is charitable. The subsidiary objects, such as printing and publishing statutes, the provision of a noting-up service and so forth, are ancillary to this primary object and do not detract from its exclusively charitable character. Indeed, the publication of the statutes of the realm is itself, I think, a charitable purpose for reasons analogous to those applicable to reporting judicial decisions.

The fact that the council's publications can be regarded as a necessary part of a practising lawyer's equipment does not prevent the council from being established exclusively for charitable purposes. The practising lawyer and the judge must both be lifelong students in that field of scholarship for the study of which The Law Reports provide essential material and a necessary service. The benefit which the council confers upon members of the legal profession in making accurate reports available is that it facilitates the study and ascertainment of the law. It also helps the lawyer to earn his livelihood, but that is incidental to or consequential on the primary scholastic function of advancing and disseminating knowledge of the law, and does not detract from the exclusively charitable character of the council's objects.[256]

The service which publication of The Law Reports provides benefits not only those actively engaged in the practice and administration of the law, but also those whose business it is to study and teach law academically, and many others who need to study the law for the purposes of their trades, businesses, professions or affairs. In all these fields, however, the nature of the service is the same: it enables the reader to study, and by study to acquaint himself with and instruct himself in the law of this country. There is nothing here which negatives an exclusively charitable purpose.

Although the objects of the council are commercial in the sense that the council exists to publish and sell its publications, they are unselfregarding. The members are prohibited from deriving any profit from the council's activities, and the council itself, although not debarred from making a profit out of its business, can only apply any such profit in the further pursuit of its objects. The council is consequently not prevented from being a charity by reason of any commercial element in its activities.

I therefore reach the conclusion that the council is a body established exclusively for charitable purposes and is entitled to be registered under the Act of 1960.[257]

[Buckley L.J. went on to hold that the Council's purposes would also be valid under the fourth head of charity on the ground that the publication of accurate law reports is beneficial to the community. Such publication assists the administration and development of the law in the courts and makes the law accessible to all members of the community, either directly or through the advice of lawyers.

Russell L.J., while not denying that the publication of accurate law reports furthered knowledge in legal science, preferred to base his holding that the Council's purposes were charitable solely on the ground that they fell within the fourth head of charity.][258]

Notes and Questions

1. It is clear from the judgments in the *Law Reporting* case that an organization which publishes law reports for profit is not charitable.

2. It is the height of irony that the Law Reports headnote in the *Law Reporting* case is patently wrong. It purports to give as the holding of the case that the purposes of the Council fell under the fourth head. Further, it states that Russell L.J. dissented, which he

---

256 *Cf. Royal College of Surgeons of England v. National Provincial Bank Ltd.*, [1952] A.C. 631 (H.L.); and *Royal College of Nursing v. St. Marylebone Borough Council*, [1959] 1 W.L.R. 1077, [1959] 3 All E.R. 663.

257 *Charities Act, 1960*, (8 & 9 Eliz. 2), c. 58.

258 This is discussed further below.

did not, and that he held the purposes to fall under advancement of education, which he did not.

3. In light of the modern approach of a broad definition of education, it is surprising that the Supreme Court of Canada held the Vancouver Society of Immigrant and Minority Women not to be charitable.[259] The Society had the following objects:

    (a) To provide educational forums, classes, workshops and seminars to immigrant women in order that they may be able to find or obtain employment or self-employment.

    (b) To carry on political activities provided such activities are incidental and ancillary to the above purposes and provided such activities do not include direct or indirect support of, or opposition to, any political party or candidate for public office.

    (c) To raise funds in order to carry out the above purposes by means of solicitation of funds from governments, corporations and individuals.

    (d) To provide services and to do all things that are incidental or conducive to the attainment of the above stated objects, including the seeking of funds from governments and/or other sources for the implementation of the aforementioned objectives.

Revenue Canada refused to register the Society because it was of the opinion that many of the activities of the Society were not charitable. The Society appealed. The Federal Court of Appeal dismissed the appeal.[260] The Society then appealed to the Supreme Court of Canada. A majority of the court dismissed the appeal. Iacobucci J., who wrote the majority decision, applied a somewhat broader test for the advancement of education than had been used in the past. In his opinion, education can include informal training that is intended to teach necessary life skills, or which provides practical information. He said:[261]

> To limit the notion of "training of the mind" to structured, systematic instruction or traditional academic subjects reflects and outmoded and underinclusive understanding of education which is of little use in modern Canadian society. . . . I the case of education, the good advanced is knowledge or training. Thus, so long as information or training is provided in a structured manner and for a genuinely educational purpose — that is, to advance the knowledge or abilities of the recipients — and not solely to promote a particular point of view or political orientation, it may properly be viewed as falling within the advancement of education.

On this basis, purpose (a) fell within the head of advancement of education and it satisfied the public benefit test. Further, purposes (b) and (c) were merely ancillary to purpose (a). However, there was a problem with purpose (d). The word "conducive" allowed the Society to engage in non-charitable activities that would not be ancillary to the other purposes. Activities such as maintaining a job skills directory, which the Society did, fell into this category. Thus, the purposes were not exclusively charitable. Iacobucci J. also held that the Society's purposes did not fall under the fourth head of charity.

The minority would have held the Society charitable on the ground that purpose (a) fell both within the head of advancement of education, as well as the head of other purposes beneficial to the community. Further, in their opinion, the other purposes were ancillary

---

259 *Vancouver Society of Immigrant & Visible Minority Women v. Minister of National Revenue*, *supra*, note 228.

260 96 D.T.C. 6232, 1996 CarswellNat 871, [1996] F.C.J. No. 307, 195 N.R. 235, [1996] 2 C.T.C. 88 (C.A.).

261 *Supra*, note 228, at D.L.R. 113.

to the first, so that the Society was exclusively charitable. Finally, the Society met the public benefit test.

Do you think the Society satisfied the various tests and should have been registered? Why?[262]

4. A testator gave money on trust:

> . . . for the purpose of educating such male children who are citizens of the Dominion of Canada as are selected by any minister of the General Church of New Jerusalem in Canada in consultation with my Trustees provided however that such applicants shall embrace the faith of the New Church and shall be acceptable to my trustees.

Is the trust charitable?[263]

5. A testator left a large part of his estate to:

> . . . the Warden and Chairman of the Academic Council . . . of the institution known as Wilton Park . . . for the benefit at the discretion of the said institution as long as Wilton Park remains a British contribution to the formation of an informed international public opinion and to the promotion of greater co-operation in Europe and the West in general . . .
>
> The testator was an academic and he originally conceived and directed "Wilton Park." That expression described regular conferences for politicians, academics, civil servants, industrialists, journalists, and others capable of influencing public opinion in the member states of the Organization for Economic Co-operation and Development. The conferences were private and were not supportive of any particular political party. They were designed to allow participants to exchange views on political, economic, and social issues. The participants paid fees to attend the conferences. The endeavour was assisted by a subvention from the British Foreign Office. The latter also provided the facilities for the conference. Is the gift charitable?[264]

6. Are any of the following trusts for the advancement of education?
(a) To provide annual treats for school children in London.[265]
(b) To provide for children's outings.[266]
(c) To provide a prize for chess to boys and young men resident in Toronto.[267]
(d) To further the Boy Scouts movement by purchasing sites for camping.[268]
(e) To the Royal Scottish Dance Society, to promote Scottish dance.[269]

7. Would a trust providing free access to the Internet be charitable under the heading of advancement of education?[270]

---

262 For a discussion of the case, see David Stevens, "Vancouver Society of Immigrant and Visible Minority Women v. M.N.R. (2000), 15 Philanthrop., No. 2, 4; Arthur B.C. Drache, "*Vancouver Immigrant Women:* The First Judicial Interpretation" (2000), 15 Philanthrop., No. 2, 14; Wolfe D. Goodman, "A Personal View of the *Vancouver Society* Decision" (2000), 15 Philanthrop., No. 2, 20.

263 *Re Doering Estate* (1948), [1949] 1 D.L.R. 267, [1948] O.R. 923 (H.C.).

264 See *Re Koeppler's Will Trusts*, [1985] 2 All E.R. 869 (C.A.).

265 *Re Mellody*, [1918] 1 Ch. 228 (Ch. Div.).

266 *Re Ward's Estate* (1937), 81 Sol. Jo. 397.

267 *Re Dupree's Deed Trusts*, [1945] Ch. 16, [1944] 2 All E.R. 443 (Ch. Div.).

268 *Re Webber*, [1954] 1 W.L.R. 1500, [1954] 3 All E.R. 712.

269 *Re Porter Estate* (1983), 52 N.B.R. (2d) 130, 137 A.P.R. 130 (Q.B.).

270 See *Vancouver Regional FreeNet Assn. v. Minister of National Revenue*, [1996] 3 F.C. 880, [1996] 3 C.T.C. 102, 96 D.T.C. 6440, 199 N.R. 223, 137 D.L.R. (4th) 206 (Fed. C.A.).

8. Would a trust to promote the preservation and enhancement of the environment and educating people on environmental issues be charitable?[271]

(ii) *Public Benefit*

In the introductory material to this chapter we discussed the requirement of public benefit in some detail. In particular, we noted that it is important to distinguish between the two elements of that requirement. Trusts for the advancement of education require a greater public component, as well as a greater benefit component than trusts for the advancement of religion. The "public" element has often been litigated in the context of education, both as regards the prohibition of a nexus between the donor and the beneficiaries, and as regards educational trusts which have political overtones. This has been dealt with sufficiently. Additional examples are found in the notes and questions below.

The "benefit" element is not so often the subject of litigation. This is because, for most educational trusts, it is, with reason, presumed. However, as we noted in our earlier discussion, it is legitimate for the court to investigate the "benefit" element and it will do so when the quality of the education proposed in the trust is called into question. *Re Pinion*,[272] reproduced below, demonstrates the importance of the "benefit" element.

RE PINION, Decd., WESTMINSTER BANK LTD. v. PINION

[1965] Ch. 85, [1964] 1 All E.R. 890
Court of Appeal

The testator, Arthur Watson Hyde Pinion, was a painter of mediocre ability, but he was wealthy. He made his own will, a "rambling and half coherent" document,[273] by which, in the events which happened, he left his studio with its paintings, painted by himself and others, together with furniture, china, glass and bric-à-brac, to the Westminster bank as trustee. The trustee was directed to offer the whole to the National Trust, with the intention that the studio and its contents be maintained as a museum. If the National Trust should decline the offer, the bank was to appoint another trustee to carry out the testator's wishes. The testator also gave the residue of his estate to the trustee to maintain the collection. The National Trust declined the offer. The bank then brought an application for an order determining whether the bequest established a valid charitable trust. The evidence showed that the collection was inferior, indeed "atrociously bad," and not likely to be of benefit to the public. Nevertheless, Wilberforce J., at first instance,[274] held that the collection included some items of historical and artistic

---

271 *Earth Fund / Fond pour la Terre v. Minister of National Revenue* (2002), 2002 FCA 498, 2002 CarswellNat 3594, 2002 CarswellNat 3919, 2002 CAF 498, 2003 D.T.C. 5016 (Eng.), 298 N.R. 391, [2003] 2 C.T.C. 10 (C.A.).
272 [1965] Ch. 85, [1964] 1 All E.R. 890 (C.A.).
273 *Ibid.*, at 104, *per* Harman L.J.
274 *Ibid.*, at 92.

interest, so that, although the benefit to the public was slight, it was a valid charitable bequest. The next-of-kin appealed.

HARMAN L.J.:

. . .

In this court the Attorney-General did not seek to support the gift as being beneficial in a general sense to the public, but confined his plea to that head of charity which is characterised as the advancement of education. He argued both here and below that no evidence was receivable on this subject. A museum, he said, is a place which the law assumes to have an educational value and purpose. . . . It would appear that a gift to an established museum is charitable. . . .[275] I conclude that a gift to found a public museum may be assumed to be charitable as of public utility if no one questions it. So in a case about religion, such as *Thornton v. Howe*,[276] the case about Joanna Southcote, the court will assume without inquiry that the teaching may do some good if not shown to be subversive of morality. Where the object is to found a school the court will not study the methods of education provided that on the face of them they are proper.[277] A school for prostitutes or pickpockets would obviously fail. A case about education is *Re Hummeltenberg*,[278] where the headnote reads:

> To be valid a charitable bequest must be for the public benefit, and the trust must be capable of being administered and controlled by the court. The opinion of the donor of a gift or the creator of a trust that the gift or trust is for the public benefit does not make it so, the matter is one to be determined by the court on the evidence before it.

The bequest in that case was connected with spiritualism and the point to which I draw attention is that the judge (the late Lord Russell of Killowen, then Russell J.) said it must be decided on the evidence. There is a passage in his judgment as follows:[279]

> It was contended that the court was not the tribunal to determine whether a gift or trust was or was not a gift or a trust for the benefit of the public. It was said that the only judge of this was the donor of the gift or the creator of the trust. . . . I respectfully disagree. If a testator by stating or indicating his view that a trust is beneficial to the public can establish that fact beyond question, trusts might be established in perpetuity for the promotion of all kinds of fantastic (though not unlawful) objects, of which the training of poodles to dance might be a mild example. In my opinion the question whether a gift is or may be operative for the public benefit is a question to be answered by the court by forming an opinion upon the evidence before it.

---

275 See *British Museum Trustees v. White* (1826), 2 Sim. & St. 594, 57 E.R. 473; *Re Holburne* (1885), 53 L.T. 212, 1 T.L.R. 517.
276 (1862), 31 Beav. 14, 54 E.R. 1042.
277 *Re Shaw's Will Trusts*, [1952] 1 Ch. 163, [1952] 1 All E.R. 49.
278 [1923] 1 Ch. 237 (Ch. Div.).
279 *Ibid.*, at 242.

Where a museum is concerned and the utility of the gift is brought in question it is, in my opinion, and herein I agree with the judge, essential to know at least something of the quality of the proposed exhibits in order to judge whether they will be conducive to the education of the public. So I think with a public library, such a place if found to be devoted entirely to works of pornography or of a corrupting nature, would not be allowable. Here it is suggested that education in the fine arts is the object. For myself a reading of the will leads me rather to the view that the testator's object was not to educate anyone, but to perpetuate his own name and the repute of his family, hence perhaps the direction that the custodian should be a blood relation of his. However that may be, there is a strong body of evidence here that as a means of education this collection is worthless. The testator's own paintings, of which there are over 50, are said by competent persons to be in an academic style and "atrociously bad" and the other pictures without exception worthless. Even the so-called "Lely" turns out to be a 20th century copy.

Apart from pictures there is a haphazard assembly — it does not merit the name collection, for no purpose emerges, no time nor style is illustrated — of furniture and objects of so-called "art" about which expert opinion is unanimous that nothing beyond the third-rate is to be found. Indeed one of the experts expresses his surprise that so voracious a collector should not by hazard have picked up even one meritorious object. The most that skilful cross-examination extracted from the expert witnesses was that there were a dozen chairs which might perhaps be acceptable to a minor provincial museum and perhaps another dozen not altogether worthless, but two dozen chairs do not make a museum and they must, to accord with the will, be exhibited stifled by a large number of absolutely worthless pictures and objects.

It was said that this is a matter of taste, and de gustibus non est disputandum, but here I agree with the judge that there is an accepted canon of taste on which the court must rely, for it has itself no judicial knowledge of such matters, and the unanimous verdict of the experts is as I have stated. The judge with great hesitation concluded that there was that scintilla of merit which was sufficient to save the rest. I find myself on the other side of the line. I can conceive of no useful object to be served in foisting upon the public this mass of junk. It has neither public utility nor educative value. I would hold that the testator's project ought not to be carried into effect and that his next-of-kin is entitled to the residue of his estate.

[Davies and Russell L.JJ. delivered concurring judgments.

In the course of his judgment, Russell L.J. said:[280]

For my part I would not admit to the favoured ranks of charity, bearing the banner of education, a disposition with such negligible qualifications to bear it. Where the evidence leaves me with the virtual certainty on balance of probabilities that no member of the public will ever extract one

---

280 *Supra*, note 272, at 111.

iota of education from the disposition, I am prepared to march it in another direction, pressing into its hands a banner lettered "De minimis non curat lex."

The court allowed the appeal.]

Notes and Questions

1. A testator, who died in 1897, left certain real property in New South Wales in trust upon successive life interests with remainder

> . . . to the Presbyterians the descendants of those settled in the Colony hailing from or born in the North of Ireland to be held in trust for the purpose of establishing a college for the education and tuition of their youth in the standards of the Westminster Divines as taught in the Holy Scriptures.

Is this gift charitable? In answering this question, consider the restrictive language of the gift.[281]

2. The Educational Grants Association Ltd. was a corporation established for the purpose of advancing education and making grants available to individuals to pursue an education. While the objects were general and on the face of it charitable, the council of management of the Association was connected with a commercial company, Metal Box Ltd., which had promoted the association. The association's income derived from the company and between 1958 and 1962, more than 75% of the income was applied for the education of children of employees of the company. Moreover, a letter inviting applications for grants was circulated only among the senior employees of the company. The association claimed exemption from income tax in respect of income applied to grants to individuals and educational institutions. The Inland Revenue Commissioners rejected the claim to the extent that the grants had been made to children of employees of the company. The Special Commissioners allowed the association's appeal, and the Inland Revenue Commissioners appealed to the court. At issue was whether the association was established exclusively for charitable purposes and whether its income was applied exclusively for such purposes as required by the English *Income Tax Act*.[282]

The court held that the association was not exclusively charitable, but was essentially a private organization, because the object was to channel funds into the hands of dependants of Metal Box employees. Hence the personal nexus defeated the otherwise charitable purpose.[283]

3. Frederick Delius was a composer, whose work was highly respected. By her will, his widow gave her residuary estate to trustees upon trust for the advancement of her late husband's musical works. The trust was not designed to operate for profit, but was to: (1) record Delius's work; (2) publish his work in a uniform edition; and (3) finance the performance in public of his work from the royalties earned. Is this a valid charitable trust?[284]

4. Are the following trusts charitable?

---

281 See *Davies v. Perpetual Trustee Co.*, [1959] A.C. 439, [1959] 2 All E.R. 128 (P.C.).

282 1952 (15 & 16 Geo. 6 & 1 Eliz. 2), c. 10, s. 447(1)(*b*).

283 See *Inland Revenue Commissioners v. Educational Grants Assn. Ltd.*, [1967] Ch. 993, [1967] 2 All E.R. 893 (C.A.).

284 See *Re Delius*, [1957] Ch. 299, [1957] 1 All E.R. 854.

(a) To assist in publishing the work of an unknown Canadian author, the choice of the work and the terms of assistance to be in the discretion of the directors of a named publishing house.[285]

(b) To present an annual award for one or both of, "A lyric, beautiful in form and in content" and "A prose original, fact or fiction, which in some way portrays the beautiful."[286]

5. A testatrix directed that "all antiques 50 years or over" owned by her be given "to suitable museums." Is the gift charitable?[287]

(d) Other Purposes Beneficial to the Community

There are a large number of items in the preamble to the *Statute of Charitable Uses*[288] which fall under the fourth head of charity. It is not necessary to repeat them. Instead, it may be more advantageous to give a modern list of purposes that have been held charitable under the fourth head. This list does not necessarily correspond in every detail to the preamble, since it is based also on cases in which purposes were decided by analogy to those contained in the preamble.

It will become apparent that many of the examples given extend benefits to the rich as well as the poor. This does not render the trust non-charitable. Only if the poor are in fact excluded may the trust not be charitable; not on the ground that it does not relieve poverty, but rather that it excludes an important segment of the community.

The following list is not intended to be either exhaustive or definitive. It purports merely to classify the preamble and the cases decided thereunder in modern form.[289] It seems that in Ontario, after the *Re Laidlaw Foundation* case,[290] reproduced below, such a list may, in any event, be otiose.

Finally, we iterate what we said earlier, namely, that the public benefit requirement appears to be stronger under the fourth head than under the first three heads of charity. The test for "a sufficient segment of the public" under the fourth head normally requires that the purpose assist the public generally, or at least a very broad segment of the public.

1. *The relief of the old and disabled.* This item corresponds with the relief of the aged and impotent people in the preamble. You will recall that trusts for the relief of the aged are often dealt with under the first head, because such trusts commonly attempt to relieve poverty among old people. However, if poverty is not an aspect of the trust, it falls under the fourth head. An example of such a trust is *Joseph Rowntree Memorial Trust Housing Association Ltd. v. A.-G.*[291] It involved charitable trustees as well as a corporation established to build and sell self-contained dwellings for elderly people. There were several schemes by which this object was to be achieved. All involved contractual arrangements with the

---

285 See *Re Shapiro* (1979), 27 O.R. (2d) 517, 107 D.L.R. (3d) 133, 6 E.T.R. 276 (H.C.).
286 See *Re Millen Estate* (1986), 22 E.T.R. 107, 30 D.L.R. (4th) 116 (B.C. S.C.).
287 *Perry v. Kovacs* (1984), 12 D.L.R. (4th) 751 (B.C. S.C.).
288 1601 (43 Eliz. 1), c. 4 (U.K.).
289 For similar attempts, see Tudor, at 90ff; Keeton and Sheridan, chapter parts.
290 *Supra*, note 29, at 573.
291 [1983] 1 All E.R. 288, [1983] Ch. 159.

beneficiaries. The court held that the purposes were charitable despite the contractual arrangements and even though a beneficiary would make a profit on a subsequent sale.

2. *The care of young persons.* This heading is represented in the preamble by a number of items, namely, "the preferment of orphans, the marriages of poor maids, and the supportation, aid and help of young tradesmen, handicraftsmen and persons decayed". In some cases these, too, may fall under the relief of poverty, if relief of poverty is the motive for the gift. If it is not, they fall under the fourth head on the ground that the care and upbringing, and the establishment in life of young persons who are defenceless, particularly if they are orphans, is *prima facie* charitable.[292]

Thus, for example, a trust for an orphans' home is charitable under this head,[293] as is a trust to enable deserving girls to marry,[294] and a trust enabling persons to emigrate.[295]

3. *Public works.* This heading is represented in the preamble by trusts to repair bridges, ports, havens, causeways, sea banks and highways. It is clear that such trusts are for the public benefit, whether they are restricted to a locality or extend to the entire country. Examples would be otiose and none will be given, except the somewhat *recherché* extension by analogy of the listed purposes in *Vancouver Regional FreeNet Assn. v. Minister of National Revenue.*[296] The court held the association to be charitable under the fourth head. The association provided free Internet access and the court held that just as the listed purposes were the essential means of communication at the time of the *Statute of Charitable Uses,* so by extension the Internet is today. Arguably, the association might be held charitable under the part of advancement of education.

4. *The benefit of a locality or the country.* This head derives by analogy from the preamble, which refers to the aid or ease of any poor inhabitants concerning the payment of fifteens and other taxes. It seems obvious that gifts which benefit a community or the nation are charitable. Thus a trust to permit residents to dredge oysters for their own benefit is charitable,[297] as is a gift "to His Majesty's government in exoneration of the national debt."[298] A gift to a foreign jurisdiction may also be charitable,[299] although this seems debatable. An organization which develops and produces radio and television programs of particular relevance to native people in a province is also charitable. The fact that the state has assumed

---

292 *Re Sahal's Will Trusts,* [1958] 1 W.L.R. 1243 at 1246, [1958] 3 All E.R. 428, *per* Danckwerts J.

293 *Harris v. Alexandra Non-Sectarian Orphanage & Children's Home in Vancouver,* [1923] 1 W.W.R. 624, [1923] 1 D.L.R. 1153 (B.C. S.C.).

294 *Re Cohen* (1919), 36 T.L.R. 16.

295 *Re Tree,* [1945] Ch. 325.

296 *Supra,* note 270.

297 *Goodman v. Saltash Corp.* (1882), 7 App. Cas. 633 (H.L.).

298 *Newland v. A.-G.* (1809), 3 Mer. 684, 36 E.R. 262.

299 *Parkhurst v. Roy* (1882), 7 O.A.R. 614 (C.A.), a gift to the government and legislature of Vermont.

special responsibility for the welfare of native people is relevant to that determination.[300]

5. *Preservation of public order and the administration of justice.* This head derives largely by analogy from the preamble. The preamble does refer (in a different context) to the setting out of soldiers. Hence, gifts to the armed forces or the police are charitable.[301] A trust to be used to train persons as officers in the Merchant Marine is charitable by analogy.[302]

A non-profit institution which publishes law reports and statutes also falls under this head. This was the holding of Russell L.J. and the alternative holding of Sachs L.J. in *Incorporated Council of Law Reporting for England and Wales v. A.-G.*[303] We have already considered this case under the part of education. Russell L.J. said:[304]

> The making of the law of this country is partly by statutory enactment (including therein subordinate legislation) and partly by judicial exposition in the decision of cases brought before the courts. It cannot be doubted that dissemination by publication of accurate copies of statutory enactments is beneficial to the community as a whole: and this is not the less so because at least in many instances the ordinary member of the public either does not attempt to, or cannot by study, arrive at a true conclusion of their import, or because the true understanding is largely limited to persons engaged professionally or as public servants in the field of any particular enactment, or otherwise interested in that field. . . . The same is to be said of the other source of our law, judicial decisions and the reasons therefor, especially in the light of our system of precedent. It is in my view just as beneficial to the community that reliable reports of judicial decisions of importance in the applicability of the law to varying but probably recurrent circumstances, or demonstrating development in the law, should be published; and all the more so if the publication be supervised by those who by training are best qualified to present the essence of a decision correctly and to distinguish the ephemeral from the significant. To state that the publication *also* supplied many professional men with the tools of their trade does not seem to me in any way to detract from the benefit that accrues to the community from the fact that the law does not remain locked in the bosom of the judiciary.

Russell L.J. held that the fact that the Council carried on the trade of publisher and seller of law reports did not defeat the charitable nature of its objects, since it was not operated for profit. His Lordship held further that the fact that the publication of law reports supplied the legal profession with the tools of their trade also did not matter, since the objects were charitable.

On the application of the *Statute of Charitable Uses*,[305] his Lordship noted[306] that the courts have variously held purposes which fall within "the spirit and

---

300 See *Native Communications Society of B.C. v. M.N.R.*, 86 D.T.C. 6353, 67 N.R. 146, [1986] 3 F.C. 471, [1986] 2 C.T.C. 170, 23 E.T.R. 210 (C.A.).

301 *I.R.C. v. City of Glasgow Police Athletic Assn.*, [1953] A.C. 380, [1953] 1 All E.R. 747 (H.C.).

302 *Re Corbyn*, [1941] Ch. 400. See also *Perry v. Kovacs* (1984), 12 D.L.R. (4th) 751 (B.C. S.C.).

303 [1972] Ch. 73, [1971] 3 All E.R. 1029 (C.A.). Case considered in *Vancouver Regional FreeNet Assn, supra,* note 270; *Positive Action against Pornography, supra,* note 123; *Toronto Volgograd, supra,* note 116; *Vancouver Society of Immigrant & Visible Minority Women, supra,* note 228.

304 *Ibid.,* at 85-86.

305 1601 (43 Eliz. 1), c. 4.

306 *Supra,* note 303, at 87-89.

intendment" of the preamble, or within "the equity" or "the mischief" of the statute to be charitable. So also, the courts have held a purpose charitable if it is charitable "in the same sense" or is "analogous to" purposes listed in the preamble, or to purposes previously held to be analogous thereto. Thus, for example, crematoria are charitable by analogy to the provision of burial grounds, which is analogous to the upkeep of churchyards, and the latter, in turn, is analogous to the repair of churches. Similarly, since the preservation of sea walls is for the safety of the public, so also, by analogy, is the provision of lifeboats and fire brigades.

His Lordship thought that the not-for-profit publication of judicial decisions is charitable in the same sense as the repair of bridges, havens, causeways and highways is. If individuals do not make provision for these, government would have to. That is, therefore, also a test of charity.

On the question whether the Council's purposes fell under the fourth head, Sachs L.J. said:[307]

> . . . I do not propose to consider the instant case on the basis of analogies. The analogies or "stepping stones" approach was rightly conceded on behalf of the Attorney-General not to be essential: its artificiality has been demonstrated in the course of the consideration of the numerous authorities put before us. On the other hand, the wide test — advancement of purposes beneficial to the community or objects of general public utility — has an admirable breadth and flexibility which enables it to be reasonably applied from generation to generation to meet changing circumstances. . . .

His Lordship held that the advancement of the administration of justice in the broad sense was clearly beneficial to the community. Further, it benefited the entire community. Hence, both the benefit and public aspects of the public benefit test were satisfied.

6. *Relief of prisoners*. The reference in the preamble to this matter is concerned largely with the release of debtors from prison by paying their debts. Later, this head was applied to hold trusts which sought the release of persons captured abroad, particularly by the Barbary pirates, charitable. Clearly, trusts to promote the release of prisoners generally would not be charitable. They would be contrary to public policy and be for political purposes. Modern organizations which seek to relieve the suffering of prisoners and to rehabilitate them would be charitable under this head.

7. *Resettlement and rehabilitation*. The preamble speaks of the maintenance of sick and maimed soldiers and mariners. This falls under the part of health, to be discussed below, but by analogy it also applies to trusts which are designed to re-establish people in life. Thus, for example, a trust for soldiers returned from a war is charitable.[308] A trust established to provide a disaster relief fund probably also falls into this category.[309] On the other hand, it has been held that an orga-

---

307 *Supra*, note 303, at 94-95.

308 *Verge v. Somerville*, [1924] A.C. 496 (P.C.); *Whitmore v. Canadian Legion of British Empire Service League (Regina Branch)*, [1940] 3 W.W.R. 359 (Sask. Q.B.).

309 *Re North Devon and West Somerset Relief Fund*, [1953] 1 W.L.R. 1260, [1953] 2 All E.R. 1032.

nization the purpose of which is to help immigrant women become established in their new country is not charitable under the fourth head.[310]

8. *Promotion of economic activity.* This derives by analogy from the preamble. Clearly a trust which promotes commerce and industry is for the benefit of the community. Provided it is not for the private benefit of an individual or an industry, it will be charitable.[311]

9. *Trusts for animals.* A trust to maintain a person's animals is not charitable, although it may be valid as a non-charitable purpose trust.[312] However, trusts which promote the maintenance and preservation of animals generally are charitable. This is because, if domesticated, the animals are useful to society. If the animals are not domesticated, the trusts benefit ecology and the balance of nature, or tend to elevate and promote feelings of humanity. On the latter point Swinfen Eady L.J. said in *Re Wedgwood*[313]

> A gift for the benefit and protection of animals tends to promote and encourage kindness towards them, to discourage cruelty, and to ameliorate the condition of the brute creation, and thus to stimulate humane and generous sentiments in man towards the lower animals, and by these means promote feelings of humanity and morality generally, repress brutality, and thus elevate the human race.

On this basis, trusts to preserve wildlife would be charitable,[314] as well as trusts to prevent cruelty to animals,[315] and trusts seeking cures for animal diseases.[316]

On the other hand, a trust which promotes anti-vivisection of animals for medical research would not be charitable. It would not benefit the public because such research is valuable and because its object is political in that it seeks to change the law.[317]

10. *Health and medicine.* Trusts which promote health and medicine are charitable by analogy to items in the preamble such as the relief of impotent people and the maintenance of sick and maimed soldiers and mariners. Hence, gifts to hospitals are charitable,[318] as are gifts designed to promote medical research and treatment.[319]

---

310 See *Vancouver Society of Immigrant & Visible Minority Women, supra,* note 228.

311 *Crystal Palace Trustees v. Minister of Town and Country Planning,* [1951] Ch. 132, [1950] 2 All E.R. 857n.

312 This is discussed in the next chapter.

313 [1915] 1 Ch. 113 at 122 (C.A.).

314 *Ibid.*

315 *Re Green's Will Trusts,* [1985] 3 All E.R. 455.

316 *University of London v. Yarrow* (1857), 1 De G. & J. 72, 44 E.R. 649.

317 *Nat. Anti-Vivisection Society v. Inland Revenue Commrs., supra,* note 33. For a recent treatment of trusts for the benefits of animals, see *Granfield Estate v. Jackson* (1999), 27 E.T.R. (2d) 50, 1999 CarswellBC 644 (S.C. [In Chambers]) in which the court reviews the relevant case law.

318 *Charlotte County Hospital v. St. Andrews (Town)* (1980), 28 N.B.R. (2d) 611, 7 E.T.R. 79, 63 A.P.R. 611 (Q.B.); *Whitman v. Eastern Trust Co.* (sub nom. *Re Hart Estate*), [1951] 2 D.L.R. 30 (N.S. S.C.).

319 *Re Stephens Estate,* [1934] O.W.N. 24 (C.A.).

It does not matter that the institution which benefits from the gift is state-supported[320] or that it charges fees to its patients.[321] A trust for health and medicine is *prima facie* charitable. Hence, the only significant issue that can arise is whether the public element is satisfied.

That issue arose is *Re Resch's Will Trusts*[322] A testator gave money "to the Sisters of Charity . . . to be applied for the general purposes of" St. Vincent's Private Hospital. The court held the gift to be charitable. The private hospital tended to admit persons who could pay for private services, but did not exclude the poor as such. It was operated in conjunction with a public hospital. Moreover, the hospital was not operated for profit, but used its income solely to meet operating costs. Lord Wilberforce said of these matters[323] that a gift to a hospital for its purposes is *prima facie* charitable because the provision of medical care is regarded as being for the benefit of the public. It is true that a gift to a hospital which is operated for profit, or does not provide benefits to the public or a sufficiently large class of the public is not charitable. However, if the hospital merely charges fees to cover its expenses and not to generate a profit, its charitable nature cannot be disputed.

His Lordship further noted[324] that it is not a criterion of charitability of a trust for relief of the sick that the sick be poor. Relief of sickness is itself sufficient to attract the sobriquet, "charitable."[325] Hence, the fact that the private hospital provided services to those who could pay, that is, the well-to-do, was not *per se* objectionable. The test remains whether there is public benefit. His Lordship held that the public element was satisfied indirectly. The need for the private hospital as a supplement to the general hospital was clear. Further, its existence provided relief and additional medical services to the general hospital and benefited the standard of medical care in the general hospital. Accordingly, the existence of the private hospital benefited all.

11. *Social and recreational purposes.* Trusts for social and recreational purposes are often thought not to be charitable because of *I.R.C. v. Baddeley*.[326] The House of Lords considered two settlements which permitted certain premises to be used for the promotion of the religious, social and physical well-being of such residents of two municipalities as were or were likely to become members of the Methodist Church and were of insufficient means otherwise to enjoy the advantages provided by the settlements.

The House of Lords held that trusts were not charitable. They did not fall under the first three heads of charity and lacked the public benefit required for the fourth. On the latter point Viscount Simonds said[327] that the intended benefi-

---

320 *Cox v. Hogan* (1925), 35 B.C.R. 286 (C.A.).

321 *Re Galbraith Estate*, [1938] 3 W.W.R. 93, [1938] 4 D.L.R. 337, 46 Man. R. 347 (K.B.).

322 [1969] 1 A.C. 514, [1967] 3 All E.R. 915 (P.C.).

323 *Ibid.*, at 540-541.

324 *Ibid.*, at 542-544.

325 This also applies to trusts for the advancement of religion and education. See *Verge v. Somerville*, [1924] A.C. 496 (P.C.).

326 *Supra*, note 83.

327 *Ibid.*, at 590-593.

ciaries were a class within a class, namely, the inhabitants of a specified area who were members of a specified church. That, in his opinion, meant that the public aspect was not satisfied. The trust was not one extended to the whole community but by its nature advantageous only to a few, such as a trust for the benefit of soldiers returned from war.[328] Rather, it was one extended to a selected few out of a greater number equally willing and able to take advantage of it.

By contrast, in *Brisbane City Council v. A.-G.*,[329] the Privy Council held that a trust to establish a park and to use it as a recreational area and show ground fell within the spirit and intendment of the *Statute of Elizabeth*.[330]

Dicta in *I.R.C. v. Baddeley* suggested that any trust for the promotion of social and recreational purposes would be void. To settle doubts on this issue, Parliament passed the *Recreational Charities Act, 1958*.[331] It declared that the provision of facilities for recreation in the interest of social welfare were deemed charitable. The Act requires that the facilities must have as object the improvement of the conditions of life of the persons for whom they are intended. Further, it requires that those persons have need of the facilities by reason of youth, age, disability, poverty, or social or economic circumstance, or that the facilities be available to all members of the public promiscuously.

The Act specifically applies to the provision of facilities at village halls, community centres, and women's institutes and the provision and maintenance of grounds and buildings to be used for recreation or leisure-time occupation. It provides that a trust which provides such facilities must satisfy the public benefit test in order to qualify as a charitable trust.

Because the Act requires, *inter alia*, that the facility should be made available to the public at large, the trust in the *Baddeley* case[332] would not have qualified under it.

There is no similar legislation in the Canadian provinces.

It seems clear that an organization which operates a community recreational facility for profit is not charitable.[333]

13. *Sports*. Trusts which promote sports have, unless associated with advancement of education, always been denied charitable status in the past. The leading case on the point is *Re Nottage*,[334] which held a trust for the provision of an annual cup to be awarded to the winner in a yacht race not to be charitable.

---

328 As in *Verge v. Somerville, supra*, note 325.

329 (1978), [1979] A.C. 411, [1978] 3 W.L.R. 299, [1978] 3 All E.R. 30 (P.C.).

330 1601 (43 Eliz. 1), c. 4.

331 1958 (6 & 7 Eliz. 2), c. 17.

332 *Supra*, note 326.

333 *Kennebecasis Valley Recreational Centre Inc. v. Minister of Municipal Affairs* (1975), 11 N.B.R. (2d) 361, 61 D.L.R. (3d) 364 (C.A.). See also *Ukrainian Youth Unity of General Roman Schuchewych-Chuprynka v. Edmonton (City)* (1997), 208 A.R. 280, 1997 CarswellAlta 836, 41 M.P.L.R. (2d) 5, 54 Alta. L.R. (3d) 31 (Q.B.).

334 [1895] 2 Ch. 649 (Ch. Div.).

More recently, this issue was dealt with in Ontario. In *Re Laidlaw Foundation*[335] the courts held that the furtherance of amateur sport is charitable. The case is reproduced below.

When we analyze the foregoing list and the examples given in it, we can conclude: (1) courts have moved away from the strict "analogy" principle and toward a "general public utility" principle; and (2) all of the items in the list can be reduced to objects of general public utility. The items are of general public utility, either because they benefit the community or a sufficient segment of it directly or indirectly by providing services or facilities which otherwise would have to be provided by the state, or else because they promote the mental, moral, and ethical improvement of the public.

When the list is seen in this light, the *Laidlaw* decision is not such a marked departure as might otherwise appear. Further, it would seem that, in Ontario, at least, some of these trusts, if they benefit the public generally, or a sufficiently important segment of it, would be charitable, even though their purposes are not analogous to purposes found in the preamble to the *Statute of Elizabeth*.

It could be argued that *Laidlaw* has altered the principle applicable to the first three heads of charity as well. In our view, that is not so. The case is concerned only with the fourth head of charity.

RE LAIDLAW FOUNDATION

(1984), 48 O.R. (2d) 549, 18 E.T.R. 77, 13 D.L.R. (4th) 491, 6 O.A.C. 181
Supreme Court of Ontario
[Divisional Court]

The Laidlaw Foundation was incorporated in Ontario for the purpose of applying the net income from its property (and the capital, with the unanimous consent of the members) in payments to or for the benefit of such charitable organizations as the directors should determine and in payment of the cost of carrying on such charitable work or objects as the directors might determine. It was, thus, a charity.

The Foundation made payments to certain amateur athletic organizations, namely, the Canadian Special Olympics, the Sports Fund for the Physically Disabled, Jeux Canada Summer Games '81, the Canadian Track and Field Association, Commonwealth Games of Canada Inc., and Olympic Trust of Canada. On the passing of the Foundation's accounts in the Surrogate Court,[336] the Public Trustee argued that the recipients were not charitable.

At first instance, Dymond Surr. Ct. J. held that the organizations were charitable. Her Honour came to this conclusion by reference to the technical meaning of the term, "charity," in law as it had developed since the *Statute of Charitable*

---

335 *Supra*, note 29.
336 The Public Trustee may require a charity to pass its accounts under s. 3 of the *Charities Accounting Act*, R.S.O. 1990, c. C.10.

Uses.[337] In her opinion, the promotion of amateur sport is for the public benefit because it promotes health and physical fitness and is, thus, preventive medicine. Further, it is educative in that it promotes discipline, perseverance, and moral qualities. Hence, sport does not have to be associated with education[338] in order to be charitable. In addition, amateur sport is promoted by governments.[339] Her Honour examined the objects and activities of each of the organizations and found that they promoted amateur sport, were for the benefit of a significant segment of the community and were exclusively charitable. Further, their ancillary purposes did not detract from their main charitable purposes.

The Public Trustee appealed.

SOUTHEY J. delivered the judgment of the Divisional Court:

. . .

While I am satisfied that the learned surrogate court judge correctly dealt with the objections to the donations in question by applying the principles derived by her from the English authorities, I think it is highly artificial and of no real value in deciding whether an object is charitable for courts in Ontario today to pay lip-service to the preamble of a statute passed in the reign of Elizabeth I. I think the better view of the law of Ontario is that stated by the Appellate Division of the Supreme Court of Ontario in *Re Orr.*[340] Meredith C.J.O., in a judgment with which three of the four other members of the court agreed, quoted the classification of charities given by Lord Macnaghten in the *Pemsel*[341] case, and referred to comments thereon by Lindley L.J. in *Re Macduff.*[342] Meredith C.J.O. then went on[343] referring to Lindley L.J.:

> The Lord Justice also pointed out[344] that Sir Samuel Romilly did not say that anything which comes under any one of these four heads must be a charity; that may be so or may not be so, but they must all come within one of them, and said that Sir Samuel Romilly did not mean, and that he was certain that Lord Macnaghten "did not mean to say that every object of public general utility must necessarily be a charity. Some may be, and some may not be."
>
> In *Re Good*[345] Farwell J. expressed the opinion that every one would agree with the Lord Justice's criticism of Lord Macnaghten's judgment, that he did not intend to say that every object of public utility is necessarily a good charity. "But there is not doubt," said he, "that many objects are charitable because they are of public utility. Some objects of public utility are charitable,

---

337 1601 (43 Eliz. 1), c. 4.
338 As in *I.R.C. v. McMullen* (1980), [1981] A.C. 1, [1980] 1 All E.R. 884 (H.L.).
339 Her Honour referred to the *Income Tax Act*, R.S.C. 1952, c. 148, as am. 1970-71-72, c. 63; the *Fitness and Amateur Sport Act*, R.S.C. 1970, c. F-25; and the *Education Act*, R.S.O. 1980, c. 129.
340 *Supra*, note 78.
341 [1891] A.C. 531 (H.L.).
342 [1896] 2 Ch. 451 at 467.
343 *Supra*, note 340, at 595-597.
344 At [1896] 2 Ch. 466, 467.
345 [1905] 2 Ch. 60 at 66.

though not all, and the question is whether within the purview of the statute of Elizabeth this particular object" (*i.e.*, the one he was dealing with) "is or is not a charity."

I have no doubt that these views of Lord Justice Lindley and Farwell J. have been accepted as correct in English cases, and that according to English law a gift is not necessarily charitable because it is for the advancement of an object of general public utility.

I do not think, however, that the English cases as to Lord Macnaghten's fourth head have any application in this Province, since the passing of *The Mortmain and Charitable Uses Act.*[346]

> [Meredith C.J.O. quoted section 2(2) of that Act, which codified Lord Macnaghten's classification, and recited the history of the legislation, which we have summarized above. He continued:]

The course of provincial legislation leads clearly, I think, to the conclusion that the Legislature of Ontario adopted this latter change in the law for the purpose of preventing the English doctrine to which I have referred from being applied in Ontario in determining whether any purpose beneficial to the community, not being the relief of poverty, education, or the advancement of religion, was in the legal sense a charitable purpose.

However that may be, there is no room for construing sub-sec. (2) of sec. 2 of the provincial Act as Lord Justice Lindley interpreted what was said by Lord Macnaghten and by Sir Samuel Romilly. It is an express declaration that the purposes which it enumerates shall be deemed to be charitable uses within the meaning of the Act; and the courts of this Province are, in my opinion, warranted in looking to it, as the courts in England look to the statute of Elizabeth, for the purpose of determining what in law is a charitable gift in the case of personalty, to which the provision does not apply. It would be strange indeed if a gift of land would be charitable because the object of it came within this provision, and a gift of personalty for the same object would not be charitable because of the rule of law adopted in England.

The same strange result could still occur under the present Ontario statute. The *Mortmain and Charitable Uses Act*[347] contained in section 1(2) the same definition of charitable uses that was in section 2(2) of the Act . . . quoted by Meredith C.J.O. in *Re Orr.*[348] That Act was in force at the time the donations in question were made, but did not apply to them because it related only to land. The *Mortmain and Charitable Uses Act* was repealed on June 15, 1982, by the *Mortmain and Charitable Uses Repeal Act, 1982*,[349] but the *Charities Accounting Act* was amended on the same date by the *Charities Accounting Amendment Act, 1982*,[350] by the addition of sections 6a, 6b, 6c and 6d. . . .

> [His Lordship quoted these sections, which contain the substance of the charitable uses provisions of the former *Mortmain and Charitable Uses Act*. They are reproduced later in this chapter. He continued:]

---

346 R.S.O. 1914, c. 103.
347 R.S.O. 1980, c. 297.
348 *Supra*, note 78.
349 S.O. 1982, c. 12.
350 S.O. 1982, c. 11, s. 1.

The decision of the Appellate Division in *Re Orr* was reversed by the Supreme Court of Canada,[351] but on the ground that the bequests were too vague and uncertain, a matter quite different from the point made by Meredith C.J.O. in the passage I have quoted above. Sir Charles Fitzpatrick C.J.[352] disapproved of the view expressed by Meredith C.J.O. . . .

None of the other judges in the Supreme Court of Canada referred to the statements made by Meredith C.J.O. as to the effect of the Ontario *Mortmain and Charitable Uses Act*, so that the disapproval of them by the Chief Justice of Canada, while entitled to the utmost respect and deference, does not form part of the judgment of the court that is binding on us. I think we are free to adopt the reasons of Meredith C.J.O. in this matter, and I do so.

If the adoption of the reasons of Meredith C.J.O. results in any change in the law, it is to provide a more liberal definition of charity. The donations in question having been held to be proper under the restricted definition, it follows that they are proper donations to charitable organizations or for payment of the cost of carrying on charitable work under the more liberal definition.

For the foregoing reasons, the appeal is dismissed. . . .

Notes and Questions

1. Does *Laidlaw* decide that the promotion of amateur sport is charitable? If so, does it apply to all sport? If not, what does it decide?[353]

2. If, as stated by Southey J. in *Laidlaw*, the statute provides a more liberal definition of charity, in particular of the fourth head, what exactly is that definition? The judgment of Meredith C.J.O. in *Re Orr*,[354] which the Divisional Court followed in *Laidlaw*, suggests a return to the definition which was current before *Morice v. Bishop of Durham*,[355] that is, that any object of general public utility not falling under the first three heads is charitable.[356] If this is so, is it wise for the law to have such an open-ended definition? How do you measure public utility in the context of charity?[357]

3. How relevant is it to the definition of charity that under the *Income Tax Act*[358] not only charities, but also Canadian amateur athletic associations are registered,[359] and donations by individuals to either type of organization qualify for a tax credit?[360] The Canadian Special Olympics, considered in *Laidlaw*, had charitable registration status, while the other organizations considered in that case were registered Canadian amateur athletic associations.

---

351 *Supra*, note 78.
352 *Ibid.*, at 671.
353 For a useful comment on *Laidlaw*, see D.W.M. Waters, Case Review, "In the Matter of the Laidlaw Foundation and in the Matter of the Charities Accounting Act" (1985), 5 Philanthrop. No. 1, 46, repr. sub nom. "Re Laidlaw Foundation: A Comment," 18 E.T.R. 120. See also D. Evans, "Sport and Charitable Status" (1986), 4 Trust. L. & P. 22.
354 *Supra*, note 78.
355 *Supra*, note 33.
356 We discussed this definition earlier in this chapter.
357 See O.L.R.C. *Report on Charities*, Chapter 7.
358 R.S.C. 1985, c. 1 (5th Supp.), as am.
359 *Ibid.*, s. 149(1)(l).
360 *Ibid.*, s. 118.1(1), (3).

While the Department of National Revenue tends to follow the provincial law of charity, it need not do so. Hence, divergencies between the federal and provincial law may appear in this manner.

4. The other Canadian jurisdictions do not have a statutory definition of charity. Does this mean that the Ontario law of charities is likely to differ from the rest of the country? Is that desirable? Should Canada have a uniform statutory definition of charity? How should it be framed? Could it be made flexible enough to meet changing needs?

5. In *Re Orr*,[361] followed in *Re Laidlaw*, Meredith C.J.O. assumed that Lord Macnaghten's classification in *Pemsel*[362] was adopted as a statutory definition of charity in Ontario to prevent the application in Ontario of the English law that an object is charitable under the fourth head if it is for the benefit of the public *and* if it is within the purview of the preamble to the *Statute of Charitable Uses*.[363] This is highly doubtful. That law was received law in Ontario and it is unlikely that the Legislature intended to change it so drastically without specific reference to it. Moreover, the adoption in Ontario of *The Mortmain, and Charitable Uses Act, 1902*[364] evidenced a desire on the part of the Ontario Legislature to follow the English model, since it copied an English Act.[365] Again, it is unlikely that the Legislature intended to adopt one English law, but reject another without saying so expressly.

What is more probable is that the Statute Law Revision Council seized upon Lord Macnaghten's classification, then recently enunciated, as a convenient statement of the law and a means whereby the re-enactment of the outdated preamble could be avoided.[366]

6. The definition of charity in the former *Mortmain and Charitable Uses Act*[367] and the *Charities Accounting Act*[368] applies only to land. Those statutes were designed to prevent charitable organizations from holding land in perpetuity except for their actual use and occupation. We have seen that in cases decided under the English predecessor of these statutes[369] the courts tended to find an object charitable in order to be able to defeat it. It is somewhat ironic that the present statute should be used for the exact opposite reason. In any event, is it legitimate to use a definition that applies to land and also to personalty?

7. The flexibility of approach to purposes falling under the fourth head offered by *Laidlaw* is not otherwise novel. In *Incorporated Council of Law Reporting for England & Wales v. A.-G.*,[370] Russell L.J. implicitly[371] and Sachs L.J. explicitly[372] rejected the artificiality of arguing by analogy to the preamble. Moreover, Sachs L.J. thought that the wide test, "advancement of purposes beneficial to the community or objects of general

---

361 *Supra*, note 78.
362 *Supra*, note 57.
363 1601 (43 Eliz. 1), c. 4.
364 S.O. 1902, c. 2.
365 The *Mortmain and Charitable Uses Act, 1888*, (51 & 52 Vict.), c. 42 (U.K.). The law of mortmain was already part of the law of Ontario before the enactment of the statute. See A.H. Oosterhoff, "The Law of Mortmain: An Historical and Comparative Review" (1977), 27 U. of T.L.J. 257 at 302ff.
366 There is no reference to this matter in *Records of the Statute Law Revision Council, 1890-1912* (Ont.), nor in the Legislative debates.
367 R.S.O. 1980, c. 297, s. 1(2).
368 R.S.O. 1990, c. C.10, s. 7.
369 *Mortmain Act, 1736*, (9 Geo. 2), c. 36.
370 [1972] Ch. 73, [1971] 3 W.L.R. 853, [1971] 3 All E.R. 1029 (C.A.).
371 *Ibid.*, at 88.
372 *Ibid.*, at 94.

public utility," in other words, Lord McNaghten's fourth head of charity, is adequate and flexible enough to determine whether an object is or is not charitable under the fourth head.[373]

8. In the *Council of Law Reporting* case[374] Sachs L.J. expressed the opinion that a statutory definition of charity would be unwise because it would cause inflexibility and would be productive of litigation and artificial distinctions.[375] Is this criticism valid of the Ontario legislation?

9. By his will, Sir Henry Strakosch, who died on October 30, 1943, directed his trustees to set aside part of his residuary estate upon trust to be applied to a fund whose purpose was designed to strengthen the bonds of unity between South Africa and Great Britain and which would also help to appease the racial tensions between the Dutch and English speaking segments of the South African community. The fund set aside amounted to about £40,000.

Evidence was admitted which tended to show that the testator's object was to promote racial and Commonwealth harmony by mean of students' education, journalistic training, and interchange of young persons between Britain and South Africa and between young South Africans of different racial origin. Is this trust charitable under the preamble?[376] Under the *Laidlaw* approach?

10. Under a deed of trust dated October 12, 1937, certain real and personal property, previously conveyed to the trustees by the settlor, was vested in the trustees for charitable purposes, namely:

> . . . for the purpose of establishing and maintaining an institute and meeting place in London to be known as "The London Welsh Association" . . . for the benefit of Welsh people resident in or near or visiting London with a view to creating a centre in London for promoting the moral social spiritual and educational welfare of Welsh people and fostering the study of the Welsh language and of Welsh history literature music and art.

This general purpose was particularized in a list of specific objects, which included permitting the property to be used for: (a) a meeting place for Welsh people in London for their social intercourse, study, reading, rest, recreation, and refreshment; (b) meetings, concerts, lectures, and other forms of instruction and discussion or entertainment connected with the Welsh language and Welsh history, literature, music and art, and similar educational purposes; and (c) a hostel for the accommodation of Welsh people in London. The term "Welsh people" was defined in the deed as meaning "persons of Welsh nationality by birth or descent or born or educated or at any time domiciled in the principality of Wales or the county of Monmouth."

The real property comprised two parcels; one part was occupied by the London Welsh Association, and the other part was rented out to tenants. The trustees of the Institute gave the rents from the premises to the London Welsh Association to be applied to some of the association's objects only. Among these activities were lectures, debates, a music club, educational classes, maintaining the headquarters of the association, maintaining badminton and table tennis clubs, and organizing dances, whist and bridge drives, and an annual dinner and garden party.

---

373 *Ibid.*
374 *Ibid.*
375 *Ibid.*, at 94-95.
376 See *Re Strakosch*, [1949] 1 Ch. 529, [1949] 2 All E.R. 6 (C.A.).

The trustees claimed exemption from income tax under section 37(1) of the British *Income Tax Act, 1918*,[377] which granted an exemption for income from lands vested in trustees for charitable purposes to the extent the income was devoted exclusively for charitable purposes.

Is this trust charitable under the preamble?[378] Would it be charitable under the *Laidlaw* approach?

11. A non-profit corporation owned and operated a cultural centre, which included an arena. The corporation's purpose was to alleviate the problems of juvenile delinquency in the region. The corporation used the arena mostly for hockey in winter, but also for a number of other events. The centre was operated by volunteers. It was funded largely by donations and by fees charged for the use of the centre and admissions to games and other functions. No other organization in the area provided similar services. A statute[379] exempts from municipal assessment and taxation real property owned and occupied by charitable societies, whether incorporated or not, used solely for charitable activities, provided no income derived from the property is paid to any member.

Is the centre a charity under the preamble? Is it charitable under *Laidlaw*? Would the building be exempt from municipal assessment and taxes?[380]

12. Are the following trusts charitable?

(a) To promote and teach the doctrines of socialism.[381]

(b) To promote the doctrines of Mr. X, regarding a single tax.[382]

(c) For the entertainment of soldiers returned from a war.[383]

(d) To promote the sport of racing pigeons.[384]

(e) For a humane society.[385]

(f) For a community hall.[386]

(g) For civil improvement.[387]

(h) To assist a fire brigade.[388]

(i) To protect the existence of a game and bird sanctuary in a developing suburban area.[389]

13. The Humanist Association of Toronto was granted charitable status by the Canada Customs and Revenue Agency. The Association had applied for charitable status,

---

377 1918 (8 & 9 Geo. 5), c. 40.

378 See *Williams' Trustees v. Inland Revenue Commissioners*, [1947] A.C. 447, [1947] 1 All E.R. 513 (H.L.).

379 *Assessment Act*, R.S.N.B. 1973, c. A-14, s. 4(1)(e), repealed 1986, c. 13, s. 2.

380 See *Centre Culturel de Saint-Quentin Inc. v. New Brunswick* (1987), 82 N.B.R. (2d) 139, 208 A.P.R. 139 (C.A.).

381 See *Re Loney* (1953), 9 W.W.R. (N.S.) 366 (Man. Q.B.).

382 *Re Knight*, [1937] O.R. 462, [1937] 2 D.L.R. 285 (H.C.).

383 *Sheppard v. Bradshaw* (1921), 50 O.L.R. 626, 64 D.L.R. 624 (H.C.).

384 *Royal National Agricultural and Industrial Association v. Chester* (1974), 48 A.L.J.R. 304.

385 *Re Toronto Humane Society* (1920), 18 O.W.N. 414 (H.C.). *Cf. Ontario (Public Trustee) v. Toronto Humane Society* (1987), 60 O.R. (2d) 236, 27 E.T.R. 40, 40 D.L.R. (4th) 111 (H.C.).

386 *Re Vernon Estate*, [1948] 2 W.W.R. 46 (B.C. S.C.).

387 *Re Eacrett Estate*, [1949] O.R. 1, [1949] 1 D.L.R. 305 (C.A.). See also *Re Etter Estate* (sub nom. *Canada Permanent Trust Co. v. Imperial (Town)*) (1967), 61 W.W.R. 427, 65 D.L.R. (2d) 398 (Sask. Q.B.), a charitable objective in a named municipality; *Re Jacques Estate* (1967), 65 W.W.R. 136, 63 D.L.R. (2d) 673 (B.C. S.C.), to finance a community project.

388 *Re Wokingham Fire Brigades Trusts*, [1951] Ch. 373, [1951] 1 All E.R. 454.

389 *Granfield Estate v. Jackson* (1999), 27 E.T.R. (2d) 50, 1999 CarswellBC 644 (S.C. [In Chambers]).

but had been turned down on the ground that it fell under none of the four heads of charity. It appealed to the Federal Court of Appeal, arguing that the Agency's decision had violated its constitutional guarantees of equality and freedom of religion. In an out-of-court settlement, the Agency granted charitable status to the Association on the ground that it was an organization "beneficial to the community as a whole".[389.1] Is this decision one that follows logically from *Laidlaw*?

5. IMPERFECT CHARITABLE TRUSTS

(a) Generally

In the preceding material we referred to the principle that, to be charitable, a trust must be devoted exclusively to charitable purposes. The early leading case on this principle is *Morice v. Bishop of Durham*,[390] discussed above. You will recall that it concerned a trust which permitted the Bishop of Durham, as trustee, to dispose of property in his discretion for "objects of benevolence and liberality." The court held that, assuming "benevolence" to be the equivalent of "charity," "liberality" was outside the definition of charity. It followed that the Bishop could, if he chose, devote all the property to objects of liberality. Since the court could only oversee the trust if it was devoted to charity, it failed.

Trust provisions of this nature are called "imperfect trust provisions" because they state the intention of the trust's creator imperfectly. The creator of the trust probably intended to devote his or her bounty to charity, but did not say so and the court will not hear extrinsic evidence of the creator's intention.

A modern example of such a trust is *Chichester Diocesan Fund & Board of Finance Inc. v. Simpsons*.[391] It concerned the will of Caleb Diplock, which directed his executors to pay the residue of the estate to "such charitable institution or institutions or other charitable or benevolent object or objects" as they should in their absolute discretion select. The executors distributed the residue among 139 charitable and benevolent organizations, of which the appellant was one. The testator's next-of-kin then questioned the validity of the trust, so the executors brought an application to determine whether it was valid as a charitable trust or void for uncertainty.

The House of Lords held that the trust was void. Lord Simonds said[392] that "benevolent" is not coterminous in meaning with "charitable." Only the latter has a recognized meaning in law. The meaning of the former is both wider and narrower than the meaning of "charitable." Further, the testator did not intend to benefit charitable objects that were also benevolent. Hence, the disjunctive "or" could not be construed as a conjunctive "and." This meant that the executors could devote the money to either or both charitable or benevolent objects. Since only the former were permitted, the gift failed in its entirety. His Lordship further

---

389.1   Tom Blackwell, "Humanists Win Victory over Status: Standing up for 'Godless Masses'". *National Post*, 14 February, 2004.
390   *Supra*, note 33.
391   *Supra*, note 83.
392   *Ibid.*, at 368-370.

noted that if "benevolent" objects were treated as charitable, then so should "philanthropic," "liberal," "patriotic," "public," and others.[393]

The Supreme Court of Canada followed the *Chichester* case in *Re Loggie, Brewer v. McCauley*.[394] The testatrix, Alexandra Loggie, directed her executors to apply the residue of her estate in their discretion "for charitable, religious, educational or philanthropic purposes . . . within the Province of New Brunswick." The judge of first instance held the trust void for uncertainty.[395] The Supreme Court of Canada, on a *per saltum* appeal, affirmed. The court declined to construe the disjunctive "or" as conjunctive and held that the word "philanthropic" vitiated the gift.[396]

Notes and Questions

1. To qualify as charitable, the purposes of an organization or trust must be exclusively charitable.[397] This exclusivity requirement, which precludes charitable organizations from pursuing a mixture of charitable and non-charitable purposes, ensures that donations made to charitable organizations are devoted solely to the pursuit of charitable purposes.[398]

The exclusivity requirement is also reflected in the *Income Tax Act*.[399] The definition of "charitable organization" contained in section 149.1(1) specifies that "all the resources" of the organization must be devoted to charitable activities carried on by the organization itself," and that "no part of the income" of the organization may personally benefit a "proprietor, member, shareholder, trustee or settlor."

2. The reason a bequest that uses the word "charitable" disjunctively with another, such as "benevolent," fails is because one or more of the objects selected by the trustees may be merely "benevolent" and not necessarily "charitable." Thus the gift is not exclusively charitable and is void for uncertainty.

It is not necessary that the word "charitable" be used disjunctively with another word for the trust to fail. Words such as "worthy" and "philanthropic" by themselves will also mean that the trust is not charitable.[400] Even if the conjunctive "and" is used, it may be construed to mean "or," thus causing the gift to fail.[401] Normally, however, if the conjunctive is used, the gift is valid because it is construed to mean that the object must be charitable as well as "benevolent," "philanthropic," or whatever other term may be used.[402]

---

393 The aftermath of the case is discussed in the chapter on breach of trust.

394 [1954] S.C.R. 645, [1955] 1 D.L.R. 415.

395 (1953), 34 M.P.R. 66 (N.B. Q.B.).

396 To the same effect, see *A.-G. v. Wahr-Hansen*, [2000] 3 All E.R. 642 (P.C.).

397 *Vancouver Society of Immigrant & Visible Minority Women v. Minister of National Revenue*, *supra*, note 228 [*Vancouver Society*].

398 *McGovern v. Attorney General* (1981), [1982] Ch. 321, [1981] 3 All E.R. 493 (Ch. Div.). See also, *Vancouver Society*, *ibid*.

399 R.S.C. 1985, c. 1 (5th Supp.). See also, *Vancouver Society*, *supra*, note 228.

400 See, *e.g.*, *Planta v. Greenshields*, [1931] 1 W.W.R. 401, [1931] 2 D.L.R. 189, 43 B.C.R. 439 (C.A.); *Re Albery*, [1964] 1 O.R. 342, 42 D.L.R. (2d) 201 (H.C.). See also *McIntosh v. McIntosh* (1982), 40 N.B.R. (2d) 101, 105 A.P.R. 101 (Q.B).

401 *Re Metcalfe Estate*, [1946] O.R. 882, [1947] 1 D.L.R. 567 (H.C.). In interpreting the testator's intention, the court construed the word "and" to mean "or".

402 *Chichester Diocesan Fund & Board of Finance Inc. v. Simpsons*, *supra*, note 83, at 352, *per* Lord Wright, dissenting; followed in *Re Shortt Estate* (1974), 2 O.R. (2d) 329, 42 D.L.R. (3d) 673 (H.C.).

3. In response to the *Chichester* case,[403] a number of jurisdictions enacted legislation to avoid the problem of imperfect trust provisions. The English legislation[404] is defective in that it applies only to trusts created before December 16, 1952.

Canadian statutes are based on a provision in the *Uniform Wills Act*.[405] The Manitoba provision is section 91 of *The Trustee Act*.[406] It provides:

> **91.**(1) Where property is, by any instrument, left in trust or by outright gift for a charitable purpose that is not void for any cause, and that is linked conjunctively or disjunctively in the instrument with a non-charitable purpose, and the non-charitable purpose is void for any cause, the charitable trust or gift is valid and operates solely for the benefit of the charitable purpose.
>
> (2) Where property is, by any instrument, left in trust or by outright gift for a charitable purpose that is not void for any cause, and that is linked conjunctively or disjunctively in the instrument with a non-charitable purpose, and the non-charitable purpose is not void, the trust or gift is valid for both purposes, and, where the instrument has not divided the property among the charitable and the non-charitable purposes, the trustee shall divide the property among the charitable and the non-charitable purposes according to his discretion.

Similar legislation exists in British Columbia,[407] Alberta,[408] and New Brunswick.[409] However, those three statutes apply only to testamentary trusts. The legislation has been criticized because it speaks of a purpose as void for uncertainty (a purpose cannot be void for uncertainty; a gift or trust can be); it refers to a purpose in the singular only; it refers to an outright gift to a purpose (which is impossible); and for other reasons.[410]

Legislation proposed for Ontario by the Ontario Law Reform Commission purports to meet these objections.[411] It also deals with the interaction of imperfect trust provisions legislation and section 16 of the *Perpetuities Act*.[412] This aspect is discussed further in the next chapter.

(b) Exceptions to the Exclusivity Rule

Apart from statute, there are three exceptions to the rule that a trust must be exclusively charitable: (1) if the charitable part can be severed from the non-charitable, the former will be valid; (2) if the main purpose of a trust is charitable, ancillary purposes which are not charitable will not cause the gift to fail; and (3) if a trust is not on its face *prima facie* charitable, but the trustee is charitable or is a person whose work is generally charitable, the gift may be held to be charitable.

---

403 *Ibid.*

404 *The Charitable Trusts (Validation) Act 1954*, (2 & 3 Eliz. 2), c. 58 (U.K.).

405 Uniform Law Conference of Canada, *Consolidation of Uniform Acts* (1978, as amended) at 53-59, s. 30.

406 R.S.M. 1987, c. T160.

407 *Law and Equity Act*, R.S.B.C. 1996, c. 253, s. 47.

408 *Wills Act*, R.S.A. 2000, c. W-12, s. 32.

409 *Wills Act*, R.S.N.B. 1973, c. W-9, s. 30.

410 Waters, at 6070-6078.

411 Ontario Law Reform Commission *Report on the Law of Trusts* (Toronto: Ministry of the Attorney General, 1984), Chapter 8; Draft Act, at 520-521, s. 81 ("O.L.R.C., *Report on Trusts*"). See also O.L.R.C. *Report on Charities*, at 415-416.

412 R.S.O. 1990, c. P.9.

The first exception, severability, applies not only to charitable trusts, but to trusts generally. In the context of charitable trusts it allows a court to save part of a gift if that part is charitable, while declaring void the part that is non-charitable. However, the court can only do so if, as a matter of construction, it is clear that specific proportions of the property were given to the two purposes. Thus, severance is possible if the gift says, "one-half each to church X and such other worthy purposes as my trustees may decide"; it is not possible if the gift is "to such charitable or worthy purposes as my trustees may decide." If there is a gift to a charitable purpose but the testator or settlor directs that part of the gift shall be applied for a non-charitable purpose, such as the maintenance of the testator's tomb, it is possible to sever the latter, however. In such a gift the non-charitable portion is dependent upon the charitable, but when the former is severed, the gift is applied solely to the charitable purpose.[413]

The second exception, main versus ancillary purposes, is somewhat more common. It was applied in *Re Laidlaw Foundation*,[414] set out above. That case considered, *inter alia*, the fact that several amateur athletic organizations had certain purposes which were not charitable in addition to their main purpose, the promotion of amateur athletics, which the court held to be charitable. The court concluded that the main purpose governed and that the ancillary purposes did not invalidate the main one. In coming to such a conclusion, a court may consider extrinsic evidence of the charity's operation.[415]

On the other hand, an organization's purposes, while otherwise charitable, may cease to be so by an overly broad "ancillary" clause. That is what happened in *Vancouver Society of Immigrant & Visible Minority Women v. Minister of National Revenue*.[416] The Supreme Court of Canada would have held the main purpose charitable as being for the advancement of education, but held that an apparent ancillary purpose, which enabled the Society to do all things "conducive" to the attainment of its objects, was too broad and would allow it do things that would not be ancillary to the main purpose. Hence, the Society was not exclusively charitable.

You must be careful, however, to distinguish between what an organization's objects are and what it actually does. In a carefully reasoned article, Maurice C. Cullity argues, correctly, we submit, that only an organization's objects are relevant in determining whether it is charitable.[417] An organization's activities are irrelevant to that issue; they are merely means to an end (the objects). Certain activities of a charity may, however, lead to proceedings against its trustees or officers, if they are beyond the charity's powers. But in determining that issue, the court should ask the question whether the activity being impugned is "a reasonable and prudent method of achieving the charitable objects" of the orga-

---

413   See, *e.g.*, *Re Coxen*, [1948] Ch. 747, [1948] 2 All E.R. 492 (Ch. Div.).
414   *Supra*, note 29. See also *Re Doering Estate*, (1948), [1948] O.R. 923, 1948 CarswellOnt 77, [1949] 1 D.L.R. 267, [1948] O.W.N. 840 (H.C.).
415   *Towle Estate v. M.N.R.* (sub nom. *Guaranty Trust Co. v. M.N.R.* (1966), [1967] S.C.R. 133, 60 D.L.R. (2d) 481, [1966] C.T.C. 755, 67 D.T.C. 5003.
416   *Supra*, note 228.
417   Maurice C. Cullity, Q.C., "The Myth of Charitable Activities" (1990-91), 10 E. & T.J. 7.

nization.[418] It should not determine that an organization is not charitable because its activities (as distinct from its objects) are not charitable. Further, Mr. Cullity is of opinion that whether an organization is charitable cannot be ascertained by determining that the greater portion of its activities (or its objects) are charitable.[419]

The third exception, gifts to persons or institutions whose work is charitable, is the subject of a number of cases. The older cases hold that if the trustee carries on both charitable and non-charitable work, the gift is not charitable. In *Blais v. Touchet*,[420] the Supreme Court of Canada took a more lenient approach. The testator was a parish priest in Saskatchewan. He wrote his will in French. In it he appointed his bishop his executor and left him all his property "pour ses oeuvres, mais pour les oeuvres qui aideraient la cause des Canadiens Français dans son diocèse." The court accepted the following literal translation of the quoted words: "for his works, but for such of the works as would aid the cause of the French Canadians in his diocese." The court held that the bishop took as trustee, that by virtue of the bishop's office the gift was limited to his charities or works arising from his religious duties as bishop, and that the quoted words did not extend the purpose beyond religion.

Notes and Questions

1. Is the construction placed upon the trust by the court in *Blais v. Touchet* correct?
2. *Re Rumball*[421] reviews cases involving fact situations similar to *Blais v. Touchet*.
3. A testator disposed of the residue of his estate in the following terms:

> I direct my Trustee to divide the residue of my Estate equally between the Roman Catholic Archiepiscopal Corporation of Winnipeg for the benefit of the Church of the Immaculate Conception in said City or otherwise as the said Corporation shall see fit and his Excellency the Roman Catholic Bishop of Victoria for such charitable purposes connected with the Roman Catholic Church on Vancouver Island as he may direct.

Is the gift to the first beneficiary valid assuming that not all the purposes of the Corporation are charitable? Is it a trust? An absolute gift? If the latter, is the purpose for which the money may be used restricted?[422]

4. A testator left the residue of his estate "to Z absolutely to be disposed of by him for worthy causes, as he considers desirable, in Exeter, Ontario."
Is the gift charitable? Was it the testator's intention to make a charitable gift? Is intention relevant? Should it be?

5. A number of Jewish families established a synagogue affiliated with the United Synagogue, a national organization which assisted new congregations. Under the rules of

---

418 *Ibid.*, at 26.
419 *Ibid.*
420 (Sub nom. *Re Touchet Estate*) [1963] S.C.R. 358, 45 W.W.R. 246, 40 D.L.R. (2d) 961.
421 (1956), [1956] Ch. 105, [1955] 3 All E.R. 71 (C.A.).
422 See *Roman Catholic Archiepiscopal Corp. of Winnipeg v. Ryan* (1957), 26 W.W.R. 69, 12 D.L.R. (2d) 23 (B.C. S.C.). The gift to the corporation was unrestricted. Compare *Jewish National Fund v. Royal Trust Co.* (1964), 43 D.L.R. (2d) 417, 1964 CarswellBC 30, 46 W.W.R. 577 (C.A.), affirmed [1965] S.C.R. 784, 1965 CarswellBC 60, 52 W.W.R. 410, 53 D.L.R. (2d) 577.

the United Synagogue, all property of a congregation had to be held in trust for "a synagogue with or without appurtenant buildings for religious education and social purposes." The chief purpose of the new congregation and its synagogue was to hold religious services and to give religious instruction to younger members of the congregation. However, it also operated a communal hall in connection with the synagogue in which a great variety of social functions were held. Is the synagogue a charity?[423]

6. In order to qualify for a charitable deduction under taxing statutes it is sometimes necessary to show not only that the purposes of the trust are exclusively charitable, but also that the objects of the trustee are exclusively charitable. This was the case under section 7(1)(d) of the former *Estate Tax Act*.[424]

Towle Estate v. M.N.R.[425] concerned a trust to establish a fund for the purpose of lending money to women medical students at a university, of which the medical alumni association of the university was to be the trustee. The court held that the trust was charitable. The association was constituted exclusively for charitable purposes, since its main objects were charitable, namely promoting and enlarging the usefulness and influence of the university and promoting the science and art of medicine. The court came to this conclusion even though the association had a number of ancillary purposes as well, such as the encouragement of good fellowship among the members of the association and promoting the interests of the medical graduates at the university.

7. In *I.R.C. v. Helen Slater Charitable Trust Ltd.*,[426] the court held that when one charitable corporation makes a donation to another, it is applying those funds for charitable purposes and the gift is exempt from income tax.

8. The letters patent of a university students' council provided that the purposes of the council were to represent the students and to develop and promote scientific, artistic, cultural, athletic, political, religious and social activities for the students, to promote the students' welfare and to advance the interest of the university in all appropriate ways. The letters patent further provided for affiliation with national and provincial student organizations and stated that the council's funds were held on trust for its purposes. Council decided to make substantial donations to aid famine relief and to support striking workers. Some students objected and called the Public Trustee. The latter sought to have the proposed payments declared *ultra vires*. Did the Public Trustee have standing in the matter?[427]

9. In *Funnell v. Stewart*[428] the testatrix's bequest was found to be charitable. She had directed the funds to be used to further the spiritual work that her own faith healing group carried out. The court found that the private religious services of the group were not in themselves charitable and were subsidiary to the public faith healing part of the group's group. This did not however, render the group non-charitable. The court found that the healing part of the group's work was charitable. Which of the following reasons do you find the most compelling? (1) Faith healing had become a recognized activity of public

---

423 See *Neville Estates Ltd. v. Madden*, [1962] Ch. 832, [1961] 3 All E.R. 769.

424 S.C. 1958, c. 29.

425 (Sub nom. *Guaranty Trust Co. v. M.N.R.*) (1966), [1967] S.C.R. 133, 60 D.L.R. (2d) 481, [1966] C.T.C. 755, 67 D.T.C. 5003.

426 [1981] 3 All E.R. 98, [1982] Ch. 49 (C.A.).

427 See *Attorney General v. Ross*, [1985] 3 All E.R. 334, [1986] 1 W.L.R. 252 (Ch. Div.). See also *Webb v. O'Doherty* (1991), 3 Admin. L.R. 731 which applied the *Ross* case in its finding that discussion of political issues was an acceptable educational activity for a charitable organization. The court, however, found that political campaigning attempting to influence public opinion was not acceptable when any educational value was peripheral to the main aim.

428 [1996] 1 All E.R. 715 (Ch. D.).

benefit; or (2) the religious nature of the faith healing movement of the group rendered the work a charitable purpose within which a sufficient element of public benefit was assumed so as to enable the organization to be recognized as charitable absent contrary evidence.

6. CHARITY AND PERPETUITY

In the introductory material to this chapter we noted that the rule against indefinite duration does not apply to charitable trusts, but that the rule against remoteness of vesting, commonly called the rule against perpetuities, does, albeit not with the same strictness as to trusts for persons and non-charitable purpose trusts.[429]

The common law rule applies in New Brunswick, Newfoundland, Nova Scotia, and Saskatchewan. The common law rule, as modified by statute, applies in British Columbia,[430] Alberta,[431] Ontario,[432] the Northwest Territories,[433] Yukon Territory,[434] and Prince Edward Island.[435] The rule has been abolished in Manitoba.[436] The Prince Edward Island Act merely changes the perpetuity period, while the other statutes enact comprehensive reforms.[437] These reforms include the principle that a gift is no longer automatically void if it may vest outside the perpetuity period, but rather is presumptively valid. The statutes permit one to "wait and see" whether the gift will vest within or outside the period. Only in the latter event, that is, if actual facts show that the gift will vest outside the period, will the gift be void.

There are four situations in which the rule applies to charities. In the following descriptions we first give the result under the common law rule. Then we consider the effect of the statutes.

1. *Future gift to charity.* When the gift is for charitable purposes, but the particular charitable object intended is not yet in existence or awaits the fulfilment of a condition precedent, the gift is valid and the property can be used initially for other charitable purposes under the *cy-près* doctrine.[438] The important question

---

429 See part 2, *supra.*

430 *Perpetuity Act*, R.S.B.C. 1996, c. 358.

431 *Perpetuities Act*, R.S.A. 2000, c. P-5.

432 *Perpetuities Act*, R.S.O. 1990, c. P.9.

433 *Perpetuities Act*, R.S.N.W.T. 1988, c. P-3.

434 *Perpetuities Act*, R.S.Y. 2002, c. 168.

435 *Perpetuities Act*, R.S.P.E.I. 1988, c. P-3.

436 By *The Perpetuities and Accumulations Act*, S.M. 1982-83-84, c. 43, s. 3. See now R.S.M. 1987, c. P33.

437 *The Perpetuities and Accumulations Act*, R.S.N.L. 1990, c. P-7, concerns employee benefit trusts only.

438 *Chamberlayne v. Brockett* (1872), 8 Ch. App. 206, [1861-73] All E.R. Rep. 271 (Ch.); *Jewish Home for the Aged v. Toronto General Trusts*, [1961] S.C.R. 465, 34 W.W.R. 638, 28 D.L.R. (2d) 48; *Re Mountain Estate* (1913), 26 O.L.R. 163, 4 D.L.R. 737 (C.A.); *Re Pearce*, [1955] 1 D.L.R. 801 (B.C. S.C.); *Scales' Wills, Re*, [1972] 2 N.S.W.R. 108. In *Re Pearce* it was alleged that the gift was on condition precedent and failed because it offended the rule against perpetuities and was not given for a charitable purpose. The court held that it was unnecessary to

the court must determine in these circumstances is whether there is an out and out gift to charity or whether the gift depends upon a future and uncertain event.

Chamberlayne v. Brockett[439] illustrates the point. A testatrix directed that the residue of her estate be invested and that the trustees make certain fixed annual payments out of the income to charity. The rest of the income was to be used to buy land in a specified municipality, as soon as the land became available, to build alms houses. Any surplus remaining was to be used for the benefit of the inmates. The court held that since the testatrix declared her intention to "return her estate in charity to God who gave it" and "therefore" she gave the estate as set out, there was a complete gift to charity immediately and that the only thing that was postponed was the particular mode of charity.

You should contrast *Chamberlayne* with *Re Mander*.[440] The testatrix wished to pay for the training for the priesthood of a person from a particular church as soon as such a person should come forward, and she gave a sum of money in trust for this purpose. The court distinguished *Chamberlayne v. Brockett* because the gift depended upon a future uncertain event and was, therefore, void for perpetuity.[441]

2. *Gift over from non-charity to charity.* When there is a gift over from a non-charity to a charity on a future event which is too remote, the gift over is void.[442]

3. *Gift over from charity to non-charity.* When the gift over is from a charity to a non-charity, and the event upon which the gift over occurs is beyond the perpetuity period, it is void. If the event is described in the form of a condition subsequent, the gift over is struck down, making the gift to the charity absolute; but if the event is described in the form of a determinable interest, the whole gift is struck down. In the latter situation, however, the court often finds a general charitable intent and applies the gift *cy-près*.

Re Randell[443] affords an example. A testatrix gave a sum of money in trust, the income from which was to be paid to the priest of a particular church, so long as he permitted the pews of that church to be occupied free of charge. If he ever called for payment for the pews, the money was to fall into residue. The court was not able to find a general charitable intent and thus the money could not be applied *cy-près*. However, the court held that the direction to let the money fall into residue, was something the law would do in any event. Accordingly, the gift was not void for perpetuity.

In *Re Bowen*[444] the court reached a different conclusion. The testatrix left money to trustees on trust to establish two schools and to continue the schools forever thereafter. But she added a proviso to the effect that if the government at

---

decide whether there was a charitable purpose. There was an immediate vesting without condition.

439   *Ibid.*
440   [1950] Ch. 547, [1950] 2 All E.R. 191.
441   To the same effect, see *Re Odelberg Estate* (1970), 72 W.W.R. 567 (Sask. Surr. Ct.).
442   See *Re Mill's Declaration of Trust*, [1950] 2 All E.R. 292 (C.A.).
443   (1888), 38 Ch. D. 213 (Ch. Div.).
444   [1893] 2 Ch. 491 (Ch. Div.).

any time in the future should establish a general system of education, then the trust should cease and the money should go to the same persons as were entitled to the residue. The court drew a distinction between a gift of property to charity for a limited time, leaving the undisposed of interest to fall into residue (as in *Re Randell*), and a gift of property to charity in perpetuity, subject to an executory gift over in favour of the residuary legatee; in the latter case, if the gift over arises upon an event that is too remote, it fails. The court held that the gift in *Bowen* was of the second type.

4. *Gift over from charity to charity*. When there is a gift over from one charity to another on the happening of an uncertain future event, the gift over is not void for perpetuity. The reason is that it makes no difference which charity is benefited, because the effect is the same; the money is applied for the benefit of the public.[445]

Under the perpetuities statutes referred to above, possibilities of reverter and possibilities of resulting trusts of real and personal property are made subject to the rule against perpetuities in the same way that rights of re-entry for condition broken are, but upon a modified perpetuity period.[446] Under the Ontario Act the period is the shorter of 21 years or a life or lives in being plus 21 years to a maximum of 40 years. The period in the other statutes varies. If the stipulated event occurs during the perpetuity period, the grantor or the testator's estate can recover the property; if it does not, the gift becomes absolute.

Thus, if an Ontario testator bequeaths money "to my trustees to pay the income to Maple Leaf Cemetery, so long as it maintains my grave in perpetuity," the estate can recover the property if, during the 21-year period after the testator's death, the Cemetery fails to maintain the grave. However, once the 21 years are up, the Cemetery's interest becomes absolute.

This has implications for charitable trusts. Thus, in Ontario, a bequest, "to my trustees, to pay the income to XYZ Ltd., provided it uses the money to maintain my family's church," confers an absolute interest upon XYZ Ltd. after 21 years (assuming it used the money for the stated purpose for the 21 years, or the estate did not demand the property back for failure to do so). This is clearly inappropriate and some of the statutes provide that, in those circumstances, the moneys shall be applied *cy-près*.[447] Clearly, if the bequest had been to the church so long as it uses the money for a specified charitable purpose, it is unobjectionable that the gift becomes absolute at the end of the perpetuity period.

---

445 *Christ's Hospital v. Grainger* (1849), 1 Mac. & G. 460, 41 E.R. 1343, [1843-60] All E.R. Rep. 204 (Ch.); *Re Tyler*, [1891] 3 Ch. 252 (C.A.); *Royal College of Surgeons of England v. National Provincial Bank Ltd.*, [1952] A.C. 631, [1952] 1 All E.R. 984 (H.L.); *Re Mountain Estate* (1912), 26 O.L.R. 163, 4 D.L.R. 737 (C.A.). This rule is codified by some of the above-mentioned statutes: Alta. Act, s. 19(4); B.C. Act, s. 23; Yukon Act, s. 19(4).

446 Alta. Act, s. 19; B.C. Act, s. 10; Ont. Act, s. 15; N.W.T. Act, s. 16; Yukon Act, s. 19.

447 Alta. Act, s. 19(3); B.C. Act, s. 13; Yukon Act, s. 19(3).

7. THE CY-PRÈS DOCTRINE

(a) Introduction

We saw that the court has the power to make or direct the making of a scheme when the purposes of a trust are exclusively charitable but the trust's creator has not defined specific purposes. This will be the case, for example, if the maker of the trust directs that the property shall be used "for charity," "for education," or for similar, undefined, but charitable purposes. We have also seen that the certainty of objects requirement does not apply to charitable trusts. Thus, the trust does not fail simply because the testator has not provided specific objects.[448] To save gifts of the kind mentioned, the court "complete" the testator's intention by the scheme. It will define the purposes to which the property should be applied.[449]

The *cy-près* doctrine is an aspect of the court's inherent scheme-making power, for under the *cy-près* doctrine the court may also make or direct the making of a scheme. However, the circumstances in which this jurisdiction arises are different. The *cy-près* jurisdiction only arises when the trust's creator has defined specific charitable purposes, but those purposes are impracticable or impossible to carry out. Professor Waters has pointed out that the courts, particularly in Canada, have confused these two aspects of the scheme-making power and often speak of *cy-près* indiscriminately.[450]

The term "*cy-près*" derives either from "*ici-près*," meaning "near this," or from "*aussi-près*," meaning "as near as possible." Both are Norman-French expressions. Modern courts have adopted the second meaning, but it is likely that the first, which gives the court more room to re-order a charitable trust, was originally applied by the ecclesiastical courts before their jurisdiction over testaments of personalty was assumed by the Court of Chancery.[451] Whichever meaning is adopted, the essence of the doctrine is clear from its name: the court is permitted to devote the property to charitable purposes as near as may be to what the trust's maker intended. The court may do this because the purposes stated by the maker of the trust cannot be carried out in the way that he or she intended by reason of impossibility or impracticability.

A distinction must be drawn between initial impossibility or impracticability and supervening impossibility or impracticability. If the purposes intended by the creator of the trust cannot be carried out, for example, because the institution he or she intended to benefit does not exist, there is an initial impossibility. If, on the other hand, the institution ceases to exist after the trust takes effect, there is a supervening impossibility. Different consequences flow from these two situations. It is therefore convenient to discuss them separately.

---

448 See Lyn L. Stevens, "Certainty and Charity — Recent Developments in the Law of Trusts" (1974), 52 Can. Bar. Rev. 372.

449 See O.L.R.C. *Report on Charities*, at 398ff.

450 Waters, at 611ff.

451 Keeton and Sheridan, at 213-214; Jones, at 73-74.

Before doing so, you should note that there are two kinds of *cy-près*:[452]

1. *The prerogative cy-près*. This arises when property is given to charity but no trust is interposed, such as a gift of property "to charity," or "to my country, Canada." The right to dispose of the property in such cases lies in the Crown and is exercisable by the Attorney-General. In practice, however, the courts exercise the prerogative *cy-près* with the consent of the Attorney-General.[453]

2. *The judicial cy-près*. This is the type we shall consider in this part. It arises when moneys are given upon charitable trust but the purposes are impossible to carry out or are impracticable. In that context we shall also discuss the use of the *cy-près* power to reform discriminatory charitable trusts.

Further Reading

Peter Luxton, "Cy-près and the Ghost of Things that Might Have Been," [1983] Conv. 107.

Jean Warburton, "The Changing Concept of General Charitable Intention" (1984), 128 Sol. J. 760.

(b) Initial Impossibility or Impracticability

There is an initial impossibility or impracticability if the specified purposes are impossible to carry out, or the named charitable institutions never existed or have ceased to exist before the trust takes effect.

There are two issues that must be determined by the courts in cases of initial failure: (1) whether the trust is impracticable or impossible, and (2) whether there is a general charitable intention.

Impracticability arises when there is no longer a need for the purposes the testator intended. For example a trust to release slaves in a country where slavery no longer exists, is impracticable.[454] Similarly, a trust to erect a parsonage for a minister is impracticable if it is unlikely that there will ever be a minister in the locality.[455]

Impracticability means that the testator's stated purposes cannot be carried out. It does not mean that practical reason dictates that the funds would be better applied to similar purposes. Thus, if a testator leaves funds for a cottage hospital and it is possible to carry out this intention, a *cy-près* scheme is not to be imposed

---

452 In fact, the term *cy-près* is used in contexts other than charitable trusts as well, namely, accumulations, conditions and perpetuities. See Anger and Honsberger, *Law of Real Property*, 2nd ed. by A.H. Oosterhoff and W.B. Rayner (Aurora: Canada Law Book Inc., 1985) at 330, 513, 538, 563.

453 See *Re Conroy Estate*, [1973] 4 W.W.R. 537, 35 D.L.R. (3d) 752 (B.C. S.C.) followed in *Montreal Trust Co. v. Richards* (1982), 14 E.T.R. 108, 1982 CarswellBC 266, [1983] 1 W.W.R. 437, 40 B.C.L.R. 114 (S.C.).

454 *Ironmongers' Co. v. A.-G.* (1844), 10 Cl. & F. 908, 8 E.R. 983 (H.L.).

455 *Re McMillan Estate* (1917), 11 O.W.N. 443 (H.C.).

merely because it makes more sense to give the money to a larger regional hospital.[456]

Impossibility arises when the trust cannot be carried out at all. Many of the cases are concerned with a named institution which never existed,[457] or which has ceased to exist.[458] Others involve moneys collected for a particular charitable purpose which is no longer required, either because there is no longer a need for it,[459] or because the state has assumed responsibility for the purpose.[460]

Whether a purpose is impracticable or impossible must be determined as of the time the trust takes effect, that is, at the time of the deed which creates an *inter vivos* trust, and at the time of the testator's death under a testamentary trust. This is so even though the determination does not take place until a later date, such as after a prior life interest.[461]

The second issue to be resolved in cases of initial failure is whether there is a general charitable intention. This issue arises because, if the testator has designated a specific purpose, it is likely that he or she intended to benefit that purpose only. Hence, if that purpose is impossible or impracticable, there will be a resulting trust to the estate. That will also be the case if a public appeal fails because insufficient funds are raised.[462] On the other hand, if the testator had a general charitable intention, then, even though he or she named a specific beneficiary, the money can be applied *cy-près*.

The question whether there is a general charitable intention often arises when the testator has named a particular institution which never existed. The court is then usually able to find a general charitable intention on the ground that the testator really intended to benefit, not the institution, but the purpose which the name of the institution signifies. Thus, if a testator gives money on trust for "The Crippled Children's Hospital" in a particular city and there never was such an

---

456 See *Re Weir Hospital Estate*, [1910] 2 Ch. 124 (C.A.); *Re Baker* (1984), 47 O.R. (2d) 415, 11 D.L.R. (4th) 430, 17 E.T.R. 168 (H.C.). Courts are reluctant to vary a trust in such a way as to alter the intent of the testator. For an explanation of the *Weir* and *Baker* cases see *Bloorview Childrens Hospital Foundation v. Bloorview MacMillan Centre* (2002), 44 E.T.R. (2d) 175, 2002 CarswellOnt 1128 (S.C.J.).

457 See, *e.g.*, *Re Barnes* (1976), 1 Alta. L.R. (2d) 147, 72 D.L.R. (3d) 651 (T.D.).

458 *Re Roberts* (1981), 9 E.T.R. 156, 120 D.L.R. (3d) 74, 36 Nfld. & P.E.I.R. 234, 101 A.P.R. 234 (P.E.I. S.C.). in which the institution ceased to exist before the bequest became payable. If a charitable society or association existed at the time of the testator's death, but ceased to exist before the legacy was paid, the fund becomes devoted to charity and will be applied *cy-près* so that the testator's intent is carried out as nearly as possible in the mode desired. *Re Roberts* was distinguished in *Stewart Estate, Re* (1999), [1999] P.E.I.J. No. 38, 1999 CarswellPEI 42, 174 Nfld. & P.E.I.R. 147, 533 A.P.R. 147, 27 E.T.R. (2d) 92 (T.D. [In Chambers]) because the beneficiary of the legacy was in existence.

459 *Re Y.W.C.A. Extension Campaign Fund*, [1934] 3 W.W.R. 49 (Sask. K.B.).

460 *Re Ulverston & District New Hospital Building Trusts*, [1956] Ch. 622, [1956] 3 All E.R. 164 (C.A.).

461 Tudor, 8th ed., at 393-394.

462 See, *e.g.*, *Y.W.C.A. Extension Campaign Fund*, *supra*, note 459.

institution, the court can find a general charitable intent in the purpose, that is, to benefit crippled children.[463]

It is also possible to find a general charitable intention by the concept of "charity by association," or "kindred objects."[464] It applies if it is clear that a testator is giving the entire estate, or all the residue, to named charities, one of which never existed.[465] However, if only one institution is named and it never existed, the court is loath to find a general charitable intention.[466]

If the institution did at one time exist, but does not exist any longer, there are two possibilities. It may either continue to exist in a changed name or form, for example, because it has amalgamated with another institution, or changed its name. In these circumstances the court is merely identifying the institution and *cy-près* is not involved.[467] Alternatively, if the institution has ceased to exist entirely before the gift takes effect, the gift can only be applied *cy-près* if a general charitable intention can be shown.[468] If there is no general charitable intention, the gift lapses.

Re Spence's Will Trusts,[469] reproduced below, is a case of initial failure in which the gift was held to lapse.

RE SPENCE'S WILL TRUSTS

(1978), [1979] Ch. 483, [1978] 3 W.L.R. 483, [1978] 3 All E.R. 92
Chancery Division

The testatrix, Beatrice Spence, made her will in 1968. She gave the residue of her estate on trust to be divided "equally between the Blind Home at Scott Street Keighley and the Old Folks Home at Hillworth Lodge Keighley for the benefit of the patients." She died in 1972.

There was no institution known as "The Blind Home" in Keighley but a local charity, in existence since 1907, known as "The Keighley and District Association for the Blind" had been operating a blind home on Scott Street for many years and it was often called the "Blind Home." The Association operated a similar home in a neighbouring town. With respect to this gift Megarry V.-C. held that the testatrix intended to benefit the patients at the home in Keighley and he approved a scheme whereby the money would be paid to the Association but

---

463 See *Montreal Trust Co. v. Richards*, [1982] 1 W.W.R. 437, 40 B.C.L.R. 114, 14 E.T.R. 108 (S.C.); *Buchanan Estate, Re* (1997), 20 E.T.R. (2d) 100, 1997 CarswellBC 2764, 101 B.C.A.C. 55, 164 W.A.C. 55, 44 B.C.L.R. (3d) 283 (C.A.).

464 *Re Knox*, [1937] Ch. 109 at 113, *per* Luxmoore J.

465 *Ibid.*

466 *Re Spence's Will Trusts* (sub nom. *Re Spence*) (1978), [1979] Ch. 483 at 495, [1978] 3 All E.R. 92.

467 See *Re Gordon*, [1965] 2 O.R. 805, 52 D.L.R. (2d) 197 (H.C.). *Re Hunter Estate*, [1973] 3 W.W.R. 197, 34 D.L.R. (3d) 602 (B.C. S.C.), a trust for a sanitarium which was transferred to the Crown and operated by the province as a mental hospital is also a case of this kind, but the court decided, erroneously, we submit, that the institution had ceased to exist.

468 *Spence's Will Trusts, supra*, note 466, at 484, *per* Megarry V.C.

469 *Ibid.*

subject to the proviso that it could only be used for the patients in the Scott Street Home.

Hillworth Lodge was originally a workhouse. It was closed in 1939 and was used to house evacuees during the war. In 1948 it became a retirement home, but it was closed down in 1971 before the testatrix died and it has since been used as offices. Old people in the area were being cared for in several different homes. The court dealt with the question whether this gift was charitable as follows:

MEGARRY V.-C.:

. . .

Now without looking at the authorities, I would have said that this was a fairly plain case of a will which made a gift for a particular purpose in fairly specific terms. The gift was for the benefit of the patients at a particular home, namely, the Old Folks Home at Hillworth Lodge, Keighley. At the date of the will there were patients at that home. When the testatrix died, there was no longer any home there, but offices instead; and so there were no longer any patients there, or any possibility of them. The gift was a gift for a charitable purpose which at the date of the will was capable of accomplishment and at the date of death was not. *Prima facie*, therefore, the gift fails unless a general charitable intention has been manifested so that the property can be applied cy-près. Buttressed by authority, Mr. Gidley Scott contended that the court would be slow to find a general charitable intention where the object of the gift is defined with some particularity, as it was here.

. . .

Mr. Mummery's . . . contention was that the will displayed a sufficient general charitable intention for the moiety to be applied cy-près. In doing this he had to contend with *Re Harwood*.[470] This, and cases which apply it, such as *Re Stemson's Will Trusts*,[471] establish that it is very difficult to find a general charitable intention where the testator has selected a particular charity, taking some care to identify it, and the charity then ceases to exist before the testator's death. This contrasts with cases where the charity described in the will has never existed, when it is much easier to find a general charitable intention.

These cases have been concerned with gifts to institutions, rather than gifts for purposes. The case before me, on the other hand, is a gift for a purpose, namely, the benefit of the patients at a particular Old Folks Home. It therefore seems to me that I ought to consider the question, of which little or nothing was said in argument, whether the principle in *Re Harwood*, or a parallel principle, has any application to such case. In other words, is a similar distinction to be made between, on the one hand, a case in which the testator has selected a

---

470 [1936] Ch. 285.
471 [1970] Ch. 16.

particular charitable purpose, taking some care to identify it, and before the testator dies that purpose has become impracticable or impossible of accomplishment, and on the other hand a case where the charitable purpose has never been possible or practicable?

As at present advised I would answer Yes to that question. I do not think that the reasoning of the *Re Harwood* line of cases is directed to any feature of institutions as distinct from purposes. Instead, I think the essence of the distinction is in the difference between particularity and generality. If a particular institution or purpose is specified, then it is that institution or purpose, and no other, that is to be the object of the benefaction. It is difficult to envisage a testator as being suffused with a general glow of broad charity when he is labouring, and labouring successfully, to identify some particular specified institution or purpose as the object of his bounty. The specific displaces the general. It is otherwise where the testator has been unable to specify any particular charitable institution or practicable purpose, and so, although his intention of charity can be seen, he has failed to provide any way of giving effect to it. There, the absence of the specific leaves the general undisturbed. It follows that in my view in the case before me, where the testatrix has clearly specified a particular charitable purpose which before her death became impossible to carry out, Mr. Mummery has to face that level of great difficulty in demonstrating the existence of a general charitable intention which was indicated by *Re Harwood*.

. . .

The other way in which Mr. Mummery sought to meet his difficulty was by relying on *Re Satterthwaite's Will Trusts*[472] (which he said was his best case), and on *Re Knox*,[473] which I think may possibly be better. The doctrine may for brevity be described as charity by association. If the will gives the residue among a number of charities with kindred objects, but one of the apparent charities does not in fact exist, the court will be ready to find a general charitable intention and so apply the share of the non-existent charity *cy-près*. I have not been referred to any explicit statement of the underlying principle, but it seems to me that in such cases the court treats the testator as having shown the general intention of giving his residue to promote charities with that type of kindred objects, and then, when he comes to dividing the residue, as casting around for particular charities with that type of objects to name as donees. If one or more of these are non-existent, then the general intention will suffice for a *cy-près* application. It will be observed that, as stated, the doctrine depends, at least to some extent, upon the detection of "kindred objects" (a phrase which comes from the judgment of Luxmoore J. in *Re Knox*)[474] in the charities to which the shares of residue are given; in this respect the charities must in some degree be *ejusdem generis*.

---

472 [1966] 1 W.L.R. 277.
473 [1937] Ch. 109.
474 *Ibid.*, at 113.

[His Lordship discussed these cases and continued:]

It will be observed that these are all cases of gifts to bodies which did not exist. In such cases, the court is ready to find a general charitable intention.[475] The court is far less ready to find such an intention where the gift is to a body which existed at the date of the will but ceased to exist before the testator died, or, as I have already held, where the gift is for a purpose which, though possible and practicable at the date of the will, has ceased to be so before the testator's death. The case before me is, of course, a case in this latter category, so that Mr. Mummery has to overcome this greater difficulty in finding a general charitable intention.

Not only does Mr. Mummery have this greater difficulty: he also has, I think, less material with which to meet it. He has to extract the general charitable intention for the gift which fails from only one other gift: the residue, of course, was simply divided into two. In *Re Knox* and *Re Hartley*[476] the gifts which failed were each among three other gifts, and in *Re Satterthwaite's Will Trusts*[477] there were seven or eight other gifts. I do not say that a general charitable intention or a genus cannot be extracted from a gift of residue equally between two: but I do say that larger numbers are likely to assist in conveying to the court a sufficient conviction both of the genus and of the generality of the charitable intention.

A further point occurred to me which I think that I should mention. There are, of course, cases where there is merely a single gift, but the court is nevertheless able to see a clear general charitable intention underlying the particular mode of carrying it out that the testator has laid down. Thus in the well-known case of *Biscoe v. Jackson*,[478] which I read in the light of *Re Wilson*,[479] the gift was to provide a soup kitchen and cottage hospital "for the parish of Shoreditch." Despite a considerable degree of particularity about the soup kitchen and the cottage hospital that were to be provided, the court found a general charitable intention to provide a benefit for the sick and poor of the parish. In that case, of course, there would have been no real difficulty in ascertaining those who were intended to benefit. Whatever the practical difficulties, at least the concept of those who were to be included is clear enough. The only real difficulty or impossibility lay in the particular method of carrying out that intention which the testator had specified. In the present case, on the other hand, the difficulty lies not only in the particular method but also in the very nature of the general charitable intention that is said to underlie that method. For the reasons that I have already given, I find it far from clear which "patients" are intended to benefit once the touch-stone of the Old People's Home at Hillworth Lodge is removed. There is no geographical or other limitation to provide a guide. Where the difficulty or impossibility not only afflicts the method but also invades the concept of the alleged general

---

475 See *Re Davis*, [1902] 1 Ch. 876, esp. at 884.
476 March 17, 1978 (unrep.).
477 *Supra*, note 472.
478 (1887), 35 Ch. D. 460.
479 [1913] 1 Ch. 314.

charitable intention, then I think that the difficulty of establishing that the will displays any general charitable intention becomes almost insuperable.

From what I have said it follows that I have been quite unable to extract from the will, construed in its context, any expression of a general charitable intention which would suffice for the moiety to be applied *cy-près*. Instead, in my judgment, the moiety was given for a specific charitable purpose which, though possible when the will was made, became impossible before the testatrix died. The gift of the moiety accordingly fails, and it passes as on intestacy.

Notes and Questions

1. Is it desirable to impose such a strict test of general charitable intention as the *Spence* case does? Canadian cases tend to be more ready to find a general charitable intention, particularly on the basis of charity by association.[480]

2. The Ontario Law Reform Commission has recommended that the *cy-près* power be widened to extend not only to impracticability and impossibility, but also any other difficulty. For that purpose it also recommends that it should be irrelevant that the donor had a general or a particular charitable intention, unless the trust instrument provides for a gift over or a reversion in the event of failure or lapse of the charitable object.[481] These recommendations apply to both initial and supervening failure. Is this proposed reform desirable?

3. We have seen that when money is raised by public appeal for a charity and there is an initial failure of the purpose, there will be a resulting trust. If there is a subsequent failure in the sense that there is a surplus, the surplus will be applied *cy-près*. The Ontario Law Reform Commission has recommended that the moneys be applied *cy-près* in both situations, unless the donor is identifiable and has indicated in writing that he wishes his money or a *pro rata* surplus returned to him.[482] Is this proposed reform desirable?

4. Can the following gifts be applied *cy-près*?

(a) A testamentary gift of a cottage as a rest facility for naval personnel.[483]

(b) A testamentary trust to construct, operate and maintain a retirement home, if the money is insufficient for the purpose.[484]

5. A sister and brother each directed that a portion of their estates be held in trust for the benefit of a tuberculosis sanatorium. This sanatorium closed 30 years after the testators died. The Public Trustee held that rather than applying the funds to other local institutions, the proper application of the *cy-près* doctrine was to direct the funds to a hospital which was dealing with a majority of the tuberculosis patients in the region. In this way, the re-direction of the trust fund maintained, as closely as possible, the charitable objects of the deceased.[485]

---

480 See generally Waters, at 619ff. See also *Fraser Estate, Re*, 32 E.T.R. (2d) 67, 2000 CarswellPEI 33, 2000 PESCTD 27, 191 Nfld. & P.E.I.R. 76, 577 A.P.R. 76 (T.D.), which outlines the circumstances in which the *cy-près* doctrine is applied and reviews the leading cases on the subject.

481 O.L.R.C. *Report on Trusts*, at 468ff., Draft Act, at 519-520, s. 76. See also O.L.R.C. *Report on Charities*, at 402ff.

482 O.L.R.C. *Report on Trusts*, Draft Act, s. 77.

483 See *Perry v. Kovacs* (1984), 12 D.L.R. (4th) 751 (B.C. S.C.).

484 *Re McSweeney Estate* (1982), 41 N.B.R. (2d) 419, 107 A.P.R. 419 (Q.B.).

484 *Lapointe v. Ontario (Public Trustee)* (1995), 7 E.T.R. (2d) 45 (Ont. Gen. Div.).

(c) Supervening Impossibility or Impracticability

If a trust is devoted exclusively to charity and the property has vested in the charity, the property cannot revert to the donor when the purpose subsequently becomes impossible or impracticable. The property then always belongs to "charity."[486] Hence, in such a situation, *cy-près* will be applied and it is irrelevant in our view whether the donor had a general or a particular intention.[487]

There are two exceptions to this principle: (1) If there is no exclusive dedication to charity, as when the donor retains an interest, or provides for a gift over to non-charity on a specified event, the donor or the beneficiary under the gift over will take, provided that the event occurs within the perpetuity period. (2) If only the income is devoted to charity, as in the case of an endowed prize, and there is a supervening impossiblity or impracticability, the capital cannot be applied *cy-près*,[488] for the charity does not have an interest in the capital.[489] Some cases allow a *cy-près* application of the capital if the donor had a general charitable intention. This is incorrect.

Professor Waters has pointed out, correctly, that the requirement of general charitable intention is otiose to cases of supervening impossibility.[490] He also argues, again correctly, we submit, that the requirement of general charitable intention is also irrelevant when the court must decide what to do with a surplus remaining after the application of moneys obtained by a public appeal. It is irrelevant in such a situation that the donors, whether they gave anonymously or by name, had a general charitable intention. Since the money has vested in charity, it is dedicated exclusively to charity and any surplus should be applied *cy-près*. However, the cases do not always support this view.[491]

The principle that a general charitable intention is not relevant in a case of supervening impossibility is discussed in *Re Fitzpatrick*,[492] reproduced below.

---

486 *Re Faraker* (sub nom. *Faraker v. Durrell*), [1912] 2 Ch. 488 (C.A.).

487 Some cases indicate that a general charitable intention may be necessary for supervening cases as well as for initial cases of impossibility or impracticality. The point is discussed in *Boy Scouts of Canada, Provincial Council of Newfoundland v. Doyle* (1997), 149 D.L.R. (4th) 22, 151 Nfld. & P.E.I.R. 91, 471 A.P.R. 91, 1997 CarswellNfld 325 (C.A.).

488 See *Re Fitzgibbon Estate* (1922), 51 O.L.R. 500, 69 D.L.R. 524 (H.C.).

489 In a limited number of cases, that is, cases in which the capital is also vested in the charity, the charity can terminate the trust under the rule in *Saunders v. Vautier* (1841), 4 Beav. 115, 49 E.R. 282, affirmed (1841), 1 Cr. & Ph. 240, 41 E.R. 482. This issue is discussed in the chapter on revocation, termination and variation. See also *Re Bell* (1980), 7 E.T.R. 129, 29 O.R. (2d) 278, 112 D.L.R. (3d) 573 (H.C.) and A.H. Oosterhoff, Annotation, *ibid.*

490 Waters, at 629. And see *Re McDougall Estate*, [1939] O.W.N. 64 (H.C.), cited by him.

491 Waters, at 629ff., citing *Re Welsh Hospital (Nethley) Fund* (sub nom. *Thomes v. A.-G.*), [1921] 1 Ch. 655; *Re North Devon and West Somerset Relief Fund Trusts*, [1953] 1 W.L.R. 1260; and *Re Northern Ontario Fire Relief Fund Trusts* (1913), 4 O.W.N. 1118, 11 D.L.R. 15 (H.C.). The latter made no reference to general charitable intention.

492 (Sub nom. *Fidelity Trust Co v. St. Joseph's Vocational School of Winnipeg*) (1984), 16 E.T.R. 221, 6 D.L.R. (4th) 644 (Man. Q.B.).

RE FITZPATRICK

[1984] 3 W.W.R. 429, 27 Man. R. (2d) 285, 16 E.T.R. 221, 6 D.L.R. (4th) 644
Manitoba Court of Queen's Bench

The testatrix, Kathleen Fitzpatrick, died in 1969. By her will she directed that the residue of her estate be held by her executors as a fund to be known as "The Kathleen Fitzpatrick Fund." The executors were directed to invest the moneys and, from the principal and interest, pay for the musical education of any boy or boys resident at St. Joseph's Vocational School of Winnipeg who should show musical talent. The selection of the boy or boys was to be made by a committee consisting of three persons, including the Reverend Sister Superior of the school.

The school was operated since 1938 by the Sisters of Providence of Kingston in Manitoba, an incorporated body. It was originally a residential vocational school for orphaned boys, but, because of changing needs, became a residential school for emotionally disturbed boys. Later, the school ceased to operate as a residential boys' school because of decreasing demand. The building was demolished and the Sisters of Providence constructed a day care facility instead. However, in 1980 they acquired a new residence elsewhere which they operated as a group home for a small number of moderately retarded teen-age boys. No selection was ever made for assistance from the testatrix's fund. The executors brought this application for advice and directions.

SIMONSEN J.:

. . .

Counsel for the parties conceded that the legacy in this instance was charitable and indeed there is ample authority in both texts and cases to support the conclusion that a gift for the advancement of musical education for boys in a particular institution was charitable and one which served a public object.

Counsel further acknowledged that there is no issue that the charitable trust was impossible or impracticable following 1979 when St. Joseph's Vocational School was terminated and the activity disbanded.

The third question involved a consideration of whether there was initial failure as distinct from supervening impossibility, it being generally acknowledged that somewhat different legal consequences arise with the two situations.

The critical date in respect of this inquiry was November 16, 1969, being the date of death, following which funds would have been available to the trustees to meet the objects specified in the legacy.

[His Lordship referred to the case law and continued:

If the charity existed at the time of death the legacy became vested in that charity and would be applied *cy-près* if there was a subsequent failure arising from disappearance of the institution. The legacy would not be defeated by supervening impossibility.

The argument has been advanced that different considerations apply when the legacy has been directed for a charitable purpose as contrasted with a devise to a charitable institution. If the devise were for a charitable purpose (not an institution) and that object became impossible, need the court find a general charitable intent before ordering a *cy-près* scheme?

. . .

The principles were expressed by the author Donovan Waters in an article:[493]

> The law in this area is not easy, but it is fairly well laid down. Before the court can approve a *cy-près* scheme, it must be shown that the testator's charitable purpose was impossible to carry out or impracticable, and that he did not have only that particular charitable purpose in mind, but a general intent to give to charitable work of that kind. It is because the testator had this so-called general charitable intent that the court will assist his intention by seeing that the property is applied to some similar purpose. If he only wanted to further the particular named charitable purpose, but impossibility or impracticability has occurred, the court will not intervene, and the property in question will revert to his estate.
>
> However, these rules only apply when the expressed charitable purpose is impossible or impractical [*sic*] on the instrument of gift taking effect, and in the case of a will, of course, this is the moment of the testator's death. It does not matter whether the charitable gift is to take place immediately or only after the completion of a prior interest. If there is a so-called initial impossibility or impracticability, the rules mentioned apply.
>
> These rules do not apply when impossibility or impracticability occurs *after* the instrument of gift has taken effect. It does not matter whether the purpose is being carried out when the impossibility or impracticability subsequently occurs, or if either of those events occurs during the time of a prior interest, while the purpose or charity is awaiting the end of that interest. When impossibility or impracticability occurs after the instrument has taken effect, a so-called supervening impossibility or impracticability has occurred.
>
> In these circumstances the court now looks to see whether the instrument of gift has given the property in question exclusively to the charitable purpose. That is to say, if there is a gift over [*sic*] any kind, then there is no so-called exclusive dedication to the charitable purpose. However, if there is an exclusive dedication, and the purpose can no longer be carried out because of impossibility or impracticability, the property is regarded as dedicated to charity, and passes to the Crown in right of the province as the ultimate protector of charity and charities. By long custom the Crown will now agree to the drawing up of a *cy-près* scheme for the approval of the court.
>
> In the circumstances of supervening impossibility of [*sic*] impracticability no general intent is required. This is because the purpose or charity was possible and practicable when the instrument of gift took effect, and whatever the scope of the donor's intent he has dedicated his property to charity. All that is required, as I have said, is an exclusive dedication.

. . .

In the present case, St. Joseph's Vocational School was in existence at the time of the testatrix's death and there were potential candidates in existence at

---

493 (1974), 52 Can. Bar Rev. 598 at 598-599.

that time. In my view, that was the critical date because the objects of the charity were in existence at the time of death. It can therefore be said the charity vested in perpetuity for the stated charitable purpose. This was not a case of initial failure but rather of supervening impossibility. In the circumstances, it is not necessary to find a general charitable intent in the legacy to permit the ordering of a *cy-près* scheme.

. . .

I do not see the terms of the legacy as being so specific that an altered mode of implementation of the charitable object would defeat the intent of the testatrix. No gift over was provided in the instrument. It was intended to bestow an educational benefit upon young people who were particularly disadvantaged. The testatrix had no husband. She had no children. She was a Roman Catholic. With all these factors in her background, it would be totally logical to bestow benefit upon students who were attending a school serving a laudable and useful public service and operated by a religious order which she respected. The gift was educational to students attending an institution which itself was charitable. There was no intent, in my view, that the gift should fail if the particular form of education had been disbanded or some other worthwhile activity replaced it.

In turning next to the question of implementation, reference should be made to the exhaustive examination of the *cy-près* doctrine in Sheridan and Delany, *The Cy-Près Doctrine*.[494] In discussing the nature of a *cy-près* order, the authors stated that it should combine the virtues of proximity, usefulness and practicability, always being mindful of the testatrix's intention. In its current operation of a group home for the mentally retarded, the Sisters of Providence continue to be engaged in the training, care, help and assistance of young disadvantaged boys. Although not functioning as an educational institution, the scope of attention and guidance given to members of the group home could readily be encompassed within the more general expression of the term "education." It has been suggested in the evidence that the mode of application *cy-près* could be to provide assistance to the Sisters of Providence in the operation of the activities in this group home for mentally retarded.

I have no doubt that the fund should be applied *cy-près*, but the material which has been presented does not contain sufficient specific information for me to make an order. Obviously, it would be desirable that the fund be employed for some educational purpose to provide greater opportunity for education and development of the young people in the home, particularly in areas of endeavour which are not adequately or fully provided for in the present educational framework.

It is common knowledge that group homes have been established in many areas of the province, and, therefore, there should be some experience available which could assist the court in formulating an appropriate scheme or mode of application of the fund. A division or branch of the Canadian Association for the

---

494 (London, 1959).

Mentally Retarded exists within the province and that organization should be requested to work with the Sisters of Providence to propose an appropriate scheme and to provide sufficient background and information to permit the court to evaluate the proposal.

Because the evidence is not complete on the issue of appropriate application of the fund, I would not preclude consideration of some other alternative scheme which would be consistent with the objects which have been expressed earlier. If in conjunction with its nursery school, the Sisters of Providence were to establish a school to teach children with disabilities or other problems requiring special attention such a programme might be equally consistent with the purposes of the legacy. If such a proposal were advanced, it should be done with the support and guidance of persons experienced in the field.

Within the framework of the views which I have expressed, I would hope and expect a further proposal to be made to the court. If counsel so desire I would be prepared to hear the further application on an appropriate *cy-près* scheme.

. . .

Notes and Questions

1. The views expressed in *Fitzpatrick* were not considered in *Re Tufford*.[495] A testator gave the residue of his estate, after a life interest, to trustees of a church cemetery to use the income for the upkeep of the cemetery. Before the testator died, the cemetery was taken over by a municipality. The Court of Appeal decided, rightly we submit, that the change in trustees did not cause a lapse, since the testator intended the gift to be applied for the upkeep of the cemetery regardless of the trustees. However, in dealing with the question of surplus income, the court held that the testator intended to dedicate the entire residue to charity forever, so that the surplus should be applied *cy-près*. It reached this decision despite the fact that only the income was given for the upkeep of the charity. No reference was made to *Re McDougall Estate*[496] or the view of Professor Waters discussed in *Fitzpatrick* and in the introduction to this part.

Which view is preferable? Why? In any event, is a gift for the upkeep of a municipal, as distinct from a church, cemetery charitable?[497]

2. The Ontario Law Reform Commission considered, but rejected, the concept of allowing variation of endowed charitable trusts by means of a modified *cy-près* power. It felt that that issue should be dealt with as part of a general review of the law of charity.[498]

Does the Commission's proposed Act, which would empower the court, *inter alia*, to enlarge the powers of the trustees to facilitate the carrying out of the testator's intention,[499] nevertheless enable the variation of such trusts?

---

495 (1984), 45 O.R. (2d) 351, 16 E.T.R. 87, 6 D.L.R. (4th) 534, 2 O.A.C. 45 (C.A.). See also *Ramsden Estate, Re* (1996), 139 D.L.R. (4th) 746, 1996 CarswellPEI 98, 14 E.T.R. (2d) 239, 145 Nfld. & P.E.I.R. 156, 453 A.P.R. 156 (T.D. [In Chambers]).

496 [1939] O.W.N. 64, [1939] 1 D.L.R. 783 (H.C.).

497 See *Re Oldfield*, [1949] 1 W.W.R. 540, [1949] 2 D.L.R. 175, 57 Man. R. 193 (K.B.); *Re Robinson* (1976), 15 O.R. (2d) 286, 75 D.L.R. (3d) 532 (H.C.).

498 O.L.R.C. *Report on Trusts*, at 471, note 185.

499 *Ibid.*, at 519, s. 76(1)(b).

3. A testator gave the income from his estate to the Governors of the Methodist College at St. John's for the support and maintenance of the college. After his death the college became part of a consolidated school board. What is to be done with the money?[500]

4. A testator left money on trust for the New Brunswick Protestant Orphans' Home. He died in 1969. The home ceased to operate as an orphans' home in 1976 and its objects were changed in 1978, but the corporation continued with the same name. Can the money be applied *cy-près*?[501]

5. A settlor transferred shares to a trustee to use the income and capital for charitable purposes, namely, to aid the cause of Christian evangelical bodies. It was a condition of the trust that the entire income and capital be disbursed for that purpose within 10 years of the settlor's death. At his death, the fund was worth £24 million and the charities in question could not handle so much money. What can be done in these circumstances?[502]

6. A testatrix directed that, after a life interest, the residue of her estate be divided equally among four named institutions. One was a home for children which an incorporated charity had operated for many years. The charity closed the home after the testatrix's death, but continued its charitable work of benefiting children. What should be done with the money?[503]

7. A testator made a gift to "The Institute for Crippled Children," however, no such institution existed. The Shriner's Hospital for Crippled Children in Montreal, the Hugh MacMillan Rehabilitation Centre (formerly the Ontario Crippled Children's Centre), and the Ontario Society for Crippled Children, each claimed the gift, either as a misdescribed beneficiary or on the basis of the *cy-près* doctrine. The court held that, as the testator had been a member of the Masonic order, the omission of a reference to the Shriner's Hospital was fatal to their claim. No link existed between the testator and the Ontario Crippled Children's Centre, and the will evidenced an intent to benefit charities in the local area. Thus the Ontario Society for Crippled Children was clearly entitled to benefit, and misdescription did not defeat the intent.[504]

8. A charitable organization may be registered as a registered charity for the purposes of the *Income Tax Act*[505] if, *inter alia*, its constitutive documents include a statement to the effect that upon dissolution its remaining assets will be distributed among other registered charities. The charity may designate the types of other charities it wishes to benefit in that event or it may do so by resolution or by-law prior to dissolution. If it does not do so, it seems that the court has power to direct a *cy-près* scheme. This is so even in the case of a charitable corporation which, although not a trustee of its corporate assets in

---

500 See *Avalon Consolidated School Board v. United Church of Canada* (1983), 42 Nfld. & P.E.I.R. 8, 122 A.P.R. 8 (Nfld. T.D.), affirmed (1984), 47 Nfld. & P.E.I.R. 261, 139 A.P.R. 261 (Nfld. C.A.).

501 See *Richards v. Central Trust Co.* (1983), 16 E.T.R. 1, 55 N.B.R. (2d) 31, 144 A.P.R. 31 (Q.B.). See also *Re Gordon Estate*, [1965] 2 O.R. 805, 52 D.L.R. (2d) 197 (H.C.).

502 See *Re J.W. Laing Trust*, [1984] 1 All E.R. 50, [1984] Ch. 143 which was cited in *Killam Estate, Re* (1999), 38 E.T.R. (2d) 50, 1999 CarswellNS 456, 185 N.S.R. (2d) 201, 575 A.P.R. 201 (S.C.) in which the spending level decided on by the trustees could not be maintained if the investment strategy was maintained.

503 See *Wilson Estate v. Loyal Protestant Assn.* (1986), 22 E.T.R. 16 (B.C. S.C.).

504 *National Trust v. Northside United Church* (1994), 5 E.T.R. (2d) 193 (Ont. Gen. Div.).

505 R.S.C. 1985, c. 1 (5th Supp.), as amended.

the strict sense, is in a position analogous to a trustee, since its assets can only be applied for the charitable purposes set out in its constitutive documents.[506]

(d) Discriminatory Trusts

There are quite a number of reported cases concerning charitable trusts which contain provisions that discriminate against one or more segments of society. In the past the Canadian courts have dealt with complaints about such provisions outside the law of charitable trusts. For example, in *Re Rattray*[507] the court held that a trust to provide scholarships for Queens University students, provided that the applicant was not "a Communist Socialist or a fellow-traveller" was valid, but that the condition was subsequent since it was not a condition of the gift but a subsequent term in the administration of the trust. Since it was uncertain, it was struck.[508]

The English courts have applied the concepts of "impossibility" and "impracticability" to discriminatory provisions in trusts when the trustees refuse to administer the trusts unless the provisions are removed. *Re Dominion Students' Hall Trust*[509] is an example. A trust had been established to maintain a hostel for male students from the British Dominions attending English universities. The trust contained a colour bar. An application to remove the colour bar was approved under the *cy-près* doctrine: the retention of the colour bar rendered the trust impossible in post-Second World War England.

The *Students' Hall Trust* case involved a supervening impossibility. *Lysaght v. Royal College of Surgeons*[510] was a case of initial impossibility. It concerned a trust establishing medical scholarships, of which the Royal College of Surgeons of England was trustee. The trust excluded students of the Jewish and Roman Catholic faiths. The College refused to carry out the trust unless the offending restriction was removed. The court held that the trust was impossible to perform as it stood, since the College was the only logical trustee. Hence the moneys were applied *cy-près* for the same purposes, but with the restriction removed.

The issue came squarely before the Ontario courts in *Canada Trust Co. v. Ontario (Human Rights Commission)*,[511] reproduced below.

---

506 See *Liverpool and District Hospital for Diseases of the Heart v. A.-G.*, [1981] Ch. 193, [1981] 1 All E.R. 994. *Cf. Ontario (Public Trustee) v. Toronto Humane Society, supra,* note 385; *Re Centenary Hospital Assn.* (1989), 69 O.R. (2d) 1, 59 D.L.R. (4th) 449, 33 E.T.R. 270 (H.C.), additional reasons at (1989), 69 O.R. (2d) 447 (H.C.). See also the discussion of this issue in the next part.

507 (1974), 3 O.R. (2d) 117, 44 D.L.R. (3d) 533 (C.A.).

508 *Cf. Re Metcalfe*, [1972] 3 O.R. 598, 29 D.L.R. (3d) 60, in which McGill University refused to accept a discriminatory gift to establish a scholarship for "a Protestant of good moral character in Ontario and who possesses academic ability."

509 [1947] Ch. 183.

510 [1966] Ch. D. 191, [1965] 2 All E.R. 888.

511 (1990), 74 O.R. (2d) 481, 69 D.L.R. (4th) 321, 38 E.T.R. 1, 37 O.A.C. 191 (C.A.).

CANADA TRUST CO. v. ONTARIO (HUMAN RIGHTS COMMISSION)

(1990), 74 O.R. (2d) 481, 69 D.L.R. (4th) 321, 38 E.T.R. 1, 37 O.A.C. 191
Supreme Court of Ontario
[Court of Appeal]

In 1923, Colonel Reuben Wells Leonard created an *inter vivos* charitable trust to be known as "The Leonard Foundation." He transferred substantial property to the trustee, the predecessor of Canada Trust, and directed that the income be used to fund educational scholarships. The trust deed recited the settlor's beliefs that: (1) the white race was best qualified by nature to be entrusted with the development of civilization; (2) the progress of the world depended upon the maintenance of the Christian religion; (3) the peace of the world and the advancement of civilization depended upon the stability of the British Empire and its stability could best be assured by the education, in patriotic institutions, of selected children whose birth and education warranted a reasonable expectation of their developing into leading and responsible citizens; and (4) the conduct of the affairs of the British Empire should be in the control of Christian persons of British Nationality. For these reasons, the settlor excluded from the management of and benefit in the Foundation all non-Christians, all non-whites, all non-British nationals and those whose parentage was not British, and all who owed allegiance to any foreign government, prince, pope or potentate, or who recognized their authority, temporal or spiritual.

The management of the Foundation was entrusted to a general committee of 25 persons who did not possess the criteria which the settlor found objectionable. The committee was charged with the selection of the recipients of the scholarships.

The sholarships were tenable at shools, colleges, and universities in Canada and Great Britain that were free of the control of adherents of the classes of persons the settlor excluded from management and benefit. Scholarships could only be awarded to students who were British subjects of the white race and of the Christian religion in its Protestant form. The settlor directed that preference be given to the children of clergymen, school teachers, military personnel who served in the armed forces, graduates of Royal Military College of Canada, and members of the Engineering Institute of Canada and the Mining and Metallurgical Institute of Canada. Of the total income expended in any year for scholarships, no more than one-fourth could be paid to female students.

The settlor empowered the trustee to apply to a judge of the Supreme Court of Ontario who possessed the qualifications required of a member of the general committee for the opinion, advice, and direction of the court on any matter concerning the trust.

The Foundation had operated and had awarded scholarships for many years. In recent years, several universities and other groups objected to the discriminatory provisions of the trust. In 1986 the Ontario Human Rights Commission filed a complaint against the Foundation, alleging that it contravened the *Human Rights*

Code, 1981.[512] In response, the trustee brought this application to the court for advice and directions.

At first instance, McKeown J. held that the trust did not violate the Act or offend public policy.[513] The Human Rights Commission appealed.

ROBINS J.A.:

> [His Lordship agreed with the judge of first instance and with Tarnopolsky J.A. that the court had jurisdiction to hear the application and that the Ontario Human Rights Commission did not have jurisdiction. He continued:]

THE PUBLIC POLICY ISSUE

A. *Can the recitals be considered in deciding this issue?*

. . .

In my opinion, the recitals cannot be isolated from the balance of the trust document and disregarded by the court in giving the advice and direction sought by the trustee in this case. The document must be read as a whole. While the operative provisions of an instrument of this nature will ordinarily prevail over its recitals, where the recitals are not clearly severable from the rest of the instrument and themselves contain operative words or words intended to give meaning and definition to the operative provisions, the instrument should be viewed in its entirety. That, in my opinion, is the situation in the case of this trust document.

The recitals here in no way contradict or conflict with the operative provisions. The settlor made constant reference to them throughout the operative part of the document. He restricted the class of persons entitled to the benefits of the trust by reference to the recitals; he set the qualification for those who might administer the trust and give judicial advice thereon by reference to the recitals; and he stipulated the universities and colleges which might be attended by scholarship winners by reference to the recitals.

Moreover, the recitals were intended to give guidance and direction to the General Committee in awarding scholarships. They go beyond the restriction in the second sentence of the fourth recital excluding "all who are not Christians of the White Race, all who are not of British Nationality or of British Parentage, and all who owe allegiance to any Foreign Government, Prince, Pope or Potentate, or who recognize any such authority, temporal or spiritual" from benefits in the Foundation. They indicate that not all white Protestants of British parentage should be eligible for the benefits of the trust but, rather, only those "whose birth and training are such as to warrant a reasonable expectation of their developing into leading citizens of the Empire" and "who are not hampered or controlled by an allegiance or pledge of obedience to any government, power or authority,

---

512 S.O. 1981, c. 53.
513 (1987), 61 O.R. (2d) 75, 27 E.T.R. 193, 42 D.L.R. (4th) 263 (H.C.).

temporal or spiritual, the seat of which government, power or authority is outside the British Empire." Those statements were intended as standards which, if not binding, were meant to be taken into account in the making of awards. I would not regard them as irrelevant. Nor would I regard any other of the recitals as irrelevant. The operative provisions were intended to be administered in accordance with the concepts articulated in the recitals. As this document is framed, its two parts are so linked as to be inextricably interwoven. In my opinion, one part cannot be divorced from the other.

Furthermore, and perhaps more fundamentally, even if the recitals are properly treated as going only to the matter of motive, I would not think they can be ignored on an application of this nature in which a trustee seeks advice with respect to public policy issues. While the Foundation may have been privately created, there is a clear public aspect to its purpose and administration. In awarding scholarships to study at publicly supported educational institutions to students whose application is solicited from a broad segment of the public, the Foundation is effectively acting in the public sphere. Operating in perpetuity as a charitable trust for educational purposes, as it has now for over half a century since the settlor's death, the Foundation has, in realistic terms, acquired a public or, at the least, a quasi-public character. When challenged on public policy grounds, the reasons, explicitly stated, which motivated the Foundation's establishment and give meaning to its restrictive criteria, are highly germane. To consider public policy issues of the kind in question by sterilizing the document and treating the recitals as though they did not exist, is to proceed on an artificial basis. In my opinion, the court cannot close its eyes to any of this trust document's provisions.

B. *Does the trust violate public policy?*

Viewing this trust document as a whole, does it violate public policy? In answering that question, I am not unmindful of the adage that "public policy is an unruly horse" or of the admonition that public policy "should be invoked only in clear cases, in which the harm to the public is substantially incontestable, and does not depend on the idiosyncratic inferences of a few judicial minds."[514] I have regard also to the observation of Professor D.W.M. Waters in his text on the *Law of Trusts in Canada*[515] to the effect that:

> The courts have always recognized that to declare a disposition of property void on the ground that the object is intended to contravene, or has the effect of contravening public policy, is to take a serious step. There is the danger that the judge will tend to impose his own values rather than those values which are commonly agreed upon in society and, while the evolution of the common law is bound to reflect contemporary ideas on the interests of society, the courts also feel that it is largely the duty of the legislative body to enact law in such matters, proceeding as such a body does by the process of debate and vote.

---

514 *Re Millar*, [1938] S.C.R. 1, [1938] 1 D.L.R. 65, *per* Crocket J., quoting Lord Aitkin in *Fender v. Mildmay*, [1937] 3 All E.R. 402, at 13 S.C.R.

515 2nd ed. (Toronto: Carswell, 1984) at 240.

Nonetheless, there are cases where the interests of society require the court's intervention on the grounds of public policy. This, in my opinion, is manifestly such a case.

The freedom of an owner of property to dispose of his or her property as he or she chooses is an important social interest that has long been recognized in our society and is firmly rooted in our law.[516] That interest must, however, be limited in the case of this trust by public policy considerations. In my opinion, the trust is couched in terms so at odds with today's social values as to make its continued operation in its present form inimical to the public interest.

According to the document establishing the Leonard Foundation, the Foundation must be taken to stand for two propositions: first, that the white race is best qualified by nature to be entrusted with the preservation, development, and progress of civilization along the best lines, and, second, that the attainment of the peace of the world and the advancement of civilization are best promoted by the education of students of the white race, of British nationality, and of the Christian religion in its Protestant form.

To say that a trust premised on these notions of racism and religious superiority contravenes contemporary public policy is to expatiate the obvious. The concept that any one race or any one religion is intrinsically better than any other is patently at variance with the democratic principles governing our pluralistic society in which equality rights are constitutionally guaranteed and in which the multicultural heritage of Canadians is to be preserved and enhanced. The widespread criticism of the Foundation by human rights bodies, the press, the clergy, the university community, and the general community serves to demonstrate how far out of keeping the trust now is with prevailing ideas and standards of racial and religious tolerance and equality and, indeed, how offensive its terms are to fair-minded citizens.

To perpetuate a trust that imposes restrictive criteria on the basis of the discriminatory notions espoused in these recitals according to the terms specified by the settlor would not, in my opinion, be conducive to the public interest. The settlor's freedom to dispose of his property through the creation of a charitable trust fashioned along these lines must give way to current principles of public policy under which all races and religions are to be treated on a footing of equality and accorded equal regard and equal respect.

Given this conclusion, it becomes unnecessary to decide whether the trust is invalid by reason of uncertainty or to consider the questions raised in this regard in para. 23 of Mr. McLeod's affidavit which I reproduced earlier. Nor is it necessary to make any determination as to whether other educational scholarships may contravene public policy.

On the material before the court, it appears that many scholarships are currently available to students at colleges and universities in Ontario and elsewhere in Canada which restrict eligibility or grant preference on the basis of such factors as an applicant's religion, ethnic origin, sex, or language. None, however, so far as the material reveals, is rooted in concepts in any way akin to those articulated

---

516 *Blathwayt v. Lord Cawley*, [1976] A.C. 397, [1975] 3 All E.R. 625 (H.L.).

here which proclaim, in effect, some students, because of their colour or their religion, less worthy of education or less qualified for leadership than others. I think it inappropriate and indeed unwise to decide in the context of the present case and in the absence of any proper factual basis whether these other scholarships are contrary to public policy or what approach is to be adopted in determining their validity should the issue arise. The court's intervention on public policy grounds in this case is mandated by the, hopefully, unique provisions in the trust document establishing the Leonard Foundation.

THE *CY-PRÈS* ISSUE

On this issue, I agree with the learned weekly court judge that the trust established by the indenture is a charitable trust. I am persuaded that the settlor intended the trust property to be wholly devoted to the furtherance of a charitable object whose general purpose is the advancement of education or the advancement of leadership through education.

It must not be forgotten that when the trust property initially vested in 1923 the terms of the indenture would have been held to be certain, valid and not contrary to any public policy which rendered the trust void or illegal or which detracted from the settlor's general intention to devote the property to charitable purposes. However, with changing social attitudes, public policy has changed. The public policy of the 1920s is not the public policy of the 1990s. As a result, it is no longer in the interest of the community to continue the trust on the basis predicated by the settlor. Put another way, while the trust was practicable when it was created, changing times have rendered the ideas promoted by it contrary to public policy and, hence, it has become impracticable to carry it on in the manner originally planned by the settlor.

In these circumstances, the trust should not fail. It is appropriate and only reasonable that the court apply the *cy-près* doctrine and invoke its inherent jurisdiction to propound a scheme that will bring the trust into accord with public policy and permit the general charitable intent to advance education or leadership through education to be implemented by those charged with the trust's administration.

The observations of Lord Simonds in *National Anti-Vivisection Society v. Inland Revenue Commissioners*[517] are apposite to this case. [H]e said:

> A purpose regarded in one age as charitable may in another be regarded differently. I need not repeat what was said by Jessel M.R. in *Re Campden Charities*.[518] A bequest in the will of a testator dying in 1700 might be held valid on the evidence then before the court but on different evidence held invalid if he died in 1900. So, too, I conceive that an anti-vivisection society might at different times be differently regarded. *But this is not to say that a charitable trust, when it has once been established can ever fail. If by a change in social habits and needs or, it may be, by a change in the law the purpose of an established charity becomes superfluous or even illegal, or if with increasing knowledge it appears that a purpose once thought beneficial is truly detrimental to*

---

517 *Supra*, note 33, at 74, emphasis added.
518 18 Ch. D. 310.

the community, it is the duty of trustees of an established charity to apply to the court or in suitable cases to the charity commissioners or in educational charities to the Minister of Education and ask that a cy-près scheme may be established. . . . A charity once established does not die, though its nature may be changed.

. . .

DISPOSITION

To give effect to these reasons, I would strike out the recitals and remove all restrictions with respect to race, colour, creed or religion, ethnic origin, and sex as they relate to those entitled to the benefits of the trust and as they relate to the qualifications of those who may be members of the General Committee or give judicial advice and, as well, as they relate to the schools, universities, or colleges in which scholarships may be enjoyed. (The provision according preferences to sons and daughters of members of the classes of persons specified in the trust document remains unaffected by this decision.)

. . .

[Tarnopolsky J.A. agreed in the result. He concluded that the trust offended public policy as reflected in a number of federal and provincial statutes, the Constitution, and international treaties to which Canada was a signatory. He opined that a charitable trust which restricts the class of beneficiaries will not be void, however, if it is designed to meliorate inequality. Hence, his Lordship did not see anything discriminatory in the preferential provisions of the trust. Similarly, he thought that trusts to promote the education of "women, aboriginal peoples, the physically and mentally handicapped, or other historically disadvantaged groups" would not offend public policy. Further, he was of opinion that the decision in the case would have no effect on trusts for individuals. Finally, his Lordship thought that the court could apply the property *cy-près*, since the testator had a general charitable intention to promote leadership through education.

Osler J. concurred with Robins J.A.

The court allowed the appeal.]

Notes and Questions

1. The case was the subject of two instructive comments.[519]

2. The court, in answering the specific questions put to it, stated that the provisions of the Leonard trust which confined management, judicial advice, schools, universities

---

519 J.C. Shepherd, "When the Common Law Fails" (1989), 9 E. & T.J. 117 (trial); and Jim Phillips, "Anti-Discrimination, Freedom of Property Disposition, and the Public Policy of Charitable

and colleges and benefits on the grounds of race, colour, ethnic origin, creed or religion, or sex were void. Further, it directed that the application form used to solicit scholarships be changed in accordance with the decision.

3. We submit that Tarnopolsky J.A. was wrong in supposing that a general charitable intention was necessary before the *cy-près* doctrine could be invoked. It was not necessary in this case, which involved a supervening impossibility or impracticability.

4. Was Tarnopolsky J.A. right when he stated that scholarships restricted for purposes designed to meliorate historical inequities are not objectionable? Is it relevant to your answer that many university scholarships are restricted on the basis of sex, language, ethnic origin, or other criteria? Or are only certain kinds of restriction objectionable?[520]

5. Would a scholarship restricted to females of, for example, Moldovan descent be charitable? Would it make any difference if (for the sake of argument) it is common knowledge that Moldovan families strongly encourage their offspring of both sexes to pursue higher education and that such students are usually highly successful?

6. Is the law of charity an appropriate means for social engineering?

7. *Re Woodhams*[521] is another case in which a restriction on musical scholarships (limited to orphans of certain homes) was deleted because the trustees (colleges of music) objected to the restriction.

8. In the United States the *cy-près* doctrine has been employed effectively to reform racially restricted charitable trusts, usually by removing the colour bar restriction.[522]

However, in *Evans v. Abney*[523] the United States Supreme Court upheld the lower Georgia courts in the exercise of their discretion not to apply *cy-près* to prevent termination of a trust which was established for the purpose of operating a segregated park. In effect, the lower courts concluded that the trust had to be terminated since its purpose had become impossible to carry out, so there was a resulting trust back to the testator's estate. The Supreme Court decided that the exercise of the Georgia court's discretion not to apply *cy-près* to prevent termination of the trust did not violate black citizens' rights to equal protection and due process under the 14th Amendment.

9. In England the *Race Relations Act, 1976*[524] now declares trusts such as the one in *Lysaght v. Royal College of Surgeons*[525] to be discriminatory and unlawful. The Act applies to discrimination on the basis of colour, race, or ethnic or national origins (including citizenship).

10. Compare the public policy reasons in the *Canada Trust Co. v. Ontario Human Rights Commission* case with the reasons in the *Ramsden Estate, Re*[526] case. *Ramsden*

Educational Trusts: A Comment on *Re Canada Trust Company and Ontario Human Rights Commission*" (1990), 9 Philanthrop. No. 3, 3.

520   See, *e.g.*, *University of Victoria Foundation v. British Columbia (Attorney General)*, 32 E.T.R. (2d) 298, (sub nom. *University of Victoria v. British Columbia (Ministry of the Attorney General)*) 185 D.L.R. (4th) 182, 2000 CarswellBC 529, 2000 BCSC 445, 73 B.C.L.R. (3d) 375, 37 C.H.R.R. D/200 (S.C. [In Chambers]), gift to University for Roman Catholic students.

521   [1981] 1 All E.R. 202 (Ch. Div.).

522   For instructive articles on the American experience in this area and the constitutional issues involved, see Note, "Sex Restricted Scholarships and the Charitable Trust" (1974) 59 Iowa L. Rev. 1000; Frank R. Parker, "Evans v. Newton and The Racially Restricted Charitable Trust" (1967), 13 Howard L.J. 223.

523   (1970) U.S. 435.

524   1976, c. 74 (U.K.), am. by the *Race Relations (Amendment) Act*, 2000, c. 34.

525   (1965), [1966] Ch. D. 191, [1965] 2 All E.R. 888, discussed above.

526   (1996), 139 D.L.R. (4th) 746, 1996 CarswellPEI 98, 14 E.T.R. (2d) 239, 145 Nfld. & P.E.I.R. 156, 453 A.P.R. 156 (T.D. [In Chambers]).

concerned a gift to the University of Prince Edward Island to establish bursaries or scholarships for Protestant student with preference to be given to those intending to become ministers. The University could not accept the gift because of its governing statute. The court purported to apply the money *cy-près*. However, this was not *cy-près*, since the gift was not impossible or impracticable. All that was lacking was a trustee. What the court in fact did was to make a scheme to carry out the charitable purpose.[527]

8. THE REGULATION OF CHARITIES

(a) The Statutory Scheme

In early times, since most charitable purposes were religious, they were controlled and administered by the church. However, when charitable uses were being employed for a variety of purposes outside the church, there was no one to complain to if the trustee misapplied the funds. The main effort to control the administration of charities after the Reformation was the *Statute of Charitable Uses*.[528] That statute introduced commissions of inquiry which had a limited jurisdiction to correct abuses or to refer a case to the Court of Chancery. The commissions were not very effective and over the next several hundred years various statutes were passed in England to improve the administration of charities. England introduced comprehensive reform of the administration of charities by the *Charities Act, 1960*.[529] Further substantial changes in the regulation of charities were made in England by the *Charities Act, 1992*,[530] and the *Charities Act, 1993*.[531]

The Canadian provinces have nothing as comprehensive as that. Indeed, apart from Ontario, there is virtually no provincial legislation on the subject, save for some isolated provisions. This means that in practice charities are regulated by the Department of National Revenue under the *Income Tax Act*.[532] This is far from ideal.

Sections 14 and 15 of the Ontario *Trustee Act*[533] empower the Supreme Court of Ontario to vest property in trustees for charitable purposes, while under section 12 of the *Public Guardian and Trustee Act*[534] the Public Guardian and Trustee may accept and administer any charitable or public trust. The latter provision has its counterpart in other provinces.[535]

---

527 See James Phillips, "Legal Developments" (1997), 14 Philanthrop., No. 2, 36.

528 1601 (43 Eliz. 1), c. 4.

529 1960 (8 & 9 Eliz. 2), c. 58 (U.K.). Minor changes were made in the *Charities Act 1985*, c. 20.

530 1992, c. 41 (U.K.).

531 1993, c. 10 (U.K.). See also the White Paper, "Charities: A Framework for the Future," H.C., Cm. 694 (1989).

532 R.S.C. 1985, c. 1 (5th Supp.), as amended. See part 2, *supra*.

533 R.S.O. 1990, c. T.23. To the same effect see *Trustee Act*, R.S.B.C. 1996, c. 464, s. 80; R.S.M. 1987, c. T160, s. 25; R.S.N.S. 1989, c. 479, s. 44; R.S.N.L. 1990, c. T-10, s. 47; R.S.S. 1978, c. T-23, ss. 32, 33; R.S.P.E.I. 1988, c. T-8, s. 22; *Trustees Act*, R.S.N.B. 1973, c. T-15, s. 35.

534 R.S.O. 1990, c. P.51.

535 See the *Public Trustee Act*, R.S.M. 1987, c. P275, s. 13; R.S.N.S. 1989, c. 379, s. 4(3)(f); R.S.N.L. 1990, c. P-46, s. 14; *Official Trustee Act*, R.S.P.E.I. 1988, c. O-4, s. 10, act repealed by 1994, c. 52, s. 80 (eff. July 14, 1994).

The *Charitable Institutions Act*[536] is concerned with the approval, maintenance and inspection of charitable corporations which operate residential premises for persons who are in need of accommodation, care and special treatment, and which are not governed by special legislation.

The *Charitable Gifts Act*,[537] prohibits a charity from holding more than a 10 per cent interest in any organization carried on for profit for longer than seven years. This Act was passed in 1949 by the Frost administration, allegedly to prevent retention of control of the Toronto Star, a Liberal paper, by the Atkinson Foundation.[538]

Under the *Charities Accounting Act*,[539] parts of which are reproduced below, all trustees for charitable purposes and charitable corporations, have a duty to inform the Public Trustee of all gifts to them as trustees for charitable purposes made by deed or will one month after a gift vests in them, and the Public Trustee has the right to order investigations and demand accountings, but there is no provision for regular supervision of charities. The Act also prohibits a charity from holding land except for its actual use and occupation.

Further Reading

Fern Levis, "The Protection of Charities in Ontario" (1972), 1 Philanthrop. (No. 1), 11.

M. Cullity, "Statutory Machinery for Supervising Charities" (1972), 1 Philanthrop. (No. 1), 22.

Public Trustee for Ontario, "Submission to the Ontario Law Reform Commission: Project on the Law of Charities" (1990), 9 Philanthrop. No. 4, 12; 10 E. & T.J. 272.

Leopold Amighetti, "The Responsibilities and Liabilities of Foundation Directors and Trustees" (1995), 13 Philanthrop. (No. 1), 3.

Kenneth R. Goodman, "Standing on Guard for Thee: The Role of the Office of the Public Guardian and Trustee" (2002), 17 Philanthrop., No. 1, 4.

Richard Bridge, "The Law of Advocacy by Charitable Corporations: The Case for Change" (2002), 21 E.T. & P.J. 92, 17 Philanthrop., No. 2, 2.

CHARITIES ACCOUNTING ACT

R.S.O. 1990, c. C.10, as amended

1. (1) Where, under the terms of a will or instrument in writing, real or personal property or any right or interest in it or proceeds from it are given to or vested in a person as executor or trustee for a religious, educational, charitable or public purpose, or are to be applied by the person for any such purpose, the person shall give written notice to,

(a) the person, if any, designated in the will or other instrument as the beneficiary or as the person to receive the gift from the executor or trustee; and

---

536 R.S.O. 1990, c. C.9.
537 R.S.O. 1990, c. C.8.
538 See the Globe and Mail, Saturday, May 5, 1973, at 3.
539 R.S.O. 1990, c. C.10.

(b) the Public Guardian and Trustee, in the case of an instrument other than a will.

(2) Any corporation incorporated for a religious, educational, charitable or public purpose shall be deemed to be a trustee within the meaning of this Act, its instrument of incorporation shall be deemed to be an instrument in writing within the meaning of this Act, and any real or personal property acquired by it shall be deemed to be property within the meaning of this Act.

(3) The notice shall be given, in the case of an instrument other than a will, within one month after it has been executed, and, in the case of a will, within the same period after the death of the testator.

. . .

(5) The notice shall state the nature of the property coming into the possession or under the control of the executor or trustee.

(6) The notice shall be accompanied by a copy of the will or other instrument; in the case of a notice under clause (1)(b), the Public Guardian and Trustee may require a notarial copy.

1.1. Sections 27 to 31[540] of the *Trustee Act* apply to,

(a) an executor or trustee referred to in subsection 1(1); and

(b) a corporation that is deemed to be a trustee under subsection 1(2).

2. (1) Every such executor or trustee shall, from time to time upon request, furnish to the Public Guardian and Trustee particulars in writing of,

(a) the condition, disposition or such other particulars as are required of the property devised, bequeathed or given or which has come into the hands of the executor or trustee;

(b) the names and addresses of the executors or trustees; and

(c) the administration or management of the estate or trust.

(2) Where such executor or trustee, either directly or indirectly through any person on the executor's or trustee's behalf or through any corporation or through a series or combination of such persons, corporations or persons and corporations, controls a corporation or the election of the directors thereof through the holding of a majority of the shares thereof or a sufficient number of shares or any class of shares thereof to enable the executor or trustee to exercise such control in fact, or in any other manner whatsoever, the corporation, the officers and manager of such corporation or any of them shall from time to time furnish to the Public Guardian and Trustee in writing such information concerning the corporation, its operation, assets, profits or losses, and finances as the Public Guardian and Trustee requests.

(3) A judge of the Superior Court of Justice, upon the application of the Public Guardian and Trustee and upon notice to the corporation concerned and to such other person or persons as a judge of the Superior Court of Justice directs, shall inquire into and determine any question relating to the failure to furnish infor-

---

540 These sections describe the investment powers of trustees.

mation to the Public Guardian and Trustee pursuant to subsection (2), and shall inquire into and determine the control of the election of directors or the ownership, control or management of, or any matter affecting, any corporation mentioned in subsection (2), or its operation, assets, profits or losses, and finances and may make such order as is considered necessary or proper...

3. Whenever required so to do by the Public Guardian and Trustee, an executor or trustee shall submit the accounts of dealings with the property coming into the hands or under the control of the executor or trustee under the terms of the bequest or gift, to be passed and examined and audited by a judge of the Superior Court of Justice.

[Section 4 confers jurisdiction on the court, upon the application of the Public Guardian and Trustee, to make such orders as are appropriate when a trustee of a charitable trust has acted contrary to the statute, the trust, or the general law.

Section 5 provides for the making of regulations and various housekeeping matters. Subsection (4) requires that notice be given to the Public Guardian and Trustee regarding any proceedings concerning a charitable trust. The Public Guardian and Trustee has the right to be heard in any such proceeding.

Section 5.1 provides for the making of regulations setting out the benefits that can be given to trustees of a charity or directors of a charitable corporation.

Section 6 authorizes the court to make an order, upon the application of any person, to direct the Public Guardian and Trustee to investigate the manner in which funds have been solicited from the public for any charitable purpose, other than for a religious or fraternal purpose, and the way in which those funds have been applied.]

7. In sections 8, 9 and 10,
"charitable purpose" means,
(a) the relief of poverty,
(b) education,
(c) the advancement of religion, and
(d) any purpose beneficial to the community, not falling under clause (a), (b) or (c);

"land" includes an interest in land other than an interest in land held as security for a debt.

[Section 8 provides that a charity may only hold land for its actual use and occupation. The Public Guardian and Trustee is empowered to vest land not so held in him or her if the land has not been used for the actual use and occupation of the charity for three years. He or she may then sell any land not required for the charity's actual use or occupation.

Section 9 permits municipalities and their local boards, universities and public hospitals to hold real and personal property upon the terms of any devise, bequest or grant to them.]

10. (1) Where any two or more persons allege a breach of a trust created for a charitable purpose or seek the direction of the court for the administration of a trust for a charitable purpose, they may apply to the Superior Court of Justice and the court may hear the application and make such order as it considers just for the carrying out of the trust under the law.

(2) An application under subsection (1) shall be upon notice to the Public Guardian and Trustee who may appear and be represented by counsel at the hearing.

(3) Where the court is of the opinion that the public interest can be served by an investigation of the matter alleged in the application, the court may make an order directing the Public Guardian and Trustee to make such investigation as the Public Guardian and Trustee considers proper in the circumstances and report in writing thereon to the court and the Attorney General.

(4) In making an investigation directed under subsection (3), the Public Guardian and Trustee has and may exercise any of the powers conferred on him or her by this Act and any of the powers of a commission under Part II of the *Public Inquiries Act*,[541] which Part applies to the investigation as if it were an inquiry under that Act.

11. This Act applies despite any provision in any will or other instrument excluding its application or giving to an executor or trustee any discretion as to the application of property, funds or the proceeds thereof to religious, educational, charitable or public purposes.

12. This Act does not apply to or affect or in any way interfere with any right or remedy that any person may have under any other Act or in equity or at common law or otherwise.

[Section 13[542] deems an order consented to by the Public Guardian and Trustee to be effective without a court hearing.]

Notes and Questions

1. Sections 7-10 were added to the Act in 1982.[543] These sections derive (with modifications) from the *Mortmain and Charitable Uses Act*,[544] which was repealed.[545] The prohibition against charities holding land except as required for their use and occupation finds its origin in the old fear of mortmain, that is, the tying up of land, the wealth of the

---

541 R.S.O. 1990, c. P.41.
542 Enacted by S.O. 1997, c. 23.
543 By S.O. 1982, c. 11, s. 1.
544 R.S.O. 1980, c. 297.
545 By S.O. 1982, c. 12, s. 1(1).

nation, in the dead hand of corporations and charities in perpetuity.[546] The Ontario Law Reform Commission has recommended that these restrictions be abolished.[547]

2. Legislation comparable to section 6 of the Ontario *Charities Accounting Act* also exists in some other provinces.[548] The Ontario Law Reform Commission has recommended that the Legislature enact legislation regulating the solicitation of funds for charitable purposes.[549]

3. Under the reforms proposed by the Ontario Law Reform Commission the court would be enabled to exercise any of the powers conferred by the proposed Act for the purpose of vesting any property in the trustees of a charity[550] and to authorize the sale of land held by trustees for a charity that is no longer required by it.[551] Notice of an application for an order under the proposed *cy-près* provisions would have to be given to the Public Trustee.[552]

4. It has been held that the Public Trustee has standing, by virtue of section 5(4) of the Ontario *Charities Accounting Act*, to notice, to appear and be heard, and to object or consent to an application to vary a charitable trust, whether or not the charity is represented.[553]

5. Section 5.1 of the Act was enacted in response to the position taken by the Public Guardian and Trustee that incorporated charities could not purchase liability insurance for directors and officers, and that a charity could not adopt an indemnification by-law governing its directors and officers, without court approval. The section allows both of these things to be done without court approval.

(b) Proposals for Reform

The Ontario Law Reform Commission has expressed the view that the current statutes governing the regulation of charities are poorly conceived and has recommended their repeal.[554] The Commission has recommended legislation which would greatly extend the regulation of charities in Ontario. The legislation would

---

546 See A.H. Oosterhoff, "The Law of Mortmain: An Historical and Comparative Review" (1977), 27 U. of T.L.J. 257.

547 O.L.R.C. *Report on Charities*, at 598-599, 636.

548 *Charitable Fund-raising Act*, R.S.A. 2000, c. C-9; *The Charities Endorsement Act*, R.S.M. 1987, c. C60; *Charities Act*, R.S.P.E.I. 1988, c. C-4; *The Charitable Fund-raising Businesses Act*, S.S. 2002, c. C-6.2. The Alberta Act replaced the *Public Contributions Act*, R.S.A. 1980, c. P-26. The Alberta Court of Appeal declared that Act to be void for violating the constitutional guarantee of freedom of expression under s. 2(b) of the *Canadian Charter of Rights and Freedoms*: see *Epilepsy Canada v. Alberta (Attorney General)* (1994), 115 D.L.R. (4th) 501, 1994 CarswellAlta 131, 20 Alta. L.R. (3d) 44, 155 A.R. 212, 73 W.A.C. 212, 23 C.R.R. (2d) 151 (C.A.), additional reasons at (1994), 115 D.L.R. (4th) 501 at 514, 20 Alta. L.R. (3d) 44 at 57, 155 A.R. 212 at 222, 73 W.A.C. 212 at 222 (C.A.), additional reasons at (1994), 1994 CarswellAlta 582, 155 A.R. 259, 73 W.A.C. 259 (C.A.), additional reasons at (1994), 1994 CarswellAlta 613, 157 A.R. 268, 77 W.A.C. 268 (C.A.). For a case involving an investigation, see *Ontario (Public Guardian & Trustee) v. AIDS Society for Children (Ontario)* (2001), 39 E.T.R. (2d) 96, 2001 CarswellOnt 1971, [2001] O.J. No. 2170 (S.C.J.)

549 O.L.R.C. *Report on Charities*, at 585ff.

550 O.L.R.C. *Report on Trusts*, at 520, s. 78.

551 *Ibid.*, s. 79.

552 *Ibid.*, s. 80.

553 *Re Baker* (1984), 47 O.R. (2d) 415, 11 D.L.R. (4th) 430, 17 E.T.R. 168 (H.C.).

554 O.L.R.C. *Report on Charities*, at 562, 635.

establish the Nonprofit Organizations Commission (the "NOC") to oversee the regulation of charities. The NOC would have administrative, educational, and investigative powers. However, it would not, at least not initially, have judicial or quasi-judicial powers, or powers to make regulations.[555]

The legislation would adopt the same terminology as that used in the *Income Tax Act*,[556] thereby ensuring uniformity. The NOC would have jurisdiction over charities and other non-profit entities.

The legislation, as envisaged by the Ontario Law Reform Commission, would require registration of all charitable associations, charitable trusts, and non-profit corporations. Further, non-profit entities which engage in fundraising or receive government grants, as well as third-party fundraisers and their employees, would be required to register. Registrants would have to file an annual return and information relating to their operation.

The NOC would also have supervisory power over fundraising, would be empowered to conduct investigations, inquiries, and audits of charities and other non-profit entities. Further, it would be empowered to advise and educate charities

A more recent report of the Law Reform Commission of British Columbia explores charitable trusts in depth and makes a number of recommendations for reform.[557]

(c) The Case Law

There has been a fair amount of judicial activity in recent years concerning the regulation of charities. The first case of note was *Ontario (Public Trustee) v. Toronto Humane Society*.[558] The Toronto Humane Society had been incorporated as a charitable organization. Its object was "to promote and develop humane public sentiment, and to secure the enactment and enforcement of suitable laws for the prevention of cruelty." At a general meeting in 1986, an "animal rights" group took control of the Society by electing six new members to the board in questionable circumstances. At a subsequent meeting of directors, five of them became officers of the Society. Two of them became paid employees of the Society and one of those remained a director. The five regarded themselves as an executive committee of the board and thereafter directed the affairs of the Society. The Society began to advocate legislative change. It actively supported an organization called the Coalition Against Pound Seizure ("CAPS"), which sought to have legislation permitting the use of impounded animals for research purposes repealed. The Society paid more than $55,000 in 1985 and more than $200,000 in 1986 to CAPS, out of a total expenditure of approximately $2 million.

The other members of the board objected to these actions and one of them and the Public Trustee brought applications seeking court review of the Society's affairs. At issue was whether the Society, being incorporated, and its directors,

---

555 *Ibid.*

556 R.S.C. 1985, c. 1 (5th Supp.).

557 *Report on Non-Charitable Purpose Trusts*, L.R.C. 128 (September 1992).

558 *Supra*, note 385. See Maurice J. Cullity, Comment, (1988-89), 9 E. & T.J. 12.

were subject to the court's supervisory jurisdiction over charities; whether the directors could receive remuneration; and whether the Society's support of CAPS was improper because it was political.

Anderson J. said the following about the court's jurisdiction:[559]

> Intervention is warranted on any one of three bases. Whatever doubts may surround the status of directors of charitable corporations, I am satisfied that it partakes sufficiently of trust to make them amenable to direction made in pursuance of the *Trustee Act*.[560] Looking at both the directors and the corporation, jurisdiction under section 6d(1) of the *Charities Accounting Act*,[561] could be invoked. Finally (in my view conclusively), there is the inherent equitable jurisdiction of the court in charitable matters.

His Lordship made an order providing for the appointment by the court of an independent person to oversee the next meeting of members and the election of a new full slate of directors at that meeting.

On the issue of the payment of remuneration of the directors, Anderson J. said:[562]

> Charitable institutions, or indeed non-profit corporations of any kind, are reasonably easy victims for any small determined group with the intention of taking control. That in itself is a sufficient potential evil. When one couples with it the capacity to pay a substantial remuneration there arises a situation which all human experience indicates should be avoided. There is not, as there would be in the case of a commercial corporation, a body of shareholders with a financial interest in scrutinizing and controlling the activities of the directors. . . . Whether one calls them trustees in the pure sense (and it would be a blessing if for a moment one could get away from the problems of terminology), the directors are undoubtedly under a fiduciary obligation to the Society and the Society is dealing with funds solicited or otherwise obtained from the public for charitable purposes. If such persons are to pay themselves, it seems to me only proper that it should be upon the terms upon which alone a trustee can obtain remuneration, either by express provision in the trust document or by the order of the court. The latter would appear to be the only practical mechanism. There is no trust document, and I have already indicated that I do not consider the ordinary corporate safeguards to be adequate. The payment of salaries to directors is a recent innovation in the affairs of the Society, and the minutes make it clear that a potential problem was recognized. It would have been a simple matter to take the opinion of the court. That is how it ought to have been done. I realize that it is common practice for commercial corporations to pay directors, as directors, and often as officers of the corporation as well. The Society is not a commercial corporation nor is it simply a non-profit corporation; it is a charitable institution.[563]

On the issue of the Society's political activities, Anderson J. noted the objections to charities pursuing political objects.[564] He agreed that the objectives of CAPS were political and, hence, not charitable. However, the objects of the Society were charitable. Further, a charity can use political means to further its

---

559 *Ibid.*, at 51.

560 R.S.O. 1980, c. 512.

561 R.S.O. 1980, c. 65, as am. 1982, c. 11; 1983, c. 61.

562 *Supra*, note 558, at 53.

563 His Lordship followed *Re French Protestant Hospital*, [1951] 1 Ch. 567, [1951] 1 All E.R. 938 (Ch.), which was to the same effect, in coming to this conclusion. See also *Re David Feldman Charitable Foundation* (1987), 58 O.R. (2d) 626, 26 E.T.R. 88 (Surr. Ct.).

564 *Supra*, note 558, at 61.

non-political purposes. In the result, his Lordship regarded the Society's political activities as ancillary to its main purposes. Further, he held that the support by the Society of CAPS had not yet reached the point where court intervention was required, although it was dangerously close to reaching that point.

In subsequent proceedings the court approved its nominee's proposals for the annual meeting.[565]

Of particular interest in the *Toronto Humane Society* case was the issue of the status of charitable corporations. Is a charitable corporation truly a trustee? Are its directors trustees? To what extent is the corporation governed by the general statute governing incorporation of non-profit corporations, and to what extent by legislation governing the supervision of charities? These issues were again before the court in *Re Centenary Hospital Assn.*,[566] reproduced below.

RE CENTENARY HOSPITAL ASSN.

(1989), 69 O.R. (2d) 1, 59 D.L.R. (4th) 449, 33 E.T.R. 270
Supreme Court of Ontario
[High Court of Justice]

The Centenary Hospital Association operated a public hospital. The hospital was incorporated under the *Corporations Act*,[567] as a corporation without share capital. The hospital owned land adjacent to the hospital and wanted to construct a medical arts building on it, integrated with the hospital, to provide offices for specialists and other health and related services. The project was, with the blessing of the Minister of Health, but subject to the approval of the Public Trustee, designed to earn income for the hospital. The Minister of Health exercises very close supervision over the operation and financial affairs of all hospitals. The Minister of National Revenue ruled that the building would be treated as an investment and not as a business. However, the Public Trustee refused his approval. He regarded the project as not charitable, but a business. He also thought that the hospital would not be occupying the land itself and would, thus, not be in actual use or occupation of the land for its charitable purposes. The association brought this application for an order determining whether the Public Trustee had any supervisory jurisdiction over the hospital and whether the building was a business or an interest in a busines.

OSLER J.:

. . .

Counsel are agreed that the purposes of public hospitals are charitable, that the Attorney-General, on whose behalf the Public Trustee claims, has responsi-

---

565 See *Ontario (Public Trustee) v. Toronto Humane Society* (1987), 61 O.R. (2d) 250 (H.C.).
566 (1989), 69 O.R. (2d) 1, 59 D.L.R. (4th) 449, 33 E.T.R. 270 (H.C.).
567 R.S.O. 1980, c. 95.

bility generally to protect charities, and that each and every object or purpose designated or pursued by a charitable organization must be of a charitable nature unless such activities are only incidental and ancillary to its charitable purposes.

Counsel for the Hospital also accepted two further propositions. A gift or bequest to a hospital for a specific charitable trust is plainly governed by the law of charity and the Public Trustee, on behalf of the Attorney-General, has a traditional supervisory jurisdiction to exercise.

. . .

Counsel for the Hospital puts forward four propositions of law. First, the Public Trustee does not have all of the common law powers and responsibilities traditionally exercised by the Attorney-General with respect to charities. Second, charitable corporations are not trustees in a strict or technical sense and may own property beneficially. Third, rules of the common law respecting charities cannot override statutes specifically applying to public hospitals. Fourth, it is impossible to characterize activities as charitable or non-charitable without reference to the purpose or object for which the activities are undertaken.

. . .

Centenary Hospital was incorporated under the *Corporations Act*[568] and counsel places great stress on the provisions of sections 274, 275 and 276 thereof. Under section 274 the corporation is given the capacity of a natural person, under section 275 it has power to construct, maintain and alter buildings necessary or convenient for its object and to acquire land necessary for its actual use and occupation, *or for carrying on its undertaking*, and under section 276 neither the corporation nor a trustee on its behalf shall acquire or hold land "not necessary for the actual use and occupation of the corporation or for carrying on its undertaking."

It is therefore submitted on behalf of the Hospital that it has full powers under the *Corporations Act* to deal with its corporate assets, including land, subject only to the restrictions on holding land that apply to all corporations, and to the directions of the Minister of Health brought into play by the operation of the *Public Hospitals Act*.[569]

That Act gives the Minister power to approve all applications to incorporate a hospital under the *Corporations Act*; to forbid the operation or use of buildings or premises for the purposes of the Hospital without the approval of the Lieutenant-Governor in Council upon the recommendation of the Minister; to prevent additional buildings or facilities by withholding his approval; and, "No land, building or other premises or place or any part thereof acquired or used for the purposes of a hospital shall be sold, leased, mortgaged or otherwise disposed of

---

568 R.S.O. 1980, c. 95.
569 R.S.O. 1980, c. 410.

without the approval of the Minister."[570] Thus, with the exception of property subject to specific trusts, the Hospital corporation has the power to deal with its assets, including its lands, in a manner as unfettered as provided for any corporation under the *Corporations Act* subject only to the necessity to obtain the approval of the Minister of Health for various activities, including the use of its lands, buildings, and other premises.

By section 29 of the *Public Hospitals Act*, the Minister is given broad powers to make regulations. These powers have been exercised and in particular section 11 of [the regulations][571] provides that an inspector appointed by the Minister is given very broad powers of audit and investigation. It is submitted that a Surrogate Court audit, the traditional means of Public Trustee control, is not necessary and cannot have been intended by the Legislature.

Counsel for the Hospital submits that, for the purpose of outside control, no case of authority in modern times has denied the distinction he makes between corporate assets wholly within the control of the directors of the corporation and assets with respect to which the corporation acts strictly as a trustee.

Ontario (Public Trustee) v. Toronto Humane Society,[572] a decision of Anderson J. of the High Court of Justice, was cited by counsel for the Public Trustee in this connection.

[His Lordship discussed this case, which is summarized above. He noted that Anderson J. held only that the society in that case was answerable for its activities in certain respects as if it were a trustee, but did not hold that it was a trustee in as full a measure as a trustee under an express trust. He also noted that Anderson J. did not address the conduct of the society's affairs generally, since those were governed by the *Corporations Act*. His Lordship also referred to *Re Incorporated Synod of Diocese of Toronto and H.E.C. Hotels Ltd.*,[573] which held that the Synod, a charitable corporation, had power to lease land to a commercial corporation. He continued:]

It is persuasive to find that the interpretation that a "charitable corporation" has power to hold land in more than one capacity is endorsed in the *Law of Trusts*,[574] an American authority but one to which respect is entitled . . .:

The truth is that it cannot be stated dogmatically that a charitable corporation either is or is not a trustee. The question is in each case whether a rule that is applicable to trustees is applicable to charitable corporations, with respect to unrestricted or restricted property. Ordinarily the rules that are applicable to charitable trusts are applicable to charitable corporations, as we have seen, although some are not. It is probably more misleading to say that a charitable corporation is not a trustee than to say that it is, but the statement that it is a trustee must be taken with some qualifications. Thus, where property is left by will to a charitable corporation, whether it may be used for the general purposes of a corporation or whether the devise or bequest is subject to

---

570 *Ibid.*, s. 4(4).
571 R.R.O. 1980, Reg. 865.
572 *Supra*, note 385.
573 (1987), 61 O.R. (2d) 737, 44 D.L.R. (4th) 161, 47 R.P.R. 177, 25 O.A.C. 85 (C.A.).
574 4th ed., by Scott and Fratcher, at 23.

restrictions as to its use, and the property is conveyed by the executor to the corporation, a corporation is not thereafter bound to account as if it were a testamentary trustee.

The same principle was recognized by the Court of Appeal for British Columbia in *Roman Catholic Archiepiscopal Corp. of Winnipeg v. Ryan*:[575]

A testator directed that a portion of his residuary estate should go "to the Roman Catholic Archiepiscopal Corporation of Winnipeg for the benefit of the Church of the Immaculate Conception in said city or otherwise as the said corporation shall see fit." There were no express words of trust associated with the gift.[576]

It was held that the gift was to the corporation absolutely and beneficially to be applied in its discretion to the objects within its corporate powers. Sheppard J.A. reached the conclusion[577] that: "In the result the intention is manifest that the corporation was to take, not as a trustee, but beneficially."

In this connection should be mentioned section 8 of the *Charities Accounting Act*[578] which provides that:

8. This Act does not apply to or affect or in any way interfere with any right or remedy that any person may have under any other Act or in equity or at common law or otherwise.

Counsel for the Hospital points once more to section 274 of the *Corporations Act* which deems a corporation to have had from its creation the capacity of a natural person, including the power to hold and deal with land. Section 274 applies "unless otherwise expressly provided in the Act or instrument creating it."

Nothing in that Act expressly provides otherwise. . . .

. . .

The corporation is to be carried on without purpose of gain for its members and, in the usual way ". . . any profits or other accretions to the corporation shall be used in promoting its objects."

It thus appears that nothing in the Act or instrument creating the Hospital derogates from the rights it is given under the *Corporations Act* to carry on its business in pursuance of its objects.

This view is reinforced by section 7 of the *Public Hospitals Act* providing, perhaps unnecessarily, in section 7 that every hospital has power to carry on its undertaking as may be authorized by the Act under which it was established.

Can it be supportable to maintain that the *Charities Accounting Act*, which, by section 1(2) deems "[a]ny corporation incorporated for a religious, educational, charitable or public purpose . . . to be a trustee within the meaning of this Act . . ."

---

575 (1957), 12 D.L.R. (2d) 23, 26 W.W.R. 69 (sub nom. *Re Delaney; Can. Trust Co. v. Roman Catholic Archiepiscopal Corp. of Winnipeg*) (B.C. C.A.).

576 *Ibid.*, D.L.R. headnote.

577 *Ibid.*, at 34.

578 R.S.O. 1980, c. 65.

and subjects it to certain initiatives by the Public Trustee, cuts down on the amplitude of the powers otherwise available to a public hospital?

[His Lordship reviewed the history of the *Charities Accounting Act* and noted that the supervision of public hospitals had never been conferred on the Public Trustee. Of the addition of s. 1a in 1951,[579] which deems charitable corporations trustees, his Lordship said:]

The activities of public hospitals were not covered by the *Charities Accounting Act* and in my view the effect of the amendment was to extend the coverage of that statute to corporations incorporated for doing the same things hitherto done by non-incorporated trustees who carried out charitable purposes. Had it been intended to give the Public Trustee, for the first time, power to supervise the financial affairs of public hospitals, quite independently of and possibly in a manner that would conflict with the powers of the Lieutenant-Governor in Council and the Minister under the *Public Hospitals Act*, it would have been plainly so stated in the legislation.

It was submitted by counsel for the Hospital, and not disputed by counsel for the Public Trustee, that in all other cases where the Public Trustee was intended to exercise powers under particular statutes, such powers were expressly conferred. It is impossible to reconcile the view that the Public Trustee has powers to supervise or question the administration of public hospitals with the express provisions in the *Public Hospitals Act* that such institutions are to have all the powers conferred by the statute under which they are incorporated and the stipulation in the *Charities Accounting Act* that that statute was not to apply to or affect any rights which any person had under any other Act.

. . .

Sections 6b, 6c, and 6d of the *Charities Accounting Act* enacted by s. 1 of the *Charities Accounting Amendment Act, 1982*[580] have in effect replaced the provisions of sections 13 and 14 of the *Mortmain and Charitable Uses Act*,[581] which were repealed in that year. Those sections did not apply to the corporate property of public hospitals incorporated under the *Corporations Act* and it is unreasonable to conclude that the *Charities Accounting Act*, as amended, is intended to have such application.

Section 6 of the *Charities Accounting Act* provides that any person may complain as to the solicitation or procurement of funds from the public for any purpose or as to the manner in which such funds have been dealt with or disposed of. This section is presumably as applicable to public hospitals as to other public institutions. In my view, it is the only section of the Act that applies. . . .

---

579 By *The Charities Accounting Amendment Act, 1951*, S.O. 1951, c. 10.
580 S.O. 1982, c. 11.
581 R.S.O. 1980, c. 297.

[Osler J. went on to say that, had he come to another conclusion, he would have held that the building did not infringe section 6b(1) of the *Charities Accounting Act*, as amended, since it would benefit patients and would provide services essential under modern health care conditions.

He referred also to, and approved, the opinion of Anderson J. in *Public Trustee v. Toronto Humane Society*,[582] who adopted a proportionality test to determine what percentage of a charity's activities could be non-charitable before it lost its charitable status. In the opinion of Osler J., the building's capital cost was not an undue proportion of the hospital's budget. He continued:]

The final question, (d), asks whether the retention by the applicant of its ownership interest and right to receive revenues from the proposed building would infringe the provisions of the *Charitable Gifts Act*.[583]

That Act provides in s. 2(1) that:

> 2.(1) Notwithstanding the provisions of any general or special Act, letters patent, by-law, will, codicil, trust deed, agreement or other instrument, wherever an interest in a business that is carried on for gain or profit is given to or vested in a person in any capacity for any religious, charitable, educational, or public purpose, such person has power to dispose of and shall dispose of such portion thereof that represents more than a ten per cent interest in such business.

Counsel for the Hospital submits four reasons why the Act has no application to the present case. First, he says it applies only to an interest in a business, where a ruling has been obtained from the Department of Revenue that what will be held by the Hospital is not an interest in the business but rather an investment. The court, of course, is not bound by this opinion but it is of interest that it has been given and the affidavit of Mr. Whiting states that it is the intention of the Hospital to see that the project is operated in such a manner as to continue to come within the ruling and will not be conducted as a business.

The second submission is that the Act is confined to gifts of business interests and in this context I understand counsel to submit that the term "vested in" in section 2(1) is roughly equivalent to what is sometimes expressed, unfortunately in my opinion, as "gifted to." A business acquired in any other way, he submits, is not caught by the section.

In the third place, it is submitted, if the Act would otherwise apply, it is excluded by section 7 of the *Public Hospitals Act* and by section 23(1)(a) of the *Corporations Act* and that in that connection the *Public Hospitals Act* should be considered as the particular statute taking precedence over the general, the *Charitable Gifts Act*.

His fourth submission, which impresses me as carrying great weight, is that if the Act applies there must necessarily be implied an exception for businesses directly related to the objects of the charity in each case. Otherwise, he submits,

582 *Supra*, note 385.
583 R.S.O. 1980, c. 63.

it would be impossible to run a hospital at all as many of its activities can be regarded as businesses.

Each of the above submissions is entitled to some weight. However, in my view, the fourth is unanswerable. It can never have been the intention of the Legislature to prevent public hospitals, whose operations are minutely supervised and overseen by the Minister of Health and those he delegates, from carrying on activities designed to improve and upgrade the quality of care delivered by the Hospital simply because certain of those activities might, in isolation, be regarded as businesses. To so interpret the statute would be utterly inconsistent with the whole scheme of the *Public Hospitals Act* and related legislation pertaining to health in Ontario.

[In supplementary reasons[584] Osler J. awarded costs against the Public Trustee on a solicitor and client basis, because the association was the victim of a difference of opinion between two government ministries, which compelled it to bring the application.]

Notes and Questions

1. Is a charitable corporation a trustee? Are its directors trustees? What exactly did *Toronto Humane Society* and *Centenary Hospital* decide?[585]

2. What is the formal difference between a charitable trust and a charitable corporation? Should different supervisory consequences flow from different forms?

3. A charitable corporation, which provides scholarships, was incorporated under a general provincial corporation statute as a corporation without share capital. The Act and the letters patent provided that the directors had to serve without remuneration and could not receive profits from their position as directors. One director was a solicitor and billed the corporation for legal services provided by him. The corporation paid him. Are such payments proper?[586]

4. Is it proper for a charitable corporation to lend money at commercial rates to a corporation controlled by one of the directors?[587]

5. What is the purpose of the *Charitable Gifts Act*?[588] Is it objectionable for a charity to own or run a business? Why or why not? Why was it not objectionable for the Centenary

---

584   *Re Centenary Hospital Assn.* (1989), 69 O.R. (2d) 447, 60 D.L.R. (4th) 768 (H.C.).

585   For a useful comment on the former, see Maurice C. Cullity, Comment (1988), 7 Philanthrop., No. 3, 12, reprinted (1988-89), 9 E. & T.J. 12; Maurice C. Cullity, "The Charitable Legal Corporation: A 'Bastard' Legal Form Revisited" (2002), 17 Philanthrop., No. 1, 17; Jane Burke-Robertson, "Liability Issues Affecting Directors and Officers in the Voluntary Sector" (2002), 17 Philanthrop., No. 2, 2. The *Centenary Hospital* case was the subject of a comment by Donovan Waters in (1990), 9 Philanthrop., No. 1, 3. And, see *Bloorview, supra* at para. 27.

586   See *Harold G. Fox Education Fund v. Ontario (Public Trustee)* (1989), 69 O.R. (2d) 242, 34 E.T.R. 113 (H.C.), additional reasons at (1989), 69 O.R. (2d) 742 at 748, 34 E.T.R. 113 at 120 (H.C.); *Ontario (Public Guardian & Trustee) v. Unity Church of Truth* (1998), 59 O.T.C. 120, 1998 CarswellOnt 1282 (Gen. Div); *French Protestant Hospital, Re,* [1951] 1 Ch. 567 (Ch. Div.), per Danckwerts J.

587   See *Re David Feldman Charitable Foundation, supra,* note 563.

588   R.S.O. 1990, c. C.8

Hospital to operate a building for profit? What do you think of counsel's argument in that case that the Act only applies to "gifts" to a charity?

6. Section 5 of the *Charitable Gifts Act* requires court approval of the consideration for and the terms of a disposition of an interest in a business mandated by section 2. It seems that the granting of a right of first refusal to acquire such an interest is not a disposition so as to attract section 5.[589]

9. THE GOVERNANCE OF CHARITABLE TRUSTS

We have not, so far, addressed issues concerning the rights and duties of charitable trustees and the governance of charitable trusts. This was deliberate. To a large extent these are the same as the rights and duties of private trustees and the governance of private trusts and we have covered those issues adequately in earlier chapters.

The Ontario Law Reform Commission has recommended that different rules apply to charitable trustees in some situations. The following is a summary of the major recommendations:[590] charitable trusts should be subject to a stricter conflict of interests and duty rule; charitable trustees should not be able to pre-take compensation; the maximum number of charitable trustees should be ten and they should be able to make decisions by a majority; the minimum number of trustees should be three; certain persons (such as bankrupts and persons convicted of an indictable offence) should be prevented from being a charitable trustee; charitable trustees should not be required to pass their accounts. While the recommendations address the issue of non-unanimous decisions by charitable trustees, they do not address the problem of a tie. It will, therefore, remain important to insert a tiebreaker provision in a charitable trust.

The Commission has also made important recommendations regarding non-profit corporations[591] and unincorporated associations,[592] organized both for charitable and other purposes. A consideration of these reforms is beyond the scope of this book.

Problems

1. Allan died last year, having made the following bequests in his will:

(a) $10,000 to the London, Ontario Revivalist Mission for the purpose of promoting physical training, recreation, and education among such persons in London, Ontario as are members of the London Revivalist Church or are likely in the opinion of the pastor to become members of that church;

(b) $10,000 to Pardon International Society for the promotion of their work in seeking to dissuade foreign governments from the use of torture as a means of punishment and in seeking to promote free speech;

---

589 See *Ballard Estate v. Ballard Estate* (1991), 3 O.R. (3d) 65, 44 O.A.C. 225, 41 E.T.R. 113, 79 D.L.R. (4th) 142 (C.A.), leave to appeal to S.C.C. refused (1991), 5 O.R. (3d) xii, 83 D.L.R. (4th) vii, 137 N.R. 385 (note), 55 O.A.C. 390 (note).

590 See O.L.R.C. *Report on Charities*, at 418ff.

591 *Ibid.*, Chapter 15.

592 *Ibid.*, Chapter 16.

(c) all my residuary estate on trust to the trustees of the Save the London Priory Fund.

The London Priory was in fact a society entitled The Priory Fund Society which, until three years ago, operated in London, Ontario, when it moved its operations to Toronto. Two years ago it was, in accordance with the rules of the Society, wound up and its assets transferred to the Ontario Priory Association.

Rebecca is Allan's executrix. Advise her on the distribution of the estate. Would there be a difference if the Priory Society had been wound up this year?

2. Sonya died this year. By her will she made the following gifts to her trustees:

(a) $20,000 in trust to pay the income only in perpetuity to St. Joseph's Roman Catholic Church in Highroad, Ontario, to be used by the priest of that church for the saying of masses for the repose of the souls of the members of my family, and for no other purpose whatsoever.

(b) $10,000 in trust to pay the income annually to the priest in charge of the parish of St. Jude's Church in London, Ontario, to be used by him for such good or religious works in his congregation as he sees fit.

There was never a Roman Catholic Church in Highroad or within ten kilometres of the village. Sonya's family originally came from that area, but she has lived all her life in British Columbia. Discuss the effect of the bequests. Disregard any conflict of laws issues.

3. Thomas, who died this year, left a will which contained the following directions to his trustees:

(a) To hold $50,000 in trust and to use the income thereon for a period of 30 years to pay the amounts levied against anyone for contravention of human rights legislation in the province.

(b) To hold $60,000 in trust and to apply the income for such of my relations as my trustees consider to be poor. They are to give preference to my first cousins.

(c) To hold the residue in trust and pay the income to universities in this province to provide scholarships solely for students studying classical Greek.

The residue of Thomas's estate was more than $10 million. The income from this amount was greatly in excess of what was needed to pay the scholarships mentioned.

Discuss the validity of these bequests, the procedure the executors must follow to determine their validity and obtain directives on distribution, and the role of the state and its officials in the proceedings.

8

NON-CHARITABLE PURPOSES

1. SCOPE

As discussed in the previous chapter, trusts for charitable purposes enjoy several advantages that other trusts do not. Lacking those advantages, trusts for non-charitable purposes normally cannot exist, primarily because there is no one to enforce them. However, there are two main ways around this problem. The first is treat the trust as a power to use the trust assets for that purpose. The person entitled to the assets in default of appointment can enforce the power negatively, by restraining its improper use. Secondly, the trust can be treated as a trust for persons, if a class of beneficiaries can be identified and the rule against perpetuities can be satisfied or avoided.

The next part of this chapter deals with the reasons why non-charitable purpose trusts are invalid and the effect of that invalidity. This is followed by discussions of different ways to give legal effect to non-charitable purposes, organized according to whether they are enforced as powers or as trusts for persons.

Further Reading

W.F. Fratcher, "Bequests for Purposes" (1971), 56 Iowa L. Rev. 773.

Law Reform Commission of British Columbia, *Report on Non-Charitable Purpose Trusts* (Vancouver, LRC 128, 1992).

Manitoba Law Reform Commission, *Non-Charitable Purpose Trusts* (Winnipeg, Report No. 77, 1992).

2. INVALIDITY

(a) Reasons for Invalidity

Charities enjoy important tax benefits. They are exempt from most forms of taxation and can encourage donations by providing tax credits for their donors. Charitable purpose trusts also enjoy several additional benefits: (1) they are enforced by or on behalf of the Crown, (2) they are exempt from the rule against perpetuities, (3) courts of equity will approve specific schemes to give practical effect to vaguely expressed charitable purposes, and (4) they can be modified *cy-*

près to avoid failure if they become impractical. This special treatment is justified by the public nature of charity. Even though charities are created by private persons ultimately for the benefit of other private persons, the legal definition of charity means that all charities provide a benefit to the public. This is not true, or at least not necessarily true, of trusts for non-charitable purposes. Therefore, although some non-charitable trusts (such as pension trusts) may receive favourable tax treatment and statutory protection from the rule against perpetuities,[1] the courts have limited their special treatment of charitable purpose trusts to those trusts which are, as a matter of law, charitable.

When non-charitable purpose trusts fail, it is usually because they lack one or more of the advantages given to charitable trusts, so (1) there is no one to enforce them, (2) they violate the rule against perpetuities, or (3) the purpose is too vague to carry out. In *Re Astor's Settlement Trusts*, below, the first and third of these objections were fatal to the trust.

RE ASTOR'S SETTLEMENT TRUSTS

[1952] 1 Ch. 534, [1952] 1 All E.R. 1067
Chancery Division

In 1945, Viscount Astor made a settlement *inter vivos* of most of the issued shares of "The Observer Limited" in trust, with the income to be used for a specified period for the following purposes:

> 1. The establishment, maintenance, and improvement of good understanding, sympathy and co-operation between nations, especially the nations of the English speaking world and also between different sections of people in any nation or community. 2. The preservation of the independence and integrity of newspapers and the encouragement of the adoption and maintenance by newspapers of fearless educational and constructive policies. 3. The promotion of the freedom, independence, and integrity of the press in all its activities and of the adoption and maintenance of the highest standards throughout the profession of journalism. 4. The control, publication, carrying on, financing, or management of any newspapers, periodicals, books, pamphlets, or publications or any businesses connected therewith or with the publication thereof. 5. The protection of newspapers (particularly country or provincial newspapers as distinct from those of the capital) from being absorbed or controlled by combines or being tied by finance or otherwise to special or limited views or interests inconsistent with the highest integrity or independence. 6. The restoration, encouragement, protection, and maintenance of the independence of the editors of and writers in newspapers and periodicals and the securing (as far as possible) for the public of full means of ascertaining by whom any newspaper is actually owned or controlled. 7. The establishment, assistance, or support of any charitable public or benevolent schemes trusts, funds, associations, or bodies for or in connection with (a) the improvement of newspapers or journalism or (b) the relief or benefit of persons (or the families or dependents of persons) actually or formerly engaged in journalism or in the newspaper business or any branch thereof or (c) any of the objects or purposes mentioned in this schedule.

It was admitted that these purposes were non-charitable and that they did not infringe the rule against perpetuities. One of the trustees, Lord Astor, made this

---

1 See, *e.g.*, *Perpetuities Act*, R.S.O. 1990, c. P.9, s. 18.

application to determine the validity of the trust. If invalid, the income would go to trustees of a second settlement for charity, so counsel for those trustees and the Attorney-General argued that the first settlement was void.

ROXBURGH J.:

The question upon which I am giving this reserved judgment is whether the non-charitable trusts of income during "the specified period" declared by clause 5 and the third schedule of the settlement of 1945 are void. Mr. Jennings and Mr. Buckley have submitted that they are void on two grounds: (1) that they are not trusts for the benefit of individuals; (2) that they are void for uncertainty.

Lord Parker considered the first of these two questions in his speech in *Bowman v. Secular Society Ltd.*[2] and I will cite two important passages. The first is:[3]

> The question whether a trust be legal or illegal or be in accordance with or contrary to the policy of the law, only arises when it has been determined that a trust has been created, and is then only part of the larger question whether the trust is enforceable. For, as will presently appear, trusts may be unenforceable and therefore void, not only because they are illegal or contrary to the policy of the law, but for other reasons.

The second is:[4]

> A trust to be valid must be for the benefit of individuals, which this is certainly not, or must be in that class of gifts for the benefit of the public which the courts in this country recognize as charitable in the legal as opposed to the popular sense of that term.

Commenting on those passages Mr. Gray observed that *Bowman v. Secular Society Ltd.* arose out of a will and he asked me to hold that Lord Parker intended them to be confined to cases arising under a will. But they were, I think, intended to be quite general in character. Further, Mr. Gray pointed out that Lord Parker made no mention of the exceptions or apparent exceptions which undoubtedly exist, and from this he asked me to infer that no such general principle can be laid down. The question is whether those cases are to be regarded as exceptional and anomalous or whether they are destructive of the supposed principle. I must later analyse them. But I will first consider whether Lord Parker's propositions can be attacked from a base of principle.

The typical case of a trust is one in which the legal owner of property is constrained by a court of equity so to deal with it as to give effect to the equitable rights of another. These equitable rights have been hammered out in the process of litigation in which a claimant on equitable grounds has successfully asserted rights against a legal owner or other person in control of property. Prima facie, therefore, a trustee would not be expected to be subject to an equitable obligation

---

2 [1917] A.C. 406 (H.L.).
3 *Ibid.*, at 437.
4 *Ibid.*, at 441.

unless there was somebody who could enforce a correlative equitable right, and the nature and extent of that obligation would be worked out in proceedings for enforcement. This is what I understand by Lord Parker's first proposition. At an early stage, however, the courts were confronted with attempts to create trusts for charitable purposes which there was no equitable owner to enforce. Lord Eldon explained, in *Attorney-General v. Brown*,[5] how this difficulty was dealt with:

> It is the duty of a court of equity, a main part, originally almost the whole, of its jurisdiction, to administer trusts; to protect not the visible owner, who alone can proceed at law, but the individual equitably, though not legally, entitled. From this principle has arisen the practice of administering the trust of a public charity: persons possessed of funds appropriated to such purposes are within the general rule; but no one being entitled by an immediate and peculiar interest to prefer a complaint, who is to compel the performance of their obligations, and to enforce their responsibility? It is the duty of the King, as *parens patriae*, to protect property devoted to charitable uses; and that duty is executed by the officer who represents the Crown for all forensic purposes. On this foundation rests the right of the Attorney-General in such cases to obtain by information the interposition of a court of equity....

But if the purposes are not charitable, great difficulties arise both in theory and in practice. In theory, because having regard to the historical origins of equity it is difficult to visualize the growth of equitable obligations which nobody can enforce, and in practice, because it is not possible to contemplate with equanimity the creation of large funds devoted to non-charitable purposes which no court and no department of state can control, or in the case of maladministration reform. Therefore, Lord Parker's second proposition would prima facie appear to be well founded. Moreover, it gains no little support from the practical considerations that no officer has ever been constituted to take, in the case of non-charitable purposes, the position held by the Attorney-General in connexion with charitable purposes, and no case has been found in the reports in which the court has ever directly enforced a non-charitable purpose against a trustee. Indeed where, as in the present case, the only beneficiaries are purposes and an at present unascertainable person, it is difficult to see who could initiate such proceedings. If the purposes are valid trusts, the settlors have retained no beneficial interest and could not initiate them. It was suggested that the trustees might proceed ex parte to enforce the trusts against themselves. I doubt that, but at any rate nobody could enforce the trusts against them. This point, in my judgment, is of importance, because in most of the cases which are put forward to disprove Lord Parker's propositions the court had indirect means of enforcing the execution of the non-charitable purpose.

> [The next part of the judgment, dealing with anomalous cases that are excepted from the general rule, is reproduced in the next section, below. Roxburgh J. continued:]

---

5 (1818), 1 Swans. 265 at 290, 36 E.R. 384, 1 Wils. Ch. 323, 37 E.R. 138.

The second ground upon which the relevant trusts are challenged is uncertainty. If (contrary to my view) an enumeration of purposes outside the realm of charities can take the place of an enumeration of beneficiaries, the purposes must, in my judgment, be stated in phrases which embody definite concepts and the means by which the trustees are to try to attain them must also be prescribed with a sufficient degree of certainty. The test to be applied is stated by Lord Eldon in *Morice v. Bishop of Durham* as follows:[6]

> As it is a maxim, that the execution of a trust shall be under the control of the court, it must be of such a nature, that it can be under that control; so that the administration of it can be reviewed by the court; or, if the trustee dies, the court itself can execute the trust; a trust therefore, which, in case of maladministration could be reformed; and a due administration directed; and then, unless the subject and the objects can be ascertained, upon principles, familiar in other cases, it must be decided, that the court can neither reform maladministration, nor direct a due administration.

Mr. Gray argued that this test was not properly applicable to trusts declared by deed, but I can see no distinction between a will and a deed in this respect.

Applying this test, I find many uncertain phrases in the enumeration of purposes, for example, "different sections of people in any nation or community" in paragraph 1 of the third schedule, "constructive policies" in paragraph 2, "integrity of the press" in paragraph 3, "combines" in paragraph 5, "the restoration... of the independence of... writers in newspapers" in paragraph 6 and "benevolent schemes" in paragraph 7. Mr. Gray suggested that in view of the unlimited discretion bestowed upon the trustees (subject only to directions from the settlors) the trustees would be justified in excluding from their purview purposes indicated by the settlors but insufficiently defined by them. But I cannot accept this argument. The purposes must be so defined that if the trustees surrendered their discretion, the court could carry out the purposes declared, not a selection of them arrived at by eliminating those which are too uncertain to be carried out. If, for example, I were to eliminate all the purposes except those declared in paragraph 4, but to decree that those declared in paragraph 4 ought to be performed, should I be executing the trusts of this settlement?

But how in any case could I decree in what manner the trusts applicable to income were to be performed? The settlement gives no guidance at all. Mr. Hunt suggested that the trustees might apply to the court ex parte for a scheme. It is not, I think, a mere coincidence that no case has been found outside the realm of charity in which the court has yet devised a scheme of ways and means for attaining enumerated trust purposes. If it were to assume this (as I think) novel jurisdiction over public but not charitable trusts it would, I believe, necessarily require the assistance of a custodian of the public interest analogous to the Attorney-General in charity cases, who would not only help to formulate schemes but could be charged with the duty of enforcing them and preventing maladministration. There is no such person. Accordingly, in my judgment, the trusts for the application of income during "the specified period" are also void for uncertainty.

---

6 (1805), 10 Ves. 522 at 539, 32 E.R. 947. See also *Re Macduff*, [1896] 2 Ch. 451 at 463.

But while I have reached my decision on two separate grounds, both, I think, have their origin in a single principle, namely, that a court of equity does not recognize as valid a trust which it cannot both enforce and control. This seems to me to be good equity and good sense.

(b) Effect of Invalidity

When a non-charitable purpose trust fails, normally the trust assets must be returned to the settlor or, if the settlor is dead, to the settlor's estate to be distributed as part of the residuary estate. If there is no will or no valid disposition of the residuary estate, then those assets are distributed according to the rules of intestacy to the settlor's next of kin. Equity's method of getting the trust assets back to the settlor or the settlor's estate is the resulting trust, studied in the next chapter. In this situation, the settlor has failed to create a valid express trust and yet did not intend to transfer the beneficial legal ownership of the trust assets to the trustees. Therefore, a resulting trust arises by operation of law to remove beneficial ownership of those assets from the trustees and return it to the settlor or her or his estate.

Sometimes, the failure affects only part of a trust, such as the income from the trust assets, a life interest in those assets, or a share of the capital. A well drafted trust provides for the complete disposition of the trust assets in the event that any portion of it turns out to be invalid. In that case, there is no resulting trust, because the beneficial ownership of the trust assets is completely and properly distributed by the express trust. If that has not been done, then normally there would be a resulting trust of the portion affected by the failure.

If a trust is created for mixed charitable and non-charitable purposes, the invalidity of the non-charitable purpose can cause the entire trust to fail. For example, in *Re Diplock*,[7] a testamentary trust for "charitable or benevolent objects" was invalid because it mixed charitable objects with benevolent (that is, good but not necessarily charitable) objects. Although the executors had distributed the estate only to charitable institutions, the possibility that it could have been used for non-charitable purposes meant that the trust was invalid and the gifts to charities were unauthorized. In response to this problem, many jurisdictions now have legislation that validates the charitable purpose trust despite the inclusion of an invalid non-charitable purpose. This is discussed in the previous chapter.

Notes and Questions

1. The playwright, George Bernard Shaw, was interested in orthography and pronunciation. He developed a forty-letter alphabet and wished to see it put into effect after he died. He and his solicitor created testamentary trusts for the following purposes: (1) to finance inquiries into the statistical and mathematical benefits of adopting the forty-letter

---

7 [1948] Ch. 465 (C.A.); affirmed *Ministry of Health v. Simpson*, [1951] A.C. 251 (H.L.); applied in *Re Loggie*, [1954] S.C.R. 645, [1955] 1 D.L.R. 415.

alphabet, (2) to employ a phonetics expert to transliterate one of his plays, *Pygmalion*, into the forty-letter alphabet, and (3) to advertise and publish the transliteration illustrating both alphabets. Any excess income was to be used to finance the launching of the forty-letter alphabet until it was generally accepted. The trusts were limited to the perpetuity period, with gifts over to various institutions.

In *Re Shaw*[8] the court held that the objects of Shaw's will trusts were not charitable because, although they might have increased knowledge generally, to be charitable a trust must be combined with provisions for teaching and education. Also, the objects were political, because they directed the launching of research on a controversial matter. As a trust for non-charitable purposes, it failed for lack of a beneficiary to enforce them. The case was settled on appeal.[9]

2. Discussed below are ways in which trusts for non-charitable purposes can be saved, either as powers of appointment or as trusts for persons. It should not be forgotten that the best option, at least for everyone involved in the trust, is the classification of its purposes as charitable, if that is possible. For example, in *Jones v. T. Eaton Co.*,[10] the Supreme Court of Canada held that "a trust fund for any needy or deserving Toronto members of the Eaton Quarter Century Club" was a charitable purpose trust for the relief of poverty, based on its generous interpretation of "needy or deserving" as meaning, in essence, more or less poor. Not only did this obviate the need to find a valid trust for persons, it entitled the trust to all the benefits of charitable status, including perpetual existence and exemption from taxation. Therefore, if one wishes to give effect to what appears to be a trust for a purpose, the following three questions should be asked in the following order: Is the purpose charitable? If not, is it a valid trust for persons? If not, is it a valid power of appointment? The first of these questions is the subject of the previous chapter. The other two questions are discussed below.

3. POWERS

There appear to be many exceptions to the general rule that a trust for a non-charitable purpose will fail, because there is no one to enforce it. On closer inspection, they turn out not to be exceptions, but cases to which the general rule does not apply, because the purpose is treated, not as the object of a trust, but as the object of a power. The first group consists of the cases that Roxburgh J. "regarded as exceptional and anomalous" in *Re Astor's Settlement Trusts*,[11] re-produced above and below. The second is the conversion of trusts for specific non-charitable purposes into powers of appointment, which is done by statute in several Canadian jurisdictions. Thirdly, the modern analysis of the *Quistclose* trust treats the payment of money to be used for a specific purpose as a trust for the payer, coupled with a power to use that money for that purpose.

---

8 [1957] 1 W.L.R. 729, [1957] 1 All E.R. 745.
9 [1958] 1 All E.R. 245n.
10 [1973] S.C.R. 635, 35 D.L.R. (3d) 97, 1973 CarswellOnt 227, 1973 CarswellOnt 227F.
11 [1952] 1 Ch. 534, at 541 [1952] 1 All E.R. 1067 (Ch. Div.) [Ch.].

(a) Anomalous Cases

English courts have upheld testamentary trusts for the care of specific animals, graves, or monuments, as well as a trust to promote fox hunting. These purposes are not charitable and they do not benefit any specific persons. Therefore, they appear to be anomalous exceptions to the general rule that a trust cannot exist unless there is someone to enforce it. However, the method by which these trusts are enforced reveals their true nature. The persons entitled to the residue of the estate, following the fulfilment or failure of the purpose, have standing to sue to prevent the misuse of the trust assets for any other purpose. As Dr. James Penner notes, "the 'enforcement' of these 'trusts' is essentially identical to the enforcement of powers of appointment."[12]

RE ASTOR'S SETTLEMENT TRUSTS

[1952] 1 Ch. 534, [1952] 1 All E.R. 1067
Chancery Division

Reproduced above are the portions of Roxburgh J.'s judgment in which he decided that a trust for non-charitable purposes was invalid. This part of his judgment considers the cases that he regarded as anomalous exceptions to the general rule.

ROXBURGH J.:

. . .

These cases I must now consider. First of all, there is a group relating to horses, dogs, graves, and monuments, among which I was referred to *Pettingall v. Pettingall*,[13] *Mitford v. Reynolds*,[14] *Re Dean*,[15] *Pirbright v. Salwey*,[16] and *Re Hooper*.[17] In *Pettingall v. Pettingall*,[18] a testator made the following bequest by his will:

"Having a favourite black mare, I hereby bequeath, that at my death, £50 per annum be paid for her keep in some park in England or Wales; her shoes to be taken off, and she never to be ridden or put in harness; and that my executor consider himself in honour bound to fulfil my wish, and see that she will be well provided for, and removable at his will. At her death all payment to cease." It being admitted that a bequest in favour of an animal was valid, two questions were made: first, as to the form of the decree on this point; and secondly, as to the disposition of the surplus not required for the mare. Knight Bruce V.C. said, that so much of the £50 as would be required to keep the mare comfortably, should be applied by the executor, and that he was entitled

---

12 J.E. Penner, *The Law of Trusts*, 3rd ed. (London: Butterworths, 2002) p. 260.
13 (1842), 11 L.J. Ch. 176.
14 (1848), 16 Sim. 105, 60 E.R. 812.
15 (1889), 41 Ch. D. 552.
16 [1896] W.N. 86.
17 [1932] 1 Ch. 38.
18 *Supra*, note 13, at 177.

to the surplus. He must give full information, whenever required, respecting the mare; and if the mare were not properly attended to, any of the parties interested in the residue might apply to the court. The decree on this point ought to be, that £50 a year should be paid to the executor during the life of the mare, or until further order; he undertaking to maintain her comfortably; with liberty for all parties to apply.

The points which I wish to make are (1) that it was there admitted that a bequest in favour of an animal was valid, and (2) that there were persons interested in residue who having regard to the decree made would have had no difficulty in getting the terms of the "bequest" enforced.

Mitford v. Reynolds related to a sepulchral monument and to horses, and there again there was a remainderman on behalf of charity to see to the enforcement of the directions, and an administration action was on foot.

In *Re Dean*, a testator devised his freehold estates, subject to and charged with an annuity of £750, and to a term of 50 years granted to his trustees, to the use of the plaintiff for life, with remainders over; and he gave to his trustees his horses, ponies and hounds; and he charged his said freehold estates with the payment to his trustees, for the term of 50 years, if any of the said horses and hounds should so long live, of an annual sum of £750. And he declared that his trustees should apply the said annual sum in the maintenance of the horses and hounds for the time being living, and in maintaining the stables, kennels and buildings inhabited by the said animals in such condition of repair as his trustees might deem fit; and in consideration of the maintenance of his horses, ponies, and hounds being a charge upon his said estate as aforesaid, he gave all his personal estate not otherwise disposed of to the plaintiff absolutely. North J. said:[19]

> Then it is said, that there is no cestui que trust who can enforce the trust, and that the court will not recognize a trust unless it is capable of being enforced by someone. I do not assent to that view. There is not the least doubt that a man may if he pleases, give a legacy to trustees, upon trust to apply it in erecting a monument to himself, either in a church or in a churchyard, or even in unconsecrated ground, and I am not aware that such a trust is in any way invalid, although it is difficult to say who would be the cestui que trust of the monument. In the same way I know of nothing to prevent a gift of a sum of money to trustees, upon trust to apply it for the repair of such a monument. In my opinion such a trust would be good, although the testator must be careful to limit the time for which it is to last, because, as it is not a charitable trust, unless it is to come to an end within the limits fixed by the rule against perpetuities, it would be illegal. But a trust to lay out a certain sum in building a monument, and the gift of another sum in trust to apply the same to keeping that monument in repair, say, for ten years, is, in my opinion, a perfectly good trust, although I do not see who could ask the court to enforce it. If persons beneficially interested in the estate could do so, then the present plaintiff can do so; but, if such persons could not enforce the trust, still it cannot be said that the trust must fail because there is no one who can actively enforce it.

This is the best case in the series from Mr. Gray's point of view, because North J. did undoubtedly uphold the particular directions, whether or not they could be "actively enforced." But putting it at its highest, he merely held that

---

19 *Supra,* note 15, at 556.

there were certain classes of trusts, of which this was one, in which that objection was not fatal. He did not suggest that it was not generally fatal outside the realms of charity.

In *Pirbright v. Salwey*, a testator, after expressing his wish to be buried in the inclosure in which his child lay in a certain churchyard, bequeathed to the rector and churchwardens of the parish church £800 Consols, the interest and dividends to be derived therefrom to be applied, so long as the law for the time being permitted, in keeping up the inclosure and decorating the same with flowers. It was held that the gift was valid for at least a period of 21 years from the testator's death, and *semble* that it was not charitable.

In *Re Hooper*,[20] a testator bequeathed to his executors and trustees money out of the income of which to provide, so far as they legally could do so, for the care and upkeep of certain graves, a vault and certain monuments. Maugham J. said:

> This point is one to my mind of doubt, and I should have felt some difficulty in deciding it if it were not for *Pirbright v. Salwey*.... That was a decision arrived at by Stirling J., after argument by very eminent counsel. The case does not appear to have attracted much attention in textbooks, but it does not appear to have been commented upon adversely, and I shall follow it.

In this case, and probably also in *Pirbright v. Salwey*, there was a residuary legatee to bring before the court any failure to comply with the directions. But I think that Maugham J. regarded them both as exceptions from general principle.

Last in this group is *Re Thompson*.[21] I have included it in this group because, although it relates to the furtherance of foxhunting and thus moves away from the subject-matter of the group and much nearer to the present case, it is expressly founded on *Pettingall v. Pettingall*, and it is indeed a most instructive case. The testator bequeathed a legacy of £1,000 to a friend to be applied by him in such manner as he should think fit towards the promotion and furthering of foxhunting and devised and bequeathed his residuary estate to Trinity Hall in the University of Cambridge. An originating summons was taken out by the executors to determine whether the legacy was valid or failed for want of a definite object or for uncertainty or on other grounds. When counsel, during the course of the argument, observed, "True, there is no cestui que trust who can enforce the application of the legacy, but that is immaterial: *Re Dean*. The object to which the legacy is to be applied is sufficiently defined to be enforced," Clauson J. interposed:[22]

> The college, as residuary legatees, seems to have an interest in the legacy, as, but for the trust for its application, they would be entitled to it. The procedure adopted by Knight Bruce V.C. in *Pettingall v. Pettingall*, cited in Jarman on Wills,[23] might be followed in this case.

And in his judgment he said:[24]

---

20 *Supra,* note 17, at 39.
21 [1934] Ch. 342.
22 *Ibid.*, at 343.
23 7th ed., Vol. 2, p. 877.
24 *Supra,* note 21, at 344.

In my judgment the object of the gift has been defined with sufficient clearness and is of a nature to which effect can be given. The proper way for me to deal with the matter will be, not to make, as it is asked by the summons, a general declaration, but following the example of Knight Bruce V.C. in *Pettingall v. Pettingall*, to order that, upon the defendant Mr. Lloyd [the friend] giving an undertaking (which I understand he is willing to give) to apply the legacy when received by him towards the object expressed in the testator's will, the plaintiffs do pay to the defendant Mr. Lloyd the legacy of £1,000; and that, in case the legacy should be applied by him otherwise than towards the promotion and furthering of foxhunting, the residuary legatees are to be at liberty to apply.

I understand Clauson J. to have held in effect that there was somebody who could enforce the purpose indicated because the college, as residuary legatees, would be entitled to the legacy but for the trust for its application and they could apply to the court to prevent any misapplication or breach of the undertaking given by Mr. Lloyd. I infer from what he said that he would not have upheld the validity of this non-charitable purpose if there had been no residuary legatee, and no possibility of making such an order as was made in *Pettingall v. Pettingall*.[25]

Lastly, I was referred to *Re Price*,[26] where a testatrix by her will gave one-half of her residuary estate to the Anthroposophical Society in Great Britain "to be used at the discretion of the chairman and executive council of the society for carrying on the teachings of the founder, Dr. Rudolf Steiner." At first sight this case would appear to be a strong card in Mr. Gray's hand. The first part of the judgment proceeds upon the footing that the purposes were not charitable. The society was the residuary legatee and there was no room for such an order as was made in *Re Thompson*. There was nobody who could have enforced the carrying out of the purposes. On closer inspection, however, it will be found that this point was not raised in argument or referred to in the judgment, and the decision was based upon *Re Drummond*[27] which is a different class of case. As the present case cannot, on any view, be assimilated to *Re Drummond*, I need not further consider *Re Price*.

Let me then sum up the position so far. On the one side there are Lord Parker's two propositions with which I began. These were not new, but merely re-echoed what Sir William Grant had said as Master of the Rolls in *Morice v. The Bishop of Durham*, as long ago as 1804: "There must be somebody, in whose favour the court can decree performance."[28] The position was recently restated by Harman J. in *Re Wood*: "A gift on trust must have a cestui que trust,"[29] and this seems to be in accord with principle. On the other side is a group of cases relating to horses and dogs, graves and monuments — matters arising under wills and intimately connected with the deceased — in which the courts have found means of escape from these general propositions and also *Re Thompson* and *Re Price* which I have endeavoured to explain. *Re Price* belongs to another field. The rest may, I think, properly be regarded as anomalous and exceptions and in no way destructive of

---

25 *Supra,* note 13, at 178.
26 [1943] Ch. 422, [1943] 2 All E.R. 505 (P.C.).
27 [1914] 2 Ch. 90.
28 (1804), 9 Ves. 399 at 405, 32 E.R. 656.
29 [1949] Ch. 498 at 501, [1949] 1 All E.R. 1100.

the proposition which traces descent from or through Sir William Grant through Lord Parker to Harman J. Perhaps the late Sir Arthur Underhill was right in suggesting that they may be concessions to human weakness or sentiment.[30] They cannot, in my judgment, of themselves (and no other justification has been suggested to me) justify the conclusion that a Court of Equity will recognize as an equitable obligation affecting the income of large funds in the hands of trustees a direction to apply it in furtherance of enumerated non-charitable purposes in a manner which no court or department can control or enforce....

Notes and Questions

1. Is the anomalous non-charitable purpose trust a true power or something akin to a power? Can the beneficiary of the residuary estate compel the trustee to perform the trust or merely restrain the misuse of trust assets? Does the residuary beneficiary have any incentive to compel performance of the trust? If the trustee refuses to perform, can he or she be replaced?

2. Enforcement of a non-charitable purpose trust negatively by the residuary estate beneficiary, in the same manner as a power of appointment, gets around the enforcement problem. Does it also solve the problem of vagueness? Most of the cases discussed above by Roxburgh J. were for clearly specified purposes, such as the care of a specific animal, grave, or monument. However, was the promotion of fox hunting, in *Re Thompson*,[31] any less vague than the purposes set out in *Re Astor's Settlement Trusts*? Although the court has no authority to make or approve a specific scheme for carrying out a vaguely expressed non-charitable purpose, is that necessary when the trust is enforced like a power? The person entitled to the residue of the estate has the right to restrain a misuse of the funds, which should be possible so long as it can be said with sufficient certainty whether or not a particular use furthers the stated purpose.

3. Roxburgh J. suggested that *Re Price*[32] may have been wrongly decided, because the trustee of the non-charitable purpose trust was the residuary beneficiary of the estate. Therefore, there was no one else entitled to the trust assets in default of appointment who would have standing to restrain the misuse of those assets. However, if the trust was, in essence, a power that did not have to be exercised and the holder of that power was entitled to the assets in default of its exercise, was the residuary bequest in *Re Price* simply a gift to the residuary beneficiary? Alternatively, if the residuary bequest was not intended to be a gift, then anything not used for the specified purpose should go back to the estate under a resulting trust (as discussed in the next chapter), to be distributed to the heirs of the testatrix according to the rules of intestacy. In that case, would the persons entitled on intestacy have standing to restrain a misuse of the assets by the residuary beneficiary?

4. In *Re Endacott*,[33] a testator gave the residue of his estate "to North Tawton Devon Parish Council for the purpose of providing some useful memorial to myself. . .". The Court of Appeal held that (1) the bequest was not a gift, but imposed a trust on the council, (2) the trust was not charitable, (3) the trust fell outside the class of anomalous non-charitable purpose trusts that had been enforced in the past, and (4) that class should not be extended. Moreover, Lord Evershed M.R. stated that, if such trusts fail as trusts, they

---

30 See *Law of Trusts*, 8th ed., p. 79.
31 *Supra,* note 21.
32 *Supra,* note 26.
33 (1959), [1960] Ch. 232, [1959] 3 All E.R. 562 (C.A.).

are not to be construed and allowed to take effect as powers. Is there a valid distinction to be drawn between the graves cases and *Re Endacott*? Do you agree with that the exceptional cases should not be extended?

5. Would *Re Endacott* have been valid if expressly drafted as a power? Should it matter whether the purpose is set up as a trust or power? Recall what Lord Wilberforce said about the difference between trusts and powers in *McPhail v. Doulton*.[34]

6. In the U.S.A., a trust to create or maintain a monument to a public figure, such as a hero, soldier, or leader of state, is regarded as beneficial to the public and therefore charitable.[35]

7. Professor Scott believed that the cases upholding trusts for anomalous non-charitable purposes are merely instances of a wider principle and that the trustee should be permitted to use the money for the specified purpose, unless it is "capricious".[36] Since the trustee is not obligated to carry out the purpose, it is called an "honorary trust", which is equivalent to a power of appointment.[37] The same view is expressed in the second *Restatement of Trusts*:[38]

> Where the owner of property transfers it in trust for a specific non-charitable purpose, and there is no definite or definitely ascertainable beneficiary designated, no enforceable trust is created; but the transferee has a power to apply the property to the designated purpose, unless such application is authorized or directed to be made at a time beyond the period of the rule against perpetuities, or the purpose is capricious.

(b) Statutory Powers of Appointment

In Alberta, British Columbia, Northwest Territories, Nunavut, Ontario, and Yukon,[39] the perpetuities legislation converts trusts for non-charitable purposes into powers of appointment valid for 21 years, provided the purposes are specific and the trusts create no enforceable equitable interests. Section 16 of the Ontario Act is reproduced below as an example.

PERPETUITIES ACT

R.S.O. 1990, c. P.9

16. (1) A trust for a specific non-charitable purpose that creates no enforceable equitable interest in a specific person shall be construed as a power to appoint the income or the capital, as the case may be, and, unless the trust is created for an illegal purpose or a purpose contrary to public policy, the trust is valid so long as and to the extent that it is exercised either by the original trustee or the trustee's successor, within a period of twenty-one years, despite the fact that the limitation

---

34 (1970), [1971] A.C. 424, [1970] 2 W.L.R. 1110, [1970] 2 All E.R. 228 (H.L.).

35 See G.T. Bogert, *Trusts*, 6th ed. (St. Paul: West Publishing, 1987) §59, p. 225.

36 Scott, §124.

37 See W.F. Fratcher, "Bequests for Purposes" (1971), 56 Iowa L. Rev. 773 at 780-783.

38 American Law Institute, *Restatement of the Law of Trusts, Second* (St. Paul: American Law Institute Publishers, 1959) §124.

39 *Perpetuities Act*, R.S.A. 2000, c. P-5, s. 20; *Perpetuity Act*, R.S.B.C. 1996, c. 358, s. 24; *Perpetuities Act*, R.S.N.W.T. 1988, c. P-3, s. 17; *Perpetuities Act*, R.S.O. 1990, c. P.9, s. 16; *Perpetuities Act*, R.S.Y. 2002, c. 168, s. 20.

creating the trust manifested an intention, either expressly or by implication, that the trust should or might continue for a period in excess of that period, but, in the case of such a trust that is to be of perpetual duration, the court may declare the limitation to be void if the court is of opinion that by so doing the result would more closely approximate the intention of the creator of the trust than the period of validity provided by this section.

(2) To the extent that the income or capital of a trust for a specific non-charitable purpose is not fully expended within a period of twenty-one years, or within any annual or other recurring period within which the limitation creating the trust provided for the expenditure of all or a specified portion of the income or the capital, the person or persons, or the person or person's successors, who would have been entitled to the property comprised in the trust if the trust had been invalid from the time of its creation, are entitled to such unexpended income or capital.

Notes and Questions

1. Do any of the trusts for anomalous non-charitable purposes, such as the care of specific animals, graves, and monuments, still exist in the provinces and territories with this legislation or have they been converted to powers of appointment? Are those trusts exempt from the statute because they are enforced, albeit negatively, by the person entitled to any assets not used for the specified purpose? Does that person have an "enforceable equitable interest" in the trust assets?

2. The only reported Canadian case in which this legislation has been interpreted is *Re Russell Estate,* below.

RE RUSSELL ESTATE

(sub nom. *Wood. v. R.*) [1977] 6 W.W.R. 273, 1 E.T.R. 285,
9 A.R. 427, 1977 CarswellAlta 240
Alberta Supreme Court (Trial Division)

The testator gave his entire estate to the "Edmonton Lodge of the Theosophical Society" upon trust for its religious, literary, and educational purposes. The society was unincorporated and had the following objects:

1. form a nucleus of the Universal Brotherhood of Humanity, without distinction of race, creed, sex, caste or colour,
2. encourage the study of comparative religion, philosophy and science,
3. investigate the unexplained laws of nature and powers latent in man, and
4. aid, support and promote the cause of Theosophy through publishing theosophical literature, hiring public speakers, and using the media for the promotion of Theosophy.

Stevenson J. ultimately decided that the will created a valid charitable purpose trust for the advancement of education. However, he first considered the possibility that the purpose was non-charitable and decided that it could not be converted to a power of appointment, by section 20 of the Alberta *Perpetuities Act*,[40] because it was not sufficiently specific. That section is virtually identical to section 16 of the Ontario Act, reproduced above.

STEVENSON J.:

. . .

The gift was clearly intended to be for the benefit of an unincorporated organization — at least for certain of its purposes — and I am of the view that it was intended to take effect as a trust and not as an absolute gift.

Reading the instrument as a whole it is intended that this trust be for the "religious, literary and educational purposes of the Lodge." A question arises as to whether or not this requirement restricts, expands or supersedes the expressed objects of the organization. It is my view that it is to be read as a gift for religious, literary and educational purposes consistent, of course, with the objectives of the Lodge.

The Validity of the Purpose Trust

Having come to the conclusion that it was the intention of the testator to establish a trust for certain purposes the validity of that gift must now be considered.

A purpose trust, unless it is charitable, fails. The reasons usually cited for the failure of such a trust are as follows: firstly, it violates the rule against perpetuities; secondly, it lacks a beneficiary; thirdly, there is an element of uncertainty or indefiniteness; and fourthly, it may be a delegation of testamentary powers.[41]

As Scott points out a mere power, where there is no attempt to create a trust, is inevitably upheld and the fourth ground does not appear to be a sound objection to a purpose trust as there can be nothing more readily classed as a delegation than a power. There is a significant trend in legislation towards finding means of upholding gifts which are neither illegal nor contrary to public policy. A gift for the benefit of the purposes of the Edmonton Lodge is neither illegal nor contrary to public policy. No one could, of course, have objected to an *inter vivos* gift to the Lodge.

A charitable trust will be upheld notwithstanding the lack of a beneficiary or the violation of the rule against perpetuities and, by definition, has sufficient certainty for the Court to administer it....

[Stevenson J. then quoted the legislation referred to above and continued:]

---

40 S.A. 1972, c. 121.
41 Scott, §123, p. 923.

I am of the view that I should first consider s. 20 of *The Perpetuities Act* since it prevents the trust from being "void for uncertainty or for any other cause" by construing it as a power.

The section in *The Perpetuities Act* (s. 20) does not appear to have been the subject of judicial interpretation although there is a like provision in Ontario. The provision appears to be based on the American Law Institutes' *Restatement of the Law of Trusts* and is a legislative recognition of the deficiencies in the existing law. I have already referred to the four usually stated objections to the enforcement of a purpose trust.

The Perpetuities Act does not, in my view, remedy only the perpetuities problem. It could have done this by simply adopting the "wait and see" principle or by imposing an arbitrary perpetuity. It does not do this but instead converts the disposition into a power. It is also clear to me that the absence of a beneficiary to enforce the power is of no significance because those who take if the power is not exercised (here next of kin) are available to ensure execution. Nor does the law recognize the objection of delegation in relation to powers of appointment or discretionary trusts.

It is interesting to note that in *Re Shaw*[42] Harman J., faced with a purpose trust, which was within the perpetuity period, expressed the wish that he could treat George Bernard Shaw's trust for the creation of a new alphabet as a power citing the *Restatement of Trusts*. Indeed, in that case, by a compromise this result was achieved with the concurrence of all parties (*Re Shaw*).[43]

The legislation appears to me to equate "specific purpose trusts" with other recognized anomalous purpose trust which have been permitted to operate as powers.

Does this gift come within the remedial section? An obvious difficulty is in the use of the term "specific". Two choices appear to be open; to define the term as being the opposite of "general" or to define it as "precise or certain". While the former interpretation may be applicable, there is nothing in the section which does away with the recognized requirement that the objects of a power must be certain. A gift in order to be protected by the section must be certain. In the case of a charitable trust the Court is able to supply certainty by its scheme making power. No authority was suggested to me which would enable the Court to settle a scheme for a power. I am also mindful of the fact that the term "specific" is ordinarily to be found defined as "made definite" or "precise";[44] I note in discussing purpose trusts that Scott sees a requirement that it be definite.[45]

If this instrument is to be construed as a power, then the executors must be able to decide that a payment is "for the religious, literary and educational purpose of the said Edmonton Lodge of The Theosophical Society in Canada." I have not been referred to any authorities discussing the appropriate criteria for "certainty"

---

42 *Supra,* note 8.
43 *Supra,* note 9.
44 See, *e.g.*, *Words and Phrases*, Vol. 39A, p. 398.
45 Scott, § 124, p. 937.

in a purpose trust and the relatively few cases in which the law recognizes a purpose trust is the obvious explanation.

The requirement of certainty under a power or a trust is discussed and equated by the House of Lords in *Re Baden's Trust Deeds*.[46] This case was applied by the Supreme Court of Canada in *Jones v. T. Eaton Co.*[47] In both cases the Courts were concerned with "certainty" in terms of determining the persons entitled. The House of Lords, and the Supreme Court of Canada, adopted as a test, the following: "the trust is valid if it can be said with certainty that any given individual is or is not a member of the class."[48] Lord Wilberforce quotes with approval a test found in the second *Restatement of Trusts*, 1959: "The class must not be so indefinite that it cannot be ascertained whether any person falls within it." Modifying the first quoted test to relate to "purposes", I do not think it can be said within certainty that any given use would qualify. I do note that Lord Wilberforce says that difficulty in ascertaining the existence or whereabouts of members of the class could be dealt with on an application for directions.

The difficulty in applying the test is compounded by the apparent conjunctive expression "religious, literary and educational purposes."

It would appear to me that what we have here is a linguistic uncertainty which vitiates the gift as distinct from the difficulty of ascertaining the existence or whereabouts of members of the class which can be appropriately dealt with on an application for directions. As Lord Upjohn says in *Re Gulbenkian's Settlement*:[49]

> ...and perhaps it is the more hallowed principle, the Court of Chancery, which acts in default of trustees, must know with sufficient certainty the objects of the beneficence of the donor so as to execute the trust.... So if the class is insufficiently defined the donor's intentions must in such cases fail for uncertainty.

In saying there is a linguistic or semantic uncertainty in connection with this portion of the will, I might be justified in considering extrinsic evidence but the most that could be said from it is that the testator knew that one of the activities of the society was the conduct of membership meetings at which theosophy was studied and considered and that goes no way towards defining the society's objects or purposes. Had the trust been simply "for the society", this difficulty would have been obviated because payment into its funds would be something which the Court, or the executors, could determine with the certainty as a compliance with the trust. In saying this, I am mindful of the fact that *Re Baden*, settled a long term controversy in equity in favour of a liberal interpretation which posed the question as being whether or not "it can be said with certainty if an individual is or is not a member of the class", in preference to the narrower view that the Court must be able to determine all possible objects.

---

46 *McPhail, supra*, note 34.
47 *Supra,* note 10.
48 *Supra,* note 34, at 456.
49 [1970] A.C. 508 at 524, [1968] 3 All E.R. 785 (H.L.).

I have reached this conclusion with some reluctance in light of the fact that the legislation is remedial and the expressed purposes are not in any way contrary to public policy. Moreover, the objection of the perpetuities period is eliminated by the introduction of the wait and see principle. Nonetheless, I do not think the Court, or the executor, has any means of judging whether in the law of private trusts an object is "religious, literary and educational". In the law of charitable trusts where the terms "religious" or "educational" are sometimes used the Court provides certainty by its scheme making power. This disposition lacks the necessary specification because of the practical impossibility in interpreting "religious, literary and educational" in relation to the various objects of the society.

Notes and Questions

1. Did Stevenson J. use the correct test to determine whether the purposes were specific, within the meaning of *The Perpetuities Act*? Should the test depend on whether purposes are sufficiently certain to be enforced positively as a trust or whether they can be enforced negatively as a power of appointment? Is there a difference between the two tests? Was it helpful to apply jurisprudence concerning the certainty of objects required for a trust for persons?

2. In *Twinsectra Ltd. v. Yardley*,[50] reproduced below, a power to use money "for the acquisition of property" was sufficiently certain to be valid. A non-charitable trust for that purpose might well have been invalid, since a court could not make a scheme directing trustees how to acquire property. However, there was no difficulty enforcing it negatively as power, because it was clear that the money had been used improperly for purposes other than the acquisition of property. Was it a "specific" purpose within the meaning of *The Perpetuities Act*?

3. The conclusions in *Re Russell Estate* have been supported by the Ontario Law Reform Commission.[51]

(c) *Quistclose* Trusts

The *Quistclose* trust takes its name from *Barclays Bank Ltd. v. Quistclose Investments Ltd.*,[52] in which money was loaned subject to a condition that it be used only to pay a dividend due to the borrower's shareholders. When the borrower became insolvent and the dividend could not be paid, the money was not available to the borrower's other creditors, but was held in trust for the lender. In the decades following that decision, a great deal of academic and judicial ink was spilled, working out the basis and terms of that trust. The strong *obiter dicta* of Lord Millett in *Twinsectra Ltd. v. Yardley*, below, has laid much of that controversy to rest. When money is loaned with a restriction on its use, the borrower holds it in trust for the lender from the outset, with a power to use it for the specified purpose.

---

50 [2002] 2 A.C. 164 (H.L.).

51 See Ontario Law Reform Commission, *Report on the Law of Trusts* (Toronto: Ministry of the Attorney-General, 1984) p. 449.

52 (1968), [1970] A.C. 567, [1968] 3 All E.R. 651, [1968] 3 W.L.R. 1097 (H.L.).

The *Twinsectra* case is the most significant development in this area of law since *Re Denley's Trusts*,[53] reproduced below (which was decided in the same year as the *Quistclose* case). *Quistclose* has been followed in many similar cases, in which money had been loaned to pay the borrower's other creditors in an unsuccessful attempt to stave off the borrower's impending insolvency. Although it had been extended to loans and payments to be used for other purposes, those extensions were tentative and almost always in the context of the recipient's insolvency. The limited reach of the *Quistclose* trust probably reflected legal uncertainty over the nature of that trust. *Twinsectra* changed all that.

It is now clear that the *Quistclose* trust can apply to gifts, loans, and other payments made on condition that the money be used only for a specific purpose, even if that purpose is abstract. The effect of this analysis is far reaching, because it applies potentially to all payments *inter vivos* in which the recipient's use of the money is restricted to specific purposes. If that transaction does not produce a trust for third persons or for charitable purposes, then the recipient holds the money in trust for the payer, with a power to use the money within the terms of the restriction. As *Twinsectra* demonstrates, the restriction can be stated in broad terms and need not be for the benefit of third persons.

The *Quistclose* trust has the potential to get around all three of the objections to non-charitable purpose trusts, discussed above: enforceability, perpetuities, and vagueness. The settlor is the beneficiary of the trust from the outset and the trustee has only a power to use the money for the specified purpose. Therefore, the settlor (as beneficiary) can enforce the trust and restrain any misuse of the money for other purposes, there are no contingent interests that might run afoul of the rule against perpetuities, and the purpose can be enforced negatively as a power even though it might be too vague to be enforced positively as a trust.

In *Twinsectra*, the majority of law lords treated the trust for the lender as an express trust, based on the fact that the lender intended to retain beneficial ownership of the money. Lord Millett treated it as a resulting trust, based on the fact that the lender did not intend to transfer beneficial ownership of the money to the borrower. The resulting trust is the subject of the next chapter. It is sufficient at this stage to know that it arises by operation of law when one person transfers an asset to another, but does not intend to benefit the recipient.

TWINSECTRA LTD. v. YARDLEY

[2002] U.K.H.L. 12, [2002] 2 A.C. 164
House of Lords

LORD HOFFMAN:

My Lords, Paul Leach is a solicitor practising in Godalming under the name Paul Leach & Co. Towards the end of 1992 he acted for a Mr. Yardley in a transaction which included the negotiation of a loan of £1m. from Twinsectra

---

53 (1968), [1969] 1 Ch. 373, [1968] 3 All E.R. 65 (Ch. Div.).

Limited. Mr. Leach did not deal directly with Twinsectra. Another firm of solicitors, Sims and Roper of Dorset ("Sims"), represented themselves as acting on
behalf of Mr. Yardley. They received the money in return for the following
undertaking:

> 1. The loan monies will be retained by us until such time as they are applied in the acquisition
> of property on behalf of our client. 2. The loan monies will be utilised solely for the acquisition
> of property on behalf of our client and for no other purpose. 3. We will repay to you the said sum
> of £1,000,000 together with interest calculated at the rate of £657.53 per day... such payment to
> be made within four calendar months after receipt of the loan monies by us.

Contrary to the terms of the undertaking, Sims did not retain the money until
it was applied in the acquisition of property by Mr. Yardley. On being given an
assurance by Mr. Yardley that it would be so applied, they paid it to Mr. Leach.
He in turn did not take steps to ensure that it was utilised solely for the acquisition
of property on behalf of Mr. Yardley. He simply paid it out upon Mr. Yardley's
instructions. The result was that £357,720.11 was used by Mr. Yardley for purposes other than the acquisition of property.

The loan was not repaid. Twinsectra sued all the parties involved including
Mr. Leach. The claim against him was for the £357,720.11 which had not been
used to buy property. The basis of the claim was that the payment by Sims to Mr.
Leach in breach of the undertaking was a breach of trust and that he was liable
for dishonestly assisting in that breach of trust in accordance with the principles
stated by Lord Nicholls of Birkenhead in *Royal Brunei Airlines Sdn. Bhd. v. Tan*.[54]

The trial judge (Carnwath J.) did not accept that the monies were "subject to
any form of trust in Sims and Roper's hands". I do not imagine that the judge
could have meant this to be taken literally. Money in a solicitor's client account
is held on trust. The only question is the terms of that trust. I should think that
what Carnwath J. meant was that Sims held the money on trust for Mr. Yardley
absolutely. That is the way it was put by Mr. Oliver Q.C., who appeared for Mr.
Leach. But, like the Court of Appeal, I must respectfully disagree. The terms of
the trust upon which Sims held the money must be found in the undertaking which
they gave to Twinsectra as a condition of payment. Clauses 1 and 2 of that
undertaking made it clear that the money was not to be at the free disposal of Mr.
Yardley. Sims were not to part with the money to Mr. Yardley or anyone else
except for the purpose of enabling him to acquire property.

In my opinion the effect of the undertaking was to provide that the money in
the Sims client account should remain Twinsectra's money until such time as it
was applied for the acquisition of property in accordance with the undertaking.
For example, if Mr. Yardley went bankrupt before the money had been so applied,
it would not have formed part of his estate, as it would have done if Sims had
held it in trust for him absolutely. The undertaking would have ensured that
Twinsectra could get it back. It follows that Sims held the money in *trust* for
Twinsectra, but subject to a *power* to apply it by way of loan to Mr. Yardley in
accordance with the undertaking. No doubt Sims also owed fiduciary obligations

---

54 [1995] 2 A.C. 378 (P.C.).

to Mr. Yardley in respect of the exercise of the power, but we need not concern ourselves with those obligations because in fact the money was applied wholly for Mr. Yardley's benefit.

The judge gave two reasons for rejecting a trust. The first was that the terms of the undertaking were too vague. It did not specify any particular property for which the money was to be used. The second was that Mr. Ackerman, the moving spirit behind Twinsectra, did not intend to create a trust. He set no store by clauses 1 and 2 of the undertaking and was content to rely on the guarantee in clause 3 as Twinsectra's security for repayment.

I agree that the terms of the undertaking are very unusual. Solicitors acting for both lender and borrower (for example, a building society and a house buyer) commonly give an undertaking to the lender that they will not part with the money save in exchange for a duly executed charge over the property which the money is being used to purchase. The undertaking protects the lender against finding himself unsecured. But Twinsectra was not asking for any security over the property. Its security was clause 3 of the Sims undertaking. So the purpose of the undertaking was unclear. There was nothing to prevent Mr. Yardley, having acquired a property in accordance with the undertaking, from mortgaging it to the hilt and spending the proceeds on something else. So it is hard to see why it should have mattered to Twinsectra whether the immediate use of the money was to acquire property. The judge thought it might have been intended to give some protective colour to a claim against the Solicitors Indemnity Fund if Sims failed to repay the loan in accordance with the undertaking....

However, the fact that the undertaking was unusual does not mean that it was void for uncertainty. The charge of uncertainty is levelled against the terms of the power to apply the funds. "The acquisition of property" was said to be too vague. But a power is sufficiently certain to be valid if the court can say that a given application of the money does or does not fall within its terms.[55] And there is no dispute that the £357,720.11 was not applied for the acquisition of property.

As for Mr Ackerman's understanding of the matter, that seem to me irrelevant. Whether a trust was created and what were its terms must depend upon the construction of the undertaking. Clauses 1 and 2 cannot be ignored just because Mr Ackerman was not particularly interested in them.

. . .

LORD MILLETT:

My Lords, there are two issues in this appeal. The first is concerned with the nature of the so-called "*Quistclose* trust" and the requirements for its creation. The second arises only if the first is answered adversely to the appellant. It is whether his conduct rendered him liable for having assisted in a breach of trust.

---

55 See *Re Baden's Deed Trusts, supra,* note 34.

. . .

Was there a Quistclose trust?

Money advanced by way of loan normally becomes the property of the borrower. He is free to apply the money as he chooses, and save to the extent to which he may have taken security for repayment the lender takes the risk of the borrower's insolvency. But it is well established that a loan to a borrower for a specific purpose where the borrower is not free to apply the money for any other purpose gives rise to fiduciary obligations on the part of the borrower which a court of equity will enforce. In the earlier cases the purpose was to enable the borrower to pay his creditors or some of them, but the principle is not limited to such cases.

Such arrangements are commonly described as creating "a *Quistclose* trust", after the well-known decision of the House in *Quistclose Investments Ltd. v. Rolls Razor Ltd.*,[56] in which Lord Wilberforce confirmed the validity of such arrangements and explained their legal consequences. When the money is advanced, the lender acquires a right, enforceable in equity, to see that it is applied for the stated purpose, or more accurately to prevent its application for any other purpose. This prevents the borrower from obtaining any beneficial interest in the money, at least while the designated purpose is still capable of being carried out. Once the purpose has been carried out, the lender has his normal remedy in debt. If for any reason the purpose cannot be carried out, the question arises whether the money falls within the general fund of the borrower's assets, in which case it passes to his trustee-in-bankruptcy in the event of his insolvency and the lender is merely a loan creditor; or whether it is held on a resulting trust for the lender. This depends on the intention of the parties collected from the terms of the arrangement and the circumstances of the case.

In the present case, Twinsectra contends that paragraphs 1 and 2 of the undertaking which Mr. Sims signed on 24 December created a *Quistclose* trust. Mr. Leach denies this and advances a number of objections to the existence of a trust. He says that Twinsectra lacked the necessary intention to create a trust, and relies on evidence that Twinsectra looked exclusively to Mr. Sims' personal undertaking to repay the loan as its security for repayment. He says that commercial life would be impossible if trusts were lightly inferred from slight material, and that it is not enough to agree that a loan is to be made for a particular purpose. There must be something more, for example, a requirement that the money be paid into a segregated account, before it is appropriate to infer that a trust has been created. In the present case the money was paid into Mr. Sims' client account, but that is sufficiently explained by the fact that it was not Mr. Sims' money but his client's; it provides no basis for an inference that the money was held in trust for anyone other than Mr. Yardley. Then it is said that a trust requires certainty of objects and this was lacking, for the stated purpose "to be applied in the purchase of property" is too uncertain to be enforced. Finally it is said that no trust in favour

---

56 [1970] A.C. 567 (H.L.).

of Twinsectra could arise prior to the failure of the stated purpose, and this did not occur until the money was misapplied by Mr. Yardley's companies.

Intention

The first two objections are soon disposed of. A settlor must, of course, possess the necessary intention to create a trust, but his subjective intentions are irrelevant. If he enters into arrangements which have the effect of creating a trust, it is not necessary that he should appreciate that they do so; it is sufficient that he intends to enter into them. Whether paragraphs 1 and 2 of the undertaking created a *Quistclose* trust turns on the true construction of those paragraphs.

The fact that Twinsectra relied for its security exclusively on Mr. Sims' personal liability to repay goes to Twinsectra's subjective intention and is not relevant to the construction of the undertaking, but it is in any case not inconsistent with the trust alleged. Arrangements of this kind are not intended to provide security for repayment of the loan, but to prevent the money from being applied otherwise than in accordance with the lender's wishes. If the money is properly applied the loan is unsecured. This was true of all the decided cases, including the *Quistclose* case itself.

The effect of the undertaking

A *Quistclose* trust does not necessarily arise merely because money is paid for a particular purpose. A lender will often inquire into the purpose for which a loan is sought in order to decide whether he would be justified in making it. He may be said to lend the money for the purpose in question, but this is not enough to create a trust; once lent the money is at the free disposal of the borrower. Similarly payments in advance for goods or services are paid for a particular purpose, but such payments do not ordinarily create a trust. The money is intended to be at the free disposal of the supplier and may be used as part of his cash-flow. Commercial life would be impossible if this were not the case.

The question in every case is whether the parties intended the money to be at the free disposal of the recipient.[57] His freedom to dispose of the money is necessarily excluded by an arrangement that the money shall be used exclusively for the stated purpose...

In the present case paragraphs 1 and 2 of the undertaking are crystal clear. Mr. Sims undertook that the money would be used *solely* for the acquisition of property *and for no other purpose*; and was to be retained by his firm until so applied. It would not be held by Mr. Sims simply to Mr. Yardley's order; and it would not be at Mr. Yardley's free disposition. Any payment by Mr. Sims of the money, whether to Mr. Yardley or anyone else, otherwise than for the acquisition of property would constitute a breach of trust.

Mr. Leach insisted that such a payment would, no doubt, constitute a breach of contract, but there was no reason to invoke equitable principles merely because

---

57 *Re Goldcorp Exchange Ltd.*, [1995] 1 A.C. 74 at 100, *per* Lord Mustill.

Mr. Sims was a solicitor. But Mr. Sims' status as a solicitor has nothing to do with it. Equity's intervention is more principled than this. It is unconscionable for a man to obtain money on terms as to its application and then disregard the terms on which he received it. Such conduct goes beyond a mere breach of contract. As North J. explained in *Gibert v. Gonard*:[58]

> It is very well known law that if one person makes a payment to another for a certain purpose, and that person takes the money knowing that it is for that purpose, he must apply it to the purpose for which it was given. He may decline to take it if he likes; but if he chooses to accept the money tendered for a particular purpose, it is his duty, and there is a legal obligation on him, to apply it for that purpose.

The duty is not contractual but fiduciary. It may exist despite the absence of any contract at all between the parties, as in *Rose v. Rose*,[59] and it binds third parties as in the *Quistclose* case itself. The duty is fiduciary in character because a person who makes money available on terms that it is to be used for a particular purpose only and not for any other purpose thereby places his trust and confidence in the recipient to ensure that it is properly applied. This is a classic situation in which a fiduciary relationship arises, and since it arises in respect of a specific fund it gives rise to a trust.

The nature of the trust

The latter two objections cannot be so easily disposed of. They call for an exploration of the true nature of the Quistclose trust, and in particular the location of the beneficial interest while the purpose is still capable of being carried out.

This has been the subject of much academic debate. The starting point is provided by two passages in Lord Wilberforce's speech in the *Quistclose* case. He said:[60]

> That arrangements of this character for the payment of a person's creditors by a third person, give rise to a relationship of a fiduciary character or trust, in favour, as a primary trust, of the creditors, and secondarily, if the primary trust fails, of the third person, has been recognised in a series of cases over some 150 years.

Later, he said:[61]

> when the money is advanced, the lender acquires an equitable right to see that it is applied for the primary designated purpose (see *Re Rogers*,[62] where both Lindley L.J. and Kay L.J. recognised this)...

These passages suggest that there are two successive trusts, a primary trust for payment to identifiable beneficiaries, such as creditors or shareholders, and a

---

58 (1884), 54 L.J. Ch. 439 at 440.
59 (1986), 7 N.S.W.L.R. 679.
60 *Supra,* note 56, at 580.
61 *Ibid.,* at 581.
62 (1891), 8 Morr. 243 (C.A.).

secondary trust in favour of the lender arising on the failure of the primary trust. But there are formidable difficulties in this analysis, which has little academic support. What if the primary trust is not for identifiable persons, but as in the present case to carry out an abstract purpose? Where in such a case is the beneficial interest pending the application of the money for the stated purpose or the failure of the purpose? There are four possibilities: (i) in the lender; (ii) in the borrower; (iii) in the contemplated beneficiary; or (iv) in suspense.

(i) *The lender.* In "The Quistclose Trust: Who Can Enforce It?",[63] I argued that the beneficial interest remained throughout in the lender. This analysis has received considerable though not universal academic support.[64] It was adopted by the New Zealand Court of Appeal, in *General Communications Ltd. v. Development Finance Corp. of New Zealand Ltd.*,[65] and referred to with apparent approval by Gummow J. in *Re Australian Elizabethan Theatre Trust.*[66] Gummow J. saw nothing special in the *Quistclose* trust, regarding it as essentially a security device to protect the lender against other creditors of the borrower pending the application of the money for the sated purpose.

On this analysis, the *Quistclose* trust is a simple commercial arrangement akin (as Professor Bridge observes) to a retention of title clause (though with a different object) which enables the borrower to have recourse to the lender's money for a particular purpose without entrenching on the lender's property rights more than necessary to enable the purpose to be achieved. The money remains the property of the lender unless and until it is applied in accordance with his directions, and insofar as it is not so applied it must be returned to him. I am disposed, perhaps pre-disposed, to think that this is the only analysis which is consistent both with orthodox trust law and with commercial reality. Before reaching a concluded view that it should be adopted, however, I must consider the alternatives.

(ii) *The borrower.* It is plain that the beneficial interest is not vested unconditionally in the borrower so as to leave the money at his free disposal. That would defeat the whole purpose of the arrangements, which is to prevent the money from passing to the borrower's trustee-in-bankruptcy in the event of his insolvency. It would also be inconsistent with all the decided cases where the contest was between the lender and the borrower's trustee-in-bankruptcy, as well as with the *Quistclose* case itself.[67]

The borrower's interest pending the application of the money for the stated purpose or its return to the lender is minimal. He must keep the money separate; he cannot apply it except for the stated purpose; unless the terms of the loan otherwise provide he must return it to the lender if demanded; he cannot refuse to return it if the stated purpose cannot be achieved; and if he becomes bankrupt

---

63 (1985), 101 L.Q.R. 269.

64 See, *e.g.*, Priestley J., "The Romalpa Clause and the Quistclose Trust" in P. Finn, ed., *Equity and Commercial Transactions* (1987) 217 at 237; M. Bridge, "The Quistclose Trust in a World of Secured Transactions" (1992), 12 O.J.L.S. 333 at 352.

65 [1990] 3 N.Z.L.R. 406 (C.A.).

66 (1991), 102 A.L.R. 681.

67 See, in particular, *Toovey v. Milne* (1819), 2 B. & Ald. 683; *Re Rogers* (1891), 8 Morr. 243.

it does not vest in his trustee in bankruptcy. If there is any content to beneficial ownership at all, the lender is the beneficial owner and the borrower is not.

In the present case the Court of Appeal adopted a variant, locating the beneficial interest in the borrower but subject to restrictions. I shall have to return to this analysis later.

(iii) *In the contemplated beneficiary.* In the *Quistclose* case itself, as in all the reported cases which preceded it, either the primary purpose had been carried out and the contest was between the borrower's trustee-in bankruptcy or liquidator and the person or persons to whom the borrower had paid the money; or it was treated as having failed, and the contest was between the borrower's trustee-in-bankruptcy and the lender. It was not necessary to explore the position while the primary purpose was still capable of being carried out and Lord Wilberforce's observations must be read in that light.

The question whether the primary trust is accurately described as a trust for the creditors first arose in *Re Northern Developments Holdings Ltd.*,[68] where the contest was between the lender and the creditors. The borrower, which was not in liquidation and made no claim to the money, was the parent company of a group one of whose subsidiaries was in financial difficulty. There was a danger that if it were wound up or ceased trading it would bring down the whole group. A consortium of the group's banks agreed to put up a fund of more than £500,000 in an attempt to rescue the subsidiary. They paid the money into a special account in the name of the parent company for the express purpose of "providing money for the subsidiary's unsecured creditors over the ensuing weeks" and for no other purpose. The banks' object was to enable the subsidiary to continue trading, though on a reduced scale; it failed when the subsidiary was put into receivership at a time when some £350,000 remained unexpended. Relying on Lord Wilberforce's observations in the passages cited above, Sir Robert Megarry V.C. held that the primary trust was a purpose trust enforceable (*inter alios*) by the subsidiaries' creditors as the persons for whose benefit the trust was created.

There are several difficulties with this analysis. In the first place, Lord Wilberforce's reference to *Re Rogers*[69] makes it plain that the equitable right he had in mind was not a mandatory order to compel performance, but a negative injunction to restrain improper application of the money; for neither Lindley L.J. nor Kay L.J. recognised more than this. In the second place, the object of the arrangements was to enable the subsidiary to continue trading, and this would necessarily involve it in incurring further liabilities to trade creditors. Accordingly the application of the fund was not confined to existing creditors at the date when the fund was established. The company secretary was given to understand that the purpose of the arrangements was to keep the subsidiary trading, and that the fund was "as good as share capital". Thus the purpose of the arrangements was not, as in other cases, to enable the debtor to avoid bankruptcy by paying off existing creditors, but to enable the debtor to continue trading by providing it with working capital with which to incur fresh liabilities. There is a powerful

---

68 Unreported, 6 October 1978.
69 *Supra,* note 67.

argument for saying that the result of the arrangements was to vest a beneficial interest in the subsidiary from the start. If so, then this was not a *Quistclose* trust at all.

In the third place, it seems unlikely that the banks' object was to benefit the creditors (who included the Inland Revenue) except indirectly. The banks had their own commercial interests to protect by enabling the subsidiary to trade out of its difficulties. If so, then the primary trust cannot be supported as a valid non-charitable purpose trust.[70]

The most serious objection to this approach is exemplified by the facts of the present case. In several of the cases the primary trust was for an abstract purpose with no one but the lender to enforce performance or restrain misapplication of the money. In *Edwards v. Glyn*,[71] the money was advanced to a bank to enable the bank to meet a run. In *Re EVTR*,[72] it was advanced "for the sole purpose of buying new equipment". In *General Communications Ltd. v. Development Finance Corp. of New Zealand Ltd.*,[73] the money was paid to the borrower's solicitors for the express purpose of purchasing new equipment. The present case is another example. It is simply not possible to hold money on trust to acquire unspecified property from an unspecified vendor at an unspecified time. There is no reason to make an arbitrary distinction between money paid for an abstract purpose and money paid for a purpose which can be said to benefit an ascertained class of beneficiaries, and the cases rightly draw no such distinction. Any analysis of the *Quistclose* trust must be able to accommodate gifts and loans for an abstract purpose.

(iv) *In suspense.* As Peter Gibson J. pointed out in *Carreras Rothmans Ltd. v. Freeman Matthews Treasure Ltd.*,[74] the effect of adopting Sir Robert Megarry V.C.'s analysis is to leave the beneficial interest in suspense until the stated purpose is carried out or fails. The difficulty with this (apart from its unorthodoxy) is that it fails to have regard to the role which the resulting trust plays in equity's scheme of things, or to explain why the money is not simply held on a resulting trust for the lender.

Lord Browne-Wilkinson gave an authoritative explanation of the resulting trust in *Westdeutsche Landesbank Girozentrale v. Islington Borough Council*,[75] and its basis has been further illuminated by Dr. Robert Chambers in his book *Resulting Trusts* published in 1997. Lord Browne-Wilkinson explained that a resulting trust arises in two sets of circumstances. He described the second as follows: "Where A transfers property to B on express trusts, but the trusts declared do not exhaust the whole beneficial interest." The *Quistclose* case was among the cases he cited as examples. He rejected the argument that there was a resulting trust in the case before him because, unlike the situation in the present case, there

70 See *Re Grant's Will Trusts*, [1980] 1 W.L.R. 360, and *cf. Re Denley's Trust Deed*, [1969] 1 Ch. 373.

71 (1859), 2 E. & E. 29, 121 E.R. 12 (C.A.).

72 [1987] B.C.L.C. 646 (C.A.).

73 *Supra,* note 65.

74 [1985] Ch. 207 at 223.

75 [1996] A.C. 669 at 708C.

was no transfer of money on express trusts. But he also rejected the argument on a wider and, in my respectful opinion, surer ground that the money was paid and received with the intention that it should become the absolute property of the recipient.

The central thesis of Dr. Chambers' book is that a resulting trust arises whenever there is a transfer of property in circumstances in which the transferor (or more accurately the person at whose expense the property was provided) did not intend to benefit the recipient. It responds to the absence of an intention on the part of the transferor to pass the entire beneficial interest, not to a positive intention to retain it. Insofar as the transfer does not exhaust the entire beneficial interest, the resulting trust is a default trust which fills the gap and leaves no room for any part to be in suspense. An analysis of the *Quistclose* trust as a resulting trust for the transferor with a mandate to the transferee to apply the money for the stated purpose sits comfortably with Dr. Chambers' thesis, and it might be thought surprising that he does not adopt it.

(v) *The Court of Appeal's analysis.* The Court of Appeal were content to treat the beneficial interest as in suspense, or (following Dr. Chambers' analysis) to hold that it was in the borrower, the lender having merely a contractual right enforceable by injunction to prevent misapplication. Potter L.J. put it in these terms:[76]

> The purpose imposed at the time of the advance creates an enforceable restriction on the borrower's use of the money. Although the lender's right to enforce the restriction is treated as arising on the basis of a "trust", the use of that word does not enlarge the lender's interest in the fund. The borrower is entitled to the beneficial use of the money, subject to the lender's right to prevent its misuse; the lender's limited interest in the fund is sufficient to prevent its use for other than the special purpose for which it was advanced.

This analysis, with respect, is difficult to reconcile with the court's actual decision insofar as it granted Twinsectra a proprietary remedy against Mr. Yardley's companies as recipients of the misapplied funds. Unless the money belonged to Twinsectra immediately before its misapplication, there is no basis on which a proprietary remedy against third party recipients can be justified.

Dr. Chambers' "novel view" (as it has been described) is that the arrangements do not create a trust at all; the borrower receives the entire beneficial ownership in the money subject only to a contractual right in the lender to prevent the money being used otherwise than for the stated purpose. If the purpose fails, a resulting trust in the lender springs into being. In fact, he argues for a kind of restrictive covenant enforceable by negative injunction yet creating property rights in the money. But restrictive covenants, which began life as negative easements, are part of our land law. Contractual obligations do not run with money or a chose in action like money in a bank account.

Dr. Chambers' analysis has attracted academic comment, both favourable and unfavourable. For my own part, I do not think that it can survive the criticism

---

76 [1999] Lloyd's Rep. Bank 438 at 456, para. 75.

levelled against it by Lusina Ho and P. St. J. Smart.[77] It provides no solution to cases of non-contractual payment; is inconsistent with Lord Wilberforce's description of the borrower's obligation as fiduciary and not merely contractual; fails to explain the evidential significance of a requirement that the money should be kept in a separate account; cannot easily be reconciled with the availability of proprietary remedies against third parties; and while the existence of a mere equity to prevent misapplication would be sufficient to prevent the money from being available for distribution to the creditors on the borrower's insolvency (because the trustee-in-bankruptcy has no greater rights than his bankrupt) it would not prevail over secured creditors. If the bank in the *Quistclose* case had held a floating charge (as it probably did) and had appointed a receiver, the adoption of Dr. Chambers' analysis should have led to a different outcome.

Thus all the alternative solutions have their difficulties. But there are two problems which they fail to solve, but which are easily solved if the beneficial interest remains throughout in the lender. One arises from the fact, well established by the authorities, that the primary trust is enforceable by the lender. But on what basis can he enforce it? He cannot do so as the beneficiary under the secondary trust, for if the primary purpose is fulfilled there is no secondary trust: the precondition of his claim is destructive of his standing to make it. He cannot do so as settlor, for a settlor who retains no beneficial interest cannot enforce the trust which he has created.

Dr. Chambers insists that the lender has merely a right to prevent the misapplication of the money, and attributes this to his contractual right to specific performance of a condition of the contract of loan. As I have already pointed out, this provides no solution where the arrangement is non-contractual. But Lord Wilberforce clearly based the borrower's obligation on an equitable or fiduciary basis and not a contractual one. He was concerned to justify the co-existence of equity's exclusive jurisdiction with the common law action for debt. Basing equity's intervention on its auxiliary jurisdiction to restrain a breach of contract would not have enabled the lender to succeed against the bank, which was a third party to the contract. There is only one explanation of the lender's fiduciary right to enforce the primary trust which can be reconciled with basic principle: he can do so because he is the beneficiary.

. . .

As Sherlock Holmes reminded Dr. Watson, when you have eliminated the impossible, whatever remains, however improbable, must be the truth. I would reject all the alternative analyses, which I find unconvincing for the reasons I have endeavoured to explain, and hold the *Quistclose* trust to be an entirely orthodox example of the kind of default trust known as a resulting trust. The lender pays the money to the borrower by way of loan, but he does not part with the entire beneficial interest in the money, and insofar as he does not it is held on

---

77 "Reinterpreting the Quistclose Trust: A Critique of Chambers' Analysis" (2001), 21 O.J.L.S. 267.

a resulting trust for the lender from the outset. Contrary to the opinion of the Court of Appeal, it is the borrower who has a very limited use of the money, being obliged to apply it for the stated purpose or return it. He has no beneficial interest in the money, which remains throughout in the lender subject only to the borrower's power or duty to apply the money in accordance with the lender's instructions. When the purpose fails, the money is returnable to the lender, not under some new trust in his favour which only comes into being on the failure of the purpose, but because the resulting trust in his favour is no longer subject to any power on the part of the borrower to make use of the money. Whether the borrower is obliged to apply the money for the stated purpose or merely at liberty to do so, and whether the lender can countermand the borrower's mandate while it is still capable of being carried out, must depend on the circumstances of the particular case.

Certainty

After this over-long exposition, it is possible to dispose of the remaining objections to the creation of a *Quistclose* trust very shortly. A trust must have certainty of objects. But the only trust is the resulting trust for the lender. The borrower is authorised (or directed) to apply the money for a stated purpose, but this is a mere power and does not constitute a purpose trust. Provided the power is stated with sufficient clarity for the court to be able to determine whether it is still capable of being carried out or whether the money has been misapplied, it is sufficiently certain to be enforced. If it is uncertain, however, then the borrower has no authority to make any use of the money at all and must return it to the lender under the resulting trust. Uncertainty works in favour of the lender, not the borrower; it cannot help a person in the position of Mr. Leach.

When the trust in favour of the lender arises

Like all resulting trusts, the trust in favour of the lender arises when the lender parts with the money on terms which do not exhaust the beneficial interest. It is not a contingent reversionary or future interest. It does not suddenly come into being like an eighteenth century use only when the stated purpose fails. It is a default trust which fills the gap when some part of the beneficial interest is undisposed of and prevents it from being "in suspense".

Conclusion

In my opinion the Court of Appeal were correct to find that the terms of paragraphs 1 and 2 of the undertaking created a *Quistclose* trust. The money was never at Mr. Yardley's free disposal. It was never held to his order by Mr. Sims. The money belonged throughout to Twinsectra, subject only to Mr. Yardley's right to apply it for the acquisition of property. Twinsectra parted with the money to Mr. Sims, relying on him to ensure that the money was properly applied or returned to it....

[The House of Lords decided unanimously that Mr. Sims held the money in trust for Twinsectra, with a power to use it for the specified purpose, and that some of it had been paid out in breach of trust. However, the majority of law lords, with Lord Millett dissenting, held that Mr. Leach was not guilty of dishonestly assisting that breach of trust.]

Notes and Questions

1. It is useful to compare *Quistclose* trusts with the anomalous non-charitable purpose trusts, discussed above. If a bequest is made for one of the acceptable purposes, such as the care of a specific animal, the recipient has the power to use the money only for that purpose and any surplus must be paid to the residuary beneficiary, who has standing to restrain any misuse of the money. If a gift *inter vivos* produces a *Quistclose* trust, the recipient has the power to use the money only for the specified purpose and any surplus must be paid back to the donor, who has standing to restrain any misuse of the money. The essential differences appear to be that anomalous non-charitable purpose trusts are testamentary and limited to a short, closed list of possible purposes, while *Quistclose* trusts are *inter vivos* and available for any non-charitable purpose that is specific and not contrary to law.

2. *Quistclose* trusts should not be affected by the perpetuities legislation, discussed above, which converts trusts for specific non-charitable purposes into powers of appointment. The creator of a *Quistclose* trust retains beneficial ownership of the money and that legislation applies only to a trust "that creates no enforceable equitable interest in a specific person".[78]

3. The *Quistclose* trust is, or at least can be, a resulting trust coupled with a power to use the money for a specific purpose. That is a relationship that can be created even though the parties did not intend to create a trust. The condition attached to the use of the money proves that the payer did not intend to benefit the recipient, which causes a resulting trust to arise by operation of law. In *Re Endacott*,[79] the Court of Appeal declared invalid a residuary bequest to create a memorial for the testator. Lord Evershed M.R. said, "the proposition. . . that if these trusts should fail as trusts they may survive as powers, is not one which I think can be treated as accepted in English law."[80] If the transaction occurred today as a gift *inter vivos* to use the money for that purpose, would it matter whether the donor intended to create a trust or a power? In either case, if the transaction fails to produce a valid express trust, the restriction on the donee's use of the money should produce a resulting trust.

4. It is important to distinguish between a payment of money for a specific purpose and a payment of money *to be used* for a specific purpose. Most loans or payments are made for a specific purpose, but that purpose does not restrict the recipient's use of the money. For example, when a bank lends money to its customers for a vacation or home improvements, the stated purpose is the reason for the loan, but does not restrict how the customers actually spend the money. A *Quistclose* trust can arise only when the use of a particular fund of money is restricted.

---

78 *Perpetuities Act*, R.S.O. 1990, c. P.9, s. 16(1).
79 *Supra,* note 33.
80 *Ibid.*, at 246.

In *Guardian Ocean Cargoes Ltd. v. Banco do Brasil S.A.*,[81] the plaintiff was negotiating the purchase of a ship, with refinancing from the seller's bank, the defendant. The plaintiff paid $600,000 to the defendant, which was to be used to pay the seller's promissory notes to the defendant when the negotiations were complete. The deal fell through five years later and the defendant was required to repay that sum to the plaintiff, with simple interest. The plaintiff's claim to a *Quistclose* trust, which would attract compound interest, was properly rejected by the English Court of Appeal. The condition attached to the payment did not require the defendant to use that money in any particular way, but merely required the defendant to do something in exchange for the money. If the negotiations had succeeded, the seller's debt to the defendant would have been reduced by the sum the plaintiff had paid to the defendant.

5. If money is paid to be used for a specific purpose, this will not create a trust if that purpose is merely the motive for the payment and not intended to be an enforceable restriction on its use. For example, in *Re Barrett*,[82] reproduced in the next chapter, a father made a large bequest to his daughter "for the purpose of enabling my said daughter to meet the immediate current expenses in connection with housekeeping." This did not restrict her use of the money, because it was interpreted as an expression of his reason for making an unconditional gift.

6. The *Quistclose* trust cases have all concerned restrictions on the use of money. Would a restriction on the use of other assets, such as land, goods, or intellectual property, produce a *Quistclose* trust? Money is used by paying it to other persons and, therefore, a restriction on its use is a restriction on its transfer. The transfer of other types of assets can also be restricted, for example, by a right of first refusal or prohibition on assignment. However, most restrictions on the use of things other than money, such as restrictive or leasehold covenants, limit the beneficial use and enjoyment of things, but not their transfer. Nevertheless, it should be possible to create a *Quistclose*-like trust of other assets, in which the recipient holds them in trust for the transferor, with a power to transfer them to others to achieve a specific purpose.

7. Does every restriction on the use of money remove the benefit of having it? If money was loaned to a business corporation to be used only for business purposes, would the corporation acquire beneficial ownership of that money? Would that restriction be enforceable by the lender? What is the effect of a condition that money *not* be used for a particular purpose? If money was paid on condition that it not be used to purchase land, what would happen to the beneficial ownership of that money?

8. In a *Quistclose* loan, the borrower holds the money in trust for the lender, with a power to use it for the specified purpose. According to Lord Millett, the borrower "has no beneficial interest in the money, which remains throughout in the lender".[83] As the sole beneficiary of that trust, presumably the lender can collapse it at any time, under the rule in *Saunders v. Vautier*,[84] and demand repayment of the money. This may be a breach of the contract of loan but, as Mr. Glister said, "the proprietary rights of the lender/beneficiary will 'trump' the contractual rights of the borrower."[85] The borrower owes a fiduciary duty to the lender to obey the trust, but could later seek damages for any loss caused by the lender's breach of contract.

---

81 [1994] 2 Lloyd's L.R. 152 (Eng. C.A.).

82 (1914), 6 O.W.N. 267 (C.A.).

83 *Twinsectra, supra,* note 50, at 193.

84 (1841), Cr. & Ph. 240, 41 E.R. 482, [1835-42] All E.R. Rep. 58 (Ch. Div.).

85 J. Glister, "*Twinsectra v Yardley*: Trusts, Powers and Contractual Obligations" (2002), 16 Tolley's Trust L. Int. 223 at 228.

9. In *Re Gillingham Bus Disaster Fund*,[86] a number of marine cadets were killed or injured when a bus drove into their marching column on December 13, 1951. A fund was collected through public appeals by the mayors of three towns to be used in part "for such worthy cause or causes in memory of the boys who lost their lives as the mayors may determine." Since the purpose was non-charitable, that part of the trust failed and the money was held on resulting trust for the donors. Would that case be decided differently today?

Further Reading

P.J. Millett, "The *Quistclose* Trust: Who Can Enforce It?" (1985), 101 L.Q.R. 269.

L.J. Priestley, "The *Romalpa* Clause and the *Quistclose* Trust" in P. Finn, ed., *Equity and Commercial Relationships* (Sydney: Law Book Co., 1987) 217.

M. Bridge, "The *Quistclose* Trust in a World of Secured Transactions" (1992), 12 Oxford J. Legal Studies 333.

D.R. Klinck, "The *Quistclose* Trust in Canada" (1994), 23 Can. Bus. L.J. 45.

R. Chambers, *Resulting Trusts* (Oxford: Clarendon Press, 1997) pp. 68-89.

J. Payne, "*Quistclose* and Resulting Trusts" in P. Birks & F. Rose, eds., *Restitution and Equity, Volume One: Resulting Trusts and Equitable Compensation* (London: Mansfield Press, 2000) 77.

L. Ho & P. St. J. Smart, "Re-interpreting the *Quistclose* Trust: A Critique of Chambers' Analysis" (2001), 21 Oxford J. Legal Studies 267.

J.E. Penner, *The Law of Trusts*, 3rd ed. (London: Butterworths, 2002) pp. 185-193.

W. Swadling, ed., *Quistclose Trusts* (Oxford: Hart Publishing, 2004).

4. TRUSTS FOR PERSONS

Sometimes, a trust for a purpose turns out to be for the benefit of an identifiable class of beneficiaries. This is not important if the purpose is charitable,[87] but can mean the difference between success and failure if the purpose is non-charitable. If the class of beneficiaries meets the test for certainty of objects and does not violate the rule against perpetuities, the non-charitable purpose trust can take effect as a valid trust for persons. Of course, this will not happen unless the settlor intended to benefit those persons. In many of the *Quistclose* trust cases, discussed above, the specified purpose was payment to the trustee's existing creditors, who formed an identifiable class of persons. However, since the settlor did not intend to confer an immediate benefit on those creditors, the transaction produced only a power to pay them and not a trust for them.

This part of the chapter is divided into three sections. The first illustrates how it is possible to find a class of trust beneficiaries even though the trust appears to be created for a particular purpose and not directly for the benefit of any particular persons. In the second section, that strategy is applied to a situation that has produced a surprisingly large number of legal difficulties in the past: gifts to unincorporated associations. The third section is a brief discussion of the modern

---

86 [1958] Ch. 300, [1958] 1 All E.R. 37, affirmed [1959] Ch. 62, [1958] 2 All E.R. 749 (C.A.).

87 See *Jones v. T. Eaton Co.*, *supra*, note 10.

perpetuities legislation, which makes it much easier to treat trusts for purposes as trusts for persons.

(a) Finding a Class of Beneficiaries

Re Denley's Trusts, below, marked a change of direction for the law in this area.[88] The court showed a remarkable willingness to treat as a class of benefici- aries the people who would benefit from the implementation of the trust's non- charitable purpose. This has since provided the means of saving a number of trusts created for good, but not charitable, purposes. This is not an exception to the normal rule that trusts for non-charitable purposes are invalid, but a situation to which that rule does not apply. The beneficiaries of the trust have standing to enforce it.

RE DENLEY'S TRUSTS

(1968), [1969] 1 Ch. 373, [1968] 3 All E.R. 65
Chancery Division

By clause 2(c) of a trust deed, H.H. Martin and Co. Ltd. conveyed real property to trustees for the purpose of creating a recreation or sports ground for the benefit of its employees. The trustees were given powers to (amongst other things) allow others to use the grounds and to make rules about the time and manner of use of the sports ground. Subject to those rules, the employees were to be entitled to the use and enjoyment of the land. If less than 75% of the employees subscribed to the sports ground, the land was not required as a sports ground, or the company went into liquidation, then the land was to go to a local hospital.

The company later wished to sell a portion of the land and use the proceeds for renovation and improvement of the remaining portion. The trustees applied to the court to determine whether they had the power to sell and to resolve some other issues.

Counsel for the hospital argued that less than 75% of the total number of employees subscribed to the sports facilities and that therefore a forfeiture oc- curred in its favour. Amongst other things, counsel for the company argued that the trust in clause 2(c) was void and that the gift over failed with it, so there was a resulting trust in favour of the company. Once the funds resulted back to the company, it could make other provisions for its employees.

Only that part of the judgment which deals with the validity of clause 2(c), the trust for a sports ground, is reproduced below.

GOFF J.:

---

88 See the note on *Re Denley's* Trusts by P.A. Lovell, "Non-Charitable Purpose Trusts — Further Reflections" (1970), 34 Conv. 77.

. . .

It was decided in *Re Astor's Settlement Trusts*[89] that a trust for a number of non-charitable purposes was not merely unenforceable but void on two grounds; first, that it was not a trust for the benefit of individuals, which I will refer to as "the beneficiary principle," and, secondly, for uncertainty.

Mr. Mills has argued that the trust in clause 2(c) in the present case is either a trust for the benefit of individuals, in which case he argues that they are an unascertainable class and therefore the trust is void for uncertainty, or that it is a purpose trust, that is, a trust for providing recreation, which he submits is void on the beneficiary principle, or, alternatively, that it is something of a hybrid, having the vices of both kinds.

I think there may be a purpose or object trust, the carrying out of which would benefit an individual or individuals, where that benefit is so indirect or intangible or which is otherwise so framed as not to give those persons any *locus standi* to apply to the court to enforce the trust, in which case the beneficiary principle would, as it seems to me, apply to invalidate the trust, quite apart from any question of uncertainty or perpetuity. Such cases can be considered if and when they arise. The present is not, in my judgment, of that character, and it will be seen that clause 2(d) of the trust deed expressly states that, subject to any rules and regulations made by the trustees, the employees of the company shall be entitled to the use and enjoyment of the land. Apart from this possible exception, in my judgment the beneficiary principle of *Re Astor's Settlement Trusts*, which was approved in *Re Endacott*,[90] — see particularly by Harman L.J.[91] — is confined to purpose or object trusts which are abstract or impersonal. The objection is not that the trust is for a purpose or object *per se*, but that there is no beneficiary or cestui que trust. The rule is so expressed in *Lewin on Trusts*,[92] and, in my judgment, with the possible exception I have mentioned, rightly so. In *Re Wood*, Harman J. said:[93]

> There has been an interesting argument on the question of perpetuity, but it seems to me, with all respect to that argument, that there is an earlier obstacle which is fatal to the validity of this bequest, namely, that a gift on trust must have a cestui que trust, and there being here no cestui que trust the gift must fail.

Again in *Leahy v. Attorney-General for New South Wales*, Viscount Simonds, delivering the judgment of the Privy Council, said:[94]

> A gift can be made to persons (including a corporation) but it cannot be made to a purpose or to an object: so also, [and these are the important words] a trust may be created for the benefit of persons as cestuis que trust but not for a purpose or object unless the purpose or object be

---

89 *Supra*, note 11.
90 *Supra*, note 33.
91 *Ibid.*, at 250.
92 16th ed. (1964), p. 17.
93 *Supra*, note 29, at 501.
94 [1959] A.C. 457 at 478, [1959] 2 W.L.R. 722, [1959] 2 All E.R. 300 (P.C.).

charitable. For a purpose or object cannot sue, but, if it be charitable, the Attorney-General can sue to enforce it.

Where, then, the trust, though expressed as a purpose, is directly or indirectly for the benefit of an individual or individuals, it seems to me that it is in general outside the mischief of the beneficiary principle.

[Goff J. referred to several cases to support this conclusion and continued:]

The trust in the present case is limited in point of time so as to avoid any infringement of the rule against perpetuities and, for the reasons I have given, it does not offend against the beneficiary principle; and unless, therefore, it be void for uncertainty, it is a valid trust.

As it is a private trust and not a charitable one, it is clear that, however it be regarded, the individuals for whose benefit it is designed must be ascertained or capable of ascertainment at any given time.[95]

It is conceded that "the employees of the company" in clause 2(c), which must mean for the time being, are so ascertained or ascertainable, but Mr. Mills submits that the inclusion in the class of "such other person or persons (if any) as the trustees may allow" is fatal, and that the qualification "secondarily" in relation to such persons does not help. In my judgment, however, this is not so, I accept Mr. Parker's submission that the provision as to "other persons" is not a trust but a power operating in partial defeasance of the trust in favour of the employees which it does not therefore make uncertain. Moreover, as it is a power, it is not necessary that the trustees should know all possible objects in whose favour it is exercisable.[96] Therefore, in my judgment, it is a valid power. If this were a will, a question might arise whether this provision might be open to attack as a delegation of the testamentary power. I do not say that would be so, but in any case it cannot be said of a settlement *inter vivos*.

Another question, perhaps of difficulty, might arise, if the trustees purported to admit not to a given individual or individuals but a class which they failed to specify with certainty, whether in such a case this would import uncertainty into and invalidate the whole trust or would be merely an invalid exercise of the power; but, as that has not in fact occurred, I need not consider it.

There is, however, one other aspect of uncertainty which has caused me some concern; that is, whether this is in its nature a trust which the court can control, for, as Lord Eldon L.C. said in *Morice v. Bishop of Durham*:[97]

> As it is a maxim, that the execution of a trust shall be under the control of the court, it must be of such a nature, that it can be under that control; so that the administration of it can be reviewed by the court; or, if the trustee dies, the court itself can execute the trust; a trust therefore, which, in case of maladministration could be reformed; and a due administration directed; and then,

---

95 See *Inland Revenue Commissioners v. Broadway Cottages Trust*, [1955] Ch. 20, [1954] 3 W.L.R. 438, [1954] 3 All E.R. 120.

96 See *Re Gulbenkian's Settlements*, [1968] Ch. 126, [1967] 3 All E.R. 15 (C.A.).

97 *Supra*, note 6, at 539.

unless the subject and the objects can be ascertained, upon principles, familiar in other cases, it must be decided, that the court can neither reform maladministration, nor direct a due administration.

The difficulty I have felt is that there may well be times when some of the employees wish to use the sports club for one purpose while others desire to use it at the same time for some other purpose of such natures that the two cannot be carried on together. The trustees could, of course, control this by making rules and regulations under clause (2d) of the trust deed, but they might not. In any case, the employees would probably agree amongst themselves, but I cannot assume that they would. If there were an impasse, the court could not resolve it, because it clearly could not either exercise the trustees' power to make rules or settle a scheme, this being a non-charitable trust.[98]

In my judgment, however, it would not be right to hold the trust void on this ground. The court can, as it seems to me, execute the trust both negatively by restraining any improper disposition or use of the land, and positively by ordering the trustees to allow the employees and such other persons (if any) as they may admit to use the land for the purpose of a recreation or sports ground. Any difficulty there might be in practice in the beneficial enjoyment of the land by those entitled to use it is, I think, really beside the point. The same kind of problem is equally capable of arising in the case of a trust to permit a number of persons — for example, all the unmarried children of a testator or settlor — to use or occupy a house or to have the use of certain chattels; nor can I assume that in such cases agreement between the parties concerned would be more likely, even if that be a sufficient distinction, yet no one would suggest, I fancy, that such a trust would be void.

In my judgment, therefore, the provisions of clause 2(c) are valid....

Notes and Questions

1. The requirement for certainty of objects was relaxed both in *Denley's Trusts, Re* and in *McPhail v. Doulton*.[99] Are there other significant similarities between the two cases?

2. When a trust for non-charitable purposes is valid as a trust for persons, the beneficiaries of that trust have all the rights normally accorded to trust beneficiaries, including the right to collapse the trust under the rule in *Saunders v. Vautier*,[100] provided all the beneficiaries are competent adults and agree to do so. This was not a problem in *Re Denley's Trusts*, because the class of beneficiaries would not close until the trust terminated at the end of the perpetuity period. The possibility of future beneficiaries would prevent the current beneficiaries from invoking the rule.

---

98 See *Re Astor's Settlement Trusts, supra*, note 11, at 547.
99 *Supra*, note 34.
100 *Supra*, note 84.

(b) Unincorporated Associations

An unincorporated association is not a legal person and, therefore, it cannot own property, hold rights, or owe duties. Rather, it is a group of persons bound together for a common purpose, whose relationship is governed by a contract (oral or written) among them. In *Conservative & Unionist Central Office v. Burrell (Inspector of Taxes)*,[101] Lawton L.J. referred to a taxing statute, which distinguished unincorporated associations from companies and partnerships, and said:

> I infer that by "unincorporated association" in this context Parliament meant two or more persons bound together for one or more common purposes, not being business purposes, by mutual undertakings, each having mutual duties and obligations, in an organisation which has rules which identify in whom control of it and its funds rests and upon what terms and which can be joined or left at will. The bond of union between the members of an unincorporated association has to be contractual.

This provides a good description of an unincorporated association but, as Dr. Penner points out,[102] little weight should be given to the requirement that it "can be joined or left at will." Although people join and leave associations voluntarily, membership can be restricted by the rules of the association and may be "by invitation only". Also, in *Keewatin Tribal Council Inc. v. Thompson (City)*,[103] Indian bands were classified as unincorporated associations even though children born to band members become members automatically at birth.

When an unincorporated association has more than a few members, it would be cumbersome if all the members had legal title to the association's assets as joint or co-tenants. Therefore, those assets are usually held by one or two members (such as the treasurer, president, or both) in trust for all of the members. In the past, undue significance has been attributed to the existence of this trust, which exists solely because it is the most convenient way for an association to hold assets. For example, there are a long series of cases dealing with the distribution of the surplus assets of associations upon their dissolution. The early cases treated the problem as a failure of express trust, possibly because the association's assets were held in trust for its members. In later cases, courts recognized the limited significance of the trust and treated the issue as a division of assets among joint or co-tenants, according to the terms of their contract. These cases are discussed in the next chapter.

The issue here is how best to treat gifts and bequests to unincorporated associations that are not charitable. *Re Russell Estate*,[104] reproduced above, shows that they can be construed in at least three different ways:

1. A simple gift to the present members of the association at the time of the gift.

---

101 (1981), [1982] 2 All E.R. 1, [1982] 1 W.L.R. 522 at 525 (C.A.).

102 J.E. Penner, *The Law of Trusts*, 3rd ed. (London: Butterworths, 2002) p. 252.

103 [1989] 5 W.W.R. 202, 1989 CarswellMan 320, [1989] 2 C.T.C. 206, 61 Man. R. (2d) 241, [1989] 3 C.N.L.R. 121 (Q.B.).

104 (sub nom. *Wood. v. R.*) [1977] 6 W.W.R. 273, 1 E.T.R. 285, 9 A.R. 427, 1977 CarswellAlta 240.

2. A gift to the present members of the association as an accretion to the assets already subject to the contract among them.
3. A trust for the purposes of the association, which will be invalid unless it is (a) a *Quistclose* trust (in which the donor has the right to restrain the misuse of the funds),[105] (b) a trust for the present members of the association,[106] or (c) a trust for the present and future members of the association that does not violate the rule against perpetuities.

Under the first construction, the transfer is an absolute gift to the members of the association as joint or co-tenants. Under the second construction, the members still receive ownership of the asset as a gift, but their rights as owners of that asset are controlled by their contract. Under the third construction, the trust is not a bare trust for the association's members, but dictates or limits the use of the trust assets according to the wishes of its settlor, the person who donated the assets to the association to be used for a specific purpose. The validity of that trust depends on whether it creates either a *Quistclose* power or a *Denley* trust for persons.

These possibilities are discussed in *Re Lipinski's Will Trusts*, below.

RE LIPINSKI'S WILL TRUSTS

(1976), [1976] Ch. 235, [1977] 1 All E.R. 33
Chancery Division

The testator died in 1969. Under clause 4(a) of his will, half of the residue of his estate was given to trustees in trust "for the Hull Judeans (Maccabi) Association in memory of my late wife to be used solely in the work of constructing the new buildings for the association and/or improvements to the said buildings". The testator had been a patron of that association, which had been founded as a cricket club in 1919, but expanded to provide social, cultural, and sporting activities for Jewish youth in Hull. The association had 26 members and 12 patrons when the testator died.

In 1972, the testator's executors applied to the court to determine the validity of the trust for the association. The Attorney General argued that the association was charitable, partly because of its objects and partly because it was affiliated with a national organization concerned with charitable objects. Oliver J. held that the objects of the national organization were not those of the association and that the association was, in essence, a sports club for the benefit of its members, despite some of the charitable objects in its constitution.

The following excerpt deals with the question of the validity of the gift on that basis.

---

105 *Burrell, supra*, note 101.
106 *Re Lipinski's Will Trusts* (1976), [1976] Ch. 235, [1977] 1 All E.R. 33 (Ch. Div.).

OLIVER J.:

. . .

I approach question 1 of the summons, therefore, on the footing that this is a gift to an unincorporated non-charitable association. Such a gift, if it is an absolute and beneficial one, is of course perfectly good.[107] What I have to consider, however, is the effect of the specification by the testator of the purposes for which the legacy was to be applied.

The principles applicable to this type of case were stated by Cross J. in *Neville Estates Ltd. v. Madden*,[108] and they are conveniently summarised in Tudor, *Charities*,[109] where it is said:

> In *Neville Estates Ltd. v. Madden* Cross J. expressed the opinion (which is respectfully accepted as correct) that every such gift might, according to the actual words used, be construed in one of three quite different ways: (a) As a gift to the members of the association at the date of the gift as joint tenants so that any member could sever his share and claim it whether or not he continued to be a member. (b) As a gift to the members of the association at the date of the gift not as joint tenants, but subject to their contractual rights and liabilities towards one another as members of the association. In such a case a member cannot sever his share. It will accrue to the other members on his death or resignation, even though such members include persons who become members after the gift took effect. If this is the effect of the gift, it will not be open to objection on the score of perpetuity or uncertainty unless there is something in its terms or circumstances or in the rules of the association which precludes the members at any given time from dividing the subject of the gift between them on the footing that they are solely entitled to it in equity. (c) The terms or circumstances of the gift or the rules of the association may show that the property in question — *i.e.*, the subject of the gift — is not to be at the disposal of the members for the time being but is to be held in trust for or applied for the purposes of the association as a quasi-corporate entity. In this case the gift will fail unless the association is a charitable body.

That summary may require, I think, a certain amount of qualification in the light of subsequent authority, but for present purposes I can adopt it as a working guide. Mr. Blackburne, for the next-of-kin, argues that the gift in the present case clearly does not fall within the first category, and that the addition of the specific direction as to its employment by the association prevents it from falling into the second category. This is, therefore, he says, a purpose trust and fails both for that reason and because the purpose is perpetuitous. He relies on this passage from the judgment of the Board in *Leahy v. Attorney-General for New South Wales*:[110]

> If the words "for the general purposes of the association" were held to import a trust, the question would have to be asked, what is the trust and who are the beneficiaries? A gift can be made to persons (including a corporation) but it cannot be made to a purpose or to an object: so also, a trust may be created for the benefit of persons as cestuis que trust but not for a purpose or object unless the purpose or object be charitable. For a person or object cannot sue, but, if it be charitable, the Attorney-General can sue to enforce it.

---

107 See, *e.g.*, *Re Clarke*, [1901] 2 Ch. 110.
108 [1962] Ch. 832 at 849, [1961] 3 All E.R. 769.
109 6th ed. (1967), at 150.
110 *Supra*, note 94, at 478-479.

Mr. Blackburne points out, first, that the gift is in memory of the testator's late wife (which, he says, suggests an intention to create a permanent memorial or endowment); secondly, that the gift is *solely* for a particular purpose (which would militate strongly against any suggestion that the donees could wind up and pocket the money themselves, even though their constitution may enable them to do so); and, thirdly, that the gift contemplates expenditure on 'improvements', which connotes a degree of continuity or permanence. All this, he says, shows that what the testator had in mind was a permanent endowment in memory of his late wife.

For my part, I think that very little turns on the testator's having expressed the gift as being in memory of his late wife. I see nothing in this expression which suggests any intention to create a permanent endowment. It indicated merely, I think, a tribute which the testator wished to pay, and it is not without significance that this self-same tribute appeared in the earlier will in which he made an absolute and outright gift to the association. The evidential value of this in the context of a construction summons may be open to doubt, and I place no reliance on it. It does, however, seem to me that nothing is to be derived from these words beyond the fact that the testator wished the association to know that his bounty was a tribute to his late wife.

I accept, however, Mr. Blackburne's submission that the designation of the sole purpose of the gift makes it impossible to construe the gift as one falling into the first of Cross J.'s categories, even if that were otherwise possible. But I am not impressed by the argument that the gift shows an intention of continuity. Mr. Blackburne prays in aid *Re Macaulay*,[111] which is reported as a note to *Re Price*,[112] where the gift was for the "maintenance and improvement of the Theosophical Lodge at Folkstone". The House of Lords held that it failed for perpetuity, the donee being a non-charitable body. But it is clear from the speeches of both Lord Buckmaster and Lord Tomlin that their Lordships derived the intention of continuity from the reference to 'maintenance'. Here it is quite evident that the association was to be free to spend the capital of the legacy. As Lord Buckmaster said in *Re Macaulay*:[113]

> In the first place it is clear that the mere fact that the beneficiary is an unincorporated society in no way affects the validity of the gift.... The real question is what is the actual purpose for which the gift is made. There is no perpetuity if the gift were for the individual members for their own benefit, but that, I think, is clearly not the meaning of this gift. Nor again is there a perpetuity if the Society is at liberty, in accordance with the terms of the gift, to spend both capital and income as they think fit.

Re Price[114] itself is authority for the proposition that a gift to an unincorporated non-charitable association for objects on which the association is at liberty to spend both capital and income will not fail for perpetuity, although the actual

---

111 [1943] Ch. 435.
112 *Supra*, note 26.
113 *Supra*, note 111, at 436.
114 *Supra*, note 26.

conclusion in that case has been criticised, the point that the trust there (the carrying on of the teachings of Rudolf Steiner) was a "purpose trust" and thus unenforceable on that ground was not argued. It does not seem to me, therefore, that in the present case there is a valid ground for saying that the gift fails for perpetuity.

But that is not the end of the matter. If the gift were to the association simpliciter, it would, I think, clearly fall within the second category of Cross J.'s categories. At first sight, however, there appears to be a difficulty in arguing that the gift is to members of the association subject to their contractual rights inter se when there is a specific direction or limitation sought to be imposed on those contractual rights as to the manner in which the subject-matter of the gift is to be dealt with. This, says Mr. Blackburne, is a pure "purpose trust" and is invalid on that ground, quite apart from any question of perpetuity. I am not sure, however, that it is sufficient merely to demonstrate that a trust is a "purpose" trust. With the greatest deference, I wonder whether the dichotomy postulated in the passage which I have referred to in the judgment of the Board in *Leahy's* case[115] is not an over-simplification. Indeed, I am not convinced that it was intended as an exhaustive statement or to do more than indicate the broad division of trusts into those where there are ascertainable beneficiaries (whether for particular purposes or not) and trusts where there are none. Indeed, that this is the case, as it seems to me, is to be derived from a later passage of the report, which is in these terms:[116]

> At the risk of repetition their Lordships would point out that, if a gift is made to individuals, whether under their own names or in the name of their society, and the conclusion is reached that they are not intended to take beneficially, then they take as trustees. If so, it must be ascertained who are the beneficiaries. If at the death of the testator the class of beneficiaries is fixed and ascertained or ascertainable within the limit of the rule against perpetuities, all is well. If it is not so fixed and not so ascertainable the trust must fail. Of such a trust no better example could be found than a gift to an Order for the benefit of a community of nuns, once it is established that the community is not confined to living and ascertained persons. A wider question is opened if it appears that the trust is not for persons but for a non-charitable purpose. As has been pointed out, no one can enforce such a trust. What follows? *Ex hypothesi* the trustees are not themselves the beneficiaries yet the trust fund is in their hands, and they may or may not think fit to carry out their testator's wishes. If so, it would seem that the testator has imperfectly exercised his testamentary power; he has delegated it, for the disposal of his property lies with them, not with him. Accordingly, the subject matter of the gift will be undisposed of or fall into the residuary estate as the case may be.

There would seem to me to be, as a matter of common sense, a clear distinction between the case where a purpose is prescribed which is clearly intended for the benefit of ascertained or ascertainable beneficiaries, particularly where those beneficiaries have the power to make the capital their own, and the case where no beneficiary at all is intended (for instance, a memorial to a favourite pet) or where the beneficiaries are unascertainable (as for instance in *Re Price*). If a valid gift may be made to an unincorporated body as a simple accretion to the funds

---

115 *Supra*, note 94, at 478.
116 *Ibid.*, at 484, *per* Viscount Simonds.

which are the subject-matter of the contract which the members have made inter se — and *Neville Estates v. Madden*[117] and *Re Recher's Will Trusts*[118] show that it may — I do not really see why such a gift, which specifies a purpose which is within the powers of the unincorporated body and of which the members of that body are the beneficiaries, should fail. Why are not the beneficiaries able to enforce the trust or, indeed, in the exercise of their contractual rights, to terminate the trust for their own benefit? Where the donee body is itself the beneficiary of the prescribed purpose, there seems to me to be the strongest argument in common sense for saying that the gift should be construed as an absolute one within the second category — the more so where, if the purpose is carried out, the members can by appropriate action vest the resulting property in themselves, for here the trustees and the beneficiaries are the same persons.

Is such a distinction as I have suggested borne out by the authorities? The answer is, I think, "Not in terms", until recently. But the cases appear to me to be at least consistent with this. For instance, *Re Clarke*,[119] *Re Drummond*,[120] and *Re Taylor*,[121] in all of which the testator had prescribed purposes for which the gifts were to be used, and in all of which the gifts were upheld, were all cases where there were ascertainable beneficiaries; whereas in *Re Wood*[122] and *Leahy's* case (where the gifts failed) there were none. *Re Price* is perhaps out of line, because there there was no ascertained beneficiary and yet Cohen J. was prepared to uphold the gift even on the supposition that (contrary to his own conclusion) the purpose was non-charitable. But as I have mentioned, the point about the trust being a purpose trust was not argued before him.

A striking case which seems to be not far from the present is *Re Turkington*,[123] where the gift was to a masonic lodge "as a fund to build a suitable temple in Stafford". The members of the lodge being both the trustees and the beneficiaries of the temple, Luxmoore J. construed the gift as an absolute one to the members of the lodge for the time being.

Directly in point is the more recent decision of Goff J. in *Re Denley's Trust Deed*,[124] where the question arose as to the validity of a deed under which land was held by trustees as a sports ground, "primarily for the benefit of the employees of [a particular] company and secondarily for the benefit of such other person or persons... as the trustees may allow to use the same". The latter provision was construed by Goff J. as a power and not a trust. The same deed conferred on the employees a right to use and enjoy the land subject to regulations made by the trustees. Goff J. held that the rule against enforceability of non-charitable "purpose or object" trusts was confined to those which were abstract or impersonal in nature where there was no beneficiary or cestui que trust. A trust which, though expressed

---

117 *Supra*, note 108.
118 [1972] Ch. 526, [1971] 3 All E.R. 401.
119 [1901] 2 Ch. 110 (the case of the Corps of Commissionaires).
120 [1914] 2 Ch. 90 (the case of the Old Bradfordians).
121 [1940] Ch. 481, [1940] 2 All E.R. 637 (the case of the Midland Bank Staff Association).
122 *Supra*, note 29.
123 [1937] 4 All E.R. 501.
124 *Supra*, note 53, at 375.

as a purpose, was directly or indirectly for the benefit of an individual or individuals was valid provided that those individuals were ascertainable at any one time and the trust was not otherwise void for uncertainty. Goff J. said:[125]

> I think there may be a purpose or object trust, the carrying out of which would benefit an individual or individuals, where that benefit is so indirect or intangible or which is otherwise so framed as not to give those persons any *locus standi* to apply to the court to enforce the trust, in which case the beneficiary principle would, as it seems to me, apply to invalidate the trust, quite apart from any question of uncertainty or perpetuity.... The objection is not that the trust is for a purpose or object *per se*, but that there is no beneficiary or cestui que trust... Where, then, the trust, though expressed as a purpose, is directly or indirectly for the benefit of an individual or individuals, it seems to me that it is in general outside the mischief of the beneficiary principle.

I respectfully adopt this, as it seems to me to accord both with authority and with common sense.

If this is the right principle, then on which side of the line does the present case fall? Mr. Morritt has submitted in the course of his argument in favour of charity that the testator's express purpose "solely in the work of constructing the new buildings for the association" referred and could only refer to the youth centre project, which was the only project for the erection of buildings which was under consideration at the material time. If this is right, then the trust must, I think, fail, for it is quite clear that that project as ultimately conceived embraced not only the members of the association, but the whole Jewish community in Hull, and it would be difficult to argue that there was any ascertainable beneficiary, I do not, however, so construe the testator's intention. The evidence is that the testator knew the association's position and that he took a keen interest in it. I infer that he was kept informed of its current plans. The one thing that is quite clear from the minutes is that from 1965 right up to the testator's death there was great uncertainty about what was going to be done. There was a specific project for the purchase of a house in 1965. By early 1966 the youth centre was back in favour. By October 1966 it was being suggested that the association should stay where it was in its rented premises. The meeting of 21st March is, I think, very significant because it shows that it was again thinking in terms of its own exclusive building and that the patrons (of whom the testator was one) would donate the money when it was needed. At the date of the will, the association had rejected the youth centre plans and was contemplating again the purchase of premises of its own; and thereafter interest shifted to the community centre. I am unable to conclude that the testator had any specific building in mind; and, in my judgment, the reference to "the ... buildings for the Association" means no more than whatever buildings the association may have or may choose to erect or acquire. The reference to improvements reflects, I think, the testator's contemplation that the association might purchase or might, at his death, already have purchased an existing structure which might require improvement or conversion, or even that it might, as had at one time been suggested, expend money in improving the premises

---

125 *Ibid.*, at 382-384.

which it rented from the Jewish Institute. The association was to have the legacy to spend in this way for the benefit of its members.

I have already said that, in my judgment, no question of perpetuity arises here, and accordingly the case appears to me to be one of the specification of a particular purpose for the benefit of ascertained beneficiaries, the members of the association for the time being. There is an additional factor. This is a case in which, under the constitution of the association, the members could, by the appropriate majority, alter their constitution so as to provide, if they wished, for the division of the association's assets among themselves. This has, I think, a significance. I have considered whether anything turns in this case on the testator's direction that the legacy shall be used "solely" for one or other of the specified purposes. Mr. Rossdale has referred me to a number of cases where legacies have been bequeathed for particular purposes and in which the beneficiaries have been held entitled to override the purpose, even though expressed in mandatory terms.

Perhaps the most striking in the present context is the case of *Re Bowes*,[126] where money was directed to be laid out in the planting of trees on a settled estate. That was a "purpose" trust, but there were ascertainable beneficiaries, the owners for the time being of the estate; and North J. held that the persons entitled to the settled estate were entitled to have the money whether or not it was laid out as directed by the testator. He said:[127]

> Then, the sole question is where this money is to go to. Of course, it is a perfectly good legacy. There is nothing illegal in the matter, and the direction to plant might easily be carried out; but it is not necessarily capable of being performed, because the owner of the estate might say he would not have any trees planted upon it at all. If that were the line he took, and he did not contend for anything more than that, the legacy would fail; but he says he does not refuse to have trees planted upon it; he is content that trees should be planted upon some part of it; but the legacy has not failed. If it were necessary to uphold it, the trees can be planted upon the whole of it until the fund is exhausted. Therefore, there is nothing illegal in the gift itself; but the owners of the estate now say: "It is a very disadvantageous way of spending this money; the money is to be spent for our benefit, and that of no one else; it was not intended for any purpose other than our benefit and that of the estate. That is no reason why it should be thrown away by doing what is not for our benefit, instead of being given to us, who want to have the enjoyment of it." I think their contention is right. I think the fund is devoted to improving the estate, and improving the estate for the benefit of the persons who are absolutely entitled to it.

I can see no reason why the same reasoning should not apply in the present case simply because the beneficiary is an unincorporated non-charitable association. I do not think the fact that the testator has directed the application "solely" for the specified purpose adds any legal force to the direction. The beneficiaries, the members of the association for the time being, are the persons who could enforce the purpose and they must, as it seems to me, be entitled not to enforce it or, indeed, to vary it.

Thus, it seems to me that whether one treats the gift as a "purpose" trust or as an absolute gift with a superadded direction or, on the analogy of *Re Turkington*

---

126 [1896] 1 Ch. 507.
127 *Ibid.*, at 510-511.

as a gift where the trustees and the beneficiaries are the same persons, all roads lead to the same conclusion.

In my judgment, the gift is a valid gift...

Notes and Questions

1. What did Oliver J. decide: was there a trust for persons or was the purpose merely a motive for making an absolute gift?[128] Either way, are the members of the association required to use the money for the purpose chosen by the testator?

2. A trust to construct buildings for an unincorporated association can be regarded as a perfectly normal trust for persons, provided it does not violate the rule against perpetuities. Compare it to a trust for the education of my children. The members of that class will be identified by the end of my life, so there is no problem with perpetuities. Although the trust dictates how my children are to enjoy its benefits, once the class is closed and my children all become competent adults, they can agree to collapse the trust under the rule in *Saunders v. Vautier*,[129] thereby frustrating its purpose. A trust which benefits the members of an association in a particular way is no different except for the number of beneficiaries.

3. In *Keewatin Tribal Council Inc. v. Thompson (City)*,[130] three apartment buildings were owned by a corporation, which was owned by 12 Indian bands. For tax reasons, the corporation executed a deed declaring that it held the buildings as bare trustee for the bands. The municipality assessed the corporation for municipal tax and argued that the bands could not be the beneficiaries of the trust because they were unincorporated associations. Jewers J. rejected that argument, adopting the reasoning in *Re Denley's Trusts*:[131]

> In the case at bar, the ultimate, albeit indirect, beneficiaries of the trust are the individual members of the bands; indeed, there are potentially very real benefits in that the children are entitled to use the properties free of charge as accommodation while attending school in Thompson. Even if this were not enough to give individual band members *locus standi*, surely the trust could, and would, be enforced by the band councils, or any one or more of them, or failing that, the chiefs, or any one or more of them. If the band councils have a status similar to that of municipalities, surely they have the necessary standing to enforce the trust. The real question is one of enforceability and nothing else. There is absolutely no problem with a charitable purpose trust, which will be enforced by the Attorney General, however impersonal its objects; similarly, there should be no problem with a non-charitable purpose trust where there are any number of persons with standing to enforce it....
>
> It follows that in Manitoba, at least, the type of trust in question is perfectly valid as a non-charitable purpose trust which neither contravenes the rule against perpetuities, for there is no such rule here, nor fails for want of beneficiaries having standing to enforce the trust.

4. Jewers J. seemed to say that the trust was valid because the band members were its beneficiaries, but then goes on to deny their interest in the trust assets:[132]

> I do not believe that the gift can be interpreted as being in favour of the individual members of the bands, either for the present or for the present and future. For one thing, the trust deed just

---

128 See J.E. Penner, *The Law of Trusts*, 3rd ed. (London: Butterworths, 2002) at 258.
129 *Supra*, note 84.
130 *Supra*, note 103.
131 *Ibid.*, at W.W.R. 217.
132 *Ibid.*, at 216.

did not say that. The gift was to the bands. Furthermore, the number of people involved is very large and it could hardly have been the intention of the settler to give an interest in these properties to such a great number of individuals so that they could each hold respective shares as tenants in common. In my opinion, the gift must be viewed as one to used for the purposes of the individual bands: in other words, a purpose trust.

Since the bands were not legal persons, a gift "to the bands" could be nothing other than a gift to its members. Why would any members of the bands have standing to enforce the trust unless they were beneficiaries of that trust? Are there any adverse consequences to the conclusion that this was a simple trust for the present and future members of the bands? The trust declared by the corporation was a bare trust. What makes it "a purpose trust" and what is its purpose?

5. Contrast *Re Lipinski's Will Trusts* with *Re Grant's Will Trusts*,[133] in which a testator left his estate "to the Labour Party Property Committee for the benefit of the Chertsey and Walton C.L.P.", with a gift over to the National Labour Party if the Chertsey headquarters should cease to be in the Chertsey district. Vinelott J. said:[134]

> Reading the gift in the will in the light of the rules governing the Chertsey and Walton C.L.P., it is, in my judgment, impossible to construe the gift as a gift made to the members of the Chertsey and Walton C.L.P. at the date of the testator's death with the intention that it should belong to them as a collection of individuals, though in the expectation that they and any other members subsequently admitted would ensure that it was in fact used for what in broad terms has been labelled "headquarters' purposes" of the Chertsey and Walton C.L.P.

Vinelott J. gave two reasons why the gift was void. First, the local party's constitution required it to transfer its property to the national party if the latter demanded it and the local party could not alter its rules unilaterally and divide the property among its members. Secondly, the gift was to trustees (the Property Committee) and not to the unincorporated association, so that a trust was clearly intended. As to the first reason, could not the local party simply have disaffiliated itself from the national party by resolution? As to the second reason, could *Denley* have been invoked to save the gift?

6. In *Conservative & Unionist Central Office v. Burrell (Inspector of Taxes)*,[135] the inspector of taxes argued that the conservative party was an unincorporated association and therefore liable to pay tax. Otherwise, it could not receive donations, since the treasurer would not be holding the money in trust for anyone. The Court of Appeal disagreed, saying that a trust for party members was unnecessary because the donors could restrain the treasurer's misuse of the money. Although the court did not connect the donors' rights to the *Quistclose* trust, the principle is the same and it should also apply to gifts to unincorporated associations that do not produce trusts for their members (at least if the gifts are *inter vivos*).

(c) The Rule Against Perpetuities

A non-charitable purpose trust cannot be saved as a trust for persons if that would violate the rule against perpetuities. If there is a remote or even fanciful

---

133 (1979), [1980] 1 W.L.R. 360, [1979] 3 All E.R. 359 (Ch. Div.).

134 *Ibid.*, at W.L.R. 374.

135 *Supra*, note 101.

possibility that new beneficiaries could join the class beyond the perpetuity period, then the trust is invalid from the start under the common law rule.

The rule was created because common law judges were concerned about uncertainty regarding the ownership of assets. Uncertainty was permitted so long as it did not last too long. For example, I can make a testamentary trust for all my grandchildren, even though that class of beneficiaries will not close and be ascertained until all my children are dead. Thus, the common law allows me to control assets through the next generation into the one after that, but no further. A trust for all my great grandchildren would fail because the ownership of the trust assets would remain uncertain too long.

At common law, the perpetuity period is defined as a life in being plus 21 years. People are lives in being if they are alive as human beings or conceived as embryos or foetuses at the time the trust is created. This definition makes sense when applied to trusts and wills that dictate the use of family assets by successive generations. The rule limited the extent to which testators could control the use of their assets after death. As Professors Lawson and Rudden said, "there comes a time when even the dead must die; and the effect of the Rule is to fix the latest date for this at the time when our grandchildren grow up."[136] Returning to the example of a testamentary trust for my grandchildren, the rule would allow me to delay vesting of beneficial ownership until they reach the age of 21, but no later.

The common law rule does not work well when the beneficiaries of the trust are not related by birth, but are employees of a corporation or members of an unincorporated association. The lives in being are the present employees or members when the trust takes effect. Since it is possible that someone born after that date (and therefore not a life in being) could join the company or association more than 21 years after all the lives in being are dead, a trust for present and future employees or members would violate the common law rule.

In both of the cases reproduced above, in which purpose trusts were declared valid as trusts for persons, the problem of perpetuities did not arise. In *Re Denley's Trusts*,[137] the trust was expressly limited to the perpetuity period of certain lives in being, named in the trust deed when it was made in 1936, plus 21 years. In *Re Lipinski's Will Trusts*,[138] the bequest was construed as a trust (or gift) for the present members of the association, who were all lives in being. If the rule against perpetuities had been violated, the employees and members would not have formed acceptable classes of trust beneficiaries.

In many Canadian jurisdictions, the problem of perpetuities is alleviated by statute, thereby greatly expanding the possibility of construing trusts for purposes as trusts for persons. In Manitoba, the rule against perpetuities has been abolished.[139] Because of this, it was possible to uphold a trust for the benefit of the

---

136 F.H. Lawson and B. Rudden, *The Law of Property*, 3rd ed. by B. Rudden (Oxford: Oxford University Press, 2002) p. 190.
137 *Supra*, note 53.
138 *Supra*, note 106.
139 *The Perpetuities and Accumulations Act*, C.C.S.M. c. P33.

present and future members of Indian bands in *Keewatin Tribal Council Inc. v. Thompson (City)*,[140] as discussed above. That trust would have been invalidated by the common law rule.

In Alberta, British Columbia, Northwest Territories, Nunavut, Ontario, and Yukon Territory,[141] the common law rule has been modified by statute. Trusts (and other dispositions of property) are not invalid just because they create interests that might remain contingent beyond the perpetuity period. They are presumptively valid until it is established that the uncertainty cannot be resolved before the perpetuity period expires. This is known as the "wait and see" rule.

If a non-charitable purpose trust benefits the present and future members of an association, the "wait and see" rule allows it to take effect as a valid trust for persons. The lives in being are all the present members of the association when the trust takes effect and the trust is allowed to operate until 21 years after all the present members are dead. In most cases, this limit would not create a problem, because the trust assets would be spent or the association discontinued before the end of the perpetuity period. If not, then the remainder will be disposed of, either by other clauses in the trust or by a resulting trust for the settlors or their estates.

The common law rule still applies in New Brunswick, Newfoundland and Labrador, Nova Scotia, and Saskatchewan. In Prince Edward Island, the perpetuity period has been modified by statute, but there is no presumptive validity for interests that might remain contingent beyond the modified period.[142] Therefore, most trusts for present and future members of an association would be void in those jurisdictions, because of the remote possibility of membership changing beyond the perpetuity period, regardless of how that period is defined.

In *Taylor v. Scurry-Rainbow Oil (Sask) Ltd.*,[143] the Saskatchewan Court of Appeal held that the common law rule can be modified by the common law and should not be applied to commercial interests in the same way it applies to control family wills and trusts. In that case, a petroleum "top lease" did not offend the policy of the rule and was therefore exempt from it. Tallis J.A. said:[144]

> Since common law rules are judge-made rules, the Court can make exceptions to such rules when changing conditions so mandate. Common law rules may be tweaked to do justice between the parties when a rigid and mechanistic application of a rule would run counter to the object and purpose of the rule.

It may be too late for a court to "tweak" the rule to save a trust for an unincorporated association, but it is not clear that anyone has seriously considered that possibility.

---

140 *Supra*, note 103.
141 *Perpetuities Act*, R.S.A. 2000, c. P-5; *Perpetuity Act*, R.S.B.C. 1996, c. 358; *Perpetuities Act*, R.S.N.W.T. 1988, c. P-3; *Perpetuities Act*, R.S.O. 1990, c. P.9; *Perpetuities Act*, R.S.Y. 2002, c. 168.
142 *Perpetuities Act*, R.S.P.E.I. 1988, c. P-3.
143 [2001] 11 W.W.R. 25, 203 D.L.R. (4th) 38, 2001 CarswellSask 539, 2001 SKCA 85, 207 Sask. R. 266, 247 W.A.C. 266 (C.A.).
144 *Ibid.*, at D.L.R. 76.

Notes and Questions

1. Under section 91(24) of the *Constitution Act, 1867*, the federal government has jurisdiction over "Lands Reserved for Indians", which includes both reserve lands and lands subject to aboriginal title.[145] Therefore, the provincial perpetuities legislation would not apply to contingent interests in that land. Nevertheless, the common law rule against perpetuities probably does not apply either, given the Supreme Court of Canada's statement that "common law real property concepts do not apply to native lands".[146] However, provincial perpetuities legislation applies to land that is owned beneficially by Indians, but not located on a reserve or subject to aboriginal title,[147] and to assets other than land.

2. Pension trusts are excepted by statute from the rule against perpetuities in Alberta, British Columbia, New Brunswick, Newfoundland and Labrador, Northwest Territories, Nunavut, Ontario, and Yukon Territory.[148]

Problems

1. Discuss the validity of the following *inter vivos* gifts:

(a) $10,000 on trust to provide facilities for the playing of rugby for my employees and others;

(b) $20,000 on trust to promote the music of "The Village Persons", a popular singing group;

(c) $15,000 on trust for the maintenance of my pet turtle;

(d) $5,000 on trust for the Ruffian's Hockey club, an unincorporated association, to improve its club house. The club has no constitution or rules.

2. Tom is a full member of the Cardinal Squash Club, an unincorporated association. His daughter, Olivia, is a student member who pays one half the subscription rate. Tom's father died, leaving $20,000 to the club in trust "for the purpose of constructing new change rooms." The members have unanimously decided to wind up the club. The $20,000 legacy has not yet been paid over. Advise Tom and Olivia regarding their rights (a) as members of the squash club and (b) as the residuary beneficiaries under Tom's father's will.

3. When Barry was accepted into law school, his sister, Rhonda, sent him a cheque for $15,000, with a letter that stated, "This is my gift to you, but it can be used only to pay your law school tuition fees and for no other purpose." Is there a trust and, if so, what are its terms?

---

145 *Delgamuukw v. British Columbia* (1997), [1997] 3 S.C.R. 1010, 153 D.L.R. (4th) 193, [1997] S.C.J. No. 108, 1997 CarswellBC 2358, 1997 CarswellBC 2359, 220 N.R. 161, 99 B.C.A.C. 161, 162 W.A.C. 161, [1998] 1 C.N.L.R. 14, [1999] 10 W.W.R. 34, 66 B.C.L.R. (3d) 285.

146 *St. Mary's Indian Band v. Cranbrook (City)*, [1997] 2 S.C.R. 657, 147 D.L.R. (4th) 385, 1997 CarswellBC 1259, 1997 CarswellBC 1258, 213 N.R. 290, 92 B.C.A.C. 161, 150 W.A.C. 161, 40 M.P.L.R. (2d) 131, [1997] 3 C.N.L.R. 282, 35 B.C.L.R. (3d) 218, [1997] 8 W.W.R. 332, additional reasons at 1997 CarswellBC 3095, 1997 CarswellBC 3096, [1997] 2 S.C.R. 678, at 392 [D.L.R.], *per* Lamer C.J.C.

147 *Keewatin Tribal Council Inc. v. Thompson (City)*, *supra*, note 103.

148 *Perpetuities Act*, R.S.A. 2000, c. P-5, s. 22; *Perpetuity Act*, R.S.B.C. 1996, c. 358, s. 4(a); *Property Act*, R.S.N.B. 1973, c. P-19, s. 3; *Perpetuities and Accumulations Act*, R.S.N.L. 1990, c. P-7, s. 2; *Perpetuities Act*, R.S.N.W.T. 1988, c. P-3, s. 19; *Perpetuities Act*, R.S.O. 1990, c. P.9, s. 18; *Perpetuities Act*, R.S.Y. 2002, c. 168, s. 22.

PART IV

REMEDIAL TRUSTS

Chapter 9

RESULTING TRUSTS

1. SCOPE

The express trust has been explored in previous chapters. This chapter marks the beginning of a fundamental shift as we begin to study those trusts that arise by operation of law. Express trusts are created directly by an intention to create a trust and an important issue in that branch of trust law is *how* express trusts are created. What must a settlor do to bring the desired trust into being? In contrast, resulting and constructive trusts are created by a variety of other events and an important (and often difficult) issue is *why* those trusts arise. The resulting trust is the subject of this chapter, while the constructive trust is discussed in the next two chapters. The resulting trust has an older lineage than the constructive trust. It dates back almost to the *Statute of Uses*[1] and derives by analogy from the older resulting use.

The first part of this chapter provides an introduction to the resulting trust, including its development, competing theories about why it arises, and what distinguishes it from express and constructive trusts. This is followed by explorations of the two main situations in which resulting trusts arise: first, when an express trust fails in whole or in part and, secondly, when there is an apparent gift from one person to another that is presumed or proved not to be intended as such. This is followed by a brief look at other situations in which resulting trusts have arisen.

Further Reading

D.W.M. Waters, "The Doctrine of Resulting Trusts in Common Law Canada" (1970), 16 McGill L.J. 187.

Malcolm L. Morris, "Rediscovering the Resulting Trust: Modern Maneuvers for a Dated Doctrine?" (1983), 17 Akron L. Rev. 43.

Peter Birks, "Restitution and Resulting Trusts" in S. Goldstein, ed., *Equity and Contemporary Legal Developments* (Jerusalem, 1992) 335.

William Swadling, "A New Role for Resulting Trusts?" (1996), 16 Legal Studies 110

Robert Chambers, *Resulting Trusts* (Oxford: Clarendon Press, 1997).

---

1 27 Hen. 8, c. 10 (1535, U.K.).

Peter Birks & Francis Rose, eds., *Restitution and Equity, Volume One: Resulting Trusts and Equitable Compensation* (London: Mansfield Press, 2000).

Robert Chambers, "Resulting Trusts in Canada" (2000), 38 Alberta L. Rev. 378.

2. INTRODUCTION TO THE RESULTING TRUST

(a) Development of the Resulting Trust

Resulting trusts derive by analogy from the resulting use. Before the *Statute of Uses*,[2] uses had become a popular way for landowners to devise land by will and avoid the feudal incidents that became due when land descended to an heir. At that time, real property could not be given away by will and, on the owner's death, would pass to the owner's heir-at-law (usually the eldest son). This created a problem for landowners who wanted to provide for other members of the family. Also, the descent to the heir was costly, since the landlord was entitled to receive certain feudal incidents (such as a year's income from the land) in exchange for recognizing the heir's right to inherit the land.

A landowner could avoid both those problems by conveying his land to trusted friends to hold it as joint tenants to the use of the landowner for life, and then to the use of whomever the landowner might direct. At that time, a conveyance of land was by *feoffment*, so the landowner (who we would call the settlor today) was the *feoffor que use*, the trusted friends were the *feoffees que use*, and the beneficiaries of the use were the *cestuis que use*. If any of the feoffees (trustees) died, the other feoffees would acquire the deceased feoffee's interest automatically as surviving joint tenants. Deceased feoffees could be replaced by further feoffments. This ensured that all of the legal owners never died so that the land never descended to an heir. The instructions given by the feoffor que use were binding on the consciences of the feoffees and operated essentially as a will directing the disposition of the feoffor's land.

The popularity of this device had two lasting consequences. The first, discussed in the first chapter, was the *Statute of Uses*. The loss of revenue to the Crown (then Henry VIII) from feudal incidents was so great, that the *Statute of Uses* was passed to execute the use and transfer legal ownership to the cestuis que use. Secondly, whenever land was conveyed for no consideration, if no uses were declared, it was assumed that the feoffment was made for the purpose of creating a use for the feoffor. This became known as the *resulting use*.

The meaning of consideration was broader then than it is now in the modern law of contract. As Professor Birks said, "A 'consideration' was once no more than a 'matter considered', and the consideration for doing something was the matter considered in forming the decision to do it."[3] The consideration for a feoffment could be the payment of the purchase price, but could be other matters, such as the desire to benefit a child. Therefore, if land was given to a stranger,

---

2 *Ibid.*

3 P. Birks, *An Introduction to the Law of Restitution*, rev. ed. (Oxford: Clarendon Press, 1989) at 223.

there would be a resulting use "for want of consideration", but if land was given to a son, there would be no use "for the consideration is apparent."[4]

When the *Statute of Uses* was enacted, the resulting use had already become a rule of law. If a feoffment was then made without consideration or a declaration of use, a resulting use would arise, the statute would execute that use, and title would be returned to the feoffor, thus nullifying the transaction. Conveyancers needed to take care to avoid a resulting use that might undo the transaction. A declaration of use for the feoffee would suffice, so it became common to convey land unto and to the use of the feoffee to ensure that there would be no resulting use and the feoffee would obtain legal title.

In the 17th century, when the Court of Chancery began to enforce the use upon a use and the modern trust was born (as discussed in the first chapter), the court also began to enforce the resulting trust by analogy to the resulting use. However, the early cases did not involve gratuitous transfers from A to B, but cases where A paid X to transfer land to B. Since X was paid in full, there was no resulting trust for X. However, B received an apparent gift at A's expense and, if there was no consideration for the gift (that is, no apparent reason for it), B would hold the land on resulting trust for A unless B proved that A really did intend to make a gift. The most famous statement of this principle is in the 18th century case of *Dyer v. Dyer*,[5] where Eyre C.B. said:

> The clear result of all the cases, without a single exception, is that the trust of a legal estate, whether freehold, copyhold, or leasehold; whether taken in the names of the purchasers and others jointly, or in the names of others without that of the purchaser; whether in one name or several; whether jointly or successive — results to the man who advances the purchase-money. This is a general proposition, supported by all the cases, and there is nothing to contradict it; and it goes on a strict analogy to the rule of the common law, that where a feoffment is made without consideration, the use results to the feoffor. It is the established doctrine of a Court of equity, that this resulting trust may be rebutted by circumstances in evidence.

Today, this principle is called the presumption of resulting trust. Except where altered by statute, it applies not just to land but to apparent gifts of any type of asset, whether made by direct transfer from A to B or by A's purchase of the asset in B's name. If B is A's wife or child, there is an assumption that A intended to make a gift. This is called the presumption of advancement. Both presumptions can be rebutted by evidence to the contrary. They are discussed below.

(b) Why Resulting Trusts Arise

Resulting trusts may be divided into two broad categories. The first occurs when a settlor transfers assets to trustees and thereby creates or intends to create an express trust. If the express trust fails to arise or fails to dispose of the entire beneficial ownership of the trust assets, the remainder normally results to the settlor or to his or her estate.

---

4 *Cook v. Fountain* (1676), 3 Sanst. 585 at 587, 36 E.R. 984, *per* Lord Nottingham L.C.
5 (1788), 2 Cox Eq. Cas. 92 at 93, 30 E.R. 42 (Ch. Div.).

Resulting trusts in the second category arise when one person (A) voluntarily transfers an asset to another person (B) or when A purchases an asset and directs the vendor to transfer the asset to B. In these situations, equity usually presumes that A did not intend that B should take the asset beneficially and, therefore, B will hold the asset on resulting trust for A unless the presumption is rebutted.

In *Vandervell's Trust (No. 2), Re,*[6] Megarry J. drew a sharp distinction between these two categories, calling the first "automatic resulting trusts" and the second "presumed resulting trusts." Although not all writers agree with these labels, resulting trusts do divide themselves readily into two categories comprising situations similar to those to which Megarry J. referred. However, there are some cases, like *Hodgson v. Marks,*[7] reproduced below, which could be placed in either category.

Megarry J. considered the first category to be automatic because he believed that this resulting trust does not depend upon the actual or presumed intention of the settlor of the express trust, but is the automatic consequence of failing to dispose of the trust assets. Although beneficial ownership of the remainder never left the settlor, legal title has been transferred to the trustee and the resulting trust is needed to enable the settlor to recover title.

By contrast, the presumed resulting trust was said to depend upon the intention of the transferor or purchaser. Not his or her actual intention, since that would lead to an express trust, but an intention that is attributed by law. Equity presumes bargains, not gifts. Therefore, when an asset is transferred gratuitously from A to B or is purchased by A for B, there could be an assumption that a trust was intended. If B cannot prove that A had an intention to give, a resulting trust is imposed.

Must it then be said that resulting trusts, at any rate presumed resulting trusts, can only be explained on the basis of intention? It may well be that A intends B to hold the property in trust for A. Indeed, in inter-spousal transfers, this is often apparent if the transfer is made to avoid A's creditors. It is also not inconceivable, although unlikely, that a settlor who transfers property to a trustee and declares a trust of a life estate only and does not dispose of the remainder, intends the trustee to hold the remainder interest on trust for the settlor. It is more likely, in the latter situation, that the settlor simply forgot to deal with the remainder.

However, it can be confusing to speak of intention in the context of resulting trusts because, in many of the resulting trusts cases, there was no actual intention on the part of the creator of the express trust, or even on the part of the transferor or purchaser. He or she has not considered the ramifications of his or her actions at all. In *Vandervell v. Inland Revenue Commissioners,*[8] the settlor thought he had disposed of his property completely and certainly did not want a resulting trust of the remainder that he failed to give away. His unforeseen interest under the resulting trust cost him dearly in income tax he had tried, but failed, to avoid.

---

6 [1974] 1 Ch. 269 at 294-295, [1974] 3 All E.R. 205 (C.A.), reversed on other grounds [1974] Ch.
    269 at 308 (C.A.).

7 [1971] Ch. 892, [1971] 2 All E.R. 684 (C.A.).

8   (1966), [1967] 2 A.C. 291, [1967] 1 All E.R. 1 (H.L.).

These problems can be resolved by recognizing that intention is important for both presumed and automatic resulting trusts. In both situations, the resulting trust responds, not directly to an intention to create a trust, but to the fact that the provider of the trust assets did not intend to benefit the recipient. This is the view taken in recent years by Lord Millett, writing judicially and extra-judicially.[9] It has been promoted by some academic lawyers,[10] but rejected by others.[11]

There are many cases in which it was clear that the provider of an asset intended to create a trust for him- or herself. This intention should be sufficient to create an express trust where no formalities are required. However, if the asset is an interest in land, the express trust will be unenforceable because of the *Statute of Frauds* or its descendants.[12] In that situation, the provider's intention to create a trust means that he or she had no intention to provide a benefit to the recipient. This absence of donative intention should attract a resulting trust.

HODGSON v. MARKS

[1971] Ch. 892, [1971] 2 All E.R. 684
Court of Appeal

Mrs. Hodgson was an elderly widow. In 1960, she transferred her house to her lodger, Mr. Evans, at his request to prevent her nephew from turning him out of the house. In 1964, Evans sold the house to Mr. Marks, who became the registered owner and granted a registered charge to the Cheltenham and Gloucester Building Society to finance the purchase. Although Hodgson was residing in the house, neither Hodgson nor Marks knew about each other's interest in it. When the problem came to light in 1965, Hodgson sued Marks and the building society claiming a right to reconveyance of the house free of the charge.

The trial judge held that Hodgson did not intend to make a gift to Evans, but had intended that he would hold the house in trust for her, and that the transfer to Evans was procured by his undue influence. Under section 53(1) of the *Law of Property Act, 1925*,[13] a trust of land was not enforceable unless manifested in writing. The judge relied on *Rochefoucauld v. Boustead*,[14] to hold that the statute

---

9 *Air Jamaica Ltd. v. Charlton*, [1999] U.K.P.C. 20, [1999] 1 W.L.R. 1399; *Twinsectra Ltd. v. Yardley*, [2002] U.K.H.L. 12, [2002] 2 A.C. 164, [2002] 2 All E.R. 377; P. Millett, "Restitution and Constructive Trusts" (1998), 114 L.Q.R. 399.

10 American Law Institute, *Restatement of the Law of Trusts, Second* (St. Paul, 1959) §404; P. Birks, "Restitution and Resulting Trusts" in S. Goldstein, ed., *Equity and Contemporary Legal Developments* (Jerusalem, 1992) 335; R. Chambers, *Resulting Trusts* (Oxford: Clarendon Press, 1997); R. Chambers, "Resulting Trusts in Canada" (2000), 38 Alberta L. Rev. 378; P. Birks, *Unjust Enrichment* (Oxford: Oxford University Press, 2003) 136-137.

11 W.J. Swadling, "A New Role for Resulting Trusts?" (1996), 16 Legal Studies 110; C.E.F. Rickett & R. Grantham, "Resulting trusts — A Rather Limited Doctrine" in P. Birks & F. Rose, eds., *Restitution and Equity, Volume One: Resulting Trusts and Equitable Compensation* (London: Mansfield Press, 2000) 39.

12 See, *e.g.*, *Statute of Frauds*, R.S.O. 1990, c. S.19, s. 9.

13 15 & 16 Geo. 5, c. 20 (U.K.).

14 [1897] 1 Ch. 196.

could not be used to prevent evidence of fraud and, therefore, Hodgson was permitted to prove the oral trust. Under section 70(1) of the *Land Registration Act, 1925*,[15] all registered land was subject to certain overriding interests, including the "rights of every person in actual occupation of the land". Although Hodgson had remained in occupation of the land throughout, the judge interpreted this section to exclude the rights of a vendor in occupation and dismissed her claim.

The Court of Appeal allowed Hodgson's appeal. Since Hodgson was in actual occupation of the land, Marks and the building society held their interests subject to her overriding interest. This part of the judgment considers the basis on which Evans held the land in trust for Hodgson.

RUSSELL L.J.:

. . .

The judge found, on the evidence, that despite the reference to love and affection as consideration in the transfer of her house to Mr. Evans, the plaintiff did not intend to make any gift to him, and that it was well understood, and indeed orally arranged between them, that the beneficial ownership was to remain in the plaintiff. This finding of fact was not challenged.

At the outset, to get the point out of the way, let me say that such a finding disposes of any question of undue influence; any such case assumes a transfer of the beneficial interest, but in circumstances which entitle the transferor to recall it.

. . .

I turn next to the question whether section 53(1) of the Law of Property Act 1925 prevents the assertion by the plaintiff of her entitlement in equity to the house. Let me first assume that, contrary to the view expressed by the judge, Mr. Marks is not debarred from relying upon the section, and the express oral arrangement or declaration of trust between the plaintiff and Mr. Evans found by the judge was not effective as such. Nevertheless, the evidence is clear that the transfer was not intended to operate as a gift, and, in those circumstances, I do not see why there was not a resulting trust of the beneficial interest to the plaintiff, which would not, of course, be affected by section 53(1). It was argued that a resulting trust is based upon implied intention, and that where there is an express trust for the transferor intended and declared — albeit ineffectively — there is no room for such an implication. I do not accept that. If an attempted express trust fails, that seems to me just the occasion for implication of a resulting trust, whether the failure be due to uncertainty, or perpetuity, or lack of form. It would be a strange outcome if the plaintiff were to lose her beneficial interest because her evidence had not been confined to negativing a gift but had additionally moved into a field

---

15 *Supra*, note 13, c. 21.

forbidden by section 53(1) for lack of writing. I remark in this connection that we are not concerned with the debatable question whether on a voluntary transfer of land by A to stranger B there is a presumption of a resulting trust. The accepted evidence is that this was not intended as a gift, notwithstanding the reference to love and affection in the transfer, and section 53(1) does not exclude that evidence.

. . .

On the above footing it matters not whether Mr. Marks was or was not debarred from relying upon section 53(1) by the principle that the section is not to be used as an instrument for fraud. Mr. Marks was in fact ignorant of the plaintiff's interest and it is forcefully argued that there is nothing fraudulent in his taking advantage of the section. I do not propose to canvass the general point further, more particularly in the light of the nature of the subject-matter with which we are dealing — an overriding interest. Quite plainly Mr. Evans could not have placed any reliance on section 53, for that would have been to use the section as an instrument of fraud. Accordingly, at the moment before the registration of Mr. Marks as registered proprietor there was in existence an overriding interest in the plaintiff, and by force of the statute the registration could only take effect subject thereto.

. . .

Accordingly, I would allow the appeal with such order as may be consequential on the establishment by the plaintiff of her overriding beneficial entitlement to the premises.

Notes and Questions

1. Are the facts that give rise to a resulting trust the same or different from the facts that give rise to an express trust? According to William Swadling, the resulting trust is created by a presumed intention to create a trust and not by the absence of intention to make a gift. He argued that *Hodgson v. Marks* does not support the contrary view because the trust in that case was not resulting, but express or constructive.[16] Either Mrs. Hodgson was permitted to prove her express trust notwithstanding the lack of writing or Mr. Evans (and his successors in title) were not allowed to benefit from his fraud.

2. If Mrs. Hodgson was allowed to enforce an oral express trust against the innocent Mr. Marks and the building society, under what circumstances would an express trust ever fail for lack of writing? What is the purpose of the writing requirements of the *Statute of Frauds* and equivalent statutes in common law jurisdictions around the world? Who are they designed to protect? On what basis would a court be justified ignoring the statute?

3. If, instead of a trust for herself, Mrs. Hodgson had intended to create an oral express trust for her nephew, would the outcome of the case have been any different?

---

16 W.J. Swadling, "A Hard Look at *Hodgson v. Marks*" in P. Birks & F. Rose, eds., *Restitution and Equity, Volume One: Resulting Trusts and Equitable Compensation* (London: Mansfield Press, 2000) 61.

(c) **Distinctions**

There is still much uncertainty and confusion about the meaning and content of the different types of trust. This is regrettable because the distinctions are of practical significance. Thus, for example, an express trust of land is unenforceable unless it is evidenced in writing,[17] whereas trusts arising by operation of law are not subject to this formal requirement.[18] Similarly, while under some of the provincial statutes of limitations,[19] as interpreted by the case law, express trustees are not protected by limitation periods, resulting and certain kinds of constructive trustees are.[20] Moreover, while persons under a disability may be precluded from being express trustees and are subject to removal if they are appointed trustees, such persons can be trustees of trusts arising by operation of law.[21] Finally, the obligations imposed upon an express trustee are normally more onerous than those expected of a resulting or constructive trustee.

The cases and commentators agree that an express trust arises from the expressed intention of its creator, but there is no such unanimity about the expressions "implied trust," "resulting trust," and "constructive trust." Indeed, some cases refer to all three as though there were no distinctions among them.[22] To some extent this confusion is fostered by statutes which also fail to distinguish between these terms.[23] Imprecise terminology leads to imprecise analysis, with resulting confusion in the law.

For the reasons given in chapter 1, the term "implied trust" is not used in this book. It should not be used to describe either resulting or constructive trusts. The courts sometimes assume that there is little difference between the latter two types of trusts either. Thus, for example, in *Hussey v. Palmer*,[24] Lord Denning said:

> Although the plaintiff alleged that there was a resulting trust, I should have thought that the trust in this case, if there was one, was more in the nature of a constructive trust; but this is more a matter of words than anything else. The two run together.

---

17 *Statute of Frauds*, R.S.O. 1990, c. S.19, s. 9.
18 *Ibid.*, s. 10. See, *e.g.*, *Chrustie v. Minister of National Revenue*, 84 D.T.C. 1465, 1984 CarswellNat 385, [1984] C.T.C. 2533 (T.C.C.).
19 *E.g.*, *The Limitation of Actions Act*, R.S.S. 1978, c. L-15, ss. 42, 43. Under the *Limitations Act, 2002*, S.O. 2002, c. 24, Sched. B, and the *Limitations Act*, R.S.A. 2000, c. L-12, no exemptions are made for claims for breach of trust.
20 See *Taylor v. Davies* (1919), [1920] A.C. 636, 1919 CarswellOnt 11, [1920] 1 W.W.R. 683, 51 D.L.R. 75 (P.C.); *Blake, Re*, [1932] 1 Ch. 54; *J.L.O. Ranch Ltd. v. Logan* (1987), 54 Alta. L.R. (2d) 130, 1987 CarswellAlta 184, 27 E.T.R. 1, 81 A.R. 261 (Q.B.).
21 See *Vinogradoff, Re*, [1935] W.N. 68.
22 See, *e.g.*, *Gissing v. Gissing* (1970), [1971] A.C. 886 at 905, [1970] 2 All E.R. 780, [1970] 3 W.L.R. 255 (H.L.) *per* Lord Diplock.
23 *E.g.*, the *Statute of Frauds*, R.S.O. 1990, c. S.19, s. 10, speaks of a trust which "arises or results by implication or construction of law", while the *Land Titles Act*, R.S.A. 2000, c. L-4, s. 47, refers to "trusts, whether expressed, implied or constructive".
24 [1972] 1 W.L.R. 1286, [1972] 3 All E.R. 744 (C.A.), at 1289 [W.L.R.].

Another example is *Rupar v. Rupar*.[25] A mother had given money to her son in order to enable him to purchase a house. The court noted that the mother's action against her son's widow in respect of the house was based "upon implied or constructive trust." Clearly the circumstances could only give rise to a resulting trust.

The terms "resulting trust" and "constructive trust" may not be capable of precise definition. This is partly because of overlap between the two and partly because the circumstances in which constructive trusts arise are numerous and diffuse. What is commonly done is to define these terms, in particular the term "resulting trust," by reference to the several situations in which they arise. While this works reasonably well in practice, it is clearly inadequate from a taxonomic point of view. Nevertheless, in order to understand the distinctions between the two, it is convenient, first of all, to consider the origins of the resulting trust and the situations in which it arises.

If resulting trusts are analysed as not being created directly by intention, then they do not differ greatly from constructive trusts. Both arise by operation of law in response to certain facts. As discussed in chapters 10 and 11 below, constructive trusts can arise when someone wrongfully acquires assets, such as an agent who profits by secretly competing with his or her principal or by taking a bribe. They can also arise when someone makes a specifically enforceable promise to transfer an asset to another, when someone detrimentally relies on an intention to benefit another, or in response to unjust enrichment. Unjust enrichment occurs when the trustee is enriched, the beneficiary has suffered a corresponding deprivation, and there is an absence of juristic reason for the enrichment.[26]

A careful consideration of the events giving rise to constructive trusts is essential for a proper understanding of those trusts. Unfortunately, it does not make it easier distinguishing them from resulting trusts. The standard Canadian definition of unjust enrichment can also apply to all cases of resulting trust. If the resulting trustee is required to return an asset because its provider did not intend to make a gift to the trustee, it can be said (at a slightly higher level of abstraction) that there is an absence of juristic reason for the enrichment of the resulting trustee at the expense of the person who transferred that enrichment to, or purchased it for, the resulting trustee and thereby suffered a corresponding deprivation.

It may be that the resulting trust is simply a subcategory of constructive trust. Regarded this way, we would then say that express trusts are created directly by intention, while all other trusts are created by operation of law in response to wrongful enrichment, unjust enrichment, and other events.[27] All trusts arising by operation of law are constructive, except that some of the trusts that respond to unjust enrichment are resulting, while trusts created by statute are called statutory trusts. Whether a trust created by unjust enrichment is constructive or resulting

---

25 (1964), 49 W.W.R. 226, 46 D.L.R. (2d) 553, 1964 CarswellBC 128 (S.C.).

26 *Becker v. Pettkus*, [1980] 2 S.C.R. 834, 117 D.L.R. (3d) 257, 1980 CarswellOnt 299, 1980 CarswellOnt 644, 34 N.R. 384, 8 E.T.R. 143, 19 R.F.L. (2d) 165, at 273-274 [D.L.R.].

27 See P. Birks, "Equity, Conscience, and Unjust Enrichment" (1999), 23 Melbourne U.L. Rev. 1; P. Birks, *Unjust Enrichment* (Oxford: Oxford University Press, 2003) 262-266.

depends primarily on the context in which it arises. If it involves a failed express trust or an apparent gift, then we usually call it a resulting trust.

(d) When a Resulting Trust Arises and When It Is Precluded

As discussed above, a resulting trust is raised in certain situations when the transferor or purchaser does not, or does not intend to, dispose of the entire beneficial interest. These situations are said to give rise to a resulting trust when the owner of the legal title transfers it to another voluntarily or purchases property and directs title to be taken in the name of another person. In fact, although it is convenient to speak of the legal title in these situations, a resulting trust, just like an express trust, may arise out of a transfer or purchase of an equitable interest in property.[28]

It should be noted that when a person lacks donative intent in whole or in part, it is incorrect to say that he or she merely transfers the legal estate but retains the equitable interest. This is because the owner of property does not have two estates, a legal and an equitable, but has an absolute, unfragmented estate and it is that estate which is transferred.[29] The resulting trust is a new equitable interest that arises because the transferor lacked donative intent and therefore the title holder has an equitable obligation to hold the property for the benefit of the transferor.[30]

It follows from this that, since the equitable obligation arises immediately upon the transfer or purchase, the resulting trust also arises at that time. It is true that the parties may not have given much thought to the matter until one of them brings an action to sort out their differences, but the resulting trust is not created by a court's declaration that B holds property upon resulting trust for A. It exists as soon as the equitable obligation arises and the judicial order is merely the court's imprimatur upon an existing state of facts. This concept may also be put this way: a resulting trust exists as soon as an equitable obligation rests upon B to hold property upon trust for A because A did not intend that B should have the beneficial interest and A did not give it to anyone else. A may need to obtain a court judgment if B resists A's request for a transfer of the property. However, the judgment merely declares the trust and does not cause it to arise.

As discussed below, Canadian courts have also recognized resulting trusts arising out of the parties' common intention in the context of matrimonial and cohabitation property disputes. It is said to arise where one (lawful or *de facto*) spouse has contributed in money or money's worth to the acquisition of assets by the other spouse. Since these contributions may occur over a period of time, it may be difficult to determine exactly when the trust arises. This may have im-

---

28 See *Vandervell's Trusts (No. 2), Re, supra,* note 6, at 296, *per* Megarry J.

29 *Cf. Commissioner of Stamp Duties (Queensland) v. Livingston* (1964), [1965] A.C. 694, [1964] 3 All E.R. 692 (Australia P.C.).

30 *D.K.L.R. Holdings Co. (No. 2) Pty. Ltd. v. Commissioner of Stamp Duties (N.S.W.),* [1980] 1 N.S.W.L.R. 510 (C.A.), at 519, *per* Hope J.A., affirmed (1982), 149 C.L.R. 431 at 464, *per* Aickin J.

portant consequences for tax and other reasons. However, we submit that this trust is not resulting, but constructive, and address this issue later in this chapter.

There are at least two situations in which a resulting trust may be precluded. The first is when a person has transferred assets for an illegal purpose. Some of the cases suggest that if the transferor resiles from the transaction before the illegal purpose can be carried into effect, he or she will be able to recover the assets. However, in a series of cases involving transfers to spouses to avoid creditors, the usual conclusion is that, if the transferor has to rebut the presumption of advancement, he or she will be precluded from recovering the assets. These cases are discussed below.

The second situation occurs when assets are given on trust for a charitable purpose, which cannot be carried out or fails to consume all of the assets. In that case, the assets may be applied *cy-près* for similar charitable purposes. If the settlor's chosen purpose is impossible at the outset, the assets will be applied *cy-près* if the settlor had a general charitable intention, but will result to the settlor if he or she had the intention to benefit only a specific charity. If the assets have been applied for the charitable purpose and that purpose fails later, any surplus will be applied *cy-près* so long as no one else has an interest in them. These matters are considered in more detail above in chapter 7.

If the trust is for a non-charitable purpose, then to the extent that the trust fails (and is not converted to a power of appointment by statute, as discussed in the previous chapter), there will be a resulting trust to the creator of the trust.

3. FAILURE OF EXPRESS TRUSTS

(a) Introduction

When an express trust fails, in whole or in part, the usual response to that failure is a resulting trust for the settlor. Otherwise, the trustees would receive an unintended benefit at the settlor's expense, because they would hold the remaining trust assets free of any trust. Although it is sometimes called an automatic resulting trust (as discussed above), a resulting trust does not automatically arise every time an express trust fails.

To begin, there is no need for a resulting trust unless the trust assets have been transferred from the settlor to the trustees. If a person declares him- or herself to be a trustee for another, and that trust fails in whole or in part, the declarant-trustee will continue to own the remaining trust assets free of the trust. A resulting trust is unnecessary and impossible, since a person cannot be a trustee solely for his or her own benefit. This is also true when an intended express trust fails to arise because it is incompletely constituted (as discussed in chapter 4). Since the trust failed because the settlor failed to transfer legal title to the intended trustees, the settlor remains the owner of the trust assets and a resulting trust will not arise.

If the settlor has transferred the trust assets to the trustees intending to create an express trust and that trust fails initially or subsequently, then normally the trustees will hold the remainder on resulting trust for the settlor. This is because the settlor did not intend to give the remaining trust assets to the trustees. Normally, the assets were transferred to them to be used only for trust purposes and they are not permitted to keep the excess for themselves. However, if the admissible evidence proves that the settlor did intend to make a gift of the surplus to the trustees, they will be allowed to keep the remainder for themselves and no resulting trust will arise.

There are also some cases which suggest that the settlor can abandon his or her interest in the trust assets and, in that case, any surplus will belong to the Crown as *bona vacantia* (ownerless goods). However, those cases fail to explain why the trustees, as legal owners of the trust assets, are not permitted to keep those assets for their own benefit. This is discussed further below.

When dealing with a possible surplus of trust assets, there are two main questions that must be answered in order to ascertain the fate of those assets: first, did an express trust fail and, secondly, did the settlor intend to give the surplus to the trustees? There will be a resulting trust for the settlor if an express trust (or attempted express trust) failed and the settlor did not intend to give the remaining trust assets to the trustees. In the vast majority of cases, these questions are easily answered and cause no concern. However, as the cases below reveal, they can be difficult.

There is a preliminary question that must be answered before the two main questions can be addressed: who is the settlor? Since both of the main questions are answered by examining the settlor's intentions, that examination cannot begin until the settlor is identified. Like the main questions, this is rarely ever difficult, but can create problems from time to time. For example, if A voluntarily transferred assets to B in trust for C and C disclaimed his or her interest, the trust would fail and the assets would result to A. Suppose, however, that B provided consideration for A's transfer. In that case, B would probably be treated as the creator of the trust, for it is as though A first transferred the assets to B and B then declared a trust in favour of C. Hence, in those circumstances, normally there would be no resulting trust since B is the declarant-trustee, already has title to the trust assets, and is permitted to retain them for his or her own benefit. For the same reason, if A paid consideration to X to transfer assets to B in trust for C and the trust failed, the assets would result to A, not X. Moreover, the property could also result to A if A paid B to declare a trust of B's assets for C's benefit and the trust failed.[31]

If more than one person pays the consideration, the property will result to them in the proportions that each contributed.

Notes and Questions

1. What happens to assets, which A has given to B upon a general power of appointment, if B appoints to C in trust for D and the trust fails? Would there be any difference

---

31 See Scott, §§422A-425.

if the power was special? What would happen in either case if there was a gift over in default of appointment?[32]

2. X is the beneficiary under a trust and he has the right to terminate it. He directs his trustee, A, to transfer the property to B in trust for C. The latter trust fails. What result?[33]

(b) Did an Express Trust Fail?

There are many different reasons why an express trust may fail, either in whole or in part. For example, it may fail because its creator made a fundamental mistake, as where he or she signs a settlement thinking that it was another document and having no intention to sign the settlement, in which case the trust is void. Alternatively, the creation of the trust may have been procured by fraud, duress, undue influence, or misrepresentation, or it may have been improvident, in which case it is voidable. A trust may also fail because it does not comply with a rule of law such as a formality prescribed by statute or the rules against perpetuities or accumulations. If there is uncertainty of objects a trust will fail.[34] Further, objects may cease to exist by reason of lapse, for example, when a beneficiary under a testamentary trust predeceases the testator or when a beneficiary disclaims his or her interest under a trust. Then again, a trust may fail because its purposes are illegal or contrary to public policy. Finally, a trust may fail because the purpose for which it was made becomes impossible.

In many of the foregoing situations, the trust will fail in its entirety. In others, for example, when one of two or more beneficiaries disclaims, there may be only a partial failure of the trust. To the extent that the trust fails and the beneficial interest is not disposed of in some other way, the normal response is a resulting trust for the settlor or his or her estate. The two main exceptions to this are, first, where the settlor intended the trustee to keep the surplus as a gift and, secondly, where the resulting trust fails for illegality. These situations are discussed below.

In some of these cases, there may actually be no surplus undisposed of by the trust or in some other way. For example, suppose that a testatrix transfers $50,000 to trustees in trust for her son, S, absolutely. If S disclaims his interest in the trust, it will result to the testatrix's estate and be disposed of by her will or according to the rules governing intestacy. Suppose, however, that the gift was in trust for S for life with the remainder to S's children in equal shares. Then, if S disclaims his life interest, there may or may not be a resulting trust. That depends on whether the remainder interest accelerates, which depends in turn on whether the testatrix intended to postpone the interest of S's children merely to S's life interest or until S's death regardless of what should happen. If she had the former intention, the remainder interest will vest in possession immediately. If the latter, it will not vest until S's death and there will then be an undisposed-of life interest

---

32 A general power of appointment is a power to dispose of property given by the owner of the property. See the chapter on trusts and powers. See also Scott, §§426-7.

33 See Scott, §428.

34 If there is no certainty of intention or subject matter, there is no trust at all.

which will result to the testator's estate.[35] The general rule appears to be that, unless the will provides otherwise, there will be an acceleration.[36] Clearly, if, in the above example, the interests of S's children were contingent, there could be no acceleration until the contingency was satisfied.

(i) *Trust or Gift?*

When faced with a possible failure of express trust, a court will, if possible, construe the transaction in a way that avoids failure. This is especially true when the disposition is testamentary. People who make wills do so intending to dispose of all the assets involved. Therefore, a construction which avoids failure is usually the best way to give effect to the settlor's intentions. One way to achieve this is to say that there was no trust, but an absolute gift. This is possible if any conditions attached to the gift can genuinely be regarded as motives for giving rather than restrictions on the donee's use of the assets. In *Barrett, Re*, below, the testator's words were ambiguous, leaving the court with a choice between a trust with a large, undisposed of surplus or an absolute gift.

BARRETT, RE

(1914), 6 O.W.N. 267, 26 O.W.R. 305
Supreme Court of Ontario
(Appellate Division)

The testator provided in paragraph 26 of his will,

> I hereby give to my daughter Sarah Frances Barrett whatever sum or sums of money may be to my credit in any bank or upon my person or in my domicile at the time of my decease for the purpose of enabling my said daughter to meet the immediate current expenses in connection with housekeeping.

At the date of the will the testator had only a small amount of money in his bank account, but when he died the account contained $17,200. Sarah claimed that she was entitled to this amount absolutely, but her brothers and sisters contested the claim. The executors brought an application to construe the will. At first instance, Middleton J. concluded that the surplus after the purpose described by the testator had been fulfilled should result to his estate:[37]

> Counsel did not refer me to any case like this, nor have I been able to find one. Had the gift been to the daughter for her own use, an expression of the motive or object or purpose of the gift would not interfere with her absolute title; but here the testator has expressed a purpose which is

---

35 See *Jacques, Re* (1985), 49 O.R. (2d) 623, 16 D.L.R. (4th) 472, 1985 CarswellOnt 694, 18 E.T.R. 65 (H.C.), reversed (1986), 55 O.R. (2d) 534, 1986 CarswellOnt 662, 23 E.T.R. 78, 29 D.L.R. (4th) 319 (C.A.).

36 See *Coulson, Re* (1977), 16 O.R. (2d) 497, 78 D.L.R. 435, 1977 CarswellOnt 385, 1 E.T.R. 1 (C.A.).

37 (1914), 5 O.W.N. 805 at 806.

not personal to the daughter. It is, I think, more than mere motive; it amounts to a trust. The testator was maintaining a household. His daughter was living with him. On his death he did not contemplate an instantaneous scattering of the family living with him; and the money on hand, either as cash in the house, or on deposit in the bank, was given to his daughter "to meet the immediate current expenses in connection with housekeeping;" not merely his household debts, but all that could fairly be regarded as falling within that designation during a reasonable time after his death, pending the family reorganisation. All money not needed for that purpose belongs to the estate as a resulting trust. *In re West*,[38] collects the more important authorities.

Sarah appealed.

MEREDITH C.J.O. delivered the judgment of the Court:

. . .

No question would probably have arisen as to the meaning of this provision but for the fact that the testator had at the time of his death at his credit in his bank the large sum of $17,200.

It is very probable that if the testator had contemplated when he made his will that so large a sum of $17,200 would be at his credit in his bank at the time of his decease he would have made a different provision as to the disposition of it from that contained in paragraph 26, but that, in my opinion, affords no reason for putting a construction on the language of the testator different from that which would be placed upon it if the fund amounted to no more than $500.

My learned brother's view was that the legatee is not entitled to the fund absolutely, but that a trust is created, and that all money not needed for the purpose which the testator mentioned "belongs to the estate as a resulting trust."

I am, with respect, unable to agree with this view, and am of opinion that the clear words of gift to the daughter are not cut down or controlled by the statement of the testator as to the purpose or object of the gift.

Such a provision in favour of a wife is spoken of by Kay J., in *Coward v. Larkman*,[39] as "the usual provision for a wife after her husband's death." The bequest in that case was of £100 to the wife "for her present wants and for housekeeping expenses," and it was not suggested that any trust was created or that the wife was not entitled to the £100 absolutely, but the contrary was taken for granted in all the Courts before which the case came.[40]

In *Hart v. Tribe*,[41] one of the questions was as to the effect of a provision of a will in these words: "I also request my sister to give her, the said Maria, my wife, the sum of £100 out of any money which may be in the house or at my banker's at the time of my decease, for her present expenses of herself and the children;" and it was held that this was an absolute gift to the wife of the £100.

---

38 [1900] 1 Ch. 84.
39 (1887), 56 L.T.R. 278 at 280.
40 *Ibid.*; (1869), 60 L.T.R. 1.
41 (1854), 18 Beav. 215, 52 E.R. 85.

. . .

I am unable to see how, if the wife in that case was entitled to the £100 absolutely, on what principle it can properly be held that the legatee in the case at bar is not entitled to receive the whole of the fund bequeathed to her or that she can be called upon to account for the mode in which she may have expended it.

While it may probably have been intended by the testator that the legatee should temporarily keep up the house in which he was living at the time of his death, and that his other unmarried daughters should continue to live with her in it, there is nothing in the language of the paragraph in question to create a duty on the part of the legatee to keep up the house or to maintain it as a residence for herself and her sisters, or to indicate that anything but a benefit personal to the legatee was intended.

What the paragraph means, I think, is, that whatever money there should be at the time of the testator's death in the places mentioned, whether it should be more or less, should belong to the legatee to enable her to meet the immediate current expenses in connection with housekeeping; and to treat the provision as meaning that a fund was created out of which the legatee was to pay the testator's household debts and "all that could fairly be regarded as falling within that designation during a reasonable time after his death, pending the family reorganisation," is to read into the will something which, with great respect for the contrary opinion of my brother Middleton, the testator has not said, and which the language he has used to express his intention does not import.

I would vary the order appealed from by substituting for the declaration contained in its third paragraph a declaration that Sarah Frances Barrett is entitled under the provisions of the 26th paragraph of the will to receive absolutely all money which the deceased at the time of his death had at his credit in any bank or upon his person or in his domicile; and, with that variation, I would affirm the order.

Notes and Questions

1. Note that *Barrett, Re* speaks of money given for a purpose. Do not confuse this case and others like it with purpose trusts, however. A purpose trust is one in which the object is a purpose, such as the advancement of education. In *Barrett, Re*, even if the judgment of Middleton J. had been upheld, the trust would not have been a purpose trust, since it would have been for the direct benefit of individuals.

2. The problem in these cases arises out of the fact that the maker of the trust has not expressed his or her intention clearly, or, it may be, has not declared a trust at all. That was the problem in *Trusts of the Abbott Fund, Re*.[42] Mr. Abbott had made adequate provision for his two deaf-mute daughters in his will, but the trust fund was lost through the defalcations of the trustee. Friends of the family issued a circular and collected a large amount of money by soliciting subscriptions from other friends and neighbours. The two women were supported from this fund until the death of the survivor, at which time there was a surplus still remaining. The subscribers were all known. The question arose whether

---

42 [1900] 2 Ch. 326.

they had intended to make an out and out gift of the fund to the two women jointly, so that the surplus would pass to the survivor's estate, or whether there was a resulting trust of the surplus that would revert to the subscribers. Stirling J. said:[43]

> I cannot believe that [the fund] was ever intended to become the absolute property of the ladies so that they should be in a position to demand a transfer of it to themselves, or so that if they became bankrupt the trustee in the bankruptcy should be able to claim it. I believe it was intended that it should be administered by ... the trustees who had been nominated in pursuance of the circular. I do not think the ladies ever became absolute owners of this fund. I think that the trustee or trustees were intended to have a wide discretion as to whether any, and if any what, part of the fund should be applied for the benefit of the ladies and how the application should be made. That view would not deprive them of all right in the fund, because if the trustees had not done their duty — if they either failed to exercise their discretion or exercised it improperly — the ladies might successfully have applied to the Court to have the fund administered according to the terms of the circular. In the result, therefore, there must be a declaration that there is a resulting trust of the moneys remaining unapplied for the benefit of the subscribers to the Abbott Fund.

3. The conclusion reached in the *Abbott* case is not the usual one. The general rule is that stated by Page Wood V.C. in *Sanderson, Re*:[44]

> [T]here are two classes of cases between which the general distinction is sufficiently clear, although the precise line of demarcation is occasionally somewhat difficult to ascertain. If a gross sum be given, or if the whole income of the property be given, and a special purpose be assigned for that gift, this Court always regards the gift as absolute, and the purpose merely as the motive of the gift, and therefore holds that the gift takes effect as to the whole sum or the whole income, as the case may be.

This principle was applied by Kekewich J. in *Andrew's Trust, Re*.[45] In that case, friends of a deceased clergyman had collected moneys for the education of the deceased's children, who were all infants. The person who was instrumental in collecting the moneys wrote to one of the trustees that the fund was intended solely for the education of the deceased's children and that it was not intended for the exclusive use of any one of them, nor for equal division among them. Various amounts had been used for the children's education. After the children reached their majority, they brought an application for advice and directions. Kekewich J. distinguished the *Abbott* case and held that the education of the children was merely the motive of the gift, the trustees being given a discretion to apply it for their benefit while they were minors, but apart from that the children were entitled absolutely. His Lordship held that, since the children were now adults, there was no longer any discretion in the trustees and, therefore, the moneys should be divided equally.

4. A testator bequeathed specific assets, as well as the residue of his estate, to his wife, "for her maintenance and for the training of my daughter ... up to university grade and for the maintenance of my aged mother." The testator's mother predeceased him. His wife survived him and died in 1970. The daughter finished her university education in

---

43 *Ibid.*, at 330-331.
44 (1857), 3 Kay & J. 497 at 503, 69 E.R. 1206, 3 Jur. (N.S.) 658, 5 W.R. 864.
45 [1905] 2 Ch. 48 (Eng. Ch. Div.).

1975. A substantial surplus remained. Is there a resulting trust to the estate? If not, how should the beneficiaries share the surplus?[46]

(ii) *The Rule in* Hancock v. Watson

Another way to avoid a resulting trust is by applying the rule of construction known either as the rule in *Lassence v. Tierney*[47] or as the rule in *Hancock v. Watson*.[48] In the latter case, Lord Davey stated the rule as follows:[49]

> [I]t is settled law that if you find an absolute gift to a legatee in the first instance, and trusts are engrafted or imposed on that absolute interest which fail, either from lapse or invalidity or any other reason, then the absolute gift takes effect so far as the trusts have failed to the exclusion of the residuary legatee or next of kin as the case may be.

Hancock v. Watson involved the following facts. The testator left the residue of his estate to trustees in trust to be divided equally among four persons, including X. However, he then went on to provide that X's portion be held in trust for her for life with remainder (in the events which happened) in trust for others. That remainder interest was void for remoteness. The portion for X was construed as an absolute gift for X, from which the invalid remainder was carved, rather than as a life interest for X, with an invalid remainder tacked on. Therefore, X took her portion free of the invalid remainder and there was no resulting trust.

This rule is examined further in *Goodhue Trusts, Re*, below.

GOODHUE TRUSTS, RE

(1920), 47 O.L.R. 178
Supreme Court of Ontario
(High Court of Justice)

In 1869 George Jervis Goodhue settled $30,000 upon trust for his daughter Harriet Amelia Thomas when she married. The money was to be held for her for life with remainder in trust for such of her issue as Harriet should by ded or will appoint and in default of appointment in trust for all her children equally at age 21 or marriage, whichever should occur first. Harriet died in 1892 and by her will she purported to deal with the corpus as though it were her own property. She gave the residue of her estate, including the $30,000, upon trust to pay her debts and to divide proceeds of a certain insurance policy into five equal parts, one each for four surviving children and one for the children of her deceased son, "this being the only portion of my estate to be divided into five parts." The balance of the residue she disposed of as follows:

---

46 See *Osaba, Re*, [1979] 1 W.L.R. 247, [1979] 2 All E.R. 393 (C.A.).
47 (1849), 1 Mac. & G. 551, 41 E.R. 1379 (Ch. Div.).
48 [1902] A.C. 14 (H.L.).
49 *Ibid.*, at 22.

> The whole residue of my estate I give and bequeath to my four living children equally to be disposed of by them respectively by last will but not otherwise and subject to the distribution and payment of the... income as hereinafter mentioned until the death of my last surviving child.... To pay monthly by cheque the net revenue and income of the residue of my estate in equal shares or proportions to my surviving children... so long as they shall live.

This was followed by provisions for the husbands of the testatrix's two daughters and the wife of one of her sons, which were to take effect on certain specified events. The will continued:

> I authorise each of my children to bequeath to any charitable object or objects or to relatives or other individuals a sum or sums of money not to exceed in the aggregate the sum of $5,000 of the share of such child of mine, thus reducing the income of such child and of his or her children, and I further empower my children to indicate and determine by last will the proportion which each of his or her children shall have of the income, that is, each of my children may divide the bequest of the income to his or her children in unequal shares or the whole to one child without assigning any reason.

The trustees of the settlement brought this application for an order determining whether the disposition made by Harriet by her will was a valid execution of the power and if not, whether they should distribute the $30,000 in accordance with the trust deed or otherwise.

The court held first that the limitations following the appointment in favour of the testatrix's four living children were void for perpetuity and probably also because they were in favour of persons who were not objects of the power. The court then continued:

MASTEN J.:

The narrow question really in controversy resolves itself into this: Does the will of Mrs. Thomas, upon its true construction, confer an absolute gift on her four children, followed by limitations which are invalid, or does the will, upon its true construction, effectively confer on those four children no more than a life estate? In other words, do the four living children take the whole interest free of any conditions or limitations, or do they take a life-interest only — and is there a failure to appoint as to the residue?

. . .

The rule of law applicable to the solution of these questions has been stated in the House of Lords in *Hancock v. Watson*[50] as follows:

> [His Lordship quoted the statement of the rule set out above, referred to the history of the rule and to the principle that the case law is only illustrative of the rule, and continued.]

---

50 *Supra,* note 48.

With a view of indicating the limits of the rule and of illustrating its application in various sets of circumstances, as well as for the purpose of suggesting various considerations which may assist the Court in reaching a conclusion, it may be useful to recapitulate a selected few of the cases which I have considered.

Kampf v. Jones[51] shews that the rule as stated in *Carver v. Bowles*[52] applies to appointments under a power in the same manner as to a devise or bequest under a will.

. . .

In *McDonald v. McDonald*,[53] the rule is thus stated by the Lord Chancellor:

> From all those cases the plain rule is derivable that, if you cannot disconnect that which is imposed by way of condition, or mode of enjoyment, from a gift, the gift itself may be found to be involved in conditions so much beyond the power that it becomes void. But where that is not so, where you have a gift to an object of the power, and where you have nothing alleged to invalidate that gift, but conditions which are attempted to be imposed as to the mode in which that object of the power is to enjoy what is given to him, there the gift may be valid, and take effect without reference to those conditions.

And Lord Hatherley in the same case[54] distinguished it—

> ...from all the cases in which you find the gift only in a continued series of limitations expressed in the instrument, without any complete severance of the share at once, and in which you find a subsequent dealing with that share and interests allotted and apportioned in it to the parties intended to be benefited; and in those cases, if those parties be out of the range of the power, the appointment becomes vitiated, because you cannot separate it from a continued series of limitations. But where we have a share taken out of the general trust-fund, and completely, and clearly, and neatly, severed from the rest of the fund, subsequent limitations do not prejudice the absolute gift.

. . .

I think that in the present case there is an absolute appointment of the settled fund, vesting it equally in the four living children, subject to certain temporary limitations as to its enjoyment, not warranted by the power, but with a power ultimately of full disposition of the corpus by last will exercisable by the appointees — and that the words appointing the corpus in favour of the four living children are distinctly severable from the subsequent limitations of income in favour of persons who are not objects of the power and to whom a gift would be against the law of perpetuities.

I have been led to this conclusion by the following among other considerations: (1) There is an expressed intention to exercise the power of appointment

---

51 (1837), 2 Keen. 756, 48 E.R. 821.
52 (1831), 2 Russ. & My. 301, 39 E.R. 409.
53 (1875), L.R. 2 Sc. App. 482 at 488-489.
54 *Ibid.*, at 490.

over the fund in question. The testatrix by her will bequeaths her estate generally to her trustees, "including the Llangorse Farm in Wales, the Como property, and also the $30,000 settled upon me with power of disposition thereof by my father." A failure to appoint was not intended by the donee of the power. (2) There is an expressed intention to divide this fund among the four living children and to exclude the fifth branch of the family. The testatrix expressly directs that the moneys received from the Phoenix Life Insurance Company be divided among the four living children and the descendants of the son who was dead, "this being the only portion of my estate to be divided into five parts." (3) There is an absolute appointment of the corpus of the fund to the four living children, by the words "the whole residue of my estate I give and bequeath to my four living children equally."

If one stopped there, no question would arise, and the appointment would be clear and absolute. They are, however, immediately followed by the words, "to be disposed of by them respectively by last will but not otherwise, and subject to the payment of the revenues, interest, and income as hereinafter mentioned," etc., setting forth the trusts. In considering this provision one must bear in mind the terms of the original settlement, viz., that the power is to appoint only among the children of the donee of the power, and that such appointment is, by the preceding words, effectively made subject to an invalid limitation or modification restraining alienation except by will; also that nowhere else in the will of Mrs. Thomas is there any attempt to modify or vary this disposition of the corpus, the modifications which are attempted relating solely to income.

Mr. Cameron adopts the only line of argument that seems open to him, viz., to argue that the attempt to bequeath for an indefinite period the whole income to grandchildren as a class is equivalent to an attempt to bequeath to them the remainder in the corpus, and that as a matter of construction it demonstrates that the prior appointment to the four living children is of a life-estate only. No doubt, the testatrix intended to modify the control and power of alienation exercisable by her children over the shares appointed to them — but did she intend to take them away? Clearly not, for she gives them power to appoint the corpus by will, and the subsequent special directions relate to income only.

(4) Lastly, it is always to be borne in mind that the testatrix is dealing with the settled fund in question along with and as part of her general estate, and the special provisions which she makes permitting gifts to charities and otherwise infringing on her general scheme of preservation may be entirely valid with regard to that part of her estate other than the settled fund in question, and for purposes of construction are not to be relied on in the same manner as though the will related only to this settled fund.

[In the result, his Lordship held that the four living children were entitled to receive from the trustees of the marriage settlement their respective shares in the property settled by Goodhue upon his daughter, free from any conditions or limitations.]

Notes and Questions

1. In *Goodhue Trusts, Re*, Masten J. gave a list of principles to be deduced from the cases respecting the rule in *Hancock v. Watson*. The list has not been reproduced, but a similar, updated list is the following, contained in *Watson v. Holland*:[55]

> (1) In each case the court must ascertain from the language of the instrument as a whole whether there has been an initial absolute beneficial gift on to which inconsistent trusts have been engrafted.[56] (2) If the instrument discloses no separate initial gift but merely a gift coupled with a series of limitations over so as to form one system of trusts, then the rule will not apply.[57] (3) In most of the cases where the rule has been held to apply, the engrafted inconsistent trusts have been separated from the absolute gift either by being placed in a separate clause or sentence or by being introduced by words implying a contrast, such as a proviso or words such as 'but so that.'[58] But this is not an essential requirement, and in an appropriate context the engrafted trusts may be introduced by the word 'and' or the words 'and so that'....[59] (4) References in parts of the instrument other than the initial gift claimed to be absolute to the share of the donee are usually treated as indicative that the share is owned by the donee,[60] though in an appropriate context even a reference to a share given to a beneficiary will not be treated as belonging to the beneficiary....[61] (5) If a donor, by the trusts which follow the initial gift, has sought to provide for every eventuality by creating what prima facie are exhaustive trusts, it is the more difficult to construe the initial gift as an absolute gift.[62]

(iii) *Unincorporated Associations*

The problems concerning failure to dispose of the complete beneficial interest have also arisen in connection with gifts to unincorporated associations, such as clubs, some churches, and various other types of organizations, which have no personality in law. They are not recognized as corporations or partnerships. This creates a number of legal difficulties, the principal one being that they cannot hold assets in their collective name.[63] Rather, they must hold land and other assets by means of trustees and, while the association continues, the trustees hold the assets for the purposes of the organization.

What happens to the assets when the association is dissolved? If the association is charitable, the surplus assets should be distributed *cy-près* to similar charitable organizations. Indeed, this is a specific requirement if the association

---

55   [1985] 1 All E.R. 290 at 300.

56   See, *e.g.*, *Lassence v. Tierney, supra*, note 47, at 562; *Burton's Settlement Trusts, Re*, [1955] Ch. 348 (C.A.), at 360.

57   See *Rucker v. Scholefield* (1862), 1 Hem. & M. 36, 71 E.R. 16.

58   See, *e.g.*, *Hancock v. Watson, supra*, note 48; *A.G. v. Lloyds Bank Ltd.*, [1935] A.C. 382 (H.L.); *Litt's Will Trusts, Re*, [1946] Ch. 154 (C.A.).

59   See *Johnson's Settlement Trusts, Re*, [1943] Ch. 341; *Norton, Re*, [1949] W.N. 23 (C.A.).

60   See *A.G. v. Lloyds Bank Ltd., supra*, note 58; *Fyfe v. Irwin*, [1939] 2 All E.R. 271 at 282-283 (H.L.); *Burton's Settlement Trusts, Re, supra*, note 56, at 356, 361.

61   See *Re Goold's Will Trusts, Lloyds Bank Ltd. v. Goold*, [1967] 3 All E.R. 652.

62   See *Lassence v. Tierney, supra*, note 47, at 567; *A.G. v. Lloyds Bank Ltd., supra*, note 58, at 395.

63   Special legislation does exist for certain organizations, such as churches, whereby they may hold property in a quasi-corporate capacity through trustees, but this is an exceptional situation. See, *e.g. Religious Organizations' Land Act*, R.S.O. 1990, c. R.23.

is a registered charity under the *Income Tax Act*.[64] However, this is not an option if the organization is non-charitable. Should the assets be distributed among the members who contributed to it, among the members remaining at dissolution, or to the Crown as *bona vacantia*? What should happen to any moneys that are given to the organization by non-members? What happens if the donors have declared trusts in respect of such gifts? Should one draw a distinction between societies for the benefit of the members and organizations which exist for the benefit of others, such as the dependants of members? Finally, does it make any difference if the association's rules make provision for distribution of the property on dissolution?

These questions are discussed in a large number of English cases, but there has, over the years, been a decided shift in the *rationes* of the decisions. The earlier cases favoured the idea that members' contributions to an unincorporated association were made on trust, so that, if the association were dissolved and money remained, that money resulted to the members. Even so, however, the cases differed on the question as to which members were entitled under the resulting trust. Thus, one case held that the moneys were divisible among the members who remained at dissolution,[65] while another held that all members, past and present, were entitled, unless the ascertainment of past members should be impossible.[66] The latter decision accords more clearly with resulting trust principles. In each of these cases, the problem arose because the society had ceased to exist and the rules failed to provide for distribution of assets.

The modern approach to this problem is not that of resulting trust, but of contract. This means, first, that if the society exists to provide benefits for members or others, the right to receive benefits as a result of making contributions is contractual. Hence, if the stipulated benefit has been paid, a member no longer has any claim to the contributions based on resulting trust.[67] Moreover, if all the members are deceased, or if there is only one member left,[68] the remaining assets may be *bona vacantia*, subject to any existing contractual claims.[69]

Secondly, the contract approach means that the relationship among the members of an unincorporated association is a contract, the terms of which are found in the rules of the association. The rules may provide for what shall happen to any assets remaining on dissolution or the remaining members may decide before dissolution to amend the rules to provide for the division of those assets. In the

---

64 R.S.C. 1985, c. 1 (5th Supp.), s. 149.1(1) (definition of "charitable organization"); also see *Registering a Charity for Tax Purposes* (Canada Customs and Revenue Agency, T4063).

65 *Printers & Transferrers Amalgamated Trades Protection Society, Re*, [1899] 2 Ch. 184 (Eng. Ch. Div.).

66 *Hobourn Aero Components Ltd. Air Raid Distress Fund, Re* (1945), [1946] 1 Ch. 86 (Eng. Ch. Div.).

67 *William Denby & Sons Ltd. Sick and Benevolent Fund, Re*, [1971] 1 W.L.R. 973 at 978, *per* Brightman J.

68 *Bucks' Constabulary Widows' and Orphans' Fund Friendly Society (No. 2), Re*, [1979] 1 W.L.R. 936, [1979] 1 All E.R. 623 at 629, *per* Walton J., who notes that one person cannot form a society, since one cannot associate with oneself. His Lordship left open the question whether there is still a society if it is moribund but has two or more members remaining.

69 *Cunnack v. Edwards*, [1896] 2 Ch. 679 (Eng. C.A.).

absence of such rules, however, the assets will be divided among the members upon dissolution. The assets will not be *bona vacantia* if there is more than one member remaining at dissolution.[70]

In *West Sussex Constabulary's Widows, Children and Benevolent (1930) Fund Trust, Re*,[71] the court held that a fund established to provide benefits to widows and other dependants of members was *bona vacantia* when the fund was dissolved, since the members had received all they had contracted for. This decision was criticised in *Re Bucks' Constabulary Widows' and Orphans' Fund Friendly Society (No. 2)*,[72] on the ground that it matters not that the society is set up for the benefit of the members or for others;[73] it is the members who control the assets and who, therefore, are entitled to the assets on dissolution. It was also held in *West Sussex* that the proceeds of collection boxes, *etc.*, were *bona vacantia*, since this money had been given out and out, but that identifiable gifts to the association were subject to a resulting trust. Moreover, it was held that the proceeds of entertainments, raffles and sweepstakes derived from contract, not from trust, so that these moneys were also *bona vacantia*. This is debatable in the context of unincorporated associations.

The better view, we submit, is that all such moneys become the assets of the association and subject to its rules and, hence, available to the members, unless moneys are given upon an express trust which fails, in which case there is a resulting trust.[74]

When moneys are divided upon dissolution, absent any rules to the contrary, the normal rule is equal division, regardless of length of membership or the amount of contributions.[75] However, honorary members are likely to be excluded from participating.[76]

Notes and Questions

1. If, as suggested above, a society's assets become *bona vacantia* if only one member remains, what happens if there are two or three?

2. If the trustees of an unincorporated association improperly transfer assets to a third party, there will be a resulting trust to the members. This occurred in *Wawrzyniak v. Jagiellicz*.[77] In 1930, the Polish Army Veterans' Association established a Toronto branch, known as Post 114, which existed as an unincorporated association. In 1950, members of Post 114 incorporated a corporation to carry on the work of Post 114. The corporation bought a clubhouse, title being taken in its name, with funds belonging to members of

---

70 *Bucks' Constabulary, Re, supra,* note 68.

71 (1970), [1971] Ch. 1, [1970] 1 All E.R. 544.

72 *Supra,* note 68.

73 The latter may be governed by legislation, such as the *Friendly Societies Act 1974*, c. 46 (U.K.), as in the *Bucks* case, although not in the *West Sussex* case.

74 See *Recher's Will Trusts, Re* (1971), [1972] 1 Ch. 526, [1971] 3 All E.R. 401, [1971] 3 W.L.R. 321, 115 Sol. Jo. 448 (Ch. Div.).

75 *Bucks' Constabulary, Re, supra,* note 68.

76 *G.K.N. Bolts & Nuts Ltd. (Automotive Division) Birmingham Works, Sports and Social Club, Re,* [1982] 1 W.L.R. 774.

77 (1988), 51 D.L.R. (4th) 639, 65 O.R. (2d) 384, 1988 CarswellOnt 598, 31 E.T.R. 45 (C.A.).

Post 114. In 1953, the corporation mortgaged the clubhouse property and used the funds to make a down payment on a farm property. In 1955, five members of Post 114 brought an action against the corporation claiming that the clubhouse and the farm belonged to the members of Post 114. The court held that the gratuitous transfer of the club's property to a third party (the corporation), which was not made in accordance with any provision of the association's constitution or which lacks unanimous approval of the members, will not vest a beneficial interest in the third party. Since neither condition was met, the third party took title subject to a resulting trust in favour of the members of the association.

3. The problems concerning unincorporated associations are also considered in the context of non-charitable purpose trusts in the previous chapter. Reference may also be made to the standard texts on this issue.[78]

(iv) *Pension Trusts*

Pension law is a relatively new field of the law that has been the subject of rapid evolution in the past decade. The demographics of our population and the billions of dollars under the control of pension plans in Canada has provided incentives for lawyers, judges, and academics to take a closer look at the legal characteristics of pension plans.[79] Is a pension plan governed by trust principles or does it represent a contract governed by its terms? The answer will be found in the wording of the plan documentation. If there has been some express or implied declaration of trust and an alienation of trust property to a trustee for the benefit of employees, then the pension plan will be impressed with a "pension trust." This characterisation has important consequences. As a trust, the pension must be administered strictly in the best interests of employees. As it is generally the employer who serves as the plan administrator, there is potential for conflict when the interests of the parties do not coincide. If no trust is created, the administration and distribution of the fund will be governed by the terms of the agreement.

The issue of entitlement to pension plan surplus has also been the subject of much litigation. A surplus arises when the value of the plan assets exceeds the value of plan liabilities. It may arise during the operation of the plan, as an "actuarial surplus," or at its termination. The fate of the surplus will depend on whether the plan is a trust or not. If it is a trust, the terms of the trust will determine whether there is a surplus and, usually, who is entitled to that surplus.

---

78 See especially Jill E. Martin, *Hanbury & Martin Modern Equity*, 16th ed. (London: Sweet & Maxwell, 2001) at 244-251. See also B. Green, "Dissolution of Unincorporated Associations" (1980), 43 Mod. L. Rev. 626.

79 See E.E. Gillese, "Pension Plans and the Law of Trusts" (1996), 75 Can. Bar Rev. 221.

SCHMIDT v. AIR PRODUCTS OF CANADA LTD.

(1994), [1994] 2 S.C.R. 611, 115 D.L.R. (4th) 631, 20 Alta. L.R. (3d) 225,
1994 CarswellAlta 138, 1994 CarswellAlta 746, 3 C.C.P.B. 1, (sub nom.
Stearns Catalytic Pension Plans, Re) 168 N.R. 81, [1994] 8 W.W.R.
305, 3 E.T.R. (2d) 1, 4 C.C.E.L. (2d) 1, 155 A.R. 81, 73 W.A.C.
81, C.E.B. & P.G.R. 8173, [1995] O.P.L.R. 283
Supreme Court of Canada

Catalytic Enterprises Ltd. ("Catalytic") started a pension plan for its employees
in 1959, which was set up as a contributory defined contribution plan held in
trust. It was amended in 1966 to become a contributory defined benefit plan and
amended again in 1978 to provide that Catalytic was entitled to any surplus in
the plan.

A "contributory" plan is one that requires contributions from employees and
the employer, while a "non-contributory" plan requires contributions only from
the employer. In a "defined contribution" plan, the benefits paid to members are
the contributions made by and on behalf of the employees, plus whatever profit
is earned from the investment of those funds. In a "defined benefit" plan, the
members are entitled to guaranteed specific benefits regardless of the value of the
fund. The employer's contributions are based on an actuary's estimate of the
amount that is needed as a present investment to meet all the potential liabilities
of the plan.

Stearns-Roger Ltd. ("Stearns") created a contributory defined benefit plan
for its employees in 1970. In 1977, this was amended to a non-contributory defined
benefit plan, with employees having the right to contribute voluntarily.

In 1983, Catalytic and Stearns merged to eventually become Air Products
Canada Ltd. ("Air Products"). At the time of the merger, both companies had
defined benefit plans that were in surplus. The plans were amalgamated as a
contributory defined benefit plan. From 1985 to 1988, Air Products transferred
no new assets to the fund, but enjoyed a "contribution holiday" by using the
actuarily determined surplus existing in the fund to pay its required contributions.

In 1988, Air Products sold most of its assets and terminated the pension plan.
The surplus in the plan, after provision was made for all the benefits to which
members were entitled, was $9,179,130. Air Products applied to the Alberta Court
of Queen's Bench for a declaration that it was entitled to the surplus. Gunter
Schmidt applied, on behalf of the employees, for declarations that the employees
were entitled to the surplus and that Air Products was required to pay a further
$1,465,400 into the pension fund to make up for the contribution holidays it
should not have taken.

The trial judge held that Air Products was entitled to the surplus derived from
the Stearns plan, that the former Catalytic employees were entitled to the surplus
derived from the Catalytic plan, and that Air Products had to pay $1,465,400 to
the pension fund because it was not entitled to take a contribution holiday by

using the surplus from the Catalytic plan.[80] An appeal by Air Products and a cross-appeal by former Stearns employees were dismissed by the Alberta Court of Appeal.[81]

On appeal to the Supreme Court of Canada, the judges agreed unanimously that Air Products was entitled to the surplus derived from the Stearns plan, because those funds were not held in trust. The former Stearns employees would receive everything to which they were entitled by contract under the plan and Air Products could keep the rest. The judges also agreed unanimously that Air Products was not required to pay any more money into the pension plan. Since the pension fund had become a defined benefit plan, Air Products was required to contribute only the amount needed to meet the potential liabilities of the plan and was entitled to take a contribution holiday whenever the pension fund contained sufficient assets to meet those liabilities.

The judges disagreed over the destination of the surplus derived from the Catalytic plan. The majority (La Forest, L'Heureux-Dubé, Gonthier, and Iacobucci JJ.) agreed with Cory J. that all the assets derived from that plan were held in trust for the employees and, therefore, the employees were entitled to the surplus. Although the original 1959 trust agreement gave the company a broad power to amend the trust, that could not be used to revoke it. Therefore, the 1978 amendment of the Catalytic plan, purporting to give the company the power to distribute the surplus to itself, was invalid.

Sopinka and McLachlin JJ. dissented in part on the basis that Air Products was entitled to the entire surplus, including the portion derived from the Catalytic plan. They each held that the 1978 amendment of that plan was valid and, therefore, Air Products was entitled to the surplus under the terms of the express trust, as amended. McLachlin J. also held that, if the amendment was invalid, Air Products would be entitled to the surplus under a resulting trust.

CORY J.:

These two cases raise the issue of entitlement to surplus moneys remaining in an employee pension fund once the fund has been wound up and all benefits either paid or provision made for their payment. There is a further related issue as to whether or when employers may refrain from contributing to ongoing pension plans which are in "surplus".

. . .

A. Surplus entitlement

---

80 *Schmidt v. Air Products of Canada Ltd.* (1990), 66 D.L.R. (4th) 230, (sub nom. *Stearns Catalytic Pension Plans, Re*) 104 A.R. 190, 1990 CarswellAlta 313, 37 E.T.R. 64 (Q.B.).

81 *Schmidt v. Air Products of Canada Ltd.* (1992), 89 D.L.R. (4th) 762, (sub nom. *Stearns Catalytic Pension Plans, Re*) 125 A.R. 224, 1992 CarswellAlta 370, 46 E.T.R. 21, 125 A.R. 224, 14 W.A.C. 224 (C.A.).

An employer who creates an employee pension plan agrees to provide pension benefits to retiring employees. At first, employers undertaking this obligation paid retired employees directly from company income. Gradually, the practice of creating separate pension funds emerged following the passage of regulations designed to protect employees from the bankruptcy or termination of the company, coupled with the realization of employers that the cost of providing pensions is reduced if money is put aside on behalf of present employees for their future benefit.

Pension funds thus began to be structured in several different ways. Investment contracts and trust funds eventually proved to be the most popular forms of pension plan funding for employers since they provided the requisite degree of "irrevocability" of contribution to entitle an employer to obtain tax relief on its pension contributions. The relatively recent phenomenon of pension plan surplus has created an inevitable tension between employers, who claim that they never lose their entitlement to moneys which they contribute to the fund but which are not needed to provide agreed benefits, and employees who assert that all pension fund moneys belong to them. It is suggested that if employers are not able to retrieve surpluses, they will be tempted to fund existing plans less generously. I cannot agree. First, unless the terms of the plan specifically preclude it, an employer is entitled to take a contribution holiday. Second, most pension plans require the level of employer contribution to be determined by an actuary. The employer will not be able to reduce the level of contribution unilaterally below that required according to standard actuarial practice. Third, employers are required by legislation to make up any unfunded liability. Finally, the fact that some employers cannot recoup surplus on termination is unlikely to influence the conduct of employers as a whole. In order to obtain registration, plans created since 1981 must make provision for distribution of surplus on termination. It is generally only in pre-existing plans that the problem of ownership of surplus arises and, as the results of these appeals demonstrate, even then employee entitlement to the surplus is not automatic.

Entitlement to the surplus will often turn upon a determination as to whether the pension fund is impressed with a trust. Accordingly, the first question to be decided in a pension surplus case is whether or not a trust exists.

1. Trust or contract?

Employer-funded defined benefit plans usually consist of an agreement whereby an employer promises to pay each employee upon retirement a pension which is defined by a formula contained in the plan. A pension fund is created pursuant to the plan, either by way of contract or by way of trust. Whether or not any given fund is subject to a trust is determined by the principles of trust law. If there has been some express or implied declaration of trust, and an alienation of trust property to a trustee for the benefit of the employees, then the pension fund will be a trust fund.

If no trust is created, then the administration and distribution of the pension fund and any surplus will be governed solely by the terms of the plan. However, when a trust is created, the funds which form the corpus are subjected to the requirements of trust law. The terms of the pension plan are relevant to distribution issues only to the extent that those terms are incorporated by reference in the instrument which creates the trust. The contract or pension plan may influence the payment of trust funds, but its terms cannot compel a result which is at odds with the existence of the trust.

Typically, when a pension fund is subject to a trust, several issues arise: Are such trusts for a purpose or are they "classic" trusts? What part of the pension fund is subject to the trust? To what extent can a settlor-employer alter the terms of a trust in order to appropriate the fund surplus for itself? Is the surplus subject to a resulting trust? Let us consider the nature of the trust in this case.

2. Purpose or "true" trust?

Air Products has suggested that the Catalytic pension fund was not subject to an express trust but instead to a trust for a purpose. Relying on dicta of the British Columbia Court of Appeal in *Hockin v. Bank of British Columbia*,[82] the company argues that a trust set up as part of a pension plan constitutes a trust whose sole purpose is to provide defined benefits to members. Once those benefits have been provided the purpose is fulfilled, the trust expires and the terms of the pension plan alone determine entitlement to any remaining fund surplus. I cannot accept this proposition.

Trusts for a purpose are a rare species. They constitute an exception to the general rule that trusts for a purpose are void.[83] The pension trust is much more akin to the classic trust than to the trust for a purpose. I agree with the following comments of the Pension Commission of Ontario in *Arrowhead Metals Ltd. v. Royal Trust Co.*,[84] cited by Adams J. in *Bathgate v. National Hockey League Pension Society*:[85]

> Purpose trusts are trusts for which there is no beneficiary; that is, they are trusts where no person has an equitable entitlement to the trust funds. Funds are deposited in trust in order to see that a particular purpose is filled; people may benefit, but only indirectly.
>
> People are clearly direct beneficiaries of pension trusts. Pension trusts are established not to effect some purpose, such as building a recreation centre, but to provide money on a regular basis to retired employees. It misconceives both the nature of a purpose trust and of a pension trust to suggest that pensions are for purposes, not persons. It is important to recognize that the characterization of pension trusts as purpose trusts results in the pension text, a contract, taking precedence over the trust agreement. That is, it makes common law principles of contract paramount to the equitable principles of trust law. It is trite law that where common law and equity conflict, equity is to prevail. In light of that rule, it seems inappropriate to do indirectly that which could not be done directly.

---

82 (1990), 71 D.L.R. (4th) 11, 38 E.T.R. 275.
83 See D.W.M. Waters, *Law of Trusts in Canada*, 2nd ed. (Toronto: Carswell, 1984) at 127-128.
84 (March 26, 1992), at 13-15.
85 (1992), 98 D.L.R. (4th) 326 at 387, 11 O.R. (3d) 449 (Gen. Div.).

To repeat, the first step is to determine whether or not the pension fund is in fact a pension trust. This will most often be revealed by the wording of the pension plan itself, but may also be implied from the plan and from the way in which the pension fund is set up. A pension trust is a "classic" or "true" trust and not a mere trust for a purpose. If there is no trust created under the pension plan, the wording of the pension plan alone will govern the allocation of any surplus remaining on termination. However, if the fund is subject to a trust, different considerations may govern.

. . .

4. Amendment of the trust

When a pension fund is impressed with a trust, that trust is subject to all applicable trust law principles. The significance of this for the present appeals is twofold. Firstly, the employer will not be able to claim entitlement to funds subject to a trust unless the terms of the trust make the employer a beneficiary, or unless the employer reserved a power of revocation of the trust at the time the trust was originally created. Secondly, if the objects of the trust have been satisfied but assets remain in the trust, those funds may be subject to a resulting trust.

The settlor of a trust can reserve any power to itself that it wishes provided the reservation is made at the time the trust is created. A settlor may choose to maintain the right to appoint trustees, to change the beneficiaries of the trust, or to withdraw the trust property. Generally, however, the transfer of the trust property to the trustee is absolute. Any power of control of that property will be lost unless the transfer is expressly made subject to it.

Employers seeking to obtain a pension surplus have frequently made the argument that they reserved a power to revoke, or to revoke partially the pension trust fund they set up for the benefit of their employees. This approach has had mixed results. The inconsistency of the decisions on the revocation of pension trusts exists on two levels. At one level, the different decisions can be explained on the basis of the wording of the particular amending clause and the limitations put upon it in each case. However, the decisions also reveal a more fundamental difference of opinion as to whether the revocation of trusts is possible when a settlor has reserved a broad power of amendment. This difference must be resolved in this case.

The differing approaches to revocation of the trust are perhaps most starkly illustrated by the cases of *Reevie v. Montreal Trust Co.*,[86] and *Hockin v. Bank of British Columbia*.[87] In both of these cases, a trust fund was established pursuant to a pension plan which contained a broad power of amendment. Each amending power was subject only to the proviso that no amendment could reduce members' entitlement to accrued benefits.

---

86 (1986), 25 D.L.R. (4th) 312, 53 O.R. (2d) 595 (C.A.).
87 *Supra*, note 82.

The court in *Reevie* relied upon a passage from Waters to the effect that it is a cardinal rule of trust law that a settlor can only revoke his or her trust when the settlor has expressly reserved the power to do so, and found that the broad amendment power reserved by Canada Dry did not amount to an express reservation. The court in *Hockin*, on the other hand, ... concluded that "[a] power to amend includes the power to revoke unless revocation is precluded by specific wording of the power to amend".[88] With respect, I cannot agree with this position.

In my view the nature and purpose of the trust as it has evolved in Canada is consistent with a more restrictive interpretation as to when the trust instrument will permit a unilateral revocation of the trust. One of the most fundamental characteristics of a trust is that it involves a transfer of property. In the words of D.W.M. Waters:[89]

> ... the trust is a mode of disposition, and once the instrument of creation of the trust has taken effect or a verbal declaration has been made of immediate disposition on trust, the settlor has alienated the property as much as if he had given it to the beneficiaries by an out-and-out gift. This almost self-evident proposition has to be reiterated because it is sometimes said that the trust is a mode of "restricted transfer." So indeed it is, but the restriction does not mean that by employing the trust the settlor inherently retains a right or power to intervene once the trust has taken effect, whether to set the trust aside, change the beneficiaries, name other beneficiaries, take back part of the trust property, or do anything else to amend or change the trust. By restriction is meant that he has transferred the property but subject to restrictions upon who is to enjoy and to what degree. The mode of future enjoyment is regulated in the act of transferring, but the transfer remains a true transfer.

The judgment of the B.C. Court of Appeal in *Hockin*, if followed to its logical conclusion, would mean that the presence of an unlimited power of amendment in a trust agreement entitles a settlor to maintain complete control over the administration of the trust and the trust property. That result is inconsistent with the fundamental concept of a trust, and cannot, in my opinion, be sustained without extremely clear and explicit language. A general amending power should not endow a settlor with the ability to revoke the trust. This is especially so when it is remembered that consideration was given by the employee beneficiaries in exchange for the creation of the trust. In the case of pension plans, employees not only contribute to the fund, in addition, they almost invariably agree to accept lower wages and fewer employment benefits in exchange for the employer's agreeing to set up the pension trust in their favour. The wording of the pension plan and trust instrument are usually drawn up by the employer. The employees as a rule must rely upon the good faith of the employer to ensure that the terms of the specific trust arrangement will be fair. It would, I think, be inequitable to accept the proposition that a broad amending power inserted unilaterally by the employer carries with it the right to revoke the trust. The employer who wishes to undertake a restricted transfer of assets must make those restrictions explicit. Moreover, amendment means change, not cancellation, which the word "revocation" connotes.

---

88 *Ibid.*, at 19.
89 *Law of Trusts in Canada*, 2nd ed. (Toronto: Carswell, 1984) at 291.

. . .

As a result I find that, at least in the context of pension trusts, the reservation by the settlor of an unlimited power of amendment does not include a power to revoke the trust. A revocation power must be explicitly reserved in order to be valid.

5. *The resulting trust*

A resulting trust may arise if the objects of the trust have been fully satisfied and money still remains in the trust fund. In such situations, the remaining trust funds will ordinarily revert by operation of law to the settlor of the fund. However, a resulting trust will not arise if, at the time of settlement, the settlor demonstrates an intention to part with his or her money outright. This is to say the settlor indicates that he or she will not retain any interest in any remaining funds.

Several Canadian cases have dealt with the resulting trust in relation to pension surplus cases. In *Re Canada Trust Co. and Cantol Ltd.*,[90] the pension plan had been terminated. The plan provided that, upon termination, assets were to be applied to four listed categories of beneficiaries. All the beneficiaries were paid in accordance with this provision, and a surplus remained in the fund. The trustee of the fund, Canada Trust, sought directions from the court as to how to deal with the surplus.

Gould J. held that the "purposes of this trust simply did not exhaust the fund and the outcome here, i.e., a surplus balance of $31,163.38, was not foreseen by the respondent. ...The situation appears to be one where a resulting trust arises by operation of the law."[91] This conclusion could well be questioned in light of another provision in the plan which provided that "no alteration, amendment or termination of the Plan or any part thereof shall permit any part of the trust fund to revert to or to be recoverable by the Company or to be used for or diverted to purposes other than the exclusive benefits of members..."[92] Perhaps the decision can be explained on the basis that the employees were not parties before the court and did not contribute to the plan which was funded solely by the employer.

In most cases, the existence of a non-reversion clause will be evidence of a permanent intention to part with the trust property and it will preclude the operation of the resulting trust. The trust agreement in *C.A.W., Local 458 v. White Farm Manufacturing Canada Ltd.* . . . contained the following clause:[93]

> No part of the capital or income of the fund shall ever revert to the company or be used for or diverted to purposes other than for the exclusive benefit of the employees and former employees under the plan except as therein and herein provided.

---

90 [1979] 6 W.W.R. 656, 103 D.L.R. (3d) 109 (B.C.S.C.).
91 *Ibid.*, at 111.
92 *Ibid.*, at 110.
93 (1988), 66 O.R. (2d) 535 at 538.

I agree with Montgomery J.'s conclusion that these provisions "effectively dispose of the respondents' arguments that the surplus is subject to the doctrine of resulting trust".[94] The employer had absolutely and irrevocably waived its interest in any surplus that might arise upon the termination of the pension fund despite the contributions it had made to that fund.

The exigencies of tax law are such that preferential tax treatment will only be afforded to registered pension plans. Registration, originally contingent upon clear evidence that the employer's contribution would be irrevocable, now requires a plan to provide that, following termination of the plan, any remaining surplus in excess of the statutory maximum level of employee benefits must revert to the employer. Therefore, the provisions of most registered pension plans will normally themselves exclude the possibility of a resulting trust's arising. That is not to say that the resulting trust will never have a place in the context of pension funds. Yet the practical reality is that the factual circumstances which could trigger the operation of a resulting trust will rarely occur in pension surplus cases.

The relevant documents in this case are such that it is not necessary to examine all of the difficult issues which can arise in relation to resulting trusts. None the less, when a resulting trust arises in respect of a contributory plan, I would be inclined to prefer the view of Nitikman J. in *Martin & Robertson Administration Ltd. v. Pension Commission of Manitoba*,[95] to that of Scott J. in *Davis v. Richards & Wallington Industries Ltd.*[96] Nitikman J. held that where employers and employees are (by virtue of their contributions) settlors of the trust, surplus funds remaining on termination can revert on a resulting trust to both employers and employees in proportion to their respective contributions. Scott J., on the other hand, held that employees cannot benefit from a resulting trust since, by the mere act of contributing to the fund, they manifest an intention to part irrevocably with their money.

I do not think that any general rule can be laid down as to the intentions of employees contributing to a pension trust. Where the circumstances of a particular case do not indicate any particular intention to part outright with money contributed to a pension fund, equity and fairness would seem to require that all parties who contributed to the fund should be entitled to recoup a proportionate share of any surplus subject to a resulting trust. However, this issue should be left to be resolved when it arises.

In most pension trust cases the resulting trust will never arise. This may be because the objects of the trust can never be said to be fully satisfied so long as funds which could benefit the employees remain in the pension trust, or because the settlor has manifested a clear intention to part outright with its contributions. The operation of the resulting trust may also be precluded by the presence of specific provisions dealing with the disposition of surplus on plan termination.

---

94 *Ibid.*, at 540.
95 (1980), 2 A.C.W.S. (2d) 249.
96 [1991] 2 All E.R. 563 (Ch. D.).

. . .

C. Summary

In the absence of provincial legislation providing otherwise, the courts must determine competing claims to pension surplus by a careful analysis of the pension plan and the funding structures created under it. The first step is to determine whether the pension fund is impressed with a trust. This is a determination which must be made according to ordinary principles of trust law. A trust will exist whenever there has been an express or implied declaration of trust and an alienation of trust property to a trustee to be held for specified beneficiaries.

If the pension fund, or any part of it, is not subject to a trust, then any issues relating to outstanding pension benefits or to surplus entitlement must be resolved by applying the principles which pertain to the interpretation of contracts to the pension plan.

If, however, the fund is impressed with a trust, different considerations apply. The trust is not a trust for a purpose, but a classic trust. It is governed by equity, and, to the extent that applicable equitable principles conflict with plan provisions, equity must prevail. The trust will in most cases extend to an ongoing or actual surplus as well as to that part of the pension fund needed to provide employee benefits. However, an employer may explicitly limit the operation of the trust so that it does not apply to surplus.

The employer, as a settlor of the trust, may reserve a power to revoke the trust. In order to be effective, that power must be clearly reserved at the time the trust is created. A power to revoke the trust or any part of it cannot be implied from a general unlimited power of amendment.

Funds remaining in a pension trust following termination and payment of all defined benefits may be subject to a resulting trust. Before a resulting trust can arise, it must be clear that all of the objectives of the trust have been fully satisfied. Even when this is the case, the employer cannot claim the benefit of a resulting trust when the terms of the plan demonstrate an intention to part outright with all money contributed to the pension fund. In contributory plans, it is not only the employer's but also the employees' intentions which must be considered. Both are settlors of the trust. Both are entitled to benefit from a reversion of trust property.

. . .

McLachlin J. (dissenting in part):

I have read the reasons of Justice Cory. I agree with his conclusions except on the question of the right to surplus on the Catalytic plan. In my view, the surplus on the Catalytic plan reverts to the employer, either on the terms of the plan or on the basis of the doctrine of resulting trust.

BACKGROUND: SITUATING THE PROBLEM

Modern private pension plans date to the late 19th century. Fundamental and pervasive societal changes — large scale industrialization coupled with the breakdown of family, village and church assistance networks — produced a need to devise methods of caring for those past working age. Employer-sponsored private pension plans, supplemented later by government plans, were the response. Today, together with personal savings, private and public pension plans provide the primary source of income for retired Canadians.

There are two main types of pension plans. In the first type, the "defined contribution" plan, the amount paid in by the contributors to the fund is set. The eventual size of the employee's annuity is determined by the rate of return on the invested contributions. It follows that a low rate of return on investment will result in a smaller pension than if the rate of return is high. While the employer contributes to the plan, the employer does not guarantee the amount of the annuity. The employee is not assured of any particular benefit. The 1959 Catalytic plan was this sort of plan.

In the other type of pension plan, the "defined benefit" plan, the employee, who may or may not contribute to the fund, is assured of a certain monetary benefit upon retirement. An actuary is employed to determine the amount of contribution which the employer must make in order to ensure that the plan can meet its present and future obligations. The market risk, assumed by the employee in a defined contribution plan, falls on the employer in a defined benefit plan. If, at any time, the plan is unable to meet its obligations, the employer is liable to make up any shortfall. For these two reasons — the guarantee of a certain benefit and the assumption by the employer of the market risk — a defined benefit plan is regarded as more advantageous to employees than a defined contribution plan.

The defined benefit plan possesses a feature which the defined contribution plan does not — a feature which is at the heart of this appeal, the actuarial surplus. A defined contribution plan can never have a surplus; everything, after deduction of taxes and expenses, must be paid out to the pensioners. However, a surplus may accumulate in a defined benefit plan when the amount in the fund exceeds the amount required to meet the defined benefits as calculated by the actuary.

In valuing the assets of a pension plan, the actuary must take into account a number of factors and make assumptions about each of them. These factors include the rate of investment return, the rate of price inflation, salary increases, rates of mortality for active and retired members, rates of employee turnover, incidence of disability and utilization of early retirement options. As might be expected, actuaries advising employers tend to err on the side of caution to produce what is called an "experience gain" rather than an "experience deficiency", since the latter would deprive pensioners of the benefits guaranteed to them.

In the early 1980s this actuarial conservatism combined with a particular set of economic factors to produce massive surpluses in many pension funds. These factors included the level of interest rates — as high as 20% at one point — which gave returns on investments in fixed value securities far in excess of those predicted. The stock market boom from 1982 to 1987 also resulted in much higher capital gains than were anticipated. Furthermore, the recession of 1981-82 caused widespread lay-offs of employees who had no vested right to pension benefits. Money contributed on their account remained in the plan and either reduced unfunded liability for other employees or fell into surplus. At the same time, employers, uncertain as to whether they could use surplus for ongoing funding, often continued to contribute to over-funded plans in years when investment returns were at their highest, increasing existing surpluses.[97] The result of these events was to increase pension surpluses in Canada which, by 1982, had already been estimated to be between $4 billion and $8 billion.[98]

So long as a pension plan remains operational, hefty surpluses pose no problem except perhaps to employers wondering whether they can use the surplus for current funding needs, taking a "contribution holiday". When a plan terminates, however, the question arises of who is entitled to the surplus. That is the problem that faces us on this appeal. It is not, we are told, an isolated one. Many plans such as this were set up in the 1960s and the decades that followed. Few contained express provisions as to distribution of surplus.

The Catalytic plan in this appeal was set up in 1959 as a defined contribution plan. As one would expect in that type of plan, all funds would ultimately be paid out to the pensioners or beneficiaries. There could be no surplus.

In 1966, however, the plan was changed to a defined benefit plan and the possibility of a surplus arose. In 1978, the plan agreement was redrafted. This restatement raised for the first time the issue of what should be done with any surplus. It empowered the company to use the surplus as it saw fit after making full provision for the accrued benefits payable to members and beneficiaries. When the plan was terminated in 1988, a large surplus was revealed. The issue was who should have it — the employees and their beneficiaries or the employer?

Implications flowing from the nature of the defined benefit plan

As noted, the employer is legally obliged under a defined benefits plan to ensure that all pension benefits owing are paid when they fall due. The employer thus bears the risk that contributions may be insufficient or that investments may not perform as well as predicted. The converse of this proposition is that the employer should be permitted to take advantage of the excess when investments do better than predicted.

From an economic policy perspective, if employers cannot retrieve surpluses, they may be inclined to request that their actuaries take a more optimistic view of the future of their investments and fund existing pensions less generously. Alternatively, they may refuse to enter into new pension regimes or, in some cases, terminate those which already exist. Inability to retrieve surpluses may also lead employers, unwilling to assume the risk of providing guaranteed benefits

---

97 Gary Nachshen, "Access to Pension Fund Surpluses: The Great Debate", in *New Developments in Employment Law* (Cowansville: Yvon Blais Inc., 1989).

98 D. Don Ezra, *The Struggle for Pension Fund Wealth* (Toronto: Pagurian Press, 1983).

without the possibility of recovering surplus funding, to choose defined contribution plans rather than defined benefit plans. Employees, no longer assured of
a specific pension and required to assume the risk of insufficient funding themselves, would be the losers.

On the other side of the coin, permitting employers to recover surplus in a
defined benefit plan is not unfair to employees. It is argued that employees should
have the surplus because they have paid for it through direct contributions or by
accepting lower wages and fewer fringe benefits. This argument overlooks the
nature of the employees' legitimate expectations under a defined benefit plan.
The employees, having bargained for specific benefits, will receive precisely
what they bargained for. The benefits, as defined by the plan, are the quid pro
quo for their services and contributions. Indeed, the intention of the parties —
and the very purpose of the plan — is that they receive these benefits. To give
the employees the surplus, however, is to give them more than they bargained
for. It is a windfall to the employees and a denial of the equitable interest which
the employer holds in the surplus.

This practical view of things is supported by the policy of the Minister of
National Revenue. Information Circular No. 72-13R7, December 31, 1981, is
based on the assumption that surplus is normally returnable to the employer. In
order to comply with registration requirements, surplus in excess of the employer's current service funding obligations in the following 24-month period
must be either refunded to the employer or applied against the employer's obligations for contributions on account of current or past service in the current and
subsequent years. Furthermore, all pension plans are to contain a provision permitting an actuarial surplus to be refunded to contributing employers of the plan.
This requirement, it may be noted, may prevent problems such as the one presented
on this appeal from arising in plans set up after the circular.

The position in other jurisdictions

The problem of surplus in defined benefit pension plans is a recent one. The
matter has, however, been considered by courts in England and the United States.
It is fair to say that they have generally come down on the side of returning the
surplus to the employers.

Courts in Great Britain have relied primarily upon principles of trust law
when attempting to resolve the question of pension surplus. In *Davis v. Richards
& Wallington Industries Ltd.*,[99] for example, Scott J. applied the doctrine of
resulting trust and concluded that a surplus in a contributory defined benefits
pension fund should be paid to the employer. He held that the result could be
otherwise only if the plan contained a provision expressly excluding return of the
funds to the employer. He rejected the argument that a resulting trust operated in

---

99   *Supra,* note 96.

favour of the employees in view of their contributions mainly on the ground that what the employees had paid for was the specific benefit received from the fund.[100]

In the United States, the courts look to the terms of the plan documents and the intent of the parties. They also tend to the view that the surplus would represent an unintended windfall profit if it were retained by the employees.[101] Provisions to the effect that amendments to the plan or trust documents may not enable an employer to divert or recover any portion of the trust funds are treated as prohibiting diversion prior to satisfaction of the plan's liabilities, but not thereafter. Once the pensioners are assured of their benefits, the surplus is recoverable by the employer.[102] Where courts in the United States have found that a surplus could not be recovered by the employer, they have done so on the basis that the wording of the plan documents unequivocally precluded such recovery.[103]

Consistency with the right to use surplus for a "contribution holiday"

It has repeatedly been held that employers are entitled to use the surplus in defined benefit plans for purposes of funding their actuarially determined contributions.[104] Cory J. arrives at the same conclusion in this case.

The obvious question immediately presents itself. If the employer is entitled to use the surplus to fund future contributions, why should the employer be denied the ability to recoup the surplus from previous funding? If, on the other hand, the fund in equity belongs to the employees in some notional sense, how can the employer usurp that interest by using the surplus to discharge its ongoing funding responsibility? Consistency suggests that both past and present funding and entitlement should be treated in the same way.

Some commentators, while recognizing the anomaly of allowing the employer to use the surplus for a contribution holiday but not to recoup past over-contributions from the surplus, argue that, from a "practical and symbolic" point of view, the two questions may be different, "since all funds paid into the pension stay there, at least notionally".[105] Cory J. makes a similar point. So, it is suggested,

---

100 See also, *Re Courage Group's Pension Schemes*, [1987] 1 W.L.R. 495 (Ch. D.).

101 *Washington-Baltimore News paper Guild Local 35 v. Washington Star Co.*, 555 F. Supp. 257 (D.C. 1983).

102 *Re C.D. Moyer Co. Trust Fund*, 441 F. Supp. 1128 (E.D. Pa. 1977); *Pollock v. Castrovinci*, 476 F. Supp. 606 (S.D.N.Y. 1979); *Washington-Baltimore Newspaper Guild, ibid.*; *Wilson v. Bluefield Supply Co.*, 819 F.2d 457 (4th Cir. 1987).

103 *Bryant v. International Fruit Products Co.*, 793 F.2d 118 (6th Cir. 1986); *Audio Fidelity Corp. v. Pension Benefit Guaranty Corp.*, 624 F.2d 513 (4th Cir. 1980).

104 *Maurer v. McMaster University* (1991), 82 D.L.R. (4th) 6, 4 O.R. (3d) 139; *Askin v. Ontario Hospital Assn.* (1991), 2 O.R. (3d) 641, 46 O.A.C. 278; *Reevie v. Montreal Trust Co. of Canada*, *supra*, note 86.

105 Bernard Adell, "Pension Plan Surpluses and the Law: Finding a Path for Reform", in *Report of the Task Force on Inflation Protection for Employment Pension Plans, Research Studies* (Toronto: The Task Force, 1988), vol. 2, at 242.

an employer's entitlement to a contribution holiday may "not automatically entitle him to ownership of the actuarial surplus, as well".[106]

Nevertheless, it remains true that as a matter of principle, there appears to be no reason why an employer permitted to use surplus for ongoing contributions should not be allowed to reclaim the result of past over-contributions from the same surplus.

Summary

Consideration of the nature of defined benefit plans leads to the conclusion that the normal and just result is that surplus in such plans (as distinguished from defined contribution plans) should revert to the employer. Against this background, I turn to the documents which govern this case and the principles of law applicable to them.

ANALYSIS

The private regime

Pension plans such as those at issue here are private arrangements bestowed by an employer on employees as a benefit of employment or set up pursuant to agreement between employer and employees. The employees may contribute (contributory plans), or the employer may bear the entire cost (non-contributory plans). The plan may be funded through insurance purchased by the employer for payment of the benefits (an insured plan), or the moneys may be placed in a trust (a "trusteed" plan). Whatever form they take, as private contractual or as trust arrangements, the law of contract or trust determines how the funds are distributed. This may be varied by legislation, but in this case that did not occur. We must look to the principles of private law for a solution to the problem of distribution of surpluses. In so far as we are concerned with an agreement, we look to the law of contract; in so far as a trust arises, we look to the law of trusts. We are not concerned with making some new law peculiar to pension surpluses.

The primary rule in construing an agreement or defining the terms of a trust is respect for the intention of the parties or, in the case of a trust, the intention of the settlor. The task of the court is to examine the language of the documents to ascertain what, on a fair reading, the parties intended. Unless there is a legal reason preventing it, the courts will seek to give effect to that intention. The search for an answer to the problem before us must therefore focus primarily on the documents relating to the plans and the intention of the parties, if any, with respect to a surplus arising under a defined benefits plan.

---

106 Nachshen, *supra*, note 97, at 77.

The documents

It is my conclusion, after studying the documents and applying them to the plan as it stood at all relevant times, that apart from the reference in the 1978 restatement which provided that surplus should go to the employer, the documents are silent on the question of surplus. There is a dispute about whether the 1978 stipulation was a valid "amendment" to the original trust documents. As I see it, and for the reasons discussed below, it was a valid amendment and, as such, ought to stand. Alternatively, even if the 1978 stipulation were disregarded, the surplus would devolve on the employer under the doctrine of resulting trust.

The crux of the debate is art. V of the 1959 trust agreement:

Modification and Termination

1. Subject as herein and in the plan provided, the Company reserves the right at any time and from time to time to amend, in whole or in part, any or all of the provisions of the plan (including this Agreement) provided that no such amendment which affects the rights, duties, compensation, or responsibilities of the Trustee shall be made without its consent, and provided further that *without the approval of the Minister of National Revenue no such amendment shall authorize or permit any part of the FUND to be used for or diverted to purposes other than for the exclusive benefit of such persons and their estates as from time to time may be designated in or pursuant to the PLAN as amended from time to time*, and for the payment of taxes or other assessments as provided in paragraph 2 of Article II hereof, and the expenses and compensation of the Trustee as provided in paragraph 4 of Article IV hereof. (Emphasis added.)

. . .

In the case at bar, there is nothing in the evidence that suggests that the parties who signed art. V intended it to apply to a surplus which might arise under a conversion of the plan to a defined benefit plan. There is no suggestion that conversion of the plan was foreseen, much less that a surplus might arise under such a scheme. Article V, by its terms, clearly applies to the specific defined contribution plan which the parties were putting in place in 1959. It refers to a specific "Plan", the 1959 plan, and, consistent with a defined contribution plan, it treats all funds as falling into one of two categories — benefits payable to the employees and expenses. Finally, to apply art. V to a surplus under the unforeseen defined benefit plan would, for the reasons enunciated earlier, produce a result which, if not anomalous, is out of step with the characteristics of a defined benefits plan and the approach which has been taken to this problem in other jurisdictions. It is not reasonable, in my opinion, to conclude that art. V applies to the surplus that could only develop after conversion of the plan years later to a defined benefit plan.

The same considerations negate the possibility of implying a term that the provisions of art. V apply to the unforeseen surplus. An attempt to imply a term to cover an unforeseen factual situation will generally fail if it is not clear that the parties would have agreed to the term, or where one or both of the parties is shown not to have known of the new situation at the time of contracting.[107] There is no suggestion that the parties who signed art. V in 1959 knew about the possibility of a surplus; nor can it be said that they would have agreed that it should go to the employees had they foreseen it. Indeed, the inference from the 1978 provision that surplus go to the employer suggests the contrary.

I am thus led to conclude that art. V, drafted in the context of a defined contribution plan, should not be read as applying to the surplus which arose under the later defined benefit plan. It follows that the 1978 provision stipulating that the surplus should go to the employer is valid and determines the issue.

Express trust

It is argued that the surplus here in question is impressed with an express trust in favour of the employees which prevents the employer from claiming it.

I note initially that this argument must be distinguished from the argument based on the doctrine of resulting trust. The doctrine of resulting trust does not deal with the classic express trust, but is rather an equitable doctrine permitting those who have an interest in funds held in the name of another to recover them. In the first case we are concerned with the interpretation of terms of an express trust document; in the latter about the application of a legal (equitable) doctrine to a given situation.

The 1959 plan created a trust. All contributions were made subject to the trust. This did not mean, however, that all contributions were payable to the employees. Under the 1959 plan, expenses and administrative fees were payable to those who earned them, and the balance was payable to the beneficiaries. Consistent with a defined contribution plan, these were the only two classes of disbursements.

When the plan was changed in 1966 to a defined benefits plan, the nature of the trust necessarily changed. For one thing, the two accounts which the trustee was obliged to hold under the 1959 plan, the employee's account and the company account, no longer made sense and were necessarily collapsed. For another, the benefits payable to the employees were redefined. The trustee's former obligation to pay out the balance in the member's share of the two accounts after expenses, was replaced with a new and different obligation to pay out the defined benefits. And finally, as the fund continued to operate in its new form, there appeared a new element; the surplus which accumulated from year to year.

It appears that when the change was first made from a defined contribution to a defined benefit plan, no thought was given to the question of surplus. Certainly the 1966 plan made no reference to surplus. In theory, the actuarial projections should be so perfect that a surplus does not arise. But in reality, as the years passed, it became evident that a surplus was being generated. This new situation needed to be addressed. The response was the 1978 stipulation that any surplus

---

107   G.H. Treitel, *The Law of Contract*, 4th ed. (London: Stevens, 1975), at 129-130.

which existed after all defined benefits and expenses had been met, was payable to the employer.

Against this background, we return to the obligations on the trustee. The situation, as I see it, was this. Under the 1966 plan the trustee was obliged to pay defined benefits to each entitled employee. The trustee was further required to pay all administrative expenses of the trust. In addition to these two obligations, however, the trustee, as the years passed, found itself holding a third fund which was attached neither by the obligation to pay out benefits nor the obligation to pay expenses — the accumulating surplus. The original trust documents did not contemplate this fund and gave no guidance as to what to do with it.

The trustee was left with the following options with respect to the surplus. Prior to the 1978 stipulation, the trustee's only option, had the question of distribution of surplus arisen, would have been to apply to the court for a ruling. Had this occurred, the appropriate ruling would have been that it go to the employer on the principles of resulting trust, for the reasons discussed below. As it happened, however, a stipulation that the surplus go to the employer was made before the question of surplus distribution arose. For the reasons discussed earlier, that stipulation was valid. It follows that the surplus goes to the employer pursuant to the 1978 amendment.

It is contended that payment of the surplus to the employer constitutes revocation of a trust and that a trust cannot be revoked without express wording so permitting. This argument, however, fails because the surplus was an unanticipated development which was never contemplated by the original trust and was not addressed by any changes to the trust until 1978. The error in the respondents' submissions, as I see it, lies in assuming that the 1959 trust provisions apply to a surplus. In fact, they do not. All contributions fell into the trust, but to stop the analysis there is to beg the critical question: what was the trustee to do with the portion of the fund which became surplus after conversion of the plan to a defined benefit plan? The answer to that question does not amount to revocation of a trust, as the respondents suggest. Rather, it amounts to fulfilling the trust.

I conclude that the terms of the trust did not require that the surplus in question be paid to the employees. In 1966, when the possibility of a surplus first arose, the trust provided no guidance as to where a surplus would go in the event of termination. The 1978 amendment made it clear that it was payable to the employer. Therefore, under the terms of the trust, the employer is entitled to the surplus.

Resulting trust

I have argued that under the terms of the governing documentation, and in particular the 1978 amendment which I consider valid, surplus contributions are returnable to the employer. If I were wrong in concluding that the documentation requires this result, the same conclusion would nevertheless flow from application of the doctrine of resulting trust.

D.W.M. Waters describes the concept of resulting trust as follows:[108]

> ... a resulting trust arises whenever legal or equitable title to property is in one party's name, but that party, because he is a fiduciary or gave no value for the property, is under an obligation to return it to the original title owner, or to the person who *did* give value for it.

The concept of resulting trust does not depend on there being an express trust in existence. However, one of its applications is in the case where residual moneys not designated to a particular person or purposes arise in an express trust. Where this happens in a charitable trust, the courts will order the residual sum cy-près, among all the creditors. Where the trust is non-charitable, the sum generally reverts to the settlor.[109]

If the 1978 amendment as to surplus is invalid, these principles suggest that the doctrine of resulting trust requires that the surplus be available to the employer. The employer was responsible for ensuring a fund sufficient to meet all defined benefits owing to employees. As it turns out, the employer paid more than required for the purpose of the trust, the provision of benefits to all eligible employees. The residual sum should therefore return to the employer.

As noted earlier, the doctrine of resulting trust has been applied to this situation in Great Britain, with the result that surplus funds in defined benefit pension plans have been ordered paid to the employer. It has also been applied in Canada. The case of *Re Canada Trust Co. and Cantol Ltd.*[110] raised similar issues as those before us. The first question was the validity of an amendment directing that surplus should revert to the employer. Gould J. found that the attempted amendment in that case was invalid. However, he went on to hold that the surplus reverted to the employer under the doctrine of resulting trust. He stated:[111]

> The method which the board has employed [directors' resolution to allow reversion] does not accomplish the purpose for which it was intended. If this method is ineffectual, how then must the money remaining in the fund be distributed?...
>
> *The purposes of this trust simply did not exhaust the fund and the outcome here, i.e., a surplus balance of $31,163.38, was not foreseen by the respondent Dependable. The situation appears to be one where a resulting trust arises by operation of the law.*

My colleague seeks to distinguish this case on two grounds. He questions Gould J.'s conclusion that there could be a resulting trust in favour of the employer because of a clause in the plan providing that no amendment "shall permit any part of the trust fund to revert to or to be recoverable by the Company". But Gould J. was not talking about reversion under an amendment (having found the attempt to amend had failed), but rather about reversion by operation of law. My colleague also points to the fact that unlike the plan at bar, the plan in *Cantol* was non-contributory. But as we have seen, even where employees contribute to a defined benefit plan, that contribution is taken to be fully satisfied by receipt of the defined

---

108 *Law of Trusts in Canada*, 2nd ed. (Toronto: Carswell, 1984), at 299 (emphasis in original).
109 See Waters, *ibid.*, at 322.
110 *Supra,* note 90.
111 *Ibid.,* at 111 (emphasis added).

benefits: *Davis v. Richards & Wallington Industries Ltd., supra.* Once the defined obligations to the employees have been paid, it is difficult to argue that the employees have an interest in the surplus on the basis of a resulting trust in their favour. It is in the nature of a defined benefit that it represents a fixed amount to which the employee is entitled from the plan. The employee accepts this fixed amount in lieu of the greater or lesser amounts he or she might obtain on a defined contribution plan. Generally, this is thought to be in the employee's interest.

To put it another way, once the stipulated benefit is paid, the employee is no longer a beneficiary — he or she has exhausted his or her rights under the plan. As Gould J. put it in *Cantol,* "[a]ll the beneficiaries have been paid off in accordance [with the trust] provisions, and no beneficiaries remain in any of the categories".[112] Moreover, the complications of holding otherwise appear significant. As Scott J. points out in *Davis,*[113] *supra,* different employees contribute different amounts, and often receive benefits disproportionate to their contributions, depending on when they started working, how long they have been working, and other factors. The task of restoring to each employee his or her fair share of any surplus would be impossible. I can do no better than echo the query of Scott J.: "How can a resulting trust work as between the various employees inter se? I do not think it can and I do not see why equity should impute to them an intention that would lead to an unworkable result."[114]

Notes and Questions

1. *Schmidt v. Air Products of Canada Ltd.* shows how it can be difficult deciding whether an express trust has failed. All judges decided that only a portion of Air Products pension funds was held in trust (the portion derived from the Catalytic pension plan). McLachlin and Sopinka JJ. held that this trust did not fail, because the surplus was disposed of according to the amendments to the plan. The rest of the court held the trust did not fail, because the amendments were invalid and the surplus was held in trust for the employees. In other words, for the majority of the court, there was no surplus. How was that outcome possible after the Catalytic pension plan was converted from a defined contribution to a defined benefit plan?

2. The majority of the court held that a general power to amend the trust does not authorize the revocation of the trust. Would it allow for the addition of new trust beneficiaries? If so, can the settlor be added as a new trust beneficiary?

3. The 1959 trust agreement establishing the Catalytic plan stated that, "In the event of termination of the Plan, the Company cannot recover any sums paid to the date thereof and each Member of the Plan shall receive the proceeds of his Member's Account and his Company Account as of the date of such termination."[115] This makes it clear that there can be no surplus and makes sense in a defined contribution plan. However, what is the

---

112 *Ibid.*
113 *Supra,* note 96, at 595.
114 *Ibid.*
115 (1994), 115 D.L.R. (4th) 631, [1994] 2 S.C.R. 611, 20 Alta. L.R. (3d) 225, 1994 CarswellAlta 138, 1994 CarswellAlta 746, 3 C.C.P.B. 1, (sub nom. *Stearns Catalytic Pension Plans, Re*) 168 N.R. 81, [1994] 8 W.W.R. 305, 3 E.T.R. (2d) 1, 4 C.C.E.L. (2d) 1, 155 A.R. 81, 73 W.A.C. 81, C.E.B. & P.G.R. 8173, [1995] O.P.L.R. 283, at 682 [D.L.R.].

effect of this statement in a defined benefit plan, once every trust beneficiary has received his or her entitlement in full and there is in fact a surplus?

4. In *Schmidt v. Air Products of Canada Ltd.*, Cory J. said, "a resulting trust will not arise if, at the time of settlement, the settlor demonstrates an intention to part with his or her money outright. This is to say the settlor indicates that he or she will not retain any interest in any remaining funds."[116] Most settlers expect that the express trust will completely dispose of the trust assets and that they will have no further interest in the trust (as settlor) once it is created. The resulting trust arises by operation of law to return the surplus to the settlor even though the settlor never expected to recover it. Can a statement that the settlor does not want the surplus back defeat a resulting trust in the absence of some assignment of that surplus to someone else? Compare the Privy Council's resolution of this issue in *Air Jamaica Ltd. v. Charlton*, below.

AIR JAMAICA LTD. v. CHARLTON

[1999] U.K.P.C. 20, [1999] 1 W.L.R. 1399
Privy Council from the Court of Appeal of Jamaica

When Air Jamaica Limited ("the Company") was privatised, its employee pension plan was discontinued, leaving a surplus in excess of $400 million. The trust deed, which established the plan as a trust, stated (in clause 13.3) that, "any balance of the Fund shall be applied to provide additional benefits for Members and after their death for their widows or their designated beneficiaries in such equitable and non-discriminatory manner as the Trustees may determine in accordance with the advice of an Actuary." If valid, this clause would have disposed of the surplus, but the Privy Council advised that it was void because it violated the common law rule against perpetuities.

Clause 4 of the trust deed stated, "No moneys which at any time have been contributed by the Company under the terms hereof shall in any circumstances be repayable to the Company." In 1994, the trust deed and the pension plan were amended to remove clause 4 and to replace clause 13.3 with a trust to pay the surplus to the company. The Privy Council advised that clause 4 invalidated the 1994 amendments, but did not prevent a resulting trust from arising. The advice of the Privy Council was given by Lord Millett. This portion of his advice deals with the destination of the surplus.

LORD MILLETT:

. . .

Prima facie the surplus is held on a resulting trust for those who provided it. This sometimes creates a problem of some perplexity. In the present case, however, it does not. Contributions were payable by the Members with matching contributions by the Company. In the absence of any evidence that this is not what happened in practice, the surplus must be treated as provided as to one half by the Company and as to one half by the Members.

---

116 *Ibid.*, at D.L.R. 660.

The Attorney-General contended that neither the Company nor the Members can take any part in the surplus, which has reverted to the Crown as *bona vacantia*. He argued that clause 4 of the Trust Deed precludes any claim by the Company, while the Members cannot claim any part of the surplus because they have received all that they are entitled to. There is authority for both propositions. Their Lordships consider that they can be supported neither in principle nor as a matter of construction.

In *In re A.B.C. Television Ltd. Pension Scheme*,[117] Foster J. held that a clause similar to clause 4 of the present Trust Deed "negatives the possibility of implying a resulting trust". This is wrong in principle. Like a constructive trust, a resulting trust arises by operation of law, though unlike a constructive trust it gives effect to intention. But it arises whether or not the transferor intended to retain a beneficial interest — he almost always does not — since it responds to the absence of any intention on his part to pass a beneficial interest to the recipient. It may arise even where the transferor positively wished to part with the beneficial interest, as in *Vandervell v. Inland Revenue Commissioners*.[118] In that case the retention of a beneficial interest by the transferor destroyed the effectiveness of a tax avoidance scheme which the transferor was seeking to implement. The House of Lords affirmed the principle that a resulting trust is not defeated by evidence that the transferor intended to part with the beneficial interest if he has not in fact succeeded in doing so. As Plowman J. had said in the same case at first instance:[119]

> As I see it, a man does not cease to own property simply by saying "I don't want it." If he tries to give it away the question must always be, has he succeeded in doing so or not?

Lord Upjohn expressly approved this.[120]

Consequently their Lordships think that clauses of this kind in a pension scheme should generally be construed as forbidding the repayment of contributions under the terms of the scheme, and not as a pre-emptive but misguided attempt to rebut a resulting trust which would arise dehors the scheme. The purpose of such clauses is to preclude any amendment that would allow repayment to the Company. Their Lordships thus construe clause 4 of the Trust Deed as invalidating the 1994 amendments, but not as preventing the Company from retaining a beneficial interest by way of a resulting trust in so much of the surplus as is attributable to its contributions.

The Members' contributions stand on a similar footing. In *Davis v. Richards & Wallington Industries Ltd.*,[121] Scott J. held that the fact that a party has received all that he bargained for is not necessarily a decisive argument against a resulting trust, but that in the circumstances of the case before him a resulting trust in favour of the employees was excluded. The circumstances that impressed him were twofold. He considered that it was impossible to arrive at a workable scheme

---

117 Unreported, 22nd May 1973.
118 *Supra,* note 8.
119 [1966] Ch. 261 at 275.
120 *Supra,* note 118, at 314.
121 [1990] 1 W.L.R. 1511.

for apportioning the employees' surplus among the different classes of employees and he declined to "impute to them an intention that would lead to an unworkable result".[122] He also considered that he was precluded by statute from "imputing to the employees an intention" that they should receive by means of a resulting trust sums in excess of the maximum permitted by the relevant tax legislation.

These formulations also adopt the approach to intention that their Lordships have already considered to be erroneous. Their Lordships would observe that, even in the ordinary case of an actuarial surplus, it is not obvious that, when employees are promised certain benefits under a scheme to which they have contributed more than was necessary to fund them, they should not expect to obtain a return of their excess contributions. In the present case, however, the surplus does not arise from over-funding but from the failure of some of the trusts. It is impossible to say that the Members "have received all that they bargained for". One of the benefits they bargained for was that the trustees should be obliged to pay them additional benefits in the event of the scheme's discontinuance. It was the invalidity of this trust that gave rise to the surplus. Their Lordships consider that it would be more accurate to say that the Members claim such part of the surplus as is attributable to their contributions because they have not received all that they bargained for.

Pension schemes in Jamaica, as in England, need the approval of the Inland Revenue if they are to secure the fiscal advantages that are made available. The tax legislation in both countries places a limit on the amount which can be paid to the individual employee. Allowing the employees to enjoy any part of the surplus by way of resulting trust would probably exceed those limits. This fact is not, however, in their Lordships' view a proper ground on which to reject the operation of a resulting trust in favour of the employees. The Inland Revenue had an opportunity to examine the Pension Plan and to withhold approval on the ground that some of its provisions were void for perpetuity. They failed to do so. There is no call to distort principle in order to meet their requirements. The resulting trust arises by operation of the general law, dehors the pension scheme and the scope of the relevant tax legislation.

Scott J. was impressed by the difficulty of arriving at a workable scheme for apportioning the surplus funds among the Members and the executors of deceased Members. This was because he thought it necessary to value the benefits that each Member had received in order to ascertain his share in the surplus. On the separate settlement with mutual insurance analysis which their Lordships have adopted in the present case, however, no such process is required. The Members' share of the surplus should be divided pro rata among the Members and the estates of deceased Members in proportion to the contributions made by each Member without regard to the benefits each has received and irrespective of the dates on which the contributions were made.

. . .

---

122 *Ibid.*, at 1544.

Notes and Questions

1. In *Air Jamaica Ltd. v. Charlton*, the Privy Council advised that clause 4 of the trust deed, which prohibited the payment of trust assets to the company, invalidated an amendment of the trust that authorized payment of the surplus to the company, but did not prevent a resulting trust from arising in favour of the company. This differs from the approaches taken by the majority and by the minority in *Schmidt v. Air Products of Canada Ltd.* Cory J., for the majority, held that amendment of the trust was invalid and that a non-reversion clause would preclude a resulting trust, while McLachlin J. thought that a clause preventing diversion of the trust fund would not prevent the company from obtaining the surplus, either by amending the express trust or through a resulting trust. Which approach do you prefer?

2. The pension surplus cases demonstrate two legitimate ways to avoid the failure of an express trust. One is to find that there is no trust, but only a contract to provide pension benefits, and the other is to allow the amendment of the express trust to deal with the unexpected surplus. A third method is to deny the existence of a surplus even though assets remain after every single member of the class of trust beneficiaries has received everything to which he is she is entitled under the terms of the trust. Although this obviates the need for a resulting trust, it does provide an unexpected windfall to the trust beneficiaries and is difficult to explain using orthodox trust principles.

(c) Did the Settlor Intend a Gift of the Surplus?

Once it is determined that there was an express trust and that it failed to dispose of all of the trust assets, the next step is to determine whether the trustees can keep the surplus for their own benefit or hold it on resulting trust for the settlor (or the settlor's estate). In the vast majority of cases, there will be a resulting trust, but that is not the automatic result of the failure of an express trust. If admissible evidence shows that the settlor intended to make a gift of the surplus to the trustees, there is no reason why a resulting trust should arise to remove that surplus from them. In other words, the trustees are enriched at the settlor's expense, but that enrichment is not unjust: the settlor's intention to give provides a juristic reason for it.

If the surplus arose because all or part of the express trust was invalid, then it is highly unlikely that the settlor intended to give that surplus to the trustees. The invalid trust provisions show that the settlor intended that the surplus would be used for the trust objects. If, however, the surplus arises after a valid express trust has been fully performed, then it is possible that settlor wanted the trustees to keep anything not needed to fulfil the trust.

MOFFIT v. MOFFIT

[1954] 2 D.L.R. 841, 13 W.W.R. (N.S.) 145, 1954 CarswellBC 91
British Columbia Supreme Court

WILSON J.:

The plaintiffs are the husband and three sons of Margaret Moffit, deceased. The defendants are the executors named in her will and the defendant Robert John Moffit, also a son of Margaret Moffit is, in his own right, substantially interested in the outcome of this litigation.

The plaintiffs, by originating summons, ask the Court to answer these questions:

1. Does the Deed of Trust made the 7th day of November, 1951, between Margaret Moffit as Grantor, Robert John Moffit as Trustee, Robert Moffit as beneficiary, and Mary Norma Moffit as Substitute Trustee, create a valid trust affecting the real estate described therein? If so, what are the terms of the trust?

2. If question Number 1 is answered in the affirmative, does the said Deed of Trust give the said Robert John Moffit any beneficial interest in the said real estate?

3. If question Number 2 is answered in the negative, will said real estate be held on a resulting trust for the personal representatives of Margaret Moffit, deceased, subject to the life interest of the said Robert Moffit?

The document which I am thus called upon to interpret contains many unusual and interesting features.

The property dealt with falls into three groups: (a) Lands owned jointly by the settlor and the trustee; (b) Lands owned by the settlor; (c) Lands owned by the trustee.

The scheme of the deed, baldly, is this:

1. That the trustee will, during the lifetime of the settlor and her husband, or the survivor of them, pay to them the net income from the trust property.

2. That if the trustee dies while the settlor and her husband, or either of them, is still alive, the trustee's wife (called the substitute trustee) will pay to the settlor and her husband or the survivor of them the income from the properties listed under heading (b) above and one-half of the income from the properties listed under heading (a) above.

3. No provision is made for the disposition of corpus or income after the death of the settlor and her husband.

The neat point I am asked to decide is this: whether or not, since the trusts do not exhaust the estate given the trustee, there is a resulting trust in favour of the executors as successors in title of Margaret Moffit, deceased, or whether, on the other hand, there is a gift to the trustee of the remainder.

All cases dealing with this subject refer to the rule stated by Lord Eldon L.C. in *King v. Denison*:[123]

---

123 (1813), 1 Ves. & B. 260 at 272-273, 35 E.R. 102.

If I give to A. and his Heirs all my real Estate, charged with my Debts, that is Devise to him for a particular Purpose, but not for that Purpose only. If the Devise is upon Trust to pay my Debts, that is a Devise for a particular Purpose, and nothing more; and the Effect of those Two Modes admits just this Difference. The former is a Devise of an Estate of Inheritance for the Purpose of giving the Devisee the beneficial interest, subject to a particular Purpose: the latter is a Devise for a particular Purpose; with no Intention to give him any beneficial interest.

This lucid exposition of the principles to be applied has never been improved upon. It is the basis of the judgments in three later cases to which I shall refer: *Croome v. Croome*,[124] *Re Foord*,[125] and *Re Rees*.[126] All of these cases deal with the interpretation of wills....

. . .

These opinions were interpreted thus by Sargant J. in *Re Foord*:[127]

While a gift to A. upon trust for the provision of a certain interest for B., without more, must, I think, be construed as a gift to A. merely to fulfil the beneficial interest of B. and must not be construed as a gift to A. of all that is not required to satisfy B.'s interest, yet looking at the case of *Croome v. Croome*, 59 L.T. 582, which I employ for the purpose of seeing the general spirit in which the Court deals with cases of this character, I find that the Court is prepared to hold that there is a beneficial gift to the first taker on slight expressions and indications of intention. The indications there were so slight that the judges of the Court of Appeal confessed that it was difficult to state in words reasons for the impression produced on their minds by the language of the testator's will.

... [T]he Court of Appeal of England appears to have given its approval to this interpretation by the following statement by Evershed M.R. in *Re Rees*:[128]

It is right to say that, as Sargant J. observed, the cases show that slight indications may well suffice to persuade the court that the intention of the testator was not to create a trust estate in the devisee but to give him a conditional gift.

So I approach the construction of this document having in mind the precepts... approved by the Court of Appeal of England. And I note that there is nothing... to indicate that the rule of construction they have stated is to be restricted to the interpretation of wills and should not also apply to the construction of deeds, such as the one before me. The fact that the deed I have to consider is made to a near relative of the settlor may, as suggested by Cotton L.J. in *Croome v. Croome*,[129] have some bearing on the subject.

I find that the principal indicia of the intention of the settlor upon which I can rely are to be found in the recital to the trust deed, considered with the will

---

124 (1888), 59 L.T. 582.
125 [1922] 2 Ch. 519.
126 [1950] Ch. 204.
127 *Supra*, note 125, at 521-522.
128 *Supra*, note 126, at 208.
129 *Supra*, note 124, at 584.

of the settlor dated July 30, 1946. This will was, at the time the trust deed was made, the effective and existing last will and testament of the settlor and both counsel agree that I am entitled to look at it. Counsel for the defendants further contends that I should also look at a later will made November 26, 1951, some 3 weeks after the execution of the trust deed, but, for the present, I shall not do.

What expressions or indications are there before me, "slight" or otherwise, to aid me in construing this document?

1. The trust property includes not only lands conveyed by the settlor, but lands owned by the trustee. This is certainly not conclusive one way or the other, since there could be a resulting trust as to the settlor's lands alone, but it is, with other circumstances I shall describe, suggestive that since the parties must have meant that one part of the lands should, on the execution of the trust, be the clear property of the trustee, they also meant that the other part of the lands should follow in the same course. It is also, considered with the rest of the document, and with the settlor's will therein referred to, suggestive of a bargain; a bargain whereby the settlor, in consideration of receiving for herself and her husband during their lives the income of the trustee's property, gave to the trustee, on the completion of the trusts, the corpus of her own property.

2. The objects of the trust are... to protect the welfare of the grantor and her husband and also to carry into effect the wishes expressed by the grantor in her last will and testament and to protect the rights of the trustee by conveying all the said properties to the trustee at or before the execution of the trust deed. Such a conveyance was made at the time the trust deed was executed. The will in existence at that time, which both counsel conceded I might examine, after some legacies of personality, gives to the trustee all the residue of her curate, which residue would include the lands in question here. Now this seems to me not a "slight indication" but evidence that the settlor was saying, in effect: "I here and now give to the trustee the property that he would by my will get in any course, subject only to his caring for my welfare and that of my husband during our lives." Otherwise I cannot see what meaning can he placed on the phrase "to protect the rights of the trustee". If the trustee does not get the corpus he, receives no rights under this trust deed — he only assumes obligations and gives away, for an indefinite period, the income from his own properties.

3. It will be noted that the substitute trustee was to perform her trust as "Executrix of the estate of the trustee or otherwise as owner of the said trust properties". The word "owner" here is suggestive, suggestive that the parties hereto thought that after the substitute trustee had, as executrix, completed administration of the property, she would, as the trustee's wife and beneficiary, become, as he had been, owner of the properties, and all of them.

The rest of the trust deed is, as counsel for the defendants concedes, consistent with either interpretation. But the passages I have cited satisfy me that the settlor intended to benefit the trustee, not merely *ex gratia*, as a son, but because she was receiving a valuable consideration, to wit, the income during her lifetime of his own properties and the unrewarded services of himself and his wife as managers, during the lifetime of herself and her husband, and for the benefit of herself and her husband, of the income from the properties. Hence I say there is no resulting trust....

Notes and Questions

1. In *Re Foord*,[130] an engineer living in China dictated a short will from his death bed to his servant, which gave $2,000 and his personal effects and furniture in China to his servant and left everything else "absolutely to my sister Margaret Juliet on trust to pay to my wife" an annuity. The bequest to the sister was more than sufficient to pay the annuity and she took out a summons to determine whether she was entitled to the surplus or held it on trust for the testator's next of kin. Sargant J. called it "a difficult case and on the border line", but decided that the surplus was intended as a gift to the sister and, therefore, no resulting trust arose. The factors that led to this conclusion were the use of the word "absolutely" in a non-technical will drafted by a non-lawyer, the description of the trustee in personal terms as "my sister" and without using her surname, Foord, and the inclusion of non-income producing assets in the bequest to her.

2. In *Re Rees*,[131] Evershed M.R. approved of *Re Foord*, but said that, "the cases show that slight indications may well suffice to persuade the court that the intention of the testator was not to create a trust estate in the devisee but to give him a conditional gift".[132] However, it is not true that there is no express trust just because the trustees are permitted to keep the surplus trust assets for their own benefit. Some transfers truly are conditional gifts, because the condition does not require the donee to use the subject of the gift in any particular way. An engagement present is a classic example. However, if the recipient is under a duty to use the subject for the benefit of another person, then the transaction is a trust even if the trustees are entitled to the surplus.[133] As Professor Waters said:[134]

> It is always open to a settlor to confer a beneficial interest upon the person who is also to be a trustee. Often, then, two questions present themselves: is the obligated person a trustee, and if he is a trustee for the purposes of carrying out the obligation concerning the property, is he also to take a beneficial interest in any excess? The apposition has been put in this way: "it is rather a gift upon condition than a gift upon trust", but this is somewhat misleading. Certainly one who is found to be a trustee is often found to have been excluded from any beneficial enjoyment, no doubt because the testator did not wish to expose his trustee to any conflict of interest and duty, but such a finding is not automatic. It is not even a presumption; it is simply a matter of construction. The question is what did the testator intend should happen to moneys left over when the trust purposes have been fulfilled.

3. What is the difference between the assumption that trustees are not intended to keep surplus trust assets for their own benefit and the presumption of resulting trust, discussed in the next section?

4. Although a resulting trust will not arise if the settlor intended to give the surplus to the trustees, this does not mean that the resulting trust depends on the settlor having

---

130 *Supra,* note 125.

131 *Supra,* note 126.

132 *Ibid.,* at 208.

133 R. Chambers, "Conditional Gifts" in N. Palmer & E. McKendrick, eds., *Interests in Goods*, 2nd ed. (London: Lloyds of London Press, 1998) 429 at 442-445.

134 D.W.M. Waters, *Law of Trusts in Canada*, 2nd ed. (Toronto: Carswell) at 86.

had an intention to get the surplus back. As Harman J. said in *Gillingham Bus Disaster Fund, Re*, in most cases the settlor never expected to recover any part of the trust assets:[135]

> The general principle must be that where money is held upon trust and the trusts declared do not exhaust the fund it will revert to the donor or settlor under what is called a resulting trust. The reasoning behind this is that the settlor or donor did not part with his money absolutely out and out but only *sub modo* to the intent that his wishes as declared by the declaration of trust should be carried into effect. When, therefore, this has been done any surplus still belongs to him. This doctrine does not, in my judgment, rest on any evidence of the state of mind of the settlor, for in the vast majority of cases no doubt he does not expect to see his money back: he has created a trust which so far as he can see will absorb the whole of it. The resulting trust arises where that expectation is for some unforeseen reason cheated of fruition, and is an inference of law based on after-knowledge of the event.

The resulting trust is the appropriate response whenever the settlor did not want to give the trust surplus to the trustees and failed to give it to anyone else. In that situation, the trustees would be unjustly enriched if they kept the surplus for themselves and, therefore, they must return it to the settlor or the settlor's estate, even if the settlor did not want to get it back. The resulting trust arises to give effect to that obligation.

4. APPARENT GIFTS

(a) Introduction

We have considered various situations in which an express trust fails and, in those situations, there is usually a resulting trust for the settlor. In the following materials, we will consider resulting trusts that do not normally arise out of express trusts, but rather upon a voluntary transfer from one person to another or upon a purchase by someone who supplies the purchase money but directs that title be taken in the name of another person. For the sake of convenience, these resulting trusts will be called voluntary transfer resulting trusts and purchase money resulting trusts, respectively.

We have argued above that these resulting trusts are as much automatic as those which arise upon the failure of an express trust. This is because the presumption of resulting trust is simply a presumption that the transferor or purchaser lacked an intention to give the beneficial ownership of the assets to the recipient. In the absence of an intention to benefit the recipient, whether established by the evidence or as a result of the presumption, there is then an automatic resulting trust to the transferor or purchaser.

The presumption is rebuttable, that is, it may be displaced by evidence of a contrary intention. As we shall see, the courts first consider the evidence to see if a contrary intention is established. The presumption will be relied on only if it is still not clear whether the recipient was intended to have beneficial ownership, as a gift, loan, or pursuant to a contract. Hence, Lord Upjohn once said that the

---

135 [1958] Ch. 300 at 310, [1958] 1 All E.R. 37, affirmed [1959] Ch. 62, [1958] 2 All E.R. 749 (C.A.).

presumption "is no more than a long stop to provide the answer when the relevant facts and circumstances fail to yield a solution."[136]

The presumption of resulting trust is raised only if the recipient is a stranger to the transferor or purchaser. For this purpose, a stranger is anyone other than the transferor's or purchaser's spouse or child, or a person to whom the transferor or purchaser stands *in loco parentis*. The presumption also applies when a person transfers assets to or purchases assets in the name of a corporation.[137] It does not apply to testamentary gifts since it is assumed that testators intend to give away all of their assets.

When the transferor or purchaser is the husband or parent of the recipient, there is a presumption of advancement, that is, that a gift was intended. This presumption is also rebuttable. However, as with the case of the presumption of resulting trust, the evidence is considered first. If the evidence establishes whether or not a gift was intended, it is not necessary to rely upon either presumption.[138]

Earlier we noted that if the evidence establishes that the recipient was intended to hold upon trust, so that the presumption need not be relied upon, the trust that arises can be an express trust. This presents difficulties when the subject of the trust is land for, while a resulting trust may be raised without evidence in writing,[139] an express trust of land is not enforceable unless it is evidenced by writing.[140] However, as *Hodgson v. Marks*[141] demonstrates, if an express trust of land is not evidenced by writing, the intention to create that trust is an important fact that may give rise to a resulting or constructive trust by operation of law. This matter is dealt with further in the materials on the constructive trust.

(b) The "Common Intention" Resulting Trust

Today, most matrimonial and cohabitation property disputes are regulated by statute or by the law of constructive trusts. Before the development of that law in the last quarter of the 20th century, many of these disputes were resolved by application of the presumptions of resulting trust and advancement. Thus, if one party (A) had contributed money to the acquisition of assets by her or his (lawful or *de facto*) spouse (B), A could obtain a declaration that B held those assets on resulting trust for A and B as co-tenants in proportion to their contributions, absent evidence that A intended to make a gift to B. If A was B's wife, she could rely on the presumption of resulting trust but, if A was B's husband, he would need evidence to displace the presumption of advancement.

---

136 *Vandervell v. Inland Revenue Commissioners, supra,* note 8, at 313.

137 See *RoyNat Inc. v. United Rescue Services Ltd.* (1982), 18 Man. R. (2d) 54, 1982 CarswellMan 16, 44 C.B.R. (N.S.) 1 (C.A.).

138 Some modern matrimonial property law statutes alter the application of the presumptions in the context of a division of matrimonial property on the breakdown of a marriage. This reform is considered later in this chapter.

139 *Chrustie v. Minister of National Revenue, supra,* note 18.

140 See, *e.g., Statute of Frauds,* R.S.O. 1990, c. S.19, s. 9.

141 [1971] Ch. 892, [1971] 2 All E.R. 684 (C.A.), reproduced above.

The orthodox position is, first, that a presumption of resulting trust can be raised only by an actual contribution to the acquisition of assets and, secondly, that the presumption of advancement applies when a wife receives assets at the expense of her husband. If a husband receives assets at the expense of his wife or the parties were not married to each other, the presumption of resulting trust applies instead. When the facts admit, these principles continue to be relevant in the resolution of matrimonial property disputes to the extent they have not been ousted by statute. Further, they continue to be relevant in resolving cohabitation property disputes and are unobjectionable so long as they are restricted to their orthodox principles.

However, the orthodox resulting trust proved inadequate for resolving matrimonial and cohabitation property disputes. In many cases, the man had title to the bulk of the family assets and the woman had not contributed money to the acquisition of those assets. However, she did contribute in other ways: perhaps by paying all or part of the mortgage over a period of time or more often by working in the house and raising the children. In order to give her a claim to land registered in the man's name, the Canadian courts developed a peculiar form of resulting trust, based on the parties' common intention, in the early 1970s. It worked this way: if both parties had a common intention that they would share land owned by one of them, the court would declare that the land was held on resulting trust for both parties in accordance with their intention. Similarly, the court would raise a resulting trust if a common intention to share the land was implied by their conduct. The courts called this resulting trust the "common intention" resulting trust. Doctrinally, such a resulting trust is impossible, for a resulting trust can arise only when one person has transferred assets to, or purchased assets for, another person and did not intend to make a gift of the property.

The "common intention" resulting trust was a purely Canadian invention. It is based upon a misreading of Lord Diplock's speech in *Gissing v. Gissing*:[142]

> Any claim to a beneficial interest in land by a person, whether spouse or stranger, in whom the legal estate in the land is not vested must be based upon the proposition that the person in whom the legal estate is vested holds it as trustee upon trust to give effect to the beneficial interest of the claimant as cestui que trust. The legal principles applicable to the claim are those of the English law of trusts and in particular, in the kind of dispute between spouses that comes before the courts, the law relating to the creation and operation of "resulting, implied or constructive trusts." Where the trust is expressly declared in the instrument by which the legal estate is transferred to the trustee or by a written declaration of trust by the trustee, the court must give effect to it. But to constitute a valid declaration of trust by way of gift of a beneficial interest in land to a cestui que trust the declaration is required by section 53(1) of the *Law of Property Act, 1925*,[143] to be in writing. If it is not in writing it can only take effect as a resulting, implied or constructive trust to which that section has no application. A resulting, implied or constructive trust — and it is unnecessary for present purposes to distinguish between these three classes of trust — is created by a transaction between the trustee and the cestui que trust in connection with the acquisition by the trustee of a legal estate in land, whenever the trustee has so conducted

---

142 *Supra*, note 22, at 904-905, 909. It is interesting to note that Martland J. expressed his agreement with these views in *Murdoch v. Murdoch* (1973), [1975] S.C.R. 423, 41 D.L.R. (3d) 367 at 376, 1973 CarswellAlta 156, 1973 CarswellAlta 119, [1974] 1 W.W.R. 361, 13 R.F.L. 185.

143 15 & 16 Geo. 5, c. 20 (U.K.).

himself that it would be inequitable to allow him to deny to the cestui que trust a beneficial interest in the land acquired. And he will be held so to have conducted himself if by his words or conduct he has induced the cestui que trust to act to his own detriment in the reasonable belief that by so acting he was acquiring a beneficial interest in the land.

. . .

Difficult as they are to solve, however, these problems as to the amount of the share of a spouse in the beneficial interest in a matrimonial home where the legal estate is vested solely in the other spouse, only arise in cases where the court is satisfied by the words or conduct of the parties that it was their common intention that the beneficial interest was not to belong solely to the spouse in whom the legal estate was vested but was to be shared between them in some proportion or other.

Lord Diplock appears to be saying that, if the spouses had a "common intention" that they should share the assets equally or in some other proportion, a trust will be raised in favour of the non-titled spouse and it does not matter whether one calls this trust resulting, implied, or constructive. The Canadian courts took this to mean that, if such a common intention could be found, a presumption of resulting trust could be raised. Moreover, since there was rarely any evidence of the proportion in which the spouses should share, an equal division was common. This approach is reflected in *Rathwell v. Rathwell*,[144] discussed in greater detail below.

In fact, however, Lord Diplock did not say this at all. He did say that the titled spouse may have created an express trust in respect of the land. For example, the husband, if he is the titled spouse, may have had the land conveyed to him upon trust for his wife and himself in certain defined proportions, or he may have made a written declaration of trust to that effect. Since it is manifest in writing, such an express trust is clearly enforceable, but is highly unlikely to occur in practice between spouses. Alternatively, the husband may have made an oral declaration of trust, or the parties may have reached an oral understanding that, although the title would be in the husband's name, the wife would have a beneficial interest in it. If the property is land, the oral trust is unenforceable.[145] Similarly the "understanding" or oral contract would be unenforceable.[146] However, Lord Diplock notes correctly that the writing requirement does not apply to trusts arising by operation of law (that is, resulting, implied, and constructive trusts) and, in certain circumstances, equity will raise such a trust out of an oral declaration or

---

144 [1978] 2 S.C.R. 436, [1978] 2 W.W.R. 101, 83 D.L.R. (3d) 289, 1978 CarswellSask 36, 1978 CarswellSask 129, 19 N.R. 91, 1 E.T.R. 307, 1 R.F.L. (2d) 1.

145 *Cf. Statute of Frauds*, R.S.O. 1990, c. S.19, s. 9.

146 As it would also be if the asset was personalty and the contract was not to be performed within the space of one year: *ibid.*, s. 4. See *Hanau v. Ehrlich*, [1912] A.C. 39 (H.L.); *Sherman v. Monarch Chrome Furniture Co.* (1958), 15 D.L.R. (2d) 6 (Ont. C.A.). However, if the contract can be performed within one year and is not for a definite period, then even though the parties expect it to last for more than a year and, even if it does in fact last longer than one year, it is not within the statute: *Richmond Wineries Western Ltd. v. Simpson* (1939), [1940] S.C.R. 1, [1940] 2 D.L.R. 481, 1939 CarswellBC 110; *Campbell v. Business Fleets Ltd.*, [1954] 2 D.L.R. 263, [1954] O.R. 87, 1954 CarswellOnt 36 (C.A.).

understanding. The reason his Lordship did not distinguish between the different types of trust is understandable in that context. He was referring merely to the trusts that are not subject to a writing requirement.

It is unfortunate that Lord Diplock did not clarify the type of trust to which he referred, because the Canadian courts took his meaning to be that a resulting trust can arise out of the parties' common intention. However, that is impossible. A resulting trust arises only out of an intention not to confer a beneficial interest, as where one party contributes to the purchase price of an asset without intending to make a gift. Lord Diplock was referring to a constructive trust and, more particularly, the constructive trust that arises out of the non-titled party's detrimental reliance upon the words or conduct of the titled party. As we shall see in subsequent chapters, such a trust had long been recognized in English law.[147]

The "common intention" resulting trust has been supplanted in large part by the constructive trust[148] and by matrimonial property law reform legislation in Canada, but it is still referred to and continues to be used in some cases. Hence, it is necessary to discuss the circumstances in which it might be raised.

Rathwell v. Rathwell[149] is a leading case in which the Supreme Court of Canada last employed the "common intention" resulting trust. The plaintiff wife and the defendant husband decided to become farmers after they were married in 1944. They had a joint bank account in which they deposited their savings and all moneys subsequently received by either of them. All expenses were paid from it, including a down payment for two quarter sections of land purchased in 1946 and most of the down payments for two subsequent purchases of land in 1947 and 1958. The husband took title to the lands.

While the parties were still cohabiting, the husband said that he and his wife were working together as a team and that their farming business was a joint venture. The wife participated in running the farm, including doing chores, milking cows, and operating machinery. Further, she provided meals, transported hired help, and kept the books and records. She also raised and educated four children.

The parties separated in 1967 and the wife then brought this action for a declaration that she had a one-half interest in the real and personal property owned by her husband and for an accounting of all income and benefits earned from that property. The Supreme Court of Canada held that the plaintiff was entitled to a property interest in the properties, but the members of the court differed about the extent of the interest. Dickson J., with whom Laskin C.J.C. and Spence J. agreed, said this about matrimonial property disputes:[150]

> In broad terms matrimonial property disputes are much alike, differing only in detail. Matrimonial property, *i.e.* property acquired during matrimony (I avoid the term "family assets"

---

147 See, *e.g.*, *Rochefoucauld v. Boustead, supra*, note 14. See also *Bannister v. Bannister*, [1948] 2 All E.R. 133 (C.A.).

148 This trust, which is discussed in the next two chapters was adopted by the Supreme Court of Canada in *Becker v. Pettkus, supra*, note 26.

149 *Supra*, note 144.

150 *Ibid.*, at 301.

with its doctrinal connotations) is ordinarily the subject-matter of the conflict. One or other, or both, of the spouses may have contributed financially to the purchase. One or other may have contributed freely given labour. The contribution may have been direct, or indirect in the sense of permitting the acquisition of an asset which would otherwise not have been acquired. Such an indirect contribution may have been in money, or it may have been in other forms as, for example, through caring for the home and family. The property is acquired during a period when there is marital accord. When this gives way to discord, problems arise in respect of property division. There is seldom prior express agreement. There is rarely implied agreement or common intention, apart from the general intention of building a life together. It is not in the nature of things for young married people to contemplate the break-up of their marriage and the division, in that event, of assets acquired by common effort during wedlock.

Dickson J. also said the following about "common intention" resulting trusts:[151]

> Resulting trusts are as firmly grounded in the settlor's intent as are express trusts, but with this difference — that the intent is inferred, or is presumed as a matter of law from the circumstances of the case. That is very old doctrine.... The law presumes that the holder of the legal title was not intended to take beneficially. There are certain situations — such as purchase in the name of another — where the law unfailingly raises the presumption of resulting trust.[152] The presumption has always been regarded as rebuttable.[153]
>
> If at the dissolution of a marriage one spouse alone holds title to property, it is relevant for the court to ask whether or not there was a common intention, or agreement, that the other spouse was to take a beneficial interest in the property and, if so, what interest? Such agreements, as I have indicated, can rarely be evidenced concretely. It is relevant and necessary for the courts to look to the facts and circumstances surrounding the acquisition, or improvement, of the property. If the wife without title has contributed, directly or indirectly, in money or money's worth, to acquisition or improvement, the doctrine of resulting trusts is engaged. An interest in the property is presumed to result to the one advancing the purchase moneys, or part of the purchase moneys....
>
> . . .
>
> The position is the same in respect of both spouses. In present social conditions the old presumption of advancement has ceased to embody any credible inference of intention.[154]
>
> The presumption of a resulting trust is sometimes explained as the fact of contribution evidencing an agreement; it has also been explained as a constructive agreement. All of this is settled law.[155] The courts are looking for a common intention manifested by acts or words that property is acquired as a trustee.
>
> If there is a contribution in money or money's worth, but absence of evidence of an agreement or common intention as to the quantum of the interest, doubts may arise as to the extent of the share of each spouse in the property. Lord Reid, in *Pettitt's* case,[156] said that the respective shares might be determined in this manner:
>
>> ... you ask what reasonable people in the shoes of the spouses would have agreed if they had directed their minds to the question of what claim the contributing spouse ought to have.
>
> This is a sensible solution and I would adopt it.

---

151 *Ibid.*, at 302-305.
152 *Dyer v. Dyer, supra,* note 5; *Barton v. Muir* (1874), 44 L.J.P.C. 193; *The Venture* (1908), 77 L.J.P.D. 105.
153 *Rider v. Kidder* (1805), 10 Ves. Jun. 360, 32 E.R. 884.
154 See *Pettit v. Pettit,* [1970] A.C. 777 at 793, 811, 815, and 824 (H.L.).
155 *Murdoch v. Murdoch, supra,* note 142; *Gissing v. Gissing, supra,* note 22; *Pettit, ibid.*
156 *Pettit, supra,* note 154, at 794.

The difficulty experienced in the cases is the situation where no agreement or common intention is evidenced, and the contribution of the spouse without title can be characterized as performance of the usual duties growing out of matrimony. There are many examples of this. There is the class of case where one spouse spends week-ends or evenings making small repairs to the family home,[157] or contributes money to such repairs.[158] There is the case where one spouse may go out to work, making contributions to family expenses enabling the other spouse to acquire and pay for the matrimonial home;[159] or the case where one spouse may work in a family business and receive no wage or title to property.[160] There is also the case where a business may be a joint effort, such as a farm and, though title may issue to one spouse only, the business only succeeds through the efforts of both husband and wife.[161] Some of these situations may be analyzed as agreement or common intention situations. Such intention is generally presumed from a financial contribution. The doctrine of resulting trusts applies. In others a common intention is clearly lacking and cannot be presumed. The doctrine of the resulting trust then cannot apply. It is here that we must turn to the doctrine of constructive trust.

Dickson J. concluded that the plaintiff should succeed in her claim to an interest in the properties under a resulting trust on the basis of the presumed common intention that arose from her contribution in money and money's worth. Further, he held that Mrs. Rathwell had a one-half interest, since her contributions derived from the joint account that was used by the parties as a pool of their resources. He went on, specifically, to state that contribution in the form of labour can be a contribution in money's worth.

Ritchie J., with whom Pigeon J. concurred, agreed that the wife was entitled to a half interest in all of the properties under a "common intention" resulting trust. Martland J., with whom Beetz and de Grandpré JJ. concurred, agreed with the finding of a common intention resulting trust, but not with the quantum of the wife's interest. In his view, the husband's contributions to the farming operation were greater than the wife's. He concluded that the wife should have a half interest in the lands purchased in 1946, but not in the other parcels.

As stated above, the "common intention" resulting trust has been replaced by statutes and the constructive trust in cases involving the division of family assets. Canadian courts have also said that it should not be used in other situations, which means that the "common intention" resulting trust may soon be extinct, if it is not already. In *Hollett v. Hollett*,[162] the plaintiff claimed that his brother, the defendant, held land on resulting trust for both of them as tenants in common. Although the defendant had paid the entire purchase price for the land, the plaintiff based his claim on their common intention that the plaintiff would be entitled to a share of the land if he reimbursed the defendant for his share of the purchase price. Green J. said:[163]

---

157   *Appleton v. Appleton*, [1965] 1 W.L.R. 25; *Pettit v. Pettit, supra,* note 154.

158   *Re Taylor and Taylor*, [1971] 1 O.R. 715, 16 D.L.R. (3d) 481.

159   *Rimmer v. Rimmer*, [1953] 1 Q.B. 63, [1952] 2 All E.R. 863 (C.A.); *Fribance v. Fribance (No. 2)*, [1957] 1 W.L.R. 384.

160   *Re Cummins*, [1971] 3 All E.R. 782.

161   *Trueman v. Trueman*, [1971] 2 W.W.R. 688, 17 D.L.R. (3d) 109 (Alta. S.C. A.D.); *Murdoch v. Murdoch, supra,* note 142; *Fiedler v. Fiedler*, [1975] 3 W.W.R. 681, 55 D.L.R. (3d) 397.

162   (1993), 106 Nfld. & P.E.I.R. 271, 31 R.P.R. (2d) 251, 1993 CarswellNfld 38, 334 A.P.R. 271, 50 E.T.R. 22 (T.D.).

163   *Ibid.,* at 264-265.

Argument in the instant case was directed to establishing evidence of a "common intention" of the parties as forming the basis of a resulting trust. Reference was made in this context to the comments in such cases as *Rathwell v. Rathwell*.[164] Proof of a common intention is not, however, the basis of resulting trust in purchase money resulting trust situations. The basis of the resulting trust in such cases is that, because persons who pay for property generally expect to get value in return, equity presumes that the person furnishing the purchase money does not intend to make a gift of the property to the grantee and therefore the grantee is presumed to hold the property (or a proportionate part thereof) on resulting trust for the payor. Proof of a common intention cannot be the basis of such a resulting trust because that would be tantamount to allowing proof of an express trust which, by section VII of the *Statute of Frauds*, is required to be evidenced in writing, where the subject matter is land. Resulting trusts are exempt from the writing requirements of the *Statute of Frauds* under Section VIII because of the very point that expression of a trust intention is not their basis. Equity supplies that which is not expressed, namely a presumed intention, and concludes that in view of the relationship of the parties, their acts express an intent to have a trust even though they did not use language to that effect.

In *Hollett v. Hollett*, the plaintiff was entitled to a share of the land because his agreement with the defendant was a specifically enforceable contract of sale. Their correspondence constituted a memorandum of the contract and, in any event, there were sufficient acts of part performance to allow the court to enforce it even in the absence of writing.

(c) Purchase Money Resulting Trusts

Suppose that A enters into an agreement to purchase land (or personal property) from V and A pays the purchase price to V. However, A then directs V to transfer the land (or to deliver or assign the personal property) to B and, in due course, B acquires title to the property. This is the typical situation of a purchase money resulting trust and it raises a presumption of resulting trust in favour of A (unless B is A's child or wife, in which case the presumption of advancement usually applies instead).

The facts may be more complex. For example, suppose A pays the purchase price to V and title is taken in the names of A and B, as joint or co-tenants. A and B will be presumed to hold their title on resulting trust for A. If title is taken in the name of B for life with remainder to A, then B is presumed to hold her or his life estate on resulting trust for A.

If A and B both contribute to the purchase price and title is taken in B's name, B is presumed to hold it on resulting trust for A and B, as co-tenants in proportion to their contributions. If title is taken in both their names as joint tenants, but A contributed more than half the purchase price, then A and B will be presumed to hold their joint legal title in trust for themselves as tenants in common in proportion to their contributions.

In all these examples, there was an apparent gift from A to B of an asset or of some interest in an asset. Since equity is suspicious of gifts, B will hold the apparent gift on resulting trust for A unless it is proven that A did intend to make a gift or the presumption of advancement applies, in which case it is presumed

---

164 *Supra*, note 144.

that A intended to make a gift. Using the language of unjust enrichment, we could say that, in each example, B is enriched at A's expense and there is an absence of juristic reason for that enrichment, unless it is proven or presumed that A intended to make a gift of the enrichment to B.

There are also cases where A and B contributed equally to the purchase of assets, title was taken in both their names as joint tenants, and they held their joint ownership on resulting trust for themselves as equal tenants in common.[165] Although a person cannot be a trustee solely for herself or himself, two or more people can be trustees for themselves so long as there is some difference between their legal ownership as trustees and their equitable ownership as beneficiaries. In this situation, the resulting trust operates to cause joint tenants to give up their rights of survivorship to each other. So, if A dies and the presumption of resulting trust is not rebutted, B will acquire sole legal title by way of survivorship, but will hold it on resulting trust for A's estate and B as tenants in common in equal shares. When business partners acquire assets as joint tenants or when people invest money as joint mortgagees, it is presumed that they did not intend to give their business assets or their investments to their partners or fellow investors when they die.[166] Equity's dislike of joint tenancies may be linked to its suspicion of gifts.

(i) *Loans*

The presumption of resulting trust is rebutted if it is proved that A intended to make a gift to B when A paid, or contributed to, the purchase price for assets transferred into B's name. It can also be rebutted if it is proved that A loaned the purchase money to B. Although A, as lender, does not intend to make a gift, the contract of loan shows that A intended B to have beneficial ownership of the purchased assets, but also to have a personal obligation to repay the loan.

This point is apparent from an English case, *Dewar v. Dewar*.[167] The defendant, a married man, purchased a house for £4,250, the sum of £3,250 being secured by a mortgage, and took title in his name. However, it was his intention that his mother and his unmarried brother, the plaintiff, live in the house as well. Hence, the mother and the plaintiff each gave the defendant £500. The mother subsequently died, leaving her estate equally to her two sons. The plaintiff then brought an action for a declaration that he had a beneficial interest in the house based proportionately upon his own contribution and one-half of that of his mother. The defendant argued that the mother's contribution was a gift and the court found this claim established on the evidence. The defendant also argued that the plaintiff's contribution was a loan. However, the court concluded that the onus to establish the nature of the payment was on the defendant and that he had failed to establish that the plaintiff intended to lend the money. Hence, the defen-

---

165 *Lake v. Craddock* (1733), 3 P. Wms. 158, 24 E.R. 1011 (Ch. Div.).
166 *Jackson, Re* (1887), 34 Ch. D. 732; *Malayan Credit Ltd v. Jack Chia-MPH Ltd.*, [1986] 1 A.C. 549 (P.C.).
167 [1975] 1 W.L.R. 1532, [1975] 2 All E.R. 728. See also *Rupar v. Rupar, supra*, note 25.

dant held title upon a resulting trust in the following proportions: 3,750/4,250 for the defendant and 500/4,250 for the plaintiff.

This does not mean that a resulting trust cannot be raised if a loan is involved. As discussed in the previous chapter, if the contract of loan restricts the borrower's use of the money, the borrower may not obtain beneficial ownership of the money, but hold it on resulting trust for the lender, with a power to use the money as agreed.[168] A loan does not raise a presumption either of resulting trust or of advancement. The natural assumption is that the lender intends the borrower to have beneficial ownership of the proceeds of loan and that the transaction is not a gift. Therefore, proof that a transaction is a loan would rebut either presumption. It is only where the evidence establishes a substantial restriction on the borrower's use of the money that a loan might give rise to a resulting trust. In that case, it is a trust based on evidence and not on a presumption that the lender did not intend to transfer beneficial ownership to the borrower.

In *MacLeod v. MacLeod*,[169] a court combined a loan with a resulting trust, but we doubt whether it was proper to do so. The plaintiffs in that case were husband and wife. They operated a day care business through a limited company before the company and the husband became bankrupt. His brother and his brother's wife (the defendants) came to the rescue. With the help of a mortgage and bank loan, they purchased from the trustee in bankruptcy the land on which the plaintiffs resided and had run their day care. It was orally agreed between the plaintiffs and defendants that the plaintiffs would reside on the property, pay all costs associated with the property, and, within one year, repay the defendants and obtain the defendants' release from liability for the mortgage and loan. The plaintiffs defaulted on that agreement, making payments late and giving the defendants a number of cheques that were declined for insufficient funds.

The plaintiffs' defaults and other family matters led to the parties falling out and to this case. The plaintiffs claimed that the defendants held the land in trust for the plaintiffs. The defendants responded that the plaintiffs' payments were rent and that their obligation to convey the land to the plaintiffs was terminated when the plaintiffs defaulted on their agreement. Burchell J. held that the defendants held the land on resulting trust for the plaintiffs, because they had purchased the land with money that they had agreed to loan to the plaintiffs. Therefore, the plaintiffs were beneficial owners of the land, entitled to a conveyance from the defendants once all their obligations under the contract of loan were satisfied.

This case cannot properly be analysed as a purchase money resulting trust. In all other cases (ignoring the "common intention" resulting trust), the assets held on resulting trust were acquired wholly or partly at the expense of the beneficiaries of that trust. In *MacLeod*, the land was not acquired by the defendants at the plaintiffs' expense. The defendants paid the down payment for the land and were personally liable to repay the mortgage and loan used to raise the balance of the purchase price. If the plaintiffs had a right to the land, it was not because

---

168 *Twinsectra Ltd. v. Yardley, supra*, note 9, at 192-193.
169 (1983), 14 E.T.R. 176, 1983 CarswellNS 115 (T.D.).

they had purchased the land *for* the defendants, but because they had agreed to purchase the land *from* the defendants.

There are two ways to achieve a similar outcome in *MacLeod*. First, the defendants made an oral contract to sell the land to the plaintiffs. Although not made in writing as required by the *Statute of Frauds*,[170] it might be possible to avoid the writing requirement through the doctrine of part performance.[171] If part performance could be used to establish a specifically enforceable contract of sale, the defendants, as vendors, would hold the land on constructive trust for the plaintiffs, as purchasers, and the plaintiffs could be entitled to relief from forfeiture.

Secondly, if the defendants did loan the money to the plaintiffs, the transaction looks exactly like a common law mortgage. The defendants, as mortgagees, advanced the loan directly to the vendor in exchange for legal title. The plaintiffs, as mortgagors, have an equity of redemption which they are entitled to exercise in the absence of foreclosure. Again, this would depend on the lack of writing being overcome by the doctrine of part performance.

In *MacLeod v. MacLeod*, the problem arose because the agreement between the plaintiffs and defendants was not made in writing. That agreement should be enforced, if at all, using the doctrine of part performance. It is not acceptable to turn to the doctrine of resulting trust as a method of enforcing oral agreements with respect to land. The resulting trust arises, not to give effect to oral contracts or oral express trusts, but to allow A to obtain restitution of assets acquired by B at A's expense. If B holds the land on resulting trust for A, it is because A did not intend to benefit B and never because B intended to benefit A.

(ii) *Contribution to the Purchase Price*

In most cases of purchase money resulting trust, the beneficiary of that trust contributed to the purchase price by paying money to the vendor. That money may have belonged to the beneficiary beforehand or have been borrowed for that purpose. For example, in *Calverley v. Green*,[172] a man and a woman purchased a house together as joint tenants. He paid one-third of the purchase price from his savings and the remaining two-thirds was raised through a joint mortgage of the house. Although she did not contribute to the down payment or to any of the mortgage payments, they held their joint title on resulting trust for themselves as tenants in common, with two-thirds for him and one-third for her. Since she was jointly liable on the mortgage, her contribution to the purchase price was one-half the value of that mortgage. Essentially, she had borrowed that amount from the mortgagee and paid it to the vendor.

The man's repayment of the mortgage after the purchase did not increase his share of the beneficial ownership of the house. He was repaying a debt due to the

---

170 R.S.N.S. 1989, c. 442, s. 7(d).
171 *Hollett v. Hollett, supra,* note 162.
172 (1984), 155 C.L.R. 242.

mortgagee and not paying the purchase price to the vendor. As Mason and Brennan JJ. said:[173]

> It is understandable but erroneous to regard the payment of mortgage instalments as payment of the purchase price of a home. The purchase price is what is paid in order to acquire the property; the mortgage instalments are paid to the lender from whom the money to pay some or all of the purchase price is borrowed.

The man may have been entitled to contribution from the woman for her share of the mortgage payments and to an equitable lien over her share of the house to secure that obligation.[174] This would be a better remedy from his perspective. If repayment of the mortgage could be treated as a contribution to the purchase of the house, only a portion of each payment would be taken into account. Most of each payment was allocated to interest and only the portion allocated to the reduction of principal could be treated as repayment of the amount borrowed to purchase the home. In contrast, the lien would secure the total amount which the woman was liable to pay, that is, one-half of all mortgage payments made by the man, including principal and interest.

As Dr. John Mee notes,[175] courts in Ireland will take contributions to mortgage payments into account when assessing beneficial ownership of the family home under a resulting trust. However, since they will also take other contributions for the benefit of the family into account, including domestic labour, these trusts arise for reasons other than a contribution to the purchase price and would be called constructive trusts in other common law jurisdictions.

The payment of a mortgage could be treated as a contribution to the purchase price if we accept Dr. Lionel Smith's argument that, when money is used to pay a debt, the value of that money can be traced back into the value of the asset purchased by acquiring that debt.[176] He argues, for example, that, if a thief steals money and uses it to buy a car, the value of the money can be traced into the value of the car regardless of whether the thief takes title to the car the day before the payment or the day after. In the former case, the thief has used the money to pay the debt incurred a day earlier when the car was purchased. If it is possible to trace back one day, why not one month, one year, or one decade?

Dr. Smith's proposal has received favourable academic and judicial attention in England.[177] If it came to be accepted by courts in Canada, it might become possible to regard the payment of a mortgage as a contribution to the purchase price for the mortgaged property. However, as discussed above, the only value that could be traced back to the purchase of property is the portion of each

---

173   *Ibid.*, at 257.
174   *Ibid.*, at 263.
175   J. Mee, *The Property Rights of Cohabitees* (Oxford: Hart Publishing, 1999) at 66-72.
176   L.D. Smith, "Tracing into the Payment of a Debt" (1995), 54 Cambridge L.J. 290; L.D. Smith, *The Law of Tracing* (Oxford: Clarendon Press, 1997) at 146-152, 353-356.
177   *Bishopsgate Investment Management Ltd. v. Homan*, [1995] Ch. 211 at 217-217 (C.A.); *Foskett v. McKeown*, [1998] Ch. 265, [1998] 2 W.L.R. 298 at 315 (Eng. C.A.); A. Burrows, *The Law of Restitution*, 2nd ed. (London: Butterworths, 2002) at 103-104; G. Virgo, *The Principles of the Law of Restitution* (Oxford: Oxford University Press, 1999) at 653.

mortgage payment attributed to the reduction of the principal amount owing. Also, this would only apply to mortgages granted for the purpose of purchasing the mortgaged asset and not for the purpose of financing improvements or for other purposes. For example, if a couple mortgaged their house to finance the purchase of a boat, repayment of the mortgage would be traceable to the value of the boat, not the house.

A valid distinction can be drawn between indebtedness to the vendor, for the balance of the purchase price, and indebtedness to a third party, for money borrowed to pay the vendor. The former is merely the delayed payment of the purchase price, but the latter is not. Canadian law currently treats these two situations differently, with a resulting trust possible only in the former situation. The distinction is blurred when the vendor accepts a mortgage back from the purchaser for the balance of the purchase price. At some point, the sale is complete and the vendor becomes a mortgagee. It is much easier to determine the shares of beneficial ownership under the resulting trust at the outset, by treating the liability to pay that mortgage as a contribution to the purchase price, than by allowing the beneficial ownership to shift incrementally over the years as that mortgage is paid by instalments.

There is an important distinction between a contribution to the acquisition of a new asset and a contribution to the improvement of an existing asset. If A buys an asset for B, without intending a gift, a resulting trust will make A the beneficial owner of that asset and compel B to transfer it to A. This does not leave B in a worse position than if the transaction never occurred. B is merely required to give up an asset that B was not intended to have for B's own benefit. In contrast, if A improves B's asset, without intending a gift, a resulting trust should not arise, because that would compel B to give up beneficial ownership of something B had before the improvement took place. B should not be forced to give up a share of any specific asset (which may have special meaning to B, such as a house inherited from B's grandparents).[178] If B is liable to A, it should only be to pay for the value of the improvement, perhaps secured by a lien on the improved asset. B then has the freedom to raise the money needed to pay A by selling the assets that B values least.

This principle applies with equal force when A contributes to the payment of a mortgage over an asset owned by B. Although it enriches B, it does not justify taking beneficial ownership of the mortgaged asset away from B. Orthodox principle would give A at most an equitable lien on the property. However, some cases suggest that A can thereby acquire an interest under a resulting trust, at least where B and A are husband and wife.[179] Although a trust is an appropriate device for dividing family assets on the breakdown of a marriage or similar relationship, it is not justified solely by contributions to the payment of the mortgage. The

---

178 P. Birks, "Proprietary Rights as Remedies" in P. Birks, ed., *The Frontiers of Liability*, vol. 2 (Oxford: Oxford University Press, 1994) 214 at 218.

179 See, *e.g.*, *Cowcher v. Cowcher*, [1972] 1 W.L.R. 425; *Thompson v. Thompson*, [1961] S.C.R. 3, 26 D.L.R. (2d) 1, 1960 CarswellOnt 52, 2 R.F.L. Rep. 257; *Rathwell v. Rathwell, supra,* note 144.

expectation of sharing those assets plays a much more important role in that situation. If a trust arises because the contributing party reasonably expected to acquire a beneficial interest in the mortgaged asset, it should be classified as a constructive trust.

Most assets are purchased with money or on credit, but a contribution to the purchase price can be any form of value accepted by the vendor in exchange for an asset. For example, in *Mumpower v. Castle*,[180] a man traded an assortment of farm animals for some land. Since some of those animals belonged to his wife, he held the land on resulting trust for both of them in proportion to their shares of the value of those animals. In *Springette v. Defoe*,[181] a woman was entitled to purchase a house from a local council at a 41% discount because she had been a council tenant for 11 years. That discount was taken into account when calculating her share of the beneficial ownership of the house under a resulting trust.

Notes and Questions

1. A and B agreed to purchase a three-story building as tenants in common, for $100,000, with $2,500 paid as a deposit, $27,500 (subject to adjustments) on closing, and the balance by mortgage back to the vendor. B was going to operate a restaurant on the ground floor and let part of the second floor, while A was going to occupy the rest of the second floor and all of the third floor. The parties intended to pay the purchase price in equal shares. However, A was not in funds when the agreement was signed or on closing because the sale of her other properties was delayed, so B agreed to pay the deposit, the balance due on closing, and the expenses of closing. On closing, the vendor refused to accept the mortgage back from A because of an outstanding execution against her. Therefore, A instructed that the deed be made to B alone. However, A joined in the mortgage back as both principal debtor and guarantor. The parties have since been in possession of the property. A has not made any payments to B, but has assigned to B a mortgage which A received on the sale of other property. Differences then arose between the parties and B took the position that A had no interest in the property. A brings an action for a declaration that she is entitled to a half interest. What result?[182]

2. A was an entrepreneur who invested in real estate and was resident in Canada. B was a successful businessman in another country. A met B and persuaded him to let A invest in real estate in Canada for B. B executed general powers of attorney in favour of A to permit him to seek out suitable property and use B's funds for its acquisition. A and B agreed in writing that A would use B's funds for the sole purpose of purchasing real property in B's name. B insisted on this agreement, since he was not interested in going into partnership with A. Shortly thereafter, A purchased an hotel and registered the title in the names of his company and B as tenants in common. A's company paid the deposit, which was returned on closing of the transaction. Half of the purchase price was paid from B's monies and the other half by the purchasers' assumption of existing mortgages. A told B that "we" have purchased a property. A operated the hotel and paid the mortgages when they fell due, using the profits from the hotel operation and his own money. Not long

---

180 104 S.E. 706 (1920, Va. C.A.).
181 (1992), 24 H.L.R. 552 (C.A.), at 555.
182 See *Chupak v. Cirka* (1982), 132 D.L.R. (3d) 351, 1982 CarswellOnt 612, 23 R.P.R. 1, 11 E.T.R. 262 (H.C.).

thereafter, B discovered what had happened. B claims the property is entirely his. Is B correct? If so, how should he proceed to recover the property?[183]

3. In some of the United States, the resulting trust (and not merely the presumption of resulting trust) have been abolished by statute,[184] while other states have statutes that expressly permit purchase moneys resulting trusts.[185]

4. In *Hough v. Champagne*,[186] the plaintiff met the defendant through the plaintiff's newspaper advertisement. They began a relationship and eventually decided to marry. The plaintiff paid all of the defendant's expenses, including tuition fees, and provided her with a weekly allowance. Before their marriage, the plaintiff purchased a house and had title put in both their names as tenants in common. About this time, the defendant secretly bought another house in her own name with her own funds. The relationship deteriorated and the plaintiff moved out of the co-owned house, having unsuccessfully tried to get the defendant to leave. The plaintiff sought declarations that the co-owned house was held on a resulting trust for him and that one half of the defendant's house was held on constructive trust for him. The court held that the plaintiff was the sole beneficial owner of the co-owned house, but had no interest in the defendant's house. Do you agree with this result?

(d) Voluntary Transfer Resulting Trusts

Most books on the law of trusts distinguish purchase money resulting trusts from voluntary transfer resulting trusts because, in the U.S.A. and most likely in England, the presumption of resulting trust does not apply to a gratuitous transfer of land. Although there has been some insecurity over this distinction in Canada, most Canadian courts chose simply to ignore it and apply the presumption generally to apparent gifts, regardless of the mode of giving. The law in other jurisdictions is discussed here because trust lawyers need to be aware of the differences and because it may help students better understand the presumption of resulting trust.

It should be noted that this issue does not affect the presumption of advancement, discussed below, which depends on the relationship between the parties and not on the method of making an apparent gift. Also, this issue does not affect the resulting trust itself, which arises whenever it is proved that an apparent donor did not intend to give, regardless of the initial presumption. Since the overwhelming majority of resulting trust cases are decided on the basis of evidence, this issue seldom has practical importance. Indeed, judicial pronouncements on the choice of presumption are rarely definitive because most decisions are based on evidence of intention and therefore discussions of the presumptions can be classified as *obiter dicta*.

---

183 See *Tim v. Lai* (1986), 5 B.C.L.R. (2d) 245, 1986 CarswellBC 207, [1986] B.C.J. No. 3171 (S.C.).

184 See Scott, §440.2.

185 Scott, §440.3.

186 (1991), 42 E.T.R. 252, 1991 CarswellOnt 308, 35 R.F.L. (3d) 27 (Gen. Div.).

(i) *England and Wales*

In England and Wales, a debate continues over the application of the presumption of resulting trust to voluntary conveyances of land. It is clear that the presumption applies when A gratuitously transfers personal property to B[187] or when A purchases any type of asset for B (unless B is A's wife or child). However, it was never clear whether the presumption of resulting trust applied to a gratuitous transfer of land. The difficulty can be traced back to the *Statute of Uses*.[188]

As discussed above, a resulting use would arise when A conveyed an estate to B, if there was no apparent consideration (such as sale or kinship) and no declaration of use, because it was presumed that B was intended to hold the estate to the use of A. The *Statute of Uses* executed all passive uses, thereby transferring legal title back to A as the beneficiary of the resulting use. Therefore, after the statute, A would need to convey the estate "unto and to the use of B" to avoid the transaction being nullified by the executed resulting use.

When the use was reborn as the trust, the presumption of resulting trust developed by analogy to the resulting use. However, it was applied to cases where A had purchased an estate for B and not where A had conveyed an estate to B.[189] There was no clear statement that the presumption of resulting trust could not apply to a gratuitous transfer, but there was no authority to say that it could. It was suggested that the declaration of use in favour of the grantee, made necessary by the *Statute of Uses*, was sufficient to rebut the presumption of resulting trust in the absence of other evidence to the contrary. However, we prefer the view of Professor Maitland that the expression of use is needed to pass legal title and has no effect on equitable ownership. The modern trust arose as a use upon a use, when the court of Chancery began to enforce the second use,[190] and the resulting trust is no different. Maitland said:[191]

> For no valuable consideration I convey land unto and to the use of A and his heirs. Here the use does not result, for a use has been declared in A's favour, so A gets the legal estate — but in analogy to the law of resulting uses, the Court of chancery has raised up a doctrine of resulting trusts. If without value by act *inter vivos* I pass the legal estate or legal rights to A and declare no trust, the general presumption is that I do not intend to benefit A and that A is to be a trustee for me. However this is only a presumption in the proper sense of that term and it may be rebutted by evidence of my intention.

The matter was complicated further by section 60(3) of the *Law of Property Act 1925*:[192]

---

187 *Fowkes v. Pascoe* (1875), [1873] 10 Ch. App. 343 (Eng. Ch. App.); *Standing v. Bowring* (1885), 16 Ch. D. 282 (C.A.); *Vinogradoff, Re, supra,* note 21; *Vandervell v. I.R.C., supra,* note 8, at 312.

188 27 Hen. 8, c. 10 (1535, U.K.).

189 See *Dyer v. Dyer, supra,* note 5, at 93, quoted above.

190 This is discussed above in chapter 1.

191 F.W. Maitland, *Equity: A Course of Lectures,* rev. ed. by John Brunyate (Cambridge, Cambridge University Press, 1936) at 79.

192 15 & 16 Geo. 5, c. 20 (U.K.).

> In a voluntary conveyance a resulting trust for the grantor shall not be implied merely by reason that the property is not expressed to be conveyed for the use or benefit of the grantee.

It is possible that this section was merely consequential to the repeal of the *Statute of Uses* in England,[193] to let conveyancers drop the expression of use in favour of the grantee without fear that its absence would have any legal significance. However, the effect of this section on the presumption of resulting trust has been debated ever since. That debate has been noticed, but not resolved, by the Court of Appeal and the House of Lords.[194]

In *Lohia v. Lohia*,[195] Strauss Q.C., sitting as a Deputy High Court Judge in the Chancery Division, decided that the presumption of resulting trust did not arise on a voluntary conveyance of land because of section 60(3) of the *Law of Property Act 1925*. He also held that there was just enough evidence to show that a voluntary conveyance of land from a son to his father had been intended to transfer beneficial ownership to the father. The Court of Appeal dismissed the appeal on the basis of the trial judge's finding of facts, but offered no support for his conclusion regarding section 60(3). Mummery L.J. said:[196]

> In my judgment the question raised... is so inextricably bound up in centuries of English legal history that it would be bold for this court to pronounce upon it without having heard very extensive argument, preferably in the context in which a decision on the point was crucial to the outcome of the case.... On the point whether the effect of the 1925 Act is to abolish the presumption of a resulting trust arising from a voluntary conveyance, I would prefer to express no concluded view, as it is unnecessary to do so for the disposition of this appeal.

One year later, in *Ali v. Khan*, a differently constituted Court of Appeal said that the trial decision in *Lohia v. Lohia*, "establishes that the presumption of a resulting trust on a voluntary conveyance of land has been abolished by s. 60(3), Law of Property Act 1925."[197] However, there was no further discussion of this issue since the case involved a transfer from a father to his daughters and the presumption of advancement in their favour was rebutted by evidence that he did not intend to convey beneficial ownership to them. Nevertheless, it probably is true that the presumption of resulting trust does not apply to a gratuitous transfer of land in England.

(ii) *U.S.A.*

In the United States, the law on this issue is not in doubt. The presumption of resulting trust applies when one person purchases an asset for another, unless precluded by statute or displaced by the presumption of advancement. However, it is almost universally accepted that it does not arise on a gratuitous transfer of

---

193 Maitland, *supra*, note 191, at 77-78.
194 *Hodgson v. Marks, supra,* note 7, at 933 (C.A.); *Tinsley v. Milligan* (1993), [1994] 1 A.C. 340 at 371, [1993] 3 All E.R. 65 (H.L.).
195 [2001] W.T.L.R. 101; noted (2001), 15 Tolley's Trust L. Int. 26.
196 [2001] E.W.C.A. Civ. 1691 at para. 24, 26.
197 [2002] E.W.C.A. Civ. 974 at para. 24, *per* Scott V.C.

either real or personal property. In that case, there is a presumption of gift, which may be rebutted.[198]

Two different reasons are given for treating purchases and transfers differently. The first is based on the parol evidence rule. Since land was almost always transferred by a deed that would contain a declaration of use for the grantee, a recital of consideration paid by the grantee, or both, courts would not admit oral evidence to contradict the written deed. This is no doubt the origin of the distinction in the U.S.A.[199] However, it fails to explain why the presumption of resulting trust does not apply to gratuitous transfers of personal property and, as Professor Scott notes,[200] it also fails to explain why that presumption does apply when A pays the purchase price and the transfer from the vendor to B contains a declaration of use for B and recital of consideration paid by B.

The second and more modern justification for the distinction is that apparent donors are more likely to have an intention to give when they make gratuitous transfers than when they pay or contribute to the purchase price.[201] The gratuitous transfer is a deliberate act by the donor that is most plausibly explained by her or his intention to give. In contrast, there are many possible reasons why a person might contribute to the purchase price other than as a gift to the recipient. Although the contributor may well have an intention to give, if it is not clearly the most likely explanation, then a presumption of resulting trust is a safer starting point.

(iii) *Canada*

The English debate over the application of the presumption of resulting trust to gratuitous transfers of land has been a cause of some concern in Canada in the past. For example, in *Neazor v. Hoyle*,[202] there is a long discussion of the English authorities, which has been omitted from the judgment reproduced below. Macdonald J.A. concluded "that by reason of the voluntary transfer..., there could well be a presumption of a resulting trust in favour of the donor",[203] after quoting the strong *obiter dictum* of Taschereau J., who did a similar review of English law in *Niles v. Lake*:[204]

> All these authorities, as well as many others which it would be superfluous to cite here, clearly indicate that a mere gratuitous transfer of property, real or personal, although it may convey

---

198 See Scott, §405; H.F. Stone, "Resulting Trusts and the Statute of Frauds" (1906), 6 Columbia L. Rev. 326 at 331-332.

199 G.T. Bogert, *Trusts*, 6th ed. (St Paul: West Publishing, 1987) §73.

200 Scott, §405.

201 *Drummer v. Pitcher* (1833), 2 My. & K. 262 at 273, 39 E.R. 944, Coop. T. Brough. 257 (Eng. Ch.); Scott, §440.

202 (1962), 32 D.L.R. (2d) 131, 37 W.W.R. 104, 1962 CarswellAlta 3 (C.A.), at 137-141 [D.L.R.].

203 *Ibid.,* at 141.

204 [1947] S.C.R. 291, [1947] 2 D.L.R. 248, 1947 CarswellOnt 123. This case concerned a joint account established by the deceased to which she contributed all the money. The court held that the other person held on a resulting trust for the estate, since there was no evidence of an intention to make a gift to the non-contributor.

the legal title, will not benefit the transferee unless there is some other indication to show such an intent, and the property will be deemed in equity to be held on a resulting trust for the transferor.

Spence J. made the same confident statement of the law in *Goodfriend v. Goodfriend*:[205]

> It is, of course, trite law, and has been since *Dyer v. Dyer*,[206] that where a person transfers his property into another's name gratuitously a resulting trust in favour of the grantor is created and the transferee must prove, in order to retain title, that a gift was intended by the transferor.

Although both pronouncements are *obiter dicta*, they are clear statements of the law by the Supreme Court of Canada. Today, when Canadian courts deal with the possibility of a resulting trust arising on an apparent gift, they do not distinguish between real and personal property nor between purchases and transfers. The presumption of resulting trust applies to all apparent gifts unless the relationship between the parties invokes the presumption of advancement.

The only jurisdiction in Canada that has legislation similar to section 60(3) of the English *Law of Property Act 1925*, quoted above, is British Columbia, where the *Property Law Act* states, "A voluntary transfer need not be expressed to be for the use or benefit of the transferee to prevent a resulting trust."[207] It does not appear that a court has considered whether this affects the presumption of resulting trust. Courts in British Columbia apply that presumption to voluntary transfers of land, without reference to this statute.[208]

NEAZOR v. HOYLE

(1962), 37 W.W.R. 104, 32 D.L.R. (2d) 131, 1962 CarswellAlta 3
Alberta Supreme Court (Appellate Division)

The respondent, Kathleen Neazor, married John Neazor in 1923, when she was 15 and he was 33 years old, after she became pregnant with their daughter. The marriage was not a happy one. The parties never lived together and entered into a formal separation agreement in 1954. Their daughter was killed in an accident in 1959 and John died in 1960.

In 1949, John transferred some farm land to his sister, the appellant, for the express purpose of preventing Kathleen from succeeding to it. He received the rents and profits from the land, but his sister paid the taxes, which were substantial, and she also kept moneys paid as compensation for an expropriation of part of the land. John made a will in 1955, leaving his entire estate to his sister.

---

205 (1971), [1972] S.C.R. 640, 22 D.L.R. (3d) 699, 1971 CarswellOnt 131, 1971 CarswellOnt 150, 6 R.F.L. 60, at 702 [D.L.R.]. This case involved a gratuitous transfer of land from a husband to his wife and, therefore, the presumption of advancement applied.

206 *Supra,* note 5.

207 R.S.B.C. 1996, c. 377, s. 19(3).

208 See *Reber v. Reber* (1988), 48 D.L.R. (4th) 376, 1988 CarswellBC 916 (S.C.); *Biljanic v. Biljanic Estate* (1995), 10 E.T.R. (2d) 148, 1995 CarswellBC 1117, 66 B.C.A.C. 131, 108 W.A.C. 131 (C.A.).

After John died, Kathleen brought an application for support from his estate under the *Family Relief Act*.[209] She was successful at first instance, being awarded the entire proceeds of the estate, including the land previously transferred to the appellant, the court holding that the appellant held the land on a resulting trust for John's estate.

MACDONALD J.A.:

. . .

The appellant contends that the land came to her as a true and completed gift *inter vivos*. On the other hand, the respondent contends that the voluntary conveyance *inter vivos* resulted in a trust for the giver.

[Macdonald J.A. discussed in great detail whether a presumption of resulting trust arose in these circumstances, with reference to English and Canadian sources. He continued:]

In the case at bar, I think that by reason of the voluntary transfer by the deceased to the appellant, there could well be a presumption of a resulting trust in favour of the donor and, if so, that the burden is on the appellant to establish as a fact that she received the beneficial interest in the lands so transferred. Has she done so?

Assuming that the equitable doctrine of a resulting trust applies, has the appellant been successful in establishing as a fact that there was a completed gift *inter vivos* and that she received the full beneficial interest in the land so transferred to her?

All of the circumstances of the case must be considered.

It is abundantly clear from the evidence that the deceased had no affection whatsoever for the respondent, while, on the other hand, he was fond of his sister. The respondent testified that the deceased "had absolutely no time" for her. From his standpoint as well as hers, the marriage must have been most unhappy and unsatisfactory. According to the respondent, the deceased had promised his father and mother to look after his sister. Read in as part of the respondent's case is the statement that the deceased wanted the appellant to have the land for the very reason that he did not want his wife to have it. By transferring the land to his sister, he would be fulfilling, in part, the said promise to his parents, and, at the same time, put the land beyond the reach of the respondent. The solicitor that prepared the transfer and registered it considered that the deceased's instructions were to give the quarter section to his sister to do what she liked with it.

Though the deceased received the rents and profits from the land following the transfer, it was the appellant who paid the taxes. There is no evidence on the point, but it is common knowledge that taxes on a quarter section of land in the area where the land is situated, are substantial.

---

209 R.S.A. 1955, c. 109.

From the evidence it appears that at any time the deceased would ask the appellant for money, she "figured" she would give it to him, for, as she put it, "a one-third share of the crop isn't much to live on and he had lots of doctor's bills". The five acres from the said one quarter section were sold by the appellant to the Municipal District for gravel, for which she received $8,300. She had refused an offer of $2,500 from the Municipal District. The deceased never suggested that she should give him that money. The fact, too, that the deceased made his will some 6 years after the transfer leaving everything to the respondent [*sic*] is further evidence of his feeling towards her.

It seems to me that although the transfer was a voluntary one, it is clear from the above that there were inducements for the deceased to part with the land.

This is not the case of a transfer to a stranger but a transfer to a sister, of land which the deceased had received as a gift from his father.

If there was an onus resting upon the appellant to show that there was a completed gift *inter vivos*, I am of the opinion that the onus has been abundantly satisfied. It follows that as far as the lands are concerned, the appellant is entitled to succeed and there will be a declaration that the lands so transferred to her were free and are free from all resulting trusts or other claims against her on behalf of the respondent or on behalf of the deceased's estate.

. . .

[Kane J.A. concurred. Johnson J.A. dissented on another ground. The appeal was allowed in respect of the land, but otherwise dismissed.]

Notes and Questions

1. An Australian court held that, when land is voluntary conveyed by deed unto and to the use of another there can be no presumption of a resulting use to the transferor, since the express use precludes it.[210] If, however, the transfer is registered under the Torrens system of land titles registration, a presumption of resulting trust is not precluded, because the object of the Torrens legislation is to enable one to ascertain the registered owner from the fact of registration. Therefore, the *Statute of Uses* does not apply to land so registered, since it could execute the use and give the legal title to a person who is not registered, and the Torrens system does not prevent the presumption of resulting use from arising.[211] Several Australian states have legislation similar to section 60(3) of the English *Law of Property Act, 1925,* discussed above.[212] The legislation in the State of Victoria also provides that it "does not limit or affect the operation of any principle or rule of equity relating to the implication of resulting trusts."[213]

2. A and B lived together for a number of years in a house owned by A. At B's request, A transferred the title to her on the understanding that if she predeceased him the house would be his. They continued to live together until B died and, in the meantime, A

---

210 *House v. Coffyn*, [1922] V.L.R. 67.

211 *Ibid.*, at 78; *Wirth v. Wirth* (1956), 98 C.L.R. 228 at 336, *per* Dixon C.J.

212 *Conveyancing Act 1919* (N.S.W.), s. 44(1); *Property Law Act 1958* (Vic.), s. 19A(3); *Property Law Act 1969* (W.A.), s. 38; *Property Law Act 1974* (Qd.), s. 7(3).

213 *Property Law Act 1958* (Vic.), s. 19A(4).

made substantial improvements to the house. B's estate claims that B was the sole beneficial owner of the house. Can A succeed against B's estate? On what basis?[214]

3. A became infatuated with B, an older man who was separated from his wife. A
had a child by B and left the child in his care, since she was employed out of the country.
A purchased a farm in Canada as a place for B and the child to live and later transferred
it to B. She sent B regular payments to care for the child and continued to do so after the
child left home. She also sent him money for maintenance of the farm. After B died, it
was discovered that his bank account contained $250,000, virtually all of which derived
from A's payments. A seeks to recover the farm and the money from B's estate. Can A
succeed? On what basis?[215]

4. Many of the cases involving voluntary transfers to another and, indeed, purchases
in the name of another, show that the transferor or purchaser intended to make a gift.
Alternatively, he or she may have intended by the transfer to place the assets beyond the
reach of her or his creditors. In view of that, is it appropriate to retain the presumption of
resulting trust, or should it be replaced with a presumption of gift?

5. S opened a savings account at a bank in her brother B's name, and deposited the
sum of $10,000 into it. She told the bank manager that B was not to be told about the
account until after she died. S received the pass book and retained it until her death. She
wanted to withdraw $500 from the account and send it to B. The bank told her that she
had no control over the account, but did allow her to issue a receipt in B's name for a bank
draft in that amount, which was sent to B. The receipt indicated that the money was to be
charged to the account. When S died, her administrator found the pass book and claimed
the money in the account. Can B recover the money?[216] Would it be relevant that the pass
book had to be produced in order to withdraw the money?

6. There is some authority that a transfer of money, as distinct from other personal
property, does not give rise to a presumption of resulting trust, but is assumed to be either
a gift or a loan.[217] There is no presumption of resulting trust when chattels are delivered
to a stranger[218] nor where the property is a non-income producing, residential leasehold
interest.[219]

(e) The Presumption of Advancement

(i) *Parents and Children*

The presumption of advancement arose out of the law respecting uses, just
like the presumption of resulting trust. Under the law respecting uses, if a father
made a voluntary conveyance to a child, their relationship was "good" as distinct

---

214 See *Copley v. Guaranty Trust Co.*, [1956] O.W.N. 621 (H.C.).

215 See *Frey v. Heintzl Estate* (1988), 24 B.C.L.R. (2d) 25, 1988 CarswellBC 75 (S.C.).

216 See *Horne v. Huston* (1919), 16 O.W.N. 173, affirmed without reasons (1919), 17 O.W.N. 2
     (C.A.).

217 See *George v. Howard* (1819), 7 Price 646 at 651, 146 E.R. 1089; *Joaquin v. Hall*, [1976] V.R.
     788. But see, *contra*, *Knight v. Biss*, [1954] N.Z.L.R. 55.

218 H. Godefroi, *The Law Relating to Trusts and Trustees*, 4th ed. (London: Stevens and Sons,
     1915), at 145.

219 See *Savage v. Dunningham*, [1974] Ch. 181. The case involved a lease that was made in favour
     of one of three persons who shared an apartment, whereas all three shared the rent and expenses
     equally. Actually this situation is one in which a purchase money resulting trust might otherwise
     arise.

from "valuable" consideration for it. Kinship was the reason for the conveyance, which would cause the use to pass to the recipient,[220] just as the purchase price was the reason that would cause the use to pass in a "bargain and sale". It came to be known as the presumption of advancement because the father was under a moral duty to advance his children in the world, that is, to get them started on the road to financial independence.

The presumption of advancement was extended to situations in which the donor stood *in loco parentis* to the donee, regardless of whether the donor was male or female, because he or she was under "the duty of a father of a child to make a provision for that child".[221] Hence, a transfer to a foster child or a child of a woman with whom the transferor was living may give rise to the presumption if it is shown that the transferor acted as a parent toward the child.[222] It used to be thought that the child had to be the father's legitimate child in order for the presumption to operate, but that is no longer the case.[223]

Formerly, the presumption of advancement did not arise when a mother transferred assets to, or purchased assets for, her child,[224] even if the mother was widowed.[225] This was because mothers were not under a father's duty to provide for their children. However, this has changed. Mothers and fathers are now under equal duties to care for their children[226] and are equally likely to intend to make gifts to them. The presumption of advancement applies to apparent gifts from mothers in Australia[227] and the U.S.A.[228] In Canada, it is now accepted that mothers and fathers should be treated equally. However, there is a debate whether apparent gifts from parents should attract the presumption of advancement or the presumption of resulting trust.

220 *Soar v. Foster* (1858), 4 K. & J. 152 at 159, 70 E.R. 64; *Johnson v. Johnson* (1926), 31 O.W.N. 313, 1926 CarswellOnt 58, 2 R.F.L. Rep. 150 (C.A.); *Hyman v. Hyman*, [1934] 4 D.L.R. 532, 1934 CarswellOnt 353 (S.C.C.), at 538 [D.L.R.].
221 *Bennet v. Bennet* (1879), 10 Ch. D. 474 (Eng. Ch. Div.), at 478, *per* Jessel M.R. Also see *Larondeau v. Laurendeau*, [1954] O.W.N. 722, [1954] 4 D.L.R. 293, 1954 CarswellOnt 315 (H.C.), at 724 [O.W.N.].
222 See *Young v. Young* (1958), 15 D.L.R. (2d) 138 (B.C. C.A.).
223 See *Soar v. Foster, supra,* note 220, at 106.
224 *Lattimer v. Lattimer* (1978), 18 O.R. (2d) 375, 82 D.L.R. (2d) 587, 1978 CarswellOnt 509, 1 E.T.R. 274 (H.C.).
225 *Bennet, supra,* note 221.
226 See, *e.g., Family Law Act*, R.S.O. 1990, c. F.3, s. 31.
227 *Nelson v. Nelson* (1995), 184 C.L.R. 538, 70 A.L.J.R. 47, 132 A.L.R. 133 (H.C.); *Brown v. Brown* (1993), 31 N.S.W.L.R. 582 (C.A.).
228 American Law Institute, *Restatement of the Law of Trusts, Second* (St. Paul, Minnesota, 1959) s. 442.

WILSON, RE

(1999), (sub nom. *Wilson (Attorney of), Re*) [1999] O.J. No. 1274,
27 E.T.R. (2d) 97, 1999 CarswellOnt 1000
Ontario General Division

FEDAK J.:

FACTUAL BACKGROUND

Lenore Kathleen Wilson suffered a debilitating stroke on September 7, 1994. After being treated in a hospital, she was transferred to a nursing home, where she continues to reside. Her son, Colin Wilson, who had earlier been appointed attorney by her, assumed responsibility for her personal affairs following the stroke. Prior to appointing her son as her attorney, Lenore Wilson had transferred ownership of various bank accounts, G.I.C.s and mutual fund accounts into the joint names of herself and Colin Wilson.

Lenore Wilson lived a frugal life, making modest withdrawals from her bank accounts to cover living expenses. After her stroke, patterns of spending on the accounts changed dramatically as Colin Wilson began to exercise his power of attorney. Colin felt he was entitled to treat the jointly held assets as his own and he accessed the funds freely. As well, Colin Wilson used an Esso credit card and a TD Visa credit card belonging to Lenore Wilson for his personal use.

Dennis Wilson, brother of Colin Wilson, was not happy with the manner in which Colin answered questions regarding Lenore Wilson's affairs, nor was he happy with the untimely manner in which Colin paid Lenore Wilson's personal bills. Dennis brought an application and received an order from the Court under section 42 of The Substitute Decisions Act requiring Colin Wilson to pass accounts. Colin continued to access the joint accounts after Dennis brought the application and even after several court appearances. Colin's Power of Attorney was finally terminated by court order on May 30, 1996 and he was ordered to account for the period from September 8, 1994 to May 30, 1996. Accounts were eventually submitted by Colin Wilson in mid-1998....

The key point of contention between the parties is whether Colin Wilson has beneficial ownership of the assets held jointly by him and Lenore Wilson. To make a determination on this issue, the Court must address the following issues: (1) Is there a presumption of advancement or a presumption of resulting trust where assets are held jointly by a mother and her child? (2) If there is a presumption of advancement, has that presumption been rebutted? (3) If there is a presumption of resulting trust, has that presumption been rebutted? Should it be found that the jointly held assets are subject to a resulting trust, it may also be necessary to deal with issues concerning the repayment of funds taken from the accounts.

. . .

THE LAW, ANALYSIS AND CONCLUSIONS

Issue 1: Is there a presumption of advancement or a presumption of resulting trust in regard to assets held jointly by Lenore Wilson and Colin Wilson?

There are two conflicting presumptions in regard to assets held jointly by two parties where one of the parties is the sole or primary contributor of the assets. The presumption of resulting trust holds that the party who has not contributed to the joint asset is holding it in trust for the individual who contributed the asset. The presumption of advancement takes the opposite view. It presumes that the contributor intended to make a gift to the other party of the legal and beneficial interest in the jointly held asset. Both of these presumptions are rebuttable.[229]

Where a person voluntarily transfers property into the name of another, or into the joint names of himself or herself and another, the law usually presumes that a gift was not intended: "Since Equity assumes bargain, and not gifts, he who has title gratuitously put into his name must prove that a gift was intended".[230] While the general rule is that transfers without consideration are presumed to create a resulting trust, in cases of special relationships the presumption of advancement is applied. Historically, the law presumed that a transfer or conveyance of property without consideration from a husband to his wife, or from a father to his child, was intended as a gift. The mother and child relationship did not give rise to the presumption, possibly due to the inferior social, economic and legal status of women.

Professor Waters suggests the presumption of advancement originated in the 18th and 19th centuries, when it was common practice for aristocratic and middle class husbands and fathers to bestow *inter vivos* gifts on their wives and children....

[S]peaking of the presumption as between a father and child, Professor Waters states that "the presumption appears to retain all its original vigour."[231] Presumably, the rationales for this position are that the love and affection between a parent and a child takes the place of consideration and that a parent has a moral and legal obligation to provide for the child. Professor Waters cites *Larondeau v. Laurendeau*,[232] for the proposition that the presumption of advancement applies not only where a father transfers property to or purchases property in the name of his child, but also arises whenever one person, male or female, places himself or herself *in loco parentis* to a child.

If the presumption of advancement applies to a female who stands *in loco parentis* to a child, then is it not reasonable and logical for the presumption of advancement to extend to a mother and child relationship? In *Edwards v. Bradley*,[233] the Supreme Court of Canada faced the issue of whether the presumption of advancement applied where a mother transferred a bank account into the joint

---

229 See J. Sopinka and S. Lederman, *The Law of Evidence in Canada* (Toronto: Butterworths, 1992) at 107-108.

230 D.W.M. Waters, *Law of Trusts in Canada*, 2nd ed. (Toronto: Carswell, 1984) at 308.

231 *Ibid.*, at 315.

232 *Supra,* note 221.

233 [1957] S.C.R. 599.

names of herself and her daughter. The daughter, one of three children, was married and lived many miles away. The court held that the presumption of resulting trust in favour of the mother was applicable unless there was evidence sufficient to overcome that presumption. Cartwright J. said:[234]

> In my opinion the result of the decisions in cases of mother and child is correctly summarized in the following passage in *Halsbury's Laws of England*:[235] "There is no presumption of a gift where the purchase or investment is made by a mother, even though living apart from her husband, or a widow, in the name of her child or in the joint names of herself and her child, though in the case of a widowed mother very little evidence to prove the intention of a gift is required..."

On the facts of the case, the Supreme Court found that there was no evidence to show that a gift was intended.

Despite this clear holding by the Supreme Court, lower courts across Canada have recognized a presumption of advancement between a mother and child.[236] In *Cohen v. Cohen*, Montgomery J. stated that "there should be a presumption of gift when a mother transfers property to a child."[237] With regard to *Edwards v. Bradley* he commented that he believed the case would be "stated differently today". And although the appeal court in *Dagle v. Dagle Estate*[238] acknowledged the clear holding in *Edwards v. Bradley*, the court held that the presumption of advancement should be extended to mothers and their children. The court noted that there was an obligation on a mother to support her children under the then current family law legislation in section 15(2) of The Divorce Act. In addition, the court referred to what Waters calls the "factor of affection" which exists between parents and their children, "something which cannot be presumed in the relationship between strangers".[239] MacDonald C.J.T.D. further noted:[240]

> The common law has never been held to be fixed in time. As times changed, so did the common law. There is no reason at this point in time where women play such an important role in the workplace that they cannot make a gift to a child resulting in the presumption of advancement.... Much has changed since the decision of Cartwright J. in the *Edwards* case in 1957.

The presumption of advancement between a mother and her child has been applied in the United States for many years.[241] The High Court of Australia recently held, in *Nelson v. Nelson*,[242] that the presumption of advancement applies in the case of gifts by a mother, as well as gifts by a father, to children. Mr. Justice Dawson observed that modern legislation governing family law matters imposes

---

234 *Ibid.*, at 604.
235 3rd ed., 1957, s. 736, at 387.
236 See, *e.g.*, *Rupar v. Rupar, supra*, note 25; *Cohen v. Cohen* (1985), 24 E.T.R. 269 (Alta. Q.B.); *Dagle v. Dagle Estate* (1990), 70 D.L.R. (4th) 201 (P.E.I.S.C.A.D.).
237 *Ibid., Cohen*, at 274.
238 (1990), 70 D.L.R. (4th) 201 (P.E.I.S.C.A.D.).
239 *Supra*, note 230, at 325.
240 *Supra*, note 238, at 209.
241 See A.W. Scott and W.F. Fratcher, *The Law of Trusts*, 4th ed. (Boston: Little, Brown and Co., 1989), vol. V, at 181-182.
242 (1995), 70 A.L.J.R. 47.

a duty upon both the mother and the father to support and maintain the child. These provisions "reflect the changed responsibility as between parents for the maintenance of their children and hence in their relationship with their children".[243] Dawson J. continued:[244]

> In modern society there is no reason to suppose that the probability of a parent intending to transfer a beneficial interest in property to a child is any the more or less in the case of a mother than in the case of a father.... In my view, whether the basis for the presumption is a moral obligation to provide for a child or the reflection of actual probabilities, there is no longer any justification for maintaining the distinction between a father and a mother. In the United States the presumption of advancement applies alike to a mother as well as a father and that should now be the situation in this country.

Toohey J. states:[245]

> In so far as the presumption of advancement derives from an obligation of support, its application to mothers who fund the purchase of property by their children is logical. In so far as the presumption operating in the case of a father and his children derives from their lifetime relationship, the same is no less true of a mother and her children.

In the same case, McHugh J. held that:[246]

> While the presumption of advancement continues to apply to transfers of property between father and child, consistency of doctrine requires that the presumption should also apply to transfers of property by a mother to her child.... But independent of any legal obligation of a mother, it would not accord with the reality of society today for the law to presume only a father has a moral obligation to support or is in a position to advance the interests of the child of the marriage.

I find the reasoning in *Nelson v. Nelson* persuasive. It leads me to agree with Montgomery J.'s opinion in *Cohen v. Cohen* that the Supreme Court of Canada would today state the law differently. To my mind, the advent of the Charter of Rights, in particular section 15, provides further justification for change in the law in Canada. It would be inconsistent with the guarantee of equality of men and women if a common law rule such as the presumption of advancement were only to apply to the father and child relationship. In *Retail, Wholesale and Department Stores Union, Local 580 v. Dolphin Delivery*,[247] McIntyre J. stated that the judiciary ought to apply and develop the principles of the common law in a manner consistent with the fundamental values enshrined in the Constitution. McIntyre J.'s view was cited with approval by Lamer C.J.C. in *Dagenais v. C.B.C.*[248]

Taking into consideration the natural affection between a mother and child, legislative changes requiring mothers to support their children, the economic

---

243 *Ibid.*, at 67.
244 *Ibid.*, at 68.
245 *Ibid.*, at 74.
246 *Ibid.*, at 82.
247 [1986] 2 S.C.R. 573 at 603.
248 [1994] 3 S.C.R. 835 at 878.

independence of women and the equality provisions of the Charter, I conclude that the presumption of advancement, rather than the presumption of resulting trust, should apply to the transfer of assets from Lenore Wilson to Colin Wilson.

[Fedak J. held that the presumption of advancement was rebutted by the evidence and, if the presumption of resulting trust applied, it would not have been rebutted. The assets had been transferred into the joint names of Lenore and Colin Wilson solely for the convenience of Lenore Wilson and not as a gift to Colin Wilson. Therefore, he held his interest in those assets on resulting trust for his mother. In reaching this conclusion, Fedak J. said:]

The creation of joint bank accounts does not in itself provide sufficient evidence to convey beneficial ownership nor is it necessarily evidence of intention to create a joint tenancy.[249]

... I find that Colin's behaviour and actions provide sufficient evidence of Lenore Wilson's true intent. Colin made no withdrawals from any of the accounts until after Lenore Wilson suffered the stroke. After the stroke, Colin withdrew over $60,000 from various accounts. He depleted the capital in the mutual fund to such an extent that Lenore Wilson's dividend income was significantly reduced. In the absence of any explanation, for his actions, I can only conclude that the fact that he did not access the accounts prior to his mother's stroke shows that he thought the accounts belonged to her, and not to him.

. . .

Therefore, I conclude that evidence adduced from a combination of facts has established on a balance of probabilities that the presumption of advancement in this case has been successfully rebutted. It is also clear on the evidence that in converting Lenore Wilson's property to his own, Colin Wilson breached his fiduciary duty as attorney for her property.

Notes and Questions

1. In *Dagle, Re,* MacDonald C.J.T.D. said, "There is no reason at this point in time when women play such an important role in the work-place that they cannot make a gift to a child resulting in the presumption of advancement."[250] Ms. Dagle made a will leaving her entire estate equally to her two sons. She then transferred real property to one of the sons. The court held that the presumption of advancement was raised on the facts and not rebutted.[251]

---

249 See *Re Mailman Estate*, [1941] S.C.R. 368; *Niles v. Lake, supra,* note 204; *Edwards v. Bradley, supra,* note 233.

250 *Dagle, supra,* note 236.

251 See also *Cohen, supra,* note 236; *Christmas Estate v. Tuck* (1995), 10 E.T.R. (2d) 47, 1995 CarswellOnt 1121, [1995] O.J. No. 3836 (Gen. Div.); *Clarke v. Hambly* (2002), 46 E.T.R. (2d) 166, [2002] B.C.J. No. 1672, 2002 CarswellBC 1690, 2002 BCSC 1074 (S.C. [In Chambers]).

2. Courts have not said clearly whether the modern presumption of advancement rests on the assumption that parents are likely to intend to make gifts to their children or on their legal and moral duties to support their children. In either case, no distinction can be drawn between fathers and mothers. However, if the source of the presumption is parental duty, then it is not clear why it applies to apparent gifts from parents to independent adult children.

3. As demonstrated by *Wilson, Re*, above, aged parents can become heavily dependent on their adult children and there may be a risk that those children will abuse their positions of trust or use undue influence to obtain large gifts from their parents. If the presumption of resulting trust arises because equity is suspicious of gifts, then this situation should attract that presumption because equity ought to be suspicious when elderly parents make large gifts to children on whom they depend. Fathers and mothers would be treated equally if the presumption of advancement applied when their children were minors or young adults, but the presumption of resulting trust applied instead when the children achieved full financial independence. Consider the position taken by Heeney J. in *McLear v. McLear Estate*, below.

McLEAR v. McLEAR ESTATE

[2000] O.J. No. 2570, 33 E.T.R. (2d) 272, 2000 CarswellOnt 2410,
[2000] O.T.C. 505
Ontario Superior Court of Justice

Georgina McLear was an elderly widow who died in 1995, leaving her entire estate by will to her son and three surviving daughters in equal shares. Another daughter had died earlier that year. The will was prepared by a lawyer a few months before the mother's death. The lawyer was not told of the existence of G.I.C.s, worth more than $80,000, that the mother had transferred into the joint names of herself and her two daughters, Marjorie Crowder and Frieda Telfer, within the last few years. Frieda Telfer was the daughter who predeceased her mother, so Ms. Crowder acquired sole legal ownership of the G.I.C.s on her mother's death.

HEENEY J.:

In this action, a self-described prodigal son has sued his sister, Marjorie Crowder, for a one-quarter share of approximately $80,000 in Canada Trust G.I.C.s that were held jointly by her and their mother at the date of their mother's death. Ms. Crowder maintains that this is her money by virtue of the joint tenancy, although she has paid out $20,000 to each of her two sisters, leaving only the Plaintiff without a share. At issue is whether the presumption of advancement or the presumption of resulting trust applies to the transfer of the G.I.C.s into joint names, and whether the evidence rebuts the applicable presumption.

. . .

THE PRESUMPTIONS

Where a person transfers his property gratuitously into another person's name, or into the names of himself and another, a resulting trust arises whereby the gratuitous transferee is deemed to hold his interest in trust for the transferor. This has been the law since at least as far back as *Dyer v. Dyer*.[252] The reason for this presumption is explained in D.W.M. Waters, *Law of Trusts In Canada*: "Since Equity assumes bargains, and not gifts, he who has title gratuitously put into his name must prove that a gift was intended."[253]

However, when the transfer is from husband to wife or from father to child, this presumption does not apply. Instead, a presumption of advancement applies, whereby there is a rebuttable presumption that a gift was intended. Note that the presumption does not arise on transfers from wife to husband, nor on transfers from mother to child.

. . .

That the presumption applies to transfers to a child from father, but not from mother, was confirmed by the Supreme Court of Canada in *Edwards Estate v. Bradley*.[254] That case is quite similar to the case at bar. Prior to her death, an elderly mother signed documents at the bank to put her account into joint names with her daughter, who was grown up, married and living many miles away in Michigan. Taking these monies out of the estate had the effect of distorting the distribution scheme of her will, which was to divide the estate in rough equality between the daughter, her two brothers and a step-son.

Cartwright J. stated that the law relating to transfers between mother and child is correctly summarized in 18 *Halsbury's Laws of England*,[255] which he quoted as follows:[256]

> There is no presumption of a gift where the purchase or investment is made by a mother even though living apart from her husband, or a widow, in the name of her child or in the joint names of herself and her child, though in the case of a widowed mother very little evidence to prove the intention of a gift is required...

Kerwin C.J., speaking for himself and Taschereau J., brought into consideration the additional factor that the transferee was independent and living away from the mother:[257]

> The circumstances of this case and particularly the fact that the respondent, a daughter of Mrs. Edwards, lived with her husband in Michigan, many miles from her mother's residence, do not permit any presumption of advancement to arise and, therefore, the ordinary rule applies that

---

252 *Supra,* note 5.
253 2nd ed. (Toronto, Carswell, 1984) at 308.
254 *Supra,* note 233.
255 3rd ed. 1957, s. 736, at 387.
256 *Supra,* note 233, at 604.
257 *Ibid.*, at 600.

there was a resulting trust in favour of the mother, unless the evidence is sufficient to overcome that presumption.

Rand J., speaking for himself and Locke J., avoided a discussion of presumptions altogether and simply reviewed the evidence to conclude that no gift had been intended by the transferor.

The Appeal Division of the P.E.I. Supreme Court considered *Edwards v. Bradley* in *Re Dagle*,[258] and concluded that it was behind the times. MacDonald C.J.T.D. quoted with approval the opinion of Montgomery J. in *Cohen v. Cohen*,[259] who felt that the statement of Cartwright J. set out above "would be stated differently today." MacDonald C.J.T.D. noted that, historically, "the presumption of advancement has been said to have arisen because of an obligation of the husband or father to provide for his wife or children". He then observed that much had changed since *Edwards v. Bradley*, including the creation of a statutory obligation upon mothers to support their children that was equivalent to the burden placed upon fathers. He then came to the following conclusion:

> The common law has never been held to be fixed in time. As times changed, so did the common law. There is no reason at this point in time where women play such an important role in the work-place that they cannot make a gift to a child resulting in the presumption of advancement.

Re Dagle and *Cohen v. Cohen* were followed in Ontario by Fedak J. in *Re Wilson (Attorney of)*.[260] After referring to these cases, as well as an Australian case, *Nelson v. Nelson*,[261] he considered s. 15 of the *Charter of Rights* which guarantees equality between men and women. He concluded that it would be inconsistent with this guarantee if the presumption of advancement were to apply only to fathers and not to mothers.

With great respect, I disagree. My views accord with those of Klebuc J. in *Cooper v. Markwart*,[262] where he says: "I have serious doubts as to whether [the] presumption of advancement continues to apply with any degree of persuasiveness ... in circumstances where an older parent has transferred property to an independent adult child who is married and lives apart from his parent." I also share the views of Dickson J. in *Rathwell v. Rathwell*: "In present social conditions the old presumption of advancement has ceased to embody any credible inference of intentions ...".[263] Dickson J. was dealing in that case with the presumption as between husband and wife, but his comments are equally applicable to parent-to-adult child transfers, once the assumptions that underlie the presumption of advancement are examined in a modern light.

The fundamental assumption that historically justified the presumption of advancement in transfers from father to child was that of financial dependency.

---

258 *Dagle, supra,* note 236.
259 *Cohen, supra,* note 236.
260 [1999] O.J. No. 1274 (Ont. Gen. Div.).
261 *Supra,* note 242.
262 [1999] S.J. No. 338 (Q.B.),
263 *Supra,* note 144, at 304 (S.C.C.).

As noted above, the court in *Re Dagle* used the fact that mothers now have an equal legal obligation to support their children as do fathers to expand the presumption of advancement to include mothers. However, in Ontario the obligation of a parent to support his or her child under s. 31 of the *Family Law Act* ceases when the child attains 18 years of age or thereafter ceases to be in full time attendance at school. Not only is there no obligation to support children beyond that point, but the reverse becomes the case. Section 32 of the Act imposes an ongoing legal obligation on an adult child to support his or her parent, in accordance with need and ability to pay. When dealing, therefore, with a fact situation involving an elderly parent and adult, independent children, it is only this child-to-parent support obligation that exists.

Waters appears to recognize the weakness of the financial dependency argument when dealing with adult children, but offers another assumption to take its place:[264]

> The presumption of advancement between father and child has not been subjected to any of the re-evaluation which in recent years has overtaken the presumption between husband and wife.... It may well be that, reflecting the financial dependency that it probably does, contemporary opinion would accord it little weight as between a father and an independent, adult child. But the factor of affection continues to exist, something which cannot be presumed in the relationship between strangers, and possibly for this reason the courts have seen no reason to challenge its modern significance.

It seems reasonable to assume that a parent has affection for a child. However, the same presumption of affection must, logically, be presumed for all of the children of that parent. This leads to a logical inconsistency in situations where the advancement of one child results in the corresponding deprivation of the other children. A gift by a parent to child A might be presumed because the parent is presumed to have affection for child A. However, the parent must be logically presumed to have equal affection for children B and C. Applying this presumption would lead one to conclude that the parent would not have arranged his affairs so as to cut out children B and C from receiving an equal share of his property. This would lead to a conclusion that child A took the property on resulting trust.

If I were given to speculate, as the court did in *Cohen*, as to what the Supreme Court of Canada might say if *Edwards v. Bradley* were decided today, I agree that they would be unlikely to decide the case on the basis of gender. So it is likely, as Fedak J. said, that mothers and fathers would be treated equally. However, it seems to me to be "bucking the trend" to suggest that the Supreme Court would expand the presumption of advancement to include mothers, given that it has been legislated out of existence in other contexts. Rather, I believe that the presumption of advancement would be applied equally to mothers and fathers with respect to dependent children, but would not apply to either mothers or fathers in situations where the children are independent adults. As noted above, the fact that the child was independent and living away from home featured very

---

264 *Supra*, note 230, at 325.

strongly in Kerwin C.J.'s reasons for finding that no presumption of advancement arose.

Just as Dickson J. considered "present social conditions" in concluding that the presumption of advancement between husbands and wives had lost all relevance, a consideration of the present social conditions of an elderly parent presents an equally compelling case for doing away with the presumption of advancement between parent and adult child. We are living in an increasingly complex world. People are living longer, and it is commonplace that an ageing parent requires assistance in managing his or her daily affairs. This is particularly so given the complexities involved in managing investments to provide retirement income, paying income tax on those investments, and so on. Almost invariably, the duty of assisting the ageing parent falls to the child who is closest in geographic proximity. In such cases, Powers of Attorney are routinely given. Names are "put on" bank accounts and other assets, so that the child can freely manage the assets of the parent.

Given these social conditions, it seems to me that it is dangerous to presume that the elderly parent is making a gift each time he or she puts the name of the assisting child on an asset. The presumption that accords with this social reality is that the child is holding the property in trust for the ageing parent, to facilitate the free and efficient management of that parent's affairs. The presumption that accords with this social reality is, in other words, the presumption of resulting trust.

Of course, there will be some situations where a gift is truly intended by the parent. Applying a presumption of resulting trust would still leave the door open to the assisting child to lead evidence to prove that the parent truly intended a gift, and was not merely making the task of managing the parent's affairs less cumbersome.

For purposes of the case at bar, however, it is not necessary for me to rewrite this chapter in the law of trusts. While I am convinced that the presumption of advancement has no relevance in transfers of property from an ageing parent of either gender to an independent, adult child, it is not necessary for me to base my decision on that opinion. The Supreme Court of Canada has, in *Edwards v. Bradley*, stated in no uncertain terms that the presumption of advancement does not apply to a transfer from a mother to an independent, adult child. The case at bar is a transfer of property from a mother to an independent, adult child. I consider myself bound by *Edwards v. Bradley*, and I choose to follow it in concluding that the presumption of resulting trust, and not the presumption of advancement, applies in this case.

The onus, therefore, is on Ms. Crowder to prove that the Canada Trust G.I.C.s were transferred by the mother into joint names with the intention of making a gift to Ms. Crowder and Frieda Telfer, or the survivor of them.

[Heeney J. held that the presumption of resulting trust was not rebutted and, if the presumption of advancement applied, it was rebutted by evidence that the mother did not intend to make a gift of the G.I.C.s to her daughters.]

Notes and Questions

1. The presumption of resulting trust has been applied to apparent gifts from parents to adult children in several recent decisions by superior courts in Canada.[265] However, many others have applied the presumption of advancement,[266] as did the Appeal Division of the P.E.I. Supreme Court in *Dagle, Re*,[267] which appears to be the only recent appellate decision on the issue.

2. F bought a foreign sweepstakes ticket in the name of his daughter, D, a minor. As a result, D won a substantial sum of money. The claims form was filled out by F and he completed it on behalf of D, although he could have completed a form to be used when the ticket was owned by several persons. The money was paid into court in the foreign jurisdiction, since D was a minor. F tried to obtain the income for D's education, but was unsuccessful. He then arranged to have the money transferred to the court in his domicile and encountered similar difficulties. F and his wife had a large family to support and limited financial resources. They reasoned that the ticket belonged to the family and that the proceeds should be available for the entire family. F would, therefore, like to have the money transferred to him. Can he do so? On what basis?[268]

3. From the facts discussed in the previous question, it will be apparent that it is difficult to obtain the income of money held in court to the credit of a minor for his or her maintenance. Indeed, that is difficult whenever money is held upon trust for a minor in the absence of express trust provisions or legislation. How should arrangements such as those be made?

4. The meaning of the phrase *in loco parentis* was considered in *Kirpalani v. Hathiramani*.[269] The testator had purchased a condominium which he registered in the name of his nephew, the defendant. Just before his death, the testator made a will naming another nephew, one of the plaintiffs, as executor and sole beneficiary of his estate. Until his death, the testator continued to pay the expenses related to the condominium, but often referred to the defendant as the "owner" of the condominium. After the testator's death, the plaintiff

---

265 *Cooper v. Markwart, supra,* note 262; *McLear v. McLear Estate*, 33 E.T.R. (2d) 272, 2000 CarswellOnt 2410, [2000] O.J. No. 2570, [2000] O.T.C. 505 (S.C.J.); *Goldson v. Goldson*, 44 E.T.R. (2d) 50, 2002 CarswellOnt 1400, [2002] O.T.C. 182 (S.C.J.), additional reasons at (2002), 2002 CarswellOnt 5752 (S.C.J.), affirmed (2004), 2004 CarswellOnt 522, 4 E.T.R. (3d) 229 (C.A.); *Thorsen Estate v. Thorsen*, 201 N.S.R. (2d) 320, 2002 CarswellNS 43, 2002 NSSC 23, 629 A.P.R. 320 (S.C.), additional reasons at 2002 CarswellNS 161, 2002 NSSC 97, 203 N.S.R. (2d) 107, 635 A.P.R. 107 (S.C.); *Robertson v. Hayton* (2003), [2003] O.J. No. 4538, 2003 CarswellOnt 4457, 4 E.T.R. (3d) 115 (S.C.J.), additional reasons at (2003), 2003 CarswellOnt 5354 (S.C.J.).

266 *Cohen v. Cohen, supra,* note 236; *Reain v. Reain* (1995), 20 R.F.L. (4th) 30, 1995 CarswellOnt 593, [1995] O.J. No. 4063 (Gen. Div.); *Smith Estate v. Smith* (1995), [1995] O.J. No. 253, 1995 CarswellOnt 2886 (Gen. Div.); *Sodhi v. Sodhi*, [1998] 10 W.W.R. 673, 53 B.C.L.R. (3d) 280, 1998 CarswellBC 107, 20 E.T.R. (2d) 242 (S.C.), affirmed (1998), 23 E.T.R. (2d) 235, 1998 CarswellBC 2419 (C.A.); *Cho Ki Yau Trust (Trustees of) v. Yau Estate* (1999), 29 E.T.R. (2d) 204, 1999 CarswellOnt 3232, [1999] O.J. No. 3818 (S.C.J.); *Wilson, Re, supra,* note 260; *Kappler v. Beaudoin* (2000), [2000] O.J. No. 3439, 2000 CarswellOnt 3329 (S.C.J.); *St. Jean v. Cocks* (2001), 38 E.T.R. (2d) 103, 2001 CarswellOnt 1138 (S.C.J.); *Clarke v. Hambly, supra,* note 251.

267 *Supra,* note 236.

268 See *B. v. B.* (1975), 65 D.L.R. (3d) 460, 1975 CarswellBC 363 (S.C.).

269 (1992), 46 E.T.R. 256, 1992 CarswellOnt 540, [1992] O.J. No. 1594 (Gen. Div.), additional reasons at (1994), 1994 CarswellOnt 3065 (Gen. Div.).

executor brought proceedings alleging that the condominium was put in the defendant's name solely for tax purposes and that the testator had intended to retain the beneficial interest. The defendant argued that the condominium was a gift to him by the testator, any presumption of resulting trust being displaced by the fact that the testator stood in *loco parentis* to the defendant. The Court held that the testator did not stand in *loco parentis* to the defendant because the testator did not provide regular and systematic assistance to the defendant or hold out to the defendant that he was to look to the testator for his future provision. The testator, although generous to the defendant, did not undertake a moral obligation to provide for the defendant. The Court found in favour of the defendant on other grounds.

5. The presumption of advancement does not arise between brother and sister,[270] unless the donor stands *in loco parentis* to the donee.[271]

(ii) *Husbands and Wives*

According to the traditional view of the presumption of advancement, it is assumed that a husband intends to give whenever he makes an apparent gift to his wife. It does not matter whether he transfers the asset to her or purchases it in her name. The presumption of resulting trust applies instead to apparent gifts from a wife to her husband,[272] between *de facto* spouses,[273] and also from a husband to a wife after their marriage has broken down.[274] However, the presumption of advancement applies when a man makes an apparent gift to a woman he intends to marry and in contemplation of that marriage.[275] As discussed below, the presumptions between husbands and wives have been amended in most Canadian jurisdictions by statute.

There is a variety of opinions regarding the basis for the presumption of advancement. It seems that it was raised because the donor was under a "natural" obligation, recognized in equity, to provide for the donee.[276] If that is so, then its

---

270 *Freeland v. Freeland* (1982), 19 Alta. L.R. (2d) 180, 1982 CarswellAlta 60, 48 A.R. 199 (Q.B.); *Bishop v. Bishop* (1983), 46 N.B.R. (2d) 405, 1983 CarswellNB 102, 121 A.P.R. 405 (Q.B.); *Halfpenny v. Holien* (1997), 37 B.C.L.R. (3d) 186, 1997 CarswellBC 1476, 19 E.T.R. (2d) 84 (S.C.).

271 *O'Brien v. Bean* (1957), 7 D.L.R. (2d) 332 (B.C. S.C.).

272 *Heseltine v. Heseltine*, [1971] 1 W.L.R. 342. *Hillier v. Hillier*, [1979] 2 W.W.R. 346, 8 R.F.L. (2d) 50, 1979 CarswellAlta 195, 17 A.R. 133 (T.D.), which holds otherwise, appears to be wrong on this point.

273 *Derhak v. Dandenault (Derhak)* (1954), 11 W.W.R. (N.S.) 37, 62 Man. R. 13, 1954 CarswellMan 6 (Q.B.); *Herviex v. Anderson* (1984), 32 Sask. R. 37, 1984 CarswellSask 53, 39 R.F.L. (2d) 315 (Q.B.), affirmed (1985), 1985 CarswellSask 98, 46 R.F.L. (2d) 320, 39 Sask. R. 184 (C.A.); *Wilson v. Munro* (1982), 13 E.T.R. 174, 1983 CarswellBC 15, 32 R.F.L. (2d) 235, 42 B.C.L.R. 317 (S.C.). See also *Copley v. Guaranty Trust Co., supra,* note 214.

274 *Shore v. Shore* (1976), 63 D.L.R. (3d) 354, 1975 CarswellBC 80, 25 R.F.L. 383 (S.C.); *Cotton v. Cotton* (1981), 126 D.L.R. (3d) 548, 32 Nfld. & P.E.I.R. 30, 1981 CarswellPEI 10, 23 R.F.L. (2d) 78, 91 A.P.R. 30 (S.C.), at 552 [D.L.R.].

275 *Ulrich v. Ulrich*, [1968] 1 W.L.R. 180, [1968] 1 All E.R. 67. The presumption applies if the marriage turns out to be voidable, but not if it is void: *Dunbar v. Dunbar*, [1909] 2 Ch. 639 (Eng. Ch. Div.).

276 See, *e.g.*, *Murless v. Franklin* (1818), 1 Swans. 13 at 17, 36 E.R. 278, *per* Lord Eldon; *Bennet v. Bennet, supra,* note 221.

restriction to cases in which the donor was the donee's husband or father is understandable in an historical context, since he was usually the only one with the financial resources to make gifts to his dependants and has always been regarded as having such an obligation.

Historically, a large gift from a husband or father could also be viewed as an advancement of a portion of his estate in advance of his death. Viewed in this way, it should not be an overly large share of his assets. This point is brought out in *Pahara v. Pahara*.[277] The husband had, by his own industry, business acumen, and wife's help, acquired a number of farm properties, stock, and implements during forty years of married life. He did not read or write English well and, for that and other reasons, title to those assets were in his wife's name. It was understood between them that those assets were held for the benefit of both and the survivor of them. However, shortly before her death, she made a will giving almost all her property to her children, requesting that they provide for their father during his lifetime. He was 67 when she died and was left virtually destitute. Although there was a presumption of advancement in favour of the wife, the court had no difficulty in finding it rebutted by the evidence. In the course of his judgment, Rand J. said:[278]

> It is really inaccurate to speak of an advancement of the entire property of a husband to his wife; an advancement is essentially a share, and here the transfers were in substance of an entire establishment.

The historical basis no longer provides sufficient support for restricting the presumption of advancement to apparent gifts from husbands and fathers. Today, women are often in as good a position to make such gifts. Indeed, spouses, parents, and children have a legal obligation to support one another at common law and by statute.[279] Moreover, legislation for the support of dependants[280] is premised on the idea that people have an obligation to make adequate provision when they die for their dependants who survive them. Further, when someone transfers property to, or purchases property in the name of, a *de facto* spouse, it is surely more likely than not that a gift was intended.

It might, therefore, be supposed that the proper modern basis for the presumption ought to be that it is more likely than not that the apparent donor intended to make a gift to the recipient. The suggested modern basis has been accepted in Australian cases[281] and has its adherents in England as well.[282]

Even if the basis for the presumption of advancement is disputed, it is not particularly difficult to prove an intention to give in those relationships in which

---

277 (1945), [1946] S.C.R. 89, [1946] 1 D.L.R. 433, 1945 CarswellAlta 126.
278 *Ibid.*, at 95.
279 See, *e.g.*, *Family Law Act*, R.S.O. 1990, c. F.3, s. 31.
280 See, *e.g.*, *Succession Law Reform Act*, R.S.O. 1990, c. S.26, Part V.
281 See *Wirth v. Wirth, supra,* note 211, at 237; *Cavalier v. Cavalier* (1971), 19 F.L.R. 199 (N.S.W. S.C.); J. Hackney, "Trusts", [1974] Annual Survey of Commonwealth Law 508 at 527.
282 See, *e.g.*, *Pettit v. Pettit, supra,* note 154, at 823-824 (H.L.); *Williams & Glyn's Bank Ltd. v. Boland* (1980), [1981] A.C. 487, [1980] 3 W.L.R. 138 at 147 (H.L.).

the presumption was not traditionally thought to arise. Indeed, the cases show that courts do not rely so much on the presumption as on the evidence. Moreover, the presumptions between spouses have lost much of their force. Thus, for example, in *Pettit v. Pettit*,[283] Lord Reid, Lord Hodson, and Lord Diplock opined that the presumptions are largely irrelevant in the context of contemporary married life. By contrast, Lord Upjohn thought that they remain important. Similarly, in *Rathwell v. Rathwell*,[284] Dickson J. stated that the presumption of advancement no longer reflects a husband's intention.[285] Consequently, between spouses, the presumptions of resulting trust and advancement are easily rebutted today.

Even though the presumptions between spouses have lost much of their significance in modern times, they remain important when evidence is not available to rebut the presumptions, either because the parties to the transaction are dead or because the evidence is inadmissible. If a husband transferred assets to his wife for a fraudulent purpose, he may not be able to lead evidence of their fraud to rebut the presumption of advancement.[286]

In *Mehta Estate v. Mehta Estate*,[287] a husband and wife were killed in an air plane crash. His estate claimed a half interest in a R.R.S.P. which he had purchased in her name. The court held that the strength of the presumptions vary from case to case. They have little value in a marital property dispute when both parties are available to give evidence of their intentions. However, there was no marital dispute, the parties were unavailable to testify, and therefore the presumption of advancement had great significance, applying absent any rebutting evidence.

Most everyone agrees that it is no longer justifiable to base the choice of presumption on the gender of the donor.[288] In the context of matrimonial property disputes, the problem is solved by statutory amendments of the presumptions in many jurisdictions. This is discussed below. However, since those statutes do not apply in all contexts and in all jurisdictions, courts should amend the rules of equity to treat husbands and wives the same. The question is whether all apparent gifts between spouses should be subject to the presumption of advancement or the presumption of resulting trust.

Three strong arguments can be made in favour of the presumption of resulting trust. First, the presumption of advancement does not apply outside marriage to people in similar relationships nor, we assume, would it apply to gay or lesbian couples who are married. Therefore, of all the people in long term domestic relationships who make apparent gifts to their (lawful or *de facto*) spouses, only

---

283 *Ibid.*

284 *Supra,* note 144, at 304.

285 Formerly it was thought that the presumption could be rebutted only by clear and cogent evidence: *Hyman v. Hyman, supra,* note 220; *Hebert v. Foulston* (1978), 7 Alta. L.R. 141, 90 D.L.R. (3d) 403, 11 A.R. 338 (C.A.).

286 This is discussed below.

287 50 E.T.R. 288, 1993 CarswellMan 118, [1993] 6 W.W.R. 457, 104 D.L.R. (4th) 24, 48 R.F.L. (3d) 121, 88 Man. R. (2d) 54, 51 W.A.C. 54 (C.A.).

288 *Cf.* L. Sarmas, "A Step in the Wrong Direction: The Emergence of Gender "Neutrality" in the Equitable Presumption of Advancement" (1994), 19 Melbourne U.L. Rev. 758, who argues that the presumptions should not be changed because they favour women and thereby help overcome an historical disadvantage.

husbands do not enjoy the benefit of the presumption of resulting trust, except where modified by statute. This amounts to unfair discrimination, not only on the basis of gender, but also on the basis of marital status and sexual orientation. It would be possible to apply the presumption of advancement to everyone in this situation, but that could create a more difficult problem: distinguishing casual relationships, which are subject to the presumption of resulting trust, from long term relationships, which would be subject to the extended presumption of advancement. It would be far simpler to apply the presumption of resulting trust when a husband is the apparent donor.

Secondly, the presumption of resulting trust can be seen as a protective device. Equity, being suspicious of gifts, double checks to make sure that apparent gifts really were intended as such. By asking a donee to prove the donor's intention to give, equity protects people from the unintended loss of their assets. Historically, everyone in society was entitled to this protection except husbands or fathers, who were economically more powerful than their wives and children and not in need of it. With the balancing of economic power between men and women, there is no longer sufficient justification for excepting husbands from the normal rule.[289] The same might be said of elderly parents, as discussed above.

Thirdly, the extension of the presumption of resulting trust to apparent gifts from husbands would be consistent with the statutory modification of the presumptions in the matrimonial property context, discussed below, and with the use of the constructive trust to distribute assets between (lawful or *de facto*) spouses on the breakdown of their relationship. When a spouse provides domestic services with the expectation of sharing the family home, a constructive trust can arise to give effect to that expectation.[290] The spouse does not have to prove that those services were provided on that basis. As Cory J. said in *Peter v. Beblow*:[291]

In today's society it is unreasonable to assume that the presence of love automatically implies a gift of one party's services to another. Nor is it unreasonable for the party providing the domestic labour required to create a home to expect to share in the property of the parties when the relationship is terminated.

If it is assumed that people in loving, long term relationships are not making gifts of their services, then it would be consistent to assume that they are not making gifts when they transfer assets to, or buy assets for, the people they love. By applying the presumption of resulting trust, instead of the presumption of advancement, to all transactions between (lawful or *de facto*) spouses, courts would be treating all inputs of value into those relationships consistently, regardless of whether the value consisted of services, money, or other assets.

---

289 See *Falconer v. Falconer*, [1970] 1 W.L.R. 1333, [1970] 3 All E.R. 449 at 452 (C.A.); *Hurst v. Benson* (1981), 9 E.T.R. 274, 1981 CarswellBC 563 (S.C.), at 283 [E.T.R.].

290 The trust is not resulting because it can arise even though the spouse did not contribute to the acquisition of the home. Constructive trusts are discussed in the next two chapters.

291 [1993] 1 S.C.R. 980, 101 D.L.R. (4th) 621, [1993] S.C.J. No. 36, 1993 CarswellBC 44, 1993 CarswellBC 1258, [1993] 3 W.W.R. 337, 23 B.C.A.C. 81, 39 W.A.C. 81, 150 N.R. 1, 48 E.T.R. 1, 77 B.C.L.R. (2d) 1, 44 R.F.L. (3d) 329, [1993] R.D.F. 369, at 633 [D.L.R.].

(f) Matrimonial Property Legislation

In most Canadian common law jurisdictions, matrimonial property legislation has changed the application of the presumptions of advancement and resulting trust to husbands and wives. It is often said that these statutes abolish the presumption of advancement, but that is not quite true. They leave room for that presumption to operate when assets are taken in the joint names of the spouses. Also, it seems that the legislative changes apply only when spouses have applied for orders under that legislation. These issues are discussed below.

The statutes that change the presumptions across Canada are very similar in each jurisdiction, but they follow two somewhat different models. Hence, the common law jurisdictions can be divided into three groups. The first is British Columbia and Manitoba. Their matrimonial property statutes do not alter the common law presumptions of resulting trust and advancement.[292] The second group consists of New Brunswick, Newfoundland and Labrador, Nova Scotia, Saskatchewan, and Yukon. Their statutes limit the presumption of advancement to assets held by the spouses as tenants in common following the severance of a joint tenancy between them.[293] The third group, Alberta, Northwest Territories, Nunavut, Ontario, and Prince Edward Island, use a more modern form of legislation that applies the presumption of advancement to assets that are jointly owned by the spouses.[294] The New Brunswick and Ontario statutes are reproduced here as representatives of the two statutory models.

Further Reading

Dennis R. Klinck, "The Unsung Demise of the Presumption of Spousal Advancement" (1985), 7 E.T.Q. 6.

MARITAL PROPERTY ACT

S.N.B. 1980, c. M-1.1

15.(1) The rule of law applying a presumption of advancement in questions of the ownership of property as between husband and wife is abolished and in place thereof the rule of law applying a presumption of a resulting trust shall be applied in the same manner as if they were not married, except that,
  (a) the fact that property is placed or taken in the name of spouses as joint tenants is *prima facie* proof that each spouse is intended to have on a severance of the joint tenancy a one-half beneficial interest in the property; and

---

292 *Family Relations Act*, R.S.B.C. 1996, c. 128; *The Marital Property Act*, C.C.S.M., c. M45.

293 *Marital Property Act*, S.N.B. 1980, c. M-1.1, s. 15; *Family Law Act*, R.S.N.L 1990, c. F-2, s. 31; *Matrimonial Property Act*, R.S.N.S. 1989, c. 275, s. 21; *The Family Property Act*, S.S. 1997, c. F-6.3, s. 50; *Family Property and Support Act*, R.S.Y. 2002, c. 83, s. 7.

294 *Matrimonial Property Act*, R.S.A. 2000, c. M-8, s. 36; *Family Law Act*, S.N.W.T. 1997, c. 18, s. 46; *Family Law Act (Nunavut)*, S.N.W.T. 1997, c. 18, s. 46; *Family Law Act*, R.S.O. 1990, c. F.3, s. 14; *Family Law Act*, R.S.P.E.I. 1988, c. F-2.1, s. 14.

(b) money on deposit in a chartered bank, savings office, credit union or trust company in the name of both spouses shall be deemed to be in the name of the spouses as joint tenants for the purposes of paragraph (a).

(2) Subsection (1) applies notwithstanding that the event giving rise to the presumption occurred before the coming into force of this section.

Notes and Questions

1. The problems with this form of legislation are discussed in *Levy, Re*.[295] Mr. Levy transferred money from his own accounts to a new joint account he established with his wife just four days before he died. She withdrew the money after he died and spent most of it. Mr. Levy's personal representative claimed that Mrs. Levy held the money upon resulting trust for the estate. The court considered the effect of s. 21(1) of the *Matrimonial Property Act*,[296] which is identical to the New Brunswick legislation set out above. The court held that the exception for jointly owned assets applied only on a severance of the joint tenancy and that there had been no severance, since death does not sever a joint tenancy. Thus, the presumption of resulting trust applied. However, Mrs. Levy was able to rebut the presumption by proving her husband's intention to make a gift of the money to her.

2. Was *Levy, Re* decided correctly? Does the legislation mean that beneficial joint ownership is to be presumed whenever assets are held jointly by spouses, or, as held by the court, only when the joint tenancy has been severed and converted to a tenancy in common? A joint tenancy is severed neither by the death of a tenant nor by a breakdown of the marriage.

3. Subsection (2) of the New Brunswick statute makes the provision retrospective. This is also true of the statutes like it and the Ontario statute, below. However, if the marriage was terminated before the legislation came into force, it probably does not apply.[297]

FAMILY LAW ACT

R.S.O. 1990, c. F.3

14. The rule of law applying a presumption of a resulting trust shall be applied in questions of the ownership of property between husband and wife, as if they were not married, except that,
   (a) the fact that property is held in the name of spouses as joint tenants is proof, in the absence of evidence to the contrary, that the spouses are intended to own the property as joint tenants; and
   (b) money on deposit in the name of both spouses shall be deemed to be in the name of the spouses as joint tenants for the purposes of clause (a).

---

295 (1981), 131 D.L.R. (3d) 15, (sub nom. *Levy v. Levy Estate*) 50 N.S.R. (2d) 14, 1981 CarswellNS 71, 25 R.F.L. (2d) 149, 12 E.T.R. 133, 98 A.P.R. 14; noted (1982-83), 12 E.T.R. 157.
296 *Ibid.,* S.N.S. 1980, c. 9.
297 *McLaren v. McLaren* (1979), 24 O.R. (2d) 481, 100 D.L.R. (3d) 163, 1979 CarswellOnt 369, 8 R.F.L. (2d) 301 (C.A.).

. . .

16.(2) Section 14 applies whether the event giving rise to the presumption occurred before or after the 1st day of March, 1986.

Notes and Questions

1. Does this model of statute solve the problems discussed in *Levy, Re*?

2. The statute does not completely abolish the presumption of advancement, but changes both presumptions to make them apply equally to men and women. The common law is changed in two respects. First, if an apparent gift from a husband to his wife is an asset or an interest in an asset held by her as sole legal owner or by both spouses as tenants in common, the presumption of resulting trust applies instead of the presumption of advancement. Secondly, if a wife makes an apparent gift to her husband of an interest in an asset owned by the spouses as joint tenants, the presumption of advancement would apply instead of the presumption of resulting trust. Is there a sufficient difference between a joint tenancy and a tenancy in common to presume that the apparent donor had an intention to give when assets are held jointly, but not when they are held as tenants in common?

3. Is the abolition of the presumption of advancement between spouses desirable? In most cases, when one spouse makes an apparent gift to the other it is usually because he or she intends to make a gift. Even if there was no such intention, but the asset is put in the other spouse's name as a matter of convenience, or worse, to put it beyond the reach of creditors, should the onus not be on the apparent donor to prove that he or she did not intend to make a gift?

4. The equivalent Alberta legislation expressly states that it applies when a court is "making a decision under this Act".[298] Therefore, the common law presumptions would be used for any other purpose. Although legislation in other jurisdictions does not contain this restriction, the same rule seems to apply, because matrimonial property legislation affects the property rights of spouses only when they trigger their rights under that legislation. This is discussed in *Clark Drummie & Co. v. Ryan*, below.

CLARK DRUMMIE & CO. v. RYAN

(1999), 170 D.L.R. (4th) 266, 209 N.B.R. (2d) 70, 1999 CarswellNB 47,
535 A.P.R. 70, 26 E.T.R. (2d) 14
New Brunswick Court of Appeal

The defendants were husband and wife. They bought a house as joint tenants in 1978 and both contributed to the purchase and payment of mortgage. In 1984, they sold it and used the proceeds to buy another house in the wife's name alone, because they believed that would protect it from the husband's creditors. The husband was a lawyer who was fired by his employers (the plaintiffs) after they discovered that he had stolen $247,603.14 from their clients. The plaintiffs reimbursed their clients, took assignments of their claims, and sued the defendants, seeking a declaration that she held one-half the house on resulting trust for him.

---

298 *Matrimonial Property Act*, R.S.A. 2000, c. M-8, s. 36(1).

RYAN J.A.:

This appeal raises issues involving the presumption of a resulting trust, of advancement and the evidence necessary to rebut either of them. The appellant, Deborah Ryan, appeals against the decision of Turnbull J. who held that her disbarred lawyer husband retained an interest in the marital home which became subject to seizure by his judgment creditor, Clark Drummie and Company, his former employer. She contends that the trial judge erred in law when he found that a presumed resulting trust in favour of her husband, thus making his interest available to execution, had not been rebutted by the common intent of the spouses and despite the fact that the creditor had based its claim on a constructive trust. Mrs. Ryan says she is not a trustee and that Clark Drummie has no cause of action against her.

. . .

Resulting Trust

In 1981, the government of New Brunswick made a major change in legislation by abolishing the presumption of advancement in questions of the ownership of property as between husband and wife in s. 15(1) of the *Marital Property Act*. In the same section the legislature provided that in place of the presumption of advancement the rule of law applying a presumption of a resulting trust shall be applied in the same manner as if the husband and wife were not married. Prior to this statutory enactment the equitable doctrines of advancement and resulting trust were rebuttable presumptions.[299] They remain rebuttable: see *Levy, Re*,[300] where the trial judge held that since the presumption of resulting trust is replacing the presumption of advancement, the presumption as between spouses should not be so strong as in the case of total strangers. In an advancement the presumption is that the purchase of property is made for the benefit of the person acquiring it rather than there being a presumption of a resulting trust in favour of the person who paid the money....

In the case before us, even though Clark Drummie's action was based on resulting and constructive trusts, the trial judge determined that the law firm should succeed on the grounds of an equitable resulting trust. The trial judge seems to have arrived at his conclusion of a resulting trust by mixing the changes in principles and presumptions in the *Marital Property Act* with creditors' rights to obtain a declaration of a spouse's beneficial interest, if any, in property and the ultimate sale of that interest. Any right given to a spouse under the Act does not constitute an interest in property owned by the other spouse unless provided for in the legislation.[301]

---

299 See *Clemens v. Clemens Estate*, [1956] S.C.R. 286 at 294-295, 1 D.L.R. (2d) 625, *per* Cartwright J.

300 *Supra*, note 295, at 27-28, *per* Hallett J.

301 See s. 47.

In *Bank of Montreal v. Kuchuk*,[302] Stratton J.A., writing for a unanimous court, Hughes C.J.N.B. and La Forest J.A. concurring, held that creditors do not have a right to make a frontal attack on the interests of a spouse under the *Marital Property Act*. Stratton J.A. said:[303]

> As stated previously, the scheme of the legislation is to continue the separate property regime between spouses until a marriage breakdown occurs. If this is correct, it would, I think, be unreasonable to suppose that the Legislature intended to permit a creditor to apply for a determination as to the ownership of the marital home when the spouses themselves could not do so until there was a legally recognizable marriage breakdown. No such marriage breakdown was asserted in the present case.

Once the rights of either spouse have crystallized as between the spouses in an application by either of them under the Act a creditor may, but not in all circumstances, attack the interest of the debtor.[304]

. . .

In the case before us, the resulting trust cannot be presumed from s. 15(1) of the *Marital Property Act* because the action is not founded on the provisions of the Act. Even so, there was evidence before the trial judge relating to the financial contribution by Mr. Ryan from the proceeds of the sale of the first home held in joint tenancy and to his continued regular contributions from his salary which he turned over to his wife. At least some of these monies found their way into paying down the mortgage. Regardless, a creditor cannot claim under the Act.[305]

. . .

The Lawyer Aspect

There is another rejoinder to the trial judge's conclusion. It relates to the unique occupation of the husband in not claiming any interest in the marital home and also concerns the marital relationship itself. Here, Mr. Ryan, a practising lawyer at all material times, knew the law and would have had to know that when the property went into his wife's name alone, his position became irrevocable. In my opinion he could not, without an agreement or conclusive evidence to the contrary, rely on the presumption of a resulting trust. Even more so for a creditor-stranger. It would be unconscionable for any lawyer to deliberately mislead and deceive his or her spouse by purporting to convey or relinquish his or her interest to the spouse while at the same time being fraudulently duplicitous about the beneficial interest the lawyer surreptitiously retains. I strongly doubt that a lawyer,

---

302 (1982), 40 N.B.R. (2d) 203, 136 D.L.R. (3d) 355 (C.A.).

303 *Ibid.,* at 218.

304 See also *George v. George* (1987), 80 N.B.R. (2d) 357, 37 D.L.R. (4th) 466, *per* Montgomery J. (Q.B.), upheld on appeal at (1987), 84 N.B.R. (2d) 355 (C.A.).

305 See *Bank of Montreal v. Kuchuk, supra,* note 302.

having conveyed or relinquished his or her interest to a spouse could, on marriage breakdown, convince a judge, except in the most unique and rare circumstance that the lawyer should be able to retain a beneficial interest in the marital home property.

Once having conveyed or committed the ownership of the marital home to a spouse, a lawyer, contending that a beneficial interest remains, puts himself or herself in the untenable position of trying to support an insupportable argument for a resulting trust by asserting that the spouse is a mere trustee of the lawyer's interest....

[The presumption of advancement applied to the husband's contribution to the purchase of the house in his wife's name and it was not rebutted. The appeal was allowed and the plaintiffs' claim against the wife was dismissed with costs.]

Notes and Questions

1. When, if ever, would a third party be able to invoke the presumptions provided by matrimonial property legislation: (1) after the marriage breaks down and the spouses are entitled to apply for the equalization or division of assets under the act, (2) after a spouse has commenced proceedings, or (3) after an order has been granted?

In *Blowes v. Blowes*,[306] a wife became bankrupt after she commenced proceedings against her husband for equalization of net family property under the *Family Law Act*.[307] The Ontario Court of Appeal held that her right to an equalization order vested in her trustee in bankruptcy for the benefit of her creditors. In *Tinant v. Tinant*,[308] the Alberta Court of Appeal said that the right to commence proceedings under the *Matrimonial Property Act*[309] would vest in the trustee in bankruptcy. It would be consistent with this if third parties were permitted to use the statutory presumptions of resulting trust and advancement once a spouse became entitled to commence proceedings under the act, but not before. Matrimonial property legislation, including its presumptions, should not affect the beneficial ownership of assets belonging to spouses who are happily married.

2. In *Clark, Drummie & Co. v. Ryan*, above, the New Brunswick Court of Appeal decided that a gift had been intended possibly because that is what an honest lawyer would have intended in the circumstances. Is it correct to resolve this issue based on an objective view of intention rather than on evidence of the husband's actual intention at the time of the purchase? Whatever his motive, if he did not intend to make a gift to his wife, this should rebut the presumption of advancement, provided that evidence is admissible. As discussed below, evidence of intention may be inadmissible if the transaction was for an illegal purpose.

---

306 (1993), 16 O.R. (3d) 318, 49 R.F.L. (3d) 27, 1993 CarswellOnt 232, 21 C.B.R. (3d) 276 (C.A.).
307 R.S.O. 1990, c. F.3.
308 15 Alta. L.R. (4th) 225, [2003] A.J. No. 856, 2003 CarswellAlta 974, 330 A.R. 148, 299 W.A.C. 148, 46 C.B.R. (4th) 150, 2003 ABCA 211 (C.A.).
309 R.S.A. 2000, c. M-8.

(g) Rebutting the Presumptions

The presumptions of resulting trust and advancement are instances of what Lord Diplock called a judicial "technique" of:[310]

> imputing an intention to a person whenever the intention with which an act is done affects its legal consequences and the evidence does not disclose what was the actual intention with which he did it... — but presumptions of this type are not immutable. A presumption of fact is no more than a consensus of judicial opinion disclosed by reported cases as to the most likely inference of fact to be drawn in the absence of evidence to the contrary.

The evidence required to rebut a presumption depends, of course, on the fact being presumed. The presumption of advancement is an inference that an apparent donor really did intend to give, while the presumption of resulting trust is an inference that no gift was intended. As discussed above, these presumptions are raised once it is established that an apparent gift was made, either by gratuitous transfer or by payment of, or contribution to, the purchase price. The choice of presumption then depends on the relationship between apparent donor and donee. Except as modified by matrimonial property legislation, discussed above, it is presumed that husbands intend to give to their wives. When statutory presumptions do apply to husbands and wives, it is presumed that gifts are intended only when they acquire assets as joint tenants. It is also presumed that parents intend to give to their children, at least until the children achieve full financial independence. In other cases, it is presumed that a gift was not intended.

Although reference is sometimes made to the "common intention" of the parties,[311] it is clearly established that it is the apparent donor's intention, and not the recipient's intention, that will rebut or confirm a presumption.[312] The recipient's intention can be relevant as circumstantial evidence of the apparent donor's intention. For example, in *Wilson, Re*, reproduced above, concerning an apparent gift from a mother to her son, Fedak J. found "that [the son's] behaviour and actions provide sufficient evidence of [the mother's] true intent."[313] The fact that the son thought that the asset belonged beneficially to his mother was relevant, not because the presumption of advancement was affected by his intention, but because it tended to prove that she did not intend to make a gift to him.

When A makes an apparent gift to B, the resulting trust depends on A's intention at the time the apparent gift is made. If A intended to make a gift, there is no resulting trust. B has obtained beneficial legal ownership of the gift and it will not be removed or diminished if A later regrets the gift or has a change of heart.[314] If A does not intend to give at the outset, a resulting trust arises. A's

---

310 *Pettit v. Pettit, supra*, note 154, at 823.
311 *Rathwell v. Rathwell, supra*, note 144; *Tinsley v. Milligan, supra*, note 194.
312 See, *e.g.*, *Biljanic v. Biljanic Estate, supra*, note 208; *Christmas Estate v. Tuck, supra*, note 251; *Dreger (Litigation Guardian of) v. Dreger*, [1994] 10 W.W.R. 293, (sub nom. *Dreger Estate, Re*) 97 Man. R. (2d) 39, 1994 CarswellMan 89, [1994] M.J. No. 520, 5 C.C.P.B. 1, 79 W.A.C. 39, 27 C.C.L.I. (2d) 25, 5 E.T.R. (2d) 250 (C.A.).
313 *Wilson, Re, supra*, note 260.
314 *Standing v. Bowring, supra*, note 187.

beneficial interest under that trust could later be released to B or assigned to a third party. Although the *Statute of Frauds* and its many descendants require that assignments of trusts be made in writing,[315] this does not apply to a disposition *inter vivos* of an interest arising under a resulting trust.[316] Therefore, if it is presumed or proven that A did not intend to make a gift to B when the apparent gift was made, it may be necessary to consider subsequent events to determine what, if anything, A did with her or his beneficial interest under the resulting trust that arose at the outset.

Subsequent events can also be relevant as circumstantial evidence of what A intended back when the apparent gift was made. For example, in *Neazor v. Hoyle*,[317] reproduced above, a brother transferred land to his sister ten years before he died. The court looked at the conduct of the parties during the years after the transfer to see whether they treated the land as belonging beneficially to the brother or the sister. That evidence was used to determine that the brother intended a gift when the transfer was made.

(i) *Rebutting the Presumption of Advancement*

At one time, the presumption of advancement was based on the assumption that a father was fulfilling his moral duty to advance his children in life. Therefore, it could be rebutted by evidence that a proper advancement had already been made.[318] The presumption has evolved to become an inference that parents and husbands intend to make gifts. Although it may still be linked to a parental or marital duty of support,[319] evidence of fulfilment or absence of that duty does not rebut the presumption. The presumption of advancement is rebutted by evidence proving that the apparent donor did not intend to give.

When there is an apparent gift from parent (A) to child (B) or from husband (A) to wife (B), any admissible evidence that proves that A did not intend to make a gift to B will suffice to rebut the presumption of advancement, thereby giving rise to a resulting trust. It is not necessary to show that A intended to create a trust for herself or himself or even that A intended to retain beneficial ownership. Indeed, the latter intention cannot exist in cases where A paid a vendor to transfer an asset to B, since A did not own the asset before B acquired title. It is not even necessary to show that A positively intended not to make a gift. It is enough to show that A never formed the intention of making a gift.

---

315 1677 (29 Cha. 2), c. 3, s. 9; *Statute of Frauds*, R.S.O. 1990, c. S.19, s. 11; see chapter 4, above.

316 *Vandervell's Trusts (No. 2), Re, supra,* note 6; see J.E. Penner, *The Law of Trusts,* 3rd ed. (London: Butterworths, 2002), at 151-154.

317 *Supra,* note 202. Also see *Clemens v. Clemens Estate, supra,* note 299; *Shephard v. Cartwright* (1954), [1955] A.C. 431, [1954] 3 All E.R. 649 (H.L.).

318 *Elliot v. Elliot* (1677), 2 Ch. Cas. 231, 22 E.R. 922; *Grey v. Grey* (1677), 2 Swans. 594 at 600, 36 E.R. 742.

319 See *McLear v. McLear Estate, supra,* note 265, reproduced above.

This last point is demonstrated by *Brown v. Brown*,[320] a majority decision of the New South Wales Court of Appeal. In 1958, a recently widowed mother lived in her own house with three of her four adult children. That house was sold and the proceeds were used to buy a larger house in the names of her two sons. The mother's contribution was almost half the purchase price, with the rest raised by a mortgage granted by the sons. When that house was sold in 1987, the mother claimed a proportionate share of the sale proceeds, but died in 1990 at age 89, while the litigation was proceeding. Evidence of what the parties intended in 1958 was scanty and unreliable.

All members of the Court of Appeal held that the presumption of advancement applied to the apparent gift from the mother to her sons in 1958. They divided on whether that presumption had been rebutted. The trial judge found that the mother "had no intention of making a loan or a gift, and that she had no agreement with her sons concerning ownership or title to the property."[321] The majority of the Court of Appeal held that this finding of fact was sufficient to rebut the presumption of advancement. Kirby P. dissented, believing that the presumption had not been rebutted, because the trial judge's "finding is not equivalent to one that the mother positively intended *not* to make a gift to her sons."[322]

We agree with the majority judgment. To rebut a presumption of advancement, a parent (or husband) need not show a positive intention not to give. It is sufficient to demonstrate an absence of intention to give. The difference between positive and negative is important. If parents had to prove that they formed the intention not to give, the presumption of advancement would not be rebutted by proof that they were unaware of the transaction or lacked the capacity to make a gift. However, any evidence establishing that parents did not form the intention to give, including evidence that they simply failed to address their minds to the issue, rebuts the inference that they did in fact intend to make a gift.

(ii) *Rebutting the Presumption of Resulting Trust*

It is no doubt true that the presumption of resulting use was a presumption that the feoffor (transferor) intended to create a use for himself. Despite suggestions to the contrary,[323] this is not the basis of the modern presumption of resulting trust, which is an inference that the apparent donor did not intend to benefit the recipient. In most cases, rebutting the presumption of advancement produces a resulting trust and rebutting the presumption of resulting trust produces a gift. However, there is a third possibility. Evidence that a transaction was a loan or sale will rebut both presumptions, because it shows that the recipient was supposed to receive beneficial ownership, but not as a gift. The beneficial interest has to be paid for.

---

320 *Supra*, note 227.
321 *Ibid.*, at 587, *per* Gleeson C.J., summarizing the findings of Bryson J.
322 *Ibid.*, at 601, emphasis in the original.
323 *Hollett v. Hollett, supra*, note 162, at 265.

The true nature of the presumption of resulting trust was demonstrated long ago in *Goodfellow v. Robertson*.[324] A resulting trust arose when a father-in-law bought land for himself using the proceeds of sale of land belonging to his son-in-law, who was suffering from an "unsoundness of mind" at the time. The case would have been decided differently if a resulting trust depended on an intention to create a trust for oneself. The son probably lacked the capacity to create a trust. However, his mental incapacity did not rebut, but confirmed the presumption of resulting trust, because it showed that the son did not intend to benefit the father.

(iii) *The Effect of Rebuttal*

It is sometimes suggested that the rebuttal of one presumption gives rise to the other presumption. For example, in *Brown v. Brown*, discussed above, Gleeson C.J. decided that the presumption of advancement was rebutted by the facts and then concluded by saying, "Since there was no operative presumption of advancement, the basic presumption of resulting trust applied."[325] In *St. Jean v. Cocks*,[326] the court approached the case as if both presumptions applied, one based on the voluntary transfer and the other based on the relationship between the parties. It decided, first, that the presumption of advancement from mother to daughter was rebutted by evidence that the mother did not intend to make a gift and, secondly, that the daughter could rebut the presumption of resulting trust. This may be prudent where a trial judge is unsure of which presumption to apply, but that was not the problem in this case. The court treated the presumption of advancement, not as an alternative to the presumption of resulting trust, but as an additional presumption.

There is no room for either presumption if there is admissible evidence of what the apparent donor intended. The presumptions are merely inferences of fact and serve no useful purpose when that fact is known.[327] As Lamm J. said in *Mackowik v. Kansas City*, "Presumptions may be looked on as the bats of the law, flitting in the twilight but disappearing in the sunshine of actual facts."[328] The presumptions of resulting trust and advancement are different inferences about the same thing: the intention of the apparent donor. If one presumption is rebutted by evidence, the other presumption cannot arise since the intention of the apparent donor is known. Also, one transaction cannot be subject to both presumptions, because it is not possible to infer that the apparent donor intended to give and, at the same time, did not intend to benefit the recipient.

It is possible to rebut each presumption only partially, if it is proven that the apparent donor intended to give some, but not all, of the apparent gift. For example, in *Napier v. Public Trustee (Western Australia)*,[329] a man bought a house in the name of his *de facto* spouse and then she died. Since he intended that she

---

324 (1871), 18 Gr. 572, 1871 CarswellOnt 79 (Ch.).
325 *Brown, supra,* note 227, at 591.
326 *St. Jean v. Cocks, supra,* note 266.
327 *Pettit v. Pettit, supra,* note 154, at 823.
328 94 S.W. 256 at 262 (1906).
329 (1980), 32 A.L.R. 153 (Australia H.C.).

should have only a life interest in the house, there was a resulting trust of the remainder. In *Riley v. Riley*,[330] it was shown that a husband intended to benefit his wife only to the extent she would have been entitled under matrimonial property legislation. Therefore, she held half of the matrimonial home, which he had transferred to her, on resulting trust for him.[331]

In both cases, the apparent donor was able to rebut the presumption of resulting trust partially by showing that he intended to give only a portion of the beneficial ownership transferred to, or purchased for, the recipient. The outcome did not depend on the choice of presumption. If the presumption of advancement had applied, it too would have been partially rebutted by the same evidence, thereby producing the same resulting trust.

(iv) *Standard of Proof*

The presumptions have become relatively weak inferences of fact that can be rebutted easily by any admissible evidence that shows that the inference probably is not true. The presumption is not a hurdle to overcome, but an assumption made in the absence of evidence. In *Brown v. Brown*, discussed above, the presumption of advancement from a mother to her sons was rebutted by evidence showing that "neither Mrs. Brown nor her sons thought through the consequences of their transaction" and "that Mrs. Brown did not have any intention concerning the potential ownership".[332] Proof of the fact that she did not think about whether her contribution was a gift was sufficient to rebut the presumption that she had intended to give.

In *Lohia v. Lohia*,[333] also discussed above, a father and his son bought property in London for £1,650 in 1955, which was worth more than £500,000 in 2001. Both contributed to the purchase price and title was taken in their joint names. In 1965, the property was registered in the sole name of the father. He did not pay money for the transfer, but nothing else was known about the transaction because no copies could be found of any documents concerning it. The father died intestate in 1971 and title was then transferred to the son and his younger brother as joint tenants. A dispute between the two brothers led to this action, with the son claiming three-quarters of the property and his brother claiming half.

The trial judge rejected the son's evidence that the transfer to his father in 1965 was a forgery and also rejected his claim that the father held half the property on resulting trust for him. The latter conclusion rested on two grounds: first, that the presumption of resulting trust does not apply to a voluntary transfer of land in England (as discussed above) and, secondly, that the likely explanation for the transfer was a family arrangement under which the father was supposed to receive beneficial ownership.

---

330 (1987), 27 E.T.R. 224, 1987 CarswellMan 120, 9 R.F.L. (3d) 204, 49 Man. R. (2d) 153 (Q.B.).
331 See also *Winter v. Winter* (1974), 3 O.R. (2d) 425, 1974 CarswellOnt 139, 45 D.L.R. (3d) 641, 16 R.F.L. 275 (C.A.).
332 *Brown, supra,* note 227, at 586, 587, *per* Gleeson C.J.
333 *Supra,* note 195.

The Court of Appeal dismissed the son's appeal on the basis of the trial judge's finding of facts. Mummery L.J. said:[334]

> The judge rightly recognised that this issue was not easy to resolve in the virtual absence of any documentary evidence. The events in question had also occurred many years previously. The judge had, however, seen and heard the appellant give his evidence and seen it tested in cross-examination. The judge expressed doubt as to the appellant's credibility on the forgery issue. In the end, whilst confessing that he felt no certainty on the point, the judge concluded that on the balance of probabilities there was some kind of family arrangement which led to the transfer being made. He said of the appellant's evidence: "I must therefore ... conclude, again on the balance of probabilities, that he was unwilling to explain the nature of the arrangements which led to the transfer."
>
> In my judgment the judge was entitled to reach this conclusion, having had the advantage of seeing and hearing the appellant give his evidence. On the basis of the very limited amount of solid information, the judge had to decide on the civil standard of proof what was the more probable explanation of how and why the father came to be registered as sole proprietor. It cannot be said, in the light of his assessment of the appellant's evidence, that the judge's inference from the available material as to the probable explanation for the transfer to the father was unsupported by any evidence or was against the weight of the evidence or was an inference which no reasonable court could have made in all the circumstances.
>
> The judge's finding as to a family arrangement under which the property was transferred to the father is also sufficient to rebut any presumption of resulting trust to the appellant which might arise from the voluntary nature of the transfer.... [I]t is therefore unnecessary to express a final conclusion on his interesting legal argument that the presumption of a resulting trust arising on a voluntary conveyance had not been abolished by Section 60(3) of the 1925 Act.

The presumption of resulting trust had been rebutted by the fact that the son's transfer to the father was pursuant to an unexplained family arrangement, which was inferred primarily from the fact that the transfer had taken place. This is almost, but not quite, the same as saying that there is no presumption of resulting trust when land is gratuitously transferred from a son to his father. However, it was significant that the father and son had previously acquired the property in equal shares that corresponded to their contributions to the purchase price and then intentionally changed legal title. Also significant was the fact that the trial judge disbelieved the evidence of the son, who was the only surviving party to that transaction. Taken together, it seems more likely than not that the transfer to the father was intended to change the beneficial ownership of the property.

In many cases of resulting trust, the standard of proof is affected by the fact that the apparent donor is dead and unable to give evidence. In *Burns Estate v. Mellon*,[335] Mr. Burns met and became friends with Ms. Mellon in 1983, when he was 78 years old and she was working at his bank. Over the next two years, they had "a lot of phone calls and three lunches" and, in 1985, he gave her a bank draft for $195,000. Burns died in 1987 and his estate sued Mellon, claiming she held the money on resulting trust. The trial judge accepted her evidence that the transfer was a gift. The estate appealed on the basis that the judge applied the wrong

---

334 [2001] E.W.C.A. Civ. 1691 at para. 19-21.
335 (2000), 48 O.R. (3d) 641, 188 D.L.R. (4th) 665, 2000 CarswellOnt 1990, 133 O.A.C. 83, 34 E.T.R. (2d) 175 (C.A.).

standard of proof and that Mellon's evidence was not corroborated as required by section 13 of the *Evidence Act*, which states:[336]

> In an action by or against the heirs, next of kin, executors, administrators or assigns of a deceased person, an opposite or interested party shall not obtain a verdict, judgment or decision on his or her own evidence in respect of any matter occurring before the death of the deceased person, unless such evidence is corroborated by some other material evidence.

The Ontario Court of Appeal dismissed the estate's appeal, pointing to two pieces of corroborating evidence. First, Burns's holograph will, made ten months after the transfer to Mellon, was "quite detailed, and no evidence was led to suggest that Burns omitted any of his assets."[337] It also forgave two loans of $100,000 he had made to his daughters. Secondly, shortly before Burns died, his daughters asked him about the transfer and he refused to explain it. These facts created an inference that he had intended to make a gift. Concerning the appropriate standard of proof, Laskin J.A. said:[338]

> In my view, however, a gift may be established under s. 13 and a presumption of resulting trust may be rebutted by proof on a balance of probabilities, recognizing that proof within the civil standard may vary depending on gravity of the issues. When a claim of gift is asserted against a deceased's estate, a trial judge is justified in carefully scrutinizing the cogency of the supporting evidence. A "healthy scepticism" may be appropriate. But it is the civil standard not the criminal standard that should be applied.

Given the weakness of the presumptions, most cases of resulting trust are decided on the basis of evidence of the apparent donor's intention and not in reliance on a presumption. However, the choice of presumption will determine the issue in the absence of evidence. This is most likely to occur in two situations: first, when the apparent donor and donee are both dead[339] and, secondly, when the evidence of intention is inadmissible because the transaction was for an illegal purpose.

(v) *Illegal Purposes*

It happens rather frequently that one person (A) makes an apparent gift to another (B) to put assets beyond the reach of A's creditors or for some other fraudulent purpose. A may have actual creditors and be unable to pay them, in which case the transfer is a fraudulent conveyance and the creditors will be able to reach the assets in B's hands,[340] or A may be concerned about possible future creditors, for example, because A is starting a risky business venture.

The effect of an apparent gift made for an illegal purpose may depend on whether the presumption of advancement or the presumption of resulting trust

---

336 R.S.O. 1990, c. E.23.
337 *Supra,* note 335, at D.L.R. 676, *per* Laskin J.A.
338 *Ibid.*, at 670.
339 See, *e.g., Mehta Estate v. Mehta Estate, supra,* note 287.
340 Under the *Fraudulent Conveyances Act*, R.S.O. 1990, c. F.29.

applies to the transaction. If A has to overcome the presumption of advancement, A must prove that no gift was intended. This is permitted if it can be done without reference to A's fraudulent intention,[341] but A may fail if the fraudulent intention is the only evidence available to rebut the presumption. Of course, if it is shown that A retained the beneficial interest throughout, A's creditors would be able to reach it. The Canadian law on this subject is in an unsatisfactory state.

The majority of cases on this issue have arisen because a husband made an apparent gift to his wife to protect it from his creditors, but secretly intended to retain beneficial ownership and recover the assets when the danger passed. If the marriage then ran into difficulties, the wife could claim the assets for herself by relying on the presumption of advancement, which the husband would be unable to rebut. This situation has been changed by matrimonial property legislation in most jurisdictions, discussed above. If the marriage has broken down, the husband can commence an action for the equalization or division of family assets and invoke the statutory presumption of resulting trust. In any event, the husband's statutory right to share the family assets or their value should provide a solution regardless of the presumptions.

If evidence of an intention to defeat creditors or some other illegal purpose appears in subsequent proceedings, how should a court deal with it? The answer to this question may depend on the outcome of the transaction. If the illegal purpose has been carried out, it is reasonable to suppose that courts would not interfere and leave the title where it falls, because a court would not want to stoop to involving itself in the enforcement of illegal schemes and because its non-interference would serve as a warning to others. If the illegal purpose has not been carried out, either because no creditors were prejudiced or because the apparent donor repented, the court could restore the assets to the apparent donor. Alternatively, it can be argued that the court should not intervene, regardless of the actual effect on creditors, because of the original illegal intent. The reported cases have taken all of these positions, but do not often deal with the problem of collusion between donor and donee. In that case, the courts may apply the principle *in pari delicto potior conditio possidentis.*[342]

At one time, the law would not permit recovery at all if the transaction was part of a fraudulent scheme, whether or not it was carried out, on the principle *ex turpi causa non oritur actio.*[343] Later cases have allowed recovery if the illegal purpose was not carried out and the action would enable the creditors to recover.[344] In effect, the apparent donor has repented of the wrongdoing and is accorded a

---

341 *Scheuerman v. Scheuerman* (1916), 52 S.C.R. 625, 28 D.L.R. 223, 1916 CarswellAlta 228, 10 W.W.R. 379, at 629 [S.C.R.], *per* Idington J.; *Krys v. Krys* (1928), [1929] S.C.R. 153, [1929] 1 D.L.R. 289, 1928 CarswellAlta 117.

342 If the parties are equally blameworthy, the party in possession is in the stronger position. See, *e.g, Muckleston v. Brown* (1801), 6 Ves. Jun. 52 at 58, 31 E.R. 934 (Ch. Div.).

343 No disgraceful matter can ground an action. See, *e.g.*, *Groves v. Groves* (1828), 2 Y. & J. 163, 148 E.R. 1136.

344 *Symes v. Hughes* (1870), L.R. 9 Eq. 475 (C.A.); *Taylor v. Bowers* (1876), 1 Q.B.D. 291, 34 L.T. 938, 24 W.R. 499 (Q.B.); *Petherpermal Chetty v. Muniandi Servai* (1908), 24 T.L.R. 462 (P.C.); *Tribe v. Tribe*, [1995] 3 W.L.R. 913 (C.A.).

locus poenitentiae.[345] However, this will happen only while the illegal purpose remains capable of fulfilment. If, for example, a husband makes an apparent gift to his wife to avoid certain creditors, they forbear to sue or the limitation periods have expired, and the husband then tries to recover the assets, his repentance comes too late. He is obviously trying to recover the assets because the purpose of the transaction has been frustrated.[346]

The basis upon which the court intervenes or refuses to intervene is the equitable principle that one who comes to equity must come with clean hands. Presumably, one who repents in time has taken the opportunity to "wash" her or his hands and that is acceptable.[347] This principle is similar to the legal principle *nemo allegans turpitudinem suam est audiendus*,[348] which is also applied in these cases, because an apparent donor can recover provided he or she does not have to rely upon evidence of illegality. Evidence of the illegal intent, if it is not central to the claim or if it is presented by the other party, will not defeat a claim in those circumstances, even though it might have done so under the clean hands doctrine.[349]

It remains now to summarize the principal Canadian cases in this area, which begin with *Scheuerman v. Scheuerman*.[350] The husband purchased the matrimonial home and had title taken in his wife's name. At the time, a creditor was pressing him to pay a debt. The creditor was later paid and, at the time of the purchase, the property was exempt from execution by statute, being less than $1,500 in value. Subsequently, differences arose between the spouses and the wife sold the house for $3,500. The case does not lay down any clear rule. Fitzpatrick C.J., Idington J., and Brodeur J. held that the husband's intention to defraud his creditor was sufficient to prevent his recovery. Duff J. appears to agree with that view, but decided the case on the ground that the onus was on the husband to prove that the fraudulent purpose had not been carried out, that is, that the creditor had not been delayed, and he did not meet the onus. Anglin J. dissented, holding that only the value of the property at the time of the transfer was relevant and, since it was then exempt, the creditor was not delayed, so the purchase was not fraudulent.

The next significant case is *Krys v. Krys*.[351] A father conveyed his homestead to his son to make sure that his (the father's) wife could not reach it, there being differences between them. No intention to defraud was pleaded or proved, but the illegal intent arose from the evidence. In those circumstances, the court distinguished *Scheuerman* and allowed the father to recover the land, since there

---

345 An opportunity to undo what has been done.

346 *Cf. Re Great Berlin Steamboat Company* (1884), 25 Ch. D. 616 (C.A.), a case of an illegal contract.

347 Some Canadian courts have taken a pharisaic attitude that one's hands must never have been defiled in the first place, leaving one forever in the situation in which Lady Macbeth found herself: Macbeth, V.i.45; *cf.* Mark 7.3,4; Luke 11.38.

348 No one alleging his or her own baseness is to be heard.

349 See, *e.g.*, *Haigh v. Kaye* (1872), 7 Ch. App. 469 (Eng. Ch. Div.).

350 *Supra,* note 341.

351 *Supra,* note 341.

was no proof that he had creditors or that any creditor had been defeated, hindered, or delayed.

Goodfriend v. Goodfriend[352] is a more recent Supreme Court decision. The husband owned a farm. He and his wife entered into a spouse-swapping arrangement with their neighbours, Mr. and Mrs. Cox. Apparently, the relationship deteriorated later and Mr. Cox threatened Mr. Goodfriend with an action for damages for alienation of affections. Mr. Goodfriend did not take the threat seriously, but Mrs. Goodfriend did. She consulted a solicitor and, on his advice, persuaded her husband to transfer the farm to her for nominal consideration in order to prevent Cox from reaching them. Later, the marriage broke up and Mrs. Goodfriend brought an action for a declaration that she owned the farm. The court held that she could not succeed. The minority judgment, written by Spence J., held that a transferor is not precluded from relying on evidence of his illegal intention if the scheme was never carried out. A fraudulent intent is not sufficient to bar the evidence and there was no evidence that any creditor was delayed. The only possible creditor was Cox, whose threatened action could no longer be maintained in law at that time,[353] and the feared execution could readily have been satisfied out of the husband's other assets. Spence J., therefore, distinguished *Scheuerman* and relied upon *Krys*.

The majority judgment in *Goodfriend*, written by Laskin J., held simply that this was a case in which the wife persuaded her husband to make the voluntary transfer, because she, rather than he, feared he might be sued, when in fact there was no danger of judgment against him. In those circumstances, the husband could recover the property. However, his Lordship reserved his opinion on what should happen when a husband makes an apparent gift to his wife to defeat anticipated creditors but later, when risk is over, seeks to recover the assets.

English courts have taken a hard line on this issue. For example, in *Tinker v. Tinker*,[354] a husband transferred property to his wife to protect it from possible future creditors that might materialize if his new garage business should fail. The marriage then deteriorated and he sought to recover the property, but was denied recovery even though there were no creditors. Denning M.R. said:[355]

> I am quite clear that the husband cannot have it both ways. So he is on the horns of a dilemma. He cannot say that the house is his own and, at one and the same time, say that it is his wife's. As against his wife, he wants to say that it belongs to *him*. As against his creditors, that it belongs to *her*. That simply will not do. Either it was conveyed to her for her own use absolutely: or it was conveyed to her as trustee for her husband. It must be one or the other. The presumption is that it was conveyed to her for her own use: and he does not rebut that presumption by saying that he only did it to defeat his creditors. I think it belongs to her.

---

352 *Supra*, note 205.

353 See *Kungl v. Schiefer*, [1962] S.C.R. 443, 33 D.L.R. (2d) 278, 1962 CarswellOnt 59, 3 R.F.L. Rep. 130.

354 (1969), [1970] P. 136, [1970] 1 All E.R. 540, 21 P. & C.R. 102 (C.A.).

355 *Ibid.*, at 141; but see *Szymczak v. Szymczak*, [1970] 3 O.R. 202, 12 D.L.R. (3d) 582, 1970 CarswellOnt 166, 3 R.F.L. 253 (S.C.), where on similar facts the husband was successful. See also *Foster v. Foster* (1978), 98 D.L.R. (3d) 390, 1978 CarswellBC 618 (S.C.); *Warenko v. Young*, [1975] 6 W.W.R. 732, 61 D.L.R. (3d) 168, 1975 CarswellMan 60 (Q.B.).

The issue has come before the Supreme Court of Canada since then,[356] but the basic questions have not been fully resolved. They are discussed in *Maysels v. Maysels*, below.

MAYSELS v. MAYSELS

(1974), 3 O.R. (2d) 321, 14 R.F.L. 286, 45 D.L.R. (3d) 337,
1974 CarswellOnt 104 (C.A.)
Supreme Court of Ontario
(Court of Appeal)

A husband and wife purchased the matrimonial home, each contributing an equal share of the purchase money. However, title was taken in the wife's name to protect it from possible future creditors. The wife executed a declaration of trust in favour of her husband, but the trial judge held it to be void, since it was made under duress. The trial judge also held that a power of attorney given by the wife to the husband did not empower him to convey the property to himself, as he tried to do. He declared that the parties owned the property equally as tenants in common. The wife appealed. In the following judgment the husband is referred to as the "grantor" and the wife as the "grantee."

KELLY J.A. delivered the judgment of the Court:

. . .

As a general rule, a Court will not lend its assistance to enforce or set aside an illegal arrangement, or at the instance of a party who intends to use it for an illegal purpose, an agreement otherwise legal. But an exception to this general rule is made where an illegal agreement which has not been carried out, has been wholly repudiated by the party seeking the Court's aid: in such a case the Court will accord to the party repudiating a *locus poenitentiae* in order to restore the parties *ad integro*. *Symes v. Hughes*[357] and *Taylor v. Bowers*[358] to which further reference will be made, are examples of this exception. However, I can find no authority for according a *locus poenitentiae* in favour of a husband whose transfer to his wife or child is presumed to be a gift.

. . .

It has long been established that, save where the grantee is the wife or child of the grantor, where a spontaneous conveyance is, as between grantor and grantee, voluntary, upon the title to the property becoming vested in the grantee

---

356 *Bingeman v. McLaughlin*, [1978] 1 S.C.R. 548, 77 D.L.R. (3d) 25; *Ibottson v. Kushner*, [1978] 2 S.C.R. 858, 84 D.L.R. (3d) 417.

357 *Supra*, note 344.

358 *Ibid*.

there arises a presumption of a resulting trust thereof of which the grantor is the beneficiary.[359]

In contrast to the foregoing, where the grantee is the wife or child of the grantor no such resulting trust in favour of the grantee arises but there does arise a presumption of advancement and that the wife or child as a donee has the beneficial interest in the property.[360]

Both the foregoing presumptions are displaceable but, in either case, the onus of displacing the presumption is upon the party who seeks to do so. The presumption as to the gift to the wife or child is more readily displaced than that of a resulting trust.

In this case, therefore, where there is a presumption of gift to the wife, the burden of adducing evidence to displace it is the obligation of the husband and until he has done so the presumption prevails.

In the light of the findings of the learned trial Judge that the wife was not a trustee for the husband and that no rights arose in favour of the husband by reason of his purported use of the power of attorney from the wife, the only way left to the husband to meet the onus on him was by adducing evidence to prove that his purpose was not to convey a benefit on his wife but to protect the property from being taken to satisfy his creditors; the learned trial Judge has found such to have been the intention. It remains to be considered whether the husband can and has thereby rebutted the presumption of gift.

The presumption as to gift being rebuttable, the husband is not precluded from adducing evidence from which the Court may find support for his contention that it was not his intention to make a gift to the wife. For example, the presumption may be successfully met by proof that at the time of the transfer the grantee knowingly became the trustee of the property for the husband and that therefore, the beneficial interest in it remained in him.[361] These cases are examples of the reliance of this Court upon an agreement between the parties or circumstances attending the transferee's conduct which could lead the Court to declare the beneficial interest to be that of the husband. In fact, when examined closely, they are seen to fall into the category of cases where the transfer is not spontaneous but has been made pursuant to an arrangement which was completely inconsistent with an intention to make a gift.

It is to be noted that in both the above-mentioned cases by reason of the grounds upon which the Court was asked to rebut the presumption of advancement, it was not necessary for the claimant to rely on any illegal act. However, in the instant case, of the grounds upon which he sought to recover the property, the only one remaining open to him requires that he advance and put reliance on his own illegal purpose in order to persuade the Court that the normal result of the bare fact of the transfer should not follow.

---

359 *Dyer v. Dyer, supra,* note 5.
360 *Christ's Hospital v. Budgin* (1712), 2 Vern. 683, 23 E.R. 1043.
361 *Davies v. Otty (No. 2)* (1865), 35 Beav. 208, 55 E.R. 875; *Krys v. Krys, supra,* note 341.

On this account I consider the instant case to fall to be decided on the grounds propounded in *Gascoigne v. Gascoigne*.[362] Here a husband had taken a lease of property in his wife's name and built a house on it with his own money; his reason for putting the house in his wife's name was that he had run into debt and borrowed money from money lenders to get out. When the husband and wife became estranged the husband sought to recover the property. In deciding that the husband should be refused a declaration that he was the beneficial owner, Lush J. said:[363]

> Now, assuming that there was evidence to support the finding that the defendant was a party to the scheme which the plaintiff admitted, but without deciding it, what the learned judge has done is this: He has permitted the plaintiff to rebut the presumption which the law raises by setting up his own illegality and fraud, and to obtain relief in equity because he has succeeded in proving it. The plaintiff cannot do this; and, whether the point was taken or not in the county court this Court cannot allow a judgment to stand which has given relief under such circumstances as that.

. . .

Galligan, J., felt bound to support the husband's claim on the authority of *Goodfriend v. Goodfriend*:[364] it is my opinion that in this he was in error due to the dissimilarity in the facts in that case from the facts found by him....

. . .

As I read *Goodfriend v. Goodfriend* there is nothing in it to support the proposition that, in the absence of any agreement between the parties, the husband who has made a spontaneous voluntary grant to his wife may set up as a means of rebutting the presumption of gift thereby arising, his intention to defeat his creditors by making the transfer.

Having in mind the foregoing, I am prepared to allow this appeal upon the ground that the husband cannot rely on his own illegal act to rebut the presumption of gift and that, the presumption not having been displaced, the wife is entitled to retain what stands in her name free of any resulting trust in favour of the husband and is presumed to have been a gift to her....

. . .

There is another feature which must be considered with respect to the husband's contention, in support of his claim to a beneficial interest in the property, that his intention was to make the property immune from the claims of his creditors. Even assuming that what he intended to do was not illegal, to be effective to carry out his intention to make the property ineligible to satisfy judgments against him, it would be necessary that he divest himself completely of any

---

362 [1918] 1 K.B. 223.

363 *Ibid.*, at 226.

364 [1971] 1 O.R. 411, 15 D.L.R. (3d) 513 (C.A.), that is, before the Supreme Court of Canada decision, [1972] S.C.R. 640, 22 D.L.R. (3d) 699, was handed down.

beneficial interest in the property as well as any interest reserving to him a power by the exercise of which he could direct to himself the beneficial interest in the property. In using the means he did in causing the property to be recorded in his wife's name, the only way in which the husband could achieve the object of defeating his creditors would be to divest himself completely of all interest in the property — in other words, to make an absolute and irrevocable transfer to his wife.

If he retains any interest by means of which he could ask the Court to revest the property in him that interest itself would be exigible and effectively prevent the accomplishment of his purpose. To cause the property to be conveyed to the wife and at the same time to have retained any beneficial interest in it might have prevented his creditors discovering he had an interest but would not be a means of preserving the property from the resources of the Court seeking to enforce the payment of a judgment against the husband. On this account it may be said that in order to carry out his avowed intention of protecting the property from his creditors, he must have intended to extinguish his own interest in or claim to the property.

. . .

[The court allowed the wife's appeal.]

Notes and Questions

1. The Supreme Court of Canada dismissed the appeal in *Maysels* without reasons.[365]

2. Kelly J.A. opined in *Maysels* that the facts in *Goodfriend v. Goodfriend*[366] were "so bizarre as to defy repetition", yet they occurred again in *Bingeman v. McLaughlin*.[367] The husband had an affair with a married woman and received strong threats from her husband. Mr. Bingeman consulted his solicitor upon his wife's advice and executed conveyances to his wife of certain lands which were previously held in joint tenancy by the parties, although they had been acquired through the husband's efforts. After the conveyances were left with the solicitor for two years, the wife registered them and then the parties separated. The court held that the evidence clearly showed that the husband had throughout exhibited an intention to make a gift to his wife. Hence, the evidence tended to confirm the presumption of advancement rather than to rebut it. In the result, therefore, the husband's application for a declaration that he was entitled to a half interest in the property failed.

3. H, a Canadian, married W, an American. They became jointly entitled as beneficiaries under a trust of American securities. H had the shares registered in W's name because, since H was an alien, the American revenue authorities would have deducted withholding tax on any income payable to him. H and W were then divorced and W sold the securities. H wants to recover half of the proceeds, but is faced with the presumption of advancement. Can he succeed?[368]

---

365 (1975), 64 D.L.R. (3d) 765n, 1975 CarswellOnt 138, 19 R.F.L. 256, 17 N.R. 111 (S.C.C.).
366 *Supra*, note 205.
367 *Supra*, note 356.
368 See *Emery v. Emery*, [1959] Ch. 410, [1959] 1 All E.R. 577 (Ch. Div.).

4. H purchased two automobiles, but had title taken in the name of W. Ltd., a corporation owned by his wife, which operated a limousine business. The reason for doing so was to take advantage of lower (that is, fleet) insurance rates. H always drove the automobiles for personal purposes and paid the operating expenses, but the company paid the insurance premiums. The company mortgaged the automobiles under certain debentures. Subsequently it went into receivership. Does the presumption of advancement apply? Can H recover the automobiles?[369]

5. F bought a boat and, to avoid paying sales tax in his home province, had it registered in the name of his daughter, D, who resided in Alberta, which does not have a provincial sales tax. D gave F a chattel mortgage to secure the sum of $45,000. D never used the boat. F died and his will gave a number of specific bequests to several of his children other than D. The residue of F's estate was shared equally by D and her brothers and sisters. D claims possession of the boat from the estate. Is D entitled?[370]

6. H used his funds to purchase the matrimonial home. He directed that title be taken in W's name. He knew that the house would be subject to equal division on a breakdown of the marriage, but he owned adjoining property and did not want both properties in his name, as that would attract a higher assessment for municipal taxes. The marriage did break down in due course. The parties live in a jurisdiction which retains the presumption of advancement. H claims a half interest in the house. Is H entitled?[371]

7. If the apparent donor does not have to overcome the presumption of advancement, but can rely on the presumption of resulting trust, he or she should be able to recover the property despite an illegal intention.[372] This was allowed in *Tinsley v. Milligan*, below.

TINSLEY v. MILLIGAN

(1993), [1994] 1 A.C. 340, [1993] 3 W.L.R. 126, [1993] 3 All E.R. 65
House of Lords

Ms. Tinsley (T) and Ms. Milligan (M) were same-sex partners. They purchased a house together, but had title registered in T's name only, in order to help M defraud the Department of Social Services.[373] They also shared bank accounts held in T's name only. Soon after the purchase, they had a falling out and T moved out of the house, while M remained in occupation. T divided the money in the accounts between the parties in roughly equal shares. Then she brought this action claiming possession and asserting full beneficial ownership of the house. M counterclaimed for an order of sale and a declaration that T held the house

---

369 Cf. *Roynat Inc. v. United Rescue Services Ltd., supra,* note 137.

370 See *Tucker Estate v. Gillis* (1986), 22 E.T.R. 73, 1986 CarswellNB 45, 70 N.B.R. (2d) 78, 179 A.P.R. 78 (Q.B.), reversed (1988), 1988 CarswellNB 375, 53 D.L.R. (4th) 688, 90 N.B.R. (2d) 391, 228 A.P.R. 391 (C.A.).

371 See *Riley v. Riley, supra,* note 330.

372 *Chettiar v. Chettiar,* [1962] A.C. 294, [1962] 1 All E.R. 494 (Malaysia P.C.); *Gorog v. Kiss* (1977), 16 O.R. (2d) 569, 78 D.L.R. (3d) 690, 1977 CarswellOnt 1058 (C.A.); *Chupak v. Cirka, supra,* note 182; *Ibottson v. Kushner, supra,* note 356; *Marks v. Marks* (1974), 18 R.F.L. 323, 1974 CarswellOnt 193 (C.A.).

373 Interestingly, before she brought the action, Ms. Tinsley was convicted of defrauding the Department, too.

upon trust for both of them in equal shares. The trial judge dismissed T's claim and declared that T held the house on trust for M and herself in equal shares.

On appeal,[374] T argued that the court should not give effect to an equitable interest arising from a trust that is unlawful by reason of the claimant's unlawful purpose. Nicholls L.J. rejected this argument. He said that the court should adopt a more flexible approach to cases of illegality. Thus, a court must balance the adverse consequences of granting relief against the adverse consequences of refusing relief. He concluded that it would be an affront to public conscience not to grant relief in this case. Lloyd L.J. adopted a different approach, but reached the same result. He distinguished the "clean hands" authorities as cases in which the equitable balance came down against T, whereas in the present case it came down in favour of M, who was seeking the assistance of equity. He held that the illegality did not taint M's claim, but was purely collateral and incidental to it.

T's appeal to the House of Lords was dismissed. All members of the House agreed with Lord Browne-Wilkinson that, "the consequence of being a party to an illegal transaction cannot depend, as the majority of the Court of Appeal held, on such an imponderable factor as the extent to which the public conscience would be affronted by recognising rights created by illegal transactions."[375] However, the House split over the question whether M's claim under a resulting trust could be defeated by evidence of her illegality.

LORD BROWNE-WILKINSON:

. . .

Neither at law nor in equity will the court enforce an illegal contract which has been partially, but not fully, performed. However, it does not follow that all acts done under a partially performed contract are of no effect. In particular it is now clearly established that at law (as opposed to in equity) property in goods or land can pass under, or pursuant to, such a contract. If so, the rights of the owner of the legal title thereby acquired will be enforced, provided that the plaintiff can establish such title without pleading or leading evidence of the illegality. It is said that the property lies where it falls, even though legal title to the property was acquired as a result of the property passing under the illegal contract itself....

[Lord Browne-Wilkinson reviewed several cases and continued:]

From these authorities the following propositions emerge.

(1) Property in chattels and land can pass under a contract which is illegal and therefore would have been unenforceable as a contract.

(2) A plaintiff can at law enforce property rights so acquired provided that he does not need to rely on the illegal contract for any purpose other than providing the basis of his claim to a property right.

---

374 *Tinsley v. Milligan*, [1992] Ch. 310, [1992] 2 All E.R. 391 (C.A.).
375 *Tinsley v. Milligan* (1993), [1994] 1 A.C. 340 at 369, [1993] 3 All E.R. 65 (H.L.).

(3) It is irrelevant that the illegality of the underlying agreement was either pleaded or emerged in evidence: if the plaintiff has acquired legal title under the illegal contract that is enough.

I have stressed the common law rules as to the impact of illegality on the acquisition and enforcement of property rights because it is the appellant's contention that different principles apply in equity. In particular it is said that equity will not aid the respondent to assert, establish or enforce an equitable, as opposed to a legal, proprietary interest since she was a party to the fraud on the Department of Social Security. The house was put in the name of the appellant alone (instead of joint names) to facilitate the fraud. Therefore, it is said, the respondent does not come to equity with clean hands: consequently, equity will not aid her.

. . .

In my judgment to draw such distinctions between property rights enforceable at law and those which require the intervention of equity would be surprising. More than 100 years has elapsed since the fusion of the administration of law and equity. The reality of the matter is that, in 1993, English law has one single law of property made up of legal and equitable interests. Although for historical reasons legal estates and equitable estates have differing incidents, the person owning either type of estate has a right of property, a right *in rem* not merely a right *in personam*. If the law is that a party is entitled to enforce a property right acquired under an illegal transaction, in my judgment the same rule ought to apply to any property right so acquired, whether such right is legal or equitable.

In the present case, the respondent claims under a resulting or implied trust. The courts below have found, and it is not now disputed, that apart from the question of illegality the respondent would have been entitled in equity to a half a share in the house.... The creation of such an equitable interest does not depend upon a contractual obligation but on a common intention acted upon by the parties to their detriment. It is a development of the old law of resulting trust under which, where two parties have provided the purchase money to buy a property which is conveyed into the name of one of them alone, the latter is presumed to hold the property on a resulting trust for both parties in shares proportionate to their contributions to the purchase price....

. . .

The presumption of a resulting trust is, in my view, crucial in considering the authorities. On that presumption (and on the contrary presumption of advancement) hinges the answer to the crucial question: does a plaintiff claiming under a resulting trust have to rely on the underlying illegality? Where the presumption of resulting trust applies, the plaintiff does not have to rely on the illegality. If he proves that the property is vested in the defendant alone but that the plaintiff provided part of the purchase money, or voluntarily transferred the property to the defendant, the plaintiff establishes his claim under a resulting trust unless either the contrary presumption of advancement displaces the presumption of resulting trust or the defendant leads evidence to rebut the presumption of resulting trust. Therefore, in cases where the presumption of advancement does not apply, a plaintiff can establish his equitable interest in the property without relying in any way on the underlying illegal transaction. In this case the respondent as defendant simply pleaded the common intention that the property should belong to both of them and that she contributed to the purchase price: she claimed that in consequence the property belonged to them equally. To the same effect was her evidence-in-chief. Therefore the respondent was not forced to rely on the illegality to prove her equitable interest. Only in the reply and the course of the respondent's cross-examination did such illegality emerge: it was the appellant who had to rely on that illegality.

Although the presumption of advancement does not directly arise for consideration in this case, it is important when considering the decided cases to understand its operation. On a transfer from a man to his wife, children or others to whom he stands *in loco parentis*, equity presumes an intention to make a gift. Therefore in such a case, unlike the case where the presumption of resulting trust applies, in order to establish any claim the plaintiff has himself to lead evidence sufficient to rebut the presumption of gift and in so doing will normally have to plead, and give evidence of, the underlying illegal purpose.

. . .

The position is well illustrated by two decisions in the Privy Council. In the first, *Sajan Singh v. Sardara Ali*[376] a plaintiff who had acquired legal title to a lorry under an illegal transaction was held entitled to succeed against the other party to the illegality in detinue and trespass.... Two years later in *Chettiar v. Chettiar*[377] the Board had to consider the case where a father, who had transferred land to his son for an illegal purpose, sought to recover it under a resulting trust. It was held that he could not, since he had to rely on his illegal purpose in order to rebut the presumption of advancement....

Further, the Board distinguished *Sajan Singh v. Sardara Ali*. It was pointed out that in *Sajan Singh v. Sardara Ali* the plaintiff founded his claim on a right of property in the lorry and his possession of it. The Board continued:[378]

> [The plaintiff] did not have to found his cause of action on an immoral or illegal act. He was held entitled to recover. In the present case the father has of necessity to put forward, and indeed, assert, his own fraudulent purpose, which he has fully achieved. He is met therefore by the principle stated long ago by Lord Mansfield:[379] "No court will lend its aid to a man who founds his cause of action upon an immoral or an illegal act".

In my judgment these two cases show that the Privy Council was applying exactly the same principle in both cases although in one case the plaintiff's claim

---

376 [1960] A.C. 167, [1960] 1 All E.R. 269.
377 *Supra*, note 372.
378 *Ibid.*, at 303.
379 *Holman v. Johnson* (1775), 1 Cowp. 341 at 343, [1775-1802] All E.R. Rep. 98.

rested on a legal title and in the other on an equitable title. The claim based on the equitable title did not fail simply because the plaintiff was a party to the illegal transaction; it only failed because the plaintiff was bound to disclose and rely upon his own illegal purpose in order to rebut the presumption of advancement. The Privy Council was plainly treating the principle applicable both at law and in equity as being that a man can recover property provided that he is not forced to rely on his own illegality.

I therefore reach the conclusion that, although there is no case overruling the wide principle stated by Lord Eldon L.C., as the law has developed the equitable principle has become elided into the common law rule. In my judgment the time has come to decide clearly that the rule is the same whether a plaintiff founds himself on a legal or equitable title: he is entitled to recover if he is not forced to plead or rely on the illegality, even if it emerges that the title on which he relied was acquired in the course of carrying through an illegal transaction.

As applied in the present case, that principle would operate as follows. The respondent established a resulting trust by showing that she had contributed to the purchase price of the house and that there was a common understanding between her and the appellant that they owned the house equally. She had no need to allege or prove why the house was conveyed into the name of the appellant alone, since that fact was irrelevant to her claim: it was enough to show that the house was in fact vested in the appellant alone. The illegality only emerged at all because the appellant sought to raise it. Having proved these facts, the respondent had raised a presumption of resulting trust. There was no evidence to rebut that presumption. Therefore the respondent should succeed. This is exactly the process of reasoning adopted by the Ontario Court of Appeal in *Gorog v. Kiss*,[380] which in my judgment was rightly decided.

Finally, I should mention a further point relied on by the appellant. It is said that, once the illegality of the transaction emerges, the court must refuse to enforce the transaction and all claims under it whether pleaded or not.[381] Therefore, it is said, it does not matter whether a plaintiff relies on or gives evidence of the illegality: the court will not enforce the plaintiff's rights. In my judgment, this submission is plainly ill-founded. There are many cases where a plaintiff has succeeded, notwithstanding that the illegality of the transaction under which she acquired the property has emerged.[382] In my judgment the court is only entitled and bound to dismiss a claim on the basis that it is founded on an illegality in those cases where the illegality is of a kind which would have provided a good defence if raised by the defendant. In a case where the plaintiff is not seeking to enforce an unlawful contract but founds his case on collateral rights acquired under the contract (such as a right of property) the court is neither bound nor entitled to reject the claim unless the illegality of necessity forms part of the plaintiff's case.

---

380   *Supra,* note 372.
381   *Scott v. Brown Doering McNab & Co.,* [1892] 2 Q.B. 724, [1891-4] All E.R. Rep. 654.
382   See, for example, *Bowmakers Ltd v. Barnet Instruments Ltd.,* [1945] K.B. 65, [1944] 2 All E.R. 579, and *Sajan Singh v. Sardara Ali, supra,* note 376.

[Lord Goff of Chieveley dissented. He would have applied the principle stated by Lord Eldon L.C. in *Muckleston v. Brown*:[383]

> ... the Plaintiff stating, he had been guilty of a fraud upon the law, to evade, to disappoint, the provision of the Legislature, to which he is bound to submit, and coming to equity to be relieved against his own act, and the defence being dishonest, between the two species of dishonesty the Court would not act; but would say "Let the estate lie, where it falls."

Lord Goff explained that this principle applied because equity will not assist a person to recover property when the person does not come to equity with clean hands. Hence, the principle is not restricted to situations in which the plaintiff must overcome the presumption of advancement. The clean hands doctrine is not applied if the illegal purpose has not been carried out, in which case the plaintiff is accorded a *locus poenitentiae*. His Lordship was sympathetic to the respondent, since the fraud was "relatively minor and all too prevalent," and the respondent had confessed her wrongdoing to the government and had made amends. Further, by allowing the appeal, the respondent would lose all her capital. However, he felt that despite these facts no exception should be made, since other cases might arise in which the fraud was major and was not discovered in consequence of a confession, but in the course of a police investigation of a serious crime.]

Notes and Questions

1. Do you agree with the majority in *Tinsley v. Milligan* or with the dissent? Was it relevant that the fraud committed by the respondent was relatively "minor"? What if the fraud or some other illegality had been major? Would the result have been the same?

2. When Lord Browne-Wilkinson referred to the "common intention" of the parties, he seemed to be mixing the presumption of resulting trust with the constructive trust of the family home. He said that Ms. Milligan could establish the facts giving rise to the presumption of resulting trust if she "simply pleaded the common intention that the property should belong to both of them and that she contributed to the purchase price" and, therefore, she "was not forced to rely on the illegality to prove her equitable interest."[384] Proof of that intention would also rebut the presumption of advancement. If evidence of that intention is admissible because it can be separated from evidence of the illegal motive for their common intention, why does it matter which presumption applies? The choice of presumption has been important in many cases because proof of a contribution to the purchase price can raise a presumption of resulting trust in the absence of any evidence of intention whatsoever.

3. In *Gorog v. Kiss*,[385] a husband and wife transferred their farm to his sister to defeat creditors of the husband and wife. In their action to recover the farm, they alleged the

---

383 *Supra,* note 342, at 68-69.
384 (1993), [1994] 1 A.C. 340 at 371-372, [1993] 3 All E.R. 65 (H.L.).
385 *Supra,* note 372. Also see *Reaney v. Reaney* (1990), 72 D.L.R. (4th) 532, 38 E.T.R. 252, 1990 CarswellOnt 279, 28 R.F.L. (3d) 52 (H.C.).

illegality of the transfer, but the court held that they did not have to do so. Proof that the sister did not provide consideration for the transfer was sufficient to raise the presumption of resulting trust. The sister then bore the onus of displacing that presumption with evidence that the husband and wife intended to make a gift to her and she could not rely on the illegal purpose to do so.

4. Which should weigh the heavier, the policy rules that a person should not benefit from her or his illegal acts and that the courts should not be seen as enforcing illegal bargains, or the policy against the unjust enrichment of the recipient? Is the choice of presumption relevant to these issues? Is it right to have so much turn on the presumption of advancement, considering that it has fallen out of favour in recent years?[386]

5. Does it make a difference if the wrongdoer is not claiming return of the property, but evidence of the wrongdoing comes to light in other proceedings? This occurred in *Kish Equipment Ltd. v. A.W. Logging Ltd.*[387] The plaintiff held a judgment against the defendant and sought to enforce it by execution against land registered in the defendant's name. The land had been transferred to the defendant by his son to avoid a claim by a third party against the land. The defendant was not a party to his son's illegal purpose. The court held that the plaintiff could not succeed, because the defendant held the property in trust for his son and the presumption had not been rebutted. Do you agree?

6. In *Nelson v. Nelson*,[388] the High Court of Australia rejected the distinction drawn by the majority in *Tinsley*, as untenable on policy grounds. However, the court also rejected the dissent's view in *Tinsley* that the court should let the estate lie where it falls, because that approach promotes one policy to the exclusion of others. The High Court concluded that the court may grant relief on the basis of public policy even if the illegal purpose has been carried out.

In *Nelson*, a mother provided the purchase money for a house, but directed that the title be registered in the names of her son and daughter. She did this to obtain a state subsidy to purchase another house, for which she was required to declare, as she did, that she did not own or have an interest in any other house. When the first house was sold, she claimed the proceeds, but her daughter objected. The court held that the presumption of advancement arose, but allowed the mother to recover because the policy of the statute under which the subsidy was conferred would not be defeated if the court enforced her claim.

The majority in *Nelson* granted relief on terms. They directed Mrs. Nelson to repay the benefit she obtained from the federal government. This is surprising, since it requires the plaintiff to do equity, not to the other party, but to someone not a party to the litigation. Two of the justices dissented on this point, holding that the court can only impose terms requiring the plaintiff to do equity to the other party.[389]

Is the approach in *Nelson* better than that in *Tinsley v. Milligan*? Why?

---

386 See *Tribe v. Tribe, supra,* note 344, at 923, *per* Nourse L.J.

387 (1986), 2 B.C.L.R. (2d) 141, 1986 CarswellBC 97 (S.C.).

388 *Supra,* note 227.

389 See N. Enonchong, "Illegality and the Presumption of Advancement", [1996] Restitution L. Rev. 78; B. Kremer, "An 'Unruly Horse' in a 'Shadowy World'?: The Law of Illegality after *Nelson v Nelson*" (1997), 19 Sydney L. Rev. 240; M. McInnes, "Advancement, Illegality and Restitution" (1997), 5 Australian Property L.J. 1.

5. OTHER RESULTING TRUST SITUATIONS

The two main situations in which resulting trusts arise are (a) when an express trust fails, leaving the trustee with a surplus, and (b) when someone receives an apparent gift. In both cases, the resulting trust arises for the same reason: one person has received an asset at the expense of another person, who did not intend to transfer beneficial ownership of that asset to the recipient. These are not the only situations in which resulting trusts have arisen. Courts have declared resulting trusts in other cases in which the same reason for equitable intervention was present. These other cases might be regarded as extensions of the two traditional categories of resulting trust.

(a) Extension of the Failed Express Trust

Twinsectra Ltd. v. Yardley,[390] reproduced in the previous chapter, shows that a *Quistclose* trust[391] can be a resulting trust. In that case, money was loaned on condition that it be used only for the purpose of buying property. According to Lord Millett, the condition restricted the borrower's use of the money to such an extent that the borrower held the money on resulting trust for the lender from the outset, with a power to use it for the specified purpose. Like other resulting trusts, it arose because the lender did not intend to transfer beneficial ownership to the borrower. However, this was not one of the two traditional situations in which resulting trusts arise. There was no failed express trust and no apparent gift.

The *Quistclose* trust is similar to a failed express trust of money in one important respect. In both cases, money was paid to another to be used only for specific purposes. If any of that money cannot be used for those purposes, it must be returned. The recipient cannot keep it for herself or himself or use it for any other purpose, because that would result in the unintended benefit of the recipient at the expense of the lender or settlor. The resulting trust arises because the basis or purpose of the transaction has failed in whole or in part, whether that failure involved an express trust or not.

In *Ames' Settlement, Re*,[392] the basis of the transaction failed, even though the express trust did not. A father settled £10,000 on trustees of a marriage settlement in trust for his son for life, with the remainder to the issue of the marriage and, in default of issue, to his son's next of kin. The son's marriage was annulled 18 years later and, when the son died, the court declared that the trustees of the marriage settlement held the surplus on resulting trust for the father's estate. The express trust had not failed, since it had completely disposed of the beneficial ownership of the marriage settlement. However, the purpose for creating that trust had failed. The annulment meant that the marriage was void *ab initio* and treated

---

390 *Supra,* note 9.
391 Named after *Barclays Bank Ltd. v. Quistclose Investments Ltd.* (1968), [1970] A.C. 567, [1968] 3 All E.R. 651, [1968] 3 W.L.R. 1097 (H.L.).
392 [1946] Ch. 217, [1946] 1 All E.R. 689.

as if it had never taken place. Vaisey J. thought it was "a simple case of money paid on a consideration which failed."[393]

Henry v. Henry[394] was a similar case. A father (A) designated his brother (B) as the beneficiary of his $50,000 life insurance policy, in trust for his son (C). This was done pursuant to A's separation agreement with his first wife, in partial fulfilment of his obligation to support C while C was a minor or student. A died in Australia shortly after C had dropped out of school at age 19. Neither B nor C was entitled to the proceeds of the policy. A created the trust solely to fulfil his obligations under the separation agreement and, when C attained the age of majority and left school, the basis for that trust was removed. Therefore, B held the proceeds on resulting trust for A's estate because, as Borins J.A. said, "It is settled law that where the object, or purpose, of an express or implied trust fails, there is a resulting trust of the trust property for the settlor, or his or her estate."[395]

It is clear that a resulting trust does not arise every time money is paid for a consideration that fails. The normal response is a debt to repay the sum as "money had and received".[396] It is not easy working out why a failure of consideration produces a debt in some cases and a resulting trust in others. The choice seems to depend on whether the recipient of the money obtained unfettered beneficial ownership of it before the consideration failed. If there was no restriction on the recipient's use of the money, then a subsequent failure of consideration creates a personal obligation to repay the value of the money received.[397] However, if the recipient's use of the money was restricted from the outset, then a failure of consideration produces a resulting trust. Usually, the restriction takes the form of an express trust, but it could be a *Quistclose* trust or any other situation in which the money "has been ring-fenced so as not to be at the disposition of the recipient."[398]

(b) Extension of the Apparent Gift

There are a number of cases slightly outside the traditional categories that are, in substance, cases of purchase money resulting trust. In these cases, a resulting trust arose because an asset was purchased for B using A's money and A did not intend to benefit B. However, there was no apparent gift, because A did not intend to contribute to the purchase price, being unaware that her or his money was being used for that purpose. This is an extension of the purchase money resulting trust from the apparent gift to cases where A's claim is even stronger. If a resulting trust can arise when A intends to buy an asset for B, but

---

393 *Ibid.*

394 (1999), 30 E.T.R. (2d) 89, 126 O.A.C. 372, 1999 CarswellOnt 3468 (C.A.).

395 *Ibid.*

396 See P. Birks, *Unjust Enrichment* (Oxford: Oxford University Press, 2003) at 249-251.

397 *Moseley v. Cressey's Co.* (1865), L.R. 1 Eq. 405; *Chillingworth v. Esche*, [1924] 1 Ch. 97 (Eng. Ch. Div.); *Guardian Ocean Cargoes Ltd. v. Banco do Brasil S.A.*, [1994] 2 Lloyd's L.R. 152 (C.A.); *Goldcorp Exchange Ltd., Re* (1994), [1995] 1 A.C. 74, [1994] 3 N.Z.L.R. 385 (P.C.).

398 Birks, *supra*, note 396, at 174; see *Nanwa Goldmines Ltd., Re*, [1955] 1 W.L.R. 1080 at 1083-1084; A. Burrows, *The Law of Restitution*, 2nd ed. (London: Butterworths, 2002) at 409-411.

does not intend to make a gift, then it should arise when A's money is taken without A's consent and used to buy an asset for B.

The first of these cases is *Ryall v. Ryall*,[399] in which assets from a deceased person's estate were used by the executor to buy land in his own name. The beneficiaries of that estate were entitled to claim the land from the executor's heir, because he held it on resulting trust. Lord Hardwicke L.C. said:[400]

> [T]he means of coming at this by way of resulting trust is excepted out of the statute of frauds; if the estate is purchased in the name of one, and the money paid by another, it is a trust notwithstanding there is no declaration in writing by the nominal purchaser.

This was followed in Ontario in *Goodfellow v. Robertson*,[401] discussed above. A resulting trust arose when money belonging to a mentally incompetent man was used to buy land for his father-in-law. Spragge C. said:[402]

> [I]t is a trust resulting by operation of law, and it does not seem to be necessary to prove that the money was advanced by its owner in order to its application in the purchase of the land. If such proof were necessary, an assenting mind on his part would necessarily have to be shewn; and in the case of the money of a lunatic, the rule could not apply. In nearly all the cases certainly the money was advanced by the nominal purchaser for the purpose of making the purchase; but there are some cases in which this was not the case; *Ryall v. Ryall* was one of these.

In *Merchants Express Co. v. Morton*,[403] the proceeds of a train robbery in the U.S.A. were used to purchase a hotel in Toronto and the victim obtained an injunction restraining the sale of the hotel, based on "the principle of resulting trust arising from the purchase of property by one with the moneys of another".[404] In *McNeil v. Sharpe*,[405] a partner improperly used partnership money to buy a house for his sister and, when the partnership became insolvent, the curator of their estate obtained the land under a resulting trust. In *Kolari, Re*,[406] a bank teller purchased assets using money she had stolen from her employer and then became bankrupt. Stortini D.C.J. allowed the employer's claim to those assets because a "resulting trust arises where property is obtained by fraud or theft".[407]

Today, a Canadian court is more likely to say that a fraud or theft produces a constructive trust. However, this creates the difficulty of finding a coherent basis for distinguishing the trusts in those cases from purchase money resulting trusts. They arise for essentially the same reason, which Millett J. (now Lord

---

399 (1739), 1 Atk. 59, 26 E.R. 39, Amb. 413, 27 E.R. 276.
400 *Ibid.,* at 59-60.
401 *Supra,* note 324.
402 *Ibid.,* at 575.
403 (1868), 15 Gr. 274, 1868 CarswellOnt 149 (Ch.).
404 *Ibid.,* at 278, *per* Spragge V.C.
405 (1913), 15 D.L.R. 73, 1913 CarswellNS 111, 47 N.S.R. 406 (S.C.), affirmed (1915), 70 D.L.R. 740, 1915 CarswellNS 84, 62 S.C.R. 504.
406 (1981), 36 O.R. (2d) 473, 1981 CarswellOnt 201, 39 C.B.R. (N.S.) 129 (Dist. Ct.).
407 *Ibid.,* at 478.

Millett) recognized when he described a trust of assets obtained by fraud as "an old-fashioned institutional resulting trust".[408]

As Spragge C. said in *Goodfellow v. Robertson*, above, it cannot matter whether the purchaser intended to contribute to the purchase price. If it did, a number of resulting trust cases in the traditional category would be called into question. For example, in *Hiebert v. Gregoire*,[409] a son had a joint account with his mother, which belonged beneficially to her. When she was 88 years old and after she had a stroke, he used money from that account to buy a term deposit in the joint names of his mother, his wife, and himself. His mother died a year later and he claimed the term deposit as a gift. Schulman J. held that the presumption of advancement was rebutted, because the mother was unaware of the transaction and it was "highly unlikely" that she had capacity to make a gift. Even though the mother did not intend to purchase the term deposit, the resulting trust was entirely appropriate because her incapacity and ignorance of the transaction proved clearly that she did not intend to make a gift.

(c) Unjust Enrichment

When the resulting trust is extended beyond its traditional categories, it encroaches into the domain that Canadians have associated with the constructive trust since *Becker v. Pettkus*.[410] Both trusts arise by operation of law in response to unjust enrichment and it is difficult to know where the resulting trust ends and the constructive trust begins. The most discernible difference is that constructive trusts respond to unjust enrichment in a wider variety of situations and to other events as well, such as wrongful enrichment, detrimental reliance, and specifically enforceable promises. Perhaps it does not matter whether a particular trust is labelled as resulting or constructive, but it is important to know when unjust enrichment gives rise to a trust, rather than a debt, a lien, rescission, or some other method of restitution, and when trusts are created by unjust enrichment, rather than by some other event.

Even within its traditional categories of failed express trusts and apparent gifts, the resulting trust responds to unjust enrichment. In every case, A has transferred an asset to, or purchased an asset for, B without intending to make a gift to B. This satisfies the test for unjust enrichment set out in *Becker v. Pettkus*,[411] since B is enriched, A has suffered a corresponding deprivation, and there is an absence of juristic reason for the enrichment. The resulting trust arises to effect restitution of that enrichment to A. This is understood in England, where Lord Millett, writing extra-judicially, said that, "the development of a coherent doctrine of proprietary restitution for subtractive unjust enrichment is impossible unless it is based on the resulting trust as traditionally understood."[412]

---

408   *El Ajou v. Dollar Land Holdings plc.* (1992), [1993] 3 All E.R. 717 (Ch. Div.), reversed on other grounds (1993), [1994] 2 All E.R. 685 (C.A.).

409   (1999), 28 E.T.R. (2d) 310, 1999 CarswellMan 362 (Q.B.).

410   *Supra*, note 26.

411   *Ibid.*, at 273-274.

412   "Restitution and Constructive Trusts" (1998), 114 L.Q.R. 399 at 410.

In Canada, we must learn to deal with the potential confusion caused by the overlap between resulting and constructive trusts. For example, in *Vancouver Trade Mart Inc. (Trustee of) v. Creative Prosperity Capital Corp.*,[413] the two corporations named in the style of cause, "Trade Mart" and "Creative", were both owned and operated by the same man. Trade Mart paid the purchase price for land bought by Creative. When Trade Mart became bankrupt, its trustee in bankruptcy sued Creative, claiming that the land was held on resulting trust or constructive trust for Trade Mart. The trial judge accepted that the purchase price paid by Trade Mart was partly a loan to Creative and partly the repayment of a previous loan from Creative. This fact both rebutted the presumption of resulting trust and was the juristic reason that negated the alleged constructive trust.

Trade Mart's trustee in bankruptcy pleaded both a resulting trust and a constructive trust, perhaps from an abundance of caution. However, the pleadings did not disclose two separate causes of action. There was one cause of action described in two different ways. There was no resulting trust, because there was no unjust enrichment. If Trade Mark had paid the purchase price without intending to benefit Creative, a resulting trust would have arisen because there would have been no juristic reason for that payment. There was really only one trust in issue, but that was obscured by our use of two different labels for that trust in some situations.

A resulting trust and a constructive trust can both arise in the same case, each responding to different facts. For example, suppose that A pays 10% of the purchase price for the family home, bought in the name of her *de facto* spouse, B, and then works inside and outside the home for many years for their mutual benefit, with the expectation of sharing beneficial ownership of the home. This should produce two trusts for A: a resulting trust of 10% of the home, based on A's contribution to the purchase price, and a constructive trust of a much greater share, based on A's contribution to the family and reasonable expectation. The constructive trust is explored in the next two chapters.

Normally, A's interest under the resulting trust would be subsumed into the greater interest under the constructive trust. However, there may be situations in which the resulting trust remains important. The resulting trust arose when the home was acquired and A's share was fixed at that time, whereas the constructive trust would emerge later and could vary over time, depending on the duration of the relationship and the relative values of each party's contribution to the family. Therefore, it is possible that A's interest under the resulting trust could have greater priority over competing claims to the home or could receive more favourable treatment if B should become bankrupt.[414]

---

413 (1998), 50 B.C.L.R. (3d) 155, 1998 CarswellBC 41, [1998] B.C.J. No. 28, 1 C.B.R. (4th) 307 (S.C.), additional reasons at (1998), 1998 CarswellBC 2528, 7 C.B.R. (4th) 3 (S.C.), affirmed (1998), 6 C.B.R. (4th) 230, 1998 CarswellBC 2655 (C.A.).

414 See *Densham, Re*, [1975] 1 W.L.R. 1519, [1975] 3 All E.R. 726 (Ch. Div.); *Bedard v. Schell*, [1987] 4 W.W.R. 699, 59 Sask. R. 71, 1987 CarswellSask 350, 26 E.T.R. 225, 8 R.F.L. (3d) 180 (Q.B.).

Problems

1. The London and District Social and Funerary Society, an unincorporated organization, is about to be wound up for lack of interest and a declining membership. It was formed years ago on the principle, "Eat, drink, and be merry, for tomorrow we die." This principle found expression in the purposes of the society which were: (a) the holding of social functions, balls, bazaars, dinners, bingo evenings, *etc.*, for the members and their families, and (b) to provide the members and their families with inexpensive but tasteful funeral services.

The Society's assets consist of investments and cash worth $84,000, which are vested in trustees whose duties under the rules of the Society are to accept receipts, invest them, and hold the moneys for the members of the Society for its purposes. They are to pay out such moneys as may be necessary to cover expenses of the Society and for funeral costs when a member or someone in his or her family dies. No moneys have yet been disbursed for funerals. The rules say nothing further about the assets.

The Society's assets are derived from contributions made by past and present members of the Society who contributed on the basis of $5 per month per family member, from donations received from time to time from members and others, and from profits made during bazaars and bingo evenings. Those functions were supposed to be restricted to members and their families, but guests could be invited by special arrangement and this happened on many occasions.

Of the original 40 members, about 12 remain. The rest either resigned or ceased to pay their contributions and take part in the Society's functions. It is known that several former members have died and their families opted for elaborate burials without calling on the Society. The remaining members consult you about winding up the Society and about who is entitled to what money and in what proportions. Please advise them.

2. Hector and Wilma have lived together as *de facto* spouses since 1996. In 1998, they bought a house, using money from a joint bank account to which both had contributed in unequal shares. Hector had managed to amass a valuable portfolio of investments, consisting of bonds and shares. The parties, therefore, agreed that, in order to equalize their assets, the house should be put in Wilma's name. By 2001, Hector's investments had greatly increased in value, so he transferred securities worth $50,000 into the joint names of himself and Caroline for life. Caroline is Wilma's daughter from a previous relationship and was 13 years old at the time. Since then, Hector has received the income on the investments transferred to Caroline and has spent it on annual holidays for Wilma, Caroline, and himself. Please advise Hector on the beneficial ownership of the house and the shares.

3. Wendy was a member of the bar and, after working for several years as an associate employed by a large law firm, she decided to start a practice of her own. A colleague who "knew about such matters" advised her that, since a lot of lawyers starting out on their own were having a tough time making ends meet, she should put some of her assets in someone else's name. So, Wendy transferred her joint share of the matrimonial home to her husband, Harold. She also transferred $50,000 worth of securities to Harold, in trust for their daughter, Caliope, who was then 15 years old. No consideration was given for the transfers. Wendy then went into practice for herself and it turned out to be a huge success. Harold died recently and his personal representatives claim that he is entitled absolutely to the house and the shares. Please discuss the rights of Wendy and Caliope.

4. John and Mary have lived together as *de facto* spouses for some time, sharing their living expenses, including the rent on their apartment, more or less equally. Their apartment building was being converted to a condominium and they decided to purchase the unit.

They agreed that the unit would be theirs equally and they both signed the purchase agreement and the mortgage. However, most of the down payment was borrowed from Mary's father. Shortly after the transaction closed, the parties separated and John left. Since then, Mary has been paying the mortgage, taxes, and condominium expenses and intends to repay her father. John has paid nothing, but claims a half interest in the condominium unit. Can he succeed?[415]

---

415 See *Ruff v. Strobel*, 86 D.L.R. (3d) 284, 1978 CarswellAlta 235, [1978] 3 W.W.R. 588, 9 A.R. 378 (C.A.).

Chapter 10

INTRODUCTION TO THE CONSTRUCTIVE TRUST

1. Scope
2. Historical Background
3. An Introduction to Unjust Enrichment and Restitution
4. Nature of the Constructive Trust
5. Procedure to Obtain a Constructive Trust Order

1. SCOPE

This chapter introduces the second type of trust arising by operation of law, the constructive trust. Traditionally, Anglo-Canadian law viewed the constructive trust as a substantive institution; that is, like the express trust, except that the intention of the parties played no role. However, there has been much judicial activity in this area in recent years. In particular, the constructive trust has been used extensively to resolve matrimonial and cohabitation property disputes. It was found that the traditional view of the constructive trust was inadequate in that context. For this reason the Canadian courts adopted the remedial constructive trust; that is, the constructive trust seen as a remedy to redress unjust enrichment.[1] This represented a substantial change in the Canadian law of trusts and restitution, the full impact of which is still being determined. As will appear from the materials in this chapter, however, the traditional constructive trust has not been superseded by the remedial constructive trust. In *Soulos v. Korkontzilas*[2] the Supreme Court of Canada held that the traditional constructive trust continues to exist side by side with the remedial constructive trust. And indeed, as we will see, the meaning of the dichotomy between substantive and remedial constructive trusts is a matter of some debate.

In this chapter we shall discuss the history of the constructive trust, its place in the panoply of remedies, and its nature. We shall also see how you can obtain a constructive trust order.

Further Reading

R.P. Austin, "Constructive Trusts" in P.D. Finn, ed., *Essays in Equity* (Sydney: The Law Book Company Limited, 1985), p. 196.

---

1 In *Pettkus v. Becker*, [1980] 2 S.C.R. 834, 19 R.F.L. (2d) 165, 117 D.L.R. (3d) 257, 34 N.R. 384, 8 E.T.R. 143.
2 [1997] 2 S.C.R. 217, 146 D.L.R. (4th) 214, 212 N.R. 1, 9 R.P.R. (3d) 1, 32 O.R. (3d) 716 (headnote only), 17 E.T.R. (2d) 89, 1997 CarswellOnt 1489, [1997] S.C.J. No. 52, 1997 CarswellOnt 1490, 246 C.B.R. (3d) 1, 100 O.A.C. 241

M.M. Litman, "The Emergence of Unjust Enrichment as a Cause of Action and the Remedy of Constructive Trust" (1988), 26 Alta. L. Rev. 407.

David M. Paciocco, "The Remedial Constructive Trust: A Principled Basis for Priorities over Creditors" (1989), 68 Can. Bar. Rev. 315.

David Hayton, "Constructive Trusts: Is the Remedying of Unjust Enrichment a Satisfactory Approach?" in T.G. Youdan, ed., *Equity, Fiduciaries and Trusts* (Toronto: The Carswell Co. Ltd., 1989), p. 205.

G. Elias, *Explaining Constructive Trusts* (Oxford: Oxford University Press, 1990).

D.W.M. Waters, "LAC Minerals Ltd. v. International Corona Resources Ltd." (1990), 69 Can. Bar. Rev. 458.

D.W.M. Waters, "The Constructive Trust in Evolution: Substantive *and* Remedial" (1991), 10 E. & T.J. 334.

A.J. Oakley, *Constructive Trusts*, 3rd ed. (London: Sweet & Maxwell Limited, 1997).

S. Hoegner, "How Many Rights (or Wrongs) Make a Remedy? Substantive, Remedial and Unified Constructive Trusts" (1997), 42 McGill L.J. 437.

D. Wright, *The Remedial Constructive Trust* (Sydney: Butterworths, 1998).

L. Smith, "Constructive Trusts and Constructive Trustees" (1999), 58 C.L.J. 294.

L. Rotman, "Deconstructing the Constructive Trust" (1999), 37 Alta. L. Rev. 133.

R. Chambers, "Constructive Trusts in Canada" (1999), 37 Alta. L. Rev. 173.

2. HISTORICAL BACKGROUND

The constructive trust derives from 17th and 18th century developments in the court of Chancery. The leading English case on constructive trusts for breach of fiduciary obligation is *Keech v. Sandford*,[3] although earlier instances exist.[4] The defendant trustee held a lease of the profits of the Romford Market in trust for the plaintiff, a minor, under an express testamentary trust. When the term of the lease expired, the trustee sought to renew it for the trust, but the lessor refused, because he would be unable to get the benefit of the covenant to pay from the plaintiff. The trustee then asked for, and obtained, a renewal in his personal capacity. The plaintiff brought proceedings to have the lease assigned to him and for an accounting of the profits made after the lease was renewed. He was successful, but had to indemnify the trustee for breach of any covenants contained in the lease. In the course of his brief judgment, Lord King L.C. stated:[5]

> I must consider this as a trust for the infant; for I very well see, if a trustee, on the refusal to renew, might have a lease to himself, few trust-estates would be renewed to *cestui que* use; though I do not say there is a fraud in this case, yet he should rather have let it run out, than to have had the

---

3 (1726), Sel. Cas. t. King 61, 25 E.R. 223 (Ch. Div.).

4 See, *e.g.*, *Holt v. Holt* (1670), 1 Ch. Cas. 190, 22 E.R. 756; *Cook v. Fountain* (1676), 3 Swans. 585, 36 E.R. 984; *Thynn v. Thynn* (1684), 1 Vern. 296, 23 E.R. 479, secret trust; *Devenish v. Baines* (1689), Prec. Ch. 3, 24 E.R. 2, secret trust; *Drakeford v. Wilks* (1747), 3 Atk. 539, 26 E.R. 539, secret trust. See also *Hutchins v. Lee* (1737), 1 Atk. 447, 26 E.R. 284, oral trust of land. For a contemporaneous analysis by a Lord Chancellor who was instrumental in the birth of the constructive trust, see ch. XIII of Lord Nottingham's *Prolegomena of Chancery and Equity* in D.E.C. Yale, ed., *Lord Nottingham's Two Treatises* (Cambridge: Cambridge University Press, 1965).

5 *Supra*, note 3, at 62.

lease to himself. This may seem hard, that the trustee is the only person of all mankind who might not have the lease: but it is very proper that rule should be strictly pursued, and not in the least relaxed; for it is very obvious what would be the consequence of letting trustees have the lease, on refusal to renew to *cestui que* use.

Chancery has always seen fit to find constructive trusts in the context of fiduciary relationships, as in *Keech v. Sandford*. Someone who acquired property in breach of trust, or otherwise by taking advantage of a fiduciary position, could not benefit from the property; he was deemed to hold the property in trust instead. The law construed it as a trust, hence, a "constructive trust." But this is not the only situation in which such trusts were found. For example, a vendor under a specifically enforceable agreement for the sale of land is regarded as holding it on a kind of constructive trust.[6] Further, the constructive trust has been used generally as a remedy to redress "equitable fraud," that is, any conduct of which equity disapproves. Hence, it is imposed to give effect to intentionally created oral trusts of land, which on their face are not enforceable because of the statutory requirement that they be evidenced by writing.[7] Another example is mutual wills; if two parties agree to make mutual wills, and they do so, then after one of them dies, the other cannot change his or her will; the trust is used to enforce the earlier agreement.[8] Similarly, there are also secret trusts, where property is left to someone in a will, subject to an oral agreement, outside the will, that he should hold it on trust.[9] There may be other miscellaneous situations in which the title holder relies upon the title in fraud of his or her undertaking made to another person.[10]

In every trust, the trustee holds property subject to obligations, owed to the beneficiary, to deal with the property for the benefit of the beneficiary. If those obligations arose by the agreement of the trustee, that is an express trust. In a constructive trust, the obligations are imposed by law. As we will see, the law may impose those obligations for a variety of reasons.

The categories of constructive trust, that is, the situations in which it was likely to arise, were largely fixed in Anglo-Canadian law by the 1970s. In that decade the courts began to search for ways in which to resolve property disputes

---

6   As we shall see in the next chapter, this is a rather infelicitous use of the concept.

7   See, *e.g.*, *Statute of Frauds*, R.S.O. 1990, c. S.19, s. 9. The statute does not apply to resulting and constructive trusts: *ibid.*, s. 10. If a title holder is met with a claim that he or she orally agreed to hold land for the benefit of the claimant, he or she can plead the statute in defence. However, courts of equity from an early date permitted evidence of the alleged trust to be adduced and if the trust was proved, would enforce it, because the statute cannot be used as an instrument of fraud: see, *e.g.*, *Hutchins v. Lee*, *supra*, note 4. The trust that is enforced in this situation is sometimes called a constructive trust: *Bannister v. Bannister*, [1948] 2 All E.R. 133 (C.A.), which provides a justification for enforcing it despite the statute. However, it is sometimes regarded as an express trust, since it is the very trust the parties intended: *Rochefoucauld v. Boustead*, [1897] 1 Ch. 196 (C.A.). On this view, the ability to avoid the requirements of the statute is perhaps explicable by detrimental reliance, which may be called 'equitable fraud.' See Section 6 in the next chapter.

8   See part 7(b) in the next chapter.

9   See part 7(a) in the next chapter.

10 *Banner Homes Group plc v. Luff Developments Ltd.*, [2000] Ch. 372, [2000] 2 All E.R. 117 (C.A.).

between spouses and other partners. Initially, the Canadian courts resolved such disputes on the basis of a "common intention resulting trust." But as we saw in the previous chapter, such a resulting trust is doctrinally impossible and is really a constructive trust. In any event, the Canadian courts discovered that it was often difficult to determine whether the parties had a common intention. Partly for that reason they gradually moved towards acceptance of the remedial constructive trust. This is a constructive trust that is imposed by the court to remedy unjust enrichment.

Laskin J., in dissent in *Murdoch v. Murdoch*,[11] was the first to adopt the American-style remedial constructive trust to resolve a matrimonial property dispute. In *Rathwell v. Rathwell*,[12] which also concerned a matrimonial property dispute, Dickson J., speaking for himself, Laskin C.J.C. and Spence J., adopted the suggestion of Laskin J. Of the remedial constructive trust he said:[13]

The constructive trust amounts to a third head of obligation, quite distinct from contract and tort, in which the court subjects —

... a person holding title to property ... to an equitable duty to convey it to another on the ground that he would be unjustly enriched if he were permitted to retain it.[14]

The constructive trust is an obligation of great elasticity and generality.

Where a common intention is clearly lacking and cannot be presumed, but a spouse does contribute to family life, the court has the difficult task of deciding whether there is any causal connection between the contribution and the disputed asset. It has to assess whether the contribution was such as enabled the spouse with title to acquire the asset in dispute. That will be a question of fact to be found in the circumstances of the particular case. If the answer is affirmative, then it will be possible to declare that the spouse with title holds that title on a constructive trust for the benefit of the non-titled spouse. The court will assess the contributions made by each spouse and make a fair, equitable distribution having regard to the respective contributions. The relief is part of the equitable jurisdiction of the court and does not depend on evidence of intention. As expressed by Professor Scott in an article entitled "Constructive Trusts":[15]

The court does not give relief because a constructive trust has been created; but the court gives relief because otherwise the defendant would be unjustly enriched; and because the court gives this relief it declares that the defendant is chargeable as a constructive trustee.

Or, as expressed by Lord Denning, M.R. in *Hussey v. Palmer*:[16]

... it is a trust imposed by law whenever justice and good conscience require it. It is a liberal process, founded upon large principles of equity to be applied in cases where the legal owner cannot conscientiously keep the property for himself alone, but ought to allow another to have

---

11 (1974), [1975] 1 S.C.R. 423, [1974] 1 W.W.R. 361, 13 R.F.L. 185, 41 D.L.R. (3d) 367.
12 [1978] 2 S.C.R. 436, [1978] 2 W.W.R. 101, 1 R.F.L. (2d) 1, 1 E.T.R. 307, 83 D.L.R. (3d) 289, 19 N.R. 91. The majority applied the "common intention resulting trust" instead of the remedial constructive trust. Dickson J. applied the "common intention resulting trust" in the alternative to the constructive trust.
13 *Ibid.*, at D.L.R. 305-307.
14 *Murdoch v. Murdoch, supra*, note 11, at D.L.R. 388, *per* Laskin J., citing Scott, at 3215.
15 (1955), 71 L.Q. Rev. 39 at 41.
16 [1972] 1 W.L.R. 1286 at 1289-1290, [1972] 3 All E.R. 744 (C.A.).

the property or the benefit of it or a share in it. The trust may arise at the outset when the property is acquired, or later on, as the circumstances may require. It is an equitable remedy by which the court can enable an aggrieved party to obtain restitution.

Lord Diplock, in a passage quoted with approval in this court in *Murdoch v. Murdoch*,[17] said that a trust is created:

> . . . whenever the trustee has so conducted himself that it would be inequitable to allow him to deny to the *cestui que trust* a beneficial interest in the land acquired.

The constructive trust, as so envisaged, comprehends the imposition of trust machinery by the court in order to achieve a result consonant with good conscience. As a matter of principle, the court will not allow any man unjustly to appropriate to himself the value earned by the labours of another. That principle is not defeated by the existence of a matrimonial relationship between the parties; but, for the principle to succeed, the facts must display an enrichment, a corresponding deprivation, and the absence of any juristic reason — such as a contract or disposition of law — for the enrichment. Thus, if the parties have agreed that the one holding legal title is to take beneficially an action in restitution cannot succeed.[18]

The emergence of the constructive trust in matrimonial property disputes reflects a diminishing preoccupation with the formalities of real property law and individual property rights and the substitution of an attitude more in keeping with the realities of contemporary family life. The manner in which title is registered may, or may not, be of significance in determining beneficial ownership.

Finally, in *Pettkus v. Becker*,[19] Dickson J., then speaking for a majority[20] applied the remedial constructive trust to a cohabitation property dispute. In the course of his judgment, his Lordship said:[21]

> The principle of unjust enrichment lies at the heart of the constructive trust. "Unjust enrichment" has played a role in Anglo-American legal writing for centuries. Lord Mansfield, in the case of *Moses v. Macferlan*,[22] put the matter in these words:

> > . . . the gist of this kind of action is, that the defendant, upon the circumstances of the case, is *obliged by the ties of natural justice and equity to refund* the money.

> It would be undesirable, and indeed impossible, to attempt to define all the circumstances in which an unjust enrichment might arise.[23] The great advantage of ancient principles of equity is their flexibility: the judiciary is thus able to shape these malleable principles so as to accom-

---

17 *Supra*, note 11, at D.L.R. 377.
18 *Peter Kiewit Sons Co. of Canada v. Eakins Construction Ltd.* [1960] S.C.R. 361, at 368-369, 22 D.L.R. (2d) 465. See also *Restatement of the Law, Restitution, Quasi-Contracts and Constructive Trusts* (St. Paul: American Law Institute Publishers, 1937), §160 ("*Restatement, Restitution*").
19 *Supra*, note 1.
20 *Ibid.*, Laskin C.J.C., Estey, McIntyre, Chouinard, and Lamer JJ. concurred.
21 *Ibid.*, at D.L.R. 273-274.
22 (1760), 2 Burr. 1005 at 1012, 97 E.R. 676 (K.B.).
23 See Austin Wakeman Scott, "Constructive Trusts" (1955), 71 L.Q. Rev. 39; Leonard Pollock, "Matrimonial Property and Trusts: The Situation from Murdoch to Rathwell" (1978), 16 Alta. L. Rev. 357.

modate the changing needs and mores of society, in order to achieve justice. The constructive trust has proven to be a useful tool in the judicial armoury.[24]

How then does one approach the question of unjust enrichment in matrimonial causes? In *Rathwell*[25] I ventured to suggest there are three requirements to be satisfied before an unjust enrichment can be said to exist: an enrichment, a corresponding deprivation, and absence of any juristic reason for the enrichment. This approach, it seems to me, is supported by general principles of equity that have been fashioned by the courts for centuries, though, admittedly, not in the context of matrimonial property controversies.

The common law has never been willing to compensate a plaintiff on the sole basis that his actions have benefited another. Lord Halsbury scotched this heresy in the case of *The Ruabon Steamship Company, Limited v. London Assurance*,[26] with these words:[27]

> . . . I cannot understand how it can be asserted that it is part of the common law that where one person gets some advantage from the act of another a right of contribution towards the expense from that act arises on behalf of the person who has done it.

Lord Macnaghten, in the same case, put it this way:[28]

> . . . there is no principle of law which requires that a person should contribute to an outlay merely because he has derived a material benefit from it.

It is not enough for the court simply to determine that one spouse has benefited at the hands of another and then to require restitution. It must, in addition, be evident that the retention of the benefit would be "unjust" in the circumstances of the case.

On these facts, the first two requirements laid down in *Rathwell* have clearly been satisfied: Mr. Pettkus has had the benefit of nineteen years of unpaid labour, while Miss Becker has received little or nothing in return. As for the third requirement, I hold that where one person in a relationship tantamount to spousal prejudices herself in the reasonable expectation of receiving an interest in property and the other person in the relationship freely accepts benefits conferred by the first person in circumstances where he knows or ought to have known of that reasonable expectation, it would be unjust to allow the recipient of the benefit to retain it.

Since then, the courts have extended the reach of the remedial constructive trust to other areas of the law. It is appropriate, therefore, to examine where this remedy fits in the scheme of restitutionary remedies, which is the goal of the next section.

Notes and Questions

1. *Pettkus v. Becker*, referred to above, involved a man and a woman, both immigrants, who lived together for almost 20 years and pooled their resources to build up an apiary business together. He took title to the property. At the end of the period he told her to "get lost." The majority in the Supreme Court of Canada had little difficulty in holding

---

24 See *Babrociak v. Babrociak* (1978), 1 R.F.L. (2d) 95 (Ont. C.A.); *Spears v. Levy* (1974), 9 N.S.R. (2d) 340, 19 R.F.L. 101, 52 D.L.R. (2d) 146 (C.A.); *Douglas v. Guaranty Trust Co.* (1978), 8 R.F.L. (2d) 98, 4 E.T.R. 65 (Ont. H.C.); *Armstrong v. Armstrong* (1978), 22 O.R. (2d) 223, 93 D.L.R. (3d) 128 (H.C.).

25 *Supra*, note 12.

26 [1900] A.C. 6 (H.L.).

27 *Ibid.*, at 10.

28 *Ibid.*, at 15.

that Mr. Pettkus was unjustly enriched at Ms. Becker's expense and that there was no juristic reason for the enrichment. Further, there was a causal connection between her contributions and the property. Accordingly, she was awarded a constructive trust for a half interest in the property.

It would appear that Ms. Becker won. But did she? By the end of 1985 she had collected only about $68,000 out of the total of approximately $95,000 due to her and most of the $68,000 was used to pay legal fees. Mr. Pettkus used every weapon in the judicial armoury to thwart realization of the judgment by Ms. Becker. Mr. Pettkus married another woman who claimed a half-interest in the properties. That required a court action to dispose of. Ms. Becker tried, in the fall of 1984, to have the beehives seized, but Mr. Pettkus appealed the seizure. That required another court proceeding. As a result of the seizure Mr. Pettkus refused to feed the bees. A court application was necessary to require him to do so, but by the time it had been obtained, most of the bees were dead. The real property was sold in the fall of 1984 for $69,000. The proceeds were paid into court and were in due course awarded to Ms. Becker.

Could Ms. Becker have avoided all this? That is difficult to say. She was awarded a half interest in the real property and the assets. The judgment was registered against the real property to prevent its disposition, but the other assets could be disposed of more readily or, in the case of the bees, simply left to die. The problem was Mr. Pettkus's intransigence and the need to ascertain the value of her half interest. It would, perhaps, be better in circumstances such as these to ask for partition or sale and a vesting order of part of the property as well as a declaration. Even if, as in this case, the trial judge dismissed the action, the evidence concerning the value of the properties would then be in the record and the appellate court could make the appropriate orders. In that way the disposition of the matter might have been speeded up, at least as regards the real property. This is not to suggest that Ms. Becker's solicitor ought to have done so in this case. The post-judgment circumstances were highly unusual, but he could not have predicted that.

The story of *Pettkus v. Becker* ended in tragedy. In November, 1986, Ms. Becker, at age 60, took her own life. In a suicide note she protested against the legal system which awarded her $150,000, but failed to ensure that she received it.[29]

2. The preceding note illustrates that, although a proprietary remedy such as the constructive trust confers additional benefits on the claimant, it is no guarantee that the claimant will be able to realize fully on the judgment if the opposite party is determined to thwart it.

3. In the 1970s and 1980s all of the Canadian common law jurisdictions enacted legislation[30] to abolish in part the concept of separate property between husband and wife and replace it with a judicial power to order the division of family assets, on a breakdown

---

29 The facts in this note were derived from a news feature by William Marsden "Palimony suit winner waits in vain for husband to pay," in the *Ottawa Citizen* of February 20, 1985; news features by Peter Cheney, "Suicide a protest of legal system says Rosa's boss," and by Linda Silver Dranoff, "How to stop tragedies like Rosa Becker's," in the *Toronto Star* of November 14, 1986; a column by Nora Underwood, "Rosa Becker's hollow victory," in *McLean's* of November 24, 1986; and from information supplied by Mr. G.E. Langlois, solicitor for Ms. Becker. See also R.J. Sharpe and K. Roach, *Brian Dickson: A Judge's Journey* (Toronto: University of Toronto Press, 2003), at 190-191.

30 The statutes are: *Family Law Act*, R.S.N.L. 1990, c. F-2; R.S.O. 1990, c. F.3; R.S.P.E.I. 1988, c. F-2.1; S.N.W.T. 1976, c. 18; *Family Property and Support Act*, R.S.Y. 2002, c. 83; *Family Relations Act*, R.S.B.C. 1996, c. 128; *Marital Property Act*, C.C.S.M. c. M45; S.N.B. 1980, c. M-1.1; *Matrimonial Property Act*, R.S.A. 2000, c. M-8; R.S.N.S. 1989, c. 275; *Family Property Act*, S.S. 1997, c. F-6.3. See also the *Civil Code of Quebec*, articles 401-492.

of the marriage.[31] While the statutes differ in detail, they provide either for a deferred sharing of property upon marriage breakdown and, in some, upon death,[32] or for a right to an equalization payment in those circumstances. Most of the statutes restrict the division to assets that are used for family purposes.

The statutes all recognize the special place of the matrimonial home by giving each spouse equal rights of possession of it during marriage. The Newfoundland statute creates community of property with respect to the matrimonial home.[33]

Some of the statutes or related statutes, also provide for the support of spouses and other dependants and for domestic contracts whereby spouses and cohabitees may regulate their property and other rights.

The Alberta and Saskatchewan Statutes[34] provide for the division of all property owned by the spouses, subject to certain exemptions.

A number of the statutes also abolished the presumption of advancement as between husbands and wives and replaced it with a presumption of resulting trust. This is discussed in the chapter on resulting trusts.

4. Many of these statutes provide for family assets to be shared on breakdown of the relationship.[35] They entitle the non-titled spouse to an equal share of the property, or its value, with a wide-ranging discretion in the judge to vary the principle of equal sharing where the facts so require. One goal of this statutory remedy was to remove the need for litigation based on resulting or constructive trusts. Those doctrines may still arise, however, in respect of assets which are outside the statutory scheme (non-family assets), or perhaps in relation to a dispute (possibly a third party) which arises while the relationship subsists (so that the statutory remedy is not triggered). The details of the different statutes are beyond the scope of this work.

5. The Ontario *Family Law Act*[36] provides for a deferred equalization scheme. Part I of the Act provides that on a breakdown of marriage a spouse is entitled to an equalization payment if the value of her or his net family property is less than the value of the net family property of the other spouse. A surviving spouse has a similar right on the death of the other spouse if the value of the latter's net family property is the greater. The claimant is awarded one-half the difference between the two values. Certain types of property, such as the capital value of property received as a gift or by inheritance, are excluded from the calculation of a spouse's net family property. The court has power to alter the amount in appropriate circumstances.[37] The rights of a surviving spouse under the Act are alternative to her or his rights under the deceased spouse's will or on his or her intestacy.[38]

---

31 In fact, the separate property regime continues until the marriage breaks up or, under some statutes, until the death of the spouse.

32 Only if an application could have been commenced before death: Alberta Act, *ibid.*, s. 6; Manitoba Act, *ibid.*, s. 18. Whether or not an application could have been commenced before death: New Brunswick Act, *ibid.*, s. 4; Newfoundland Act, *ibid.*, s. 71; Nova Scotia Act, *ibid.*, s. 12; Saskatchewan Act, *ibid.*, s. 30. The other statutes permit an application brought before a spouse's death to be continued.

33 *Family Law Act* (Nfld.), s. 8, *supra*, note 30.

34 *Supra*, note 30.

35 *Family Law Act*, R.S.N.L. 1990, c. F-2, s. 29; *Family Law Reform Act*, R.S.O. 1980, c. 152, s. 8 (subsequently rep. by S.O. 1986, c. 4, s. 71); *Marital Property Act*, S.N.B. 1980, c. M-1.1, s. 42; *Matrimonial Property Act*, R.S.N.S. 1989, c. 275, s. 18; S.S. 1997, c. F-6.3.

36 R.S.O. 1990, c. F.3. Similar is R.S.P.E.I. 1988, c. F-2.1.

37 *Ibid.*, s. 5(6).

38 *Ibid.*, s. 6(7), (8).

One would have thought that the Ontario Act was intended to oust the "common law" doctrine of constructive trust completely. However, in a landmark case, *Rawluk v. Rawluk*,[39] a majority of the Supreme Court of Canada held otherwise. Mr. and Mrs. Rawluk had been married for almost 30 years when they separated in 1984. While married, they worked together in two businesses. They acquired several parcels of real property, but the husband took title to most of them. The wife applied for an equalization payment under the *Family Law Act*.[40] Section 4 of the Act requires that the parties' respective properties be valued at the date of the separation. However, the properties owned by the husband had risen substantially in value between the date of the separation and the date of the trial in 1986. The wife sought to share in the increase by claiming a one-half interest in the properties under a constructive trust.

Mr. Justice Cory, with whom Dickson C.J.C. and Wilson and L'Heureux-Dubé JJ. concurred, held that the Act did not constitute a complete code for determining ownership of matrimonial property and did not expressly or impliedly prevent the use of the constructive trust for that purpose. In fact, he opined, the Act permitted its use, since it enhanced the Act's purpose of equalizing the parties' assets and treating marriage as a partnership of equals. Since section 10 permits a spouse to ask a court to determine questions of ownership while the marriage subsists, his Lordship felt that a spouse should not be precluded from raising a similar issue after a breakdown of the marriage. His Lordship concluded that the definition of "property" in section 4 of the Act was wide enough to include both legal and equitable interests. Further, and most significantly, he held that a property interest arising under a constructive trust arises not when the court declares it, but at the time the unjust enrichment first arose.

Madam Justice McLachlin, with whom La Forest and Sopinka JJ. concurred, wrote a strong dissent. She was of opinion that the Act provides a complete code for determining ownership of matrimonial property and that it was designed to provide a statutory remedy for unjust enrichment as between spouses.[41] The fact that a spouse can obtain a constructive trust order before marriage breakdown is not relevant. The Legislature has substituted the right to an equalization payment upon a breakdown of marriage for a constructive trust order. Further, and again significantly, her Ladyship was strongly of the view that a constructive trust which deserves the name "remedial" cannot be said to arise when the duty to make restitution arises, but only when the court confers the remedy. This is apparent from the fact that the constructive trust is only one remedy to redress unjust enrichment and a court may, and in most situations should, deny it in favour of a personal remedy.

Consider the respective positions of the majority and the minority in *Rawluk* apart from the emotive context of an application for an equalization payment. Which position on the nature of the constructive trust makes more sense? When does the constructive trust arise? What implications does your answer have apart from someone in the position of Mrs. Rawluk?

---

39 [1990] 1 S.C.R. 70, 65 D.L.R. (4th) 161, 23 R.F.L. (3d) 337, 71 O.R. (2d) 480, 36 E.T.R. 1, 103 N.R. 321.

40 *Supra*, note 36.

41 See now *Family Law Act*, R.S.P.E.I. 1988, c. F-2.1, s. 15.

3. AN INTRODUCTION TO UNJUST ENRICHMENT AND RESTITUTION

(a) Overview

In order to appreciate the nature of the remedial constructive trust fully, it is necessary to give a brief outline of the law of unjust enrichment.[42]

Unjust enrichment can be used in a loose or non-technical sense, as well as in a more defined sense. The loose sense is not much use in legal analysis. For example, if a defendant negligently harms a plaintiff in a traffic accident, or causes him a loss through a breach of contract, we might say that until the damages are paid, the defendant is unjustly enriched at the plaintiff's expense. To use the phrase so widely would be simply to refer to every kind of legal liability.

The core case of unjust enrichment, used in a more technical sense, arises where there is no other theory of liability available. The best example is a mistaken payment. For example, A owes B $50. He pays the debt, but then due to some mistake, he sends another cheque for $50. It has always been the law that B is obliged to repay $50. This obligation does not depend on any wrongdoing by B; it is not a wrongful act to be paid by mistake. Nor is there any contract governing this overpayment. The obligation is not explicable by tort or by contract. It is explicable by the independent cause of action in unjust enrichment. As laid down in *Pettkus v. Becker*,[43] the elements of this cause of action are "an enrichment, a corresponding deprivation and absence of any juristic reason for the enrichment." The enrichment is the receipt of $50; the corresponding deprivation is the loss of $50 by the plaintiff; and there is no juristic reason for a payment by mistake. So it can be concluded that the defendant has been unjustly or unjustifiably enriched. Then it follows that he must make restitution of the $50. Restitution is the remedy for unjust enrichment.

This kind of case is sometimes called "autonomous unjust enrichment," because it is based on an autonomous cause of action, or "subtractive unjust enrichment," because the defendant's enrichment comes "by subtraction" from the plaintiff.

There is another kind of case which is sometimes discussed as part of restitution or unjust enrichment. A defendant may acquire a benefit through some conduct which amounts to a wrongful act against the plaintiff. In *Keech v. Sandford*,[44] the defendant acquired a valuable asset (a leasehold interest in land) through conduct which was, as against the plaintiff, a breach of the defendant's

---

42 A more detailed account of this area of law may be found in texts on restitution and unjust enrichment. See, *e.g.*, P. Birks, *Unjust Enrichment* (Oxford: Oxford University Press, 2003); A.S. Burrows, *The Law of Restitution,* 2nd ed. (London: Butterworths, 2002); Peter D. Maddaugh and John D. McCamus, *The Law of Restitution*, 2nd ed. (Aurora: Canada Law Book Inc., 2004) ("Maddaugh and McCamus"); R. Goff and G. Jones, *The Law of Restitution*, 6th ed. (London: Sweet & Maxwell Ltd., 2002), ch. 1, 2 ("Goff and Jones"); George E. Palmer, *The Law of Restitution* (Boston: Little, Brown and Co., 1978), ch. 1 ("Palmer").

43 *Supra*, note 1.

44 *Supra*, note 3.

duty of loyalty. This is "unjust enrichment" in a different sense. It is not autonomous unjust enrichment. The plaintiff does not need to satisfy the three-part test from *Pettkus;* indeed, the plaintiff could not do so, because there has been no real "corresponding deprivation"; the benefit did not come from the plaintiff. For the same reason, this is not a case of "subtractive unjust enrichment." Rather, it could be called "unjust enrichment by wrongdoing." Usually, when a defendant commits a wrongful act, the plaintiff seeks *compensation* for loss caused. But if the defendant has actually profited from the wrongdoing, then in at least some cases, the plaintiff is allowed to take away that wrongful gain.[45] Maddaugh and McCamus explain the matter as follows:[46]

> Cases of unearned windfalls are those in which the benefit obtained by the defendant has been acquired through a transfer of value from the plaintiff to the defendant. In these circumstances, the benefit has been conferred "at the expense of" the plaintiff in the sense that it has been obtained by a reduction of the plaintiff's wealth. Birks refers to this phenomenon as "unjust enrichment by subtraction from the plaintiff".[47] Where the benefit has been acquired through breach of a duty owed to the plaintiff, as in cases of breach of fiduciary obligation, the acquisition may be said to be "at the expense of" the plaintiff in the sense that it has been made possible through the infliction of an injury upon or the infringement of an interest of the plaintiff. Birks refers to this phenomenon as "unjust enrichment by doing wrong to the plaintiff."[48]

The terminology of this area of the law is contested and is still in a state of flux. One view is that the terminology of unjust enrichment can usefully be used to cover both cases of autonomous unjust enrichment, and cases in which defendants are required to give up the profits of wrongdoing.[49] Another view is that the distinction established by Birks must be taken to the following logical conclusion. There is the autonomous cause of action in unjust enrichment, and the remedy for that is restitution. Cases of profitable wrongdoing, however, are not based on the autonomous cause of action in unjust enrichment; instead the defendant is liable for the act of wrongdoing. To avoid confusion, these cases should not, therefore, be called "unjust enrichment." Birks himself has now moved to this view.[50] There is a third view which takes this even further. Not only should we not use the phrase "unjust enrichment" to describe cases in which a defendant must give up the profits of wrongdoing; we should not even use the word "restitution." The word "restitution" means "giving back" and is appropriate for cases

---

45 J. Berryman, "The Case for Restitutionary Damages over Punitive Damages: Teaching the Wrongdoer that Tort Does Not Pay" (1994), 73 Can. Bar Rev. 320.

46 Maddaugh and McCamus, at 3-7.

47 P.B.H. Birks, *An Introduction to the Law of Restitution* (Oxford: Clarendon Press, 1985), at 25 ("Birks").

48 *Ibid.*

49 This is the approach in A.S. Burrows, *The Law of Restitution,* 2nd ed. (London: Butterworths, 2002), at 4-5, and also in Maddaugh and McCamus, 35, where the authors note the dangers of confusion. Note that on this view, unjust enrichment is a "principle" rather than a cause of action, since in cases where a defendant must give up the profit of wrongdoing, the cause of action is clearly the wrong.

50 P. Birks, "Misnomer" in W. Cornish *et al.*, eds., *Restitution: Past, Present and Future* (Oxford: Hart Publishing, 1998) 1.

of subtractive or autonomous unjust enrichment, where a defective transfer must be reversed. Cases of profitable wrongdoing, however, are not usually cases of giving back; as in *Keech v. Sandford,* the gain usually came from a third hand. The defendant is not giving back, but rather is giving *up* the gain. Hence, on this view, we should refer to the "disgorgement" of wrongful gains. In other words, where there is a wrong, the plaintiff may seek compensation of loss suffered, or disgorgement of any gain acquired by the defendant.[51]

Terminology aside, when restitution or disgorgement is to be granted, there are a number of ways in which this can be done. The following sections distinguish personal remedies from proprietary remedies. A personal remedy alleges a debt, while a proprietary remedy alleges a right of property in a particular asset. If I mistakenly pay you $100 by handing over a $100 bill, I have a right to restitution. A personal remedy entails that you owe me $100, which (like any debt) can be satisfied out of any asset that you have. An allegation that you hold the $100 bill on trust for me (or that I still own it at common law) would be an allegation of a proprietary remedy. A proprietary right has a specific subject matter; if the $100 bill is gone, so is the right. But personal rights are much weaker in insolvency situations, where a defendant does not have enough assets to answer his or her debts. Personal claims abate proportionately in bankruptcy (if the debtor has $10 and owes $100, every creditor will get 10% of what he or she is owed). Proprietary rights survive in the bankruptcy of the defendant and so are preferable in insolvency situations.[52]

Proprietary rights, in turn, can be either beneficial rights, or rights by way of security. Legal ownership and the beneficiary's interest under a trust are beneficial rights, which entitle the holder to all the benefits of the asset. A bank's mortgage over a house is a proprietary right by way of security. If the house goes up in value, the bank does not benefit; the homeowner does. But the bank does hold a proprietary right to secure the repayment of the mortgage debt; this right will survive in a bankruptcy of the homeowner, and will allow the bank to satisfy the mortgage debt out of the proceeds of sale of the house, in priority to any other creditor. Security rights are associated with a personal obligation, and disappear when the obligation is discharged.

This allows us to identify another advantage of some proprietary claims, those which are beneficial. Where the property in question has risen in value, the benefit of this will accrue to the plaintiff, be he a legal owner or the beneficiary of a trust. Conversely, if the property has gone down in value, the value of the plaintiff's right will be less.[53] Finally, in an action seeking to enforce a proprietary claim, the plaintiff may obtain an order to preserve the property pending trial.[54]

---

51 For this view, see L. Smith, "The Province of the Law of Restitution" (1992), 71 Can. Bar Rev. 672; M. McInnes, "The Measure of Restitution" (2002), 52 Univ. of Toronto L.J. 163.

52 Other advantages of proprietary remedies are discussed in L. Smith, *The Law of Tracing* (Oxford: Clarendon Press, 1997), at 24-29.

53 As noted, this is not the case for rights which are by way of security for a personal obligation. Security rights, like beneficial proprietary rights, can arise by consent and also by operation of law.

54 *E.g. Rules of Civil Procedure* (Ont.), Rule 45.01(1). Another procedural advantage is that it is

Notes and Questions

1. Most unjust enrichment scholars are of the view that a defendant can be made legally liable in unjust enrichment even when that defendant has not done anything wrong, which is unusual in private law. For a discussion of the merits of this see L. Smith, "Restitution: The Heart of Corrective Justice" (2001), 79 Texas L.R. 2115; S. Smith, "Justifying the Law of Unjust Enrichment" (2001), 79 Texas L.R. 2177.

2. The liability of a wrongdoing defendant to give up a gain can be based solely on the wrongdoing, even if the enrichment did not come subtractively from the plaintiff. At the same time, however, it may be that it did come from the plaintiff, and it may even be that the same facts are susceptible to analysis either as a liability to give up a wrongful gain, or a liability to give back an unjust enrichment. This is no different from concurrent liability in breach of contract and tort.[55]

3. There is an ongoing development of the common law as to which wrongs allow a plaintiff to choose disgorgement of the defendant's gain, as an alternative to compensation of the plaintiff's loss. Breach of the fiduciary duty of loyalty is a clear example of a wrong which allows disgorgement. Breach of confidence is another example. Breaches of intellectual property rights, and the tort of conversion, also permit this. More recent decisions have allowed plaintiffs to claim disgorgement of the profits of a breach of contract, at least in some cases.[56]

4. It may be that some cases can be understood as subtractive unjust enrichment even if the enrichment did not come from the plaintiff; this might be so where the defendant "intercepts" some value that would otherwise been acquired by the plaintiff.

In *LAC Minerals*, La Forest J. said:[57]

> In my view the facts present in this case make out a restitutionary claim, or what is the same thing, a claim for unjust enrichment. When one talks of restitution, one normally talks of giving back to someone something that has been taken from them (a restitutionary proprietary award), or its equivalent value (a personal restitutionary award). As the Court of Appeal noted in this case, Corona never in fact owned the Williams property, and so it cannot be "given back" to them. However, there are concurrent findings below that but for the interception by LAC, Corona would have acquired the property. In *Air Canada v. British Columbia*,[58] I said that the function of the law of restitution "is to ensure that where a plaintiff has been deprived of wealth that is either in his possession *or would have accrued for his benefit*, is restored to him. The measure of restitutionary recovery is the gain the [defendant] made at the [plaintiff's] expense". In my view the fact that Corona never owned the property should not preclude it from pursuing a restitutionary claim.[59] LAC has therefore been enriched at the expense of Corona.

---

easier to commence litigation against a person who is not within the jurisdiction, where there is a proprietary claim to property within the jurisdiction: *e.g. Rules of Civil Procedure* (Ont.), Rule 17.02(a).

55 See for example *Guinness plc v. Saunders,* [1990] 2 A.C. 663, discussed in L. Smith, "The Province of the Law of Restitution" (1992), 71 Can. Bar Rev. 672, 692-694.

56 See *A.G. v. Blake,* [2001] 1 A.C. 268; *Amertek Inc. v. Canadian Commercial Corp.* (2003), 229 D.L.R. (4th) 419 (Ont. S.C.J.).

57 [1989] 2 S.C.R. 574, 61 D.L.R. (4th) 14 at 45, 6 R.P.R. (2d) 1, 44 B.L.R. 1, 35 E.T.R. 1, 69 O.R. (2d) 287.

58 (1989), 59 D.L.R. (4th) 161 at 193-4.

59 See Birks, at 133-9.

This idea is however somewhat controversial. If the plaintiff had some entitlement to the asset, then the case is an ordinary "subtraction" case. If the plaintiff did not have any entitlement to it, then it is not clear that the law of unjust enrichment should create one.[60] This issue is discussed further in Section 3 of the next chapter.

(b) Restitution at Common Law

Not every claim for restitution (or disgorgement) is made via a constructive trust, a creature of equity. Most restitutionary claims are personal, and arise at law.

Claims at common law developed through an action called *indebitatus assumpsit,* which was used to enforce both consensual debts and also debts arising by operation of law (as in unjust enrichment).[61] There were four sub-species of *indebitatus assumpsit* which could be used to enforce what are now considered claims in unjust enrichment:[62]

1. The action for money had and received, which lay to recover money paid by the plaintiff to the defendant under mistake or compulsion, or for a consideration (a mutually understood reason) which failed. In appropriate cases, the action was also used to recover the profits a defendant had made through a wrongful act against the plaintiff, for example, by selling the plaintiff's goods.
2. The action for money paid, which lay where the plaintiff paid money to a third party and the defendant received a benefit therefrom. For example, the plaintiff paid the defendant's monthly rent.
3. The action for *quantum meruit*, which lay to recover a reasonable price for services supplied by the plaintiff to the defendant. In many cases, this might be based on a genuine implied contract, as where the parties did not fix a price for some work, but clearly intended that a reasonable price be paid. But in other cases, for example where the contract was void or unenforceable, no such implied contract can explain the liability, which is actually based on unjust enrichment. *Quantum meruit,* which only means "as much as he deserved," does not distinguish between these two analytical bases for the claim.
4. The action called *quantum valebat*, which lay to recover a reasonable price for goods supplied by the plaintiff to the defendant. This is similar to *quantum meruit,* except that it deals with goods rather than services.

---

60 L. Smith, "A Critique of Birks's Theory of Interceptive Subtraction" (1991), 11 O.J.L.S. 481; M. McInnes, "Interceptive Subtraction, Unjust Enrichment and Wrongs — A Reply to Professor Birks" (2003), 62 Cambridge L.J. 697; P. Birks, *Unjust Enrichment* (Oxford: Oxford University Press, 2003), at 66-72.

61 For details of the history, see Maddaugh and McCamus, ch. 1; J.H. Baker, *An Introduction to English Legal History,* 4th ed. (London: Butterworths, 2002), ch. 21.

62 There were seven variations in all, called the "common counts." The other three (for money lent, for money due upon an account stated, and for use and occupation of land; see Baker, *ibid.,* at 348) were less important in the development of the law of unjust enrichment.

Because all of these claims were sub-species of *indebitatus assumpsit,* which in turn was a sub-category of trespass, they were all claims for a sum of money. This is why they were all personal claims.

The common law also recognizes a limited number of proprietary claims, which may serve a restitutionary function. These claims, like all beneficial proprietary claims, identify some particular asset and allege that the asset belongs to the plaintiff. The clearest example is the action called detinue, which directly asserts legal ownership (or at least a right to possession) of a tangible moveable thing. Where it is successful, however, the common law position was that the *defendant* had the option of returning the thing or paying its value.[63] By statutory intervention in the mid-nineteenth century, the court was given the power to order the defendant to return the thing. In imitation of the Chancery practice, this power was (and is) exercised where the thing was not readily replaceable.

Under the rules of court or a statute, the plaintiff may have access to a pre-trial procedure called "replevin".[64] This label can be confusing; it was originally confined to claims against landlords who had wrongfully seized goods for non-payment of rent. In the U.S., it has been widened to refer to all claims to recover a tangible movable thing. In Canada it usually retains this intermediate sense of a pre-trial procedure in which the sheriff, as officer of the court, takes possession of the thing in dispute and delivers it to the plaintiff, *pending the trial.* When people say that replevin is not a cause of action but only a procedure, they mean that the plaintiff must still go to trial and through some cause of action (probably detinue) establish that the thing is really his. If he fails, he would be liable to the defendant for his unlawful invocation of replevin (which is why a plaintiff using replevin must usually post security).

In the case of land, there have always been actions for the direct assertion of the right to occupy land; if successful, such an action will allow the defendant to be ejected. It is also arguable that the action for money had and received, mentioned above, can serve as a proprietary claim to the traceable proceeds, in the defendant's hands, of property belonging to the plaintiff.[65]

As the equitable proprietary remedies generally provide more relief to a claimant, the legal remedies are seldom used outside of the context of land.

(c) Restitution in Equity

Equity achieves some kinds of restitution through the mechanism of accounting. Many parties were and are liable in equity to render an account; this does not necessarily mean that they have done anything wrong.[66] Every trustee must account for what he has done with the trust property. Partners and agents are also

---

63 *General & Financial Facilities Ltd. v. Cooks Cars (Romford) Ltd.,* [1963] 1 W.L.R. 644 (C.A.).

64 See for example *Courts of Justice Act,*R.S.O. 1990, c. C.43, s. 104; *Rules of Civil Procedure* (Ont.), Rule 44.

65 L. Smith, "Restitution: The Heart of Corrective Justice" (2001), 79 Texas L.R. 2115, 2159-2174.

66 P. Millett, "Equity's Place in the Law of Commerce" (1998), 114 L.Q.R. 214, 225-226; R. Chambers, "Liability" in P. Birks and A. Pretto, eds., *Breach of Trust* (Oxford: Hart Publishing, 2002), 1 at 16-20.

accountable. The court scrutinizes the accounts and profits are part of the trust, or the partnership property, as the case may be. Where the goal was to take away a profit from wrongdoing—for example, from a breach of copyright—equity could order an "accounting of profits," even though such a party would not have been accountable in the absence of the wrongdoing. The account is a judicially overseen process by which the amount of the profit was determined. Once the amount of the profit is determined, it must be disgorged.[67] Where an accounting of profits is ordered outside of a trust relationship, the accounting of profits creates a debt; it is a personal claim. But if the accounting by a trustee shows a profit from trust property, that property is also held in trust.

Equity also requires compensation for wrongful conduct, such as a trustee's breach of trust which caused loss to the trust. In the case of an accountable party, the amount of the loss to be compensated is also determined through the accounting process.[68] This claim enables the beneficiary to recover the loss with interest. The traditional name for this remedy is equitable compensation. The orthodox view is that it must not be confused with common law damages, since the equitable rules governing compensation favour the trust beneficiary in a number of ways.[69] On this view, for example, the damage principles of foreseeability and remoteness do not apply in assessing compensation in breach of trusts cases.[70] Nonetheless, there are indications in Canada that the legal and equitable claim for damages are merging.[71] This is discussed later.[72]

Because compensation and disgorgement both arise out of the process of rendering an account, they are alternative. The first is based upon a disapproval or reprobation of the fiduciary's conduct; the second adopts the conduct. For example, if the defendant misappropriated trust property, the plaintiff can disapprove by disallowing any deduction in the accounts for the removal of the property; the effect will be that when the account is completed, the defendant will have to replace the property or its value in order to make the account balance. Alternatively, if the defendant used the property profitably, then the plaintiff can treat that transaction as one made for his benefit, and require it (with the profit) to be entered in the account. The result will be that the defendant will hold the

---

67 Long ago, the common law also had an action of account, but it was superseded by the pro-
    ceeding in equity because the latter afforded the plaintiff relief more readily. *A.G. v. Dublin
    Corp.* (1827), 1 Bli. N.S. 312 at 327, 4 E.R. 888 (H.L.), *per* Lord Redesdale. See *Restatement,
    Restitution*, Part I, Introductory Note, p. 5.

68 Traditionally there were two kinds of accounting which might be required of an accountable
    party: a "common account" and an "account on the basis of wilful default." An accountable party
    is liable to render a common account without any allegation of wrongdoing. The other account
    was ordered on the basis that the accountable party had committed a particular kind of wrong,
    namely, the failure to receive all the assets that the party should have received. See R. Chambers,
    "Liability" in P. Birks and A. Pretto, eds., *Breach of Trust* (Oxford: Hart Publishing, 2002), 1 at
    18-20.

69 *Bartlett v. Barclays Bank Trust Co. Ltd. (Nos. 1 and 2)*, [1980] Ch. 515 at 543. See also *Re Bell's
    Indenture*, [1980] 1 W.L.R. 1217; *Re Dawson*, [1966] 2 N.S.W.R. 211.

70 Ford and Lee, §17020.

71 See, *e.g., Canson Enterprises Ltd. v. Boughton & Co.*, [1991] 3 S.C.R. 534, 85 D.L.R. (4th) 129.

72 Chapter 15, part 2.

property and the profit as trust property. While the beneficiary may be entitled to either remedy, he or she must elect one or the other. The beneficiary cannot approbate and reprobate the same action of the fiduciary.[73] A beneficiary may take the profit if this remedy will give a greater recovery, as where the trust would have been unable to make the profit itself because the particular profit arose out of an investment which was not an authorized trust investment.[74] By contrast, a beneficiary will want to claim compensation if the fiduciary made no profit but incurred a loss, or if it is difficult to prove the amount of the profit or whether and the extent to which it was caused by the breach of trust. When rendering his account, the trustee may deduct the outgoings, such as maintenance, but is chargeable with occupation rent if he or she has been in occupation of the property.

The accounting of profits provides a way to create a personal liability to disgorge a profit, even against a party who would not be accountable if he had behaved lawfully. Much better known are the equitable proprietary remedies. Again, the crucial difference is that these proprietary remedies assert not a debt, but right of property in a particular asset. These remedies are:

1. The resulting trust, discussed in the previous chapter. Arguably, it is a more appropriate remedy to effect restitution than the constructive trust, where restitution is used to refer to the objective of restoring value whence it came.[75]

2. The constructive trust, the effect of which is usually to have specific property restored to the plaintiff. It lies not only against the original property, but also against its traceable proceeds. Like any trust, it can be asserted against a third person to whom the property has been transferred and who is not a *bona fide* purchaser of the legal estate for value without notice. This trust can be deployed as a way of bringing about the disgorgement of wrongful profits.[76] For the time being, at least, it is also often the label used when a trust is imposed to effect restitution in the sense of giving back. And the constructive trust is used for other goals as well, as in mutual wills and secret trusts.

3. The equitable lien, which is gives the plaintiff a proprietary security interest to secure a personal claim. Thus, for example, if the defendant has misappropriated trust property worth $10,000, and then combined it with his own $10,000 and invested the $20,000 in land, the plaintiff can claim a 50% trust interest in the land. If, however, the land has now dropped to a market value of $14,000, this would give the plaintiff a claim worth only $7,000. In this situation, the plaintiff would instead be allowed to assert a personal claim for recovery of the $10,000, and to secure that claim by asserting a lien over the land. If the debt is not paid, the lien will allow a forced sale of the land, just like a bank's mortgage. The lien is proprietary, inasmuch as it is enforceable against donees or in bankruptcy; but it is not a beneficial interest, only a security interest, so the plaintiff cannot obtain

---

73 *Heathcote v. Hulme* (1819), 1 Jac. & W. 123, 37 E.R. 322.

74 See *MacMillan Bloedel Ltd. v. Binstead* (1983), 14 E.T.R. 269 (B.S.S.C.), a useful case on the details of an account.

75 See Robert Chambers, *Resulting Trusts* (Oxford: Clarendon Press, 1995), 104ff.; Lionel D. Smith, *The Law of Tracing* (Oxford: Clarendon Press, 1997), 294, 300, 357.

76 Smith, *ibid.*, 357.

more than payment of the debt.

The equitable lien was used in *LAC Minerals Ltd. v. International Corona Resources Ltd.*[77] The defendant had a constructive trust imposed against it, over a gold mine it had acquired through a breach of confidence against the plaintiff. But the defendant was also granted a lien over the mine, for the money it had laid out in improving the property and in acquiring it. Similarly, in *Georg v. Hassanali*[78] the court imposed an equitable lien on property, in respect of which it declined to impose a constructive trust, to secure the monetary award it made.[79]

4. Subrogation, which lies in equity when the plaintiff's property has been used by the plaintiff or by another to discharge some other party's obligation, can be a proprietary remedy. In subrogation, the plaintiff stands in the place of the discharged creditor; he is said to be "subrogated to" the latter's position. For example, subrogation can arise where A pays money to B, who holds land subject to a mortgage debt owing to C, and B uses it as agreed to discharge the debt to C; unknown to A, another party X has registered a different kind of security against B's land. If A merely registers a mortgage now, he will lose priority to X, since securities are ranked in order of registration. By showing his mistake about X's security, however, A could establish that he should be subrogated to the position of C, the discharged mortgagee. Then he would take over the rights C used to hold. This will give him priority over X.[80]

Subrogation also arises where two people are liable to pay the same debt, for example, where there is a primary debtor and a guarantor of the debt. If the guarantor pays the debt, she will be subrogated to the rights of the discharged creditor against the primary debtor. This may have proprietary effects, if the discharged creditor held proprietary security rights. It may also be purely personal, if the discharged creditor had only personal rights.[81]

There are certain advantages to equitable proprietary rights, beyond the crucial feature of insolvency priority, and the other features which apply to proprietary rights generally. Claims to property held in trust may be barred only by laches, so the limitation period may be much longer than for personal claims.[82] There may also be other kinds of bars to a personal action which do not apply to

---

77 *Supra,* note 57.

78 (1989), 18 R.F.L. (3d) 225 (Ont. H.C.J.).

79 See also *Orobko v. Orobko* (1992), 76 Man. R. (2d) 296, 45 E.T.R. 156 (C.A.); *Henderson v. Henderson* (2000), 73 B.C.L.R. (3d) 124, 184 D.L.R. (4th) 128 (C.A.).

80 See *Brown v. McLean* (1889), 18 O.R. 533. The effect is as if C directly assigned his mortgage to A, preserving its priority over X; this indeed is probably what would have occurred, had A been aware of X. There is no harm to X, at least where he has not relied to his detriment on his apparent priority after the discharge of C's mortgage.

81 The case of indemnity insurance is similar. If a tortfeasor D damages P's property, but P has insurance provided by I, P can sue either D or I. If P recovers from I, then I is subrogated to and takes over P's rights against D. All of these forms of subrogation may be sourced in common law or statute (or even in contract in the case of indemnity insurance) rather than in equity. See C. Mitchell, *The Law of Subrogation* (Oxford: Clarendon Press, 1994), especially at 44-45.

82 See *Pullan v. Koe,* [1913] 1 Ch. 9, in which trust property was recovered 34 years after it was misdirected.

a proprietary action.[83]

Since proprietary remedies give priority over the defendant's general creditors, a proprietary claim may afford the plaintiff full or substantial recovery on the defendant's insolvency while a personal claim would not, since, in obtaining judgment, the plaintiff would rank *pari passu* with the defendant's other creditors. This may be illustrated by reference to certain cases.

In *Waselenko v. Touche Ross Ltd.*,[84] the applicants paid approximately one-half of the cost of a house being built for them under contract by the respondent builder, after which the latter was put into receivership. The contract stipulated that the builder would hold title until the house was completed. The receiver refused to complete because the cost of completion exceeded the balance payable. An application for a declaration that the receiver held the house upon constructive trust for the applicants was granted. The receiver and the creditors would have been unjustly enriched if the applicants could only have sued in breach of contract.[85]

In *Thorne Riddell Inc. v. Rolfe*[86] the bankrupt syndicator sold units in a proposed shopping centre to client developers on the basis of a prospectus. The prospectus referred to the property as being 19 acres, whereas, in fact, the syndicator had bought 29.4 acres with the clients' money. Misstatements in the prospectus were intended to conceal the situation, so as to enable the syndicator to obtain a secret profit from the surplus land. The development did not proceed and the 29.4 acres were sold under court order, which stated that the proceeds should be a fund in substitution for the land. In an action to determine entitlement to the fund, it was held that the syndicator was a fiduciary and the benefit he acquired out of the misuse of his position, therefore, belonged to his principals,

---

83 It In *Sinclair v. Brougham*, [1914] A.C. 398 (H.L.), depositors deposited money with a building society (a kind of credit union) which was running a banking business that was beyond its legal capacity to run. The contracts of deposit being void, it was held that no personal claim in restitution could be made out. However the depositors were apparently allowed to succeed in a proprietary claim. The case is difficult to understand and has been overruled as regards the non-availability of a personal claim to restitution: *Westdeutsche Landesbank Girozentrale v. Islington L.B.C.*, [1996] A.C. 669, [1996] 2 All E.R. 961 (H.L.).

84 (1982), 24 Sask. R. 260, [1983] 2 W.W.R. 352 (Q.B.), aff'd (1985), 45 Sask. R. 196, [1985] 3 W.W.R. 38 (C.A.).

85 Note however that a simple breach of contract does not usually give the victim a proprietary claim to any property transferred earlier to the other party (although rescission of the contract probably does: *Small v. Attwood* (1832), You. 407, 159 E.R. 1051, reversed on another point (1838), 6 Cl. & F. 232, 7 E.R. 684 (H.L.); *Re Eastgate*, [1905] 1 K.B. 465, followed in *Tilley v. Bowman*, [1910] 1 K.B. 745; *Daly v. Sydney Stock Exchange* (1986), 160 C.L.R. 371, at 387-390; *El Ajou v. Dollar Land Holdings plc*, [1993] 3 All E.R. 717, at 734, reversed on another point [1994] 2 All E.R. 685 (C.A.)). In *Waselenko*, the plaintiffs did not get a trust over the money they had paid, but rather were granted an interest in the house that they wanted to buy. The case may be best explained by reference to the concept of the purchaser's lien, a lien arising by operation of law to secure repayment of an advance payment for the purchase of specific property (other than goods); see the nearly identical case of *Hewitt v. Court* (1983), 149 C.L.R. 639, where the law governing this lien is reviewed.

86 [1984] 6 W.W.R. 240 (B.C.S.C.).

the client developers. In order to achieve that result, a constructive trust in their favour was imposed, which gave them priority over the bankrupt syndicator's general creditors.[87]

In *Chase Manhattan Bank N.A. v. Israel-British Bank (London) Ltd.,*[88] one bank paid another and then mistakenly paid again. The recipient was insolvent. It was held that a mistaken payment is held on trust for the payor; so long as the payment could be traced, the current traceable proceeds were also held on trust with the consequent priority for the payor.[89]

While a proprietary remedy is, therefore, an extremely useful remedy when the defendant has become bankrupt, it may not be imposed simply to give the plaintiff a remedy that would otherwise be unavailable. This is clear from *Barnabe v. Touhey.*[90] Some partners in a law firm left to establish their own firm, using moneys from the old firm. Eventually the new partnership went bankrupt. Partners from the old firm alleged that some of the money from the old firm was now held by a bank, or by the leaving partners, on constructive trust. The judge of first instance awarded a constructive trust over all the property of the new partnership. However, that judgment was reversed on appeal. The Ontario Court of Appeal held that a constructive trust was inappropriate in the circumstances. The plaintiffs had not established unjust enrichment. Even if they had, a trust was impossible, because there was no specific property which was subject to the alleged trust. The trial judge's order ignored this basic requirement of any trust. In the course of its brief judgment, the court said:[91]

> While a constructive trust, if appropriately established, could have the *effect* of the beneficiary of the trust receiving payment out of funds which would otherwise become part of the estate of a bankrupt divisible among his creditors, a constructive trust, otherwise unavailable, cannot be imposed for that *purpose*. This would amount to imposing what may be a fair result as between the constructive trustee and the beneficiary, to the unfair detriment of all other creditors of the bankrupt.

(d) Choice of Remedy

Can the plaintiff choose the remedy, or is the choice restricted? No definitive answer can be given to this question. It is clear that if the claim is one which traditionally fell within the jurisdiction of equity, such as claims against fiduciaries, the plaintiff is entitled to make an equitable claim. If, however, the claim is typically one that was within the jurisdiction of the common law, the traditional

---

87 See also *Carreras Rothmans Ltd. v. Freeman Mathews Treasure Ltd. (in liq.)*, [1975] 1 All E.R. 155. This *"Quistclose"* trust is perhaps best understood as a resulting trust: see *Twinsectra Ltd. v. Yardley,* [2002] 2 A.C. 164, [2002] 2 All E.R. 377 (H.L.).

88 [1981] Ch. 105, [1979] 3 All E.R. 1025, [1980] 2 W.L.R. 202; followed in *Harper v. Royal Bank of Canada* (1994), 18 O.R. (3d) 317, 114 D.L.R. (4th) 749 (Div. Ct.), although the matter of tracing may have been overlooked. *Chase* is extracted in the next chapter.

89 See also *Ellingsen (Trustee of) v. Hallmark Ford Sales Ltd.* (2000), 190 D.L.R. (4th) 47 (B.C.C.A.).

90 (1995), 26 O.R. (3d) 477 (C.A.).

91 *Ibid.*, at 479 (emphasis in the original).

view is that a legal remedy must be sought, unless it is shown that the legal remedy would be inadequate.[92] But, the plaintiff does not always have to show this. For example, in the context of the sale of land, it is rare that a plaintiff is required to sue for damages for breach of the agreement of sale and denied the right to sue for specific performance.[93] Nevertheless, it must be remembered that all equitable remedies are discretionary. Hence, the court will refuse the equitable remedy if that is appropriate.[94]

The traditional view is that if the personal remedy is adequate, the proprietary remedy should be denied. This view appears to have found favour in Canada. In *LAC Minerals Ltd. v. International Corona Resources Ltd.*,[95] La Forest J. stated that the constructive trust is not the appropriate remedy in the great majority of cases but that a personal remedy is usually sufficient.[96] He also listed a number of criteria the court should take into account in deciding whether to award a constructive trust. As the case is reproduced in the next chapter, this issue will be explored further there,[97] but it may be noted that in *Peter v. Beblow*[98] McLachlin

---

92 As, for example, when the action is to recover the title to a chattel which is not unique, but which has been obtained from the plaintiff by fraud and the defendant is insolvent. An action at law for conversion is then inadequate because of the defendant's insolvency. Hence an action in equity for specific restitution, that is, the constructive trust, can be maintained. See Austin Wakeman Scott and William Franklin Fratcher, *The Law of Trusts*, 4th ed. (Boston: Little, Brown and Company, 1987-91), at §462.3 ("Scott").

93 Examples of cases in which specific performance was denied because the remedy in damages was adequate are: *Chaulk v. Fairview Construction Ltd.* (1977), 3 R.P.R. 116, 14 Nfld. & P.E.I.R. 13, 33 A.P.R. 13 (Nfld. C.A.); and *McNabb v. Smith* (1981), 124 D.L.R. (3d) 547, 30 B.C.L.R. 37, 20 R.P.R. 146 (S.C.), affirmed (1982), 132 D.L.R. (3d) 523, 44 B.C.L.R. 295 (C.A.). See also *Heron Bay Investments Ltd. v. Peel Elder Development Ltd.* (1976), 2 C.P.C. 338 (Ont. H.C.).

94 The discretionary nature of specific performance, even for land contracts, was affirmed in *Semelhago v. Paramadevan*, [1996] 2 S.C.R. 415, 136 D.L.R. (4th) 1, paras. 20-22.

95 *Supra*, note 57.

96 *Ibid.*, at D.L.R. 51.

97 Some examples may be given to support the point just made, however. In *Ruff v. Strobel*, 86 D.L.R. (3d) 284, 1978 CarswellAlta 235, [1978] 3 W.W.R. 588, 9 A.R. 378 (C.A.), the constructive trust remedy was denied because the legal, personal remedies were adequate. The plaintiff and the defendant lived together briefly and took title to a condominium unit in their joint names. However, the plaintiff paid the down payment and all subsequent obligations. The court held that the plaintiff ought to have pursued such remedies as contribution and partition. Similarly, in *Barnaby v. Petersen Estate* (1996), 15 E.T.R. (2d) 139 (B.C. S.C.), the court denied the plaintiff a constructive trust because of the short term relationship between her and the deceased. However, since the deceased had been unjustly enriched by her efforts, she was given a monetary award. See also *Guzzo v. Catlin Estate* (1989), 33 E.T.R. 163, 38 B.C.L.R. (2d) 31 (C.A.). The view that a proprietary remedy should not be used where the personal remedy is adequate is also implicit in the judgment of Goulding J. in *Chase Manhattan Bank N.A. v. Israel-British Bank (London) Ltd.* (1979), [1981] Ch. 105, [1979] 3 All E.R. 4025 (Ch. Div.). Money had been paid by the plaintiff to the credit of the defendant bank by mistake. When the defendant became insolvent, the personal remedy to recover the money was inadequate and, hence, the plaintiff was granted a constructive trust over the traceable proceeds of the money.

98 [1993] 1 S.C.R. 980, 101 D.L.R. (4th) 621 at 650, [1993] 3 W.W.R. 337, 150 N.R. 1, 48 E.T.R. 1.

J. also held that a constructive trust should not be imposed unless monetary compensation is inadequate.

This issue was explored in *Semiahmoo Indian Band v. Canada*.[99] The Crown had accepted the absolute surrender of a portion of an Indian reserve for the purpose of a federal work. However, the Crown did not proceed with the work and did not make use of the land for 30 years. The court held that the Crown breached its fiduciary duty to the band by not making the surrender conditional upon the land being returned if not used and by failing to restore surplus land. The court also held that the appropriate remedy was the constructive trust with compensation, and that an account of profits was inappropriate, since the Crown had not made use of the land.

The discretionary nature of judicial remedies is the subject of a great deal of controversy. Some argue that it is inconsistent with the ideal of the rule of law.[100]

Notes and Questions

1. The majority judgment in *Pettkus v. Becker*[101] did not distinguish carefully between unjust enrichment and constructive trust; they were treated as interchangeable. The distinction has since been clarified. This began to emerge with *Sorochan v. Sorochan*,[102] and was discussed by M.M. Litman in "The Emergence of Unjust Enrichment as a Cause of Action and the Remedy of Constructive Trust".[103] See also *Lac Minerals Ltd. v. International Corona Resources Ltd.*,[104] *Rawluk v. Rawluk*,[105] and *Peter v. Beblow*.[106] If a defendant is required to make restitution of an unjust enrichment, this can be achieved in different ways. The defendant might be required to pay a sum of money measured by the value of the defective transfer; that is a personal remedy. Alternatively, he might be required to return the enrichment in specie. This second possibility is usually activated by the constructive trust. So there are two steps. The liability in unjust enrichment is established by the proof of the three elements of the cause of action in unjust enrichment. There then follows a second inquiry, into how restitution should be made.

The most recent decision in this line, *Peter v. Beblow,* provides guidance on how this second inquiry should be conducted. The majority judgment sets down the following test, both for family law disputes and for commercial ones. First, the plaintiff must show that a money award would be inadequate. This represents the continuation of an ancient equitable principle for those remedies which supplement the common law, as in cases of specific performance or injunctions. The court may consider the probability that a money award will be paid, and any "special interest" which the plaintiff holds in the disputed property. Second, the plaintiff must show that there is a link between the plaintiff's

---

99   (1997), 148 D.L.R. (4th) 523, 215 N.R. 241, 131 F.T.R. 319 (note), 1997 CarswellNat 1316, 1997 CarswellNat 2683, [1998] 1 F.C. 3, [1998] 1 C.N.L.R. 250 (C.A.).

100 See for example P. Birks, "Rights, Wrongs and Remedies" (2000), 20 O.J.L.S. 1; D.W.M. Waters, "Liability and Remedy: An Adjustable Relationship" (2001), 64 Sask. L. Rev. 429; S. Evans, "Defending Discretionary Remedialism" (2001), 23 Sydney L.R. 463.

101 *Supra,* note 1.

102 [1986] 2 S.C.R. 38, 29 D.L.R. (4th) 1.

103 (1988), 26 Alta. L. Rev. 497.

104 *Supra,* note 57.

105 *Supra,* note 39.

106 *Supra,* note 99.

contribution and the property over which the plaintiff now claims a trust. The trust cannot be imposed over some arbitrarily selected property. This is discussed in more detail in the next note.

2. In *Rathwell*, Mr. Justice Dickson indicated that there must be a substantial and direct connection between the plaintiff's deprivation and the acquisition of the property by the defendant. He confirmed this opinion when Chief Justice in *Pettkus*. The idea is that the plaintiff is not entitled to a trust over any asset belonging to the defendant, but rather to any asset which the plaintiff's efforts helped place in the ownership of the defendant. This could have been understood to suggest that there can be no constructive trust if the plaintiff's contributions were made *after* the property was acquired by the defendant.

The point arose for decision in *Sorochan v. Sorochan*.[107] The parties were not married, but lived together for 42 years and had six children together. During their relationship they jointly farmed three quarter sections. The defendant man held title to these and had acquired them before the plaintiff woman moved in with him. She did all the domestic chores and raised the children. She also worked extensively on the farm. In fact, during an extensive period she was solely responsible for the operation of the farm, since the defendant was also a travelling salesman and was, therefore, often absent. She received no remuneration for her work. The Supreme Court held that the three requirements of unjust enrichment (an enrichment, a corresponding deprivation, and an absence of any juristic reason for the enrichment) were satisfied. The court concluded that the plaintiff was entitled to a remedy and that the remedy should be a one-third interest in the farm under a constructive trust. However, the court was met with the argument that the constructive trust can only be awarded if there is a causal connection between the deprivation and the *acquisition* of the property by the defendant. It could not be applied in this case, so it was argued, since the defendant already owned the farm when the relationship began. The Alberta Court of Appeal had accepted that argument,[108] holding that it derived from *Pettkus*. Mr. Justice Dickson, who delivered the court's judgment, said this about the argument:[109]

> It is understandable that this issue could be a source of confusion. Since the early constructive cases involved situations where there was some acquisition of property, there was a tendency to treat a particular manifestation of a general principle as the rule itself. In the same paragraph from which the Alberta Court of Appeal derived the acquisition requirement in *Pettkus*, however, one also finds articulations of the causal connection test in more general terms. It is suggested simply that there should be a "clear link between the contribution and the disputed asset".[110] The question of a connection between the deprivation and the property is further explained as "an issue of fact". That is, courts must ask whether the contribution is "sufficiently substantial and direct" to entitle the plaintiff to an interest in the property in question.
>
> In a number of cases, this more general formulation of the causal connection test has been adopted and courts have held that constructive trusts can be imposed in situations where the contribution does not relate to the acquisition of property....

[His Lordship referred to a number of cases and continued:]

---

107 *Supra,* note 103.
108 (1984), 36 Alta. L.R. (2d) 119, 44 R.F.L. (2d) 144.
109 *Supra,* note 108, at 8, 10.
110 *Supra,* note 1, at 277.

These cases reveal the need to retain flexibility in applying the constructive trust. In my view, the constructive trust remedy should not be confined to cases involving property acquisition. While it is important to require that some nexus exist between the claimant's deprivation and the property in question, the link need not always take the form of a contribution to the actual acquisition of the property. A contribution relating to the preservation, maintenance or improvement of property may also suffice. What remains primary is whether or not the services rendered have a "clear proprietary relationship", to use Professor McLeod's phrase.[111] When such a connection is present, proprietary relief may be appropriate. Such an approach will help to ensure equitable and fair relief in the myriad of familial circumstances and situations where unjust enrichment occurs. As stated in *Pettkus*:[112] "The equitable principle on which the remedy of constructive trust rests is broad and general; its purpose is to prevent unjust enrichment in whatever circumstances it occurs."

In the present case, Mary Sorochan worked on the farm for 42 years. Her labour directly and substantially contributed to the maintenance and preservation of the farm preventing asset deterioration or divestment. There is, therefore, a "clear link" between the contribution and the disputed assets.

The Supreme Court of Canada again had to consider the matter of causal connection in *Peter v. Beblow*.[113] The parties lived together for 12 years. Ms. Peter raised her own and Mr. Beblow's children, managed the house and improved the property where they lived. Both contributed financially to the household budget. When they separated, she brought an action for a constructive trust in respect of the house. The Supreme Court agreed that she had made out her claim in unjust enrichment, that a constructive trust was the appropriate remedy and that she should be awarded the house. McLachlin J. stressed the fact that there is no difference between recognizing the kinds of services provided by Ms. Peter and other kinds of contributions. Both are equally capable of supporting a claim in unjust enrichment. She also expressed the opinion that the question whether the enrichment is unjust must be considered under the third part of the test: absence of a juristic reason for the enrichment.[114]

With respect to the question of causal connection, Cory J., with whom L'Heureux-Dubé and Gonthier JJ. agreed, said:[115]

The difficulty of establishing a causal connection between unjust enrichment arising from the provision of domestic services and the property has been the subject of scholarly debate.[116] As Professor Ralph Scane put it the difficulty with looking for a causal connection in such cases is "that [the] unjust enrichment created by receipt of the benefit of [domestic] services ... seeps throughout all of the assets of the defendant".[117] Thus, the contributions which indirectly created accumulated family wealth for the parties cannot be traced to any one property. However, I do

---

111 Annotation, 42 R.F.L. (2d) 154 at 155.

112 *Supra,* note 1, at 276.

113 *Supra,* note 99.

114 *Ibid.,* at 644.

115 *Ibid.,* at 637. Note also what Cory J.A., as he then was, said on the same subject in *Murray v. Roty* (1983), 41 O.R. (2d) 705, at 711, 147 D.L.R. (3d) 438, at 444, which was seemingly approved by the Supreme Court of Canada in *Sorochan v. Sorochan, supra,* note 103, at 49.

116 See, for example, Ralph E. Scane "Relationships 'Tantamount to Spousal', Unjust Enrichment and Constructive Trusts" (1991), 70 Can. Bar Rev. 260; Keith B. Farquhar, "Causal Connection in Constructive Trusts" (1986-88), 8 E. & T. Q. 161; Berend Hovius and Timothy G. Youdan, The Law of Family Property (Toronto: Carswell, 1991); Ian Narev, "Unjust Enrichment and De Facto Relationships" (1991), 6 Auckland U.L. Rev. 504.

117 *Op. cit.,* at 289.

not think that the required link between the deprivation suffered and the property in question is as difficult to establish as it may seem.

This court has specifically recognized that indirect financial contributions to the maintenance of property will be sufficient to establish the requisite property connection for the imposition of a constructive trust. In *Pettkus v. Becker*,[118] the fact that Ms Becker paid the rent, purchased the food and clothing and looked after other living expenses, enabled Mr. Pettkus to save his entire income, a goodly amount of money which he later used to purchase property. Even though Ms Becker's financial contributions did not directly finance the purchase of the property, it was held that her indirect financial contribution was sufficient to entitle her to a proprietary interest in the property purchased by Mr. Pettkus upon the dissolution of the relationship.

It seems to me that in a family relationship the work, services and contributions provided by one of the parties need not be clearly and directly linked to a specific property. As long as there was no compensation paid for the work and services provided by one party to the family relationship then it can be inferred that their provision permitted the other party to acquire lands or to improve them. In this case the work of the appellant permitted the respondent to pay off the mortgage and, as well, to purchase a houseboat and a cabin cruiser. In the circumstances, the trial judge was justified in applying the constructive trust to the property which he felt would best redress the unjust enrichment and would treat both parties in a just and equitable manner.

However, McLachlin J., with whom La Forest, Sopinka and Iacobucci JJ. agreed, insisted that there must be a more direct connection between the contribution and the property. She said:[119]

Where a monetary award is insufficient in a family situation, this is usually related to the fact the claimant's efforts have given her a special link to the property, in which case a constructive trust arises.

For these reasons, I hold the view that in order for a constructive trust to be found, in a family case as in other cases, monetary compensation must be inadequate and there must be a link between the services rendered and the property in which the trust is claimed.

Ironically, though, the majority went on to dispose of the case in a way which seems more consistent with the minority opinion than with the majority's own view. McLachlin J. went on to say:

The parties and the Court of Appeal appear to have treated the house as a single asset rather than as part of a family enterprise. This led to the argument that the appellant could not be entitled to full ownership in the house because the respondent had contributed to its value as well. The approach I would take—and the approach I believe the trial judge implicitly to have taken—is to consider the appellant's proper share of all the family assets. This joint family venture, in effect, was no different from the farm which was the subject of the trust in *Pettkus v. Becker*. . . .
It seems clear that the maintenance of the family enterprise through work in cooking, cleaning, and landscaping helped preserve the property and saved the respondent large sums of money which he was able to use to pay off his mortgage and to purchase a houseboat and a van. The appellant, for her part, had purchased a lot with her outside earnings. All these assets may be viewed as assets of the family enterprise to which the appellant contributed substantially.
The question is whether, taking the parties' respective contributions to the family assets and the value of the assets into account, the trial judge erred in awarding the appellant a full interest in the house. In my view, the evidence is capable of supporting the conclusion that the house

---

118 *Supra*, note 1.
119 *Supra*, note 99, at 650.

reflects a fair approximation of the value of the appellant's efforts as reflected in the family assets. Accordingly, I would not disturb the award.[120]

This approach treats all of the family assets as a pool; contributions by Ms. Peter which allowed Mr. Beblow to save money and pay off the mortgage on the house were treated as contributions to the house. The house was treated as part of the pool, and not really as a separate asset; because Ms. Peter contributed to the pool, a trust over the house (which was a part of the pool that had a value approximating the value of her contributions) was justified.[121] Is this not exactly the approach for which the minority was arguing, and which the majority purported to reject?

3. Consider in this regard the situation in which the parties have orally agreed that they shall share their assets in some proportion. Consider also the situation in which the parties have not reached an oral agreement, but the plaintiff has a reasonable expectation, based on the defendant's conduct or statements, that she or he is entitled to an interest in certain property. Is the agreement or the reasonable expectation frustrated because there is no causal connection with specific property? Should it be?

In *Sorochan*, Chief Justice Dickson also referred to the argument, often made, that a reasonable expectation of the plaintiff that she or he is entitled to an interest in the property is relevant in determining whether a constructive trust should be granted.[122] He stated that a reasonable expectation of *benefit* is part and parcel of the question whether there is absence of a juristic reason for the defendant's enrichment; but when the court turns to whether restitution should be made by a money order or a constructive trust, a relevant question was whether the plaintiff had a reasonable expectation of acquiring a proprietary interest in a specific asset. Mary Sorochan did have a reasonable expectation that she would obtain an interest in Alex Sorochan's land and he was aware of her expectation.

4. Chief Justice Dickson also intimated in *Sorochan* that a constructive trust might be denied if the property has increased in value during the relationship, but the increase was solely attributable to inflation. There was, however, no evidence in the case that this was so.

5. It is, of course, possible that the property has decreased in value between the date of valuation and the date of the trial because of a downturn in the economy. Who should bear the loss in those circumstances? This is what happened in *McDonald v. McDonald*.[123] The parties had been married for almost 30 years when they separated in 1983. They had operated a tobacco farm during their marriage and the wife had contributed to the operation to such an extent as to warrant awarding her a half interest in the farm property under a constructive trust. However, she did not make the application for a constructive trust order; he did. The value of the farm had declined from $1,800,000 at valuation date to $1,647,000 at the date of trial because of the drastic decline in smoking. The court held that either the non-titled or the titled spouse can ask for a constructive trust order. Further, it held,

---

120 *Ibid.*, at 653-654.

121 For another example of this asset-pooling approach, see *Nasser v. Mayer-Nasser* (2000), 32 E.T.R. (2d) 230, 5 R.F.L. (5th) 100 (Ont. C.A.). See also *Harrison v. Kalinocha* (1994), 90 B.C.L.R. (2d) 273, 112 D.L.R. (4th) 43 (C.A.), in which the plaintiff's obtained a "constructive trust" which was really a lien over the assets of the defendant to secure a payment of $35,000, being half of the gain in value of both parties' assets during the relationship. Here the requirement of any link to particular property has effectively been dropped. Similar is *Hantel v. Hilscher* (1996), 182 A.R. 285 (Q.B.), affirmed (2000), 255 A.R. 187, 7 R.F.L. (5th) 108 (C.A.).

122 *Supra*, note 103, at 12.

123 (1988), 11 R.F.L. (3d) 321 (Ont. H.C.J.).

following *Rawluk*,[124] that the constructive trust should be imposed. In consequence, the plaintiff wife was required to share in the decrease in value of the farm.

Amsterdam v. Amsterdam[125] is to the same effect. The wife held title to the matrimonial home. It declined in value between the valuation date and the date of trial because of a downturn in the economy. The court awarded the husband a half interest in it under a constructive trust. It held that failure to do so would lead to an unjust and inequitable result.

Is a principle of unjust enrichment, which reverses unjustifiable transfers of wealth, suitable for shifting a loss from one party to another? If the idea of unjust enrichment can cover loss-shifting, it is likely to become meaningless, as every case in which the legal system intervenes could be said to be based on unjust enrichment. The technical sense of the term covers the reversal of transfers which are legally defective. On that view, a different principle is required to explain loss-shifting.

6. In *Peter v. Beblow*,[126] the minority judges would have moved the law in the direction of recognizing that the principles which govern cohabitational property disputes are different from those governing commercial cases. The majority, however, insisted that the law of unjust enrichment, including the availability of the constructive trust, is the same in cohabitational property disputes as in purely commercial cases. Note, however, the following points:

(a) As noted in note 2 above, different principles seem to apply for the availability of the trust, as far as identifying its subject matter. The majority in *Peter* resolved the case in a way that was more consistent with the minority's statement of the law than with the majority's.

(b) The courts frequently affirm that a money order is the normal remedy for an unjust enrichment, and a constructive trust is exceptional. In *LAC Minerals Ltd. v. International Corona Resources Ltd.*[127] La Forest J. stated that the constructive trust is not the appropriate remedy in the great majority of cases; a personal remedy is usually sufficient. In cohabitational property disputes, the courts also state that constructive trusts are only for unusual cases, but in fact such awards are absolutely routine and probably are awarded more often than money awards, at least where the relationship was of a substantial duration.

(c) In *Peter v. Beblow*,[128] the majority set out a requirement for a constructive trust which does not appear in commercial cases. This is that the plaintiff must have made a *substantial* contribution to the asset claimed; this is a threshold requirement, which would appear to confine plaintiffs who have made small contributions to money claims.[129]

(d) In cohabitational cases, the availability of the constructive trust is sometimes said to depend on whether the plaintiff had a reasonable expectation of acquiring a proprietary

---

124 At the Ontario Court of Appeal level: 10 R.F.L. (3d) 113.

125 (1991), 31 R.F.L. (3d) 153 (Ont. Ct, Gen Div.). See also *Salib v. Cross* (1993), 15 O.R. (3d) 521 (Gen. Div.) and the discussion in *Arndt v. Arndt* (1993), 15 O.R. (3d) 389, 107 D.L.R. (4th) 1 (C.A.) and *Harrison v. Kalinocha, supra,* note 122, at 50-51 (C.A.).

126 *Supra,* note 99.

127 *Supra,* note 57, at 51.

128 *Supra,* note 99.

129 "A minor or indirect contribution is insufficient": *ibid.*, at 621, 650. The meaning of "indirect" here is unclear, because this is stated as an additional requirement to the requirement of showing a clear link to the property claimed. The minority judges in *Peter* interpreted *Pettkus v. Becker* as a case of the award of a constructive trust over property to which the plaintiff had contributed indirectly.

interest[130] (although this was not stated as a requirement for the trust in *Peter v. Beblow*[131]). This requirement does not appear in other contexts.

(e) The possibility of imposing a "reverse constructive trust," discussed in the previous note, has never been raised except in cohabitational property disputes.

It is strongly arguable that cohabitational cases are and should be decided on different principles. They are not simply about reversing transfers of wealth, or else the focus would be on accounting for the value of benefits conferred on the other party. Rather, they are about the breakdown of intimate relationships of sharing. The cases generally (at least in longer term relationships) focus on the fair division of the remaining assets, which is not the same as reversing transfers of wealth, but is more like the kind of analysis that would apply on the breakup of a commercial partnership. This approach, unlike unjust enrichment properly so called, can certainly encompass loss sharing. In effect it is the approach now adopted by statute in every province.[132]

4. NATURE OF THE CONSTRUCTIVE TRUST

(a) Introduction

In the previous chapter we noted that, while an express trust arises because of a manifest intention on the part of its creator to establish it, and while resulting trusts are sometimes explained on the basis of presumed-in-fact intention, constructive trusts have nothing to do with intention, but arise strictly by operation of law. Various examples were there given to distinguish the three concepts and they need not be repeated here. It is now necessary to consider the nature of the constructive trust.

The constructive trust is a vehicle of equity whereby one person is required, by operation of law, to hold some property for the benefit of another. But when will a constructive trust be imposed? It is here that we encounter real difficulties, because traditionally, in Anglo-Canadian law, the constructive trust was not based upon any general theory. It was imposed in a variety of situations to redress fraud, undue influence and other reprehensible conduct on the part of the person who holds title to or has possession or control of property. It was also applied, in the absence of fraud, as a response to breach of fiduciary obligations. Indeed, until recently, the constructive trust was largely employed in Anglo-Canadian and Commonwealth law in the fiduciary context. Hence, it was used against express trustees, personal representatives, agents, corporate executives, solicitors, joint venturers and others. As a result, the constructive trust was sometimes thought of as a substantive institution, like the express trust, in which the parties stood in a fiduciary relationship and which imposed various rights and obligations upon the parties. But there were also situations in which the trust was imposed which were

---

130 *Sorochan v. Sorochan, supra,* note 103, at 12; see also *Re Burke* (1992), 104 Nfld. & P.E.I.R. 305, 329 A.P.R. 305 (Nfld. S.C.T.D.); *Treanor v. Smith* (1992), 44 R.F.L. (3d) 165 (Ont. Gen. Div.).

131 *Supra,* note 99.

132 For fuller analysis, see P. Parkinson, "Beyond *Pettkus v. Becker:* Quantifying Relief for Unjust Enrichment" (1993), 43 U.T.L.J. 217; S. Gardner, "Rethinking Family Property" (1993), 109 L.Q.R. 263.

based neither on fiduciary obligations nor on reprehensible conduct; trusts might be imposed where property was transferred by mistake, and undue influence does not necessarily constitute wrongful conduct.[133] Both mistaken transfers and those under undue influence can be seen as cases of unjust enrichment.

All trusts properly so called have the following characteristics: the trustee holds property, and owes certain kinds of obligations with respect to that particular property.[134] An express trust is one in which those obligations were voluntarily assumed by the trustee. Otherwise, the trust arises by operation of law and is either resulting or constructive. All constructive trusts, therefore, have the following features in common: the trustee holds property and owes certain kinds of obligations with respect to that particular property; they are obligations which have effects on third parties, and which were not voluntarily undertaken. But even though there are these elements common to all constructive trusts, there are also important differences among constructive trusts. In particular, the obligation owed by the defendant may come from any one of a number of sources.[135] In the law of obligations, we distinguish contract, tort, unjust enrichment; we classify obligations by their source. Some obligations arise from consent; some arise by operation of law from wrongdoing, and some arise by operation of law from unjust enrichment. Every constructive trust has at its core an obligation, and that obligation has a source, which in turn can be understood as the source of the trust. It is, therefore, possible to classify or organize constructive trusts according to the legally significant event or events which gave rise to the trust. Some constructive trusts arise to reverse unjust enrichment; some arise to effect the disgorgement of a gain which was acquired by the defendant through a wrongful act against the plaintiff. Still others arise to perfect an intention, usually an intention of the person who transferred property to the trustee. This comes very close to an express trust. This issue will be explored in the next chapter, where constructive trusts are organized in this threefold manner.[136]

In comparing the American law to the English law, many authors have contrasted the American "remedial" constructive trust to the English "institutional" view. In what follows, we shall examine this distinction. In either case, the constructive trust is a proprietary remedy. We shall also discuss when the

---

133 In other words, the plaintiff's ability to recover, or to set aside a transaction, on the basis of undue influence is arguably based on the fact that the plaintiff did not fully consent to it, rather than on any finding of bad behaviour on the part of the defendant. It is a case of unjust enrichment, in the strict sense of a legally defective transfer of wealth. See the discussion in *Goodman Estate v. Geffen*, [1991] 2 S.C.R. 353, 81 D.L.R. (4th) 211.

134 See L. Smith, "Transfers" in P. Birks and A. Pretto (eds.), *Breach of Trust* (Oxford: Hart Publishing, 2002) 111.

135 See R. Chambers, "Constructive Trusts in Canada" (1999), 37 Alta. L. Rev. 173.

136 As is noted there, this classification may not be exhaustive. Detrimental reliance can play an important role: *Banner Homes Group plc v. Luff Developments Ltd.*, [2000] Ch. 372 (C.A.). For another example, a judicial order to transfer specific property may create a constructive trust of that property, even though the order did not purport to do so: *Re Morris*, 260 F.3d 654 (6th Cir. 2001); *Mountney v. Treharne*, [2003] Ch. 135, [2002] 3 W.L.R. 1760 (C.A.). Here the source of the obligation which founds the trust is the court order.

constructive trust arises, its relationship to tracing, and the position of the trustee and the beneficiary under a constructive trust.

(b) Institutional vs. Remedial

The remedial view of the constructive trust was developed in the United States, largely as the result of pioneering work of Ames, Pound and others. They argued that one role of the trust is to prevent unjust enrichment of a party holding property, by affording specific restitution of that property to the plaintiff.[137]

For example, in a leading case, *Beatty v. Guggenheim Exploration Co.*[138] Cardozo C.J., said:

> [a] constructive trust is the formula through which the conscience of equity finds expression. When property has been acquired in such circumstances that the holder of the legal title may not in good conscience retain the beneficial interest, equity converts him into a trustee.

In *Meinhard v. Salmon*,[139] with reference specifically to trusts arising on breach of fiduciary obligations, he said:

> A constructive trust is then the remedial device through which preference of self is made subordinate to loyalty to others.

If by "remedial," it is only meant to underline that the trust arises by operation of law and not by the intention of the trustee, then most every constructive trust all over the world is remedial; so this does not help us to understand the difference between "remedial" and "institutional."

Pound "defined" the constructive trust as follows:[140]

> A group of cases involving constructive trusts invite consideration of what such a "trust" really is. An express trust is a substantive institution. Constructive trust, on the other hand, is purely a remedial institution. As the chancellor acted *in personam*, one of the most effective remedial expedients at his command was to treat a defendant as if he were a trustee and put pressure upon his person to compel him to act accordingly. Thus constructive trust could be used in a variety of situations, sometimes to provide a remedy better suited to the circumstances of the particular case, where the suit was founded on another theory, as in cases of reformation, of specific performance, of fraudulent conveyance, and of what the civilian would call exclusion of unworthy heirs, and sometimes to develop a new field of equitable interposition, as in what we have come to think the typical case of constructive trust, namely, specific restitution of a received benefit in order to prevent unjust enrichment.

American commentators often say, building on this kind of observation, that a constructive trust is not "really" a trust at all. It is a totally different, *sui generis*

---

137 See, *e.g.*, Roscoe Pound, "The Progress of the Law, 1918-19, Equity" (1920), 33 Harv. L. Rev. 420 at 421; Ames, "Following Misappropriated Property" (1906), 19 Harv. L. Rev. 511. But neither of them argued that all constructive trusts reverse what would otherwise be an unjust enrichment. See the extract from Pound in the text immediately below.

138 (1919), 225 N.Y. 380 at 386, 122 N.E. 378 (Ct. Apps.).

139 (1928), 249 N.Y. 458 at 467, 164 N.E. 545 (Ct. Apps.).

140 *Loc. cit.*

concept, which bears no relation to the express trust.[141] But it is not clear what this might mean. There is one clear difference. An express trust imports a fiduciary relationship; a constructive trust does not[142] (even though it may be imposed, *inter alia*, in circumstances involving a fiduciary relationship). This may be part of what is meant by the contrast between "remedial" and "institutional" constructive trusts. But Commonwealth law agrees with this. It does not take the position that a person who holds property subject to a constructive trust owes fiduciary obligations of loyalty; such duties must be assumed voluntarily.[143] In the same way, a person who holds property subject to a constructive trust does not owe other obligations which an express trustee owes, such as duties of management. The duty of a person who holds property subject to a constructive trust is simply to convey the property, either to the beneficiary or to a properly appointed trustee.[144]

So one could understand the claim that a constructive trust is not a trust in this way: a trust is only properly called a trust where the trustee owes the fiduciary duties of loyalty, or other personal duties of trusteeship.[145] But most commentators, including in the U.S. where the term "constructive trust" is still used, do not confine the word "trust" to such situations. The essence of the trust idea is the proprietary protection of the obligations which the trustee owes to the beneficiary in relation to the trust property.[146] It is for this reason that the constructive trust has one crucial feature in common with the express trust, that it gives the beneficiary priority in the bankruptcy of the trustee. This seems to be the basis on which we can say that a constructive trust *is* a trust, both in the U.S. and elsewhere.

Another way in which we might try to make sense of the distinction between "remedial" and "institutional" constructive trusts is on the basis that a remedial trust is one that arises according to a judicial discretion, while an institutional one arises by operation of law from defined factual circumstances, as the facts occur. To take an analogy, a right to damages arises by operation of law upon the negligent or deliberate infliction of bodily injury; the judge's role is essentially declaratory. On the other hand, according to a traditional view of equitable remedies, a decree of specific performance is different. A promisee has a *right* to

---

141 Scott, §462.1.

142 *Restatement, Restitution*, §160, comment *a*.

143 *Lonhro plc v. Fayed (No. 2)*,[1992] 1 W.L.R. 1, 12; R. Chambers, *Resulting Trusts* (Oxford: Clarendon Press, 1997), 194-200; L. Smith, "Constructive Fiduciaries?" in P. Birks, ed., *Privacy and Loyalty* (Oxford: Clarendon Press, 1997) 249, 263-267.

144 R.H. Maudsley, "Constructive Trusts" (1977), 28 N.I.L.R. 123 at 124.

145 It may be possible to understand the speech of Lord Browne-Wilkinson in *Westdeutsche Landesbank Girozentrale v. Islington L.B.C.*, [1996] A.C. 669 (H.L.) as making this terminological choice.

146 *Hardoon v. Belilios*, [1901] A.C. 118, 123 (P.C.): "All that is necessary to establish the relation of trustee and cestui que trust is to prove that the legal title was in the plaintiff and the equitable title in the defendant."; *Guerin v Canada* [1984] 2 S.C.R. 335, 13 D.L.R. (4th) 321, 361: *per* Wilson J.: "A trust arises, as I understand it, whenever a person is compelled in equity to hold property over which he has control for the benefit of others (the beneficiaries) in such a way that the benefit of the property accrues not to the trustee, but to the beneficiaries."; P. Millett, "Restitution and Constructive Trusts" in in W. Cornish *et al.*, eds, *Restitution: Past, Present and Future* (Oxford: Hart, 1998) 199 at 204.

compensatory damages for breach of contract; if he or she seeks specific performance, there is only a hope that the judge will exercise the discretion accordingly. One might conclude, therefore, that an institutional constructive trust is like a right to damages, while a remedial constructive trust is like a decree of specific performance. As we noted above, the status of wide judicial discretion is contested.[147] And even in the U.S., the courts do not insist that constructive trusts are discretionary.[148]

(c) The Variety of Constructive Trusts

Because the constructive trust came to be regarded as a remedy in the United States, its treatment was included in the *Restatement of Restitution*,[149] rather than in the *Restatement of Trusts*,[150] although the latter does deal with constructive trusts arising out of express trusts. The *Restatement of Restitution* defines the circumstances under which a constructive trust arises as follows:[151]

> Where a person holding title to property is subject to an equitable duty to convey it to another on the ground that he would be unjustly enriched if he were permitted to retain it, a constructive trust arises.

Further, Professor Scott says:[152]

> When a person holds the title to property which he is under an obligation to convey to another, and when that obligation does not arise merely because he has voluntarily assumed it, he is said to hold the property on a constructive trust for the other and he is called a constructive trustee of the property. He is not compelled to convey the property because he is a constructive trustee; it is because he can be compelled to convey it that he is a constructive trustee.

These formulations make it clear that constructive trusts can arise for different reasons. If a person has an obligation, relating to specific property, to hold the property for the benefit of another person, there will be a trust. If that obligation was voluntarily undertaken, the trust is express; otherwise, it is resulting or constructive. The obligation to convey property, which makes the trust, *may* arise from unjust enrichment, as in the case of a mistaken payment.[153] But unjust

---

147 See for example P. Birks, "Rights, Wrongs and Remedies" (2000), 20 O.J.L.S. 1; D.W.M. Waters, "Liability and Remedy: An Adjustable Relationship" (2001), 64 Sask. L. Rev. 429; S. Evans, "Defending Discretionary Remedialism" (2001), 23 Sydney L.R. 463.

148 See *Re Morris,* 260 F.3d 654 (6th Cir. 2001) at 668, stressing that a constructive trust, to be effective in bankruptcy, must be one which arises from the facts.

149 American Law Institute, *Restatement of the Law of Restitution: Quasi-Contracts and Constructive Trusts* (St. Paul: American Law Institute Publishers, 1937).

150 American Law Institute, *Restatement of the Law of Trusts* (St. Paul: American Law Institute Publishers, 1936). See now American Law Institute, *Restatement of the Law, Second, Trusts 2nd* (St. Paul: American Law Institute Publishers, 1959), ("*Restatement, Trusts 2d*"). See also Austin Wakeman Scott, "Constructive Trusts" (1955), 71 L.Q. Rev. 39 at 41.

151 *Restatement, Restitution*, §160, quoted in *Knox v. Knox*, 222 Minn. 477, 25 N.W. 2d 255 (1946).

152 Scott, §462.

153 *Chase Manhattan Bank N.A. v. Israel-British Bank (London) Ltd., supra*, note 89, extracted in the next chapter.

enrichment is not the only explanation for trusts arising by operation of law. Obligations to hold specific property for the benefit of another, which will form the basis of a constructive trust of that property, may arise for other reasons. Examples include breaches of fiduciary obligation;[154] the perfection of intention;[155] detrimental reliance;[156] and even a court judgment ordering the transfer of property, which order does not expressly impose a trust.[157] In the next chapter, constructive trusts are organized by the principal legal events which create them, namely unjust enrichment, wrongful gains, and the perfection of intention.

Just because Canadian courts have recognized that constructive trusts may arise to reverse unjust enrichments, it does not follow that every other kind of constructive trust has ceased to exist. This argument has found favour in some of the cases. In *Rawluk v. Rawluk*[158] the issue was whether the doctrine of the constructive trust had survived the enactment of the *Family Law Act*[159] and, if it had, whether a constructive trust could be imposed. The constructive trust that was being discussed was one to reverse unjust enrichment, and that is what the majority imposed. However, McLachlin J., speaking for the minority, discussed the historical development of the constructive trust. Ultimately, she concluded that it was unnecessary to decide whether any other constructive trust survived the introduction of the remedial constructive trust in Canada. In *Atlas Cabinets & Furniture Ltd. v. National Trust Co. Ltd.*,[160] Lambert J.A. strongly supported the argument that the traditional constructive trust still existed.

In *Soulos v. Korkontzilas* the Supreme Court of Canada accepted the argument.

SOULOS v. KORKONTZILAS

[1997] 2 S.C.R. 217, 146 D.L.R. (4th) 214, 9 R.P.R. (3d) 1, 17 E.T.R. (2d) 89, 212 N.R. 1, 1997 CarswellOnt 1489, [1997] S.C.J. No. 52, 1997 CarswellOnt 1490, 246 C.B.R. (3d) 1, 100 O.A.C. 241
Supreme Court of Canada

A real estate broker acted as agent for a purchaser of commercial property and made an offer on certain property on behalf of the purchaser. The owner signed back the offer, but the purchaser rejected the counter-offer. The owner told the broker the price he would accept, but the broker did not tell the purchaser. Rather, he arranged to purchase the property in his wife's name. The purchaser then sued, claiming damages for breach of fiduciary duty. In the alternative he

---

154 *Soulos v. Korkontzilas, supra,* note 2. Breaches of confidence, and other wrongs, may also create constructive trusts, as discussed in the following chapter.
155 This is developed in the next chapter as the explanation for a wide range of constructive trusts.
156 For example, *Banner Homes Group plc v. Luff Developments Ltd.,* [2000] Ch. 372, [2000] 2 All E.R. 117 (C.A.).
157 *Re Morris, supra,* note 137; *Mountney v. Treharne, supra,* note 137.
158 *Supra,* note 39.
159 By S.O. 1986, c. 4; now R.S.O. 1990, c. F.3.
160 (1990), 68 D.L.R. (4th) 161 at 169-70 (B.C.C.A.).

sought a declaration that the broker's wife held the property upon a constructive trust for him. When the value of the property dropped, he abandoned his claim for damages. The purchaser claimed that the property had special value to him, because one of the tenants was a bank and his ethnic community would attach special significance to the fact that he would be the landlord of a bank. There was a clear breach of fiduciary duty and Anderson J., the trial judge, so found.[161] However, the trial judge denied the constructive trust, holding that it is an alternative to damages and the purchaser had not suffered damages. The Ontario Court of Appeal, by a majority, allowed the purchaser's appeal.[162] The broker appealed to the Supreme Court of Canada.

MCLACHLIN J.:

. . .

[13] The difference between the trial judge and the majority in the Court of Appeal may be summarized as follows. The trial judge took the view that in the absence of established loss, Mr. Soulos had no action. To grant the remedy of constructive trust in the absence of loss would be "simply disproportionate and inappropriate," in his view. The majority in the Court of Appeal, by contrast, took a broader view of when a constructive trust could apply. It held that a constructive trust requiring reconveyance of the property could arise in the absence of an established loss in order to condemn the agent's improper act and maintain the bond of trust underlying the real estate industry and hence the "integrity of the laws" which a court of equity supervises.

[14] The appeal thus presents two different views of the function and ambit of the constructive trust. One view sees the constructive trust exclusively as a remedy for clearly established loss. On this view, a constructive trust can arise only where there has been "enrichment" of the defendant and corresponding "deprivation" of the plaintiff. The other view, while not denying that the constructive trust may appropriately apply to prevent unjust enrichment, does not confine it to that role. On this view, the constructive trust may apply absent an established loss to condemn a wrongful act and maintain the integrity of the relationships of trust which underlie many of our industries and institutions.

[15] It is my view that the second, broader approach to constructive trust should prevail. This approach best accords with the history of the doctrine of constructive trust, the theory underlying the constructive trust, and the purposes which the constructive trust serves in our legal system.

V

[16] The appellants argue that this court has adopted a view of constructive

---

161 (1991), 4 O.R. (3d) 51 (Gen. Div.), additional reasons (1991), 19 R.P.R. (2d) 205, 4 O.R. (3d) 51 at 71, 2 C.P.C. (3d) 70 (Gen. Div.).
162 (1995), 25 O.R. (3d) 257, 126 D.L.R. (4th) 637, 47 R.P.R. (2d) 221, 84 O.A.C. 390 (C.A.).

trust based exclusively on unjust enrichment in cases such as *Pettkus v. Becker*.[163] Therefore, they argue, a constructive trust cannot be imposed in cases like this where the plaintiff can demonstrate no deprivation and corresponding enrichment of the defendant.

[17] The history of the law of constructive trust does not support this view. Rather, it suggests that the constructive trust is an ancient and eclectic institution imposed by law not only to remedy unjust enrichment, but to hold persons in different situations to high standards of trust and probity and prevent them from retaining property which in "good conscience" they should not be permitted to retain. This served the end, not only of doing justice in the case before the court, but of protecting relationships of trust and the institutions that depend on these relationships. These goals were accomplished by treating the person holding the property as a trustee of it for the wronged person's benefit, even though there was no true trust created by intention. In England, the trust thus created was thought of as a real or "institutional" trust. In the United States and recently in Canada, jurisprudence speaks of the availability of the constructive trust as a remedy; hence, the remedial constructive trust.

[18] While specific situations attracting a constructive trust have been identified, the older English jurisprudence offers no satisfactory limiting or unifying conceptual theory for the constructive trust. As D.W.M. Waters puts it,[164] the constructive trust "was never any more than a convenient and available language medium through which . . . the obligations of parties might be expressed or determined." The constructive trust was used in English law "to link together a number of disparate situations . . . on the basis that the obligations imposed by law in these situations might in some way be likened to the obligations which were imposed upon an express trustee."[165]

[19] The situations in which a constructive trust was recognized in England include constructive trusts arising on breach of a fiduciary relationship, as well as trusts imposed to prevent the absence of writing from depriving a person of proprietary rights, to prevent a purchaser with notice from fraudulently retaining trust properties, and to enforce secret trusts and mutual wills.[166] The fiduciary relationship underlies much of the English law of constructive trust. As Waters writes:[167] "the fiduciary relationship is clearly wed to the constructive trust over the whole, or little short of the whole, of the trust's operation." At the same time, not all breaches of fiduciary relationships give rise to a constructive trust. As L.S. Sealy states:[168]

---

163 *Supra*, note 1.

164 D.W.M. Waters, *The Constructive Trust: The Case for a New Approach in English Law* (London: University of London, Athlone Press, 1964), at 39.

165 John L. Dewar, "The Development of the Remedial Constructive Trust" (1982-84), 6 E. & T. Q. 312, at 317, citing Waters, *supra*.

166 See Dewar, *ibid.*, at 334.

167 *Supra*, note 165, at 33.

168 L.S. Sealy, "Fiduciary Relationships," [1962] Camb. L.J. 69, at 73 (emphasis in original).

The word "fiduciary," we find, is *not* definitive of a single class of relationships to which a fixed set of rules and principles apply. Each equitable remedy is available only in a limited number of fiduciary situations; and the mere statement that John is in a fiduciary relationship towards me means no more than that in some respects his position is trustee-like; it does not warrant the inference that any particular fiduciary principle or remedy can be applied.

Nor does the absence of a classic fiduciary relationship necessarily preclude a finding of a constructive trust; the wrongful nature of an act may be sufficient to constitute breach of a trust-like duty.[169]

[20] Canadian courts have never abandoned the principles of constructive trust developed in England. They have, however, modified them. Most notably, Canadian courts in recent decades have developed the constructive trust as a remedy for unjust enrichment. It is now established that a constructive trust may be imposed in the absence of wrongful conduct like breach of fiduciary duty, where three elements are present: (1) the enrichment of the defendant; (2) the corresponding deprivation of the plaintiff; and (3) the absence of a juristic reason for the enrichment.[170]

[21] This court's assertion that a remedial constructive trust lies to prevent unjust enrichment in cases such as *Pettkus v. Becker* should not be taken as expunging from Canadian law the constructive trust in other circumstances where its availability has long been recognized. The language used makes no such claim. A.J. McClean[171] describes the ratio of *Pettkus v. Becker* as "a modest enough proposition." He goes on: "It would be wrong . . . to read it as one would read the language of a statute and limit further development of the law."

[22] Other scholars agree that the constructive trust as a remedy for unjust enrichment does not negate a finding of a constructive trust in other situations. David M. Paciocco states:[172] "the constructive trust that is used to remedy unjust enrichment must be distinguished from the other types of constructive trusts known to Canadian law prior to 1980." Paciocco asserts that unjust enrichment is not a necessary condition of a constructive trust:[173]

. . . in the largest traditional category, the fiduciary constructive trust, there need be no deprivation experienced by the particular plaintiff. The constructive trust is imposed to raise the morality of the marketplace generally, with the beneficiaries of some of these trusts receiving what can only be described as a windfall.

[23] Dewar holds a similar view:[174]

While it is unlikely that Canadian courts will abandon the learning and the classifications which have grown up in connection with the English constructive trust, it is submitted that the adoption

---

169 See Dewar, *supra*, note 166, at 322-323.

170 *Pettkus v. Becker, supra*, note 1.

171 "Constructive and Resulting Trusts — Unjust Enrichment in a Common Law Relationship — *Pettkus v. Becker*" (1982), 16 U.B.C.L. Rev. 156 at 170.

172 "The Remedial Constructive Trust: A Principled Basis for Priorities over Creditors" (1989), 68 Can. Bar Rev. 315 at 318.

173 *Ibid.*, at 320.

174 *Supra*, note 173, at 332.

of the American style constructive trust by the Supreme Court of Canada in *Pettkus v. Becker* will profoundly influence the future development of Canadian trust law.

Dewar goes on to state:[175] "In English and Canadian law there is no general agreement as to precisely which situations give rise to a constructive trust, although there are certain general categories of cases in which it is agreed that a constructive trust does arise." One of these is to correct fraudulent or disloyal conduct.

[24] M.M. Litman[176] sees unjust enrichment as a useful tool in rationalizing the traditional categories of constructive trust. Nevertheless he opines that it would be a "significant error" to simply ignore the traditional principles of constructive trust. He cites a number of Canadian cases subsequent to *Pettkus v. Becker*,[177] which impose constructive trusts for wrongful acquisition of property, even in the absence of unjust enrichment and correlative deprivation, and concludes that the constructive trust "cannot always be explained by the unjust enrichment model of constructive trust."[178] In sum, the old English law remains part of contemporary Canadian law and guides its development. As La Forest J.A. (as he then was) states in *White v. Central Trust Co.*,[179] cited by Litman,[180] the courts "will not venture far onto an uncharted sea when they can administer justice from a safe berth."

[25] I conclude that the law of constructive trust in the common law provinces of Canada embraces the situations in which English courts of equity traditionally found a constructive trust as well as the situations of unjust enrichment recognized in recent Canadian jurisprudence.

VI

[26] Various principles have been proposed to unify the situations in which the English law found constructive trust. . . . Goff and . . . Jones,[181] suggest that unjust enrichment is such a theme. However, unless "enrichment" is interpreted very broadly to extend beyond pecuniary claims, it does not explain all situations in which the constructive trust has been applied. As McClean states:[182] "however satisfactory [the unjust enrichment theory] may be for other aspects of the law of restitution, it may not be wide enough to cover all types of constructive trust." McClean goes on to note the situation raised by this appeal: "In some cases, where such a trust is imposed the trustee may not have obtained any benefit at all; this could be the case, for example, when a person is held to be a trustee de

---

175 *Supra*, note 166, at 332-333.
176 "The Emergence of Unjust Enrichment as a Cause of Action and the Remedy of Constructive Trust" (1988), 26 Alta. L. Rev. 407 at 414.
177 *Supra*, note 164.
178 *Ibid.*, at 416.
179 (1984), 17 E.T.R. 78 at 90, 7 D.L.R. (4th) 236, 54 N.B.R. (2d) 293 (C.A.).
180 *Supra*, note 177.
181 Robert Goff and Gareth Jones, The Law of Restitution, 3rd ed. (London, Sweet & Maxwell, 1986), at 61.
182 *Supra*, note 172, at 168.

son tort. A plaintiff may not always have suffered a loss." McClean concludes:[183] "Unjust enrichment may not, therefore, satisfactorily explain all types of restitutionary claims."

[27] McClean, among others, regards the most satisfactory underpinning for unjust enrichment to be the concept of "good conscience" which lies at "the very foundation of equitable jurisdiction":[184]

> "Safe conscience" and "natural justice and equity" were two of the criteria referred to by Lord Mansfield in *Moses v. MacFerlan*[185] in dealing with an action for money had and received, the prototype of a common law restitutionary claim. "Good conscience" has a sound basis in equity, some basis in common law, and is wide enough to encompass constructive trusts where the defendant has not obtained a benefit or where the plaintiff has not suffered a loss. It is, therefore, as good as, or perhaps a better, foundation for the law of restitution than is unjust enrichment.

[28] Other scholars agree with McClean that good conscience may provide a useful way of unifying the different forms of constructive trust. Litman adverts to the "natural justice and equity" or "good conscience" trust "which operates as a remedy for wrongs which are broader in concept than unjust enrichment" and goes on to state that this may be viewed as the underpinning of the various institutional trusts as well as the unjust enrichment restitutionary constructive trust.[186]

[29] Good conscience as the unifying concept underlying constructive trust has attracted the support of many jurists. Edmund Davies L.J. suggested that the concept of a "want of probity" in the person upon whom the constructive trust is imposed provides "a useful touchstone in considering circumstances said to give rise to constructive trusts."[187] Cardozo J. similarly endorsed the unifying theme of good conscience in *Beatty v. Guggenheim Exploration Co.*:[188]

> A constructive trust is the formula through which the conscience of equity finds expression. *When property has been acquired in such circumstances that the holder of the legal title may not in good conscience retain the beneficial interest, equity converts him into a trustee.*

[30] Lord Denning M.R. expressed similar views in a series of cases applying the constructive trust as a remedy for wrong-doing.[189] In *Binions [v. Evans]*,[190] referring to the statement by Cardozo J.,[191] Denning M.R. stated that the court would impose a constructive trust "for the simple reason that it would be utterly inequitable for the plaintiffs to turn the defendant out contrary to the stipulation

---

183 *Ibid.*, at 168-169.
184 *Ibid.*, at 169.
185 *Supra*, note 22.
186 *Supra*, note 177, at 415-416.
187 *Carl Zeiss Stiftung v. Herbert Smith & Co. (No. 2)* (1968), [1969] 2 All E.R. 367, [1969] 2 Ch. 276 (C.A.).
188 (1919), 122 N.E. 378 at 380, 225 N.Y. 380 (emphasis added).
189 See *Neale v. Willis* (1968), 19 P. & C.R. 836 (C.A.); *Binions v. Evans*, [1972] Ch. 359, [1972] 2 All E.R. 70 (C.A.); *Hussey v. Palmer*, [1972 1 W.L.R. 1286, [1972] 3 All E.R. 744 (C.A.).
190 *Ibid.*
191 *Binions, ibid.*

subject to which they took the premises."[192] In *Hussey [v. Palmer]*,[193] he said the following of the constructive trust:[194] "By whatever name it is described, it is a trust imposed by law whenever justice and good conscience require it."

[31] Many English scholars have questioned Lord Denning's expansive statements on constructive trust. Nevertheless, he is not alone: Bingham J. similarly referred to good conscience as the basis for equitable intervention in *Neste Oy v. Lloyd's Bank Plc*.[195]

[32] The New Zealand Court of Appeal also appears to have accepted good conscience as the basis for imposing a constructive trust in *Elders Pastoral Ltd. v. Bank of New Zealand*,[196] cited the following passage from Bingham J.'s reasons in *Neste Oy*:[197]

> Given the situation of [the defendants] when the last payment was received, any reasonable and honest directors of that company (or the actual directors had they known of it) would, I feel sure, have arranged for the repayment of that sum to the plaintiffs without hesitation or delay. It would have seemed little short of sharp practice for [the defendants] to take any benefit from the payment, and it would have seemed contrary to any ordinary notion of fairness that the general body of creditors should profit from the accident of a payment made at a time when there was bound to be a total failure of consideration. Of course it is true that insolvency always causes loss and perfect fairness is unattainable. The bank, and other creditors, have their legitimate claims. *It nonetheless seems to me that at the time of its receipt [the defendants] could not in good conscience retain this payment and that accordingly a constructive trust is to be inferred.*

Cooke P. concluded simply:[198] "I do not think that in conscience the stock agents can retain this money." Elders has been taken to stand for the proposition that even in the absence of a fiduciary relationship or unjust enrichment, conduct contrary to good conscience may give rise to a remedial constructive trust.[199] Although the Judicial Committee of the Privy Council rejected the creation of a constructive trust on grounds of good conscience in *Re Goldcorp Exchange Ltd.*,[200] the fact remains that good conscience is a theme underlying constructive trust from its earliest times.

[33] Good conscience addresses not only fairness between the parties before the court, but the larger public concern of the courts to maintain the integrity of institutions like fiduciary relationships which the courts of equity supervised. As La Forest J. states in *Hodgkinson v. Simms*:[201]

---

192 *Ibid.*, at 368.
193 *Ibid.*
194 *Hussey*, *supra*, note 189, at 1289-1290.
195 [1983] 2 Lloyd's Rep. 658 (C.A.).
196 [1989] 2 N.Z.L.R. 180. Cooke P., at 185-186.
197 *Supra*, note 196, at 666 (emphasis added).
198 In *Elders Pastoral*, *supra*, note 197, at 186.
199 See *Mogal Corp. v. Australasia Investment Co. (In Liquidation)* (1990), 3 N.Z.B.L.C. 101,783.; John Dixon, "The Remedial Constructive Trust Based on Unconscionability in the New Zealand Commercial Environment" (1995), 7 Auck. U.L. Rev. 147, at 157-158.
200 [1994] 2 All E.R. 806.
201 [1994] 3 S.C.R. 377 at 453, 117 D.L.R. (4th) 161, [1994] 9 W.W.R. 609, 97 B.C.L.R. (2d) 1, 5 E.T.R. (2d) 1, 171 N.R. 245.

The law of fiduciary duties has always contained within it an element of deterrence. This can be seen as early as *Keech [v. Sandford . . .].*[202] In this way the law is able to monitor a given relationship society views as socially useful while avoiding the necessity of formal regulation that may tend to hamper its social utility.

The constructive trust imposed for breach of fiduciary relationship thus serves not only to do the justice between the parties that good conscience requires, but to hold fiduciaries and people in positions of trust to the high standards of trust and probity that commercial and other social institutions require if they are to function effectively.

[34] It thus emerges that a constructive trust may be imposed where good conscience so requires. The inquiry into good conscience is informed by the situations where constructive trusts have been recognized in the past. It is also informed by the dual reasons for which constructive trusts have traditionally been imposed: to do justice between the parties and to maintain the integrity of institutions dependent on trust-like relationships. Finally, it is informed by the absence of an indication that a constructive trust would have an unfair or unjust effect on the defendant or third parties, matters which equity has always taken into account. Equitable remedies are flexible; their award is based on what is just in all the circumstances of the case.

[35] Good conscience as a common concept unifying the various instances in which a constructive trust may be found has the disadvantage of being very general. But any concept capable of embracing the diverse circumstances in which a constructive trust may be imposed must, of necessity, be general. Particularity is found in the situations in which judges in the past have found constructive trusts. A judge faced with a claim for a constructive trust will have regard not merely to what might seem "fair" in a general sense, but to other situations where courts have found a constructive trust. The goal is but a reasoned, incremental development of the law on a case-by-case basis.

[36] The situations which the judge may consider in deciding whether good conscience requires imposition of a constructive trust may be seen as falling into two general categories. The first category concerns property obtained by a wrongful act of the defendant, notably breach of fiduciary obligation or breach of duty of loyalty. The traditional English institutional trusts largely fall under but may not exhaust (at least in Canada) this category. The second category concerns situations where the defendant has not acted wrongfully in obtaining the property, but where he would be unjustly enriched to the plaintiff's detriment by being permitted to keep the property for himself. The two categories are not mutually exclusive. Often wrongful acquisition of property will be associated with unjust enrichment, and vice versa. However, either situation alone may be sufficient to justify imposition of a constructive trust.

[37] In England the law has yet to formally recognize the remedial constructive trust for unjust enrichment, although many of Lord Denning's pronounce-

---

202 (1726), Sel. Cas. t. King 61, 25 E.R. 223 (Ch. Div.). See also *Canadian Aero Services Ltd. v. O'Malley*, [1974] S.C.R. 592 at 607, 610, 40 D.L.R. (3d) 371, 11 C.P.R. (2d) 206; *Canson Enterprises Ltd. v. Boughton & Co. supra*, note 71, at 547, *per* McLachlin J.

ments pointed in this direction. The courts do, however, find constructive trusts in circumstances similar to those at bar. Equity traditionally recognized the appropriateness of a constructive trust for breach of duty of loyalty *simpliciter*. The English law is summarized by Goff and Jones:[203]

> A fiduciary may abuse his position of trust by diverting a contract, purchase or other opportunity from his beneficiary to himself. If he does so, he is deemed to hold that contract, purchase, or opportunity on trust for the beneficiary.

Peter Birks[204] agrees. He suggests that cases of conflict of interest not infrequently may give rise to constructive trust, absent unjust enrichment. Birks distinguishes between anti-enrichment wrongs and anti-harm wrongs.[205] A fiduciary acting in conflict of interest represents a risk of actual or potential harm, even though his misconduct may not always enrich him. A constructive trust may accordingly be ordered.

[38] Both categories of constructive trust are recognized in the United States; although unjust enrichment is sometimes cited as the rationale for the constructive trust in the U.S., in fact its courts recognize the availability of constructive trust to require the return of property acquired by wrongful act absent unjust enrichment of the defendant and reciprocal deprivation of the plaintiff. Thus the authors of *Scott on Trusts*[206] state that the constructive trust "is available where property is obtained by mistake or by fraud or by other wrong." Or as Cardozo C.J. put it, "[a] constructive trust is, then, the remedial device through which preference of self is made subordinate to loyalty to others."[207] *Scott on Trusts*,[208] states that there are cases "in which a constructive trust is enforced against a defendant, although the loss to the plaintiff is less than the gain to the defendant or, indeed, where there is no loss to the plaintiff."

[39] Canadian courts also recognize the availability of constructive trusts for both wrongful acquisition of property and unjust enrichment. Applying the English law, they have long found constructive trusts as a consequence of wrongful acquisition of property, for example, by fraud or breach of fiduciary duty. More recently, Canadian courts have recognized the availability of the American-style remedial constructive trust in cases of unjust enrichment.[209] However, since *Pettkus v. Becker* Canadian courts have continued to find constructive trusts where property has been wrongfully acquired, even in the absence of unjust enrichment. While such cases appear infrequently since few choose to litigate absent pecuniary loss, they are not rare.

---

203 *The Law of Restitution*, 3rd ed., *supra*, note 182, at 643.
204 *An Introduction to the Law of Restitution* (Oxford: Clarendon Press, 1985), at 330, 338-343.
205 *Ibid.*, at 340.
206 3rd ed. (Boston: Little, Brown, 1967), vol. 5, at 3410.
207 *Meinhard v. Salmon* (1928), 164 N.E. 545 at 548, 62 A.L.R. 1, cited in *Scott on Trusts*, *supra*, at 3412.
208 *Supra*, note 207, at 3418.
209 *Pettkus v. Becker*, *supra*, note 1.

[40] Litman notes[210] that in "the post-*Pettkus v. Becker* era there are numerous cases where courts have used the institutional constructive trust without adverting to or relying on unjust enrichment." The imposition of a constructive trust in these cases is justified not on grounds of unjust enrichment, but on the ground that the defendant's wrongful act requires him to restore the property thus obtained to the plaintiff.

[41] Thus in *Ontario (Wheat Producers' Marketing Board) v. Royal Bank*,[211] a constructive trust was imposed on a bank which received money with actual knowledge that it belonged to someone other than the depositor.

[42] Again, in *MacMillan Bloedel Ltd. v. Binstead*,[212] a constructive trust was imposed on individuals who knowingly participated in a breach of fiduciary duty despite a finding that unjust enrichment would not warrant the imposition of a trust because the plaintiff company could not be said to have suffered a loss or deprivation since its own policy precluded it from receiving the profits. Dohm J. (as he then was) stated that the constructive trust was required "not to balance the equities but to ensure that trustees and fiduciaries remain faithful and that those who assist them in the breaches of their duty are called to account."[213]

[43] I conclude that in Canada, under the broad umbrella of good conscience, constructive trusts are recognized both for wrongful acts like fraud and breach of duty of loyalty, as well as to remedy unjust enrichment and corresponding deprivation. While cases often involve both a wrongful act and unjust enrichment, constructive trusts may be imposed on either ground: where there is a wrongful act but no unjust enrichment and corresponding deprivation; or where there is an unconscionable unjust enrichment in the absence of a wrongful act, as in *Pettkus v. Becker*.[214] Within these two broad categories, there is room for the law of constructive trust to develop and for greater precision to be attained, as time and experience may dictate.

[44] The process suggested is aptly summarized by McClean:[215]

> The law [of constructive trust] may now be at a stage where it can distill from the specific examples a few general principles, and then, by analogy to the specific examples and within the ambit of the general principle, create new heads of liability. That, it is suggested, is not asking the courts to embark on too dangerous a task, or indeed on a novel task. In large measure it is the way that the common law has always developed.

VII

[45] In *Pettkus v. Becker*[216] this court explored the prerequisites for a constructive trust based on unjust enrichment. This case requires us to explore the prerequisites for a constructive trust based on wrongful conduct. Extrapolating

---

210 *Supra*, note 177, at 416.
211 (1984), 9 D.L.R. (4th) 729, 46 O.R. (2d) 362, 4 O.A.C. 391 (C.A.).
212 (1983), 14 E.T.R. 269, 22 B.L.R. 255 (S.C.).
213 *Ibid.*, at 302.
214 *Supra.*, note 1.
215 *Ibid.*, at 167-170.
216 *Ibid.*

from the cases where courts of equity have imposed constructive trusts for wrongful conduct, and from a discussion of the criteria considered in an essay by Roy Goode[217] I would identify four conditions which generally should be satisfied:

(1) The defendant must have been under an equitable obligation, that is, an obligation of the type that courts of equity have enforced, in relation to the activities giving rise to the assets in his hands;

(2) The assets in the hands of the defendant must be shown to have resulted from deemed or actual agency activities of the defendant in breach of his equitable obligation to the plaintiff;

(3) The plaintiff must show a legitimate reason for seeking a proprietary remedy, either personal or related to the need to ensure that others like the defendant remain faithful to their duties; and

(4) There must be no factors which would render imposition of a constructive trust unjust in all the circumstances of the case; *e.g.*, the interests of intervening creditors must be protected.

VIII

[46] Applying this test to the case before us, I conclude that Mr. Korkontzilas' breach of his duty of loyalty sufficed to engage the conscience of the court and support a finding of constructive trust for the following reasons.

[47] First, Mr. Korkontzilas was under an equitable obligation in relation to the property at issue. His failure to pass on to his client the information he obtained on his client's behalf as to the price the vendor would accept on the property and his use of that information to purchase the property instead for himself constituted breach of his equitable duty of loyalty. He allowed his own interests to conflict with those of his client. He acquired the property wrongfully, in flagrant and inexcusable breach of his duty of loyalty to Mr. Soulos. This is the sort of situation which courts of equity, in Canada and elsewhere, have traditionally treated as involving an equitable duty, breach of which may give rise to a constructive trust, even in the absence of unjust enrichment.

[48] Second, the assets in the hands of Mr. Korkontzilas resulted from his agency activities in breach of his equitable obligation to the plaintiff. His acquisition of the property was a direct result of his breach of his duty of loyalty to his client, Mr. Soulos.

[49] Third, while Mr. Korkontzilas was not monetarily enriched by his wrongful acquisition of the property, ample reasons exist for equity to impose a constructive trust. Mr. Soulos argues that a constructive trust is required to remedy the deprivation he suffered because of his continuing desire, albeit for nonmonetary reasons, to own the particular property in question. No less is required, he asserts, to return the parties to the position they would have been in had the breach not occurred. That alone, in my opinion, would be sufficient to persuade

---

217 "Property and Unjust Enrichment," in Andrew Burrows ed., *Essays on the Law of Restitution* (Oxford: Clarendon Press, 1991).

a Court of Equity that the proper remedy for Mr. Korkontzilas' wrongful acquisition of the property is an order that he is bound as a constructive trustee to
convey the property to Mr. Soulos.

[50] But there is more. I agree with the Court of Appeal that a constructive
trust is required in cases such as this to ensure that agents and others in positions
of trust remain faithful to their duty of loyalty:[218] If real estate agents are permitted
to retain properties which they acquire for themselves in breach of a duty of
loyalty to their clients provided they pay market value, the trust and confidence
which underpins the institution of real estate brokerage will be undermined. The
message will be clear: real estate agents may breach their duties to their clients
and the courts will do nothing about it, unless the client can show that the real
estate agent made a profit. This will not do. Courts of equity have always been
concerned to keep the person who acts on behalf of others to his ethical mark;
this court should continue in the same path.

[51] I come finally to the question of whether there are factors which would
make imposition of a constructive trust unjust in this case. In my view, there are
none. No third parties would suffer from an order requiring Mr. Korkontzilas to
convey the property to Mr. Soulos. Nor would Mr. Korkontzilas be treated unfairly. Mr. Soulos is content to make all necessary financial adjustments, including
indemnification for the loss Mr. Korkontzilas has sustained during the years he
has held the property.

[Her Ladyship, therefore, held that a constructive trust should be imposed.
La Forest, Gonthier, Cory and Major JJ., concurred.
Sopinka J. wrote a dissenting judgment, with which Iacobucci J., concurred.
Sopinka J. was of opinion that since the imposition of the constructive trust
lies within the discretion of the trial judge, the court should show deference
to the decision at trial, unless the trial judge had erred in principle. In his
opinion, there was no such error. The constructive trust, according to the case
law can only be imposed for unjust enrichment and the broker was not unjustly
enriched because the purchaser did not suffer any damages.]

Notes and Questions

1. Do you agree with the decision? Is it possible to argue that there was unjust
enrichment, not in the sense of a monetary gain, but in the sense of a wrong done to the
plaintiff?[219] Was the case about restitution ("giving back") or disgorgement ("giving up")?

2. Does the decision mean that a constructive trust is remedial when it is imposed to
redress unjust enrichment, but that it is non-remedial when there is no unjust enrichment?
Or does it allow us to dispense with "remedial" vs. "non-remedial" and simply say that
trusts arise by operation of law for a variety of legal reasons, all of which can be said in
some general way to be based on "good conscience"?

---

218 See *Hodgkinson v. Simms, supra,* note 202, *per* La Forest J.
219 See the discussion on this point in part 3(a), *supra.*

3. Compare the majority judgment in *Soulos* with what was said in *Peter v. Beblow*.[220] Is the test for imposing a constructive trust in the case of unjust enrichment in the strict sense (a defective transfer of wealth from plaintiff to the defendant, which must be reversed) different from the test which applies to the availability of a constructive trust over the profits of wrongdoing?

4. It is generally taken for granted in Canada that the imposition of a constructive trust, to reverse an unjust enrichment, or to take away the profit of wrongdoing, is a matter that lies in the discretion of the court. Prof. Waters has argued that specific restitution should never be automatic even in the situations in which the constructive trust was traditionally imposed.[221] When the court considers what remedy to impose to correct unjust enrichment or other wrong in a particular case, it should have regard to the relationship between the parties, the gravity of the defendant's actions, whether the property originally derived from the plaintiff, whether the defendant is insolvent, *etc.* It should also take into account the effect of the order upon third parties. Thus, for example, it should have regard to the rights of the defendant's general creditors.[222] Moreover, in general, it should be wary of employing the constructive trust in the commercial setting where the parties can protect their rights by contract.[223] Recent cases dealing with unjust enrichment, and especially those dealing with the disgorgement of the profits of wrongdoing,[224] suggest that the imposition of the remedy lies in the court's discretion. Whether it should be imposed in a given situation depends upon whether it is just that the plaintiff be awarded the additional rights that flow from this proprietary remedy.

On the other hand, the discretionary nature of judicial remedies is the subject of a great deal of controversy. Some argue that it is inconsistent with the ideal of the rule of law.[225] And many cases of the imposition of the constructive trust do not make any reference to discretion, but seem to assume that the trust arises by operation of law as the relevant facts occur.[226] Perhaps, as Professor Waters has noted,[227] the term "constructive trust" is at fault, because it is ambiguous. It may be desirable, at least in Canada, to signal the breach we have made with the past (albeit in typical Canadian fashion, ambivalently)

---

220 *Supra*, note 99.

221 D.W.M. Waters, "The Constructive Trust in Evolution: Substantive *and* Remedial" (1991), 10 E. & T.J. 334 at 380.

222 See generally, David M. Paciocco, "The Remedial Constructive Trust: A Principled Basis for Priorities over Creditors" (1989), 68 Can. Bar Rev. 315.

223 See *Lac Minerals Ltd. v. International Corona Resources Ltd.*, *supra*, note 57, *per* Sopinka J., dissenting.

224 Like *Soulos*, *supra*, note 2, and *Lac Minerals*, *ibid.*

225 See for example P. Birks, "Rights, Wrongs and Remedies" (2000), 20 O.J.L.S. 1; D.W.M. Waters, "Liability and Remedy: An Adjustable Relationship" (2001), 64 Sask. L. Rev. 429; S. Evans, "Defending Discretionary Remedialism" (2001), 23 Sydney L.R. 463.

226 This is true, for example, of secret trusts, discussed in the next chapter, and also many of the cases discussing trusts arising to reverse unjust enrichment in circumstances of mistake: *Chase Manhattan Bank N.A. v. Israel-British Bank (London) Ltd.*, *supra*, note 89, followed in *Harper v. Royal Bank of Canada*, *supra*, note 89; *Kimwood Enterprises Ltd. v. Roynat Inc.* (1985), 31 Man. R. (2d) 105, 15 D.L.R. (4th) 751 (C.A.). No discretion is claimed where beneficiaries assert a trust interest in traceable proceeds of trust property: *Ontario (Securities Commission) v. Greymac Credit Corp.* (1986), 55 O.R. (2d) 673, 30 D.L.R. (4th) 1 (C.A.), aff'd [1988] 2 S.C.R. 172, 52 D.L.R. (4th) 767; nor is discretion asserted in the simple case in which a trustee transfers trust property in breach of trust to a third party who is not a bona fide purchaser of a legal interest for value without notice.

227 D.W.M. Waters, "The Constructive Trust in Evolution: Substantive *and* Remedial" (1991), 10 E. & T.J. 334 at 372.

by calling the constructive trust something else, like "specific restitution." That way the historical baggage that encumbers the term "constructive trust" could be relinquished.

(d) A Proprietary Remedy

We have seen that the constructive trust is imposed upon a person who has title to, or possession or control of property. It is, therefore, a remedy that affects property. There can be no constructive trust unless there is property to which it can attach.[228]

Equity also imposes personal obligations to make compensation. However, the cases and texts often speak of the person who is liable to pay compensation as being "liable to account as a constructive trustee." We submit that this is incorrect terminology.[229] The duty to render an account falls on every express trustee.[230] It does not turn on wrongdoing, but is part of the office of trustee and of the rights of beneficiaries. If a person who is not an express trustee is subjected to a requirement to render an account, the language of constructive trusteeship may be added, not because property is held in trust, but because it provides a link to the established accountability of express trustees. This duty to account may be imposed on a non-trustee where he or she knowingly assists an express trustee in a fraudulent breach of trust, with a resulting loss to the trust estate. Here the accounting to which the defendant is subjected is imposed by the court to determine the loss. In the case of an express trustee, the normal obligation to render an account of what was done with the trust property may reveal that a loss was caused in breach of trust (say, by an unauthorized or careless investment). In both cases, the liability to compensate is a personal one; the accounting is a way of measuring it. Similarly, a fiduciary's accounts may reveal an unauthorized gain; and an accounting of profits may be imposed on a non-fiduciary to measure a gain.

Because of the confusing phrase "liable to account as a constructive trustee," the cases and texts often speak indiscriminately of the duty to account as the equivalent of the constructive trust. They will, for example, state that a constructive trust arises when a person is under an equitable duty to account to another and call the first person a constructive trustee. Ford and Lee state that the constructive trust takes two forms: under one a personal liability to account is imposed; under the other, property held by one person is impressed with a constructive trust in favour of another person.[231] Similarly, Professor Waters speaks of a constructive trust as encompassing not only the duty to make restitution of specific property, but also the duty to account.[232]

The circumstances in which a fiduciary can make an unauthorized profit are legion. These include the case of a fiduciary who has made a profit out of some

---

228 *Restatement, Restitution,* §160, comment *i*. In this sense a constructive trust is similar to an express trust which cannot exist without a trust *res* either.

229 L. Smith, "Constructive Trusts and Constructive Trustees" (1999), 58 C.L.J. 294.

230 Waters, at 871-876.

231 Ford and Lee, §22000.

232 Waters, at 391-2.

opportunity which came to the fiduciary in the course of his or her duties to the beneficiaries and which the fiduciary ought to have acquired for the beneficiaries, or alternatively, to have declined if the opportunity was not one which the trust or the principal could acquire.[233] Similar cases frequently arise in corporate law, where directors and officers owe fiduciary obligations to their corporation.[234] In these situations, the fiduciary is said to be liable to account "as a constructive trustee."

In many cases, it is not clear whether the court means that the fiduciary is personally liable to disgorge the gain which the accounting reveals; or, whether the court means that the gain itself is held on a true constructive trust.

Let us consider some of the possibilities. If a trustee has simply misappropriated trust property, the trust survives; the property is still held in trust for the beneficiary. If the trustee no longer has the property, the beneficiary may still be able to establish that it is held on a constructive trust by the transferee; this will be resolved by asking whether the transferee can establish the defence of *bona fide* purchase of a legal interest for value without notice of the trust. Alternatively, the beneficiary may choose to claim a trust over any traceable proceeds of the trust property which the trustee received, if the accounting or other evidence can be used to identify any traceable proceeds. In this case, the beneficiary will be able to elect whether to treat the proceeds as trust property or not. If a principal gives an agent $100,000 and directs him or her to purchase property with it for the principal and the agent does so, but also makes a profit with the money, for example, through a short-term investment, the agent can be declared to hold the profit on a constructive trust. That profit is a traceable product of the $100,000.[235]

But what if the trustee, or other fiduciary such as an agent, makes a profit which is *not* a traceable product of property which belonged, legally or beneficially, to the beneficiary or principal? The case of taking a bribe from a third party is a good example. Clearly, here, an accounting of profits can be required; the faithless fiduciary can be compelled to surrender the profit to the beneficiary or the principal. But is the bribe held on constructive trust for the beneficiary or principal?

This issue arose clearly in an English case, *Lister & Co. v. Stubbs*.[236] Stubbs was an employee of the plaintiff company who was charged with purchasing materials for use in the business. He received large amounts in secret commissions from Varley and Co., a trade customer of the plaintiff, for placing orders with it. Stubbs invested some of these moneys in land and in securities and the plaintiff sought to follow the money into these investments. In other words, it sought to impress the product of the money with a constructive trust, a proprietary remedy. In order to prevent Stubbs from dealing with and disposing of the property, it brought proceedings for an interlocutory injunction. The plaintiff was unsuccess-

---

233 *Keech v. Sandford, supra,* note 3; *Boardman v. Phipps,* [1967] 2 A.C. 46, [1966] 3 All E.R. 721 (H.L.).

234 E.g. *Canadian Aero Services Ltd. v. O'Malley, supra,* note 203.

235 Lionel D. Smith, *The Law of Tracing* (Oxford: Clarendon Press, 1997), at 143-144.

236 (1890), 45 Ch. D. 1 (C.A.).

ful. The Court of Appeal held that the relationship between the parties was that of debtor and creditor and not of trustee and beneficiary because the money did not belong to the plaintiff in equity until a court so declared. Hence, while Stubbs would be accountable to the plaintiff, he did not hold the property upon a constructive trust.

Lister was effectively overruled by the Privy Council in *A.G. for Hong Kong v. Reid.*[237] Reid was Crown Counsel in Hong Kong, although he was a New Zealand national. He accepted bribes in return for obstructing the prosecution of certain criminals and was convicted and ordered to pay the amount of the bribes. He had invested some of the money in real property in New Zealand and the Attorney General for Hong Kong registered caveats against the title. The Attorney General claimed that the properties, which had increased in value, were held upon constructive trust for the Crown. The defence did not deny that Reid breached his fiduciary duty to the Crown when he accepted the bribes and became a debtor in equity to the Crown for the amount of the bribes. However, it was argued that he was only liable for the amount of the original bribes, not the increased value of the property in which they were invested because he could not be both debtor and trustee (of a constructive trust). However, the Board held that there is no reason why equity cannot provide two remedies, so long as there is no double recovery. Lord Templeman said:[238]

> When a bribe is accepted by a fiduciary in breach of his duty then he holds that bribe in trust for the person to whom the duty was owed. If the property representing the bribe decreases in value the fiduciary must pay the difference between that value and the initial amount of the bribe because he should not have accepted the bribe or incurred the risk of loss. If the property increases in value, the fiduciary is not entitled to any surplus in excess of the initial value of the bribe because he is not allowed by any means to make a profit out of a breach of duty.

His Lordship said of *Lister*:[239]

> The decision in *Lister & Co. v. Stubbs* is not consistent with the principles that a fiduciary must not be allowed to benefit from his own breach of duty, that the fiduciary should account for the bribe as soon as he receives it and that equity regards as done that which ought to be done. From these principles it would appear to follow that the bribe and the property from time to time representing the bribe are held on a constructive trust for the person injured. A fiduciary remains personally liable for the amount of the bribe if, in the event, the value of the property then recovered by the injured person proved to be less than that amount.

In *Soulos v. Korkontzilas,*[240] the Supreme Court of Canada did not make reference to the tension between *Lister* and *Reid,* and held that the gain acquired by a fiduciary in breach of his duties of loyalty could, in appropriate circumstances, be held on constructive trust for the principal. This seems closer to the holding in *Reid,* although the Supreme Court of Canada adopted a rather open-

---

237 [1994] 1 All E.R. 1 (P.C.). And see D.W.M. Waters, "Proprietary Relief: Two Privy Council Decisions — A Canadian Perspective" (1995), 25 C.B.L.J. 90.
238 *A.G. for Hong Kong v. Reid, ibid.,* at 5.
239 *Ibid.,* at 9.
240 *Supra,* note 2.

ended four-part test for deciding whether a trust was appropriate, while the Privy Council in *Reid* was of the view that the trust arose by operation of law automatically.[241]

(e) When the Constructive Trust Arises

When does the constructive trust arise? When the court decrees it, or when the defendant became obligated to make restitution? If the constructive trust is a remedy imposed to redress unjust enrichment, but which lies in the discretion of the court, you might suppose that it arises only when the court decrees it. If, like an obligation to pay damages for a tort, it arises by operation of law as the facts occur which give rise to it, then the court's role is merely to declare it.

The question is of some moment for a number of reasons. If the constructive trust does not arise until so decreed, the plaintiff cannot be said to have an interest in the property from the outset, and this may have significance for tax purposes, bankruptcy, and other reasons. An example may illustrate the point. Suppose that a man and woman live together, the woman contributes in money's worth to the acquisition of property, the title to which is in the man's name, and the court concludes that he would be unjustly enriched if he were to retain the property. Hence, it impresses the property with a constructive trust in favour of both. If the trust comes into being when an obligation on his part to make restitution occurs, when did that obligation arise? The courts do not generally address this question, being content to assume that on the totality of the evidence over the years there was such an obligation, and impress the constructive trust upon the assets in existence when the decree is made. But what about earlier property which was, for example, dissipated by the man, or withdrawn and invested in securities? Would the woman have an action for compensation in respect of the former and can she follow the latter? Further, how is the woman's liability for tax purposes, including capital gains determined? These are questions yet to be resolved.

And what if the husband became bankrupt before the court order was made? Property held in trust by a bankrupt person is not divisible among his creditors.[242] But in *Bedard v. Schell*,[243] the court held that a discretionary remedial constructive trust is not a "trust" within the meaning of that legislation, because it only arises when the court order is made.

Bogert takes the view that a constructive trust only arises when the court decrees it, but states that the property interest then dates back to the time that the defendant was under a duty to make restitution.[244] Scott, however, regards this as a fiction and insists that a constructive trust comes into being when the duty to

---

241 Although the holding in *Soulos* seems closer to *Reid* than to *Lister*, the Court in *Soulos* adopted this four-part test from an article by Goode. Goode's goal was to formulate a test which would explain some of the constructive trusts seen in the cases, while at the same time being consistent with the holding that there was no trust in *Lister*, a holding which Goode supports.

242 *Bankruptcy and Insolvency Act*, R.S.C. 1985, c. B-3, s. 67(1)(a).

243 (1987), 59 Sask. R. 71, [1987] 4 W.W.R. 699. See also *Nelson v. Nelson*, 2001 ABQB 888.

244 G.G. Bogert, *The Law of Trusts and Trustees*, 2nd ed. rev. (St. Paul, West Publishing Co., 1979), §472 ("Bogert").

make restitution arises and that the plaintiff has an interest in the property from that date.[245] The constructive trust on Scott's view, therefore, exists even though in the particular circumstances of the case it will not be enforced, either because the remedy at law, or the personal equitable remedy, is adequate, or for some other reason.[246] This view is consistent with the fundamental idea that every trust arises out of an obligation to deal with particular property for the benefit of someone. If the constructive trust arises out of an obligation to make restitution by transferring particular property, then it must arise when that obligation arises, which is at the time of the unjust enrichment.

Palmer disagrees with Scott, arguing that the constructive trust is purely remedial and that it does not somehow "exist" from the moment the unjust enrichment occurs. He is of the opinion that it is nonsensical to speak of a constructive trust as being in existence if the court will not enforce it in certain circumstances.[247]

It appears that the English and Canadian cases may have adopted Professor Scott's view. The point seems to have been specifically addressed first in *Chase Manhattan Bank N.A. v. Israel-British Bank (London) Ltd.*[248] This case, which is extracted in the next chapter, involved a large payment between banks. By mistake, the payment was made twice, and then the defendant recipient bank became insolvent. The plaintiff was clearly entitled to be repaid the mistaken payment. If, however, it was only entitled to a personal judgment, it would be an unsecured creditor, and would get little or none of its money back because of the defendant's insolvency. The plaintiff wanted instead to establish that it was the beneficiary of a constructive trust of the mistaken payment. If it could, and if it could locate the payment or its traceable proceeds, then to that extent it would recover all of the payment. It was held that the plaintiff was entitled to a trust, although the question of whether it could actually locate the payment or its traceable proceeds was not resolved. The holding was that the trust arose at the time the mistaken payment was made, not at the time of the judicial order.

The issue was also addressed in *Re Sharpe*.[249] Mrs. Johnson advanced £17,000 to her nephew, Sharpe, to enable him to purchase a house for £17,000. In consideration for the advance, Mrs. Johnson would live with Mr. and Mrs. Sharpe in the house and they would care for her. Sharpe became bankrupt and his trustee in bankruptcy entered into an agreement to sell the house to a third party. The trustee then brought application for an order for vacant possession. Browne-Wilkinson J. held that Mrs. Johnson had an irrevocable licence to occupy the house which was not merely contractual, but arose under a constructive trust

---

245 Scott, §462.4.

246 *Restatement, Restitution*, §160, comment *e*.

247 Palmer, §1.4. Note, however, that where a contract to transfer specific property is specifically enforceable (as in the case of contracts to transfer an interest in land), the specifically enforceable obligation to transfer has always made a constructive trust from the time the contract was made, even though the plaintiff would not know for certain that the obligation would be specifically enforceable until a court order was so made.

248 *Supra,* note 89.

249 [1980] 1 W.L.R. 219, [1980] 1 All E.R. 198 (Ch. Div.).

which bound the trustee in bankruptcy. The third party was not before the court due to a procedural oversight.

On the question when a constructive trust comes into being, his Lordship held that the interest of someone in the position of Mrs. Johnson does not just arise when the court declares it to exist, but when the original transaction took place. Otherwise, she would not have any right which can be remedied on breach. In this respect, *Re Sharpe* followed a number of cases involving similar licences.[250] Although the question when a constructive trust arises was not discussed in those cases, Brown-Wilkinson J. held that it was inherent in those decisions that the equitable interest predates the order of the court.

In *Canadian Imperial Bank of Commerce v. Croteau*[251] the court also held that a constructive trust arose before bankruptcy and survived the bankruptcy. A husband and wife had been married and lived together for many years. The parties intended to share all their assets equally throughout their marriage. However, title to the matrimonial home was in the husband's name.[252] When he encountered financial difficulties, he transferred it to his wife. This occurred within one year of his bankruptcy. On an application to set aside the transfer, the court was satisfied that the wife had a one-half interest in the home under a constructive trust,[253] retroactive to before the bankruptcy.

The issue came before the Supreme Court of Canada in *Rawluk v. Rawluk*.[254] The case involved a matrimonial property dispute following the spouses' separation. The husband owned farm property and a business; the wife ran the house, raised the family, and played a considerable role in the management of the farm and business. Under the provisions of the *Family Law Act*,[255] the wife was entitled to an equalization payment equal to one-half the difference between the value of the parties' respective net family properties, valued at the date of separation. However, the husband's various properties had appreciated in value between the date of separation and the date of trial and Mrs. Rawluk claimed that she was entitled to share in that appreciation under a constructive trust. The majority of the Supreme Court agreed with her argument, holding that the Act had not ousted the constructive trust. Further, they held that the constructive trust, although a remedy, confers rights as of the date a duty to make restitution arises. Cory J., speaking for the majority, followed Professor Scott's view on this point. He said:[256]

---

250 *Binions v. Evans, supra*, note 190; *D.H.N. Food Distributors Ltd. v. Tower Hamlets London Borough Council*, [1976] 1 W.L.R. 852, [1976] 3 All E.R. 462 (C.A.).

251 (1985), 47 R.F.L. (2d) 45, 50 O.R. (2d) 629 (H.C.).

252 Matrimonial property reform legislation, which might have conferred a half interest on the wife, did not apply.

253 The court does not actually identify the trust but follows *Pettkus v. Becker, supra*, note 1, which sanctioned the constructive trust as a remedy for unjust enrichment in "common intention" situations. The headnote, which refers to a resulting trust is, therefore, wrong, at least in describing the wife's interest before the transfer of the house to her. It is probably the case that when the house was transferred to her, she held it as to a one half interest on a resulting trust for the husband.

254 *Supra*, note 39.

255 S.O. 1986, c. 4; now R.S.O. 1990, c. F.3.

256 *Supra*, note 234, at D.L.R. 176-177.

It is important in this respect to keep in mind that a property interest arising under a constructive trust can be recognized as having come into existence not when the trust is judicially declared but from the time when the unjust enrichment first arose. As Professors Oosterhoff and Gillese state, "the date at which a constructive trust arises . . . is now generally accepted to be the date upon which a duty to made restitution occurs."[257] Professor Scott has stated that:[258]

> The beneficial interest in the property is from the beginning in the person who has been wronged. The constructive trust arises from the situation in which he is entitled to the remedy of restitution, and it arises as soon as that situation is created. . . . It would seem that there is no foundation whatever for the notion that a constructive trust does not arise until it is decreed by a court. It arises when the duty to make restitution arises, not when that duty is subsequently enforced.

I agree completely with the position taken on this issue by the authors of these helpful texts.

As well in *Hussey v. Palmer*,[259] Lord Denning M.R. noted that a constructive trust "may arise at the outset when the property is acquired, or later on, as the circumstances may require." As a result, even if it is declared by a court after the parties have already separated, a constructive trust can be deemed to have arisen when the duty to make restitution arose. It should therefore be considered as part of the property owned by the beneficiary at valuation date.

It must be emphasized that the constructive trust is remedial in nature. If the court is asked to grant such a remedy and determines that a declaration of constructive trust is warranted, then the proprietary interest awarded pursuant to that remedy will be deemed to have arisen at the time when the unjust enrichment first occurred. But, as Professor Scott made clear, the fact the proprietary interest is deemed to have arisen before the remedy was granted is not inconsistent with the remedial characteristics of the doctrine.

By contrast, McLachlin J., speaking for the minority, opined that the constructive trust is truly a remedy and can, therefore, not come into existence until the court declares it. She allowed that the property interest so created may extend back to the date when the duty to make restitution arose. She said:[260]

> Although the constructive trust is remedial, that is not to say that the remedial concept of constructive trust does not give rise to property interests. When the court declares a constructive trust, at that point the beneficiary obtains an interest in the property subject to the trust. That property interest, it appears, may be taken as extending back to the date when the trust was "earned" or perfected. In *Hussey v. Palmer*,[261] in a passage referred to by Dickson J. in *Rathwell v. Rathwell*[262] and relied on by the Court of Appeal in this case, Lord Denning postulated that the interest may arise at the time of declaration or from the outset, as the case may require. Scott views the trust as being in force from the outset, with a discretion in the court as to whether it should be enforced.[263] Another American scholar regards it as coming into existence only on an order being made, but having retrospective operation.[264]

257 Oosterhoff and Gillese, *A.H. Oosterhoff: Text, Commentary and Cases on Trusts*, 3rd ed. (Toronto: Carswell, 1987), at 579.
258 Scott, at 323-324.
259 [1972] 1 W.L.R. 1289 at 1290, [1972] 3 All E.R. 744 (C.A.) (quoted by Dickson J. in *Rathwell v. Rathwell, supra*, note 12, at 306.
260 *Rawluk, supra*, note 39, at D.L.R. 185-186.
261 *Supra*, note 260.
262 *Loc. cit., supra*, note 12.
263 Scott, §462.2.
264 Bogert, §472.

The significance of the remedial nature of the constructive trust is not that it cannot confer a property interest, but that the conferring of such an interest is discretionary and dependent on the inadequacy of other remedies for the unjust enrichment in question. The doctrine of constructive trust may be used to confer a proprietary remedy, but does not automatically presuppose a possessory property right. Thus, even where the tests for constructive trust are met — unjust enrichment, corresponding deprivation, and no juridical justification for the enrichment and justification — the property interest does not automatically arise. Rather, the court must consider whether other remedies to remedy the injustice exist which make the declaration of a constructive trust unnecessary or inappropriate.

Presumably, it would be for the court to decide whether the constructive trust should extend back in a particular situation.[265] On the issue of the date the constructive trust arises her Ladyship said:[266]

Against this background, I return to the first of the two questions I posed at the outset. Is the doctrine of constructive trust as it has developed in Canada a substantive doctrine of trust, automatically conferring a property interest where the basic criteria for the trust are made out? Or is it a remedy, to be applied where necessary to remedy unjust enrichment?

The answer must be that in Canada constructive trust, at least in the context of unjust enrichment, is not a doctrine of substantive property law, but a remedy. It follows that a constructive trust cannot be regarded as arising automatically when the three conditions set out in *Pettkus v. Becker* are established. Rather, the court must go on to consider what other remedies are available to remedy the unjust enrichment in question and whether the proprietary remedy of constructive trust is appropriate.

. . .

In my opinion, the doctrine of constructive trust does not permit the court to retrospectively confer a property interest solely on the basis of contribution of one spouse and enrichment of the other. A further inquiry must be made, namely, whether, given the presence of another remedy, the remedy of constructive trust is necessary or appropriate. . . .

Thus, although Cory J., writing for the majority in *Rawluk*, spoke of the constructive trust as remedial, he regarded it as existing from the time the duty to make restitution arose. The effect of his judgment, therefore, was that the plaintiff had a property interest in her husband's properties, which the majority recognized, but did not create. In other words, the majority were really treating the constructive trust as a substantive trust.

We submit that the question when a constructive trust arises is not yet settled. If the constructive trust is truly a remedy, as the Supreme Court said in *Pettkus v. Becker*,[267] albeit a remedy which is granted because necessary to redress unjust enrichment, a concept of substantive law, can it then itself be something substantive? Or must it either always be a remedy or a substantive trust? Must it be one or the other, or can it be both? Until the Supreme Court grapples squarely with

---

265 See *Westdeutsche Landesbank Girozentrale v. Islington L.B.C., supra,* note 84, at 714-715, *per* Lord Browne-Wilkinson.

266 *Rawluk, supra,* note 39, at 188.

267 *Supra,* note 1.

this issue, we will continue to be in a quandary about the nature of the constructive trust.[268]

(f) Constructive Trusts and Tracing

The traditional view is that when an express trustee or other fiduciary wrongfully misappropriates trust property and transfers the property to a third person, the beneficiary is entitled to follow the property and show that it is still held on constructive trust, so long as the third person is not a *bona fide* purchaser for value of the legal estate without notice. (which is a defence that the third party must establish). Alternatively, if the beneficiary can show what proceeds the trustee received for the property, then the beneficiary can show that these traceable proceeds are held by the trustee on trust for the beneficiary. In American law there is no requirement that the wrongdoer be a fiduciary in order to permit the plaintiff to trace in equity.[269] In Anglo-Canadian law the requirement, if not yet abolished, has been eroded to such an extent that it is now largely irrelevant, for the courts are willing to raise a fiduciary relationship,[270] to treat it as a fiction if the circumstances warrant it,[271] or even to disregard it altogether.[272] Tracing, if successful, leads to a proprietary remedy, for it enables the plaintiff to have the property or its product impressed with a constructive trust[273] or made subject to an equitable lien. The choice of remedy is normally the plaintiff's.[274]

If the property or its product has increased in value, the plaintiff will want to recover the property itself; that is, he or she will want a constructive trust. This may be over the whole traceable product, where it was acquired with the plaintiff's assets, or over a share, where it was acquired only in part with the plaintiff's assets. For example, if a painting is bought for $2,000, using $1,000 of misappropriated trust money, the beneficiary can assert that it is held on trust for her as to 50%; if the painting is now worth $5,000, this claim will capture part of the rise in value.

If the property has fallen in value, the plaintiff will want to obtain personal judgment against the defendant and a lien on the property to secure the judgment in part. For example, assume that the same painting is now worth only $1,200.

---

268 *Cf.* the illuminating remarks on this point by D.W.M. Waters, "The Constructive Trust in Evolution: Substantive *and* Remedial" (1991), 10 E. & T.J. 332 at 352ff. See also *LeClair v. LeClair Estate* (1998), 48 B.C.L.R. (3d) 245, 159 D.L.R. (4th) 638 (C.A.).

269 See, *e.g.*, Scott, §507.

270 See, *e.g.*, *Goodbody v. Bank of Montreal* (1974), 4 O.R. (2d) 147, 47 D.L.R. (3d) 335 (H.C.).

271 *Chase Manhattan Bank N.A. v. Israel-British Bank (London) Ltd.*, *supra*, note 89.

272 *Simpsons-Sears Ltd. v. Fraser* (1974), 7 O.R. (2d) 61, 54 D.L.R. (3d) 225 (H.C.); *B.C. Teachers' Credit Union v. Betterley* (1976), 61 D.L.R. (2d) 755 (B.C. S.C.). See further Lionel D. Smith, *The Law of Tracing* (Oxford: Clarendon Press, 1997), at 120ff., 342ff., who argues that a fiduciary relationship is not required.

273 Arguably, the remedy should be a resulting trust, since the purpose is to restore value whence it came. See Smith, *ibid.*, at 294, 300, 357; Robert Chambers, *Resulting Trusts* (Oxford: Clarendon Press, 1997), at 104ff., 212-214.

274 *Re Hallett's Estate* (1880), 13 Ch. D. 696 at 709 (C.A.), *per* Jessel M.R.; *Foskett v. McKeown*, [2001] 1 A.C. 102, [2000] 3 All E.R. 97 (H.L.).

The plaintiff would not want to claim a 50% share and so end up with an asset worth only $600. Instead, he or she could sue in breach of trust for the $1,000 misappropriation, and could secure this claim by asserting a lien over the whole painting. Even if the trustee becomes bankrupt, the plaintiff should be able to recover the secured part of the claim, that is $600; the remaining $400 will be unsecured.

If the defendant is a third party and not the original trustee or other wrongdoer, the plaintiff can only succeed in showing that the property received by the defendant remains subject to the trust if the defendant is a volunteer (*i.e.*, did not give value), or if he or she took with notice of the trust. Even a defendant who is a volunteer, but took without notice of the trust, is not personally liable if he or she no longer has the property when the claim is made.[275] The liability, not being based on wrongdoing, attaches only to the property; it is not a personal liability. Some authors now argue that even a totally innocent recipient of trust property is strictly liable, without wrongdoing or notice, from the moment of receipt, although he or she can raise the defence of change of position.[276]

Since tracing leads to a proprietary remedy, it is advantageous to the plaintiff, particularly where the defendant is insolvent; and it may be important for other reasons as well, such as the case of the rise in value discussed above. The traditional view is that all of these principles regarding following, tracing and claiming apply just as much in a case of a constructive trust as in the case of an express trust.[277] Professor Waters has pointed out that if the constructive trust is to be regarded as purely a remedy, in other words, as no longer based on a pre-existing property right, then a person will no longer have a *right* to trace.[278] As he also points out, however, the court is entitled to grant proprietary relief to a claimant who is, in fact, able to "trace" specific property into the hands of the defendant.[279] Further, it should do so if the equities warrant it. Hence, a different approach to the constructive trust will not destroy the tracing remedy, but will make it discretionary.[280] By contrast, Lionel Smith argues that the constructive

---

275 See *Re Diplock*, [1948] Ch. 465 at 521 (C.A.). Another part of the judgment did hold that the defendants were personally liable for the amounts received, and this part was affirmed sub nom. *Ministry of Health v. Simpson*, [1951] A.C. 251 (H.L.). This personal claim, however, is generally understood to be based on the maladministration of the estates of deceased persons, which are not trusts. This issue is addressed in Chapter 15.

276 This is said to be based on unjust enrichment, which does not depend on wrongdoing, but arguably this position reads too much into the nature of the beneficiary's interest. For discussion and criticism of this approach, see L.D. Smith, "Unjust Enrichment, Property and the Structure of Trusts" (2000), 116 Law Quarterly Review 412. It may, however, be arguable that the innocent recipient becomes liable in unjust enrichment, not in receiving the property, but in spending it if that expenditure enriches the defendant: L. Smith, *supra*, note 65, at 2172-4.

277 For example, in *A.G. for Hong Kong v. Reid, supra*, note 238, there was a constructive trust over the bribe taken in Hong Kong; this was traceable into land in New Zealand.

278 D.W.M. Waters, "The Constructive Trust in Evolution: Substantive *and* Remedial" (1991), 10 E. & T.J. 334 at 370.

279 *Ibid.*

280 *Ibid.*, at 371.

trust should not be regarded as discretionary in these circumstances, since its purpose is to restore value whence it came.[281]

(g) The Trustee and the Beneficiary under a Constructive Trust

(i) *The Beneficiary*

We have seen that a beneficiary under an express trust (other than a discretionary trust) has a property interest in the trust property and the trustee is endowed with extensive powers of management. Under a resulting trust, by contrast, the trustee does not normally have any duties except to convey the property to the beneficiary, but the beneficiary has an interest under a resulting trust akin to that of a beneficiary under an express trust, although, usually, he or she will be able to call for a conveyance immediately.

The position of the parties under a constructive trust is both similar and dissimilar to that of the parties under a resulting trust. This is because the constructive trust is remedial. Assuming that it comes into being when the equitable duty to make restitution arises,[282] the beneficiary has an interest in the property from that date onward, although the court may in the particular circumstances of a case decide not to enforce the constructive trust.

Professor Scott uses the example of a person, A, whose money is wrongfully taken and used by B to purchase land.[283] The constructive trust then arises at the time of B's wrongful conduct, but A has two remedies, one at law to recover the money converted and one in equity to reach the land. Assuming that B is solvent, the former remedy would probably be more appropriate. Moreover, when A dies, the claim passes to his or her personal representatives for the benefit of A's next-of-kin. Hence, Scott argues that A's interest in the land is less than that of the beneficiary under an express trust, for A's interest would not descend to the heirs; nor would it be sufficient to entitle A's wife to a dower claim in the land.

A similar situation obtains where the alternative personal claim is equitable, such as an accounting. If the plaintiff is entitled to an accounting and that remedy is adequate, a constructive trust should not be imposed.[284]

Under traditional Anglo-Canadian law, which insists upon a pre-existing property interest, it is likely that the beneficiary would be regarded as having an interest in the property coterminous with that of the beneficiary under an express trust. This would appear to be the result of *Re Gardner*.[285] The case concerned a beneficiary under a secret trust who died before the testatrix. The case held that the secret trust, a constructive trust, arose at the time of the trustee's undertaking

---

281 Which is why it ought, perhaps, to be regarded as a resulting trust. See Robert Chambers, *Resulting Trusts* (Oxford: Clarendon Press, 1997), 104ff., 212-14; Lionel D. Smith, *The Law of Tracing* (Oxford: Clarendon Press, 1997), 357.

282 A matter about which there continues to be dispute, as we have seen.

283 Scott, §462.5.

284 See, *e.g.*, *David v. Russo* (1983), 119 Ill. App. 3d 290, 456 N.E. 2d 342.

285 [1923] 2 Ch. 330.

to give the property to the beneficiary. Hence, the beneficiary died possessed of an interest in the property which passed to his estate.

If the constructive trust is regarded as a true remedy, of course, the beneficiary has no pre-existing property interest. He or she only acquires a property interest when the court makes an order granting specific restitution.

(ii) *The Trustee*

Normally the only obligation of a constructive trustee is to convey the property to the beneficiary once a constructive trust decree is made, or, if the beneficiary is under a disability, to hold it until the trustee is replaced. In the meantime, however, the trustee has no active duties of management. Nor, it would seem, is the trustee required to keep the property separate from his or her own, although the beneficiary may later be allowed to trace the property.

There may be situations, however, in which the constructive trustee is more like an express trustee in that he or she is required to hold the property for the beneficiaries in the same way as an express trustee. Examples of such a constructive trust are those arising under secret trusts and mutual wills. Here the terms of the trust are likely be very similar to an express trust that was intended; the trust is constructive because the express trust is incapable of enforcement due to some lack of formality. For exactly this reason, some argue that these are really express trusts. We will address this issue in the next chapter.

It must be remembered that the trustee of a constructive trust does not stand in a fiduciary relationship to the beneficiary of the trust, unlike the express trustee. Fiduciary duties of loyalty arise by voluntary undertaking. The circumstances which give rise to a constructive trust may involve a fiduciary relationship. They often do, but this is not a necessary precondition of the constructive trust.[286]

5. PROCEDURE TO OBTAIN A CONSTRUCTIVE TRUST ORDER

Assuming that the circumstances are such that the court, in its discretion, may make a constructive trust order, how do you obtain such an order? And, if you obtain the order, what does it mean?

To obtain a constructive trust order, the plaintiff normally institutes an action for a declaration that the defendant holds certain property upon a constructive trust for the plaintiff. All superior courts have a wide power to grant declarations of legal and equitable rights.[287]

When the constructive trust is alleged to arise to reverse an unjust enrichment, it is then up to the plaintiff to show that the defendant has been unjustly enriched; he or she would do so by proving the circumstances giving rise to a duty to make restitution. If the case involves a matrimonial or cohabitational property dispute, the plaintiff must also show a causal connection between the contribution made

---

286 Scott, §462.1.
287 See, *e.g.*, *Courts of Justice Act*, R.S.O. 1990, c. C.43, s. 97.

by the plaintiff and the acquisition of the property by the defendant, and the absence of any juristic reason for the enrichment, such as an agreement between the parties that the defendant should hold title beneficially. If the trust is said to arise to take away the profits of wrongdoing, then the plaintiff must prove the wrong (such as a breach of fiduciary obligation) and the gain derived by the defendant. Further, the plaintiff must show that it is just that the proprietary remedy be awarded in the circumstances. Moreover, the plaintiff may have to overcome certain defences, such as acquiescence and laches, limitations, estoppel, change of circumstances, and adequacy of the legal or personal remedy.

If the plaintiff makes out his or her case, a declaration will issue. But what does that mean? If the property is real property, a copy of the judgment or a caveat may be registered on title so as to prevent disposition by the defendant to a *bona fide* purchaser for value of the legal estate without notice. If, however, the property is personalty, the plaintiff does not have the same opportunity to protect his or her interest.

Assuming that the plaintiff is granted a declaration that the defendant holds the property upon a constructive trust for the plaintiff, or for him- or herself and the plaintiff in certain specific proportions, how does the plaintiff realize upon the judgment?

If the declaration is in favour of the plaintiff to the exclusion of the defendant, the property is the plaintiff's in equity. If, however, the judgment declares that the parties have a proportionate interest in the property, it is submitted that they become equitable tenants in common. Hence, they should be able to apply for partition or sale under partition legislation[288] if the property is land, or apply to the court to have the property divided or sold and the proceeds divided if the property is personalty.

This necessarily raises the question, why not ask the court to vest the property in the plaintiff, or the plaintiff and the defendant as the case may be, and to partition or sell the property in the latter case in the same action in which the constructive trust decree is sought? This can indeed be done, but it does not appear to be the practice. It depends on a statutory jurisdiction. Without that, the limit of the reach of a court of equity was to *order* the defendant to transfer the property to the plaintiff; this order effectively creates or declares the constructive trust. But the order has to be complied with. Traditionally, if the defendant did not comply, he could be jailed for contempt, or his assets could be seized; this is called sequestration. But the court of chancery could not, of its own motion, change the location of legal title.

The court has some powers under the *Trustee Acts* to make "vesting orders".[289] These powers also extend to constructive trusts;[290] but their function is to allow the court to vest property *in a trustee* to facilitate the trust, as where the court appoints a new trustee. They do not generally allow the court to vest property in

---

288 See, *e.g., Partition Act,* R.S.O. 1990, c. P.4.

289 See for example *Trustees Act,* R.S.N.B. 1973, c. T-15, ss. 15-23; *Trustee Act,* R.S.O. 1990, c. T.23, ss. 10, 13; R.S.B.C. 1996, c. 464, ss. 33, 43-49, 51-59, 61, 65, 67.

290 This is provided in the definition section of every *Trustee Act.*

a beneficiary to terminate the trust.[291] More usefully, in many provinces there is a wide and general jurisdiction, under the successor legislation to the Judicature Acts, to make vesting orders in favour of any person and in respect of any property.[292] This allows the court effectively to terminate the constructive trust, by making the beneficiary into the legal owner.

It is probably wise, especially in matrimonial and cohabitation property disputes, for the plaintiff to ask not simply for a declaration that the defendant holds the property upon a constructive trust for the plaintiff, or for both parties in certain proportions, but, if a proprietary remedy is desired, also for an order vesting the property in the plaintiff, or in the parties as tenants in common, and for an order for partition or sale in the latter case.

Although the plaintiff should be able to have a constructive trust order executed immediately, the court retains a discretion to postpone it, since it is an equitable remedy. In *Clark Drummie & Co. v. Ryan*[293] the court postponed execution of a resulting trust in the special circumstances of that case. A law firm held a judgment against a former associate to recover moneys stolen by him. It obtained an order against the associate and his wife. Title to their house was in her name, but he had contributed to its acquisition and maintenance. The court held that the wife held the house on a resulting trust, as to one half, for the husband, and the law firm sought an order for partition and sale in order to get paid what was owing to it under the judgment against the husband. The wife did not know of the theft and was trying to keep the family together and to raise the children in the house which she was maintaining out of her own resources. The court directed that the resulting trust order not be enforced until the defendants' youngest child reached the age of majority. At that time the property should be sold, or the wife could purchase the husband's interest, and the law firm's judg-

291 In Ontario, *Trustee Act*, R.S.O. 1990, c. T.23, s. 10(1)(f) for land and s. 13(1)(b)(iv)-(v) for intangible property allow vesting orders *against* trustees and in favour of a beneficiary. The jurisdiction arises 14 days after the trustee's default. Using these provisions, a declaration of constructive trust with consequential orders for transfer of the trust property could be followed, in the case of a failure to transfer, by a vesting order in favour of the plaintiff. Even here, though, not every kind of property is covered. *Cf. Trustee Act*, R.S.B.C. 1996, c. 464, ss. 63, 64, 66 for intangible property, requiring 28 days' default.

292 *Courts of Justice Act*, R.S.O. 1990, c. C.43, s. 100: "A court may by order vest in any person an interest in real or personal property that the court has authority to order be disposed of, encumbered or conveyed." Cf. *Law and Equity Act*, R.S.B.C. 1996, c. 253, s. 37; *Law of Property Act*, R.S.A. 2000, c. L-7, s. 76; *The Court of Queen's Bench Act*, C.C.S.M., c. C280, s. 37 (1); *The Queen's Bench Act, 1998*, S.S. 1998, c. Q-1.01, s. 12; *Supreme Court Act*, R.S.P.E.I. 1988, c. S-10, s. 33; *Judicature Act*, R.S.N.W.T. 1988, c. J-1, s. 13; *Judicature Act*, R.S.Y. 2002, c. 128, s. 6. This requires us to know over what property the court has such authority. But if the court has a general authority to issue an injunction, including a mandatory injunction to transfer property, it seems to follow that the court has authority to order that the property be conveyed.

293 (1997), 146 D.L.R. (4th) 311, 17 E.T.R. 162, 188 N.B.R. (2d) 91, 48 A.P.R. 91, 1997 CarswellNB 179 (Q.B.), reversed on other grounds (1999), 1999 CarswellNB 47, 170 D.L.R. (4th) 266, 209 N.B.R. (2d) 70, 535 A.P.R. 70, 26 E.T.R. (2d) 14 (C.A.). Note that, on appeal, it was held that the husband did not in fact have any interest in the house at all to which the law firm could have access via its judgment against him.

ment paid out of the husband's share of the proceeds. We submit that the court would have a similar discretion with respect to a constructive trust judgment.

If the court declares an equitable lien, this could be registered in the case of land, to be sure that the lien will bind any subsequent purchaser of the land. In the case of personal property, the lien would normally carry with it a power of sale held by the creditor in order to obtain payment of the secured debt, although another application to the court might be necessary to activate the power. The best route would be to have the initial order declaring the lien also spell out what enforcement rights the creditor should have.[294]

If a proprietary remedy is not desired, a *quantum meruit* claim is all that need be sought, any reference to a constructive trust being superfluous and confusing of the issue. Unless the defendant is insolvent, normally only a personal remedy will be needed.

---

294 See for example *Re Gareau Estate* (1995), 9 E.T.R. (2d) 25 (Ont. Gen. Div.). Improper payments were traced into purchase payments on houses. The judge ordered that the repayment be secured by a lien on the houses. (He called it a constructive trust, but since it was not a beneficial interest in the houses but rather an interest to secure a debt, it was actually a lien.) In order that innocent defendants would not have to sell their homes to make restitution, he decreed that the lien be

11

THE CONSTRUCTIVE TRUST APPLIED

1. SCOPE

The constructive trust applies in a broad range of circumstances and for a variety of reasons. Professor Waters once explained:[1]

> There was never a theme behind the use of the constructive trust by Chancery. It was never more than a medium through which for the Chancery mind the obligations of the parties might be expressed or determined.

From a pedagogic perspective, the primary challenge created by that fact is organizational. Constructive trusts are difficult to master largely because they are numerous and often seemingly unrelated. And indeed, to some extent, the effect of the subject's history is inescapable. The concept of the constructive trust is, on any reckoning, something of a grab bag. It is, nevertheless, possible to make that grab bag more manageable. The most promising strategy is to compartmentalize, by arranging the various species of constructive trusts according to their triggering events.

Of course, some arrangements are more helpful than others. For instance, it traditionally has been said that some constructive trusts arise in response to "equitable fraud."[2] Unfortunately, that proposition tends to obscure more than it illuminates. At law, "fraud" bears a specific meaning. It refers to conduct by which one person consciously deceives another.[3] The issue is taken seriously. The plaintiff must plead and prove legal fraud, and an unfounded allegation may be met with an award of costs. "Equitable fraud" is far different. It does not require

---

1 D.W.M. Waters, *The Constructive Trust* (London: Athlone Press, 1964) at 39.
2 The list includes secret trusts and mutual wills, as well as those constructive trusts that are triggered by oral trusts of land, undue influence and unconscionability.
3 *Derry v. Peek* (1889), 14 App. Cas. 337, 38 W.R. 33, [1886-90] All E.R. Rep. 1 (H.L.).

specific pleading⁴and its scope extends far beyond intentional misrepresentations. It is, in essence, merely a failure to act as equity would like one to act. Lord Haldane L.C. offered the following explanation in *Nocton v. Lord Ashburton*.⁵

> [W]hen fraud is referred to in the wider sense in which the books are full of the expression, used in Chancery in describing cases which were within its exclusive jurisdiction, it is a mistake to suppose that an actual intention to cheat must always be proved. A man may misconceive the extent of the obligation which a Court of Equity imposes on him. His fault is that he has violated, however innocently because of his ignorance, an obligation which he must be taken by the Court to have known, and his conduct has in that sense always been called fraudulent, even in such a case as a technical fraud on a power. It was thus that the expression "constructive fraud" came into existence. The trustee who purchases the trust estate, the solicitor who makes a bargain with his client that cannot stand, have all for several centuries run the risk of the word fraudulent being applied to them. What it really means in this connection is, not moral fraud in the ordinary sense, but breach of the sort of obligation which is enforced by a Court that from the beginning regarded itself as a Court of conscience.

Equity therefore conceives of "fraud" as a broad residual category, encompassing virtually every case other than those in which relief is granted for mistake, breach of confidence or breach of fiduciary duty.⁶ The sheer breadth of the concept substantially, if not fatally, undermines its analytical value.

As we saw in Chapter 10, the Supreme Court of Canada has twice attempted to organize constructive trusts, with mixed results on both occasions. It began, in 1980, with the proposition that "unjust enrichment lies at the heart of the constructive trust."⁷ That approach proved unworkable, not least because, as explained below, "unjust enrichment" is an ambiguous phrase, referring to two quite distinct phenomena.⁸

---

4 See *Brown v. Storoschuk* (1946), [1946] 3 W.W.R. 641, [1947] 1 D.L.R. 227, 1946 CarswellBC 85 (C.A.).

5 [1914] A.C. 932 (U.K. H.L.) at 954. See also *Goldin, Re* (2003), 2003 CarswellOnt 2626, (sub nom. *Goldin (Trustee of) v. Bennett & Co.*) 229 D.L.R. (4th) 736, 65 O.R. (3d) 691, (sub nom. *Goldin (Bankrupt), Re*) 174 O.A.C. 117 (C.A.), leave to appeal refused (2004), 2004 CarswellOnt 576, 2004 CarswellOnt 577 (S.C.C.).

6 L.A. Sheridan, *Fraud in Equity* (London: Pitman & Sons Limited, 1957), p. 210. According to an old jingle, Thomas More said that "Three things are to be helped in Conscience; Fraud, Accident and Things of Confidence." The third category consists of confidential and fiduciary obligations; the second refers to mistake; the first encompasses everything else.

7 *Becker v. Pettkus* (1980), 117 D.L.R. (3d) 257, 1980 CarswellOnt 299, 1980 CarswellOnt 644, [1980] 2 S.C.R. 834, 117 D.L.R. (3d) 257, 34 N.R. 384, 8 E.T.R. 143, 19 R.F.L. (2d) 165, at 273 [D.L.R.]. See also *International Corona Resources Ltd. v. Lac Minerals Ltd.*, (sub nom. *LAC Minerals Ltd. v. International Corona Resources Ltd.*) (1989), 61 D.L.R. (4th) 14, [1989] 2 S.C.R. 574, 1989 CarswellOnt 126, 1989 CarswellOnt 965, [1989] S.C.J. No. 83, 6 R.P.R. (2d) 1, 44 B.L.R. 1, 35 E.T.R. 1, 69 O.R. (2d) 287, 101 N.R. 239, 36 O.A.C. 57, 26 C.P.R. (3d) 97, at 48, 51 [D.L.R.]; *Brissette Estate v. Westbury Life Insurance Co.* (1992), 96 D.L.R. (4th) 609, 1992 CarswellOnt 544, 1992 CarswellOnt 999, [1992] S.C.J. No. 86, [1992] I.L.R. 1-2888, 47 E.T.R. 109, 13 C.C.L.I. (2d) 1, 142 N.R. 104, 58 O.A.C. 10, [1992] 3 S.C.R. 87, at 614 [D.L.R.].

8 The Supreme Court of Canada occasionally has confused the two meanings of unjust enrichment. *International Corona Resources Ltd. v. Lac Minerals Ltd.*, an extract of which appears below, is illustrative.

In *Soulos v. Korkontzilas*,[9] which we examined in the Chapter 10, the Supreme Court of Canada rejected exclusive reliance on unjust enrichment and suggested instead that all constructive trusts are referable to a two-part principle of "good conscience." Once again, however, there is cause for concern. As McLachlin J. conceded, the concept of good conscience, in itself, is too vague to be applied directly. Further guidance must be drawn from the cases. Moreover, some species of constructive trust do not appear to fit under either branch of the good conscience principle. For instance, the trust that is imposed over property that is subject to a specifically performable contract of sale cannot convincingly be explained on the basis of either unjust enrichment or wrongdoing.

Although McLachlin J.'s scheme in *Soulos* provides an useful starting point, it does leave room for refinement. This chapter consequently adopts a somewhat different approach. The various species of constructive trusts are arranged under three categories of triggering events.[10]

- *Unjust enrichment* — A trust sometimes is imposed to reverse an unjust enrichment that the defendant received at the plaintiff's expense. That may be true, for instance, if the plaintiff conferred a benefit upon the defendant as a result of a mistake, incapacity or illegitimate pressure. In Canada, another (somewhat controversial) application of the claim in unjust enrichment involves the resolution of cohabitational property disputes. There is, however, some need for caution. As suggested in an earlier chapter, it may be that all restitutionary trusts ought to be classified as resulting, rather than constructive. If so, the size and complexity of the constructive trust grab bag can be reduced considerably.
- *Wrongs* — Some constructive trusts unequivocally are imposed to compel the defendant to proprietarily disgorge a benefit acquired through wrongdoing. That most obviously is true with respect to enrichments acquired by breach of confidence or breach of fiduciary duty. However, the same explanation also extends to some benefits acquired through death.
- *Perfecting Intentions* — Finally, despite frequent attempts to fit them under the rubrics of unjust enrichment or wrongdoing, some constructive trusts are best explained as instances in which equity perfects intentions. In some situations, especially if there is an element of detrimental reliance, equity will impose a trust to ensure that an intended disposition in fact occurs. That appears to be true in cases involving: (i) specifically performable contracts of sale, (ii) oral trusts of land, (iii) incomplete gifts, (iv) proprietary estoppel, (v) secret trusts, and (vi) mutual wills.

---

9 (1997), 146 D.L.R. (4th) 214, 1997 CarswellOnt 1489, [1997] S.C.J. No. 52, 1997 CarswellOnt 1490, 212 N.R. 1, 9 R.P.R. (3d) 1, 46 C.B.R. (3d) 1, 32 O.R. (3d) 716 (headnote only), 100 O.A.C. 241, 17 E.T.R. (2d) 89, [1997] 2 S.C.R. 217.
10 See especially R. Chambers, "Constructive Trusts in Canada" (1999), 37 Alberta L. Rev. 173; G. Elias, *Constructive Trusts* (Oxford: Clarendon Press, 1990).

The preceding scheme should be read subject to two important caveats. First, as Professor Waddams has demonstrated, it occasionally may be impossible to assign a particular rule exclusively to a single category.[11] In developing the law in an area, the courts may be influenced by many factors operating concurrently. Consequently, while the preceding scheme will be used for the purposes of discussion, it may be that, at some level, some species of constructive trust (*e.g.* those that apply in the context of secret trusts) simultaneously reflect notions of unjust enrichment, wrongdoing, perfected intentions and detrimental reliance.

Second, it is important to appreciate that the scheme used in this chapter is a working hypothesis. Although it accepts and applies the substantive rules that Canadian courts traditionally have used to determine the availability of constructive trusts, it has not, as an organizing model, received judicial imprimatur. That lack of express recognition does not, however, diminish the scheme's usefulness. As a practical matter, constructive trusts must be organized in *some* way. Presented simply as a mass of raw materials, the case law is unmanageable, if not impenetrable. The different species of trusts appear to arise almost at random. There is little hope of developing the law in a more coherent direction unless it is possible not only to predict (on the brute force of precedent) *when* a constructive trust will occur, but also to explain *why* it will arise.

The chapter concludes with an examination of "constructive trustees." As we shall see, that phrase is something of a misnomer. A constructive trustee is not a trustee of a constructive trust, or indeed, any trust at all. A constructive trustee is, instead, a person who has been held personally (rather than proprietarily) liable for interfering with a trust to which he or she was a stranger. There are three categories of constructive trustee, which again can be classified according to their triggering events: (i) knowing assistance is a form of wrongdoing, (ii) knowing receipt most likely is a form of unjust enrichment, and (iii) trustee *de son tort* is a form of wrongdoing.

2. UNJUST ENRICHMENT

(a) Introduction

Although it is not true, as suggested in *Becker v. Pettkus*,[12] that *all* constructive trusts are referable to unjust enrichment, it (probably) is true, as recognized in *Soulos v. Korkontzilas*,[13] that *some* constructive trusts are triggered by that type of event.

In the interests of analytical clarity, that proposition must immediately be refined. As explained in the last chapter, "unjust enrichment" is an ambiguous phrase. It has two meanings.

---

11 S.M. Waddams, *Dimensions of Private Law: Categories and Concepts in Anglo-Canadian Legal Reasoning* (Cambridge: Cambridge University Press, 2003).

12 *Supra*, note 7, at 273. See also *Lac Minerals Ltd.*, *supra*, note 7, at 48, 51 (S.C.C.); *Brissette Estate*, *supra*, note 7, at 614.

13 *Supra*, note 9.

- *Unjust Enrichment By Wrongdoing* — "Unjust enrichment" sometimes is used, quite loosely, to describe a situation in which the court, having found the breach of a civil obligation (*e.g.* trespass to land, breach of fiduciary duty), quantifies relief not by reference to the plaintiff's loss (*i.e.* compensation), but rather by reference to the defendant's gain (*i.e.* restitution, or, perhaps more precisely, disgorgement).[14] In this context, the significance of "unjust enrichment" is purely remedial. It says nothing about the underlying cause of action.
- *Autonomous Unjust Enrichment*[15] — The second definition of "unjust enrichment" involves the three-part cause of action that Dickson J. formulated in *Becker v. Pettkus*. The court must be satisfied that: (i) the defendant received an enrichment, (ii) the plaintiff suffered a corresponding deprivation, and (iii) there is an absence of any juristic reason for the enrichment. If those elements are established, then the defendant may attempt to avoid liability by invoking a defence. To the extent that that the defendant cannot do so, the remedy is restitution. The defendant must give the benefit back to the plaintiff. In this context, then, the significance of "unjust enrichment" is both substantive and remedial. It governs the cause of action and its associated remedies.

Although we will encounter the concept of unjust enrichment by wrongdoing later in this chapter, we will focus in this section on the autonomous action in unjust enrichment.

The relevance of constructive trusts in the present context is easily explained, at least in outline. Where successful, the autonomous action in unjust enrichment invariably results in the remedy of restitution. Having received a benefit that cannot be retained, the defendant must give it back to the plaintiff. Restitution, however, may be effected either personally or proprietarily. The defendant may be subject to an obligation to restore the monetary value of the impugned enrichment, or, somewhat exceptionally, he or she may be required to transfer a particular asset *in specie*. And finally, proprietary restitution most often takes the form

---

14 The two varieties of "unjust enrichment" sometimes are distinguished by referring to "enrichments by wrongdoing" and "enrichments by subtraction." As that scheme suggests, a gain is relevant in the first category as long as it was acquired as a result of a wrong that the defendant committed against the plaintiff. In contrast, the defendant's gain is relevant in the second category only if it was economically subtracted from the plaintiff. Consequently, while the remedy in the first category occasionally is restitutionary in effect (when, by chance, the wrong allowed the defendant to subtract a benefit from the plaintiff, as opposed to a third party), its purpose is always disgorgement because the defendant must broadly *give up* all of his wrongful gains. In contrast, the remedy in the second category invariably is restitutionary in effect and purpose because the defendant merely is required to *give back* the benefit that he acquired from the plaintiff. See L.D. Smith, "The Province of the Law of Restitution" (1992), 71 Can. Bar Rev. 672; M. McInnes, "The Measure of Restitution" (2002), 52 U. of Toronto L.J. 163.

15 The action is "autonomous" because it is not dependent upon the proof of wrongdoing (*e.g.* trespass to land or breach of fiduciary duty).

of a trust.[16] The defendant may be required to administratively hold an asset for the benefit of the plaintiff, with a view to transferring it back.

Although easily stated in the abstract, the relationship between unjust enrichments and constructive trusts raises a number of difficult issues. *Chase Manhattan Bank N.A. v. Israel-British Bank (London) Ltd.*,[17] which appears below, provides an introduction to the area.

Further Reading

D.M. Paciocco, "The Remedial Constructive Trust: A Principled Basis for Priorities Over Creditors" (1989), 68 Can. Bar Rev. 315.

R.M. Goode, "Property and Unjust Enrichment" in A.S. Burrows, ed., *Essays on the Law of Restitution* (1991).

B.E. Cotton, "The Equitable Lien: New Life in an Old Remedy?" (1994), 16 Adv. Q. 385.

J. Beatson, "Proprietary Claims in the Law of Restitution" (1995), 25 C.B.L.J. 66.

D.W.M. Waters, "Proprietary Relief: Two Privy Council Decisions — A Canadian Perspective" (1995), 25 C.B.L.J. 90.

R. Chambers, "Constructive Trusts in Canada" (1999), 37 Alta. L. Rev. 173.

R. Chambers, "Resulting Trusts in Canada" (2000), 38 Alta. L. Rev. 378.

L.D. Smith, "Unjust Enrichment, Property, and the Structure of Trusts" (2000), 116 L.Q. Rev. 412.

A.S. Burrows, "Proprietary Restitution: Unmasking Unjust Enrichment" (2001), 117 L.Q. Rev. 412.

C. Rotherham, *Proprietary Remedies in Context* (Oxford: Hart, 2002) chs. 6 and 15.

CHASE MANHATTAN BANK N.A. v. ISRAEL-BRITISH BANK (LONDON) LTD.

(1979), [1981] Ch. 105, [1980] 2 W.L.R. 207, [1979] 3 All E.R. 1025 (Ch. Div.).

The plaintiff, a New York bank, owed a debt of $2M to the defendant, an English bank. On July 3, 1974, the plaintiff mistakenly paid that amount twice to another New York bank, on account for the defendant. The defendant knew, or ought to have known, of that error by July 5, 1974. A short time later, the defendant became insolvent. The plaintiff undoubtedly was entitled to restitution of the overpayment. Significantly, however, if relief was not available proprietarily, then, given the defendant's financial status, the plaintiff would not be able to entirely satisfy judgment.

---

16 Other forms of proprietary restitution include liens over mistakenly improved property (*e.g. Cooper v. Phibbs* (1867), L.R. 2 H.L. 149; *Sel-Rite Realty Ltd. v. Miller*, [1994] 8 W.W.R. 172, 1994 CarswellAlta 132, 20 Alta. L.R. (3d) 58, 39 R.P.R. (2d) 177 (Q.B.)), rights of subrogation that lead to the acquisition of property rights (*e.g. Lord Napier and Ettrick v. Hunter*, [1993] A.C. 713 (U.K. H.L.); *Banque Financière de la Cité v. Parc (Battersea) Ltd.*, [1999] 1 A.C. 221 (U.K. H.L.)) and rights to rescission that lead to the revesting of property rights (*e.g. Car and Universal Finance Ltd. v. Caldwell*, [1965] 1 Q.B. 525).

17 (1979), [1981] Ch. 105, [1980] 2 W.L.R. 207, [1979] 3 All E.R. 1025 (Ch. Div.).

GOULDING J.:

The plaintiff's claim, viewed in the first place without reference to *any* system of positive law, raises problems to which the answers, if not always difficult, are at any rate not obvious. If one party P pays money to another party D by reason of a factual mistake, either common to both parties or made by P alone, few conscientious persons would doubt that D ought to return it. But suppose that D is, or becomes, insolvent before repayment is made, so that P comes into competition with D's general creditors, what then? If the money can still be traced, either in its original or through successive conversions, and is found among D's remaining assets, ought not P to be able to claim it, or what it represents, as his own? If he ought, and if in a particular case the money has been blended with other assets and is represented by a mixed fund, no longer as valuable as the sum total of its original, what priorities or equalities should govern the distribution of the mixed fund? If the money can no longer be traced, either separate or in mixture, should P have any priority over ordinary creditors of D? In any of these cases, does it make any difference whether the mistake was inevitable, or was caused by P's carelessness, or was contributed to by some fault, short of dishonesty, on the part of D?

At this stage I am asked to take only one step forward, and to answer the initial question of principle, whether the plaintiff is entitled in equity to trace the mistaken payment and to recover what now properly represents the money. The subsequent history of the payment and the rules for ascertaining what now represents it have not been proved or debated before me. They will have to be established in further proceedings if the plaintiff can clear the first hurdle today.

This initial question in the action appears not to be the subject of reported judicial decision in England. Let me read a few lines from *Goff and Jones, The Law of Restitution*.[18] The authors say:

> Whether a person who has paid money under a mistake of fact should be granted a restitutionary proprietary claim can arise in a number of contexts. It will be most important when the payee is insolvent and the payer seeks to gain priority over the payee's general creditors. The English courts have never had to consider this question. But in the United States it has arisen on a few occasions. A leading case is *In re Berry*.[19]

That was a case decided in the Circuit Court of Appeals, Second Circuit. I shall read a passage from the judgment of the court, delivered by Judge Coxe:[20]

> Stripped of all complications and entanglements we have this naked fact that Raborg & Manice by mistake paid Berry & Co. $1,500, which they did not owe and which Berry & Co. could not have retained without losing the respect of every honourable business man. It is conceded on all hands that had not insolvency and bankruptcy intervened Raborg & Manice could have recovered the money on an implied assumpsit in the event that Berry & Co. declined to return it after knowledge of the facts — a highly improbable contingency. Of course such an action would lie.

---

18 2nd ed., (1978), 89.
19 (1906) 147 Fed. 208.
20 *Ibid.*, at 210.

On no possible theory could the retention of the money by Berry & Co. be justified; it was paid to them and received by them under mistake, both parties believing that Raborg & Manice owed the amount. If the $1,500 had been placed in a package by Raborg & Manice and delivered to a messenger with instructions to deposit it in their bank, and the messenger, by mistake, had delivered it to Berry & Co., it will hardly be pretended that the latter would acquire any title to the money, and yet the actual transaction in legal effect gave them no better right. It is urged that to compel restitution now will work injustice to the general creditors of the bankrupts, but this contention loses sight of the fact that the money in dispute never belonged to the bankrupts, and their creditors, upon broad principles of equity, have no more right to it than if the transaction of November 25 had never taken place. If the trustees succeed on this appeal the creditors will receive $1,500, the equitable title to which was never in the bankrupts. There can be no doubt of the fact that the payment to Berry & Co. was a mistake and that by reason of this mistake that trustees have in their possession $1,500 which, otherwise, they would not have. The proposition that Raborg & Manice who have done no wrong, shall be deprived of their property and that it shall be divided among creditors to whom it does not fairly belong, is not one that appeals to the conscience of a court of equity.

. . .

The effect of the American case law, developed in a number of different states, as well as the federal jurisdiction, is summarised in the important book of Professor A.W. Scott, *The Law of Trusts*:[21]

Similarly where chattels are conveyed or money is paid by mistake, so that the person making the conveyance or payments is entitled to restitution, the transferee or payee holds the chattels or money upon a constructive trust. In such a case, it is true, the remedy at law for the value of the chattels or for the amount of money paid may be an adequate remedy, in which case a court of equity will not ordinarily give specific restitution. If the chattels are of a unique character, however, or if the person to whom the chattels are conveyed or to whom the money is paid is insolvent, the remedy at law is not adequate and a court of equity will enforce the constructive trust by decreeing specific restitution. The beneficial interest remains in the person who conveyed the chattel or who paid the money, since the conveyance or payment was made under a mistake.

In my opinion, on the evidence that I have heard . . . the foregoing passages correctly represent the law of the State of New York. I believe they are also in accord with the general principles of equity as applied in England, and in the absence of direct English authority I should wish to follow them.

. . .

[T]he relevant municipal law of New York is not, in my view, in serious doubt. I find it, shortly stated in my own words, to be as follows:
(a) If one party P transfers property to another party D by reason of a mistake of fact, P has in general a right to recover it and D a duty to restore it. (b) P in general has a right to sue in equity for an order that D return the property, or its traceable proceeds, to P. Sometimes this requires actual transfer by D, sometimes the court can use the alternative remedy of reformation, *i.e.* rectification of instruments, to produce the same result. P is said to retain an equitable title to the

---

21 3rd ed. (1967), vol. 5. p. 3428.

property notwithstanding it may have been legally transferred to D, and D is treated as a constructive trustee thereof. (c) In many cases P has also a common law right of action in *quasi-contract* to recover damages in respect of his loss. (d) The court will not, in its equitable jurisdiction, order specific restitution under (b) above where common law damages under (c) furnish adequate relief. (e) Accordingly where the property in question is money, equitable relief is not available to restore the sum paid by mistake if the payee D is solvent. But when D is insolvent P is entitled to a decree in equity for the purpose of tracing the money paid and recovering it or the property representing it. (f) Modern analysis concentrates attention less on the protection of P than on preventing the unjust enrichment of D, thus bringing the law of mistake into a broad jurisprudence of restitutionary rights and remedies.

. . .

[T]he view I have formed on the American material as a whole [is] that the plaintiff is right in alleging that the defendant became a trustee for the plaintiff of the sum paid by mistake. . . . I have held, after examining *In re Diplock*,[22] that under English municipal law a party who pays money under a mistake of fact may claim to trace it in equity, and that this right depends on a continuing right of property recognized in equity. I have found, on the evidence presented by the parties, that a similar right to trace is conferred by New York municipal law, and that there too the party paying by mistake retains a beneficial interest in the assets. No doubt the two systems of law in this field are not in all respects identical, but if my conclusions are right no conflict has arisen between them in the present case. . . .

Subject to any discussion of the wording, I will declare that on July 3, 1974, the defendant became trustee for the plaintiff . . . and I will direct an inquiry what has become of that sum, and what assets (if any), in the possession or power of the defendant, now represent the said sum or any part thereof or any interest or income thereof.

Notes and Questions

1. Historically, restitution generally was available if money was paid pursuant to a mistake of fact (as in *Chase Manhattan*), but not if it was paid under a mistake of law.[23] That distinction has now been abolished. Relief generally is available in either instance, as long as the plaintiff's error caused the payment.[24]

---

22 [1948] Ch. 465.

23 *Bilbie v. Lumley* (1802), 2 East. 469, 102 E.R. 448 (K.B.); *Nepean Hydro-Electric Commission v. Ontario Hydro* (1982), 132 D.L.R. (3d) 193, 1982 CarswellOnt 116, 1982 CarswellOnt 721, [1982] 1 S.C.R. 347, 16 B.L.R. 215, 41 N.R. 1.

24 *Air Canada v. British Columbia* (1989), 59 D.L.R. (4th) 161, 1989 CarswellBC 67, 1989 CarswellBC 706, [1989] S.C.J. No. 44, [1989] 4 W.W.R. 97, [1989] 1 S.C.R. 1161, 95 N.R. 1, 36 B.C.L.R. (2d) 145, 41 C.R.R. 308, 2 T.C.T. 4178, [1989] 1 T.S.T. 2126; *Canadian Pacific Air Lines Ltd. v. British Columbia* (1989), 59 D.L.R. (4th) 218, 1989 CarswellBC 68, 1989 CarswellBC 705, [1989] 1 S.C.R. 1133, 2 T.C.T. 4170, [1989] 4 W.W.R. 137, 36 B.C.L.R. (2d)

2. Although Goulding J. followed the decision in *In Re Berry*, some American courts subsequently have adopted a different approach.[25] To what extent does the recent American case law affect the validity of Goulding J.'s decision?

3. The reasoning in *Chase Manhattan* was also questioned in *Westdeutsche Landesbank Girozentrale v. Islington London Borough Council*.[26] Goulding J. believed that, assuming other conditions could be met, a trust could be imposed on the basis of the defendant's *receipt* of the mistaken payment, and not merely upon the defendant's *knowledge* of the plaintiff's error. In *Westdeutsche*, in contrast, Lord Browne-Wilkinson said in *obiter* that the imposition of a trust was dependent upon the defendant's conscience being affected. On that approach, the defendant could not have become trustee of the money immediately upon receipt, but only two days later, when it realized, or should have realized, the plaintiff's error. That approach has been heavily criticized.[27]

4. In *Chase Manhattan*, Goulding J. also discussed at considerable length an apparent rule that restricts the availability of constructive trusts following equitable tracing to situations involving fiduciary relationships. Modern Canadian courts have not, however, been much impressed by that purported rule and generally no longer treat it as binding.[28]

5. Goulding J. drew a distinction between: (i) a situation in which the plaintiff's error is so fundamental as to prevent legal title from passing, and (ii) a situation in which the error, while not so fundamental as to prevent legal title from passing, does prevent the defendant from acquiring full beneficial ownership in equity, such that the asset is held on trust. Is it possible and appropriate to draw such a distinction?[29] In the former situation, the plaintiff sometimes is said to enjoy a "pure proprietary claim," whereas in the latter there is said to be a "restitutionary proprietary claim."[30]

6. Although Goulding J.'s approach has not been firmly adopted into Canadian law, it has been applied, or cited with approval, in a number of cases.[31]

185, [1989] 1 T.S.T. 2153, 96 N.R. 1, varied on reconsideration 1989 CarswellBC 717, 1989 CarswellBC 1257, 102 N.R. 75, [1989] 2 S.C.R. 1067, 63 D.L.R. (4th) 768; *Kleinwort Benson Ltd. v. Lincoln City Council*, [1999] 2 A.C. 349 (U.K. H.L.).

25 *Dow Corning Corp., Re*, 192 Bankruptcy R. 428 (U.S. Bank. Ct., 1996), noted in A. Kull, "Restitution in Bankruptcy" (1998), 72 Am. Bankruptcy L.J. 265.

26 [1996] A.C. 669 (U.K. H.L.). Compare *Polly Peck Ltd. (No. 2), Re*, [1998] 3 All E.R. 812 (C.A.) at 827; *Bank of America v. Arnell*, [1999] Lloyd's Rep. Bank. 399 (Q.B.).

27 P. Birks, "Trusts Raised to Reverse Unjust Enrichment: The *Westdeutsche* Case" [1996] Restitution L. Rev. 3; P. Millett, "Restitution and Constructive Trusts" (1998), 114 L.Q. Rev. 399; R. Chambers, "Restitution, Trusts and Compound Interest" (1996), 20 Melbourne U.L. Rev. 1192.

28 *Goodbody v. Bank of Montreal* (1974), 47 D.L.R. (3d) 335, 1974 CarswellOnt 308, 4 O.R. (2d) 147 (H.C.); *British Columbia Teachers' Credit Union v. Betterly* (1975), 61 D.L.R. (3d) 755, 1975 CarswellBC 318 (S.C.); *Becker v. Pettkus, supra*, note 7.

29 A. Tettenborn, "Remedies for the Recovery of Money Paid by Mistake" (1980), 39 Cambridge L.J. 272.

30 A. Burrows, *The Law of Restitution*, 2nd ed. (London: Butterworths, 2002) at 67. Compare *Foskett v. McKeown*, [2001] 1 A.C. 102 (H.L.).

31 *Peter v. Beblow* (1993), 101 D.L.R. (4th) 621, [1993] S.C.J. No. 36, 1993 CarswellBC 44, 1993 CarswellBC 1258, [1993] 3 W.W.R. 337, 23 B.C.A.C. 81, 39 W.A.C. 81, [1993] 1 S.C.R. 980, 150 N.R. 1, 48 E.T.R. 1, 77 B.C.L.R. (2d) 1, 44 R.F.L. (3d) 329, [1993] R.D.F. 369, at 638 [D.L.R.]; *Phoenix Assurance Co. of Canada v. Toronto (City)* (1981), 129 D.L.R. (3d) 351, 1981 CarswellOnt 741, 35 O.R. (2d) 16 (H.C.), additional reasons at (1981), 1981 CarswellOnt 191, 33 O.R. (2d) 457, 38 C.B.R. (N.S.) 299, 124 D.L.R. (3d) 738 (H.C.), affirmed (1982), 1982 CarswellOnt 240, 39 O.R. (2d) 680, 48 N.R. 240n, 46 C.B.R. (N.S.) 80, 142 D.L.R. (3d) 767n (C.A.), leave to appeal refused (1983), 142 D.L.R. (3d) 767n (S.C.C.); *Canadian Imperial Bank of Commerce v. Twin Richfield Oils Ltd.* (1992), 88 D.L.R. (4th) 596, 1992 CarswellAlta 280,

(b) Constructive Trust or Resulting Trust?

Assuming that a particular species of autonomous unjust enrichment gives rise to the imposition of a restitutionary trust, the first question pertains to classification. Is the operative trust better regarded as constructive or as resulting? The issue is unsettled. Commentators traditionally have presumed the former. That approach finds some support in *Chase Manhattan*. After stating that the laws of New York and England were "in accord," Goulding J. concluded that, in the circumstances, a constructive trust could be imposed under the laws of the former. However, he also relied upon the House of Lords' decision in *Sinclair v. Brougham*[32] in finding, somewhat cryptically, that the plaintiff could, as a matter of English law, enjoy "a continuing right of property recognized in equity."[33] Interestingly, in *Sinclair* itself, Lord Haldane classified the applicable trust as resulting.

The possibility that the applicable trust is resulting, rather than constructive, is also supported by the fact that the circumstances of *Chase Manhattan* are similar to (and perhaps indistinguishable from) those that underlie the classic gratuitous transfer resulting trust. And indeed, as discussed in an earlier chapter, while the issue has not yet been entertained by Canadian courts,[34] it may be that every trust raised to reverse an unjust enrichment ought to be classified as resulting.

(c) Guidelines for Proprietary Restitution

The second question arising from *Chase Manhattan* is even more difficult. Regardless of the remedy's precise classification, when should a trust be imposed to effect restitution of an unjust enrichment?[35] Although the Supreme Court of Canada has addressed that question on a number of occasions, it has done so only in the context of cohabitational property disputes, where gender politics undoubtedly (and arguably quite correctly) have affected the analysis.[36] Moreover, the Court has not yet decided a case in which the defendant's insolvency was a live issue. It therefore remains to be seen, especially in a commercial context, how the Court will balance the competing interests.

---

11 C.B.R. (3d) 103, 129 A.R. 161, 45 E.T.R. 189 (Q.B.), at 610 [D.L.R.]; *Harper v. Royal Bank* (1994), 114 D.L.R. (4th) 749, 1994 CarswellOnt 2201, 18 O.R. (3d) 317, 71 O.A.C. 237 (Div. Ct.), at 751 [D.L.R.]. But see *Barnabe v. Touhey* (1994), 18 O.R. (3d) 370, 1994 CarswellOnt 659, 4 E.T.R. (2d) 22 (Gen. Div.), reversed (1995), 26 O.R. (3d) 477, 1995 CarswellOnt 1167, 10 E.T.R. (2d) 68, 37 C.B.R. (3d) 73 (C.A.).

32 [1914] A.C. 398 at 421.

33 *Supra*, note 17, at 1040.

34 Compare *Westdeutsche Landesbank Girozentrale, supra*, note 26, *per* Lord Browne-Wilkinson (H.L.); *Air Jamaica v. Joy Charlton*, [1999] 1 W.L.R. 1399 (P.C.) *per* Lord Millett; *Twinsectra Ltd. v. Yardley*, [2002] 2 A.C. 164 (H.L.) *per* Lord Millett.

35 The issue of choice of remedy was discussed more broadly in the last chapter. The focus of the present discussion is on the availability of proprietary "restitution" for "unjust enrichment," as both of those terms have been narrowly defined.

36 See especially *Becker v. Pettkus, supra*, note 7.

Those interests obviously affect the parties themselves. As in *Chase Manhattan*, the issue of proprietary restitution may arise because the plaintiff seeks to avoid the burden of the defendant's insolvency. Alternatively, the plaintiff's claim to a trust may stem from a desire to acquire ownership of property that is, for some reason, particularly attractive. An asset may, for instance, be unique or it may have increased in value since the time of its transfer.[37] By the same token, however, the defendant may resist the imposition of a trust on the ground that it is relatively more intrusive. It is one thing to be required to pay over a certain sum of money; quite another to be required to give up a specific asset to which one may be, for some reason, particularly attached.

Significantly, however, when formulating the rules governing the imposition of proprietary restitution, the courts must look beyond the immediate parties and have regard for other interests. General creditors clearly will be concerned by any order that reduces the pool of assets that is available for the satisfaction of debts in the event of the defendant's insolvency. So too, the legislature may oppose judicially-created trusts on the ground that they disrupt statutory schemes that were carefully crafted to address the issue of insolvency.[38] And finally, all else being equal, society as a whole has an interest in a system that minimizes the costs associated with the resolution of restitutionary claims and the effects of insolvency. Consequently, a complicated regime that turns largely on judicial discretion may be undesirable insofar as it inhibits settlements and encourages litigation.

(i) *Cases*

The autonomous action in unjust enrichment applies across a wide range of circumstances. The defendant's enrichment may consist of the receipt of money, land, goods or services. Furthermore, the reasons for reversing enrichments are varied.[39]

---

37 A personal obligation to provide restitution typically is measured at the time of enrichment, rather than the time of trial, with the result that an increase in value accrues to the defendant. See *Jones & Sons (Trustee) v. Jones*, [1997] Ch. 159 (C.A.) at 168 *per* Millett L.J.; R.B. Grantham & C.E.F. Rickett, "Disgorgement for Unjust Enrichment?" (2003), 62 Cambridge L.J. 159 at 164; S. Hedley & M. Halliwell, eds., *The Law of Restitution* (London: Butterworths, 2002) at 9; G. Virgo, *The Principles of the Law of Restitution* (Oxford: Oxford University Press, 1998) at 95-96; *cf.* A. Burrows, *The Law of Restitution*, 2nd ed. (London: Butterworths, 2002) at 28.

38 Compare *British Columbia v. National Bank of Canada* (1994), 119 D.L.R. (4th) 669, 1994 CarswellBC 639, 99 B.C.L.R. (2d) 358, [1995] 2 W.W.R. 305, 30 C.B.R. (3d) 215, 6 E.T.R. (2d) 109, 52 B.C.A.C. 180, 86 W.A.C. 180, 2 G.T.C. 7348 (C.A.), leave to appeal refused 34 C.B.R. (3d) 302 (note), 9 E.T.R. (2d) 117 (note), 9 B.C.L.R. (3d) xxxi (note), 126 D.L.R. (4th) vii (note), [1995] 9 W.W.R. lxxix (note), 63 B.C.A.C. 159 (note), 104 W.A.C. 159 (note), 196 N.R. 240 (note) (S.C.C.), at 693 [119 D.L.R.] and *Ellingsen, Re,* (sub nom. *Ellingsen (Trustee of) v. Hallmark Ford Sales Ltd.*) (2000), 190 D.L.R. (4th) 47, 2000 CarswellBC 1684, [2000] B.C.J. No. 1682, 2000 BCCA 458, 7 B.L.R. (3d) 12, 19 C.B.R. (4th) 166, (sub nom. *Ellingsen (Bankrupt), Re*) 142 B.C.A.C. 26, 233 W.A.C. 26, 1 P.P.S.A.C. (3d) 307 (C.A.).

39 The phrase "absence of juristic reason" seems to suggest that the relevant inquiry pertains to factors justifying the defendant's retention of an enrichment (*e.g.* donative intention, contractual performance). In practice, however, Canadian courts generally follow the English approach,

- In most cases, restitution is available because the plaintiff's intention was *impaired* in the sense of being either vitiated or conditional. A *vitiated* intention occurs if the plaintiff did not truly intend to enrich the defendant. That is true, for instance, if the plaintiff acted pursuant to a mistake (as in *Chase Manhattan*), was legally incapable of forming an intention (as in the case of infancy) or formed no intention at all (as in a case of theft). An intention is also impaired if it was the function of illegitimate external forces, such as undue influence, duress or unconscionability.[40] A *conditional* intention arises, in contrast, if the plaintiff fully intended for the defendant to receive a benefit, but further intended for that benefit to be retained only if a specified event occurred.[41] If that event does not materialize, the condition fails and the benefit must be returned. That is true, for instance, of a wedding gift given in contemplation of a marriage that never takes place.

- An enrichment may also be reversed on the ground of *free acceptance*. Although the relationship between that concept and the concept of impaired intention has never been adequately explained, Dickson J. did firmly establish free acceptance in *Becker v. Pettkus*.[42]

> [W]here one person . . . prejudices herself in the reasonable expectation of receiving an interest in property and the other person . . . freely accepts benefits conferred by the first person in circumstances where he knows or ought to have known of that reasonable expectation of receiving an interest in property, it would be unjust to allow the recipient of the benefit to retain it.

Although that test was initially developed in the context of cohabitational property disputes, where it continues to be most frequently applied,[43] it has been used in commercial cases as well.[44]

- Finally, enrichments sometimes are reversed for discrete and clearly-defined policy reasons. For instance, restitution may be available to vindicate the

---

which requires the plaintiff to prove a positive reason for *reversing* an enrichment (*e.g.* mistake, failure of condition). See M. McInnes, "Unjust Enrichment — Restitution — Absence of Juristic Reason" (2000), 79 Can. Bar Rev. 459; L.D. Smith, "The Mystery of Juristic Reason" (2000), 12 Supreme Court L. Rev. (2d) 211. The situation may, however, be dramatically altered by the recent decision in *Garland v. Consumers' Gas Co.*, 2004 S.C.C. 25.

40 Although the plaintiff may have consciously chosen to confer a benefit upon the defendant, the intention is considered vitiated insofar as it was the product of illegitimate external pressure, rather than the plaintiff's free will.

41 That concept traditionally was addressed under the label of "failure of consideration." That phrase unfortunately suggests a contractual analysis and, for that reason, is better avoided. Although the relevant condition quite often is the performance of a contractual undertaking, it need not be. See *Chillingworth v. Esche*, [1924] 1 Ch. 97; *Ames' Settlement, Re*, [1946] Ch. 217.

42 *Supra*, note 7, at 274.

43 *Sorochan v. Sorochan* (1986), 29 D.L.R. (4th) 1, 1986 CarswellAlta 714, 1986 CarswellAlta 143, [1986] 2 S.C.R. 38, [1986] 5 W.W.R. 289, 69 N.R. 81, 46 Alta. L.R. (2d) 97, 74 A.R. 67, 23 E.T.R. 143, 2 R.F.L. (3d) 225, [1986] R.D.I. 448, [1986] R.D.F. 501; *Peter v. Beblow, supra*, note 31.

44 *Brisebois v. Modern Music Co.* (1993), 50 E.T.R. 305, 1993 CarswellOnt 570 (Gen. Div.); *Gill v. Grant* (1988), 30 E.T.R. 255, 1988 CarswellBC 641 (S.C.).

constitutional principle that prohibits unauthorized taxation,[45] or as a means of encouraging emergency intervention.[46]

As a matter of precedent, restitutionary trusts (whether classified as resulting or constructive) have been imposed across almost the entire breadth of unjust enrichment. They have been applied with respect to every form of enrichment, including services,[47] and most species of "unjust factor." Proprietary relief has, for instance, been granted in response to freely accepted services in the family context, as well as for enrichments received by reason of mistake,[48] incapacity,[49] ignorance,[50] compulsion[51] and failure of condition.[52]

Unfortunately, while trusts have been imposed in response to many types of unjust enrichments, the cases do not readily yield any clear pattern. The decision to award restitution proprietarily, rather than personally, often appears to be fortuitous and *ad hoc*. In developing a more coherent regime, Canadian courts may wish to consider the academic literature. We will briefly consider two sets of proposals.[53] The first seeks a principled relationship between the autonomous action in unjust enrichment and proprietary restitution. The second, which arrives

---

45 *Woolwich Building Society v. Inland Revenue Commission (No. 2)*, [1993] A.C. 70 (U.K. H.L.); *Air Canada v. British Columbia, supra*, note 24, *per* Wilson J. (S.C.C.); *Eurig Estate, Re* (1998), 165 D.L.R. (4th) 1, 1998 CarswellOnt 3950, 1998 CarswellOnt 3951, [1998] S.C.J. No. 72, 40 O.R. (3d) 160 (headnote only), (sub nom. *Eurig Estate v. Ontario Court (General Division), Registrar*) 231 N.R. 55, 23 E.T.R. (2d) 1, 114 O.A.C. 55, [1998] 2 S.C.R. 565, [2000] 1 C.T.C. 284.

46 *Matheson v. Smiley*, [1932] 2 D.L.R. 787, 1932 CarswellMan 13, [1932] 1 W.W.R. 758, 40 Man. R. 247 (C.A.).

47 *Becker v. Pettkus, supra*, note 7.

48 *Canada (Attorney General) v. Northumberland General Insurance Co.* (1987), 36 D.L.R. (4th) 421, 1987 CarswellOnt 725, 58 O.R. (2d) 592, 26 C.C.L.I. 252 (H.C.), affirmed (1988), 1988 CarswellOnt 723, 34 C.C.L.I. 1, 52 D.L.R. (4th) 383, 65 O.R. (2d) 735 (C.A.).

49 *Goodfellow v. Robertson* (1871), 18 Gr. 572, 1871 CarswellOnt 79 (Ch.).

50 *Merchants Express Co. v. Morton* (1868), 15 Gr. 274, 1868 CarswellOnt 149 (Ch.); *Kolari, Re* (1981), 36 O.R. (2d) 473, 1981 CarswellOnt 201, 39 C.B.R. (N.S.) 129 (Dist. Ct.).

51 *Zaidan Group Ltd. v. London (City)* (1987), 36 D.L.R. (4th) 443, 1987 CarswellOnt 639, 43 R.P.R. 276, 25 E.T.R. 283, 58 O.R. (2d) 667, 35 M.P.L.R. 148 (H.C.), affirmed (1988), 49 D.L.R. (4th) 681, 1988 CarswellOnt 589, 37 M.P.L.R. 261, 48 R.P.R. 253, 30 E.T.R. 59, 64 O.R. (2d) 438, 28 O.A.C. 365 (C.A.), reversed on other grounds (1990), 64 D.L.R. (4th) 514, 1990 CarswellOnt 474, 71 O.R. (2d) 65, 35 E.T.R. 162, 36 O.A.C. 384, 47 M.P.L.R. 1 (C.A.), affirmed 1991 CarswellOnt 550, 1991 CarswellOnt 1030, 5 O.R. (3d) 384, [1991] 3 S.C.R. 593, 50 O.A.C. 1, 7 M.P.L.R. (2d) 235, 129 N.R. 227, 85 D.L.R. (4th) 448, 44 E.T.R. 193; *Phoenix Assurance Co. of Canada v. City of Toronto, supra*, note 31.

52 *Ellingsen, Re, supra*, note 38; *Waselenko v. Swertz Brothers Construction Ltd. (Receiver of)* (1982), [1983] 2 W.W.R. 352, 1982 CarswellSask 229, (sub nom. *Waselenko v. Touche Ross Ltd.*) 14 E.T.R. 125, 24 Sask. R. 260, 34 R.F.L. (2d) 404 (Q.B.), affirmed [1985] 3 W.W.R. 38, 1985 CarswellSask 180, 18 E.T.R. 217, 45 Sask. R. 196 (C.A.); *Kenron Homes Ltd., Re* (January 17, 1985), Doc. 7943, [1985] S.J. No. 81 (C.A.); *Yorkshire Trust Co. v. Empire Acceptance Corp.* (1983), 44 B.C.L.R. 334, 1983 CarswellBC 109, 13 E.T.R. 189 (S.C.).

53 There are others. Professor Cope, for example, has suggested that a constructive trust for unjust enrichment should, like specific performance for a contract, be available only if the asset in question is land or a unique chattel, such that monetary relief would not be an adequate remedy: *Constructive Trusts* (Sydney: Law Book Co., 1992) at 487.

at substantially similar results but for somewhat different reasons, focuses on the issue of insolvency.

(ii) *A Principled Approach*

The principled approach starts with the following proposition.[54]

> There are two minimum requirements which should be met before a trust is a possible response to unjust enrichment: (a) that the unjust enrichment is an asset capable of being the subject matter of a trust and (b) that the defendant did not acquire the full beneficial ownership of that asset before the plaintiff's right to restitution arose.

According to that approach, it is necessary to examine the nature of both the defendant's enrichment and the plaintiff's reason for claiming restitution.

As a matter of logic, there cannot be a restitutionary trust unless the defendant holds an asset upon which a trust can be impressed. That limitation applies simply by virtue of the remedy's nature. Proprietary relief is impossible in the absence of property. Going further, however, it is suggested that a restitutionary trust should be possible only with respect to property that consists of the very enrichment that the defendant received from the plaintiff, or the traceable proceeds of that enrichment.[55]

> Unless an unjust enrichment continues to exist as all or part of the value of an asset in the defendant's hands, there is no justification for creating a property right to effect restitution of that unjust enrichment. There simply is no connection between the unjust enrichment and the defendant's asset and no reason why one asset should be chosen, in preference to any other, to satisfy the obligation to make restitution. The same is true of other obligations, such as payments due under a contract or to compensate for losses caused by a tort. The creation of property rights requires justification and unrelated indebtedness will not do.[56]

---

54 R. Chambers, "Constructive Trusts in Canada" (1999), 37 Alberta L. Rev. 173 at 208.

55 See P. Birks, "Proprietary Rights as Remedies", in P. Birks, ed., *The Frontiers of Liability*, vol. 2 (Oxford: Oxford University Press, 1994) 214 at 218; R. Goode, "Proprietary Restitutionary Claims", in W. Cornish *et al.*, eds., *Restitution: Past, Present & Future* (Oxford: Hart, 1998) 63. Canadian courts occasionally have emphasized the need for the plaintiff to demonstrate that the defendant received and (traceably) retained an enrichment that is capable of being the subject matter of a trust. See *Canadian Commercial Bank v. R.T. Holman Ltd.* (1986), 57 Nfld. & P.E.I.R. 129, 1986 CarswellPEI 13, 59 C.B.R. (N.S.) 79, 170 A.P.R. 129 (S.C.); *Michelin Tires (Canada) Ltd. v. R.*, [2001] 3 F.C. 552, 2001 CarswellNat 846, 2001 CarswellNat 2629, [2001] F.C.J. No. 707, 2001 G.T.C. 3536, 2001 FCA 145, (sub nom. *Michelin Tires (Canada) Ltd. v. Minister of National Revenue (Customs & Excise)*) 271 N.R. 183, 205 F.T.R. 305 (note) (C.A.), leave to appeal refused (2001), 2001 CarswellNat 2734, 2001 CarswellNat 2735, 291 N.R. 197 (note) (S.C.C.), at 560 [F.C.]; *Federated Co-Operatives Ltd. v. R.*, 273 N.R. 281, 2001 CarswellNat 1451, 2001 FCA 217, 2001 D.T.C. 5414, [2001] 3 C.T.C. 269 (C.A.); *cf. Forest Oil Corp. v. R.* (1996), [1997] 1 F.C. 624, 1996 CarswellNat 2002, 1996 CarswellNat 2648, (sub nom. *Forest Oil Corp. v. Minister of National Revenue*) 126 F.T.R. 119, 4 G.T.C. 6269 (T.D.), additional reasons at 1998 CarswellNat 234, 144 F.T.R. 62, [1998] 2 C.T.C. 381 (T.D.).

56 Chambers, *supra*, note 54, at 199.

If that is true, then proprietary restitution generally should not be possible with respect to beneficial services.[57] After all, unlike money, land and goods, services cannot be restored *in specie*. And while the defendant may have other assets that are theoretically capable of being held on trust, the plaintiff is not, by the mere provision of services, sufficiently connected to them so as to justify the creation of property rights.

The most obvious objection to that analysis is that it is contrary to precedent. Canadian courts habitually impose a constructive trust if one cohabitee provided services that facilitated the preservation or improvement of an asset that the other cohabitee held prior to the relationship.[58] It may be, however, that while a constructive trust is warranted in such circumstances, it is better explained not on the basis of unjust enrichment, but rather as a means of perfecting the parties' intentions and protecting the plaintiff's detrimental reliance.[59] That possibility is explored below.

Assuming that the defendant received and (traceably) retained an enrichment that is capable of being the subject matter of a trust, the principled approach further limits the availability of proprietary restitution to situations in which the defendant did not acquire full beneficial ownership of the relevant asset before the plaintiff's right to restitution crystallized. That means, to begin, that a trust generally should be available if the plaintiff's intention was vitiated by ignorance, error or illegitimate pressure. In *Chase Manhattan*, for instance, the plaintiff never truly intended to confer the benefit upon the defendant. The defendant consequently had no right to retain it.

The situation is more complicated where the plaintiff's intention was impaired, not in the sense of being vitiated, but rather in the sense of being conditional. In such circumstances, a further distinction needs to be drawn depending upon whether or not, when initially intending to effect the transfer, the plaintiff also intended for the defendant to immediately receive full beneficial use of the asset.[60] If so, then proprietary restitution should not be possible. If the plaintiff was prepared at the outset to allow the defendant to dispose of the asset and merely become subject to a debt upon the condition's failure, then the mere fact that the defendant fortuitously continues to hold the asset when the condition does fail is not sufficient to justify the creation of a property right in the plaintiff's favour. In contrast, if, despite the intended transfer, the plaintiff never intended the defendant to enjoy full beneficial ownership over the asset, then proprietary restitution should be available. Since the plaintiff never agreed to relinquish full control over the asset, the enrichment should be recoverable *in specie* when the condition for the defendant's retention fails.

---

57 An exception would be justified with respect to services that *create* an asset, but not to those that merely *improve* an asset or allow the owner of an asset to *retain* it: Chambers, *ibid.*, at 209.

58 See, for example, *Peter v. Beblow*, *supra*, note 31.

59 Chambers, *supra*, note 54, at 201-207.

60 Although the distinction may be fine and, in some cases, difficult to draw, it effectively already is drawn for the purpose of identifying *Quistclose* trusts: *Barclays Bank Ltd. v. Quistclose Investments Ltd.*, [1970] A.C. 567 (H.L.). See also *Twinsectra Ltd.*, *supra*, note 34.

(iii) *Priority in Insolvency*

The principled approach determines the availability of a restitutionary trust formalistically, by reference to the nature of the defendant's unjust enrichment. It is not overtly driven by external considerations, such as insolvency.[61] Other commentators, in contrast, have argued that the imposition of a trust should very much be dictated by such considerations. A minority view, as seen in *Chase Manhattan*, holds that, in the interest of effective restitution, the plaintiff's inability to fully satisfy a personal judgment against the defendant may justify the availability of a proprietary order.[62] The more common view, however, is that restitution *prima facie* should be personal, and that proprietary relief should be reserved for special circumstances in which the claimant should not be required to bear the burden of the defendant's insolvency.

A typical line of argument classifies unjust enrichment claimants according to whether they are more analogous to secured or unsecured creditors.[63] A plaintiff who acted pursuant to a vitiated intention (*e.g.* because of mistake, ignorance, incapacity or illegitimate pressure) normally is akin to a secured creditor insofar as he or she never intended to assume the risk of the defendant's insolvency.[64] A trust consequently is appropriate. In contrast, if relief is sought on the basis of a qualified intention, then, unless the relevant set of conditions fettered the defendant's interest in the asset, the plaintiff assumed a position akin to an unsecured

---

61 "[I]t is difficult to understand why an event, which is wholly unrelated to the unjust enrichment that generates the trust, should affect the creation or continuation of that property right": Chambers, *supra*, at 212. Professor Birks similarly has also questioned the allocation of property rights on the basis of an inquiry that asks:

> . . .who deserves priority against an insolvent defendant and who should join the queue of unsecured creditors waiting to share the residual dividend, if any. Quite apart from the fact that property determines many other issues too, that question is for those charged from time to time with reforming insolvency laws, not for a court presiding over a particular disaster which nobody deserved. The complex rationality of "women and children first" is not to be re-examined as each ship goes down.

"Restitution of Unjust Enrichment", in A. Burrows & E. Peel, eds., *Commercial Remedies: Current Issues and Problems* (Oxford: Oxford University Press, 2003) 131 at 167.

62 American Law Institute, *Restatement of the Law of Restitution: Quasi-Contracts and Constructive Trusts* (St. Paul: American Law Institute Publishers, 1937) at 645ff. See also *Peter v. Beblow*, *supra*, note 31, at 652 (S.C.C.); *Zaidan Group Ltd. v. City of London, supra*, note 51, at 447.

63 A. Burrows, *The Law of Restitution*, 2d ed. (London: Butterworths, 2002) at 64ff.; A. Burrows, "Proprietary restitution: Unmasking Unjust Enrichment" (2001), 117 L.Q.R. 412 at 423ff. P.D. Maddaugh & J.D. McCamus, *The Law of Restitution* (Aurora, Ont.: Canada Law Book, 1990) at 94ff.

64 There are, however, exceptions. Consider a case in which the plaintiff paid money pursuant to a contract that he or she wrongly believed was valid. The plaintiff's error may warrant restitution, but, if the putative contract did not secure the parties' performance, there is no justification for granting the advantages that proprietary relief would offer in the event of the defendant's insolvency. Regardless of the agreement's invalidity, the facts reveal that the plaintiff was willing to transfer the impugned benefit to the defendant in exchange for a purely personal obligation to provide counter-performance. See *Sinclair v. Brougham, supra*, note 32; *cf. Taypotat v. Surgeson*, [1985] 3 W.W.R. 18, 1985 CarswellSask 55, 18 E.T.R. 195, 55 C.B.R. (N.S.) 218, 37 Sask. R. 205 (C.A.).

creditor. In such circumstances, it is appropriate to restrict recovery to the enforcement of a personal judgment. There is no need to provide greater protection than the plaintiff had arranged for himself or herself.

One possible objection to that analysis is that the unjust enrichment claimant is no different than many (perhaps most) civil litigants. The mistaken payer may not assume the risk of the defendant's insolvency, but nor does the victim of a tort. Indeed, the latter may be the more sympathetic character. Whereas the plaintiff in *Chase Manhattan* could have avoided its own error through greater care,[65] there was relatively little that, say, May Donoghue could have done to avoid the contaminated bottle of ginger beer.[66] And yet, tort claimants do not enjoy priority over their defendant's general creditors. Nevertheless, it may be possible to draw a sensible distinction. The plaintiff in an unjust enrichment case not only suffers a loss, but, unlike the typical tort victim, also confers an enrichment upon the defendant. Priority for the tort victim necessarily would deprive the defendant's general creditors of assets to which they normally would be entitled. In contrast, priority for the unjust enrichment claimant merely precludes the defendant's general creditors from enjoying the benefit of an asset that never should have been at the defendant's disposal. In that sense, proprietary relief for the unjust enrichment claimant leaves the defendant's general creditors none the worse for wear.[67]

Notes and Questions

1. Although the various forms of illegitimate pressure that are recognized in equity are examined elsewhere in greater detail,[68] it is possible to briefly comment on them in these notes. To begin, there is, in the present context, a natural temptation to organize the concepts of undue influence and unconscionability under the rubric of wrongdoing insofar

---

65 Restitution is available regardless of the plaintiff's carelessness in creating the error that resulted in the mistaken payment: *Kelly v. Solari* (1841), 9 M. & W. 54, 152 E.R. 24 (Exch.); *RBC Dominion Securities Inc. v. Dawson* (1994), 111 D.L.R. (4th) 230, 1994 CarswellNfld 308, [1994] N.J. No. 22, 114 Nfld. & P.E.I.R. 187, 356 A.P.R. 187 (C.A.). Likewise, relief is available even if the defendant was innocent of the operative error: *Air Canada v. Ontario (Liquor Control Board)* (1997), 148 D.L.R. (4th) 193, 1997 CarswellOnt 1979, 1997 CarswellOnt 1980, 214 N.R. 1, 102 O.A.C. 1, 33 O.R. (3d) 479 (headnote only), [1997] 2 S.C.R. 581, 5 G.T.C. 7251; *Central Guaranty Trust Co. v. Dixdale Mortgage Investment Corp.* (1994), 121 D.L.R. (4th) 53, 1994 CarswellOnt 760, 43 R.P.R. (2d) 137, 77 O.A.C. 253, 24 O.R. (3d) 506 (C.A.).

66 *Donoghue v. Stevenson*, [1932] A.C. 562 (H.L.).

67 Exceptions may exist. For example, a creditor may have extended unsecured credit in the mistaken belief that the defendant was fully entitled to dispose of the assets in his or her possession, including those representing the enrichment received from the plaintiff. It therefore has been suggested that, insofar as it prejudiced other creditors, the plaintiff's negligence perhaps should bar the imposition of a trust. See D.M. Paciocco, "The Remedial Constructive Trust: A Principled Basis for Priorities Over Creditors" (1989), 68 Can. Bar Rev. 315 at 348-349.

68 S.M. Waddams, *The Law of Contracts*, 4th ed. (Toronto: Canada Law Book, 1999) c. 14.

as the defendant may have improperly taken advantage of the plaintiff.[69] It is suggested, however, that those concepts may be better addressed within the autonomous action for unjust enrichment as explanations as to why the plaintiff's intention was impaired.[70] Lord Diplock offered a similar explanation of duress.[71]

> The use of economic duress to induce another person to part with property or money is not a tort *per se*; the form that duress takes may, or may not, be tortious. . . . Where the particular form taken by the economic duress used is itself a tort, the restitutional remedy for money had and received by the defendant to the plaintiff's use is one which the plaintiff is entitled to pursue as an alternative remedy to an action for damages in tort.

Consequently, while some forms of improper pressure involve wrongful acts, and thereby support concurrent claims for wrongdoing, the important point for present purposes is that, as a result of the circumstances, including the defendant's behaviour, the plaintiff's apparent decision to part with an asset was impaired and hence capable of supporting a restitutionary action.

2. If a person acquires property from another through undue influence, duress or compulsion in an *inter vivos* transaction, the transaction may be avoided in equity by the injured party.[72] The doctrine applies only to *inter vivos* transactions because similar situations arising in the context of wills are dealt with by analogous, but distinct, doctrines of probate. In the latter situation, the iniquitous party does not receive the property, since the will of the testator is denied probate.[73]

If the parties are in a fiduciary or confidential relationship, most authorities agree that equity raises a rebuttable presumption of undue influence. It does so because it is more likely than not, in those relationships, that the transferor was unable to exercise his or her own will and was overborne by the fiduciary.[74] The presumption is most easily rebutted by proof that the transferor had independent legal advice.[75]

---

69 *Barclays Bank plc v. O'Brien*, [1994] 1 A.C. 180 (U.K. H.L.); *Royal Bank of Scotland plc v. Etridge (No. 2)*, [2001] 3 W.L.R. 1021 (U.K. H.L.) (undue influence as a wrong); *Harry v. Kreutziger* (1978), 95 D.L.R. (3d) 231, 1979 CarswellBC 487, 9 B.C.L.R. 166 (C.A.), at 241 [D.L.R.]; *Portman Building Society v. Dusangh*, [2000] Lloyds Rep. Bank. 197 (C.A.) (unconscionability as "moral fraud").

70 *Agnew v. Länsförsäkringsbolagens*, [2001] 1 A.C. 223 (U.K. H.L.), at 264; *C.I.B.C. Mortgages plc v. Pitt*, [1994] 1 A.C. 200 (U.K. H.L.), at 209; *Bridgeman v. Green* (1757), Wilm. 58, 97 E.R. 22.

71 *Universe Tankships Inc. of Monrovia v. International Transport Workers' Federation, the Universe Sentinel*, [1983] 1 A.C. 366 (U.K. H.L.), at 386. See also *Dimskal Shipping Co. S.A. v. International Transport Workers' Federation, The Evia Luck*, [1992] 2 A.C. 152 (U.K. H.L.), at 166; P. Birks & N.Y. Chin, "On the Nature of Undue Influence", in J. Beatson & D. Friedmann, eds., *Good Faith and Fault in Contract* (Oxford: Oxford University Press, 1995) 57; R.B. Grantham & C.E.F. Rickett, *Enrichment & Restitution in New Zealand* (Oxford: Hart, 1998) 85ff.; A. Burrows, *The Law of Restitution*, 2d ed. (London: Butterworths, 2002), chs. 5-8.

72 See Finn, §172.

73 See A.H. Oosterhoff, *Oosterhoff on Wills and Succession: Text, Commentary and Cases*, 5th ed. (Toronto: Carswell, 2001), ch. 5, parts 4 and 5, for a discussion of these doctrines.

74 *Bradley v. Crittenden*, [1932] 3 D.L.R. 193, 1932 CarswellAlta 75, [1932] S.C.R. 552, at 194 [D.L.R.] *per* Duff A.C.J.

75 See *Davis v. Walker* (1902), 5 O.L.R. 173 (C.A.), which held that the presumption applies to gifts *mortis causa*. See *contra Slovchenko v. Toronto Dominion Bank* (1963), 42 D.L.R. (2d) 484, 1963 CarswellOnt 153, [1964] 1 O.R. 410 (H.C.); *Rushford v. Hunchuk* (1970), 16 D.L.R. (3d) 731, 1970 CarswellSask 45, [1971] 1 W.W.R. 628 (Q.B.).

If the parties do not stand in a fiduciary or confidential relationship, the transaction may still be avoided, but there is not normally a presumption in favour of the transferor. In order to raise the presumption, the plaintiff must prove that the relationship between the parties had an inherent potential for domination and (at least in commercial transactions) that he or she was unduly disadvantaged by the transaction under review.[76] There is also not normally a presumption of undue influence in inter-family transfers.[77] Instead the undue influence must be proved.[78]

In redressing undue influence, the courts normally do not speak of trusts. In most cases, there is no apparent need to do so because the transaction can be effectively avoided simply through a declaration of invalidity and, if necessary, an order directing the reconveyance of property. Alternatively, the court may revest title in the transferor.

The proprietary nature of relief is demonstrated by cases in which the property comes into the hands of a third party, either directly or indirectly, as a result of the pressure applied by the party exerting the undue influence. In such circumstances, the transferor is entitled to follow the property (or its traceable proceeds)[79] and, unless the third party was a *bona fide* purchaser of the legal estate for value and without notice, recover it *in specie*. Consequently, although such terminology is not always used, the third party may be regarded as holding the property on constructive (or resulting) trust.[80]

It is important to appreciate that the transferor's interest generally is regarded for priority purposes as a mere equity and therefore does not bind a third person who is a *bona fide* purchaser of either a legal or an equitable interest without notice.[81] Apart from priorities, the equity is regarded as a property interest, which can be devised[82] and assigned.[83]

---

76 *Goodman Estate v. Geffen* (1991), 81 D.L.R. (4th) 211, [1991] S.C.J. No. 53, 1991 CarswellAlta 91, 1991 CarswellAlta 557, [1991] 5 W.W.R. 389, 42 E.T.R. 97, [1991] 2 S.C.R. 353, 125 A.R. 81, 14 W.A.C. 81, 80 Alta. L.R. (2d) 293, 127 N.R. 241.

77 See *Wegrzynek v. Kinash*, [1978] 3 W.W.R. 210, 1978 CarswellSask 48, 3 E.T.R. 270 (Q.B.); *Peckford v. Dingle* (1972), 2 Nfld. & P.E.I.R. 61, 1971 CarswellNfld 21 (T.D.). But see *Geffen*, *ibid.*

78 See, *e.g.*, *British Columbia Public Trustee v. Skoretz* (1972), 32 D.L.R. (3d) 749, 1972 CarswellBC 292, [1973] 2 W.W.R. 638 (S.C.), nursing home operator; *Tannock v. Bromley* (1979), 10 B.C.L.R. 62, 1979 CarswellBC 7 (S.C.), hypnotherapist; *Marsh Estate, Re* (1991), 41 E.T.R. 225, 1991 CarswellNS 95, 104 N.S.R. (2d) 266, 283 A.P.R. 266 (C.A.), brother-in-law to frail elderly widow; *Brocklehurst's Estate, Re*, [1978] 1 Ch. 14 (C.A.); *Garland v. Clarke* (1982), 41 Nfld. & P.E.I.R. 75, 119 A.P.R. 75, 1982 CarswellNfld 185 (Dist. Ct.). See also *Cornish v. Midland Bank*, [1985] 3 All E.R. 513 (C.A.), which held that a bank which was negligent in explaining the effect of a mortgage to a customer, was liable in damages, but the mortgage itself would not be set aside unless the customer could show that the bank had taken unfair advantage of her. The latter would raise the presumption of undue influence.

79 *Goddard v. Carlisle* (1821), 9 Price 169, 147 E.R. 57; *Lancashire Loans Ltd. v. Black*, [1934] 1 K.B. 380 (C.A.), at 416-7.

80 A.J. Oakley, *Constructive Trusts*, 2nd ed. (London: Sweet & Maxwell Limited, 1987) at 14; Scott, §§768-9; *cf.* R. Chambers, *Resulting Trusts* (Oxford: Clarendon Press, 1997) at 135; G. Jones, *Goff & Jones: The Law of Restitution*, 6th ed. (London: Sweet & Maxwell, 2002) at 343, 360.

81 *Lancashire Loans Ltd. v. Black*, *supra*, note 79; *Phillips v. Phillips* (1862), 4 De G. F. & J. 208, 45 E.R. 1164; *Latec Investments Ltd. v. Hotel Terrigal Pty. Ltd. (in liq.)* (1965), 113 C.L.R. 265 (Australia H.C.).

82 *Stump v. Gaby* (1852), 2 De G. M. & G. 623, 42 E.R. 1015.

83 *Dickinson v. Burrell* (1866), L.R. 1 Eq. 337.

3. Aside from cases of undue influence, equity has long been willing to interfere in unconscionable transactions. It traditionally regarded a transaction as unconscionable if property was transferred at a gross undervalue and it would set aside such a transaction even if there was no undue influence or inequality of bargaining power.[84] The modern cases, however, require inequality of bargaining power arising from ignorance, need or distress, as well as substantial unfairness in the transaction.[85]

Equity's jurisdiction in this area has largely been supplanted by statute,[86] but where it remains operative the normal remedy is to set the transaction aside.[87] As in the case of undue influence, the constructive trust is relevant in this area if the transferee is insolvent or transfers the property to another person who is not a *bona fide* purchaser for value of the legal estate without notice.

4. On the basis of fraudulent misrepresentations and forgeries, M obtains a line of credit for $3M from a bank. M draws upon the line of credit to buy several paintings, some of which he gives as gifts to his wife. The bank did not take security in any of the art. M subsequently became bankrupt. The bank claimed a constructive trust over the paintings on the basis of the autonomous action in unjust enrichment. What relief, if any, should be available to the bank?[88]

5. H, an automobile dealership, purportedly sold a truck to E. Part of the price was paid by way of a trade-in, but the remainder was to be financed by a lender on terms that were to be settled in the future. Despite the outstanding terms, H gave possession of the vehicle to E and, so as to allow him to arrange insurance, signed ownership documents. H did not register security under the P.P.S.A. because some of the terms of the sale agreement remained outstanding. The lender subsequently refused to advance financing and E became bankrupt. H claimed a constructive trust over the truck on the basis of the autonomous action in unjust enrichment. What relief, if any, should the court have granted?[89]

6. N, an insurance company, was in financial difficulty. It received money from A, who wished to purchase an insurance contract. N was then forced to cease operations, but it did not publicly disclose that fact for one week. During the interim, it received money from B, who wished to purchase an insurance premium. N's assets were insufficient to satisfy claims by both A and B. B, however, claims a constructive trust on the basis that, unlike A, it made its payment pursuant to the mistake of fact that N was still in operation at the time of payment. Is B entitled to proprietary restitution and the priority that it would create over A?[90]

7. After stealing money from her employer, K became subject to a number of claims. Her employer claimed priority on the basis that, as a result of the theft, K held the money

---

84   *Coles v. Trecothick* (1804), 9 Ves. 234, 32 E.R. 592.

85   *Harry v. Kreutziger, supra,* note 69, at 237.

86   See, *e.g.,* the *Unconscionable Transactions Relief Act,* R.S.O. 1990, c. U.2.

87   *Collins v. Forest Hill Investment Corp. Ltd.* (1967), 63 D.L.R. (2d) 492, [1967] 2 O.R. 351 (Co. Ct.).

88   *Baltman v. Coopers & Lybrand Ltd.* (1996), 43 C.B.R. (3d) 33, 1996 CarswellOnt 4337, (sub nom. *Melnitzer (Bankrupt), Re*) 15 O.T.C. 221 (Bktcy.), additional reasons at (1997), 1997 CarswellOnt 2766, 47 C.B.R. (3d) 121 (Bktcy.), varied (1998), 1998 CarswellOnt 1663 (C.A.).

89   *Ellingsen (Trustee of) v. Hallmark Ford Sales Ltd., supra,* note 38. See J.S. Ziegel, "The Unwelcome Intrusion of the Remedial Constrcutive Trust in Personal Property Security Law" (2001), 34 C.B.L.J. 460; S. Barkehall Thomas, "Constructive Trust Protects Unpaid Vendor" [2001] Restitution L. Rev. 93.

90   D.M. Paciocco, "The Remedial Constructive Trust: A Principled Basis for Priorities Over Creditors" (1989), 68 Can. Bar Rev. 315 at 344-345.

on trust for it. Did K, as a result of the theft, obtain title to the money? If not, is it possible for her to hold that money on trust?[91]

Does it help to say that "the constructive trust can be used as a remedial device to accomplish specific restitution whenever that result is appropriate, regardless of title, since the trust is merely a fiction" and that "the requirement of a nominal title in the constructive trustee should be abandoned 'as an unwarranted hangover of the historical connection between the constructive trust and the express trust'"?[92] If theft does not affect title, why would the plaintiff not simply rely on legal remedies? Which legal remedies are available in such circumstances? Do those remedies provide priority over competing creditors?

3. WRONGFUL GAINS #1 — BREACH OF CONFIDENCE

A trust may be imposed to effect proprietary restitution under the autonomous action in unjust enrichment. A constructive trust may also be imposed to compel proprietary disgorgement of a benefit that the defendant acquired through wrong-doing. Because of the size of the topic, we have divided our examination of that rule into three sections, dealing with: (i) breach of confidence, (ii) breach of fiduciary duty, and (iii) culpable homicide.

For the purposes of breach of confidence, we will focus in this section on *International Corona Resources Ltd. v. Lac Minerals Ltd.*[93] By way of preface, however, it will be useful to first outline the nature of the cause of action and its associated remedies.

(a) Elements of the Claim

The cause of action in breach of confidence requires proof of three elements.

- *Confidential Information* — The information must be confidential in nature. In other words, it must not generally be known to the relevant segment of the public. But it need not pertain to a new discovery, such that it could be patented. Nor is confidentiality necessarily lost merely because the information is known to a small number of people. Confidentiality sometimes is a question of degree. On the other hand, information will not be considered confidential if it consists merely of the ordinary skills that a person acquires in the course of employment. Nor will it be protected as being confidential if such a result would be illegal or against public policy.
- *Confidential Circumstances* — The information must have been imparted to the defendant in circumstances that imported a duty of confidence. The obligation may have arisen expressly (*e.g.* as a result of a contractual stipulation) or impliedly (*e.g.* as when a person finds a notebook, clearly marked

---

91 *Re Kolari, supra,* note 50; *Goodbody v. Bank of Montreal, supra,* note 28; *Blackhawk Downs Inc. v. Arnold* (1972), 38 D.L.R. (3d) 75, 1972 CarswellOnt 85, [1973] 3 O.R. 729, 17 C.B.R. (N.S.) 284 (H.C.); *Hamilton Provident & Loan Society v. Gilbert* (1884), 6 O.R. 434.

92 D.M. Paciocco, "The Remedial Constructive Trust: A Principled Basis for Priorities Over Creditors" (1989), 68 Can. Bar Rev. 315 at 329 (footnotes omitted).

93 *Supra,* note 7.

"diary," on a bus). Moreover, the duty of confidence may apply not only to the initial recipient, but also to subsequent parties. It may also apply with respect to information that the recipient initially believed was ordinary, but prior to disclosure discovered was confidential.

- *Detriment* — The defendant must have acted upon the information without authority and to the plaintiff's detriment. The final part of that requirement is somewhat controversial. In *LAC Minerals*, La Forest J. echoed the orthodox view that the cause of action is complete only upon "detriment" to the plaintiff. Other judges have held, however, that the requirement may be satisfied by proof of the emotional or psychological distress that may accompany the disclosure of an intimate secret,[94] or that disclosure of a secret may be detrimental *per se*.[95]

As long as the constituent elements of the cause of action are established, breach of confidence may arise in virtually any setting. It is not inherently limited to particular contexts. The cases consequently run the gamut from details of a model's drug addiction,[96] to recipes for Clamato juice,[97] to information acquired by a spy on behalf of a government.[98]

(b) Nature of the Claim

Breach of confidence historically was regarded as an equitable cause of action.[99] In *Lac Minerals Ltd.*, La Forest J. agreed with that characterization. Sopinka J., however, suggested that breach of confidence had become *sui generis*.[100]

> The foundation for the action for breach of confidence does not rest solely on one of the traditional jurisdictional bases for action of contract, tort or property. The action is *sui generis* relying on all three of them to enforce the policy that confidences must be respected.

The issue of characterization is thought to be important primarily insofar as it affects the range of remedial options. Sopinka J. accordingly went on to say that

---

94   *Argyll (Duchess) v. Argyll (Duke)*, [1967] Ch. 302.

95   *Attorney-General v. Guardian Newspapers Ltd. (No. 2) (Spycatcher)*, [1990] 1 A.C. 109 (U.K. H.L.) at 256, *per* Lord Keith.

96   *Campbell v. Mirror Group Newspapers Ltd.*, [2004] U.K.H.L. 22.

97   *Cadbury Schweppes Inc. v. FBI Foods Ltd.* (1999), 167 D.L.R. (4th) 577, 1999 CarswellBC 77, 1999 CarswellBC 78, [1999] S.C.J. No. 6, 83 C.P.R. (3d) 289, 235 N.R. 30, 42 B.L.R. (2d) 159, 117 B.C.A.C. 161, 191 W.A.C. 161, 59 B.C.L.R. (3d) 1, [1999] 5 W.W.R. 751, [1999] 1 S.C.R. 142, [2000] F.S.R. 491.

98   *Attorney-General v. Guardian Newspapers Ltd. (No. 2) (Spycatcher)*, *supra*, note 95.

99   *Ibid.*

100 *Supra*, note 7. See also *Apotex Fermentation Inc. v. Novopharm Ltd.* (1998), 162 D.L.R. (4th) 111, 1998 CarswellMan 318, 80 C.P.R. (3d) 449, 129 Man. R. (2d) 161, 180 W.A.C. 161, [1998] 10 W.W.R. 455, 42 C.C.L.T. (2d) 133 (C.A.).

the "multi-faceted jurisdictional basis for the action provides the Court with considerable flexibility in fashioning a remedy."[101]

The Supreme Court of Canada had occasion to revisit the matter in *Cadbury Schweppes Inc. v. FBI Foods Ltd.*[102] While Binnie J. declined the opportunity to settle the issue of classification, he did confirm that there is "ample jurisdiction to fashion appropriate relief out of the full gamut of available remedies."[103] He further said that the applicable remedy in any given dispute ought to be "dictated by the facts of the case rather than strict jurisdictional or doctrinal considerations."[104] The goal in each instance is to vindicate the societal interest in maintaining secrets and to redress the factual consequences of the defendant's breach or threatened breach.

(c) Remedies for Breach of Confidence

A breach of confidence consequently may be met by virtually the whole range of private law remedies. To begin, a court quite often will provide direct protection by imposing an injunction to prevent the continued or threatened disclosure of information.[105] The availability of such relief is influenced by a number of factors, including the nature of the information, the quality of the defendant's breach (*e.g.* whether it was deliberate or inadvertent), the adequacy of monetary relief, the balance of convenience as between the parties and the public interest.

Along similar lines, a court may order the return or destruction of confidential information, such as plans,[106] or, if the defendant acquired a patent as a result of the confidential information, compel an assignment of the patent to the plaintiff.[107]

Monetary relief may be awarded in addition to, or in lieu of, other remedies.[108] Once again, there are a number of possibilities. Compensation may be available with respect to a loss that the plaintiff suffered as a result of the defendant's breach. Moreover, reflecting the variety of circumstances in which a breach may

---

101 Whether such flexibility is, in fact, appropriate and desirable is an open question. Compare J.D. Davies, "Duties of Confidence and Loyalty" [1990] Lloyd's Maritime & Commercial L.Q. 4; P. Birks, "The Remedies for Abuse of Breach of Confidential Information" [1990] Lloyd's Maritime & Commercial L.Q. 460.

102 *Supra*, note 97.

103 *Ibid.*, at 589.

104 *Ibid.*

105 R.J. Sharpe, *Injunctions and Specific Performance* (looseleaf edition) ¶5.130ff.

106 *Floydd v. Cheney*, [1970] 1 All E.R. 446.

107 *Shellmar Products Co. v. Allen-Qualley* (1929), 36 F.2d 623.

108 Equity's ability to award damages historically was limited under *Lord Cairns' Act, 1858* to situations in which they were sought in lieu of injunctive relief. If an injunction for some reason was unarguable (*e.g.* because confidential information already had been disclosed), then it sometimes was said that damages similarly were unavailable. In *Cadbury Schweppes Inc. v. FBI Foods Ltd.*, however, Binnie J. said that, "having regard to the evolution of equitable principles ... we should clearly affirm that, in this country, the authority to award financial compensation for breach of confidence is inherent in the exercise of general equitable jurisdiction and does not depend upon the niceties of *Lord Cairns' Act* or its statutory successors": *supra*, at 604.

occur, compensation may be calculated in a number of different ways. For instance, in *Seager v. Copydex (No. 2)*,[109] Lord Denning recognized three categories.

- The first category arises if there was "nothing very special" about the information, such that it did not involve a particularly inventive step and could have been developed simply by hiring a competent consultant. Compensation may be quantified by reference to a reasonable consulting fee.
- The second category arises if the information was "something special," such that it involved an inventive step and could not be obtained simply be hiring a competent consultant. Compensation may be calculated in excess of a mere consultant's fee, by reference to the price that would be paid between a willing buyer and a willing seller.
- The final category arises if the information was "very special indeed." In that situation, the plaintiff has the right to demand damages equal in value to a royalty that, under a proper arrangement, would have been paid as between the parties.

Compensation is the appropriate remedy when a court is concerned with the loss that the plaintiff suffered as a result of the defendant's breach. Sometimes, however, a court is concerned not with the plaintiff's loss, but rather with the defendant's gain. If so, then the appropriate measure of relief is "restitution" (or, perhaps more accurately, disgorgement). Again, there are several possibilities. "Restitutionary damages" may be awarded with respect to a benefit that the defendant enjoyed in the form of saved expenses.[110] That may be true, for instance, with respect to at least the first and second categories in *Seager v. Copydex (No. 2.)*. It is possible to view those measures of relief not only from the perspective of what the plaintiff lost, but also from the perspective of what the defendant saved or gained (*i.e.* the expense of hiring a consultant or the price of purchasing the information).

Alternatively, gain-based relief may be measured not by reference to an expense that the defendant saved, but rather by reference to a positive enrichment that he or she acquired as a result of breach. In other words, profits may be stripped. If liability takes the form of a personal obligation to give up the value of the ill-gotten gain, then it is common to speak of an "account of profits."[111] Such relief is well-established in Anglo-Canadian law. In contrast, only Canadian law alternatively allows disgorgement to be ordered proprietarily, by means of a constructive trust. *International Corona Resources Ltd. v. Lac Minerals Ltd.* is the leading case. It is, unfortunately, also a very difficult case.

---

109 [1969] 2 All E.R. 718, [1969] 1 W.L.R. 809 (C.A.), adopted in *Cadbury Schweppes Inc. v. FBI Foods Ltd.*, *supra*, note 97, at 606.

110 *Universal Thermosensors Ltd. v. Hibben*, [1992] 1 W.L.R. 840.

111 *Attorney-General v. Guardian Newspapers Ltd. (No. 2) (Spycatcher)*, *supra*, note 95; *Peter Pan Manufacturing Corpn. v. Corsets Silhouette Ltd.*, [1964] 1 W.L.R. 96.

Further Reading

G. Jones, "Restitution of Benefits Obtained in Breach of Another's Confidence" (1970), 86 L.Q. Rev. 463.

F. Gurry, *Breach of Confidence* (Oxford: Oxford University Press, 1984).

F. Gurry, "Breach of Confidence" in P.D. Finn, ed., *Essays in Equity* (Sydney: The Law Book Company Limited, 1985) 110.

P.Y. Atkinson and R.A. Spence, "Fiduciary Duties Owed by Departing Employees — The Emerging 'Unfairness' Principle" (1983-84), 8 Can. Bus. L.J. 501.

D.W.M. Waters, "*LAC Minerals Ltd. v. International Corona Resources Ltd.*" (1990), 69 Can. Bar Rev. 455.

R. Brait, "The Unauthorized Use of Confidential Information" (1991), 18 Can. Bus. L.J. 323.

P.M. Perell, "Breach of Confidence to the Rescue" (2002), 25 Adv. Q. 199.

D. Freedman, "The Great Canadian Juice War" (1999), 58 Cambridge L.J. 288

A. Abdullah & Tey-Tsun Hang, "To Make the Remedy Fit the Wrong" (1999), 115 L.Q. Rev. 376.

INTERNATIONAL CORONA RESOURCES LTD. v.
LAC MINERALS LTD.

(sub nom. *LAC Minerals Ltd. v. International Corona Resources Ltd.*) 61 D.L.R. (4th) 14, 1989 CarswellOnt 126, 1989 CarswellOnt 965, [1989] S.C.J. No. 83, 6 R.P.R. (2d) 1, 44 B.L.R. 1, 35 E.T.R. 1, 69 O.R. (2d) 287, 101 N.R. 239, 36 O.A.C. 57, [1989] 2 S.C.R. 574, 26 C.P.R. (3d) 97
Supreme Court of Canada

Corona, a junior mining company, had confidential information indicating that certain properties in northern Ontario, which were owned by Mrs. Williams, sat atop gold deposits of inestimable value. Corona shared that information with LAC Minerals, a senior mining company, with a view to acquiring the land and developing the project by means of a joint venture. LAC instead used the information to purchase the Williams land for itself. It then spent a considerable amount of money on the early stages of mining operations.

Corona brought actions against LAC in both breach of fiduciary duty and breach of confidence. By way of relief, Corona sought both monetary relief and proprietary relief.

At trial, R.E. Holland J. found that LAC had breached both a fiduciary duty and a duty of confidence, and that, but for those wrongs, Corona "would *probably* have acquired the. . .property."[112] He further held that the appropriate remedy for breach of fiduciary duty was a constructive trust, subject to a lien in favour of LAC for the cost of improvements and the amount paid to Mrs. Williams, less royalty payments. The trial judge also directed an account of the profits earned by LAC from the Williams property and ordered LAC to pay those profits with

---

112 *Lac Minerals Ltd.*, *supra*, note 7 at 546 (H.C.) (emphasis added).

interest to Corona. He did not determine the appropriate remedy for breach of confidence separately. Finally, in the event that an appellate court found that proprietary relief was inappropriate, Holland J. assessed damages at $700 million, the value of the mine at the date of judgment, determined on the basis of a discounted cash flow approach.

The Ontario Court of Appeal affirmed.[113] It agreed that LAC was liable for both breach of confidence and breach of fiduciary duty. It also held that the constructive trust was the appropriate remedy in the circumstances for breach of confidence as well as for breach of fiduciary duty.

In the Supreme Court of Canada, there was a sharp difference of opinion regarding the existence of a fiduciary duty and the appropriate remedy. All five members of the panel agreed that LAC was in breach of confidence, but the majority (McIntyre, Lamer and Sopinka JJ.) concluded that there was no breach of fiduciary duty. The majority, differently constituted (Lamer, Wilson and La Forest JJ.), further held that the appropriate remedy in the circumstances was a constructive trust. The main judgments were delivered by La Forest and Sopinka JJ.

La Forest J.:

Breach of confidence

I can deal quite briefly with the breach of confidence issue. I have already indicated that LAC breached a duty of confidence owed to Corona. The test for whether there has been a breach of confidence is not seriously disputed by the parties. It consists in establishing three elements: that the information conveyed was confidential, that it was communicated in confidence, and that is was misused by the party to whom it was communicated. In *Coco v. A.N. Clark (Engineers) Ltd.*,[114] Megarry J. (as he then was) put it as follows:

> In my judgment, three elements are normally required if, apart from contract, a case of breach of confidence is to succeed. First, the information itself, in the words of Lord Greene, M.R. in the *Saltman* case[115] must "have the necessary quality of confidence about it." Secondly, that information must have been imparted in circumstances importing an obligation of confidence. Thirdly, there must be an unauthorized use of that information to the detriment of the party communicating it.

This is the test applied by both the trial judge and the Court of Appeal. Neither party contends that it is the wrong test. LAC, however, forcefully argued that the courts below erred in their application of the test. LAC submitted that "the real issue is whether Corona proved that LAC received confidential information from it and [whether] it should have known such information was confidential."

---

113 *Lac Minerals Ltd., supra,* note 7 (C.A.).
114 [1969] R.P.C. 41 at 47 (Ch.).
115 *Saltman Engineering Co. Ltd. v. Campbell Engineering Co. Ltd.* (1948), 65 R.P.C. 203 at 215 (C.A.).

Sopinka J. has set out the findings of the trial judge on these issues, and I do not propose to repeat them. They are all supported by the evidence and adopted by the Court of Appeal. I would not interfere with them. Essentially, the trial judge found that the three elements set forth above were met: (1) Corona had communicated information that was private and had not been published. (2) While there was no mention of confidence with respect to the site visit, there was a mutual understanding between the parties that they were working towards a joint venture and that valuable information was communicated to LAC under circumstances giving rise to an obligation of confidence. (3) LAC made use of the information in obtaining the Williams property and was not authorized by Corona to bid on that property. I agree with my colleague that the information provided by Corona was the springboard that led to the acquisition of the William's property. I also agree that the trial judge correctly applied the reasonable man test. The trial judge's conclusion that it was obvious to Sheehan, LAC's vice-president for exploration, that the information was being communicated in circumstances giving rise to an obligation of confidence, following as it did directly on a finding of credibility against Sheehan, is unassailable.

In general, then, there is no difference between my colleague and me that LAC committed a breach of confidence in the present case. Where we differ — and it is a critically important difference — is in the nature and scope of the breach. The precise extent of that difference can be seen by a closer examination of the findings and evidence on the third element of the test set forth above, and I will, therefore, set forth my views on this element at greater length.

[His Lordship set out part of the judgments of the trial judge and of the Court of Appeal. He noted that the trial judge found on a balance of probabilities that, but for LAC's actions, Corona would have acquired the Williams' property and that LAC, therefore acted to Corona's detriment. He also noted that the Court of Appeal affirmed this finding. Since the trial judge was considering the issue of misuse of confidential information, Justice La Forest accordingly concluded that the trial judge found as a fact that LAC received and misused confidential information. He continued:]

If, as we saw, each of the three elements of the above-cited test are made out, a claim for breach of confidence will succeed. The receipt of confidential information in circumstances of confidence establishes a duty not to use that information for any purpose other than that for which it was conveyed. If the information is used for such a purpose, and detriment to the confider results, the confider will be entitled to a remedy.

There was some suggestion that LAC was only restricted from using the information imparted by Corona to acquire the Williams property for its own account, and had LAC acquired the claims on behalf of both Corona and LAC, there would have been no breach of duty. This, as I have noted, seems to me to misconstrue the finding of the trial judge. What is more, the evidence, in my view, does not support that position.

[His Lordship noted that the evidence did not support the suggestion that LAC could acquire the Williams property either on its own account, or for itself and Corona jointly. Further, the evidence disclosed that LAC was aware that it owed a duty to act in good faith toward Corona and that this duty comprehended an industry-recognized practice not to acquire a property which the party with which it was negotiating was seeking to acquire. He continued:]

This entire inquiry appears, however, to be misdirected. In establishing a breach of duty of confidence, the relevant question to be asked is what is the confidee entitled to do with the information, and not to what use he is prohibited from putting it. Any use other than a permitted use is prohibited and amounts to breach of duty. When information is provided in confidence, the obligation is on the confidee to show that the use to which he put the information is not a prohibited use. In *Coco v. A.N. Clark (Engineers) Ltd.,*[116] Megarry J. said this in regard to the burden on the confidee to repel a suggestion of confidence:

> In particular, where information of commercial or industrial value is given on a business-like basis and with some avowed common object in mind, such as a joint venture or the manufacture of articles by one party for the other, I would regard the recipient as carrying a heavy burden if he seeks to repel a contention that he was bound by an obligation of confidence.

In my view, the same burden applies where it is shown that confidential information has been used and the user is called upon to show that such use was permitted. LAC has not discharged that burden in this case.

I am therefore of the view that LAC breached a duty owed to Corona by approaching Mrs. Williams with a view to acquiring her property, and by acquiring that property, whether or not LAC intended to invite Corona to participate in its subsequent exploration and development. Such a holding may mean that LAC is uniquely disabled from pursuing property in the area for a period of time, but such a result is not unacceptable. LAC had the option of either pursuing a relationship with Corona in which Corona would disclose confidential information to LAC so that LAC and Corona could negotiate a joint venture for the exploration and development of the area, or LAC could, on the basis of publicly available information, have pursued property in the area on its own behalf. LAC, however, is not entitled to the best of both worlds.

In this regard, the case can be distinguished from *Coco v. A.N. Clark (Engineers) Ltd.,* in that here the confidential information led to the acquisition of a specific, unique asset. Imposing a disability on a party in possession of confidential information from participating in a market in which there is room for more than one participant may be unreasonable, such as where the information relates to a manufacturing process or a design detail. In such cases, it may be that the obligation on the confidee is not to use the confidential information in its possession without paying compensation for it or sharing the benefit derived from it.

---

116 *Supra,* note 114, at 48.

Where, however, as in the present case, there is only one property that Corona was seeking, the duty of confidence is a duty not to use the information. The fact that LAC is precluded from pursuing the Williams property does not impose an unreasonable restriction on LAC. Rather, it does the opposite by encouraging LAC to negotiate in good faith for the joint development of the property.

Fiduciary obligation

Having established that LAC breached a duty of confidence owed to Corona, the existence of a fiduciary relationship is only relevant if the remedies for a breach of a fiduciary obligation differ from those available for a breach of confidence. In my view, the remedies available to one head of claim are available to the other, so that provided a constructive trust is an appropriate remedy for the breach of confidence in this case, finding a fiduciary duty is not strictly necessary. In my view, regardless of the basis of liability, a constructive trust is the only just remedy in this case. None the less, in light of the argument, I think it appropriate to consider whether a fiduciary relationship exists in the circumstances here.

[His Lordship noted that there were three distinct usages of the term "fiduciary." The first refers to certain recognized relationships such as solicitor and client, directors and corporation, and guardian and ward, in which a fiduciary duty is presumed to rest on one of the parties to the relationship. The second refers to situations in which a fiduciary obligation arises as a matter of fact out of the specific circumstances of a relationship not typically regarded as fiduciary, such as a commercial relationship. The third and wrong usage refers to situations in which a person is called a fiduciary because it is thought necessary to do so to attract an appropriate remedy, such as the constructive trust.

His Lordship quoted an excerpt from a judgment of Wilson J. in *Frame v. Smith*[117] with approval. In that excerpt her Ladyship noted that a fiduciary relationship possesses three characteristics:

(1) The fiduciary has scope for the exercise of some discretion or power.

(2) The fiduciary can unilaterally exercise that power or discretion so as to affect the beneficiary's legal or practical interests.

(3) The beneficiary is peculiarly vulnerable to the fiduciary holding the discretion or power.

La Forest J. was of opinion that LAC was subject to fiduciary obligations in the second sense, that is, because of the circumstances of the case. In other words, on the facts of the case the relationship of the parties was such as to create a fiduciary relationship. His Lordship concluded that a fiduciary relationship had been created between Corona and LAC because (a) a relationship of trust and confidence had developed between them; (b) it was industry practice not to act to the other party's detriment when in serious negotiations; and (c) in the circumstances Corona was vulnerable to LAC because it was

---

117 [1987] 2 S.C.R. 99, 42 D.L.R. (4th) 81 at 98-9.

susceptible to harm from LAC's actions. He did not, however, regard vulnerability to be a necessary ingredient of every fiduciary relationship. Further, he concluded that the existence of a fiduciary obligation should not be denied because the parties could have regulated their affairs by means of a confidentiality agreement. He continued:]

Remedy

The appropriate remedy in this case can not be divorced from the findings of fact made by the courts below. As I indicated earlier, there is no doubt in my mind that but for the actions of LAC in misusing confidential information and thereby acquiring the Williams property, that property would have been acquired by Corona. That finding is fundamental to the determination of the appropriate remedy. Both courts below awarded the Williams property to Corona on payment to LAC of the value to Corona of the improvements LAC had made to the property. The trial judge dealt only with the remedy available for a breach of a fiduciary duty, but the Court of Appeal would have awarded the same remedy on the claim for breach of confidence, even though it was of the view that it was artificial and difficult to consider the relief available for that claim on the hypothesis that there was no fiduciary obligation.

The issue then is this. If it is established that one party (here LAC) has been enriched by the acquisition of an asset, the Williams property, that would have, but for the actions of that party been acquired by the plaintiff (here Corona), and if the acquisition of that asset amounts to a breach of duty to the plaintiff, here either a breach of fiduciary obligation or a breach of a duty of confidence, what remedy is available to the party deprived of the benefit? In my view the constructive trust is one available remedy, and in this case it is the only appropriate remedy.

In my view the facts present in this case make out a restitutionary claim, or what is the same thing, a claim for unjust enrichment. When one talks of restitution, one normally talks of giving back to someone something that has been taken from them (a restitutionary proprietary award), or its equivalent value (a personal restitutionary award). As the Court of Appeal noted in this case, Corona never in fact owned the Williams property, and so it cannot be "given back" to them. However, there are concurrent findings below that but for its interception by LAC, Corona would have acquired the property. In *Air Canada v. British Columbia*,[118] I said that the function of the law of restitution "is to ensure that where a plaintiff has been deprived of wealth that is either in his possession *or would have accrued for his benefit*, it is restored to him. The measure of restitutionary recovery is the gain the [defendant] made at the [plaintiff's] expense". In my view the fact that Corona never owned the property should not preclude it from the [*sic*] pursuing

---

118 *Supra*, note 24, at 193-4.

a restitutionary claim[119]. LAC has therefore been enriched at the expense of Corona.

That enrichment is also unjust, or unjustified, so that the plaintiff is entitled to a remedy. There is, in the words of Dickson J. in *Pettkus v. Becker*[120], "an absence of any juristic reason for the enrichment". The determination that the enrichment is "unjust" does not refer to abstract notions of morality and justice, but flows directly from the finding that there was a breach of a legally recognized duty for which the courts will grant relief. Restitution is a distinct body of law governed by its own developing system of rules. Breaches of fiduciary duties and breaches of confidence are both wrongs for which restitutionary relief is often appropriate. It is not every case of such a breach of duty, however, that will attract recovery based on the gain of the defendant at the plaintiff's expense. Indeed this has long been recognized by the courts.

. . .

In breach of confidence cases as well [as in breach of fiduciary cases], there is considerable flexibility in remedy. Injunctions preventing the continued use of the confidential information are commonly awarded. Obviously that remedy would be of no use in this case where the total benefit accrues to the defendant through a single misuse of information. An account of profits is also often available. Indeed in both courts below an account of profits to the date of transfer of the mine was awarded. Usually an accounting is not a restitutionary measure of damages. Thus, while it is measured according to the defendant's gain, it is not measured by the defendant's gain at the plaintiff's expense. Occasionally, as in this case, the measures coincide. In a case quite relevant here, this court unanimously imposed a constructive trust over property obtained from the misuse of confidential information.[121] More recently, a compensatory remedy has been introduced into the law of confidential relations. Thus in *Seager v. Copydex Ltd. (No. 2)*[122], an inquiry was directed concerning the market value of the information between a willing buyer and a willing seller. The defendant had unconsciously plagiarized the plaintiff's design. In those circumstances it would obviously have been unjust to exclude the defendant from the market when there was room for more than one participant.

. . .

In view of this remedial flexibility, detailed consideration must be given to the reasons a remedy measured by LAC's gain at Corona's expense is more appropriate than a remedy compensating the plaintiff for the loss suffered. In this case, the Court of Appeal found that if compensatory damages were to be awarded, those damages in fact equalled the value of the property. This was premised on the finding that but for LAC's breach, Corona would have acquired the property. Neither at this point nor any other did either of the courts below find Corona

---

119 See Birks, *An Introduction to the Law of Restitution* (1985), at 133-9.
120 *Supra*, note 7, at 274.
121 *Pre-Cam Exploration & Development Ltd. v. McTavish* (1966), 57 D.L.R. (2d) 557, 50 C.P.R. 299, [1966] S.C.R. 551.
122 *Supra*, note 109.

would only acquire one half or less of the Williams property. While I agree that, if they could in fact be adequately assessed, compensation and restitution in this case would be equivalent measures, even if they would not, a restitutionary measure would be appropriate.

The essence of the imposition of fiduciary obligations is its utility in the promotion and preservation of desired social behaviour and institutions. Likewise with the protection of confidences. In the modern world the exchange of confidential information is both necessary and expected. Evidence of an accepted business morality in the mining industry was given by the defendant, and the Court of Appeal found that the practice was not only reasonable, but that it would foster the exploration and development of our natural resources. The institution of bargaining in good faith is one that is worthy of legal protection in those circumstances where that protection accords with the expectations of the parties. The approach taken by my colleague, Sopinka J., would, in my view, have the effect not of encouraging bargaining in good faith, but of encouraging the contrary. If by breaching an obligation of confidence one party is able to acquire an asset entirely for itself, at a risk of only having to compensate the other for what the other would have received if a formal relationship between them were concluded, the former would be given a strong incentive to breach the obligation and acquire the asset. In the present case, it is true that had negotiations been concluded, LAC could also have acquired an interest in the Corona land, but that is only an expectation and not a certainty. Had Corona acquired the Williams property, as they would have but for LAC's breach, it seems probable that negotiations with LAC would have resulted in a concluded agreement. However, if LAC, during the negotiations, breached a duty of confidence owed to Corona, it seems certain that Corona would have broken off negotiations and LAC would be left with nothing. In such circumstances, many business people, weighing the risks, would breach the obligation and acquire the asset. This does nothing for the preservation of the institution of good faith bargaining or relationships of trust and confidence. The imposition of a remedy which restores an asset to the party who would have acquired it but for a breach of fiduciary duties or duties of confidence acts as a deterrent to the breach of duty and strengthens the social fabric those duties are imposed to protect. The elements of a claim in unjust enrichment having been made out, I have found no reason why the imposition of a restitutionary remedy should not be granted.

This court has recently had occasion to address the circumstances in which a constructive trust will be imposed in *Hunter Engineering Co. v. Syncrude Canada Ltd.*[123] There, the Chief Justice discussed the development of the constructive trust over 200 years from its original use in the context of fiduciary relationships, through to *Pettkus v. Becker*,[124] where the court moved to the modern approach with the constructive trust as a remedy for unjust enrichment. He identified that *Pettkus v. Becker*, set out a two-step approach. First, the court determines whether a claim for unjust enrichment is established, and then, secondly,

---

123 57 D.L.R. (4th) 321, [1989] 1 S.C.R. 426, 35 B.C.L.R. (2d) 145.
124 *Supra*, note 7.

examines whether in the circumstances a constructive trust is the appropriate remedy to redress that unjust enrichment. In *Hunter v. Syncrude*, a constructive trust was refused, not on the basis that it would not have been available between the parties (though in my view it may not have been appropriate), but rather on the basis that the claim for unjust enrichment had not been made out, so no remedial question arose.

In the case at hand, the restitutionary claim has been made out. The court can award either a proprietary remedy, namely that LAC hand over the Williams property, or award a personal remedy, namely a monetary award. While, as the Chief Justice observed, "the principle of unjust enrichment lies at the heart of the constructive trust",[125] the converse is not true. The constructive trust does not lie at the heart of the law of restitution. It is but one remedy, and will only be imposed in appropriate circumstances. Where it could be more appropriate than in the present case, however, it is difficult to imagine.

[His Lordship noted that it was virtually impossible to assess the actual monetary damage to Corona. He continued:]

To award only a monetary remedy in such circumstances when an alternative remedy is both available and appropriate would, in my view, be unfair and unjust.

There is no unanimous agreement on the circumstances in which a constructive trust will be imposed. Some guidelines can, however, be suggested. First, no special relationship between the parties is necessary. I agree with this comment of Wilson J. in *Hunter v. Syncrude:*[126]

Although both *Pettkus v. Becker*[127] and *Sorochan v. Sorochan*[128] were "family" cases, unjust enrichment giving rise to a constructive trust is by no means confined to such cases[129]. Indeed, to do so would be to impede the growth and impair the flexibility crucial to the development of equitable principles.

. . .

Secondly, it is not the case that a constructive trust should be reserved for situations where a right of property is recognized. That would limit the constructive trust to it institutional function, and deny to it the status of a remedy, its more important role. Thus, it is not in all cases that a pre-existing right of property will exist when a constructive trust is ordered. The imposition of a constructive trust can both recognize and create a right of property.

---

125 *Ibid.*, at 273.
126 *Supra*, note 123, at 383.
127 *Supra.*
128 *Supra*, note 43.
129 See *Deglman v. Guaranty Trust Co. of Canada*, [1954] 3 D.L.R. 785, [1954] S.C.R. 725.

[His Lordship referred to Goff and Jones,[130] who state that a proprietary claim should be granted when it is just to grant the plaintiff the additional benefits that flow from the recognition of a proprietary right. He continued:]

I do not countenance the view that a proprietary remedy can be imposed whenever it is "just" to do so, unless further guidance can be given as to what those situations may be. To allow such a result would be to leave the determination of proprietary rights to "some mix of judicial discretion. . .subjective views about which party 'ought to win'. . .and 'the formless void of individual moral opinion'".[131]

As Deane J. further noted:[132]

> Long before Lord Seldon's anachronism identifying the Chancellor's foot as the measure of Chancery relief, undefined notions of "justice" and what was "fair" had given way in the law of equity to the rule of ordered principle which is of the essence of any coherent system of rational law. The mere fact that it would be unjust or unfair in a situation of discord for the owner of a legal estate to assert his ownership against another provides, of itself, no mandate for a judicial declaration that the ownership in whole or in part lies, in equity, in that order.

Much of the difficulty disappears if it is recognized that in this context the issue of the appropriate remedy only arises once a valid restitutionary claim has been made out. The constructive trust awards a right in property, but that right can only arise once a right to relief has been established. In the vast majority of cases a constructive trust will not be the appropriate remedy. Thus, in *Hunter*,[133] had the restitutionary claim been made out, there would have been no reason to award a constructive trust, as the plaintiff's claim could have been satisfied simply by a personal monetary award; a constructive trust should only be awarded if there is reason to grant to the plaintiff the additional rights that flow from recognition of a right of property. Among the most important of these will be that it is appropriate that the plaintiff receive the priority accorded to the holder of a right of property in a bankruptcy. More important in this case is the right of the property holder to have changes in value accrue to his account rather than to the account of the wrongdoer. Here as well it is justified to grant a right of property since the concurrent findings below are that the defendant intercepted the plaintiff and thereby frustrated its efforts to obtain a specific and unique property that the courts below held would otherwise have been acquired. The recognition of a constructive trust simply redirects the title of the Williams property to its original course. The moral quality of the defendants' [*sic*] act may also be another consideration in determining whether a proprietary remedy is appropriate. Allowing the defendant to retain a specific asset when it was obtained through conscious wrongdoing may so offend a court that it would deny to the defendant the right

---

130 Lord Goff of Chieveley and Gareth Jones, *The Law of Restitution,* 3rd ed. (London: Sweet & Maxwell, 1986), at 78.

131 *Per* Deane J. in *Muschinski v. Dodds* (1985), 160 C.L.R. 583 at 616.

132 *Ibid.,* at 616.

133 *Supra,* note 123.

to retain the property. This situation will be more rare, since the focus of the inquiry should be upon the reasons for recognizing a right of property in the plaintiff, not on the reasons for denying it to the defendant.

Having specific regard to the uniqueness of the Williams property, to the fact that but for LAC's breaches of duty Corona would have acquired it, and recognizing the virtual impossibility of accurately valuing the property, I am of the view that it is appropriate to award Corona a constructive trust over that land.

. . .

SOPINKA J. (dissenting in part):

[Like La Forest J., Sopinka J. quoted and approved the three criteria of fiduciary relationships enumerated by Wilson J., in *Frame v. Smith*[134]. However, he was of opinion that normally fiduciary relationships ought not to be found in arm's-length commercial transactions, since the parties have the opportunity to prescribe their obligations in contract. Further, he believed vulnerability or dependency of one party to be essential to a fiduciary relationship and concluded that Corona was not vulnerable, or that, if it was, it had placed itself gratuitously in that position. Hence, in his opinion, there was no fiduciary relationship or breach thereof.

Sopinka J., did agree with the lower courts that Corona had made out a breach of confidence by LAC. He continued:]

Constructive trust or damages

The foundation of action for breach of confidence does not rest solely on one of the traditional jurisdictional bases for action of contract, equity or property. The action is *sui generis* relying on all three to enforce the policy of the law that confidences be respected.[135]

This multi-faceted jurisdictional basis for the action provides the court with considerable flexibility in fashioning a remedy. The jurisdictional basis supporting the particular claim is relevant in determining the appropriate remedy.[136] A constructive trust is ordinarily reserved for those situations where a right of property is recognized. As stated by the learned authors of Goff & Jones:[137]

In restitution, a constructive trust should be imposed if it is just to grant the plaintiff the additional benefits which flow from the recognition of a right of property.

---

134 *Supra*, note 117, at 98-9.
135 See Gurry, at 25-6, and Goff & Jones, at 664-7.
136 See *Nichrotherm Electrical Co. Ltd. v. Percy*, [1957] R.P.C. 207 at 213-4; Gurry, 26-7; and Goff & Jones, at 664-5.
137 *Ibid.*, at 209.

Although confidential information has some of the characteristics of property, its foothold as such is tenuous.[138] I agree in this regard with the statement of Lord Evershed in *Nichrotherm*,[139] that:

> . . .a man who thinks of a mechanical conception and then communicates it to others for the purpose of working out means of carrying it into effect does not, because the idea was his (assuming that it was), get proprietary rights equivalent to those of a patentee. Apart from such rights as may flow from the fact, for example, of the idea being of a secret process communicated in confidence or from some contract of partnership or agency or the like which he may enter into with his collaborator, the originator of the idea gets no proprietary rights out of the mere circumstance that he first thought of it.

As a result, there is virtually no support in the cases for the imposition of a constructive trust over property acquired as a result of the use of confidential information. In stating that such a remedy is possible, the Court of Appeal referred to Goff & Jones.[140] The discussion of proprietary claims commences[141] with the statement which I have quoted above and thereafter all references to constructive trust pertain to an accounting of profits. No reference is made to any case in which a constructive trust is imposed on property acquired as a result of the use of confidential information.

In Canada as in the United Kingdom, the existence of the constructive trust outside of a fiduciary relationship has been recognized as a possible remedy against unjust enrichment.[142]

In Canada this device has been sporadically employed where the unjust enrichment occurred in the context of a pre-existing special relationship between the parties. Thus in *Pettkus v. Becker*,[143] Dickson J. (as he then was) spoke of "a relationship tantamount to spousal". In *Nicholson v. St. Denis*,[144] MacKinnon J.A. refused the remedy in the absence of "a special relationship" between the parties. In *Unident Ltd. v. Delong*,[145] Hallet J., quoting MacKinnon J.A., refused restitution where a special relationship could not be shown.

In *Pre-Cam Exploration & Development Ltd. v. McTavish*,[146] an employee acting on information which he obtained entirely in the course of his employment, staked certain claims which would otherwise have been staked by the employer. This court affirmed the decision of the trial judge who held that the employee was a trustee of the claims for his employer. In his reasons for the court, Judson J. stated[147] that:

---

138 See Goff & Jones, at 665.
139 *Supra*, note 136, at 209.
140 Goff & Jones, at 659-74.
141 *Ibid.*, at 673.
142 See Waters, at 386-97.
143 *Supra*, note 7.
144 (1975), 57 D.L.R. (3d) 699, 8 O.R. (2d) 315 (C.A.) (leave to appeal to the Supreme Court of Canada refused).
145 (1981), 131 D.L.R. (3d) 225, 50 N.S.R. (2d) 1 (S.C.T.D.).
146 *Supra*, note 121.
147 *Ibid.*, at 560.

. . .it was a term of his employment, which McTavish on the facts of this case understood, that he could not use this information for his own advantage. The use of the term "fraud" by the learned Chief Justice at trial was fully warranted.

In these circumstances, Judson J. referred to the use of the constructive trust. I do not consider that that decision lays down any principle that makes the remedy of a constructive trust an appropriate remedy for misuse of confidential information except in very special circumstances.

Although unjust enrichment has been recognized as having an existence apart from contract or tort under a heading referred to as the law of restitution, a constructive trust is not the appropriate remedy in most cases. As pointed out by Professor Waters,[148] although unjust enrichment gives rise to a number of possible remedies:

> . . .the best remedy in the particular circumstances is that which corrects the unjust enrichment without contravening other established legal doctrines. In most cases, as in *Deglman v. Guar. Trust Co. of Can. and Constantineau*[149] itself, a personal action will accomplish that end, whether its source is the common law or equity, providing as it often will monetary compensation.

While the remedy of the constructive trust may continue to be employed in situations where other remedies would be inappropriate or injustice would result, there is no reason to extend it to this case.

The conventional remedies for breach of confidence are an accounting of profits or damages. An injunction may be coupled with either of these remedies in appropriate circumstances. A restitutionary remedy is appropriate in cases involving fiduciaries because they are required to disgorge any benefits derived from the breach of trust. In a breach of confidence case, the focus is on the loss to the plaintiff and, as in tort actions, the particular position of the plaintiff must be examined. The object is to restore the plaintiff monetarily to the position he would have been in if no wrong had been committed.[150] Accordingly, this object is generally achieved by an award of damages, and a restitutionary remedy is inappropriate.

[Sopinka J. went on to discuss the formula for measuring damages. He held that the measure should be the same as for economic torts, namely the sum of money that would put the plaintiff in the same position it would have been in had it not sustained a wrong. His Lordship felt that the "wrong" was only that LAC acquired the Williams property to the exclusion of Corona. Had LAC acquired Williams for the proposed joint venture, there would have been no "wrong" done to Corona.

In assessing the damages, Sopinka J. found that, but for the breach, Corona and LAC probably would have entered into an agreement under which prop-

---

148 Waters, *supra*, at 394.
149 *Supra*, note 129.
150 See *Dowson & Mason Ltd. v. Potter*, [1986] 2 All E.R. 418 (C.A.), and *Talbot v. General Television Corp. Pty. Ltd.*, [1980] V.R. 224.

erty interests and development costs would have been shared equally. Having accepted the trial judge's valuation of the mine at $700 million, Sopinka J. accordingly fixed damages at $350 million. From that figure, he made an appropriate deduction with respect to the costs that LAC had in fact incurred in connection with the project, including the purchase price paid to Mrs. Williams.

Sopinka J., however, denied the account of profits also directed by the trial judge, since an account is a restitutionary remedy which he held to be inappropriate.

The appeal was dismissed.]

Notes and Questions

1. Do you think that LAC was subject to a fiduciary duty? Why or why not?

2. All courts, including all members of the Supreme Court of Canada, held that LAC was in breach of confidence. Describe breach of confidence and explain how it differs from breach of fiduciary duty. Can the two overlap? What happens if they do?

3. La Forest J.'s approach to the imposition of a constructive trust has been criticized for distorting the principle of "unjust enrichment."[151] The defendant in *International Corona Resources Ltd. v. Lac Minerals Ltd.* was held liable under the cause of action in breach of confidence. The remedial options for that action include both loss-based and gain-based relief. The latter may be awarded either personally (*e.g.* in the form of an account of profits) or proprietarily (*e.g.* in the form of a constructive trust).[152]

Seeds of confusion were sown, however, by Dickson J.'s statement in *Becker v. Pettkus* that "the principle of unjust enrichment lies at the heart of the constructive trust."[153] Although that belief has since been scotched,[154] it seemed to La Forest J. that a constructive trust consequently was available only if there was an "unjust enrichment." As explained in the last part, however, "unjust enrichment" is an ambiguous phrase. It refers to at least two distinct concepts.

The first form of "unjust enrichment" consists of the cause of action of that name that the Supreme Court of Canada formulated in *Becker v. Pettkus*. That cause of action requires proof of three elements: (i) an enrichment to the defendant, (ii) a corresponding deprivation to the plaintiff, and (iii) the absence of any juristic reason for the enrichment. The remedy is always restitution. The defendant is required to give back (either personally or proprietarily) the benefit that he or she acquired from the plaintiff. The gist of the claim is that, regardless of any wrongdoing, a transfer of wealth occurred between the parties that ought to be reversed. Because the focus is on an enrichment that the defendant obtained from the plaintiff, it is common to speak of an "unjust enrichment by subtraction." The defendant's gain must correspond to the plaintiff's loss.[155]

151 L.D. Smith, "The Province of the Law of Restitution" (1992), 71 Can. Bar Rev. 672 at 687ff.; M. McInnes, "The Canadian Principle of Unjust Enrichment: Comparative Insights Into the Law of Restitution" (1999), 37 Alberta L. Rev. 1 at 28ff.

152 *Pre-Cam Exploration and Development Ltd. v. McTavish, supra*, note 121.

153 *Supra*, note 7, at 273.

154 *Soulos v. Korkontzilas, supra*, note 9.

155 *Air Canada v. British Columbia, supra*, note 24, at 193, *per* La Forest J. (S.C.C.).

"Unjust enrichment by wrongdoing" is a much different concept. It does *not* involve the three-part, *Becker v. Pettkus* cause of action. Rather, it involves a situation in which, having established a cause of action that entails the breach of a civil obligation (*e.g.* trespass to land, breach of contract, breach of fiduciary duty, breach of confidence), the plaintiff eschews compensation for loss and seeks instead to compel the defendant to give up an ill-gotten gain. Significantly, because the action is not unjust enrichment, and because the plaintiff therefore need not establish a corresponding deprivation, the defendant may be required to disgorge benefits that he acquired from any source, including a third party. The defendant's plus need not correspond to the plaintiff's minus.

The first difficulty, therefore, is that, having decided that a constructive trust presumes the existence of an unjust enrichment, La Forest J. assumed that "unjust enrichment" must be defined in terms of the cause of action of that name. He overlooked the concept of unjust enrichment by wrongdoing. Curiously, then, he effectively required the plaintiff to prove two different causes of action. The threshold issue of liability was satisfied by proof of the cause of action in breach of confidence. The plaintiff thereby became entitled to a wide range of remedies. At the remedial stage of analysis, however, La Forest J. premised the availability of one particular remedy (*i.e.* proprietary disgorgement of an ill-gotten gain in the form of a constructive trust) upon proof of the cause of action in unjust enrichment. That approach, needless to say, was unprecedented.

The second difficulty with La Forest J.'s analysis is that, even if the plaintiff was required to satisfy the elements of the action in unjust enrichment, there appeared to be a difficulty regarding the second element of that claim (*i.e.* that the defendant's enrichment must correspond to the plaintiff's deprivation). LAC Minerals' enrichment consisted of the acquisition of the gold-bearing property. That property was not, however, subtracted from Corona. Instead, it was purchased from a third party, Mrs. Williams. La Forest J. circumvented that problem by considerably expanding the scope of the concept of "corresponding deprivation." As previously explained, that requirement typically is satisfied by proof that a benefit passed directly from the plaintiff to the defendant. Under the doctrine of "interceptive subtraction," the courts historically extended proof to situations in which the defendant acquired from a third party a benefit that otherwise would have accrued to the plaintiff. That is true, for instance, if the defendant usurped the plaintiff's position as landlord and received rent from a tenant in circumstances that discharged the tenant's obligation.[156] Significantly, however, while the doctrine of interceptive subtraction has never been fully explained, it generally is thought to be applicable only if the third party was *legally obligated* to confer the benefit upon the plaintiff and the defendant's usurpation discharged that obligation.[157] On the facts of *International Corona Resources Ltd. v. Lac Minerals Ltd.*, of course, Mrs. Williams was not under any obligation to sell her land to the plaintiff. The most that could be said, on the basis of the trial judge's findings of fact, was that, but for LAC Minerals' wrongful behaviour, Corona "would

---

156 *Lyell v. Kennedy* (1889), 14 App. Cas. 437; *Official Custodian for Charities v. Mackey (No. 2)*, [1985] 1 W.L.R. 1308 (Eng. Ch. Div.).

157 G. Virgo, *The Principles of the Law of Restitution* (Oxford: Oxford University Press, 1999) at 109-113; R.B. Grantham & C.E.F. Rickett, *Enrichment & Restitution in New Zealand* (Oxford: Hart, 2000) at 20. See also M. McInnes, "Interceptive Subtraction, Unjust Enrichment and Wrongs — A Reply to Professor Birks" (2003), 62 Cambridge L.J. 697; L.D. Smith, "Three-Party Restitution: A Critique of Birks' Theory of Interceptive Subtraction" (1991) 11 Oxford J. of Legal Stud. 481.

probably have acquired the. . .property."[158] There is, of course, a substantial difference between a factual probability, as established on the facts, and a legal certainty, as traditionally required under the doctrine of interceptive subtraction.

4. As explained in the last chapter, McLachlin J. used *Soulos v. Korkontzilas*[159] to establish four criteria governing the availability of a constructive trust for wrongful gains. Should those criteria be applied in the context of a breach of confidence? If so, could they have been satisfied on the facts of *Lac Minerals Ltd.?* What does McLachlin J.'s four-part test say with respect to the approach that La Forest J. adopted in *Lac Minerals Ltd.?*

5. How would the test outlined in *Soulos v. Korkontzilas* affect the availability of constructive trusts in the context of other forms of wrongdoing? Suppose, for instance, that as a result of committing the tort of deceit against the plaintiff, the defendant reaped a substantial profit. If the ill-gotten gain was subtracted from the plaintiff, it might be recoverable under the action in unjust enrichment. But what if part of the benefit was obtained, as a result of the wrong against the plaintiff, from a third party? Should the tort of deceit support the remedy of disgorgement, as an alternative to compensation? And if so, should disgorgement be available proprietarily in the form of a constructive trust?[160]

6. As previously noted, English courts have yet to impose a constructive trust as a means of compelling proprietary disgorgement of a benefit that the defendant acquired through breach of confidence. Professor Burrows has suggested some of the reasons for that position.[161]

> In principle, proprietary restitution would be justified if the correct analysis is that confidential information is a form of property, owned in equity by the claimant, and which the claimant can then trace in equity into its substitute product. Without that subtraction from the claimant's wealth there seems no justification for giving the claimant priority on the defendant's insolvency. If one were to take that analysis (which seems rather artificial) there would be no need to view the claim for proprietary restitution as based on the wrong of breach of confidence. It would be most naturally explained as lying within unjust enrichment by subtraction with the unjust factor being ignorance or powerlessness.

Based on his judgment in *International Corona Resources Ltd. v. Lac Minerals Ltd.*, how would La Forest J. respond to Burrows' suggestion that a constructive trust is justifiable only if the defendant's gain can be identified as the traceable product of the plaintiff's property in the confidential information? Based on her judgment in *Soulos*, how would McLachlin J. respond to Burrows' concern regarding the fact that a constructive trust provides the plaintiff with priority in the event of the defendant's insolvency? Was McLachlin J.'s advice on that point followed in *Lac Minerals Ltd.?*

7. La Forest J and Sopinka J. adopted very different positions regarding the appropriate remedy in *Lac Minerals Ltd.?* Which approach is preferable?

8. Assuming that Sopinka J. was right in awarding damages for breach of confidence, was he right in concluding that an account of profits was not appropriate because such relief is "restitutionary"? Were the damages that Sopinka J. favoured "compensation," or were they "common law damages"? What is the difference between those two concepts?

---

158 *Lac Minerals Ltd.*, *supra*, note 7, at 546 (emphasis added). The trial judge also said that the defendant "deprived [the plaintiff] of the opportunity of obtaining the property" (at 546), and that, "[o]n the balance of probabilities. . .but for the actions of [the defendant], [the plaintiff] would have acquired the. . .property" (at 542-543).

159 *Supra*, note 9.

160 See *Halifax Building Society v. Thomas*, [1996] Ch. 217 (C.A.).

161 A. Burrows, *The Law of Restitution*, 2nd ed. (London: Butterworths, 2002), at 503-504.

9. A was employed by S Ltd. as its general manager to sell its products in North America. The products were manufactured by machines which were designed and built from drawings owned by S Ltd. In his contract of employment, A agreed to devote all his efforts to S Ltd. and to keep all knowledge acquired by him in the course of his employment secret. While employed, he solicited S Ltd.'s customers and sold competing products to them. He also had machines made from the drawings, which were similar to S Ltd.'s machines. Then he terminated his employment with S Ltd. and incorporated A Ltd. Through it he sold virtually identical products to those sold by S Ltd.

S Ltd. wishes to bring action against A and A Ltd. What causes of action does it have? What remedies can it seek? What will be the likely outcome of its action?[162]

10. A person who has misused confidential information may be deprived of remedies otherwise available. *Computer Workshops Ltd. v. Banner Capital Market Brokers Ltd.*[163] is an example. The defendant had engaged the plaintiff to supply computers to it. In the course of performing the contract, the plaintiff learned about a unique configuration of the defendant's software system. It would have taken the plaintiff six months to develop the configuration on its own. The plaintiff agreed to supply a computer software system which incorporated the unique configuration to a competitor of the defendant. The defendant learned of it and terminated its contract with the plaintiff. The plaintiff's action for damages for breach of contract was dismissed, *inter alia*, because it breached its duty of confidence.

11. *Speed Seal Products Ltd. v. Paddington*[164] affords an example of another remedy available for breach of confidence. The defendant had worked for the plaintiff for several months on the design of couplings for use on pipes on oil rigs. Then he left his employment and established his own business to manufacture and sell oil rig couplings. He applied for a patent and described the couplings in a marketing brochure. The plaintiff alleged that the defendant's couplings were based on confidential information acquired by him while employed by the plaintiff. The plaintiff sought an injunction to prevent the further publishing of the confidential information. It was successful, since that afforded the plaintiff real protection and because an injunction was the appropriate remedy in the circumstances.

12. In *Aber Resources Ltd. v. Winspear Resources Ltd.*,[165] the parties were, in contrast to those in *International Corona Resources Ltd. v. Lac Minerals Ltd.*, in fact part of a joint venture. A constructive trust was imposed on the basis of "unconscionability" and the elements in unjust enrichment when the defendant wrongfully excluded the plaintiff from participating in a particular project.

---

162 See *Schauenburg Industries Ltd. v. Borowski* (1979), 25 O.R. (2d) 737, 50 C.P.R. (2d) 69, 101 D.L.R. (3d) 701, 1979 CarswellOnt 166, 8 B.L.R. 164 (H.C.). See also *Investors Syndicate Ltd. v. Versatile Investments Inc.* (1983), 42 O.R. (2d) 397, 1983 CarswellOnt 1270, 73 C.P.R. (2d) 107, 149 D.L.R. (3d) 46 (C.A.); and *Investors Syndicate Ltd. v. Vandenberg* (1986), 1986 CarswellOnt 828, 10 C.C.E.L. 153 (Ont. H.C.). In both cases a salesman for the plaintiff took his client information cards with him when he left his employment and joined a competitor. The plaintiff was protected by restrictive covenants and obtained injunctions to prevent soliciting former clients and disclosing the information to the competitor.

163 (1988), 64 O.R. (2d) 266, 1988 CarswellOnt 107, 39 B.L.R. 64, 50 D.L.R. (4th) 118, 21 C.P.R. (3d) 116 (H.C.), affirmed (1990), 1990 CarswellOnt 1445, 74 D.L.R. (4th) 767, 33 C.P.R. (3d) 416, 1 O.R. (3d) 398 (C.A.).

164 [1986] 1 All E.R. 91 (C.A.).

165 33 E.T.R. (2d) 1, 2000 CarswellBC 772, [2000] B.C.J. No. 742, 2000 BCSC 463, 19 B.L.R. (3d) 142 (S.C.).

4. WRONGFUL GAINS #2 — BREACH OF FIDUCIARY DUTY

(a) Introduction

With the possible exception of the constructive trust that is imposed to effect an equitable distribution of property upon the dissolution of a cohabitational relationship, the most common form of constructive trust is the one that is used to compel disgorgement of a benefit that was acquired through a breach of fiduciary duty. Unfortunately, as we shall see, the Canadian law on fiduciary duties is problematic in a number of respects.

(i) *Relationships Supporting Fiduciary Obligations*

It is notoriously difficult to identify the situations in which fiduciary relationships will be recognized. "[T]here are few legal concepts more frequently invoked but less conceptually certain."[166] That has always been true. The difficulties are particularly pronounced in Canada, however, because the courts in recent years have extended the concept far beyond its historical limits.

Although we will return below to the question of *what* fiduciary obligations entail, it is useful, for the purpose of identifying *when* they will be imposed, to consider the functional explanation of fiduciary relationships, as traditionally conceived.

One of the central functions of a legal system is to create rules that facilitate inter-personal relationships. Just as society has need for various types of relationships, so too it has need for various sets of rules. Sometimes, the nature of the desired relationship is such that the law must take a relatively light hand. For instance, it traditionally has been thought appropriate to largely leave the marketplace to its own devices and to impose legal sanctions for only the most egregious forms of commercial impropriety. The rule in *Allen v. Flood*[167] accordingly states that, so long as he or she does not otherwise act unlawfully, a business person generally is entitled to deliberately, even maliciously, drive a competitor to ruin.

Outside of the marketplace, the facilitation of healthy relationships often requires somewhat greater consideration for one another. And in exceptional circumstances, it may require one person to entirely subvert his or her own interests and to act selflessly for another. It is within a sub-set of that type of relationship that the fiduciary concept is traditionally applied.

The desire to protect and reinforce the integrity of social institutions and enterprises is prevalent throughout fiduciary law. The reason for this desire is that the law recognized the importance of instilling in our social institutions and enterprises some recognition that not all relationships are

---

166 *Lac Minerals Ltd.*, *supra*, note 7, at 26, *per* La Forest J.
167 [1898] A.C. 1 (H.L.).

characterized by a dynamic of mutual autonomy, and that the marketplace cannot always set the rules.[168]

Equity long ago recognized the existence of relationships in which one person, called the fiduciary,[169] exercised a discretion to make legal decisions that affected the legal position of another person, called the principal or beneficiary. People may want to enter into such a relationship for a variety of reasons. The principal, for instance, may simply find it impossible, inconvenient or impractical to personally exercise the decisions in question. In any event, equity also recognized that the viability of such relationships depended upon the principal's ability to rely confidently upon the fiduciary. There is little point in reposing a discretion in another person if it is also necessary to constantly monitor that person's decision-making process. Equity's response is to impose a set of proscriptions. With respect to decisions that the fiduciary is entitled to exercise for the purpose of affecting the principal's legal status, the fiduciary must act wholly in the principal's best interests.

Against that backdrop, the classic illustrations of the fiduciary concept are easily understood. Agents owe fiduciary obligations to their principals,[170] just as trustees of express trusts owe them to their beneficiaries.[171] The primary function of an agent is to enter into legal relationships on a principal's behalf. An agent may, for instance, create an agreement under which the principal becomes contractually obliged to sell widgets to a third party. Such an arrangement will work effectively only if the principal has the legal system's assurance that, when creating contracts, the agent will not selfishly serve his or her own ends (*e.g.* by reducing the widgets' purchase price in exchange for a bribe). The analysis is much the same in the trusts context. The whole purpose of an express trust is to assure the settlor that the trustee will administratively hold property on behalf of the beneficiary. In that capacity, the trustee generally has both the authority and obligation to manage the property, for instance, by investing it. That arrangement simply will not work if there is a substantial risk that the trustee will prefer his or her own interests to those of the beneficiary (*e.g.* by personally usurping investment opportunities that become available to the trust).

Other traditional applications of the fiduciary concept are similarly explicable. One partner is capable of binding others to legal obligations. Consequently, a partner must act in the best interests of the partnership, rather than in his or her

---

168 *Hodgkinson v. Simms* (1994), 117 D.L.R. (4th) 161, [1994] S.C.J. No. 84, 1994 CarswellBC 438, 1994 CarswellBC 1245, [1994] 9 W.W.R. 609, 49 B.C.A.C. 1, 80 W.A.C. 1, 22 C.C.L.T. (2d) 1, 16 B.L.R. (2d) 1, 6 C.C.L.S. 1, 57 C.P.R. (3d) 1, 5 E.T.R. (2d) 1, [1994] 3 S.C.R. 377, 95 D.T.C. 5135, 97 B.C.L.R. (2d) 1, 171 N.R. 245, at 186 [D.L.R.] per La Forest J. See also Lord Wedderburn, "Trust, Corporation and the Worker" (1985), 23 Osgoode Hall L.J. 203 at 221("Fiduciary obligation is imposed by private law, but its function is public, and its purpose social"); P.D. Finn, "The Fiduciary Principle", in T. Youdan, ed., *Equity, Fiduciary and Trusts* (Toronto: Carswell, 1989) 1 at 26 (fiduciary principle used to "maintain the integrity, credibility and utility of relationships perceived to be of importance in society").

169 The word "fiduciary" is derived from the Latin *fiducia*, meaning trust or reliance.

170 *Johnston v. Johnston* (1872), 19 Gr. 133, 1872 CarswellOnt 19 (Ch.).

171 *Keech v. Sandford*, (1726), Sel. Cas. t. King 61, 25 E.R. 223 (Ch. Div.).

own best interests.[172] One joint venturer may be subject to obligations in favour of another.[173] Likewise, because a company's legal status is determined by decisions made by its directors, those directors are subject to fiduciary obligations.[174] Much the same is true of, say, employees holding confidential information.[175] The situation is only slightly different as between solicitors and clients. True, a solicitor does not normally enjoy the ability to make decisions directly on behalf of the client. Given the nature of the relationship, however, a decision nominally made by a client very often is a direct function of the solicitor's "advice." Equity recognizes the reality of the situation.[176]

The categories of fiduciary relationships, like the categories of negligence, are, however, never closed. They are capable of being extended by analogy to situations in which the relevant criteria are satisfied. In Canada, those criteria were established in *Frame v. Smith*, where Wilson J. said that a fiduciary relationship was one in which:[177]

(1) The fiduciary has scope for the exercise of some discretion or power.
(2) The fiduciary can unilaterally exercise that power or discretion so as to affect the beneficiary's legal or practical interests.
(3) The beneficiary is peculiarly vulnerable to or at the mercy of the fiduciary holding the discretion or power.

Subsequent cases have debated the universality of that test, especially its third criterion. In *International Corona Resources Ltd. v. Lac Minerals Ltd.*, La Forest J. suggested that an element of vulnerability was not essential to every fiduciary relationship, but Sopinka J., writing for the majority on point, held otherwise.[178]

---

172 *Gordon v. Holland* (1913), 10 D.L.R. 734, 1913 CarswellBC 181, 4 W.W.R. 419 (P.C.); *Molchan v. Omega Oil & Gas Ltd.* (1988), 47 D.L.R. (4th) 481, 1988 CarswellAlta 17, 1988 CarswellAlta 549, [1988] 3 W.W.R. 1, 57 Alta. L.R. (2d) 193, 83 N.R. 25, [1988] 1 S.C.R. 348, 87 A.R. 81, reconsideration refused (1988), 49 D.L.R. (4th) vii (S.C.C.). Of course, in contrast to some other types of fiduciaries, a partner may profit from the fiduciary relationship insofar as he or she may benefit personally from any decision that affects the best interests of the partnership as a whole.

173 *Chitel v. Bank of Montreal* (2002), 45 E.T.R. (2d) 167, 2002 CarswellOnt 1824, [2002] O.J. No. 2170, 26 B.L.R. (3d) 83 (S.C.J.).

174 *Canadian Aero Service Ltd. v. O'Malley* (1973), 40 D.L.R. (3d) 371, 1973 CarswellOnt 236, 1973 CarswellOnt 236F, [1974] S.C.R. 592, 11 C.P.R. (2d) 206.

175 *Physique Health Club Ltd. v. Carlsen* (1996), 141 D.L.R. (4th) 64, 1996 CarswellAlta 958, [1996] A.J. No. 1004, 45 Alta. L.R. (3d) 383, 25 C.C.E.L. (2d) 231, 70 C.P.R. (3d) 426, 193 A.R. 196, 135 W.A.C. 196, [1997] 4 W.W.R. 609 (C.A.), reconsideration refused (1997), 1997 CarswellAlta 1014, 209 A.R. 239, 160 W.A.C. 239 (C.A.), leave to appeal refused [1997] S.C.C.A. No. 40, 212 A.R. 26 (note), 168 W.A.C. 26 (note), [1997] 2 S.C.R. xiii (S.C.C.).

176 *Read v. Cole* (1915), 52 S.C.R. 176, 1915 CarswellBC 210, 9 W.W.R. 1137, 26 D.L.R. 564.

177 *Supra*, note 117, at 98-99.

178 *Supra*, note 7.

The tables were turned five years later in *Hodgkinson v. Simms*.[179] Sopinka J. (McLachlin J. concurring) continued to maintain his position.[180]

> This then is the hallmark to which a court looks in determining whether a fiduciary relationship exists; is one party dependent upon or in the power of the other. In determining if this is the case, the court looks to the characteristics referred to by Wilson J. in *Frame v. Smith*. Does one party possess power or discretion over the property of the other? In the final analysis, can the powerless party be said to be "peculiarly vulnerable" or "at the mercy of" the party who holds the power?
>
> . . .
>
> Phrases like "unilateral exercise of power," "at the mercy of the other's discretion" and "has given over that power" suggest a total reliance and dependence on the fiduciary by the beneficiary. The courts and writers have used them advisedly, concerned for the need for clarity and aware of the Draconian consequences of the imposition of a fiduciary obligation. Reliance is not a simple thing. . . . To date, the law has imposed a fiduciary obligation only at the extreme of total reliance.

La Forest J. nevertheless was able to attract a majority to his view. He regarded Wilson J.'s three-part test as containing "indicia that help recognize a fiduciary relationship rather than the ingredients that define it."[181] Accordingly, while acknowledging that *Frame v. Smith* provides "a useful guide,"[182] he also found that it "encounters difficulties in identifying relationships described by a slightly different use of the term 'fiduciary,' *viz.*, situations in which fiduciary obligations, though not innate to a given relationship, arise as a matter of fact out of the specific circumstances of that particular relationship."[183] And in that regard, he concluded that special vulnerability need not invariably be demonstrated. At a minimum, all that is required for the imposition of fiduciary obligations is a relationship of trust and confidence in which the plaintiff relies upon the defendant.[184]

All of that undoubtedly is important. The truly significant point, however, is not so much the precise formulation of the test, as the judicial attitude underlying its application. And in that regard, Canadian courts have gone well beyond both the historical precedents and the approach adopted in other jurisdictions. That proposition is true in a number of respects.

Non-Economic Interests Fiduciary relationships traditionally were concerned with decisions taken for the protection and advancement of economic interests. In exercising a discretion regarding investments, for instance, the trustee was required to act exclusively in the best interests of the beneficiary. The beneficiary did not want the trust *res* squandered or misused. Canadian courts, in contrast, frequently apply fiduciary obligations in connection with non-economic interests.[185] That approach firmly took root during a remarkable five month period in

---

179 *Supra*, note 168. See also L.D. Smith, *infra*, note 199.
180 *Ibid.*, at 218.
181 *Ibid.*, at 176.
182 *Ibid.*
183 *Ibid.*
184 *Ibid.*, at 184.
185 R. Joyce, "Fiduciary Law and Non-Economic Interests" (2003), 28 Monash U. L. Rev. 239.

1992, when the Supreme Court of Canada's new-found enthusiasm for the equitable principle led it to impose fiduciary obligations in a trio of cases dealing with physical, sexual and psychological interests. In *Norberg v. Wynrib*,[186] an elderly physician exploited a young woman's addiction to prescription pills to extract sexual favours from her. While the majority of the court imposed liability on orthodox grounds (the torts of battery and negligence), McLachlin and L'Heureux-Dubé JJ. concurred on the basis that the doctor had breached a fiduciary duty that he owed to his patient. Only that analysis, they believed, conveyed the essence of the wrong, which was the exploitation of vulnerability. A few months later, a similar line of thought was endorsed unanimously in *M. (K.) v. M. (H.).*[187] The defendant had sexually assaulted his daughter while she was a minor. La Forest J. referred to the test formulated in *Frame v. Smith* and said:[188]

> Even a cursory examination of these indicia establishes that a parent must owe fiduciary obligations to his or her child. Parents exercise great power over their children's lives, and make daily decisions that affect their welfare. In this regard, the child is without doubt at the mercy of her parents.

Interestingly, the plaintiff's motivation for framing the action in breach of fiduciary duty lie largely in the belief that whereas a claim for the common law tort of battery was barred by the lapse of time under the *Limitations Act*, no such difficulty attended upon the equitable claim.[189] Finally, the Supreme Court of

---

186 92 D.L.R. (4th) 449, [1992] S.C.J. No. 60, 1992 CarswellBC 155, 1992 CarswellBC 907, [1992] 4 W.W.R. 577, [1992] 2 S.C.R. 226, 12 C.C.L.T. (2d) 1, 9 B.C.A.C. 1, 19 W.A.C. 1, 138 N.R. 81, 68 B.C.L.R. (2d) 29, [1992] R.R.A. 668, additional reasons at 1992 CarswellBC 338, 1992 CarswellBC 908, [1992] 2 S.C.R. 318, 74 B.C.L.R. (2d) 2, [1992] 6 W.W.R. 673. The minority analysis was adopted in *T. (L.) v. M. (W.K.)* (1993), 110 D.L.R. (4th) 64, 1993 CarswellNB 157, 143 N.B.R. (2d) 241, 366 A.P.R. 241 (Q.B.).

187 96 D.L.R. (4th) 289, 1992 CarswellOnt 841, 1992 CarswellOnt 998, [1992] S.C.J. No. 85, 142 N.R. 321, (sub nom. *M. c. M.*) [1992] 3 S.C.R. 6, 57 O.A.C. 321, 14 C.C.L.T. (2d) 1. See also R. Flannigan, "Fiduciary Regulation of Sexual Exploitation" (2000), 79 Can. Bar Rev. 301.

188 *Ibid.*, at 325. See also *B. (K.L.) v. British Columbia*, [1998] 10 W.W.R. 348, 1998 CarswellBC 404, [1998] B.C.J. No. 470, 51 B.C.L.R. (3d) 1, 41 C.C.L.T. (2d) 107 (S.C.), additional reasons at (1998), [1998] B.C.J. No. 1909, 1998 CarswellBC 1763, 163 D.L.R. (4th) 550, 24 C.P.C. (4th) 234 (S.C.), reversed 2001 CarswellBC 722, [2001] B.C.J. No. 584, 2001 BCCA 221, 87 B.C.L.R. (3d) 52, 4 C.C.L.T. (3d) 225, [2001] 5 W.W.R. 47, 197 D.L.R. (4th) 431, 151 B.C.A.C. 52, 249 W.A.C. 52, 23 C.P.C. (5th) 207 (C.A.), leave to appeal allowed (2001), 2001 CarswellBC 2758, 2001 CarswellBC 2759, 285 N.R. 400 (note), 169 B.C.A.C. 191 (note), 276 W.A.C. 191 (note) (S.C.C.), affirmed [2003] S.C.J. No. 51, 2003 CarswellBC 2405, 2003 CarswellBC 2406, 18 B.C.L.R. (4th) 1, 19 C.C.L.T. (3d) 66, 230 D.L.R. (4th) 513, [2003] 11 W.W.R. 203, 309 N.R. 306, 44 R.F.L. (5th) 245, 187 B.C.A.C. 42, 307 W.A.C. 42, 38 C.P.C. (5th) 199, 2003 SCC 51, 2004 C.L.L.C. 210-014; (fiduciary relationship between provincial government and children in foster care); *Lafrance Estate v. Canada (Attorney General)*, (sub nom. *Bonaparte v. Canada (Attorney General)*) 64 O.R. (3d) 1, [2003] O.J. No. 1046, 2003 CarswellOnt 994, 30 C.P.C. (5th) 59, 169 O.A.C. 376, [2003] 2 C.N.L.R. 43 (C.A.), additional reasons at (2003), 2003 CarswellOnt 2484 (C.A.) (breach of fiduciary duty through creation of residential schools).

189 Instrumental manipulation of fiduciary principles is not limited to Canadian courts. See *Reading v. Attorney General*, [1949] 2 K.B. 232, affirmed [1951] A.C. 507, [1951] 1 All E.R. 617 (H.L.), at 236 [K.B.] (fiduciary relationship recognized as between military sergeant and government,

Canada's recognition of non-economic interests extended, in *McInerney v. Mac-Donald*,[190] to the imposition of a fiduciary duty upon physicians to make medical records available to patients.

While widely accepted within Canadian legal circles, those developments have been questioned and criticized abroad. It has been suggested, for instance, that a fiduciary analysis is an entirely inappropriate response to incest. Even though a parent undoubtedly may be a fiduciary in some respects, it does not follow that every wrong that he or she commits against the child is a breach of fiduciary duty.[191] Classically conceived, a fiduciary was required to exercise good faith and loyalty while discharging an obligation or authority to make certain decisions affecting the beneficiary's legal interests. A fiduciary, in other words, was prohibited from making *illegitimate use* of a *legitimate power*. A parent does not, however, have a legitimate power to make decisions regarding a child's sexuality. There is, consequently, no question of exercising a particular type of discretion properly or improperly. Furthermore, the mere fact that a parent is motivated by a selfish desire for sexual gratification cannot elevate otherwise tortious conduct into an equitable wrong.[192]

Australian courts have rejected *M. (K.) v. M. (H.)* on similar grounds. In *Paramasivam v. Flynn*,[193] the Federal Court of Australia reviewed the case law, both historical and modern, and concluded that incest does not constitute a breach of fiduciary duty. It conceded that sexual assault by a parent or guardian "can readily be described in terms of abuse of a position of trust or confidence, or even in terms of . . . allowing personal interest . . . to displace a duty to protect the [plaintiff's] interests."[194] However, it also observed that fiduciary obligations traditionally were confined to the protection of economic interests, and furthermore doubted the wisdom of super-imposing equitable obligations on the operation of established legal claims (*e.g.* battery).

The High Court of Australia was even more cutting in its comments. *Breen v. Williams*[195] mirrored *McInerney v. MacDonald* insofar as the plaintiff sought to invoke fiduciary principles as a means of gaining access to medical records held by her physician. The judicial reaction to that claim was, however, far different. Dawson and Toohey JJ. suggested that the Canadian position is

---

"in a very loose, or at any event very comprehensive, sense," so as to allow disgorgement of benefit that sergeant acquired by using position and uniform to assist smugglers in Cairo).

190 (1992), 93 D.L.R. (4th) 415, 1992 CarswellNB 63, 1992 CarswellNB 247, [1992] S.C.J. No. 57, 137 N.R. 35, 126 N.B.R. (2d) 271, 317 A.P.R. 271, 7 C.P.C. (3d) 269, 12 C.C.L.T. (2d) 225, [1992] 2 S.C.R. 138.

191 The difference between a breach of a fiduciary duty and a breach of a duty by a fiduciary is examined in greater detail below.

192 J. Penner, "Exemptions", in P. Birks & A. Pretto, eds., *Breach of Trust* (Oxford: Hart, 2002) 241 at 245-247.

193 (1998), 160 A.L.R. 203 (F.C.A.).

194 *Ibid.*, at 219.

195 (1996), 186 C.L.R. 71 (H.C.A.). The High Court similarly adopted a cautious and restrictive approach to the recognition of fiduciary relationships in *Hospital Products Ltd. v. United States Surgical Corp.* (1984), 156 C.L.R. 41 (H.C.A.) (no fiduciary relationship between distributor and manufacturer).

"achieved by assertion rather than analysis and, whilst it may effectuate a preference for a particular result, it does not involve the development or elucidation of any accepted doctrine."[196] The High Court readily recognized, of course, that a breach of fiduciary duty may arise in a medical context if, for instance, a physician prescribes treatment in a private facility in which he or she holds an undisclosed financial stake. The court nevertheless emphatically refused to extend equitable protection to a patient's non-economic interest in receiving access to medical records.

Commercial Relationships There is no denying that fiduciary principles frequently apply in what may be described as "commercial contexts." The relationships that exist between partners and co-partners, agents and principals, and directors and companies, for example, play out largely, if not exclusively, in the marketplace. Furthermore, in the modern world, express trusts increasingly are used for commercial purposes. It nevertheless is true to say that the courts traditionally were loath to impose fiduciary obligations as between commercial parties. The explanation is obvious. The essence of a fiduciary relationship is selfless service in the interests of another. Nothing could be further from the classic conception of commerce.

The tendency of Canadian courts to view the fiduciary principle as a panacea nevertheless has resulted in that principle's expansion into the marketplace. As we saw in our discussion of breach of confidence, *International Corona Resources Ltd. v. Lac Minerals Ltd.*[197] involved a situation in which a small mining company, in the hope of developing a joint venture, informed a large mining company of the location of potentially valuable land. The larger entity took advantage of the situation by purchasing the properties for itself. Sopinka J., writing for the majority on point, allowed relief for breach of confidence, but rejected a fiduciary analysis. In his view, "equity's blunt tool must be reserved for situations that are truly in need of the special protection that equity affords."[198] That rarely will be true in a commercial context, where the parties are presumed capable of safeguarding their own interests, and where neither is especially vulnerable to the discretion of the other. Significantly, however, La Forest J., dissenting on point, believed that recognition of a fiduciary relationship was appropriate on the facts.

The broader approach prevailed five years later in *Hodgkinson v. Simms.*[199] The plaintiff, a sophisticated stockbroker, sought tax planning and sheltering advice from the defendant, an accountant who specialized in such matters. The plaintiff accepted the defendant's recommendation to invest in certain MURBs.[200] At the time that it was given, the advice was sound. Subsequently, however, the

---

196 *Ibid.*, at 95.

197 *Supra*, note 7.

198 *Ibid.*, at 61.

199 *Supra*, note 168, critiqued in L.D. Smith, "Fiduciary Relationships — Arising in Commercial Contexts — Investment Advisors" (1995), 74 Can. Bar Rev. 714. See also *Burns v. Kelly Peters & Associates Ltd.*, 41 D.L.R. (4th) 577, 1987 CarswellBC 210, 41 C.C.L.T. 257, 16 B.C.L.R. (2d) 1, [1987] 6 W.W.R. 1, [1987] I.L.R. 1-2246 (C.A.).

200 *I.e.* Multi-unit residential buildings.

real estate market unexpectedly experienced a sharp decline and the plaintiff lost a considerable amount of money on the investment. The plaintiff also subsequently discovered that, at the time of giving the advice, the defendant had a financial stake in the MURBs, such that he received a commission on each investor that he attracted. In dissent, Sopinka J. (McLachlin and Major JJ. concurring) held that the defendant was liable for breach of contract insofar as he did not disclose his interest, but not for breach of fiduciary duty. Sopinka J. further held that because the loss of investment value did not satisfy either branch of *Hadley v. Baxendale*,[201] it was too remote to be recoverable as contractual damages. In contrast, La Forest J., writing for the majority, held that the defendant had committed a breach of fiduciary duty and consequently was fully liable for the plaintiff's loss. On the issue of the existence of fiduciary obligations, La Forest J. distinguished between arm's length commercial relationships, as arose in *Lac Minerals Ltd.*, and professional advisor relationships, as arose in *Hodgkinson*. In the latter, the requisite element of trust and confidence may exist even if, as on the facts, the advisee retains ultimate control over the decision-making process and merely relies upon the advisor's guidance.

Summary To say that Canadian law has gone well beyond both the traditional concept of fiduciary relationships and the modern approach taken in other jurisdictions is not, of course, to say that mistakes necessarily have been made. It may well be that the special level of protection afforded by fiduciary obligations is warranted with respect to, say, sexual exploitation, disclosure of medical records and the integrity of financial advice. There is, nevertheless, cause for concern. The sheer volume of fiduciary relationships is almost overwhelming. Legend has it that Chief Justice Mason of the High Court of Australia once remarked that in Canada there are only three classes of people: those who are fiduciaries, those who are about to become fiduciaries, and judges.[202] Moreover, expansions of the fiduciary principle have not always been accompanied by the level of analysis that such developments warrant.[203] Few concepts have stirred the Canadian judicial imagination in quite the same way. There is, consequently, a very real

---

201 (1854), 9 Ex. 341, 156 E.R. 145.

202 E. Cherniak, "Comment on Paper by Professor Jeffrey G. MacIntosh", in *Special Lectures of the Law Society of Upper Canada 1990: Fiduciary Duties* (Toronto: DeBoo, 1991) at 275. The real punch line awaits delivery. Given current trends in Canadian legal literature, the day may well come when someone accuses a judge of breaching a fiduciary duty while discharging professional obligations. See E. Gibson, "The Gendered Wage Dilemma", in K. Cooper-Stephenson & E. Gibson, eds., *Tort Theory* (Toronto: Captus, 1993) 185 at 203-204 (judges guilty of violating human rights legislation when quantifying compensation for loss of income by reference to "discriminatory" actuarial evidence).

203 *A. (C.) v. C. (J.W.)* (1998), 166 D.L.R. (4th) 475, 1998 CarswellBC 2370, [1998] B.C.J. No. 2587, 113 B.C.A.C. 248, 184 W.A.C. 248, 42 R.F.L. (4th) 427, 43 C.C.L.T. (2d) 223, 60 B.C.L.R. (3d) 92, 13 Admin. L.R. (3d) 157 (C.A.), at 496 [D.L.R.] *per* McEachern C.J.B.C. ("The law in this respect has been extended by our highest court not predictably or incrementally but in quantum leaps so that judges, lawyers and citizens alike are often unable to know whether a given situation is governed by the usual laws of contract, negligence or other torts, or by fiduciary obligations whose limits are difficult to discern").

danger that, released from its historical origins, the fiduciary principle is becoming an unruly horse of public policy,[204] pressed into service whenever existing doctrines are perceived to be inapplicable or inadequate.

(ii) *The Nature of Fiduciary Obligations*

It is difficult, perhaps impossible, to succinctly state the nature of a fiduciary's obligations. The general proposition is that a fiduciary must act in the beneficiary's best interests. As we shall see, however, that proposition may have many manifestations, depending upon the circumstances. It is, for instance, common to refer to the "conflict rule" and the "profit rule." The former states that a fiduciary must avoid situations in which his or her personal interests conflict with the beneficiary's interests. The latter states, somewhat more specifically, that a fiduciary must not profit from his or her position.

Those statements are, however, insufficient to fully convey the nature, and in particular, the stringency, of the fiduciary's obligations. In that respect, it is crucial to understand that the rules were developed largely *pour encourager les autres*. They were intended to be prophylactic — not merely sanctioning past transgressions, but, more significantly, deterring future disloyalty. It is useful to consider a few illustrations.

Gaudron and McHugh JJ., of the High Court of Australia, drew a lesson from Matthew 6:24.[205]

> The law of fiduciary duty rests not so much on morality or conscience as on the acceptance of the implications of the biblical injunction that "[n]o man can serve two masters." Duty and self-interest, like God and Mammon, make inconsistent calls on the faithful. Equity solves the problem in a practical way by insisting that fiduciaries give undivided loyalty to the persons whom they serve.

Chief Justice Cardozo, while on the New York Court of Appeal, described the fiduciary obligation of a "co-adventurer."[206]

> Joint adventurers, like co-partners, owe to one another, while the enterprise continues, the duty of the finest loyalty. Many forms of conduct permissible in a workaday world for those acting at arm's length, are forbidden to those bound by fiduciary ties. A trustee is held to something stricter than the morals of the market place. Not honesty alone, but the punctilio of an honor the most sensitive, is then the standard of behavior. As to this there has developed a tradition that is unbending and inveterate. Uncompromising rigidity has been the attitude of courts of equity when petitioned to undermine the rule of undivided loyalty by the "disintegrating erosion" of particular exceptions. . . . Only thus has the level of conduct for fiduciaries been kept at a level higher than that trodden by the crowd. It will not consciously be lowered by any judgment of this court.

---

204 *Richardson v. Mellish* (1824), 2 Bing 229 at 252.
205 *Breen, supra*, note 195, at 108.
206 *Meinhard v. Salmon*, 249 N.Y. 456, 164 N.E. 545 (Ct. Apps., 1928), at 546.

Lord Herschell used equally strong language in *Bray v. Ford*.[207]

> It is an inflexible rule of a Court of Equity that a person in a fiduciary position, such as the respondent's is not, unless otherwise expressly provided, entitled to make a profit; he is not allowed to put himself in a position where his interest and duty conflict. It does not appear to me that this rule is, as has been said, founded upon principles of morality. I regard it rather as based on the consideration that, human nature being what it is, there is danger, in such circumstances, of the person holding a fiduciary position being swayed by interest rather than by duty, and thus prejudicing those whom he was bound to protect. It has, therefore, been deemed expedient to lay down this positive rule. But I am satisfied that it might be departed from in many cases, without any breach of morality, without any wrong being inflicted, and without any consciousness of wrong-doing.

In the discussion of *Boardman v. Phipps*[208] that appears below, we will see a dramatic illustration of the proposition that equity will not countenance a breach of fiduciary duty even if the defendant acted morally and without conscious wrongdoing — indeed, even if the defendant acted at great personal risk and to the beneficiary's financial advantage.

Degrees of Fiduciary Duties At the same time, it is important to appreciate that, within a generally strict scheme, it is possible to recognize varying shades of obligation. Professor Scott explained:[209]

> Some fiduciary relationships are undoubtedly more intense than others. The greater the independent authority to be exercised by the fiduciary, the greater the scope of his fiduciary duty. Thus, the trustee is under a stricter duty of loyalty than is an agent upon whom limited authority is conferred or a corporate director who can act only as a member of the board of directors or a promoter acting for investors in a new corporation. All of these, however, are fiduciaries and are subject to the fiduciary principle of loyalty, although not to the same extent.

Proscriptive and Prescriptive Obligations Although the point has been frequently overlooked by modern Canadian courts, it is also important to note that, as traditionally conceived, fiduciary obligations were *proscriptive*, rather than *prescriptive*. In other words, they negatively prohibited the fiduciary from behaving in certain ways, rather than positively requiring certain actions to be taken.[210]

The line between prescriptions and proscriptions, like the line between acts and omissions, is sometimes difficult to draw. Part of the explanation lies in the

---

207 [1896] A.C. 44 (U.K. H.L.), at 51-52. See also *Toronto (City) v. Bowes* (1854), 4 Gr. 489, 1854 CarswellOnt 26 (U.C. Ch.), affirmed (1856), 1856 CarswellOnt 42, 6 Gr. 1 (U.C. C.A.), affirmed (1858), 14 E.R. 770, 11 Moo. P.C. 463 (Canada P.C.) at 503 [4 Gr.].

208 (1966), [1967] 2 A.C. 46, [1966] 3 All E.R. 721 (H.L.).

209 A.W. Scott, "The Fiduciary Principle" (1949), 37 Cal. L. Rev. 539 at 541.

210 "To foster fidelity, the law does not prescribe loyal conduct, rather it prohibits disloyal conduct, including conduct that merely tends to be disloyal": P.D. Maddaugh, "Definition of Fiduciary Duty" in *Special Lectures of the Law Society of Upper Canada 1990: Fiduciary Duties* (Toronto: DeBoo, 1991) 15 at 28; "Essentially, however, fiduciary obligations prescribe what is impermissible to do, not what ought to be done": P. Parkinson, "Fiduciary Obligations", in P. Parkinson, ed., *The Principles of Equity* (Sydney: Law Book Company, 1996) 325 at 331-332; A.J. McClean, "The Theoretical Basis of the Trustee's Duty of Loyalty" (1969), 7 Alberta L. Rev. 218.

fact that essentially the same rule may take either form, depending upon its phrasing. A rule regarding incest, for instance, may be stated positively ("act in the child's best interests") or negatively ("don't act in a way that harms the child"). The distinction nevertheless may prove significant in some circumstances. One reason why the High Court of Australia in *Breen v. Williams*[211] refused to follow the Supreme Court of Canada's decision in *McInerney v. MacDonald*[212] was the belief that a physician's obligation to provide access to medical records amounts to the imposition of a positive duty in the patient's favour.[213]

It appears that the Supreme Court of Canada has now begun to recognize the significance of that point. *B. (K.L.) v. British Columbia*[214] involved claims arising from sexual abuse that the plaintiffs suffered while in foster homes. Relief was sought on the basis of, *inter alia*, the government's alleged breach of fiduciary duty in failing to protect against such abuse. The court easily found that the circumstances supported a fiduciary relationship as between the parties, but denied that the government had committed any breach. The crucial question concerned the *content* of the fiduciary duty.

Working by analogy to the obligations that are imposed upon parents and guardians, McLachlin C.J.C. held that the government's duty was merely to *avoid* certain harmful courses of action. She expressly refused to follow several lower court decisions, which had required parents to *act in the best interests of their children*. She considered such an obligation to be untenable for two reasons: (i) it would constitute result-based liability, rather than fault-based liability, insofar as it would be violated anytime that a child's best interests were not served, regardless of the steps taken by the fiduciary, and (ii) it would be unworkable insofar as it often is impossible to determine a child's best interests with sufficient certainty (*i.e.* there are different, equally legitimate views on parenting). McLachlin C.J.C. preferred instead to explain the content of the fiduciary duty as an obligation "to act loyally, and to not put one's own or others' interests ahead of the child's in a manner that abuses the child's trust."[215] That duty is breached, for instance, when a parent exercises undue influence over a child's economic inter-

---

211 *Supra*, note 195, at 83, 93-95, 113, 135-138.

212 *Supra*, note 190.

213 See also D.W.M. Waters, "The Reception of Equity in the Supreme Court of Canada (1875-2000)" (2000), 80 Can. Bar. Rev. 620 at 685 ("One has the fear at the moment that Canadian courts have drifted into this 'best interests' formulation of fiduciary obligation without realising quite what they are saying. 'Best interests' does inevitably mean . . . that any number of diversity of specific positive duties could be imposed upon the person who is found to be a fiduciary").

214 2003 SCC 51, [2003] S.C.J. No. 51, 2003 CarswellBC 2405, 2003 CarswellBC 2406, 18 B.C.L.R. (4th) 1, 19 C.C.L.T. (3d) 66, 230 D.L.R. (4th) 513, [2003] 11 W.W.R. 203, 309 N.R. 306, 44 R.F.L. (5th) 245, 187 B.C.A.C. 42, 307 W.A.C. 42, 38 C.P.C. (5th) 199, 2004 C.L.L.C. 210-014. See also *B. (M.) v. British Columbia*, 2003 SCC 53, 2003 CarswellBC 2409, 2003 CarswellBC 2410, [2003] S.C.J. No. 53, 18 B.C.L.R. (4th) 60, 19 C.C.L.T. (3d) 1, 230 D.L.R. (4th) 567, [2003] 11 W.W.R. 262, 309 N.R. 375, 44 R.F.L. (5th) 320, 187 B.C.A.C. 161, 307 W.A.C. 161; *G. (E.D.) v. Hammer*, 2003 SCC 52, [2003] S.C.J. No. 52, 2003 CarswellBC 2407, 2003 CarswellBC 2408, 18 B.C.L.R. (4th) 42, 19 C.C.L.T. (3d) 38, 230 D.L.R. (4th) 554, [2003] 11 W.W.R. 244, 187 B.C.A.C. 193, 307 W.A.C. 193, 310 N.R. 1, 2004 C.L.L.C. 210-011.

215 *Ibid.* at para. 49.

ests, engages in sexual exploitation or fails to stop another person from acting as a sexual predator. On the facts of *(B.) (K.L.)*, however, the government had not acted with insufficient loyalty. Although it negligently failed to place the plaintiffs into safe homes, it had not placed anyone's interests ahead of the plaintiffs.[216]

The distinction between prescriptive and proscriptive duties has also been explained on the basis of the latter's parasitic nature.[217] Properly understood, a (proscriptive) fiduciary duty cannot exist on its own. Loyalty in the abstract is meaningless. The concept makes sense only in connection with the discharge of a different, positive duty. The trustee's position is illustrative. A trustee is subject to a number of distinct obligations. There is, for instance, a positive obligation to use skill and care in the management of the trust property. There is also a negative, fiduciary obligation to refrain from disloyalty while acting in discharge of the positive obligation. The fiduciary duty, in other words, is ancillary. It is a super-added obligation that negatively limits the manner in which the trustee may carry out his or her other tasks.[218]

Breaches of Fiduciary Duties and Other Duties As suggested in the preceding paragraph, not every breach by a fiduciary is a breach of a fiduciary duty. Recognition of that fact is especially important in Canada where, relative to other jurisdictions, fiduciary obligations are much more likely to exist alongside obligations sounding in tort or contract.[219] Southin J. (as she then was) forcefully made the point in *Girardet v. Crease & Co.*:[220]

> Counsel for the plaintiff spoke of this case in his opening as one of breach of fiduciary duty and negligence. It became clear during his opening that no breach of fiduciary duty is in issue. What is in issue is whether the defendant was negligent in advising on the settlement of a claim for injuries suffered in an accident. The word "fiduciary" is flung around now as if it applied to all breaches of duty by solicitors, directors of companies and so forth. . . . That a lawyer can commit a breach of special duty of a trustee, *e.g.*, by stealing his client's money, by entering into a contract with the client without full disclosure, by sending a client a bill claiming disbursements never made and so forth is clear. But to say that simple carelessness in giving advice is such a breach

---

216 *Critchley, supra*, note 203.

217 P. Birks, "The Content of Fiduciary Obligation" (2002), 16 Trust Law Intl. 34.

218 A useful comparison can be drawn between a trustee and a financial advisor. Both individuals are subject to a positive duty to use skill and care for the benefit of another person. The basic obligation is essentially the same in both situations. The difference arises from the fact that a fiduciary obligation parasitically is imposed invariably in the case of a trustee, but only occasionally in the case of a financial advisor. Consequently, while the positive obligation must be discharged in either event, the manner of its performance may be relatively unfettered in the latter context.

219 *Hodgkinson v. Simms, supra*, note 168, at 216 *per* McLachlin & Sopinka JJ. ("not every act in a so-called fiduciary relationship is encumbered with fiduciary obligation").

220 (1987), 11 B.C.L.R. (2d) 361, 1987 CarswellBC 42, [1987] B.C.J. No. 240 (S.C.), at 362 [B.C.L.R.], quoted with approval in *Bristol and West Building Society v. Mothew*, [1996] 4 All E.R. 698 (C.A.), at 710. See also *Fasken Campbell Godfrey v. Seven-Up Canada Inc.* (1997), 142 D.L.R. (4th) 456, 1997 CarswellOnt 8 (Gen. Div.), affirmed (2000), 47 O.R. (3d) 15, 2000 CarswellOnt 89, [2000] O.J. No. 122, 182 D.L.R. (4th) 315, 128 O.A.C. 249 (C.A.), leave to appeal refused (2000), 2000 CarswellOnt 3844, 2000 CarswellOnt 3845, [2000] S.C.C.A. No. 143, 262 N.R. 390 (note), 143 O.A.C. 396 (note), at 483 [142 D.L.R.].

is a perversion of words. The obligation of a solicitor of care and skill is the same obligation of any person who undertakes for reward to carry out a task. One would not assert of an engineer or physician who had given bad advice and from whom common law damages were sought that he was guilty of a breach of fiduciary duty. Why should it be said of a solicitor?

Unfortunately, not all judges are so attentive to the distinct character of discrete obligations. *Szarfer v. Chodos*[221] provides an illustration of the tendency of Canadian courts to over-extend the scope of breach of fiduciary duty. The plaintiff retained the defendant, a lawyer, to act on his behalf in a wrongful dismissal action. In the course of preparing that file, the defendant learned that the plaintiff was experiencing marital difficulties, due in part to impotency. By chance, the plaintiff's wife worked temporarily in the defendant's office as a secretary. She and the defendant entered into an adulterous relationship. When the plaintiff discovered the affair, he suffered psychological problems that necessitated an expensive course of treatment. The question was whether or not the defendant could be held responsible for that loss. The court answered in the affirmative and awarded $30,000. That decision is, however, controversial. The defendant undoubtedly had acted badly, but on orthodox analysis, his wrong arguably was moral, rather than legal. The Ontario legislature had abolished the inaptly-named tort of "criminal conversation,"[222] and various related doctrines, precisely because it was thought inappropriate to treat a wife as her husband's chattel or to attribute blame in the event of marital breakdown. Callaghan A.C.J.H.C. therefore fixed instead upon the fiduciary relationship that exists between a solicitor and client, and found that the defendant had used information acquired in his professional capacity "in order to obtain the delights and benefits of the affair."[223] That was, however, an unprecedented invocation of the "no-conflict" rule, not least because it applied in connection with the plaintiff's psychological interests.

(iii) *Remedies for Breach of Fiduciary Duty*

The distinction between fiduciary and non-fiduciary breaches is important for a number of reasons. Most obviously, different claims entail different elements of proof. There may also be tactical advantages to one type of action over another. In *M. (K.) v. M. (H.)*,[224] for example, the plaintiff framed her action in breach of fiduciary duty, rather than battery, in an effort to escape a limitation period. Ultimately, however, the primary object of civil litigation is to obtain relief. The

---

221 (1986), 27 D.L.R. (4th) 388, 1986 CarswellOnt 766, 36 C.C.L.T. 181, 54 O.R. (2d) 663 (H.C.), affirmed (1988), 54 D.L.R. (4th) 383, 1988 CarswellOnt 1059, 66 O.R. (2d) 350 (C.A.).

222 The action was in tort, not criminal law, and it did not require proof of any conversation. *Family Law Reform Act*, R.S.O. 1980, c. 152, s. 69.

223 *Szarfer, supra*, note 221, at 402.

224 *Supra*, note 187.

plaintiff wants a remedy.[225] And in that regard, breach of fiduciary duty may be particularly attractive, especially in comparison to tort or breach of contract. Whereas claims at law typically are restricted to compensatory damages, the equitable action may support a host of alternatives, including disgorgement, specific enforcement and proprietary relief. Moreover, even in regards to seemingly similar remedies, equity may be more generous. While both jurisdictions will order monetary reparation of losses, equity takes a more relaxed approach to issues of causation,[226] proof,[227] mitigation and time of assessment.[228]

---

225 In light the Supreme Court of Canada's application of fiduciary principles to incest, however, it is interesting to note that victims of sexual abuse sometimes sue, not in the hope of receiving monetary relief, but rather in the hope of vindicating their sense of vulnerability and violation. See *Myers (Wiebe) v. Haroldson*, [1989] 3 W.W.R. 604, 1989 CarswellSask 246, 48 C.C.L.T. 93, 76 Sask. R. 27, 69 C.R. (3d) 387 (C.A.); B. Feldthusen, "The Civil Action for Sexual Battery: Therapeutic Jurisprudence?" (1993), 25 Ottawa L. Rev. 203.

226 McLachlin J. has said that common law principles of causation, remoteness and foreseeability do not apply with respect to equitable compensation. The court should instead be guided by a "common sense view of causation": *Canson Enterprises Ltd. v. Boughton & Co.* (1991), 85 D.L.R. (4th) 129, 1991 CarswellBC 269, 1991 CarswellBC 925, [1991] S.C.J. No. 91, [1992] 1 W.W.R. 245, 9 C.C.L.T. (2d) 1, 39 C.P.R. (3d) 449, 131 N.R. 321, 61 B.C.L.R. (2d) 1, 6 B.C.A.C. 1, 13 W.A.C. 1, [1991] 3 S.C.R. 534, 43 E.T.R. 201, at 163 [D.L.R.]. See also *Target Holdings Ltd. v. Redferns*, [1996] A.C. 421 (H.L.). La Forest J. similarly rejected the application of the common law's general rules of causation, preferring instead the peculiarly strict "but-for" causal test that applies under the tort of deceit: *Hodgkinson v. Simms*, *supra*, note 168, at 201. On the related issue of contributory negligence, however, the Supreme Court of Canada used *Canson Enterprises* to follow the New Zealand Court of Appeal and hold that rules of contributory negligence do apply by analogy to equitable claims: *Day v. Mead*, [1987] 2 N.Z.L.R. 443 (C.A.). That approach has been trenchantly criticized as "clearly wrong," both as a matter of precedent and, in light of the equitable approach to causation, as a matter of principle: R.P. Meagher, W.M.C. Gummow & J.R.F. Lehane, *Equity: Doctrines and Remedies*, 3rd ed. (Sydney: Butterworths, 1992), at 637-638.

227 In calculating compensation for loss of an investment opportunity, equity applies a presumption, not found at law, that but-for the defendant's breach, the plaintiff would have put the property to its most valuable use: *Guerin v. R.* (1984), 13 D.L.R. (4th) 321, 1984 CarswellNat 813, 1984 CarswellNat 693, [1984] 6 W.W.R. 481, [1984] 2 S.C.R. 335, 55 N.R. 161, [1985] 1 C.N.L.R. 120, 20 E.T.R. 6, 36 R.P.R. 1, 59 B.C.L.R. 301. Another equitable doctrine applies if a beneficiary entered into a transaction after a fiduciary failed to disclose a material fact. It will be presumed that, but-for the non-disclosure, the transaction would not have occurred: *Brickenden v. London Loan & Savings Co.*, [1934] 3 D.L.R. 465 (P.C.); *cf. Swindle v. Harrison*, [1997] 4 All E.R. 705 (C.A.) (limiting rule to cases of fraudulent non-disclosure). Consistent with the original formulation of the *Brickenden* rule, Australian courts refuse to allow the defendant to adduce evidence to the contrary: *Maguire v. Makaronis* (1997), 188 C.L.R. 449 (H.C.A.). Canadian courts, in contrast, merely shift a rebuttable burden onto the defendant.

228 At law, compensation typically is reduced to the extent that the plaintiff failed to mitigate a loss. For that reason, damages generally are calculated at the time of breach, rather than the time of trial. The nature of fiduciary relationships, however, demands a different rule. Mitigation is a principle of individual responsibility. But within a fiduciary relationship, responsibility for the beneficiary's interests primarily rests with the fiduciary. Consequently, the notion of mitigation takes effect only if the plaintiff, "after due notice and opportunity, fails to take the most obvious steps to alleviate his or her losses." It is only at that point that the plaintiff becomes "the author of his own misfortune": *Canson Enterprises Ltd. v. Boughton & Co.*, *supra*, note 226, at 162, *per* McLachlin J.

The types of responses that historically were available for a breach of fiduciary duty were, however, somewhat restricted, partially because of the traditional interpretation of the underlying obligation. Writing in reference to current English law, Dr. Worthington explains that the *prescriptive* duties that apply in, say, tort and contract require the defendant to ensure that the plaintiff enjoys a particular "end-position" (*e.g.* to be free of a particular harm or to obtain a particular benefit). In the event of breach, relief consequently is typically calculated to monetarily place the plaintiff into that "end-position." Fiduciary duties, in contrast, are said to be *proscriptive*. Their purpose is not to compel the defendant to ensure that the plaintiff enjoys a particular "end-position," but rather to limit the manner in which the defendant can exercise a discretion that affects that plaintiff. And since such obligations are not directed toward particular "end-positions," relief must be calculated somewhat differently. Dr. Worthington further explains:

> Equity's strategy . . . is clever. It focuses throughout on the defendant, not the claimant. It identifies the type of conduct that is likely to put the claimant most at risk, and bans, or *proscribes*, it. If the defendant acts in breach of these proscriptions, Equity again ignores the claimant (it has no prescribed end-position that might assist in defining remedies). Instead, its strategy is to return the *defendant* to the position he was in before his breach. It strips the defendant of profits made; it undoes decisions improperly reached; it unwinds irregular deals. The risk of wasted effort is the most effective weapon the law can muster to deter the defendant from engaging in the proscribed behaviour.[229]

It is not clear, however, that Canadian courts view themselves as being constrained by such considerations. As we shall see throughout the remainder of this part, the appropriate remedy for a breach of fiduciary duty is thought to depend very much upon the nature and consequences of the defendant's wrong. It is, however, possible to briefly outline the most significant possibilities.

- *Injunction* — The best remedy is always prevention. Injunctive relief consequently is available to restrain a threatened breach of fiduciary duty.[230]
- *Declaration* — A court may issue a declaration, confirming the plaintiff's rights and the defendant's obligations.[231]
- *Rescission* — Assuming that it is possible to restore the defendant to his prior position, the plaintiff may be entitled to rescind an improper transaction.[232] That might be true, for instance, if a trustee purchased property from the trust. However, even if rescission is available, the beneficiary may choose to affirm a transaction and seek compensation instead.

---

229 S. Worthington, *Equity* (Oxford: Clarendon Press, 2003) 118 (emphasis in original).

230 *Pacifica Shipping Co. Ltd. v. Andersen*, [1986] 2 N.Z.L.R. 328.

231 R.P. Meagher, W.M.C. Gummow & J.R.F. Lehane, *Equity: Doctrines and Remedies*, 3rd ed. (Sydney: Butterworths, 1992), c. 19.

232 *Hogar Estates Ltd. v. Shebron Holdings Ltd.* (1979), 101 D.L.R. (3d) 509, 1979 CarswellOnt 1499, 25 O.R. (2d) 543 (H.C.); *Baskerville v. Thurgood*, (sub nom. *582872 Saskatchewan Ltd. v. Thurgood*) (1992), 93 D.L.R. (4th) 694, 1992 CarswellSask 323, [1992] S.J. No. 327, [1992] 5 W.W.R. 193, 100 Sask. R. 214, 18 W.A.C. 214, 46 E.T.R. 28 (C.A.); P.M. Perell, "Rescission" in *Special Lectures of the Law Society of Upper Canada 1995: Law of Remedies — Principles and Proof* (Toronto: Carswell, 1995) 255.

- *Punishment* — Though the possibility historically was rejected,[233] and more recently has been questioned in other jurisdictions,[234] Canadian courts now have the power to respond to particularly reprehensible breaches of fiduciary obligations by awarding punitive damages. They most often do so in cases involving sexual assault or incest.[235]
- *Compensation* — Monetary reparation is available with respect to losses that the plaintiff suffered as a result of a breach of fiduciary duty.[236] Indeed, as previously mentioned, equitable compensation is even more generous than common law damages in some respects.
- *Disgorgement* — Disgorgement (or "restitution") is available with respect to benefits that the defendant acquired through breach. Depending upon the circumstances, the remedy may be personal or proprietary or both.[237] Personal disgorgement typically is referred to as an "account of profits." Proprietary disgorgement usually takes the form of a constructive trust. Alternatively, a lien may add proprietary weight to the enforcement of a primarily personal judgment. Confusingly, however, judges sometimes refer to the defendant as a "constructive trustee," regardless of the form that disgorgement takes.

As a final observation, it must be stressed that while choices occasionally need to be made, neither the plaintiff nor the court enjoys an entirely free hand in selecting remedies. In *Re Coomber*, Fletcher Moulton L.J. famously said:[238]

> [T]he Courts have again and again, in cases where there has been a fiduciary relation, interfered and set aside acts which, between persons in a wholly independent position, would have been perfectly valid. Thereupon in some minds there arises the idea that if there is any fiduciary relation whatever any of these types of interference is warranted by it. They conclude that every kind of fiduciary relation justifies every kind of interference. Of course that is absurd. The nature of the fiduciary relation must be such that it justifies the interference.

---

233 *Fern Brand Waxes Ltd. v. Pearl*, [1972] 3 O.R. 829, 1972 CarswellOnt 917, 29 D.L.R. (3d) 662 (C.A.); *Worobel Estate v. Worobel* (1988), 67 O.R. (2d) 151, 1988 CarswellOnt 603, 31 E.T.R. 290 (H.C.).

234 *Harri v. Digital Pulse Pty. Ltd.*, [2003] N.S.W.C.A. 10.

235 *Norberg v. Wynrib, supra*, note 186, *per* McLachlin J. (S.C.C.); *M. (K.) v. M. (H.), supra*, note 187. See also, in a commercial context, *Huff v. Price* (1990), 51 B.C.L.R. (2d) 282, 1990 CarswellBC 267, 46 C.P.C. (2d) 209, 76 D.L.R. (4th) 138 (C.A.), additional reasons at (1990), 1990 CarswellBC 774, 76 D.L.R. (4th) 138 at 176 (C.A.), leave to appeal refused (1991), 56 B.C.L.R. (2d) xxxviii (note), (sub nom. *Charpentier v. Huff*) 4 B.C.A.C. 80 (note), 9 W.A.C. 80 (note), 136 N.R. 409 (note) (S.C.C.).

236 *Nocton v. Lord Ashburton*, [1914] A.C. 932 (H.L.). See also I.E. Davidson, "The Equitable Remedy of Compensation" (1982), 13 Melbourne U. L. Rev. 349; J. Berryman, "Equitable Compensation for Breach by Fact-Based Fiduciaries: Tentative Thoughts on Clarifying Remedial Goals" (1999), 37 Alberta L. Rev. 95; P.M. Perell, "Compensation and the Scope of Equity's Remedial and Restitutionary Generosity" (1999), 37 Alberta L. Rev. 114.

237 In *Keech v. Sandford, supra*, note 171, a trustee breached his fiduciary duty by renewing a lease for his own benefit, rather than on behalf of the beneficiary. He was required to both hold the lease on trust for the beneficiary and account for the profits that he had made from the acquisition.

238 [1911] 1 Ch. 723 (C.A.), at 728-729.

Further Reading

G. Jones, "Unjust Enrichment and the Fiduciary's Duty of Loyalty" (1968), 84 L.Q. Rev. 472.

E.J. Weinrib, "The Fiduciary Obligation" (1975), 25 U. of T.L.J 1.

P.D. Finn, *Fiduciary Obligations* (Sydney: Law Book Co., 1977).

R. Flannigan, "The Fiduciary Obligation" (1989), 9 Oxford J. of Legal Studies 285.

M. Gautreau, "Demystifying the Fiduciary Mystique" (1989), 68 Can. Bar Rev. 1.

T.G. Youdan, ed., *Equity, Fiduciaries and Trusts* (Toronto: Carswell, 1989).

Special Lectures of the Law Society of Upper Canada 1990: Fiduciary Duties (Toronto: DeBoo, 1991).

P.D. Finn, "Fiduciary Law and the Modern Commercial World", in E. McKendrick, ed., *Commercial Aspects of Trusts and Fiduciary Obligations* (Oxford: Oxford University Press, 1992) 7.

D.W.M. Waters, *Equity, Fiduciaries and Trusts 1993* (Toronto: Carswell, 1993).

J.D. McCamus, "Prometheus Unbound: Fiduciary Obligation in the Supreme Court of Canada" (1997), 28 Can. Busi. L.J. 107.

L. Hoyano, "The Flight to Fiduciary Haven", in P. Birks, ed., *Privacy and Loyalty* (Oxford: Oxford University Press, 1997) 169.

P. Parkinson, "Fiduciary Obligation", in P. Parkinson, ed., *The Principles of Equity* (Sydney: LBC Information Services, 1996) 325.

D.W.M. Waters, "The Reception of Equity in the Supreme Court of Canada (1875-2000)" (2000), 80 Can. Bar. Rev. 620.

P. Birks, "The Content of Fiduciary Obligation" (2002), 16 Trust Law Intl. 34.

M.D.J. Conaglen, "Equitable Compensation for Breach of Fiduciary Dealing Rules" (2003), 119 L.Q. Rev. 246.

L. Smith, "The Motive, Not the Deeds" in J. Getzler, ed., *Rationalizing Property, Equity and Trusts: Essays in Honour of Edward Burn* (London: Butterworths, 2003), 53.

S. Worthington, *Equity* (Oxford: Clarendon Press, 2003) 117-131.

Notes and Questions

1. When should a fiduciary relationship be recognized? Has the Supreme Court of Canada gone too far in its extension of traditional principles?

2. Describe the obligations to which a person is subject by virtue of being a fiduciary. How do those obligations differ from obligations commonly encountered in tort or contract? Has the Supreme Court of Canada's expansion of fiduciary obligations been a function of policy or of principle?

3. As explained in the text, fiduciary obligations traditionally have been conceived in terms of proscriptive duties that prohibit disloyalty in the performance of *other* types of obligations. That is to say, a fiduciary duty is ancillary or adjectival, and it serves a prophylactic purpose insofar as it discourages the fiduciary from acting in conflict with the beneficiary's interests.

There are, however, competing perspectives. Professor Burrows, for instance, argues that a fiduciary duty consists of a positive obligation to advance the beneficiary's interests. On that view, prophylactic obligations prohibiting disloyalty serve to encourage the fiduciary to act for the beneficiary's benefit.[239]

---

239 A. Burrows, "We Do This At Common Law But That in Equity" (2002), 22 Oxford J. of Leg. Studies 1 at 8-9.

Dr. Lionel Smith has added another perspective.[240] While agreeing with Burrows that prophylactic obligations are not fiduciary duties in themselves (but rather exist to prevent fiduciary duties from being breached), he rejects the suggestion that the essence of a fiduciary duty is the obligation to positively advance the beneficiary's interests. He argues instead that the essence of a fiduciary duty is the obligation to act with a proper *motive*. He insists that the focus should not be on results (*e.g.* whether the fiduciary's interests conflicted with the beneficiary's interests, or whether the fiduciary advanced the beneficiary's interests), but rather on motivation (*i.e.* whether the fiduciary acted in what he *believed* to be the beneficiary's best interests). Within that scheme, prophylactic obligations remain important insofar as they preclude the fiduciary from denying an improper motive in certain circumstances. Having promised to act loyally, it would be a kind of disloyalty for the fiduciary to put the beneficiary to proof of an improper motive.

4. The explanation for the recent expansion in Canadian law undoubtedly is attributable, in large measure, to the advantages that the fiduciary analysis may confer upon the claimant. Professor Hoyano has identified a long list of potential advantages:[241]

(a) *Circumventing common law barriers to establishing liability*, such as negating apparent consent to a battery, or defeating any exclusion of liability or liquidated damages clauses in a contract between the parties;

(b) *Overcoming procedural hurdles*, such as avoiding limitation periods applicable to common law actions, or obtaining access to evidence prior to commencing an action;

(c) *Establishing a breach of a duty* where the evidence falls short of the subjective dishonesty required for deceit, or of breach of a common law standard of care, through the construction of evidential presumptions and shifting the burden of proof of certain exculpatory facts to the fiduciary;

(d) *Surmounting other evidential problems*, such as proof of harm to the plaintiff, and forging a causal link between that loss and the defendant's breach of duty;

(e) Seeking to *hold a fiduciary responsible for losses caused by events and parties beyond the fiduciary's control*;

(f) *Obtaining remedial advantages*, such as
   (1) attempting to gain access to a greater quantum of monetary compensation:
      (a) by sweeping all losses into the sequelae of the breach of duty, by dispensing with the common law limitations of foreseeability and remoteness of loss;
      (b) by seeking to avoid the mitigation principle operating against the plaintiff in common law wrongs;
      (c) by avoiding reduction of damages for contribution to the breach or loss by the plaintiff, as the beneficiary's behaviour is irrelevant to determining whether the fiduciary acted disloyally;
      (d) by accumulating damages for breach of fiduciary duty plus common law wrongs, or by splitting the breaches of fiduciary duty into separate components;
      (e) by obtaining exemplary damages, which are only rarely awarded for common law wrongs;

---

240 L. Smith, "The Motive, Not the Deed", in J. Getzler, ed., *Rationalizing Property, Equity and Trusts: Essays in Honour of Edward Burn* (London: Butterworths, 2003), 53.

241 L. Hoyano, "The Flight to Fiduciary Haven", in P. Birks, ed., *Privacy and Loyalty* (Oxford: Oxford University Press, 1997) 169 at 174ff. (footnotes omitted).

(2) Seeking a monetary award in excess of the compensatory measure, by forcing the fiduciary to disgorge any profits gained from the breach, or otherwise to reverse an unjust enrichment at the expense of the plaintiff;

(3) Obtaining proprietary remedies, such as equitable tracing of the plaintiff's property into hands of subsequent transferees (other than a *bona fide* purchaser without notice) or into substituted property, or creation of a constructive trust, which confer on the plaintiff the advantages of:

(a) obtaining any accretion of value in the asset;

(b) gaining access to any profits earned by that asset; and

(c) obtaining priority over unsecured creditors in an insolvency situation.

5. As explained in the text and in preceding note, breach of fiduciary duty is often an attractive cause of action insofar as it avoids many of the remedial restrictions that affect other types of claim. That is not to say, however, that relief will always be forthcoming. *Authorson (Litigation Guardian of) v. Canada (Attorney General)*[242] provides a disturbing counter-example.

Joseph Authorson was the representative plaintiff in a class action brought against the federal government. Like the other members of the class, he was a veteran of the Canadian Armed Forces who, because of disability, was incapable of administering his own finances. The Department of Veterans Affairs consequently took control of his money and in doing so assumed fiduciary obligations. In breach of those fiduciary obligations, it failed to invest the money or add interest. It nevertheless resisted liability on the basis of s. 5.1(4) of the *Department of Veterans Affairs Act*, which stated that "[n]o claim shall be made . . . for or on account of interest on moneys held or administered by the Minister."

The Supreme Court of Canada, reversing the lower courts, held that while the government *prima facie* was liable for breach of fiduciary duty, the legislation provided a defence. It further held that the legislation did not, contrary to the plaintiff's allegation, violate his right under the *Canadian Bill of Rights* to the "enjoyment of property, and the right not to be deprived thereof except by due process of law." The federal government had immunized itself, after the fact, from the consequences of its own wrongdoing.

6. A solicitor acted for both sides in a mortgage transaction. The solicitor undertook to ensure that the mortgage would be the sole mortgage on the property and that the balance of the purchase price would be provided by the purchasers personally. The purchasers had a loan with a bank secured by a second charge on their existing property and, while most of it would be repaid on the sale of that property, the bank required that the small portion remaining be secured by a second charge on the new property. The solicitor negligently failed to inform the mortgagee of this fact. When the purchasers defaulted, the mortgagee was unable to recoup the total amount of its loan because the real estate market had crashed. The mortgagee therefore sued the solicitor for breach of his duty of care and for breach of fiduciary duty. What is the proper result in such circumstances?[243]

In the remainder of this section, we will examine eight species of breach of fiduciary duty, involving:

---

242 (2003), 227 D.L.R. (4th) 385, 2003 CarswellOnt 2773, 2003 CarswellOnt 2774, [2003] S.C.J. No. 40, 306 N.R. 335, 175 O.A.C. 363, 4 Admin. L.R. (4th) 167, 66 O.R. (3d) 734 (note), C.E.B. & P.G.R. 8051, 2003 SCC 39, 36 C.C.P.B. 29.

243 See *Bristol and West Building Society v. Mothew, supra*, note 220.

- purchase of trust property,
- sale to the trust,
- use of confidential information,
- corporate and other opportunities,
- secret commissions and bribes,
- conflicting duties,
- self-hiring, and
- miscellaneous situations.

Throughout, we will place special emphasis on the issue of remedies, particularly the constructive trust.

(b) Purchase of Trust Property

(i) *Statement of the Rule*

In an arm's length transaction, it is irrelevant that the purchaser exploited special information, not available to the vendor, so as to secure a very good deal. The vendor has no grounds for rescinding the agreement, recovering the property or securing other relief. The situation is much different, however, if the purchaser owed fiduciary obligations to the vendor. A fiduciary is precluded from taking advantage of the relationship. One manifestation of that proposition is the "self-dealing rule," which prevents a trustee from purchasing trust property. The transaction will be reversed and the trustee will hold the property on constructive trust for the beneficiary.

The rule applies not only where the fiduciary actually manages specific property for another, as a trustee might do, but also where he or she has been engaged to perform services with respect to specific property. It therefore extends to real estate agents and brokers who either purchase the property they were engaged to sell[244] or purchase property they ought to have acquired for their principals.[245] Auctioneers,[246] trustees in bankruptcy,[247] stockbrokers,[248] and solicitors who sell property on behalf of clients[249] are also caught by the rule.[250]

---

244 *D'Atri v. Chilcott* (1975), 55 D.L.R. (3d) 30, 1975 CarswellOnt 357, 7 O.R. (2d) 249 (H.C.). And see *Wood v. St. Jules* (1976), 69 D.L.R. (3d) 481, 1976 CarswellOnt 839, 12 O.R. (2d) 529 (C.A.); *Robert D. Berto Ltd. v. Cushley* (1977), 78 D.L.R. (3d) 713, 1977 CarswellOnt 1084, 16 O.R. (2d) 604 (Dist. Ct.).

245 *Soulos v. Korkontzilas, supra,* note 9.

246 *Kitson v. Hardwicke* (1872), L.R. 7 C.P. 473 at 478.

247 *Ex parte Lacey* (1802), 6 Ves. 625 at 626, 31 E.R. 1228, *per* Lord Eldon.

248 *Oelkers v. Ellis,* [1914] 2 K.B. 139.

249 *Holman v. Loynes* (1854), 4 De G.M. & G. 270, 43 E.R. 510.

250 Of course, in such cases the principal may also have other remedies, such as a right to refuse to pay the commission (*Len Pugh Real Estate Ltd. v. Ronvic Construction Co.* (1973), 41 D.L.R. (3d) 48, 1973 CarswellOnt 286, 1 O.R. (2d) 539 (Co. Ct.), varied (1974), 53 D.L.R. (3d) 71, 6 O.R. (2d) 454 (C.A.)); or a right to recover damages for negligence or misrepresentation: *Bango v. Holt,* 21 D.L.R. (3d) 66, 1971 CarswellBC 161, [1971] 5 W.W.R. 522 (S.C.); *Avery v. Salie* (1972), 25 D.L.R. (3d) 495, 1972 CarswellSask 48, [1972] 3 W.W.R. 759 (Q.B.); *Kragh-*

Finn has organized the fiduciaries caught by the rule into five classes: (i) fiduciaries to sell, such as real estate agents, (ii) fiduciaries to manage, such as trustees, stewards and managing agents, (iii) adviser fiduciaries, such as solicitors who are asked to advise on the sale or management of clients' property, (iv) "overseer" fiduciaries, such as inspectors appointed in bankruptcies, and (v) the fiduciary's agents and employees, such as solicitors employed by trustees.[251] In addition, if the fiduciary sells the property to a family member, it will be presumed that the transaction was for the fiduciary's own benefit.[252] Further, if the fiduciary sells the property to a third party on the understanding that he or she can repurchase it, the fiduciary will be required to hold the property for the trust or the principal, even though the original sale was in all other respects proper.[253]

(ii) *Codification*

The rule has been codified in some situations. For example, a real estate broker or salesperson who wishes to acquire real property (directly or indirectly) must first deliver a written statement of disclosure and obtain a written receipt from the vendor. If the broker is the listing agent, or if the salesperson is employed by the listing agent, the statement must give full disclosure of all facts within the purchaser's special knowledge that may affect the resale value, as well as the particulars of any negotiations or agreement by the purchaser with any other person for a resale.[254] Moreover, those statutory obligations merely represent threshold requirements and are not exhaustive of the rule. Consequently, even if there has been technical compliance with the statute, the purchaser may still be found to have breached the rule.[255]

Likewise, in the absence of court approval, an inspector in a bankrupt estate is precluded from acquiring any property from the estate, either directly or indirectly.[256]

The *Securities Act*[257] includes an extensive disclosure regime. For instance, a registered dealer cannot transact as a principal without first providing written notice of the intention to do so. Similarly, a duty of disclosure is imposed upon a

---

Hansen v. Kin-Com Construction & Developments Ltd. (1979), 13 R.P.R. 22, 1979 CarswellBC 640 (S.C.).

251 Finn, ch. 20. See also J.C. Shepherd, *The Law of Fiduciaries* (Toronto: The Carswell Company Limited, 1981), chs. 2, 10 ("Shepherd").

252 *Daly v. Brown* (1907), 39 S.C.R. 122, 1907 CarswellNB 116; *International Equities Ltd., Re*, [1943] 4 D.L.R. 806, 1943 CarswellOnt 327, [1943] O.W.N. 735 (C.A.).

253 *Re Postlethwaite, Postlethwaite v. Rickman* (1888), 59 L.T. 58.

254 See, *e.g.*, *Real Estate and Business Brokers Act*, R.S.O. 1990, c. R.4, s. 31.

255 *George W. Rayfield Realty Ltd. v. Kuhn* (1980), 30 O.R. (2d) 271, 1980 CarswellOnt 1386, 115 D.L.R. (3d) 654 (H.C.), affirmed (1981), 1981 CarswellOnt 1206, 31 O.R. (2d) 160, 118 D.L.R. (3d) 192 (C.A.), denial of commission because the agent was the principal of the purchaser corporation; *Beckett v. Karklins* (1974), 50 D.L.R. (3d) 21, 1974 CarswellOnt 498, 5 O.R. (2d) 211 (H.C.), purchase avoided because the purchaser under the option became a broker after the option was granted, but before he negotiated an extension of the option.

256 *Bankruptcy and Insolvency Act*, R.S.C. 1985, c. B-3, Part V, s. 120(1).

257 R.S.O. 1990, c. S.5, s. 39.

person[258] who, by virtue of a special relationship with the issuer, has special information regarding securities.

Directors and officers are also bound by extensive statutory disclosure requirements with respect to material contracts involving their corporation.[259] A sale generally is valid only if proper disclosure is made, the director or officer abstained from voting on the matter, and the transaction was reasonable and fair to the corporation.[260]

(iii) *Application and Exceptions*

The rule applies only to property with respect to which the purchaser stood in a fiduciary relationship. Consequently, for instance, if the purchaser managed Blackacre, but not Whiteacre, then the latter may be purchased as long as no other invalidating factors (*e.g.* undue influence) are in operation. Lord Blackburn explained:[261]

> If he purchases from his client in a matter totally unconnected with what he was employed in before, no doubt an attorney may purchase from one who has been his client, just as any stranger may do, honestly telling the truth and without any fraudulent concealment, being in no respect bound to do more than any other purchaser would do. But when he is purchasing from a person property with respect to which the confidential relation has existed or exists, it becomes wrong of him to purchase without doing a great deal more than would be expected from a stranger.

Although the rule may apply regardless of the transaction's substantive fairness or the fiduciary's honesty,[262] it is not, contrary to occasional suggestion, absolute.[263] It does admit of some exceptions. A sale will not be caught if it was created before the purchaser entered into the fiduciary relationship. Nor will relief be available if the beneficiary consented to the transaction after receiving full disclosure and payment of the price. (This exception will be discussed in the notes and questions at the end of this part.) Finally, a court may give its consent to a transaction if the beneficiaries are not all *sui juris* or have not unanimously consented to the disposition. Courts are reluctant to do so, however, especially if there are objections.[264] Consequently, this exception tends to be limited to situations in which no other purchaser is available.[265]

---

258 *Ibid.*, s. 76.
259 *Canada Business Corporations Act*, R.S.C. 1985, c. C-44, s. 120(1); *Business Corporations Act*, R.S.O. 1990, c. B.16, s. 132(1).
260 *Canada Business Corporations Act, ibid.* subs. (7); *Business Corporations Act, ibid.*, subs. 7(b).
261 *McPherson v. Watt* (1877), 3 App. Cas. 254 (H.L.), at 270-1.
262 *Ex parte James* (1803), 8 Ves. 337 at 345, 32 E.R. 385, *per* Lord Eldon.
263 *Lacey, supra*, note 247, at 626.
264 *Tennant v. Trenchard* (1869), L.R. 4 Ch. App. 537.
265 See Finn, ¶453.

(iv) *Remedies*

A variety of remedies are available in the event of breach. The beneficiary *prima facie* has a right to rescind the transaction.[266] If the fiduciary still has the property, it will be held upon a constructive trust for the beneficiary.[267] If the fiduciary sold the property to a *bona fide* purchaser for value, the property itself will be irrecoverable but the fiduciary will hold the sale proceeds on constructive trust.[268] Depending upon the circumstances, the beneficiary may also be entitled to an account of any profits made without interest,[269] or occupation rent.[270] Alternatively, the beneficiary may allow the transaction to stand and recover compensation for any loss.[271] Certain beneficiaries may also have other remedies, either at law or under statute.

As demonstrated by *Tornroos v. Crocker*,[272] however, the circumstances must be carefully examined in order to determine whether or not a fiduciary obligation applies with respect to a particular transaction, and if so, whether or not it has been breached. Of course, if either question is answered in the negative, then there will be no basis for awarding relief.

TORNROOS v. CROCKER

[1957] S.C.R. 151, 7 D.L.R. (2d) 104, 1957 CarswellBC 193
Supreme Court of Canada

Crocker, Dietrich and Tornroos each held an equal number of shares in a limited company. Under the articles of association, the shareholders held *pro rata* pre-emptive rights of purchase in the event that any shareholder wished to sell. Tornroos died in 1940. His will contained three important provisions. First, it appointed his widow, Crocker and Dietrich as executors and trustees. Second , it directed them to sell the estate assets and place the proceeds into trust investments. Third, it prohibited the trust from purchasing shares in the company.

Dietrich died three months after Tornroos. In 1945, Crocker exercised his pre-emptive right and purchased Dietrich's shares from Dietrich's widow. (Crocker then caused the shares to be taken in the name of Croquip Ltd.) Crocker retired from the Tornroos trust in 1948.

In 1958 the plaintiff, who had become trustee of the Tornroos trust, brought this action. He argued that Crocker should have applied to the court under the "emergency" or "salvage" doctrine for authority to purchase one-half of the

---

266 *Stahl v. Miller*, 56 S.C.R. 312, 1918 CarswellBC 20, [1918] 2 W.W.R. 197, 40 D.L.R. 388; *Upper Canada College v. Jackson* (1852), 3 Gr. 171, 1852 CarswellOnt 11 (U.C. Ch.).
267 *Taylor v. Davies*, [1920] A.C. 636; *Daly v. Brown, supra*, note 252.
268 *Gilbert v. Store* (1914), 17 D.L.R. 189, 1914 CarswellSask 182, 6 W.W.R. 719 (S.C.).
269 *Silkstone & Haigh Moor Coal Co. v. Edey*, [1900] 1 Ch. 167.
270 *James, supra*, note 262.
271 *Daly, supra*, note 252.
272 [1957] S.C.R. 151, 7 D.L.R. (2d) 104, 1957 CarswellBC 193.

Dietrich shares. He further argued that since that had not happened, Crocker breached his fiduciary duty as trustee to the Tornroos estate and consequently held one-half of the Dietrich shares on constructive trust for the Tornroos estate.

The action was dismissed at trial,[273] but reversed by the British Columbia Court of Appeal.[274] The plaintiff then appealed to the Supreme Court of Canada.

KELLOCK J. delivered the judgment of the Court:

. . .

It is, of course, well settled that a trustee may not place himself in a situation where his interest and his duty conflict. The question which arises at the threshold of this litigation is, therefore, whether the appellant Crocker, as trustee of the Tornroos estate, had any duty toward the estate in connection with the purchase of any part of the Dietrich shares.

It is common ground, as already pointed out, that the trustees were debarred by the direction of the testator himself from investing any of the funds of the estate in these shares. To have done so would have been a breach of trust on the part of the trustees. . . . Leaving aside any question as to whether or not the estate could have financed the purchase or whether such an investment would have been considered suitable at the time owing to its undoubted speculative character, in my opinion the authorities are clear that in the circumstances of this case, there is no foundation for a contention that the Court, if it had been applied to, had jurisdiction to authorize the purchase on the basis of "salvage."

. . .

The [salvage] rule was authoritatively expressed by Romer L.J. in *In re New; In re Leavers; In re Morley*[275] as follows:

> As a rule, the Court has no jurisdiction to give, and will not give, its sanction to the performance by trustees of acts with reference to the trust estate which are not, on the face of the instrument creating the trust, authorized by its terms. . . . But in the management of a trust estate, and especially where that estate consists of a business or shares in a mercantile company, it not infrequently happens that some peculiar state of circumstances arises for which provision is not expressly made by the trust instrument, and which renders it most desirable, and it may be even essential, for the benefit of the estate and in the interest of all the cestuis que trust, that certain acts should be done by the trustees which in ordinary circumstances they would have no power to do. *In a case of this kind, which may reasonably be supposed to be one not foreseen or anticipated by the author of the trust, where the trustees are embarrassed by the emergency that has arisen* and the duty cast upon them to do what is best for the estate, and the consent of all the beneficiaries cannot be obtained by reason of some of them not being sui juris or in existence, then it may be right for the Court, and the Court in a proper case would have jurisdiction, to sanction on behalf of all concerned such acts on behalf of the trustees as we have above referred to. (The italics are mine.)

---

273 (1955), 14 W.W.R. 344, [1955] 2 D.L.R. 815, 1955 CarswellBC 7 (S.C.).
274 (1956), 3 D.L.R. (2d) 9 (B.C. C.A.).
275 [1901] 2 Ch. 534 at 544.

. . .

The jurisdiction of the Court on the ground of salvage being as above defined, it is impossible to contend in the case at bar that the offer of the Dietrich shares presented a situation which, in the language of Romer L.J., might "reasonably be supposed to be one not foreseen or anticipated" by the testator, or one where his trustees were "embarrassed by the emergency".

In drawing his will, the testator clearly had present to his mind his share-holding in the company in question, as he specifically mentions these shares. He must equally be taken to have been well aware of the provisions of the articles of the company, of which he was one of the founders, and that in the event of the death of either Dietrich or Crocker occurring while his own estate was undergoing administration, the shares of either might be offered for sale, in which event his trustees would be entitled to buy. In settling the terms of his will and giving directions to his trustees, it is plain he did not desire that his estate should exercise the right to purchase but was content that his own shares should continue as a minority holding in a company controlled by the one or other of his former business associates, in whom he had such confidence that he desired they should be his trustees. That being so, the case is entirely outside the rule in *New's* case.[276] Accordingly, there was no duty resting upon the appellant Crocker as suggested by the majority in the Court of Appeal.

It may be pointed out, also, that had any duty as trustee rested upon Crocker with respect to the Dietrich shares on the footing that the estate had something to sell or assign, it would have involved him in a purchase from an estate of which he was trustee, if he had brought about an agreement "to pay the estate to surrender its rights or to allow them to lapse so that he could get control", as the majority in the Court below considered he ought to have endeavoured to do.

In truth, however, the estate had nothing either to sell or to assign, and Crocker, in purchasing the shares as he did, was exercising nothing but a con-tractual right vested in himself personally under the articles of association to buy all the shares offered where there was no other competing shareholder. The respondents admit that the appellant was entitled to buy one-half of the Dietrich shares but it is plain that he was entitled to buy all of those shares when no other shareholder appeared in the market. The fact that the Tornroos estate could not be a buyer was not due to anything for which the appellant Crocker, by reason of any act or default of his, as trustee, was responsible. Crocker, accordingly, had a right to buy upon the footing of the articles or if, as was contended, the time for acceptance of the Dietrich offer had gone by, then just as any other member of the public.

[The court allowed the appeal.]

---

[276] *Ibid.*

Notes and Questions

A. Generally

1. Crocker's contractual right of purchase arose before he became a trustee. A pre-emptive right may, however, also be conferred by will, in which case the situation is different.

This point arose in *Wright v. Morgan*.[277] The testator directed in his will that his two farms be valued and offered for sale to his eldest son, Harry. After the testator's death, Harry sold his rights under the will to his brother, Douglas, who was a trustee of the estate. Douglas arranged for the required valuations and the sale to him, then resigned his position and exercised the right to purchase the farms. The terms of the sale were advantageous to Douglas. Certain beneficiaries brought action to have the transaction set aside and to require Douglas to account for the profits. The action was successful. In the course of the Board's opinion, Viscount Dunedin said:[278]

> [T]heir Lordships hold that the position of Douglas as a trustee and as the assignee of the option to purchase was one which would involve a conflict of duty and interest. It was of moment when the sale should take place, because the option could only be exercised when the trustees had decided that now was the moment to sell. The best moment for the trust was the moment when prices generally were high. The best moment for a purchaser was when prices generally were low, and such prices would be naturally reflected in the value fixed by the valuers. So also as to the terms of payment, the best term for the trust was cash down; the best term for the purchaser was some easier arrangement. Their Lordships do not think it necessary to go into the actual terms of payment here, although it is perhaps startling to find that the whole transaction was carried out by the payment in cash of quite an infinitesimal sum. The criterion, however, is not what was done, but what might be done. Their Lordships, therefore, come to the conclusion that this case falls within the general rule, and that the sale being, as carried out, a sale of trust property to a trustee, cannot be allowed to stand. . . .

2. *Wright v. Morgan* suggests that another exception to the purchase rule occurs when the settlor or testator permits the purchase. This is indeed so, but the trustee must nevertheless strictly observe the conditions laid down by the settlor or testator.[279] Beyond that, it is submitted that he or she must still ensure that the transaction is fair and reasonable in the sense that its terms are as good as might be obtained in an arms-length transaction. In cases of doubt, court approval should be sought.

3. Quite a different approach from *Wright v. Morgan* is apparent in *Holder v. Holder*.[280] The testator owned two farms. He worked one with his son Victor and leased the other to Victor and another person. Subsequently, Victor worked both farms and paid

---

277 [1926] A.C. 788 (P.C.).

278 *Ibid.*, at 798.

279 *Ballard Estate v. Ballard Estate* (1991), 79 D.L.R. (4th) 142, 1991 CarswellOnt 533, 3 O.R. (3d) 65, (sub nom. *Ballard Estate, Re*) 44 O.A.C. 225, 41 E.T.R. 113 (C.A.), leave to appeal refused (1991), [1991] S.C.C.A. No. 239, 5 O.R. (3d) xii, 83 D.L.R. (4th) vii, 137 N.R. 385 (note), 55 O.A.C. 390 (note).

280 [1968] Ch. 353, [1968] 1 All E.R. 665 (C.A.). See also *Fleetwood Mac Promotions Ltd. v. Clifford Davis Management Ltd.*, [1975] F.S.R. 150; *Guaranty Trust Co. of Canada v. Berry*, 7 E.T.R. 287, 115 D.L.R. (3d) 513, 19 C.P.C. 157, 33 N.R. 271, 1980 CarswellOnt 447, 1980 CarswellOnt 647, [1980] 2 S.C.R. 931; *cf. Hollinger v. Heichel*, [1941] 1 W.W.R. 97, 1941 CarswellAlta 5 (T.D.).

rent to his father. The testator's will directed that the freeholds be sold and the proceeds divided among his widow and children. Victor was one of the executors. He purported to renounce before probate was granted, but before he renounced he had, with the other two executors, opened an account for the estate and co-signed some cheques drawn on it. The other executors had the farms valued and sold by auction. Victor purchased them at a fair price, but his brother, the plaintiff, claimed that Victor was prevented from buying them because of his conflict of interest. The trial judge agreed and ordered a resale. Victor appealed. Victor admitted that his renunciation was ineffective because he had acted as executor, but the court was of the opinion that he ought not to have made this admission. The Court of Appeal allowed the appeal. All three members of the court examined the policy of the rule and quoted extensively from the cases which favoured automatic avoidance, but concluded that the rule did not apply on the facts, partly because they found that the plaintiff had acquiesced in the transaction and partly because Victor never in fact occupied the dual position of vendor and purchaser. He acquired his knowledge about the farms *qua* lessee, not *qua* executor. Moreover, his interest and duty were not in conflict. He had never made a secret of his intention to purchase. Thus, the beneficiaries did not look to him to protect their interests. Accordingly, said Harman L.J., since "the reasons behind the rule do not exist I do not feel bound to apply it."[281] The other two members of the court agreed, but went somewhat further. Thus, Dankwerts L.J., in referring to Lord Eldon's statement of the rule in *Ex parte Lacey*,[282] stated:[283]

[t]he reason given by Lord Eldon, that it is impossible to ascertain what knowledge the trustee may have, seems less persuasive in the light of Lord Bowen's famous dictum[284] that "the state of a man's mind is as much a fact as the state of his digestion," and the almost daily experience of any judge engaged in ascertaining the knowledge and intentions of a party to proceedings.

Sachs L.J. opined that the rule was not nowadays as rigid as when Lord Eldon formulated it and agreed with Lord Justice Dankwerts' comments regarding the alleged inability of a court to ascertain the state of mind of a trustee. His Lordship said in this context:[285]

I am inclined to the view that an irrebuttable presumption as to the state of his knowledge may no longer accord with the way in which the courts have now come to regard matters of this type. Thus the rigidity of the shackles imposed by the rule on the discretion of the court may perhaps before long be reconsidered as the courts tend to lean more and more against such rigidity of rules as can cause patent injustice. . . . The rule, after all, appears on analysis to be one of practice as opposed to one going to the jurisdiction of the court.

    4. What is the effect of *Holder v. Holder*? Has it reversed a centuries-old rule of law as some have claimed? It is submitted that the case does not go that far. In one sense it can be regarded as having been decided strictly on its facts. In another and, it is submitted, the correct sense, it can be regarded as demonstrating a willingness by the court to examine all the facts before applying a supposedly automatic rule. Hence, the rule itself has not been abrogated, but its severity has been much lessened.

---

281 *Holder, ibid.*, at 392.
282 *Supra*, note 247, at 626.
283 *Holder, supra*, note 280, at 398.
284 In *Edgington v. Fitzmaurice* (1885), 29 Ch. D. 459 (C.A.) at 483.
285 *Holder, supra*, note 280, at 402-3.

B. Purchase of a Beneficiary's Interest

1. The rule prohibiting a fiduciary from purchasing trust property generally is regarded as virtually absolute. However, the same cases that laid down that rule also recognized that a fiduciary may purchase property from a beneficiary.[286] The difference between the two situations is simple. A trustee who purchases trust property essentially acts as both vendor and purchaser. In contrast, a trustee who buys from a beneficiary transacts with a different person and that is permissible.

Of course, a conflict of interest may arise even in the latter situation. The trustee remains a fiduciary toward the beneficiary and in that capacity may have acquired special information about the property. And indeed, the differences between the two situations are not as great as they might seem. Because of the trustee's advantageous position, the courts scrutinize purchases from beneficiaries very carefully.[287] The trustee is subject to the "fair dealing rule." He or she bears the burden of showing that the beneficiary received full disclosure of all material facts, independent advice and a fair price. If that burden is not satisfied, the beneficiary enjoys the same remedies that are available in the event of a trustee's purchase of trust property.

2. The rule is illustrated by *Crighton v. Roman*.[288] Roman, Crighton and Featherstone entered into a joint venture. Roman, who was the managing partner, acquired certain mining claims in Saskatchewan for the joint venture for $10,000. Roman contributed one-half of the purchase price and Crighton and Featherstone one-quarter each. Title to the claims was taken in the name of Peacock, a solicitor, in trust for Roman. On Roman's instructions Peacock: (a) sold the claims to North Denison Mines Ltd. for $15,000 and the allotment of 100,000 fully paid-up shares in its capital stock, (b) distributed the $15,000 one-half to Roman one-quarter each to Crighton and Featherstone, and (c) transferred the shares to Roman's company, New Concord Development Corporation Ltd. The shares were later exchanged for fully paid-up shares in Consolidated Denison Mines Ltd. on the basis of one fully paid share of the stock of that company for every three and one-half shares of North Denison.

The mining claims turned out to be valuable. Crighton and the executor of Featherstone's estate brought action against Roman for transfer to each of them of 25,000 shares of North Denison. The court held that Roman stood in the position of a trustee purchasing the beneficiaries' interest in the trust property. Cartwright J., quoting Halsbury,[289] held[290] that a trustee may do so if he or she is able to show:

> (1) that there has been no fraud or concealment or advantage taken by him of information acquired by him in the character of trustee; (2) that the *cestui que trust* had independent advice, and every kind of protection, and the fullest information with respect to the property; and (3) that the consideration was adequate.

Roman failed to meet the onus. The court consequently found that he held the 25,000 shares in North Denison Mines (or the equivalent thereof in Consolidated Denison Mines) on constructive trust for each of his partners. The court also held Roman accountable for the dividends earned on the shares.[291]

---

286 See, *e.g.*, *Ex parte Lacey*, *supra*, note 247.
287 Finn, ¶430.
288 [1960] S.C.R. 858, 25 D.L.R. (2d) 609, 1960 CarswellOnt 65.
289 2nd ed., vol. 33, at 284-5.
290 *Crighton*, note 288, at 618.
291 *Ibid.*, at 620n.

3. A and B were executors and beneficiaries of an estate which owned certain shares. X offered to purchase the shares. A and B persuaded the other beneficiaries to sell their interests in the estate to them without disclosing the offer and then sold the shares to X at a substantial profit. When the other beneficiaries discovered the matter they sought to make A and B accountable. How should the matter be resolved?[292]

4. A and B were executors of an estate. C was the sole beneficiary. The trust property was land. Although he never formally resigned from the trust, B declared his intention to do so and in fact stopped acting as executor. C, who was quite familiar with the property, wanted to have it sold. B offered to buy it. A contract was made between A and B, with C consenting as third party. C also released the executors from all claims against them in respect of the transaction. Later, however, C discovered that B had made false representations about the property and demanded repayment of $2,000. B refused. A couple of years later C claimed a right to either set aside the transaction or receive compensation. Do the facts reveal a purchase of trust property or a purchase of a beneficiary's interest? In either case, what is the result?[293]

C. Renewals of Leases and Related Problems

1. The problem that arises when a trustee renews a lease on his or her own behalf is simply one manifestation of the larger issue regarding conflicts of interest and purchases from trusts.[294] Nevertheless, lease renewals are often treated as an area unto themselves.

Keech v. Sandford[295] is the leading case on both the narrow issue of renewed leases and the broader issue of constructive trusts for breach of fiduciary duty. A lease of a market had been held on trust. Since the lessor refused to renew the lease in favour of the beneficiary, the trustee took a lease for himself. As a precedent, *Keech v. Sandford* has a number of drawbacks. Lord King, who decided the matter, was not a particularly distinguished holder of the Great Seal.[296] The reporting series in which the decision appears is not highly regarded. And most significantly, it is not clear from the stated facts that the original lease was renewable. The case nevertheless is of great importance insofar as it established that, in such circumstances, the trustee must hold the lease on constructive trust and account for the profits that he had received. The case also established that the basis of relief is not fraud in the usual sense (for the trustee may not have acted fraudulently), but rather the need to strongly deter breach of fiduciary duty.

2. The rule most often has been applied to leases that are renewable by custom and where a minor is the beneficiary. However, it also encompasses leases that are not customarily or expressly renewable.[297] Moreover, it extends to all fiduciaries, as well as to persons who are not technically fiduciaries, but who stand in a "special position" toward another party, such as co-tenants and mortgagees.[298] Arguably, however, that last extension of the rule is not defensible unless the person who acquires the renewal actually assumes to act for the other person, in which case fiduciary obligations arise.[299]

---

292 See *Field v. Banfield*, [1933] O.W.N. 39 (H.C.).

293 See *Hollinger v. Heichel, supra*, note 280.

294 S. Cretney, "The Rationale of Keech v. Sandford" (1969), 33 Conv. 161.

295 *Supra*, note 171. A very similar case is *Knowles' Will Trusts, Re*, [1948] 1 All E.R. 866 (C.A.).

296 Cretney, *op. cit.*, note 294, at 162-3.

297 See *Biss, Re*, [1903] 2 Ch. 40 at 60.

298 Finn, ¶603ff.

299 *Ibid.*, ¶605. See also *Quong v. Pong*, [1927] S.C.R. 271, 1927 CarswellOnt 56, [1927] 3 D.L.R. 128, affirming 56 O.L.R. 616, [1925] 2 D.L.R. 1192 (C.A.).

3. The rule also applies if a fiduciary purchases a reversion.[300] Initially, that appeared to be true only if the lease was renewable by custom or contract,[301] but the English Court of Appeal has since held that the renewability of the lease is irrelevant.[302]

4. The difficulty with the rule is that it is absolute. It does not merely raise a presumption against the fiduciary. It automatically requires the fiduciary to hold the property upon trust for the beneficiary. In that regard, the rule is inconsistent with the rules that apply with respect to the purchase of trust property, which allow the fiduciary to retain the property by proving either that there was no breach or that the beneficiary consented to the transaction. The more flexible rules perhaps ought to apply across the board.

(c) Sale to the Trust

The rule that prohibits a trustee from effectively acting on both sides of a transaction generally cuts both ways. It precludes the trustee from selling (or lending[303]) to the trust, just as it prevents purchases from the trust. The rule is, however, slightly more forgiving in the former situation insofar as a transaction will be regarded as valid as long as the trustee provided full disclosure.[304]

The sale rule sometimes causes difficulties. Quite often, a modern corporate trustee would be able, by means of inter-departmental transfers, to make advantageous investments on behalf of a trust if it was entitled to sell assets to the trust from its own resources.[305] *Osadchuk v. National Trust Co.*[306] nevertheless stands in the way of such transactions. The appellant trust company obtained letters of administration in the Osadchuk estate in July of 1919. At that time, the value of the estate was approximately $5,494. In October and December of 1919, the trust company advanced $1,700 and $1,300 of its own funds to third parties on the security of two mortgages. It took the mortgages in its own name. In March of 1920, the trust company debited the estate with these amounts and claimed that it allocated the mortgages to the estate. The mortgages turned out badly and were almost a total loss. The sole beneficiaries of the estate were minors in 1919. In 1941, after they attained the age of majority, they brought an action for a general accounting in the estate and of the sums invested in the two mortgages in particular. The court held that the transaction amounted to a sale to the trust and was void.

If a sale is improper, the beneficiary can have it set aside if *restitutio in integrum* remains possible.[307] If not, the beneficiary is entitled to compensation

---

300 *Phillips v. Phillips* (1884), 29 Ch. D. 673.

301 *Bevan v. Webb*, [1905] 1 Ch. 620.

302 *Protheroe v. Protheroe*, [1968] 1 W.L.R. 519, followed in *Thompson's Trustee in Bankruptcy v. Heaton*, [1974] 1 W.L.R. 605, [1974] 1 All E.R. 1239.

303 *Davis v. Kerr* (1890), 17 S.C.R. 235, 1890 CarswellQue 25.

304 *Massey v. Davies* (1794), 2 Ves. Jun. 317, 30 E.R. 651; *cf. Harrison v. Harrison* (1868), 14 Gr. 586, 1868 CarswellOnt 66 (U.C. Ch.) (beneficiary consented to acquisition of property but was unaware the trustee was the owner — sale set aside).

305 Waters, at 723.

306 [1943] S.C.R. 89, [1943] 1 D.L.R. 689, 1943 CarswellSask 90.

307 Which would not be the case if, for example, the property has been resold or consumed. See Finn, ¶520.

for any losses. Interestingly, however, it has been said that if rescission is impossible, the court will not alternatively order disgorgement of any gain that the trustee received under the transaction unless the trustee's original acquisition of the property was itself tainted by a breach of fiduciary duty.[308] The explanation is that if the fiduciary's original acquisition was legitimate, then the property never belonged to the beneficiary. In contrast, if the fiduciary's original acquisition was illegitimate, then it belonged equitably to the beneficiary from the outset, such as to provide access to the full range of remedies, including an account of profits and a constructive trust.[309] However, while that explanation may be persuasive with respect to a constructive trust, which provides the beneficiary with equitable ownership, it fails to identify a reason for refusing personal disgorgement. The fact remains that, in making the sale to the trust, the trustee committed a wrong. In other situations, wrongdoers may be compelled to disgorge ill-gotten gains even if no property is involved.[310]

Notes and Questions

1. Does *Osadchuk* impose too great a restraint upon the corporate trustee?

A different rule has been applied in the United States. Corporate trustees are allowed to allocate investments from their corporate pools to individual trusts under their management. However, that rule applies only if a trustee purchases investments specifically for the trust pool and if none of the investments in that pool can be purchased by the corporate trustee in its private capacity.[311] If the trustee could allocate some the investments to itself, there would be a danger that it might allocate the better ones to itself. Is it relevant that in the United States a corporate trustee may still be tempted to favour one trust over another?

2. Trust companies are, by statute, permitted to maintain common trust funds[312] and pooled trust funds.[313]

3. If a corporate trustee (or indeed any trustee) can demonstrate that an investment was purchased with trust funds and in the name of the estate, and if the investment was otherwise proper, the trustee will not be liable if a loss results. It consequently is important for a trustee to follow proper procedures and to keep proper records, so that the information can be put into evidence if the transaction is later attacked.[314]

---

308 *Burland v. Earle*, [1902] A.C. 83 (P.C.); Finn, ¶¶521-525; Shepherd, p. 176. For instance, the circumstances may be such that the trustee initially acquired the property for himself when he should have acquired it on behalf of the trust.

309 Finn, *loc. cit.*; Shepherd, pp. 182-3.

310 *Attorney General v. Blake*, [2001] 1 A.C. 268 (H.L.); *Bank of America Canada v. Mutual Trust Co.* (2002), 211 D.L.R. (4th) 385, 2002 CarswellOnt 1114, 2002 CarswellOnt 1115, [2002] S.C.J. No. 44, 2002 SCC 43, 49 R.P.R. (3d) 1, 287 N.R. 171, 159 O.A.C. 1, [2002] 2 S.C.R. 601, at 293 [D.L.R.] (disgorgement of profits earned through breach of contract).

311 A.W. Scott and W.F. Fratcher, *The Law of Trusts*, 4th ed. (Boston: Little, Brown and Company, 1987-91), ¶170.14 ("Scott"). See also the Editorial Note to the *Osadchuk* case, *supra*, note 306, at 689-90.

312 *Loan and Trust Corporations Act*, R.S.O. 1990, c. L.25, s. 173.

313 *Ibid.*

314 See *Laing v. Trusts & Guarantee Co.*, [1944] 3 W.W.R. 401, [1944] 4 D.L.R. 419, 1944 CarswellMan 42 (C.A.).

4. As previously noted, a trustee may not lend money to the trust, except with the consent of all the beneficiaries[315] or with the prior consent of the court.[316] This rule prohibits a corporate trustee from investing trust moneys in its own securities, such as guaranteed investment certificates and debentures. Such transactions are, in effect, loans to the trust.[317] This practice may, in any event, be prohibited by legislation.[318]

(d) Use of Confidential Information

As we saw in a previous section, a constructive trust may be imposed over property acquired through breach of confidence. That is true regardless of the precise context. In this section, we examine the rules governing the abuse of confidential information acquired through a fiduciary relationship. In such circumstances, the action generally is framed as breach of fiduciary duty, rather than breach of confidence. Although similar, the two actions proceed on somewhat different footings. In a case of breach of confidence, the court intervenes because secret information has been misused. In a case of breach of fiduciary duty, in contrast, equity intervenes because there is a conflict between the defendant's personal interests on the one hand and his or her fiduciary obligations on the other. The misuse of secret information is simply one manifestation of that conflict. There are also some remedial differences between the two species of claim. As we earlier saw, breach of confidence may be met with a range of responses, carefully tailored to the circumstances. Consequently, while an intentional breach may trigger an account of profits, an unintentional breach may merely result in relief calculated on a *quantum meruit* basis. In contrast, a fiduciary who misuses confidential information will likely be subjected to the more thorough remedy, even if the breach was honest.[319]

Confidential information is often acquired by means of a fiduciary relationship. A corporate officer may learn about a planned take-over bid and invest heavily in the company's shares; a mining prospector, having received information from co-venturers, may subsequently use it to stake an individual claim; a partner may exploit confidential information in order to acquire property in which the partnership was interested; and so on. In all such cases, unless the information was obtained in a personal capacity, the defendant may be liable to, *inter alia*, provide compensation with respect to the plaintiff's losses or disgorge a wrongful gain (either personally or, by means of a constructive trust, proprietarily).

The leading case, *Boardman v. Phipps*,[320] warrants extended examination. C.W. Phipps created a testamentary trust. The trust property included shares in a company called Lester & Harris Ltd. That company was performing poorly and

---

315 *Lerner, Re*, 6 W.W.R. (N.S.) 187, [1952] 4 D.L.R. 605, 1952 CarswellMan 39 (Q.B.).

316 *Higgins v. Higgins* (1932), 4 M.P.R. 365 (N.B.).

317 See *Pick, Re* (1965), 52 W.W.R. 136, 1965 CarswellSask 23 (Surr. Ct.); *Ferrier v. Reid* (1966), 55 W.W.R. 299, 1966 CarswellBC 21 (S.C.).

318 See, *e.g.*, *Trustee Act*, R.S.B.C. 1996, c. 464, s. 17(2).

319 G. Jones, "Restitution of Benefits Obtained in Breach of Another's Confidence" (1970), 86 L.Q. Rev. 463 at 487.

320 *Supra*, note 208.

the trust shares consequently were not as valuable as they might have been. Tom Phipps, a beneficiary of the trust, and Mr. Boardman, a solicitor to the trustees, used proxies held by the trust to attend a shareholders' meeting. On the basis of information obtained at that meeting, Phipps and Boardman formed the opinion that the company was being mis-managed. They also formed the opinion that it would be desirable to purchase the outstanding shares in Lester & Harris, take control of the company and improve its fortunes.

Because of the investment terms imposed by C.W. Phipps, the testamentary trust was prohibited from purchasing shares in Lester & Harris. Boardman and Phipps therefore formulated a plan under which they would buy the necessary shares themselves. They received *some* consent for that plan from two of the three trustees (the third trustee, the settlor's widow, being in poor mental and physical health). It appears, however, that Mr. Fox, the active trustee, did not fully appreciate that Phipps and Boardman would be purchasing shares for their own account.

Initially at least, the plan worked well. Tom Phipps and Mr. Boardman purchased a large number of shares in Lester & Harris, took control of the company and vastly improved its financial position. The immediate result was two-fold: (i) the trust benefited insofar as the value of its shares in Lester & Harris increased, and (ii) Phipps and Boardman benefited insofar as the value of their personal shares increased as well.

A problem nevertheless subsequently arose. John Anthony Phipps (the plaintiff) was a beneficiary of the Phipps trust with a 5/18ths interest. He claimed that Tom Phipps and Mr. Boardman (the defendants) had committed a breach of fiduciary duty by using confidential information obtained from the trust for personal gain. He further claimed that they held 5/18ths of their shares on constructive trust for him and that they should account for 5/18ths of their profits to him.

The claim was in many respects unsympathetic. The defendants: (i) acted honestly insofar as they believed that they were entitled, by the trustees' consent, to proceed as planned, (ii) purchased the shares in Lester & Harris only after determining that the trust could not do so, (iii) acted in the best interests of the trust, and (iv) spent considerable time and effort, and incurred substantial financial risks, carrying out the plan.

Wilberforce J. nevertheless allowed the claim.[321] He found that the defendants occupied fiduciary positions because they acted as self-appointed agents to the trust. He further found that they had breached their fiduciary obligations. He accordingly held that the defendants: (i) held 5/18ths of the shares on constructive trust for the plaintiff, and (ii) were personally liable to account for the profits that they had earned on those shares. Wilberforce J. was not, however, entirely unforgiving. He permitted the defendants an allowance for their "work and skill."[322]

> But, in addition to expenditure, should not the defendants be given an allowance or credit for their work and skill? This is a subject on which authority is scanty; but Cohen J. in *In re Macadam*[323]

---

321 *Phipps v. Boardman*, [1964] 1 W.L.R. 993, [1964] 2 All E.R. 187.
322 *Ibid.*, at W.L.R. 1018, All E.R. 208.
323 (1945), [1946] Ch. 73, [1945] 2 All E.R. 664.

gave his support to an allowance of this kind to trustees for their services in acting as directors of a company. It seems to me that this transaction, *i.e.*, the acquisition of a controlling interest in the company, was one of a special character calling for the exercise of a particular kind of professional skill. If Boardman had not assumed the role of seeing it through, the beneficiaries would have had to employ (and would, had they been well advised, have employed) an expert to do it for them. If the trustees had come to the court asking for liberty to employ such a person, they would in all probability have been authorised to do so, and to remunerate the person in question. It seems to me that it would be inequitable now for the beneficiaries to step in and take the profit without paying for the skill and labour which has produced it.

. . .

Without in any way binding the court [conducting the inquiry] as to what it should do on the evidence that may be presented, I think that I ought, from the knowledge gained in the course of this trial, to express the opinion that payment should be on a liberal scale.

The Court of Appeal affirmed. Pearson L.J. explained:[324]

[T]he defendants were acting with the authority of the trustees and were making ample and effective use of their position representing the trustees and wielding the power of the trustees, who were substantial minority shareholders, to extract from the directors of the company a great deal of information as to the assets and resources of the company. . . . [T]his information enabled the defendants to appreciate the true value of the company's shares and to decide that a purchase of the shares held by the director's group at a price offered would be a very promising venture. The defendants made their very large profit, not only by their own skill and persistence and risk-taking, but also by making use of their position as agents for the trustees.

The House of Lords split three to two in dismissing the further appeal. The majority, comprising Lords Hodson, Guest and Cohen, applied the conflict rule strictly. They agreed with Wilberforce J. that Boardman and Tom Phipps were self-appointed agents to the trust and as such were subject to fiduciary obligations. They breached those obligations by using information gained from the trust for personal gain. Consequently, the House (apparently) confirmed the relief awarded at trial (including the defendants' "allowance"). The majority regarded the conflict rule as being virtually absolute. The defendants would have been permitted to purchase the shares only if they received either unanimous consent from the beneficiaries or court approval. Since neither of those conditions were met, the defendants were liable, regardless of how much the "equities" appeared to be in their favour.

The minority, comprising Viscount Dilhorne and Lord Upjohn, would have allowed the appeal. Viscount Dilhorne agreed that Boardman and Tom Phipps were fiduciaries, but concluded that there had not been a conflict of interest. The defendants did not acquire the shares solely because of their position or in the course of their duties as agents for the trust. They initially acted as agents for the trust, but when the trust, represented by Fox, made it clear that it would not purchase the shares under any circumstances, the defendants were able to act on their own account. The information they obtained from the company did not belong to the trust, since the acquisition of the shares was outside the scope of the trust and outside the scope of the agency created by the employment of the

---

324 [1965] Ch. 992 at 1022.

defendants. Consequently, they were not obliged to advise the trust to apply to the court for permission to invest in the shares, nor did they have to obtain the beneficiaries' consent.

In agreeing with Viscount Dilhorne, Lord Upjohn emphasized the fact that the trust could not have invested in the shares since they were not authorized investments. He also stressed that no court would have sanctioned their acquisition by the trust in the circumstances.

The implications of the conflicting views of the majority and the minority are explained further in the Notes and Questions.

Notes and Questions

1. It is not particularly helpful to call confidential information "property." It was so regarded at trial and by all three members of the Court of Appeal. Only two members of the majority in the House of Lords (Lords Hodson and Guest) treated the information obtained by Boardman and Tom Phipps as property, while Lord Cohen did not think that information could be treated as property. Of the dissenting judges, Viscount Dilhorne thought that information could be property in certain circumstances, but did not think that it was in this case, while Lord Upjohn emphatically denied that confidential information is property.

In Canada, confidential information has been regarded both as trust property[325] and as not being the equivalent of property.[326] In *Cadbury Schweppes Inc. v. FBI Foods Ltd.*,[327] Binnie J. regarded the "characterization of confidential information as property [as] controversial."

Shepherd argues that the trust *res* in cases involving misuse of information (as well as in all other breaches of fiduciary relationships) is the power conferred on the fiduciary coupled with the duty to use the power in the best interests of the fiduciary. He regards the power as being a species of property.[328]

2. It must not be thought, as a result of *Boardman v. Phipps*, that a fiduciary need only obtain the consent of the (capacitated) trustees in order to act on his own account. The trustees are unable to give such consent; only the beneficiaries can do so. If consent cannot be obtained from the beneficiaries, court approval must be obtained.

3. What exactly was the remedy obtained in *Boardman v. Phipps*? Were Boardman and Tom Phipps required to hold the shares on constructive trust and personally account for their profit (as Wilberforce J. held) or did they hold both the shares and the profits on constructive trust? Unfortunately, the House of Lords was ambiguous. Their Lordships did not clearly distinguish between personal and proprietary relief, and, with the exception of Lord Guest, spoke of "accountability" only. They did affirm Wilberforce J.'s decision and therefore generally are assumed to have agreed that while the shares should be held on trust, the profits should not. However, there is also a suggestion in the trial judgment that the profits should also be held on trust.[329] If that was intended, then the remedy

---

325 *Carlsen v. Gerlach* (1979), 3 E.T.R. 231, 16 A.R. 553, 1979 CarswellAlta 185, 9 M.P.L.R. 229 (Dist. Ct.).

326 *Pine Pass Oil & Gas Ltd. v. Pacific Petroleums Ltd.* (1968), 70 D.L.R. (2d) 196 (B.C. S.C.).

327 *Supra*, note 97.

328 Shepherd, pp. 96ff., 110ff., 326ff. And see also ch. 5 in which he discusses various competing theories as a basis for the fiduciary obligation, including the property theory.

329 *Boardman, supra*, note 321, at 1018. *Cf.* the Court of Appeal at [1965] Ch. 1006.

arguably was too harsh. It may be more appropriate to restrict the more invasive remedy to situations in which the defendant acted dishonestly.[330]

4. Should Boardman and Tom Phipps have been liable at all, given that they acted honestly, in the best interests of the trust, using their own extensive skill and knowledge and in respect of information which the trust could not utilize, since the shares were not proper trust investments? In other words, is the equitable principle too strict? Even if liability was properly imposed, would it not have been preferable to apportion the profit between Boardman and Tom Phipps on the one hand and the plaintiff on the other?

5. An honest fiduciary is given some advantages. In *Boardman v. Phipps*, the defendants were allowed liberal remuneration for their services.[331] The court has an inherent jurisdiction to authorize such remuneration.[332] Furthermore, where required to account, the honest fiduciary may be subjected to a lower rate of interest than the dishonest.[333]

6. A came across indications of asbestos in Northern Manitoba and staked four claims. Due to lack of money, however, the claims were allowed to lapse. A subsequently discussed the matter with B, a well-known prospector. The parties agreed that B would stake and record the asbestos mineral claims and that A would supply the necessary information to B to locate them. Under that agreement, B would receive a 25% interest in the claims as a result. B went to stake the claims, but returned to say that there was no asbestos in the area. B then sought out C and recommended the area for investigation because of its mineral possibilities. As a result, B went back to the area on behalf of himself and C and staked a large number of claims. B held a one-quarter interest in them. Four years later, chrome was discovered in the area. A brings an action against B for a declaration that B holds his interest in the claims as to 75% thereof upon constructive trust for A. How should the dispute be resolved?[334]

(e) Corporate and Other Opportunities

In *Boardman v. Phipps*,[335] the defendants were liable because they obtained a profit on the basis of information that they had acquired from the trust. It was irrelevant that the defendants had acted honestly or that the trust was incapable of acquiring the profits for itself. The same principles often are applied, outside the trust context, with respect to information regarding corporate opportunities. We will examine three cases: *Regal (Hastings) Ltd. v. Gulliver, Peso Silver Mines Ltd. (N.P.L.) v. Cropper* and *Canadian Aero Services Ltd. v. O'Malley*.

(i) *Regal (Hastings) Ltd. v. Gulliver*[336]

For present purposes, the facts of *Regal (Hastings) Ltd. v. Gulliver*[337] can be slightly simplified. The plaintiff company wanted to purchase two cinemas, but

---

330 G. Jones, *Goff & Jones: The Law of Restitution*, 6th ed. (London: Sweet & Maxwell, 2002) 731-732.

331 Compare *Guiness plc v. Saunders*, [1990] 2 A.C. 663 (H.L.).

332 J. Martin, *Hanbury and Martin: Modern Equity*, 14th ed. (London: Sweet & Maxwell Ltd., 1993), p. 577 ("Hanbury and Martin").

333 *Ibid.*, at 596.

334 See *McLeod v. Sweezey*, [1944] S.C.R. 111, [1944] 2 D.L.R. 145, 1944 CarswellMan 64.

335 *Supra*, note 208.

lacked the £5,000 needed to do so. So as to ensure that the opportunity would not be lost, a new subsidiary was created with £5,000 in shares. The plaintiff purchased £2,000 in shares and the plaintiff's directors purchased the rest. After acquiring the cinemas, the subsidiary performed very well and the value of its shares increased. The directors consequently enjoyed substantial profits.

The plaintiff subsequently came under the control of a new board of directors. They caused the plaintiff to sue the former directors for breach of fiduciary duty. The House of Lords upheld the claim and ordered the defendants to personally account for (*i.e.* disgorge) their profits. (Interestingly, proprietary relief was not sought.) It was irrelevant that the directors had acted in good faith and had paid fair value for the shares, that the plan had conferred a benefit upon the company insofar as the value of its shares in the subsidiary increased, or that the company could not have afforded to take up the opportunity for itself. Some commentators regard the decision in *Regal* as harsh.

(ii) *Peso Silver Mines Ltd. v. Cropper*[338]

Regal may usefully be contrasted with *Cropper*. Cropper was a mining executive with wide knowledge of mining and prospecting. He and others incorporated Peso Silver Mines Ltd. in 1961, with Cropper as its managing director. In 1961 and 1962 the company acquired a large number of mineral claims in the Yukon which strained its financial resources. In the spring of 1962, a prospector offered to sell the company additional mining claims in the Yukon, some contiguous and some a short distance from the company's holdings. The company received approximately two or three such offers a week. The claims in question were speculative and the company rejected the offer. It was found at trial that the board acted honestly and in the best interests of the company in doing so.

Subsequently, after the matter had passed from his mind (as found by the court), Cropper was approached by a consulting geologist regarding the mineral claims recently offered to the company. Cropper, the geologist and another person bought the claims as a speculative venture. Title was taken in the name Cross Bow Mines Ltd., in which the three partners held equal shares. This company also acquired title to the lands between its original claims and those owned by Peso. Cross Bow subsequently transferred the properties to Mayo Silver Mines Ltd. to develop the claims in return for shares. Cropper and his partners also acquired shares in Mayo for cash.

In November of 1963, Charter Oil Co. Ltd. purchased one million shares in Peso Silver Mines. A new board was created for Peso, consisting mostly of nominees of Charter Oil, but also Cropper. Frictions soon developed and the new chairman asked Cropper to hand over his interests in Cross Bow and Mayo at cost. When Cropper refused, the board rescinded his appointment as officer and he resigned as director. Peso then brought action for a declaration that Cropper held the shares in Cross Bow and Mayo upon trust for Peso and for an order

---

338 [1966] S.C.R. 673, 56 W.W.R. 641, 58 D.L.R. (2d) 1, 1966 CarswellBC 90.

directing him to deliver the shares to Peso, or requiring him to account for their proceeds.

The claim was dismissed. In the British Columbia Court of Appeal, Bull J.A. wrote for the majority:[339]

> Consideration must now be given as to whether the facts of the case at bar are such as to bring them fairly within the principles of law set out above. That these principles are strict, and in many situations can inflict inequities and hardship, cannot be denied, but they are of the nature that James, L.J., referred to in *Parker v. McKenna*[340] as an "inflexible rule, and must be applied inexorably by this Court. . . ." Notwithstanding, in this modern day and country when it is accepted as commonplace that substantially all business and commercial undertakings, regardless of size or importance, are carried on through the corporate vehicle with the attendant complexities involved by interlocking, subsidiary and associated corporations, I do not consider it enlightened to extend the application of these principles beyond their present limits. That the principles, and the strict rules applicable to trustees upon which they are based, are salutory [*sic*] cannot be disputed, but care should be taken to interpret them in the light of modern practice and way of life.

The Supreme Court of Canada held, distinguishing *Regal*, that Cropper did not obtain his shareholdings "by reason of the fact that he was a director of the appellant and in the course of execution of that office." Cropper stood in a fiduciary position toward Peso when he took up the opportunity, but his duty had been discharged when he and his co-directors in good faith and for sound business reasons rejected the offer. Moreover, when the consulting geologist approached him about the matter later, Cropper was not acting in his capacity as director of Peso, but as a member of the public.

One may debate the correctness of certain findings of fact in the *Peso* case. The more important question is whether the law was stated correctly. Is it appropriate to impose liability only if the fiduciary acquires knowledge of the opportunity *qua* fiduciary and in the execution of that office and not otherwise? This way of formulating the test certainly let Cropper escape liability and perhaps rightly so. But does the test as formulated not put too much temptation in the way of fiduciaries to the possible detriment of their principals? And, is it not right, in appropriate situations, to hold the honest but foolish fiduciary liable (even though, perhaps, not to the same extent as a dishonest one) just because he or she is a fiduciary?

CANADIAN AERO SERVICE LTD. v. O'MALLEY

(1973), [1974] S.C.R. 592, 40 D.L.R. (3d) 371,
1973 CarswellOnt 236, 1973 CarswellOnt 236F, 11 C.P.R. (2d) 206
Supreme Court of Canada

The plaintiff company was attempting to secure a contract from the Guyanese

---

339 (1965), 54 W.W.R. 329, 56 D.L.R. (2d) 117, 1965 CarswellBC 144 (C.A.), at 154-5 [D.L.R.].
340 (1874), 10 Ch. App. 96, at 124 (C.A.).

and Canadian governments to provide topographical mapping and aerial photographing of regions of Guyana. The defendants, O'Malley and Zarzycki, who were directors and officers of the plaintiff company, were involved in the plaintiff's efforts. However, they later resigned their positions and formed a new company, Terra Surveys, for the purpose of tendering a competing bid. Terra's bid was successful and the new company earned substantial profits. The plaintiff company sued the individual defendants, as well as Terra, seeking disgorgement of the profits resulting from the contract.

LASKIN J.:

Like Grant J., the trial Judge, I do not think it matters whether O'Malley and Zarzycki were properly appointed as directors of Canaero or whether they did or did not act as directors. What is not in doubt is that they acted respectively as president and executive vice-president of Canaero for about two years prior to their resignations. To paraphrase the findings of the trial Judge in this respect, they acted in those positions and their remuneration and responsibilities verified their status as senior officers of Canaero. They were "top management" and not mere employees whose duty to their employer, unless enlarged by contract, consisted only of respect for trade secrets and for confidentiality of customer lists. Theirs was a larger, more exacting duty which, unless modified by statute or by contract (and there is nothing of this sort here), was similar to that owed to a corporate employer by its directors. I adopt what is said on this point by Gower, *Principles of Modern Company Law*[341] as follows:

> . . .these duties, except in so far as they depend on statutory provisions expressly limited to directors, are not so restricted but apply equally to any officials of the company who are authorised to act on its behalf, and in particular to those acting in a managerial capacity.

The distinction taken between agents and servants of an employer is apt here, and I am unable to appreciate the basis upon which the Ontario Court of Appeal concluded that O'Malley and Zarzycki were mere employees, that is servants of Canaero rather than agents. Although they were subject to supervision of the officers of the controlling company, their positions as senior officers of a subsidiary, which was a working organization, charged them with initiatives and with responsibilities far removed from the obedient role of servants.

It follows that O'Malley and Zarzycki stood in a fiduciary relationship to Canaero, which in its generality betokens loyalty, good faith and avoidance of a conflict of duty and self-interest. Descending from the generality, the fiduciary relationship goes at least this far: a director or a senior officer like O'Malley or Zarzycki is precluded from obtaining for himself, either secretly or without the approval of the company (which would have to be properly manifested upon full disclosure of the facts), any property or business advantage either belonging to

---

341 3rd ed. (1969) at 518.

the company or for which it has been negotiating; and especially is this so where the director or officer is a participant in the negotiations on behalf of the company.

An examination of the case law in this Court and in the Courts of other like jurisdictions on the fiduciary duties of directors and senior officers shows the pervasiveness of a strict ethic in this area of the law. In my opinion, this ethic disqualifies a director or senior officer from usurping for himself or diverting to another person or company with whom or with which he is associated a maturing business opportunity which his company is actively pursuing; he is also precluded from so acting even after his resignation where the resignation may fairly be said to have been prompted or influenced by a wish to acquire for himself the opportunity sought by the company, or where it was his position with the company rather than a fresh initiative that led him to the opportunity which he later acquired.

It is this fiduciary duty which is invoked by the appellant in this case and which is resisted by the respondents on the grounds that the duty as formulated is not, nor should be, part of our law and that, in any event, the facts of the present case do not fall within its scope.

This Court considered the issue of fiduciary duty of directors in *Zwicker v. Stanbury*,[342] where it found apt for the purposes of that case certain general statements of law by Viscount Sankey and by Lord Russell of Killowen in *Regal (Hastings) Ltd. v. Gulliver*.[343] These statements reflecting basic principle which is not challenged in the present case, are represented in the following passages, *per* Viscount Sankey:

> In my view, the respondents were in a fiduciary position and their liability to account does not depend upon proof of *mala fides*. The general rule of equity is that no one who has duties of a fiduciary nature to perform is allowed to enter into engagements in which he has or can have a personal interest conflicting with the interests of those whom he is bound to protect. If he holds any property so acquired as trustee, he is bound to account for it to his *cestui que* trust. The earlier cases are concerned with trusts of specific property: *Keech v. Sandford*[344] *per* Lord King L.C. The rule, however, applies to agents, as, for example, solicitors and directors, when acting in a fiduciary capacity.

Per Lord Russell of Killowen:

> In the result, I am of opinion that the directors standing in a fiduciary relationship to Regal in regard to the exercise of their powers as directors, and having obtained these shares by reason and only by reason of the fact that they were directors of Regal and in the course of the execution of that office, are accountable for the profits which they have made out of them. The equitable rule laid down in *Keech v. Sandford*,[345] and *Ex p. James*,[346] and similar authorities applies . . . in full force. It was contended that these cases were distinguishable by reason of the fact that it was impossible for Regal to get the shares owing to lack of funds, and that the directors in taking the shares were really acting as members of the public. I cannot accept this argument. It was impossible for the *cestui que* trust in *Keech v. Sandford* to obtain the lease, nevertheless the trustee was

---

342 [1953] 2 S.C.R. 438, [1954] 1 D.L.R. 257.
343 *Supra*, note 336, at 381, 389.
344 *Supra*, note 262.
345 *Ibid*.
346 (1803), 8 Ves. 337.

accountable. The suggestion that the directors were applying simply as members of the public is a travesty of the facts. They could, had they wished, have protected themselves by a resolution (either antecedent or subsequent) of the Regal shareholders in general meeting. In default of such approval, the liability to account must remain.

I need not pause to consider whether on the facts in *Regal (Hastings) Ltd. v. Gulliver* the equitable principle was overzealously applied.[347] What I would observe is that the principle, or, indeed, principles, as stated, grew out of older cases concerned with fiduciaries other than directors or managing officers of a modern corporation, and I do not therefore regard them as providing a rigid measure whose literal terms must be met in assessing succeeding cases. In my opinion, neither the conflict test, referred to by Viscount Sankey, nor the test of accountability for profits acquired by reason only of being directors and in the course of execution of the office, reflected in the passage quoted from Lord Russell of Killowen, should be considered as the exclusive touchstones of liability. In this, as in other branches of the law, new fact situations may require a reformulation of existing principle to maintain its vigour in the new setting.

The reaping of a profit by a person at a company's expense while a director thereof is, of course, an adequate ground upon which to hold the director accountable. Yet there may be situations where a profit must be disgorged, although not gained at the expense of the company, on the ground that a director must not be allowed to use his position as such to make a profit even if it was not open to the company, as for example, by reason of legal disability, to participate in the transaction. An analogous situation, albeit not involving a director, existed for all practical purposes in the case of *Boardman v. Phipps*,[348] which also supports the view that liability to account does not depend on proof of an actual conflict of duty and self-interest.

. . .

What these decisions indicate is an updating of the equitable principle whose roots lie in the general standards that I have already mentioned, namely, loyalty, good faith and avoidance of a conflict of duty and self-interest. Strict application against directors and senior management officials is simply recognition of the degree of control which their positions give them in corporate operations, a control which rises above day accountability to owning shareholders and which comes under some scrutiny only at annual general or at special meetings. It is a necessary supplement, in the public interest, of statutory regulation and accountability which themselves are, at one and the same time, an acknowledgment of the importance of the corporation in the life of the community and of the need to compel obedience by it and by its promoters, directors and managers to norms of exemplary behavior.

---

347 See, for example, Gower, *op. cit.* 535-7.
348 *Supra*, note 208.

. . .

That the rigorous standard of behavior enforced against directors and executives may survive their tenure of such offices was indicated as early as *Ex p.
James*,[349] where Lord Eldon, speaking of the fiduciary in that case who was a
solicitor purchasing at a sale, said:[350]

> With respect to the question now put, whether I will permit *Jones* to give up the office of solicitor,
> and to bid, I cannot give that permission. If the principle is right, that the solicitor cannot buy, it
> would lead to all the mischief of acting up to the point of the sale getting all the information that
> may be useful to him, then discharging himself from the character of solicitor, and buying the
> property. . . . On the other hand I do not deny, that those interested in the question may give the
> permission.

. . .

Submissions and argument were addressed to this Court on the question
whether or how far Zarzycki copied Canaero's documents in preparing the Terra
proposal. The appellant's position is that Zarzycki was not entitled to use for
Terra what he compiled for Canaero; and the respondents contended that, although
Zarzycki was not entitled to use for Terra the 1965 report or proposal as such that
he prepared for Canaero, he was entitled to use the information therein which
came to him in the normal course and by reason of his own capacity. It was the
respondents' further submission that Zarzycki did not respond in 1966, on behalf
of Terra on the basis of his 1965 report as an officer of and for Canaero; and they
went so far as to say that it did not matter that O'Malley and Zarzycki worked on
the same contract for Terra as they had for Canaero, especially when the project
was not exactly the same.

In my opinion, the fiduciary duty upon O'Malley and Zarzycki, if it survived
their departure from Canaero, would be reduced to an absurdity if it could be
evaded merely because the Guyana project had been varied in some details when
it became the subject of invited proposals, or merely because Zarzycki met the
variations by appropriate changes in what he prepared for Canaero in 1965, and
what he proposed for Terra in 1966. I do not regard it as necessary to look for
substantial resemblances. Their presence would be a factor to be considered on
the issue of breach of fiduciary duty but they are not a *sine qua non*. The cardinal
fact is that the one project, the same project which Zarzycki had pursued for
Canaero, was the subject of his Terra proposal. It was that business opportunity,
in line with its general pursuits, which Canaero sought through O'Malley and
Zarzycki. There is no suggestion that there had been such a change of objective
as to make the project for which proposals were invited from Canaero, Terra and
others a different one from that which Canaero had been developing with a view
to obtaining the contract for itself.

---

349 *Supra*, note 262.
350 *Ibid.*, at 352, 390-1.

Again, whether or not Terra was incorporated for the purpose of intercepting the contract for the Guyana project is not central to the issue of breach of fiduciary duty. Honesty of purpose is no more a defence in that respect than it would be in respect of personal interception of the contract by O'Malley and Zarzycki. This is fundamental in the enforcement of fiduciary duty where the fiduciaries are acting against the interests of their principal. Then it is urged that Canaero could not in any event have obtained the contract, and that O'Malley and Zarzycki left Canaero as an ultimate response to their dissatisfaction with that company and with the restrictions that they were under in managing it. There was, however, no certain knowledge at the time O'Malley and Zarzycki resigned that the Guyana project was beyond Canaero's grasp. Canaero had not abandoned its hope of capturing it.

. . .

Although it was contended that O'Malley and Zarzycki did not know of the imminence of the approval of the Guyana project, their ready run for it, when it was approved at about the time of their resignations and at a time when they knew of Canaero's continuing interest, are factors to be considered in deciding whether they were still under a fiduciary duty not to seek to procure for themselves or for their newly-formed company the business opportunity which they had nurtured for Canaero.

Counsel for O'Malley and Zarzycki relied upon the judgment of this Court in *Peso Silver Mines Ltd. (N.P.L.) v. Cropper*,[351] as representing an affirmation of what was said in *Regal (Hastings) Ltd. v. Gulliver* respecting the circumscription of liability to circumstances where the directors or senior officers had obtained the challenged benefit by reason only of the fact that they held those positions and in the course of execution of those offices. In urging this, he did not deny that leaving to capitalize on their positions would not necessarily immunize them, but he submitted that in the present case there was no special knowledge or information obtained from Canaero during their service with that company upon which O'Malley and Zarzycki had relied in reaching for the Guyana project on behalf of Terra.

There is a considerable gulf between the *Peso* case and the present one on the facts as found in each and on the issues that they respectively raise. In *Peso*, there was a finding of good faith in the rejection by its directors of an offer of mining claims because of its strained finances. The subsequent acquisition of those claims by the managing director and his associates, albeit without seeking shareholder approval, was held to be proper because the company's interest in them ceased. ... What is before this Court is not a situation where various opportunities were offered to a company which was open to all of them, but rather a case where it had devoted itself to originating and bringing to fruition a particular business deal which was ultimately captured by former senior officers who had been in charge of the matter for the company. Since Canaero had been invited to

351 *Supra*, note 338.

make a proposal on the Guyana project, there is no basis for contending that it could not, in any event, have obtained the contract or that there was any unwillingness to deal with it.

It is a mistake, in my opinion, to seek to encase the principle stated and applied in *Peso,* by adoption from *Regal (Hastings) Ltd. v. Gulliver,* in the straightjacket of special knowledge acquired while acting as directors or senior officers, let alone limiting it to benefits acquired by reason of and during the holding of those offices. As in other cases in this developing branch of the law, the particular facts may determine the shape of the principle of decision without setting fixed limits to it. So it is in the present case. Accepting the facts found by the trial Judge, I find no obstructing considerations to the conclusion that O'Malley and Zarzycki continued, after their resignations, to be under a fiduciary duty to respect Canaero's priority, as against them and their instrument Terra, in seeking to capture the contract for the Guyana project. They entered the lists in the heat of the maturation of the project, known to them to be under active Government consideration when they resigned from Canaero and when they proposed to bid on behalf of Terra.

In holding that on the facts found by the trial Judge, there was a breach of fiduciary duty by O'Malley and Zarzycki which survived their resignations I am not to be taken as laying down any rule of liability to be read as if it were a statute. The general standards of loyalty, good faith and avoidance of a conflict of duty and self-interest to which the conduct of a director or senior officer must conform, must be tested in each case by many factors which it would be reckless to attempt to enumerate exhaustively. Among them are the factor of position or office held, the nature of the corporate opportunity, its ripeness, its specificness and the director's or managerial officer's relation to it, the amount of knowledge possessed, the circumstances in which it was obtained and whether it was special or, indeed, even private, the factor of time in the continuation of fiduciary duty where the alleged breach occurs after termination of the relationship with the company, and the circumstances under which the relationship was terminated, that is whether by retirement or resignation or discharge.

. . .

There remains the question of the appropriate relief against O'Malley and Zarzycki, and against Terra through which they acted in breach of fiduciary duty. In fixing the damages at $125,000, the trial Judge based himself on a claim for damages related only to the loss of the contract for the Guyana project, this being the extent of Canaero's claim as he understood it. No claim for a different amount or for relief on a different basis, as, for example, to hold Terra as constructive trustee for Canaero in respect of the execution of the Guyana contract, was made in this Court. Counsel for the respondents, although conceding that there was evidence of Terra's likely profit from the Guyana contract, emphasized the trial Judge's finding that Canaero could not have obtained the contract itself in view of its association with Spartan Air Services Limited in the submission of a proposal. It was his submission that there was no evidence that that proposal would have been accepted if Terra's had been rejected and, in any event, there was no evidence of Canaero's likely share of the profit.

Liability of O'Malley and Zarzycki for breach of fiduciary duty does not depend upon proof by Canaero that, but for their intervention, it would have obtained the Guyana contract; nor is it a condition of recovery of damages that Canaero establish what its profit would have been or what it has lost by failing to realize the corporate opportunity in question. It is entitled to compel the faithless fiduciaries to answer for their default according to their gain. Whether the damages awarded here be viewed as an accounting of profits or, what amounts to the same thing, as based on unjust enrichment, I would not interfere with the quantum.

Further Reading

S.M. Beck, "The Saga of Peso Silver Mines: Corporate Opportunity Reconsidered" (1971), 49 Can. Bar Rev. 80.

S.M. Beck, "The Shareholders' Derivative Action" (1974), 52 Can. Bar Rev. 159.

S.M. Beck, "The Quickening of Fiduciary Obligation: Canadian Aero Services v. O'Malley" (1975), 53 Can. Bar Rev. 771.

W.J. Braithwaite, "Unjust Enrichment and Directors' Duties: Abbey Glen Property Ltd. v. Stumborg" (1979), 3 Can. Busi. L.J. 210.

P.C. Wardle, "Post-Employment Competition — Canaero Revisited" (1990), 69 Can. Bar Rev. 233.

D. Klinck, "Things of Confidence: Loyalty, Secrecy and Fiduciary Obligation" (1990), 54 Sask. L. Rev. 73.

R. Goode, "The Recovery of a Director's Improper Gains: Proprietary Remedies for Infringement of Non-Proprietary Rights", in E. McKendrick, ed., *Commercial Aspects of Trusts and Fiduciary Obligations* (Oxford: Oxford University Press, 1992) 137.

H. Glasbeek, "More Direct Director Responsibility: Much Ado About. . .What?" (1995), 25 Can. Busi. L.J. 416.

Notes and Questions

1. Explain the remedy awarded in *Canaero*. Is that remedy best described as compensation, restitution or disgorgement? Notice that Laskin J. did not calculate relief by reference to losses that the plaintiff suffered or profits that the plaintiff would have enjoyed if it had realized the corporate opportunity in question. Instead, he proceeded by reference to the defendant's gain.

Laskin J. concluded by saying that the remedy could be "viewed as an accounting of profits or, what amounts to the same thing, as based on unjust enrichment." Recall our earlier discussion of the principle of "unjust enrichment." How did Laskin J. use that term?

Was relief in *Canaero* personal or proprietary? Did Laskin J. impose a constructive trust? Should he have done so?

2. While the problem in *Canaero* concerned corporate opportunity, there may be an overlap in such cases with use of confidential information, as that concept was previously explained. For instance, in taking advantage of an opportunity, a person may solicit clients appearing on a list obtained from a former employer. If the defendant was a director or senior manager of her or his former employer, the issue of confidential information need not be raised because the defendant will be liable for breach of a fiduciary duty. If, however, he or she was a lower echelon employee, it is unlikely that the defendant would be regarded as a fiduciary. Nevertheless, quite apart from any contract between the parties, such an employee is prevented from divulging her or his former employer's trade secrets and confidential information, or what has been called his "objective knowledge." An employee is, however, entitled to use "subjective knowledge" — *i.e.* aptitudes, skills and abilities acquired or developed while employed.[352] In other words, general information inevitably acquired by an employee as part of her or his experience as an employee becomes part of her or his general stock of knowledge and is not subject to the duty of confidence. But information which is improved with the badge of confidence, that is, the type of information that an ordinary, honest and intelligent person would recognize as belonging to the employer, is subject to the duty.[353]

Of course, once the information becomes public knowledge, as it did in *Canaero*, it ceases to be confidential and is no longer protected.[354] The one exception to this appears to be that the former employee cannot use the information, even after it has become public, as a "springboard" to gain an advantage over his or her former employer.[355]

3. It follows from *Canaero* that it is a breach of fiduciary duty for senior management employees, after they leave their employment, to solicit the company's clients.[356] But whether a fiduciary relationship exists and whether it has been breached is a question of fact in each case and the court will look for an actual conflict of interest. Otherwise an employee could never switch jobs within the same industry.[357]

---

352 See *Ormonoid Roofing & Asphalts Ltd. v. Bitumenoids and Ors* (1930), 31 S.R. (N.S.W.) 347.

353 *United Sterling Corporation Ltd. v. Felton and Mannin*, [1974] R.P.C. 162.

354 *Industrial Furnaces Ltd. v. Reaves*, [1970] R.P.C. 605 at 618, *per* Graham J. But see *Speed Seal Products Ltd. v. Paddington et al.*, *supra*, note 164, in which the plaintiff obtained an interlocutory injunction against the defendants, the first of whom was its former employee who had made a trade secret public by applying for a patent in respect of it.

355 *Terrapin Ltd. v. Builders' Supply Co. (Hayes) Ltd.*, [1967] R.P.C. 375 at 391, *per* Roxburgh J.; *Potters-Ballotini Ltd. v. Weston-Baker*, [1977] R.P.C. 202 (C.A.), at 206-7, *per* Lord Denning M.R.; *Schauenburg Industries Ltd.*, *supra*, note 162, at 747.

356 *W.J. Christie & Co. v. Greer* (1981), 9 Man. R. (2d) 269, 121 D.L.R. (3d) 472, 1981 CarswellMan 83, 14 B.L.R. 146, [1981] 4 W.W.R. 34, 59 C.P.R. (2d) 127 (C.A.). See also *Moore International (Can.) Inc. v. Carter* (1982), 40 B.C.L.R. 322, 1982 CarswellBC 297 (S.C.), additional reasons at (1982), 41 B.C.L.R. 396, 1982 CarswellBC 358 (S.C.), affirmed (1984), 1984 CarswellBC 267, 56 B.C.L.R. 207, 1 C.P.R. (3d) 171, B.C. Corps. L.G. 78,262 (C.A.); *Commercial Transport (Northern) Ltd. v. Watkins* (1983), 73 C.P.R. (2d) 207, 1983 CarswellOnt 137, 22 B.L.R. 249 (H.C.), holding that senior management's fiduciary duty in this respect continues until new managerial talent is in place; *White Oaks Welding Supplies v. Tapp* (1983), 42 O.R. (2d) 445, 149 D.L.R. (3d) 159, 1983 CarswellOnt 915, 73 C.P.R. (2d) 98 (H.C.). *Cf. Mercury Marine Ltd. v. Dillon* (1986), 11 C.P.C. (2d) 235, 1986 CarswellOnt 405, 56 O.R. (2d) 266, 30 D.L.R. (4th) 627, 12 C.P.R. (3d) 158 (H.C.); *R.W. Hamilton Ltd. v. Aeroquip Corp.* (1988), 65 O.R. (2d) 345, 1988 CarswellOnt 114, 40 B.L.R. 79, 22 C.P.R. (3d) 135 (H.C.); *Quantum Management Services Ltd. v. Hann* (1989), 69 O.R. (2d) 26, 1989 CarswellOnt 124, 43 B.L.R. 93, 25 C.P.R. (3d) 218 (H.C.), affirmed (1992), 1992 CarswellOnt 1707, 45 C.P.R. (3d) 498, 11 O.R. (3d) 639 (C.A.).

357 *Chevron Standard Ltd. v. Home Oil Co.*, 22 A.R. 451, [1980] 5 W.W.R. 624, 11 B.L.R. 53, 50 C.P.R. (2d) 182, 1980 CarswellAlta 258 (Q.B.), affirmed 1982 CarswellAlta 44, [1982] 3 W.W.R. 427, 19 Alta. L.R. (2d) 1, 64 C.P.R. (2d) 11, 35 A.R. 550 (C.A.).

Nevertheless, the *Canaero* principles apply to employees as well as to directors and management. The corporate opportunity doctrine depends on whether the corporation is in need of protection having regard to all the surrounding circumstances.[358]

4. As the cases suggest, it sometimes is difficult to determine whether or not a breach of fiduciary duty has occurred through the appropriation of an opportunity. Professor VanDuzer has summarized the factors that a court will consider in answering that question.[359] He divides those factors into two categories.

The first category pertains to the nature and strength of the corporation's interest: (i) *maturity* — how much had the corporation done to obtain the opportunity? how close did it come to securing the opportunity? (ii) *specificity* — had the opportunity in question been specifically identified by the corporation or was it simply one of many that existed in the area? (iii) *significance of the opportunity* — was the opportunity particularly unusual or valuable from the corporation's perspective? (iv) *public or private opportunity* — was the opportunity freely available in the market or was it specifically addressed to the corporation? did the fiduciary have access to the opportunity other than through the corporation? (v) *rejection* — did the corporation in good faith reject the opportunity before it was taken up by the fiduciary?

The second category pertains to the relationship of the fiduciary to the opportunity in question: (i) *position of the fiduciary* — how high in the corporate structure did the fiduciary stand? (ii) *relationship between the fiduciary and the opportunity* — did the opportunity arise within the fiduciary's scope of authority? did the fiduciary negotiate the opportunity for the corporation? (iii) *knowledge as a fiduciary* — to what extent did the fiduciary acquire knowledge of the opportunity by virtue of his or her position in the corporation? (iv) *involvement in competing business* — did the fiduciary acquire the opportunity through the vehicle of another company that resembled or competed with the aggrieved corporation? (v) *use of position* — was the fiduciary's position within the corporation critical to the acquisition of the opportunity? (vi) *time after termination* — did the fiduciary acquire the opportunity after leaving the corporation? if so, why and when did that departure occur?

5. *Canaero* may be compared to the later Australian case, *Warman International Ltd. v. Dwyer*.[360] Dwyer was the general manager of Warman. Warman was an agent for the distribution of products supplied by an Italian company. Dwyer secretly negotiated with the Italian company to transfer the agency and other business to new companies to be incorporated by him. He left his job with Warman in 1988 when the Italian company ended the agency arrangement with Warman and entered into an arrangement with Dwyer, his wife and his new companies. The Italian company had a stake in one of those companies. The businesses were successful. The court held that Dwyer clearly breached his fiduciary duty to Warman and that Dwyer's companies were equally liable with him. The trial judge held that Warman was entitled to an account of profits, but the Queensland Court of Appeal held that it was only entitled to recover its losses flowing from the breach of duty. The High Court only addressed the question whether Warman was entitled to an account of profits and, if so, on what basis. It was agreed that Warman would otherwise be entitled to compensation for the loss it sustained. In a unanimous judgment, the court held that the defendants were liable to account. In the process they made a number of

---

358 *Sheather v. Associates Financial Services Ltd.* (1979), 15 B.C.L.R. 265, 1979 CarswellBC 307 (S.C.).

359 J.A. VanDuzer, *The Law of Partnerships and Corporations* (Toronto: Irwin, 1997), at 231-232.

360 (1995), 128 A.L.R. 201 (Aust. H.C.). See also *Chan v. Zacharia* (1984), 154 C.L.R. 179 (Aust. H.C.).

comments that repeat the substance of what Laskin J. said in *Canaero*. Thus, for example, they pointed out that the liability of a fiduciary to account does not depend upon detriment to the plaintiff, or the dishonesty and lack of *bona fides* of the fiduciary.[361] They went on to say:[362]

> A fiduciary must account for a profit or benefit if it was obtained either (1) when there was a conflict or possible conflict between his fiduciary duty and his personal interest, or (2) by reason of his fiduciary position or by reason of his taking advantage of opportunity or knowledge derived from his fiduciary position. The stringent rule that the fiduciary cannot profit from his trust is said to have two purposes: (1) that the fiduciary must account for what has been acquired at the expense of the trust, and (2) to ensure that fiduciaries generally conduct themselves "at a level higher than that trodden by the crowd".[363] The objectives which the rule seeks to achieve are to preclude the fiduciary from being swayed by considerations of personal interest and accordingly misusing the fiduciary position for personal advantage.

However, the court drew a distinction between the liability to account for specific assets and for a business to which the fiduciary has contributed skill, money and effort. With respect to the latter situation, the court said:[364]

> [T]he stringent rule requiring a fiduciary to account for profits can be carried to extremes and . . . in cases outside the realm of specific assets, the liability of the fiduciary should not be transformed into a vehicle for the unjust enrichment of the plaintiff.

Warman, thus, raises some interesting concerns about the overzealous application of the rules. These comments may yet serve for reconsideration and refinement of the rules in Canada.

6. In *Abbey Glen Property Corp. v. Stumborg*,[365] the company brought action against former directors for breach of their fiduciary duty. The directors had profited from certain land transactions with a third person. Subsequently they sold their shares in the company to new management. It was held that they were accountable to the company. It did not matter that the third person refused to deal with the company and that the company could not itself have profited from the opportunity. Nor did it matter that the new shareholders would gain a windfall since the right of an accounting belonged to the company.

7. Some of the corporate opportunity cases suggest that directors who seek to take up an opportunity, but who cannot vote *qua* director in a directors' meeting because of the conflict of interest, can declare their interest and abstain from voting. If the other directors then vote to approve the transaction which confers the opportunity on the abstaining directors, the transaction will be unimpeachable if the directors' action is ratified by the shareholders. It has, however, been pointed out that this solution is illusory where the effect of the shareholders' vote is that the majority appropriates the company's assets to themselves at the expense of the minority. The majority of shareholders cannot give away the company's assets.[366]

---

361 *Ibid.*, at 208.

362 *Ibid.*, at 209.

363 *Meinhard v. Salmon, supra*, note 206, at 546, *per* Cardozo C.J.

364 *Warman*, note 360, at 211-12.

365 [1978] 4 W.W.R. 28, 4 B.L.R. 113, 9 A.R. 234, 85 D.L.R. (3d) 35, 1978 CarswellAlta 236 (C.A.).

366 *Cook v. Deeks*, [1916] 1 A.C. 554. See S. Beck, "The Saga of Peso Silver Mines: Corporate Opportunity Reconsidered" (1971), 49 Can. Bar Rev. 80 at 114ff.

Ratification is no longer effective in any event under the *Canada Business Corporations Act*,[367] and statutes based thereon. The Act provides that, while approval by the shareholders may be taken into account in an application for an order permitting a representative action or other relief, the application shall not be stayed or dismissed by reason only that an alleged breach of a right or duty owed to the corporation has been approved by the shareholders.[368]

8. The fiduciary duties of directors and officers have largely been codified by modern corporations statutes. Thus, the *Canada Business Corporations Act*[369] provides:

> 117. (1) A resolution in writing, signed by all the directors entitled to vote on that resolution at a meeting of directors or committee of directors, is as valid as if it had been passed at a meeting of directors or committee of directors.
>
> (2) A copy of every resolution referred to in subsection (1) shall be kept with the minutes of the proceedings of the directors or committee of directors.
>
> (3) Unless a ballot is demanded, an entry in the minutes of a meeting to the effect that the chairperson of the meeting declared a resolution to be carried or defeated is, in the absence of evidence to the contrary, proof of the fact without proof of the number or proportion of the votes recorded in favour of or against the resolution.

9. Can a director be liable for breach of fiduciary duty to the company when the engagement entered into is not of a commercial or business nature, but of an amorous kind?

Company X was owned by Mr. Misener. His wife was a director, secretary and shareholder of company X. She subsequently had an affair with the manager of another company, who caused his own company to purchase the assets of company X. Mrs. Misener then left her husband to live with her lover. In the course of the matrimonial proceedings that followed, Mr. Misener claimed that his wife had breached her fiduciary duties to company X. The court rejected the claim.[370] Mrs. Misener made no profit from the alleged conflict between her personal interests and her fiduciary duties, and the appellant company did not suffer any actual or potential loss as a result of her actions.

10. In *MacMillan Bloedel Ltd. v. Binstead*,[371] the plaintiff, a forest products company, regularly disposed of surplus logs. Its employee, the defendant Binstead, was manager of the log trading section. While so employed, Binstead held a secret one-third interest in A-M Log Sales Ltd., whose shareholders of record were Anderson and MacKinnon. The latter also owned A-M Log Brokerage Ltd. Both companies traded extensively with the plaintiff through Binstead. Binstead, Anderson and MacKinnon then incorporated AMCO Ltd., with the latter two individuals holding a third of the shares in trust for Binstead. AMCO established a sawmill operation and it acquired an interest in certain other companies, Delta Cedar Products Ltd. and Delta Chip Ltd., with surplus funds from A-M Log

---

367 R.S.C. 1985, c. C-44.

368 *Canada Business Corporations Act, ibid.*, s. 242(1).

369 *Ibid.*, s. 117. *Cf. Business Corporations Act*, R.S.O. 1990, c. B.16, s. 134, *Company Act*, R.S.B.C. 1996, c. 62, ss. 118, 119; *The Corporations Act*, R.S.M. 1987, c. C225, s. 117; *The Business Corporations Act*, R.S.S. 1978, c. B-10, s. 117.

370 *Misener v. H.L. Misener & Son Ltd.* (1977), 21 N.S.R. (2d) 92, 2 B.L.R. 106, 77 D.L.R. (3d) 428, 1977 CarswellNS 13, 3 R.P.R. 265 (C.A.).

371 (1983), 14 E.T.R. 269, 1983 CarswellBC 540, [1983] B.C.J. No. 802, 22 B.L.R. 255 (S.C.). See also *Redekop v. Robco Construction Ltd.* (1978), 89 D.L.R. (3d) 507, 1978 CarswellBC 127, 7 B.C.L.R. 268, 5 B.L.R. 58 (S.C.), to the same effect.

Sales Ltd. A fourth person involved was Morgan, an accountant, who advised Binstead in respect of his interests.

MacMillan Bloedel brought action against all the named individuals and corporations. It had not suffered any loss, since the logs were surplus to its requirement. The claim nevertheless was successful. The court held that Binstead stood in a fiduciary relationship to his employer and that his interest in A-M Log Sales Ltd. conflicted with his fiduciary duty. All of the other defendants, except Morgan, were held liable on the basis that they had knowingly assisted Binstead in his breach of duty. The case of a stranger who knowingly assists a trustee in a fraudulent breach of trusts is considered later in this chapter.

The remedy consisted of a constructive trust imposed over all of the shares in AMCO Ltd., as well as disgorgement of the profits that the defendant had earned through their equitable wrongs.

The case is very useful for the detailed examination of the accounts and illustrates the difficulties encountered in an action for an accounting.

11. A customs broker was an employee, director and shareholder of a custom brokerage firm. He sold his shares to the other shareholders, resigned his position, and went to work for a competitor. Shortly thereafter, he contacted all his former customers and a number of them switched their business to his new employer. The first customs broker wants to sue its former employee. Will it be successful?[372]

12. There are a large number of Canadian cases involving agreements to share in mineral and oil and gas claims. Most of them involve a form of joint venture and, consequently, a fiduciary relationship. They all concern some form of opportunity.

Midcon Oil & Gas Co. v. New British Dominion Oil Co.[373] is an example. Midcon and New British agreed to exploit together a gas reservation in which the latter held certain rights. Midcon was to drill a well in return for a one-half interest while New British was to become operator, which meant that it was to market the gas. Since there was no ready market for the gas at the time, New British promoted a new manufacturing company in which it took a substantial interest and which would be the primary consumer of the gas. The other major consumer was to be the city in which the new manufacturing concern was located. New British negotiated long-term agreements with the new company and the city, which were approved by Midcon as required by the agreement between the two parties. The prices obtained under the agreements were higher than could otherwise have been obtained. The action by Midcon for a declaration that New British held its interest in the manufacturing company upon a constructive trust for Midcon failed.

Locke J., speaking for the majority in the Supreme Court of Canada, concluded that the parties were merely tenants in common of the mineral leases and therefore not fiduciaries. His Lordship held that New British did owe Midcon a duty to act in good faith, but concluded that that duty had been fulfilled. Furthermore, he held that if the parties were fiduciaries, the claim should fail because New British did not acquire its interest in the manufacturing company by reason of the existence of the gas field or by reason of the fact that it was operator under the agreement, but because it was the primary promoter of

---

372 See *Anderson, Smyth & Kelly Customs Brokers Ltd. v. World Wide Customs Brokers Ltd.*, 39 Alta. L.R. (3d) 411, 1996 CarswellAlta 395, [1996] A.J. No. 475, 20 C.C.E.L. (2d) 1, [1996] 7 W.W.R. 736, 96 C.L.L.C. 210-045, 184 A.R. 81, 122 W.A.C. 81, 68 C.P.R. (3d) 45 (C.A.).
373 [1958] S.C.R. 314, 12 D.L.R. (2d) 705, 1958 CarswellAlta 70.

the manufacturing company. His Lordship distinguished the leading cases on fiduciary liability.[374]

Rand J., speaking for the minority, held that New British was a fiduciary and acquired its interest in the manufacturing company by reason of the fiduciary relationship.

13. Joint venture agreements may themselves preclude the imposition of a constructive trust. That was true in *Pine Pass Oil & Gas Ltd. v. Pacific Petroleums Ltd.*[375] The plaintiff held certain Crown oil exploration permits which it transferred to the defendant in return for a seven and one-half per cent interest in the net revenues from production. The agreement referred to such lands as should "at any time hereafter be comprised within any. . .lease or licence issued pursuant to" the permits. The defendant obtained licenses for the permits, discovered oil and gas in the area, selected one lease from the permit area for production, as required by the applicable legislation, and brought in a producing well. Under the legislation, a one-half mile wide corridor around the selected lease revested in the Crown which then was required to sell the permits in the corridor by public auction. The defendant submitted the highest bid at the auction and thereby acquired fresh permits, which in due course led to other producing wells. The plaintiff brought an action for a declaration that the defendant held the additional properties upon an express or constructive trust for it as to a seven and one-half per cent interest. The action was dismissed.

Ruttan J. concluded that the corridor wells were outside the scope of the defendant's fiduciary obligation, because the leases in the corridor were not acquired by the defendant pursuant to the permits held originally by the plaintiff, but rather by reason of direct dealing between the Crown and the defendant. Consequently, although the defendant acquired the necessary information by reason of his fiduciary position, the plaintiff had effectively given up its right to that information except to the extent specified in the agreement.

14. The preceding two cases may be contrasted with *Pre-Cam Exploration & Development Ltd. v. McTavish.*[376] The plaintiff, Murtach, owned 15 mineral claims. He engaged Pre-Cam to do exploratory work on them and "to follow-up any anomalous conditions that might be found to extend from this block of claims in any direction." McTavish, an employee of Pre-Cam, was charged with the work. While so engaged, he discovered that the mineralized zone extended beyond the 15 claims. Accordingly he terminated his employment with Pre-Cam and staked the adjoining area in his own name. It was held that McTavish held the additional claims on constructive trust for Murtach. In the course of his judgment, Judson J. said:[377]

> [n]either Pre-Cam nor McTavish, its servant, could acquire these connected claims against the interest of Murtack. . . . I think that it was a term of his employment, which McTavish on the facts of this case understood, that he could not use this information for his own advantage. . . . The constructive trust is imposed in a case of this kind because of the mere use of confidential information for private advantage against the interest of the person who made the acquisition of the information possible.

---

374 Namely, *Keech v. Sandford, supra,* note 171; *Ex parte James, supra,* note 262; and *Regal (Hastings) Ltd. v. Gulliver, supra,* note 336.

375 *Supra,* note 326.

376 *Supra,* note 121.

377 *Ibid.,* at 555.

15. A general partner in a limited partnership can make a profit from information he obtains while in the course of his duties, if an express agreement so provides.[378]

(f) Secret Commissions and Bribes

(i) *Generally*

Writing extra-judicially, Lord Millett once explained and distinguished bribes and secret commissions in the following terms.[379]

> In common parlance a bribe is a gift of money with the corrupt purpose of securing a favour from the recipient. It is, however, not necessary that the money should have been paid for a corrupt purpose for it to be recoverable by the recipient's principal. It is sufficient that it was paid in the course of a transaction in which the recipient was acting for a principal who was unaware of the payment. A payment which is not corrupt is best described as a secret commission.

The receipt of a bribe or secret commission involves the same sort of conflict of interest that occurs when a fiduciary takes up an opportunity personally, rather than on behalf of the principal. Because of the element of dishonesty that lies at the heart of a bribe, however, the situation is often regarded as relatively more culpable. It therefore is not surprising that equity has, in the present context, adopted quite stringent rules for stripping away the defendant's gain.[380] In that regard, Romer L.J. said that:[381]

> . . .the court will not inquire into the donor's motive in giving the bribe, nor allow evidence to be gone into as to the motive. Secondly the court will presume in favour of principal and as against the briber and the agent bribed, that the agent was influenced by the bribe; and this presumption is irrebuttable.

It has been argued that the presumption ought to be rebuttable, for there may be rare cases in which it can be shown that the fiduciary was not influenced by the bribe.[382] The preceding quotation nevertheless remains applicable.

Notwithstanding equity's generally unforgiving attitude, it must not be assumed that *every* secret commission triggers liability. For instance, no action arises if a franchisor takes a kickback, as long as the parties to the franchise agreement were at arms-length and independently advised.[383]

---

378 See *Molchan v. Omega Oil & Gas Ltd.* (1985), 21 D.L.R. (4th) 253, 1985 CarswellAlta 189, [1986] 1 W.W.R. 398, 63 A.R. 369, 40 Alta. L.R. (2d) 251 (C.A.), affirmed 1988 CarswellAlta 17, 1988 CarswellAlta 549, [1988] 3 W.W.R. 1, 57 Alta. L.R. (2d) 193, 83 N.R. 25, [1988] 1 S.C.R. 348, 87 A.R. 81, 47 D.L.R. (4th) 481, reconsideration refused (1988), 49 D.L.R. (4th) vii (S.C.C.).

379 P. Millett, "Bribes and Secret Commissions" [1993] Restitution L. Rev. 7.

380 Oddly, the rule is of relatively recent vintage, dating back only to 1869. Before that date a fiduciary could keep a bribe: Shepherd p. 260.

381 *Hovenden & Sons v. Milhoff* (1900), 83 L.J. 41 at 43 (C.A.).

382 Shepherd, at 260-2.

383 *Cf. Jirna Ltd. v. Mister Donut of Canada Ltd.* (1973), 40 D.L.R. (3d) 303, 1973 CarswellOnt 580, 1973 CarswellOnt 581, [1975] 1 S.C.R. 2, 12 C.P.R. (2d) 1.

Another counter-example arose in *Swain v. The Law Society*.[384] The English Law Society entered into a contract with a firm of insurance brokers for a compulsory indemnity insurance plan for its members. Under the contract, the Law Society received a portion of the commissions earned by the brokers. An action was brought by two solicitors claiming that the Law Society held the commissions it received upon a constructive trust. The House of Lords held that the Society held the money free of trust because, *inter alia*, in imposing the scheme pursuant to statute, the Law Society was exercising its powers not only in the interests of the profession, but also for the benefit of the public. Because it was performing a public duty, it could not be liable for breach of trust.

It is also important to be wary of over-extending the principle that generally precludes a fiduciary from receiving a bribe or secret commission. Obviously, a public official, such a police officer[385] or military personnel, should not be entitled to retain the benefit of a payment that was received as inducement to act improperly. Arguably, however, there is no need to press fiduciary analysis into service. Liability may be based simply upon the defendant's misuse of public office.[386]

Reading v. A.G.[387] is illustrative. Reading was an army sergeant on active duty in Egypt during World War II. While stationed in Alexandria, he provided assistance to a rum-running operation by driving trucks loaded with illicit spirits into Cairo. He did so while wearing his army uniform in order to avoid inspection of the cargo. He was paid approximately £20,000 for his efforts. In due course, the army seized that money and court-martialled Reading. Seemingly incorrigible, he sued to recover the fund. That action failed before both Denning J.[388] and the Court of Appeal.[389] A further appeal to the House of Lords was also dismissed. Lord Porter based his decision on the proposition that, even in the absence of any compensable loss, an employer or principal can recover a secret commission or bribe from an employee or agent. His Lordship also stated that liability is not premised upon proof of a fiduciary relationship. Nevertheless, he also agreed with Asquith L.J. in the Court of Appeal[390] that the phrase "fiduciary relationship" is broad and flexible enough to capture a case in which an employee or agent, like Reading, abuses the authority attached to his or her position in order to secure the receipt of a bribe.[391]

---

384 [1982] 3 W.L.R. 261 (H.L.).

385 *A.G. v. Goddard* (1929), 98 L.J.K.B. 743 (police officer accountable for value of bribes paid by bordello operators to avoid prosecution).

386 Finn, ¶¶497-8, at 215

387 *Supra*, note 189.

388 [1948] 2 K.B. 268.

389 *Reading, supra*, note 189.

390 *Ibid.*, at 236.

391 The characterization of Reading as a fiduciary nevertheless is often considered controversial because, *inter alia*, his obligations pertained, contrary to orthodox analysis, to the principal's non-economic interests. The significance of economic and non-economic interests was examined above.

(ii) *Remedies*

In recent years, the discussion of bribes and secret commissions has focussed on remedial issues. Of course, both the briber and the wayward fiduciary may be held criminally responsible if the payment was corrupt.[392] On the civil side, the options are more plentiful and more controversial. If a compensable loss can be established, reparation is available from either the briber or the fiduciary.[393] Alternatively, the principal may ignore its loss and elect[394] to obtain relief with respect to the fiduciary's gain.[395] The scheme of gain-based relief is, however, curious in a number of respects.

To begin, gain-based relief is available not only against the fiduciary, but also against the briber. In the leading case of *Mahesan v. Malaysia Government Housing Society*, Lord Diplock confirmed earlier precedents that imposed liability for the value of the bribe under "an action for money had and received." He adopted that analysis "whatever conceptual difficulties it may raise."[396] And indeed, the conceptual difficulties appear to be considerable. Today, we recognize the action for money had and received as a vehicle through which a person may be compelled to provide restitution or disgorgement. Such relief makes perfectly good sense with respect to the person who *received* a bribe — but it seems wholly inapplicable to the person who *paid* a bribe. Having already paid the bribe to the fiduciary, the briber has nothing to give back or give up to the principal.[397]

---

392 *Criminal Code*, R.S.C. 1985, c. C-46, ss. 119-125, 139, 426. See, *e.g.*, *R. v. Kelly*, 92 D.L.R. (4th) 643, 1992 CarswellBC 154, 1992 CarswellBC 906, [1992] 4 W.W.R. 640, 73 C.C.C. (3d) 385, 9 B.C.A.C. 161, 19 W.A.C. 161, 68 B.C.L.R. (2d) 1, 137 N.R. 161, [1992] 2 S.C.R. 170, 14 C.R. (4th) 181. The accused, part owner of a firm providing investment advice, entered into an agreement with a developer whereby the developer would pay commissions to the firm for multiple-use residential buildings (MURBs) the accused sold to the firm's clients. He was convicted under s. 496 for corruptly accepting a reward, as agent, as consideration for an act relating to the affairs of his principals.

393 *Mahesan v. Malaysia Government Housing Society*, [1979] A.C. 374 (P.C.); *Nova Scotia (Attorney General) v. Christian* (1974), 49 D.L.R. (3d) 742, 1974 CarswellNS 146, 9 N.S.R. (2d) 209 (C.A.). Depending upon the circumstances and the defendant, the cause of action may be the tort of deceit, the tort of inducing breach of contract, the equitable action for breach of fiduciary duty or the equitable action for knowing assistance.

394 The principal must make a choice as between relief calculated with respect to its own loss *or* relief calculated with respect to the fiduciary's gain: *Mahesan, ibid.*; *Tang Man Sit v. Capacious Investments Ltd.*, [1996] A.C. 514 (P.C.). The need for election, however, might be questioned. As a matter of deterrence, for instance, it would be more effective to allow for the accumulation of remedies. See P. Birks, "Inconsistency Between Compensation and Restitution" (1996), 112 L.Q Rev. 375; A. Burrows, *Understanding the Law of Obligations: Essays on Contract, Tort and Restitution* (Oxford: Hart 1998) 40-44.

395 Not surprisingly, in contrast to the defendants in *Boardman v. Phipps*, a fiduciary in receipt of a bribe is not entitled to remuneration for services rendered, even if those services contributed to the generation of the impugned gain: *Stapleton v. American Asbestos Co.* (1912), 6 D.L.R. 340 (Quebec P.C.); *Bayley v. Trusts & Guarantee Co.* (1930), [1931] 1 D.L.R. 500, 66 O.L.R. 254 (C.A.).

396 *Ibid.*, at 383.

397 The action for money had and received is also curious in another respect, even when applied as against the recipient of the improper payment. The cause of action is breach of fiduciary duty,

Even with respect to a fiduciary who received a bribe, the scheme of gain-based relief traditionally has been riddled with anomalies and inconsistencies. Equity historically drew a distinction between money and property bribes. With respect to the latter, the principal was entitled to demand payment of the value of the bribe or, if the property traceably survived, a constructive trust.[398] In contrast, if the bribe took the form of money, proprietary relief was denied and the principal was confined to the enforcement of a personal judgment against the fiduciary.[399]

For many years, the leading case for that last proposition was *Lister & Co. v. Stubbs*.[400] The plaintiff employed the defendant to act as its agent in the purchase of goods. The defendant placed orders with Varley & Co. in exchange for a bribe of £5541. He then placed that money into investments and land. The plaintiff brought an action to recover £5541 plus damages. Pending the trial of that action, it also sought an interlocutory injunction restraining the defendant from disposing of the assets that he had purchased with the bribe. The Court of Appeal refused to issue such an order. Lindley L.J. explained that the relationship between the parties:[401]

> . . .is that of debtor and creditor; it is not that of trustee and *cestui que trust*. We are asked to hold that it is — which would involve consequences which, I confess, startle me. One consequence, of course, would be that, if Stubbs were to become bankrupt, this property acquired by him with the money paid to him by Messrs. Varley would be withdrawn from the mass of his creditors and be handed over bodily to Lister & Co. Can that be right? Another consequence would be that, if the Appellants are right, Lister & Co. could compel Stubbs to account to them, not only for the money with interest, but for all the profit which he might have made by embarking in trade with it. Can that be right?

To Lindley L.J., it seemed inconceivable that the principal enjoyed a proprietary interest in the fiduciary's bribe, such that the plaintiff could enjoy both priority in the event of the defendant's insolvency and the benefit of any secondary profits generated by means of the bribe. As we saw in Chapter 2, however, *Lister & Co. v. Stubbs* has effectively been overruled in English law by *A.G. for Hong Kong v. Reid*.[402]

Reid worked for the government of Hong Kong as the Acting Director of Public Prosecutions. In that capacity, he received $12.4 million in bribes to obstruct the prosecution of certain criminals. He invested that money in three properties in New Zealand. His misconduct eventually was detected and, follow-

---

which sounds in equity. In such circumstances, it makes sense for the court to compel disgorgement of the wrongful gain by means of the equitable remedy of account of profits. It is not entirely clear, however, why relief alternatively has been effected by means of the common law action for money had and received. See A. Burrows, *The Law of Restitution*, 2d ed. (London: Butterworths, 2002) at 497.

398   *Eden v. Ridsdale Railway Lamp & Lighting Co.* (1889), 23 Q.B.D. 368 at 372 *per* Lindley L.J. (C.A.).

399   If neither money nor property was received but some other benefit, such as an indemnity or relief from liability, the beneficiary can recover its value from the fiduciary: Finn, ¶510.

400   (1890), 45 Ch. D. 1.

401   *Ibid.*, at 15.

402   [1994] 1 A.C. 324 (P.C.).

ing a criminal trial, he was imprisoned. The government of Hong Kong then instituted civil proceedings and claimed that it was entitled to the benefit of a constructive trust over the New Zealand properties. Lord Templeman agreed.[403]

> The decision in *Lister & Co v. Stubbs* is not consistent with the principles that a fiduciary must not be allowed to benefit from his own breach of duty, that the fiduciary should account for the bribe as soon as he receives it and that equity regards as done that which ought to be done. From these principles it would appear to follow that the bribe and the property from time to time representing the bribe are held on a constructive trust for the person injured. A fiduciary remains personally liable for the amount of the bribe if, in the event, the value of the property then recovered by the injured person proved to be less than that amount.

There is much to be said for that decision. It would seem curious that the defendants in *Boardman v. Phipps*, who acted honestly and for the beneficiaries' benefit, would (apparently[404]) be subject to proprietary relief, whereas Reid, who betrayed his employer and subverted the course of justice, would merely be personally liable to disgorge the value of his gain.

A.G. for Hong Kong v. Reid nevertheless is controversial in a number of respects. First, Lord Templeman's invocation of the maxim that "equity deems to be done that which ought to be done" appears to beg the question. Applied to the facts, the maxim merely states that *if* Reid should have received the bribe on behalf of the government, then he can be treated as if he had done so. It is, of course, perverse to suggest that Reid should have received the bribe at all.[405] But beyond that, the application of the maxim presumes a reason as to why Reid, having received the money, *ought* to have held it on behalf of the government, rather than merely be subject to a personal liability to disgorge its value.

Second, moving from logic to policy, it is not clear that, in the circumstances, the claimant warranted the benefits of a constructive trust — most significantly, the enjoyment of any increase in value and priority in the event of insolvency. Granted, as to the former, it may well have been desirable, as a matter of deterrence, to strip Reid of both the value of his initial bribe *and* the value of his profitable investments. Fiduciaries must know that faithlessness will not pay, even indirectly. The same end could be achieved, however, simply by quantifying a personal obligation by reference to both factors.

The plaintiff's ability to use a constructive trust to obtain priority over the defendant's general creditors is even more contentious. In the event of Reid's insolvency, why should the government of Hong Kong have been entitled to remove the New Zealand properties from the estate, thereby greatly diminishing the assets available to other creditors? It might be suggested that those creditors have only themselves to blame insofar as they should have taken security on their debts. That statement presumes, however, that all debts arise voluntarily and that

---

403 *Ibid.*, at 336.

404 As discussed in the notes accompanying the discussion of *Boardman v. Phipps*, there is some question as to whether relief in that case truly was proprietary.

405 The maxim typically applies with respect to acts that the defendant should, in fact, have performed. For instance, a contractual undertaking may be treated as having been fulfilled on the day that it should have been fulfilled.

security is always a viable option. But sometimes, as in the case of a tort victim, that simply is not true.[406]

It previously was suggested, in our discussion of the autonomous action in unjust enrichment, that a constructive trust may defensibly take priority over general creditors if the plaintiff suffered a deprivation that corresponded to the defendant's gain. In that situation, it is arguable that the defendant's creditors should not be entitled to satisfy their debts on the basis of property the defendant never should have received from the plaintiff. In the present context, however, the property in question came not from the plaintiff, but rather from a third party. Consequently, there is no possibility of building a constructive trust upon a pre-existing "proprietary base."[407] Moreover, any relief that the plaintiff does receive is a pure windfall. Having suffered an incalculable and hence non-compensable loss (*i.e.* the non-prosecution of alleged criminals), the government of Hong Kong enjoyed the benefit of $12.4 million that it never previously held and never could have obtained in the ordinary course of events.

Although the point has yet to be decided, it is quite likely that Canadian courts will eventually follow *A.G. for Hong Kong v. Reid*. The result reached by Lord Templeman fits neatly with the Supreme Court of Canada's broad, remedial approach to the constructive trust. There may, however, be a problem insofar as McLachlin J., in *Soulos v. Korkontzilas*,[408] endorsed Professor Goode's four-part test for the imposition of a constructive trust over wrongful gains.[409] Goode's second criterion requires poof that the defendant acquired the impugned asset by means of "deemed or actual agency activities." Such proof may be possible in cases like *Soulos* or *International Corona Resources Ltd. v. Lac Minerals Ltd.*,[410] but it certainly seems odd to describe the receipt of a bribe as a "deemed agency gain." Furthermore, Goode's fourth criterion requires proof that there are no factors, such as the interests of intervening creditors, that would render the imposition of proprietary relief unjust. Very often, of course, the whole point of seeking a constructive trust will be to defeat unsecured creditors.

Further Reading

A.J. Oakley, "The Bribed Fiduciary as Constructive Trustee" (1994), 53 Cambridge L.J. 31.

---

406 Furthermore, even if security was an option, a creditor may have been induced to take an unsecured debt by the perception that the defendant, whose assets were swollen by the proceeds of the bribe, was credit-worthy and quite likely to satisfy his obligations. It is not obvious why the burden of the mis-perception should be placed entirely upon the creditor, as opposed to being shared by the plaintiff.

407 P. Birks, "Personal Restitution in Equity" [1988] Lloyd's Mari. & Comm. L.Q. 128; R. Goode, "Proprietary Restitutionary Claims", in W. Cornish *et al.*, eds., *Restitution: Past, Present & Future* (Oxford: Hart, 1998) 63.

408 *Supra*, note 408, at 230. McLachlin J. did not refer to either *Lister & Co. v. Stubbs* or *A.G. for Hong Kong v. Reid*.

409 "Property and Unjust Enrichment", in A. Burrows, ed., *Essays on the Law of Restitution* (Oxford: Oxford University Press, 1991) 215 at 237-244.

410 *Supra*, note 7.

P. Birks, "Property in the Profits of Wrongdoing" (1994), 24 U. of Western Australia L. Rev. 8.

D. Crilley, "A Case of Proprietary Overkill" [1994] Restitution L. Rev. 57.

R. Pearce, "Personal and Proprietary Claims Against Bribees" [1994] Lloyd's Mari. & Comm. L.Q. 189.

S. Gardner, "Two Maxims of Equity" (1995), 54 Cambridge L.J. 60.

T. Allen, "Bribes and Constructive Trusts" (1995), 58 Modern L. Rev. 87.

Notes and Questions

1. Should a bribe or its traceable proceeds be held on constructive trust or should the party in breach merely be subject to a personal obligation to disgorge the value of the ill-gotten gain?

2. What if the person bribed is honest, reports the bribe and hands over the money to his or her employer? Is there a difference in this regard between a private employee and a public official?[411]

3. *Ruiter Engineering & Construction Ltd. v. 430216 Ontario Ltd.*[412] illustrates some of the issues that may be raised, both substantively and remedially, by the receipt of a bribe. The facts can be slightly simplified for present purposes. The plaintiff retained Alternate Design Group to enter into a contract on its behalf for the construction of a restaurant. Alternate Design contracted with the defendant for that purpose. Unbeknownst to the plaintiff, however, Alternate Design also agreed with the defendant to provide on-site supervision for the project in exchange for $18,500. Although the evidence was somewhat unclear, it appears that the construction contract was marked up by the amount of the bribe. It also appears that, but-for the arrangement between the defendant and Alternate Design, the defendant would have provided on-site supervision itself and simply charged the amount directly to the plaintiff. In essence, then, the plaintiff would have paid the same price in any event. The bribe simply allowed Alternate Design to effectively take part of the contract for itself.

The defendant paid $10,800 of the promised bribe to Alternate Design. The defendant also completed construction of the restaurant and claimed $30,000 from the plaintiff under the contract. Having discovered the bribe, however, the plaintiff refused payment.[413]

The trial judge held that since Alternate Design provided services at fair value in exchange for the disputed payment, there was no question of a bribe or secret commission. The Court of Appeal disagreed. It cited *Industries & General Mortgage Co. Ltd. v. Lewis* for the fact that equity takes a broad view of "bribes."[414]

> For the purposes of the civil law a bribe means the payment of a secret commission, which only means (i) that the person making the payment makes it to the agent of the other person with whom he is dealing; (ii) that he makes it to that person knowing that that person is acting as the agent of the other person with whom he is dealing; and (iii) that he fails to disclose to the other person

---

411 See *Ring v. Newfoundland* (1989), 75 Nfld. & P.E.I.R. 270, 234 A.P.R. 270, 1989 CarswellNfld 170 (T.D.).

412 (1989), (sub nom. *Ruiter Engineering & Construction Ltd. v. 441734 Ont. Ltd.*) 57 D.L.R. (4th) 140, 67 O.R. (2d) 587, 1989 CarswellOnt 121, 32 C.L.R. 23, 41 B.L.R. 213, 35 O.A.C. 230 (C.A.).

413 The party who paid the bribe was the plaintiff on the main claim for payment under the contract, but defendant on the counterclaim pertaining to the bribe.

414 [1949] 2 All E.R. 573 (K.B.), at 575.

with whom he is dealing that he has made that payment to the person whom he knows to be the other person's agent. Those three are the only elements necessary to constitute the payment of a secret commission or bribe for civil purposes.

It further quoted from *Stoney Point Canning Co. v. Barry*:[415]

The fundamental principle in all these cases is that one contracting party shall not be allowed to put the agent of the other in a position which gives him an interest against his duty. The result to the agent's principal is the same whatever the motive which induced the other principal to promise the commission. The former is deprived of the services of an agent free from the bias of an influence conflicting with his duty, for which he had contracted and to which he was entitled.

Having found that the payment to Alternate Design did constitute a bribe, the Court of Appeal then considered remedies available to the plaintiff against the defendant. It recognized the possibility of compensatory damages, but found that the plaintiff had not suffered any loss.

The court also recognized that "a surreptitious dealing between a third party and a principal's agent may be the basis for rescinding a contract." However, it found that such relief was unavailable on the facts because the plaintiff had received the full benefit of the contract and was unable to provide counter-restitution to the defendant.

Finally, the court held that the plaintiff enjoyed a "restitutionary" claim against the defendant "for money had and received." It said, quoting the *Restatement of the Law of Restitution*, that the:[416]

. . .principle underlying this claim is that of unjust enrichment. Whether the [plaintiff] has suffered any loss is irrelevant. The basis of liability is not "harm done to the beneficiary in the particular case, but . . . a broad principle of preventing a conflict of opposing interests in the minds of fiduciaries, whose duty it is to act solely for the benefit of their beneficiaries."

Having found that the purpose of that underlying principle is to "strip the defendant of his unlawful gain or profit," the court concluded that the relevant gain was "the amount that the contract was increased ($18,500) minus the amount actually paid to Alternate Design ($10,800) = $7,700." The deduction was allowed on the ground that, without it, "restitutionary" relief would "carry the deterrent purpose of the principle of unjust enrichment . . . beyond its necessary limit."

Bearing in mind that the relevant claim was against the party who paid the bribe, rather than the party who received the bribe, explain the application of the principle of unjust enrichment. Was the defendant unjustly enriched?[417] If so, in what sense? Was it appropriate for the court to reduce liability by the amount actually paid by the defendant to Alternate Design? Did the court award personal or proprietary relief? Was there any scope for the application of a constructive trust?

---

415 (1917), 36 D.L.R. 326, 55 S.C.R. 51, 1917 CarswellOnt 19, at 342 [D.L.R.].

416 At 809-810.

417 In answering that question, you should note that the Court of Appeal relied upon *Mahesan v. Malaysia Government Housing Society*, note 393, which was discussed above.

(g) Conflicting Duties

The discussion to this point has focused on situations involving a conflict between the obligations owed to the principal and the fiduciary's self-interest. In this section, we turn to situations in which the fiduciary owes obligations to two or more people. It may be possible for the fiduciary to faithfully serve each principal. Often, however, by serving the interests of one principal, the fiduciary will act contrary to the interests of another.

Double fiduciary employments are common. For instance, a company director may sit on interlocking boards or a solicitor may act for both sides in a real estate transaction. Conflicting duties are a particular danger for real estate agents. While an agent typically avoids difficulties by acting for the vendor only, that option is not available where he or she initially was retained by the purchaser to locate a desirable property. In that situation, should the agent disclose secret information that hurts one party but helps the other?

It appears that while the law does not absolutely prohibit double fiduciary employments, it does recognize that one cannot serve two masters[418] and therefore provides relief for conflicts that do arise. That obviously will be true if a fiduciary actually breaches an obligation to one of the parties. Moreover, a conflict will be deemed to arise if a fiduciary has failed to obtain the informed consent of both sides to the double employment.[419]

Various remedies are available, depending upon the facts.

- If neither beneficiary knew of the double employment, neither will be able rescind the transaction. But if only one knew, then the other will be entitled to rescind as long as the fiduciary was paid by the knowledgeable party to effect the transaction[420] or the fiduciary had an interest in the knowledgeable party's business or affairs.[421]
- If the fiduciary's failure to fulfil a duty causes one party to suffer a loss, then monetary reparation will be available as damages at law[422] or as compensation in equity.[423]
- A different form of relief will be triggered by a breach of fiduciary duty if only one beneficiary knew of the double employment and if that party paid a fee to the fiduciary. In that case, the non-knowledgeable party is entitled to compel the fiduciary to disgorge the fee as if it was a bribe.[424]

---

418 *Boulting et al. v. Association of Cinematograph, Television and Allied Technicians*, [1963] 2 Q.B. 606 at 638. *Cf.* Mt. 6:24; Lk 16:13.

419 *Fullwood v. Hurley*, [1928] 1 K.B. 498. A beneficiary who knew of a double employment will not later be heard to complain: *Haslam v. Hier Evans*, [1902] 1 Ch. 765.

420 *Grant v. Gold Exploration & Development Syndicate*, [1900] 1 Q.B. 233.

421 *Transvaal Lands Co. v. New Belgium (Transvaal) Land & Development Co.*, [1914] 2 Ch. 488.

422 *Groom v. Crocker*, [1939] 1 K.B. 194.

423 *North and South Trust Co. v. Berkeley*, [1971] 1 W.L.R. 470.

424 *Andrews v. Ramsay & Co.*, [1903] 2 K.B. 635.

- A non-knowledgeable beneficiary who agreed to pay a fee to the fiduciary can refuse to make payment and still retain the benefit of any transaction that occurred.[425]
- Finally, if neither beneficiary knew of the double employment, they can both refuse to pay any promised fees to the fiduciary.[426]

Obviously, a fiduciary cannot excuse a breach of duty to one beneficiary on the ground that the breach was necessary in order to fulfil a duty to the other beneficiary.[427] At the same time, however, a fiduciary is not required to fulfil a fiduciary duty to one party if doing so would constitute a breach toward another.[428] Consequently, a fiduciary who enters into a position of conflict may be caught between a rock and a hard place.

Although it is not objectionable for a fiduciary to seek double employment, the courts have occasionally inveighed against it, particularly with respect to solicitors acting for both sides in a conveyancing transaction.[429] Beyond obtaining informed consent from both beneficiaries, how is a solicitor (or any fiduciary) expected to act in difficult situations? The Rules of the Law Society of Upper Canada[430] provide some assistance. They provide that: a solicitor may act for both sides in a real estate transaction after informing both sides; no information received can be treated as confidential as between the parties; and if a conflict occurs the solicitor must discharge herself or himself and is unable thereafter to act for either side in that transaction.[431]

It often happens that one of the clients in a real estate transaction is a major client of the solicitor, such as a developer or an institutional leader. If a problem subsequently develops, the solicitor will be tempted to act for the developer in the ensuing litigation. He or she may, however, be restrained from doing so.[432] Montgomery J. explained:[433]

> Parties to a concluded lawsuit should feel that they have been fairly dealt with. How can they have confidence in a just result when their former solicitor acts for the other side in a matter where he advised both parties?

Double representation is a problem that can easily arise when solicitors move from the firm representing one party to the firm representing the other. Unless

---

425 *Ibid.*

426 *Harrods Ltd. v. Lemon*, [1931] 2 K.B. 157.

427 *Moody v. Cox and Hatt*, [1917] 2 Ch. 71 at 81 *per* Lord Cozens-Hardy M.R.

428 *Berkeley, supra*, note 423.

429 See, *e.g.*, *Spector v. Ageda*, [1973] Ch. 30 at 47; *Smith v. Mansi*, [1962] 3 All E.R. 857 at 859-60.

430 Law Society of Upper Canada, *Professional Conduct Handbook* (1996, as am.).

431 *Ibid.*, Rule 5, comment 5. And see Rule 4, comment 6; Rule 8, comment 3.

432 *Flynn Development Ltd. v. Central Trust Co.* (1985), 51 O.R. (2d) 57, 1985 CarswellOnt 1095 (H.C.).

433 *MTS International Services Inc. v. Warnat Corp. Ltd.* (1980), 31 O.R. (2d) 221, 1980 CarswellOnt 427, 18 C.P.C. 212, 118 D.L.R. (3d) 561 (H.C.) at 222 [O.R.].

adequate safeguards against disclosure are taken, the latter firm may be removed by the court.[434]

In other circumstances the court may advise fiduciaries to disqualify themselves in conflict situations, or may remove the fiduciary, as in the case of its own appointees, such as receivers, or trustees.[435]

Notes and Questions

1. Friendly Trust Co. is trustee for Trust A and Trust B. Both trusts are engaged in redeveloping real estate in the inner core of a municipality. Because of planning restrictions, only one property suitable for such redevelopment has become available. Friendly Trust acquires the property for Trust A. The adult beneficiaries of Trust A and Trust B know of the common trusteeship, but both trusts also have infant beneficiaries. What rights does Trust B have?

2. A is a director of both company X and company Y. She is paid a finder's fee by each company for locating suitable markets for the companies' products. The companies compete and the markets are limited. Company Y enters into a contract with Z Ltd. for the sale of its products. Z Ltd. was introduced to Company Y by A. What rights does Company X have?

3. S, a real estate salesman, acted for P on a number of occasions. S presented P's offer to purchase real property owned by V. In the offer, S Ltd. (S's real estate broker and employer) was described as "agent of the vendor," which is common practice. The offer contained a clause requiring V to pay for various planning fees, which would cost V approximately $20,000. V directed S to remove the clause, but he failed to do so. Subsequently V refused to close because of the offending clause. P sued V for damages and recovered. What rights does V have against S?[436]

(h) Self Hiring

A trust often has a substantial interest in a corporation or partnership. If so, the trustees may be tempted, for the benefit of the trust, to appoint themselves as directors or to become partners. Although that practice is not objectionable, trustees who receive fees as directors or partners must, pursuant to the conflict of duty and interest rules, account for them to the trust unless there has been informed consent or the trust instrument authorizes the receipt of such payments.[437] The same rule applies to such things as discounts, commissions and rebates that are paid to an agent, even if they are not in the nature of bribes.[438] An exception is made, however, if the profit is merely a small tip or gratuity — the fiduciary is allowed to keep it.[439]

---

434 *MacDonald Estate v. Martin* (1990), 77 D.L.R. (4th) 249, 1990 CarswellMan 384, [1990] S.C.J. No. 41, 1990 CarswellMan 233, [1991] 1 W.W.R. 705, 121 N.R. 1, (sub nom. *Martin v. Gray*) [1990] 3 S.C.R. 1235, 48 C.P.C. (2d) 113, 70 Man. R. (2d) 241.

435 The power to remove a trustee is discussed in the chapter on appointment retirement and removal of trustees.

436 See *Len Pugh Real Estate Ltd. v. Ronvic Construction Ltd., supra*, note 250.

437 See *Re Macadam, Dallow v. Codd, supra*, note 323; *Gee, Re*, [1948] 1 All E.R. 498.

438 *Hippisley v. Knee Brothers*, [1905] 1 K.B. 1.

439 *The Parkdale*, [1897] P. 53.

The problem of "self-hiring" occurs when solicitors or other professional trustees employ themselves to perform services for the trust. Since that situation falls within the conflict rule, fees cannot be charged for such services, unless there is express provision for it.[440] In this context, it may be noted that it is improper for a solicitor to insert a clause into a client's will that directs the executor to retain the services of the solicitor in the administration of the estate without the client's express and unsolicited instructions.[441]

(i) Miscellaneous Examples

We have examined a number of situations in which relief (including a constructive trust) may be imposed in response to a breach of fiduciary duty. There are many others. It is impossible to discuss them all. By way of conclusion, however, we can briefly mention some.

Municipal officials may be subject to liability if they make a profit on property owned by them as a consequence of municipal actions in which they took part. In *Hawrelak v. Edmonton (City)*,[442] however, the mayor of the City of Edmonton was held not to be accountable for profits because they arose not by reason of his office, but rather as a result of the city's previously established policies.

Franchisors may also be held to be fiduciaries, but only where there is a real disparity in the bargaining power of the parties. If both parties are experienced in business and represented by counsel throughout their negotiations, the courts will be loath to interfere with agreements that have been reached.[443]

Partners owe each other fiduciary duties and are required to hold all partnership profits on trust for the partnership.[444]

It has also been held that a mortgage broker is a fiduciary with respect to his or her finder's fee and must account for it to the mortgagor, unless the broker makes full disclosure and the mortgagor expressly consents to the fee.[445]

Limited owners such as life tenants, lessees and mortgagees are not normally regarded as fiduciaries toward other persons having an interest in the property. However, a mortgagee will be regarded as a trustee of rents and profits after entering into possession, and of surplus proceeds after selling under a power of

---

440 *Thompson v. Northern Trust Co.*, [1924] 2 W.W.R. 237, [1924] 1 D.L.R. 1135, 1924 CarswellSask 57 (K.B.), varied [1925] 4 D.L.R. 184 (Sask. C.A.); *Meighen v. Buell* (1878), 25 Gr. 604, 1878 CarswellOnt 58 (Ch.); *Re Winding Up of Commercial Bank* (1899), 8 Nfld. L. Rev. 257; *Bray v. Ford, supra*, note 207.

441 The Law Society of Upper Canada, *Professional Conduct Handbook* (1978, as am.), Rule 13, comment 16.

442 (1975), [1976] 1 S.C.R. 387, [1975] 4 W.W.R. 561, 54 D.L.R. (3d) 45, 4 N.R. 197, 1975 CarswellAlta 38, 1975 CarswellAlta 136.

443 See *Jirna v. Mister Donut of Canada Ltd., supra*, note 383.

444 *Davis v. Ouellette* (1981), 27 B.C.L.R. 162, 1981 CarswellBC 58 (S.C.).

445 *Advanced Realty Funding Corp. v. Bannink* (1979), 27 O.R. (2d) 193, 9 B.L.R. 161, 12 R.P.R. 17, 106 D.L.R. (3d) 137, 1979 CarswellOnt 174 (C.A.).

sale. Furthermore, a mortgagee who sells the property at a gross undervalue will be liable to compensate the mortgagor.[446]

It is, however, debatable whether all of these situations truly involve fiduciary relationships. As we previously explained, there is a tendency to categorize situations as fiduciary simply as a means of accessing equitable relief, such as constructive trusts. The attendant danger is that fiduciary analysis may improperly usurp perfectly adequate actions and remedies, such as conversion, deceit and misrepresentation.

Notes and Questions

1. *Snepp v. U.S.*[447] arguably illustrates the over-extension of fiduciary principles. Snepp, a former CIA agent, published a book about his experiences. Under his contract with the CIA, he was required to clear the subject matter of any such book. He failed to do so. The majority of the United States Supreme Court held that the contract placed a fiduciary obligation upon him. Having breached that obligation, Snepp held the resulting profits on constructive trust for the government. The dissenting judgment held, however, that Snepp merely breached his contract by not submitting the book for clearance and that, since it did not contain confidential information, he did not breach his fiduciary duty of confidentiality and no damage was suffered. Hence no constructive trust could be imposed.

On similar facts in *Attorney General v. Blake*,[448] the House of Lords refused to recognize a breach of fiduciary duty. Although the court acknowledged that the defendant, as a government spy, initially had been subject to fiduciary obligations, the situation changed as soon as he was imprisoned for acting as a double agent for the Soviets. Blake nevertheless was subject to a personal obligation to disgorge profits earned from the publication of his memoirs. The underlying cause of action was, however, breach of contract, rather than breach of fiduciary duty.

2. P, a potential purchaser of income-producing real estate, approached R Ltd., a realtor, knowing of its expertise in that particular branch of the business and intending to rely on its advice. R Ltd. relied on information supplied by the listing agent, X, who got the information from the vendor, Y. The information was to the effect that a licence permitting the conversion of a particular property to a duplex had expired, but was renewable. Y knew that it was not renewable and also knew that P was looking for a duplex. R Ltd. did not check out the listing information. Neither did X. P completed the transaction and then discovered that the property could not be converted to a duplex.

If you were acting for P, against whom would you bring your action? How would you argue your case — in contract, fiduciary relationship, tort or something else?[449]

3. A developer constructed a condominium complex. Prior to the registration of the declaration and the description of the condominium (which creates the condominium corporation), it sold extra parking spaces. The janitor's suite was described as a common

---

446 See, *e.g.*, *Frost Ltd. v. Ralph* (1980), 115 D.L.R. (3d) 612, 1980 CarswellNfld 122, 40 Nfld. & P.E.I.R. 207, 115 A.P.R. 207 (T.D.), affirmed (1982), 1982 CarswellNfld 66, 40 Nfld. & P.E.I.R. 204, 115 A.P.R. 204, 140 D.L.R. (3d) 572 (C.A.); *cf. Cuckmere Brick Co. Ltd. v. Mutual Finance Ltd.*, [1971] 2 All E.R. 633 at 643 *per* Salmon L.J.; *Siskind v. Bank of Nova Scotia* (1984), 46 O.R. (2d) 575, 1984 CarswellOnt 1256, 10 D.L.R. (4th) 101 (H.C.).

447 (1980), 100 S. Ct. 763.

448 *Supra*, note 310.

449 See *Bango v. Holt*, *supra*, note 250.

element with restricted access. The developer retained title to it and leased it to the condominium corporation, but was prepared to sell it to the corporation.

Under the applicable legislation, the common elements, including parking spaces, hallways and so on, vest in the unit owners as tenants in common,[450] but the condominium corporation has a duty to control, manage and administer them[451] and has a right to sue in respect of them on its own behalf and on behalf of the unit owners.[452]

What are the condominium corporation's rights against the developer?[453]

5. WRONGFUL GAINS #3 — DEATH

(a) Introduction

A constructive trust may be triggered by wrongdoing. We have examined that proposition in connection with property acquired through breach of confidence or breach of fiduciary duty. In this section, we examine a third group of cases, involving benefits wrongfully acquired through death.

For present purposes, it is important to stress the element of wrongdoing. Equity is responding to the fact that, for instance, the defendant murdered the deceased or improperly induced the deceased to draft a will in certain terms. As we shall see in a later section, other species of constructive trust (*e.g.* those falling under the rubrics of "secret trusts" and "mutual wills") that are imposed in connection with death are triggered not by wrongdoing, but rather by equity's desire to perfect intentions and to protect detrimental reliance.

(b) Acquisition of Property by Murder

Crime should not pay. Consequently, a person who commits murder is not allowed to retain assets acquired through the victim's death. Although property is allowed to pass to the wrongdoer, it is immediately impressed with a constructive trust in favour of the person who would have received it if the victim had outlived the murderer.[454]

That rule applies whenever the killer otherwise would become entitled to property by reason of the deceased's death. Consequently, it applies when a

---

450 *Condominium Act, 1998*, S.O. 1998, c. 19, s. 11(2).

451 *Ibid.*, s. 90.

452 *Ibid.*, s. 23(1).

453 See *York Condominium Corp. No. 167 v. Newrey Holdings Ltd.* (1981), 32 O.R. (2d) 458, 1981 CarswellOnt 1131, 122 D.L.R. (3d) 280 (C.A.), leave to appeal refused 32 O.R. (2d) 458n, 38 N.R. 129, 122 D.L.R. (3d) 280n, [1981] 1 S.C.R. xi.

454 That process is illustrated by the Australian case of *Rasmanis v. Jurewitch*, [1976] 1 N.S.W.R. 650 (C.A.). A husband, wife and X were joint tenants of real property. The husband murdered his wife. It was held that he took one-half of her interest upon constructive trust for X. The effect was that the husband and X held a one-third interest as tenants in common. This was necessary, for if X should predecease the husband, the latter should not become entitled to that one-third interest. However, the husband was not denied his right to succeed to X's one-third interest if X should predecease him. In other words, the joint tenancy continued in respect of the other two-thirds.

beneficiary murders a testator,[455] an heir murders a person who dies intestate,[456] a joint tenant kills the other joint tenant,[457] a beneficiary of social insurance benefits kills the insured[458] or a beneficiary of an insurance policy kills the insured.[459] Similarly, a person who commits murder to prevent the execution of a will, and who thereby benefits from the death, holds the property upon constructive trust for the intended beneficiaries.[460] Likewise, a person who is entitled to a remainder, and who kills a life tenant, holds the accelerated portion of the interest upon constructive trust. The application of that rule requires the court to ascertain the life expectancy that the tenant should have enjoyed.[461]

The preceding rules do not apply, however, if the killer was insane,[462] nor if there was no intentional killing.[463]

A court may also refuse to apply the rules even though the circumstances appear to demand otherwise. *Rosenfeldt v. Olson*[464] is a notorious illustration. The R.C.M.P. had been investigating the disappearance and murders of children in the lower mainland of British Columbia. In the course of the lengthy investigation, Clifford Olson was charged with the murder of one of those children, but Crown counsel was concerned that the evidence was circumstantial and might not lead to a conviction. Olson then offered to give the R.C.M.P. a statement and lead them to the bodies of ten children in exchange for a $100,000 payment to his wife, Joan, and their child. In view of the paucity of evidence and the high level of public concern, the Attorney General of British Columbia agreed.

Olson's lawyer, Schantz, advised him to have the money put in trust with provision that Olson could not benefit from it, so as to prevent the R.C.M.P. from recovering it. Schantz could not act as trustee himself because he was representing

---

455 *McKinnon v. Lundy* (1895), 24 S.C.R. 650, 1895 CarswellOnt 17.
456 *Nordstrom v. Baumann* (1961), [1962] S.C.R. 147, 37 W.W.R. 16, 31 D.L.R. (2d) 255, 1961 CarswellBC 154; *Missirlis, Re* (1970), [1971] 1 O.R. 303, 15 D.L.R. (3d) 257 (Surr. Ct.); *Gore, Re* (1971), [1972] 1 O.R. 550, 23 D.L.R. (3d) 534, [1972] I.L.R. 1-448, 1971 CarswellOnt 246 (H.C.); *Charlton, Re* (1968), [1969] 1 O.R. 706, 3 D.L.R. (3d) 623, 1968 CarswellOnt 331 (C.A.).
457 *Gore, Re, ibid.; Schobelt v. Barber* (1966), [1967] 1 O.R. 349, 60 D.L.R. (2d) 519, 1966 CarswellOnt 179 (H.C.); *Singh Estate v. Bajrangie-Singh* (1999), 29 E.T.R. (2d) 302, [1999] O.J. No. 2703, 1999 CarswellOnt 2230 (S.C.J.).
458 *R. v. National Insurance Commissioner, Ex parte Connor*, [1981] 1 All E.R. 769 (Q.B.).
459 *Cleaver v. Mutual Reserve Fund Life Association*, [1892] 1 Q.B. 147 (Q.B.); *Gore, Re, supra*, note 456; *Brissette Estate v. Westbury Life Insurance Co., supra*, note 7.
460 *Latham v. Father Devine*, 299 N.Y. 22, 85 N.E. 168 (1942).
461 See Scott, ¶493.1.
462 *Re Houghton, Houghton v. Houghton*, [1915] 2 Ch. 173; *Re Pitts, Cox v. Kilsby*, [1931] 1 Ch. 546; *Nordstrom v. Baumann, supra*, note 456; *Manitoba (Public Trustee) v. LeClerc* (1981), 8 Man. R. (2d) 267, 123 D.L.R. (3d) 650, 1981 CarswellMan 248 (Q.B.).
463 See *Gray v. Barr*, [1971] 2 Q.B. 554, [1971] 2 All E.R. 954 (C.A.), at 581 [Q.B.] and at 964 [All E.R.], *per* Salmon L.J.; *R. v. National Insurance Commissioner, Ex parte Connor, supra*, note 458, at 774, *per* Lord Lane L.C.
464 (1986), 25 D.L.R. (4th) 472, 1986 CarswellBC 52, 1 B.C.L.R. (2d) 108, 22 E.T.R. 83, [1986] 3 W.W.R. 403 (C.A.), leave to appeal refused (1986), 72 N.R. 77 (note) (S.C.C.), reversing (1984), 59 B.C.L.R. 193, [1985] 2 W.W.R. 502, 20 E.T.R. 133, 16 D.L.R. (4th) 103, 1984 CarswellBC 437 (S.C.). See John D. McCamus, "Recovery of the Indirect Profits of Wrongful Killing: The New Constructive Trust and the Olson Case" (1986), 20 E.T.R. 165.

Olson. He therefore asked another lawyer, McNeney, to be trustee. A trust deed was then drawn up on terms that McNeney would pay the money out for the benefit of Joan Olson and her son if Clifford Olson met his part of the bargain. Olson complied by disclosing the location of the bodies and making the promised statement. He was subsequently convicted of murdering eleven children.

On instructions ostensibly from Joan, but effectively from Clifford Olson, McNeney paid $10,000 to Schantz for fees earned while acting for Clifford in another matter, $8,000 to Joan Olson's father in payment of a debt owed by Clifford Olson, $3,000 to Joan Olson's brother, $2,000 to his law firm for work in the establishment and administration of the trust, and $10,000 to a condominium corporation of which he was president as a deposit on the purchase of a condominium unit for Joan Olson. McNeney and his firm secreted the balance of the funds by establishing an account in the Bahamas under the control of McNeney's partner, Morrison.

The parents of seven of the children obtained default judgment for damages against Clifford Olson and then asked a court to issue a declaration that the money in trust was impressed with a constructive trust. They initially succeeded. Trainor J. applied the principles formulated by the Supreme Court of Canada in *Becker v. Pettkus*,[465] found that Olson had been unjustly enriched and plaintiffs correspondingly deprived, and imposed a constructive trust.

The British Columbia Court of Appeal, however, reversed. It correctly held that the plaintiffs could not satisfy the second element of the cause of action in unjust enrichment, which requires proof that they suffered an economic deprivation corresponding to Olson's gain. The money that was paid into the trust came not from the victims' parents, but rather from the R.C.M.P. Moreover, there was no way in which the victims or their parents could have become entitled to that fund in the normal course of events.

It is, however, unfortunate that the court failed to consider the possibility of a constructive trust arising not under the autonomous action in unjust enrichment, but rather under the concept of unjust enrichment by wrongdoing. (The difference between those two conceptions of unjust enrichment was examined earlier in this chapter.) Had the court done so, it might well have concluded that the wrongful gain should be disgorged to the plaintiffs.[466]

Further Reading

T.G. Youdan, "Acquisition of Property by Killing" (1973), 89 L.Q. Rev. 235.

Norman M. Tarnow, "Unworthy Heirs: The Application of the Public Policy Rule in the Administration of Estates" (1980), 58 Can. Bar Rev. 582, repr. (1981), 5 E. & T. Q. 376.

G. Jones, "Stripping a Criminal of the Profits of Crime" (2000), 1 Theoretical Inquiries in Law 59.

---

465 *Supra*, note 7.

466 Alternatively, however, the court might have concluded that since payment of the money was not a *direct* result of the children's murder, it was too remote to be recoverable: G. Virgo, *The Principles of the Law of Restitution* (Oxford: Oxford University Press, 1999), at 566.

G. Virgo, *The Principles of the Law of Restitution* (Oxford: Oxford University Press, 1999) 570-588.

Notes and Questions

1. A widow pleaded guilty to causing the death of her husband by criminal negligence. She had not intended to kill him. In subsequent proceedings to determine her right to benefits under her husband's pension plan, the court held that it would be an abuse of process to re-open the question of her guilt. Since she was criminally responsible for her husband's death, she was disentitled to the benefits.[467]

2. A penitentiary inmate convicted of arranging his wife's murder has been receiving survivor benefits for himself and his daughter and a lump sum burial payment under the *Canada Pension Plan*.[468] A government minister is studying the matter to determine if the money can be recovered and whether legislative amendments are needed to prevent a reoccurrence of such payments. The *Canada Pension Plan* provides burial payments and survivor benefits to the surviving spouse and children of a deceased participant. How would you advise the Minister?[469]

3. The forfeiture rule has been modified by statute in England. Under the *Forfeiture Act 1982*[470] the court may make an order modifying the effect of the forfeiture rule which prevents a person who has unlawfully killed another from acquiring any interest in the latter's property if application is made within three months of the former's conviction.[471] The Act does not apply where a person is convicted of murder.[472] For a case which interprets the Act, see *K (deceased), Re*.[473]

4. *Dhaliwall v. Dhaliwall*[474] presents a useful solution to a difficult problem. The testatrix named her husband executor and sole beneficiary of her will if he survived her by 30 days. If he did not survive her for 30 days, she directed that the estate be paid to her children when the youngest attained age 21. The husband killed his wife. The court held that he was not entitled to probate and should be deemed to have died immediately before the testatrix. The normal solution would have been to declare an intestacy and exclusion of the husband. Approximately the same result would have been achieved in this case if that solution had been adopted. However, the court's order clearly carried out the testatrix's intention, for it did not change the terms of the gift over. Furthermore, the court's approach was especially appropriate given that the persons taking under the gift over were not the testator's intestate heirs.

---

467 See *Ontario (Municipal Employees Retirement Board) v. Young* (1985), 21 E.T.R. 1, 1985 CarswellOnt 707, 49 O.R. (2d) 78, 15 D.L.R. (4th) 475 (H.C.), additional reasons at (1985), 1985 CarswellOnt 1638, 49 O.R. (2d) 704, 16 D.L.R. (4th) 160 (H.C.).

468 R.S.C. 1985, c. C-8.

469 *Cf. R v. National Insurance Commissioner, Ex parte Connor, supra*, note 458.

470 1982, c. 34 (U.K.).

471 *Ibid.*, s. 2(1), (3).

472 *Ibid.*, s. 5.

473 [1985] 2 All E.R. 833 (C.A.).

474 [1986] 6 W.W.R. 278, 1986 CarswellBC 235, 6 B.C.L.R. (2d) 62, 30 D.L.R. (4th) 420, 23 E.T.R. 271 (S.C.).

(c) Other Instances of Wrongful Acquisition on Death

The law of probate may preclude a person from wrongfully acquiring property upon another's death. For instance, a will may be refused probate if there is proof that it was induced by fraud, duress or undue influence.[475]

It may be, however, that the wrongful conduct did not come to light until after probate had been granted, or that the disputed property was not included in the probate estate. In those situations, a constructive trust will be imposed upon the person who improperly induced the will and thereby obtained the impugned benefit.[476] The trust operates in favour of the testator's estate. Similar principles apply if a legatee wrongfully prevented a testator from revoking a gift.[477] In that situation, the trust will be in favour of the estate if the testator did not intend to make another will, or in favour of the person who would have benefited if a will had been executed as intended.[478]

If a testator's heir wrongfully induces the revocation of a will, and the heir takes on the resulting intestacy, the affected property will be impressed with a constructive trust in favour of the people who otherwise would have benefited.[479] Likewise if an heir wrongfully prevents the creation of a will and thereby obtains a benefit.[480]

Similar principles apply where a person wrongfully induces the owner of an insurance policy to substitute her or his name for that of the existing beneficiary,[481] or, being the beneficiary under the policy, wrongfully prevents the owner from changing the beneficiary designation.[482]

6. PERFECTING INTENTIONS #1 — *INTER VIVOS* TRANSFERS

(a) Introduction

We opened this chapter by equating the concept of the constructive trust to a grab bag insofar as it encompasses a large number of seemingly unrelated applications. We then suggested, for reasons of both pedagogy and practical justice, the need to organize the contents of that grab bag. There may be something historically charming in the idea of the common law as "a heap of good learning"[483]

---

475 *Danchuk v. Calderwood* (1996), 15 E.T.R. (2d) 193, [1996] B.C.J. No. 2383, 1996 CarswellBC 2555 (S.C.), additional reasons at (1997), 1997 CarswellBC 1483 (S.C. [In Chambers]). The undue influence of a housekeeper over a testator with senile dementia resulted in the last will of the testator being refused probate and the previous will of the testator being accepted for probate.

476 See, *e.g.*, *Teele v. Graves*, 425 So. 2d 1117 (Ala., 1983).

477 *Doe ex d. Greatrex and Hoffman v. Harris* (1837), 6 Ad. & E. 209, 112 E.R. 78.

478 See, *e.g.*, *White v. Mulvania*, 575 S.W. 2d 184 (Mo., 1979).

479 *Thynn v. Thynn* (1684), 1 Vern. 296, 23 E.R. 479.

480 See, *e.g.*, *Lieberman v. Rogers*, 40 Conn. Super. 116, 481 A.2d 1295 (1984).

481 *Richards v. Richards*, 58 Wis. 2d 290, 206 N.W.2d 134 (1973).

482 *Nobel v. Andrea*, 141 S.C. 168, 139 S.E. 403 (1927). See further Scott, §§489-490.2

483 T. Wood, *An Institute of the Law of England*, (1722) preface.

— a collection of rules accumulated not through a methodically deductive process, as has occurred in civilian jurisdictions, but rather through the gradual accumulation of discrete decisions reached largely on pragmatic grounds. The complexity of modern law demands, however, that an effort be made to recognize categories inherent in that heap. There is no question of changing substantive rules (at least not directly). The task, rather, is first to identify, at a fundamental level, the various grounds upon which constructive trusts may be imposed, and second to group like cases together. The goals of that exercise are to make the subject more accessible and to enhance the prospects for rational development.

We have already identified two large pockets within the grab bag of constructive trusts: unjust enrichment[484] and wrongdoing. A great deal nevertheless remains: specifically performable contracts of sale, oral trusts of land, incomplete gifts, proprietary estoppel, secret trusts and mutual wills. Several strategies have in the past been used to explain those species of constructive trust. One approach is simply to leave them as a miscellany. The heap is just a heap. Another approach, barely more ambitious, is to place them under the rubric of "equitable fraud," a label so broad and variegated as to be almost meaningless.[485] A third approach, potentially quite dangerous, is to force the remaining species of constructive trust into the categories of unjust enrichment and wrongdoing.

The strategy adopted in this chapter is different. It suggests that the constructive trusts in question are *perfectionary*. They arise because, in some circumstances, equity wants to ensure the perfection, or fulfilment, of stated intentions. The constructive trust is a means by which people are held to their words. A supporting rationale, present in many, but not all, of the cases, is *detrimental reliance*. In some circumstances, equity imposes a constructive trust to protect the position of a person who has taken the representations of another person at face value.

Further Reading

R. Chambers, "Constructive Trusts in Canada" (1999), 37 Alberta L. Rev. 173.
G. Elias, *Constructive Trusts* (Oxford: Clarendon Press, 1990).

Notes and Questions

1. The categories of constructive trust, like the categories of negligence, remain open. As Millett L.J. said in *Lonrho plc v. Fayed (No. 2)*, there is an "inherent flexibility and capacity to adjust to new situations by reference to the mainsprings of equitable jurisdiction."[486] New species of constructive trust consequently may be added from time to time as the perceived need arises. A recent example, seen in England, but not yet adopted in Canada, concerns the "*Pallant v. Morgan* equity."

---

484 It may be, however, that unjust enrichment trusts are better viewed as resulting, rather than constructive.
485 As we saw in the introduction to this chapter.
486 [1992] 1 W.L.R. 1 (C.A.) at 9.

Pallant v. Morgan[487] itself involved a situation in which both parties were interested in purchasing a particular piece of land. Since the land was to be sold at auction, the parties, acting through agents, entered into an arrangement whereby the plaintiff agreed to refrain from bidding so as to keep the price down, and the defendant agreed to divide the land after buying it. The court found that that arrangement effectively cut the purchase price in half. Nevertheless, having acquired the land, the defendant refused to divide it with the plaintiff. The plaintiff sought specific performance, but that claim was refused on the basis that the terms of the agreement were insufficiently certain. At the same time, however, Harman J. stated that it would be "tantamount to sanctioning fraud"[488] to deny relief altogether. He accordingly found that, in purchasing the land, the defendant's agent had acted on behalf of *both* parties. The land therefore being jointly held, Harman J. ordered a sale and division of the proceeds.

Pallant v. Morgan traditionally was interpreted narrowly as creating a right of equitable relief where a claim to specific performance was for some reason (*e.g.* uncertainty of terms) unavailable.[489] Recently, however, it received a much broader reading in *Banner Homes Group plc v. Luff Developments Ltd. (No. 2).*[490]

Banner Homes Group concerned two land developers who had informally agreed to create a joint venture for the purpose of developing a particular piece of land. The parties realized that they had not entered into a binding contract, but expected to do so in the future. A company owned by the defendant acquired the land as planned, but the defendant subsequently announced that it had changed its mind and that it did not want the plaintiff to be involved. The trial judge, while sympathetic to the plaintiff and displeased with the defendant's course of conduct, denied relief largely on the basis of the absence of an enforceable agreement.

Drawing upon *Pallant v. Morgan*, however, the English Court of Appeal effectively enforced the proposed joint venture. It declared that the shares in the company that had purchased the land were held by the defendant on constructive trust for itself and the plaintiff, and that the plaintiff was obliged to make payment accordingly. In reaching that conclusion, Chadwick L.J. found that the plaintiff had detrimentally relied upon the parties' agreement by refraining from attempts to purchase the land for itself. Significantly, however, he further stated that relief might have been available even in the absence of any *detrimental* reliance.

> It may be just as inequitable to allow the defendants to treat the property as his own when it has been acquired by the use of some advantage which he has obtained under the agreement or understanding as it is to allow him to treat the property as is own when the plaintiff has suffered some detriment under the arrangement or understanding.[491]

The apparent effect of that decision is that a constructive trust may be imposed if: (i) there was an "agreement," "arrangement" or "understanding" — though not necessarily an enforceable contract — that one party would acquire property and that the other party would subsequently receive an interest in it, and (ii) the non-acquiring party somehow relied upon that plan. As to the second element, it further appears that reliance may be

---

487 [1953] 1 Ch. 43.

488 *Ibid.*, at 48.

489 J. McGhee, *Snell's Equity*, 30th ed. (London: Sweet & Maxwell, 2000), at ¶40-35; R. Megarry & H.W.R. Wade, *The Law of Real Property*, 5th ed. (London: Stevens, 1984), at 625.

490 [2000] Ch. 372 (C.A.).

491 *Ibid.*, at 141.

sufficient as long as it either: (i) is detrimental to the non-acquiring party, or (ii) beneficial to the acquiring party.

Should a constructive trust be imposed in such circumstances? In particular, should such relief be available even in the absence of *detrimental* reliance by the non-acquiring party? What is the significance of detrimental reliance, such that it normally is present in the other situations examined in this section?

(b) Specifically Enforceable Contracts for Sale

A constructive trust attaches to property that is subject to a specifically performable contract for sale. The leading authority is *Lysaght v. Edwards*,[492] where Jessel M.R. explained:

> It appears to me that the effect of a contract for sale has been settled for more than two centuries. . . . [T]he moment you have a valid contract for sale the vendor becomes in equity a trustee for the purchaser of the estate sold, and the beneficial ownership passes to the purchaser, the vendor having a right to the purchase-money, a charge or lien on the estate for the security of that purchase-money, and a right to retain possession of the estate until the purchase-money is paid, in the absence of express contract as to the time of delivering possession.

In such circumstances, the constructive trust represents the culmination of a series of equitable doctrines. The doctrine of specific performance holds that, where damages would not provide an adequate remedy for a breach of contract, equity will compel specific performance of a contractual obligation. The equitable doctrine of conversion further states that equity deems as done that which ought to be done. Consequently, since the vendor under a specifically performable contract for sale ought to transfer the property *in specie* to the purchaser, that transfer is deemed to have occurred. The constructive trust recognizes and facilitates that conclusion. The vendor holds the property on trust for the purchaser pending actual execution of the sale.[493]

(i) *Scope of Application*

That scheme most often is applied in connection with contracts for the sale of land, simply because, in other contexts, monetary damages generally provide a satisfactory remedy for the vendor's breach.[494] Nevertheless, the authorities confirm that, just as contracts for the sale of rare or unique chattels may attract

---

492 (1876), 2 Ch. D. 499 (C.A.), at 506. See also *Rayner v. Preston* (1881), 18 Ch. D. 1 (C.A.).

493 For applications in Canadian law, see, *e.g.*, *Buchanan v. Oliver Plumbing & Heating Ltd.* (1959), 18 D.L.R. (2d) 575, 1959 CarswellOnt 167, [1959] O.R. 238 (C.A.); *Aquarius T.V. Ltd., Re* (1975), 21 C.B.R. (N.S.) 144, 1975 CarswellBC 21 (S.C.); *Rich v. Krause* (1974), [1975] 1 W.W.R. 87, 1974 CarswellBC 237 (S.C.).

494 Although it traditionally was said that specific performance (almost) invariably was available with respect to contracts for the sale of land, the Supreme Court of Canada recently adopted a less extensive position: *Semelhago v. Paramadevan*, [1996] 2 S.C.R. 415, 136 D.L.R. (4th) 1, 1996 CarswellOnt 2737, 1996 CarswellOnt 2738, [1996] S.C.J. No. 71, 197 N.R. 379, 3 R.P.R. (3d) 1, 28 O.R. (3d) 639 (note), 91 O.A.C. 379.

the doctrine of specific performance, so too they may result in the imposition of a constructive trust.[495]

Moreover, although that analysis typically is applied to contracts of sale, it may also apply to leases. Granted, it is common to refer in such circumstances to an "equitable lease,"[496] rather than to a "constructive trust of a lease," but the effect is the same — the purchaser/lessee receives an equitable interest in the property.

Although it generally is said that a constructive trust arises as soon as a specifically performable contract for sale is created, the situation may, in fact, be slightly more complicated. The imposition of the trust is postponed until it has been ascertained that the agreement is specifically enforceable. That occurs, perhaps just before the transaction is about to close, when all of the conditions of the contract, including title, are met. At that point, however, the trust arises and dates back to the date when the agreement was first created.[497]

(ii) *The Triggering Event*

The timing of the trust holds the key to understanding its nature. In theory, and often in practice, the trust arises at the outset. In most cases, it applies without incident and simply falls away once the property has been transferred to the purchaser and the transaction has been completed. That fact reveals that while the trust tends to be noticed only if a breach of contract subsequently occurs, its existence cannot be explained in terms of wrongdoing.[498] There typically is no wrong at all — the sale is completed as anticipated.

For similar reason, unjust enrichment cannot provide an explanation. At the time of the trust's creation, none of the elements of that cause of action can be satisfied. The vendor has not yet received anything from the purchaser and therefore has not been enriched; the purchaser has not yet parted with anything and therefore has not suffered a corresponding deprivation; and since nothing has yet gone awry, there is no injustice.[499]

---

495 *Holyroyd v. Marshall* (1862), 10 H.L.C. 191 at 209; *Oughtred v. I.R.C.,* [1960] A.C. 206 (H.L.); *Neville v. Wilson,* [1996] 3 All E.R. 171 (C.A.).

496 *Walsh v. Lonsdale* (1882), 21 Ch. D. 9 (C.A.). Much the same analysis applies with respect to a specifically performable promise to create a security interest. In that situation, however, it would be misleading to refer to, say, a "constructive trust of a mortgage." The word "trust" is not otherwise used to describe security interests. The proper terminology consequently is "equitable mortgage" or "equitable charge."

497 *Martin Commercial Fueling Inc. v. Virtanen* (1997), 144 D.L.R. (4th) 290, 1997 CarswellBC 600, [1997] B.C.J. No. 581, 8 R.P.R. (3d) 1, [1997] 5 W.W.R. 330, 31 B.C.L.R. (3d) 69, 90 B.C.A.C. 161, 147 W.A.C. 161 (C.A.).

498 Other rights similarly lie dormant in many contracts of sale. A "purchaser's lien" allows a purchaser to exercise rights against a property if the vendor breaches the contract, fails to complete the transfer and refuses to refund a prepayment. In contrast to the constructive trust, that lien merely constitutes a security interest and, moreover, applies only to the extent of the pre-payment. It does not constitute ownership of the entire asset.

499 It is pointless to say that, by virtue of the doctrines of specific performance and conversion, the vendor is enriched by the retention of property that equitably belongs to the purchaser. That

The best explanation appears to be that equity imposes the trust in order to perfect contractually-stated intentions and affirm its commitment to autonomy.

> The power to dispose of one's options in favour of another person is an integral aspect of the fundamental capacity of the individual to make and realize such dispositive or other plans as he pleases. We would not take the capacity seriously — we would begin to say that there should be no power to dispose at all — if we took the bare plea "I have changed my mind" seriously.[500]

The vendor promised to transfer title to the purchaser; the circumstances are such that the transfer ought to occur in reality and not merely through the proxy of monetary relief; equity therefore treats the promise as already having been fulfilled. The fact that the ensuing constructive trust may well *protect* the purchaser against wrongdoing or unjust enrichment cannot alter the fact that it was imposed for a much different purpose.

(iii) *Operation and Consequences*

The constructive trust that applies in these circumstances is unusual in some respects. The beneficiary of a trust typically is entitled to all of the benefits associated with the trust property. In this instance, however, the vendor retains the right to both possession and profits pending performance of the contract. On the other hand, consistent with orthodox principles, the vendor does become subject to obligations to maintain the property and to refrain from dealing with it in a way that would adversely affect the purchaser. Likewise, risk passes to the purchaser as soon as the contract is created and the trust arises. It is common, however, for the parties' agreement to transfer that risk back to the vendor pending completion of the transaction.

What does the constructive trust provide to the purchaser that the right of specific performance does not? Perhaps the most dramatic answer is that the right of beneficial ownership substantially increases the range of remedies that is available to the purchaser. For instance, if the vendor becomes insolvent, the purchaser has the right to call for legal title and need not pursue mere personal relief along with the other creditors.

Consider also a case in which, despite the existence of a specifically performable agreement for sale with the plaintiff, the defendant sells a piece of land to a *bona fide* purchaser for value without notice. In the circumstances, the plaintiff cannot have the property itself. And while the situation has begun to change,[501] the orthodox position remains that monetary relief under the cause of action for

---

analysis simply begs the question that it purports to answer — *i.e.* why the vendor holds the property on trust for the purchaser. In any event, there is, at the time of the trust's creation, no injustice.

500 G. Elias, *Trusts* (Oxford: Clarendon Press, 1990), at 9.

501 *Attorney General v. Blake, supra,* note 310; *cf. Bank of America Canada v. Mutual Trust Co. supra,* note 310, at 393.

breach of contract is confined to compensation of the plaintiff's loss.[502] More specifically, the defendant is not required to disgorge any profits made from the breach. Significantly, however, because of the existence of the constructive trust, the vendor committed not only a breach of contract, but also a breach of fiduciary duty. And, as we previously discussed, disgorgement is available, both personally or proprietarily, for breach of a fiduciary duty. The end result is that the plaintiff is entitled to assert ownership of the proceeds generated by wrongful sale. Walton J. explained that result in *Lake v. Bayliss*.[503]

> [W]hat has happened is that the vendor has sold the trust property, and [the plaintiff] is entitled under those circumstances to follow the trust property and say that when it comes to the final performance of the contract that he will take the proceeds of the sale instead of the property. . . . [The vendor] remained a trustee right down to the moment of resale, and accordingly is bound to hold the purchase price as trust property to transfer to the purchaser. . . .

Further Reading

D.W.M. Waters, "Constructive Trust — Vendor and Purchaser" (1961), 14 Curr. Leg. Prob. 76.

Notes and Questions

1. Should a constructive trust attach to the subject of a specifically performable contract for sale? Although the equitable doctrines of specific performance and conversion can be offered in support of such a conclusion, the fact remains that the imposition of a trust is a function of a policy, rather than logical necessity. Is that policy compelling?

2. According to the purported doctrine of "mutuality," if specific performance is available to one party, it must be available to the other party as well.[504] As a result, courts sometimes find that a purchaser's obligation to pay money is specifically enforceable, even though monetary damages would provide an adequate remedy to the vendor in the event of breach. Assuming all of that to be true, does it follow that, once a contract is created, constructive trusts attach not only to property in the vendor's possession, but also to money in the purchaser's possession? What difficulty would often stand in the way of that conclusion?

3. Is it fair that a purchaser under the rule in *Lysaght v. Edwards* takes priority over other creditors in the event of the vendor's insolvency? What considerations might justify such a result?

4. P agreed to purchase a business as a going concern from V. V refused to close and P brought an action for specific performance. Pending the court's decision, V remained

---

502 *Baud Corp., N.V. v. Brook* (1978), (sub nom. *Asamera Oil Corp. v. Sea Oil & General Corp.*) 89 D.L.R. (3d) 1, 1978 CarswellAlta 268, 1978 CarswellAlta 302, [1979] 1 S.C.R. 633, [1978] 6 W.W.R. 301, 23 N.R. 181, 12 A.R. 271, 5 B.L.R. 225, varied 1979 CarswellAlta 201, 1979 CarswellAlta 279, [1979] 3 W.W.R. 93, 14 A.R. 407, 25 N.R. 451, 97 D.L.R. (3d) 300, (sub nom. *Baud Corp., N.V. v. Brook (No. 2)*) [1979] 1 S.C.R. 677 (S.C.C.), at 8 [89 D.L.R.]; *Robinson v. Harman* (1848), 1 Ex. 850, 154 E.R. 363 at 365.

503 [1974] 1 W.L.R. 1073 (Ch. D.), at 1075-1076. See also *Bunny Industries Ltd v. F.S.W. Enterprises*, [1982] Qd. R. 712 (F.C.).

504 R.J. Sharpe, *Injunctions and Specific Performance* (Toronto: Canada Law Book, looseleaf ed.), at ¶7.840ff.

in possession by agreement with P whereunder he was not to convert any profits to his own use. After a court ordered specific performance, V claimed to be entitled to remuneration with respect to services performed in running the business during the interim. Is he entitled to such relief?[505]

(c) Oral Trusts of Land

As we saw in Chapter 4, the *Statute of Frauds* (and its successors) holds that trusts of land that are not evidenced in writing are unenforceable. That rule does not, however, apply with respect to resulting or constructive trusts. The legislation was directed at situations in which one person fraudulently claims that another person agreed to hold certain property on express trust. The writing requirement was thought to erect an evidentiary barrier against such improprieties. In practice, however, the provision often creates as many problems as it solves. The danger now lies not in the fraudulent *assertion* of a trust, but rather in the fraudulent *denial* of one. Having orally agreed to hold Blackacre on trust for the plaintiff, the defendant may subsequently decide to keep the property. Moreover, the defendant appears to have the Act on his side — it says that the plaintiff's claim is unenforceable. Equity, however, will not allow any statute,[506] let alone the *Statute of Frauds*, to be an instrument of fraud.[507]

The difficult question, however, pertains to the appropriate remedy. A leading modern case is *Rochefoucauld v. Boustead*.[508] The plaintiff, the Comtesse de la Rochefoucauld, owned certain lands in Ceylon, subject to a mortgage. After she defaulted on the mortgage, she entered into an oral arrangement with the defendant. It was agreed that he would purchase the property at a mortgage sale and thereby become legal owner, but also that he would hold title on trust for her, subject to her undertaking to reimburse him for the purchase price and other expenses. Although the plan was put into motion, the defendant subsequently denied the plaintiff's interest and claimed to hold the property absolutely. In

---

505 See *Rangi v. Gill* (1982), 14 E.T.R. 94, [1983] 2 W.W.R. 524, 42 B.C.L.R. 59, 1982 CarswellBC 367 (S.C.).

506 A constructive trust similarly may be imposed to prevent the fraudulent use of other statutes. For instance, under a statutory land titles system, registered interests are generally indefeasible. Consequently, a purchaser may obtain clear title even if he or she acted with actual notice of an unregistered interest. Such notice does not amount to fraud. The situation will be different, however, if, at the time of acquisition, the purchaser contractually agreed to obtain the interest subject to an unregistered interest. Although the extent of the doctrine has not yet been determined, it is clear that equity may impose a constructive trust in order to perfect the parties' intentions and prevent the perpetration of fraud: *Lyus v. Prowsa Developments Ltd.*, [1982] 1 W.L.R. 1044; *Ashburn Anstalt v. Arnold*, [1989] Ch. 1 (C.A.).

507 The *Statute of Frauds* applies not only to trusts of interests in land, but also, *inter alia*, to sales of interests in land. Relief similarly is available in such circumstances. If the purchaser can satisfy the doctrine of part performance, equity will order specific performance of the agreement, notwithstanding the statute. Compare *Thompson v. Guaranty Trust Co.* (1973), 39 D.L.R. (3d) 408, 1973 CarswellSask 106, 1973 CarswellSask 143, [1974] S.C.R. 1023, [1973] 6 W.W.R. 746; *cf. Deglman v. Guaranty Trust Co. of Canada, supra*, note 129.

508 [1897] 1 Ch. 196 (C.A.).

defence of that position, he pleaded both the *Statute of Frauds*[509] (insofar as the agreement was not in writing) as well as the *Statute of Limitations*[510] (insofar as 21 years had lapsed since he had purchased the land).

The Court of Appeal held that certain correspondence between the parties provided sufficient evidence for the purposes of the *Statute of Frauds*. It nevertheless went on to hold that oral evidence was admissible to prove the defendant's fraud. As Lindley L.J. said:[511]

> It is further established by a series of cases, the propriety of which cannot now be questioned, that the Statute of Frauds does not prevent the proof of a fraud; and that it is a fraud on the part of a person to whom land is conveyed as a trustee, and who knows it was so conveyed, to deny the trust and claim the land himself. Consequently, notwithstanding the statute, it is competent for a person claiming land conveyed to another to prove by parol evidence that it was so conveyed upon trust for the claimant, and that the grantee, knowing the facts, is denying the trust and relying upon the form of conveyance and the statute, in order to keep the land himself. This doctrine was not established until some time after the statute was passed.

On the limitations defence his Lordship said:[512]

> The next defence is the *Statute of Limitations*. The trust which the plaintiff has established is clearly an express trust within the meaning of that expression as explained in *Soar v. Ashwell*.[513] The trust is one which both plaintiff and defendant intended to create. This case is not one in which an equitable obligation arises although there may have been no intention to create a trust. The intention to create a trust existed from the first. The defendant is not able in this case to claim the benefit of s. 8 of the *Trustee Act*,[514] and the statute which is applicable is the *Judicature Act*,[515] which enacts as follows:
>
>> No claim of a *cestui que* trust against his trustee for any property held on an express trust, or in respect of any breach of such trust, shall be held to be barred by any *Statute of Limitations*.
>
> The *Statutes of Limitations*, therefore afford no defence if the plaintiff's action is to be regarded as one brought by a *cestui que* trust against his trustee seeking for an account of trust property.

Rochefoucauld v. Boustead is a difficult decision. The court said that the defendant held the property on "express trust." It is, however, difficult to agree. Such a conclusion flies in the face of the *Statute of Frauds*. Consequently, it may be better to interpret the court merely as having treated the defendant *as if* he was a trustee under an express trust in order to avoid the operation of the limitation periods. That interpretation draws support from *Soar v. Ashwell*,[516] which simi-

---

509   29 Car. 2, c. 3 (1677, U.K.).
510   That is, the *Trustee Act, 1888*, 51 and 52 Vict. c. 59.
511   *Boustead, supra*, note 508, at 206.
512   *Ibid.*, at 208.
513   [1893] 2 Q.B. 390.
514   *Supra.*
515   36 & 37 Vict. c. 66.
516   *Supra*, note 513.

larly regarded certain types of "constructive trustees"[517] as trustees of express trusts, thereby denying them the protection of the limitation periods.

(i) *The Nature and Basis of the Trust*

If, as the *Statute of Frauds* seems to demand, the trust is not express, then it must be either resulting or constructive.

Equity could have chosen the former option. The resulting trust that arises upon the failure of an express trust provides a ready model. The problem with that analysis, however, is that it is relatively inflexible. As previously explained, "resulting" is the English translation of the Latin word *"resalire,"* which means to "jump back." A resulting trust invariably sends property back from whence it came. In some situations, that solution would work well. *Bannister v. Bannister,* which appears below, is illustrative. In other situations, however, a resulting trust would be unsatisfactory. Consider a situation in which X transfers Blackacre to the defendant on the oral understanding that the property will be held on trust for the plaintiff. X subsequently dies and the defendant refuses to honour the agreement. To whom should Blackacre belong? There are three main possibilities. First, equity could allow the property to beneficially remain with the defendant — but that would reward fraud. Second, equity could send the property back to (the estate of) X by way of a resulting trust — but, since X is deceased, there is no assurance that Blackacre would then find its way to the plaintiff, as desired. Third, equity could send the property forward to the plaintiff — but that is not an outcome that a resulting (jumping back) trust can achieve.

In light of the available responses, it consequently is important that the failure of the express trust in the present situation is different than the failure of express trust that classically gives rise to a resulting trust. In the latter situation, the express trust fails because, for instance, there is uncertainty of objects or subject matter. Those sorts of defects irreparably go to the very heart of the express trust. It simply is impossible to send the property forward as intended.[518] And since the property obviously cannot stay with the transferee, it must go back to the transferor. There are no other possibilities. In contrast, an express trust that fails for want of writing is not inherently defective — it merely is unenforceable. Consequently, there exists the possibility of sending the property forward to its intended beneficiary.

That possibility is realized through the imposition of a constructive trust, which, unlike a resulting trust, is not logically restricted to sending property back

---

517 *Viz.,* trustees *de son tort* and constructive trustees who participate with express trustees in fraud upon the trust or who convert trust property to their own use.

518 An express trust may also fail, for instance, on grounds of public policy pertaining to, say, illegality or immorality. In that situation, equity could, conceivably, send the property forward to the intended beneficiary by way of a constructive trust. There is no uncertainty regarding intention, objects or subject matter. Significantly, however, the policy that precludes the enforcement of the express trust will also preclude the creation of a forward-moving constructive trust.

to its transferor.[519] It then becomes necessary to identify the fact that triggers the imposition of that constructive trust.

- The causative event cannot be unjust enrichment because the remedy for that cause of action is always restitution — the transferee invariably is required to give a benefit *back* to the transferor (either personally or proprietarily).
- The causative event might be wrongdoing, insofar as the recipient of the property refuses to hold it on trust for the intended beneficiary. The primary difficulty with that analysis lies in the identification of the operative wrong. There may be a breach of contract. But if so, the promise generally will have been given by the transferee to the transferor, such that the intended beneficiary (the party seeking relief) lacks privity. Moreover, obligations that the transferee might owe directly to the intended beneficiary (*e.g.* fiduciary obligations) would seem to presume the existence of a trust — the very fact for which an explanation is being sought. Furthermore, the constructive trust occasionally has been imposed even in the absence of fraud, where neither party denies the existence of the unenforceable express trust.[520]
- The best explanation therefore may be that, just as in the case of a specifically enforceable contract for sale, equity imposes a constructive trust in order to perfect intentions. The transferee agreed to hold property, received from the transferor, on trust for the beneficiary. A trust arises, out of respect for autonomy, to ensure that that undertaking is fulfilled. The trust may also be buttressed by the doctrine of detrimental reliance insofar as the transferee's promise induced the transferor to part with the property or create a contract to that effect.

Further Reading

T.G. Youdan, "Formalities for Trusts of Land, and the Doctrine in *Rochefoucauld v. Boustead*", (1984), 43 Cambr. L.J. 306.

BANNISTER v. BANNISTER

[1948] 2 All E.R. 133
Court of Appeal

In 1943 the defendant agreed to sell two adjoining cottages, Nos. 30 and 31, to the plaintiff, her brother-in-law, for £250, if he would let her live in No. 30 rent-free for the rest of her life. The plaintiff agreed. The value of the cottages at the time was £400. Subsequently, differences arose between them and the plaintiff sought to evict the defendant, alleging that she was merely a tenant at will. At

---

519 See, *e.g.*, *Neale v. Willis* (1968), 19 P. & C.R. 836, 112 S.J. 521 (C.A.); *Langille v. Nass* (1917), 51 N.S.R. 429, 36 D.L.R. 368 (C.A.).

520 See, *e.g.*, *Bouchard v. R.*, [1983] C.T.C. 173, 83 D.T.C. 5193, 1983 CarswellNat 146 (Fed. T.D.) (discussed below in the notes following *Bannister v. Bannister*).

trial, the court found in favour of the defendant on the basis of a constructive trust. The plaintiff appealed.

SCOTT L.J. delivered the judgment of the Court:

[His Lordship listed the plaintiff's three objections to the judgement below: (1) the defendant's interest was at most a tenancy at will; (2) even if was a life interest, it could only take effect as a tenancy at will because the interest was not evidenced by writing, contrary to ss. 53 and 54 of the *Law of Property Act, 1925*;[521] and (3) a constructive trust could only be raised by a finding of actual fraud on the part of the plaintiff.

His Lordship held that the interest created was a life interest determinable on the defendant ceasing to occupy No. 30. He continued:]

As will be seen from what is said below, the second objection (based on want of writing) in effect stands or falls with the third, and it will, therefore, be convenient to deal with that next. It is, we think, clearly a mistake to suppose that the equitable principle on which a constructive trust is raised against a person who insists on the absolute character of a conveyance to himself for the purpose of defeating a beneficial interest, which, according to the true bargain, was to belong to another, is confined to cases in which the conveyance itself was fraudulently obtained. The fraud which brings the principle into play arises as soon as the absolute character of the conveyance is set up for the purpose of defeating the beneficial interest, and that is the fraud to cover which the *Statute of Frauds*[522] or the corresponding provisions of the *Law of Property Act, 1925*,[523] cannot be called in aid in cases in which no written evidence of the real bargain is available. Nor is it, in our opinion, necessary that the bargain on which the absolute conveyance is made should include any express stipulation that the grantee is in so many words to hold as trustee. It is enough that the bargain should have included a stipulation under which some sufficiently defined beneficial interest in the property was to be taken by another. The above propositions are, we think, clearly borne out by the cases to which we were referred of *Booth v. Turle*. . . .[524] We see no distinction in principle between a case in which property is conveyed to a purchaser on terms that the entire beneficial interest in some part of it is to be retained by the vendor (as in *Booth v. Turle*) and a case, like the present, in which property is conveyed to a purchaser on terms that a limited beneficial interest in some part of it is to be retained by the vendor. We are, accordingly, of opinion that the third ground of objection to the learned county court judge's conclusion also fails. His finding that there was no fraud in the case cannot be taken as meaning that it was not fraudulent in the plaintiff to insist on the absolute character of the conveyance for the purpose of defeating the beneficial interest which he

---

521 15 & 16 Geo. 5, c. 20.
522 22 Car. 2, c. 3 (1677).
523 *Supra*, note 521.
524 (1873), L.R. 16 Eq. 182.

had agreed the defendant should retain. The conclusion that the plaintiff was fraudulent, in this sense, necessarily follows from the facts found, and, as indicated above, the fact that he may have been innocent of any fraudulent intent in taking the conveyance in absolute form is for this purpose immaterial. The failure of the third ground of objection necessarily also destroys the second objection based on want of writing and the provisions of ss. 53 and 54 of the *Law of Property Act, 1925*.[525]

Notes and Questions

1. In *Bannister*, the same person was both the settlor and the beneficiary of the unenforceable express trust. Consequently, the outcome would have been the same whether the property had been sent back by way of resulting trust or forward by way of constructive trust.

In other situations, however, the choice between a resulting trust and a constructive trust will be significant. *Densham, Re*[526] provides an example. A piece of land was purchased. The wife contributed one-ninth, and the husband eight-ninths, of the purchase price. Title, however, was taken in his name alone, on the oral understanding that he would hold the property for both parties jointly. The wife relied on that agreement to her detriment. The husband's financial situation deteriorated and a question arose as to the creditors' rights to the property. The court recognized that the wife held a half interest by way of constructive trust, but further held that since that interest arose by way of a voluntary settlement, it was void as against the creditors. In contrast, the court held that the wife also enjoyed a one-ninth share on resulting trust by virtue of her contribution toward the purchase price, and further that that interest could not similarly be impugned.

2. There are cases in which, like *Bannister*, either a resulting trust or a constructive trust would have the same effect. They usually speak of a resulting trust,[527] but sometimes the judgments do not make it clear whether relief is granted on that basis or on the basis of the constructive trust.[528]

3. *Brown v. Storoschuk*[529] affords another example of a failure to classify the trust. Brown, a successful farmer, employed Storoschuk for some years. Storoschuk was anxious to buy his own farm and learned of a suitable property in the neighbourhood, but lacked the money to buy it. He told Brown about the farm. Brown was anxious to retain Storoschuk, so he bought the property on Storoschuk's behalf on the understanding that Storoschuk would continue to work for him for three years and pay off the purchase price. Later, after the farm had greatly increased in value, Brown refused to honour the agreement. The court held that the doctrine in *Rochefaucauld v. Boustead*[530] applied. Brown therefore held

---

525 *Supra.*

526 [1975] 1 W.L.R. 1519.

527 See, *e.g.*, *Hodgson v. Marks*, [1971] Ch. 892 (C.A.); *Beaton v. Hayman* (1970), 16 D.L.R. (3d) 537, 1970 CarswellNS 158, 3 N.S.R. (2d) 325 (T.D.); *David v. Szoke* (1973), 39 D.L.R. (3d) 707, 1973 CarswellBC 309 (S.C.).

528 See, *e.g.*, *Pahara v. Pahara* (1945), [1946] S.C.R. 89, [1946] 1 D.L.R. 433, 1945 CarswellAlta 126; *Childers v. Childers* (1857), 1 De. G. & J. 482, 44 E.R. 810; *Davies v. Otty (No. 2)* (1867), 35 Beav. 208, 55 E.R. 875; *Haigh v. Kaye* (1872), L.R. 7 Ch. 469.

529 *Supra*, note 4.

530 *Supra*, note 508.

the farm in trust for Storoschuk and was required to convey it, subject to Storoschuk's paying the balance owing.[531]

4. X leased a golf driving range from Y. He unsuccessfully attempted to buy the reversion. Then he agreed orally with Z, the owner of a licensed restaurant, that Z would purchase the reversion, X paying part of the purchase price, and Z would subsequently convey the land to X. Z reached an oral agreement with Y to purchase the land. Then Z told X that he was going to insist on a restrictive covenant in the deed to X prohibiting the use of the land for a licensed restaurant. X disagreed. Z completed the purchase from Y and refused to transfer the land to X. Is X entitled to a conveyance?[532]

5. As noted above, the constructive trust that is being enforced in these cases works forwards. That is illustrated in *Neale v. Willis*.[533] X agreed with his mother-in-law that, upon her lending him money for the purpose, he would buy a house in his and his wife's name jointly. In fact, X took title in his own name. The Court of Appeal held that a constructive trust arose in favour of the wife's interest. Lord Denning said that *Bannister v. Bannister*:[534]

> ...shows that if a person who takes a conveyance to himself, which is absolute in form, nevertheless has made a bargain that he will give a beneficial interest to another, he will be held to be a constructive trustee [of the property] for the other.[535]

6. The same thing happened in *Langille v. Nass*.[536] A husband and wife had granted a certain parcel of land to three persons "in trust," without mentioning the trust objects. It was common ground that the property had been given to permit the building of a community hall for religious and social purposes. Money for the building had been raised and it was built. Unfortunately, members of the community then disagreed about the use of the hall and the trustees took sides in the matter. The court held that evidence of the donors' intention was admissible to prevent fraud, despite the statute. The effect of the decision was that the constructive trust worked forwards.

7. In many cases on oral trusts of land, such as *Rochefoucauld v. Boustead*[537] and *Brown v. Storoschuk*,[538] the transferee's apparently absolute title is in fact a security interest. He or she holds title until paid the amount of the loan. Consequently, while a trust may be declared to prevent fraud, the transferee has a lien on the property for unpaid money. The prevention of fraud is not the only situation in which the trust arises, however. For example, it can also be raised if a person transfers property to another person in order to qualify the transferee to vote.[539]

---

531 Sidney Smith J.A. dissented, holding that in order to take the case out of the statute, fraud had actually to be pleaded. See also *Drummond v. Drummond* (1964), 50 W.W.R. 538, 1964 CarswellBC 193 (S.C.).

532 See *Gilmurray v. Corr*, [1978] N.I. 99 (Ch. D.).

533 *Supra*, note 519.

534 [1948] 2 All E.R. 133 (C.A.).

535 *Supra*, note 519, at 839. See also *Breitenstein v. Munson* (1914), 6 W.W.R. 188, 19 B.C.R. 495, 1914 CarswellBC 181, 16 D.L.R. 458 (S.C.).

536 *Supra*, note 519.

537 *Supra*, note 508.

538 *Supra*, note 4.

539 *Western Trust Co. v. Lang*, [1919] 1 W.W.R. 651, 12 Sask. L.R. 94, 1919 CarswellSask 29 (K.B.).

8. Must the transferee be aware of the trust at the outset? If so, is it also necessary that a fraudulent intention was formed at that time?[540] Is a fraudulent intention on the part of the trustee required before the doctrine can be invoked?

9. Can the doctrine apply if a person declares herself or himself to be a trustee of land for another, but later denies that declaration?[541]

10. *Bouchard v. R.*[542] is one of the more interesting situations in which the fraud doctrine has arisen. The taxpayer and his wife purchased a house for $23,000 and entered into an agreement that they would convey it to their son and daughter-in-law upon payment of the $23,000. The son and his wife took possession, renovated the property and lived in it. Seven years later, they had paid off the loan and the property was conveyed to them. During those seven years, the taxpayer treated the payments made by his son and daughter-in-law as rent and claimed capital cost allowance. This was largely because his returns were prepared and filed by his accountant. The Minister assessed the taxpayer for capital gains tax. The taxpayer contested the assessment and alleged an oral trust in favour of his son and daughter-in-law. The court declared the oral evidence admissible on the basis of *Rochefoucauld v. Boustead*[543] and set aside the assessment, holding that it was contrary to public policy to refuse to permit the taxpayer to prove the trust. Notice that the taxpayer did not deny the trust, so that there was no fraud on his part. Is this an appropriate use of the constructive trust?[544]

11. So far we have assumed that an oral trust of land, while valid,[545] is unenforceable because of failure to comply with the statutory formalities. But that is so only if the defendant expressly pleads the statute. If the statute is not pleaded, the trust is enforceable.[546]

(d) Incomplete Gifts

In Chapter 4, we examined equity's approach to gifts. Equity will not perfect an imperfect gift.[547] However, if the donor has done everything possible to perfect a gift, then equity will treat it as having been perfected. The classic case is *Rose, Re*.[548] Mr. Rose wished to place certain shares into trust. On March 30th, he properly executed a share transfer in the trustees' favour. The company did not,

---

540 See D. Browne, *Ashburner's Principles of Equity*, 2nd ed. (London: Butterworth & Co. Limited, 1933), at 99. *Cf.* the doctrine of secret trusts, *infra*.

541 See *Morris v. Whiting* (1913), 15 D.L.R. 254, 1913 CarswellMan 327, 5 W.W.R. 936, 24 Man. R. 56 (K.B.).

542 *Supra*, note 520.

543 *Supra*, note 508.

544 The *Bouchard* case also held, following *McKinnon v. Harris* (1909), 14 O.W.R. 876, 1909 CarswellOnt 594, 1 O.W.N. 101 (C.A.), at 878 [O.W.R.], *per* Meredith J.A., that in determining whether an oral trust has been established, the court should ask itself the following, among possibly other, questions: (1) is the claim supported by probability? (2) is it supported by evidence in writing in any form? (3) is it supported by indisputable facts? (4) is it supported by disinterested testimony? (5) is the parol evidence quite satisfactory and convincing?

545 *Rochefoucauld v. Boustead, supra*, note 508; and see *Gardner v. Rowe* (1828), 5 Russ. 258, 38 E.R. 1024.

546 *Bjorklund v. Gillott*, [1955] 5 D.L.R. 466 at 469, *per* Wilson J.; *Bouchard v. R., supra*, note 520, at 181.

547 *Milroy v. Lord* (1862), 4 De G.F. & J. 264, 45 E.R. 1185.

548 [1952] Ch. 499. See also *Mascall v. Mascall* (1984), 50 Plan. & Comp. 119 (C.A.).

however, register that transfer until June 30th. Because Mr. Rose died a short time later, a question arose regarding beneficial ownership of the shares as of April 10th. A tax would be incurred if, but only if, Mr. Rose was the beneficial owner on that date.[549] The Court of Appeal held that once Mr. Rose had done everything possible to effect the transfer, he held the shares on trust for the intended donee (*i.e.* the trustees of the intended express trust). The tax consequently was not incurred.

The ultimate trust undoubtedly was an express trust that arose directly from the settlor's intention. The classification of the interim trust is more complicated. It arose not from the settlor's direct intention,[550] but rather by operation of law. It therefore was either a resulting trust or a constructive trust, but not an express trust. It could not be a resulting trust, however, because it sent property forward to the intended recipient, rather than backward to the transferor. It therefore must have been a constructive trust.

The explanation for that constructive trust is also complicated. It cannot be unjust enrichment. Mr. Rose had not been enriched by anyone — he merely retained possession of the shares pending registration of their transfer. Moreover, there was nothing unjust in that retention. Nor can the constructive trust be explained on the basis of wrongdoing. Mr. Rose had done nothing wrong — to the contrary, he was in the process of conferring a gift. The best explanation appears to be that equity imposed the trust in order to respect the donor's autonomy and perfect his intention. And interestingly, it did so despite the absence of any detrimental reliance by the donee.[551]

(e) Proprietary Estoppel

The ideas of perfecting stated intentions and protecting detrimental reliance are well illustrated in some instances of proprietary estoppel. That doctrine applies if, with the encouragement or acquiescence of the owner, a person detrimentally relies on the belief that he or she enjoys an interest in a piece of land. *Baker v. Inwards*[552] is a classic case. The plaintiff was encouraged by his father to build a bungalow on the father's land. There was an understanding between the parties that the plaintiff would be permitted to live in the house as long as he wished. Unfortunately, the father died and his will left the property to someone else. He

---

549 A similar sort of question would have arisen if, for instance, the company had declared a dividend at some point between March 30 and June 30. The dividend would have belonged to the person beneficially entitled to the shares.

550 Mr. Rose never intended to declare himself to be trustee for the interim. But see *Pennington v. Waine*, [2002] 1 W.L.R. 2075 (C.A.) (ambiguously suggesting that the interim trust arises from the settlor's intention and hence is express); see also A. Doggett, "Explaining *Re Rose*: The Search Goes On?" (2003), 62 Cambridge L.J. 263.

551 Compare *Restatement of the Law of Restitution* at 668-669 (American law requires proof that either the donor died believing that the gift had been completed or the donee detrimentally relied on the belief that the gift would be completed).

552 [1965] 2 Q.B. 29 (C.A.).

had forgotten to insert the appropriate provision in favour of his son. Lord Denning M.R. came to the plaintiff's rescue.

> So in this case, even though there is no binding contract to grant any particular interest to the licensee, nevertheless the court can look at the circumstances and see whether there is an equity arising out of the expenditure of money. All that is necessary is that the licensee should, at the request or with the encouragement of the landlord, have spent the money in the expectation of being allowed to stay there. If so, the court will not allow that expectation to be defeated where it would be inequitable so to do. In this case, it is quite plain that the father allowed an expectation to be created in the son's mind that this bungalow was to be his home. It seems to me, in light of that inquiry, that the father could not . . . have turned to his son and said: "You are to go. It is my land, my house." Nor could he at anytime thereafter so long as his son wanted it as his home.
>
> . . . It is for the court to say in what way the equity can be satisfied. . . . I am quite clear in this case it can be satisfied by holding that the [son] can remain there as long as he desires to as his home.

As the end of the quoted passage suggests, the court may select from a range of remedies when responding to proprietary estoppel. Depending upon the circumstances, the plaintiff may, for instance, be awarded monetary compensation (perhaps secured by a lien), a lease,[553] an undivided share,[554] a right of purchase[555] or even a transfer of legal title.[556] The defendant may also be required to hold the property on constructive trust for the plaintiff.[557] The imposition of constructive trusts in aid of the doctrine of proprietary estoppel has, however, been criticised severely in England.[558]

---

553 *Yaxley v. Gotts*, [2000] 1 All E.R. 711 (C.A.).

554 *Lim Teng Huan v. Ang Swee Chuan*, [1992] 1 W.L.R. 113 (P.C.).

555 See, *e.g.*, *Conveyancing and Law of Property Act*, R.S.O. 1990, c. C.34, s. 37(1).

556 *Dillwyn v. Llewelyn* (1862), 4 De G. F. & J. 517, 45 E.R. 1285 (H.C.); *Pascoe v. Turner*, [1979] 1 W.L.R. 431 (C.A.).

557 *Hussey v. Palmer*, [1972] 1 W.L.R. 1286 (C.A.). See also *Binions v. Evans*, [1972] Ch. 359 *per* Lord Denning M.R. (C.A.); *D.H.N. Foods Ltd. v. Tower Hamlets London Borough Council*, [1976] 1 W.L.R. 852 (C.A.).

558 Various concerns have been expressed, most of which can be overcome in Canada. (1) It is said that a constructive trust imposed in aid of a licence for life may create a strict settlement under the *Settled Land Act 1925*, 15 & 16 Geo. 5, c. 18, which would give the licensee the right to have the land conveyed to him or her and to sell it: see *Dodsworth v. Dodsworth* (1973), 228 E.G. 115 (C.A.); *contra Binions, ibid.*, at 366, *per* Lord Denning M.R. This problem does not exist in Canada. (2) It is further said that such licences create interests in land that cannot be protected as land charges or under the registered land system in England: see J. Martin, ed., *Hanbury and Martin: Modern Equity*, 16th ed. (London: Sweet & Maxwell Ltd., 2001) at 902ff. In Canada, the interest could be protected by a deposit on title in deeds registration systems (*e.g.*, *Registry Act*, R.S.O. 1990, c. R.20, ss. 105-110. Under land titles systems, the interest might be considered an overriding interest (*e.g. Land Titles Act*, R.S.O. 1990, c. L.5, s. 44(1), para. 3), or it may be protected by caveat (*ibid.*, s. 128(1)). (3) Finally, it is said that without documentary evidence, it may be necessary for the owner of the interest to obtain and register an order declaring the interest. In Canada, under a deeds registration system, an equitable interest binds a subsequent purchaser if there is either actual notice or registration (*e.g.*, *Registry Act, supra*, ss. 70-74). Under a land titles system the interest, unless it is an overriding interest, must be registered; actual notice is ineffective against a subsequent *bona fide* purchaser for value (*e.g.*, *Land Titles Act, supra*, s. 78(5), but see *Dominion Stores Ltd. v. United Trust Co.*

(f) Cohabitational Property Disputes

In Canadian law, cohabitational property disputes generally are thought to provide the primary example of constructive trusts imposed to reverse unjust enrichments. As previously suggested, however, there are difficulties with that view. Most significantly, although the remedy for unjust enrichment must, in principle, be restitution,[559] the relief awarded in the family context typically entails the fulfilment of expectations. As a matter of social policy, that is entirely understandable. Cohabitational relationships are, by their nature, forward-looking. The parties start with the assumption of a lifelong commitment in which benefits and burdens are equally shared (even if those benefits and burdens take different forms — *e.g.* household services by one party, financial income by the other). Moreover, although it generally is imprudent to express such sentiments at the outset, there is an expectation that the same scheme of sharing will carry over to the distribution of assets in the event of separation.

Against that backdrop, the remedy of restitution (and hence the action in unjust enrichment) seems almost uniquely ill-suited to the resolution of cohabitational property disputes. Restitution looks backward. At most, it merely restores the parties' respective *status quo ante*. Strictly applied, that measure of relief would pervert the very nature of intimate relationships. The plaintiff in the typical case did not choose to cohabitate on a "money back guarantee" basis. She acted instead with a partnership model in mind.

Consequently, while the suggestion may seem heretical, the constructive trust imposed in the family context perhaps responds not so much to unjust enrichment as to the desire to perfect intentions and protect detrimental reliance. The trust, in other words, reflects equity's willingness to take inter-personal relationships seriously.[560]

7. PERFECTING INTENTIONS #2 — TRANSFERS UPON DEATH

(a) Secret Trusts

(i) *Introduction*

As its name suggests, a secret trust is, in some respect, secret or unknown. A will is drafted that leaves property to a certain person. That person secretly agrees with the testator to hold the property for the benefit of someone else. Under a *fully-secret trust*, the will discloses neither the existence of the trustee nor the name of the beneficiary. To outward appearances, there does not seem to be any trust at all. Under a *semi-secret trust*, the will discloses the existence of the trustee,

---

(1976), [1977] 2 S.C.R. 915, 1976 CarswellOnt 383, 1976 CarswellOnt 404, 71 D.L.R. (3d) 72, 1 R.P.R. 1, 11 N.R. 97).

559 M. McInnes, "The Measure of Restitution" (2002), 52 U.T.L.J. 163.

560 R. Chambers, "Constructive Trusts in Canada" (1999), 37 Alberta L. Rev. 173.

but does not identify the beneficiary. There obviously is a trust, but its effect is not generally known.

A secret trust may arise for many reasons. A knowledgeable, but indecisive, testator who wishes to circumvent the formal requirements of the wills legislation may leave everything to a solicitor, and simply call from time to time with an updated list of desired beneficiaries. More often, however, the testator is motivated by a desire for goodwill or harmonious relations. A testamentary gift that favours one sibling over another, or that reveals the existence of an illegitimate child or secret lover, may generate ill-will or hostility amongst family members and close friends. Better to postpone the storm until after one is gone. Alternatively, a testator may be motivated by a desire for secrecy even after death. Once admitted to probate, a will becomes a public document, available to anyone for a fee. A secret trust allows a testator to conceal the fact that he or she effectively left property to, say, a political organization with unpopular views.

From a legal perspective, the problem with secret trusts is that they do not satisfy the testamentary provisions of the *Statute of Frauds* or its successor legislation. Modern *Wills Acts* state that testamentary dispositions generally must be in writing and signed by the testator in the presence of two witnesses. Under a secret trust, the disposition in favour of the intended trustee is written and hence *prima facie* valid, but the terms of intended trust are un-stated and hence invalid.

Equity responds to that situation in much the same way that it responds to the situation (examined earlier) in which a settlor purports to orally create an *inter vivos* trust of land. The trustee is permitted to acquire title under the initial testamentary disposition. The wills legislation prevents the intended express trust from taking effect,[561] but a constructive trust, in precisely the same terms as the failed express trust, is immediately impressed upon the property in the trustee's hands. A cynic might view the exercise as something of a charade. The *Wills Act* is formally honoured, but substantively evaded. The statute is allowed to operate, but equity fixes upon the recipient's conscience and enforces the promise that had been given to the testator.

That is not to say, however, that the choice between an express testamentary trust and a judicially-imposed constructive trust is a matter of indifference. As we shall see, there are practical differences, especially in terms of the elements of proof. Consequently, unless there is a pressing need for secrecy, it generally is prudent to comply with the statutory requirements.

As a final prefatory comment, it should be noted that the reasoning employed in connection with secret testamentary trusts extends, by analogy, to other situations. For instance, a constructive trust may be imposed if the deceased was

---

561 Notwithstanding the statutory provisions, some commentators insist that equity enforces the express trust that arose from the settlor's intention: A.J. Oakley, ed., *Parker & Mellows: The Modern Law of Trusts*, 7th ed. (London: Sweet & Maxwell, 1998), at 62ff.; *cf* L.A. Sheridan, "English and Irish Secret Trusts" (1951), 67 L.Q. Rev. 314 (semi-secret trusts are express, fully-secret trusts are constructive). With respect, however, the difficulties with that view seem insuperable. It is one thing to impose a trust outside the operation of a statute; quite another to directly disregard statutory invalidity.

induced to die intestate, or to refrain from re-drafting a will, by a promise of the person who subsequently inherited property from the estate.[562]

(ii) *Nature and Basis of the Constructive Trust*

Why does equity act as it does? Assuming that the requisite promise has been established, it obviously would be fraud for the immediate recipient of the property to retain it contrary to the undertaking. The property therefore must be sent either backward to the estate or forward to the intended beneficiary. The former option is undesirable because the donor, being dead, no longer is in a position to implement the desired disposition through proper means. The intended beneficiary ultimately might prevail, but only rarely and fortuitously (*e.g.* by being the party entitled to succeed upon intestacy). Equity therefore imposes a trust to send the property forward as intended.

The precise explanation for that trust is controversial. At first glance, at least, unjust enrichment might seem a promising possibility insofar as the trustee undoubtedly is enriched by the receipt of the property. There are, however, two difficulties with that analysis. The first stems from the fact that the corresponding deprivation lies not with the intended beneficiary, but rather with the testator.[563] That is important because, as previously explained, the remedy for unjust enrichment invariably is restitution.[564] A benefit must be given *back* to the person from whom it was acquired. Consequently, in the present context, a restitutionary remedy would, contrary to equity's wish to effect practical justice, return the property to the estate, rather than send it forward to the intended beneficiary. The second difficulty with an unjust enrichment analysis lies in the need to identify an injustice. Granted, a secret trust often comes before a court after a trustee

---

562 See, for example, *Sellack v. Harris* (1708), 2 Eq. Cas. Abr. 46. For ease of discussion, the party providing the property for the purpose of establishing a trust shall be referred to as the "testator" even when that term is not, strictly speaking, applicable. Likewise, the terms "trustee" and "beneficiary" should be read, where necessary, as "would-be trustee" and "would-be beneficiary."

563 The courts generally require proof of a *direct subtraction*, such that the defendant's benefit was taken from the plaintiff. Exceptionally, however, they are satisfied by proof of an *interceptive subtraction*, such that the defendant received from a third party a benefit that ought to have accrued to the plaintiff. It therefore might be said, in the present context, that the trustee was interceptively enriched by the receipt of property that ought to have passed from the testator to the intended beneficiary. The problem with that analysis, however, is that, while somewhat unsettled, the doctrine of interceptive subtraction generally is thought to require proof that the plaintiff was *legally entitled* to demand the benefit from the third party. And it is the very existence of that legal entitlement that currently is in issue. The right cannot be self-generating. See G. Virgo, *The Principles of the Law of Restitution* (Oxford: Oxford University Press, 1999) at 109-113; R.B. Grantham & C.E.F. Rickett, *Enrichment & Restitution in New Zealand* (Oxford: Hart, 2000) at 20. See also M. McInnes, "Interceptive Subtraction, Unjust Enrichment and Wrongs — A Reply to Professor Birks" (2003), 62 Cambridge L.J. 697; L.D. Smith, "Three-Party Restitution: A Critique of Birks' Theory of Interceptive Subtraction" (1991), 11 Oxford J. of Legal Stud. 481; *cf. Air Canada v. British Columbia*, *supra*, note 24, *per* La Forest J. (S.C.C.).

564 M. McInnes, "The Measure of Restitution" (2002), 52 U.T.L.J. 163.

purports to retain the property beneficially. It is clear, however, that a constructive trust arises at the moment of the testator's death, before the trustee may have actually engaged in any fraudulent behaviour. Furthermore, the trust applies even if the trustee concedes that he or she is not entitled to the benefit of the property and merely seeks the court's advice as to the true beneficiary.[565]

It is also common to ascribe the constructive trust to wrongdoing — more specifically, the trustee's fraud in attempting to retain the property beneficially. Lord Westbury's comments in *McCormick v. Grogan*[566] are illustrative.

> My Lords, the jurisdiction which is invoked here by the Appellant is founded altogether on personal fraud. It is a jurisdiction by which a Court of Equity, proceeding on the ground of fraud, converts the party who has committed it into a trustee for the party who is injured by that fraud. Now, being a jurisdiction founded on personal fraud, it is incumbent on the Court to see that a fraud, a *malus animus*, is proved by the clearest and most indisputable evidence.[567] It is impossible to supply presumption in the place of proof, nor are you warranted in deriving those conclusions in the absence of direct proof, for the purpose of affixing the criminal character of fraud, which you might by possibility derive in a case of simple contract. . . . You are obliged, therefore, to shew most clearly and distinctly that the person you wish to convert into a trustee acted *malo animo*. You must shew distinctly that he knew that the testator or the intestate was beguiled and deceived by his conduct. If you are not in a condition to affirm that without any misgiving, or possibility of mistake, you are not warranted in affixing on the individual the *delictum* of fraud, which you must do before you convert him into a trustee.

There are, however, difficulties with that explanation too. First, as previously explained, a constructive trust may arise prior to, or in the absence of, any actual fraud. Second, although a fully-secret trust creates a danger of actual fraud, a semi-secret trust does not. By revealing the existence of a trust (though not its terms), the will itself ensures that the trustee will not be able to improperly retain the property. Consequently, unless the explanation is to vary depending upon whether the trust is fully-secret or semi-secret (an unattractive proposition), no secret trust can be explained on the basis of wrongdoing. Third, since the constructive trust works in favour of the beneficiary, one would expect, on general private law principles, to find that the operative wrong was committed against that party as well. The dis-honoured undertaking, however, was given not to the intended beneficiary, but rather to the deceased.[568] Moreover, while it may be tempting to say that the trustee breached a fiduciary obligation owed to the

---

565 *Blackwell v. Blackwell*, [1929] A.C. 318 (H.L.); *Boyes, Re* (1884), 26 Ch. D. 531.

566 (1869), L.R. 4 H.L. 82 at 97.

567 To the extent that Lord Westbury was suggesting the need for something more than proof on a balance of probabilities (the usual civil standard of proof), Megarry V.C. subsequently disagreed: *Snowdon, Re*, [1979] Ch. 528, [1979] 2 All E.R. 172. The more lenient view is even more clearly correct if the constructive trust is imposed, not to redress actual fraud, but to perfect intentions and protect detrimental reliance.

568 But see *Beswick v. Beswick*, [1968] A.C. 58 (H.L.); *Contracts (Rights of Third Parties) Act 1999*, c. 31 (U.K.); *Law Reform Act*, S.N.B. 1993, c. L-1.2, s. 4.

intended beneficiary, the existence of such an obligation seems to presume the existence of the very same trust for which an explanation is being sought.[569]

The best explanation may be that a constructive trust arises to perfect intentions and to protect detrimental reliance. The trustee promised to hold property received from the testator on trust for the beneficiary. In reliance upon that promise, the testator died with a will drafted in certain terms. Equity therefore imposes a constructive trust in order to effectively enforce the promise and ensure that the proper person enjoys the benefit of the property.

Further Reading

P. Matthews, "The True Basis of the Half-Secret Trust?", [1979] Conv. 360.

T.G. Youdan, "Formalities for Trusts of Land and the Doctrine in *Rochefoucauld v. Boustead*" (1984), 43 Cambridge L.J. 306.

B. Perrins, "Secret Trusts: The Key to the *Dehors*?" [1985] Conv. 248.

P.A. Johnson, "Secret Trusts: A Look at the Basis, Method and Consequences of their Enforcement" (1985), 7 E. & T.Q. 176.

D. Wilde, "Secret and Semi-Secret Trusts: Justifying the Distinctions Between the Two" [1995] Conv. 366.

P. Critchley, "Instruments of Fraud, Testamentary Dispositions and the Doctrine of Secret Trusts" (1999), 115 L.Q. Rev. 631.

R. Chambers, "Constructive Trusts in Canada" (1999), 37 Alberta L. Rev. 173.

Notes and Questions

1. The secret trusts doctrine has been applied to *inter vivos* transactions that take effect as will substitutes. *Clauda v. Lodge*[570] is an example. Certain property was held in joint tenancy by A and B. A promised B that on B's death he would pay a certain sum out of the property to C. The court held that A's promise created an enforceable fully-secret trust since to hold otherwise would be a fraud upon B.

2. If a gift is made to more than one person, but an agreement is made with one only, the others are not necessarily bound. Whether they are depends upon whether the property is given to them as tenants in common or as joint tenants. In the latter situation, the answer also depends upon whether the communication took place before or after the will was made. In *Stead, Re*[571] Farwell J. summarized the rules on this point as follows:

---

569 The tort of negligence has been used to provide relief to a person who would have inherited property but-for a solicitor's carelessness in drafting a deceased's will. In such circumstances, the relevant duty of care is owed directly to the disappointed beneficiary: *White v. Jones*, [1995] 2 A.C. 207 (H.L.); *Earl v. Wilhelm*, 1 C.C.L.T. (3d) 215, 2000 CarswellSask 49, 183 D.L.R. (4th) 45, 2000 SKCA 1, [2000] 4 W.W.R. 363, 189 Sask. R. 71, 216 W.A.C. 71, 31 E.T.R. (2d) 193 (C.A.), leave to appeal refused (2000), 2000 CarswellSask 627, 2000 CarswellSask 628, 266 N.R. 394 (note), 213 Sask. R. 156 (note), 260 W.A.C. 156 (note) (S.C.C.). There has never been any suggestion, however, that the tort of negligence can support the imposition of a constructive trust.

570 [1952] 4 D.L.R. 570 (B.C. S.C.). Compare *Stephenson, Re*, [1939] 1 W.W.R. 278, 47 Man. R. 211, [1939] 2 D.L.R. 32, 1939 CarswellMan 17 (Q.B.), affirmed 47 Man. R. 211 at 219, [1939] 3 D.L.R. 716, 1939 CarswellMan 52, [1939] 2 W.W.R. 636 (C.A.).

571 [1900] 1 Ch. 237 at 241.

If A induces B either to make, or to leave unrevoked, a will leaving property to A and C as tenants in common, by expressly promising, or tacitly consenting, that he and C will carry out the testator's wishes, and C knows nothing of the matter until after A's death, A is bound, but C is not bound;. . . the reason stated being, that to hold otherwise would enable one beneficiary to deprive the rest of their benefits by setting up a secret trust. If, however, the gift were to A and C as joint tenants, the authorities have established a distinction between those cases in which the will is made on the faith of an antecedent promise by A and those in which the will is left unrevoked on the faith of a subsequent promise. In the former case, the trust binds both A and C,. . . the reason. . .being that no person can claim an interest under a fraud committed by another; in the latter case A and not C is bound,. . . the reason. . .being that the gift is not tainted with any fraud in procuring the execution of the will. Personally I am unable to see any difference between a gift made on the faith of an antecedent promise and a gift left unrevoked on the faith of a subsequent promise to carry out the testator's wishes; but apparently a distinction has been made by the various judges who have had to consider the question.

These rules were applied in *Blackwell v. Blackwell*[572] and *Hardy, Re.*[573]

    3. *Hardy, Re*[574] applied the rule to executors. The testator appointed A and B his executors and trustees. He directed them to convert his estate into cash and invest the proceeds. Until the death of the survivor of A and B, he directed the application of the income in a specified way and he gave the survivor a general power to appoint the corpus by will, with a gift over on failure to appoint. Before making the will, the testator told A, his lawyer and the drafter of the will, that he would tell him the appointees later and A agreed to carry out the instructions. No such instructions were ever given. A renounced his executorship and died. B then purported to appoint to members of his family and died. The court held that the power was given to A and B *virtute officii*, which meant that it was a fiduciary power, so that B could not use it for his own personal benefit, since that would be in breach of his fiduciary duties. The court also held that the testator could have given further instructions later and that B was bound by A's undertaking, since A and B as executors took jointly and the communication took place before the will. Further, the secret trust doctrine applied to the situation, since, in effect, A and B took absolutely, that being the nature of a general power of appointment, and it was a fully secret trust. In the result, therefore, B's actions in appointing to members of his family were invalid.

    4. *Hardy, Re* suggests that a secret trustee can take beneficially under a secret trust if that was intended. However, in *Rees, Re*[575] the English Court of Appeal held that this is not always so. The testator left his estate to his two executors, A and B, "absolutely, they well knowing my wishes concerning the same." B, the surviving executor, was the testator's solicitor and the drafter of, or a member of the firm that drafted, the will. He testified that the testator had told both himself and A that they were to make a number of payments to various persons and objects and keep the balance themselves. B, thus, claimed the balance as survivor. The court held that: (a) the gift, properly construed, was not a conditional gift (in which case B could have succeeded),[576] but a trust, (b) to admit B's evidence would tend to establish a conditional gift contrary to the will, (c) trustees should not place themselves in a position where their interest and duty conflict, and (d) it would be contrary to the public interest to give the property to the solicitor as drafter of the will under a secret trust.

---

572 *Supra*, note 565.
573 (1952), 29 M.P.R. 358, [1952] 2 D.L.R. 768, 1952 CarswellNS 9 (C.A.).
574 *Ibid.*
575 [1950] Ch. 204, [1949] 2 All E.R. 1003 (C.A.).
576 See *Foord, Re*, [1922] 2 Ch. 519.

Do you agree with this reasoning?

5. If a secret trust has been established in favour of a charity it may be subject to taxation even though the relevant statute exempts gifts to charities. Whether the gift is subject to tax depends upon the wording of the statute. If the statute exempts testamentary gifts to charities, the gift will be taxable if the secret trustee takes apparently absolutely on the face of the will, since the trust is regarded as not testamentary.[577]

In the United States, the courts appear to regard the trust to be testamentary at least for tax purposes.[578]

A Canadian case has held that because the secret trust beneficiaries would have been taxable if they had been named in the will, they were taxable under a statute which imposed taxes on interests passing on death.[579]

6. Legislation imposing formalities on the making of wills generally provides that a beneficial gift to a person who witnesses a will or to his or her spouse is void.[580]

A testatrix gave her entire estate to her husband, H, but continued,

> . . .it being a condition of this will that H leave the balance of my estate on his death by his will for the purposes he knows I desire it to be used for.

The testatrix had told H before making the will that she wanted him to leave $25,000 to her housekeeper, M. H was happy to oblige, but M was a witness to the will.

Is M entitled to the $25,000 after H dies?[581]

7. A is the intended beneficiary under a secret trust. He predeceases the creator of the trust, but the trustee does subsequently acquire the money. Is A's estate entitled to the property? This raises a question as to when the interest of a secret trust beneficiary vests.

The issue arose in *Gardner, Re*.[582] The textatrix drafted a will that left her estate to her husband for life (but that did not deal with the remainder interest). A short time later, she secured his promise to hold her estate for A, B and C. B, the testatrix and her husband subsequently died in that order.

A question arose as to B's entitlement. The general rule holds that a testamentary gift lapses if the donee dies before the testatrix. Romer J. nevertheless held that B's interest did not lapse, but went to her own estate, because the operative trust took effect outside the will when the husband agreed to the testatrix's proposal. (The result might have been different if the testatrix's wishes had been to benefit such of A, B and C as should survive her husband.)

Gardner, Re is a difficult decision and quite possibly wrong. A secret trust normally is thought to take effect upon death. If that is correct, then B's share should have lapsed. Romer J. avoided that problem by finding that the trust arose immediately upon the husband's assent to the testatrix's proposal. But it is difficult to see how that could be so. As we discussed in an earlier chapter with respect to the issue of constitution, a trust cannot exist until the trust property has been ascertained or rendered ascertainable.[583] That is

---

577 See *Cullen v. A-G for Ireland* (1865), L.R. 1 H.L. 190.

578 See Scott, ¶55.7.

579 See *MacMillan v. Kennedy*, [1942] 2 W.W.R. 497, [1942] 3 D.L.R. 170, 1942 CarswellAlta 44 (C.A.).

580 See, *e.g.*, *Succession Law Reform Act*, R.S.O. 1990, c. S.26, s. 12.

581 See *Young, Re* (1950), [1951] Ch. 344, [1950] 2 All E.R. 1245; *Armstrong Estate v. Weisner* (1969), 7 D.L.R. (3d) 36, 1 N.S.R. 1965-69 58 (T.D.).

582 [1920] 2 Ch. 523 (C.A.), first application; [1923] 2 Ch. 230, second application.

583 See *Beardmore Trusts, Re* (1951), [1952] 1 D.L.R. 41, 1951 CarswellOnt 304, [1951] O.W.N. 728 (H.C.).

equally true for express, resulting or constructive trusts. Of course, at the time of the agreement in *Gardner, Re*, the content of the testatrix's estate could not be known.[584]

A further problem with *Gardner, Re* is that the court's reasoning is difficult to reconcile with the orthodox view that a secret trust does not take effect until death, and therefore is revocable during the testatrix's lifetime. The testatrix can revoke the will, draft a new one, or simply scrap the agreement made with the would-be trustee. But if, as suggested in *Gardner, Re*, the trust takes effect immediately upon the creation of the agreement, then it is difficult to see how the beneficiaries' interests could later be revised or eliminated.

Regardless of B's entitlement, was the trust in *Gardner, Re* fully-secret or half-secret? Is your answer different with respect to the husband's life interest and the remainder that he obtained by way of intestacy upon the testatrix's death?

8. The general view is that secret trusts take effect upon death, but are not testamentary because they do not operate under the wills legislation. Nevertheless, secret trusts may be treated as being testamentary for some purposes. *Maddock, Re*[585] is illustrative. The testatrix left the residue of her personal estate to X and X undertook a secret trust with respect to part of it. The testatrix's debts were substantial. In those circumstances, the residuary personal estate would have to abate and, if there were more than one beneficiary of the residuary personal estate, the several gifts would abate rateably. If X sat by and said nothing, therefore, her interest would abate along with the interests of the secret trust beneficiaries. However, the court held that in these circumstances, and to prevent possible fraud by the secret trustee, the secret trust beneficiaries' interests should be treated as special legacies. Hence they would abate, but only after the general residuary personal estate (that is, X's interest) was exhausted by payment of the debts, as in fact it was.[586] Hence, to that extent the secret trust was regarded as testamentary.

9. T makes an otherwise enforceable semi-secret trust, naming A as trustee. After T's death, A makes a memorandum setting out the objects according to T's instructions and dies. Is A's statement admissible in evidence to prove the identities of the beneficiaries as an exception to the hearsay rule?[587]

(iii) *Fully-Secret Trusts*

As previously indicated, equity draws a distinction between fully-secret trusts and semi-secret trusts. Although it might be assumed that the same rules apply in each instance, there are, as we shall see, at least two substantial differences: one pertaining to the timing of communication and the other to the consequences of failure.

Both types of secret trusts require proof of three elements: (i) communication by the testator to the trustee regarding the intended trust, (ii) acceptance of the

---

584 An attempt might be made to interpret the agreement in *Gardner, Re* as an agreement to constitute a trust in the future (*i.e.* upon the testatrix's death). That approach, however, raises another difficulty, also discussed in an earlier chapter, regarding the enforcement of covenants.

585 [1902] 2 Ch. 220 (C.A.).

586 On the principles of abatement, see Oosterhoff, *Wills*, pp. 499ff.

587 See *Gardner's Will Trusts, Re*, [1936] 3 All E.R. 938; and see Comment (1937), 15 Can. Bar Rev. 101.

trust by the trustee, and (iii) the timing of those communications.[588] All three elements demand further attention.

First, the testator (or an agent[589]) must inform the trustee of the proposed secret trust. In that respect, it is important to revisit the distinction, encountered in an earlier chapter, between words imposing an obligation to hold property on behalf of another person and mere precatory words, which express a desire or hope, but which are not intended to impose an obligation. A trust is possible in the former situation, but not the latter.[590]

Second, the trustee must have agreed to hold the property on trust for the beneficiaries. Actual acceptance obviously will suffice, but so too will silent acquiescence.[591]

Third, the parties' agreement must have occurred before the testator's death. Because the rule for semi-secret trusts is different, it bears emphasizing that the agreement for a fully-secret trust need not have occurred before the will was drafted. In terms of the content of the agreement, it appears to be sufficient for the testator to secure the trustee's general assent to a trust. As long as such an agreement exists, it is acceptable for the testator to hand the trustee a sealed letter containing the details of the trust, along with instructions to open the letter upon death.[592] "[A] ship which sails under sealed orders is sailing under orders though the exact terms are not ascertained by the captain till later."[593] In contrast, it is not sufficient for the testator, having secured the trustee's assent to some vague plan, to subsequently formulate the details and reduce them to writing. Nor is it sufficient for the testator to merely inform the trustee where to find a letter upon death, without securing agreement to the proposed trust.[594] In that situation, there is no agreement prior to death.

Re Boyes[595] illustrates these principles. The testator appointed his friend and solicitor, Carritt, his sole executor and gave all his estate to him absolutely. The testator had told Carritt that he wanted him to hold the property according to directions that he would communicate by letter. Carritt agreed to do so. Unfortunately, the testator never gave Carritt further directions. After the testator's death, two letters were found written by him in which he directed that substantially

---

588 *Champoise v. Champoise-Prost Estate*, 33 E.T.R. (2d) 213, 2000 CarswellBC 1405, [2000] B.C.J. No. 1364, 2000 BCCA 426, 77 B.C.L.R. (3d) 228, 140 B.C.A.C. 112, 229 W.A.C. 112 (C.A.).

589 *Moss v. Cooper* (1861), 1 John & H. 352.

590 See *Irvine v. Sullivan* (1869), L.R. 8 Eq. 673; *Spencer's Will, Re* (1887), 57 L.T. 519; *Glasspool v. Glasspool Estate* (1999), 25 E.T.R. (2d) 8, 1999 CarswellBC 151, [1999] B.C.J. No. 172, 1999 BCCA 30 (C.A.).; *Milsom v. Holien* (2001), 40 E.T.R. (2d) 77, 2001 CarswellBC 1545, 2001 BCSC 868 (S.C.); *Brynelsen Estate v. Verdeck* (2002), 44 E.T.R. (2d) 26, 2002 CarswellBC 530, 2002 BCCA 187, 165 B.C.A.C. 279, 270 W.A.C. 279 (C.A.).

591 See *Russell v. Jackson* (1852), 10 Hare 204, 68 E.R. 900; *Charlton v. Cipperley* (1984), 32 Alta. L.R. (2d) 289, 19 E.T.R. 66, 12 D.L.R. (4th) 582, 54 A.R. 269, 1984 CarswellAlta 90 (C.A.).

592 *Boyes, Re, supra*, note 565; *Keen, Re*, [1937] Ch. 236, [1937] 1 All E.R. 452 (C.A.).

593 *Keen, Re, ibid.*, at 242.

594 *McCormick v. Grogan, supra*, note 566.

595 *Supra*, note 565.

all the property should go to Mrs. Brown. The testator's next of kin brought action for a declaration that they were entitled to the estate. The court held that the testator could not evade the *Statute of Wills*[596] by imposing a trust upon his devisee or legatee unless he communicated the objects to him before his death.

If the requirements for a secret trust are not met, the would-be trustee often is entitled to take the property absolutely.[597] That is true, for instance, if the testator failed to communicate the desire for a fully-secret trust, or if, having been informed of such a desire, the would-be trustee refused to participate in the arrangement. In such circumstances, the property need not be held on trust for the beneficiaries, nor need it be returned to the deceased's estate.[598] There are two, related explanations for that rule. First, since the trust is fully-secret, it receives no mention in the will. Consequently, there is nothing outwardly fraudulent in the would-be trustee's beneficial retention of the property. Second, if the testator did not receive the would-be trustee's assent to the proposed trust, it is natural to presume, given the terms of the will, that the gift was intended to take effect absolutely. If the testator did not want that result to occur, he or she should have re-drafted the will before passing away.[599] Of course, there may be situations in which neither of those explanations is entirely convincing (*e.g.* where the testator died very shortly after the would-be trustee rejected the proposed trust, or where the testator erroneously believed that the would-be trustee had agreed to the proposed trust).

In some circumstances, however, the would-be trustee is not entitled to retain the property beneficially. As *Boyes, Re* illustrated, that is true if, for instance, the testator secured assent to a general plan, but never supplied the details. In that situation, it is clear that neither party contemplated an absolute gift, with the result that the would-be trustee must return the property to the estate.

The fully-secret trust is examined further in *Ottaway v. Norman*,[600] reproduced below.

OTTAWAY v. NORMAN

(1971), [1972] Ch. 698, [1972] 2 W.L.R. 50, [1971] 3 All E.R. 1325
Chancery Division

Harry Ottaway devised his house and contents to Miss Hodges upon her agreement to devise them to the plaintiffs, his son and daughter-in-law.

The testator died in 1963. Miss Hodges made a will in which she left the house and its contents to the defendant, Mr. Norman, and his wife, "or to such of them as survive me and if both survive me as joint tenants beneficially." She left

---

596 7 Will. 4 & 1 Vict., c. 26 (1837).
597 *Wallgrave v. Tebbs* (1855) 20 J.P. 84; *Proby v. Landor* (1860), 28 Beav. 540, 54 E.R. 460.
598 *Boyes, Re, supra*, note 565; *McCormick v. Grogan, supra*, note 566.
599 *Hayman v. Nicoll*, [1944] S.C.R. 253, [1944] 3 D.L.R. 551 (S.C.C.).
600 (1971), [1972] Ch. 698, [1972] 2 W.L.R. 50, [1971] 3 All E.R. 1325 (Ch.).

the residue of her estate equally to the plaintiffs and the defendant and his wife, and named the defendant as her executor.

The plaintiffs brought this action against Miss Hodges' estate, claiming that, because of her promise to the testator, Miss Hodges held the house, its contents and the residue of the testator's estate on constructive trust for them.

BRIGHTMAN J.:

It will be convenient to call the person upon whom such a trust is imposed the "primary donee" and the beneficiary under that trust the "secondary donee." The essential elements which must be proved to exist are: (i) the intention of the testator to subject the primary donee to an obligation in favour of the secondary donee; (ii) communication of that intention to the primary donee; and (iii) the acceptance of that obligation by the primary donee either expressly or by acquiescence. It is immaterial whether these elements precede or succeed the will of the donor. I am informed that there is no recent reported case where the obligation imposed on the primary donee is an obligation to make a will in favour of the secondary donee as distinct from some other form of *inter vivos* transfer. But it does not seem to me that there can really be any distinction which can validly be taken on behalf of the defendant in the present case. The basis of the doctrine of the secret trust is the obligation imposed on the conscience of the primary donee and it does not seem to me that there is any materiality in the machinery by which the donor intends that that obligation shall be carried out.

Mr. Buckle, for Mr. Norman, relied strongly on *McCormick v. Grogan*.[601] In that case, the testator in 1851 had left all his property by a three line will to his friend Mr. Grogan. In 1854 the testator was struck down by cholera. With only a few hours to live he sent for Mr. Grogan. He told Mr. Grogan in effect that his will and a letter would be found in his desk. The letter named various intended beneficiaries and the intended gifts to them. The letter concluded with the words:

I do not wish you to act strictly on the foregoing instructions, but leave it entirely to your own good judgment to do as you think I would, if living, and as the parties are deserving.

An intended beneficiary whom Mr. Grogan thought it right to exclude sued.

[Brightman J. then quoted part of the extract from Lord Westbury in *McCormick v. Grogan* that appeared above in connection with the "wrongdoing" explanation of the constructive trust, and continued:]

Founding himself on Lord Westbury, Mr. Buckle sought at one stage to deploy an argument that a person could never succeed in establishing a secret trust unless he could show that the primary donee was guilty of deliberate and conscious wrong doing of which he said there was no evidence in the case before me. That proposition, if correct, would lead to the surprising result that if the

---

601 *Supra*, note 566.

primary donee faithfully observed the obligation imposed on him there would not ever have been a trust at any time in existence. The argument was discarded, and I think rightly. Mr. Buckle then fastened on the words "clearest and most indisputable evidence" and he submitted that an exceptionally high standard of proof was needed to establish a secret trust. I do not think that Lord Westbury's words means more than this: that if a will contains gift which is in terms absolute, clear evidence is needed before the court will assume that the testator did not mean what he said. It is perhaps analogous to the standard of proof which this court requires before it will rectify a written instrument, for there again a party is saying that neither meant what they have written.

[His Lordship then reviewed the evidence and the arguments thereon and continued:]

Having heard the evidence I have no doubt in my mind that I have received an accurate account of all essential facts from William and Mrs. Dorothy Ottaway (the plaintiffs). I find as a fact that Mr. Harry Ottaway intended that Miss Hodges should be obliged to dispose of the bungalow in favour of the plaintiffs at her death; that Mr. Harry Ottaway communicated that intention to Miss Hodges; and that Miss Hodges accepted the obligation. I find the same facts in relation to the furniture, fixtures and fittings which passed to Miss Hodges under clause 4 of Mr. Harry Ottaway's will. I am not satisfied that any similar obligation was imposed and accepted as regards any contents of the bungalow which had not devolved on Miss Hodges under clause 4 of Mr. Harry Ottaway's will.

I turn to the question of money. In cross-examination William said the trust extended to the house, furniture and money:

> Everything my father left to Miss Hodges was to be in the trust. The trust comprised the lot. She could use the money as she liked. She had to leave my wife and me whatever money was left.

In cross-examination Mrs. Dorothy Ottaway said that her understanding was that Miss Hodges was bound to make a will giving her and her husband the bungalow, contents and any money she had left. "She could please herself about the money. She did not have to save it for us. She was free to spend it." It seems to me that two questions arise. First, as a matter of fact, what did the parties intend should be comprised in Miss Hodges's obligation? All money which Miss Hodges had at her death including both money which she had acquired before Mr. Harry Ottaway's death and money she acquired after his death from all sources? Or, only money acquired under Mr. Harry Ottaway's will? Secondly, as a matter of law, if such an obligation existed would it create a valid trust? On the second question I am content to assume for present purposes but without so deciding that if property is given to the primary donee on the understanding that the primary donee will dispose by his will of such assets, if any, as he may have at his command at his death in favour of the secondary donee, a valid trust is created in favour of the secondary donee which is in suspense during the lifetime of the primary donee, but attaches to the estate of the primary donee at the moment of the latter's death.

There would seem to be at least some support for this proposition in an Australian case to which I was referred.[602] I accept that the parties mentioned money on at least some occasions when they talked about Mr. Harry Ottaway's intentions for the future disposition of Ashcroft. I do not, however, find sufficient evidence that it was the intention of Mr. Harry Ottaway that Miss Hodges should be compelled to leave all her money, from whatever source derived, to the plaintiffs. This would seem to preclude her giving even a small pecuniary legacy to any friend or relative. I do not think it is clear that Mr. Harry Ottaway intended to extract any such far-reaching undertaking from Miss Hodges or that she intended to accept such a wide obligation herself. Therefore the obligation, if any, is in my view, to be confined to money derived under Mr. Harry Ottaway's will. If the obligation is confined to money derived under Mr. Harry Ottaway's will, the obligation is meaningless and unworkable unless it includes the requirement that she shall keep such money separate and distinct from her own money. I am certain that no such requirement was ever discussed or intended. If she had the right to mingle her own money with that derived from Mr. Harry Ottaway, there would be no ascertainable property upon which the trust could bite at her death. . . .

There is another difficulty. Does money in this context include only cash or cash and investments, or all movable property of any description? The evidence is quite inconclusive. In my judgment the plaintiffs' claim succeeds in relation to the bungalow and in relation to the furniture, fixtures and fittings which devolved under paragraph 4 of Mr. Harry Ottaway's will subject, of course, to normal wastage, fair wear and tear, but not to any other assets.

Notes and Questions

1. Brightman J.'s *dictum* in *Ottaway v. Norman* that the standard of proof in secret trusts cases "is perhaps analogous to the standard of proof which this court requires before it will rectify a written instrument" was not followed by Megarry V.C. in *Re Snowden*.[603]

2. Brightman J. also stated in *dictum* that if property is given to A on the understanding that A may use it, but must dispose of whatever is left at A's death to B, there may be a valid trust for B which is in suspense while A is living.

Is such a trust possible? Is there certainty of trust property? Is such certainty required? Does this mean that the trust cannot be express, but can be constructive?

3. A testator left a legacy to A absolutely, A having undertaken with the testator that he would hold it on trust for B. Subsequently, the testator increased the legacy, but did not inform A of the increase. Is the secret trust enforceable in whole or in part?[604]

4. A testator made his will and appointed E his executor. Later, he told E that he left some property to him in the will because he wanted E to discharge some of the testator's obligations secretly. E agreed to do so. The testator wrote the names of the beneficiaries in a letter addressed to E, which he put in a locked box with the will and gave the key to the box to E. Is E obliged to carry out his undertaking?[605]

---

602   *Birmingham v. Renfrew* (1937), 57 C.L.R. 666 (Austr. H.C.).
603   *Supra*, note 567.
604   See *Colin Cooper, Re*, [1939] Ch. 811.
605   See *McDonald v. Moran* (1938), 12 M.P.R. 424 (P.E.I.).

5. By her will, a testatrix appointed her solicitor and long-time friend her executor and trustee, and directed him to "pay, transfer and deliver all the residue of my estate to my said Executor to deal with as he may in his discretion decide upon." Before the will was executed, the testatrix told the solicitor that he was to distribute the residue under that clause to three persons. After the will was executed, he learned the names of the three persons. Were the elements of a secret trust established?[606]

(iv) *Semi-Secret Trusts*

As previously noted, a will containing a semi-secret trust reveals that the legatee is to take as trustee, but does not disclose the objects of the trust. Superficially, at least, the requirements for a semi-secret trust are the same as those that govern a fully-secret trust — *i.e.* (i) communication by the testator, (ii) acceptance by the trustee, and (iii) timeliness of communications. There is, however, an important difference with respect to the third requirement.

The courts have held, illogically, that while the parties' agreement must occur before the testator's death in the case of a fully-secret trust, it must occur before the drafting of the will in the case of a semi-secret trust. That distinction is based upon *dicta* in *Blackwell v. Blackwell*[607] and *Keen, Re*.[608] In the first of these cases Viscount Sumner said:[609]

> The limits, beyond which the rules as to unspecified trusts must not be carried, have often been discussed. A testator cannot reserve to himself a power of making future unwitnessed dispositions by merely naming a trustee and leaving the purposes of the trust to be supplied afterwards, nor can a legatee give testamentary validity to an unexecuted codicil by accepting an indefinite trust, never communicated to him in the testator's lifetime. . . . To hold otherwise would indeed be to enable the testator to "give the go-by" to the requirements of the *Wills Act*,[610] because he did not choose to comply with them. It is communication of the purpose to the legatee, coupled with acquiescence or promise on his part, that removes the matter from the provision of the Wills Act and brings it within the law of trusts, as applied in this instance to trustees, who happen also to be legatees.

In drawing that distinction, the court confused the imposition of a constructive trust with the doctrine of incorporation by reference. That doctrine permits a testator to incorporate an unattested document into a will if: (i) the document is in existence when the will is executed, (ii) the will refers to it as an existing document, and (iii) the document is sufficiently described so that it can be identified.[611] If these conditions are satisfied, a court of probate can grant probate of the will and the incorporated document. The doctrine precludes admission of an informal document which the testator describes as one yet to be made, because

---

606 See *Jankowski v. Pelek Estate* (1995), 10 E.T.R. (2d) 117, 1995 CarswellMan 447, [1996] 2 W.W.R. 457, 131 D.L.R. (4th) 717, 107 Man. R. (2d) 167, 109 W.A.C. 167 (C.A.).

607 *Supra*, note 565.

608 *Supra*, note 592.

609 *Supra*, note 565, at 339.

610 7 Will. 4 & 1 Vict., c. 26 (1837).

611 See, *e.g.*, *Allen v. Maddock* (1858), 11 Moo. P.C. 427, 14 E.R. 757 (P.C.); *Warren, Re* (1930), 38 O.W.N. 358 (H.C.); *Poole, Re*, [1929] 1 D.L.R. 418 (P.E.I. S.C.).

to admit it would allow the testator to change the will without complying with the statutory formalities.[612] If the will is unclear on whether an existing or future document is contemplated, but is construed as referring to a future document only, evidence to show that the document was in existence when the will was made is inadmissible, because such evidence would contradict the will.[613] This issue is explored further in *Mihalopulos, Re*,[614] reproduced below.

The doctrine of incorporation by reference has no necessary connection with semi-secret trusts.[615] Although semi-secret trusts frequently involve the use of documents, they may also arise from entirely oral communications between the testator and the trustee. The constructive trusts associated with semi-secret trusts, like those associated with fully-secret trusts, consequently arise not on the basis of incorporated documents, but rather on the basis of equity's two-fold desire to perfect the parties' shared intention and protect the testator's detrimental reliance. In either instance, the constructive trust arises outside the will.[616]

Moreover, if the concern underlying the timing requirement for semi-secret trusts is thought to arise from the need to respect the provisions of the wills legislation, it is curious that a different, more lenient rule applies for fully-secret trusts. If anything, fully-secret trusts seem to flout the statutory requirements even more egregiously. They conceal not only the beneficiaries' identity, but also the very existence of a trust.

A second distinction between fully-secret and semi-secret trusts pertains to the consequences of failure. As previously mentioned, if a fully-secret trust fails, the would-be trustee often is allowed to retain the property beneficially. A contrary rule applies in connection with semi-secret trusts. Since the will, on its face, reveals that the property was to be obtained on trust, and not beneficially, the would-be trustee cannot keep the property. The asset returns instead to the estate.[617]

MIHALOPULOS, RE

(1956), 19 W.W.R. 118, 5 D.L.R. (2d) 628, 1956 CarswellAlta 37
Alberta Supreme Court
[Trial Division]

John Mihalopulos had assets in Canada and in Greece. By his will he appointed separate executors for these assets. He directed his Canadian executors

---

612 See *Currie, Re* (1978), (sub nom. *Labatt v. Minister of National Revenue*) 21 O.R. (2d) 709, 3 E.T.R. 196, 91 D.L.R. (3d) 559, 1978 CarswellOnt 522 (H.C.).

613 *Keen, Re*, *supra*, note 592. See further Oosterhoff, *Wills*, p. 141.

614 (1956), 19 W.W.R. 118, 5 D.L.R. (2d) 628, 1956 CarswellAlta 37 (T.D.).

615 It is possible to argue a case on the basis of incorporation by reference and in the alternative on the basis of semi-secret trust, as shown below in *Mihalopulos, Re*.

616 See *Blackwell*, *supra*, note 565.

617 *Keen*, *supra*, note 592.

to convert his Canadian assets into cash and to pay the cash to his Greek executors as trustees. The latter were instructed by the will as follows:

> 4 (g) And the remainder of my said Canadian Estate shall be distributed by my said trustees to such charities as they will find designated by me to share in this bequest among my papers.

After the testator's death, an unsigned document written in Greek in the testator's handwriting was found among his effects. It was dated the same date as the will and directed the Greek executors to apply the money for certain specified charitable and philanthropic purposes in Greece.

The two witnesses and the surviving Canadian executor deposed that they did not know that the document was in existence when the will was made and one of the witnesses stated that from what the testator said to him at the time it was not in existence.

An application was made by the executors for advice and directions.

EGBERT J.:

> [His Lordship noted that while a holograph document can be a valid codicil to an attested will, the document could not so operate in this case because it was unsigned. He continued:]

The question then is, whether, by virtue of para. 4(g) of the will, the document in question was incorporated into and became part of the will itself.

It seems clear from the authorities that if a document is to be deemed as having been incorporated into a will, two conditions must be satisfied. (1) It must be clear that the testator in the will referred to some document then in existence; and (2), the document in question must be beyond doubt the document referred to.[618] As to the first of these conditions the affidavits. . .show that neither the witnesses to the will nor the executors knew of the existence of the document in question, and Mr. Vallance goes so far as to say that at the time of the execution of the will it was his understanding and belief, induced from information given to him by the testator, that he had not written any other document at that time. I think it is clear that the onus is on the person seeking to have incorporated some other documents into a will to prove compliance with the above conditions.[619] Here no such proof is submitted, and such evidence as is available indicates that the document in question did not exist at the time of the execution of the will. As to the second condition, it will be observed that by the wording of para. 4(g) of the will no particular document is referred to by the testator — the Greek trustees are to distribute the remainder of the Canadian estate "to such charities as they will find designated by me to share in this bequest among my papers". It would

---

618 *Jarman on Wills*, 8th ed., p. 154; *Re Watkins* (1865), L.R. 1 P. & D. 19; *Allen v. Maddock, supra,* note 611; *Singleton v. Tomlinson* (1878), 3 App. Cas. 404; *Re Smart,* [1902] P. 238; *University College of North Wales v. Taylor,* [1908] P. 140; *Smart v. Prujean* (1801), 6 Ves. 560, 31 E.R. 1195.

619 *Singleton, ibid.*

appear that the testator was referring to some written document that would be found among his other papers, but there is nothing to indicate that such document was then in existence, and nothing by which the particular document — if there were more than one — could be identified. It will be observed that the document in question consists of five numbered paragraphs, and then follows the number "6" with no writing after it. It would appear as if the deceased had intended to write something further but had never completed the document. In any event, there is nothing in the will to identify this particular document as the "designation" there referred to.

In my view, the document fails to satisfy either of the requisite conditions above set forth — there is no evidence that it was in existence at the time of the execution of the will — in fact, the available evidence is to the contrary — and it cannot be said that the document is beyond doubt the document referred to in the will. There is no doubt in my mind that the testator attempted and intended to reserve to himself the right to make future unattested dispositions of trust property which, prior to the present provisions of the *Wills Act*[620] as to holograph instruments, would have been impossible.[621] It might, by virtue of the aforesaid provisions, have been possible for him to do so through the medium of a signed but unattested document which would operate as a holograph codicil. But certainly he could not do so by means of a document both unsigned and unattested.

Counsel for the Greek executors. . .urges that the question before the Court cannot be determined without hearing further evidence as to whether or not the document was in existence before the will was executed, and that for the purpose of determining this question of its pre-existence parol evidence is admissible. . . . In *Allen v. Maddock*[622] it was made clear that parol evidence will be excluded where it is clear that the document is not in existence at the time of the making of the will, or where the description is so vague as to be incapable of being applied to any instrument in particular. In this case the description of the instrument contained in the will is, in my view, too vague to be applicable to any particular instrument, and so under the rule laid down in *Allen v. Maddock* parol evidence on the question of the time when the instrument came into existence is inadmissible. . . . Whether or not parol evidence is admissible, there is no suggestion that any parol evidence is available which would establish that the document was in existence at the time of the making of the will.

. . .

There is another ground on which it was suggested that effect could be given to the document, namely, that it created a valid and effective trust. The Courts have on occasion invoked the doctrine of trusts in order to prevent the provisions of the *Wills Act*[623] from protecting a fraud, *e.g.*, where a testator leaves property absolutely to a legatee on a secret trust communicated to and accepted by the legatee. No such situation arises here; there is no suggestion that anyone is

---

620 R.S.A. 1942, c. 210.
621 *Blackwell v. Blackwell, supra*, note 565, at 330.
622 (1858), 11 Moo. P.C. 427, 14 E.R. 757 (P.C.).
623 *Supra*, note 620.

attempting to perpetrate a fraud; nor is there any evidence that the terms of the document in question were ever communicated to or accepted by anyone. Certainly they were not communicated to the Canadian executors nor to the witnesses to the will, and there is no evidence that they were communicated to the Greek trustees. In *Johnson v. Ball*,[624] it was attempted to create certain trusts by a letter signed subsequent to the execution of the will. The Vice-Chancellor pointed out that it was impossible to give effect to the letter as a declaration of trust since that would admit the document as part of the will. He pointed out the difference between these circumstances and the case where the will refers to a trust created by the testator by communication with the legatee antecedent to or contemporaneously with the will.

> [His Lordship then quoted the excerpt from Viscount Sumner's speech in *Blackwell v. Blackwell*[625] already set out and continued:]

In my view it is clear from the evidence that the document in question was written by the testator after the execution of the will. It is argued, however, that despite this the trust attempted to be set up by the document may, in fact, have been set up in some other way by the testator prior to the execution of the will, and have at that time been communicated to and accepted by the trustees, and that accordingly an opportunity should be given to the Greek trustees to establish this if it is the fact.

Not only do I doubt very much if the Greek trustees could furnish such evidence, but in the light of the decision in *Re Keen*,[626] I am of the opinion that the evidence would not, in any event, be helpful. In that case a testator by his will gave to his trustees the sum of £10,000

> . . .to be held upon trust and disposed of by them among such person, persons, or charities as may be notified by me to them or either of them during my lifetime.

The testator had on the execution of an earlier will containing a similar clause told one of his trustees that he desired to provide for a person whose name was to be kept secret, and that he had written the name and address of the proposed beneficiary on a sheet of paper enclosed in a sealed envelope which he handed to the trustee to be kept with his will and not opened until after his death. No further communication was ever made regarding the envelope by the testator. After his death it was opened and found to contain a paper bearing the words "£10,000 to G". The Court of Appeal held that on the true construction of the will it reserved power to the testator to dispose of his property by a future unattested disposition contrary to the provisions of the *Wills Act*[627] and that the trust sought to be established by parol evidence was one inconsistent with the terms of the will, the notification of it to the trustee being anterior to the will. The trust therefore failed

---

624 (1851), 5 De G. & Sm. 85, 64 E.R. 1029.
625 *Supra*, note 565, at 339.
626 *Supra*, note 592.
627 7 Will. 4 & 1 Vict., c. 26 (1837).

and the legacy fell into residue. Lord Wright M.R. in the course of his judgment, and after having referred to the conditions on which parol evidence is admissible to supplement the terms of a will, pointed out that in this case the trust sought to be established by parol evidence would be inconsistent with the express terms of the will.[628]

> In the present case, while clause 5 refers solely to a future definition or to future definitions of the trust subsequent to the date of the will, the sealed letter relied on as notifying the trust was communicated. . .before the date of the will. . . . [T]he notification sought to be put in evidence was anterior to the will and hence not within the language of clause 5, and inadmissible simply on that ground as being inconsistent with what the will prescribes.

In this case, as in the *Keen* case, the will, in my opinion clearly contemplates a future notification of the trust. Reading the will as a whole, and reading it in the light of the evidence as to the non-existence of the designation of trust at the time of execution of the will, there seems no doubt that the will contemplated a future designation and so as in the *Keen* case, was an attempt to reserve to the testator a power to make future disposition of his property by unattested and unsigned instruments, contrary to the provisions of the *Wills Act*. Moreover since the will contemplates some future designation of the trust, and the parol evidence suggested would be of an anterior designation, as in the *Keen* case, such evidence must be excluded as being inconsistent with what the will provides.

Notes and Questions

1. Suppose that the will did not refer in terms to an antecedent or a future communication, nor to whether it would be in writing or oral. Instead there was an oral communication after the will and before the testator's death, which the trustee accepted. What is the result?

2. We discussed the problem of precatory language in connection with fully-secret trusts. A similar problem may arise in connection with semi-secret trusts. *Hayman v. Nicoll*[629] is instructive. The testatrix bequeathed money to her daughter Ina, "in full confidence that she will dispose of the same in accordance with the wishes I have expressed to her." Ina died without having disclosed the trust and apparently without carrying out her mother's wishes, whatever they may have been. Her brothers and sisters then brought action for a declaration that Ina's administrator held the money upon a resulting trust for the testatrix' estate. The Supreme Court of Canada held that the will did not create a semi-secret trust, because the testatrix had used precatory words, while other parts of the will demonstrated that she knew how to create an express trust by imperative language. Hence, Ina took absolutely. On the question whether there was communication and acceptance of a fully-secret trust, the court held that there was insufficient evidence to establish either.[630]

3. In certain circumstances, the probate doctrine of republication may save a gift referred to in an unattested document that was not in existence when the will, which purports to incorporate it, was made. Since the cases apply incorporation by reference principles to semi-secret trusts, the same result obtains in the latter context. The doctrine

---

628 *Supra*, at Ch. 248.
629 *Supra*, note 599.
630 See also *Donovan v. Donovan* (1920), 18 O.W.N. 318, to the same effect.

of republication runs as follows. Absent a contrary intention, when a testator makes a codicil to his or her will, the will is republished, so that it notionally takes a new date — *i.e.* the date of the codicil. Consequently, if the will referred to an existing document to be incorporated, but that document was not, in fact, in existence when the will was made, but came into existence before the date of the codicil, the document can be incorporated. On the other hand, if the will refers to a future document, evidence cannot be admitted to prove that the document was in fact in existence when the codicil was made, since this would contradict the will.[631]

4. Secret trusts are used on occasion to fund pre-existing *inter vivos* trusts. *Johnson Estate, Re*[632] is illustrative. The testator gave money to the University of British Columbia upon trust to help students obtain university educations. By a codicil to his will, he left the residue of his estate to the university "to be added to the trust created by me in my lifetime." Technically this was a "pour-over trust." However, the court treated it as a secret trust (apparently fully-secret, since the court spoke of a communication before death, not before the will was made), on the ground that the testator had communicated his intentions to the university during his lifetime and the University's officers had agreed to his scheme. (In fact, the communication took place before the date of the codicil.)

It is submitted that if the doctrine of secret trusts applied, it was a semi-secret trust, but that the doctrine need not have been used at all. Instead, the trust could have been treated as a referential or pour-over trust. A pour-over trust is a device whereby a testator funds an existing *inter vivos* trust by means of a testamentary disposition. In other words, he or she "pours over" money or other property from the will into the existing trust. The trust need not be one made by the testator. A referential trust is a device by which a testator incorporates an existing trust (whether *inter vivos* or testamentary, and whether created by the testator or someone else) into the will. When that occurs, the trust becomes, to the extent that the testator funds it, testamentary. By contrast, under the pour-over doctrine, the *inter vivos* trust is not incorporated in the will and does not become testamentary. The implications of this will be discussed shortly.

5. When there is a gift by will to a trust, the courts normally treat the matter as involving the doctrine of incorporation by reference — *i.e.* they seek to incorporate the trust into the will. A problem may then arise if the trust is not yet in existence. This occurred in *Currie, Re*.[633] A testatrix, domiciled in Ontario, in an attempt to avoid Ontario succession duties, bequeathed securities to a trust situated in Alberta if it should be in existence at the time of her death. In fact, the trust did not come into existence until two days after the date of the testamentary disposition, so that the attempt failed.

6. Another problem is that an *inter vivos* trust may be revocable or subject to change. In that case, an issue may arise as to whether the testator was attempting to reserve a power to change the will by unattested codicil. That issue arose in a trio of English cases, *Jones, Re*,[634] *Edwards' Will Trusts, Re*[635] and *Schintz' Will Trusts, Re*.[636]

Jones, Re was the first case. The testator left a legacy to the trustees of an *inter vivos* trust previously established by him with nominal funding, "or any substitution therefor or modification thereof or addition thereto which I may hereafter execute." The power of revocation prevented the incorporation of the existing trust, as well as admission of

---

631 *Smart, Re, supra*, note 618; *Keen, Re, supra*, note 592.
632 (1961), 30 D.L.R. (2d) 474 (B.C. S.C.).
633 *Supra*, note 612.
634 [1942] Ch. 328.
635 [1948] Ch. 440, [1948] 1 All E.R. 821 (C.A.).
636 [1951] Ch. 870, [1951] 1 All E.R. 1095.

evidence tending to show that the trust had not, in fact, been amended. *Quaere* the result if the will had said instead, "unless I substitute another trust."[637]

Edwards' Will Trusts, Re distinguished *Jones, Re*. The will gave property to the trustees of the existing trust "so far as [it is] subsisting and capable of taking effect." Clause 2 of the *inter vivos* trust enabled the settlor to name the beneficiaries by signed memorandum, while clause 3 provided that subject to clause 2 the trust fund should be held upon trust for specified persons. The court held that the trust was properly identified and could, thus, be incorporated. However, clause 2 could not be given effect as far as the testamentary addition to the trust was concerned, since it reserved to the testator the power to make unattested alterations to his will. However, clause 3 was not objectionable and the bequest could, thus, be held upon its trusts.

Schintz' Will Trusts, Re followed *Edwards*. The *inter vivos* trust reserved a power to the settlor to declare new trusts for his wife, children and other relatives, but not for himself, "and for that purpose wholly or partially to revoke and make void the trusts. . ." The subsequent will created a testamentary trust for the settlor's issue, but required the interest of one child to be transferred to the trustees of the *inter vivos* trust upon the trusts thereof "and upon the deed or deeds (if any) which may hereafter be executed by me under the power of revocation and declaration of new trusts thereby reserved to me. . ." The court held, unconvincingly, we submit, that, as in *Edwards*, the existing trust could be incorporated, although the clause reserving a power to revoke was invalid for the purpose of the will. The court reached this conclusion by holding the testator's language to be merely descriptive of the *inter vivos* trust and not an attempt to incorporate either the existing document, or whatever amendment might be substituted for it in future, and because the *inter vivos* trust reserved only a limited power to revoke, instead of an unlimited one as in *Jones*.

7. The problem with the referential trusts cases is that they defeat the testator's intention. In virtually all of these cases, one suspects that the testator did not at all intend to give the *inter vivos* trust testamentary effect.[638] He or she simply wanted to pour over funds from the estate into the previously created and nominally funded trust.

The doctrine that should be used to give effect to such attempts is not the secret trusts doctrine, nor the doctrine of incorporation by reference (unless it is clear that the testator intends the trust to be incorporated), but rather the probate doctrine of facts of independent significance. This doctrine permits the court to admit extrinsic evidence to identify the object or subject matter of a testamentary gift. Thus, for example, if a testator devises "my farm" to "my farmhand," evidence to identify the property and the beneficiary is admissible. Both are facts of independent significance, for even though the testator may have changed farms and farm hands since he made his will, he or she probably did not do so in order to change the will.[639] In the same way, an existing *inter vivos* trust is a fact of independent significance. While the Canadian courts use the doctrine to identify property and beneficiaries, they have not used it to identify existing trusts. In the United States, the

---

637 See *Jones, Re, supra*, note 634, at 331, *per* Simonds J.

638 It should be noted that the *inter vivos* trust remains effective as such. Only to the extent that it is funded by the will does it become testamentary. However, the fact that the trust remains an *inter vivos* institution to the extent that it was funded other than by will is usually academic, since the object of the scheme is to establish the trust with nominal funding and to feed it from the estate with substantial funds when the testator no longer has need of the money and at a time when he or she is likely to have amassed sufficient moneys to give practical effect to the earlier *inter vivos* trust.

639 See, *e.g.*, *Stubbs v. Sargon* (1837), 2 Keen. 255, 48 E.R. 626.

courts do so in order to allow the pour-over trust to work. Moreover, many American courts have applied the doctrine to situations in which the trust was revocable and was, in fact, amended. In some states which have difficulty with the latter step, legislation has overcome the problem.[640] Legislation to this effect was also promulgated in Canada[641] by the Conference of Commissioners on Uniformity of Legislation.[642] To date it has been adopted only in one jurisdiction,[643] but is likely to be adopted in others.

The legislation permits a testator to transfer property to the trustees of an *inter vivos* trust created by the testator or another person, or a testamentary trust made by a person who has predeceased the testator. The fact that the trust is revocable, or was amended after the date of the testator's will or his or her death, is irrelevant. Further, the property transferred becomes part of the trust to which it is paid and is not held under a testamentary trust created by the testator, unless the will says otherwise.

8. The difference between recognizing an *inter vivos* trust and recognizing a testamentary trust may be significant. Consider a situation in which a beneficiary predeceases the testator. If the trust has been incorporated into the will so that it becomes testamentary, the gift to the beneficiary (to the extent conferred by the will) lapses — *i.e.* it fails and does not go to the beneficiary's estate, unless the testator has provided otherwise by a substitutionary gift to the beneficiary's estate, or unless the beneficiary falls within the class of close relations of the testator in respect of whom a statutory anti-lapse provision applies.[644] By contrast, if the will is regarded as transferring property to an existing trust, as in *Playfair, Re*,[645] so that the *inter vivos* trust does not become testamentary, the fact that a beneficiary under the *inter vivos* trust dies after the trust was created but before the testator, does not invalidate the poured-over gift. The beneficiary's estate will be entitled to it.[646]

---

640 See Scott, ¶¶54.1, 56.4, 358. The reverse situation, namely where *inter vivos* funds are poured over into a testamentary trust, is common in Canada in the context of life insurance. Thus, for example, the proceeds of a policy of insurance on the testator's life and owned by her or him may be poured over into a trust created by the will. See, *e.g.*, the *Insurance Act*, R.S.O. 1990, c. I.8, ss. 190-193. And see *Succession Law Reform Act*, R.S.O. 1990, c. S.26, Part III, respecting the designation of beneficiaries under pension plans.

641 See *Uniform Testamentary Additions to Trust Act*, in *Uniform Acts of the Uniform Law Conference of Canada* (1978, as am.), p. 47-1.

642 *Proceedings of the Forty-ninth Annual Meeting of the Conference of Commissioners on Uniformity of Legislation in Canada* (1967), Appendix U, p. 207. The Conference is now called the Uniform Law Conference of Canada.

643 *Wills Act*, R.S.Y. 1986, c. 179, ss. 27, 28 (enacted in 1965 on the basis of an earlier draft of the uniform legislation).

644 See, *e.g.*, *Succession Law Reform Act*, R.S.O. 1990, c. S.26, s. 31; and see Oosterhoff, *Wills*, ch. 12.

645 [1951] Ch. 4.

646 See further E.J. Mockler, "'Pour-Over' from a Will to an *Inter Vivos* Trust" (1975), 24 U.N.B.L.J. 50; H.A. Leal, Q.C., "The Revocable Trust and Pour Over Wills" (1966), 1 Real Prop. Prob. & Tr. J. 286; G.E. Palmer, "Testamentary Disposition to the Trustee of an *Inter-Vivos* Trust" (1951), 50 Mich. L. Rev. 33; A.N. Polasky, "'Pour-Over' Wills And the Statutory Blessing" (1959), 98 Tr. & Est. 949.

(b) Mutual Wills

(i) *Reciprocal Wills and Mutual Wills*

People (typically spouses or partners) often collaborate on wills. For instance, A and B may each draft wills that give a life estate to the survivor, with the remainder to C. Alternatively, A and B may each leave everything to the other, or to C if the other should predecease.[647]

Depending upon the parties' intentions, such wills may be either *reciprocal* or *mutual*. The distinction is important. Reciprocal wills simply mirror each other in a way that does not import legal obligations. Consequently, each party is free, at any time before or after the other's death, to revoke his or her will.[648]

Mutual wills are significantly different. In the typical case, the parties draft wills that mirror each other *and* they agree to have wills containing certain provisions when they die.[649] The cases occasionally are inconsistent, but it appears that the precise effect of that agreement depends upon its terms. The agreement may say that each party is free to revoke during the other's life, but that the power of revocation is lost if the first party dies with a will containing the stipulated provisions. Alternatively, the agreement may require both parties, upon death, to have wills containing the stipulated provisions. In that situation, if one party revokes while the other party is still alive, the innocent party may be entitled to sue, on the basis of anticipatory breach, for damages or specific enforcement.[650] In any event, if the first to die leaves behind an appropriate will, then equity will, if necessary, impose a trust in order to effectively hold the survivor to the agreement.

The operation of that trust again depends upon the terms of the parties' agreement. Although the cases are not entirely consistent, a few observations can be made. If the parties agreed that a particular asset ultimately would be given to C, then a constructive trust may arise immediately upon the death of the first party, such that the survivor enjoys a life estate, with the remainder interest in C.[651] If, as typically occurs, the parties simply agreed that the survivor's entire estate ultimately would be given to C, then it is difficult to see how a trust can

---

647 T.G. Youdan, "The Mutual Wills Doctrine" (1979), 29 U of T.L.J. 390 at 391.

648 *Edell v. Sitzer* (2001), 55 O.R. (3d) 198, [2001] O.J. No. 2909, 2001 CarswellOnt 5020, 40 E.T.R. (2d) 10 (S.C.J.).

649 *Bell v. Bell* (1998), 24 E.T.R. (2d) 169, 1998 CarswellBC 1357 (S.C.); *Shewchuk v. Preteau* (2000), 31 E.T.R. (2d) 127, 2000 CarswellMan 11, 142 Man. R. (2d) 154, 212 W.A.C. 154 (C.A.). On the nature of the requisite agreement, see J. Cassidy, "*Osborne v. Osborne*: An Equitable Agreement or a Contract in Law: Merely a Matter of Nomenclature?" (2003), 27 Melbourne U. L. Rev. 217.

650 Youdan, *supra* at 406ff.; *Robinson v. Ommanney* (1883), 23 Ch. D. 285. Such relief may be denied, however, if the will was revoked by law as a result of the marriage: C.E.F. Rickett, "Extending Equity's Reach Through the Mutual Wills Doctrine?" (1991), 54 Modern L. Rev. 581.

651 *Hagger, Re*, [1930] 2 Ch. 190; *Green, Re*, [1951] Ch. 148, [1950] 2 All E.R. 913.

arise on the death of the first party.[652] After all, the contents of the survivor's estate, and hence the subject matter of the trust, cannot be known until the survivor's death. Moreover, the parties may have intended the survivor to have the unfettered use of the property during his or her lifetime. Consequently, the trust may arise only if and when the second party dies without a will in appropriate form.[653]

Those principles most commonly apply to situations in which two people draft mutual wills as part of an agreement. The same principles extend, however, to other situations as well. There may be more than two people involved in the agreement. Moreover, rather than draft separate wills on similar terms, the parties may create a single joint will.[654] Or they may agree to retain wills already in existence. Or, if they are joint tenants, they may agree to not sever the tenancy, thereby allowing the survivor to acquire the entire estate through the right of *jus accrescendi* and subsequently dispose of the property to C.[655] The same principles may also apply if the parties agree to die intestate, thereby facilitating a particular distribution of their assets.[656]

(ii) *Basis of the Doctrine*

The doctrine originates with *Dufour v. Pereira*.[657] A married couple made a joint will that contained evidence that they had agreed not to alter it. The will gave a life estate to the survivor, with the remainder to certain beneficiaries. The husband died without breaching the agreement, but the wife subsequently made a new will that was not in compliance. After the wife died, the intended beneficiaries of the joint will sought to impress a trust upon her estate.[658] The report of

---

652 Compare *Dale, Re*, [1994] Ch. 31; J. Martin, *Hanbury & Martin: Modern Equity*, 16th ed. (London: Sweet & Maxwell, 2001), at 322-323 (suggesting that the trust arises upon the death of the first party).

653 It commonly is said that mutual wills preclude the survivor from revoking his or her will. That is not, strictly speaking, true. Because the constructive trust generally takes effect only upon the survivor's death, the relevant question is not whether he or she revoked a will at some point, but rather whether he or she died with a will in appropriate form: *cf. Oldham, Re*, [1924] All E.R. Rep. 288, [1925] Ch. 75 (Ch. Div.). Indeed, the rule could hardly be otherwise. As discussed below, a will is revoked by law upon marriage: see, *e.g., Succession Law Reform Act*, R.S.O. 1990, c. S.26, ss. 16, 17(2). It could not be, for instance, that a widow commits a breach of a mutual will agreement merely because she remarries after her husband's death. Of course, the parties may also agree that their arrangement comes to an end upon remarriage: see *Marsland, Re*, [1939] Ch. 820 (C.A.).

654 Interestingly, there is no such thing, from a legal perspective, as a joint will. In the eyes of the law, a joint will is, in fact, two separate wills on identical terms: *Gillespie, Re* (1968), [1969] 1 O.R. 585, 3 D.L.R. (3d) 317, 1968 CarswellOnt 322 (C.A.), at 595 [O.R.], *per* Laskin J.A.

655 See *McGeachy v. Russ*, [1955] 3 D.L.R. 349, 1955 CarswellBC 35, 15 W.W.R. 178 (S.C.).

656 See T.G. Youdan, "The Mutual Wills Doctrine" (1979), 29 U. of T.L.J. 390 at 404.

657 (1769), 1 Dick. 419, 21 E.R. 332.

658 That is the usual means by which mutual wills come before a court: see, *e.g., Patamsis Estate v. Bajoraitis* (1994), 2 E.T.R. (2d) 200, 1994 CarswellOnt 648 (Gen. Div.), additional reasons at (1994), 1994 CarswellOnt 4395, 2 E.T.R. (2d) 200n (Gen. Div.).

the case is brief, but in the course of his judgment Lord Camden said of the agreement:[659]

> It is a contract between the parties which cannot be rescinded, but by the consent of both. The first that dies, carries his part into execution. Will the Court afterwards permit the other to break the contract? Certainly not.

Hargrave subsequently reported that Lord Camden said:[660]

> The instrument itself is the evidence of the agreement: and he that dies first does by his death carry the agreement on his part into execution. If the other then refuses, he is guilty of a fraud, can never unbind himself and becomes a trustee of course. For no man shall deceive another to his prejudice. By engaging to do something that is in his power, he is made a trustee for the performance, and transmits that trust to those who claim under him.

(iii) *Explanation for the Trust*

The precise explanation for the trust is somewhat controversial. It clearly is not resulting because it does not cause property to jump back from whence it came. Moreover, while there is some debate as to whether it is express or constructive,[661] it generally is thought to be the latter. As we have seen in other contexts, however, to say that a trust is constructive is to open the door to a further inquiry regarding the operative triggering event.

In some circumstances, at least, it might be possible to make out a claim in unjust enrichment.[662] The survivor's estate may be enriched by the inclusion of the other party's property, and that enrichment may be unjust insofar as the survivor's will does not conform to the parties' agreement.[663] A (resulting) trust could then carry the property back to the estate of the party that died first, and out through his or her will to the intended beneficiaries. As a matter of precedent, however, that is not how mutual wills work.[664]

---

659 *Ibid.*, at Dick. 421.
660 Hargrave, *Juridical Arguments*, 304, cited in *Green, Re, supra*, note 651, at 153. The *Dufour* case was also considered in *Lord Walpole v. Lord Orford* (1797), 3 Ves. 402, 30 E.R. 1076, in which counsel referred to the notes which Lord Camden apparently took and which were recognized by Lord Loughborough, counsel in *Dufour*, as authentic: *ibid.*, at Ves. 412, 418.
661 *Gillespie, Re, supra*, note 654, at 593, *per* Laskin J.A.
662 This analysis would not, however, explain a trust that is imposed upon the death of the first party with respect to a particular asset — prior to the "injustice" of the survivor's failure to die with a will in appropriate form. Nor can this analysis explain why the operative trust attaches not only to property initially held by the party that first died, but also to property initially held by the survivor. The latter property did not move from one party to another and hence cannot constitute an enrichment and corresponding deprivation. That point was noticed by the Court of Appeal in *University of Manitoba v. Sanderson Estate*, which appears below.
663 In other words, the unjust factor, or reason for reversing the enrichment, may be failure of a condition (or, as traditionally phrased, "failure of consideration").
664 It might be suggested that the survivor's estate is unjustly enriched at the expense of the intended beneficiaries (rather than the party that first died) and that the trust consequently carries the property to them. The problem with that analysis, however, is that it presupposes that the intended beneficiaries already are entitled to the property — the very point for which an

An attempt might also be made to explain the trust in terms of wrongdoing, specifically, the survivor's failure to facilitate the distribution of the assets as agreed. There are, however, several difficulties with that analysis. First, if the parties' agreement pertains to a particular asset, a trust may arise immediately upon the death of the first party, prior to any possible breach by the survivor. Second, any breach that does occur would seem to be committed against the other party with whom the agreement was made — not against the intended beneficiaries of that agreement. Though not entirely inflexible,[665] the general rule precludes third party beneficiaries from claiming relief for breach of contract.[666]

Alternatively, it sometimes is suggested that the trust is triggered by the survivor's fraud against the intended beneficiaries themselves. Once again, however, a trust may arise immediately upon the death of the first party and before any fraud by the survivor. Moreover, the term "fraud" often seems inappropriate to the circumstances. The survivor's failure to die with an appropriate will may be due to the fact that he or she married after entering into the agreement. A person often fails to realize that marriage automatically revokes an existing will. Consequently, he or she may die believing, honestly though erroneously, that the requirements of the mutual wills have been satisfied.

The best explanation may be that equity imposes a constructive trust in order to perfect the parties' intentions and protect the detrimental reliance of the party that died first. That party presumably would have made other arrangements if he or she had known that the survivor would not honour the agreement.

University of Manitoba v. Sanderson Estate, which appears below, explores a number of issues arising from mutual wills.

Further Reading

Robert Burgess, "A Fresh Look at Mutual Wills" (1970), 34 Conv. (N.S.) 230.

William A. Lee, "Contracts to Make Wills" (1971), 87 L.Q. Rev. 358.

L.A. Sheridan, "The Floating Trust: Mutual Wills" (1977), 15 Alta L. Rev. 211.

T. G. Youdan, "The Mutual Wills Doctrine" (1979), 29 U. of T.L.J. 390.

C.E.F. Rickett, "A Rare Case of Mutual Wills and its Implications" (1982), 8 Adelaide L. Rev. 178.

C.E.F. Rickett, "Mutual Wills and the Law of Restitution" (1989), 105 L.Q. Rev. 534.

C.E.F. Rickett, "Extending Equity's Reach Through the Mutual Wills Doctrine?" (1991), 54 Modern L. Rev. 581.

---

explanation is being sought. Any unjust enrichment that may arise against the intended beneficiaries "is not the source of the constructive trust, but is caused by a distribution of the estate contrary to the constructive trust, which arose independently in response to another event": R. Chambers, "Constructive Trusts in Canada" (1999), 37 Alberta L. Rev. 173 at 194.

665 *Cf. Beswick v. Beswick*, [1968] A.C. 58 (H.L.); *Contracts (Rights of Third Parties) Act 1999*, c. 31 (U.K.); *Law Reform Act*, S.N.B. 1993, c. L-1.2, s. 4.

666 Once a trust has been established (*e.g.* on the basis of perfecting intentions or protecting detrimental reliance), there is no question of enforcing third party rights. The intended beneficiaries of the mutual wills become the beneficiaries of the trust and consequently are entitled to enforcement in the normal way.

R. Chambers, "Constructive Trusts in Canada" (1999), 37 Alberta L. Rev. 173.

J. Cassidy, *Mutual Wills* (Sydney: Federation Press, 2000).

K. Farquhar, "Mutual Wills — Some Questions Recently Answered" (2000), 19 Estates, Trusts & Pension J. 327.

UNIVERSITY OF MANITOBA v. SANDERSON ESTATE

155 D.L.R. (4th) 40, 1998 CarswellBC 121, 155 D.L.R. (4th) 40,
20 E.T.R. (2d) 148, 102 B.C.A.C. 186, 166 W.A.C. 186, [1998] 7 W.W.R. 83,
47 B.C.L.R. (3d) 25
British Columbia Court of Appeal

In 1970, Mr. and Mrs. Sanderson entered into an agreement which provided that (a) they would make wills in the form attached to the agreement; (b) they would not alter or revoke the wills during their joint lives except with the written consent of both; (c) the survivor would not alter or revoke his or her will; and (d) if either will should be revoked by operation of law, the survivor would make a new will leaving the residue upon the same terms as in the original wills. The wills, which were made on the same date as the agreement, declared that (a) the spouses had agreed to execute mirror wills and not to alter or revoke them; and (b) the wills were made in consideration of the agreement.

The wills left the estate of the first spouse to die in trust for the survivor for life, or until remarriage. The trustees were given a discretion to use the income and capital for the benefit of the survivor. The wills left the residue to the University of Manitoba in trust to establish a perpetual bursary fund for undergraduate student teachers. Mr. and Mrs. Sanderson made two mirror codicils in 1973 and 1977. In 1984, Montreal Trust Co., their named executor, wrote the spouses suggesting a review of their wills. Mr. Sanderson replied asking that the wills be kept in force.

Mrs. Sanderson died in 1985. Almost all of her assets were owned jointly with her husband. Accordingly, he became entitled to them by right of survivorship. This obviated the need to have her will probated. Mr. Sanderson made a new will in 1985, soon after his wife died. It was inconsistent with the original will in that it left part of the residue to certain named persons and the balance to the University of Manitoba. He died in 1994. Montreal Trust Co. obtained probate of the 1985 will.

The University brought an action for a declaration that Montreal Trust Co. held the assets of the husband's estate for its sole benefit. Arkell J. dismissed the action for the reasons stated below.[667] The University appealed.

ROWLES J.A:

. . .

---

667 (1996), 17 E.T.R. (2d) 78, 1996 CarswellBC 2813 (S.C.).

Trial Judge's reasons for dismissing the claim

[19] In dismissing the University's claim, the trial judge reasoned as follows: (1) the immediate effect of the Agreement and the mutual wills made in 1970 was to sever any joint tenancy of property and convert it into a tenancy in common; (2) "either or both parties were at liberty to withdraw from the arrangement in the future and to obtain other joint properties if necessary or deemed advisable by them", (3) any joint property that came into existence after the Agreement was made in 1970 was not severed by the Agreement and the mutual wills; (4) almost all Mr. and Mrs. Sanderson's property was purchased jointly after the second codicil was signed in 1977; (5) their property was held jointly or in both names at the time of Mrs. Sanderson's death; (6) when Mrs. Sanderson died in 1985, Mr. Sanderson was entitled at law to that property by right of survivorship or "right of transfer"; (7) Mrs. Sanderson's will was not probated; (8) "The assets that [Mr. Sanderson] received were not received by him under the terms of the will of Mrs. Sanderson"; (9) Mr. Sanderson therefore could not be said to have received or gained any benefit from his wife's estate. The trial judge concluded:

> The 1970 will of Mrs. Sanderson, as I have already indicated, was never probated, and Mr. Sanderson, the deceased, never received any benefit or unjust enrichment under the terms of the will. He only acquired those assets that were his by law as a joint owner. There was no benefit conferred upon him without juridical reason that would give rise to equitable estoppel under a constructive trust. There is no fraud and no need for the equitable remedy of a constructive trust.

[20] The trial judge also found:

> Montreal Trust was involved in the preparation of Mr. Sanderson's will of 1985. Montreal Trust knew of the 1970 agreement, the 1970 wills, and the two subsequent codicils.
>
> Since Montreal Trust and its solicitors had the knowledge of the 1970 agreement and wills and proceeded to prepare a new will in 1985 for Mr. Sanderson, it can be inferred that the original agreement had been modified, altered or perhaps even cancelled by the acquisition of the joint assets with the consent and acquiesence of Mrs. Sanderson.

. . .

Issues on appeal

[22] The appellant argues that the learned trial judge erred: (1) in finding that the Agreement between the Sandersons had been modified, altered or cancelled by them prior to Mrs. Sanderson's death; (2) in finding that Mr. Sanderson had to receive a benefit before the court could find a constructive trust. . . .

[23] The appeal raises these issues:

1. Was the Agreement not to revoke their mutual wills revoked by the Sandersons during their joint lives?
2. Does the obligation of the survivor not to revoke his mutual will depend on his receiving a benefit under the will of the first to die?

. . .

Issue 1: Was the Agreement not to revoke their mutual wills revoked by the Sandersons during their joint lives?

[24] It is uncontentious that an agreement not to revoke mutual wills may be revoked by the parties prior to the death of the first. In this case, the trial judge found that there was a revocation of the Agreement by conduct of the parties inconsistent with the Agreement. Specifically, the judge found that joint revocation by conduct could be inferred from the parties' purchase of jointly held assets and from Montreal Trust's participation in Mr. Sanderson's preparing his 1985 will.

. . .

[30] In my respectful view, the trial judge was in error when he concluded that there was a revocation of the Agreement by conduct of the parties inconsistent with that Agreement. While it is true that mutual conduct inconsistent with a contract may be taken to show that the contract is no longer enforceable, that conduct must be quite clear. Here the evidence would have to show that, by the purchase of assets in their joint names, the Sandersons intended to supersede the operation of their mutual wills.

[31] From the evidence in this case it is not at all clear what effect, if any, the Sandersons intended their subsequent purchase of jointly held assets to have in relation to their Agreement. The creation of a right of survivorship in their assets is not necessarily inconsistent with the operation of the mutual wills, and it has no bearing on the Agreement, which was simply not to revoke the wills.

[32] It is also my respectful view that the inferences drawn by the trial judge from Montreal Trust's involvement in the preparation of Mr. Sanderson's 1985 will are unsupportable. Montreal Trust's participation in the preparation of Mr. Sanderson's will after Mrs. Sanderson's death does not provide any foundation for drawing an inference that the Sandersons intended to revoke or modify their Agreement before Mrs. Sanderson's death.

[33] I am also of the view that the trial judge was in error in finding that the agreement not to revoke, which was contained in both the Agreement and the mutual wills, could be revoked by conduct or implication.

[34] The Agreement contained a provision allowing it to be revoked by written consent of both parties. In my opinion, anything less, such as conduct of the parties which might be construed as inconsistent with the continuance of the Agreement, could not be taken to revoke the contract in light of the clear mechanism for revocation contained within it.

[35] Quite apart from whether the Agreement could be revoked by conduct inconsistent with it, the mutual wills could not be so revoked. There are only a limited number of ways to revoke a will and the inconsistent conduct said to have occurred in this case is not one of them.

[36] The mutual wills clearly contain the parties' agreement not to revoke within them. Short of clear evidence that they were revoked prior to Mrs. San-

derson's death, I must conclude that the agreement not to revoke the mutual wills was still in force at the time of Mrs. Sanderson's death in 1985.

Issue 2. Does the obligation of the survivor not to revoke his mutual will depend on his receiving a benefit under the will of the first to die?

[37] The appellant argues that there are two conditions which must be met before the court will impose a trust as a consequence of joint or mutual wills: (1) a mutual agreement not to revoke the joint or mutual wills, and (2) the first to die must have died without revoking or changing his or her will in breach of the agreement.

[38] The question is whether there is a third condition, that is, a benefit flowing to the survivor from the will of the first to die. The appellant argues that a benefit is not required for equity to hold the survivor to his promise.

[39] The respondents' argument is to the contrary. The respondents contend that because the will of Mrs. Sanderson was never probated and Mr. Sanderson took no benefit under her will, the learned trial judge was correct in not imposing a constructive trust on any property of the Sandersons.

[40] In the respondents' submission, in all cases in which there is a constructive trust imposed in circumstances of mutual wills, the will of the first to die has been probated. Support for that proposition is said to be found in *Dufour v. Pereira*;[668] *Re Gillespie*;[669] *Pratt v. Johnson*;[670] *Re Kerr*;[671] *Re Cleaver*;[672] *Re O'Connell Estate*;[673] and *Re Grisor*.[674]

[41] The respondents further contend that even if Mrs. Sanderson's will had been admitted to probate, there would have been no basis for imposing a constructive trust because Mr. Sanderson received no benefit under Mrs. Sanderson's will, Mrs. Sanderson's assets having come to him by survivorship. In support of the proposition that a benefit must be received before a constructive trust may be imposed, the respondents referred to *Pratt v. Johnson*,[675] in which Locke J. quoted with approval the following passage from of *Snell's Principles of Equity*:[676]

> Until the death of the first to die either may withdraw from the arrangement, but thereafter it is irrevocable, at least if the survivor accepts the benefits conferred on him by the other's will.

Other cases said to support that proposition are *Denyssen v. Mosert*;[677] *Re Payne*;[678] and *Birmingham v. Renfrew*.[679]

---

668 *Supra*, note 657, at 421.
669 *Supra*, note 654.
670 (1958), [1959] S.C.R. 102.
671 [1948] 3 D.L.R. 668 (Ont. H.C.J.), affirmed [1949] O.W.N. 70 (C.A.).
672 [1981] 2 All E.R. 1018.
673 (1981), 9 E.T.R. 57 (N.S.S.C., A.D.).
674 (1979), 26 O.R. (2d) 57 (H.C.J.).
675 *Supra*, note 670.
676 (24th ed.), at 156.

[42] The respondents argue that the requirement of unjust enrichment is fundamental to the use of a constructive trust and that the three elements referred to in *Peter v. Beblow*[680] must be satisfied before a constructive trust is imposed: (1) an enrichment; (2) a corresponding deprivation; and (3) the absence of a juristic reason for the enrichment. The respondents submit that none of these requirements is met in this case because: (1) Mr. Sanderson took no benefit under the will of Mrs. Sanderson; (2) there was no deprivation to Mrs. Sanderson; and (3) even if Mr. Sanderson's taking assets of Mrs. Sanderson on her death constitutes an "enrichment", there is a "juristic reason" for it because of his entitlement by right of survivorship as joint tenant.

[43] According to the respondents, the unjust enrichment justification for the imposition of a constructive trust in the mutual wills context is set out in *Re Cleaver*,[681] where Nourse J. said:

> The principle of all these cases is that a court of equity will not permit a person to whom property is transferred by way of gift, but on the faith of an agreement or clear understanding that it is to be dealt with in a particular way for the benefit of a third person, to deal with that property inconsistently with that agreement or understanding. If he attempts to do so after having received the benefit of the gift equity will intervene by imposing a constructive trust on the property which is the subject matter of the agreement or understanding.

[44] With respect, I do not agree that either the probate of the will of the first to die, or a benefit flowing to the survivor from the will of the other, is a necessary condition for relief to be granted to the University on trust principles.

[45] This is a case in which there was an express agreement made that the mutual wills would not be revoked or altered during the joint lives of the parties to the agreement and that after the death of the first, the will of the survivor would not be altered or revoked. There was an exchange of promises and Mrs. Sanderson did not revoke her will, although she had the legal right to do so, before her death.

[46] The guiding principles to be applied in this case are to be found in *Dufour v. Pereira*,[682] in which the enforcement of an agreement in a joint will was held to be within equity's jurisdiction to prevent fraud. Equity considers it a fraud upon the deceased, who has acted upon and relied upon the mutually binding nature of the agreement, for the survivor to change the will and break the agreement. As the deceased cannot intervene to enforce the obligation, equity will enforce the survivor's obligation, despite the survivor's subsequent intentions.

[47] A very full account of *Dufour v. Pereira* appears in F. Hargrave, *Juridical Arguments and Collections*.[683] In that account, Mr. Hargrave quotes from a manuscript copied from Lord Camden L.C.' s own handwriting and, in view of the fullness of the account, it is to be preferred over the other report of the case. (In

---

679 *Supra*, note 602.
680 *Supra*, note 31, at 987, *per* McLachlin J.
681 *Supra*, note 672, at 1024.
682 *Supra*, note 657.
683 Vol. 2, (London: 1799), at 304-11.

Pratt v. Johnson[684] Locke J. expresses a preference for the account in Hargrave's *Juridical Arguments*.)

[48] In *Dufour*, a husband and wife had made a joint will in which the residuary estate of the first to die was to be held for the survivor for his or her life with remainders over. On the death of the husband, the wife (who was one of his executors) proved his will. She had the benefit of his residuary estate together with her separate property for many years. On her death it was found that her last will was not in accord with the joint will and her estate had been left to her daughter, the defendant, Mrs. Pereira. The plaintiffs, who were the beneficiaries under the joint will, claimed that the wife's personal estate was held in trust for them.

[49] The significance in equity of the agreement that the mutual will should not be revoked after the death of one of the parties clearly emerges from Lord Camden L.C.'s judgment as it appears in the account in Hargrave's *Juridical Arguments*:[685]

[Her Ladyship quoted extensively from this text, and continued:]

[50] The essence of Lord Camden L.C.'s opinion on the question, "how far the mutual will shall operate as a binding engagement, independent of any confirmation by accepting the legacy under it", is contained in the following passage:[686]

> ... he, that dies first, does by his death carry the agreement on his part into execution. If the other then refuses, he is guilty of a fraud, can never unbind himself, and becomes a trustee of course. For no man shall deceive another to his prejudice. By engaging to do something that is in his power, he is made a trustee for the performance, and transmits that trust to those that claim under him.

That passage contains no suggestion that the first to die must have conferred a benefit on the survivor by his will for equity to intervene.

[51] Lord Camden L.C.'s opinion on the question, "whether the survivor can depart from this engagement, after she has accepted a benefit under it", is stated in this passage:[687]

> I have perhaps given myself more trouble than was necessary upon this point; because, if it could be doubtful, whether after the husband's death his wife could be at liberty to revoke her part of the mutual will, it is most clear, that she has estopped herself to this defence, by an actual confirmation of the mutual will, — not only by proving it, but by accepting and enjoying an interest under it. She receives this benefit, takes possession of all her husband's estates, submits to the mutual will as long as she lives, and then breaks the agreement after her death.

---

684 *Supra*, note 670, at 110.
685 *Supra*, note 683, at 306-11.
686 *Ibid.*, at 310.
687 *Ibid.*, at 311.

The emphasis here is on the survivor proving the joint will and thereafter accepting and enjoying a benefit under it but those matters are not essential to the principles enunciated by Lord Camden L.C. on the first question. Proving the will and taking a benefit under it is simply evidence to support the survivor's acceptance of the joint will and the binding nature of the agreement within it. What is fundamental in *Dufour* is the finding that there was an agreement. The taking of the benefit under a joint or mutual will tends to support such a finding but it is not an essential element to the imposition of a trust on the estate of the survivor.

[52] Unlike the present case in which there is an express agreement between the testators not to revoke their mutual wills, the authorities to which the respondents referred all concern the question of whether there was, in fact, such an agreement.

[53] In one of these cases, *Re Hagger*,[688] Clauson J. of the Chancery Division in England explicitly rejected any benefit requirement, although the observation was obiter since a benefit was taken in that case:

> To my mind *Dufour v. Pereira* decides that where there is a joint will such as this, on the death of the first testator the position as regards that part of the property which belongs to the survivor is that the survivor will be treated in this Court as holding the property on trust to apply it so as to carry out the effect of the joint will. As I read Lord Camden's judgment in *Dufour v. Pereira* that would be so, even though the survivor did not signify his election to give effect to the will by taking benefits under it.

[54] That an agreement is essential to the application of the principles in *Dufour v. Pereira* is clear from the decision in *Gray v. Perpetual Trustee Co.*,[689] the headnote to which accurately states what was decided:

> The fact that a husband and wife have simultaneously made mutual wills, giving each to the other a life interest with similar provisions in remainder, is not in itself evidence of an agreement not to revoke the wills; in the absence of a definite agreement to that effect there is no implied trust precluding the wife from making a fresh will inconsistent with her former will, even though her husband has died and she has taken the benefits conferred by his will.

[55] In *Pratt v. Johnson*,[690] a husband and wife made a joint will which contained these provisions:

> We desire that all property real and personal of which we may die possessed at the time of the decease of either of us shall be held by the survivor during his or her life to use as such survivor may see fit.
>
> Upon the decease of the survivor it is our desire that our property both real and personal shall be divided as follows:
>
> To [five named beneficiaries] equally amongst them share and share alike.

[56] At the time of the husband's death, the will remained unaltered and no other will had been made, but thereafter the wife made a will disposing of her

---

688 *Supra*, note 651, at 195.
689 [1928] A.C. 391 (P.C.).
690 *Supra*, note 670, at 104-105.

property to a differently constituted group of beneficiaries. The trial judge granted a declaration that the late Johanna Johnson "was bound by trust to leave her estate including all assets received by her from Arni Johnson, deceased, in accordance with the joint will of herself and the said Arni Johnson, deceased". Appeals to the provincial appellate court and the Supreme Court of Canada were dismissed. In the Supreme Court, Mr. Justice Locke, giving the majority judgment, said this:[691]

> The question to be decided is, in my opinion, not as to whether there was evidence of an agreement between the husband and wife not to make a disposition of the property referred to in the joint will in a manner inconsistent with its terms, but rather whether there was evidence of an agreement between them that the property in the hands of the survivor at the time of his or her death should go to the said five beneficiaries and, since nothing was done by Johanna Johnson to alter the terms of the joint will until after the death of her husband, the property received by her from the executor of her husband's estate and such estate of her own of which she died possessed were impressed with a trust in favour of the five named beneficiaries. . . .

[57] While the question of whether the survivor must receive a benefit before the survivor's property and any property received from the deceased spouse will be impressed with a trust was not directly before the Court in *Pratt v. Johnson*, I see nothing in the majority decision to suggest that a benefit was considered an essential element to the imposition of a trust.

[58] It is also my respectful view that the remedy of constructive trust grounded on the principle of unjust enrichment is not analogous to the principles enunciated in *Dufour v. Pereira*[692] and that the trial judge erred when he concluded that an unjust enrichment was required. A constructive trust arising from an unjust enrichment is imposed on property gained at the expense of another for no juristic reason, whereas the obligation created by an agreement not to revoke mutual wills binds not only that portion of the survivor's estate which may have come from the estate of the first to die, but also his or her own property.

[59] In my opinion, the requisite conditions for the imposition of a trust on the property of Mr. Sanderson have been met in this case and the University is entitled to succeed on the appeal.

[Cumming and Gibbs JJ.A., concurred. The court allowed the appeal.]

Notes and Questions

1. What is the basis for the imposition of a constructive trust in a mutual will situation?

2. The trial judge in *Sanderson* stated that when the parties made their agreement, any property then owned by them as joint tenants was converted into a tenancy in common. However, he concluded that the parties modified or revoked their agreement because they subsequently acquired a number of assets as joint tenants. It is, indeed, the generally accepted view that an agreement to make mutual wills converts a joint tenancy into a tenancy in common, at least if the property is subject to the agreement. That is because

---

691 *Ibid.*, at 106-107.
692 *Supra*, note 657.

the agreement (and the wills made pursuant thereto) are inconsistent with the survivor taking by survivorship, since the parties have made other arrangements for the succession of the property.[693]

The Court of Appeal took a different view. It held that the agreement had not been revoked by the parties' conduct in buying property in their joint names. One therefore might assume that jointly-owned property would remain converted. However, in para. 31 of her judgment, Rowles J.A. noted that the creation of a right of survivorship is not necessarily inconsistent with the operation of the mutual wills. At first blush, this might suggest that she was departing from the generally accepted view. But not so. She was referring to property acquired after the creation of the agreement. It may or may not be converted depending upon the terms of the agreement. If the parties intended to make subsequently acquired property subject to the agreement, presumably it would be converted, but not otherwise. The question regarding which assets are subject to the agreement is discussed in a later note.

3. You will have noticed from the material that parties often use a joint will. As explained in the introductory text, the common law does not recognize a joint will. A joint will is actually the separate wills of the two parties. However, in *Gillespie, Re*,[694] Kelly J.A., writing for the majority of the court, concluded that a joint will makes it easier to find an agreement: the fact that both parties sign the document suggests an agreement. Laskin J.A. dissented. In his view, the alleged agreement must be proved on a balance of probabilities whether the parties used a joint will or separate wills, because the consequences of finding an agreement can be quite onerous on the survivor. Laskin J.A. quoted[695] the following excerpt from the judgment of Latham C.J. in *Birmingham v. Renfrew*[696] on this point:

> Those who undertake to establish such an agreement assume a heavy burden of proof. It is easy to allege such an agreement after the parties to it have both died, and any court should be very careful in accepting the evidence of interested parties upon such a question. Perhaps most husbands and wives make wills "by agreement" but they do not bind themselves not to revoke their wills. They do not intend to undertake or impose any kind of binding obligation. The mere fact that two persons make what may be called corresponding wills in the sense that the existence of each will is naturally explained by the existence of the other will is not sufficient to establish a binding agreement not to revoke wills so made.

With this in mind, which opinion on the effect of a joint will is to be preferred, that of Kelly J.A. or that of Laskin J.A.? Explain your answer.

4. *Ohorodnyk, Re*[697] also involved a joint will. A husband and wife made a joint will in which each gave his estate to the survivor absolutely. However, they then went on to state that upon the death of the survivor, the remainder should be divided equally between five named persons, resident behind the Iron Curtain. The husband died first and his wife then made a new will inconsistent with the joint will. On an application to construe the will, the solicitor who drafted the will testified that it was his belief that the parties agreed that the joint will should be irrevocable, but that the survivor was to be allowed to dispose

---

693 See *Gillespie, Re, supra*, note 654, at 589, *per* Kelly J.A.

694 *Ibid.*

695 *Ibid.*, at 594.

696 *Supra*, note 603, at 674-5.

697 (1979), 24 O.R. (2d) 228, 4 E.T.R. 233, 97 D.L.R. (3d) 502, 1979 CarswellOnt 593 (H.C.), affirmed (1980), 26 O.R. (2d) 704, 6 E.T.R. 215, 102 D.L.R. (3d) 576, 1980 CarswellOnt 524 (C.A.).

of the property inherited from the deceased and her own property as she saw fit. The judge of first instance held that the will and the solicitor's evidence indicated that the survivor did not receive a life estate, but an absolute interest, so that there was nothing left to go to the named persons.

The Court of Appeal held, in a brief judgment, that a mutual wills agreement could be spelled out of the will itself and, since it was therefore not ambiguous, the solicitor's evidence ought not to have been admitted. The court agreed that the survivor took an absolute interest.

Was the conclusion that the will did not confer a life estate with remainder, but an absolute interest, correct?[698] Was the decision of the Court of Appeal that the extrinsic evidence was not admissible correct?[699]

5. *Grisor, Re*[700] should also be considered on this point. A husband and wife made a joint will in which the survivor received a life estate in all property in their possession "at the time of the decease of either of us," to be used as the survivor saw fit, except that he or she could not sell or encumber certain real property and the business situate thereon, and had to continue the business as a going concern. The will continued by giving a remainder interest to the testators' children equally. The real property and the business were in fact owned solely by the husband. The wife died first. The husband then sold the property and died. The children claimed the proceeds of sale.

The court held that a mutual wills agreement gives rise to a constructive trust and that such an agreement should be inferred from the joint distribution scheme of the will. However, the court also said that the real property and the business were not subject to the trust, which binds only such property as belonged to the first testator and not property which belonged to the survivor and did not come to him by the joint will.

Is this decision correct: (i) with respect to the agreement being inferred from the joint will, and (ii) with respect to property subject to the agreement?[701]

6. An issue concerning the property subject to the agreement also arose in *Gillespie, Re*. In that case, however, the parties conceded and the courts held that the agreement covered only the property owned by the wife at her death and the husband's property owned by him at that point. It did not encompass any property acquired by the husband thereafter. That result is explained on the basis that if the survivor is unable to dispose of property acquired after the first person died, he would be unable to deal with it by way of *inter vivos* or testamentary gift. Thus, for example, if he remarried, he would be unable to leave any property to his second spouse.

In *Pratt v. Johnson*,[702] the Supreme Court of Canada held that the joint will did permit the surviving wife to deal freely with all the assets (both her husband's and her own, whether acquired before or after his death) during her life, but that the remainder of all those assets was subject to the trust. Hence, her subsequently-acquired assets were subject to the agreement.

7. A related question is whether the parties can dispose of their assets while both are living, or whether those assets are subject to the trust. This, of course, also depends upon the terms of the agreement, but if it is silent on the point, it is arguable that a disposition by one party of a substantial portion of the assets would be a breach of the agreement and

---

698 On this point see T.G. Youdan, "Some Comments on Re Ohorodnyk and the Mutual Wills Doctrine" (1979), 4 E.T.R. 249.

699 See T.G. Youdan, Annotation, (1980), 6 E.T.R. 216.

700 *Supra*, note 674.

701 See M.M. Litman, Annotation (1979), 5 E.T.R. 296.

702 *Supra*, note 670.

would be actionable by the other. An analogous case is *Synge v. Synge*,[703] in which the defendant had promised that when he died he would leave certain real property to the plaintiff in consideration of her marrying him. When he subsequently sold the property, thereby putting it out of his power to perform the contract, she was held entitled to recover damages for the breach.

It would seem that such substantial gifts by the survivor might also be a breach of the agreement. The point was addressed by Dixon J. in *Birmingham v. Renfrew*[704] in the following *dictum*:[705]

> The purpose of an arrangement for corresponding wills must often be, as in this case, to enable the survivor during his life to deal as absolute owner with the property passing under the will of the party first dying. That is to say, the object of the transaction is to put the survivor in a position to enjoy for his own benefit the full ownership so that, for instance, he may convert it and expend the proceeds if he choose. But when he dies he is to bequeath what is left in the manner agreed upon. It is only by the special doctrines of equity that such a floating obligation, suspended, so to speak, during the lifetime of the survivor can descend upon the assets at his death and crystallize into a trust. No doubt gifts and settlements, *inter vivos*, if calculated to defeat the intention of the compact, could not be made by the survivor and his right of disposition, *inter vivos*, is, therefore, not unqualified. But, substantially, the purpose of the arrangement will often be to allow full enjoyment for the survivor's own benefit and advantage upon condition that at his death the residue shall pass as arranged.

Analogous cases involving contracts to leave property by will hold that the promisor is precluded from making a disposition of property which is in substance testamentary and which has the effect of dissipating the assets subject to the agreement, unless the agreement provides otherwise.[706] American cases on mutual wills are to the like effect.[707]

8. A joint will made by H and W left their entire estates to the survivor for life, with remainder to A, B, C, D, E, F and G. The gift to A, B and C was conditional upon their surviving H and W. D, E and F survived W, but predeceased H. Are their estates entitled to share in the property that was the husband's whose will conformed to the agreement? Does this depend upon the terms of the agreement?[708]

9. The main point decided by *Sanderson*, that the survivor does not need to benefit from the will of the first to die, would also apply if the survivor disclaimed her or his interest under the will of the first to die. The point was also foreshadowed by a *dictum* in *Gillespie, Re*.[709] The Ontario Court of Appeal did not have to decide the question, but Kelly J.A. stated that he would have been prepared to hold that the trust became binding on the husband when his wife died, even if he had not benefited from her estate.[710]

10. Related to the issue discussed in the preceding note is the question as to when the constructive trust, imposed in consequence of a mutual wills agreement, arises. Does it arise when the agreement is made, when the first person dies, or when the survivor dies?

---

703 [1894] 1 Q.B. 466 (C.A.).

704 *Supra*, note 602.

705 *Ibid.*, at 689.

706 See *Fortescue v. Hennah* (1812), 19 Ves. 67, 34 E.R. 443; *Palmer v. Bank of New South Wales* (1975), 7 A.L.R. 671 (Austr. H.C.).

707 See L.A. Sheridan, "The Floating Trust: Mutual Wills" (1977), 15 Alta. L. Rev. 211 at 230-240.

708 See *Hagger, supra*, note 651.

709 *Supra*, note 654.

710 *Ibid.*, at 589.

It is unlikely that the trust arises when the agreement is made, since the parties can revoke by joint agreement or individually, provided they give notice to the other party.[711] Nevertheless, as we have seen, the parties may have contractual rights during their joint lives.

The more likely date is when the first party dies, since he or she dies in the belief that the agreement has been adhered to, and this appears to be the generally accepted view.[712]

The last date was, however, selected in *Fiegehen, Re*.[713] A husband and wife made mutual wills under which the survivor received a life interest with remainder to specified persons. One of those entitled in remainder was the Watch Tower Bible and Trust Society, which was a lawful organization when the agreement was made and when the husband died in 1931, but which was declared unlawful in 1939 under regulations passed in support of Canada's involvement in the Second World War. Hence the Society's interest under the husband's will came under the control of the Custodian of Enemy Property. The wife died in 1942, having made a new will contrary to the agreement. Rose C.J.H.C. held that the agreement required performance on the wife's part only on her death. At that time, the Society was unlawful, so that it could not compel compliance with the agreement. It followed that the Custodian of Enemy Property did not have a vested interest in remainder in the wife's property from the date of the husband's death and could not enforce the agreement on the wife's death.

Which approach is to be preferred, that of *Fiegehen, Re* or that which holds that the trust crystallizes when the first party dies? Why?

8. THE STRANGER AS CONSTRUCTIVE TRUSTEE

(a) The Nature of a Constructive Trustee

In each of the situations examined so far, equity has imposed a constructive (or resulting) trust on property in the defendant's possession. The court's order is proprietary. Its purpose is to ensure that the proper person enjoys the benefit of the asset in question.

The situations examined in this final section are significantly different. They typically involve three parties: (i) the beneficiary of an existing trust, (ii) the trustee of that trust, and (iii) a stranger to that trust. As a result of improperly dealing with the existing trust, the stranger incurs liability as a "constructive trustee." That phrase seems to suggest that relief once again is proprietary. And indeed, courts occasionally act as if that was true. Properly understood, however, a constructive trustee is not really a trustee. The remedy is personal, rather than proprietary. The stranger merely is required to pay an appropriate amount of money.

Why, then, is the stranger in such circumstances referred to as a "constructive trustee"? The answer to that question stems from the nature of a trust.[714] The settlor of the underlying trust chose not to give property directly to the beneficiary,

---

711   *Dufour v. Pereira, supra*, note 657, at 420-421; *Pratt v. Johnson, supra*, note 670, at 391-2, *per* Locke J.

712   *Dufour v. Pereira, ibid.*; *Pratt v. Johnson, ibid.*; *Hagger, Re, supra*, note 651.

713   [1942] O.W.N. 575, 1942 CarswellOnt 340 (H.C.).

714   L. Smith, "Constructive Trusts and Constructive Trustees" (1999), 58 Cambridge L.J. 294.

preferring instead to give it to trustees to hold on the beneficiary's behalf.[715] One incident of that arrangement is that if something goes wrong, the beneficiary *prima facie* is entitled to sue only the trustees and no one else.

As discussed elsewhere in this book, the beneficiary's rights against the trustees are generous. Liability generally is strict in the sense that trustees may be held accountable for a breach of their obligations even if they did not intentionally or carelessly act contrary to the beneficiary's interests. Moreover, the beneficiary enjoys a wide selection of remedies, including compensation and disgorgement, which may be awarded either personally or proprietarily.

Notwithstanding the breadth of those rights, the beneficiary occasionally may want to sue a stranger to the trust, either in addition to, or instead of, the trustees.[716] From a historical perspective, however, such an action appeared to be barred by the rule that limited the beneficiary to claims against the trustees. As they did in so many areas, the early courts overcame that problem through the use of a fiction. The stranger was characterized as a "constructive trustee" — *i.e.* a pretend trustee. Although everyone understood that the stranger was not really a trustee, the ruse allowed that person to be treated as if he or she was one so as to facilitate the beneficiary's claim.

Like all legal fictions, the concept of a constructive trustee carries the risk of being taken at face value. That danger is exacerbated by the fact that situations supporting that concept often are subject to alternative analysis. Trust property improperly finds its way into a stranger's possession. Assuming that the other elements of the relevant actions can be established, there are at least two avenues of relief.[717] The stranger might be held liable as a constructive trustee. If so, he or she will be personally obligated to pay an appropriate amount of money. Alter-

---

715 The typical situation involves interference with an express trust. In some circumstances, however, accessory liability may also arise with respect to dealing with property held on a constructive or resulting trust: *Twinsectra Ltd. v. Yardley, supra*, note 34.

716 The trustees may not have sufficient assets to satisfy judgment or they may have disappeared. So too, an action against the stranger may be more valuable. For instance, the stranger may have profited from the breach in a way that the trustees did not. Finally, although there is little case law on point, an action may lie against the stranger even if the trustees are protected from liability by an exemption clause. To the contrary, it might be argued that insofar as a constructive trusteeship is a form of accessory liability, it necessarily is precluded, as a matter of logic, if the primary wrongdoers (*i.e.* the trustees) are immune from liability. See S. Gardner, "Knowing Assistance and Knowing Receipt: Taking Stock" (1996), 112 L.Q. Rev. 56 at 68.

   If the beneficiary successfully sues both the trustees and the stranger, liability is joint and several. See *Abbey Glen Property Corp. v. Stumborg* (1975), 65 D.L.R. (3d) 235, 1975 CarswellAlta 108, [1976] 2 W.W.R. 1 (T.D.), affirmed 1978 CarswellAlta 236, [1978] 4 W.W.R. 28, 4 B.L.R. 113, 9 A.R. 234, 85 D.L.R. (3d) 35 (C.A.), at 281-283 [65 D.L.R.]; *Canada Safeway Ltd. v. Thompson*, [1951] 3 D.L.R. 295 (B.C. S.C.), at 323.

   Perhaps surprisingly, a right of action against the stranger may also lie with the trustees, even if they were themselves implicated in the underlying breach. The right to monetary relief is itself a trust asset and it remains the continuing duty of the trustees to act in the beneficiary's best interests by capitalizing that chose in action. Of course, the stranger need not fully satisfy judgment twice, once to the beneficiary and again to the trustee. See *Selangor United Rubber Estates Ltd. v. Cradock (No. 3)*, [1968] 2 All E.R. 1073 at 1152.

717 Of course, if the trustees are culpably implicated in the misappropriation, they may be sued as well.

natively, if the stranger still retains the trust property (or its traceable proceeds), the court may impose a constructive trust.[718] If so, the stranger will be a trustee — a true trustee — and will be required to hold the property on the beneficiary's behalf.

There is, therefore, a substantial difference between a constructive trustee and a trustee of a constructive trust. But not surprisingly, those two concepts are often confused. The overlapping language invites such error. Consequently, if a judge merely finds that the defendant is "liable as a constructive trustee," it may be difficult to say with confidence whether the intended remedy is personal or proprietary.

You should remain alert to that problem as you read through this part. You should also consider whether it would be preferable to adopt a more transparent set of labels. "Constructive trust" could be confined to situations in which a true trust[719] is constructed (or imposed) by law. A stranger's personal liability could be described as just that and the phrase "constructive trustee" could be dropped altogether.[720] There is growing support for that proposal. In *Paragon Finance v. D.B. Thakerar & Co.*,[721] Millett L.J. said that in a case of personal liability:

> . . .the expressions "constructive trust" and constructive trustee are misleading, for there is no trust and usually no possibility of a proprietary remedy; they are "nothing more than a formula for equitable relief."

(b) Categories of Constructive Trustees

Depending upon the circumstances, a stranger may become liable as a constructive trustee in one of three ways. The classic statement belongs to Lord Selborne L.C. in *Barnes v. Addy*.[722]

> Now in this case we have to deal with certain persons who are trustees, and with certain other persons who are not trustees. That is a distinction to be borne in mind throughout the case. Those who create a trust clothe the trustee with a legal power and control over the trust property, imposing on him a corresponding responsibility. That responsibility may no doubt be extended in equity to others who are not properly trustees, if they are found either making themselves

---

718 It has been held that a beneficiary is not entitled to maintain an action for the recovery of trust property if the trustee is willing and able to bring such a claim: *Nelson House Indian Band v. Young* (1999), 169 D.L.R. (4th) 606, 1999 CarswellMan 47, [1999] M.J. No. 63, 134 Man. R. (2d) 134, 193 W.A.C. 134, [1999] 6 W.W.R. 405, 25 E.T.R. (2d) 252, (sub nom. *Nelson House Indian Band v. Frost*) [1999] 4 C.N.L.R. 86, 35 C.P.C. (4th) 252 (C.A.); *Sharpe v. San Paulo Rlwy. Co.* (1873), 8 Ch. App. 597 (C.A.); *Norfolk v. Roberts* (1912), 28 O.L.R. 593, 1912 CarswellOnt 656, 23 O.W.R. 538, 4 O.W.N. 419 (H.C.), reversed (1913), 28 O.L.R. 593 at 600, 13 D.L.R. 463, 4 O.W.N. 1231 (C.A.), affirmed (1914), 50 S.C.R. 283, 23 D.L.R. 547, 1914 CarswellOnt 430.

719 Other than a resulting trust.

720 P. Birks, "Trusts in the Recovery of Misapplied Assets: Tracing, Trusts and Restitution" in E. McKendrick, ed., *Commercial Aspects of Trusts and Fiduciary Obligations* (Oxford: Oxford University Press, 1992) 149 at 153-156.

721 [1999] 1 All E.R. 400 at 409, quoting *Selangor United Rubber Estates Ltd. v. Cradock (No. 3)*, *supra*, note 716 at 1097 *per* Ungoed Thomas J.

722 (1874), 9 Ch. App. 244 (C.A.), at 251-2.

trustees *de son tort*, or actually participating in any fraudulent conduct of the trustee to the injury of the *cestui que trust*. But, on the other hand, strangers are not to be made constructive trustees merely because they act as the agents of trustees in transactions within their legal powers, transactions, perhaps of which a Court of Equity may disapprove, unless those agents receive and become chargeable with some part of the trust property or unless they assist with knowledge in a dishonest and fraudulent design on the part of the trustees. Those are the principles, as it seems to me, which we must bear in mind in dealing with the facts of this case. If those principles were disregarded, I know not how anyone could, in transactions admitting of doubt as to the view which a Court of Equity might take of them, safely discharge the office of solicitor, of banker, or of agent of any sort to trustees. But, on the other hand, if persons dealing honestly as agents are at liberty to rely on the legal power of the trustees, and are not to have the character of trustees constructively imposed upon them, then the transactions of mankind can safely be carried through; and I apprehend those who create trusts do expressly intend, in the absence of fraud and dishonesty, to exonerate such agents of all classes from the responsibilities which are expressly incumbent, by reason of the fiduciary relation, upon the trustees.

As suggested by Lord Selborne, a stranger may be held liable as a constructive trustee on three grounds: (i) trustee *de son tort*, (ii) knowing assistance in a breach of trust, and (iii) knowing receipt of trust property. Those possibilities will be addressed in this section. Trustee *de son tort* will be considered last because its guiding principles are somewhat different from those pertaining to knowing assistance and knowing receipt.

Further Reading

C. Harpum, "The Stranger as Constructive Trustee" (1986), 102 L.Q. Rev. 114 and 267.

R. Sullivan, "Strangers to the Trust" (1988), 8 E. & T. Q. 217.

C. Harpum, "The Basis of Equitable Liability" in P. Birks, ed., *The Frontiers of Liability* vol. 1 (Oxford: Oxford University Press, 1994), 9.

T. Allen, "Fraud, Unconscionability and Knowing Assistance" (1995), 74 Can. Bar Rev. 29.

S. Gardner, "Knowing Assistance and Knowing Receipt: Taking Stock" (1996), 112 L.Q. Rev. 56.

D. Stevens, "Knowing Assistance and Knowing Receipt in the Supreme Court of Canada" (1998), 14 Business & Finance L. Rev. 407.

L.D. Smith, "Unjust Enrichment, Property and the Structure of Trusts" (2000), 116 L.Q. Rev. 412.

E. Bant & P. Creighton, "Recipient Liability in Western Australia" (2000), 29 U. of Western Australia L. Rev. 205.

J. Penner, *The Law of Trusts*, 3d ed. (London: Butterworths, 2002), 364*ff*.

M. McInnes, "Knowing Receipt and the Protection of Trust Property" (2002), 81 Can. Bar Rev. 171.

C. Mitchell, "Assistance", in P. Birks & A. Pretto, eds., *Breach of Trust* (Oxford: Hart, 2002), 139.

P. Birks, "Receipt", in P. Birks & A. Pretto, eds., *Breach of Trust* (Oxford: Hart, 2002), 213.

C. Mitchell, "Banks, Dishonesty and Negligence" in *Dirty Money: Civil and Criminal Aspects of Money Laundering* (Cowansville, Que.: Yvon Blais, 2003), 133.

(c) Knowing Assistance in a Breach of Trust

The first head of constructive trusteeship centres on the case in which a stranger participates in a breach of trust. Four issues arise for consideration: (i) the nature of the underlying relationship, (ii) the nature of relief, (iii) the nature of the stranger's knowledge, and (iv) the nature of the underlying breach.

(i) *The Nature of the Underlying Relationship*

It typically is said that liability is incurred if a stranger knowingly participates in a breach of an express trust. The rule can, however, be stated more broadly. Liability may arise for participation in a breach of any fiduciary duty, whether or not that duty arose in the context of an express trust.[723] Consequently, the same principles apply if, in breach of a fiduciary obligation, an employee, officer or director misappropriates a company asset, even though that property is not being held on trust for the company.[724] Going even further, it may be that any type of equitable relationship will do, even if it is not fiduciary in nature. If so, a constructive trustee may be recognized in connection with, say, a breach of confidence,[725] or a breach of a resulting or constructive trust in which the trustee does not owe any fiduciary obligations.[726]

(ii) *The Nature of Relief*

A stranger who is held liable for knowing assistance is subject to a personal obligation to pay money. In most cases, that obligation is quantified by reference to the loss that the plaintiff suffered as a result of the defendant's breach. *Air Canada v. M & L Travel Ltd.*, which appears below, is illustrative. However, if, as a result of participating in the breach, the defendant obtained a benefit, the plaintiff has the option of demanding disgorgement, rather than compensation. In

---

723 *Cook v. Deeks, supra*, note 366; *Satnam Ltd. v. Dunlop Heywood Ltd.*, [1999] 3 All E.R. 652 (C.A.); *cf. Petrotrade Inc. v. Smith*, [2000] 1 Lloyds Rep. 486 (C.A.) (confining dishonest assistance liability to cases involving assistance in the misapplication of property), criticized in C. Mitchell, "Civil Liability for Bribery" (2001), 117 L.Q. Rev. 207.

724 So too, for instance, if a stranger knowingly participates in the breach of a fiduciary duty arising in connection with a partnership: *Jiwan v. Jiwan* (2001), 37 E.T.R. (2d) 238, 2001 CarswellBC 311, 2001 BCSC 270 (S.C.); *Alers-Hankey v. Solomon* (2000), 75 B.C.L.R. (3d) 232, 2000 CarswellBC 616, [2000] B.C.J. No. 602, 2000 BCCA 196, 136 B.C.A.C. 93, 222 W.A.C. 93 (C.A.). See also P.M. Perell, "Intermeddlers or Strangers to the Breach of Trust or Fiduciary Duty" (1999), 21 Adv. Q. 94.

725 *Cf. Rodaro v. Royal Bank* (2000), [2000] O.J. No. 272, 2000 CarswellOnt 281 (S.C.J.), reversed on other grounds (2002), 59 O.R. (3d) 74, 2002 CarswellOnt 1047, [2002] O.J. No. 1365, 22 B.L.R. (3d) 274, 157 O.A.C. 203, 49 R.P.R. (3d) 227 (C.A.), at ¶¶936-937 [O.J. No. 272].

726 *Gordon v. Winnipeg Canoe Club* (1999), 172 D.L.R. (4th) 423, 1999 CarswellMan 164, [1999] M.J. No. 165, [1999] 6 W.W.R. 697, 134 Man. R. (2d) 213, 193 W.A.C. 213, 8 C.C.L.I. (3d) 310, 26 E.T.R. (2d) 235 (C.A.), leave to appeal refused (2000), 2000 CarswellMan 180, 2000 CarswellMan 181, 254 N.R. 200 (note), 153 Man. R. (2d) 160 (note), 238 W.A.C. 160 (note) (S.C.C.), at 436 [D.L.R.]. See also L. Smith, "Constructive Fiduciaries?" in P. Birks, ed., *Privacy and Loyalty* (Oxford: Clarendon Press, 1997) 249 at 267.

that case, the remedial obligation will be quantified by reference to the defendant's gain, rather than the plaintiff's loss.[727]

(iii) *The Nature of the Stranger's Knowledge*

It would be undesirable and impractical to impose liability on *every* stranger who participated in a breach of trust. Such a rule would cast the net far too wide. No one would be willing to interact with a trust, for fear of being held liable. Liability consequently is premised upon the stranger's culpable state of mind.

In that regard, it sometimes is said that a stranger should be liable if, at the time of acting, he or she had "notice" of the underlying breach of trust. "Notice" is not, however, an appropriate test. The concept of notice was developed in equity in order to determine the priority of successive property interests. A person (often referred to as a subsequent purchaser)[728] who deals with property that is already subject to an equitable interest does not acquire priority to that interest if she or he acted with notice of it. Equity distinguishes three kinds of notice: actual, imputed and constructive.

- *Actual notice* is self-defining. It arises if a subsequent purchaser acts with actual notice that someone else has an equitable interest in the property.
- *Imputed notice* is the notice possessed by a person's agent. The agent's notice is, absent fraud on the agent's part, imputed to the principal.[729]
- *Constructive notice* may occur in the absence of actual or imputed notice. It arises if the subsequent purchaser was alerted to facts that ought to have triggered inquiries and led to the discovery of the prior interest.[730]

While appropriate for determining the priority of successive interests, the rules regarding notice are too onerous to govern the imposition of liability for

---

727 *Warman Intl Ltd. v. Dwyer, supra*, note 360; *Fyffes Group Ltd. v. Templeman*, [2000] 2 Lloyd's Rep. 643 (Q.B.), at 660-668; *United States Surgical Corp. v. Hospital Products Intl. Pty. Ltd.* (1982), 2 N.S.W.L.R. 766 (S.C.), at 817.

728 The expression "subsequent purchaser" includes anyone who, for value, acquires an interest in or a security right against property. Volunteers do not enjoy priority.

729 *Purdom v. Northern Life Assurance Co.*, (sub nom. *Fidelity Trust Co. of Ontario v. Purdom*) [1930] S.C.R. 119, (sub nom. *Fidelity Trust Co. v. Purdom*) [1930] 1 D.L.R. 1003, 1929 CarswellOnt 52; *Ficke v. Spence*, 15 Sask. L.R. 282, [1922] 1 W.W.R. 1271, 65 D.L.R. 249, 1922 CarswellSask 74 (K.B.).

730 The doctrine of constructive notice is now largely irrelevant in the context of real property because of the recording statutes which, with some exceptions (principally fraud, gratuitous transactions and short-term leases), abolish the doctrine and impose the concept of statutory notice. This means, in effect, that a person generally is deemed to have actual notice of any instrument affecting land with which she or he is dealing if it is registered, but not otherwise. With respect to personal property and the principle of *nemo dat quod non habet* ("one who has no title cannot give title"), the doctrine of constructive notice has been affected by provisions of the *Sale of Goods Act* (R.S.O. 1990, c. S.1, ss. 22-25), the *Factors Act* (R.S.O. 1990, c. F.1) and the *Personal Property Security Act* (R.S.O. 1990, c. P.10). The doctrine of constructive notice is modified with respect to bills, notes, cheques and other negotiable instruments by the *Bills of Exchange Act* (R.S.C. 1985, c. B-4).

knowing assistance. A more appropriate question for that purpose pertains not to notice, but rather to knowledge.

Having said that, it remains necessary to precisely define the requisite knowledge. Actual knowledge obviously will suffice.[731] A stranger may be held liable for participating in what he or she actually knew to be a breach of trust. But what of knowledge less than actual knowledge? Should it be enough that a reasonable person in the stranger's position would have recognized the underlying breach? Alternatively, should it be enough that the stranger shut his or her eyes to the facts, or wilfully or recklessly proceeded without making appropriate inquiries? The first formulation, which is objective, is less forgiving. The second ("Nelsonian"[732]) formulation, which is subjective, is more lenient. Which is preferable?

That question was addressed in *Air Canada v. M & L Travel Ltd.*, which is reproduced below. Although some Canadian courts previously applied the objective test,[733] the Supreme Court of Canada recently endorsed the more subjective approach.

The situation in England is more complex. As in Canada, the objective test[734] initially found favour, before giving way to a more subjective approach.[735] In 1995, however, Lord Nicholls, writing for the Privy Council in *Royal Brunei Airlines v. Tan*,[736] charted a new course. He decided that the relevant question pertains not to notice or knowledge, but rather to dishonesty. On that view, the action should be styled "dishonest assistance," rather than "knowing assistance." In 2002, the House of Lords agreed. The test articulated by the majority in *Twinsectra Ltd. v. Yardley*,[737] however, turns on a controversial interpretation of *Royal Brunei*. Lord Hutton's two-stage "combined test" requires the plaintiff to

---

731 *Anderson, Smyth & Kelly Customs Brokers Ltd. v. World Wide Customs Brokers Ltd., supra*, note 372.

732 The designation is derived from the remarks of Admiral Horatio Nelson at the Battle of Copenhagen in 1801. His superior officer, Admiral Hyde Parker, signalled him to "leave off action" in order to give Nelson the opportunity to retire, as the fighting was fierce. Nelson, convinced that he could destroy the enemy, chose to ignore the signal, stating "I have only one eye — I have a right to be blind sometimes." Then, putting his telescope to his blind eye (having lost sight in that eye in action at Corsica), he said, "I really do not see the signal." He went on to defeat the Danish fleet, thereby causing the dissolution of the League of the Northern Powers: Christopher Lloyd, *Nelson and Sea Power* (London: The English Universities Press Ltd., 1973), 100-1. See further on the two approaches to constructive knowledge: *Belmont Finance Corp. v. Williams Furniture Ltd.*, [1979] Ch. 250, [1979] 1 All E.R. 118, at 267 [Ch.], *per* Buckley L.J.

733 *MacDonald v. Hauer* (1976), [1977] 1 W.W.R. 51, 72 D.L.R. (3d) 110, 1976 CarswellSask 95 (C.A.).

734 *Selangor United Rubber Estates v. Cradock (No. 3), supra*, note 716; *Karak Rubber Co. Ltd. v. Burden (No. 2)*, [1972] 1 W.L.R. 602, [1972] 1 All E.R. 1210; and *Rowlandson v. National Westminster Bank*, [1978] 1 W.L.R. 798; *Baden, Delvaux and Lecuit v. Société Generale pour Favoriser le Développement du Commerce et de l'Industrie en France S.A.*, [1983] B.C.L.C. 325. See also *Consul Development Pty. Ltd. v. D.P.C. Estates Pty. Ltd.* (1975), 132 C.L.R. 373 (H.C.A.).

735 See, *e.g.*, *Carl-Zeiss Stiftung v. Herbert Smith & Co. (No. 2)*, [1969] 2 Ch. 276, [1969] 2 All E.R. 367 (C.A.).

736 [1995] 2 A.C. 378, [1995] 3 W.L.R. 64 (P.C.).

737 [2002] 2 A.C. 164 (H.L.).

prove: (i) that "the defendant's conduct was dishonest by the ordinary standards of reasonable and honest people," and (ii) that the defendant "himself realised that by those standards his conduct was dishonest."[738] The first part of that test is objective; the second is subjective. In a forceful dissent, Lord Millett insisted that, as long as the impugned conduct was dishonest as judged by ordinary standards, it should be irrelevant that the defendant failed to appreciate that his behaviour was unacceptable. Both *Royal Brunei Airlines v. Tan* and *Twinsectra Ltd. v. Yardley* are discussed at length in the notes following the extract of *Air Canada v. M & L Travel Ltd.* that appears below.

(iv) *The Nature of the Underlying Breach*

Assuming for the purposes of Canadian law that the defendant must have acted with a certain degree of knowledge, a final question arises: To what fact must that knowledge pertain? As seen below in *Air Canada v. M & L Travel Ltd.*, Iacobucci J. followed tradition and held that the plaintiff must prove that the defendant acted with the knowledge that the trustees were engaged in a "fraudulent and dishonest design."

Although English law previously followed that same path, it recently has charted a different course. In *Royal Brunei Airlines v. Tan*, the Privy Council held that as long as the stranger acted dishonestly, accessory liability should arise even if the trustees' underlying breach occurred in good faith. The House of Lords agreed with that decision in *Twinsectra Ltd. v. Yardley*. Those judgments are examined in greater detail in the notes following *Air Canada v. M & L Travel Ltd.*

AIR CANADA v. M & L TRAVEL LTD.

[1993] 3 S.C.R. 787, 50 E.T.R. 225, 108 D.L.R. (4th) 592, 67 O.A.C. 1, 159 N.R. 1, 15 O.R. (3d) 804 (note), 1993 CarswellOnt 568, 1993 CarswellOnt 994
Supreme Court of Canada

Martin owned M & L Travel Ltd., a travel agency. In 1977, the appellant, Valiant, acquired a 50 percent interest in the company. He borrowed money to make the investment and the parties agreed that he could withdraw the monthly instalments required to repay the loan from the company's operating account.

Martin was president and Valiant was vice-president of the company. They obtained an operating line of credit for $15,000 from a bank. Both guaranteed the loan and authorized the bank to withdraw moneys from the company's general account at any time to pay the loan. Both officers had signing authority, but Martin ran the business.

In 1978, the company entered into a passenger sales agency agreement with the International Air Transport Association (IATA), which entitled it to sell tickets

---

738 *Ibid.*, at 172.

and receive commissions. In March of 1979, the company entered into a passenger sales agency agreement with Air Canada, which entitled it to issue tickets directly to the public. This agreement provided that the funds collected from ticket sales were the property of Air Canada and that M & L would hold the funds in trust and remit them, less commissions, twice a month to Air Canada. Martin had set up trust accounts for the deposit of airline funds, but never used them. Instead, those moneys were deposited in the company's general operating account, together with funds from all other sources.

A dispute arose between Martin and Valiant in April of 1979. Martin thought that Valiant had agreed to stop making payments on his loan for the time being, but found cancelled cheques for the instalment payments. He took these to his lawyer and stopped payment on the last instalment. When Valiant discovered this, he changed the locks on the doors, and called the bank and stopped payment on all cheques and withdrawals. At that time the company owed Air Canada approximately $25,000.

While the dispute continued, both parties sought to pay Air Canada, but their efforts were unsuccessful. The bank sent a demand notice to the parties and when it was not honoured, withdrew the moneys owing on the operating line of credit from the company's general account. Air Canada then brought this action against M & L, Martin and Valiant for the amount owing to it for ticket sales. The trial judge awarded judgment against M & L, but dismissed the claim against Martin and Valiant. The Ontario Court of Appeal allowed Air Canada's appeal and also awarded judgment against Martin and Valiant.[739] Valiant appealed from that judgment.

IACOBUCCI J.:

. . .

III. ISSUES

[19] As mentioned at the outset, there are two main issues raised in this case. First, was the relationship between M & L and the respondent one of trust, or one of debtor and creditor? Second, if the relationship was one of trust, then under what circumstances can the directors of a corporation be held personally liable for breach of trust by the corporation, and are those circumstances present in this case?

IV. ANALYSIS

1. The Nature of the Relationship between M & L and Air Canada

[Iacobucci J. concluded that the relationship was one of trust and not debtor and creditor. Although the agreement with Air Canada did not require M &

---

739 (1991), 2 O.R. (3d) 184, 77 D.L.R. (4th) 536, 1991 CarswellOnt 984, 43 O.A.C. 215 (C.A.).

L to keep the airline moneys separate, it clearly spoke of a trust. He continued:]

2. *Personal Liability of the Directors as Constructive Trustees*

(a) *General Principles*

[31] Having found that the relationship between M & L and the respondent airline was a trust relationship, there is no question that M & L's actions were in breach of trust. M & L failed to account to the respondent for the monies collected through sales of Air Canada tickets. What remains to be decided is whether the directors of M & L should be held personally liable for the breach of trust on the basis that they were constructive trustees. Whether personal liability is imposed on a stranger to a trust depends on the basic question of whether the stranger's conscience is sufficiently affected to justify the imposition of personal liability.[740] The authorities reflect distinct approaches to answer this question depending on the circumstances of the case, and it is to these that I shall now turn.

[Iacobucci J. noted that the directors could not be held liable as trustees *de son tort*, because they did not take possession of the trust property, or assume the office of trustees.]

[34] Second, strangers to the trust can also be personally liable for breach of trust if they knowingly participate in a breach of trust. The starting point for a review of the bases of this kind of personal liability is *Barnes v. Addy*,[741] which involved an estate, for which three trustees had been designated by the testator. The will allowed for the appointment of new trustees without the consent of any other party, but did not allow for a decrease in the number of trustees. Two of the trustees died and a rift developed between the family and the third trustee, who wished to retire. He instructed his solicitor to prepare an instrument appointing Barnes, who was the husband of one of the beneficiaries, as sole trustee. The solicitor advised him against having only one trustee, but prepared the instrument on the instructions of his client. Barnes' solicitor approved the appointment. Barnes invested the trust funds for his own purposes and went bankrupt. The beneficiaries sued the previous trustee, his solicitor and Barnes' solicitor for breach of trust. The action against the solicitors was dismissed on the basis that they had no knowledge of, or any reason to suspect, a dishonest design in the transaction, and that they did not receive any trust property.

[35] Lord Selborne L.C. set out the ways in which a non-trustee can become responsible for a trust:

---

740 *Re Montagu's Settlement Trusts*, [1987] Ch. 264 at 285.
741 *Supra*, note 722.

[Iacobucci J. quoted part of the quotation from Lord Selborne's judgment set out above and continued:]

In addition to a trustee *de son tort*, there were traditionally therefore two ways in which a stranger to the trust could be held personally liable to the beneficiaries as a participant in a breach of trust: as one in receipt and chargeable with trust property and as one who knowingly assisted in a dishonest and fraudulent design on the part of the trustees. The former category of constructive trusteeship has been termed "knowing receipt" or "knowing receipt and dealing", while the latter category has been termed "knowing assistance".

[36] The former category of "knowing receipt" of trust property is inapplicable to the present case because it requires the stranger to the trust to have received trust property in his or her personal capacity, rather than as an agent of the trustees.[742] As I have already noted, the courts below found that the directors of M & L did not personally control the trust funds in the present case, and this finding was not challenged before us.

[37] Thus the only basis upon which the directors could be held personally liable as constructive trustees is under the "knowing assistance" head of liability. To repeat, in *Barnes v. Addy*,[743] Lord Selborne L.C. stated that persons who "assist with knowledge in a dishonest and fraudulent design on the part of the trustees" will be liable for the breach of trust as constructive trustees.[744] This basis of liability raises two main issues: the nature of the breach of trust and the degree of knowledge required of the stranger.

(b) *Degree of Knowledge of the Stranger*

[38] The latter point may be quickly addressed. The knowledge requirement for this type of liability is actual knowledge; recklessness or wilful blindness will also suffice.[745] In [*Carl-Zeiss-Stiftung v. Herbert Smith & Co.*[746]], Sachs L.J. stated that to be held liable the stranger must have had "both actual knowledge of the trust's existence and actual knowledge that what is being done is improperly in breach of that trust — though, of course, in both cases a person wilfully shutting his eyes to the obvious is in no different position than if he had kept them open." Whether the trust is created by statute or by contract may have an impact on the question of the stranger's knowledge of the trust. If the trust was imposed by

---

742 *Baden, Delvaux, supra*, note 734, appeal dismissed, [1985] B.C.L.C. 258 (C.A.); *International Sales & Agencies Ltd. v. Marcus* (1981), [1982] 3 All E.R. 551 (Q.B.); *Karak Rubber Co. v. Burden (No. 2), supra*, note 734, at 1234-1235; *Belmont Finance Corp. v. Williams Furniture Ltd., supra*, note 732, at 129, 134; Underhill and Hayton, *Law Relating to Trusts and Trustees* (14th ed. 1987), at 360; Philip H. Pettit, *Equity and the Law of Trusts* (6th ed. 1989), at 159-160. See, *contra, Lee v. Sankey* (1873), L.R. 15 Eq. 204.

743 *Supra*, note 722, at 252.

744 See also, *Soar v. Ashwell, supra*, note 513.

745 *Belmont Finance, supra*, note 732, at 130, 136; *Montagu's Settlement Trusts, supra*, note 740, at 271-272, 285; *Carl-Zeiss-Stiftung, supra*, note 735, at 379.

746 *Carl-Zeiss-Stiftung, ibid.*

statute, then he or she will be deemed to have known of it. If the trust was contractually created, then whether the stranger knew of the trust will depend on his or her familiarity or involvement with the contract.

[39] If the stranger received a benefit as a result of the breach of trust, this may ground an inference that the stranger knew of the breach.[747] The receipt of a benefit will be neither a sufficient nor a necessary condition for the drawing of such an inference.

[40] The reason for excluding constructive knowledge (that is, knowledge of circumstances which would indicate the facts to an honest person, or knowledge of facts which would put an honest person on inquiry) was discussed in *Re Montagu's Settlement Trusts*.[748] Megarry V.-C. held[749] that constructive notice was insufficient to bind the stranger's conscience so as to give rise to personal liability. While cases involving recklessness or wilful blindness indicate a "want of probity which justifies imposing a constructive trust", Megarry V.-C. held[750] that the carelessness involved in constructive knowledge cases will not normally amount to a want of probity, and will therefore be insufficient to bind the stranger's conscience.[751]

(c) *Nature of the Breach of Trust*

[41] With regard to the first issue, the nature of the breach of trust, the authorities can be divided into two lines. Most of the English authorities have followed the *Barnes v. Addy* standard which requires participation by the stranger in a dishonest and fraudulent design.[752] An extensive review of the authorities was undertaken by Ungoed-Thomas J. in the *Selangor* case. He concluded as follows:[753]

> I come to the third element, "dishonest and fraudulent design on the part of the trustees". I have already indicated my view, for reasons already given, that this must be understood in accordance with equitable principles for equitable relief.
>
> I therefore cannot accept the suggestion that, because an action is not of such a dishonest and fraudulent nature as to amount to some crime, that it is not fraudulent and dishonest in the eyes of equity — or that an intention eventually to restore or give value for property — which it

---

747 *Shields v. Bank of Ireland*, [1901] I.R. 22, at 228; *Gray v. Johnston* (1868), L.R. 3 H.L. 1 at 11 per Lord Cairns, L.C.; *Selangor United Rubber Estates Ltd. v. Cradock (No. 3)*, *supra*, note 716, at 1101, [1968] 1 W.L.R. 1555; *Coleman v. Bucks & Oxon Union Bank*, [1897] 2 Ch. 243 at 254; D.W.M. Waters, *Law of Trusts in Canada* (2nd ed., 1984), at 401; *Fonthill Lumber Ltd. v. Bank of Montreal*, [1959] O.R. 451 (C.A.), at 468; *Groves-Raffin Construction Ltd. v. Canadian Imperial Bank of Commerce* (1975), 64 D.L.R. (3d) 78 (B.C. C.A.), at 116-117.

748 *Supra*, note 740, at 271-273, 275-285.

749 *Ibid.*, at 255.

750 *Ibid.*, at 285.

751 See also, *Gorman v. Karpnale Ltd.* (1986), [1992] 4 All E.R. 331 (Q.B.), at 341-349, 351-357, reversed in part (1988), [1992] 4 All E.R. 409 (C.A.), at 416-418, reversed in part on other grounds (1990), [1992] 4 All E.R. 512, [1991] 2 A.C. 548, [1991] 3 W.L.R. 10 (H.L.).

752 *Carl-Zeiss-Stiftung*, *supra*, note 735, at 379; *Belmont Finance*, *supra*, note 732, at 135; Pettit, *supra*, note 742, at 154-156; Underhill, *supra*, note 742, at 355-357.

753 *Supra*, note 716, at 1104-1105 [footnote omitted].

was suggested might provide a good defence to a criminal charge — would of itself make its appropriation and use in the meantime, with its attendant risks and deprivation of the true owner, unobjectionable in equity, and thus make what would otherwise be dishonest and fraudulent free from such objection.

It was suggested for the plaintiff company that "fraudulent" imports the element of loss into what is dishonest, so that the phrase means dishonest resulting in loss to the claimant. It seems to me unnecessary and, indeed, undesirable to attempt to define "dishonest and fraudulent design", since a definition *in vacuo*, without the advantage of all the circumstances that might occur in cases that might come before the court, might be to restrict their scope by definition without regard to, and in ignorance of, circumstances which should patently come within them. The words themselves are not terms of art and are not taken from a statute or other document demanding construction. They are used in a judgment as the expression and indication of an equitable principle and not in a document as constituting or demanding verbal application and, therefore, definition. They are to be understood "according to the plain principles of a court of equity" to which SIR RICHARD KINDERSLEY, V.-C., referred,[754] and these principles, in this context at any rate, are just plain, ordinary commonsense. I accept that "dishonest and fraudulent", so understood, is certainly conduct which is morally reprehensible; but what is morally reprehensible is best left open to identification and not to be confined by definition.

[42] In *Belmont Finance*,[755] Goff L.J. discussed the approach taken on this issue by Ungoed-Thomas J. in *Selangor*:

> If and so far as Ungoed-Thomas J. intended, as I think he did, to say that it is not necessary that the breach of trust in respect of which it is sought to make the defendant liable as a constructive trustee should be fraudulent or dishonest, I respectfully cannot accept that view. I agree that it would be dangerous and wrong to depart from the safe path of the principle as stated by Lord Selborne LC[756] to the uncharted sea of something not innocent (and counsel for the plaintiff conceded that mere innocence would not do) but still short of dishonesty.

> In my judgment, therefore, it was necessary in this case . . . to prove, that the breach of trust by the directors [who were the trustees] was dishonest.

[43] In the same case, Buckley L.J. stated:[757]

> I do not myself see that any distinction is to be drawn between the words "fraudulent" and "dishonest"; I think they mean the same thing, and to use the two of them together does not add to the extent of dishonesty required. . . .

> The plaintiff has contended that in every case the court should consider whether the conduct in question was so unsatisfactory, whether it can be strictly described as fraudulent or dishonest in law, as to make accountability on the footing of constructive trust equitably just. This, as I have said, is admitted to constitute an extension of the rule as formulated by Lord Selborne LC.[758] That formulation has stood for more than 100 years. To depart from it now would, I think, introduce an undesirable degree of uncertainty to the law, because if dishonesty is not to be the criterion, what degree of unethical conduct is to be sufficient? I think we should adhere to the formula used by Lord Selborne LC. So in my judgment the design must be shown to be a dishonest one, that is to say, a fraudulent one.

---

754 In *Bodenham v. Hoskins* (1852), 21 L.J.Ch. 864, at 873; [1843-60] All E.R. Rep. at 697.
755 *Supra*, note 732, at 135.
756 In *Barnes v. Addy, supra*, note 722.
757 *Supra*, note 722, at 130.
758 In *Barnes v. Addy, supra*, note 722.

[44] In the oft-cited case of *Baden, Delvaux*,[759] Peter Gibson J. reviewed the authorities on this point:

> As to the second element the relevant design on the part of the trustee must be dishonest and fraudulent. In *Selangor*,[760] Ungoed-Thomas J. held that this element must be understood with equitable principles for equitable relief and that conduct which is morally reprehensible can properly be said to be dishonest and fraudulent for the purposes of that element. But in *Belmont Finance Corp. Ltd. v. Williams Furniture Ltd.*,[761], the Court of Appeal made clear that it is not sufficient that there should be misfeasance or a breach of trust falling short of dishonesty and fraud. For present purposes there is no distinction to be drawn between the two adjectives "fraudulent" and "dishonest".[762] It is common ground between the parties that I can take as a relevant description of fraud "the taking of a risk to the prejudice of another's rights, which risk is known to be one which there is no right to take."[763]

[45] The English "fraudulent" and "dishonest design" analysis was adopted by the Saskatchewan Court of Appeal in *MacDonald v. Hauer*.[764] In that case, one of the trustees opened a margin account in his own name for the purpose of securities trading. He pledged securities belonging to the estate for which he was trustee with a broker as security for the margin, and gave his business associate Hauer his power of attorney on the account. The profits on the account were to be shared equally between the trustee and Hauer. The estate's securities were eventually sold by Hauer. Bayda J.A. (as he then was) found Hauer liable in equity for breach of trust as a constructive trustee. Relying on *Barnes v. Addy*,[765] Bayda J.A. held[766] that the three essential elements for finding a stranger to a trust to be a constructive trustee were: "(1) assistance by the stranger of a nominated trustee (2) with knowledge (3) in a dishonest and fraudulent design on the part of the nominated trustee (or fraudulent or dishonest disposition of the trust property)", although it should be noted that Bayda J.A. appears later in his analysis also to rely on a passage from *Selangor*, supra, which is characteristic of the second approach, discussed below.

[46] *Barnes v. Addy* was also followed in *Scott v. Riehl*.[767] In that case, the two defendants were the directors of a construction company. The directors had failed to comply with the provisions of the *Mechanics' Lien Act, 1956*,[768] requiring certain monies to be held in trust. All monies received were deposited into one bank account, which was always overdrawn. The director and president of the corporation, Riehl, "knew that monies deposited, such as those received from the plaintiffs, must [not] be used for the general purposes of the company in abuse of the trust created by s. 3 of the Act. He knowingly created, maintained and

---

759 *Supra*, note 734, at 406.
760 *Supra*, note 716, at 1098, 1104.
761 *Supra*, note 732.
762 *Ibid.*, at 267.
763 *R. v. Sinclair*, [1968] 3 All ER 241.
764 *Supra*, note 733.
765 *Supra*, note 722.
766 *MacDonald v. Hauer*, *supra*, note 733, at 121.
767 (1958), 15 D.L.R. (2d) 67 (B.C. S.C.).
768 S.B.C. 1956, c. 27.

operated this unlawful system. The company was the instrument of its operation, but he was the director".[769] Wilson J. (as he then was) concluded as follows:[770]

> . . . on the facts here Riehl as, agent received and misdirected trust funds. The acts of reception and application of these particular monies may not physically have been his, but they were entirely directed by him, with the possible, although not proven, collusion of the defendant Schumak. Riehl received a benefit, through the payment of his salary out of the account into which these trust funds were paid. His complicity in the misappropriation of these funds is proven; it was not an act of negligence or a mistake of judgment but a wrongful act knowingly done. In these circumstances not only the principal but the agent is liable.
>
> I have not ignored the numerous cases cited to me by defence counsel in which it has been held that directors are not personally responsible to strangers for acts done by them on behalf of the company but are at most responsible to the company. I only say that none of these cases goes so far as to say that where a fraudulent breach of trust known by the director to be fraudulent, is done by the company at his direction, so that he is not only a party to but the instigator of the fraudulent breach of trust and benefits from the breach of trust he is not to be held liable.

[His Lordship also discussed *Wawanesa Mutual Insurance Co*,[771] and continued:]

[48] There is, however, a second line of Canadian authority, holding that a person who is the controlling or directing mind of a corporate trustee can be liable for an innocent or negligent breach of trust if the person knowingly assisted in the breach of trust. That is, in these cases, proof of fraud and dishonesty has not been required. In *Horsman Brothers Holdings Ltd. v. Panton*[772], which involved similar facts to those in *Scott v. Riehl*,[773] counsel for the beneficiary of the statutory trust conceded that the breach of trust was "innocent", that is, that the defendant directors had no knowledge that they were committing a breach of trust by conducting the corporation's affairs in the way in which they did. However, he relied upon the decision in *Scott v. Riehl* in support of the contention that the defendant directors should nonetheless be personally liable for the corporate breach of trust. Craig J. held as follows:[774]

> Counsel for the defendants seeks to distinguish the *Riehl* case on the ground that Wilson J. was dealing with a "fraudulent" breach of trust whereas in this case I am dealing with an "innocent" breach of trust. I am not sure that Wilson J. was dealing with a "fraudulent" breach of trust in the Riehl case, but, even if he were, I think that his remarks are equally applicable to an "innocent" breach of trust. If a person deals with the funds, which are within the meaning of s. 3, in a manner inconsistent with the trust, he breaches the trust, even though he may do so "innocently".
>
> . . .
>
> Accordingly, I find that the defendants did breach the trust provisions of s. 3 and that they are liable to the plaintiff for this breach.

---

769 *Supra*, at 70.
770 *Ibid.*, at 73-74.
771 (1969), 69 W.W.R. 612, 7 D.L.R. (3d) 283 (Sask. Q.B.).
772 [1976] 3 W.W.R. 745 (B.C. S.C.).
773 *Supra*, note 767.
774 At 750-751.

[His Lordship next discussed *Trilec Installations Ltd. v. Bastion Construction Ltd.*,[775] *Henry Electric Ltd. v. Farwell*,[776] *Andrea Schmidt Construction Ltd. v. Glatt*,[777] and *Austin v. Habitat Development Ltd.*,[778] which were all to the same effect.]

[56] The modified standard found in many of the Canadian cases involving directors of a closely held corporation reflects a difficulty with the application of the strict *Barnes v. Addy* standard to cases in which the corporate trustee is actually controlled by the stranger to the trust. In *Barnes v. Addy*,[779] Lord Selborne L.C. expressed concerns regarding the imposition of liability on strangers to the trust in the absence of participation in a fraudulent and dishonest design: "those who create trusts do expressly intend, in the absence of fraud and dishonesty, to exonerate such agents of all classes from the responsibilities which are expressly incumbent, by reason of the fiduciary relation, upon the trustees." Later in his reasons, Lord Selborne L.C. reiterated this position:[780] "if we were to hold that [a solicitor] became a constructive trustee by the preparation of such a deed, . . . not having enabled any one, who otherwise might not have had the power, to commit a breach of trust, we should be acting . . . without authority. . .".

[57] Generally, there are good reasons for requiring participation in a fraudulent and dishonest breach of trust before imposing liability on agents of the trustees:

> Unlike the stranger who takes title, an agent who disposes of trust property has no choice in the matter. He is contractually bound to act as directed by his principal the trustee. It is one thing to tell an agent that he must breach his contract rather than participate in a fraud on the part of his principal. It is quite another to tell him that he must breach his contract any time he believes his principal's instructions are contrary to the terms of the trust. This is to tell the agent that he must first of all master the terms of his principal's undertaking and, secondly, enforce his own understanding of what that undertaking entails. In effect, it burdens him with the duties of trusteeship upon the mere receipt of trust property as agent. As we have seen, however, properly understood, the role of agent is distinct from that of trustee. An agent is not to be made a trustee de son tort unless he voluntarily repudiates the role of agent and takes on the job of a trustee. So long as he chooses to remain an agent, his loyalties are to his principal, the trustee, and he should be free to follow the latter's instructions short of participating in a fraud.[781]

[58] It must be remembered that it is the nature of the breach of trust that is under consideration at this point in the analysis, rather than the intent or knowledge of the stranger to the trust. That is, the issue here is whether the breach of trust was fraudulent and dishonest, not whether the appellant's actions should be so characterized. *Barnes v. Addy* clearly states that the stranger will be liable if he

---

775 (1982), 135 D.L.R. (3d) 766 (B.C.C.A.).

776 (1986) 5 B.C.L.R. (2d) 273, 29 D.L.R. (4th) 481 (C.A.).

777 (1979), 25 O.R. (2d) 567, 104 D.L.R. (3d) 130 (H.C.J.), affirmed (1980), 28 O.R. (2d) 672, 112 D.L.R. (3d) 371 (C.A.).

778 (1992), 94 D.L.R. (4th) 359 (N.S.C.A.).

779 *Supra*, note 722, at 252.

780 *Ibid.*, at 253.

781 Ruth Sullivan, "Strangers to the Trust" [1986] Est. and Tr. Q. 217 at 246 [footnote omitted].

or she knowingly assisted the trustee in a fraudulent and dishonest breach of trust. Therefore, it is the corporation's actions which must be examined. The appellant's actions will also be relevant to this examination, given the extent to which M & L was controlled by the defendant directors. The appellant's conduct will be more directly scrutinized when the issue of knowledge is under consideration. It is unnecessary, therefore, to find that the appellant himself acted in bad faith or dishonestly.

[59] Where the trustee is a corporation, rather than an individual, the inquiry as to whether the breach of trust was dishonest and fraudulent may be more difficult to conceptualize, because the corporation can only act through human agents who are often the strangers to the trust whose liability is in issue. Regardless of the type of trustee, in my view, the standard adopted by Peter Gibson J. in the *Baden, Delvaux* case,[782] following the decision of the English Court of Appeal in *Belmont Finance*,[783] is a helpful one. I would therefore "take as a relevant description of fraud 'the taking of a risk to the prejudice of another's rights, which risk is known to be one which there is no right to take'." In my opinion, this standard best accords with the basic rationale for the imposition of personal liability on a stranger to a trust which was enunciated in *Re Montagu's Settlement Trusts*,[784] namely, whether the stranger's conscience is sufficiently affected to justify the imposition of personal liability. In that respect, the taking of a knowingly wrongful risk resulting in prejudice to the beneficiary is sufficient to ground personal liability. This approach is consistent with both lines of authority previously discussed.

[60] In the instant case, as a party to the contract between itself and the respondent, M & L knew that the Air Canada monies were held in trust for the respondent, and were not for the general use of M & L. Trust accounts were set up by M & L in 1978, but never used. M & L also knew that any positive balance in its general account was subject to the Bank's demand. By placing the trust monies in the general account which were then subject to seizure by the Bank, M & L took a risk to the prejudice of the rights of the respondent beneficiary, Air Canada, which risk was known to be one which there was no right to take.[785] Therefore, the breach of trust by M & L was dishonest and fraudulent from an equitable standpoint.

[61] It is clear that the appellant participated or assisted in the breach of trust. As was the case in *Horsman Brothers*,[786] the appellant dealt with the funds in question: in particular, he stopped payment on all cheques, and then opened a trust account and attempted to withdraw the stop payment orders and to transfer the funds into the new trust account in order to pay the respondent. The breach of trust was directly caused by the conduct of the defendant directors. As Griffiths J.A. observed,[787] "[t]he movement of these directors, acting solely in their own

---

782 *Supra*, note 734.
783 *Supra*, note 732.
784 *Supra*, note 740
785 *Baden, Delvaux*, *supra*, note 734; *Scott v. Riehl*, *supra*, note 767.
786 *Supra*, note 772.
787 At 204.

interest to stop payment on cheques, not only prevented payment on cheques issued to Air Canada, but precipitated the seizure by the bank of the only funds available in the unprotected general account." In such circumstances, the directors are personally liable for the breach of trust as constructive trustees provided that the requisite knowledge on the part of the directors is proved.

[62] With respect to the knowledge requirement, this will not generally be a difficult hurdle to overcome in cases involving directors of closely held corporations. Such directors, if active, usually have knowledge of all of the actions of the corporate trustee. In the instant case, the analysis is somewhat more difficult to resolve, as the appellant was not as closely involved with the day-to-day operations as was the other director, Martin. However, the appellant knew of the terms of the agreement between M & L and the respondent airline, as he signed that agreement. The appellant also knew that the trust funds were being deposited in the general bank account, which was subject to the demand loan from the Bank. This constitutes actual knowledge of the breach of trust. That is, even if the appellant could argue that he had no subjective knowledge of the breach of trust, given the facts of which he did have subjective knowledge, he was wilfully blind to the breach, or reckless in his failure to realize that there was a breach. Furthermore, the appellant received a benefit from the breach of trust, in that his personal liability to the Bank on the operating line of credit was extinguished. Therefore, he knowingly and directly participated in the breach of trust, and is personally liable to the respondent airline for that breach.

[His Lordship dismissed the appeal.

La Forest, Sopinka, Gonthier, Cory and Major JJ., concurred. McLachlin J. wrote a short concurring judgment.]

Notes and Questions

1. In the penultimate paragraph of his judgment, Iacobucci J. said that the directors were "personally liable for the breach of trust as constructive trustees." Is that statement inherently contradictory? How can the defendants be held "personally liable" as "constructive trustees"?

2. Iacobucci J. held that liability for knowing assistance requires proof of two things. First, the plaintiff must prove that the defendant had actual knowledge of the underlying breach, or was reckless or wilfully blind to the facts. Second, the plaintiff must prove that the underlying breach was part of the trustees' "fraudulent and dishonest design." Iacobucci J. further indicated, however, that as long as the defendant acted knowingly, there was no need for proof that he or she also acted dishonestly or in bad faith. In other words, fraud and dishonesty must be established with respect to the trustees' behaviour, but not the defendant's.

What reasons did Iacobucci J. provide in support of each of those propositions? Are those reasons persuasive? As discussed in the next two notes, Iacobucci J.'s approach has not fared well in the Privy Council and the House of Lords, where it has been held that liability should triggered by: (i) the defendant's *dishonest* participation — and not by his or her *knowing* participation, (ii) in *any* breach by the trustees — and not only in a *fraudulent and dishonest* breach by the trustees.

3. The facts in *Royal Brunei Airlines v. Tan*[788] resembled those in *Air Canada*. The airline appointed a travel agency to act as its general travel agent for the sale of passenger and cargo transportation. Tan was the managing director and principal shareholder of the travel agency. The agreement with the travel agency required it to hold all moneys received by it for sales on behalf of the airline in trust for the airline and to account for the moneys to the airline within 30 days. The agency paid the moneys it collected into its general account from which it paid expenses and its bank overdraft. When the agency became insolvent, Royal Brunei sued Tan personally, arguing that he was a constructive trustee because he had knowingly assisted in a fraudulent and dishonest design on the part of the agency, which was a trustee for the airline.

> The Privy Council held Tan liable. The agency had committed a breach of trust when it used the moneys it was to hold in trust in the operation of its business, and Tan, by causing or permitting the agency to do so, had dishonestly assisted in the breach. Both the agency and Tan had acted dishonestly. In the process of finding Tan liable, the Privy Council restated some basic principles. It said that for a stranger to be liable, there must be a breach of trust or other fiduciary obligation and the stranger must have dishonestly procured or assisted in that breach. At the same time, the Board said that while the stranger's dishonesty is essential to liability, the plaintiff need not prove that the trustee's breach was also dishonest, although that is usually the case. Lord Nicholls of Birkenhead, who delivered the opinion, explained.[789]
>
> It must be noted at once that there is a difficulty with the approach adopted on this point in the *Belmont* case.[790] Take the simple example of an honest trustee and a dishonest third party. Take a case where a dishonest solicitor persuades a trustee to apply trust property in a way the trustee honestly believes is permissible but which the solicitor knows full well is a clear breach of trust. The solicitor deliberately conceals this from the trustee. In consequence, the beneficiaries suffer a substantial loss. It cannot be right that in such a case the accessory liability principle would be inapplicable because of the innocence of the trustee. In ordinary parlance, the beneficiaries have been defrauded by the solicitor. If there is to be an accessory liability principle at all, whereby in appropriate circumstances beneficiaries may have direct recourse against a third party, the principle must surely be applicable in such a case, just as much as in a case where both the trustee and the third party have been dishonest. Indeed, if anything, the case for liability of the dishonest third party seems stronger where the trustee is innocent, because in such a case the third party alone was dishonest and that was the cause of the subsequent misapplication of the trust property.
>
> The position would be the same if, instead of *procuring* the breach, the third party dishonestly *assisted* in the breach. Change the facts slightly. A trustee is proposing to make a payment out of the trust fund to a particular person. He honestly believes he is authorised to do so by the terms of the trust deed. He asks a solicitor to carry through the transaction. The solicitor well knows that the proposed payment would be a plain breach of trust. He also well knows that the trustee mistakenly believes otherwise. Dishonestly he leaves the trustee under his misapprehension and prepares the necessary documentation. Again, if the accessory principle is not to be artificially constricted, it ought to be applicable in such a case.
>
> These examples suggest that what matters is the state of mind of the third party sought to be made liable, not the state of mind of the trustee. The trustee will be liable in any event for the breach of trust, even if he acted innocently, unless excused by an exemption clause in the trust instrument or relieved by the court. But *his* state of mind is essentially irrelevant to the question whether the *third party* should be made liable to the beneficiaries for the breach of trust. If the

---

788 *Supra*, note 736.
789 *Ibid.*, at 384-5.
790 *Supra*, note 732.

liability of the third party is fault-based, what matters is the nature of his fault, not that of the trustee. In this regard dishonesty on the part of the third party would seem to be a sufficient basis for his liability, irrespective of the state of mind of the trustee who is in breach of trust. It is difficult to see why, if the third party dishonestly assisted in a breach, there should be a further prerequisite to his liability, namely that the trustee also must have been acting dishonestly. The alternative view would mean that a dishonest third party is liable if the trustee is dishonest, but if the trustee did not act dishonestly that of itself would excuse a dishonest third party from liability. That would make no sense.

Lord Nicholls defined dishonesty as:[791]

... not acting as an honest person would in the circumstances. This is an objective standard. At first sight this may seem surprising. Honesty has a connotation of subjectivity, as distinct from the objectivity of negligence. Honesty, indeed, does have a strong subjective element in that it is a description of a type of conduct assessed in the light of what a person actually knew at the time, as distinct from what a reasonable person would have known or appreciated. Further, honesty and its counterpart dishonesty are mostly concerned with advertent conduct, not inadvertent conduct. Carelessness is not dishonesty. Thus for the most part dishonesty is to be equated with conscious impropriety. However, these subjective characteristics of honesty do not mean that individuals are free to set their own standards of honesty in particular circumstances. The standard of what constitutes honest conduct is not subjective. Honesty is not an optional scale, with higher or lower values according to the moral standards of each individual. If a person knowingly appropriates another's property, he will not escape a finding of dishonesty simply because he sees nothing wrong in such behaviour.

His Lordship then went on to discuss situations in which there is some doubt about whether the stranger was dishonest and notes that this is the reason that dishonesty must be measured objectively. On this point he concluded:[792]

To inquire, in such cases, whether a person dishonestly assisted in what is later held to be a breach of trust is to ask a meaningful question, which is capable of being given a meaningful answer. This is not always so if the question is posed in terms of "knowingly" assisted. Framing the question in the latter form all too often leads one into tortuous convolutions about the "sort" of knowledge required, when the truth is that "knowingly" is inapt as a criterion when applied to the gradually darkening spectrum where the differences are of degree and not kind.

His Lordship went on to note that negligent conduct is not sufficient to render a stranger liable. A stranger would be negligent when assisting in a breach of trust of which the stranger would have become aware had he or she exercised reasonable diligence. Most strangers in this situation are agents of the trustee who owe the trustee a duty to exercise reasonable care and skill. That being so, there is no reason to impose liability on them towards the beneficiaries. Strangers who owe no duty of reasonable care and skill to the trustee should not have that duty imposed on them toward the beneficiaries.

His Lordship summarized the principles as follows:[793]

Drawing the threads together, their Lordships' overall conclusion is that dishonesty is a necessary ingredient in accessory liability. It is also a sufficient ingredient. A liability in equity to make good resulting loss attaches to a person who dishonestly procures or assists in a breach

791 *Ibid.*, at 389.
792 *Ibid.*, at 391.
793 *Ibid.*, at 392.

of trust or fiduciary obligation. It is not necessary that, in addition, the trustee or fiduciary was acting dishonestly, although this will usually be so where the third party who is assisting him is acting dishonestly. "Knowingly" is better avoided as a defining ingredient of the principle, and in the context of this principle the *Baden*[794] scale of knowledge is best forgotten.

In what ways do *Air Canada* and *Royal Brunei* differ? Which set of reasons is more persuasive?

4. The House of Lords addressed the same issues in *Twinsectra Ltd. v. Yardley.*[795] The plaintiff agreed to lend £1,000,000 to Yardley. Under the terms of that loan, Yardley was allowed to use the money for only one purpose: the purchase of land. The claimant paid the money to Sims, a solicitor who was associated with Yardley, but who was not acting for him in this matter. Sims gave his undertaking that he would not release the money to Yardley except in accordance with the loan conditions. In breach of that undertaking, Sims released the money to Leach, who was working as Yardley's solicitor. Leach in turn released the money to Yardley. Yardley improperly used £357,000 of the fund to pay off a debt. The claimant was unable to recover that amount and therefore brought a number of actions. For present purposes, the relevant claim was against Leach. The claimant argued that Yardley had received the money on trust, that Yardley had paid away £357,000 of that money in breach of trust, and that Leach was liable for dishonestly assisting in that breach.

At first instance, Carnwath J. held that the loan arrangement did not involve a trust. Although that finding was sufficient to dispose of the claim, the trial judge went on to find that while Leach was "misguided" and had shut his eyes to the implications of Sims' undertaking, he had not acted dishonestly. The Court of Appeal reversed on both issues and imposed liability. In the House of Lords, there was unanimous agreement that the loan money was impressed with a trust, and that Leach had in fact assisted in a breach of that trust. Moreover, each member of the panel agreed that English law should follow the formulation of the action for dishonest assistance that Lord Nicholls articulated in *Royal Brunei*. Unfortunately, the House was split as to the proper interpretation of Lord Nicholls' occasionally cryptic comments.

The majority decision is represented by Lord Hutton's judgment. He began by recognizing three possible tests of dishonesty.

> [T]here are three possible standards which can be applied to determine whether a person has acted dishonestly. There is a purely subjective standard, whereby a person is only regarded as dishonest if he transgresses his own standard of honesty, even if that standard is contrary to that of reasonable and honest people. This has been termed the "Robin Hood test" and has been rejected by the courts. . . . Secondly, there is a purely objective standard whereby a person acts dishonestly if his conduct is dishonest by the ordinary standards of reasonable and honest people, even if he does not realise this. Thirdly, there is a standard which combines an objective test and a subjective test, and which requires that before there can be a finding of dishonesty it must be established that the defendant's conduct was dishonest by the ordinary standards of reasonable and honest people and that he himself realised that by those standards his conduct was dishonest. I will term this "the combined test."[796]

---

794   *Baden v. Société Générale pour Favoriser le Développement du Commerce et de l'industrie en France S.A.*, [1992] 4 All E.R. 161.

795   *Supra*, note 34.

796   *Ibid.*, at 171-172.

Lord Hutton then held, as a matter of interpretation, that Lord Nicholls' test of dishonesty was of the third variety. He accordingly concluded that:

> . . .dishonesty requires knowledge by the defendant that what he was doing would be regarded as dishonest by honest people, although he should not escape a finding of dishonesty because he sets his own standards of honesty and does not regard as dishonest what he knows would offend the normally accepted standards of honest conduct.[797]

Lord Hutton further supported that view with a policy argument.

> A finding by a judge that a defendant has been dishonest is a grave finding, and it is particularly grave against a professional man, such as a solicitor. Notwithstanding that the issue arises in equity law and not in a criminal context, I think that it would be less than just for the law to permit a finding that a defendant had been "dishonest" in assisting in a breach of trust where he knew of the facts which created the trust and its breach but had not been aware that what he was doing would be regarded by honest men as being dishonest.[798]

Applying the "combined test" of dishonesty, Lord Hutton referred to the trial judge's findings of fact and held that since Leach had not actually realized that what he was doing violated ordinary standards of honesty, he could not be held liable.

Lord Millett delivered a forceful dissent. While agreeing that English law should follow *Royal Brunei*, he rejected Lord Hutton's interpretation of Lord Nicholls' earlier opinion. He began by noting that the second branch of Lord Hutton's "combined test" essentially adopts the criminal law test of dishonesty[799] — a test that Lord Nicholls appeared to have expressly rejected in *Royal Brunei*. For the purposes of accessory liability in equity, Lord Millett preferred a test that was based on the defendant's conduct (as judged by his actual knowledge of the relevant facts) and concluded that "it is not necessary that he should actually have appreciated that he was acting dishonestly; it is sufficient that he was."[800]

Lord Millett offered several arguments in favour of his approach. He noted, for instance, that as opposed to criminal liability, which is premised upon a *mens rea*, civil liability "does not ordinarily require a guilty mind. Civil liability is usually predicated on the defendant's conduct rather than his state of mind; it results from his negligent or unreasonable behaviour or, where this is not sufficient, from intentional wrongdoing."[801] As an example, Lord Millett noted the tort of inducing breach of contract, which parallels the equitable action for accessory liability, and which does not require proof of dishonesty in a subjective sense.

> It would be most undesirable if we were to introduce a distinction between the equitable claim and the tort, thereby inducing the claimant to attempt to spell a contractual obligation out of a fiduciary relationship in order to avoid the need to establish that the defendant had a dishonest state of mind. It would, moreover, be strange if equity made liability depend on subjective dishonesty when in a comparable situation the common law did not. This would be a reversal of the general rule that equity demands higher standards of behaviour than the common law.[802]

---

797 *Ibid.*, at 174.
798 *Ibid.*
799 *R. v. Ghosh*, [1982] Q.B. 1053 (C.A.).
800 [2002] 2 A.C. 164, at 198.
801 *Ibid.*, at 197.
802 *Ibid.*, at 201.

On the facts, Lord Millett believed that liability was appropriate. While Leach did not know that the funds were impressed with a trust at the outset, he did know that the plaintiff had given the money to Sims on the understanding that it could be made available to Yardley for the exclusive purpose of purchasing land. Leach nevertheless assisted Sims in breaking that undertaking by treating the money as if it was at Yardley's free disposal. (Lord Millett interpreted the trial judge's finding that Leach had "deliberately shut his eyes to the implications" to simply mean that Leach believed that the breach was not his problem, but rather Sims'.) Accordingly, just as Leach would have been liable in tort if the arrangement between the plaintiff and Sims had been entirely contractual in nature, so too he should be liable for assisting in a breach of the trust that existed between those parties.

Whose approach is preferable: Lord Hutton's or Lord Millett's? How does Iacobucci J.'s approach in *Air Canada* compare with each?

5. Similar issues arose in *Commercial Union Life Assurance Co. of Canada v. John Ingle Insurance Group Inc.*[803] The plaintiff operated a travel health insurance business. Because it was experiencing difficulties, it invited the individual defendant to join as director, chairman and chief executive officer. In due course, the individual defendant acquired control of a new corporation that had been created to run the enterprise. That corporation collected premiums and remitted a share to the plaintiff under the terms of an agreement. In time, however, the relationship deteriorated. The plaintiff demanded payment of certain funds, but the corporation, under the individual defendant's control, refused. Indeed, the individual defendant not only stopped remitting premiums, he also "then set up a competing business, transferred the funds and used them to fund the start-up costs of his competing business."[804]

The Ontario Court of Appeal found that the premiums collected by the corporation were impressed with a statutory trust under the *Insurance Act*, as well as an express trust under the terms of the parties' arrangement. It further found that the corporation had committed "a fraudulent, or dishonest, breach of trust"[805] by refusing to remit money to the plaintiff as required, and that the individual defendant, as the directing mind of the corporation, was liable for knowing assistance in the fraudulent scheme to withhold the trust funds.

In an attempt to avoid liability, the individual defendant invoked *Twinsectra* and argued that the plaintiff was required to prove that he had acted with conscious dishonesty. Weiler J.A. appeared to reject that argument on the ground that the individual defendant *had* acted in such a manner.[806] A paragraph earlier in her judgment, however, she referred to *Air Canada* and stated that since the individual defendant had "subjective knowledge," and had "knowingly and directly participated in the breach of trust," it was "unnecessary to determine whether [he] had a dishonest state of mind when he engaged in this conduct."[807]

Are Weiler J.A.'s reasons entirely consistent with Canadian law? Did Iacobucci J. in *Air Canada* require proof of "subjective dishonesty," as the majority of the House of Lords did in *Twinsectra*?

---

803 (2002), 217 D.L.R. (4th) 178, 2002 CarswellOnt 2707, [2002] O.J. No. 3200, 162 O.A.C. 203, 61 O.R. (3d) 296, 50 C.C.L.I. (3d) 6 (C.A.), additional reasons at (2002), 2002 CarswellOnt 2928 (C.A.).

804 *Ibid.*, at 201.

805 *Ibid.*, at 200.

806 *Ibid.*, at 202.

807 *Ibid.*

6. *Grinnell Fire Protection Systems Co. v. Bank of Montreal*[808] is an example of a bank which benefited from a breach of trust, but which also had knowledge of the breach. C Corp. was the general contractor on a building project and the plaintiff was a subcontractor. C Corp. had a general purpose account with the defendant bank. All monies from all projects were paid into the account and all accounts were paid from it. C Corp. also had a revolving line of credit with the bank. C Corp. failed to pay the plaintiff for its work and went bankrupt. It was a trustee under a statutory provision which made all payments received by a contractor on account of the contract price a trust fund in favour of, *inter alia*, subcontractors.[809] The bank applied many of the progress payments paid to C Corp. to itself to reduce the line of credit. The plaintiff sued the bank for the amount owing to it, alleging breach of trust by C Corp. and its officers, and assistance in the breach by the bank. The court found the bank liable. It was aware of the trust and of the fact that C Corp. was not complying with the trust and was breaching its trust. The bank avoided making inquiries to determine whether the subcontractors were being paid. Had it done so, it would have discovered the breach. Hence, the bank assisted C Corp. with knowledge in its fraudulent and dishonest dealings with the trust funds.[810]

7. *Winslow v. Richter*[811] is an example of a solicitor to a trustee who knowingly assisted the trustee in disposing of trust property to the detriment of the beneficiary. The defendant solicitor acted for a wife on a separation and prepared the separation agreement. The husband represented himself. The agreement provided that the plaintiff husband would transfer his interest in the matrimonial home to his wife, but that when she sold it he would receive half of the net proceeds. When the wife sold the house a year later, the solicitor acted for her on the sale and received the net proceeds in trust. She paid these out to the wife without telling the plaintiff. He brought this action for damages. The action was not properly pleaded, but the court treated it as if the plaintiff had pleaded that the defendant was a constructive trustee toward the plaintiff and dismissed the defendant's motion to dismiss the action. The court held that the defendant did not stand in a fiduciary relationship toward the plaintiff, but that the wife was a trustee toward the plaintiff. She breached her trust and the defendant knowingly assisted her in disposing of the trust property contrary to the trust. The defendant was not merely negligent (which would not have rendered her liable), but acted with wilful blindness or actual knowledge, since she drew the separation agreement.

8. Do partners in a firm of solicitors become liable as constructive trustees when one partner knowingly assists in the misappropriation of trust moneys which pass through the firm's trust account?[812]

What would be the firm's liability if one of its members is a trustee, the trust is handled though the firm and the trustee steals money from the trust?[813]

9. A solicitor received written notice from a creditor of his client that the client had, for good consideration, made an assignment of a certain sum of money which the client anticipated he would recover in a personal injury action being conducted on his behalf by the solicitor. In due course the client fraudulently misrepresented to his solicitor that the

---

808 (1986), 21 C.L.R. 44, 1986 CarswellBC 721 (S.C.).

809 *Builder's Lien Act*, R.S.B.C. 1989, c. 40, s. 2(1), see now *Builders Lien Act*, R.S.B.C. 1996, c. 41, s. 2(1).

810 See also *Groves-Raffin Construction Ltd.*, *supra*, note 747, to the same effect.

811 (1989), 39 B.C.L.R. (2d) 83, 35 E.T.R. 100, 61 D.L.R. (4th) 549, 1989 CarswellBC 148, (S.C.).

812 See *Bell's Indenture, Re*, [1980] 1 W.L.R. 1217, [1980] 3 All E.R. 425.

813 *Ontario (Public Trustee) v. Mortimer* (1985), 49 O.R. (2d) 741, 16 D.L.R. (4th) 404, 1985 CarswellOnt 697, 18 E.T.R. 219 (H.C.).

creditor had been satisfied. The solicitor, without checking with the creditor, paid the net proceeds recovered in the action to the client.

Is the solicitor liable in an action by the creditor? If so, on what basis?[814]

10. Thieves stole bearer bonds from the plaintiff. The thieves sold the bonds and invested the proceeds in other securities. When they were arrested and charged, the thieves engaged the defendants as their lawyers and transferred the securities to the defendants in payment of their legal services. Can the plaintiff recover the securities from the defendants?[815]

11. O Board is a statutory board with exclusive authority to buy wheat in the province and to appoint agents to act for it. The Board appointed A Ltd., a feed mill, as its agent to buy wheat. Under the regulations, the agent receives wheat on behalf of the Board (at which time it becomes the Board's property) and makes an initial payment to the farmer. The agent then informs the board and is reimbursed. The agent can also purchase wheat it has received from the Board by making an offer to that effect. Payment is then required on the 15th day of the next month, after which interest becomes payable.

A Ltd. encountered financial difficulties and R Bank, which held security from A Ltd. appointed B as its agent to manage the business. B negotiated with all of A Ltd.' s major trade creditors except the Board. A Ltd. then received large quantities of wheat from farmers, paid the initial payments, informed the Board and was reimbursed. Thereafter A Ltd. purported to sell the wheat to C Ltd. without making an offer to the Board first and was paid by C Ltd. B did inform the Board later, but meanwhile took advantage of the interest-free credit terms under the agency agreement. B was aware of the regulations, the agency agreement and the reasons for the delay in reporting. Some of the moneys paid by C Ltd. to A Ltd. are still held by it; some have been used by R Bank to repay A Ltd.' s indebtedness to it.

The Board discovered the situation and wants to recover the moneys paid by C Ltd. to A Ltd. What will be the basis of the action and the likely outcome?[816]

12. The Supreme Court of Canada's decision in *M. & L. Travel* has been applied on a number of occasions.[817]

814 *Triple A Holdings Ltd. v. Tick* (1971), 24 D.L.R. (3d) 100, 1971 CarswellBC 306 (S.C.).

815 *Newton v. Porter*, 69 N.Y. 133 (1877).

816 *Ontario (Wheat Producers' Marketing Board) v. Royal Bank* (1983), 41 O.R. (2d) 294, 1983 CarswellOnt 615, 15 E.T.R. 12, 145 D.L.R. (3d) 663 (H.C.), affirmed (1984), 1984 CarswellOnt 1365, 46 O.R. (2d) 362, 9 D.L.R. (4th) 729, 4 O.A.C. 391 (C.A.). See also *Lockeport (Town) v. J.F. Isenor Construction Ltd.* (1981), 47 N.S.R. (2d) 667, 90 A.P.R. 667, 1981 CarswellNS 171 (T.D.), affirmed (1982), 1981 CarswellNS 242, 53 N.S.R. (2d) 562, 109 A.P.R. 562 (C.A.).

817 *Sorrel 1985 Ltd. Partnership v. Sorrel Resources Ltd.* (2000), [2001] 1 W.W.R. 93, 2000 CarswellAlta 1023, 2000 ABCA 256, 85 Alta. L.R. (3d) 27, 10 B.L.R. (3d) 61, 277 A.R. 1, 242 W.A.C. 1 (C.A.); *Haida Nation v. British Columbia (Minister of Forests)* (2002), 216 D.L.R. (4th) 1, 2002 CarswellBC 2067, [2002] B.C.J. No. 1882, 2002 BCCA 462, 5 B.C.L.R. (4th) 33, [2002] 10 W.W.R. 587, [2002] 4 C.N.L.R. 117, 172 B.C.A.C. 75, 282 W.A.C. 75 (C.A.), leave to appeal allowed (2003), 2003 CarswellBC 696, 2003 CarswellBC 697, 310 N.R. 200 (note) (S.C.C.); *Alers-Hankey v. Solomon, supra*, note 724; *Glenko Enterprises Ltd. v. Keller* (2000), [2001] 1 W.W.R. 229, 2000 CarswellMan 467, [2000] M.J. No. 444, 2000 MBCA 7, 5 C.L.R. (3d) 1, 150 Man. R. (2d) 1, 230 W.A.C. 1 (C.A.).

(d) Knowing Receipt

(i) *Isolating the Cause of Action*

The action for knowing receipt involves a stranger who improperly acquires trust property.[818] Because of the risk of confusion, that species of claim must be carefully identified and isolated.

To begin, it is important to distinguish a stranger who is liable for knowing receipt from one who is liable as a trustee *de son tort*. In either situation, the stranger exercises authority over trust property. There are, nevertheless, several significant differences. First, the trustee *de son tort* purports to administer the trust property on behalf of the beneficiary. The stranger who is liable for knowing receipt, in contrast, purports to acquire the property on his or her own behalf. Second, as we shall see, the constituent elements of the applicable causes of action differ. Third, for the purposes of limitation periods, a trustee *de son tort* is regarded as an express trustee, with the result that time does not run against him or her.[819] In contrast, a stranger who is held liable as a "constructive trustee" as a result of knowing receipt is not treated as an express trustee and consequently may be protected by the lapse of a limitation period. This distinction is no longer significant in jurisdictions which now treat all constructive trustees alike for limitation purposes,[820] but it remains significant in most Canadian provinces. This issue is discussed in the chapter on breach of trust.

It is also important to distinguish between the different forms of liability that may be visited upon a stranger who improperly receives trust property for his or her own benefit.[821] If the property not only was received, but also (traceably) retained, the stranger may hold it on constructive trust. (That may also be true of a subsequent recipient who continues to hold possession of the asset.) Alternatively, a stranger who continues to hold trust property may be held personally liable as a "constructive trustee" under an action in knowing receipt. In contrast, however, a stranger who received, but no longer retains, misdirected assets can be held personally, but not proprietarily liable. Without trust property, there cannot be a constructive trust. Nevertheless, a personal action for *receipt* (as opposed to *retention*) remains possible.

---

818 The same principles may apply if property is improperly received by way of breach of fiduciary duty, whether or not the property in question was held on trust. Liability consequently may be imposed upon a third party who receives company property that was misapplied by a director: *Houghton v. Fayers*, [2000] Lloyds Rep. Bank. 145 (C.A.); *Bank of Credit and Commerce Intl. (Overseas) Ltd. v. Akindele*, [2001] Ch. 437, [2000] 4 All E.R. 221 (C.A.).

819 *Soar v. Ashwell, supra*, note 513; *Taylor v. Davies, supra*, note 267.

820 As in England. See the *Limitation Act 1980*, c. 58 (U.K.), s. 21(3).

821 The rights available to a beneficiary upon a breach of trust are considered in more detail in a later chapter.

(ii) *Bona Fide Purchase for Value Without Notice*

The scheme outlined in the previous paragraph is subject to an important caveat.[822] A stranger who acquires the legal estate in trust property for value, *bona fide* and without notice of a breach of trust, takes free of the beneficiaries' equitable interests.[823] The beneficiaries have neither a proprietary remedy[824] nor a personal remedy against the stranger (although they may have rights against the defalcating trustee). Moreover, since the *bona fide* purchase of a legal interest is said to extinguish pre-existing equitable interests, the purchaser generally can pass clear title onto subsequent recipients — including volunteers and people who obtain their interests with notice of the beneficiaries' prior rights.[825] An exception to that scheme applies only if the subsequent recipient was the trustee or a party to the breach.[826] In that instance, the beneficiaries' interest is revived and the property once again is held on their behalf.[827]

Two more observations can be added in the interests of clarity. First, the preceding rules apply to the *bona fide* purchase of *legal* interests. A *bona fide* purchase of an *equitable* interest generally does not have the same effect. *Qui prior est tempore potior est jure.*[828] Equitable interests normally take priority in the order that they were created.[829]

Second, while the *bona fide* purchase of a legal interest extinguishes pre-existing *equitable* interests, it normally does not have the same effect on pre-

---

822 The discussion in this sub-section is confined to the rules developed by the courts of law and equity. In many circumstances, priority of successive interests are now governed by legislation and statutory registration schemes.

823 *Pilcher v. Rawlins* (1871), L.R. 7 Ch. 259. Observe that the test involves (actual or constructive) notice, rather than knowledge, when the question pertains to priority of successive interests, rather than to accessory liability. Unfortunately, judges do not always draw a distinction between notice and knowledge.

824 *Harrison v. Mathieson* (1916), 36 O.L.R. 347, 30 D.L.R. 150 (C.A.).

825 *Wilkes v. Spooner*, [1911] 2 K.B. 473; *Durbin v. Monserat Investments Ltd.* (1978), 87 D.L.R. (3d) 593, 1978 CarswellOnt 540, 20 O.R. (2d) 181, 5 R.P.R. 15 (C.A.); but see *Thomson v. Harrison*, 60 O.L.R. 484, [1927] 3 D.L.R. 526 (Co. Ct.).

826 *Barrow's Case* (1880), 14 Ch. D. 432.

827 R. Chambers, *An Introduction to Australian Property Law* (Sydney: LBC Information Services, 2001), c. 29.

828 He or she who is first in time is preferred in law.

829 Equity's scheme is, in fact, somewhat more complicated than the maxim might suggest. As a general rule, successive equitable interests take priority in order of their creation. However, an exception *may* (though not necessarily *will*) arise if the newer interest was acquired for value, in good faith and without notice of the older interest. If those requirements are satisfied, then it is necessary to consider the nature of the older interest. If the older interest is a "mere equity," then the newer interest will take priority. If the older interest is not a "mere equity," then the newer interest generally will take priority if the holder of the older interest failed to take reasonable steps to protect it. A different rule applies, however, if the older interest consisted of beneficial title under an express trust. Express trust beneficiaries are not expected to take steps to protect their rights — that is, after all, the job of the trustee. Consequently, in a competition between successive equitable interests, the beneficiaries under an express trust will lose priority to a newer interest only if they did something that misled the holder of the new interest into believing that the trust did not exist. See Chambers, *supra*.

existing *legal* interests. Indeed, under the rule of *nemo dat quod non habet*,[830] it generally is impossible for a person to obtain title from anyone other than the true owner. Given a choice between maintaining the integrity of legal title and protecting *bona fide* purchases, the common law typically prefers the former. As a result, for instance, a person who honestly and reasonably pays fair market value to a car thief does not obtain clear title to the vehicle. To the contrary, he or she commits the tort of conversion. There is, however, one very significant exception to that scheme.[831] The *bona fide* purchase of the legal estate in *money* does extinguish pre-existing legal interests so as to confer clear title upon the purchaser. The explanation for that rule lies in commercial reality. Money is effective as currency only if it can be passed easily in the marketplace.[832]

(iii) *The Nature of the Claim*

Although the claim for knowing receipt clearly exists, its precise nature is a matter of debate. Broadly speaking, there are two possibilities.[833] Knowing receipt may be a species of wrongdoing. Some see it, for instance, as the equitable analogue of the tort of conversion.[834] If that is true, then perhaps liability is triggered by the stranger's breach of an obligation to refrain from interfering with the beneficiary's property rights. Alternatively, knowing receipt may be a species of unjust enrichment. If that is true, then liability is not triggered by the stranger's wrongdoing *per se*, but rather, following the general cause of action in unjust enrichment,[835] because: (i) the stranger was enriched, (ii) the beneficiary suffered the corresponding deprivation, and (iii) there was an absence of any juristic reason for that enrichment.

In contrast to English courts, which, despite some debate, continue to view knowing receipt as an equitable wrong,[836] the Supreme Court of Canada has characterized the action as an instance of unjust enrichment.

---

830 No one can give what he or she does not have.

831 There are, in fact, a number of exceptions to the general rule of *nemo dat quod non habet*. See J.S. Ziegel & A.J. Duggan, *Commercial and Consumer Sales Transactions*, 4th ed. (Toronto: Emond Montgomery, 2002), c. 14; R. Goode, *Commercial Law*, 2nd ed. (London: Butterworths, 1995), c. 14.

832 D. Fox, "Bona Fide Purchase and the Currency of Money" (1996), 55 Cambridge L.J. 547.

833 As a third possibility, it may be that two distinct heads of liability ought to be drawn out of the traditional concept of knowing receipt: one a species of wrongdoing, the other a species of unjust enrichment. See Lord Nicholls, "Knowing Receipt: The Need for a New Landmark", in W. Cornish *et al.*, eds., *Restitution: Past, Present & Future* (Oxford: Oxford University Press, 1998) 231; P. Birks, "Receipt", in P. Birks & A. Pretto, eds., *Breach of Trust* (Oxford: Hart, 2002) 212.

834 L.D. Smith, "W(h)ither Knowing Receipt" (1998), 114 L.Q. Rev. 394; L.D. Smith, "Unjust Enrichment, Property and the Structure of Trusts" (2000), 116 L.Q. Rev. 412.

835 *Becker v. Pettkus*, *supra*, note 7. The cause of action in unjust enrichment was discussed earlier in this chapter.

836 *Carl-Zeiss Stiftung v. Herbert Smith & Co. (No. 2)*, *supra*, note 735. There is support for the view that since dishonest assistance and knowing receipt are both forms of wrongdoing, they should simply be regarded as different manifestations of a unitary action for improper participation in breach of an equitable obligation: *Fyffes Group Ltd. v. Templeman*, *supra*, note 727.

(iv) *The Elements of Proof*

Significantly, however, as discussed in the notes that follow the extract of *Citadel General Assurance Co. v. Lloyds Bank Canada*[837] that appears below, the Supreme Court of Canada's formulation of the constituent elements of the action for knowing receipt is controversial. Liability in unjust enrichment generally is "strict" in the sense that it is triggered by the mere fact that the plaintiff did not intend to confer a benefit upon the defendant. In the present context, that would suggest that relief should be available simply because the beneficiary did not consent to the disposition of the trust property to the stranger. Nevertheless, in *Citadel Assurance*, La Forest J. further required the beneficiary to demonstrate that the stranger had at least constructive knowledge that trust funds were being misdirected.

Likewise, English courts have struggled to settle the constituent elements of the civil wrong of knowing receipt. Some authorities have required proof of the recipient's dishonesty,[838] others have been satisfied by proof of constructive knowledge,[839] and recently the Court of Appeal has said that the touchstone of liability is unconscionability.[840] Those possibilities are further examined the notes that follow the extract of *Citadel Assurance* that appears below.

(v) *The Nature of Relief*

Following general principles, if the action in knowing receipt is a species of unjust enrichment, then the response must be restitution.[841] The stranger is required to give back the value that he or she received at the beneficiary's expense. In contrast, if the action is a species of equitable wrongdoing, then (as in the case of knowing or dishonest assistance) the response should be either compensation of the beneficiary's loss or disgorgement of the stranger's gain. In any event,

---

As Lord Nicholls observed extra-judicially, "receipt of property is incidental, in the sense that it is merely the form which the dishonest participation takes": "The Need for a New Landmark" in W. Cornish *et al.*, eds., *Restitution: Past, Present & Future* (Oxford: Hart, 1998) 231 at 244. That view has been endorsed by the High Court of Australia: *Consul Development Pty. Ltd. v. DPC Estates Pty. Ltd.*, *supra*, note 734, at 397 (H.C.A.); *Warman Intl. Ltd. v. Dwyer*, *supra*, note 360. See also J. Edelman, *Gain-Based Damages: Contracts, Tort, Equity and Intellectual Property* (Oxford: Hart, 2002), 201.

837 (1997), 152 D.L.R. (4th) 411, 1997 CarswellAlta 823, 1997 CarswellAlta 824, [1997] S.C.J. No. 92, 206 A.R. 321, 156 W.A.C. 321, 19 E.T.R. (2d) 93, 35 B.L.R. (2d) 153, 47 C.C.L.I. (2d) 153, [1997] 3 S.C.R. 805, 219 N.R. 323, [1999] 4 W.W.R. 135, 66 Alta. L.R. (3d) 241. See also the companion case of *Gold v. Rosenberg* (1997), 152 D.L.R. (4th) 385, 1997 CarswellOnt 3273, 1997 CarswellOnt 3274, [1997] S.C.J. No. 93, 219 N.R. 93, 35 O.R. (3d) 736, 19 E.T.R. (2d) 1, 104 O.A.C. 1, 35 B.L.R. (2d) 212, [1997] 3 S.C.R. 767, which is discussed in the notes that follow.

838 *Bank of America v. Arnell*, *supra*, note 26.

839 *Belmont Finance Corp. v. Williams Furniture Ltd. (No. 2)*, *supra*, note 732, at 274 (C.A.); *Houghton v. Fayers*, *supra*, note 817.

840 *Bank of Credit and Commerce International (Overseas) Ltd. v. Akindele*, *supra*, note 818.

841 M. McInnes, "The Measure of Restitution" (2002), 52 U.T.L.J. 163.

since the question pertains to the stranger's liability as a "constructive trustee," the form of relief is personal rather than proprietary.

CITADEL GENERAL ASSURANCE CO. v. LLOYDS BANK CANADA

(1997), [1997] 3 S.C.R. 805, 19 E.T.R. (2d) 93, 152 D.L.R. (4th) 411, 219 N.R. 323, 206 A.R. 321, 1997 CarswellAlta 823, 1997 CarswellAlta 824, [1997] S.C.J. No. 92, 156 W.A.C. 321, 35 B.L.R. (2d) 153, 47 C.C.L.I. (2d) 153, [1999] 4 W.W.R. 135, 66 Alta. L.R. (3d) 241
Supreme Court of Canada

Citadel General Assurance Company and Citadel Life Assurance Company (collectively "Citadel") underwrote insurance sold by Drive On Guaranteed Vehicle Payment Plan (1982) Limited ("Drive On") to auto dealers. Auto dealers collected premiums when they sold cars and remitted them to Drive On. After it collected the premiums, Drive On paid commissions and settled any current claims under the contracts of insurance. It remitted the balance of the premiums to Citadel on a monthly basis.

Drive On was a wholly-owned subsidiary of International Warranty Company Limited ("International Warranty"). The two companies both used the respondent bank (the "Bank") and they had the same signing officers. Drive On used one bank account for all of its transactions. The only deposits to the account were insurance premiums it collected and transfers from International Warranty. The Bank's senior officers knew that Drive On deposited insurance premiums into its account. After April 1, 1987, Drive On's account was usually in an overdraft position. On April 8, International Warranty's signing officers instructed the Bank to transfer funds between International Warranty's and Drive On's accounts to cover overdrafts on either accounts.

In April 1987 Drive On and Citadel agreed that from June 1, 1987 Citadel would adjudicate and pay all claims on insurance contracts sold by Drive On. This increased the premiums payable to Citadel. Citadel also discovered that Drive On had not been depositing the premiums into a trust account, but Drive On said that it would establish one if necessary.

On June 5, International Warranty's signing officers instructed the Bank to transfer all funds in Drive On's account at the end of each business day to the International Warranty account. This resulted in a reduction of International Warranty's overdraft.

On August 7, 1987, Drive On paid the June premiums to Citadel. Drive On told Citadel in late August that it could not pay the July and August premiums. Accordingly, the parties agreed that, effective September 1, all premiums would be forwarded directly to Citadel. Drive On also gave Citadel a promissory note for the July and August premiums. Drive On made a number of payments under the promissory note until it and International Warranty went out of business in December.

Citadel obtained judgment against Drive On for the balance owing on the note, $633,622.84, but was unable to collect on the judgment. Citadel therefore sued the Bank for the same amount and obtained judgment at trial. However, the Alberta Court of Appeal allowed the Bank's appeal.

LA FOREST J.:

[His Lordship held that the relationship between Drive On and Citadel was one of trust. The issue was not really in dispute. The relationship between the parties was governed by s. 124(1) of the *Insurance Act*,[842] which provides:

124.(1) An agent or broker who acts in negotiating, renewing or continuing a contract of insurance with an insurer licensed under this Act, and who receives any money or substitute for money as a premium for such a contract from the insured, shall be deemed to hold the premium in trust for the insurer.

La Forest J. held that the repayment arrangements between the parties did not revoke the trust, as the promissory note merely confirmed the amount owing to Citadel. His Lordship noted that, apart from the statutory trust, the arrangement satisfied the three certainties requirement. The fact that the trust funds were commingled with other funds also did not revoke the trust.

La Forest also held that Drive On clearly breached its trust when it failed to remit the premiums in July and August. The sole question, therefore, was whether the Bank could be held liable to Citadel as a constructive trustee. His Lordship noted that it could not be held liable as a trustee *de son tort*, since it had not assumed the office or function of trustee, or administered trust funds on behalf of Citadel. Nor could the Bank be personally liable for "knowing assistance," as in *Air Canada v. M. & L. Travel Ltd.*[843] The trial judge did not find that the Bank had actual knowledge of the breach of trust, nor that the Bank was reckless or willfully blind to the obvious. Rather, the trial judge restricted his findings to constructive knowledge, based on the Bank's duty to make inquiries of Drive On in the circumstances.]

[24] The only basis upon which the Bank may be held liable as a constructive trustee is under the "knowing receipt" or "knowing receipt and dealing" head of liability. Under this category of constructive trusteeship it is generally recognized that there are two types of cases. First, although inapplicable to the present case, there are strangers to the trust, usually agents of the trustees, who receive trust property lawfully and not for their own benefit but then deal with the property in a manner inconsistent with the trust. These cases may be grouped under the heading "knowing dealing". Secondly, there are strangers to the trust who receive

---

842 R.S.A. 1980, c. I-5.
843 [1983] 3 S.C.R. 787, 50 E.T.R. 225, 108 D.L.R. (4th) 592 (S.C.C.), set out above.

trust property for their own benefit and with knowledge that the property was transferred to them in breach of trust. In all cases it is immaterial whether the breach of trust was fraudulent.[844] The second type of case, which is relevant to the present appeal, raises two main issues: the nature of the receipt of trust property and the degree of knowledge required of the stranger to the trust.

2. Liability for Knowing Receipt

(a) The Receipt Requirement

[25] Liability on the basis of "knowing receipt" requires that strangers to the trust receive or apply trust property for their own use and benefit.[845] As Iacobucci J. wrote in *Air Canada v. M & L Travel Ltd.*,[846] the "knowing receipt" category of liability "requires the stranger to the trust to have received trust property in his or her personal capacity, rather than as an agent of the trustees". In the banking context, which is directly applicable to the present case, the definition of receipt has been applied as follows:

> The essential characteristic of a recipient . . . is that he should have received the property for his own use and benefit. That is why neither the paying nor the collecting bank can normally be made liable as recipient. In paying or collecting money for a customer the bank acts only as his agent. It sets up no title of its own. It is otherwise, however, if the collecting bank uses the money to reduce or discharge the customer's overdraft. In doing so it receives the money for its own benefit. . . .[847]

[26] Thus, a distinction is traditionally made between a bank receiving trust funds for its own benefit, in order to pay off a bank overdraft ("knowing receipt"), and a bank receiving and paying out trust funds merely as agent of the trustee ("knowing assistance").[848]

[27] . . . Although the Bank was instructed . . . to make the transfers [from Drive On's account to International Warranty's account], the Bank did not act as mere agent in the circumstances. The Bank's actions went beyond the mere collection of funds and payment of bills on Drive On's behalf. The Bank, by applying the deposit of insurance premiums as a set-off against International Warranty's overdraft, received a benefit. This benefit, of course, was the reduction in the amount owed to the Bank by one of its customers. It follows that the Bank received the trust funds for its own use and benefit.

---

844 *Halsbury's Laws of England* (4th ed. 1995), vol. 48, at para. 595; Pettit, *Equity and the Law of Trusts* (7th ed., 1993), at 168; Underhill and Hayton, *Law Relating to Trusts and Trustees* (14th ed. 1987), at 357.

845 *Agip (Africa) Ltd. v. Jackson*, [1990] 1 Ch. 265, affirmed [1992] 4 All E.R. 451 (C.A.); *Halsbury's Laws of England, supra*, at paras. 595-96; Philip H. Pettit, *Equity and the Law of Trusts* (7th ed., 1993), at 168.

846 *Supra*, note 843, at 810-11.

847 P.J. Millett, "Tracing the Proceeds of Fraud" (1991), 107 L.Q. Rev. 71 at 82-83 [footnotes omitted].

848 See *Underhill, supra*, at 361.

[The Bank argued that it had not received trust property, since it was merely a debtor of the two companies, and it merely transferred credits from one account to another. La Forest J. rejected this argument. He held that a debt obligation is a chose in action, which is property that can be the subject matter of a trust.]

[30] Nonetheless, the respondents' arguments reflect a difficulty with the traditional conception of "receipt" in "knowing receipt" cases. In my view, the receipt requirement for this type of liability is best characterized in restitutionary terms. In *LAC Minerals Ltd. v. International Corona Resources Ltd.*,[849] I stated that a restitutionary claim, or a claim for unjust enrichment, is concerned with giving back to someone something that has been taken from them (a restitutionary proprietary award) or its equivalent value (a personal restitutionary award). As well, in *Air Canada v. British Columbia*,[850] I stated that the function of the law of restitution "is to ensure that where a plaintiff has been deprived of wealth that is either in his possession or would have accrued for his benefit, it is restored to him. The measure of restitutionary recovery is the gain the [defendant] made at the [plaintiff's] expense." In the present case, the Bank was clearly enriched by the off-setting of debt obligations, or transferring of credits between the Drive On and International Warranty accounts. That is, the amount due to the Bank was reduced. As well, the Bank's enrichment deprived Citadel of the insurance premiums collected on its behalf. Moreover, the fact that the insurance premiums were never in Citadel's possession does not preclude Citadel from pursuing a restitutionary claim. After all, the insurance premiums would have accrued to Citadel's benefit. The Bank has been enriched at Citadel's expense. Thus, in restitutionary terms, there can be no doubt that the Bank received trust property for its own use and benefit.

(b) The Knowledge Requirement

[31] The first requirement for establishing liability on the basis of "knowing receipt" has been satisfied. The Bank received the trust property for its own benefit and, in doing so, was enriched at the beneficiary's expense. The second requirement relates to the degree of knowledge required of the Bank in relation to the breach of trust. With regard to this knowledge requirement, there are two lines of authorities. According to one line of jurisprudence, the knowledge requirement for both "knowing assistance" and "knowing receipt" cases should be the same. More specifically, constructive knowledge should not be the basis for liability in either type of case. A second line of authority suggests that a different standard should apply in "knowing assistance" and "knowing receipt" cases. More specifically, the authorities favour a lower threshold of knowledge in "knowing receipt" cases.

---

849 *Supra*, note 7, at 669.
850 *Supra*, note 24, at 1202-3.

[32] A leading case in relation to the first line of authority is *In re Montagu's Settlement Trusts.*[851] That case involved a dispute arising out of a 1923 settlement in which the future tenth Duke of Manchester had made an assignment of certain chattels to a number of trustees. The trustees were under a fiduciary duty to select and make an inventory of the chattels after the ninth Duke of Manchester died. The selection and inventory did not occur and the tenth Duke took absolutely whatever chattels he wanted. Megarry V.-C. held that the Duke was not liable as a constructive trustee because he did not know that the chattels were subject to a trust. In discussing the degree of knowledge required of the Duke, Megarry V.-C. emphasized that liability in "knowing receipt" cases is personal in nature and arises only if the stranger's conscience is sufficiently affected to justify imposing a constructive trust. Although cases involving actual knowledge, recklessness, and wilful blindness justify imposing a constructive trust, Megarry V.-C. doubted[852] whether the carelessness associated with constructive knowledge cases could sufficiently bind the stranger's conscience.

[His Lordship next discussed *Polly Peck International plc v. Nadir (No. 2)*,[853] which followed *In re Montagu's Settlement Trusts.* He continued:]

[34] The English approach favouring exclusion of constructive knowledge received the approval of the Manitoba Court of Appeal in *C.I.B.C. v. Valley Credit Union Ltd.*[854] In that case, a business obtained a line of credit from the plaintiff bank. Under the bank's general security agreement, the customer became trustee of monies paid to it with respect to accounts receivable or sales of inventory. The customer subsequently opened an account with the defendant credit union and used this account to deposit trust monies. The bank became aware of the other account, eventually called the customer's loans, and brought an action against the credit union to recover the funds in the customer's account. Philp J.A. refused to find the credit union liable as a constructive trustee. Without distinguishing between the categories of "knowing assistance" and "knowing receipt", Philp J.A. doubted whether the carelessness associated with constructive knowledge was sufficient to impose liability on the bank as a constructive trustee. Relying in part on *In re Montagu's Settlement Trusts,*[855] he stated:[856]

> I do not think that it can be said that it has been authoritatively decided in Canada that carelessness or negligence is sufficient to impute constructive knowledge to a stranger, and to impose upon him liability as a constructive trustee. I think that it is a doubtful test, particularly in the case of a bank. The relationship between a bank and its customer is contractual and a principal obligation of the bank is to pay out as directed the moneys its customer has deposited. It seems to me that that obligation should be a paramount one, save in special factual circumstances sufficient to hold the bank privy to its customer's breach.

---

851 *Supra*, note 740.
852 *Ibid.*, at 285.
853 [1992] 4 All E.R. 769 (C.A.).
854 [1990] 1 W.W.R. 736.
855 *Supra*, note 740.
856 *Supra*, note 854, at 747.

It should be noted, however, that later in his reasons Philp J.A. applied the test for constructive knowledge, but found that it had not been met in the circumstances.

> [La Forest J. also discussed *Bullock v. Key Property Management Inc.*,[857] which was to the same effect, as was the decision of the Court of Appeal in the *Citadel* case itself.]

[37] According to a second line of authority, however, constructive knowledge is sufficient to find a stranger to the trust liable on the basis of "knowing receipt". A leading English authority, in terms of formulating the test for constructive knowledge in breach of trust cases, is *Selangor*.[858] There, a company director carried out a fraudulent takeover bid by using the company's funds to purchase its own shares. Two banks were involved in the takeover. One bank acted on behalf of the director by paying, for a fee, those shareholders who had agreed to sell. The bank's fee was paid for by way of an advance from a second bank, where the company's account had been transferred. The second bank was repaid with trust funds drawn from the company's account. In addressing the banks' liability, Ungoed-Thomas J. did not distinguish between receipt and assistance cases. He presumed[859] that there was only one category of liability for strangers to the trust who, unlike trustees de son tort, "act in their own right and not for beneficiaries". Relying on this single category of liability, Ungoed-Thomas J. held:[860]

> The knowledge required to hold a stranger liable as constructive trustee in a dishonest and fraudulent design, is knowledge of circumstances which would indicate to an honest, reasonable man that such a design was being committed or would put him on enquiry, which the stranger failed to make, whether it was being committed.

Ungoed-Thomas J. found both banks liable as constructive trustees.

> [La Forest J. next discussed *Groves-Raffin Construction Ltd. v. Bank of Nova Scotia*[861] and *Carl B. Potter Ltd. v. Mercantile Bank of Canada*,[862] both of which applied *Selangor*, and continued:]

[40] A similar test of constructive knowledge was applied by the Ontario Court of Appeal in *Arthur Andersen Inc. v. Toronto-Dominion Bank*.[863] In that case, the defendant bank was sued by a trustee appointed under the *Construction Lien Act*.[864] The bank had agreed to administer the accounts of a number of

---

857 (1997), 33 O.R. (3d) 1 (C.A.).
858 *Selangor United Rubber Estates Ltd. v. Cradock (No. 3)*, *supra*, note 716.
859 *Ibid.*, at 1095.
860 *Ibid.*, at 1104.
861 *Supra*, note 747.
862 [1980] 2 S.C.R. 343.
863 (1994), 17 O.R. (3d) 363, leave to appeal refused, [1994] 3 S.C.R. v.
864 R.S.O. 1990, c. C.30.

associated construction companies, in accordance with a "mirror accounting system" Among other things, this system eliminated the need to monitor overdrafts in individual accounts and permitted the informal transfer of debits and credits between all of the operating companies' accounts. The trial judge's findings implied that the funds in the accounts were transferred in breach of the trust requirements under the *Construction Lien Act*. Considering the liability of the bank as a constructive trustee, Grange and McKinlay JJ.A. thus wrote in their joint reasons:[865]

> We consider that the law on this point can be summarized thus: in the absence of sufficient facts or circumstances indicating that there is a good possibility of trust beneficiaries being unpaid there is no duty of inquiry on a bank to determine whether the trades have been paid or will be able to be paid.

>   . . .

> Only if a bank is aware of facts which would indicate that trades would not be paid in the normal course of business should it be charged with a duty of special inquiry.

It should be noted that Grange and McKinlay JJ.A. formulated this test without distinguishing between receipt and assistance cases. However, their comment that the "Bank can only be liable for a breach of trust, and that breach would have to involve making use for its own benefit of money held on a trust for trade creditors",[866] suggests that the case fell under the "knowing receipt" head of liability.

> [La Forest J. then discussed *Glenko Enterprises Ltd. v. Ernie Keller Contractors Ltd.*,[867] which followed the same test.]

[42] There are also a number of recent English authorities supporting the view that constructive knowledge is sufficient to impose liability on the basis of "knowing receipt". In *Agip (Africa) Ltd.*[868] Millett J. made a number of comments regarding "knowing receipt" cases, even though the case before him was of the "knowing assistance" category. With regard to the degree of knowledge required in "knowing receipt" cases, he wrote:[869]

> The first [category of "knowing receipt" cases] is concerned with the person who receives for his own benefit trust property transferred to him in breach of trust. He is liable as a constructive trustee if he received it with notice, actual or constructive, that it was trust property and that the transfer to him was a breach of trust; or if he received it without such notice but subsequently discovered the facts.

---

865 *Supra*, note 863, at 381-82.
866 *Ibid.*, at 381-82.
867 (1996), 134 D.L.R. (4th) 161 (Man. C.A.).
868 *Supra*, note 845.
869 *Ibid.*, at 291.

However, Millett J.' s comments must be read in light of a later passage,[870] where he refused to express an opinion as to whether constructive knowledge sufficed in "knowing receipt" cases.

. . .

[44] Millett J. reiterated the views he expressed in *Agip (Africa) Ltd.*[871] in *El Ajou v. Dollar Land Holdings plc.*[872] That case involved a massive share fraud carried out by three Canadians in Amsterdam between 1984 and 1985. The plaintiff, the largest single victim of the fraud, claimed to be able to trace some of the proceeds of the fraud from Amsterdam through locations in Geneva, Gibraltar, Panama, back to Geneva, and then to London, where they were invested in a joint venture to carry out a property development project. In this "knowing receipt" case, Millett J. was prepared to assume that constructive knowledge was a sufficient basis for liability. [H]e stated:[873]

> In the absence of full argument I am content to assume, without deciding, that dishonesty or want of probity involving actual knowledge (whether proved or inferred) is not a precondition of liability; but that a recipient is not expected to be unduly suspicious and is not to be held liable unless he went ahead without further inquiry in circumstances in which an honest and reasonable man would have realized that the money was probably trust money and was being misapplied.

[45] According to the second line of authority, then, the degree of knowledge required of strangers to the trust should be different in assistance and receipt cases. Generally, there are good reasons for requiring different thresholds of knowledge under the two heads of liability. As Millett J. wrote in *Agip (Africa) Ltd.*:[874]

> The basis of liability in the two types of cases is quite different; there is no reason why the degree of knowledge required should be the same, and good reason why it should not. Tracing claims and cases of "knowing receipt" are both concerned with rights of priority in relation to property taken by a legal owner for his own benefit; cases of "knowing assistance" are concerned with the furtherance of fraud.

[46] In other words, the distinction between the two categories of liability is fundamental: whereas the accessory's liability is "fault-based", the recipient's liability is "receipt-based". In an extrajudicial opinion, Millett J. described the distinction as follows:[875]

> . . . the liability of the accessory is limited to the case where the breach of trust in question was fraudulent and dishonest; the liability of the recipient is not so limited. In truth, however, the distinction is fundamental; there is no similarity between the two categories. The accessory is a

---

870 *Ibid.*, at 293.
871 *Ibid.*
872 [1993] 3 All E.R. 717 (Ch.).
873 *Ibid.*, at 739.
874 *Supra*, note 845, at 292-93.
875 "Tracing the Proceeds of Fraud", *supra*, at 83 [footnotes omitted].

person who either never received the property at all, or who received it in circumstances where his receipt was irrelevant. His liability cannot be receipt-based. It is necessarily fault-based, and is imposed on him not in the context of the law of competing priorities to property, but in the application of the law which is concerned with the furtherance of fraud.

[47] S. Gardner makes a similar point in "Knowing Assistance and Knowing Receipt: Taking Stock":[876]

> . . . it is questionable whether knowing receipt is about wrongfully causing loss at all. There may be more than one other thing that it could be about, but most modern opinion takes it to be a restitutionary liability, based on the fact that the defendant has acquired the plaintiff's property

The same view was expressed by the Privy Council in *Royal Brunei Airlines Sdn. Bhd. v. Tan*:[877] "Different considerations apply to the two heads of liability. Recipient liability is restitution-based; accessory liability is not". These comments are also cited with approval by Iacobucci J. in *Gold*.[878]

[48] Given the fundamental distinction between the nature of liability in assistance and receipt cases, it makes sense to require a different threshold of knowledge for each category of liability. In "knowing assistance" cases, which are concerned with the furtherance of fraud, there is a higher threshold of knowledge required of the stranger to the trust. Constructive knowledge is excluded as the basis for liability in "knowing assistance" cases.[879] However, in "knowing receipt" cases, which are concerned with the receipt of trust property for one's own benefit, there should be a lower threshold of knowledge required of the stranger to the trust. More is expected of the recipient, who, unlike the accessory, is necessarily enriched at the plaintiff's expense. Because the recipient is held to this higher standard, constructive knowledge (that is, knowledge of facts sufficient to put a reasonable person on notice or inquiry) will suffice as the basis for restitutionary liability. Iacobucci J. reaches the same conclusion in *Gold*, where he finds[880] that a stranger in receipt of trust property "need not have actual knowledge of the equity [in favour of the plaintiff]; notice will suffice".

[49] This lower threshold of knowledge is sufficient to establish the "unjust" or "unjustified" nature of the recipient's enrichment, thereby entitling the plaintiff to a restitutionary remedy. As I wrote in *LAC Minerals*,[881] "the determination that the enrichment is 'unjust' does not refer to abstract notions of morality and justice, but flows directly from the finding that there was a breach of a legally recognized duty for which the courts will grant relief". In "knowing receipt" cases, relief flows from the breach of a legally recognized duty of inquiry. More specifically, relief will be granted where a stranger to the trust, having received trust property for his or her own benefit and having knowledge of facts which would put a reasonable person on inquiry, actually fails to inquire as to the possible misap-

---

876   (1996), 112 L.Q. Rev. 56, at 85.
877   *Supra*, note 736, at 70.
878   *Supra*, note 837, at para. 41.
879   *Air Canada v. M & L Travel Ltd.*, *supra*, note 843, at 811-13.
880   *Supra*, note 837, at para. 46.
881   *Supra*, note 7, at 670.

plication of trust property. It is this lack of inquiry that renders the recipient's enrichment unjust.

[50] Some commentators go further and argue that a recipient may be unjustly enriched regardless of either a duty of inquiry or constructive knowledge of a breach of trust. According to Professor Birks, a recipient of misdirected funds should be liable on a strict, restitutionary basis. In his article "Misdirected Funds: Restitution from the Recipient",[882] he argues that a recipient's enrichment is unjust because the plaintiff did not consent to it, not because the defendant knew that the funds were being misdirected. In particular, he writes,[883] that "[t]he 'unjust' factor can be named 'ignorance', signifying that the plaintiff, at the time of the enrichment, was absolutely unaware of the transfer from himself to the defendant". Birks, however, lessens the strictness of his approach by allowing a defendant to take advantage of special defences, including a defence arising out of a *bona fide* purchase for value.[884]

[51] In my view, the test formulated by Professor Birks, while not entirely incompatible with my own, may establish an unjust deprivation, but not an unjust enrichment. It is recalled that a plaintiff is entitled to a restitutionary remedy not because he or she has been unjustly deprived but, rather, because the defendant has been unjustly enriched, at the plaintiff's expense. To show that the defendant's enrichment is unjustified, one must necessarily focus on the defendant's state of mind not the plaintiff's knowledge, or lack thereof. Indeed, without constructive or actual knowledge of the breach of trust, the recipient may very well have a lawful claim to the trust property. It would be unfair to require a recipient to disgorge a benefit that has been lawfully received. In those circumstances, the recipient will not be unjustly enriched and the plaintiff will not be entitled to a restitutionary remedy.

[52] In the banking context of the present case, it is true that s. 206(1) of the *Bank Act*[885] negates any duty on the part of a bank to see to the execution of any trust, whether express, implied or constructive, to which a deposit is subject. In accordance with this provision, a bank is not under a duty to regularly monitor the activities of its clients simply because the funds deposited by those clients are impressed with a statutory trust. Nonetheless, this provision does not render a bank immune from liability as a constructive trustee or prevent the recognition of a duty of inquiry on the part of a bank. Indeed, in certain circumstances, a bank's knowledge of its customer's affairs will require the bank to make inquiries as to possible misapplication of trust funds. As discussed earlier, the degree of knowledge required is constructive knowledge of a possible breach of trust. It follows that a bank which is enriched by the receipt of trust property and has knowledge of facts that would put a reasonable person on inquiry is under a duty to make inquiries of its customer regarding a possible breach of trust. If the bank

---

882 [1989] L.M.C.L.Q. 296.

883 *Ibid.*, at 341.

884 See also P. Birks, "Overview: Tracing, Claiming and Defences", in P. Birks, ed., *Laundering and Tracing* (1995), 289, at 322 et seq.

885 R.S.C. 1985, c. B-1.

fails to make the appropriate inquiries, it will have constructive knowledge of the breach of trust. In these circumstances, the bank will be unjustly enriched and, therefore, required to disgorge the benefit it received at the plaintiff's expense.

[53] The respondents argued that imposing liability on a banker who merely has constructive notice of a breach of trust will place too great a burden on banks, thereby interfering with the proper functioning of the banking system. While this may be true in assistance cases where a banker merely pays out and transfers funds as the trustee's agent, the same argument does not apply to receipt cases where a banker receives the trust funds for his or her own benefit. Professor Harpum addresses this point in "The Stranger as Constructive Trustee":[886]

> Although there should be a reluctance to allow the unnecessary intrusion of "the intricacies and doctrines connected with trusts" into ordinary commercial transactions, considerations of speed and the importance of possession which normally justify the exclusion of these doctrines, are less applicable to a banker who chooses to exercise his right of set-off than they are to other commercial dealings. Where a banker combines accounts, he alone stands to gain from the transaction. Because of that benefit, more should be expected of him than if he gained nothing.

In "knowing receipt" cases, therefore, it is justifiable to impose liability on a banker who only has constructive knowledge of a breach of trust.

[54] In the present case, it has already been established that the Bank was enriched at Citadel's expense by the receipt of insurance premiums collected by Drive On and subject to a statutory trust in favour of Citadel. The only remaining question is whether the Bank had the requisite degree of knowledge to render the enrichment unjust, thereby entitling the plaintiff insurer to a remedy.

[55] On this issue, it is clear from the trial judge's findings that the Bank was aware of the nature of the funds being deposited into, and transferred out of, Drive On's account. On discovery, two of the Bank's employees stated that they knew Drive On's sole source of revenue was the sale of insurance policies. The Bank also knew that premiums collected by Drive On were payable to the plaintiff insurer. The Bank's knowledge of the nature of Drive On's deposits must also be considered in conjunction with the activities in Drive On's account. It is recalled that in April 1987 the Bank began transferring funds between the Drive On and International Warranty accounts to cover overdrafts in either account. As well, in June 1987, the Bank was directed to empty the Drive On account on a daily basis, again to facilitate the transfer of funds to the International Warranty account.

[56] In light of the Bank's knowledge of the nature of the funds, the daily emptying of the account was in the trial judge's view "very suspicious". In these circumstances, a reasonable person would have been put on inquiry as to the possible misapplication of the trust funds. Notwithstanding the fact that the exact terms of the trust relationship between Citadel and Drive On may have been unknown to the Bank, the Bank should have taken steps, in the form of reasonable inquiries, to determine whether the insurance premiums were being misapplied. More specifically, the Bank should have inquired whether the use of the premiums to reduce the account overdrafts constituted a breach of trust. By failing to make

---

886 (1986), 102 L.Q. Rev. 114 at 138 [footnotes omitted].

the appropriate inquiries, the Bank had constructive knowledge of Drive On's breach of trust. In these circumstances, the Bank's enrichment was clearly unjust, thereby rendering it liable to Citadel as a constructive trustee.

[57] I make one additional point regarding the nature of the Bank's liability in the present case. As already established, recipient liability is restitution-based. The imposition of liability as a constructive trustee on the basis of "knowing receipt" is a restitutionary remedy and should not be confused with the right to trace assets at common law or in equity. The principles relating to tracing at law and in equity were thus set out by the English Court of Appeal in *Agip (Africa) Ltd.*:[887]

> Tracing at law does not depend upon the establishment of an initial fiduciary relationship. Liability depends upon receipt by the defendant of the plaintiff's money and the extent of the liability depends on the amount received. Since liability depends upon receipt the fact that a recipient has not retained the asset is irrelevant. For the same reason dishonesty or lack of inquiry on the part of the recipient are irrelevant. Identification in the defendant's hands of the plaintiff's asset is, however, necessary. It must be shown that the money received by the defendant was the money of the plaintiff. Further, the very limited common law remedies make it difficult to follow at law into mixed funds.

> . . .

> Both common law and equity accepted the right of the true owner to trace his property into the hands of others while it was in an identifiable form. The common law treated property as identified if it had not been mixed with other property. Equity, on the other hand, will follow money into a mixed fund and charge the fund.

[58] In my view, a distinction should be made between the imposition of liability in "knowing receipt" cases and the availability of tracing orders at common law and in equity. Liability at common law is strict, flowing from the fact of receipt. Liability in "knowing receipt" cases is not strict; it depends not only on the fact of enrichment (i.e. receipt of trust property) but also on the unjust nature of that enrichment (i.e. the stranger's knowledge of the breach of trust). A tracing order at common law, unlike a restitutionary remedy, is only available in respect of funds which have not lost their identity by becoming part of a mixed fund. Further, the imposition of liability as a constructive trustee is wider than a tracing order in equity. The former is not limited to the defence of purchaser without notice and "does not depend upon the recipient still having the property or its traceable proceeds".[888]

[59] Despite these distinctions, there appears to be a common thread running through both "knowing receipt" and tracing cases. That is, constructive knowledge will suffice as the basis for imposing liability on the recipient of misdirected trust funds. Notwithstanding this, it is neither necessary nor desirable to confuse the traditional rules of tracing with the restitutionary principles now applicable to "knowing receipt" cases. This does not mean, however, that a restitutionary

---

887 *Supra*, note 845, at 463-64, 466.
888 *In re Montagu's Settlement Trusts, supra*, note 740, at 276.

remedy and a tracing order are mutually exclusive. Where more than one remedy is available on the facts, the plaintiff should be able to choose the one that is most advantageous. In the present case, the plaintiff did not seek a tracing order. It is therefore unnecessary for me to decide whether such a remedy would have been available on the facts of the present appeal, and I have not explored the issue.

[La Forest J., therefore, allowed the appeal.

Gonthier, Cory, McLachlin, Iacobucci and Major JJ., concurred.

Sopinka J. concurred subject to his reasons in *Gold v. Rosenberg*.[889]]

Notes and Questions

1. La Forest J. held that knowing receipt is an equitable species of the action in unjust enrichment. Within that framework, he more specifically held that liability requires proof of two elements: (i) the stranger's receipt of trust property for his or her own benefit, and (ii) the stranger's knowledge of the beneficiary's rights. Both of those requirements raise difficult issues.

2. On the facts of *Citadel*, the stranger was the bank. On what basis did La Forest J. conclude that the bank had received trust property for its "own use and benefit"? Why was it important that International Warranty's account was overdrawn? If that account had not been overdrawn, would the bank have enjoyed the requisite receipt?

Foley v. Hill[890] stands for the general proposition that a deposit of money into a bank account provides the bank with clear title to those notes and coins. In exchange, the bank creates a chose in action in favour of the account holder. In light of that rule, upon what basis can a court ever conclude, on La Forest J.'s analysis, that a bank in receipt of trust funds has not received the money for its "own use and benefit"?[891]

3. La Forest J. drew a distinction between knowing assistance, "which is concerned with the furtherance of fraud," and knowing receipt, which is concerned with unjust enrichment. He further held, in light of that distinction, that it was appropriate to impose liability more readily in the latter context.[892]

> More is expected of the recipient who, unlike the accessory, is necessarily enriched at the plaintiff's expense. Because the recipient is held to this higher standard, constructive knowledge...will suffice as a basis for liability. . . . This lower threshold of knowledge is sufficient to establish the "unjust" or "unjustified" nature of the recipient's enrichment

Significantly, however, La Forest J. insisted that the standard could not be lowered even further such that, regardless of the recipient's knowledge of the beneficiary's interest,

---

889 *Supra*, note 837.

890 [1848] 11 H.L. 28.

891 M. Bryan, "The Receipt-Based Constructive Trust: A Case Study of Personal and Proprietary Restitution in the Supreme Court" (1999), 37 Alberta L. Rev. 73.

892 The existence of an enrichment and a corresponding deprivation generally is thought to lower the threshold to judicial intervention: see J.P. Dawson, *Unjust Enrichment: A Comparative Analysis* (Boston, Little Brown & Co., 1951), at 7; L.L. Fuller & W.R. Perdue, "The Reliance Interest in Contract Damages" (1936), 46 Yale L.J. 52 at 56.

restitution could be ordered simply on the basis that the beneficiary did not consent to the disposition of the trust property.

> [Strict liability] may establish an unjust deprivation, but not an unjust enrichment. It is recalled that a plaintiff is entitled to a restitutionary remedy not because he or she has been unjustly *deprived* but, rather, because the defendant has been unjustly *enriched*, at the plaintiff's expense. To show that the defendant's enrichment is unjustified, one must necessarily focus on the defendant's state of mind, not the plaintiff's knowledge or lack thereof.

That statement is difficult to square with general restitutionary principles. Liability in unjust enrichment *prima facie* is strict. Given the existence of an enrichment and a corresponding deprivation, it normally is enough that the plaintiff did not truly intend to confer a benefit upon the defendant. More specifically, liability is triggered immediately upon receipt of an unintended benefit, even if the defendant is unaware of the plaintiff's interest (and, indeed, even if the defendant is unaware of the enrichment itself).[893] Three months before La Forest J. delivered judgment in *Citadel Assurance*, the Supreme Court of Canada re-affirmed those principles in *Air Canada v. Ontario (Liquor Control Board)*.[894] While technically distinguishable (*e.g.* because one arose in equity and the other arose in law), the decisions in *Citadel Assurance* and *Air Canada* appear to be essentially irreconcilable.

If restitutionary relief with respect to misdirected trust assets was available under a regime of strict liability, it no longer would be appropriate to refer to the action as "knowing receipt." As to the threshold issue of liability (as opposed to the question of defences), the recipient's knowledge would be irrelevant. The claim would, instead, simply be addressed under the more general rubric of "unjust enrichment."

4. In rejecting the suggestion that liability for knowing receipt ought to involve a strict liability regime of unjust enrichment, La Forest J. was principally concerned that "without any constructive or actual knowledge of the breach of trust, the recipient may very well have a lawful claim to the trust property" and that it might be "unfair to require a recipient to disgorge a benefit that has been lawfully received." Unfortunately, that analysis appears to overlook the fact that even within a regime of strict liability, the defendant may be entitled to the protection of a defence.[895]

In unjust enrichment, two defences are especially important. First, the recipient of a misdirected enrichment is entirely relieved of responsibility if he or she obtained that benefit by way of a *bona fide* purchase.[896] Second, even if the recipient received the enrichment as a volunteer, liability will be reduced to the extent to which he or she in good faith incurred an exceptional expenditure in reliance upon that enrichment.[897] For instance, if, having received a mistaken payment of $10,000, the defendant spent $6000 on a trip to Jamaica that he or she otherwise never would have taken, the plaintiff's measure of recovery will be reduced to $4000. (Not so, however, if the recipient incurred

---

893 M. McInnes, "The Measure of Restitution" (2002), 52 U.T.L.J. 163.

894 *Supra*, note 65.

895 M. McInnes, "Knowing Receipt and the Protection of Trust Property" (2002), 81 Can. Bar Rev. 171.

896 A. Burrows, *The Law of Restitution*, 2nd ed. (London: Butterworths, 2002), at 585ff.

897 *Storthoaks (Rural Municipality) v. Mobil Oil Canada Ltd.* (1975), 55 D.L.R. (3d) 1, 1975 CarswellSask 56, 1975 CarswellSask 97, [1976] 2 S.C.R. 147, [1975] 4 W.W.R. 591, 5 N.R. 23; P. Birks, "Change of Position: The Nature of the Defence and Its Relationship to Other Restitutionary Defences", in M. McInnes, ed., *Restitution: Developments in Unjust Enrichment* (Sydney: LBC Information Services, 1996), c. 3.

the expense knowing of the plaintiff's error, nor if the defendant would have taken the same trip in any event.)

The result of such defences is that, even if, as in law, unjust enrichment in equity was strict (in the sense that it was triggered by the plaintiff's impaired intention, rather than the defendant's knowledge of that impairment), liability would never positively hurt the defendant. It would, at most, return the defendant to the position that he or she enjoyed immediately before receiving the benefit of the misappropriated asset.[898]

5. In exercising a choice between two models of unjust enrichment, one based on a stranger's "knowing receipt" of misdirected trust property and the other based on a regime of strict liability that is subject to the defences of *bona fide* purchase and change of position, a court might wish to consider a situation along the following lines.

The defendant intended to spend $5000 on a vacation and to pay for that trip with $5000 that he kept in a shoebox. Shortly before his departure, he received $5000 as a gift from his friend. Although the defendant had no reason to suspect anything improper, the friend had actually stolen that money from a trust of which he was a trustee and the plaintiff was the beneficiary. The defendant used all of the apparent gift, and none of the money in his shoebox, to pay for the vacation. When he returned from abroad, he learned of the plaintiff's claim. Although the defendant still has $5000 in his shoebox, he refuses to make amends to the plaintiff.

Is the defendant liable to the plaintiff to restore the value that he had received from the plaintiff's trust account? Answer that question on the basis of: (i) the test that La Forest J. formulated in *Citadel Assurance*, and (ii) a regime of unjust enrichment in which liability is strict but subject to defences. As a matter of fairness, should liability be imposed? Would the defendant be any worse for wear if he was required to provide restitution? Is it appropriate that he should, in effect, be entitled to have taken his vacation at the plaintiff's expense?

Are there any other claims that the plaintiff could pursue? What cause of action, if any, does the plaintiff have against the dishonest trustee? Will that action necessarily provide the plaintiff with full satisfaction? Would it be possible for the plaintiff to successfully sue people to whom the defendant paid the misappropriated funds (*e.g.* travel agents, hotels and restaurants)?

6. It is important to understand, especially in the sort of situation that was involved in the last note, that La Forest J.'s test of knowing receipt requires the recipient to possess the requisite knowledge within a particular period of time. Liability obviously is possible if misdirected trust property was actually acquired with knowledge of the beneficiary's interest. So too if, despite a lack of knowledge at the moment of receipt, the recipient subsequently acquired knowledge while still in possession of the property. In *Citadel Assurance*, La Forest J. cited *Agip (Africa) Ltd. v. Jackson*,[899] for that proposition. Significantly, however, liability is not possible if the defendant had disposed of the trust property by the time that he or she became fixed with knowledge of the plaintiff's rights.

7. Notwithstanding the availability of restitutionary defences, some commentators have suggested that, even though liability in unjust enrichment generally is strict at law, a knowledge requirement is appropriate for the equitable species of unjust enrichment that operates under the label of "knowing receipt." For instance, there is a concern that under a rule of strict liability, "[b]ankers, stockbrokers, lawyers and others will routinely be required to go to trial to establish their defences, no matter how honest and careful are

---

898 M. McInnes, "Enrichments and Reasons for Restitution: Protecting Freedom of Choice" (2003), 48 McGill L.J. 419.

899 *Supra*, note 845, at 291.

their procedures."[900] Bradley Crawford Q.C. has gone even further, arguing in favour of a test of actual knowledge, on the basis that the test of constructive knowledge exposes banks to an unreasonable burden of inquiry.[901] A higher threshold of liability has also been defended on the ground that equitable property rights are, by their nature, more vulnerable than their legal counterparts and that the extension of strict liability to the former would undermine the very essence of the institution of trust.[902]

8. What did La Forest J. mean in the last three paragraphs of his judgment in *Citadel Assurance* where he tried to distinguish between "the imposition of liability as a constructive trustee on the basis of 'knowing receipt'" and "the right to trace assets at common law or equity"? What is a "tracing order"? The nature and consequences of tracing are examined in a later chapter.

9. While it has not yet entirely worked out the details, Canadian law clearly has adopted an unjust enrichment model of recipient liability. The situation is quite different in England, where knowing receipt continues to be regarded as a wrong of misappropriation. In that respect, it serves much the same role in equity that conversion serves in the common law. There is, however, a noticeable difference between knowing receipt and conversion. Whereas the equitable action traditionally has required proof that the defendant acquired the asset with knowledge of the plaintiff's pre-existing interest, liability may arise under the common law action even if the defendant had no reason to suspect anything untoward. The explanation for that difference lies in the package of protection that each jurisdiction extends to property owners.

Equity offers a *vindicatio*. A dispossessed equitable owner generally is entitled to point to misappropriated property in the stranger's hands and, regardless of the stranger's level of knowledge (but subject to the defence of *bona fide* purchase), to demand its return *in specie*. The generosity and breadth of that proprietary action took pressure off equity's personal claim. It was thought acceptable to confine knowing receipt to cases in which the stranger could be ascribed with fault, insofar as he or she received trust property with (constructive) knowledge of the beneficiary's pre-existing interest.

A different regime operates at law. With very limited exceptions (*e.g.* the action in ejectment that allows for the recovery of land), a dispossessed legal title holder does not enjoy a right of restoration *in specie*. There is no general *vindicatio* at law. As a result, it is necessary to generously protect property rights through personal actions that lead instead to the payment of money. The tort of conversion originally required proof that the defendant had dishonestly misappropriated the plaintiff's goods. In time, however, the allegation of dishonesty became non-traversable and conversion effectively was transformed from a fault-based claim into one of strict liability.[903] It remains true today that liability may be

---

900 K. Barker & L.D. Smith, "Unjust Enrichment", in D. Hayton, ed., *Law's Future* (Oxford: Hart, 2000), 410 at 426.

901 B. Crawford, Q.C., "Constructive Thinking? The Supreme Court's Extension of Constructive Trusts to Banks on the Basis of Constructive Notice of a Breach of Trust by a Customer" (1999), 31 Can. Business L.J. 1.

902 L.D. Smith, "Unjust Enrichment, Property and the Structure of Trusts" (2000), 116 L.Q. Rev. 412. Compare P. Birks, "Receipt", in P. Birks & A. Pretto, eds., *Breach of Trust* (Oxford: Hart, 2002), 212.

903 It is important to distinguish between two different meanings of "strict liability." As applied to the cause of action in unjust enrichment, that phrase indicates that the reason for restitution pertains entirely to the plaintiff and that, as long as he or she received an enrichment, the defendant may be held liable despite doing nothing wrong. In contrast, "strict liability" in tort law means that, as long as the defendant breached an obligation (*e.g.* converting the plaintiff's

imposed upon an "innocent" convertor — *i.e.* one who acted in a manner that was inconsistent with the plaintiff's property rights, but without any form of culpable knowledge.[904]

10. Although English courts have traditionally regarded knowing receipt as an equitable wrong of misappropriation, there are some indications that they eventually may join the Supreme Court of Canada in recognizing an action in unjust enrichment. Professor Birks previously argued that the historical precedents ought to be reinterpreted in such a way as to jettison the fault (knowledge) requirement and establish a strict restitutionary claim.[905] Having found little judicial support for that proposal, however, he now argues that the general concept of knowing receipt ought to be divided into two separate branches: a knowledge-based wrong of misappropriation and a strict liability action in unjust enrichment.[906] Lord Nicholls, writing extra-judicially, has agreed.[907] Moreover, there are some signs that the judiciary may be receptive to such an approach.[908]

11. There are, however, commentators who remain sceptical about placing knowing receipt within a model of unjust enrichment.[909] They argue, *inter alia*, that it is in the nature of equitable property interests to be more vulnerable than legal property interests. Such interests may be defeated by *bona fide* purchase without notice; trust beneficiaries are not entitled to sue in conversion if a person interferes with trust property;[910] and trust beneficiaries are not owed the same duties of care as legal owners.[911] On that view, it is not surprising, and may not be inappropriate, to regard knowing receipt as a species of wrongdoing and to premise liability upon proof of fault.

12. Even if English courts continue to view the liability of the recipient of misdirected trust property through the lens of wrongdoing, rather than unjust enrichment, they must

---

property), liability may be imposed even though the defendant did not commit the wrong intentionally or carelessly.

904 See J.G. Fleming, *The Law of Torts*, 9th ed. (Sydney: LBC Information Services, 1998), at 61; P. Birks, "Personal Property: Proprietary Rights and Remedies" (2000), 11 King's College L.J. 1 at 6-10; M. McInnes, "Knowing Receipt and the Protection of Trust Property" (2002), 81 Can. Bar Rev. 171 at 172.

905 See, for example, "Misdirected Funds: Restitution from the Recipient," [1989] Lloyd's Maritime & Commercial L.Q. 296 and "Persistent Problems in Misdirected Money: A Quintet," [1993] Lloyd's Maritime & Commercial L.Q. 218.

906 P. Birks, "Receipt", in P. Birks & A. Pretto, eds., *Breach of Trust* (Oxford: Hart, 2002), 213.

907 Lord Nicholls, "Knowing Receipt: The Need for a New Landmark", in W. Cornish *et al.*, eds., *Restitution: Past, Present & Future* (Oxford: Hart, 1998), 230.

908 See, for example, *Twinsectra Ltd. v. Yardley*, *supra*, note 34, at 194 *per* Lord Millett (H.L.) ("Liability for 'knowing receipt' is receipt-based. It does not depend on fault. The cause of action is restitutionary and is available only where the defendant received the money in breach of trust for his own use and benefit. . . . There is no basis for requiring actual knowledge of the breach of trust, let alone dishonesty, as a condition of liability. Constructive notice is sufficient, and may not even be necessary. There is powerful academic support for the proposition that the liability of the recipient is the same as in other cases of restitution, that is to say strict but subject to the change of position defence."). See also *Koorootang Nominees Pty. Ltd. v. A.N.Z.*, [1998] 3 V.R. 16 (S.C.).

909 See especially L.D. Smith, "W(h)ither Knowing Receipt" (1998), 114 L.Q. Rev. 394; K. Barker & L. Smith, "Unjust Enrichment", in D. Hayton, ed., *Law's Futures* (Oxford: Hart, 2000), 411; L.D. Smith, "Unjust Enrichment, Property and the Structure of Trusts" (2000), 116 L.Q. Rev. 412.

910 *M.C.C. Proceeds Inc. v. Lehman Bros. Intl. (Europe)*, [1998] 4 All E.R. 675 (C.A.).

911 *Leigh and Sullivan Ltd. v. Aliakmon Shipping Co. Ltd. (The Aliakmon)*, [1986] A.C. 785 at 812 (H.L.); *Parker-Tweedale v. Dunbar Bank plc (No. 1)*, [1991] Ch. 12 (C.A.).

precisely identify the nature of the wrong. Unfortunately, as La Forest J. noted in *Citadel Assurance*, the cases are inconsistent. While Megarry V.C. in *Montagu's Settlement Trusts, Re*[912] required proof of the stranger's dishonesty, the Court of Appeal on other occasions was satisfied by proof that the recipient possessed constructive knowledge of the beneficiary's equitable interest in the disputed asset.[913]

A recent decision of the English Court of Appeal clouds the issue even further. In *Bank of Credit and Commerce International (Overseas) Ltd. v. Akindele*,[914] Nourse L.J. rejected both a regime of strict liability, on the grounds that it would be "commercially unworkable," and a requirement of dishonesty. However, rather than unequivocally adopt a standard of constructive knowledge, he ultimately held that liability was triggered by the defendant's "unconscionability." That approach has been criticized by some commentators. Professor Birks, for instance, has said:[915]

> "Unconscionable" gives no guidance. At one extreme it is unconscionable to not repay what you were not intended to receive. At the other extreme , it is unconscionable to be dishonest. "Unconscionable," indicating unanalysed disapprobation, thus embraces every position in the controversy.

Likewise, in *Royal Brunei Airlines v. Tan*, Lord Nicholls said that if "unconscionable" means something different than dishonesty, "it is not clear what that something different is."[916]

13. As matters currently stand in both Canada and England, an innocent recipient[917] of misdirected trust property cannot be held personally liable as a "constructive trustee." (He or she nevertheless may be required to hold the asset on constructive trust unless the property was obtained by way of a *bona fide* purchase.) It has been suggested, however, that the courts may, and arguably should, develop an action in unjust enrichment that, subject to defences (*e.g.* change of position and *bona fide* purchase), renders the recipient strictly liable to personally restore the value of the misdirected asset.

Indirect support for that proposition can be drawn from what is known as "the *Diplock* claim." That concept takes its name from *Diplock v. Wintle*.[918] Caleb Diplock died leaving a will that directed his executors to apply the residue of his estate "for such charitable institution or institutions or other charitable or benevolent object or objects" as they saw fit. The executors accordingly distributed money to 139 charities. Subsequently, however, it was determined that the disposition was invalid because (for reasons explained elsewhere in this book) the bequest was not exclusively charitable and hence "imperfect." A question then arose regarding the ability of Caleb Diplock's next-of-kin (to whom the residue of his estate should have been paid) to recover the value of the misdirected funds from the

---

912 *Supra*, note 740.

913 *Belmont Finance Corp. v. Williams Furniture Ltd. (No. 2)*, [1980] 1 All E.R. 393; *Houghton v. Fayers*, [2000] B.C.L.C. 511.

914 *Supra*, note 818.

915 "Receipt" in P. Birks & A. Pretto, eds., *Breach of Trust* (Oxford: Hart, 2002) 213 at 226. Compare S. Barkehall-Thomas, "Goodbye Knowing Receipt: Hello Unconscientious Receipt" (2001), 21 O.J.L.S. 239.

916 *Supra*, note 736, at 392.

917 That is, a recipient who did not have actual or constructive knowledge of the beneficiaries' interest, or who, under *Akindele*, did not act unconscionably.

918 [1948] Ch. 465 (C.A.), affirmed (sub nom. *Ministry of Health v. Simpson*) [1951] A.C. 251 (H.L.).

charities.[919] The situation was complicated by the fact that some of the charities had, in good faith reliance upon their enrichments, irretrievably spent the money in ways that they otherwise would not have done.

The House of Lords established a number of rules. First, the charities were strictly liable to restore the value of the money that they had received. It was irrelevant that they had received the funds without actual or constructive knowledge of the next-of-kin's interest, nor that they had not acted unconscionably. Second, the charities were not entitled to invoke the defence of change of position with respect to the exceptional expenditures that they had incurred in reliance upon their enrichments. Third, however, the next-of-kin were entitled to exercise their rights against the charities only to the extent that they were unable to satisfy judgment against the executors, who had improperly disposed of the money.

It is important to understand that the case did not involve the receipt of misdirected *trust* property.[920] A personal representative does not hold the deceased's estate on trust (although it is, of course, common for the representative, in the administration of the estate, to establish trusts according to the deceased's wishes). The *Diplock* claim consequently is distinguishable from the sort of claim that arose in, say, *Citadel Assurance*.

Nevertheless, the two types of claim are closely related and it has been argued that the general notion of strict restitutionary liability that equity applies in connection with the misadministration of estates should extend by analogy to the misappropriation of trust property.[921] It has been further argued that if the courts were to adopt such an approach, it would be desirable to modify two aspects of the *Diplock* claim. First, although a general defence of change of position did not exist at the time that *Diplock* was decided, it has since been accepted into Canadian and English law.[922] It therefore should be available in response to any restitutionary claim. Second, subject to the general rule against double-recovery, it should not be necessary for the aggrieved parties to exhaust their rights against the people who misdirected the property (*e.g.* the personal representative or trustee) before seeking relief from the people who received the benefit.

There are, however, also a number of commentators who argue that the *Diplock* claim should be confined to the context of the administration of estates,[923] or that the unusual features of the *Diplock* claim (*e.g.* the need to exhaust other avenues of relief before turning to the recipients) are defensible and ought to be retained even if the claim is allowed to extend to other contexts.[924]

---

919 As discussed in a later chapter on "Breach of Trust," the next-of-kin in *Diplock* also sought proprietary relief with respect to the misdirected assets.

920 The same rules have, however, occasionally been applied outside of the context of misdirected estate assets. See, for example, *Baker Ltd. v. Medway Building & Supplies Ltd.*, [1958] 2 All E.R. 532, affirmed [1958] 3 All E.R. 540 (C.A.) (liability with respect to funds that an auditor, in breach of a fiduciary duty, directed from a company to a third party).

921 Lord Nicholls, "Knowing receipt: The Need for a New Landmark" in W. Cornish *et al.*, eds., *Restitution: Past, Present & Future* (Oxford: Hart, 1998) 231 at 241; P. Birks, "Misdirected Funds: Restitution From the Recipient" [1989] Lloyd's Maritime & Commercial L.Q. 296; A. Burrows, *The Law of Restitution*, 2nd ed. (London: Butterworths, 2002), 203-206, 38-39.

922 *Rural Municipality of Storthoaks v. Mobil Oil Canada Ltd.*, *supra*, note 897; *Gorman v. Karpnale Ltd.* (1990), [1991] 2 A.C. 548, [1991] 3 W.L.R. 10, [1992] 4 All E.R. 512 (H.L.).

923 C. Harpum, "The Basis of Equitable Liability" in P. Birks, ed., *The Frontiers of Liability* (Oxford: Oxford University Press, 1994), 9 at 22-24.

924 L.D. Smith, "Three-Party Restitution: A Critique of Birks' Theory of Interceptive Subtraction" (1991), 11 Oxford J.L.S. 481.

14. At the same time that it released *Citadel Assurance*, the Supreme Court of Canada also delivered judgment in the companion case of *Gold v. Rosenberg*.[925] Regrettably, this was not a unanimous decision. A testator, who died in 1985, named his son, Rosenberg, and his grandson, Gold, his executors and equal beneficiaries of the residue of his estate. The residue consisted primarily of commercial real estate held by two companies, Primary Developments Ltd. ("Primary") and Existing Enterprises Ltd. ("Existing"). Rosenberg had been closely involved with the running of the companies while his father was alive. After the testator died, Gold gave Rosenberg a general power of attorney, which permitted Rosenberg to continue to operate the companies. Rosenberg also operated his own commercial real estate companies, including Trojan Self-Storage Mini-Warehouse Ltd. ("Trojan"). The estate, Primary, Existing, Trojan, and Rosenberg, all used the Toronto-Dominion Bank (the "Bank") for their banking, and a single accounts manager oversaw all of their accounts.

In order to repay loans made by the Bank to himself and to one of his companies, and to obtain a larger loan for Trojan, Rosenberg agreed, in July of 1989, to: (1) cause Primary to guarantee the new loan; (2) cause Primary to give a second collateral mortgage over property owned by it; (3) cause Existing to postpone a mortgage held by it over property owned by Trojan in favour of a new mortgage to be given to the bank by Trojan. A law firm acted as counsel to the estate, Primary, Existing, Rosenberg, Trojan and, on certain matters, the Bank. It provided an opinion letter to the Bank saying that the guarantee was valid. The Bank advanced the loan to Trojan before Gold signed certain documents to carry the agreement into effect, including the directors' resolution authorizing Primary's guarantee. In November of 1989, Gold revoked the power of attorney. In 1993 he sued Rosenberg, Primary, the Bank and the law firm, claiming a declaration that the guarantee was invalid.

The trial judge treated the case as one of knowing assistance, and held that: (1) Rosenberg had committed a fraudulent and dishonest breach of trust; and (2) the Bank had actual knowledge of the breach. Hence the trial judge imposed a constructive trust on the Bank in favour of Gold of those assets of the estate representing his 50 percent beneficial interest, by declaring the guarantee unenforceable, together with the collateral mortgage and postponement agreement. The law firm was also held liable. It did not appeal. The Ontario Court of Appeal allowed the Bank's appeal. It held that Rosenberg's breach of trust was not fraudulent or dishonest, since Gold signed the directors' resolution knowing the risk it imposed on the estate. In any event, the Bank was not liable, since it was entitled to rely on the opinion letter that the guarantee was valid. Hence the Bank did not have actual knowledge of the breach, it was not willfully blind to the breach and it did not recklessly disregard the breach. Gold appealed.

In the Supreme Court of Canada, a majority, comprising La Forest, Cory, Iacobucci and Gonthier JJ., held that this was a knowing receipt case. A minority, comprising Sopinka, McLachlin and Major JJ. thought that it was a knowing assistance case, but held that even if it was regarded as a knowing receipt case, the Bank acted reasonably in the circumstances and could, therefore, not be held liable. This minority was joined by Gonthier J. on the point of reasonableness. Thus, in the end result, the court dismissed the appeal.

In what were, therefore, dissenting reasons, Iacobucci J. held that the Bank could not be held liable for knowing assistance for essentially the same reasons as the Court of Appeal. However, this was not a case of knowing assistance, but of knowing receipt. The Bank received trust property in the form of the guarantee, supported by the collateral

---

925 *Supra*, note 837.

mortgage on real estate belonging to Primary (and, therefore, to the estate). Even if the argument that a guarantee is not property because it is contract security were accepted, the giving of the guarantee conferred a benefit on the Bank and constituted a corresponding deprivation to the estate. That was sufficient to bring the case within the knowing receipt category. His Lordship then applied the constructive knowledge (which he also called "notice") test, as also applied by La Forest J. in *Citadel*, and held that the facts were sufficiently suspicious to require the Bank to make reasonable inquiries to ensure Rosenberg was not acting in breach of trust. The Bank, through its account manager, knew: (1) all the relevant details about the testator's will and the estate; (2) that Gold had left the management of the estate to Rosenberg; (3) the details of Rosenberg's banking arrangements; (4) that Gold had not yet signed the directors' resolution when the loans were advanced to Trojan; and (5) that these dealings were not to the advantage of the estate or Gold. Since the Bank failed to make further inquiries, it was fixed with notice of the breach. The opinion letter did not absolve it from making the inquiries, because the Bank knew that the law firm was acting for all parties and could, therefore, not have given Gold independent advice.

Sopinka J., who wrote the majority judgment, thought that a guarantee supported by a collateral mortgage could not be regarded as trust property, since a guarantee is only contractual security. However, assuming it was trust property and that, therefore, this was a knowing receipt case, the bank acted reasonably in the circumstances. In other words, an honest and reasonable person in the position of the Bank would not be put on inquiry. This was because the Bank knew: (1) that Gold had given Rosenberg a power of attorney to manage the estate; (2) Primary had executed a guarantee and collateral mortgage; (3) a solicitor for the estate and for the guarantor had warranted the validity of the guarantee; (4) the accountants for the estate and Primary gave financial advice about the guarantee; (5) Gold had signed the resolution approving the granting of the guarantee; and (6) Rosenberg's share of the estate far exceeded the amount of the guarantee. In the circumstances, therefore, the Bank did not need to require that Gold obtain independent legal advice.

Which of the two approaches is correct? Was this a knowing receipt case? Did the Bank act reasonably?

15. The executor of an estate opened a bank account in his name as "executor of A, deceased." The executor then drew on the account over a period of three years by issuing cheques, signed by him as "executor of A, deceased," in favour of a turf accountant.[926] The executor would take these cheques to the turf accountant after banking hours and receive cash for them, and the turf accountant would later cash them at the bank. The executor is now insolvent. Does the estate have an action against the turf accountant?[927]

16. The Supreme Court of Canada's decision in *Citadel Assurance* has been applied on a number of occasions.[928] In *Banton v. CIBC Trust Corp.*, however, the Ontario Court

---

926 A "bookie" in the North American vernacular.
927 *Nelson v. Larholt* (1947), [1948] 1 K.B. 339, [1947] 2 All E.R. 751.
928 See, for example, *Waxman v. Waxman* (2002), 25 B.L.R. (3d) 1, 2002 CarswellOnt 2308 (S.C.J.), additional reasons at (2002), 2002 CarswellOnt 3047, [2002] O.J. No. 3533 (S.C.J.), additional reasons at (2003), 2003 CarswellOnt 52, [2003] O.J. No. 87, 30 C.P.C. (5th) 121 (S.C.J.), varied (April 30, 2004), Doc. CA C38611, C38616, C38624 (Ont. C.A.); *Silverman Jewellers Consultants Canada Inc. v. Royal Bank* (2001), (sub nom. *A & A Jewellers Ltd. v. Royal Bank of Canada*) 53 O.R. (3d) 97, 2001 CarswellOnt 633, 143 O.A.C. 375 (C.A.); *Ontario (Director, Real Estate & Business Brokers Act) v. NRS Mississauga Inc.* (2003), 226 D.L.R. (4th) 361, 2003 CarswellOnt 1239, 40 C.B.R. (4th) 127, 49 E.T.R. (2d) 256, 8 R.P.R. (4th) 13, (sub nom.

of Appeal failed to cite *Citadel Assurance*, curiously preferring to resolve the issue of knowing receipt instead on the basis of American authorities.[929]

(e) Trustees *De Son Tort*

A person who, although not appointed a trustee, intermeddles in a trust by assuming some or all of the obligations of the trustee, is regarded as a constructive trustee of the trust property for the beneficiaries. In *Mara v. Browne*[930] A.L. Smith L.J. described such a person as follows:

> . . .if one, not being a trustee and not having authority from a trustee, takes upon himself to intermeddle with trust matters or to do acts characteristic of the office of trustee, he may thereby make himself what is called in law a trustee of his own wrong — i.e., a trustee de son tort, or, as it also termed, a constructive trustee.

As in other areas that we have examined, the choice of terminology is not necessarily the most illuminating. Lord Millett recently suggested:[931]

> Substituting dog Latin for bastard French, we would do better to describe such persons as *de facto* trustees.

A trustee *de son tort* therefore is a person who knows that he or she is dealing with trust property and who receives, or later acquires, it with such knowledge. The trustee's liability is based, not on dishonesty[932] (although the trustee may also be dishonest), but on the fact that he or she takes control of trust property and purports to act for the beneficiaries. He or she will be liable in the same way as the express trustee would have been for any breach of trust.[933] This means that the trustee will hold any identifiable trust property on behalf of the beneficiaries, be accountable to the trust for any profits and be liable in an action for compensation for any loss. The fact that property is actually held on trust distinguish the trustee *de son tort* from the other types of constructive trustees.

The rules regarding trustees *de son tort* are an illustration of a broader equitable principle that treats a person who improperly assumes the responsibilities of a fiduciary as a fiduciary. The term "trustee *de son tort*" was adopted by

---

Director of Real Estate and Business Brokers v. NRS Mississauga Inc.) 170 O.A.C. 259, 64 O.R. (3d) 97 (C.A.), additional reasons at (2003), 2003 CarswellOnt 1888, 42 C.B.R. (4th) 280, 1 E.T.R. (3d) 220 (C.A.), leave to appeal refused (2003), 2003 CarswellOnt 5191, 2003 CarswellOnt 5192 (S.C.C.).

929 (2001), 197 D.L.R. (4th) 212, 2001 CarswellOnt 828, [2001] O.J. No. 1023, (sub nom. *Banton v. Banton*) 142 O.A.C. 389, 53 O.R. (3d) 567, 38 E.T.R. (2d) 167 (C.A.), leave to appeal refused (2001), 2001 CarswellOnt 3069, 2001 CarswellOnt 3070, 276 N.R. 395 (note), 155 O.A.C. 198 (note) (S.C.C.), critiqued in M. McInnes, "Knowing Receipt and The Protection of Trust Property" (2002), 81 Can. Bar Rev. 171.

930 [1896] 1 Ch. 199 at 209 (C.A.).

931 *Dubai Aluminium Company Ltd. v. Salaam*, [2003] 2 A.C. 366 (H.L.), at 403.

932 *Preston, Re* (1906), 13 O.L.R. 110 (Div. Ct.). In fact, many trustees *de son tort* are honest and are simply trying to administer the trust.

933 *Maguire v. Maguire* (1921), 50 O.L.R. 162, 64 D.L.R. 204 (H.C.).

analogy from the term "executor *de son tort*."[934] Likewise, a person who purports to act as an agent is liable to account to the "principal" in the same way as a true agent.[935]

In order to be liable as a trustee *de son tort*, the person who assumes to act as trustee must have the estate, be in a position to call for it, or at least have control of the trust property so as to be in a position to dispose of it. *Barney, Re*[936] illustrates this point. The testator appointed his widow his trustee and she continued to operate the testator's business. Two of the testator's friends agreed to help her by checking the business accounts regularly and an arrangement was made with the bank whereby the bank would not honour the trustee's cheques unless the two friends' initials appeared on them. The two friends were held not liable as trustees *de son tort* in proceedings by the testator's children because they did not have title to the property.

This case may be contrasted with *Maguire*.[937] The deceased was a guardian for the plaintiff, her nephew. The plaintiff persuaded her to lend a sum of money from his estate to a third party. She consulted the individual defendant, the plaintiff's older brother and, at his suggestion, gave him the money to lend to the third party. The individual defendant lent the money to the third party as intended, taking back a note which he turned over to his aunt. The third party defaulted and was judgment-proof. The plaintiff then sued his brother and his aunt's estate. The latter was not liable because the plaintiff had executed a release in favour of his aunt after he reached the age of majority. The brother was held to be a trustee *de son tort* because he received trust money with notice, had possession of it and purported to act as trustee. He then breached the trust by lending the money without security. In the end the brother was held not liable because the plaintiff, in effect, adopted the transaction by not bringing action for five years after reaching the age of majority.

Notes and Questions

1. A trustee decided to put trust money into a joint account with X on the ground that the moneys would be more secure that way. X was not required to co-sign any of the trustee's cheques. When a loss occurred, the beneficiaries sued X. What is the result?[938]

2. A died intestate in respect of certain real property which B had been managing for him. After A's death B continued to collect the rents without telling the lessees of A's death. B placed the funds in a separate account. In due course A's heirs were located and they wish to bring action against B to recover the funds. What cause of action do A's heirs have?[939]

---

934 The latter is described in *O'Reilly (No. 2), Re* (1981), 28 O.R. (2d) 481, 111 D.L.R. (3d) 238, 1980 CarswellOnt 531, 7 E.T.R. 185 (H.C.), affirmed (1981), 33 O.R. (2d) 352, 123 D.L.R. (3d) 767n, 1981 CarswellOnt 1306 (C.A.), at 485-6 [28 O.R.].
935 *Blyth v. Fladgate*, [1891] 1 Ch. 337.
936 [1892] 2 Ch. 265.
937 *Supra*, note 933.
938 *Constantine v. Ioan* (1969), 67 W.W.R. 615, 1969 CarswellBC 23 (S.C.).
939 *Lyell v. Kennedy, supra*, note 156.

3. A died possessed of real property of his own and real property in respect of which he was a trustee for others under the will of X. He devised the former to his sister, B. B assumed to act as trustee under X's will and sold some real property belonging to that trust. She allowed C to take the proceeds and to apply them for his own use in breach of trust. After B's death, X's beneficiaries sued B's estate. What is the result?[940]

4. I Ltd. lent money on mortgages. It did not do so directly, but acted through V Ltd., a mortgage broker. V Ltd. would make proposals of suitable investment opportunities to I Ltd. and, if the latter agreed, it would advance money to V Ltd. V Ltd. would then lend I Ltd.'s money and money of other investors to the borrower and take a mortgage in return, which it held in trust for the investors in the proportions in which they had contributed. Typically, therefore, I Ltd. did not advance the full amount of a mortgage, but participated in it with others. RD was the president and major shareholder of V Ltd. and made all policy decisions. BD was another director of V Ltd.

I Ltd. agreed to participate in the usual fashion in a mortgage to Mr. L. There was to be a first mortgage in favour of V Ltd. on certain property (lot A) owned by Mrs. L, together with a charge on Mrs. L's interest as unpaid vendor in another property (lot B).

Later Mrs. L exchanged her interest in lot B for another property (lot C) and V Ltd.'s charge on lot B was discharged and replaced with a charge on lot C. The defendants did not have a fraudulent intention in doing so.

Mr. and Mrs. L then defaulted on the loan and V Ltd. went into liquidation. I Ltd. and the other investors released the mortgage in consideration of an amount much less than that owing. I Ltd. brings an action for breach of trust against V Ltd., RD and BD. What is the appropriate result?[941]

5. A bank lent K $180,000 as a deposit on a share purchase on the understanding that the funds would be held in trust by K's lawyer, B, and would be returned if the purchase did not take place. Subsequently, B informed K that $100,000 of money held in the trust account was going to be used to cover fees owed by K to the law firm. The bank brought an action for the return of the funds. What is the appropriate result?[942]

Problems

1. Jennifer Brown, a highly successful puppeteer, hired Ian Carson, an entertainment lawyer, to assist her in her business dealings. For the most part, Carson's responsibilities consisted of conducting negotiations and drafting contracts on behalf of his client. Unbeknownst to Brown, however, Carson was a close friend of Wayland Lewis, who was Brown's primary competitor in puppetry field. Lewis and Carson together devised a scheme under which Carson informed Lewis of the fee that Brown intended to demand for a particular performance, thereby allowing Lewis to undercut his competitor by offering his services at a lower price. During the life of that scheme, Lewis received puppetry contracts worth $200,000. Although the evidence on point is somewhat equivocal, the evidence indicates that, in the normal course of events, half of that business certainly would have gone to Brown. For his part in the scheme, Carson received $50,000 from Lewis at the outset. Carson placed that money into a separate bank account, where it remains to this day. It has not been mixed with any other funds.

---

940 *Life Association of Scotland v. Siddal* (1861), 3 De. G. F. & J. 58, 45 E.R. 800.

941 *Island Realty Investments Ltd. v. Douglas* (1985), 19 E.T.R. 56, 1985 CarswellBC 614, [1985] B.C.J. No. 1118 (S.C.).

942 *Royal Bank v. Fogler, Rubinoff* (1991), 43 E.T.R. 131, 1991 CarswellOnt 544, 84 D.L.R. (4th) 724, 5 O.R. (3d) 734, 50 O.A.C. 209, 50 O.A.R. 209 (C.A.).

Lewis performed the contracts in question and received payment of $200,000. That money, however, is gone. Lewis died a short time ago, leaving behind an apparently empty estate — it contains neither assets nor debts (disregarding for the moment any possible judgment debt that may be owed to Brown). Lewis evidently spent all of his money on travel shortly before his death.

Discuss the rights and obligations that exist between the parties.

2. Davis Dewey, an extraordinarily successful artist, died in 1990. As he neared the end of his life, he became concerned with the ultimate distribution of his fortune. He therefore drafted a valid will in 1987 that (purportedly) created a number of testamentary dispositions, including the following: "The series of drawings known as *Sketches of Spain* shall be given to Bess Porgy."

Dewey drafted his will in June of 1987. In March of that year, he had written a letter to Porgy. The relevant passage said, in whole, "I'm writing to you in confidence. Although I plan to name you as a beneficiary in my will, I must fully explain my intentions. I want you to sell the sketches and distribute the proceeds equally amongst the friends that I hold near to my heart — including yourself."

Because of a postal strike, Porgy did not receive that letter until August of 1987. She immediately responded by saying, "I'm touched by your proposal and I would, of course, be happy to comply with your wishes."

Following Dewey's death, Porgy acquired the *Sketches of Spain* from his estate and sold them for $1,000,000. After preparing a list of the testator's acquaintances, she separately contacted Ron Hancock and Herbie Carter (who, along with Dewey, formed the "big three" of the Canadian art scene in the 1960s), fully explained the situation and paid $100,000 to each. Hancock and Carter pooled their gifts together and invested in a venture that unfortunately failed. Today, neither man has anything to show for the money that he received.

A question has arisen regarding the proper distribution of the proceeds from the sale of *Sketches of Spain*. Although Porgy is prepared to give away the rest of the money, she has not yet done so. That delay can be traced to the fact that she learned, after Hancock and Carter's venture failed, that while Dewey had been very close to Hancock since the 1960s, he died in the midst of a private feud with Carter. Neither Porgy nor Hancock knew of that feud until very recently.

Discuss the rights and obligations that exist between the parties.

3. A sole trustee proposes to invest trust funds in a particular manner. Although he honestly believes that he is entitled to do so, he seeks the advice of a solicitor out of an abundance of caution. The solicitor recognizes that the intended investment is actually prohibited under the terms of the trust. Nevertheless, for some ulterior motive, she fails to disclose that fact and actually helps the trustee make the investment.

The investment fails utterly and the trust suffers a sizable loss. The invested property no longer is traceable. Although the trustee is impecunious, the solicitor is quite wealthy. Must the solicitor compensate the trust beneficiaries with respect to their loss? Should she be required to do so? Are the answers to those questions the same in Canada as in England?

4. Pam keeps $5000 in her cookie jar. That money is not subject to a trust. While Pam is on vacation, a thief enters her home and steals the money. The thief then gives it to his friend, Dave, as a gift. Dave is unaware of the circumstances underlying the gift. When Pam returns from vacation, she discovers what has happened. As the thief has disappeared, she brings an action in unjust enrichment for personal restitution against Dave, who has not spent the money. Analyse Pam's claim against Dave. Is there any reason why it should not succeed? Would your answer be any different if the money had be held on trust for Pam?

5. Theo held a gold coin worth $50 000 on trust for Pam. In breach of trust, he gave that coin to his friend, Dave, in an effort to prevent Dave from becoming bankrupt. The effort failed — Dave later declared bankruptcy. Theo has disappeared, but Dave remains and he still has the coin in his possession. Pam has discovered the facts and seeks relief from Dave. Should she seek relief on the basis that Dave: (i) was a trustee *de son tort*, (ii) was guilty of knowing assistance, or (iii) was guilty of knowing receipt? Is there any other basis upon which she should seek relief?

6. Tom, who had fallen on hard times, held $500,000 on trust for Pam. The terms of the trust permitted only safe investments that yielded guaranteed, but minimal, returns. Because Pam paid relatively little attention to the operation of the trust, Tom believed that he could obtain an improper benefit for himself without being detected.

Tom entered into an agreement with Xavier, a friend of his who worked as an financial adviser. Tom transferred the trust money to Xavier. Xavier promised that he would place the $500,000 in high risk investments that potentially offered large returns. According to the terms of that agreement, after one year, Xavier would return to Tom all of the money representing the original trust funds (*i.e.* $500,000 plus the income received on the investments). Tom would then place an appropriate amount back into Pam's trust account and retain the additional profits for himself. For his part in the scheme, Xavier was paid $50,000 by Tom at the outset.

In breach of his promises, Xavier squandered the entire $550,000 on unsuccessful gambling junkets to unidentifiable casinos in Europe. The money is untraceable.

The scheme eventually was uncovered. Tom was devastated by the adverse publicity and committed suicide. His estate contains virtually no assets. Xavier, in contrast, has assets in excess of $1,000,000. Advise Pam. What cause of action should she use? What measure and form of relief should she seek?

7. For tax reasons, Pam does not wish to hold legal title to a certain piece of real property. She therefore transfers title into Dave's name. In exchange, Dave orally agrees that he will hold the property on trust for Pam's sister. Subsequently, however, Dave asserts his legal title and refuses to allow Pam's sister to enjoy the benefit of the house. Will a resulting trust based on unjust enrichment serve Pam's purpose? Will a constructive trust serve Pam's purpose? If so, upon what event is such a trust based?

8. Pam drafted a will that left her house to Dave. She later showed him the document and explained that its terms were misleading. She wanted him to enjoy the property for five years, but to then give it as a gift to her nephew, Xavier. Dave agreed to that arrangement. Pam died six years ago. Dave took immediate possession of the house, but now refuses to give it up to Xavier. Can Xavier enforce a constructive trust?

What if the precise wording of the will was "I leave my house to Dave"?

What if the precise wording of the will was "I leave my house to Dave. He shall enjoy the use of the property for five years, after which time he shall hold it on trust as agreed"?

If a constructive trust arose, when and why did it attach to the property?

PART V

THE ADMINISTRATION OF TRUSTS

12

THE APPOINTMENT, RETIREMENT, AND REMOVAL OF TRUSTEES

1. SCOPE

In order for a trust to work, it must be administered. This is a continuing process and is the function of the trustee. Administration of the trust would be impeded if there were a vacancy in the office of the trustee. A vacancy is not fatal to the trust itself, since one of equity's maxims is that a trust does not fail for want of a trustee. As a corollary to the maxim, courts of equity always assumed jurisdiction to fill a vacancy or to appoint another trustee. Modern statutes have codified this law.

This chapter begins with an examination of how and when trustees are appointed. In particular, it differentiates between judicial and non-judicial appointments of trustees, and between the appointment of new and substitute trustees. Then, it discusses the conditions under which a trustee may retire. The chapter concludes with a discussion of the circumstances in which trustees can be discharged or removed from office.

2. APPOINTMENT

(a) Introduction

There are two distinct aspects to the issue of appointment of trustees: the occasions on which trustees are appointed and the manner in which they are appointed. In other words, you need to know both when and how trustees are appointed. This part is devoted to a discussion of how trustees are appointed.

First trustees are normally appointed by the settlor or testator in the document that creates the trust. However, if the named trustees renounce, are unable to act, or predecease the testator, it may be necessary to appoint others. If the trust instrument named another trustee who is willing and able to act, the office will devolve upon that person. However, if there is no such alternate (or substitute), the mechanisms discussed below are available for the appointment of other persons.

Sometimes, it becomes necessary to appoint trustees during the continuance of the trust as well. For example, first trustees may die or retire, or it may be decided that additional trustees are necessary for the proper functioning of the trust. In these circumstances, trustees will be appointed either in substitution for, or in addition to, existing trustees.

The following materials deal with the different methods of appointing trustees. The methods apply to all appointments, whether made at the outset or during the continuance of the trust.

(b) Non-judicial Appointment of Trustees

(i) *Substitute Trustees*

As mentioned, first trustees are normally appointed by the trust instrument. Thereafter, the creator has no further say about appointments unless he or she has reserved such a power. If the trust instrument addresses the issues of appointment, removal, or discharge of trustees, its terms will govern. If it does not, the non-judicial power to appoint substitute trustees created by legislation in all Canadian common law jurisdictions except Prince Edward Island and New Brunswick applies, subject to any contrary intention in the trust document. Section 3 of the Ontario *Trustee Act*,[1] set out below, is representative of such legislation although you should be aware that the circumstances in which appointments can be made differ slightly in each statute.

In Ontario, the circumstances which call for the substitution of a new trustee are: the need to replace a trustee who dies or wishes to be discharged; or the need to remove a trustee because he or she remains outside Ontario for more than 12 months, refuses to act, is unfit or incapable of acting, is convicted of an indictable offence, is bankrupt or is insolvent.

In Ontario, the non-judicial power of substitution is exercisable by the person nominated in the trust instrument to appoint new trustees. If no such provision exists or if the person so named is unable or unwilling to act, the surviving or continuing trustee may appoint a replacement by will. However, if there is no surviving or continuing trustee, the personal representative of the last surviving or continuing trustee has power to administer the trust.

As *Re Brockbank*,[2] below, illustrates, the power of appointment in surviving or continuing trustees is a fiduciary power exercisable only with due regard for the interests of the trust and the beneficiaries. If the beneficiaries are *sui juris* and together absolutely entitled, they may end the trust.[3] They cannot, however, compel the trustees to appoint their nominee; the trustees must exercise independent judgment in making such an appointment.

---

1 R.S.O. 1990, c. T.23.
2 [1948] Ch. 206, [1948] 1 All E.R. 287.
3 See Chapter 6, part 4, *supra*.

TRUSTEE ACT

R.S.O. 1990, c. T.23

3. (1) Where a trustee dies or remains out of Ontario for more than twelve months, or desires to be discharged from all or any of the trusts or powers reposed in or conferred on the trustee, or refuses or is unfit to act therein, or is incapable of acting therein, or has been convicted of an indictable offence or is bankrupt or insolvent, the person nominated for the purpose of appointing new trustees by the instrument, if any, creating the trust, or if there is no such person, or no such person able and willing to act, the surviving or continuing trustees or trustee for the time being, or the personal representatives of the last surviving or continuing trustee, may by writing appoint another person or other persons (whether or not being the persons exercising the power) to be a trustee or trustees in the place of the trustee dying, remaining out of Ontario, desiring to be discharged, refusing or being unfit or incapable.

(2) Until the appointment of new trustees, the personal representatives or representative for the time being of a sole trustee, or where there were two or more trustees, of the last surviving or continuing trustee, are or is capable of exercising or performing any power or trust that was given to or capable of being exercised by the sole or last surviving trustee.

4. Subject to the terms of any instrument creating a trust, the sole trustee or the last surviving or continuing trustee appointed for the administration of the trust may appoint by will another person or other persons to be a trustee or trustees in the place of the sole or surviving or continuing trustee after his or her death.

Comparable Legislation

Trustee Act, R.S.A. 2000, c. T-8, s. 14 (am. by R.S.A. 2000, c. 16 (Supp.), s. 59(c)); R.S.B.C. 1996, c. 464, s. 27 (subs. (2)(c) am. by S.B.C. 1999, c. 6, s. 26); R.S.M. 1987, c. T160, s. 8 (am. by S.M. 1993, c. 29, s. 206(3)); R.S.N.S. 1989, c. 479, s. 16; R.S.N.L. 1990, c. T-10, s. 11; R.S.N.W.T. 1988, c. T-8, s. 7; R.S.S. 1978, c. T-23, s. 15; R.S.Y. 2002, c. 223, s. 10; *Trustees Act*, R.S.N.B. 1973, c. T-15, s. 6 (am. by S.N.B. 1979, c. 41, s. 123(2); S.N.B. 1980, c. 32, s. 42(1), (2)).

Concerning the power of a surviving trustee see: *Trustee Act*, R.S.A. 2000, c. T-8, s. 29; R.S.B.C. 1996, c. 464, s. 12; R.S.M. 1987, c. T160, s. 6; R.S.O. 1990, c. T.23, s. 25; R.S.N.S. 1989, c. 479, s. 17; R.S.N.L. 1990, c. T-10, s. 27; R.S.N.W.T. 1988, c. T-8, s. 25; R.S.S. 1978, c. T-23, s. 73; R.S.Y. 2002, c. 223, s. 28; *Trustees Act*, R.S.N.B. 1973, c. T-15, s. 12.

RE BROCKBANK; WARD v. BATES

[1948] Ch. 206
[Chancery Division]

The testator left the residue of his estate in trust for his widow for life and, on her death, to his children. The trustees of the will were W and B.

W wished to retire and the widow and children wanted Lloyds Bank to be appointed the replacement trustee. B, the defendant and co-trustee, refused to concur.

W and the beneficiaries applied to the court asking that it direct B to concur in appointing Lloyds Bank as sole trustee of the will. In the alternative, they sought a court appointment of Lloyds Bank as the sole trustee.

VAISEY J.:

This case involves a question which is said to be novel. It is possible, I think, that the reason for the novelty is that the courage required for the raising of it has hitherto been lacking. The two alternative grounds of relief claimed are sought to be justified by the following argument: It is said that where all the beneficiaries concur, they may force a trustee to retire, compel his removal, and direct the trustees, having the power to nominate their successors, to appoint as such successors such persons or person or corporation as may be indicated by the beneficiaries, and it is suggested that the trustees have no option but to comply.

I do not follow this. The power of nominating a new trustee is a discretionary power, and, in my opinion, is no longer exercisable and, indeed, can no longer exist if it has become one of which the exercise can be dictated by others. But then it is said that the beneficiaries could direct the trustees to transfer the trust property either to themselves absolutely, or to any other person or persons or corporation, upon trusts identical with or corresponding to the trusts of the testator's will. I agree, provided that the trustees are adequately protected against any possible claim for future death duties and are fully indemnified as regards their costs, charges, and expenses. But the result of such a transaction (that is to say a transaction which involves the repetition of the former trusts) would be to establish a new settlement, with (as it seems to me) two consequences which would be to the disadvantage of the beneficiaries: First, it would probably attract an *ad valorem* stamp duty and, secondly, the benefit of the exemption from estate duty given by section 14 of the *Finance Act, 1914*, on the death of the widow, as a surviving spouse, would be lost.

It seems to me that the beneficiaries must choose between two alternatives: either they must keep the trusts of the will on foot, in which case those trusts must continue to be executed by trustees duly appointed pursuant either to the original instrument or to the powers of s. 36 of the *Trustee Act, 1925*, and not by trustees arbitrarily selected by themselves; or they must, by mutual agreement, extinguish and put an end to the trusts with the consequences which I have just indicated.

The claim of the beneficiaries to control the exercise of the defendant's fiduciary power of making or compelling an appointment of the trustees is, in my judgment, untenable. The court itself regards such a power as deserving of the greatest respect and as one with which it will not interfere, as is shown by the case of *Re Gadd*[4] of which it will suffice if I read the headnote:

---

4 (1883), 23 Ch. D. 134, [1891-4] All E.R. Rep. 1070, 31 W.R. 417 (C.A.).

A decree for the administration of the trusts of a will directed "that some proper person be appointed" a trustee of the will in the place of a deceased trustee. The power of appointing new trustees was given by the will to the surviving trustee, who was the defendant. The plaintiff took out a summons to have A.B. appointed trustee, and the defendant a summons to have C.D. appointed. The summonses were adjourned into court and Bacon V.-C., appointed the nominee of the plaintiff. Held, on appeal, that the decree did not take away from the defendant the power of appointing new trustees, though after decree he could only exercise it subject to the supervision of the court; that if he nominated a fit and proper person such person must be appointed, and the court would not appoint someone else on the ground that such other person was in the opinion of the court more eligible, and that if he nominated a person whom the court did not approve the court would not itself make the choice, but would call on him to make a fresh nomination. Held, therefore, that the appointment of A.B. must be discharged.

This point is emphasized in *Re Higginbottom*,[5] of which I will again read the headnote:

The court has no jurisdiction, under the Trustee Acts, to appoint new trustees of a will against the wishes of an existing sole trustee desirous of exercising his statutory power of appointing new trustees under section 31 of the *Conveyancing and Law of Property Act, 1881*,

— that corresponds with section 36 of the *Trustee Act, 1925*, —

even though the application to the court is made by a majority of the beneficiaries, and the existing trustee has himself no beneficial interest.

Kekewich J. in his judgment says: "The non-interference by the court with the legal power of appointment of new trustees is established by several cases." He cites *Re Gadd*[6] and other cases to which I need not more particularly refer.

If the court, as a matter of practice and principle, refuses to interfere with the legal power of appointment of new trustees, it is, in my judgment, *a fortiori* not open to the beneficiaries to do so. As I have said, they can put an end to the trust if they like; nobody doubts that; but they are not entitled, in my judgment, to arrogate to themselves a power which the court itself disclaims possessing, and to change trustees whenever they think fit at their whim or fancy — for it follows from Mr. Cross' argument for the present plaintiffs (as appeared from his reply to a question I put to him during the course of the hearings) that whenever the beneficiaries choose to say that they do not like their trustee, they can order him to retire and order him to appoint anyone they like to succeed him. That seems to me to show a complete disregard of the true position. As I have said, as long as the trust subsists, the trust must be executed by persons duly, properly, and regularly appointed to the office.

No doubt, in many cases trustees would gladly exercise their powers of appointment so as to accord with the wishes of their beneficiaries, whether unanimous or not; but the unfortunate thing is that here the defendant was approached in a manner which was the very reverse of conciliatory. He was not asked, but was told, to do what the beneficiaries wanted and, though I need not refer to the

5 [1892] 3 Ch. D. 1342, [1891-4] All E.R. Rep. 1070.
6 *Supra*, note 4.

correspondence in detail, it was, in my judgment, couched in terms which were both peremptory and provocative.

The trouble now is that the defendant, as a professional man, if he is to be thrown out of his trust, will inevitably be placed under the stigma of having his proceedings as trustee brought before the court and then it will be pointed out that the result of those proceedings is that he has been expelled from his trusteeship.

No case whatever is made out for depriving the defendant of his statutory power and still less is any case made out for removing him from the trusteeship, as is asked for by the originating summons. The summons does not ask in the alternative that the defendant should remain as trustee with the nominee of the plaintiffs; it asks that he should be displaced in favour of a sole trustee. It has been suggested at the Bar that the plaintiffs did not mean to expel or procure the removal of the defendant from the trusteeship, but only to procure the appointment of the bank as trustee with him. All I can say is that that is in flat contradiction of what I find in the originating summons.

Let me say at once that if the beneficiaries had called upon the defendant to transfer to them the trust property, subject, of course, to his being sufficiently protected against all possible claims, there would have been no sort of answer to the application. But he was never asked to do that. What he was asked to do was to execute what I think would have been a fictitious appointment, the appointment of a new trustee, which would purport and appear to be something done of his own volition, while all the time he was in fact being told, "You have no option and no choice; you must do exactly what you are told." That is, I think, a misconception of the position; but whether the plaintiffs will follow what I think is the very unwise course of setting up a new trust, which will have the general consequences to which I have alluded, I do not know, and I cannot stop them doing that if they think it is right to do it: so much the better for the exchequer. They may elect to have the property made over to them or they may think it better, having regard to the age of the tenant for life, to allow the trust to run its course under a trusteeship duly and properly constituted. I think it would be improper for me to recommend the plaintiffs what course they ought to take. I have pointed out what seem to me to be the objections to one of the courses suggested, which I think I was entitled to do, because it was represented to me by Mr. Cross that this was actually a case in which I, as a judge, should appoint the bank to be a new trustee on the ground that it was "expedient" to do so. To appoint a bank, who charge an acceptance fee, who charge a withdrawal fee and who charge an income fee, as a trustee of a trust, of which all that remains to be done is to pay the income to a lady of 83 years and on her death to divide the capital, seems to me to be a very improvident way of dealing with the position.

[The court dismissed the application.]

(ii) *Additional Trustees*

Section 3 of the Ontario *Trustee Act*,[7] as we have seen, provides for the non-judicial appointment of substitute trustees. It provides that, when a trustee dies, retires or is removed, another person *or persons* may be appointed to replace such trustee. The ability to appoint more than one person, thus, allows for an increase in the number of trustees. An increase is also possible under s. 6(a), which is set out below.[8]

However, if no replacement is sought, there is no mechanism in the Ontario legislation for the non-judicial appointment of additional trustees. Unless there is an express power in the instrument to appoint additional trustees, an application to the court is required.

All other Canadian common law jurisdictions, except Manitoba, New Brunswick and Prince Edward Island, follow the Ontario legislation in this respect. In Manitoba, the non-judicial appointment of additional trustees is permitted, but not mandatory.[9] New Brunswick and Prince Edward Island do not permit non-judicial appointments at all, so in those jurisdictions there must always be a court application for the appointment of trustees whether as substitutes for or in addition to existing trustees.[10]

Notes and Questions

1. No one can be compelled to undertake a trust.[11] Thus, a person who is named as trustee in a trust instrument may renounce.

2. It has been noted that a non-judicial power of appointment can be exercised when a trustee wishes to be discharged. The statutory provision is probably wide enough to apply to a trustee who wants to be discharged from only a part of the trust. For example, if part of a trust fund is set aside to provide for a beneficiary's life interest and the trustee is prepared to carry on in relation to the appropriated funds, but not for the main fund, the non-judicial power of appointment can probably be invoked.

3. A person named as a trustee in an *inter vivos* trust instrument normally accepts the office of trustee by executing the trust instrument. However, execution of the instrument is not a prerequisite to assumption of the office. A trustee who does any act, however slight, that carries out the trust, he or she is presumed to have accepted the office.

4. The Ontario Law Reform Commission has recommended that the non-judicial appointment and removal of substitute trustees be extended.[12]

(c) Judicial Appointment of Trustees

The courts in common law jurisdictions in Canada have an inherent jurisdiction to appoint and dismiss trustees. This inherent jurisdiction has, for the most

---

7 R.S.O. 1990, c. T.23.
8 In part 2(d)(ii).
9 See R.S.M. 1987, c. T160, s. 10.
10 See R.S.N.B. 1973, c. T-15, s. 29 and R.S.P.E.I. 1988, c. T-8, s. 4.
11 *Re Richardson*, [1958] Ch. 508, [1958] 1 All E.R. 538.
12 See Ontario Law Reform Commission Report, at 172-184.

part, been codified by statute. While such legislation does not eliminate the courts' inherent powers, it does cover most situations, thus rendering resort to the courts' inherent jurisdiction virtually unnecessary.

The legislation empowers the courts to appoint both substitute and additional trustees. Note the difference between the appointment of substitute and additional trustees. When appointing an additional trustee, the court need only consider the suitability of the proposed trustee and whether the circumstances warrant an increase in the number of trustees. Substitution requires that an existing trustee be removed and that a new trustee be appointed.[13] For example, one factor the court must bear in mind when appointing one trustee in place of another is whether the original appointment was for a corporate trustee. In such a case, it may be inappropriate to replace the corporate trustee with an individual trustee.[14]

As the Ontario statutory provisions are representative of those of the other common law jurisdictions, they are set out below. Arguably, court appointments should be used only if it is doubtful that the statutory non-judicial power of appointment can be exercised, if there is no person capable of making a non-judicial appointment, if security of title might be in issue, or if an actual increase in the number of trustees is desired. In practice, however, resort to court appointments is frequent, as it may offer more protection to those making the application, and in the case of substitution, those leaving the office of trustee.

The principles guiding the court in appointing trustees were set out by Turner L.J. in *Re Tempest*.[15]

It was said in argument, and has been frequently said, that in making such appointments the court acts upon and exercises its discretion; and this, no doubt, is generally true; but the discretion which the court has and exercises in making such appointments, is not, as I conceive, a mere arbitrary discretion, but a discretion in the exercise of which the court is, and ought to be, guided by some general rules and principles, and, in my opinion, the difficulty which the court has to encounter in these cases lies not so much in ascertaining the rules and principles by which it ought to be guided, as in applying those rules and principles to the varying circumstances of each particular case. The following rules and principles may, I think, safely be laid down as applying to all cases of appointments by the Court of new trustees.

First, the Court will have regard to the wishes of the persons by whom the trust has been created, if expressed in the instrument creating the trust, or clearly to be collected from it. I think this rule may be safely laid down, because if the author of the trust has in terms declared that a particular person, or a person filling a particular character, should not be a trustee of the instrument, there cannot, as I apprehend, be the least doubt that the Court would not appoint to the office a person whose appointment was so prohibited, and I do not think that upon a question of this description any distinction can be drawn between express declarations and demonstrated intention. The analogy of the course which the Court pursues in the appointment of guardians affords, I think, some support to this rule. The Court in those cases attends to the wishes of the parents, however informally they may be expressed.

Another rule which may, I think, safely be laid down is this — that the Court will not appoint a person to be trustee with a view to the interest of some of the persons interested under the trust, in opposition either to the wishes of the testator or to the interests of others of the *cestuis que trusts* [sic]. I think so for this reason, that it is the essence of the duty of every trustee to hold an

---

13 For removal of a trustee see, Removal, part 4, *infra*.

14 *Re Bushell* (1984), 46 O.R. (2d) 326, 17 E.T.R. 65 (H.C.).

15 (1866), 1 Ch. App. 485, 487 (C.A.).

even hand between the parties interested under the trust. Every trustee is in duty bound to look to the interests of all, and not of any particular member or class of members of his *cestuis que trusts* [sic].

A third rule which, I think, may safely be laid down, is, — that the Court in appointing a trustee will have regard to the question, whether his appointment will promote or impede the execution of the trust, for the very purpose of the appointment is that the trust may be better carried into execution.

It would appear that the principles which guide the appointment of additional trustees are the same as those for substitution of trustees. The main consideration is what is best for the trust. The court thus takes into account the benefits the appointment of additional trustees will confer and whether the appointment will remove existing problems.

Re Moorhouse,[16] set out below, illustrates one difference between a judicial and a non-judicial power to appoint trustees; namely, that when a court is asked to appoint a new trustee in substitution for an existing trustee, it may select a trustee against the wishes of the existing trustees.[17]

TRUSTEE ACT

R.S.O. 1990, c. T.23

5.(1) The Superior Court of Justice may make an order for the appointment of a new trustee or new trustees, either in substitution for or in addition to any existing trustee or trustees, or although there is no existing trustee.

(2) An order under this section and any consequential vesting order or conveyance does not operate as a discharge from liability for the acts or omissions of the former or continuing trustees.

. . .

WHO MAY APPLY

16.(1) An order under this Act for the appointment of a new trustee, or concerning any land or personal estate, subject to a trust, may be made upon the application of any person beneficially interested therein, whether under disability or not, or upon the application of any person duly appointed as a trustee thereof.

Comparable Legislation

Trustee Act, R.S.A. 2000, c. T-8, s. 16 (am. by R.S.A. 2000, c. 16 (Supp.), s. 59(c)); R.S.B.C. 1996, c. 464, ss. 30, 31; R.S.M. 1987, c. T160, s. 9 (am. by S.M. 1993, c. 29, s. 206(4)); R.S.N.S. 1989, c. 479, s. 16; R.S.P.E.I. 1988, c. T-8, s. 4; R.S.N.L. 1990, c. T-10, s. 33; R.S.N.W.T. 1988, c. T-8, s. 6; R.S.S. 1978, c. T-23, s. 14; R.S.Y. 2002, c. 223, s. 10; *Trustees Act*, R.S.N.B. 1973, c. T-15, s. 29.

---

16 [1946] O.W.N. 789, 4 D.L.R. 542 (H.C.).
17 *Re Brockbank; Ward v. Bates*, [1948] Ch. 206.

RE MOORHOUSE

[1946] O.W.N. 789, [1946 4 D.L.R. 542
Ontario Supreme Court
High Court of Justice

An executor and trustee applied to the court asking that her lawyer be appointed in her place.

BARLOW J.:

. . .

Walter Hoare Moorhouse died on or about the 24th October 1921, leaving a last will and testament by which he appointed Mary Elizabeth Butler Moorhouse and the Premier Trust Company his executors. Probate of the said last will and testament was granted on the 4th January 1922 to the Premier Trust Company and Mary Elizabeth Moorhouse, who have since that time administered the estate and the trusts set out in the said will.

Mary Elizabeth Butler Moorhouse is the life-tenant and is now about 90 years of age. Upon her death the estate will be distributed.

. . .

Mary Elizabeth Butler Moorhouse does not ask to retire unconditionally as trustee. She only asks to be discharged if Eric G. Moorhouse is appointed in her place and stead. If he is not to be appointed by the court she wishes to continue. This condition takes from the court its discretion as to the appointment of a new trustee. *The Trustee Act*,[18] section 5(1) is as follows:

> The Supreme Court may make an order for the appointment of a new trustee or new trustees, either in substitution for or in addition to any existing trustee or trustees, or although there is no existing trustee.

This not only places in the court the power to appoint, but also there goes with it a discretion as to the person to be appointed.

[The court then reproduced section 3 of the Ontario *Trustee Act*.]

This gives power to the surviving or continuing trustees or trustee to appoint a new trustee.

Where there is a continuing trustee, I do not find in the *Trustee Act* any power permitting one trustee to retire and to dictate the person to be appointed in his or her place or stead. If a trustee wishes to retire, he must retire unconditionally, leaving it to the continuing trustee or to the court to appoint a new trustee, if it appears advisable. It therefore follows that Mary Elizabeth Butler Moorhouse has no power to appoint Eric G. Moorhouse a trustee in her place and stead, and

---

18 R.S.O. 1937, c. 165.

furthermore she ought not to be permitted to hamper the court in its discretion by attempting to dictate whom the court should appoint.

Furthermore, Eric G. Moorhouse is the personal solicitor of Mary Elizabeth Butler Moorhouse, who is now a trustee and the life-tenant. If he were to be appointed trustee, it may very well be that his interest as trustee and his interest as solicitor for the life-tenant would come in conflict. For this reason alone he ought not to be appointed.[19]

[The court dismissed the application.]

Notes and Questions

1. A new trustee, whether appointed non-judicially or by the court, has the same powers, authorities and discretions as if he or she had been the original trustee.[20]

2. In *Moorhouse*, could the retiring trustee have appointed her solicitor under a non-judicial power of appointment? If not, why not?[21]

3. Can you think of any advantages to having the court appoint a new trustee as opposed to making a non-judicial appointment?

4. What would happen if existing trustees advised the court that they would not act with the person the court proposed to appoint?[22]

5. *Construction Labour Relations, an Alberta Assn., Sheet Metal (Provincial) Trade Division v. S.M.W., Local No. 8*[23] explores the principles the court will follow on the appointment of additional trustees. The applicant was an employers' organization. In an effort to gain influence over the administration of the trust fund, it sought to have additional trustees appointed by the court. The organization was responsible for bargaining collectively with the trade unions but was not permitted to appoint trustees. The trust agreement, entered into twenty-two years earlier, stipulated that there be equal representation of both employers and unions on the board of trustees, with a minimum of four trustees. Since the agreement's inception, a number of employers ceased to exist, leaving only two capable of appointing trustees. Hence, a maximum of four trustees could be appointed to the board. The applicant claimed the ability to appoint future trustees, however, the trust agreement stated that only an employer or an employer's successor could appoint a trustee. The employers' organization did not meet either of these conditions and thus could not appoint trustees. Although the circumstances surrounding the trust had changed significantly, the court refused to name additional trustees as it did not find that the beneficiaries were being prejudiced. In arriving at its conclusion, the court was influenced by the fact that the required minimum number of trustees remained and the administration of the trust had not suffered. The court concluded that there was no good reason to appoint additional trustees.

---

19 See *Kemp's Settled Estates, Re* (1883), 24 Ch. D. 485; *Lewin on Trusts*, 14th ed., 1939, p. 445; and *Allen v. Norris* (1884), 27 Ch. D. 333.

20 See, for example, *Trustee Act*, R.S.O. 1990, c. T.23, s. 7.

21 See *Merry Estate v. Merry Estate* (2002), (sub nom. *Meredith v. Plaxton*) 62 O.R. (3d) 427, 202 CarswellOnt 3993, 48 E.T.R. (2d) 72 (S.C.J.).

22 See *Re Tempest* (1886), 1 Ch. App. 485, 487 (C.A.).

23 (1994), (sub nom. *Construction Labour Relations v. S.M.W., Local 8*) 111 D.L.R. (4th) 569, 1994 CarswellAlta 452, 2 C.C.P.B. 25, 150 A.R. 314 (Q.B.).

(d) Number of Trustees

(i) *Maximum*

At common law, there is no maximum number of persons who may be trustees of a trust. However, it is wise to establish a maximum so that the trust does not become unworkable. Because trustees must act jointly, as a general rule all acts must be agreed to unanimously and the greater the number of trustees the more difficult it is to obtain unanimity.

Legislation in Manitoba, set out below, has established four as a maximum number of trustees; no other Canadian jurisdiction appears to have a statutory restriction on the number of trustees that may be appointed.[24]

TRUSTEE ACT

R.S.M. 1987, c. T160

Powers of appointment of trustees

10. On the appointment of a trustee for the whole or any part of a trust property,

(*a*) the number of trustees may, subject to the restrictions imposed by this Act on the number of trustees, be increased; and

(*b*) a separate set of trustees, not exceeding four, may be appointed for any part of the trust property held on trusts distinct from those relating to any other part or parts of the trust property, notwithstanding that no new trustees or trustee are or is to be appointed for other parts of the trust property, and any existing trustee may be appointed or remain one of the separate set of trustees; or, if only one trustee was originally appointed, then, one separate trustee may be so appointed; and

(*c*) it is not obligatory to appoint more than one new trustee where only one trustee was originally appointed, or to fill up the original number of trustees where more than two trustees were originally appointed; and

(*d*) any assurance or thing requisite for vesting the trust property, or any part thereof, in a sole trustee, or jointly in the persons who are the trustees, shall be executed or done.

(ii) *Minimum*

Whether trustees are appointed non-judicially or by the court, legislation in Canadian common law jurisdictions decrees that there be a certain minimum

---

24 As to the number of trustees see: *Trustee Act*, R.S.A. 2000, c. T-8, s. 14(5); R.S.B.C. 1996, c. 464, s. 27(2) (am. by S.B.C. 1999, c. 6, s. 26); R.S.N.L. 1990, c. T-10, s. 11; R.S.N.S. 1989, c. 479, s. 16(1); R.S.N.W.T. 1988, c. T-8, s. 6; R.S.S. 1978, c. T-23, s. 16; R.S.Y. 2002, c. 223, s. 11.

numbers of trustees. The Ontario *Trustee Act*,[25] set out below, is representative of such legislation.

In most Canadian jurisdictions, there must be a minimum of two trustees. However, in Ontario and Manitoba, the legislation allows for trusts with a single trustee if only one was originally appointed; if more than one was originally appointed, a trustee can be discharged provided that the sole remaining trustee is a trust corporation.[26]

TRUSTEE ACT

R.S.O. 1990, c. T.23

6. On the appointment of a new trustee for the whole or any part of trust property,

(*a*) the number of trustees may be increased; and

(*b*) a separate set of trustees may be appointed for any part of the trust property held on trusts distinct from those relating to any other part or parts of the trust property, even though no new trustees or trustee are or is to be appointed for other parts of the trust property, and any existing trustee may be appointed or remain one of such separate set of trustees or, if only one trustee was originally appointed, then one separate trustee may be so appointed for the first-mentioned part; and

(*c*) it is not obligatory to appoint more than one new trustee where only one trustee was originally appointed or to fill up the original number of trustees where more than two trustees were originally appointed but, except where only one trustee was originally appointed, a trustee shall not be discharged under section 3 from the trust unless there will be a trust corporation or at least two individuals as trustees to perform the trust; and

(*d*) any assurance or thing requisite for vesting the trust property, or any part thereof, in the person who is the trustee, or jointly in the persons who are the trustees, shall be executed or done.

Comparable Legislation

Trustee Act, R.S.A. 2000, c. T-8, s. 14(5); R.S.B.C. 1996, c. 464, s. 27(2) (am. by S.B.C. 1999, c. 6, s. 26); R.S.M. 1987, c. T160, s. 10; R.S.N.L. 1990, c. T-10, s. 11(2); R.S.N.S. 1989, c. 479, s. 16(2); R.S.N.W.T. 1988, c. T-8, s. 8; R.S.S. 1978, c. T-23, s. 16; R.S.Y. 2002, c. 223, s. 11.

---

25 R.S.O. 1990, c. T.23.
26 *Ibid.*, s. 6(c).

3. RETIREMENT

If the trust instrument expressly provides for the retirement of the trustees, its terms will govern. In the absence of such express provisions, legislation in all Canadian jurisdictions enables a trustee to retire with the consent of his or her co-trustees. The consent must be by deed. Section 2 of the Ontario *Trustee Act*,[27] reproduced below, is representative of such legislation.

Note that the retirement provisions of the Ontario legislation do not apply to personal representatives. Personal representatives cannot resign; they must file a deed with the appropriate court and obtain an order of removal.[28] *Re McLean*,[29] below, illustrates the differences between the retirement of a trustee and the removal of an executor.

TRUSTEE ACT

R.S.O. 1990, c. T.23

Retirement of Trustees

2. (1) Where there are more than two trustees, if one of them by deed declares a desire to be discharged from the trust, and if the co-trustees and such other person, if any, as is empowered to appoint trustees, consent by deed to the discharge of the trustee, and to the vesting in the co-trustees alone of the trust property, then the trustee who desires to be discharged shall be deemed to have retired from the trust, and is, by the deed, discharged therefrom under this Act without any new trustee being appointed.

(2) This section does not apply to executors or administrators.

Comparable Legislation

Trustee Act, R.S.A. 2000, c. T-8, s. 15 (am. by R.S.A. 2000, c. 16 (Supp.), s. 59(c)); R.S.B.C. 1996, c. 464, s. 28; R.S.M. 1987, c. T160, s. 7; R.S.N.L. 1990, c. T-10, s. 11(2); R.S.N.S. 1989, c. 479, s. 17; R.S.N.W.T. 1988, c. T-8, s. 12; R.S.P.E.I. 1988, c. T-8, s. 33; R.S.S. 1978, c. T-23, s. 20; R.S.Y. 2002, c. 223, s. 5.

---

27 R.S.O. 1990, c. T.23.
28 *Re Cooper (No. 1)* (1976), 21 O.R. (2d) 574, 90 D.L.R. (3d) 710 (H.C.).
29 (1982), 135 D.L.R. (3d) 667, 37 O.R. (2d) 164, 11 E.T.R. 293 (H.C.).

RE MCLEAN

(1982), 135 D.L.R. (3d) 667
Ontario Supreme Court
High Court of Justice

A testator who died in 1954 appointed three persons as "Executors of this my Will and Trustees of my Estate." In 1975 one of the trustees resigned and was replaced. In 1977 two additional trustees were appointed by the court and in 1978 the number of trustees was varied by court order to a minimum of three and a maximum of five.

In 1980, Bennett, one of the original appointees under the will, resigned his position as trustee by deed with the consent of his co-trustees. Bennett continued as executor, but then became incapable. Consequently, the estate brought an application for his removal as executor and to confirm his resignation as trustee or to remove him in that capacity.

The question was whether an order removing Bennett as trustee was necessary. The Official Guardian took the position that it was, whereas the estate argued that Bennett's resignation was effective under section 2 of the *Trustee Act*.[30]

OSBORNE J.:

. . .

It is common practice for a testator to appoint the same person to act as both executor and trustee. Wills rarely divide the function of that person between the two roles in any specific way. The confusion of roles is compounded by the fact that under the *Trustee Act*[31] the personal representative holds the assets of the estate in trust. The definition section of the *Trustee Act* provides, in part, as follows:

1. In this Act,

. . .

(k) "personal representative" means an executor, an administrator, and an administrator with the will annexed;

. . .

(q) "trust" does not mean the duties incident to an estate conveyed by way of mortgage; but, with this exception, includes implied and constructive trusts and cases where the trustee has some beneficial estate or interest in the subject of the trust, and extends to and includes the duties incident to the office of personal representative of a deceased person, and "trustee" has a corresponding meaning and includes a trustee however appointed and several joint trustees;

However, despite the general practice in drafting wills, there are definite differences between the functions of executors and trustees. These differences are discussed in Waters,[32] as follows:

---

30 R.S.O. 1980, c. 512.
31 *Ibid.*
32 *Law of Trusts in Canada* (1974), at 34-36.

> The task of the personal representative of the deceased is to gather in the assets of the deceased, to discharge funeral and testamentary expenses and debts, and to distribute the remaining assets among the persons entitled.
>
> . . .
>
> . . . there are certain differences between the two offices which, though less extensive than the similarities, do reflect the fact that, while a trust is essentially a means whereby property can be enjoyed by a succession of persons over a period of time, the personal representative is merely concerned to wind up the affairs of another and distribute his effects.

Waters,[33] goes on to observe that this distinction in roles is maintained in the legislation:

> The *Devolution of Estates Act* and *Trustee Act* reflect this more limited role of the representative in the type of powers and duties which are given him; the *Trustee Act* also confers powers and imposes duties upon trustees as such; but these assume the continuity of trust ownership and beneficial enjoyment. For example, both parties may sell, lease and mortgage the property held by them, but while the trustee does so as an investment policy, the personal representative is concerned merely in making real estate productive prior to its distribution, or in employing it as a means of raising money to pay off the deceased's debts and expenses.

This difference between the executor's role and the trustee's role is also reflected in section 2 of the *Trustee Act*, which permits a trustee to retire by deed, but which specifically excludes executors and administrators from resort to this option. The case of *Re Heintzman*[34] involved an application by the co-trustees, a trust company and the widow of the testator, to permit the resignation of the trust company and the appointment of two of the adult children of the testator as replacement trustees. A variation of the trust was also sought to permit the adult children, who were contingent beneficiaries, to act as trustees. The application was granted by Trainor J. who stated in *obiter*[35] the following:

> The trusts have been set up under the will. The executors' work is completed. In these circumstances, it would appear that the estate might have achieved an identical result by proceeding under sections 3 [am. 1978, c. 22, s. 1], 5 and 6 of the *Trustee Act* without the necessity of seeking court approval under section 37 of the Act.

The *Heintzman* case deals with resignation and replacement of trustees under section 3 of the *Trustee Act*, not under section 2. It does not deal with whether the resignation as trustee affected the office of executor, but it does reinforce the position that the offices are different in function and in time.

> [His Lordship found further support for the position that the offices of personal representative and trustee are different in *Re Cockburn's Will Trusts*;[36] *Re Ponder*,[37] and *Harvell v. Foster*.[38]]

---

33 *Ibid.*, at 36.
34 (1981), 31 O.R. (2d) 724, 120 D.L.R. (3d) 295, 9 E.T.R. 12 (H.C.).
35 See at O.R. 727, at D.L.R. 298.
36 [1957] Ch. 438, [1957] 2 All E.R. 522.
37 [1921] 2 Ch. 59.
38 [1954] 2 Q.B. 367, [1954] 2 All E.R. 736 (C.A.).

The Official Guardian relied upon *Foxwell v. Kennedy*,[39] to establish the principle that the offices of executor and trustee are indivisible, unless the will established two separate positions. In the absence of the will establishing two separate and distinct positions, it was the Official Guardian's position that a person who was acting in the combined role of executor and trustee cannot resign as trustee without court approval, unless the will so provides. Mr. Perry submitted that in this way the courts are able to maintain appropriate control over estates generally.

In *Foxwell v. Kennedy*, the will appointed A, B and C "hereinafter called my trustees, to be the executors and executrices of this my will."[40] The terms "executor" and "trustee" were then used interchangeably throughout the will. Probate was granted to C since B renounced, as A was a minor. Upon reaching her majority, A also renounced probate. A later sued C and others, raising several claims, the only relevant one being that although she had renounced probate, she had not renounced her right to act as trustee. The issue was dealt with in the following terms.[40a]

> ... I think the testator did not contemplate two distinct offices in the sense that either of those named could elect to reject the executorial rights and responsibilities and accept only the office of trustee. In other words, I think, taking the will as a whole, the testator constituted the persons named, or those of them who might accept the whole of the burden, his representatives to perform the combined duties of a trustee-executor.

The court held that A had no rights as a trustee because of her renunciation of probate. The appeal to the Divisional Court was dismissed, with Riddell J. stating as follows at p. 204:

> It is, in my view, clear that the testator did not intend to create two sets of persons, *viz.*, (1) executors and (2) trustees, but that he used the expression "executors," executrices, and trustees" as meaning the one class. ...

[In *Foxwell v. Kennedy* the court relied upon *Re Gordon*[41] and *Re Birchall*.[42] The court went on to distinguish the three cases as follows.]

The obvious factual differences between *Foxwell v. Kennedy, Re Gordon* and *Re Birchall* and this case, is that the three English cases involved persons appointed to the joint office of executor and trustee who either renounced or did not participate in probate, but did not specifically disclaim the trusts. The failure to act as an executor was considered as evidence of disclaimer of the trust.

In this case, Mr. Bennett accepted probate and participated in the administration of the estate. He acted as trustee until his resignation was tendered and accepted. It seems clear that refusal to act as an executor may well justify a

---

39 (1911), 24 O.L.R. 189 (Div. Ct.).
40 *Ibid.*, at 191.
40a *Ibid.*, at 192.
41 (1877), 6 Ch. D. 531.
42 (1889), 40 Ch. D. 436.

conclusion that the trust has been disclaimed. A person who refuses to act from the outset might be taken to have no desire to become involved in the estate, at all. In addition, the trustee's function cannot be performed until after the executor's function is carried out; thus it may be unfair to permit a person who has sloughed off the duties of executors to then act as trustee.

Neither *Re Gordon* nor *Re Birchall* go so far as to establish that the offices of trustee and executor are indivisible unless the will provides otherwise. It seems to me that if authority for this proposition exists it must be found within *Foxwell v. Kennedy* itself.

In *Foxwell v. Kennedy* the wording of the appointment was vague and uncertain. The testator made no real distinction between the roles of executor and trustee, and did not seem to realize that the functions of an executor, and the functions of a trustee were separate. It would appear to me that this imprecise wording was the cornerstone of the *Foxwell v. Kennedy* decision since it was impossible to find that in fact two separate offices had been created. Here, this problem does not arise. The will clearly appoints executors of the will, and trustees of the estate. The fact that the same persons are designated to fulfil both positions does not go to dilute the conclusion that the positions are separate.

Section 2 of the *Trustee Act* establishes a procedure whereby a trustee may resign by deed, while executors may only be removed from their office by the court pursuant to section 37. This reflects the common law principle that the functions of an executor and trustee are different and separate. After the executor has fully administered the estate, the role of trustee is assumed. This, however, does not mean that the person appointed to fulfil both functions, ceases to be an executor merely because that function has been performed. The cases of *Re Cockburn's Will Trusts* and *Re Heintzman* recognize this principle, although they do not deal specifically with whether a person appointed to both offices can resign as trustee without impairing the office of executor. *Foxwell v. Kennedy* and the cases relied upon it, seem to indicate that a renunciation of probate is material evidence going to the issue of the presence or absence of a disclaimer of a trusteeship. In addition, where a testator has, by imprecise wording, created one indistinguishable office, as opposed to appointing the same person to two separate offices, that person cannot renounce probate without giving up the trusteeship as well.

In my view the case law does not suggest that a person cannot resign as a trustee and continue as an executor. When one person is appointed to both offices, the roles continue to be distinct, and the procedures set out in section 2(1) of the *Trustee Act* may be resorted to with respect to the trustee function. To give effect to the Official Guardian's suggestion that the roles are inseparable, when performed by the same person, would be to circumvent the intention of the *Trustee Act*, and to make the section 2(1) procedure available only when different people are appointed to the two offices, that being a rare occurrence. It may well be preferable that the court be able to exercise control over persons acting in both capacities, as Mr. Perry submits. That, however, will require legislative intervention, given the current state of the *Trustee Act*.

The Legislature was quite aware that the general practice was to appoint the same person to both functions, but nevertheless chose to give greater flexibility to trustees regarding their period of service, than to executors. The legislative intention seemed to be that the functions are divisible, and that one person can resign as trustee without affecting his or her office as executor. It seems to be neither necessary nor appropriate to discuss the reasons for this statutory approach.

In the end result, therefore, Stewart Gordon Bennett's resignation as trustee is confirmed as at November 24, 1980. Stewart Gordon Bennett is removed as executor, effective now.

. . .

Notes and Questions[a]

1. Can a sole or last surviving trustee retire? If so, in whom does the trust property vest?[43]

2. What happens if a trustee wants to retire and his or her co-trustees refuse to consent? Can the co-trustees withhold consent? If so, on what grounds?[44]

3. Who bears the legal costs associated with a trustee's retirement?[45]

4. Must a trustee give reasons for wishing to retire? Does it matter whether the trustee is retiring under section 2 (or the equivalent) or through the court? Should it? What reasons should be considered satisfactory and what not?[46]

5. Must a retiring trustee be replaced?

6. A trustee's resignation can trigger a non-judicial appointment[47] in all Canadian jurisdictions except Alberta, Prince Edward Island, and New Brunswick.[48]

7. A retiring trustee has no power to appoint his or her replacement.[49]

8. In *McLean*, Osborne J. affirmed that once an executor has fully administered the estate, it is assumed that the executor has then assumed the role of trustee, but he did not expand on what is meant by "fully administered." What factors should the court consider in assessing whether an executor has completed the administration of an estate?[50]

4. REMOVAL OF TRUSTEES

If the trust instrument specifies a mechanism for removing a trustee from office, its terms will govern. In the absence of such a power, trustees can be

43 *Mitchell v. Richey* (1867), 13 Gr. 445 (Ont. Ch.); but see also *Courtney v. Courtney* (1846), 3 J. & Lat. 519.

44 See Waters, *Trusts*, at 679-680.

45 See Waters, *Trusts*, at 679-681.

46 *Mitchell v. Richey*, *supra*, note 43.

47 Pursuant to sections 3 and 4 of the *Trustee Act*, R.S.O. 1990, c. T.23 or equivalent legislation, set out in part 2(b), *infra*; see also *McLachlin v. Usborne* (1884), 7 O.R. 297 (Ch.).

48 Alberta, New Brunswick, and Prince Edward Island require a court appointment.

49 *Re Moorhouse*, [1946] O.W.N. 789, [1946] 4 D.L.R. 542 (H.C.).

50 See *Booty v. Hutton* (1999), 140 Man. R. (2d) 186, 30 E.T.R. (2d) 159, [1999] M.J. No. 410, 1999 CarswellMan 447, [2000] 1 W.W.R. 81 (Q.B.) and *Singer v. Singer Estate* (2000), 280 A.R. 127, 2000 CarswellAlta 1580, 2000 ABQB 944, [2001] 6 W.W.R. 192, 90 Alta. L.R. (3d) 387 (Surr. Ct.), affirmed (2002), 2002 CarswellAlta 1600, 2002 ABCA 294, [2003] 3 W.W.R. 31, 9 Alta. L.R. (4th) 10, 320 A.R. 143, 288 W.A.C. 143 (C.A.).

removed by use of the non-judicial power to appoint trustees,[51] or application to the court.

The non-judicial power of appointment enables removal by substituting a new trustee for an existing one. The grounds for removal through the use of the non-judicial power of appointment are spelled out in legislation and are dealt with above.[52]

The court can remove a trustee by exercise of its inherent jurisdiction or through powers conferred on it under legislation.[53] Because of the wording of the legislation, the court may only exercise its statutory power of removal when appointing a replacement. If a court wishes to remove a trustee without naming a replacement, it can only do so under its inherent jurisdiction.

Whether removing a trustee pursuant to its inherent jurisdiction or statutory powers, the court must be guided by the principle that a trustee will be removed when his or her continuance would jeopardize the assets of the trust, put the welfare of the beneficiaries at risk, or prevent the trust from being properly executed.[54]

The following actions, inactions, and conditions, render a trustee subject to removal: misconduct,[55] lack of *bona fides*,[56] an inability or unwillingness to carry out the terms of the trust,[57] incapacity, personally benefiting from the trust,[58] acting to the detriment of beneficiaries,[59] or any other ground that shows that the trustee is not fit to control another's property.[60]

Although the law on the grounds for removal appears clear, its application to any given set of circumstances has not been as apparent. The Ontario Court of Appeal in *Bathgate v. National Hockey League Pension Society*[61] dismissed an

---

51 Created by ss. 3 and 4, *Trustee Act*, R.S.O. 1990, c. T.23 and equivalent legislation as set out in part 2(b), *supra*.

52 *Ibid.*

53 See, for example, *Trustee Act*, R.S.O. 1990, c. T.23, s. 5 and comparable legislation set out in part 2(c), above.

54 This statement is based upon the principles enunciated in *Letterstedt v. Broers* (1884), 9 App. Cas. 371 at 386, [1881-85] All E.R. Rep. 882 (P.C.).

55 *Re Commonwealth Investors Syndicate Ltd.* (1986), 69 B.C.L.R. 346, 61 C.B.R. (N.S.) 147 (S.C.), additional reasons at (1986), 62 C.B.R. (N.S.) 308 (S.C.).

56 *Ibid.*

57 *Hickey Estate, Re* (2002), 46 E.T.R. (2d) 193, 2002 CarswellNfld 228, [2002] N.J. No. 225, 216 Nfld. & P.E.I.R. 334, 647 A.P.R. 334 (T.D.).

58 *Small v. Packard*, [1925] 1 W.W.R. 897 (Sask. K.B.); *Hall v. Hall* (1983), 45 B.C.L.R. 154 (S.C.).

59 *Ibid.* And see *Gubbe v. Sardella*, [2001] O.T.C. 402, 39 E.T.R. (2d) 62, 2001 CarswellOnt 1941 (S.C.J.), in which the court removed the trustee because he was not acting in the best interests of the beneficiaries.

60 *Re Joss*, [1973] 2 O.R. 128, 33 D.L.R. (3d) 152 (H.C.). See *Re Confederation Treasury Services Ltd.* (1995), 37 C.B.R. (3d) 237 (Ont. Bktcy.) in which the court discusses responsibilities of a trustee and grounds for removal.

61 (1994), 2 E.T.R. (2d) 1, 1 C.C.P.B. 209, 69 O.A.C. 269, 2 C.C.E.L. (2d) 94, 110 D.L.R. (4th) 609 (C.A.). See also *Manitoba Health Organizations Inc. v. Byron*, 127 Man. R. (2d) 100, 22 E.T.R. (2d) 228, 1998 CarswellMan 172, 17 C.C.P.B. 161, [1998] 9 W.W.R. 364 (Q.B.); *Oates v. Baker Estate* (1993), [1993] B.C.J. No. 1293, 1993 CarswellBC 1956 (S.C.); *Blitz Estate, Re*,

application for removal of trustees, finding that there had been no apparent dishonesty, misconduct, or lack of reasonable fidelity in carrying out their duties despite the fact that the trustees had paid out trust funds improperly. The trust consisted of pension money for hockey players. After allowing for payment of pensions, surplus funds remained. The trustees elected to pay the surplus funds to the hockey clubs rather than to the players, without first obtaining a court declaration as to entitlement. The court held that the surplus funds belonged to the hockey players, not the hockey clubs. In light of the uncertainty over ownership of the funds, it seems that the trustees had not acted prudently in disposing of the trust assets. However, the court did not view imprudence as a sufficient ground for removal.

While misconduct of the trustee is not a prerequisite to removal, something more than mere friction is normally necessary. For example, before making an order for removal of a trustee because of friction with co-trustees, the court must be satisfied that the continued administration of the trust is impossible or improbable.[62] Similarly, as illustrated by *Conroy v. Stokes*,[63] below, friction between a trustee and a beneficiary is not necessarily a sufficient ground for removal.[64]

CONROY v. STOKES

[1952] 4 D.L.R. 124, 6 W.W.R. 204
British Columbia Supreme Court
Court of Appeal

Peter Conroy appointed two trustees by his will. Two of the five beneficiaries under the will applied to the court to have the trustees removed, as they were dissatisfied with the manner in which the trustees were administering the estate. The judge of instance held that "it was in the interests of all parties under the circumstances that the trust administration should be placed in the hands of an independent administrator." The trustee appealed.

BIRD J.A.:

This appeal is taken from an order of Wood J., made upon originating summons, whereby trustees appointed under the last will of the late Peter Conroy deceased, were removed from that office, and a new trustee appointed. The order under review which was opposed by the said trustees, was made on the application

---

35 E.T.R. (2d) 172, 2000 CarswellBC 2122, 2000 BCSC 1596 (S.C.); *Reid Martin v. Reid* (1999), 35 E.T.R. (2d) 267, 1999 CarswellOnt 4722, 11 R.F.L. (5th) 374 (Div. Ct.).

62 *Re Consiglio Trusts (No. 1)*, [1973] 3 O.R. 326, 36 D.L.R. (3d) 659 (C.A.).

63 [1952] 4 D.L.R. 124, 6 W.W.R. (N.S.) 204 (B.C. C.A.).

64 But see *Re Davis* (1983), 14 E.T.R. 83 (Ont. C.A.) where friction between the trustee and beneficiaries was held to prevent the trustee from being able to exercise the broad discretion that she had been given, with the result that the trustee was removed.

of two of five *cestuis que trust*. The majority of the beneficiaries had expressed no dissatisfaction with the administration of the estate by the trustees so removed.

Counsel for the respondent invokes the *Trustee Act*,[65] in support of the order made, and submits that on the facts this is a case wherein it is "expedient to appoint a new trustee" in substitution for the existing trustees, and that the learned judge below correctly exercised the discretion given him by that section.

The learned trial judge has recited in his reasons for judgment the various grounds for the applicants' dissatisfaction with the administration of the trustees, which need not be repeated here. Suffice to say that the learned judge does not find misconduct or breach of trust on the part of the trustees, or that the acts or omissions complained of are such as to endanger the trust property, but founds the order for removal of the trustees appointed by the testator upon the sole ground that friction had developed between the applicants and the trustees, relative to the latter's conduct of the affairs of the estate, arising out of dissension between the applicants and the widow of the testator, the latter being his second wife, and the former the children of this first wife. The learned judge held therefore "it is in the interest of all parties under the circumstances that the administration should be placed in the hands of an independent administrator."

In *Forster v. Davies*[66] Turner L.J. said that:

> the mere fact of there being a dissension between one of the several *cestuis que trust* and the trustee is [not] a sufficient ground for this court removing that trustee from the trust, because the consequence of that would be that one *cestui que trust* might at any time raise a quarrel with the trustee and thereupon come to this court to discharge the trustee and remove him from the trust upon the ground of the impossibility of their acting together. It would be the duty of the court, as I conceive, in all cases of that description, to inquire and ascertain from whose fault that dissension or that cessation of friendly intercourse has arisen.

The evidence before the learned judge below was not directed to determining the origin of that dissension, nor was any finding made as to where the fault lay, though it does appear that the applicants, soon after the death of the testator, expressed dissatisfaction with the provisions of the will, as is indicated by the fact that they or one of them, had instituted proceedings under the *Testator's Family Maintenance Act*,[67] in effect, to vary the terms of the will. In the circumstances, the evidence adduced here does not permit of any conclusion as to the persons upon whom rests the responsibility of the dissension.

In *Letterstedt v. Broers*[68] their Lordships of the Judicial Committee held that the main principle upon which the jurisdiction of Courts of Equity has been exercised to remove old trustees and substitute new ones in cases requiring such a remedy, is the welfare of the beneficiaries of the trust estate.

There Lord Blackburn said:[69]

---

65 R.S.B.C. 1948, c. 345, s. 23.
66 (1861), 4 De G.F. & J. 133 at 139, 45 E.R. 1134 (Ch. Div.).
67 R.S.B.C. 1948, c. 336.
68 (1884), 9 App. Cas. 371 at 386, [1881-85] All E.R. Rep. 882 (P.C.).
69 *Ibid.*, at 385.

It is not disputed that there is a jurisdiction "in cases requiring such a remedy," as is said in Story's Equity Jurisprudence, s. 1287, but there is very little to be found to guide us in saying what are the cases requiring such a remedy; so little that their Lordships are compelled to have recourse to general principles.

Story says,[70]

But in cases of positive misconduct Courts of Equity have no difficulty in interposing to remove trustees who have abused their trust; it is not indeed every mistake or neglect of duty, or inaccuracy of conduct of trustees, which will induce Courts of Equity to adopt such a course. But the acts or omissions must be such as to endanger the trust property or to shew a want of honesty, or a want of proper capacity to execute the duties, or a want of reasonable fidelity.

Again:[71]

In exercising so delicate a jurisdiction as that of removing trustees, their Lordships do not venture to lay down any general rule beyond the very broad principle above enunciated, that their main guide must be the welfare of the beneficiaries.

And again:[72]

It is quite true that friction or hostility between trustees and the immediate possessor of the trust estate is not of itself a reason for the removal of the trustees. But where the hostility is grounded on the mode in which the trust has been administered, where it has been caused wholly or partially by substantial overcharges against the trust estate, it is certainly not to be disregarded.

Here the acts or omissions complained of do not, in my opinion, support a conclusion that the conduct of the trustees has endangered the trust property, or show a want of honesty or of proper capacity to execute the duties, or a want of reasonable fidelity. The failure of the trustees to account to the beneficiaries annually or to pass their account annually, are perhaps matters for criticism on the basis of neglect of duty, but such omissions, as is said by Story, are not such as to induce the court to remove trustees unless persisted in. Moreover, it appears that since the initial complaint in this regard by the applicants, the trustees have remedied the omissions except in respect of moving the court to confirm the Registrar's report on the passing of the accounts for the years 1950 and 1951, which we are told have been submitted to the beneficiaries, passed by the Registrar, and, but for these proceedings, would have been the subject of an application for confirmation by the court.

Counsel for the respondent questions the authority of the trustees to sell the Nanaimo real property. In my opinion the terms of the will confer full power and authority upon the trustees to sell at their discretion. The sale appears to have been made by the trustees at a price which was highly advantageous to the estate; and is not otherwise seriously criticized by the applicants, except from the point of view that they were not consulted prior to its consummation. This transaction,

---

70 Section 1280.
71 *Ibid.*, at 387.
72 *Ibid.*, at 389.

in my view, provides no reasonable ground for criticism of the conduct of the trustees.

In the circumstances I find nothing in the evidence to support a conclusion that the "welfare of the beneficiaries," and that phrase I think must be taken to mean the "benefit of the beneficiaries collectively," has been impaired by any act or omission of the trustees.

Consequently, I think, with great respect, that the discretion of the learned trial judge has been exercised on wrong principles, and that he has omitted to apply the correct and guiding principles laid down in the decisions cited. In these circumstances the order made below cannot be sustained.[73]

Since in my opinion no sufficient grounds have been shown for the removal of the trustees appointed by the will of the testator, the appeal must be allowed and a direction given that the trustees so appointed be re-instated in their office.

. . .

Notes and Questions

1. For further reading on this topic, see Rodney Hull, "Removal of Trustees and Personal Representatives."[74]

2. Can you apply to have yourself removed as trustee?

3. In which of the following situations should a trustee be removed? Give reasons for your answers.

(a) The bankruptcy or liquidation of a trustee.[75]

(b) The trustee's conviction of a crime.

(c) The trustee taking up permanent residence outside the jurisdiction of the trust.

(d) The attempt by a trustee to purchase an asset of the trust or beneficiary.

(e) The trustee makes a personal claim against the trust property.[76]

(f) There is hopeless disagreement between the trustee and beneficiary.

(g) There is hostility between the trustee and one or more of the beneficiaries.[77]

(h) The trustee has a professional relationship with one of the beneficiaries.[78]

(i) The trustee fails to take steps to protect the trust property.[79]

(j) The sole trustee of the estate is also one of the beneficiaries.[80]

---

73 *Creasey v. Sweny*, [1942] 2 D.L.R. 552, 57 B.C.R. 457; *Taylor v. Vancouver General Hospital*, [1945] 4 D.L.R. 737, 62 B.C.R. 42; *B.C. Electric & Bridge River Power Cos. v. Humboldt Timber Holdings Ltd.*, [1950] 1 W.W.R. 1017 (B.C. C.A.).

74 (1982), 6 E. & T.Q. 54.

75 *Newbank Group Inc. (Trustee of) v. Handelman (Trustee of)* (1991), 4 O.R. (3d) 626, 1991 CarswellOnt 198, 6 C.B.R. (3d) 240 (Gen. Div.); *Assaf v. Assaf Estate* (1998), 22 E.T.R. (2d) 306, 1998 CarswellOnt 1626 (Gen. Div.), set aside/quashed (1999), 31 E.T.R. (2d) 157, 1999 CarswellOnt 4308 (C.A.).

76 *Mardesic v. Vukovich Estate* (1988), 30 B.C.L.R. (2d) 170 (S.C.).

77 *Re Bowerman* (1978), 20 O.R. (2d) 374, 87 D.L.R. (3d) 597 (Surr.Ct.).

78 *Tannis Trading Inc. v. Camco Food Services Ltd.* (1988), 63 O.R. (2d) 775, 49 D.L.R. (4th) 128, 67 C.B.R. (N.S.) 1 (S.C.).

79 *Ibid.*

80 *Ballentine v. Ballentine* (2000), 35 E.T.R. (2d) 165, 2000 CarswellOnt 3813 (S.C.J.), additional reasons at (2001), 2001 CarswellOnt 105, 37 E.T.R. (2d) 169 (S.C.J.), affirmed (2001), 2001 CarswellOnt 1950, 38 E.T.R. (2d) 165 (C.A.).

(k)   A trustee refuses to effect a transfer of a trust, advocated by the remainder of the trustees.[81]

(l)   The trustee has an interest as creditor[82] or debtor[83] to the estate.

(m) The trustee unreasonably delayed administering the estate.[84]

(n)   There is hostility between the trustees.[85]

4. Are the grounds for removal the same for non-judicially appointed trustees, trustees in bankruptcy, and court appointed trustees?[86]

5. Who should pay the costs of a court application to have a trustee removed?[87] Does it make a difference if the removal proceedings result from the trustee committing a serious breach of trust and refusing to resign after being asked to do so by the beneficiaries?

6. The summary proceedings provided by legislation should not be used to remove a trustee against his or her will when there are facts in dispute.[88]

7. By statute, courts are empowered to remove personal representatives.[89] As *Re Moorhouse*,[90] *Re McLean*,[91] and *Re McIntyre*[92] illustrate, when a person is both executor and trustee, different steps must be taken to ensure discharge from both positions.

8. The principles to be applied in applications for removal of executors are the same as those for the removal of trustees.[93] The grounds for removal are the same, as well.[94]

9. Does a court have jurisdiction to remove trustees and executors who have taken steps to administer the estate, but have not obtained letters probate from the court?[95]

---

81 *Ocean Man Trust, Re* (1992), 46 E.T.R. 224, 1992 CarswellSask 70, 103 Sask. R. 304 (Q.B.), reversed (1993), [1993] S.J. No. 367, 1993 CarswellSask 88, 50 E.T.R. 150, 113 Sask. R. 179, 52 W.A.C. 179 (C.A.).

82 *Cooper v. Fenwick* (1994), [1994] O.J. No. 2148, 1994 CarswellOnt 3949 (Gen. Div.); *Berner Estate v. Berner Estate*, [2000] O.T.C. 118, 2000 CarswellOnt 652, [2000] O.J. No. 662 (S.C.J.).

83 *Owen Family Trust, Re* (1989), 33 E.T.R. 213, 1989 CarswellBC 495 (S.C.).

84 *Loftus v. Clarke Estate*, 40 E.T.R. (2d) 242, 2001 CarswellBC 1710, 2001 BCSC 1136 (S.C.).

85 *Mailing v. Conrad* (2003), 48 E.T.R. (2d) 238, 2003 CarswellOnt 627 (S.C.J.).

86 See *Confederation Treasury Services Ltd., Re* (1995), 37 C.B.R. (3d) 237, [1995] O.J. No. 3993, 1995 CarswellOnt 1169 (Bktcy.); *YBM Magnex International Inc., Re* (2000), 275 A.R. 352, 2000 CarswellAlta 1068, [2000] A.J. No. 1118, 9 B.L.R. (3d) 296 (Q.B.), affirmed 293 A.R. 337, 2001 CarswellAlta 1794, 2001 ABCA 305, 257 W.A.C. 337, 23 B.L.R. (3d) 293 (C.A.).

87 *Thompson v. Lamport*, [1945] S.C.R. 343, 1945 CarswellOnt 97, [1945] 2 D.L.R. 545.

88 *Popoff v. Actus Management Ltd.* (1986), 20 E.T.R. 1, [1985] 5 W.W.R. 660, 41 Sask. R. 308 (Q.B.).

89 *Trustee Act*, R.S.A. 2000, c. T-8, ss. 14, 16 (am. by R.S.A. 2000, c. 16 (Supp.), s. 59(c)); R.S.B.C. 1996, c. 464, s. 31; R.S.M. 1987, c. T160, s. 10; R.S.N.L. 1990, c. T-10, s. 11; R.S.N.S. 1989, c. 479, s. 16(1); R.S.N.W.T. 1988, c. T-8, s. 6; R.S.O. 1990, c. T.23, s. 37 (am. S.O. 2000, c. 26, Sched. A, s. 15(2)); R.S.S. 1978, c. T-23, s. 15; R.S.P.E.I. 1988, c. T-8, s. 34; R.S.Y. 2002, c. 223, s. 10; *Trustees Act*, R.S.N.B. 1973, c. T-15, s. 29(1).

90 [1946] O.W.N. 789, 1946 CarswellOnt 301, [1946] 4 D.L.R. 542 (H.C.).

91 (1982), 37 O.R. (2d) 164, 135 D.L.R. (3d) 667, 1982 CarswellOnt 614, 11 E.T.R. 293 (H.C.).

92 (1905), 9 O.L.R. 408 (C.A.) reproduced in part in Chapter 13.

93 *Powers v. Powers Estate* (1988), 68 Nfld. & P.E.I.R. 336, 209 A.P.R. 336, 47 D.L.R. (4th) 471 (Nfld. T.D.)

94 See, for example, *Trustee Act*, R.S.O. 1990, c. T.23, s. 37 (am. by S.O. 2000, c. 26, Sched. A, s. 15(2)).

95 *Carmichael v. Carmichael Estate* (2000), (sub nom. *Carmichael Estate, Re*) 46 O.R. (3d) 630, 2000 CarswellOnt 71, 184 D.L.R. (4th) 175, 31 E.T.R. (2d) 33 (S.C.J.).

10. Trustees are obliged to keep an even hand between beneficiaries.[96] This principle is particularly important when the beneficiaries have competing interests as, for example, between life-tenants and those entitled to the remainder interest. If trustees fail to exercise their discretion to encroach in favour of life-tenants because of a deadlock among the trustees, the court may intervene by giving the casting vote or, if the continued administration of the trust is improbable, by removing the trustees. However, the court will do so only if non-removal is manifestly prejudicial to the beneficiaries' interest.[97]

11. A co-executor and trustee had been the business partner of the testator. He wished to continue running the business in a manner of which the beneficial owners of a one-half interest under the will did not approve. The court removed the trustee based on a finding of conflict of interest and being of the view that his continuance would prevent the trust from being properly executed.[98]

Problems

1. The testator appointed N, T, and his wife, W, his executors. W was the life-tenant and the testator's issue living at her death took the remainder interest. Ninety-two per cent of the estate's assets consisted of shares in a private company in which the estate held a majority position. The deceased was president of the company and upon his death N succeeded him. Under N's direction the company did well and paid substantial dividends. An advantageous offer for the shares of the company was received by N and T. They wished to accept the offer, but W was opposed. All other capacitated beneficiaries also opposed the sale and the Official Guardian did not urge acceptance of the offer.

Advise N and T on how to proceed.[99]

Should the court intervene to break such a deadlock between the administrators of an estate? If so, what factors should it consider in determining which course to follow?[100]

2. A testator appointed his wife as trustee of his estate, and directed that at her death she should appoint her replacement. Prior to her death, however, the wife sought to nominate two trustees in her place.
(a) Can the wife validly appoint her replacement during her life?
(b) Could the wife achieve the result she wants by applying to the court?
(c) Could the rule in *Saunders v. Vautier*[101] be used to achieve the result the wife wants?[102]

---

96 But see *Crawford v. Jardine* (1997), 48 O.T.C. 23, 20 E.T.R. (2d) 182, 1997 CarswellOnt 4962 (Gen. Div.), in which Dilks J. held that the court will not intervene when there has been an egregious breach of the even-hand rule if the settlor clearly expressed his or her intention that the trustees were not required to be even-handed.

97 *Re Blow* (1977), 18 O.R. (2d) 516, 2 E.T.R. 209, 82 D.L.R. (3d) 721 (H.C.).

98 *Re Anderson* (1928), 35 O.W.N. 7 (H.C.).

99 See *Re Price* (1979), 5 E.T.R. 194 (Ont. H.C.).

100 *Billes, Re* (1983), 42 O.R. (2d) 110, 1983 CarswellOnt 613, 14 E.T.R. 247, 148 D.L.R. (3d) 512 (H.C.).

101 (1841), 4 Beav. 115, 49 E.R. 282 (Ch. Div.), affirmed (1841), 1 Cr. & Ph. 240, 41 E.R. 482, [1935-42] All E.R. Rep. 58 (Ch. Div.).

102 *McLachlin v. Usborne* (1884), 7 O.R. 297 (Ch.).

13

DUTIES OF TRUSTEES

1. SCOPE

Trustees are subject to many duties, all of which are onerous in nature. The trust instrument and legislation create specific duties for trustees, but the general duties which all trustees must perform arise by virtue of the fact that they are fiduciaries.

Trustees have title to, and control over, property belonging to another person; thus, they must act solely in the best interests of that other person. This obligation of trustees, to serve solely the beneficiaries, is known as the "duty of loyalty." It is the duty of loyalty that underlies all of the duties discussed in this chapter: the obligation to perform duties personally, the duty to invest the trust assets, the obligation to act impartially, the duty to account and the duty to provide information. The obligation of trustees to avoid placing themselves in situations of conflict of interest also arises from the duty of loyalty but that prohibition is dealt with elsewhere.

This chapter begins by considering the initial duties that a trustee must perform. It then considers the rights of trustees to seek the court's advice. Following that, we discuss the standard of care to which trustees are held. Thereafter, we explore the circumstances in which trustees may delegate their duties, the trustees' obligation to invest and enhance trust funds, the duty to be impartial, that is, to treat beneficiaries even-handedly, and, finally, the obligation to ensure that beneficiaries are kept apprised of what is happening in the administration of the trust.

2. POWERS AND DUTIES AND THEIR EXERCISE

(a) Initial Duties

Upon appointment, trustees must: (a) ascertain the terms of the trust; (b) acquaint themselves with the state of the trust property; (c) invest the trust property in accordance with the provisions of the trust instrument or statute; (d) ensure that the trust property is in proper custody; and, (e) if the appointment is of a replacement trustee, the new trustee must take all reasonable steps to ensure that there were no prior breaches of trust. If there are such indications, then the trustee must take action to recoup for the trust any losses that may have been incurred.[1]

In short, the trustees' obligations are to collect the assets for the trust, ensure their safety, and then preserve and enhance their value. Failure to do any of those things amounts to a breach of trust. For example, in *Bentley v. Canada Trust Co.*,[2] the trustee was held to have breached its duty by failing to safeguard the trust property adequately. The plaintiff signed and returned a registered retirement savings plan agreement to Canada Trust. The plaintiff never attended at the offices of Canada Trust. The plaintiff's wife forged his signature in letters directing Canada Trust to redeem shares under the plan. The court held that Canada Trust could have met with the plaintiff in person and required him to sign a signature card or could have made inquiries regarding the forged requests for redemption. Having failed to do these things, Canada Trust as trustee was held to have breached its obligations to safeguard the trust property. Convenience and reduced expense could not justify relaxing the trustee's standard of care in preserving and protecting the trust property in the circumstances.

There has been an interesting development in the pension trusts field in the context of the trustee's duty to safeguard the trust property. In *Froese v. Montreal Trust Co. of Canada*,[3] the court held that this duty encompasses a non-contractual common law duty to warn beneficiaries of any threats to the trust. The court held that the custodial trustee of private pension plan funds should have warned plan members of the employer's failure to make contributions required under the plan. It remains to be seen whether this duty to warn will be accepted in general trust law.[4]

(b) Trustees Must Act Jointly

Unless the trust instrument provides otherwise, trustees of private trusts must act jointly; that is, their decisions must be unanimous.[5] The requirement of unanimity exists for every decision of the trustees; whether the decision relates to the

---

1 A trustee who fails to establish the value of the trust fund at its creation may be liable for breach of trust. See *Re Carley Estate* (1994), 2 E.T.R. (2d) 142 (Ont. Gen. Div.).

2 (1992), 48 E.T.R. 111 (B.C. S.C.).

3 (1996), 137 D.L.R. (4th) 725, 20 B.C.L.R. (3d) 193, 26 B.L.R. (2d) 1 (C.A.), leave to appeal refused (1997), 208 N.R. 244, [1996] S.C.C.A. 399.

4 See *Seaboard Life Insurance Co. v. Bank of Montreal*, 2002 BCCA 192, 23 B.L.R. (3d) 163, 2002 CarswellBC 630, [2002] B.C.J. No. 599, 166 B.C.A.C. 64, 271 W.A.C. 64 (C.A.) in which the court extended the reasoning in *Froese* to the relationship between a bank, as custodial trustee of preferred shares, and the beneficial owner of the shares. See also *Ford v. Laidlaw Carriers Inc.* (1993), 1 E.T.R. (2d) 117, 1993 CarswellOnt 552, [1993] O.J. No. 2941, 50 C.C.E.L. 165, 1 C.C.P.B. 97, C.E.B. & P.G.R. 8163 (Gen. Div.), affirmed in part (1994), [1994] O.J. No. 2663, 1994 CarswellOnt 1807, 12 C.C.P.B. 179 (C.A.), leave to appeal refused (1995), [1995] S.C.C.A. No. 34, 12 C.C.P.B. 179n, 191 N.R. 400 (note). In *Laidlaw* the court found that the trustee of employee benefits and pension plans breached its fiduciary duty to the beneficiaries of the plans by conveying inaccurate information about the pay-out procedure to them under the plans.

5 A majority of the trustees of a charitable trust may make decisions for the trust.

exercise of a power or a duty is irrelevant for the purpose of determining how the trustees are to make decisions in relation to the exercise of the power or duty. In consequence of the unanimity requirement, if one trustee fails to agree with his or her co-trustees, there is a deadlock.

(c) Seeking the Court's Advice

One mechanism for the resolution of deadlocks is for trustees to apply to the court for direction on the exercise of their powers. Section 60 of the Ontario *Trustee Act*,[6] set out below, illustrates how this may be done. You should note, however, that the provision is of limited utility. Because the courts are reluctant to interfere with the exercise of discretion by the trustees, the court will often only advise whether a power or duty must be exercised. The court may even direct the trustees to act (*i.e.*, exercise the power or duty) but, normally, it will not direct trustees how to act, that is, how to exercise any particular power or duty. So, for example, if the trustees are agreed that a power should be exercised but disagree about the circumstances in which to act, the courts will not resolve this disagreement by issuing a direction.[7]

Re Wright,[8] below, illustrates the principles the courts use in situations of deadlock.

Further Reading

M.C. Cullity, "Judicial Control of Trustees' Discretions" (1975), 25 U. of T.L.J.

M.C. Cullity, "Trustees' Duties, Powers and Discretions — Exercise of Discretionary Powers," *Recent Developments in Estate Planning and Administration*, 1980, at 13.

TRUSTEE ACT

R.S.O. 1990, c. T.23[9]

APPLICATIONS TO COURT FOR ADVICE

60. (1) A trustee, guardian or personal representative may, without the institution of an action, apply to the Ontario Court (General Division) for the opinion, advice or direction of the court on any question respecting the management or administration of the trust property or the assets of a ward or a testator or intestate.

(2) The trustee, guardian or personal representative acting upon the opinion, advice or direction given shall be deemed, so far as regards that person's responsibility, to have discharged that person's duty as such trustee, guardian or personal representative, in the subject-matter of the application, unless that person has

---

6 R.S.O. 1990, c. T.23.

7 See *Re Wright* (1976), 14 O.R. (2d) 698, 74 D.L.R. (3d) 504 (H.C.), *infra.*

8 (1976), 14 O.R. (2d) 698, 74 D.L.R. (3d) 504 (H.C.).

9 Amended by S.O. 2000, c. 26, Sched. A, s. 15(2).

been guilty of some fraud, wilful concealment or misrepresentation in obtaining such opinion, advice or direction.

Comparable Legislation

Trustee Act, R.S.A. 2000, c. T-8; R.S.B.C. 1996, c. 464, ss. 86, 87; R.S.M. 1987, c. T160, s. 84; R.S.N.L. 1990, c. T-10, s. 26; R.S.N.W.T. 1988, c. T-8, s. 50; R.S.P.E.I. 1988, c. T-8, s. 52; R.S.S. 1978, c. T-23, s. 79; R.S.Y. 2000, c. 223, s. 48.

RE WRIGHT

(1976), 14 O.R. (2d) 698, 74 D.L.R. (3d) 504
Supreme Court of Ontario
High Court of Justice

The testator, William Henry Wright, died in 1951. At that time the estate was worth $7.7 million. At the time of the application the estate had increased in value to $35.8 million. 52.2 percent of the estate consisted of shares in the Crown Life Insurance Company and those shares represented 20 percent of the outstanding shares of that company.

The testator directed payment of the annual income to certain "main beneficiaries", namely, his sister and three of her children, and the lineal legitimate descendants of those children. The capital was to be distributed among the main beneficiaries living either 21 years after the death of the last survivor of those main beneficiaries who were living at the testator's death, or when the last survivor of the main beneficiaries shall have died, whichever event should occur first. There were also gifts to spouses of deceased main beneficiaries and a gift over to a named charity if all main beneficiaries should die within 21 years of the testator's death. In the normal course of events, distribution was not likely to occur until about the year 2040.

The annual income at the time of the application was approximately $2 million. The market value of the shares was $42.50 per share. They paid a dividend of $1.50 per annum. Thus the shares generated a yield of only approximately 2.8 percent to the estate.

The executors, who were Canada Permanent Trust Company and three main beneficiaries, had resolved that it was in the best interests of the estate to sell the shares. They obtained investment analyses from two firms, which indicated that the shares were currently selling at the lower end of their historic range and that a price of $70 per share was their realistic value. The executors appointed a brokerage firm to try to sell the shares for $73 per share. A former executor was until recently an officer and director of the brokerage firm and he and his family were also major shareholders of Crown Life. Another major shareholder of Crown Life made an offer of $49 per share which the executors rejected. Then it made another offer at $55 per share, but on terms that permitted it to take up and pay for the shares over a four year period. Independent advice from two investment firms indicated that the second offer was only equivalent to a present price of $49 per share. The advice further indicated that the stock market was depressed and that while the offer was fair in current market conditions, a higher price could be obtained in better market conditions.

Canada Permanent Trust Co. thought that the second offer should be accepted. It took the view that the retention of the low-yield shares prevented the executors from maintaining an even hand between the interests of the life tenants and those interested in the capital. However, none of the income beneficiaries wanted to sell at the offered price. Neither did the Official Guardian, who represented minor, unascertained, and unborn beneficiaries. Moreover, the other executors also did not want to sell at the offered price. Canada Permanent Trust brought an application seeking the court's advice.

The will contained the following powers:

I Give, Devise and Bequeath and Appoint to my Trustees all the rest, residue and remainder of my Estate both real and personal and mixed, of every nature and kind and wheresoever situate, and all property over which I have I have any power of appointment, upon the following trusts, namely:

(a) To sell, call in and convert into money the residue and remainder of my Estate not consisting of money, at such time or times, in such manner and upon such terms and either for cash or credit, or for part cash and part credit, as my Trustees may in their discretion decide upon, with full power and discretion to postpone such conversion of such Estate or any part or parts thereof, for such length of time as they may think best, and I hereby declare that my Trustees may retain any part of my Estate in the form in which it may be at my death (notwithstanding that it may not be in the form of an investment in which Trustees are authorized to invest trust funds and whether or not there is a liability attached to any such part of my Estate) for such length of time as my Trustees in their discretion deem advisable; and upon conversion to invest my Estate in such investments and securities as are permissible in law for the investment of trust funds, provided, however, that my Trustees may in their discretion and for such time as is by them thought advisable retain the moneys of my Estate on deposit at current rates of interest, such deposits, however, to be equally distributed between at least my corporate trustee, if authorized to receive deposits, and any two Chartered Banks in the Dominion of Canada.

(b) I request that in the making of any investment of my Estate my Trustees shall have regard for the security of the capital and shall make investment with such security in mind rather than with the object of securing larger interest or income at the risk of less security for the repayment of the capital.

(c) In connection with any shares, securities and other interests in companies and enterprises which I hold at the time of my death, it not being my desire that any such company or enterprise should be unduly or unnecessarily inconvenienced or injured by reason of my death or that any of my investments or properties should be got in or realized at undue sacrifice, I empower my Trustees, having regard to the reasonable accomplishment of this desire, of which they are to be the sole judge from time to time, to join in any amalgamation, re-organization, pooling agreement, sale, compromise or other scheme or arrangement, and so act and deal with exchange or surrender such shares, securities or other interests as in the sole and absolute discretion of the Trustees they may deem to be in the best interests of my Estate. The powers herein given are under no circumstances to be read as extending the powers of my Trustees to make investments in securities other than securities permitted in law for the investment of trust funds.

CRAIG J.:

. . .

The cases cited by counsel indicate that powers and discretion of executors and trustees with respect to the sale, retention and investment conferred by a will, may be divided into three categories:

(1) where there is an absolute trust to sell or convert to which is added a discretionary power to retain. In such a case the basic duty is to convert;
(2) where there is an absolute trust to retain to which is added a discretionary power to convert. In such a case the basic duty is to retain;
(3) where there is a power to sell or convert with an equal power to retain.

These cases are *Re Hilton, Gibbes v. Hale-Hinton,*[10] *Royal Trust Co. v. Crawford;*[11] *Re Haasz.*[12]

Counsel for the applicant submits that:

. . . the disposition of the shares of Crown Life Insurance Company will carry into effect the direction contained in paragraphs 7(a), (b) and (c) of the will of the deceased to the effect that the estate should be converted into investments and securities as are permissible in law for the investment of trust funds.

This would place the powers contained in the will within category (1) above. His second point in this connection is that "in the absence of unanimity among the executors, the shares of Crown Life Insurance Company ought to be sold."

Aside from the powers of retention contained in the will, the question arises as to whether these shares are investments authorized by s. 27(1)(c) of *The Trustee Act.*[13] Counsel for the applicant made the submission that since these shares exceed 35% of the market value of the whole estate, they are not so authorized because of the provisions of s. 27(2) of the said Act. Since no argument was presented to the contrary by counsel for any of the respondents, I assume that the retention of these shares since the death of the deceased does not meet all of the conditions of ss. 27(2), (3) and (4) (and s. 27 has been amended since 1951) so as to bring them within the class of investments authorized for trust funds by *The Trustee Act.*

If it is necessary to my decision, I interpret the powers contained in this will as coming within category (3) above. The executors are given a power to convert at their sole discretion and an equal power to retain. In fact it may be a difficult presentation for the applicant to say that, upon the true interpretation of the will, there is a primary duty to convert, when the evidence before me indicates that the executors have been unanimous in retaining these shares for 25 years.

---

10 [1909] 2 Ch. 548.
11 [1955] S.C.R. 184, [1955] 2 D.L.R. 225.
12 [1959] O.W.N. 395, 21 D.L.R. (2d) 12 (C.A.).
13 R.S.O. 1970, c. 470.

However, it is my further opinion that, whether the powers contained in this will come within category (1) or (3) above, the Court should not intervene on the facts of this case to force the sale of the shares at a price considered to be too low by the majority of the executors.

The individual executors and trustees did concur in the decision to sell these shares if a buyer for them can be found who will pay what they consider to be a fair price. In the year 1973 all executors concurred in the sale of 70,580 shares at a price of $78 per share. They reject the present offer dated October 15, 1976, upon the following considerations. (I quote these considerations in full from the statement of fact and law of Mr. Sheard, not because I agree or disagree with them but because there cannot be any doubt about the *bona fides* of the decision reached by these respondents.)

1. . . .

(*a*) The offer is not substantially different from the previous offer of $49.00 per share that the trustees, including Canada Permanent, unanimously rejected as too low. The offer is not for $22,000,000 cash but for that amount spread over a period of three years. This works out to a cash offer of approximately $49.00 a share.

(*b*) At the present time the market for Crown Life shares is extremely depressed. The stock market as a whole is at its lowest point in nearly a year. The market for Crown Life shares is limited and is subject to control by other major shareholders more closely associated with Crown Life; the present offeror appears to be part of the group having effective control of the Crown Life shares. After holding these shares all these years, this does not seem the appropriate time to sell them.

(*c*) These respondents are not satisfied that the best efforts have been made to find a purchaser willing to pay the highest price for the benefits of the estate and believe the agency for the sale of these shares should be placed with a firm such as Wood Gundy Ltd. which is not so closely associated with those who may effectively control Crown Life and the market for its shares. Such an independent firm should be given inadequate time to find a purchaser possibly under more advantageous market conditions.

When Burns Fry Ltd. were selected as agents, Charles F.W. Burns was still a trustee of the estate and it was natural, and indeed inevitable, to give the agency to the firm with which he was then, or had previously been closely associated. Once he resigned as a trustee of the estate and as a director of Canada Permanent the situation changed and he was no longer under any obligation to the estate or its beneficiaries. Clearly Burns Fry Ltd. would not be likely to seek a purchaser who was not acceptable to Mr. Burns and his family interests. In fact the present offeror Minas Basin, is already a substantial shareholder of Crown Life and represented on its board and there are indications that Minas Basin acts together with Burns family interests in exercising effective control of the shares of Crown Life. The scope and intensity of the efforts to interest possible purchasers may therefore have been unduly limited and, in the opinion of these respondents, the agency should now be given to an independent firm.

(*d*) Both firms of assessors consider the offered price is too low. Lindsay McKelvey & Co. Ltd. in its report dated February 27th, 1976 considered the then market price of $54-55 was only 7 times earnings in a normal year and at the lower end of the stock's history range. Eckler Brown Segal & Co. Ltd. consider $70 per share to be an objective value of the shares.

(*e*) There is no pressure on the Trustees to obtain increased income for the beneficiaries. Any increase in such income would largely go in increased income taxes.

This is a case where the executors and trustees are in agreement to sell these shares, and they only differ as to the adequacy of the price, also bearing in mind that they were unanimous in rejecting an offer of $49 per share in June of 1976. If the Wood Gundy opinion is correct, this is a similar offer on a price per share basis.

I adopt the language of Middleton J. in the case of *Re Fulford*[14] as follows:

> The executors are protected from all liability if they honestly and with due care exercise the discretion vested in them. But the responsibility is theirs, and cannot be shifted upon the Court. The executors cannot come to the Court and ask whether the present is a good time or a bad time to sell stock or anything else, or ask whether a price offered is sufficient or insufficient. The advice which the Court is authorised to give is not of that type or kind; it is advice as to legal matters or legal difficulties arising in the discharge of the duties of executors, not advice with regard to matters concerning which the executors' judgment and discretion must govern.

These views were repeated [elsewhere].[15]

Counsel for the applicant relies upon the case of *Re Haasz*, mentioned above. It was a case where the trustees could not agree to sell and the court did intervene to order a sale. That case is quite distinguishable from the case at bar. Morden J.A. states:[16]

> It is well-settled that in their execution of their powers, absolute and discretionary, executors must be unanimous. Broadly speaking, where executors agree in the exercise of a discretionary power conferred upon them by the will, the Court will not interfere with or overrule their unanimous decision so long as they act *bona fide* and fairly as between the beneficiaries.[17] I must say that if in the administration of this estate the executors had been unanimous in deciding to sell or to retain the Erie shares, then in the absence of evidence of bad faith or unfairness to or as between the beneficiaries, the Court would not, at the instance of a beneficiary, interfere with the exercise of their discretion. However that is not the situation here. The executors do not agree upon either the sale or the retention of the shares.

I also adopt the language used in the case of *Tempest v. Lord Camoys*,[18] referred to with approval by Middleton J. in the case of *Re Sievert*[19] as follows:

> In an earlier case, *Tempest v. Lord Camoys* the same learned Judge had expressed similar views, and his decision was affirmed by the Court of Appeal, consisting of Jessel M.R., Brett and Cotton L.JJ., one of the strongest Courts ever constituted, which affirmed the principle that the Court has no power, save in the case of *mala fides* or a refusal to discharge the duty undertaken, to put a control on the exercise of the discretion which the testator has left to the trustees.

---

14 (1913), 29 O.L.R. 375, 14 D.L.R. 844 at 850 (H.C.).
15 By Kelly J. in *Re Davis*, [1936] O.W.N. 146; again by Middleton J.A. in *Re Boukydis* (1927), 60 O.L.R. 561, [1927] 3 D.L.R. 558 at 559 (C.A.); and by Masten J.A. in *Re Warden* (1928), 34 O.W.N. 146.
16 *Supra*, note 12, at D.L.R. 19.
17 *Gisborne v. Gisborne* (1877), 2 App. Cas. 300 at 306 (H.L.); *Re Sievert* (1921), 67 D.L.R. 199, 51 O.L.R. 305 (C.A.); and *Re McLaren* (1921), 69 D.L.R. 599, 51 O.L.R. 538 (C.A.).
18 (1882), 21 Ch. D. 571.
19 (1921), 51 O.L.R. 305, 67 D.L.R. 199 at 200 (C.A.).

For these reasons the application is dismissed. Costs of all parties shall be paid out of the estate on a solicitor-and-client basis forthwith after taxation.

Notes and Questions

1. For further reading, see the comment by Donovan Waters on *Re Wright.*[20]

2. The principle upon which the court acted in *Re Wright*, that is, that if there is no deadlock the court will not exercise the trustees' discretion for them, is undoubtedly sound. Does that mean that trustees should never apply to the court in cases such as this? Under s. 60, of the Ontario *Trustee Act*, reproduced above, or the equivalent, they have the right to ask the court to determine what kind of power they have, that is, whether they have a duty to convert with a power to retain, a duty to retain with a power to convert, or a power to convert or retain as the trustees see fit.

We submit, that in any event, trustees may be well-advised to seek the court's advice in cases of this kind so as to forestall a future action by the beneficiaries for breach of trust.[21] This may have been one of the reasons why the corporate trustee made the application in this case, since it had only recently suffered defeat in *Fales v. Canadian Permanent Trust Co.; Wohlleben v. Canada Permanent Trust Co.,*[22] below.

3. When hostility among the trustees causes a deadlock and the administration of the trust is brought to a halt, the court can remove one or more trustees.[23]

4. In *Kordyban v. Kordyban,*[24] the court held that its jurisdiction to break a deadlock between trustees is not so broad that is will intervene to accomplish what is just and equitable. It reiterated that there are only two bases for intervention: the intentions of the testator and the interests of the beneficiaries. In considering the latter factor, the court found that intervention is not confined to the question of the express terms of the trust, nor is it confined to situations where there has been an unjust deprivation of a right.[25]

5. The creator of a trust can stipulate that trustee decisions be made by a majority.[26]

---

20 (1978), 56 Can. Bar Rev. 128.

21 It was held in *Linsley v. Kirstiuk* (1986), 28 D.L.R. (4th) 495 (B.C. S.C.) that failure to seek such advice was grounds for not relieving a trustee from liability under the statutory excusing power.

22 (1976), [1977] 2 S.C.R. 302, [1976] 6 W.W.R. 10, (sub nom. *Wohlleben v. Canada Permanent Trust Co.*) 70 D.L.R. (3d) 257, 1976 CarswellBC 240, 1976 CarswellBC 317, 11 N.R. 487.

23 A fuller discussion of this matter, including references to cases, can be found in Chapter 10, part 4, *infra*.

24 1 B.C.L.R. (4th) 45, 44 E.T.R. (2d) 85, 2002 CarswellBC 813, 2002 BCSC 475 (S.C.), additional reasons at 2004 CarswellBC 298, 2004 BCSC 184, 5 E.T.R. (3d) 176 (S.C.), affirmed 2003 CarswellBC 803, 2003 BCCA 216, 13 B.C.L.R. (4th) 50, 50 E.T.R. (2d) 116, [2003] 6 W.W.R. 606, 181 B.C.A.C. 75, 298 W.A.C. 75 (C.A.), additional reasons at 2003 CarswellBC 2019, 19 B.C.L.R. (4th) 19, 186 B.C.A.C. 77, 306 W.A.C. 77, 2003 BCCA 455 (C.A.).

25 See also, *Engelman Estate, Re* (1985), 21 E.T.R. 134, 1985 CarswellBC 620 (S.C.), reversed (1986), 1986 CarswellBC 587, 23 E.T.R. 30 (C.A.) in which the court gave a direction to the trustees about the way they ought to exercise the power. The court intervened even though in the absence of the direction the beneficiaries would nonetheless have received the benefit bestowed on them by the will. Neither of them would have been prejudiced and not making the direction would still have been consistent with the terms of the will.

26 For an example of a trust which permitted decisions to be made by a majority, see *Ballard Estate v. Ballard Estate* (1991), 79 D.L.R. (4th) 142, 3 O.R. (3d) 65, 41 E.T.R. 113, 1991 CarswellOnt 533, (sub nom. *Ballard Estate, Re*) 44 O.A.C. 225 (C.A.), leave to appeal refused (1991), [1991] S.C.C.A. No. 239, 5 O.R. (3d) xii, 83 D.L.R. (4th) vii, 137 N.R. 385 (note), 55 O.A.C. 390 (note).

6. Should the law be reformed to allow trustees to act by majority vote instead of requiring unanimity?

7. Should beneficiaries have a right to oppose decisions made by trustees?[27]

8. Can trustees apply under s. 60 of the Ontario *Trustee Act, supra,* for advice or direction on matters that affect beneficiaries' rights?[28]

9. The Ontario Law Reform Commission has recommended that a new provision be created by statute that would enable trustees to apply to the court for an order resolving deadlocks in such manner as the court sees fit.[29]

10. One of the factors that trustees must have regard to in deciding whether to convert or retain is their duty to maintain an even hand between successive beneficiaries.[30]

11. If a will gives property to beneficiaries absolutely, but gives the executors a discretion to postpone distribution, the discretion is a restriction on the gift, which is void for repugnancy.[31]

12. Testators and settlors commonly give wide powers of investment and management to trustees. There are limits, however, to what powers can be given. For example, a power given to trustees under a testamentary trust to determine conclusively which receipts are income and which capital is invalid.[32] The settlor or testator can validly give the trustees the power to capitalize income or to encroach on capital.

Similarly, a privative clause in a trust instrument will not be effective to prevent the court from reviewing the exercise of the trustee's discretion, when the trustees have (i) failed to exercise their discretion at all; (ii) acted dishonestly; (iii) failed to exercise the level of prudence to be expected from reasonable business persons; and (iv) failed to hold the balance evenly between beneficiaries, or acted in a manner prejudicial to the interests of a beneficiary.[33]

3. STANDARD OF CARE

The standard of care required of a trustee in administering a trust is that which a person of ordinary prudence would use in managing his or her own affairs.[34] In Canada, the question has arisen whether a higher standard of care is owed by a professional trustee than by a non-professional. While *Fales v. Canadian Per-*

---

27 See Ont. Law Ref. Comm., *Report on the Law of Trusts* (Toronto: Ministry of the Attorney General, 1984), at 75 ("O.L.R.C. Report").

28 See *Tecumseh Public Utilities Comm. v. MacPhee*, [1931] 1 D.L.R. 538, 66 O.L.R. 231 (C.A.); and *Re Bailey* (1982), 38 B.C.L.R. 227, 137 D.L.R. (3d) 563, 12 E.T.R. 242 (S.C.); but contrast *Re Engelman Estate* (1985), 21 E.T.R. 134 (B.C. S.C.), reversed (1986), 23 E.T.R. 30 (B.C. C.A.).

29 O.L.R.C. Report at 72.

30 *Haasz, Re*, [1959] O.W.N. 395, 21 D.L.R. (2d) 12 (C.A.); *Jeffery, Re*, [1948] 4 D.L.R. 704, 1948 CarswellOnt 66, [1948] O.R. 735 (H.C.); *Boe v. Alexander* (1987), 15 B.C.L.R. (2d) 106, 1987 CarswellBC 182, 41 D.L.R. (4th) 520, 28 E.T.R. 228 (C.A.), leave to appeal refused (1988), 22 B.C.L.R. (2d) xxx, 28 E.T.R. xxxvi, 87 N.R. 299 (note) (S.C.C.).

31 *Re Lysiak* (1975), 7 O.R. (2d) 317, 55 D.L.R. (3d) 161 (H.C.).

32 See *Re Wynn*, [1952] Ch. 271, [1952] 1 All E.R. 341 and *Re Bronson*, [1958] O.R. 367, 14 D.L.R. (2d) 51 (H.C.). Cf. *Re Zive* (1977), 26 N.S.R. (2d) 477, 77 D.L.R. (3d) 669 (T.D.).

33 *Rivett v. Hospitals of Ontario Pension Plan* (1995), [1995] O.J. No. 3270, 1995 CarswellOnt 1139, 9 C.C.P.B. 284, C.E.B. & P.G.R. 8251 (Gen. Div.).

34 *Fales, supra,* note 22.

manent Trust Co.,[35] below, suggests that there is no such distinction in the standard of care owed, we submit that the courts' use of the statutory excusing power has just such an effect.[36]

The *Fales* case illustrates not only the general standard of care to which a trustee is held but also how inextricably the standard of care is bound up with the various rights and duties of a trustee such as indemnification, contribution, the duty to convert, and statutory relief for breach of trust. Only that portion of the case relating to the standard of care is set out below as the other aspects of the case are dealt with elsewhere.

Further Reading

B. Dillon, "The Trustee's Standard of Care," 7 E. & T.Q. 334.

A.H. Oosterhoff, "Trustees' Powers of Investment" (Study for the Ontario Law Reform Commission, 1970).

FALES v. CANADIAN PERMANENT TRUST CO.; WOHLLEBEN v. CANADA PERMANENT TRUST CO.

[1977] 2 S.C.R. 302, [1976] 6 W.W.R. 10,
70 D.L.R. (3d) 257
Supreme Court of Canada

The testator, Kai Wohlleben, had been an officer and one of the four major shareholders of a small, but sound and profitable corporation, Boyles Bros. Drilling Company Ltd. His will gave a life interest to his wife and directed that the residue be divided equally among their four children on his wife's death. The will appointed his wife and Canada Permanent Trust Co. executors and trustees and directed his trustees to sell, call in and convert the estate into money and invest the proceeds in investments authorized by law for the investment of trust funds. The will contained a power to postpone conversion, as well as a power to join in any corporate reorganization. For the latter purpose, the trustees were authorized to accept shares or securities in any other corporation in exchange for shares held by them.

The shareholders, including the estate, were approached with a proposal to merge the company with a larger company, Inspiration Limited, which was in the same line of business. Inspiration was a subsidiary of Power Corporation of Canada Limited, a major Canadian conglomerate. The proposal contemplated an exchange of the Boyles shares for common and preferred shares and notes of Inspiration. Canada Permanent recognized that the shares of Inspiration were speculative and noted that Inspiration's profit and loss picture was "not inspiring", but agreed to approve the merger if the broker that had presented the proposal

---

35 *Ibid.*

36 This was the effect of the legislation in *Linsley v. Kirstiuk* (1986), 28 D.L.R. (4th) 495 (B.C. S.C.).

was willing to underwrite, at a set price, the sale of the preferred shares the Boyles shareholders would receive, and if Mrs. Wohlleben and the other shareholders approved.

Eventually the merger was approved and went ahead in 1966, even though the broker refused to underwrite the sale of the preferred shares and Power Corp. refused to guarantee Inspiration's notes. Canada Permanent informed Mrs. Wohlleben of Inspiration's final offer, but did not disclose its internal memoranda and correspondence about the merger to her. In 1967 the broker underwrote a public issue of preferred shares at a price lower than their par value and the estate had opportunity to sell at that price. Canada Permanent disclosed the offer to Mrs. Wohlleben without recommendation and she declined. During 1967 the value of Inspiration's common and preferred shares declined steadily and it suffered a loss for the year. In January 1968 Canada Permanent recommended the sale of some of the common shares, but none were sold . Inspiration did not pay the June 1, 1968 dividend on the preferred shares and in September disclosed that it had suffered a significant loss. Canada Permanent made a notation to check into the matter, but took no other action. In December, 1968 Inspiration failed to pay the instalment due on the notes. The value of its shares continued to decline.

In May, 1969 Canada Permanent suggested to Mrs. Wohlleben that the estate should sell some of the preferred shares, but no action was taken. Internal memoranda of Canada Permanent in June and July recommended sale of the shares, but the recommendations were not communicated to Mrs. Wohlleben. There was some discussion of a corporate reorganization and recapitalization in November of 1969, but those plans fell through when Power Corp. withdrew its support. Inspiration made an assignment in bankruptcy in January, 1970. While there was a measure of recovery on the notes, the shares became valueless on the bankruptcy.

The four children sued Canada Permanent. It claimed indemnity and contribution from Mrs. Wohlleben. Mrs. Wohlleben counterclaimed for the loss to her life interest as a result of Canada Permanent's mismanagement. The children chose not to sue their mother. The decisions at trial and on appeal are summarized in the judgment below.

Dickson J.:

. . .

I

In the main action three issues faced Munroe J. during a 13-day trial: (i) whether the exchange of Boyles Bros. shares for Inspiration shares was authorized by the terms of the will; (ii) if so, was Canada Permanent, in entering into the transaction, guilty of a breach of its duty to make proper inquiry and to exercise reasonable skill and care; (iii) was there a breach of duty in failing to sell the Inspiration shares before the bankruptcy of that company?

Mr. Justice Munroe[37] held that (i) the exchange was authorized by the terms of the will, not as a permanent investment but as a satisfactory vehicle for the

---

37 44 D.L.R. (3d) 242, [1974] 3 W.W.R. 84 (B.C. S.C.).

divestment of Boyles Bros. shares; (ii) Canada Permanent incurred no liability to the plaintiffs by reason of having entered into the exchange arrangement; (iii) Canada Permanent made no real attempt to sell or persuade its co-trustee to agree to a sale of Inspiration shares notwithstanding the unsatisfactory and gradually worsening financial condition of Inspiration; (iv) failure to sell the shares in timely fashion resulted in a breach of duty rendering Canada Permanent liable to the plaintiffs for damages, which should be assessed at $250,408, based upon the average price at which Inspiration shares traded during the period in which, in the opinion of the Judge, the shares should have been sold. The Judge dismissed Canada Permanent's claim for contribution from Mrs. Wohlleben, and her counterclaim for interest and income on her interest in the estate. He refused Canada Permanent relief under section 98 of the *Trustee Act*.[38] This section provides that, if it appears that a trustee is or may be personally liable for any breach of trust, but has acted honestly and reasonably, and ought fairly to be excused for breach of trust, then the Court may relieve him from personal liability.

The Court of Appeal for British Columbia, following seven days of argument, allowed the appeal brought by Canada Permanent to the extent that the damages were reduced from $250,408 to $206,398.80.[39] The Court agreed that Canada Permanent had committed a breach of trust by negligently failing to sell all or any of the estate's preferred and common shares of Inspiration Limited while there was a ready market. The Court considered, however, that there was a time immediately following acquisition when it was not imprudent to hold the shares, and that the period of averaging should extend until the shares were delisted. This change in the base period resulted in a reduction in the damages to be awarded. A cross-appeal, in which the plaintiffs, their contentions that there was no power in the will to make the exchange of shares, and that Canada Permanent was guilty of breach of trust in acquiring the speculative and hazardous shares of Inspiration Limited, was dismissed. Canada Permanent was again unsuccessful in its claim for relief under section 98 of the *Trustee Act* but succeeded on the appeal in obtaining a reversal of the trial Judge's dismissal of the third party proceedings brought against Mrs. Wohlleben for contribution. The Court of Appeal considered Mrs. Wohlleben guilty of breach of trust for failure to join in liquidation of the Inspiration Limited shares at advantageous times and ordered that she contribute a moiety of the damages sustained by plaintiffs in the period to September 1, 1969, amounting to $31,127.52. Her cross-appeal for interest and income was dismissed.

In this Court the appellant residuary beneficiaries seek an increase in the damages awarded to them. The third party, Mrs. Wohlleben, asks that she not be held liable to contribute in any way for the breach of trust by Canada Permanent and that she be awarded her lost interest and income by reason of such breach. Canada Permanent asks that the Court of Appeal be reversed in its decision to relieve Mrs. Wohleeben in part from the consequences of her breach of trust or in the alternative, if relief is afforded her, that the Court declare a different method

---

38 R.S.B.C. 1960, c. 390.
39 55 D.L.R. (3d) 239, [1975] 3 W.W.R. 400 (B.C. C.A.).

of calculating the amount of reduction. Canada Permanent also seeks a declaration that the Court of Appeal erred in failing to relieve it from the consequences of any breach of trust.

. . .

V

Traditionally, the standard of care and diligence required of a trustee in administering a trust is that of a man of ordinary prudence in managing his own affairs[40] and traditionally the standard has applied equally to professional and non-professional trustees. The standard has been of general application and objective though, at times, rigorous. There has been discussion of the question whether a corporation which holds itself out, expressly or impliedly, as possessing greater competence and ability than the man of ordinary prudence should not be held to a higher standard of conduct than the individual trustee. It has been said by some that a higher standard of diligence and knowledge is expected from paid trustees:[41] and upon dicta found in *National Trustees Co. of Australasia v. General Finance Co. of Australasia*[42] a case which did not turn upon the imposition of a greater or lesser duty but upon the relief to which a corporate trustee might be entitled under the counterpart of section 98 of the *Trustee Act* of British Columbia, to which I have earlier referred.

In the case at bar the trial Judge held that the law required a higher standard of care from a trustee who charged a fee for his professional services than from one who acted gratuitously. Mr. Justice Bull, delivering the judgment of the Court of Appeal, was not prepared to find, and held it unnecessary to find that a professional trustee, by virtue of that character and consequential expertise, had a greater duty to a *cestui que trust* than a lay trustee.

The weight of authority to the present, save in the granting of relief under remedial legislation such as section 98 of the *Trustee Act*, has been against making a distinction between a widow, acting as trustee for her husband's estate, and a trust company performing the same role. Receipt of fees has not served to ground, nor to increase exposure to, liability. Every trustee has been expected to act as the person of ordinary prudence would act. This standard, of course, may be relaxed or modified up to a point by the terms of a will and, in the present case, there can be no doubt that the co-trustees were given wide latitude. But however wide the discretionary powers contained in the will, a trustee's primary duty is preservation of the trust assets, and the enlargement of recognized powers does not relieve him of the duty of using ordinary skill and prudence, nor from the application of common sense.

Whether the testator intends a power of postponement to mean retention permanently or only until the trustees can sell advantageously will depend upon

---

40 *Learoyd v. Whiteley* (1887), 36 W.R. 721, 12 App. Cas. 727 at 733 (H.L.); Underhill's *Law of Trusts and Trustees*, 12th ed., art. 49; *Restatement of the Law of Trusts*, 2nd ed., para. 174.

41 Underhill's *Law of Trusts and Trustees*, art. 49 relying upon *obiter* of Harman J. in *Waterman's Will Trusts v. Sutton; Lloyds Bank v. Sutton*, [1952] 2 All E.R. 1054 at 1055 (Ch. Div.).

42 [1905] A.C. 373 (P.C.).

construction of the trust instrument: *Inman v. Inman*.[43] The right to hold may be held to be ancillary and subsidiary to the basic duty to convert and to invest.[44] Such was the construction, I think properly, placed upon the will in the instant case by the trial Judge and by the Court of Appeal. What is a reasonable delay in selling will depend upon the particular circumstances but where the duty of the trustee is to sell, call in and convert to investments authorized for trustees a heavy burden rests upon a trustee, where loss is suffered by reason of retention of speculative non-trustee securities, to show that the delay in selling was reasonable and proper in all the circumstances.

A trustee must also be alert to changes in the fortunes of the companies represented in the portfolio of the trust estate. It is not expected that he will sell hastily at a sacrifice, since a power to postpone and retain will generally entitle him to hold for an advantageous sale, but such a power has never had the effect of converting non-trustee securities into trustee securities.

During argument there was some discussion as to the obligation of one trustee to keep a co-trustee informed. In my view where an asset of the character of the Inspiration shares is involved, constituting the principal asset of the estate, a duty rested upon Canada Permanent to keep its co-trustee as fully informed as possible as to any information touching upon the shifting fortunes of inspiration.

VI

Applying the foregoing principles to the facts of this case, I do not think it can be doubted that Canada Permanent breached the duty which it owed the residuary beneficiaries of the Wohlleben estate. It is not necessary to decide whether a higher standard of diligence should be applied to the paid professional trustee, for Canada Permanent failed by any test. No one in that organization would seem to have brought his mind to bear upon the relative merits, and dangers, of retention and disposition of the shares with which we are concerned. It is not with the prescience of hindsight that one may conclude that the Inspiration shares should have been sold during the period of two and one-half years following acquisition. Notwithstanding recognition by Canada Permanent during the negotiations antedating the exchange that the Inspiration shares would be speculative and that it would be desirable to extract an undertaking from Pembertons to take them off the hands of the shareholders of Boyles Bros. who received them, the trust officers in Vancouver sat idly by and allowed the shares progressively to decline in worth until they became valueless. Despite gathering storm clouds and successive presages of disaster, no attempt was made to market the shares. The vigilance, prudence and sagacity which the law expects of trustees was never apparent. After the acquisition, the Vancouver trust officers charged with supervision of the account, initially Mr. Donnelly and later Mr. Jakeway, would seem never to have consulted a senior officer of the company concerning the shares of the Inspiration. There was no communication between Vancouver and Toronto as to retention or sale. The Vancouver advisory committee, the head office man-

---

43 [1915] 1 Ch. 187.
44 *Royal Trust Co. v. Crawford*, [1955] 2 D.L.R. 225, [1955] S.C.R. 184.

agement, the head office investment committee, the board of directors were available but never consulted. Internal procedures proved inadequate and sterile. Apart from the annual review of the Vancouver investment committee which produced cryptic, handwritten, practically illegible notations, there would appear to have been no meetings at which sale was considered. No minutes are in evidence.

To a certain extent, the trustees may have been lulled into a state of inertia by the presence of Power Corporation as controlling shareholder of Inspiration and by the belief, which proved to be ill-founded, that Power Corporation would never allow a subsidiary to suffer the ignominy of bankruptcy. But after due allowance for all of that, there is simply no explanation for the languor shown in retaining shares in a venture known to be speculative, for an extended period, during which period the market afforded ample opportunity for profitable sale. Canada Permanent was never seized with a sense of urgency, yet the shares constituted over 60 per cent of the assets of a substantial estate.

The refusal of Mrs. Wohlleben to respond affirmatively to three or four half-hearted suggestions for sale is not sufficient to protect her co-trustees. At no time did Canada Permanent make an intelligent analysis followed by a firm recommendation, supported by reasons. At most, Mrs. Wohlleben was told the obvious truism that it was not wise to have too many eggs in one basket. Although familiar with the passed dividends and the note defaults it was not until November 1969, when Inspiration was in extremis, that Mrs. Wohlleben became aware of the grave financial condition of Inspiration. Canada Permanent had not forwarded to her the earlier annual reports or interim reports received by it. In any event, it would not have been enough for Canada Permanent merely to have acquiesced in the refusal of its co-trustee to sell; if after a recommendation and proper explanation Mrs. Wohlleben remained adamant, the proper course would have been to have applied to the Court for advice and directions.

. . .

[After finding that Canada Permanent breached the trust, the court assessed the damages at the average price of the shares over the period from their acquisition until they could have been sold advantageously. The court then went on to determine whether Canada Permanent should be excused. This aspect of the case is discussed in the chapter on Breach of Trust.]

Notes and Questions

1. For an analysis of *Fales*, see the case comment by Donovan Waters.[45]

2. In *Fales*, why was Canada Permanent Trust Co. wrong to accept Mrs. Wohlleben's "adamant" refusal to sell the Boyles Bros. shares? Why did the court say that the trust company ought to have gone to the court for advice and direction? Do you see any disadvantages to such an approach?

---

45 (1977), 55 Can. Bar Rev. 342.

3. Is the standard of care owed by a trustee tested objectively or subjectively?[46] What difference does it make?

4. *Kinakh v. Kurta*[47] examines this question. The testator's will directed that the residue of an estate was to remain invested until the fifth anniversary of his death, at which time it was to be divided among the plaintiffs. One of the estate assets was a house. The trustees rented the house out for less than market rent to ensure that it did not remain vacant during the five-year period. Ten months before the five-year anniversary, one of the trustees leased the house for a five-year term without consulting the plaintiffs. The plaintiffs sued for breach of trust.

The court held that the trustees met their standard in relation to "the less than market" rent. In relation to the five-year lease, the court decided that the defendants breached their duty by acting unreasonably and imprudently, although they were not dishonest.

5. An act which constitutes a breach of the standard of care may be actionable as negligent misrepresentation, as well.[48]

6. Should the Public Trustee be held to the same standard of care as all other trustees? Why or why not?[49]

7. It has been suggested[50] that an alternative standard of care might be that which the prudent business person or prudent trustee would take in dealing with the property of another. What difference, if any, would such a formulation make to the existing standard of care?

8. Given the existing standard of care, is it possible to find that the conduct of only one of two co-trustees amounts to a breach of the standard? In answering this question, recall that trustees must act jointly.[51]

9. Is it fair to expect lay trustees to meet the standard of care of an ordinary prudent business person?

10. After taking into account the effect of the statutory excusing power, is it accurate to say that the standard of care owed by a professional is the same as for a lay trustee?[52]

---

46 See *Fales v. Canadian Permanent Trust Co.*, *supra*, note 22; *Y. (C.F.), Re*, 291 A.R. 303, 2001 CarswellAlta 771, 2001 ABQB 470, 40 E.T.R. (2d) 310 (Q.B.). But see *O'Hagan v. O'Hagan*, 72 B.C.L.R. (3d) 100, 183 D.L.R. (4th) 30, 2000 CarswellBC 198, [2000] 3 W.W.R. 643, 2000 BCCA 79, 31 E.T.R. (2d) 3, 134 B.C.A.C. 104, 219 W.A.C. 104 (C.A.) which appears to introduce a subjective element by applying the standard of what a reasonable business person "of advanced years" would consider prudent.

47 (1995), 8 E.T.R. (2d) 183, 103 Man. R. (2d) 22 (Q.B.).

48 *Blair v. Can. Trust Co.* (1986), 9 B.C.L.R. (2d) 43, 32 D.L.R. (4th) 515, 38 C.C.L.T. 300 (S.C.). See *Queen v. Cognos Inc.*, [1993] 1 S.C.R. 87, 1993 CarswellOnt 801, 1993 CarswellOnt 972, [1993] S.C.J. No. 3, 45 C.C.E.L. 153, 93 C.L.L.C. 14,019, 99 D.L.R. (4th) 626, 60 O.A.C. 1, 14 C.C.L.T. (2d) 113, 147 N.R. 169 for an explanation of negligent misrepresentation an its connection with the standard of care.

49 See *Wood v. British Columbia (Public Trustee)* (1986), 70 B.C.L.R. 373, 25 D.L.R. (4th) 356 (C.A.).

50 B. Dillon, "The Trustee's Standard of Care," (1985-86), 7 E. & T.Q. 334.

51 See *Linsley v. Kirstiuk*, *supra*, note 36.

52 See *Bartlett v. Barclays Bank Trust Co.*, [1980] 1 All E.R. 139 (Ch. Div.); and *Ford v. Laidlaw Carriers Inc.* (1993), 1 E.T.R. (2d) 117, 1993 CarswellOnt 552, [1993] O.J. No. 2941, 50 C.C.E.L. 165, 1 C.C.P.B. 97, C.E.B. & P.G.R. 8163 (Gen. Div.), varied on other grounds (1994), [1994] O.J. No. 2663, 1994 CarswellOnt 1807, 12 C.C.P.B. 179 (C.A.), leave to appeal refused (1995), [1995] S.C.C.A. No. 34, 12 C.C.P.B. 179n, 191 N.R. 400 (note), in which a higher standard of care was imposed on professional trustees.

11. The Ontario Law Reform Commission proposes[53] that the standard of care be codified for trustees. It further recommends that professionals who possess, or because of their profession, business or calling ought to possess, a particular level of knowledge or skills relevant to the administration of the trust, must employ that particular level of knowledge or skill in the administration of the trust.[54]

12. If the higher standard proposed by the Ontario Law Reform Commission is implemented, is it fair to apply such a standard to a particular professional who does not advertise or hold himself or herself out as having special skills?

13. The fact that a trustee is paid for his or her services is irrelevant, we submit, to the standard of care owed since statutes in all Canadian jurisdictions provide that trustees, whether professional or not, are entitled to remuneration.[55]

14. If a higher standard of care is owed by a professional trustee, ought that standard of care extend to accountants and solicitors who work as trustees?[56]

4. DELEGATION OF DUTIES

As a general rule, trustees may not delegate any of their powers or duties to other people. The rationale for the rule is simple. When trustees accept office, they accept the obligation to manage property for another person and they will not be allowed to shift that obligation to other people.

Delegation is permitted in the following circumstances: (a) if expressly authorized by statute or the trust instrument; (b) if the duties are not required to be performed personally; (c) if it is clearly necessary, that is, there is no other practicable way for the trustee to perform; and (d) if it is common business practice to delegate the particular power or duty. This last exception has also been stated thus: if, in the ordinary course of affairs, it would be prudent for a person to delegate performance of certain duties, a trustee may delegate those duties.[57]

If delegation is permitted, trustees may use agents but they are still responsible for making all decisions. In other words, ultimate responsibility for decision making rests with the trustees; all that they are entitled to do is have the agent perform a particular duty or give advice. Trustees, while permitted to delegate some of their duties, may not delegate all of them as that would amount to an abdication of responsibility.[58]

Proper delegation requires a trustee carefully to select and supervise agents. In selecting an agent, the trustee must ensure that the agent is used to perform work which the agent normally performs and the trustee must exercise his or her own judgment in selecting and determining the agent's suitability.[59] The trustee

---

53 O.L.R.C. Report, Vol. 1, Chapter 2, part 2.

54 *Ibid.*

55 But see *Wagner v. Van Cleef* (1991), 5 O.R. (3d) 477, 43 E.T.R. 115, 53 O.A.C. 161 (Div. Ct.) which suggests that a lower standard of care is owed by a trustee who acts gratuitously.

56 See O.L.R.C. Report, Vol. 1, Chapter 2, part 2. And see *Kulyk Estate, Re* (1997), 17 E.T.R. (2d) 308, 1997 CarswellOnt 1899, 33 O.T.C. 260 (Gen. Div.).

57 *McLellan Properties Ltd. v. Roberge*, [1947] S.C.R. 561, [1947] 4 D.L.R. 641; *Wagner v. Van Cleef, supra,* note 55.

58 *Wagner v. Van Cleeff, supra,* note 55.

59 *Fry v. Tapson* (1884), 28 Ch. D. 268.

must meet the general standard of care in selecting agents. In other words, the trustee must take the care that a person of ordinary prudence would show in choosing an agent. Proper supervision requires the trustee to monitor the agent's activities carefully and to terminate the delegation when circumstances show that it ought not to continue. A trustee who puts assets in the hands of an agent and takes no steps to ensure that the assets are properly dealt with has breached the duty to supervise.[60] The same obligation also applies to the delegation of duties to co-trustees.[61]

If a trustee is entitled to delegate, and does so properly, the trustee is not liable for any losses that result to the trust from the delegation. On the other hand, in the event of improper delegation, the trustee is liable for any and all losses to the trust. Thus, in a decision, since reversed by statute,[62] the court held that the investment of trust money in mutual funds is an abdication of responsibility, because it is a delegation of the trustee's function of making investment decisions and therefore improper.[63] The court distinguished between investing in a mutual fund and relying on an investment advisor because, in the latter situation, the trustee retains the right to reject the advice. Trustees will be liable, as well, for any costs associated with an improper delegation and his or her compensation may be reduced accordingly.[64]

Legislation also enables trustees to employ agents in certain circumstances. Section 20 of the Ontario *Trustee Act*,[65] set out below, is representative of such legislation.[66] The case of *Speight v. Gaunt*[67] which follows, illustrates when agents can be used and when liability will ensue for an agent's defaults.

TRUSTEE ACT

R.S.O. 1990, c. T.23

20. (1) A trustee may appoint a solicitor as agent to receive and give a discharge for any money or valuable consideration or property receivable by the trustee under the trust.

(2) A trustee may appoint a manager or a branch manager of a bank listed in Schedule I or II to the *Bank Act* (Canada) or a solicitor to be the trustee's agent

60 *Low v. Gemley* (1890), 18 S.C.R. 685; *Wagner v. Van Cleeff, supra*, note 55.

61 *Crowe v. Craig* (1897), 29 N.S.R. 394, 1897 CarswellNS 13 (C.A.).

62 *Trustee Act*, R.S.O. 1990, c. T.23, s. 27(2), (3), re-enacted S.O. 1998, c. 18, Sched. B, s. 16(1), am. S.O. 2001, c. 9, Sched. B, s. 13(2).

63 *Haslam v. Haslam* (1994), 114 D.L.R. (4th) 562, 1994 CarswellOnt 654, 3 E.T.R. (2d) 206 (Gen. Div.). See also *O'Brien Estate v. O'Brien* (1996), (sub nom. *O'Brien Estate, Re*) 21 O.T.C. 264, 1996 CarswellOnt 4885 (Gen. Div.), additional reasons at (1997), 1997 CarswellOnt 4247, [1997] O.J. No. 4112 (Gen. Div.)

64 *Re McCusker Estate* (1988), 63 Alta. L.R. (2d) 106, 91 A.R. 150 (Surr. Ct.).

65 R.S.O. 1990, c. T.23.

66 And see *Trustee Act, ibid.*, ss. 27(3), 27.1, and 27.2, reproduced in the next section.

67 (1883), 9 App. Cas. 1 (H.L.).

to receive and give a discharge for any money payable to the trustee under or by virtue of a policy of assurance or otherwise.

(3) A trustee shall not be charged with a breach of trust by reason only of having made or concurred in making any such appointment.

(4) Nothing in this section exempts a trustee from any liability that would have been incurred if this Act had not been passed, in case the trustee permits any money, valuable consideration, or property to remain in the hands or under the control of the banker or solicitor for a period longer than is reasonably necessary to enable the banker or solicitor to pay or transfer the same to the trustee.

Comparable Legislation

Trustee Act, R.S.A. 2000, c. T-8, s. 23; R.S.B.C. 1996, c. 464, s. 7; R.S.M. 1987, c. T160, s. 35; R.S.N. 1990, c. T-10, s. 7; R.S.N.S. 1989, c. 479, s. 23; R.S.N.W.T. 1988, c. T-8, s. 20; R.S.S. 1978, c. T-23, s. 44 (am. by S.S. 1998, c. 40, s. 11); R.S.Y.T. 2002, c. 223, s. 23.

SPEIGHT v. GAUNT

(1883), 9 App. Cas. 1
House of Lords

The testator, John Speight, a stuff manufacturer, left a large estate to his friend Isaac Gaunt (and another, since retired) as his trustees, in trust for his widow and several minor children. Gaunt, another stuff manufacturer, accepted the trust out of friendship and acted gratuitously. He had no special knowledge of investments.

Gaunt wanted to invest £15,000 from the trust fund at a good yield so he approached John Cooke & Son, a stockbroker whom the testator himself had always used, and instructed Richard Cooke to purchase certain municipal stock, which was an authorized investment. Cooke undertook to act and in due course presented Gaunt with a "bought-note" pretending that he had purchased the securities. Gaunt gave Cooke the £15,000 in order to pay the seller of the securities. In fact, Cooke never bought the securities but appropriated the money to cover losses he had incurred in the stock market. Cooke went bankrupt and Speight's widow and children brought this action against Gaunt to recover the moneys, arguing that he has was guilty of a breach of trust.

LORD BLACKBURN:

. . .

The authorities cited by the late Master of the Rolls, I think shew that as a general rule a trustee sufficiently discharges his duty if he takes in managing trust affairs all those precautions which an ordinary prudent man of business would take in managing similar affairs of his own. There is one exception to this: a trustee must not choose investments other than those which the terms of his trust permit, though they may be such as an ordinary prudent man of business would select for his own money; and it may be that however usual it may be for a person who wishes to invest his own money, and instructs an agent, such as an attorney, or a stockbroker, to seek an investment, to deposit the money at interest with the agent till the investment is found, that is in effect lending it on the agent's own personal security, and is a breach of trust. No question as to this arises here, Mr. Gaunt did nothing of that kind. Subject to this exception, as to which it is unnecessary to consider further, I think the case of *Ex parte Belchier*[68] establishes the principle that where there is a usual course of business the trustee is justified in following it, though it may be such that there is some risk that the property may be lost by the dishonesty or insolvency of an agent employed.

The transactions of life could not be carried on without some confidences being bestowed. When the transaction consists in a sale where the vendor is entitled to keep his hold on the property till he receives the money, and the purchaser is entitled to keep his money till he gets the property, it would be in all cases inconvenient if the vendor and purchaser were required to meet and personally exchange the one for the other; when the parties are, as is very often the case, living remote from each other, it would be physically impossible.

Men of business practically ascertain how much confidence may be safely bestowed, or rather whether the inconvenience and hampering of trade which is avoided by this confidence is too heavy a premium for insurance against the risk thus incurred. When a loss such as that which occurred in *Ex parte Belchier* occurs from having bestowed such confidence, they doubtless reconsider all this; and when a new practice, such as that of making bankers' cheques payable to order and crossing them arises, as it has done within living memory, no doubt it is made use of in many cases to avoid incurring that risk, which was formerly practically inevitable. So that what was at one time the usual course, may at another time be no longer usual.

Judges and lawyers who see brought before them the cases in which losses have been incurred, and do not see the infinitely more numerous cases in which expense and trouble and inconvenience are avoided, are apt to think men of business rash. I think that the principle which Lord Hardwicke lays down is that, while the course is usual, a trustee is not to be blamed if he honestly, and without knowing anything that makes it exceptionally risky in his case, pursues that usual course. And I think that, independent of the high authority of Lord Hardwicke, this is founded on principle. It would be both unreasonable and inexpedient to make a trustee responsible for not being more prudent than ordinary men of business are.

The question as it seems to me is whether Mr. Gaunt has done more than this.

It is to be remembered that in the state of things which existed in February 1881, Mr. Gaunt was not only authorized to invest in securities such as were authorized by the trust, but was bound to do so if he could.

For this purpose it was necessary to ascertain what securities of that sort could be obtained, and what were the most favourable terms, to make the bargain with those who furnished the securities, and when the proper time came to

68 Amb. 218.

exchange the money for the documents of title to the securities. Stockbrokers professionally manage all this class of business, and the very large number of persons who pursue this trade is quite sufficient to shew that it is usual to employ them.

. . .

Was then Mr. Gaunt justified in employing a stockbroker and giving them authority to procure the desired securities on the London Stock Exchange if that was the best way to get them? I think he was. It was argued by Mr. Millar that he was not; for that in fact the securities of the different corporations were not in the market and could only be obtained from the documents of which copies are in evidence and so learn that he had no more to do than make his offer, and when it was accepted pay the money into a bank named by the corporation, which was, Mr. Millar argued, so simple an operation that anyone could do it without a stockbroker at all. This is not quite accurate, for we know from the evidence that Leeds has issued a large quantity of debenture stock which from time to time was sold by the holders, and if sold would necessarily be sold somewhat below the price which would have to be given to the corporation, and therefore, as is explained by Mr. Rhodes (Question 756), it would have been proper to inquire if they were for sale on the market. But it is true that it was not likely that so large a quantity as £5000 would be got at once. We also know that Halifax and Huddersfield had no debenture stocks at all, though they had borrowed and were borrowing money on mortgages for a fixed term of years, which would be equally good securities. And though someone might be found who wished to transfer a mortgage not yet due, that would not be likely. But Mr. Gaunt did not know this: and there is neither principle nor authority for saying that he ought to have inquired, and might have learned, and is to be responsible for not doing so. For independent of the unreasonableness of requiring a trustee to leave his own business, and do part of what a stockbroker is generally employed to do, there would be great risk of a trustee missing the most profitable way of obtaining the investment, which a stockbroker would not. I think, therefore, Mr. Gaunt was justified in employing John Cooke & Son.

. . .

It is not suggested that Mr. Gaunt was not *bona fide* and honestly doing what he thought right. And in my opinion the whole question in the cause is whether it is made out that he neglected his duty as a trustee not to expose the property of his *cestui que trust* to unusual risks so far as to be guilty of a breach of trust. And the answer to that question, according to the authorities cited, and as I think on principle, greatly depends on the evidence of what was, at that time, the usual course of business.

. . .

Now when a purchase has been made on the London Stock Exchange, it is necessary that the money should be ready in London, to be paid in exchange for the transfers, from the date of the settling-day till the transfers are all delivered, in order to keep the buying broker out of cash advance, and the evidence is, I think, that it is the usual course of business to do this by giving to the buying broker a cheque for the money, so that he may be in funds to take up the transfers when ready. If the broker appropriated the money to any other purpose it would be an act of dishonesty on his part, but all men may be dishonest; and even if he is not dishonest, there is a possibility that he may fail before the stocks are ready, and that the money advanced can be no longer recovered *in specie*. There is, so far, some risk incurred by trusting the broker for a few days with the money.

. . .

Mr. McMillan says that, except in very rare instances, it was, up to the time of Mr. Cooke's failure, usual to pay the money to the broker. He suggests, what I think is probable, that the confidence in brokers was shaken by that failure, and I think it very likely that until that confidence is restored there will be more caution, perhaps to the extent of vexatious timidity; and it may very possibly become unusual, at least where the sum is large, to pay, as Mr. Gaunt did in this case; and if the usage change, a trustee who should pay in this way after it had ceased to be usual so to do, may be responsible. As to that I give no opinion. But we must look to what was usual at the time he acted; and I think that the effect of the evidence is to bring the usual course very near to that which was the usual course in *Ex parte Belchier*. There the broker, who had sold the tobacco, might have brought the purchaser and the vendor together, and let the vendor receive the money in exchange for the dock warrants or whatever it was than represented the goods; the only reason why that was not usual was that it was cumbersome, not convenient, not that it was impossible. Yet Lord Hardwicke thought that the defendant was justified in following the usual course. And I agree with the judges of the Court of Appeal that Mr. Gaunt, without improper want of caution, might here believe that Cooke had bought on the London Stock Exchange and might put the money in his hands on the pay-day.

. . .

[The Earl of Selborne L.C., Lord Watson, and Lord Fitzgerald concurred.]

Notes and Questions

1. For further reading in the area, see R.E. Scane, "Trustees Duties, Powers and Discretions — Power to Delegate and Duty to Account."[69]

2. A trustee wants to employ a property appraiser to value property for the purpose of granting a mortgage. Is it proper for the trustee to rely on his or her solicitor's recommendation of an appraiser?[70]

3. Give several examples of circumstances in which it would be permissible for a trustee to delegate duties because they are of the sort that a trustee is not required to perform personally.

---

69 Law Society of Upper Canada Special Lectures, *Recent Developments in Estate Planning and Administration*, 1980, at 43.

70 See *Fry v. Tapson* (1884), 28 Ch. D. 268.

4. Executors may employ agents "where the circumstances make it reasonable to do so."[71] How is this different, if at all, from the ability of a trustee to delegate? Ought this statement of the rule to be adopted for trustees?

5. Is it acceptable for a trustee to grant a general power of attorney over trust property to an agent?[72]

6. Agents are not liable to the trust for losses that result if they act *bona fide*. Are the trustees who selected the agents liable in such a situation?[73]

7. The Manitoba legislation gives trustees broader powers of delegation than does the Ontario legislation.[74] In Manitoba, trustees may employ agents for all tasks regardless of whether necessity or the usual course of business justifies it.

8. The Ontario Law Reform Commission[75] has recommended that a new statutory provision be enacted to permit delegation of all administrative tasks. Such delegation would be governed by the general standard of care, that is, careful selection and supervision of the agent by the trustee.

9. The Ontario Law Reform Commission[76] has also recommended that trustees be enabled, by legislation, to grant a power of appointment to any person for a period of up to 12 months over such duties and powers as are vested in them as trustees.

10. Trustees may delegate their functions relating to investment of trust property to an agent.[77] This is dealt with in the next section.

5. INVESTMENT OF TRUST FUNDS

(a) Generally

Trustees are under a duty to invest the trust funds in authorized investments. Investments are authorized by the trust instrument or by statute. The statutory powers are dealt with below. Failure to invest the trust property will cause the trustees to be personally liable for any loss that the trust suffers.[78]

Regardless of the source of investment powers, when investing a trustee must be guided by at least three principles. First, the trustee must be even-handed between beneficiaries interested in income and those interested in capital. Second, the trustee must act honestly. And, third, the trustee must not select speculative or unduly risky investments.

A properly drawn trust instrument normally contains wide powers of investment even though modern statutes permit a wide variety of trust investments. However, the trust instrument can limit the scope of possible investments if so desired.[79] If the investment powers are too narrow, trustees may make application

---

71 *Re McCusker Estate* (1988), 63 Alta. L.R. (2d) 106, 91 A.R. 150 (Surr. Ct.).

72 See *Wagner v. Van Cleeff, supra*, note 55.

73 See *Barabash Estate, Re*, [1999] A.J. No. 1012, 1999 CarswellAlta 1433, 1999 ABQB 656 (Q.B.), additional reasons at 1999 CarswellAlta 1434, 1999 ABQB 807 (Q.B.).

74 R.S.M. 1970, c. T160, s. 37.

75 O.L.R.C. Report at 80.

76 *Ibid.*, at 81.

77 *Trustee Act*, R.S.O. 1990, c. T.23, ss. 27.1, 27.2, added by S.O. 2001, c. 9, Sched. B, s. 13(5).

78 See *Re Proniuk* (1984), 59 A.R. 97, 18 E.T.R. 31 (Surr. Ct.); *Jamieson Estate, Re* (November 4, 1996), Doc. 71228, [1996] A.J. No. 1324 (Surr. Ct).

79 See, for example, *Trustee Act*, R.S.O. 1990, c. T.23, s. 68.

to the court under the *Variation of Trusts Act*,[80] to have them broadened. When considering such applications, the court will have regard to: the breadth of the proposed investment powers; the efficacy of provisions for advising and controlling trustees in the exercise of the extended powers; the desirability, when the proposed extended powers of investment are to be very wide, of a scheme dividing the trust fund into two parts, one to be confined to safe investments and the other to be used for investments involving a greater risk; the standing of the particular trustees and the size of the trust fund.[81]

(b) The Standard of Care Owed

We have seen that the standard of care that is owed, in general, by trustees is that they use the same degree of diligence in managing the trust property as that which a person of ordinary prudence would use in managing his or her own affairs.[82]

In the context of investments, the standard of care has been modified to allow for the fact that investment decisions affect both those persons entitled to present income and those who are to enjoy the capital at some future time. The modified standard also reflects the fact that not all people are willing to accept the same degree of risk. This refined standard, which requires that a trustee use the same degree of diligence in managing the trust property as that which a person of ordinary prudence would use in managing the affairs of another person, is illustrated in *Learoyd v. Whiteley*,[83] below.

LEAROYD v. WHITELEY

(1887), 12 App. Cas. 727
House of Lords

The testator directed his trustees to invest £5,000 "in or upon real securities in England or Wales" and to hold the same in trust for E for life, with remainder to her children.

The trustees wished to invest part of the money on a mortgage of a freehold brick yard. They employed local appraisers who advised them that the premises were good security for £3,500, and that when the mortgagors made improvements worth £1,700, as they intended to do, the premises would be good security for £4,500. The trustees invested £3,500 on the mortgage.

The business later failed. The trustees sold the property under their power of sale but it brought only £3,300. The beneficiaries then brought an action against the trustees to recover the loss. They were successful at trial and in the Court of Appeal; the trustees then appealed to the House of Lords.

---

80 R.S.O. 1990, c. V.1 and equivalent legislation.
81 See *Trustees of the British Museum v. Attorney General*, [1984] 1 All E.R. 337 (Ch. Div.).
82 *Fales v. Canadian Permanent Trust Co.*, *supra*, note 34.
83 (1887), 12 App. Cas. 727, 36 W.R. 72 (H.L.).

LORD WATSON:

. . .

As a general rule the law requires of a trustee no higher degree of diligence in the execution of his office than a man of ordinary prudence would exercise in the management of his own private affairs. Yet he is not allowed the same discretion in investing the moneys of the trust as if he were a person *sui juris* dealing with his own estate. Business men of ordinary prudence may, and frequently do, select investments which are more or less of a speculative character; but it is the duty of a trustee to confine himself to the class of investments which is permitted by the trust, and likewise to avoid all investments of that class which are attended with hazard. So long as he acts in the honest observance of these limitations, the general rule already stated will apply.

The Courts of Equity in England have indicated and given effect to certain general principles for the guidance of trustees in lending money upon the security of real estate. Thus it has been laid down that in the case of ordinary agricultural land the margin ought not to be less than one-third of its value; whereas in cases where the subject of the security derives its value from buildings erected upon the land, or its use for trade purposes, the margin ought not to be less than one-half. I do not think these have been laid down as hard and fast limits up to which trustees will be invariably safe, and beyond which they can never be in safety to lend, but as indicating the lowest margins which in ordinary circumstances careful investor of trust funds ought to accept. It is manifest that in cases where the subjects of the security are exclusively or mainly used for the purposes of trade, no prudent investor can be in a position to judge of the amount of margin necessary to make a loan for a term of years reasonably secure, until he has ascertained not only their present market price, but their intrinsic value, apart from those trading considerations which give them a speculative and it may be a temporary value.

Upon the general law applicable to this case I have only to observe further that whilst trustees cannot delegate the execution of the trust, they may, as was held by this House in *Speight v. Gaunt*[84] avail themselves of the services of others wherever such employment is according to the usual course of business. If they employ a person of competent skill to value a real security, they may, so long as they act in good faith, safely rely upon the correctness of his valuation. But the ordinary course of business does not justify the employment of a valuator for any other purpose than obtaining the data necessary in order to enable the trustees to judge of the sufficiency of the security offered. They are not in safety to rely upon his bare assurance that the security is sufficient, in the absence of detailed information which would enable them to form, and without forming, an opinion for themselves. At all events if they choose to place reliance upon his opinion without the means of testing its soundness they cannot, should the security prove defective, escape from personal liability, unless they prove that the security was such as would have been accepted by a trustee of ordinary prudence, fully informed of

---

84 (1883), 9 App. Cas. 1 (H.L.).

its character, and having in the view the principles to which I have already adverted.

By the terms of Benjamin Whiteley's will his trustees are authorized to invest trust moneys upon real securities in England and Wales. It is not disputed that in lending £3,500 upon the security of Barstow & Hartley's brickfield, in terms of the mortgage of the 12th of January 1878, the appellants acted in good faith. Of that sum £3,000 only belonged to Whiteley's trust, a circumstance which does not alter the character of the security, because it has not been shewn that the trust money was made a charge in priority to the balance of £500.

The course which was followed by the appellants in entering into the transaction of January 1878 is very compendiously stated by Mr. Learoyd, in whose evidence, so far as it related to matters within his personal knowledge, Mr. Carter generally concurred. In his examination in chief Mr. Learoyd was referred to a report by Messrs. Uttley & Gray, dated the 8th of October 1877, and interrogated: "(Q.) Did you and Mr. Carter on that report form an opinion that it was a proper security for the investment? — (A.) We did after further inquiries." Being interrogated in cross-examination: "What other inquiries did you make about the brick properties? — (A.) I instructed our solicitor to make inquiries respecting the respectability of the parties."

It plainly appears from these answers that the appellants had no information regarding the subjects mortgaged except what was contained in the report of their valuators.

In my opinion the report of Uttley & Gray is not such a document as a lender of ordinary prudence would have ventured to act upon. It discloses the fact that there were only ten acres of land, and that a not inconsiderable portion of the subjects consisted of buildings and fixed machinery used for brick making. But it does not state either the cumulo value of the subjects or the separate values of the land, the buildings, and the machinery. It does, no doubt, contain the statement that the valuators thought the land, premises, and freehold fixtures would afford good security for £3,500; but trustees who choose to act upon such an opinion must take the risk of the security proving insufficient.

In these circumstances, I think it has been established that, at the time of taking the security, the appellants altogether failed to exercise that ordinary amount of care which the law required of them. Notwithstanding such failure, they would still have had a good answer to the respondents' claim had they been able to shew that if they had made full inquiries, and had obtained all necessary particulars from the valuators, they would have been justified as men of ordinary prudence in accepting the security. Unfortunately the evidence led by the appellants themselves appears to me to negative any inference of that kind. Their witness and valuator, Mr. Uttley, states that in 1877 he valued the subjects as a going brick-work at £7,200, of which £2,000 was for the land, and the remaining £5,200 for buildings and machinery. He did not in 1877 form any estimate of their value upon a sale by the mortgagees, and not as a going concern. Being asked on cross-examination what difference that would have made on his estimate he said, "I should say 10 per cent, would represent the difference not as a going concern. Everything was in order." The answer is by no means satisfactory. It assumes that the works would be kept in the same good order; and it leaves out of account the possibility of depression in the brick-making trade, a factor which I do not think a prudent valuator would omit from his calculations. But, taking his estimate as he gave it, a deduction of 10 per cent, leaves a margin of £520 below the minimum amount which ought to be allowed in order to cover the possible depreciation of subjects affected, to the extent of five-sevenths of their value, by the fluctuations of trade.

Upon the question of interest I agree with the reasoning of Cotton L.J. I do not think the tenant for life can now be required to repay or give credit for any part of the sums paid to her before August 1884, as the actual income of the trust estate.

[The concurring speeches of Lord Halsbury L.C. and Lord Fitzgerald have been omitted. The appeal was dismissed.]

(c) Under Statute

The trustee's duty and powers to invest, when not governed by the trust instrument, are governed by statute. Sections 26 and 27 of the Ontario *Trustee Act*[85] formerly contained a statutory "legal list" of investments. Similar provisions were or remain in force in other provinces. However, ss. 26 and 27 were replaced in 1998 by the "prudent investor" standard set out in the revised s. 27. Section 27, set out below, illustrates the types of investments that a trustee may make. In addition, it outlines the statutory standard of care that the trustee must satisfy and certain criteria that the trustee must consider. Other powers relevant to investment are contained in ss. 27.1-29, also set out below.

TRUSTEE ACT

R.S.O. 1990, c. T.23; am. S.O. 1998, c. 18, Sched. B, s. 16(1);
S.O. 2001, c. 9, Sched. B, s. 13(2)-(5)

INVESTMENTS

27. (1) In investing trust property, a trustee must exercise the care, skill, diligence and judgment that a prudent investor would exercise in making investments.

(2) A trustee may invest trust property in any form of property in which a prudent investor might invest.

(3) Any rule of law that prohibits a trustee from delegating powers or duties does not prevent the trustee from investing in mutual funds, pooled funds or segregated funds under variable insurance contracts, and sections 27.1 and 27.2 do not apply to the purchase of such funds.

---

85 R.S.O. 1990, c. T.23.

(4) If trust property is held by co-trustees and one of the co-trustees is a trust corporation as defined in the *Loan and Trust Corporations Act*, any rule of law that prohibits a trustee from delegating powers or duties does not prevent the co-trustees from investing in a common trust fund, as defined in that Act, that is maintained by the trust corporation and sections 27.1 and 27.2 do not apply.

(5) A trustee must consider the following criteria in planning the investment of trust property, in addition to any others that are relevant to the circumstances:

1. General economic conditions.
2. The possible effect of inflation or deflation.
3. The expected tax consequences of investment decisions or strategies.
4. The role that each investment or course of action plays within the overall trust portfolio.
5. The expected total return from income and the appreciation of capital.
6. Needs for liquidity, regularity of income and preservation or appreciation of capital.
7. An asset's special relationship or special value, if any, to the purposes of the trust or to one or more of the beneficiaries.

(6) A trustee must diversify the investment of trust property to an extent that is appropriate to,

(a) the requirements of the trust; and

(b) general economic and investment market conditions.

(7) A trustee may obtain advice in relation to the investment of trust property.

(8) It is not a breach of trust for a trustee to rely on advice obtained under subsection (7) if a prudent investor would rely on the advice under comparable circumstances.

(9) This section and section 27.1 do not authorize or require a trustee to act in a manner that is inconsistent with the terms of the trust.

(10) For the purposes of subsection (9), the constating documents of a corporation that is deemed to be a trustee under subsection 1(2) of the *Charities Accounting Act* form part of the terms of the trust.

27.1 (1) Subject to subsections (2) to (5), a trustee may authorize an agent to exercise any of the trustee's functions relating to investment of trust property to the same extent that a prudent investor, acting in accordance with ordinary investment practice, would authorize an agent to exercise any investment function.

(2) A trustee may not authorize an agent to exercise functions on the trustee's behalf unless the trustee has prepared a written plan or strategy that,

(a) complies with section 28; and

(b) is intended to ensure that the functions will be exercised in the best interests of the beneficiaries of the trust.

(3) A trustee may not authorize an agent to exercise functions on the trustee's behalf unless a written agreement between the trustee and the agent is in effect and includes,

(a) a requirement that the agent comply with the plan or strategy in place from time to time; and

(b) a requirement that the agent report to the trustee at regular stated intervals.

(4) A trustee is required to exercise prudence in selecting an agent, in establishing the terms of the agent's authority and in monitoring the agent's performance to ensure compliance with those terms.

(5) For the purpose of subsection (4),

(a) prudence in selecting an agent includes compliance with any regulation made under section 30; and

(b) prudence in monitoring an agent's performance includes,

    (i)   reviewing the agent's reports,

    (ii) regularly reviewing the agreement between the trustee and the agent and how it is being put into effect, including considering whether the plan or strategy of investment should be revised or replaced, replacing the plan or strategy if the trustee considers it appropriate to do so, and assessing whether the plan or strategy is being complied with,

    (iii) considering whether directions should be provided to the agent or whether the agent's appointment should be revoked, and

    (iv) providing directions to the agent or revoking the appointment if the trustee considers it appropriate to do so.

27.2 (1) An agent who is authorized to exercise a trustee's functions relating to investment of trust property has a duty to do so,

(a) with the standard of care expected of a person carrying on the business of investing the money of others;

(b) in accordance with the agreement between the trustee and the agent; and

(c) in accordance with the plan or strategy of investment.

(2) An agent who is authorized to exercise a trustee's functions relating to investment of trust property shall not delegate that authority to another person.

(3) If an agent is authorized to exercise a trustee's functions relating to investment of trust property and the trust suffers a loss because of the agent's breach of the duty owed under subsection (1) or (2), a proceeding against the agent may be commenced by,

(a) the trustee; or

(b) a beneficiary, if the trustee does not commence a proceeding within a reasonable time after acquiring knowledge of the breach.

28. A trustee is not liable for a loss to the trust arising from the investment of trust property if the conduct of the trustee that led to the loss conformed to a plan or strategy for the investment of the trust property, comprising reasonable assessment of risk and return, that a prudent investor could adopt under comparable circumstances.

29. If a trustee is liable for a loss to the trust arising from the investment of trust property, a court assessing the damages payable by the trustee may take into account the overall performance of the investments.

Comparable Legislation

Trustee Act, R.S.A. 2000, c. T-8, s. 2 (am. by S.A. 2001, c. 28, s. 2); R.S.B.C. 1996, c. 464, ss. 15.1-15.6, 17.1, 19, 21-23 (ss. 15.1-15.6 en. by S.B.C. 2002, c. 33, s. 23; s. 17.1

en. by S.B.C. 2002, c. 33, s. 24); R.S.M. 1987, c. T160, ss. 68-75; R.S.N.L. 1990, c. T-10, ss. 3, 6-10 (s. 3 am. by S.N.L. 2000, c. 28, s. 1; ss. 6-8 am. by S.N.L. 2000, c. 28, s. 3; s. 9 am. by S.N.L. 2000, c. 28, s. 4); R.S.N.S. 1989, c. 479, ss. 3-14 (s. 3 am. by S.N.S. 1992, c. 8, s. 37; S.N.S. 1994-95, c. 19, s. 1; S.N.S. 2002, c. 10, s. 45; ss. 3A-3F en. by S.N.S. 2002, c. 10, s. 45; ss. 4, 5 am. by S.N.S. 1994-95, c. 19, s. 1; s. 6 rep. by S.N.S. 1994-95, c. 19, s. 1); R.S.N.W.T. 1988, c. T-8, ss. 2, 3; R.S.P.E.I. 1988, c. T-8, ss. 2, 3 (s. 2 am. by S.P.E.I. 1990, c. 63; S.P.E.I. 1991, c. 46; S.P.E.I. 1992, c. 68, s. 1; S.P.E.I. 1994, c. 59, s. 75 (Sched. 3); S.P.E.I. 1996, c. 46; S.P.E.I. 1997, c. 51; s. 3 am. by S.P.E.I. 1997, c. 51, s. 1); R.S.S. 1978, c. T-23, s. 3-10 (s. 3 am. by S.S. 1980-81, c. 31, s. 3; S.S. 1998, c. C-45.2, s. 476(2) (Sched.); S.S. 1998, c. 40, s. 3; ss. 3.1-3.3 en. by S.S. 1998, c. 40, s. 3; s. 4 am. by S.S. 1998, c. 40, s. 4; s. 5 am. by S.S. 1998, c. 40, s. 5; s. 6 am. by S.S. 1980-81, c. 31, s. 4; S.S. 1998, c. C-45.2, s. 476(2) (Sched.); s. 9 am. by S.S. 1998, c. 40, s. 6; s. 10 am. by S.S. 1998, c. 40, s. 7); R.S.Y. 2002, c. 223, ss. 2-7; *Trustees Act*, R.S.N.B. 1973, c. T-15, ss. 2-4 (s. 2.1 en. by S.N.B. 2000, c. 29, s. 1).

Notes and Questions

1. For further reading in the area see A.H. Oosterhoff, "Trustees' Powers of Investment"[86] and the Honourable Madame Justice Bertha Wilson, "Trustees' Investment Powers."[87]

2. Are trustees obliged to invest in the full range of investments authorized by the trust instrument? Are they allowed to narrow the range for political, social, or ethical reasons?[88]

3. Because the legal lists formerly contained in many statutes are too restrictive, the Uniform Law Conference of Canada promulgated a model Act to abolish the legal list and substitute a power to invest according to the general standard of care.[89] All provincial statutes have now been amended to abolish the legal list and to substitute a prudent investor standard in its place. The statutes of some provinces, such as those of Alberta, Saskatchewan, Prince Edward Island, and Newfoundland contain a list of investment criteria that must be considered by the trustee which is similar to the list contained in the Ontario Act. Other statutes simply adopt the prudent investor standard without a list of criteria.

4. England has also adopted a new trust investment regime. Section 3(1) of the Trustee Act, 2000[90] allows a trustee to "make any kind of investment that he could make if he were absolutely entitled to the assets of the trust". Is this power too wide, perhaps? Or is it constrained by the general rule of prudence?[91]

5. There was a tendency on the part of the courts to exonerate more readily a trustee who invested under the statutory legal list than one who invested under wider powers conferred by the trust instrument.[92] Was that practice correct?

6. An example of a clause conferring wide investment powers is:

---

86 Study for the Ont. Law Ref. Comm., 1970.

87 Law Society of Upper Canada, Special, *Recent Developments in Estate Planning and Administration*, 1980, at 1.

88 See *Cowan v. Scargill* (1984), [1984] 2 All E.R. 750, [1985] Ch. 270 (Ch. Div.).

89 (1978), *Uniform Acts of the Uniform Law Conf. of Canada*, p. 48-51.

90 C. 29 (U.K.).

91 See A. Hicks, "The Trustee Act 2000 and the Modern Meaning of Investment" (2001), Trust Law International 203.

92 See A.H. Oosterhoff, *"Trustees' Powers of Investment"* (Study for the Ontario Law Reform Commission, 1970).

I declare that my trustees, when making investments for my estate, shall not be limited to investments authorized by law for trustees but may make any investments which they, in their absolute discretion considerable advisable.

7. The creator of a trust who is uncertain about the trustees' ability to handle a wide discretion in investing, can direct that they retain a named investment adviser.

8. Trustee legislation provides that trustees are entitled to insure buildings, up to three-fourths of the value of the buildings.[93] Because the reasonably prudent person would insure, this power in fact amounts to a duty.

9. A trustee under a will was empowered to invest "in such investments as she thinks fit." The trustee lent money: (a) on the security of deposits of jewellery; and (b) without security. Are such loans in fact investments? If not, is the trustee liable for breach of trust? Is there a difference between situations (a) and (b)?[94]

6. IMPARTIALITY

(a) Introduction

Trustees must act impartially when dealing with beneficiaries. That is, they may not give preferential treatment to any one beneficiary or group of beneficiaries unless so authorized by the trust instrument. Trustees who show partiality to beneficiaries because of the terms the trust instrument must take care that their interpretation of the instrument is correct; actions based on honest but erroneous interpretations that have the effect of failing to hold an even hand among beneficiaries amount to a breach of trust.[95]

The rules relating to investments are designed to ensure that impartiality is achieved because they strike a balance between providing income for life-tenants and preserving capital for those with the remainder interest. However, situations do arise in which the interests of the life-tenant and those entitled to the remainder come into conflict. For example, if a trustee invests in high income producing securities, the life-tenant may benefit at the expense of those entitled to the remainder interest because high returns are often achieved at the expense of capital appreciation. Or, if the trustee pays the expenses associated with the administration of the trust from income, the life-tenant would be penalized and the holders of the remainder interest correspondingly benefited.

This part of the chapter deals with how the obligation to act even-handedly is fulfilled. In it we consider the consequences of a failure to act impartially; apportionments between capital and income generally and as regards corporate distributions; and allocation of expenditures. In addressing generally the question of apportionment of income between successive beneficiaries, we will explore

---

93 See, for example, *Trustee Act*, R.S.O. 1990, c. T.23, s. 21.

94 See *Khoo Tek Keong v. Ch'ng Joo Keong*, [1934] A.C. 529, 1934 CarswellFor 4, [1934] 3 W.W.R. 737 (Straits Settlements P.C.). See also *Horan v. Beattie Estate* (1999), [1999] O.J. No. 4739, 1999 CarswellOnt 4750 (S.C.J.).

95 *Boe v. Alexander* (1985), 21 E.T.R. 246 (B.C. S.C.), affirmed (1987), 15 B.C.L.R. (2d) 106, 41 D.L.R. (4th) 520, 28 E.T.R. 228 (C.A.), leave to appeal to S.C.C. refused (1988), 22 B.C.L.R. (2d) xxx, 28 E.T.R. xxxvi.

the duty to convert unauthorized assets into authorized ones and to apportion the assets between capital and income.

Keep in mind, as you work through this section, that it is common practice today to exclude some or all of the rules governing apportionment and allocation of outgoings in the trust instrument. This is done for two reasons. First, the rules may block trustees from making decisions that reflect tax considerations; second, because application of the rules often makes administration of the trust unjustifiably complicated.

Unless the rules relating to even-handedness are excluded, failure to act impartially is a breach of trust, as *Re Smith*,[96] below, illustrates.

RE SMITH

[1971] O.R. 584, 16 D.L.R. (3d) 130[97]
Supreme Court of Ontario
[High Court of Justice]

Frank Smith inherited a substantial fortune, consisting primarily of 52,000 shares in Imperial Oil Limited on terms which required him, if he had a son, to bequeath the shares to his son. Peter Smith was his son and Frank bequeathed the shares to him. He left the residue of his estate to his wife, Virginia. However, the residue was small and he requested Peter to pay one-quarter of the annual income from the shares to his mother, Virginia, for her life.

Peter did more than his father asked. When he reached the age of majority in 1966, he created an *inter vivos* trust, with Canada Trust as trustee, and transferred one-quarter of the shares to the trustee. The trustee was directed to pay the net annual income to Virginia for her life and, if Peter should predecease his mother, to transfer the trust fund to her. If Virginia should predecease Peter, the trustee had to transfer the trust fund to him. The trust deed empowered the trustee, in its sole discretion, to retain the trust fund in its present form, whether producing income or not. The shares placed in the *inter vivos* trust had a market value of $689,000 when the trust was created, and at the date of the hearing they were worth more than one million dollars. The shares had meanwhile been split four for one.

The annual dividends paid by Imperial Oil on the shares since 1966 were approximately $2\frac{1}{2}$ percent of market value, which generated an income of $27,000 for Virginia. Virginia, who was used to a very high standard of living while her husband was alive, found this income to be inadequate. Her solicitor wrote Canada Trust requesting it to diversify the portfolio, having regard to Virginia's need for additional income. Canada Trust spoke with Peter, who was not anxious to have the shares in Imperial Oil sold, since he would lose the anticipated capital gain

---

96 [1971] 1 O.R. 584, 16 D.L.R. (3d) 130 (H.C.).
97 Affirmed [1971] 2 O.R. 541, 18 D.L.R. (3d) 405 (C.A.).

on the shares. Virginia then brought proceedings against Canada Trust for the relief described in the judgment below.

KEITH J.:

. . .

The relief sought on this application set out in the notice of motion is as follows:

1. Determining the following questions which have arisen in the administration of the said trust:
    (a) Whether the trustee is in breach of its duty as a trustee to maintain an even hand between the life-tenant and remainderman by refusing to exercise its power to invest in securities which would produce a reasonable return for the life-tenant having regard to her financial circumstances;
    (b) Whether the trustee is in breach of its duty to exercise prudence and reasonable care in the investment of the trust assets by failing to diversify the investments of the trust; and
    (c) Whether the trustee has properly exercised its discretion with respect to the investment of the trust assets;
2. Removing the trustee for breach of trust, or, in the alternative, removing the trustee if it fails within a reasonable time hereafter to carry out its duties under the trust as to the investment of trust assets and as to the exercise of its discretion; . . .

Turning first to Q. 1(a), it is impossible for me to come to any other conclusion than that the trustee has failed to maintain an even hand between the life-tenant and the remaindermen, the remaindermen being the applicant and her son, each being contingently entitled to the *corpus* of the trust in the event of the death of the other. Although it was conceded that, by reason of the actual disparity in ages, a son has longer life expectancy in the ordinary course of things than a mother, this seems of no consequence to me since neither party has any lease on life. Persons of all ages are subject to unexpected termination of their lives at any moment.

It is perfectly clear from the very fact of the necessity of bringing this application that the trustee has chosen to ignore the request of the life-tenant for a variation of the investment portfolio which would afford her a very much enhanced income during her lifetime. The evidence of John W. Rothwell, the trust officer of the trustee responsible for this particular trust, conceded that, for at least the past several years, good quality bonds within the investment powers of the trustee are available with a yield of between 8 per cent and 9 per cent per annum, and that the rate of interest on prime residential mortgages, at the time of his examination in November 1970, was 10 per cent. He also conceded that the applicant borrowed money from the Canada Trust Company and was charged 9 per cent for a personal loan which she contracted because, as she alleges, the income from the trust was insufficient.

It was at no time urged by the trustee that the retention of the Imperial Oil Ltd. stock was intrinsically advisable. Counsel appeared for the remainderman, Peter Smith, in opposition to any change of investment. The only reason that counsel gave for this is that for some unspecified reason or purpose Peter Smith considers it to be in his interest that the present investments be retained.

This evidence is supported further by the fact that his own solicitors are the ones who wrote to the applicant's solicitors on September 18, 1969, and, in so doing, stated that they were going to consult Peter Smith to seek his views.

In the result, I find that the trustee has not maintained an even hand as between the life-tenant and her son in his position as a contingent remainderman.

Unless there is some provision in the trust agreement which prevents the trustee from doing so, it seems to me inescapable that the trustee is in breach of his well-recognized duty to maintain such an investment. In this connection, reference should be made to *Lewin on Trusts*;[98] *Raby v. Ridehalgh*;[99] *Stuart v. Stuart*;[100] Underhill's *Law of Trusts and Trustees*;[101] *Re Armstrong*.[102]

On behalf of the trustee whose argument in this connection counsel for the respondent Peter Smith adopts, it is urged that it was always the intention of the settlor that the shares of Imperial Oil Ltd. should be kept intact and undisturbed as being the prime asset in the trust fund. In support of this, the said respondent has filed with the court his affidavit sworn October 23, 1970, in which, among other things, he swears that, in instructing his lawyer to prepare a trust agreement, "It was my intention and I so directed Mr. Poole, to retain ownership in the Trust of the 13,000 shares of Imperial Oil common which I transferred to the trust." In my opinion, this proffered evidence is wholly inadmissible. The language of the written trust agreement, already quoted, is clear and unambiguous. It contains no suggestion of the sort now sought to be imposed on it.

In view of the deference which the trustee has heretofore displayed to the opinions of Peter Smith, it is impossible to restore confidence in the trustee with respect to the future administration of this trust, and a new trustee must be appointed.

. . .

[On the subsequent application to appoint a new trustee, the court appointed Canada Permanent Trust Company as the replacement trustee on consent of all the parties. Because of Canada Trust's "obduracy . . . in its determination to respect only the wishes of the settlor . . ." the court directed that Canada Trust pay Virginia's costs on a solicitor and client basis.]

---

98   16th ed. (1964), at 356.
99   (1835), 7 De G.M. & G. 104, 44 E.R. 41.
100 (1841), 3 Beav. 430, 49 E.R. 169.
101 11th ed., art. 45(1), at 273; 38 Hals. 3rd ed., at 972, para. 1683.
102 (1924), 55 O.L.R. 639 (C.A.).

Notes and Questions

1. Can surplus funds in a pension trust be used to enhance the benefits paid to one group of beneficiaries but not to all beneficiaries?[103]

2. Should aggravated or punitive damages be awarded against trustees who breached their duty to act reasonably?[104]

(b) Apportionments Between Capital And Income

(i) *Generally*

In order to maintain an even hand between successive beneficiaries, ideally all assets will be authorized investments. The trustees then can simply pay the income to the life-tenant and retain the capital for those entitled to the remainder. Unfortunately, trust property often consists of unauthorized investments and, therefore, the trustees must determine:

1. whether a duty to convert a particular asset into an authorized investment exists;
2. if so, whether the asset must be apportioned between income and capital; and
3. if so, how the apportionment is to be calculated.

Lottman v. Stanford,[105] below, deals with these questions.

LOTTMAN v. STANFORD

[1980] 1 S.C.R. 1065, 6 E.T.R. 34, 107 D.L.R. (3d) 28, 31 N.R. 1
Supreme Court of Canada

The testator, Sam Lottman, left an estate with a gross value of about $341,000. Some $285,000 of this consisted of real property, which was leased to a son and realized less than the annual taxes in rent. By clause III(g) of his will, the testator left the income from the residue of his estate to his wife, but gave his trustees power to encroach on the capital on her behalf for "medical, hospital or nursing expenses, or other expenses of a similar emergent nature". Upon his wife's death the capital was to be distributed equally among the couple's four children. Clause III(d) directed the trustees:

---

103 See *Anova Inc. Employee Retirement Pension Plan (Administrator of) v. Manufacturers Life Insurance Co.* (1994), 121 D.L.R. (4th) 162, 11 C.C.P.B. 67 (Ont. Gen. Div.); *Rittel v. Imprimeries Quebecor Inc.* (1994), 113 D.L.R. (4th) 166, 94 B.C.L.R. (2d) 12, 43 B.C.A.C. 222, 69 W.A.C. 222 (C.A.), leave to appeal refused (1994), 95 B.C.L.R. (2d) xxxiii, 116 D.L.R. (4th) vii (note), 179 N.R. 75 (note) (S.C.C.).

104 See *Nicholas v. Metropolitan Life Insurance Co. of Canada*, [2003] B.C.J. No. 734, 2003 CarswellBC 1268, 1 C.C.L.I. (4th) 239, [2003] I.L.R. I-4248, 2003 BCSC 506, C.E.B. & P.G.R. 8499 (note) (S.C.).

105 [1980] 1 S.C.R. 1065, 107 D.L.R. (3d) 28, 6 E.T.R. 34, 31 N.R. 1.

> To sell, call in and convert into money all of my personal estate at such time and in such manner and upon such terms as my Trustees in their absolute discretion determine, with power to them to postpone such conversion of the whole or any party of such estate for such length of time as they shall think best;

During the three years since her husband's death, Mrs. Lottman received $7,000 by way of income from the trust. She was not satisfied with the income and brought an application seeking various kinds of relief, in particular, a direction that the trustees forthwith carry out the trust for sale in clause III(d) of the will, and a declaration that she was entitled to be paid six per cent of the value of the unconverted assets (the value being determined one year after her husband's death) from the time of her husband's death until her death.

MCINTYRE J.:

This appeal concerns the application in Ontario of the rule in *Howe v. Lord Dartmouth; Howe v. Countess Aylesbury.*[106] Adopting the words found in Hanbury's Modern Equity,[107] Kerwin C.J.C., in *Royal Trust Co. v. Crawford,*[108] expressed it in these terms:

> Where residuary personalty is settled on death for the benefit of persons who are to enjoy it in succession, the duty of the trustees is to convert all such parts of it as are of a wasting or future or reversionary nature, or consist of unauthorized securities, into property of a permanent and income bearing character.

The Ontario Court of Appeal applied the rule in the case at Bar directing the conversion by the trustees under the will of the deceased Sam Lottman of what it found to be non-productive real property. This appeal is against the judgment.

. . .

The motion came on for hearing in weekly court and on June 13th, 1977, Galligan J. gave judgment dismissing the motion.[109] He left open the question of whether the rule in *Howe v. Lord Dartmouth* applied in Ontario to real property but he held it could not apply to the facts of this case because, in his view, the real property in question was neither unproductive nor wasting.

In the Court of Appeal, McKinnon and Wilson JJ.A. (Weatherston J.A. dissenting), the appeal was allowed.[110] It was held, applying the rule in *Howe v. Lord Dartmouth* to the real property concerned, that the executors were under a duty to convert and a sale of the real property was directed. The executors were further directed to invest the proceeds of sale in authorized investments and to pay the appellant widow the income therefrom during her lifetime. It was also

---

106 (1802), 7 Ves. Jun. 137, 32 E.R. 56.

107 (4th ed.), at 241.

108 [1955] S.C.R. 184 at 185, [1955] 2 D.L.R. 225.

109 (1977), 1 E.T.R. 11 (Ont. H.C.).

110 (1978), 2 E.T.R. 1 (Ont. C.A.).

ordered that pending conversion of the real property the widow would have a charge upon the property

> such charge being seven per cent of the value of the said properties as of one year from the date of the testator's death and payable from the date of the testator's death to the date of the actual conversion, less the amount of any income actually paid to the appellant during the specified period from the properties in question.

In argument before this Court, counsel for the appellant took the position that the sole issue was whether the rule in *Howe v. Lord Dartmouth* applied to compel a conversion of real property in Ontario. It was said further that even if the rule applied to real property it could not affect this case since no finding could reasonably be made that the land was either wasting or non-productive. The respondent widow adopted the judgments of the majority of the Court of Appeal, particularly that of Wilson J.A. She contended that on a reasonable interpretation of the will one could find the power to convert and, failing that, the equitable duty of the trustee to act even-handedly between the life-tenant and the remaindermen required the conversion of the unproductive realty and justified the application of the rule.

In her judgment, Wilson J.A. said:[111]

> The two rules of equity, the rule in *Howe v. Lord Dartmouth*, and its corollary, the rule in *Re Chesterfield's (Earl) Trusts*[112] do not proceed on any presumed intention of the testator that the property must be converted. These rules prescribe that, where the residue of an estate is left to persons in succession, *i.e.*, to a life-tenant and remaindermen, such parts of the estate as are of a wasting character or a reversionary or unproductive nature must be realized by the trustees and the proceeds invested in authorized investments unless the will shows a contrary intention.

She accepted the view, well-settled in the authorities, that the rule in *Howe v. Lord Dartmouth* requires a trustee to deal even-handedly between a life-tenant and a remainderman by converting wasting or unproductive assets and investing the proceeds of conversion in trustee or where authorized in the will, other permitted investments. This step enables all interests to be protected and the assets preserved so that the benefits provided for in the will may pass in succession to the respective beneficiaries. She disposed of the contention of the remaindermen that the rule had no application to real property in these words:

> It is true that the English courts have confined the application of the rule in *Howe v. Lord Dartmouth* to personal estate: *Re Woodhouse*; *Public Trustee v. Woodhouse*.[113] Accordingly, a life-tenant under an English will has no claim to any part of the proceeds of sale of unproductive real estate. Conversely, even if the will directs a sale of the real estate, the life-tenant in England is entitled to all of the income produced by it until it is sold. There is no apportionment in either case. Mr. Shead, however, directed us to a number of Ontario authorities in which the rule was

---

111 *Ibid.*
112 (1883), 24 Ch. D. 643.
113 [1941] Ch. D. 332, [1941] 2 All E.R. 265 (Ch. Div.).

applied to unproductive real estate.[114] Even if our courts were on a frolic of their own in applying the rule to real estate, which indeed it seems they were, it was in my opinion a frolic which reflected a contemporary Canadian attitude to property. Real estate is not a "sacred cow" in Canada as it was in England when these equitable rules were developed. Sale of the family hereditaments is not fraught with the same trauma and disgrace. I see no reason why in the current social context in Canada a trustee's powers and duties in relation to realty should be any different from his powers and duties in relation to personalty. I would therefore in an appropriate case apply the rule to the unproductible or under-productive real estate. Real estate may, I believe, be properly viewed by the trustees as under-productive if the income received from it and the rate of return on authorized investments is so disparate that it is unfair to the life-tenant that it be retained.

While expressing some qualification on another question not now in contention on this appeal, McKinnon J.A. agreed with Wilson J.A.

The rule in *Howe v. Lord Dartmouth*, as has been pointed out, is a rule requiring the trustee of an estate settled in succession to deal even-handedly between the life-tenant and the remaindermen. It operates to compel, where its operation is not excluded by the testator, a conversion of wasting or unproductive personalty and the investment of the proceeds of such conversion in trustee investments. By this means the life-tenant is assured of an income from the assets of the estate and the capital of the estate is preserved for the remainder interests upon the demise of the life-tenant. The corollary to that rule is the rule in *Re Earl of Chesterfield's Trusts*. It relates to the apportionment between capital and income of the proceeds of the conversion between the life-tenant and the remaindermen and is called into play as a result of a conversion of estate assets resulting either from the application of the rule in *Howe v. Lord Dartmouth* or from an express provision in the will. However, with the greatest of deference, I do not agree with Wilson J.A. that the rule may be applied in this case.

It will be observed that clause III(d) of the will contains a direction to convert the personal estate at the discretion of the trustees. Clause III(g) directs the investment of the residue. There is therefore no room for the operation of the rule which is wholly unnecessary where a specific direction to convert is given: see *Re Stekl; Lauer v. Stekl*.[115] In the case at Bar, the personal estate is subject to a direction requiring conversion and, in that respect, recourse to the rule is therefore unnecessary. As far as the real property is concerned, the rule in *Howe v. Lord Dartmouth* has never been extended to real property. All the authorities and text writers to which I have been referred and which I have been able to discover emanating from common law jurisdictions (excepting the United States of America) confine its operation to personalty. Wilson J.A., in the passage above-quoted, recognized this proposition, but was of the view that an exception had been made in the province of Ontario. She cited various authorities but again, and with the utmost respect, I am of the opinion that none of the cases she cited is authority

---

114 *Re Cameron* (1901), 2 O.L.R. 756 (Q.B.); *Toronto Gen. Trusts Corp. v. Clarke* (1903), 6 O.L.R. 551; *Re Prime* (1924), 25 O.W.N. 522 (H.C.); *Re Pears* (1926), 31 O.W.N. 235 (C.A.); *Re Rutherford*, [1933] O.R. 707, [1933] 4 D.L.R. 222 (C.A.).

115 [1974] 6 W.W.R. 490, 47 D.L.R. (3d) 286 (sub nom. *Re Lauer and Stekl*) (B.C. C.A.), affirmed [1976] 1 S.C.R. 781, [1976] 2 W.W.R. 382, 16 N.R. 559, 54 D.L.R. (3d) 159n.

for the proposition that the rule in *Howe v. Lord Dartmouth* applies to real property in Ontario. *Re Cameron*[116] was a case turning upon the application of the rule in the *Earl of Chesterfield's Trusts* [case] regarding the appointment between income and capital and insofar as conversion of real property was concerned it resulted not from the operation of any rule of equity but from the direction in the will to set apart the sum of $50,000 out of the estate; *Re Clarke; Toronto Gen. Trust Corp. v. Clarke*[117] was a case where the will gave a power to sell both real and personal property; *Re Pime*[118] was a case where the will provided an express duty to convert real and personal property; *Re Pears (No. 1)*[119] was a case where the will gave a power to convert the residue with a power to postpone leaving no room for the application of the rule; *Re Rutherford*[120] was a case where the will gave an express duty to convert. A further case mentioned in argument, *Re Bingham*,[121] adds no force to the contention that the rule has been applied in Ontario, for a direction in the will in that case authorized the conversion of "so much of my property as may be necessary for the purpose of carrying into effect the provisions of this my will." These cases are not illustrations of the application of the rule in *Howe v. Lord Dartmouth* requiring the conversion of real property. In each case the conversion, insofar as it applied to real property, resulted from a direction in the will. These cases all deal with the apportionment between capital and income of the proceeds of such conversion and, insofar as they depart from older authority, they do so by applying principles of apportionment of the nature applied in *Re Earl Chesterfield's Trusts*, to the proceeds of real property contrary to the law in that regard in England: see *Re Woodhouse; Public Trustee v. Woodhouse*.[122]

The question then arises whether new ground should be broken here and whether the operation of the rule in *Howe v. Lord Dartmouth* should be extended to real property. Wilson J.A.'s views are expressed in her judgment and reproduced above. I am not, however persuaded that we should on this point venture into the field of judicial legislation so boldly. To begin with, the restriction of the rule in *Howe v. Lord Dartmouth* to personal property is itself a rule of long standing. It must be presumed that those engaged in the preparation of wills and the settlement of trusts under wills know and understand, and have known and understood, its operation and effect and have planned and set in motion many trusts under wills upon the premise that the rule will continue to apply in relation to personal estate but not real estate. Great inconvenience could be caused to many existing trust arrangements by a sudden extension and, in my view, this is not a step which should be taken in this fashion. This is not to say that old rules may never be changed, but rules dealing with estate administration of this nature should not be changed unless there is a positive reason for so doing. In such case,

---

116 (1901), 2 O.L.R. 756 (Q.B.).
117 (1903), 6 O.L.R. 551 (Chambers).
118 (1924), 25 O.W.N. 522 (H.C.).
119 (1926), 31 O.W.N. 235 (C.A.).
120 [1933] O.R. 707, [1933] 4 D.L.R. 222 (C.A.).
121 66 O.L.R. 121, [1931] 1 D.L.R. 248 (C.A.).
122 [1941] Ch. D. 332, [1941] 2 All E.R. 265.

it should be done by the Legislature which at the same time has the power to enact the necessary transition and protective provisions to avoid interference with existing trusts and with rights and obligations acquired and undertaken upon the reasonableness expectation that there would be some degree of certainty in the law.

Furthermore, it should be borne in mind that we are here dealing with equitable rules relating to estate administration and not with dependent's relief legislation which enables a court to alter testamentary provisions in order to do justice between the testator and members of his family. Other legislative provisions deal with such matters and in Ontario may be found in the *Succession Law Reform Act, 1977*.[123] Courts must not twist rules such as that expressed in the case of *Howe v. Lord Dartmouth* to interfere with testamentary dispositions for the purpose of remedying supposed injustice. I would not extend the rule beyond its present limits. Such a step should be left to the Legislature when and if it should consider it advisable.

In view of the foregoing, it is unnecessary to deal with the questions raised as to whether the real property in question is productive or wasting.

The remaining point involves the claim by the widow for what may be termed a notional income in the form of a percentage of the value of the unconverted real property. The case of *Re Lauer and Stekl* is relied upon to support this claim. *Re Lauer and Stekl* cannot assist the widow here. In that case, the trustees were under a duty to convert all the assets of the estate, with a power of postponement. That case held that in such a situation the life-tenant was entitled to a notional income-based on a percentage of the value of the unconverted real property during the period of postponement. It has no operation here where there is no duty upon the trustees to convert the realty and, therefore, the rights of the widow, subject to any power in the trustees to encroach upon capital of the estate for her benefit, are limited to the receipt of the actual income earned by the real property.

[The Court allowed the appeal.]

Notes and Questions

1. Which approach in *Lottman* is preferable, that of the majority of the Ontario Court of Appeal or that of the Supreme Court of Canada?

2. Is the reason the court gives in *Lottman* for not changing the rule a good one? Note that the court has on other occasions interfered with the established rules of property law, even when there were substantial policy questions involved.[124]

3. Why should the Court have declined to change the rule in the *Lottman* case when, in *Lauer v. Stekl*,[125] it had imposed a duty to apportion unproductive real property under

---

123 (Ont.), S.O. 1977, c. 40, particularly ss. 64 to 88.

124 See, for example, *Pettkus v. Becker*, [1980] 2 S.C.R. 834, 19 R.F.L. (2d) 165, 8 E.T.R. 143, 34 N.R. 384, 117 D.L.R. (3d) 257.

125 (1974), 47 D.L.R. (3d) 286 (B.C. C.A.), affirmed [1976] 1 S.C.R. 781. But, see *Ball v. Ball-Ryder* (1997), 17 E.T.R. (2d) 63 (Ont. Gen. Div.) in which the trust instrument conferred

an express trust for conversion, thereby departing from the English rule? As a result there is now the further anomaly that unproductive realty must be apportioned if there is an express trust for sale, but not if there is no such trust.[126]

4. A trust held certain real property, which generated most of the income paid to the life-tenant, and an interest in a mortgage in land. The mortgage went into default and the mortgagees foreclosed. They held onto the land until they received an adequate offer. During this period, the asset earned no income for the trust. When the property was sold, the life-tenant claimed that the sale proceeds should be apportioned. The Ontario Court of Appeal held that the rule in *Howe v. Lord Dartmouth* applied because the property at issue was a mortgage, which is personalty and not real property. As such, the even-hand rule applied. The trustees breached their duty by failing to obtain a reasonable income from the property. They should have converted this unproductive asset.[127]

5. Is the even-hand rule affected when the trust owns depreciable property?

It has always been the rule that if the trustees are carrying on a business authorized by the trust they may, and perhaps should, establish a depreciation reserve from income payable to a life tenant in accordance with good business accounting practices.[128] The reason for setting up a depreciation reserve is that a life tenant, who is to receive income from a business in fact receives the profits from the business and profit is not determined until after the depreciation allowance has been made. If the trustees fail to establish a depreciation reserve, they may be liable in an action by those who hold the remainder interest and who would benefit from such a reserve. Until recently, however, the cases held that a depreciation reserve is not proper if the trust is not carrying on a business.[129] In those circumstances the testator was presumed to have intended the life-tenant to receive the actual income from the property.

However, in *Re Zive*,[130] Hart J. held that a depreciation reserve should be established in respect of income-producing real property even though no business was being carried on if the assets are depreciating to the point that those holding the remainder interest are suffering an actual disadvantage compared with the life-tenant. The basis of the decision was the even-hand rule even though the strict conversion and apportionment rules were expressly excluded by the testator.

The Zive estate contained a large number of rental properties. The trustees were under a duty to convert, but had a power to retain. They chose to retain most of the properties under an arrangement between the life-tenants and those entitled in remainder. The trustees retained part of the income for the first four years of the trust in order to pay taxes and

---

a power to convert real property, but did not impose a duty to convert. The court compared the trust instrument with that in the *Lauer v. Stekl* case.

126　See further Smith, "Does the Trustee's 'Duty of Impartiality' Extend to Real Property" (1981), 59 Can. Bar Rev. 687; Hogg, "Trusts — Life Tenants and Remaindermen — 'Even Hand' rule — Rule in *Howe v. Earl of Dartmouth* — non-applicability to real property in Ontario" (1981), 5 E. & T.Q. 181.

127　See *Josephs v. Canada Trust Co.* (sub nom. *Josephs v. Josephs Estate*) (1992), 90 D.L.R. (4th) 242, 7 O.R. (3d) 403, 45 E.T.R. 162, 52 O.A.C. 254 (Gen. Div.), reversed (1993), 15 O.R. (3d) 319, 106 D.L.R. (4th) 384 (C.A.).

128　See *Chartered Trust Co. v. Robertson*, [1953] 2 S.C.R. 1, [1953] C.T.C. 444, [1953] 4 D.L.R. 225, 1953 CarswellOnt 126; *Hunter, Re*, [1958] N.Z.L.R. 654.

129　See *Re Hunter, ibid.*; *Re Lauer and Stekl*, 40 D.L.R. 407, [1973] 6 W.W.R. 249 (B.C. S.C.), reversed [1974] 6 W.W.R. 490, 47 D.L.R. (3d) 286 (B.C. C.A.), affirmed [1976] 1 S.C.R. 781, [1976] 2 W.W.R. 382, 16 N.R. 559, 54 D.L.R. (3d) 159n.

130　(1977), 26 N.S.R. (2d) 651, 40 A.P.R. 651, 77 D.L.R. (3d) 669 (T.D.), noted (1977), 4 E. & T.Q. 1.

other debts and this enabled them to retain most of the properties. In return they claimed capital cost allowance and allocated it to the life-tenants so that they would not have to pay income tax on the income retained by the trustees. They continued this practice after the life-tenants began to receive the full income. The trustees then applied to the court to determine whether they should set up a depreciation account.

Hart J. held that such a reserve should be established and charged annually against the revenue account, since current maintenance did not cover the deterioration of the properties. His Lordship further held that the allocation of capital cost allowance to the income beneficiaries, while proper for income tax purposes under which they get the advantage of a tax shelter, was not proper under trust law and it is the latter, specifically the even-hand rule, that governs. The problem arises because when the properties are sold there is a real possibility that there will be a recapture of capital cost allowance (which represents income tax saved by the life-tenants) and that would result in a loss to those entitled in remainder. The depreciation reserve should, therefore, be held by the trustees to provide for a possible later recapture. The trustees were also required to recover from the life-tenants 50% of the capital cost allowance previously allocated to them less interest on the income they left in the trust during its first four years. The trustees could do so either by withholding income or requiring the life-tenants to give security for the purpose.

6. *Re Katz*[131] represents, in some respects, a retrenchment from *Re Zive*. Although the Katz will contained no express trust to convert, Maloney J. appears to have concluded that the trustees were under a duty to convert. The trustees were given an express power to retain. The strict conversion and apportionment rules were excluded, including, therefore, the extension of those rules in *Lauer v. Stekl*. The income-producing real estate was not as large as in *Zive* but had appreciated greatly in value. The trustees established a depreciation reserve which reduced the life-tenant's income from almost 7% to approximately 4.5% in three years. When she objected, the trustees sought the advice of the court.

Maloney J. held that in the absence of an express or implied power to establish a depreciation reserve, because the trustees were not carrying on a business, because of the increased value of the properties, and because in the circumstances the life-tenant would lose substantial income, the trustees should not have established the reserve. Indeed, the even-hand rule precluded it.

7. Which of the two decisions, *Zive* or *Katz*, is preferable?

8. See A.H. Oosterhoff, "The Application of the Rule in *Howe v. Earl of Dartmouth* to Residuary Real Property"[132] for additional reading on this topic.

(ii) *Corporate Distributions*

In general, when trustees make prudent investment choices, few difficulties arise over the question whether a particular receipt represents income or capital. However, when the receipt comes in the form of a capital distribution, the classification of the receipt as income or capital may not be readily apparent. The creator of the trust is free to stipulate who is to receive any particular kind of corporate distribution. Alternatively, the settlor or testator can authorize the trustees to allocate corporate distributions in their discretion, subject to their duty of impartiality. Failing such directions, the courts have laid down rules for deter-

---

131 (1980), 29 O.R. (2d) 81, 112 D.L.R. (3d) 529, 7 E.T.R. 222 (Ont. H.C.), noted (1981), E. & T.Q. 195 and 277.

132 (1980), 5 E. & T.Q. 127.

mining entitlement. As *Re Waters*,[133] below, illustrates, dividends or other money payments are treated as income for the benefit of the life-tenants. If, however, corporate profits are retained and capitalized, any distributions therefrom must be treated as capital which are for the benefit of the holders of the remainder interest. Thus, stock dividends, bonus shares and the right to purchase stock are all classified as capital.

RE WATERS

[1956] S.C.R. 889, [1956] C.T.C. 217,
56 D.T.C. 1113, 4 D.L.R. (2d) 673
Supreme Court of Canada

An estate held a substantial interest in a limited company which had a large undistributed surplus on hand. In order to pass it on to the shareholders, the company paid a tax of 15% on the surplus and capitalized the rest by issuing redeemable preference shares. Some of the shares were redeemed and the proceeds were received tax-free by the former shareholders under s. 95 of *The Income Tax Act*.[134] The question was whether the estate received the shares and the proceeds upon redemption as income or as capital. At first instance and on appeal to the Ontario Court of Appeal, it was held that they were received as capital.

RAND J.:

The question here is between a life-tenant and a remainderman whose interests are in shares of the capital stock of a company incorporated under the Ontario *Companies Act*. The dispute arises through the fact that at the death of the testator the company had accumulated a large amount of earnings which thereafter were capitalized into redeemable preference stock over the beneficial ownership of which the issue is joined.

The nature of a life interest in property depends upon the kind of property. If land, it will be possession and use or income of rents; if money or obligations, it will be income or interest; where the asset is common stock of a commercial company, the income consists of dividends. The large amount of accumulated earnings, in this case, was, at the death, reflected in the value of the stock; the testator might have made it clear that the shares, in the value based on the assets then existing, were to be treated as capital and the income thereafter to be related to subsequent earnings only; but he did not do that; what he did was to bequeath the "income."

The question, in such circumstances, of what is income has been before the courts in a number of cases and the principles applicable have been considered in both the House of Lords and the Judicial Committee. From them the following

---

133 [1956] S.C.R. 889, [1956] C.T.C. 217, 56 D.T.C. 1113, 4 D.L.R. (2d) 673.
134 S.C. 1948, c. 52 (enacted S.C. 1950, c. 40, s. 32).

considerations, among others, emerge. A joint stock company, having modern powers and, in the absence of special provisions, bound to the preservation in its capital asset structure of property representing its share capital, is in absolute control of the profits which its business produces. They may be distributed as dividends, kept in reserves, applied to restore lost capital assets or be capitalized by appropriating them as assets representing or fulfilling payment of unpaid existing or newly issued share capital.

In *Hill v. Permanent Trustee Co. of New South Wales*,[135] Lord Russell of Killowen summarizes some settled propositions dealing with payments of money to shareholders and speaks of the "capitalization" of accumulated profits as follows:

> (4.) Other considerations arise when a limited company with power to increase its capital and possessing a fund of undivided profits, so deals with it that no part of it leaves the possession of the company, but the whole is applied in paying up new shares which are issued and allotted proportionately to the shareholders, who would have been entitled to receive the fund had it been, in fact, divided and paid away as dividend.

And:[136]

> Their Lordships desire to adopt the language used by Eve J., and to say in regard to the funds out of which the sums of $19,380 and $8,360 were paid by the Buttabone Company to the trustee company: "Unless and until the fund was in fact capitalized it retained its characteristics of a distributable property ... no charge in the character of the fund was brought about by the company's expressed intention to distribute it as capital. It remained an uncapitalized surplus available for distribution either as dividend or bonus on the shares, or as a special division of an ascertained profit . . . and in the hands of those who received it in retained the same characteristics.

Knowledge of that control over this type of property is to be attributed to the testator: it is with this actually or imputedly in mind that he confers the life interest: he knows or is held to know that the receipt of income or capital will depend on the acts of the company.

When accumulated earnings are capitalized, the precise theory according to which the transformation takes place is by no means clear. If a dividend has been declared which the shareholder has the option of receiving either in cash or in paid up new shares, the latter alternative is to be deemed to consist of two steps: the creation of a real credit in the amount of the dividend to the shareholder, a debt owing by the company to him; and the application of that debt by way of release as payment for the new stock. The right to receive the dividend and its constructive receipt constitute a payment of income to the shareholder which belongs to the life-tenant to whom the substituted stock goes as to a purchaser. On this stock he will be liable to tax as for income: *Swan Brewery Co. v. R.*[137]

On the other hand, the capitalization of the accumulation directly without the option of a dividend presents difficulty in theoretical conception. In substance the

---

135 [1930] A.C. 721 at 731, [1930] All E.R. Rep. 87 (P.C.).
136 *Ibid.*, at 735.
137 [1914] A.C. 231 (P.C.).

interest of the shareholder represented by the original stock merely changes its form; from being X percentage of Y it becomes X plus A percentage of Y plus B. Nothing is withdrawn from the company and no immediate additional value passes to the shareholder. The company by declaration appropriates an asset available for dividends to the capital asset structure and creates for the shareholder a new capital stockholding, with the same fractional interest in a new total capital asset as before.

In *Bouch v. Sproule*,[138] the question was considered. Although the reasons, following the facts, are less than assured on the matter of an alternative right to elect for the dividend, they seem to me to hold that what was to be determined was the intention of the company as that was evidenced by its corporate acts interpreted in the total circumstances. Lord Herschell says:[139]

> I cannot, therefore, avoid the conclusion that the substance of the whole transaction was, and was intended to be, to convert the undivided profits into paid-up capital upon newly-created shares.
>
> Upon the whole, then, I am of opinion that the company did not pay, or intend to pay, any sum as dividend, but intended to and did appropriate the undivided profits dealt with as an increase of the capital stock in the concern.

Lord Watson [says]:[140]

> But in a case like the present, where the company has power to determine whether profits reserved, and temporarily devoted to capital purposes, shall be distributed as dividend or permanently added to its capital, the interest of the life-tenant depends, in my opinion, upon the decision of the company.

And:[141]

> In these circumstances it was undoubtedly within the power of the company, by raising new capital to the required amount, to set free the sums thus spent out of the reserve fund and undivided profits for distribution among the shareholders. It was equally within the power of the company to capitalize these sums by issuing new shares against them to its members in proportion to their several interests. I am of opinion that the latter alternative was, in substance, that which was followed by the company.

And:[142]

> If I am right in my conclusion the substantial bonus which was meant to be given to each shareholder was not a money payment but a proportional share of the increased capital of the company.

In the present case a new element is introduced by the provisions of the *Income Tax Act* as amended, enabling a company by paying a tax, in this case 15

---

138 (1887), 12 App. Cas. 385 (H.L.).
139 *Ibid.*, at 399.
140 *Ibid.*, at 401.
141 *Ibid.*, at 402-403.
142 *Ibid.*, at 405.

per cent, on earnings accumulated up to 1949, to capitalize the remaining fund by the issue of a stock dividend free from income tax in the hands of the shareholders. The earnings, if distributed as dividends, would have been taxable. This power furnishes a means by which, through the issue, as authorized by the appropriate company law, of redeemable preference shares, an amount of money equal to that of the earnings converted will reach the shareholders by the redemption; the nature of that payment, capital or income, will depend on the proper interpretation of what the company has done.

. . .

I take the principle laid down to be that unless the earnings as such actually or constructive pass from the company to the shareholder there is, for all purposes, capitalization. But the argument is that the machinery of capitalization and redemption can be used to effect a transfer of the earnings as such to the shareholders.

Here, the retention of the preferred shares as part of the capital stock is sufficient of itself to negative the conclusion that the shares belong to the life interest as dividends: but I have reached the same conclusion on a broader ground.

When earnings are "capitalized," they cease at that moment to be "earnings"; they become part of the capital assets; and if the transaction has not the elements of dividend and purchase, they *prima facie*, are not income. Mr. Henderson urged very plausibly that the company's intention was to release those earning and pass them to the shareholders as such in a single act consisting of several parts. The fallacy lies in overlooking what has taken place. The company undoubtedly intends by its total act to pass money to the shareholders; but if what the company does converts the earnings into capital, the "intention" of the company must take account of the fact; it "intends" the fact; and to carry the intention to a conclusion it intends to distribute capital assets by means of an authorized reduction in capital stock. Here form is substance; and the moment form has changed the character of the earnings as assets, the intention follows that change.

In the absence of a statutory provision, a stock dividend, so called, would not appear to be "income"; and the exemption from taxation provided for the shares here simply suspends the provision of the *Income Tax Act* imposing tax. From the standpoint of tax, it is indifferent to the company and the shareholder whether the ultimate receipt of money is capital or income; in neither case is it taxable. But its form is fixed and determined; and in the absence of special directions in the will, we are not at liberty to disregard what the testator is to be deemed to have foreseen as the possible action of the company.

[The Court dismissed the appeal.]

Notes and Questions

1. It is open to a testator to stipulate that the proceeds of redeemable preference shares be treated as income, not capital.[143]

---

143   *Re Carson*, [1963] 1 O.R. 373, 37 D.L.R. (2d) 292 (H.C.).

2. The Ontario Law Reform Commission has recommended that statutory provision should be made to permit trustees, in their discretion, to allocate receipts (including corporate distributions) between income and capital.[144]

3. In *Royal Trust v. Crawford*,[145] dividends of approximately $325,000 were treated partly as interest and partly as capital. On construction of the will, the court held that the life-tenant was not meant to take all income *in specie* and therefore could not take the full amount of the dividends as income.

4. Consider the following situations.

(a) A $20,000 dividend is paid from an undistributed surplus. Is the dividend interest or capital?

(b) A company redeems preference shares from undistributed income. Are the proceeds of redemption income or capital?

(c) Dividends are paid on common shares but out of a tax paid surplus. Do such dividends constitute income or capital?[146]

5. In *Waters*, the distribution was of capital, not income, despite the original intention of the company. The manner in which the original desired result is carried out is important and has legal implications because it may determine the legal effect of the transaction. The original intention may therefore be superseded and therefore be irrelevant. In *Fehr v. Fehr*[147] the Manitoba Court of Appeal recently adopted the same reasoning.

(c) Allocation of Outgoings

Ideally, the trust instrument will specify whose beneficial interest is to bear what expenses. If the document does not expressly stipulate how outgoings are to be allocated, the trustees must look for the settlor's or testator's implied intention — an exercise which can lead to difficult questions of construction. If the intention is still unclear after construction, the trustees must turn to the common law for guidance.

The general rule is that outgoings which relate to the income of a trust are borne by the income beneficiaries whereas expenses of a capital nature are borne by those with the remainder interest. Examples of the former kinds of expenses are taxes, insurance, and ongoing repairs to property. Expenses which fall into the latter category are the costs of major improvements to trust property and expenses related to the administration of the trust. Of course, if certain costs related to the administration of the trust are related exclusively to the life-tenant's interest, then his or her interest is made to bear such expenses. Administration costs are *prima facie* allocated to those entitled to the remainder because, by using capital to meet such costs, the life-tenant loses income which would have been produced by the expended capital and so he or she indirectly shares the burden.

---

144 Ont. Law Ref. Comm. Report at p. 299. The OLRC's recommendations were recently incorporated in the British Columbia Law Institute Report on *Total Return Investing by Trustees*, B.C.L.I. Report No. 16, August 2001.

145 [1955] S.C.R. 184, [1955] 2 D.L.R. 225.

146 See *Re Fleming* (1973), 37 D.L.R. (3d) 512, [1973] 3 O.R. 588 (H.C.), and note by R.E. Scane (1973-74), 1 E. & T.Q. 105.

147 [2003] M.J. No. 154, 2003 CarswellMan 182, 40 R.F.L. (5th) 71, 177 Man. R. (2d) 1, 304 W.A.C. 1, 2003 MBCA 68, [2003] 8 W.W.R. 440 (C.A.).

It should be apparent that the speed with which debts are paid will directly affect the amount that is paid to the life-tenant. A simple example will illustrate this point. If an estate has assets of $10,000 and debts of $5,000, immediate payment of the debts means that the life-tenant receives the income from only $5,000, whereas if payment is deferred for a year, the life-tenant will receive income on the full $10,000. The rule in *Allhusen v. Whittel*[148] is designed to alleviate this problem by striking a balance between the life-tenant and the holders of the remainder interest with respect to the payment of debts out of residue. The rule charges the life-tenant with interest on the amount later used to pay debts so that the life-tenant is placed in the same position as if the debts had been paid on death. Thus, the rule requires calculation of the average income of the estate from the date of death to the date of payment, taken net after deduction of income tax. The life-tenant is charged with interest so that when the debt is paid, it is partly from income and partly from capital.

The difficulties in making such calculations should be apparent. For that reason, some jurisdictions have ousted the rule except when it is expressly invoked by the settlor or testator. Section 49 of the Ontario *Trustee Act*[149] is representative of such legislation.

TRUSTEE ACT

R.S.O. 1990, c. T.23

49. (1) Unless a contrary intention appears from the will,

(a) the personal representative of a deceased person, in paying the debts, funeral and testamentary expenses, estate, legacy, succession and inheritance taxes or duties, legacies, or other similar disbursements, shall not apply or be deemed to have applied any income of the estate in or towards the payment of any part of the capital of any such disbursements or of any part of the interest, if any, due thereon at the date of death of such person;

(b) until the payment of the debts, funeral and testamentary expenses, estate, legacy, succession and inheritance taxes or duties, legacies, or other similar disbursements mentioned in clause (a), the income from the property required for the payment thereof, with the exception of any part of such income applied in the payment of any interest accruing due thereon after the date of death of the deceased, shall be treated and applied as income of the residuary estate,

---

148 (1867), L.R. 4 Eq. 295, 36 L.J. Ch. 929 (Eng. Ch.). For a consideration of the rule in Canada, see *Lotzkar v. Lotzkar Estate* (1965), [1966] S.C.R. 69, 54 D.L.R. (2d) 47, 1965 CarswellBC 192. The Supreme Court of Canada found that the rule did not apply because the provisions in the will indicated that the testator intended that the rule should not apply. He designated a specific capital fund for the payment of debts and succession duties. The terms of the will therefore displaced the application of the rule.

149 R.S.O. 1990, c. T.23.

but, in any case where the assets of the estate are not sufficient to pay the disbursements in full, the income shall be applied in making up such deficiency.

(2) Subsection 1 shall be deemed always to have been part of the law of Ontario.

(3) Notwithstanding subsections 1 and 2, in any case in which the personal representative has before the coming into force of this section applied any rule of law or of administration different from the provisions of subsection 1, such application is valid and effective.

Comparable Legislation

Trustee Act, R.S.B.C. 1996, c. 464, s. 10; R.S.M. 1987, c. T160, s. 32.

Notes and Questions

1. A trust invests in a mortgage security. How should losses arising from the investment be allocated?[150]

2. If trust property is mortgaged to raise money for repairs and improvements, how should the burden of repayment be allocated?

3. If a business is carried on as part of the trust property, how should annual losses and profits be treated?

4. Whose interest should bear the cost of an audit?

5. The Ontario Law Reform Commission has recommended that the courts be empowered to confer additional administrative powers on trustees and to direct how costs involved in the exercise of powers are to be allocated.[151]

6. The Commission has recommended also that powers be conferred on trustees to determine, in their discretion, the equitable allocation of outgoings. Such discretion is to be exercised in accordance with the general standard of care. This recommendation is based on the fact that existing case law rules may be ambiguous, conflicting, inflexible, or nonexistent.[152]

7. Under s. 21(1) of the Ontario *Trustee Act*[153] the costs of insuring property (up to three-fourths of the value of the property) are to be paid from income. There is comparable legislation in all Canadian jurisdictions except Prince Edward Island.

8. When an estate has insufficient funds to pay testamentary gifts, the gifts abate in the following order: (1) residuary personalty; (2) the residuary (not specifically devised) real property; (3) general bequests; (4) demonstrative bequests; (5) specific bequests; (6) specifically devised real property.[154]

---

150 See *Re Plumb* (1896), 27 O.R. 601 (H.C.) and *Re Moore* (1885), 54 L.J. Ch. 432; *Toronto General Trusts Corp. v. Clarke* (1903), 6 O.L.R. 551 (H.C.).

151 Ont. Law Ref. Comm. Report at p. 265. See also the British Columbia Law Institute *Report on Statutory Powers of Delegation by Trustees*, July 2000.

152 *Ibid.*, at 268.

153 R.S.O. 1990, c. T.23.

154 *Legge Estate, Re*, 203 N.S.R. (2d) 1, 2001 CarswellNS 395, 2001 NSSC 156, 635 A.P.R. 1 (Prob. Ct.).

7. THE DUTY TO ACCOUNT AND TO PROVIDE INFORMATION

(a) The Duty to Account

Trustees must keep proper accounts of how they deal with the trust property; as well, they must be ready to produce them for inspection and examination by the beneficiaries.[155] However, as *Sandford v. Porter*,[156] below, illustrates, while beneficiaries have a right to inspect the accounts, the trustee is allowed a reasonable time to assemble the accounts after the beneficiary requests them. If a trustee causes expense through neglect or refusal to furnish accounts, the trustee must bear the expense personally.[157]

Trustees may pass accounts in the manner stipulated by the trust instrument. In the absence of such express provisions, trustees may pass accounts in accordance with statute. An example of such legislation is s. 23 of the Ontario *Trustee Act*,[158] set out below. Note that the legislation makes the procedure that trustees must follow the same as that for passing executors' and administrators' accounts. Thus, the application must contain an inventory of the trust property, an account showing what the original estate consisted of, an account of all money received and disbursed, an account of all property remaining, a statement of the compensation requested and such other accounts as the court may require.[159]

SANDFORD v. PORTER

(1889), 16 O.A.R. 565
Ontario Court of Appeal

A creditor demanded copies of the accounts of the assignee of a debtor. He then brought an action for an account against the assignee. However, the creditor did not express any desire or make any attempt to inspect the accounts and did not wait a reasonable time for the preparation of copies of the accounts.

MacLennan J.A.:

. . .

I do not think there was anything here that could properly be called misconduct. The litigation in which the trustee was involved ended about the 1st of April.

---

155 A trustee will not be reimbursed for the cost of preparing accounts nor for certain legal fees. See *Re Carley Estate* (1994), 2 E.T.R. (2d) 142 (Ont. Gen. Div.), additional reasons at (1994), 4 E.T.R. (2d) 102 (Ont. Gen. Div.).

156 (1889), 16 O.A.R. 565 (C.A.).

157 *Re Smith*, [1952] O.W.N. 62 (H.C.), reversed on other grounds [1952] O.W.N. 170 (C.A.).

158 R.S.O. 1990, c. T.23 (am. by S.O. 2000, c. 26, Sched. A, s. 15(2)).

159 See, for example, *Estates Act*, R.S.O. 1990, E.21, ss. 48-50 (s. 49 am. by S.O. 1997, c. 23, s. 8(2), which repealed s. 49(5)-(7)).

As the result of this litigation he obtained for the estate certain promissory notes which yielded a sum of $1,430, which constituted the greatest part of the assets which came to his hands. It does not appear how soon after the 1st of April this sum was recovered. On the 15th of May the plaintiffs' solicitors demanded an account for some clients, not saying for whom, and on the 18th they furnished the names. On the 25th they were told that a statement was being prepared and that it would be furnished in a few days; and again on the 2nd of June they were told that the costs due by the estate were being revised, without which the statement could not be sent, but that it would be sent in the same week. In spite of this information the plaintiffs commenced their action on the same day, the 2nd of June. The statement was delivered on the 7th. There was here certainly no culpable neglect by the trustee, no neglect at all that I can see. The plaintiffs' solicitors knew very well all about the litigation in which the trustee had been involved, for they had been the solicitors in the replevin action. They knew the principal item of the estate had only lately been recovered, and that there must be a large bill of costs to be adjusted. When therefore they were told that a statement was being prepared and would be ready in a few days, and again that the costs were being revised, and that they would have the statement was so delivered, I think there is not the slightest ground for saying that there was any culpable neglect by the trustee.

It seems to have been thought by the solicitors of the plaintiffs that it was the duty of a trustee, upon demand for an account, to lay aside everything else, and to sit down and make out an account for them, at the peril of a suit for an account and costs. But the law is not so unreasonable.

The duty of a trustee or other accounting party is to have his accounts always ready, to afford all reasonable facilities for inspection and examination, and to give full information whenever required; but as a general rule he is not obliged to prepared copies of his accounts for the parties interested. Cases may be imagined where it would be reasonable to require, and when it might be the duty of the trustee to furnish, statements of account, as, for example, when the *cestui que trust* or the principal lives at a distance from where the trust affairs are being carried on, or in a foreign country. In such a case it would be the duty of a trustee to give all reasonable information and explanations by letter; and even, if requested, but of course at the expense of the *cestui que trust*, to prepare and transmit accounts and statements. But every case must depend on its own circumstances, and must be governed by reason and common sense. Every one would see how unreasonable and absurd it would be to say it was the duty of an executor of a large estate which had been going on for a number of years, to furnish, on demand, to a person interested, it might be in only a small share of the residue, a copy of the estate accounts. In such a case the accounts might fill one or more large ledgers, and other usual books of account. In such a case the legatee is interested in, and entitled to see and examine, all the entries from first to last. He may examine them and take copies or extracts and he is entitled to reasonable explanation from the trustee of whatever requires explanation, but he cannot require the trustee to make copies and extracts for him. Mr. Holman cited *Kemp v. Burn*[160] as an authority for the proposition, that a trustee was bound, on demand, to prepare and deliver accounts to his *cestui que trust*, and that if he did not do so, he would be made to pay the costs of a suit for an account. But that was a case in which the trustee refused to allow the solicitor for the *cestui que trust* to see the accounts, because he thought he wanted them for some ulterior object of his own and not in the interest of his client, and it was held he was not justified in such refusal.

The true rule, as I understand it, is laid down by Mr. Lewin, *Law of Trusts*[161] where he says,

> The *cestui que trust* has a right to call upon the trustee for accurate information as to the state of the trust. Thus in a trust for sale and payment of debts, the party entitled subject to the trust may say to the trustees, what estates have you sold? What is the amount of the moneys raised? What debts have been paid? etc. It is, therefore, the bounden duty of the trustee to keep clear and distinct accounts of the property he administers and he exposes himself to great risks by the omission. It is the first duty of an accounting party to be constantly ready with his accounts.

No doubt expressions are used in some of the cases indicating that it is a trustee's duty to render accounts. But I have found no case in which it was distinctly laid down, that the rendering of an account meant the preparation by the trustee of a copy of a trust account, and its delivery to the *cestui que trust*. There is, however, clear authority the other way.

. . .

TRUSTEE ACT

R.S.O. 1990, c. T.23

Passing of Accounts

23. (1) A trustee desiring to pass the accounts of dealings with the trust estate may file the accounts in the office of the Ontario Court (General Division), and the proceedings and practice upon the passing of such accounts shall be the same and have the like effect as the passing of executors' or administrators' accounts in the court.

(2) Where the compensation payable to a trustee has not been fixed by the instrument creating the trust or otherwise, the judge upon the passing of the accounts of the trustee has power to fix the amount of compensation payable to the trustee and the trustee is thereupon entitled to retain out of any money held the amount so determined.

---

160 4 Giff. 348.
161 8th ed., at 691.

Comparable Legislation

Trustee Act, R.S.A. 2000, c. T-8, ss. 14-15 (am. by R.S.A. 2000, c. 16 (Supp.), s. 59(c)); R.S.B.C. 1996, c. 464, s. 99; R.S.M. 1987, c. T160, ss. 85-88.

(b) The Duty to Provide Information

Trustees must regularly give beneficiaries accurate and full information and explanations of the state of the trust. They must also make available trust documents for inspection by the beneficiaries.[162] However, traditionally, they were not required to give their reasons for making a decision involving the exercise of their discretion.[163] English courts have extended this rule into the pension trusts area. *Wilson v. Law Debenture Trust Corp.*[164] is an example. A company sold a division and the affected employees transferred to the purchaser. The vendor company's pension plan was funded through a trust. The trust deed provided that the trustees were to transfer such of the trust assets as they deemed appropriate to the purchaser's newly established pension plan. The trustees transferred an amount equal only to the past service reserve of the transferred employees, leaving the whole of the surplus in the vendor's plan. The employees sought disclosure of the documents that might indicate the trustees' reasons for making such a decision. The court refused the application, saying that the principles of trusts generally were to be applied to pension trusts and, in the absence of evidence of impropriety, the trustees were under no obligation to disclose documents containing evidence of their reasons for the manner in which they exercised their discretion. It is questionable whether the rule is appropriate in the pension trusts context.

The basis upon which beneficiaries are often said to be entitled to information and to inspect trust documents is that they are the actual owners of the trust property and the documents therefore belong to them. This conclusion is derived in part from a *dictum* of Lord Wrenbury in *O'Rourke v. Darbishire.*[165] The case is discussed in *Schmidt v. Rosewood Trust Ltd.,*[166] reproduced below. Modern cases have disputed the proprietary theory as the basis for access to information, as is evident from the *Schmidt* case.

The issue is often explored in the context of instruments containing discretionary trusts or powers of appointment. In neither of those do the beneficiaries have a property interest in the trust, so the question of the basis upon which the beneficiaries are entitled to information may be more problematic. Further, such instruments typically involve documents which relate to the administration of the trust and to the exercise of the trustee's discretion and it is often difficult to know

---

162 *Barkin v. Royal Trust Co.* (2002), [2002] O.J. No. 661, 2002 CarswellOnt 669, 45 E.T.R. (2d) 1 (S.C.J.), additional reasons at (2002), 2002 CarswellOnt 1237, 45 E.T.R. (2d) 8 (S.C.J.), additional reasons at (2002), 2002 CarswellOnt 1399, 45 E.T.R. (2d) 6 (S.C.J.). This right extends to contingent beneficiaries. See *Ballard Estate, supra*, note 26.
163 *Re Beloved Wilkes' Charity* (1851), 3 Mac. & G. 440, 42 E.R. 440.
164 [1995] 2 All E.R. 337 (Ch.).
165 [1920] A.C. 581, [1920] All E.R. Rep. 1 (H.L.) at 626-7 [A.C.].
166 [2003] UKPC 26 (March 27, 2003).

what, if any, documents a beneficiary is entitled to see. The issue arose in *Londonderry's Settlement, Re*,[167] which illustrates such difficulties. It involved a trust which empowered the trustees, with the consent of certain persons called "appointors", to distribute income among the members of a defined class of persons and, in default among the settlor's children, of whom the defendant was one. In addition, the trustees had power to appoint the capital during the lifetime of the last survivor of the class, with a trust in default of appointment to the settlor's next of kin. The trustees obtained advice from their solicitors and corresponded with the solicitors and the appointors. The defendant, who was dissatisfied with the amounts the trustees proposed to distribute to her, sought disclosure of a large number of documents. On the trustees' application for directions, the court held that the trustees were not bound to disclose:

(1) The agenda of the meetings of the trustees of the settlement, (2) correspondence passing between the individuals for the time being holding office as trustees of or appointors under the settlement, (3) correspondence passing between the said trustees and appointors or any of them on the one hand and the beneficiaries under the settlement on the other hand, and (4) minutes of meetings of the trustees or appointors and other documents disclosing the deliberations of the trustees as to the manner in which they should exercise the discretionary powers . . . or disclosing the reasons for any particular exercise of such powers or the material upon which such reasons were or might have been based.

However,

the trustees were bound to disclose to the defendant at her request any written advice from their solicitors or counsel as to the manner in which the trustees were in law entitled to exercise such powers.

Of the three judges on the appeal, Salmon L.J. took the view that the basis of disclosure is that the beneficiary is the owner of trust documents. *Londonderry* is also discussed in *Schmidt*.

SCHMIDT v. ROSEWOOD TRUST LTD.

[2003] UKPC 26 (March 27, 2003)[168]
Privy Council

The deceased, Vitali Schmidt, was, as the board concluded, co-settlor of two off-shore *inter vivos* trusts based in the Isle of Man, called the Angora Trust and the Everest Trust. Some US$105 million was settled on the two trusts. The defendant, Rosewood, was the trustee. The deceased was the senior executive director of Lukoil, the largest Russian oil company, and he apparently created the trusts with other executives from the company. In doing so they employed a

---

167 (1964), [1965] Ch. 918, [1964] 3 All E.R. 855, [1965] 2 W.L.R. 229, 108 Sol. Jo. 896 (C.A.).
168 http://www.privy-council.org.uk/files/other/vadim%20schmidt%20jud.rtf

variety of corporate vehicles to ensure secrecy. The purpose of such trusts is explained in the opening paragraphs of the judgment.

The deceased died unexpectedly and intestate. The appellant, his son, Vadim, was appointed his administrator. The appellant was entitled to share the estate with his mother and paternal grandmother. He believed that his efforts to trace his father's assets was being frustrated by some of his father's co-directors, so he brought proceedings in the Isle of Man in 1998 against Rosewood and others, alleging breach of trust and fiduciary duty and obtained an *ex parte* order requiring the defendants to make extensive disclosure of information. In 1999 he brought these proceedings by petition in which he alleged that the disclosure made in the 1998 proceedings was defective, and sought fuller disclosure, not by way of discovery in the 1998 proceedings, but in consequence of the discretionary interest he held under the trusts and that his father had. The appellant had been paid some US$14.6 million as his father's administrator pursuant to the 1998 proceedings, but did not accept that sum as a compromise of his claims and believed that it represented only a small fraction of what his father was entitled to under both trusts.

While there were some differences between the two trusts, the beneficiaries were The Royal National Lifeboat Institution ("RNLI")[169] and persons named in a schedule, who included the deceased and other Lukoil executives. The trusts contained wide powers of appointment, exercisable by the trustees with the consent of the protector (who was the deceased in one of the trusts). The Everest trust also contained a wide power to add beneficiaries. The objects of the powers were the named beneficiaries. Clause 4(2) provided that on the death of a beneficiary the trustee should hold the portion of the trust fund to which the deceased was entitled on trust for such persons as the deceased had notified the trustee in writing, failing which, for the closest relatives of the deceased. The deceased had in fact written to the trustees expressing his wish that on his death any portion of the trusts he might be entitled to should be held on trust for the appellant.

The appellant's petition was heard at first instance by Deemster Cain. The Deemster made an order requiring the trustee to make extensive disclosure of documents and to provide information. The trustee appealed to the Staff of Government Division. It allowed the appeal on the ground that the appellant was not a beneficiary under the two settlements and that his father was no more than a mere object of a power under the settlements and was, thus, not entitled to trust documents or information. The appellant appealed to the Privy Council.

The advice of the Board was delivered by LORD WALKER OF GESTING-THORPE:

---

169 It was purely a nominal beneficiary and would be replaced by the trustees in the exercise of their powers of appointment.

Introduction.

1. It has become common for wealthy individuals in many parts of the world (including countries which have no indigenous law of trusts) to place funds at their disposition into trusts (often with a network of underlying companies) regulated by the law of, and managed by trustees resident in, territories with which the settlor (who may be also a beneficiary) has no substantial connection. These territories (sometimes called tax havens) are chosen not for their geographical convenience (indeed face to face meetings between the settlor and his trustees are often very inconvenient) but because they are supposed to offer special advantages in terms of confidentiality and protection from fiscal demands (and, sometimes from problems under the insolvency laws, or laws restricting freedom of testamentary disposition, in the country of the settlor's domicile). The trusts and powers contained in a settlement established in such circumstances may give no reliable indication of who will in the event benefit from the settlement. Typically it will contain very wide discretions exercisable by the trustees (sometimes only with the consent of a so-called protector) in favour of a widely-defined class of beneficiaries. The exercise of those discretions may depend on the settlor's wishes as confidentially imparted to the trustees and the protector. As a further cloak against transparency, the identity of the true settlor or settlors may be concealed behind some corporate figurehead.

2. All these considerations may encourage a settlor to entrust substantial funds to an apparently secure and confidential off-shore shelter. But the very same features may, as this case strikingly illustrates, present problems to the close relatives of a settlor who dies unexpectedly . . .

[After describing the background to the litigation, the terms of the trusts, and certain constructional difficulties, his Lordship discussed the significant ways in which settlements have changed in the twentieth century. The changes were largely driven by high rates of taxation. In addition, modern trusts typically confer wide discretions on the trustees. These take the form of either discretionary trusts or mere powers. In consequence, courts have had to wrestle with the rights of beneficiaries under such discretionary trusts and the rights of donees of mere powers. His Lordship discussed *McPhail v. Doulton*[170] in which the House of Lords applied the certainty test that applies to powers to discretionary trusts. Lord Wilberforce in that case noted that the distinction between discretionary trusts and mere powers is narrow and artificial and that the validity of a disposition should not depend on whether one classifies the disposition as a discretionary trust or as a mere power.

Lord Walker then went on to discuss the differences between powers of appointment and discretionary trusts. These differences were addressed elsewhere in this book.[171] He continued:]

170 [1971] A.C. 424 (H.L.). This case is discussed in ch. 4.
171 In chs. 3 and 4.

Disclosure to discretionary beneficiaries: a proprietary basis?

43. Much of the debate before the Board addressed the question whether a beneficiary's right or claim to disclosure of trust documents should be regarded as a proprietary right. Mr Brownbill argued that it should be classified in that way, and from that starting point he argued that no object of a mere power could have any right or claim to disclosure, because he had no proprietary interest in the trust property. Mr. Brownbill submitted that this point has been conclusively settled by the decision of the House of Lords in *O'Rourke v Darbishire*.[172] It is therefore useful to go straight to that case to see what it did decide.

44. The facts of the case were unusual. Sir Joseph Whitworth, a man of considerable wealth, had died in 1887. In 1884 he had made a will appointing three executors and leaving his residuary estate to charity. By a codicil made in 1885 he altered his will to leave his ultimate residue to his executors for their own benefit, with a precatory expression of his wishes that it should be used for charitable purposes. Two further codicils executed in 1886 extended the scope of the first codicil's gift to the executors. Sir Joseph's intestate successors would have been Mrs Uniacke (as to realty) and Mrs Uniacke and Mrs McGowan (as to personalty). Mrs McGowan threatened to challenge the will and codicils, but in 1889 there was a compromise between all interested parties. Then in 1916, after Mrs Uniacke, Mrs McGowan and the executors had all died, Mrs Uniacke's administrator (Mr O'Rourke) sought to challenge both the will and codicils and the compromise, alleging fraud by Mr Darbishire (who was one of the executors and had been Sir Joseph's solicitor). Mr O'Rourke sought to obtain disclosure of documents containing legal advice given to Sir Joseph during his lifetime, and to his executors after his death.

45. The House of Lords dismissed Mr O'Rourke's appeal, primarily because he had not made out even a *prima facie* case that the will and codicils were invalid, or that the communications had been promoting fraud. Viscount Finlay[173] referred to Mr O'Rourke's reliance on a "proprietary right" and Lord Sumner[174] referred to "what has been called the 'proprietary' ground". Lord Parmoor said:[175]

> A cestui que trust, in an action against his trustees, is generally entitled to the production for inspection of all documents relating to the affairs of the trust. It is not material for the present purpose whether this right is to be regarded as a paramount proprietary right in the cestui que trust, or as a right to be enforced under the law of discovery, since in both cases an essential preliminary is either the admission, or the establishment, of the status on which the right is based.

46. It is on what was said by Lord Wrenbury that Mr Brownbill most relied. Lord Wrenbury said:[176]

---

172 *Supra*, note 165.
173 At 603.
174 At 617.
175 At 619-20.
176 At 626-7.

If the plaintiff is right in saying that he is a beneficiary and if the documents are documents belonging to the executors as executors, he has a right to access to the documents which he desires to inspect upon what has been called in the judgments in this case a proprietary right. The beneficiary is entitled to see all trust documents because they are trust documents and because he is a beneficiary. They are in this sense his own. Action or no action, he is entitled to access to them. This has nothing to do with discovery. The right to discovery is a right to see someone else's documents. The proprietary right is a right to access to documents which are your own.

On the facts of the case, what Lord Wrenbury said was very apposite. If Mr O'Rourke was right in his claim, the executors had had no proper legal or equitable title to Sir Joseph's estate. The grant of probate to them should have been revoked and Mr O'Rourke (together with the representatives of Mrs McGowan) would have been entitled to the whole of the estate, including any documents which formed part of it.

. . .

48. In *In re Cowin*[177] a beneficiary with a vested future interest in one-eighth of a testator's residuary trust fund, subject to his mother's interest during widowhood, wished to mortgage his interest and for that reason sought inspection of the title deeds to the trust property. North J made an order for inspection but rejected the notion that the beneficiary had an absolute right. He quoted[178] from the then current edition of Lewin:[179]

All documents held by the trustee in that character must be produced by him to the *cestuis que trust*, who are in equity the true owners.

But North J clearly considered that the particular interest of an individual beneficiary might in some circumstances run counter to the collective interest of the beneficiaries as a body. He said:[180]

I do not say that he is entitled as of right, but only that he is entitled under the circumstances, because there might be a state of circumstances under which the right to production would not exist.

Chitty J took a similar approach in *In re Tillott*,[181] noting that a trustee is not bound to give a beneficiary information about a share in which he has no interest.

49. In *In re Londonderry's Settlement*[182] the Court of Appeal had to consider one of the most important limitations on the right to disclosure of trust documents, that is the need to protect confidentiality in communications between trustees as to the exercise of their dispositive discretions, and in communications made to the trustees by other beneficiaries. That issue can alternatively be seen as an inquiry whether such confidential communications are indeed trust documents. The judgments of the three members of the court (Harman, Danckwerts and

---

177 (1886), 33 Ch. D. 179.
178 At 185.
179 8th ed., at 975.
180 At 187.
181 [1892] 1 Ch 86 at 89.
182 [1965] Ch 918.

Salmon LJJ) are not easy to reconcile. All three referred to *O'Rourke v Darbishire* but Harman and Danckwerts LJJ found that Lord Wrenbury's general observations gave little assistance on the issue which concerned them. Only Salmon LJ[183] expressly adopted the proprietary basis of the principle.

50. Lord Wrenbury's observations in *O'Rourke v Darbishire* have also been cited in several Australian cases, and they were referred to by Lord Lowry in *A T & T Istel Ltd v Tully*.[184] The Board does not find it surprising that Lord Wrenbury's observations have been so often cited, since they are a vivid expression of the basic distinction between the right of a beneficiary arising under the law of trusts (which most would regard as part of the law of property) and the right of a litigant to disclosure of his opponent's documents (which is part of the law of procedure and evidence). But the Board cannot regard it as a reasoned or binding decision that a beneficiary's right or claim to disclosure of trust documents or information must always have the proprietary basis of a transmissible interest in trust property. That was not an issue in *O'Rourke v Darbishire*.

51. Their Lordships consider that the more principled and correct approach is to regard the right to seek disclosure of trust documents as one aspect of the court's inherent jurisdiction to supervise, and if necessary to intervene in, the administration of trusts. The right to seek the court's intervention does not depend on entitlement to a fixed and transmissible beneficial interest. The object of a discretion (including a mere power) may also be entitled to protection from a court of equity, although the circumstances in which he may seek protection, and the nature of the protection he may expect to obtain, will depend on the court's discretion.[185] Mr Brownbill's submission to the contrary effect tends to prove too much, since he would regard the object of a discretionary trust as having a proprietary interest even though it is not transmissible (except in the special case of collective action taken unanimously by all the members of a closed class).

52. Their Lordships are therefore in general agreement with the approach adopted in the judgments of Kirby P and Sheller JA in the Court of Appeal of New South Wales in *Hartigan Nominees Pty Ltd. v. Rydge*.[186] That was a case concerned with disclosure of a memorandum of wishes addressed to the trustees by Sir Norman Rydge (who was in substance, but not nominally, the settlor). Kirby P said:[187]

> I do not consider that it is imperative to determine whether that document is a 'trust document' (as I think it is) or whether the respondent, as a beneficiary, has a proprietary interest in it (as I am also inclined to think he does). Much of the law on the subject of access to documents has conventionally been expressed in terms of the 'proprietary interest' in the document of the party seeking access to it. Thus, it has been held that a cestui que trust has a 'proprietary right' to seek

183 At 937.

184 [1993] A.C. 45 at 65.

185 See Lord Wilberforce in *Gartside v. Inland Revenue Commissioners*, [1968] A.C. 553 at 617-8 and in *McPhail v Doulton*, *supra*, note 170, at 456-7; Templeman J. in *In re Manisty's Settlement*, [1974] Ch. 17 at 27-8; and Warner J. in *Mettoy Pension Trustees Ltd. v. Evans*, [1990] 1 W.L.R. 1587 at 1617-8.

186 (1992), 29 N.S.W.L.R. 405.

187 At 421-2.

all documents relating to the trust.[188] This approach is unsatisfactory. Access should not be limited to documents in which a proprietary right may be established. Such rights may be *sufficient*; but they are not *necessary* to a right of access which the courts will enforce to uphold the cestui que trust's entitlement to a reasonable assurance of the manifest integrity of the administration of the trust by the trustees. I agree with Professor H A J Ford's comment, in his book (with Mr W A Lee) *Principles of the Law of Trusts*,[189] that the equation of rights of inspection of trust documents with the beneficiaries' equitable rights of property in the trust assets 'gives rise to far more problems than it solves':

> ... The legal title and rights to possession are in the trustees: all the beneficiary has are equitable rights against the trustees. ... The beneficiary's rights to inspect trust documents are founded therefore not upon any equitable proprietary right which he or she may have in respect of those documents but upon the trustee's fiduciary duty to keep the beneficiary informed and to render accounts. It is the extent of that duty that is in issue. The equation of the right to inspect trust documents with the beneficiary's equitable proprietary rights gives rise to unnecessary and undesirable consequences. It results in the drawing of virtually incomprehensible distinctions between documents which are trust documents and those which are not; it casts doubts upon the rights of beneficiaries who cannot claim to have an equitable proprietary interest in the trust assets, such as the beneficiaries of discretionary trusts; and it may give trustees too great a degree of protection in the case of documents, artificially classified as not being trust documents, and beneficiaries too great a right to inspect the activities of trustees in the case of documents which are, equally artificially, classified as trust documents.

53. Mahoney JA[190] favoured the proprietary basis but recognised that it extended to information of a non-documentary kind. Sheller JA[191] considered that inquiry as to an applicant's proprietary interest was "if not a false, an unhelpful trail". All three members of the court expressed reservations about the reasoning and conclusions in *In re Londonderry's Settlement*.

54. It will be observed that Kirby P said that for an applicant to have a proprietary right might be sufficient, but was not necessary. In the Board's view it is neither sufficient nor necessary. Since *In re Cowin* well over a century ago the court has made clear that there may be circumstances (especially of confidentiality) in which even a vested and transmissible beneficial interest is not a sufficient basis for requiring disclosure of trust documents; and *In re Londonderry's Settlement* and more recent cases have begun to work out in some detail the way in which the court should exercise its discretion in such cases. There are three such areas in which the court may have to form a discretionary judgment: whether a discretionary object (or some other beneficiary with only a remote or wholly defeasible interest) should be granted relief at all; what classes of documents should be disclosed, either completely or in a redacted form; and what safeguards should be imposed (whether by undertakings to the court, arrangements for professional inspection, or otherwise) to limit the use which may be made of documents or information disclosed under the order of the court.

55. The proprietary basis of a beneficiary's right to disclosure was fully argued before the Staff of Government Division, which . . . accepted the submis-

---

188 See *O'Rourke v Darbishire, supra,* note 165, at 601, 603.
189 2nd ed. (Sydney: Law Book Co., 1990), at 425.
190 At 435.
191 At 444.

sion (made on behalf of the appellant) that a proprietary interest, although often found, was not necessary. On this part of the case the Board agrees with the conclusion reached by the Staff of Government Division, and does not accept the criticisms of it put forward by Mr Brownbill. It has nevertheless been necessary to look at the authorities in some detail, because they lead on to part of the Staff of Government Division's judgment . . . in which the court reached the conclusion that Deemster Cain had no jurisdiction to make the order for disclosure which he did make. In reaching that conclusion the court distinguished (or treated as unhelpful) a number of cases, of which the most important are *Chaine-Nickson v The Bank of Ireland*,[192] *Spellson v George*,[193] *Hartigan Nominees Pty Ltd v Rydge*,[194] *A-G of Ontario v Stavro*,[195] and *Murphy v Murphy*.[196]

[His Lordship discussed these cases, which confirmed his thesis that proprietary basis of the beneficiary's right to disclosure is an inappropriate one. He continued:]

Conclusion.

66. Their Lordships have already indicated their view that a beneficiary's right to seek disclosure of trust documents, although sometimes not inappropriately described as a proprietary right, is best approached as one aspect of the court's inherent jurisdiction to supervise (and where appropriate intervene in) the administration of trusts. There is therefore in their Lordships' view no reason to draw any bright dividing-line either between transmissible and non-transmissible (that is, discretionary) interests, or between the rights of an object of a discretionary trust and those of the object of a mere power (of a fiduciary character). The differences in this context between trusts and powers are (as Lord Wilberforce demonstrated in *McPhail v Doulton*) a good deal less significant than the similarities. The tide of Commonwealth authority, although not entirely uniform, appears to be flowing in that direction.

67. However the recent cases also confirm (as had been stated as long ago as *In re Cowin* in 1886) that no beneficiary (and least of all a discretionary object) has any entitlement as of right to disclosure of anything which can plausibly be described as a trust document. Especially when there are issues as to personal or commercial confidentiality, the court may have to balance the competing interests of different beneficiaries, the trustees themselves, and third parties. Disclosure may have to be limited and safeguards may have to be put in place. Evaluation of the claims of a beneficiary (and especially of a discretionary object) may be an important part of the balancing exercise which the court has to perform on the

---

192 [1976] I.R. 393.
193 (1987), 11 N.S.W.L.R. 300.
194 (1992), 29 N.S.W.L.R. 405.
195 (1994), 119 D.L.R. (4th) 750.
196 [1999] 1 W.L.R. 282.

materials placed before it. In many cases the court may have no difficulty in concluding that an applicant with no more than a theoretical possibility of benefit ought not to be granted any relief.

68. It would be inappropriate for the Board to go much further in attempting to give the High Court of the Isle of Man guidance as to the future conduct of this troublesome matter. But their Lordships can, without trespassing on the High Court's discretion, summarise their views on the different components of the appellant's claims:

(1) It seems to be common ground that during Mr Schmidt's lifetime substantial distributions were made for his benefit, all or most by allocation of funds to the two companies (Gingernut and Petragonis) which were regarded as being (in some sense) Mr Schmidt's. The appellant as Mr Schmidt's personal representative does not accept that these funds have been fully accounted for. His contention is that in respect of allocated funds Mr Schmidt ceased to be a mere discretionary object, and became absolute owner. On the face of it the appellant (as personal representative) seems to have a powerful case for the fullest disclosure in respect of these funds.

(2) The appellant as personal representative would also, on the face of it, have a strong claim to disclosure of documents or information relevant to the issue whether, but for breaches of fiduciary duty (such as for instance overcharging) more funds would have been available for distribution to Mr Schmidt, and would or might have been allocated to him in practice. The Board express no view whatever as to whether the appellant has a case for overcharging or any other breach of fiduciary duty. But claims of that sort have been put forward in the 1998 proceedings, and the possibility must be noted in order to make the position clear.

(3) As regards the appellant's personal claims under the Angora Trust since his father's death, his status as beneficiary of any sort depends on the issue of construction discussed [earlier in the case].

(4) As regards the Everest Trust, the appellant is . . . a possible object of the very wide power in clause 3.3, but an object who may be regarded (especially in view of the Everest letter) as having exceptionally strong claims to be considered.

69. Their Lordships will therefore humbly advise Her Majesty that the appeal should be allowed, the order of Deemster Cain restored and the matter remitted to the High Court of the Isle of Man for further consideration in the light of the Board's judgment.

. . .

Notes and Questions

1. For an instructive comment on *Schmidt*, see Lionel Smith "Access to Trust Information: Schmidt v. Rosewood Trust Ltd." (2003), 23 E.T. & P.J. 1.

2. The effect of *Schmidt* is that beneficiaries no longer have a right to information. Rather, the court has assumed a discretion to confer access to information depending upon the circumstances of the case. Is this a desirable development? Will it lead to more litigation?

3. Does *Schmidt* mean that beneficiaries may be able to require trustees to give reasons for the exercise or non-exercise of discretionary powers?

4. Can a beneficiary compel a trustee to pass his or her accounts?

5. It would appear that a beneficiary can gain access to all documents by commencing an action against the trustee for an alleged breach of trust. The beneficiary is then entitled to ask for discovery of documents.

6. In providing access to trust documents, trustees must afford all reasonable facilities for inspection.[197]

Problems

1. A testator directed the sale of real estate, subject to a discretionary power to retain. The testator's son, the life-tenant under the will, occupied a certain house rent-free. The personal representative proposed to sell it. The son objected. What result?[198]

2. A settlor wished to bestow property successively on those of his descendants who, *inter alia*, married "approved" Jewish wives. If any question arose as to whether a woman met the qualifications for approval (namely, Jewish faith and Jewish blood) the matter was to be decided by the Chief Rabbi of London.[199]

    a) A descendant marries an approved wife. Should the trustees distribute? Must they?

    b) Was a gift or a trust created? In either event has a valid power been bestowed upon the Chief Rabbi?

3. M and N are trustees of a trust under which they have a power to appoint income in favour of A, B, and C.

    a) A has demanded to see the minutes of meetings at which the trustees have considered the exercise of their discretion.

    b) B has demanded that the trustees give him a copy of the trust instrument.

    c) C has demanded that the trustees assign her interest under the trust to trustees for her own children.

    d) C has also demanded that the trustees advise her whether the rule in *Saunders v. Vautier*[200] applies.

Advise M and N.

4. Alice, who died recently, bequeathed her residuary estate to her executors and trustees, William and Joan, upon trust for Cecilia for life with remainder to Dawn. The residuary estate included:

    a) a leasehold interest with three years to run;

    b) 1,000 common shares in ABC Ltd., a company which has not paid a dividend upon its common shares in the four years immediately preceding the death of Alice;

    c) the right to receive $25,000 on the death of her (Alice's) father;

    d) a copyrighted piece of music.

Advise William and Joan about their obligations.

---

197 *Eglin v. Sanderson* (1862), 3 Giff. 434, 66 E.R. 479.

198 *Re Miller* (1981), 9 E.T.R. 37 (Ont. H.C.) and *Re Hopkins* (1982), 35 O.R. (2d) 403, 11 E.T.R. 27, 132 D.L.R. (3d) 671 (H.C.), affirmed (1983), 39 O.R. (2d) 673, 13 E.T.R. 31, 41 D.L.R. (3d) 660 (C.A.).

199 *Re Tuck's Settlement Trusts*, [1978] Ch. 49, [1978] 1 All E.R. 1047 (C.A.).

200 (1841), 4 Beav. 115, 49 E.R. 282, affirmed (1841), 1 Cr. & Ph. 240, 41 E.R. 482, [1835-42] All E.R. Rep. 58.

5. Anna, an Austrian citizen, flew to Ottawa to attend the funeral of her sister, Beth, who had immigrated to Canada many years earlier. While in Ottawa there were legal matters to attend to and Anna retained Michel, a respected Ottawa lawyer, to handle them. After returning to Austria, Anna was advised that an administrator would have to be appointed for Beth's estate. She recommended the appointment of Vadia, an inhabitant of Ottawa and a person of Austrian extraction, whom she knew she would be able to converse with in her own language.

Vadia agreed to act and was duly appointed. Vadia did not advise anyone that she was unfamiliar with the obligations of an administrator. Vadia retained Michel and gave him a general power of attorney over all the assets of the estate. Once or twice, Vadia asked Michel about the progress of the administration of the estate but was told that "these things take time." Michel absconded after misappropriating the estate funds.

Anna has come to you for advice. Specifically, she wishes to know on what grounds, if any, she can sue Vadia, what the likelihood of success is and what she might hope to recover for the estate.[201]

6. A woman dies leaving a will in which she names her husband as sole executor and trustee of her estate. The will provides that the husband is to have a life interest and her two children are to share the remainder equally. The will contains an unfettered power of encroachment in favour of the husband. The husband purports to exercise the power of encroachment and transfer all the capital of the estate to himself. Is he able to do this? On what basis? What grounds do the children have for arguing against the use of the capital in that fashion?[202]

---

201 See *Wagner v. Van Cleeff, supra*, note 55.
202 See *Saunders v. Halom* (1986), 8 B.C.L.R. (2d) 117, [1987] 1 W.W.R. 557, 32 D.L.R. (4th) 503, 25 E.T.R. 186 (C.A.) and *Coakwell Estate v. Saskatchewan (Public Trustee)* (1987), 63 Sask. R. 220 (Q.B.).

14

THE POWERS AND RIGHTS OF TRUSTEES

1. SCOPE

Thus far, we have concentrated on how the office of trustee is filled and the job that the trustees must perform once in office. In this chapter, we explore the powers that trustees need to carry out the trust effectively and efficiently. These powers are of two kinds: administrative and dispositive. Administrative powers enable trustees to manage the trust property. Dispositive powers enable the trustees to transfer trust assets to the beneficiaries. The two can look remarkably similar as, for example, when trustees transfer a trust asset. If it is transferred to a beneficiary, the transfer is an exercise of a dispositive power, whereas if the transfer is to a third party, it is an exercise of an administrative power.

The nature and types of administrative and dispositive powers are the subject-matter of the following two parts. We then discuss the circumstances in which the court will interfere with the exercise of the trustees' discretion. The chapter concludes with an examination of the rights of trustees to payment, indemnification, and set-off.

2. ADMINISTRATIVE POWERS

(a) Generally

Trustees are given administrative powers to enable them to manage the trust property and thereby fulfil the terms of the trust. They obtain their administrative powers primarily from two sources: the trust instrument and legislation. Many of the standard, general, and more basic powers necessary for the proper functioning of the trust are conferred upon trustees by legislation. These legislative powers can be excluded or amended by the creator of the trust.[1]

Those powers necessary for the effective functioning of a given trust should be conferred by the trust instrument itself. The administrative powers created by the trust instrument should be specific and tailored to achieve the purpose of the

---

1 See, for example, *Trustee Act*, R.S.O. 1990, c. T.23, ss. 67, 68.

trust. To draft administrative powers properly you must bear in mind the nature of the trust property and the types of beneficial interests created and their duration.

If additional administrative powers are needed — that is, powers in addition to those given by the trust instrument and conferred by legislation — the trustee can make application to the court in two ways. First, trustees can apply to the court for enlargement of their powers pursuant to the court's inherent jurisdiction. The scope of this jurisdiction is limited to emergency or salvage circumstances in which it can be demonstrated that the lack of a particular power will jeopardize the trust. Second, an application for the grant of additional powers may be brought under the *Variation of Trusts Act*[2] or equivalent legislation. You will recall that such an application usually requires that all beneficiaries who are *sui juris* consent to the proposed variation and that the court approve the variation on behalf of any incapacitated, minor, unborn, or unascertained beneficiaries. Apart from the difficulties that can arise in obtaining the consent of the beneficiaries, court applications are expensive and inconvenient, so it is best to ensure that the trust document is drafted to provide the trustee with all the requisite powers. Moreover, should the application for additional powers be held to be unreasonable, the trustee may be sanctioned in costs personally.[3]

The powers given to trustees by legislation are basically the same throughout Canada. Examples of such powers are:[4]

1. to determine the mode of sale when a power or duty of sale is created by the trust instruments.[5]
2. to dedicate or sell lands for municipal highway purposes.[6]
3. to insure property up to three-fourths of its value.[7]
4. to enable trustees who hold renewable leases to renew them.[8]
5. to issue receipts.[9]
6. to invest in authorized investments.[10]
7. to reimburse the trustees for expenses incurred in the administration of the trust.[11]
8. to pay moneys into court.[12]
9. to compromise claims by or against the trust.[13]

---

2   R.S.O. 1990, c. V.1.

3   *Re Lotzkar; Montreal Trust Co. of Canada v. James* (1985), 19 E.T.R. 135, 66 B.C.L.R. 265 (S.C.).

4   For ease of reference, all of the following powers will be cited only from the Ontario, R.S.O. 1990, c. T.23.

5   *Trustee Act*, R.S.O. 1990, c. T.23, s. 17.

6   *Ibid.*, s. 19, am. by S.O. 2000, c. 26, Sched. A, s. 15(2).

7   *Ibid.*, s. 21.

8   *Ibid.*, s. 22.

9   *Ibid.*, s. 24.

10 *Ibid.*, s. 27(2), am. by S.O. 1998, c. 18, Sched. B, s. 16(1).

11 *Ibid.*, s. 33, repealed by S.O. 1998, c. 18, Sched. B, s. 16(1). However, trustees have a similar power under s. 23.1, added by S.O. 2001, c. 9, Sched. B., s. 13(1).

12 *Ibid.*, s. 36, am. by S.O. 1992, c. 32, s. 27; 1994, c. 27, s. 43(2); 1998, c. 18, Sched. B., s. 16(3); 2000, c. 26, Sched. A, s. 15.

13 *Ibid.*, s. 48.

10. to apply to the court for its opinion, advice, or direction on any question respecting the management or administration of trust property.[14]

(b) Proposals for Reform

The Ontario Law Reform Commission has recommended that new administrative powers be given to trustees by legislation.[15] In keeping with existing legislation, settlors and testators would be able to exclude or vary all such powers. A summary of the recommended powers follows. We suggest that these powers should be considered for inclusion when drafting trust instruments.

1. Deposit of trust funds. The current provisions should be extended to enable trustees to deposit funds with all depositories empowered by law to accept money on deposit.
2. Power of sale. (The current provisions speak only to the mode of sale.) The Commission recommends that trustees be given a power to sell trust assets unless such a power is specifically excluded or modified by the trust instrument. The power of sale would permit trustees to sell property on credit if appropriate security were given.[16]
3. Exchange and partition. Such a power should be expressly bestowed upon trustees.
4. Power to lease. The existing power to renew leases should be extended to permit trustees to lease or renew leases on any trust property.
5. Power to maintain and repair. Trustees should be given a general power to manage, maintain, repair, renovate, improve, or develop trust property.[17]
6. Power to insure. (The power to insure is currently limited to loss or damage of up to three-fourths of the value of the property.) The recommendation is that the provision be extended so that insurance can be obtained against all risks or liability and the three-fourths value limitation be dropped.
7. Power to carry on business. Specific powers should be included to enable trustees to carry on a business, change its form, dispose of, or wind up a business.[18]
8. Shareholding obligations. Specific statutory powers should enable trustees to exercise all rights and powers and satisfy all liabilities incidental to the ownership of shares.
9. Surrender of property. Pursuant to the trustee's duty of impartiality, trustees are obligated to sell wasting or hazardous assets. It is questionable whether this duty extends to enable trustees to surrender property. The Commission recommends that a power of surrender be created.

---

14 *Ibid.*, s. 60, am. by S.O. 2000, c. 26, Sched. A, s. 15(2).
15 Ontario Law Reform Commission, *Report on the Law of Trusts* (Toronto: Ministry of the Attorney General, 1984) at 233-250 ("O.L.R.C. Report").
16 Such a provision can be found in *The Trustee Act*, R.S.M. 1987, c. T160, s. 24, as amended by S.M. 1993, c. 48, s. 104.
17 This power has been prescribed in the *Trustee Act*, R.S.B.C. 1996, c. 464, s. 11.
18 *Ibid.*, s. 23.

10. Acquisition of dwelling house. A statutory power should be introduced to enable trustees to purchase, rent, or erect accommodation for use by beneficiaries. If an income beneficiary exists, his or her prior permission would be required.

11. Power to borrow money. A general provision permitting trustees to borrow money should be inserted and, as security, they should be entitled to mortgage, pledge, or otherwise charge the trust property.

12. Settlement and contestation of claims. The current provisions permitting trustees to contest and settle claims should be continued and expanded.

13. Power to pay outgoings. Trustees should be empowered to pay from the trust property any taxes, assessments, charges, premiums, or other out-goings incurred in the administration of the trust.

14. Appropriation and valuation of property *in specie*. Currently, trustees may only distribute property *in specie* if the trust instrument so provides or if all the beneficiaries are capacitated and agree. The Commission recommends that the trustees be empowered to appropriate property *in specie* in or towards satisfaction of the share or interest of any beneficiary with the consent of that beneficiary.

15. Execution of administrative powers. Express power should be given to the trustees to do all supplementary or ancillary acts or things and execute all instruments necessary or desirable to enable them to act.

16. Enlargement of powers. The Commission recognized that situations might arise in which the interest of the trust would be better served if the trustees could exercise a power that was not authorized by the trust instrument nor contained in the proposed list. In such circumstances, the Commission recommends that a mechanism should be available to permit an enlargement of trustee powers if the court feels it is expedient.

Notes and Questions

1. The *Settled Estates Act*[19] confers other administrative powers upon trustees in two situations. The first arises when land is limited to persons in succession as, for example, in a grant "to A for life, remainder to B in fee simple." The second arises when land is limited in trust to persons in succession as, for example, where land is conveyed "unto and to the use of T1 and T2 to hold in trust for A for life, remainder in trust for B in fee simple."

Whereas the specific administrative powers enumerated above are conferred upon the trustees of a settlement unless expressly excluded, the purpose of the *Settled Estates Act* is to empower the court, upon application, to authorize more extensive powers of disposition than would otherwise exist. Moreover, such powers can be conferred under the Act whether or not the land is held in trust. The Act provides, however, that the court shall not make an order "beyond the extent to which, in the opinion of the court, the same might have been authorized in and by the settlor."[20]

---

19 R.S.O. 1990, c. S.7.
20 *Ibid.*, s. 28.

3. DISPOSITIVE POWERS

(a) Generally

A dispositive power is an authority to allocate (*i.e.*, dispose of) trust property to one or more beneficiaries. Familiar examples of dispositive powers are discretionary trusts and the powers of appointment, encroachment, maintenance, and advancement. Powers of maintenance, advancement and encroachment are discussed below; discretionary trusts and powers of appointment are discussed elsewhere.[21]

Notes and Questions

1. Discretionary trusts involve dispositive powers in that the trustees have the power to choose who among a class of beneficiaries is to take or how much each beneficiary is to take or both.

2. The term "dispositive power" can be misleading. Although termed a power, the authorization may be mandatory in flavour, thereby making it imperative that the trustee exercise it. Alternatively, the authorization may simply enable the trustee, in his or her discretion, to act.[22]

3. Through a power of encroachment, trustees can seriously deplete the capital of a trust fund. Is such a power reconcilable with the duty to maintain an even hand among beneficiaries?[23]

(b) Power of Maintenance

A power of maintenance is the authority to apply income for the immediate and recurring needs of a beneficiary; capital may, in certain circumstances, also be so applied.[24] Powers of maintenance are normally used to provide for basic physical needs such as food, shelter, clothing, and medical care.[25] In some provinces, legislation also allows the power of maintenance to be used to provide for

---

21 In Chapter 3, *supra*.

22 The different consequences that flow from a power that is mandatory and from one that is discretionary is discussed further in part 3(d), *infra*.

23 See part 3(d), *infra*; and see *Carley Estate, Re* (1994), 2 E.T.R. (2d) 142, 1994 CarswellOnt 646, [1994] O.J. No. 900 (Gen. Div.), additional reasons at (1994), 1994 CarswellOnt 662, [1994] O.J. No. 1981, 4 E.T.R. (2d) 102 (Gen. Div.), in which the trustees exercised their power of encroachment to pay the debts of the income beneficiary. The will had limited the trustees' power of encroachment to what was in the best interest of the beneficiaries. The court interpreted this to include the payment of the debts of the income beneficiary. The court found, however, that the trustees' power to encroach on the capital of the trust was limited by the rights of capital beneficiaries under the even-hand principle.

24 *Crane v. Craig* (1886), 11 P.R. 236 (Ont. H.C.); *Re Green* (1908), 9 W.L.R. 630 (Sask. Chambers).

25 *Cook v. Noble* (1886), 12 O.R. 81 (H.C.).

the education of beneficiaries.[26] Many of the provinces and territories also allow for a more general application of trust property for the beneficiaries' benefit or advancement. Generally, the statutory power of maintenance only addresses the needs of minors, but it has been broadened in Alberta[27] and Prince Edward Island[28] to include adults. Even if the legislation is silent, the trust instrument may provide that other needs may be met through a power of maintenance.

Unlike other Canadian provinces and territories, Ontario has no statutory power of maintenance.[29] Trustees must, therefore, rely upon either an express power of maintenance in the trust instrument or the inherent jurisdiction of the court to bestow such a power. *Re McIntyre*; *McIntyre v. London and Western Trusts Company*,[30] below, is illustrative of the general principles guiding the court in granting such powers.

RE McINTYRE; McINTYRE v. LONDON AND WESTERN TRUSTS CO.

(1905), 9 O.L.R. 408
Supreme Court of Ontario
[Court of Appeal]

A testator died leaving a considerable estate. By his will he left his homestead to his son, Hugh, for ten years, subject to a payment of $100 a year to his widow. Subject to that, he left the homestead to his minor twin sons, Mowat and Ross. He also left them $4,000 each, which they were to have when they attained the age of 25. After making certain other provisions, he left the balance of his estate to his heirs.

No express provision was made for the maintenance of Mowat and Ross. The issues for the court were whether the minors were entitled to maintenance and, if so, how the maintenance was to be generated.

Moss C.J.O.:

. . .

As the result of proceedings subsequently taken for the purpose of ascertaining and adjusting the rights of the persons entitled to benefits under the will, the Master at London made his report, dated December 9th, 1903.

---

26 *Trustee Act*, R.S.A. 2000, c. T-8, ss. 33-37; R.S.B.C. 1996, c. 464, ss. 24, 25; R.S.M. 1987, c. T160, s. 29; R.S.N.L. 1990, c. T-10, s. 26; R.S.N.S. 1989, c. 479, s. 30; R.S.N.W.T. 1988, c. T-8, ss. 27, 28 [am. by S.N.W.T. 1998, c. 17, s. 28(2), (3)]; R.S.P.E.I. 1988, c. T-8, ss. 39, 40; R.S.S. 1978, c. T-23, ss. 52-54 (s. 53 am. by S.S. 1983, c. 80, s. 22(2); S.S. 1992, c. 62, s. 33(2); s. 54 am. by S.S. 1983, c. 80, s. 22(3)); R.S.Y. 2002, c. 223, ss. 30, 31; *Trustees Act*, R.S.N.B. 1973, c. T-15, s. 14 (am. by S.N.B. 1986, c. 4, s. 54(2); S.N.B. 2000, c. 29, s. 2 (Fr.)).
27 *Trustee Act*, R.S.A. 2000, c. T-8, ss. 34, 35.
28 *Trustee Act*, R.S.P.E.I. 1988, c. T-8, s. 40.
29 The statutory powers of maintenance are different for each province and territory.
30 (1905), 9 O.L.R. 408 (C.A.).

The report finds that the executors have in hand belonging to the infants Mowat and Ross, as their present share of the residue of the estate, the sum of $2,000.

It further states that it is not necessary or proper for the executors to set apart for payment of the legacies of $4,000 each payable to Mowat and Ross, the sum of $8,000, inasmuch as these legacies are contingent on the infants attaining 25 years of age, and that the proper amount to be set apart will be the sum of $4,442.16 which invested at 4 per cent, and compounded yearly until the infants attain their majority will produce $8,000.

These findings and the directions given consequent thereon determined in effect that neither for the purposes of maintenance, nor otherwise, do the legacies of $4,000 carry interest until the day named for payment.

On appeal Street J. held that the legacies carried interest from the testator's death for the purpose of maintenance and he varied the report in this and other respects as stated in his order. Against this there is an appeal on behalf of the plaintiff, supported by others interested in the residuary estate.

As I have already pointed out there is no express provision for the maintenance of the two infants during their minority. But the appellants contend that the other devises and bequests in favour of the infants contained in the will are a sufficient provision for their maintenance.

The well-settled rule is that when a legacy is given to a minor by a parent or by a person *in loco parentis* payable at a future period, if no other provision is made for maintenance interest will be allowed for that purpose even though by the terms of the will the legacy is contingent on the legatee living to the period which is mentioned for payment of the legacy.

In *Haughton v. Harrison*,[31] Lord Hardwicke stated the rule,

If a legacy be left upon no condition but to be paid at the age of 21, and not given over, it is a legacy vested and transmissible; but still no interest can be demanded unless in the case of a child, who had no other maintenance or provision, for a parent is bound by nature to support a child.

Again he stated it in *Heath v. Perry*[32] and in *Hearle v. Greenbank*.[33] In the latter case he observed, "But in all these cases the ground the court goes on is giving interest by way of maintenance." And in that case he held that inasmuch as the testatrix had allotted maintenance for her daughter from the general funds of her personal estate and there could be no allowance of interest on a contingent legacy to the daughter.

So in *Wynch v. Wynch*,[34] Lord Kenyon M.R. said,

It is very clear that when a father gives a legacy to a child, whether it be a vested legacy, or not, it will carry interest from the death of the testator, as a maintenance for the child; but this will be only where no other fund is provided for such maintenance; for it is equally clear, that where

---

31 2 Atk. 320.
32 (1744), 3 Atk. 101.
33 3 Atk. 695 at 717.
34 (1788), 1 Cox 133.

other funds are provided for the maintenance, then if the legacy be payable at a future day, it shall not carry interest, until the day of payment, comes, as in the case of a legacy to a perfect stranger.

. . .

In *Binkley v. Binkley*,[35] Spragge V.-C. said

It is clear law, and it is undisputed, that a legacy by a parent to an infant child, payable upon coming of age, or upon that event or marriage, the will being silent as to interest upon the legacy, stand upon a different footing from a legacy to a stranger; the latter not carrying interest; while in the case of a legacy to a child, the child is entitled to maintenance to the extent, if necessary of interest upon the legacy — this as a general rule — it is otherwise when other provision is made by the will for the maintenance of the infant.

To the same effect, Mowat V.-C., in *Spark v. Perrin*,[36] and Proudfoot V.-C., in *Rees v. Fraser*.[37]

In the very recent case *Re Bowlby, Bowlby v. Bowlby*,[38] the question to what extent is a child, to whom a legacy payable *in futuro* or contingent is given, entitled to the interest which the legacy bears or carries — whether to the whole interest as such or only to so much as may be necessary for maintenance — was fully discussed in argument and considered by the Court of Appeal. Although Vaughan Williams L.J. argued strongly that the effect of giving interest at all was to entitle the infant to the whole, the conclusion of the court was that, by the practice of the court, the infant is only allowed so much as is necessary for maintenance, thus affirming the view expressed by Spragge V.-C., in *Binkley v. Binkley*, that a child is entitled to maintenance to the extent, if necessary, of the interest upon the legacy.

I think that is the correct rule where the will makes no other provision or provides no other fund for the maintenance of the infant legatee.

But where there is in the will an express provision for maintenance from some other source, and the amount is specified, the legacy will not bear interest for the purpose of maintenance even though the provision made should be deemed insufficient for the purpose. This is upon the principle that as interest is allowed in other cases because it will not be assumed that the father intended no maintenance, there is no ground for the assumption where a provision is made.

So that where the amount of maintenance is specified that is in general the limit.[39]

Where there is a general provision for maintenance and no amount specified there seems to be no absolute bar to recourse, if necessary, to interest upon the contingent legacy. Much less should there be where there is no express provision of any kind. The amount of the allowance in such cases must be governed by a

---

35 15 Gr. 519.
36 17 Gr. 519.
37 26 Gr. 233.
38 [1904] 2 Ch. 685.
39 *Simpson on Infants*, 2nd ed., at 304.

consideration of the other circumstances, and a due regard to such other sources or funds as may be properly resorted to for maintenance.

Although in the present case it may be surmised that in making the provisions and arrangements in his will with reference to the payment to his widow by his son Hugh of $100 a year for the use of the homestead farm for 10 years until the infants should have possession, and in giving the other benefits to his widow out of the same farm the testator was intending to provide for the infants' maintenance by their mother until they could maintain themselves on the farm, he has not given expression to that intention.

Upon the construction of the will I think there is no provision for maintenance out of the farm. The gift of an immediate share in the residue indicates a fund or source from which maintenance is derivable, but not in such form as to preclude recourse for maintenance to the interest upon the legacies. But in my opinion it should be taken into consideration in dealing with the allowance to be made for maintenance out of interest of the legacies. I think, therefore, that the Master was wrong in determining that no part of the interest on the legacies could be devoted to the maintenance of the infants. I think that to the extent necessary for their maintenance, having regard to their shares of the residue, and the income derivable therefrom, they are entitled to have recourse to interest on their legacies, but only to that extent. It follows that the order of Lount J. was proper at the time it was made, and that the whole sum of $8,000 must be set apart to provide maintenance if necessary.

The order of Street J. in this case does not in terms give to the infants the whole interest upon the legacies. The amount allowed by Lount J. is continued, subject to being increased or reduced by a judge. But that sum was manifestly arrived at without reference to the income from the infants' shares in the residue, and the question of the proper amount to be allowed, having regard to such shares and the time when they were ascertained, should be now settled by the Master unless otherwise agreed upon.

It is said that the decision of Kekewich J. in *Re Moody, Woodroffe v. Mood*,[40] shows that the infants' interests in the residue is not to be taken into account. But I do not think so. The learned judge was dealing with the argument that the gift of a share in the residue without any provision for maintenance, was a bar to a claim for maintenance out of contingent legacies. He excluded the 43rd sec. of the *Conveyancing Act*,[41] and treated the gift of a share in the residue as not subject to any provision for maintenance, and so treating it he held that it was not a bar for maintenance out of the income of the legacies. But he did not consider, and apparently was not called upon to consider, the question whether in fixing the maintenance, the infants' rights in the residue were to be taken into consideration. And in the light of the discussion in *Re Bowlby, Bowlby v. Bowlby*,[42] his declaration that the infants were entitled to interest *qua* interest would probably only apply to the circumstances of that case.

---

40 [1895] 1 Ch. 101.
41 1881, Imp. 44-45 Vict, ch. 41.
42 *Supra*, note 38.

I think that subject to any variation that may be needed in accordance with what I have stated, the order of Street J. should be affirmed, but under the circumstances the costs of the appeal should be borne by the estate.

Notes and Questions

1. Legislation may enable trustees, indirectly, to obtain the power to make maintenance payments for beneficiaries who are minors; see, for example, s. 60 of the *Children's Law Reform Act*,[43] which enables the court to order the disposition of a minor's property for the purpose of support, education or benefit of the minor; consent of the life estate holder is required for such an application.

2. The courts are reluctant to allow maintenance to be paid from capital.[44] Can you explain why?

3. Is the power of maintenance restricted to the beneficiary's minority? Should it be?[45]

4. Can a trustee refuse to exercise a power of maintenance clearly spelled out in the trust instrument? If so, under what circumstances? Does a beneficiary have any recourse in such a case?[46]

5. What role does the settlor's or testator's intention play in determining whether the court will confer a power of maintenance? What other factors are relevant?[47]

6. The Ontario Law Reform Commission has recommended[48] that a statutory power of maintenance be created for minors regardless of whether their interests are vested or contingent. The Commission further recommended that such interests should be deemed to carry the intermediate income from the date that the interest arises unless the income is expressly disposed of otherwise.

7. If a minor has a vested life interest in trust property but enjoyment is postponed to age 25, is the minor entitled to receive maintenance from the intermediate income on the interest?[49]

8. Does a trustee have a general obligation to notify beneficiaries of the exercise of powers when practical and give them an opportunity to comment?[50]

(c) Power of Advancement

A power of advancement is an authority to pay capital to, or for the benefit of, a minor so that he or she may take advantage of some opportunity that will

---

43 R.S.O. 1990, c. C.12, am. by S.O. 2001, c. 9, Sched. B, s. 4(7).

44 See *Crane v. Craig, supra*, note 24; *Re Green supra*, note 24; *Rundle, Re* (1914), (sub nom. *Trusts & Guarantee Co. v. Rundle*) 32 O.L.R. 312 (C.A.), affirmed (1915), 1915 CarswellOnt 25, 52 S.C.R. 114, 26 D.L.R. 108; *Re Mason*, [1946] 4 D.L.R. 299 (N.S. S.C.).

45 See *Singer v. Singer* (1916), 52 S.C.R. 447, 27 D.L.R. 220; *Cook v. Noble, supra*, note 25; *Re Wright*, [1954] O.R. 755, [1955] 1 D.L.R. 213 (H.C.); and *Re McCallum*, [1956] O.W.N. 321, 2 D.L.R. (2d) 618 (H.C.).

46 See *Re Davis* (1983), 14 E.T.R. 83 (Ont. C.A.).

47 See *Re McIntyre, infra*. See also *Fuller v. Evans*, [2000] 1 All E.R. 636 (Ch. D.).

48 O.L.R.C. Report at 321-323.

49 See *Watson v. Conant*, [1964] S.C.R. 312, 44 D.L.R. (2d) 346 and *Re Baragar*, [1973] 1 O.R. 831, 32 D.L.R. (3d) 529 (C.A.). *Cf. Berry v. Geen*, [1938] A.C. 575, [1938] 2 All E.R. 362 (H.L.); and *Re Geering* (1962), [1964] Ch. 136, [1962] 3 All E.R. 1043.

50 See *X. v. A*, [2000] 1 All E.R. 490 (Ch. D).

further him or her in life.[51] Thus, advancement means to "set up" a beneficiary in life. That may be accomplished, for example, by purchasing a business for the beneficiary or paying a substantial debt owed by the beneficiary.

The courts have an inherent power to order that an advance be made to a beneficiary. However, they can only do so if the interest is vested absolutely and payment is postponed only because of a prior interest or because of the minority of the beneficiary. For this reason, a well-drawn trust typically includes an express power of advancement and often the trustee may exercise the power even if the beneficiary's interest is contingent or vested subject to divestment. If the advancement is properly made, but the interest was contingent, the money cannot be recovered from the beneficiary's estate if the interest never vests.[52] The advancement does not have to be brought into hotchpot, that is, it is not taken into account in determining the beneficiary's ultimate entitlement from the estate, unless the will so provides.[53]

Only Manitoba[54] and Prince Edward Island[55] have express statutory powers of advancement.[56] These can be exercised whether the beneficiary's interest is contingent or not.

Notes and Questions

1. While maintenance normally entails small, periodic payments, advancement is usually a one-time payment of a significant sum.[57]

2. What is the difference between encroachment and advancement?

3. The Ontario Law Reform Commission has recommended that a statutory power of advancement be created under which a trustee could apply, sell, mortgage, or charge any capital asset for the advancement in life of a minor.[58]

4. If B receives $10,000 from trust capital to start a business, has B received an advancement? If the business flounders, can B get further advancements to pay off outstanding debts, buy new inventory or meet payroll demands?[59]

5. Can a power of advancement be used to provide a beneficiary with post-secondary education? Would it make a difference if the education was for purposes of obtaining professional qualifications such as dentistry or education? If a power of advancement cannot be so used (and no express provision is made in the trust instrument to allow for it), what can a trustee do to assist a beneficiary who would otherwise be unable to pursue further education?

---

51 O.L.R.C. Report (1984), at 317-318. See *Brooke v. Brooke* (1911), 3 O.W.N. 52 at 54; *Patterson v. Royal Trust Co.*, 36 D.L.R. (3d) 590, 1973 CarswellMan 35, [1973] 4 W.W.R. 490 (Q.B.).

52 *Patterson v. Royal Trust Co., ibid.*

53 *Ibid.*

54 *Trustee Act*, R.S.M. 1987, c. T160, s. 32.

55 *Trustee Act*, R.S.P.E.I. 1988, c. T-8, s. 40.

56 Alberta empowers trustees to apply income for the advancement of a beneficiary. R.S.A. 2000, c. T-8, s. 34(1).

57 See *Patterson v. Royal Trust Co., supra*, note 51 for a detailed consideration of the meaning of the term "advancement."

58 O.L.R.C. Report at 367-368.

59 See *Brooke v. Brooke, supra*, note 51, and *Re Cross Estate* (1965), 51 W.W.R. 377 (B.C. Chambers).

(d) Power of Encroachment

A power of encroachment is a particular type of power of appointment in the sense that the settlor or testator confers upon a designated individual the power to distribute capital to an income beneficiary. The beneficiary does not have to be in receipt of income at the time of the advancement. The power is normally given to the trustee, but may be conferred upon another beneficiary, such as the life tenant. In either case, issues may arise about the extent of the power. This is resolved primarily by an interpretation of the language creating the power. *Fox v. Fox Estate*,[60] reproduced in the next section, is an example of a case involving a power to encroach and examines, among other things, the extent of the power.

Notes and Questions

1. Depending upon the capital source, the exercise of a power to encroach will normally reduce the income stream to the income beneficiaries. Thus, while one beneficiary may receive a significant capital sum, the income of other income beneficiaries will be reduced in consequence. This possibility should be carefully considered by the donor of the power and the drafter of the instrument.

4. JUDICIAL INTERFERENCE WITH THE TRUSTEES' DISCRETION

In the preceding chapter we discussed duties of trustees, whereas in this chapter we are concerned with powers that have been given to trustees. You will recall that duties must be carried out, even if the trustee is also given a discretion in the exercise of the duty. In contrast, a power does not have to be exercised. We have seen that the courts will sometimes interfere with the exercise by trustees of a discretion they have been given, whether the discretion is coupled with a duty or not. We shall now consider when and on what basis the courts will do so.

Any discretion given to a trustee (or to another person) may be misused. The misuse may take various forms. For example, the holder of the power may appoint outside the class of beneficiaries named as potential appointees. Doing so constitutes a fraud on the power and the estate or trust can recover the property so appointed. It may also be that the holder of the power appoints a person who is named as a potential appointee, but the holder of the power has misinterpreted the power and paid out money when it should not have been paid. The holder of the power may also have taken extraneous factors into account in making an appointment. *Fox v. Fox Estate*,[61] reproduced below, is an example of a case in which a trustee took extraneous factors into account. Yet again, the trustee may not have considered whether to exercise a power, or the trustees may be deadlocked over the exercise of their discretion.

---

60 (1996), 28 O.R. (3d) 496, 10 E.T.R. 229, 1996 CarswellOnt 317, 88 O.A.C. 201 (C.A.), leave to appeal refused (1996), 207 N.R. 80 (note), 97 O.A.C. 320 (note) (S.C.C.).

61 *Ibid.*

If a power is totally discretionary and the donor of the power has given the trustees an absolute and uncontrolled discretion to exercise it, the court will not interfere with the exercise of their discretion, assuming there is no *mala fides* and the trustees have considered whether the power should be exercised.[62] The court is more likely to interfere if a power is coupled with a duty. Thus, for example, if a deadlock arises in relation to a duty and the majority of trustees wish to act, the court is more likely to direct that the trustees act because of the imperative nature of duties. But, if the stalemate arises in relation to the exercise of a power, different considerations prevail. As Jessel M.R. said:[63]

> It is settled law that when a testator has given a pure discretion to trustees as to the exercise of a power, the Court does not enforce the exercise of the power against the wishes of the trustees, but it does prevent them from exercising it improperly. The Court says that the power, if exercised at all, is to be properly exercised. This may be illustrated by the case of persons having a power of appointing new trustees. Even after a decree in a suit for administering this trust have been made they may still exercise the power, but the Court will see that they do not appoint improper persons.
>
> But in all cases where there is a trust or duty coupled with the power the Court will then compel the trustees to carry it out in a proper manner and within a reasonable time.

While it is generally conceded that courts will not intervene when trustees are deadlocked over the exercise of a power, if the failure of the trustees to exercise the power would frustrate the intention of the testator or harm the interests of the beneficiaries, the courts will intervene.[64]

If the exercise of a power has been considered but not acted upon, the court will do nothing.[65] Whether a discretion has been considered is not always clear. For example, in *Poche v. Pihera*,[66] an executor was found to have failed to consider the exercise of a discretion to convert non-income producing investments to income producing investments despite evidence that she had discussed the same with an assistant public trustee and a stock broker.

If the exercise of a power has not been considered at all, the court will interfere.[67] If the power has been exercised, the court will not interfere unless the

---

62 *Gisborne v. Gisborne* (1877), 2 App. Cas. 300 (U.K. H.L.).

63 *Tempest v. Lord Camoys* (1882), 21 Ch. D. 571 (Eng. Ch. Div.) at 578.

64 See *Billes, Re* (1983), 42 O.R. (2d) 110, 1983 CarswellOnt 613, 14 E.T.R. 247, 148 D.L.R. (3d) 512 (H.C.); *Haasz, Re*, [1959] O.W.N. 395, 21 D.L.R. (2d) 12 (C.A.); *Engelman Estate, Re* (1985), 21 E.T.R. 134, 1985 CarswellBC 620 (S.C.), reversed (1986), 1986 CarswellBC 587, 23 E.T.R. 30 (C.A.); *Hinton v. Canada Permanent Trust Co.* (1979), 5 E.T.R. 117, 1979 CarswellOnt 596 (H.C.); *Kordyban v. Kordyban*, 1 B.C.L.R. (4th) 45, 44 E.T.R. (2d) 85, 2002 CarswellBC 813, 2002 BCSC 475 (S.C.), additional reasons at 2004 CarswellBC 298, 2004 BCSC 184, 5 E.T.R. (3d) 176 (S.C.), affirmed 2003 CarswellBC 803, 2003 BCCA 216, 13 B.C.L.R. (4th) 50, 50 E.T.R. (2d) 116, [2003] 6 W.W.R. 606, 181 B.C.A.C. 75, 298 W.A.C. 75 (C.A.), additional reasons at 2003 CarswellBC 2019, 19 B.C.L.R. (4th) 19, 186 B.C.A.C. 77, 306 W.A.C. 77, 2003 BCCA 455 (C.A.).

65 *Tempest v. Lord Camoys, supra*, note 63.

66 (1983), (sub nom. *Poche v. Poche*) 50 A.R. 264, 1983 CarswellAlta 291, 16 E.T.R. 68, 6 D.L.R. (4th) 40 (Surr. Ct.).

67 *Klug v. Klug*, [1918] 2 Ch. 67 (Eng. Ch. Div.).

decision to exercise it was made in bad faith, oppressively, corruptly or otherwise improperly.[68]

If there is a conflict between a duty and a power as, for example, when trustees are given a duty to convert and a power to retain, the court will not intervene. If there is no unanimity, the duty to sell prevails over the power to retain.[69] However, if there are equally balanced powers as, for example, a power to convert and a power to retain, the court will intervene in cases of deadlock on the basis that the trustees are under a duty to exercise one power or the other and until they do so they fail to discharge their duty. If the court did not intervene, the testator's intentions would be frustrated and the interests of the beneficiaries affected adversely.[70]

The courts' inherent jurisdiction to supervise the exercise of the trustees' discretion cannot be displaced.[71] Therefore, provisions in the trust instrument which purport to relieve trustees from liability will not prevent the courts from intervening when the trustees are grossly negligent.[72]

Further Reading

M.C. Cullity, "Judicial Control of Trustees' Discretions" (1975), 25 U.T.L.J.

M.C. Cullity, "Trustees' Duties, Powers and Discretions — Exercise of Discretionary Powers", *Recent Developments in Estate Planning and Administration*, 1980, p. 13.

FOX v. FOX ESTATE

(1996), 28 O.R. (3d) 496, 10 E.T.R. (2d) 229, 1996 CarswellOnt 317,
88 O.A.C. 201
Ontario Court of Appeal[73]

The testator, Ralph Fox, was survived by his wife, Miriam, and his only child, Walter. Walter had married a couple of months before his father's death. The testator's will provided:

4. During the lifetime of my said wife, if she shall survive me, to hold the residue of my estate upon the following trusts:

---

68 *Haasz, Re*, [1959] O.W.N. 395, 21 D.L.R. (2d) 12 (C.A.); *Gisborne v. Gisborne* (1877), 2 App. Cas. 300 (U.K. H.L.), at p. 306; *Sievert, Re* (1921), 67 D.L.R. 199, 51 O.L.R. 305 (C.A.); *McLaren, Re* (1921), 69 D.L.R. 599, 51 O.L.R. 538 (C.A.).

69 *Haasz, ibid.*

70 *Billes, Re* (1983), 42 O.R. (2d) 110, 1983 CarswellOnt 613, 14 E.T.R. 247, 148 D.L.R. (3d) 512 (H.C.); *Haasz, ibid.*

71 *Boe v. Alexander* (1985), 21 E.T.R. 246, 1985 CarswellBC 622 (S.C.), affirmed on reconsideration (October 18, 1985), Doc. Vancouver C824399 (B.C. S.C.), affirmed (1987), 28 E.T.R. 228, 1987 CarswellBC 182, 15 B.C.L.R. (2d) 106, 41 D.L.R. (4th) 520 (C.A.), leave to appeal refused (1988), 22 B.C.L.R. (2d) xxx, 28 E.T.R. xxxvi, 87 N.R. 299 (note) (S.C.C.).

72 *Ibid.* See also *Poche v. Pihera, supra*, note 66.

73 Application for leave to appeal to the Supreme Court of Canada dismissed with costs (1996), 207 N.R. 80 (note), 97 O.A.C. 320 (note) (S.C.C.). S.C.C. Bulletin, 1996, p. 2157.

(a) To pay to my said wife, for her own use and benefit absolutely, 75% of the net income derived therefrom, and to pay the remaining 25% thereof as follows:

    (i) For so long as my said son shall be living, to my said son,

    (ii) After the death of my said son, to or for my said son's issue, or some one or more of them, in such proportions as my Trustee may, in its absolute discretion, consider advisable from time to time.

    (iii) After the death of the last survivor of my said son and his issue, to my said wife, for her own use and benefit absolutely.

(b) Out of the capital thereof, to pay such amount or amounts as my Trustee may in its absolute discretion, consider advisable to or for my said son.

(c) Out of the capital thereof, to pay such amount or amounts as my Trustee may, in its absolute discretion, consider advisable from time to time to or for the benefit of my said son's issue or such one or more of them as my Trustee may select from time to time.

5. After the death of the survivor of me and my said wife, subject as hereinafter provided, to hold the residue of my estate upon trust to pay the net income therefrom to my said son until he attains the age of twenty-five years, and at that time or at the death of the survivor of me and my said wife, whichever be later, to pay, transfer and convey unto my said son the residue of my estate; provided that if my said son shall die before attaining the age of twenty-five years, either in my lifetime or after my death, the residue of my estate shall, after the death of the last survivor of me and my said wife and my said son, (hereinafter referred to as "the time of determination") be held in trust, in equal shares per stirpes, for the issue of my said son living at the time of determination, or, if there be no issue of my said son living at the time of determination . . .

Walter married a couple of months before his father died. There were two children of the marriage, Ralph and Shayne. The marriage was unhappy and ended in divorce in 1986. In 1989, Walter married his secretary. This caused serious problems in the family, since the Fox family were Jewish and Walter's new wife was not. Miriam objected to the marriage and made a new will disinheriting Walter. Then she exercised her power of encroachment in favour of her grandchildren.

Walter brought an application for an order reviewing Miriam's exercise of the power of encroachment, removing her as executrix, and directing her to account. The judge of first instance ordered an accounting, but dismissed the application to remove Miriam as executrix.[74] She found that Miriam had used the power in order to deprive Walter of his right to the residue because she disapproved of his marriage outside the faith. However, the judge of first instance held that, since she had not acted *mala fide*, Miriam acted properly in exercising the power. Walter appealed.

---

74 (1994), 5 E.T.R. (2d) 174, 1994 CarswellOnt 666 (Gen. Div.), additional reasons at (1994), 1994 CarswellOnt 4516, 5 E.T.R. (2d) 174 at 188 (Gen. Div.).

GALLIGAN J.A.:

. . .

The principal question [at first instance] concerned Miriam's reason for exercising her power to encroach. A second concomitant question was whether the exercise of the power was a proper one. The first issue was factual; the second was legal.

The trial judge's finding on the factual issue is clear. She found that Miriam used her power to encroach in order "to deprive the applicant of his interest in the bulk of the residue of the estate *because he had married a gentile*".[75] There was overwhelming evidence to support that finding even though Miriam denied that this was her motive. The trial judge found that Miriam's motive was "perhaps coupled" with her concern for the welfare of her grandchildren but that her dislike of Walter's marriage was throughout "her prime motivation in encroaching as she did".

Unquestionably, concern for the welfare of her grandchildren would be a proper motive to encroach on their behalf. Initially, I was of the view that because Miriam's primary motive was "perhaps coupled" with a concern for her grand-children's welfare, that the latter concern might support the exercise of the power of encroachment. However . . . I have concluded that I must examine the legal issue in the light of an unassailable finding of fact that Miriam's disapproval of Walter's proposed marriage to a gentile was her motivation for exercising her power to encroach.

[His lordship noted that the discretion conferred on the executrix was absolute and continued:]

The entire question of the degree of control which the courts can and should exercise over a trustee who holds an absolute discretion is filled with difficulty. The leading case, or at least the case to which reference is almost always made, is *Gisborne v. Gisborne*.[76] It stands for the proposition that so long as there is no *mala fides* on the part of a trustee the exercise of an absolute discretion is to be without any check or control by the courts.

The courts, however, have not always equated *mala fides* with fraud. I am spared an extensive review of authority by a very learned paper written by Professor Maurice Cullity, "Judicial Control of Trustees' Discretions".[77] I think it can safely be said in the light of Professor Cullity's analysis of the authorities that some conduct which does not amount to fraud will be categorized as *mala fides* so as to bring it within the scope of judicial supervision. I am in respectful agreement with Professor Cullity when he expresses the opinion that the term

---

75 *Ibid.*, at 191 (emphasis added).
76 (1877), 2 App. Cas. 300 (H.L.).
77 (1975), 25 U.T.L.J. 99.

mala fides is sufficiently broad "to make the use of the term undesirable".[78] Nevertheless, the term is still used. While I am not bold enough to attempt to define its outside limits, I think the cases do support Professor Cullity's conclusion that the courts may interfere if a trustee's decision is influenced by extraneous matters.[79] I make particular reference to the judgment of Steele J. in *Hunter Estate v. Holton*:[80]

> Trustees must act in good faith and be fair as between beneficiaries in the exercise of their powers. There is no allegation of bad faith in the present case. A court should be reluctant to interfere with the exercise of the power of discretion by a trustee. I adopt the following criteria in *Re Hastings-Bass . . .,*[81] as being applicable to the court's review of the exercise of such power:
>
> > To sum up the preceding observations, in our judgment, where by the terms of a trust . . . a trustee is given a discretion as to some matter under which he acts in good faith, the court should not interfere with his action notwithstanding that it does not have the full effect which he intended, *unless* (1) what he has achieved is unauthorised by the power conferred upon him, or (2) *it is clear that he would not have acted as he did (a) had he not taken into account considerations which he should not have taken into account,* or (b) had he not failed to take into account considerations which he ought to have taken into account.[82]

In this case, in my view, the fact that her son intended to marry a gentile was completely extraneous to the duty which the will obviously imposed upon Miriam, namely, to be concerned about the welfare of her grandchildren. This extraneous consideration demonstrated sufficient *mala fides* to bring her conduct within any reasonable interpretation of that term.

The circumstances bear some similarity to those in *Klug v. Klug.*[83] In that case a trustee refused to exercise a discretion allowing her to pay money for the advancement or benefit of her daughter because her daughter had married without her consent. In those circumstances Neville J. held:[84]

> . . . it is the duty of the Court to interfere and, in the exercise of its control over the discretion given to the trustees, to direct a sum to be raised out of the capital sufficient to pay . . .

The duty which rested with the trustee was to pay moneys for the advancement or benefit of the children if the trustee saw fit to do so. While Neville J. did not specifically state that the mother's displeasure at her daughter's marriage was an extraneous circumstance, it seems to me that the situation was analogous to this one. In the context of all the facts, disapproval of the marriage was extraneous to the child's advancement or benefit. The court interfered with the trustee's discretion in that case and I think this court ought to do the same.

---

78 *Ibid.,* at 119.
79 *Ibid.,* at 117.
80 (1992), 7 O.R. (3d) 372 at 379, 46 E.T.R. 178 (Gen. Div.).
81 [1975] Ch. 25 at 41, [1974] 2 All E.R. 193 (C.A.).
82 Emphasis added.
83 *Supra,* note 67.
84 *Ibid.,* at 71.

There is another reason why the discretion which Miriam exercised in this case was improper and must be set aside. It is abhorrent to contemporary community standards that disapproval of a marriage outside of one's religious faith could justify the exercise of a trustee's discretion. It is now settled that it is against public policy to discriminate on grounds of race or religion. This is made clear in the reasons delivered by Robins J.A. in *Canada Trust Co. v. Ontario Human Rights Commission*:[85]

> To say that a trust premised on these notions of racism and religious superiority contravenes contemporary public policy is to expatiate the obvious. The concept that any one race or any one religion is intrinsically better than any other is patently at variance with the democratic principles governing our pluralistic society in which equality rights are constitutionally guaranteed and in which the multicultural heritage of Canadians is to be preserved and enhanced. The widespread criticism of the Foundation by human rights bodies, the press, the clergy, the university community and the general community serves to demonstrate how far out of keeping the trust now is with prevailing ideas and standards of racial and religious tolerance and equality and, indeed, how offensive its terms are to fair-minded citizens.
>
> To perpetuate a trust that imposes restrictive criteria on the basis of the discriminatory notions espoused in these recitals according to the terms specified by the settlor would not, in my opinion, be conducive to the public interest. The settlor's freedom to dispose of his property through the creation of a charitable trust fashioned along these lines must give way to current principles of public policy under which all races and religions are to be treated on a footing of equality and accorded equal regard and equal respect.

In that case, Robins J.A. was discussing the restraint which public policy puts upon the freedom of the settlor to dispose of his property as he saw fit. If a settlor cannot dispose of property in a fashion which discriminates upon racial or religious grounds, it seems to me to follow that public policy also prohibits a trustee from exercising her discretion for racial or religious reasons.

I am of the view that in this case it would be contrary to public policy to permit a trustee effectively to disinherit the residual beneficiary because he dared to marry outside the religious faith of his mother. While there were decisions in the past which have upheld discriminatory conditions in wills, in response to a query from the bench, counsel in this case were not prepared to argue that any court would today uphold a condition in a will which provides that a beneficiary is to be disinherited if he or she marries outside of a particular religious faith. I find compelling Mr. Eastman's argument that if a testator could not do so then his trustee could not do it for him.

Counsel for the grandchildren argued that if Ralph were still alive there would have been nothing to prevent him from revoking his will and making a new one in which he left nothing to Walter. She argued, therefore, that in the exercise of her absolute power to encroach Miriam should be able to do that for him. Even if it were accepted that Ralph, if alive, would have disinherited Walter because of his intention to marry out of Ralph's religious faith, that argument cannot succeed.

---

85 (1990), 74 O.R. (2d) 481 at 495-96, 69 D.L.R. (4th) 321 (C.A.).

It is of course a given, assuming testamentary capacity, that a person is entitled to dispose of property by will in any fashion that he or she may wish. The exercise of a testator's right of disposition is not subject to supervision by the court. But a trustee's exercise of discretion is subject to curial control. Admittedly, because he would not be subject to judicial supervision, Ralph, if alive, could have disinherited Walter for reasons which would have contravened public policy. However, Ralph is not alive and is not preparing a new will. Miriam, while acting as a trustee, on the other hand is subject to judicial control and that control can and must prevent her from exercising her discretion in a fashion which offends public policy.

With great deference to the experienced trial judge who held a different view, it is my opinion that Miriam's exercise of discretion to the prejudice of Walter because he married outside of Miriam's and his own religious faith was unlawful and must be set aside. It follows that as a result of her improper dealing with the assets of the estate Miriam can no longer remain the executrix.

For these reasons it is my opinion that this appeal should succeed. I have read the reasons for judgment prepared by McKinlay J.A. and I agree that the appeal should also be allowed for the reasons which she has given. I would dispose of the appeal in the fashion which she proposes.

[McKinlay J.A. concurred. She agreed that if the sole reason Miriam exercised the power the way she did was because of her objections to Walter's marriage, then the judgment of Galligan J.A. was correct. However, in her view it was not clear that that was the sole reason. Accordingly, it was necessary to interpret the power and Miriam's exercise of it. Her ladyship was of the opinion that the obvious intent of the testator was to give his son an income from the estate and the remainder absolutely on his mother's death. The power to encroach in favour of the son's issue had to be viewed in that light. She held that Miriam did not consider the terms of the will, had no understanding of her duties as executrix, and assumed that she was entitled to dispose of the property as if it were her own. Accordingly, the exercise of the power was invalid for that reason.

Catzman J.A. agreed that Miriam dealt with the property as if it were her own and that the power to encroach did not entitle her to encroach in the way she did. However, he was of the opinion that Miriam's disapproval of her son's marriage was not the sole basis for her exercise of the power. Another basis was her concern for the financial welfare of her grandchildren. That basis would have been a legitimate reason for exercising the power in favour of her grandchildren. He did not decide whether the first basis had the effect of also invalidating the second, but expressed the opinion that the courts should be loath to interfere with the exercise of a trustee's discretion if it is exercised for a valid motive even if the trustee also acts out of an invalid motive.

The court allowed the appeal, removed Miriam as executrix, and directed that the moneys and property improperly transferred to her grandchildren should be restored to the estate.]

Notes and Questions

1. If a trustee exercises a power from a proper motive as well as from a base motive, does the latter invalidate the former? Should it?

2. If a power not coupled with a duty is given to trustees to be exercised in their absolute discretion, assuming that the trustees are willing to exercise the power and they are not acting *male fide*, the courts have consistently said that they will not interfere with the trustees' exercise of their discretion and lack the power to do so. Indeed, in the leading case, *Gisborne v. Gisborne*,[86] Lord Cairns stated that the court recognizes that it is the trustees who must exercise the discretion and the court had no right to control the exercise by the trustees of their discretion.

Does this, perhaps, not put the trustees in a difficult position? If they ask the court for advice about how to exercise their discretion, the court will not give it, since the matter is entirely within the trustees' discretion.[87] However, if they go ahead and exercise their discretion they may be told afterwards that they have erred and be liable. Should trustees not be entitled to seek advice about different courses of action?

3. Another instructive case on the exercise by the trustees of their discretion is *Edell v. Sitzer*.[88] Paul Sizter and his wife had two children, Michael and Jodi. Michael worked in his father's business. Paul developed an estate freeze under which Michael would acquire shares in the business and other assets would be transferred to Jodi. Under the estate freeze, two trusts were created, one for Michael, and one for Jodi. Each trust gave the trustees (Paul and his wife) a power to distribute capital in the following terms:

> The Trustees shall have the right at any time or times before the Distribution Date to pay to or for some one or more of the said children and more remote issue of Paul Sitzer and Geraldine Sitzer who are then living and are at least eighteen (18) years of age, to the exclusion of any other or others, such amount or amounts out of the capital of the Trust Property in such proportions as the Trustees in their unfettered discretion shall determine advisable or expedient.

Paul's relationship with Jodi had been acrimonious for years and deteriorated after Paul's wife died. Eventually, he became estranged from Jodi. Then he became concerned about the future financial security of the family business, since Jodi's trust had an interest in the shares of the holding company that owned the business. Accordingly, he exercised the power of encroachment in Jodi's trust to transfer those shares to Michael's trust. He made an offer of settlement to Jodi which would have provided substantial benefits to her and her family, but she rejected the offer and sued her father. Among other things, she alleged that the encroachment was invalid because, properly interpreted, it only authorized payments of money, and because Paul had acted *male fide* to punish her.

The court dismissed the action. Cullity J. held that the exercise of the power of encroachment was valid. A power of encroachment, as well as other dispositive powers, can be exercised by *in specie* distributions. This was true especially of this power, since Jodi's trust held shares in the holding company. Thus, it was not reasonable to interpret

---

86 (1877), 2 App. Cas. 300 (U.K. H.L.) at 306, 307.

87 *Cf. Wright, Re* (1976), 14 O.R. (2d) 698, 74 D.L.R. (3d) 504, 1976 CarswellOnt 567 (H.C.).

88 (2001), 55 O.R. (3d) 198, 40 E.T.R. (2d) 10, [2001] O.J. No. 2909, 2001 CarswellOnt 5020 (S.C.J.).

the power narrowly. The court further held that Paul did not abuse his discretion. While he was angry with Jodi, he was not motivated by improper considerations in exercising the power. Rather, his motive was to ensure that Jodi and her issue be prevented from interfering in the operation of the family business to the detriment of all concerned. Further, the power of encroachment was wide and gave the trustees power to change the initial capital allocations if the trustees determined that that would be in the best interests of one or more of the beneficiaries.

5. RIGHTS OF TRUSTEES

(a) Payment

At common law, trustees were expected to perform their duties gratuitously unless the trust instrument expressly provides for their remuneration. In Canada, however, legislation empowers the courts to compensate trustees for their efforts in administering trusts.[89] Thus, it is common for all trustees to be paid. In Ontario, for example, a trustee may apply for compensation either at the time of passing the accounts or, pursuant to s. 61 of the *Trustee Act*,[90] set out below, at any other time. Section 61 permits the court to award a "fair and reasonable allowance" to the trustee as compensation. The usual practice of the courts in awarding compensation is to apply the "tariff guidelines," that is, to award compensation as a percentage of capital and income.[91] However, as explained in *Laing Estate v. Laing Estate*,[92] reproduced below, the court will then check this amount against such considerations as the size and complexity of the trust, the care, responsibility and risks assumed by or required of the trustee, the time spent in administering the trust, the skill and ability displayed, and the results obtained and success achieved through the efforts of the trustees.[93] In addition, on the application of

---

89 These same principles have been held to apply to directors of a charitable corporation even though the directors were not, strictly speaking, trustees. See *Public Trustee v. Toronto Humane Society* (1985), 40 D.L.R.(4th) 111, 60 O.R. (2d) 236 (H.C.).

90 R.S.O. 1990, c. T.23 (am. by S.O. 2000, c. 26, Sched. A, s. 15(2)).

91 See, *e.g.*, *Cohen, Re* (1977), 1 E.T.R. 80, 1977 CarswellOnt 391 (Surr. Ct.) in which 5% of capital, 5% of income and 2/5 of 1% of the gross value of assets as a management fee were permitted; see *Yale v. Mokelky* (1984), 37 Sask. R. 292, 1984 CarswellSask 511 (Surr. Ct.) which followed the percentages used in *Atkinson Estate, Re* (1951), [1952] O.R. 685, [1952] 3 D.L.R. 609, 1952 CarswellOnt 66 (C.A.), affirmed (sub nom. *National Trust Co. v. Public Trustee*) [1953] 2 S.C.R. 41, 1953 CarswellOnt 136, [1953] 3 D.L.R. 497; contrast, however, *Hooke, Re* (1969), 72 W.W.R. 229, 1969 CarswellSask 99, 9 D.L.R. (3d) 525 (C.A.) and *O'Kelly v. Canada Permanent Trust Co.* (1971), [1972] 1 W.W.R. 41, 1971 CarswellSask 77 (C.A.).

92 (1998), (sub nom. *Laing Estate v. Hines*) 167 D.L.R. (4th) 150, 1998 CarswellOnt 4037, [1998] O.J. No. 4169, (sub nom. *Laing Estate, Re*) 113 O.A.C. 335, 41 O.R. (3d) 571, 25 E.T.R. (2d) 139 (C.A.).

93 *Toronto General Trusts Corp. v. Central Ontario Railway* (1905), 6 O.W.R. 350, 1905 CarswellOnt 449 (H.C.); *Hughes, Re* (1918), 43 O.L.R. 594 (H.C.), affirmed (1918), 42 O.L.R. 345, 14 O.W.N. 5 (Master); *Anderson, Re*, 55 O.L.R. 527, [1924] 4 D.L.R. 441 (H.C.), reversed (1924), 56 O.L.R. 228, [1925] 1 D.L.R. 371 (C.A.); and *Verbonac, Re* (1984), 31 Sask. R. 161, 1984 CarswellSask 252 (Surr. Ct.). See, also, Brian A. Schnurr, "Quantifying Executors' Compensation: Law and Procedure" (1991), 11 E. & T.J. 134.

the trustee, the court may award an additional sum for the management of the trust based on special circumstances.[94]

There has been a fair bit of litigation about the principles that should be used in fixing compensation. Some courts have been critical of the application of the tariff guidelines on the ground that this is not compatible with what s. 61 requires[95] since it limits the court to making an award that is "fair and reasonable" in the circumstances.[96] For the same reason, some courts have required the trustee to provide sufficient particulars of the magnitude of the estate, the diversity of assets, the time spent, and skills required.[97] This was also an issue in *Laing*. Because information about the details of the estate and its administration is contained in an application to pass accounts, it is more common to have compensation set at that time than by means of a separate application pursuant to section 61 of the *Trustee Act*.[98]

TRUSTEE ACT

R.S.O. 1990, c. T.23, am by S.O. 2000, c. 26, Sched. A, s. 15(2)

ALLOWANCE TO TRUSTEES AND PERSONAL REPRESENTATIVES

61. (1) A trustee, guardian or personal representative is entitled to such fair and reasonable allowance for the care, pains and trouble, and the time expended in and about the estate, as may be allowed by a judge of the Ontario Court (General Division).

(2) The amount of such compensation may be settled although the estate is not before the court in an action.

---

94 *Jeffery Estate, Re* (1990), 39 E.T.R. 173, 1990 CarswellOnt 503 (Surr. Ct.). See *Trustee Act*, R.S.B.C. 1996, c. 464, s. 88(3) which permits a trustee to make an application for a care and maintenance fee. The provision sets the maximum amount of the fee at 0.4% of the average market value of the assets.

95 See, *e.g.*, *Atkinson Estate, Re* (1951), [1952] O.R. 685, [1952] 3 D.L.R. 609, 1952 CarswellOnt 66 (C.A.), affirmed (sub nom. *National Trust Co. v. Public Trustee*) [1953] 2 S.C.R. 41, 1953 CarswellOnt 136, [1953] 3 D.L.R. 497.

96 See for *e.g.*, *Gerow, Re* (1974), 8 N.B.R. (2d) 90, 1974 CarswellNB 31 (Prob. Ct.); *Laing Estate v. Laing Estate, supra,* note 92.

97 *Welbourn, Re*, [1979] 3 W.W.R. 113, 4 E.T.R. 122, 1979 CarswellAlta 202, 96 D.L.R. (3d) 76, 23 A.R. 91 (Surr. Ct.); *Sproule, Re*, 17 A.R. 58, (sub nom. *Sproule v. Montreal Trust Co. (No. 2)*) [1979] 4 W.W.R. 670, 95 D.L.R. (3d) 458, 1979 CarswellAlta 218 (C.A.), additional reasons at (1979), 95 D.L.R. (3d) 458 at 471 (C.A.); *Matteotti v. Matteotti* (1982), 48 A.R. 225, 1982 CarswellAlta 83, 19 Alta. L.R. (2d) 369 (Q.B.). See *Safian Estate v. Safian* (1995), (sub nom. *Gerrand v. Safian*) 134 Sask. R. 229, 1995 CarswellSask 454, 9 E.T.R. (2d) 155, 101 W.A.C. 229 (C.A.), in which the Court of Appeal held that the trial judge was entitled to request that the executors provide the court with an estimate of the amount of time they had expended in completing the administration of the estate. Cameron J.A. held that the trial judge appropriately drew an adverse inference from the executors' refusal to provide an estimate. He inferred that the time expended by the executors bore no reasonable relation to the compensation they sought. But see, *Laing Estate, supra,* note 96, reproduced below.

98 R.S.O. 1990, c. T.23.

(3) The judge, in passing the accounts of a trustee or of a personal representative or guardian, may from time to time allow a fair and reasonable allowance for care, pains and trouble, and time expended in or about the estate.

(4) Where a barrister or solicitor is a trustee, guardian, or personal representative, and has rendered necessary professional services to the estate, regard may be had in making the allowance to such circumstances, and the allowance shall be increased by such amount as may be considered fair and reasonable in respect of such services.

(5) Nothing in this section applies where the allowance is fixed by the instrument creating the trust.

Comparable Legislation

Trustee Act, R.S.A. 2000, c. T-8, s. 44 (am. by R.S.A. 2000, c. 16 (Supp.), s. 59(a)); R.S.B.C. 1996, c. 464, s. 88 (am. by R.S.B.C. 1996 (Supp.) c. 464, s. 1); R.S.M. 1987, c. T160, s. 90; R.S.N.S. 1989, c. 479, s. 62; R.S.N.W.T. 1988, c. T-8, ss. 49-53; R.S.P.E.I. 1988, c. T-8, s. 31; R.S.S. 1978, c. T-23, ss. 80-84 (s. 82 am. by S.S. 1992, c. 62, s. 33(3)); R.S.Y. 2002, c. 223, s. 49; *Trustees Act*, R.S.N.B. 1973, c. T-15, s. 38 (am. by S.N.B. 1975, c. 63, s. 1; S.N.B. 1979, c. 41, s. 123(2); S.N.B. 1987, c. 6, s. 115, repealing s. 38(5)).

LAING ESTATE v. LAING ESTATE

(1998), (sub nom. *Laing Estate v. Hines*) 167 D.L.R. (4th) 150, 41 O.R. (3d) 571, 1998 CarswellOnt 4037, [1998] O.J. No. 4169, (sub nom. *Laing Estate, Re*) 113 O.A.C. 335, 25 E.T.R. (2d) 139
Ontario Court of Appeal

The deceased left a large and complex estate. His executor brought an application under s. 61 of the *Trustee Act*[99] for an order passing his accounts and awarding compensation in the amount of $211,968.33. That amount was calculated on the basis of the "tariff guidelines" normally used to calculate an executor's compensation. Wright J. refused to apply the guidelines in part because the executor was not able to provide details of the time spent in administering the estate. He reduced the compensation to $75,000. The Divisional Court allowed the executor's appeal, holding that the tariff guidelines should be applied.[100] Beneficiaries of the estate appealed to the Court of Appeal.[101]

---

99 R.S.O. 1990, c. T.23.

100 The reasons of the Divisional Court are reported at (1996), (sub nom. *Logan v. Laing Estate*) 11 E.T.R. (2d) 268, 1996 CarswellOnt 775, (sub nom. *Laing Estate, Re*) 89 O.A.C. 321 (Div. Ct.).

101 The appeal was heard together with appeals in *Flaska Estate, Re* (1998), [1998] O.J. No. 4171, 1998 CarswellOnt 4059 (C.A.), additional reasons at (1999), 1999 CarswellOnt 178 (C.A.), and *Gordon Estate, Re* (1998), 1998 CarswellOnt 2207, (sub nom. *Gordon & Kent v. Panet*) 111 O.A.C. 125, 24 E.T.R. (2d) 308 (Div. Ct.), additional reasons at (1998), 1998 CarswellOnt 3732, 114 O.A.C. 312 (Div. Ct.), reversed (1998), 1998 CarswellOnt 4036, 125 O.A.C. 272

By the Court:

. . .

II

[2] There are two questions of law of general importance raised on this appeal:

* What are the principles to be applied in determining "fair and reasonable" compensation under s. 61(1) of the *Trustee Act*?
* What is the appropriate standard of appellate review of an audit judge's assessment of what constitutes fair and reasonable compensation?

. . .

The Applicable Principles

[4] Section 61(1) of the *Trustee Act* provides:

> 61(1) A trustee, guardian or personal representative is entitled to such fair and reasonable allowance for the care, pains and trouble, and the time expended in and about the estate, as may be allowed by a judge of the Ontario Court (General Division).

[5] The language of the statute is, of necessity, broad. Modern judicial efforts to structure the assessment required under s. 61(1) so as to yield results which were fair to the trustee and the beneficiaries and reasonably predictable can be traced as far back as at least *Re Toronto General Trusts Corp. and Central Ontario Railway*,[102] where Teetzel J. said:[103]

> From the American and Canadian precedents, based upon statutory provision for compensation to trustees, the following circumstances appear proper to be taken into consideration in fixing the amount of compensation: (1) the magnitude of the trust; (2) the care and responsibility springing therefrom; (3) the time occupied in performing its duties; (4) the skill and ability displayed; and (5) the success which has attended its administration.

[6] The five factors set out by Teetzel J. have been recognized as appropriate considerations in determining "fair and reasonable" compensation under s. 61 of the *Trustee Act*.[104]

[7] In a further effort to bring predictability to the assessment of a trustee's compensation, the practice developed of determining the trustee's compensation as a percentage of the probate value of the estate. These percentages are sometimes referred to as the "tariff guidelines". These guidelines are not sanctioned by statute

---

(C.A.). The reasons in *Laing* reflect the submissions made and the conclusions reached in all the appeals.

102 (1905), 6 O.W.R. 350 (H.C.).

103 *Ibid.*, at 354.

104 See, *e.g.*, *Re Mortimer*, [1936] O.R. 438 at 441, [1936] 3 D.L.R. 380 (C.A.).

or regulation, but were developed by the estates bar and judges of the former Surrogate Court.[105] Those guidelines are described in *Re Jeffery Estate*.[106]

> There are many later cases which show that, in Ontario at least, a practice has developed of awarding compensation on the basis of 2½ per cent percentages against the four categories of capital receipts, capital disbursements, revenue receipts and revenue disbursements, along with, in appropriate cases, a management fee of 2/5 of 1 per cent per annum on the gross value of the estate . . .

[8] The issue to be determined here is the manner in which the factors identified in *Re Toronto General Trusts and Central Ontario Railway*[107] and the tariff guidelines are to be meshed so as to yield an amount which is "fair and reasonable" in all the circumstances. Having reviewed the six factums filed in these appeals, considered the oral submissions and examined the relevant authorities, it appears that all parties favour the approach set down by Killeen J. in *Re Jeffery Estate*:[108]

> To me, the case law and common sense dictate that the audit judge should first test the compensation claims using the "percentages" approach and then, as it were, cross-check or confirm the mathematical result against the "five-factors" approach set out in Re Toronto General Trusts and Central Ontario Railway, supra. Usually, counsel will, in argument, set out a factual background against which the five factors can be brought to bear on the case at hand. Additionally, the judge will consider whether an extra allowance should be made for management, based on special circumstances. The result of this testing process should enable the judge to determine whether the claims are excessive or not and, in the result, will enable the judge to make adjustments as required. The process is not scientific but is not intended to be: in the estate context, it is a search for an award which reflects fairness to the executor; in a real sense, the search is for an appropriate quantum meruit award in a unique setting.

[9] Adams J. and Steele J. (in dissent), in their reasons, clearly followed the approach set out in *Re Jeffery Estate*. Certain passages in the reasons of Corbett J.[109] suggest some departure from that approach. We agree with and adopt the approach taken in *Re Jeffery Estate*. In our view, it best achieves the appropriate balance between the need to provide predictability while, at the same time, tailoring compensation to the circumstances of each case.

The Standard of Appellate Review

[10] The fixing of compensation under s. 61(1) of the *Trustee Act* is far from an exact science. As Adams J. observed,[110] it "is an issue over which reasonable minds may differ". Appellate review of that assessment must be restrained so that

---

105 B. Schnurr, Quantifying Executor's Compensation; Canadian Bar Association, Continuing Legal Education, November 8, 1991, pp. 5-7.
106 (1990), 39 E.T.R. 173 (Ont. Surr. Ct.) at 178.
107 *Supra.*
108 *Supra*, at 179.
109 *E.g.*, at 282-3.
110 In the Divisional Court, *ibid.*, at 284.

it does not become merely the substitution of one reasonable assessment for another reasonable assessment. In *Re Smith*,[111] Pickup C.J.O. observed:

> ... but the Court of Appeal should interfere if there is any error in principle, or if, in its opinion, the amount allowed is grossly insufficient or excessive.

[11] In addition to appellate review to determine compliance with the applicable principles and to ensure that the result is not grossly insufficient or excessive, an appellate court may review findings of fact upon which an assessment under s. 61(1) of the *Trustee Act* is based. It will interfere with those findings only where they can be said to be unreasonable.[112]

[12] If an appellate court determines that the audit judge has made an unreasonable finding of fact, erred in principle, or reached a manifestly wrong result, it should, if possible, go on to determine the appropriate compensation. In doing so, the appellate court will accept any findings of fact made by the assessment judge which the appellate court has not found to be unreasonable. On occasion when the appellate court finds reversible error, it will be necessary to order a new hearing.

[13] In his written submissions, Mr. Mercer . . . suggested that the Supreme Court of Canada had sanctioned a broader ambit of review in *Re Atkinson*.[113] It is true that Kerwin J., for the majority . . . rejected as unsound the contention that the Court of Appeal could interfere with the decision of the Surrogate Court judge only if it found that he had erred in principle.[114] In *Atkinson*, however, the Court of Appeal had directed a reference to the master when the case first came before that court.[115] The master had heard several days of evidence and, as required, returned that evidence, the exhibits and his report to the Court of Appeal. The court then determined the matter based on that expanded record. In those circumstances, the court could hardly be limited to an examination of the record before the Surrogate Court judge. *Re Atkinson* is, however, the exception and should not be confused with the rule as described in *Re Smith*.[116]

III

Did the Divisional Court err in holding that Wright J. erred in principle?

[14] The Divisional Court was divided on this question. Corbett J. and Adams J. found error in principle. Steele J. could find none. It is apparent from the reasons of Wright J. that he was primarily concerned with the respondent's inability to provide even a relatively accurate estimate of the time spent on the administration of the estate. Wright J. was also concerned about the absence of any documentation

---

111 [1953] O.R. 185 (C.A.) at 189.
112 *Equity Waste Management of Canada v. Halton Hills (Town)* (1997), 35 O.R. (3d) 321 (C.A.) at 335-6.
113 [1953] 2 S.C.R. 41, [1953] 3 D.L.R. 497.
114 *Ibid.*, at 44.
115 [1952] O.R. 685 at 692, [1952] 3 D.L.R. 609.
116 *Supra.*

evidencing the time spent in the administration of the estate. He focussed on these inadequacies in allowing the respondent only about 35% of the amount he would have been entitled to under the tariff guidelines. In fixing the respondent's compensation, it appears that Wright J. was motivated, in part, by a desire to encourage trustees in large estates to keep detailed records of time spent on the administration of the estate.

[15] There can be no doubt that time spent is one of the relevant factors in fixing compensation. Nor could one argue with the proposition that trustees of large estates would be well advised to thoroughly document their time spent on work related to the estate. We cannot, however, agree that time spent on the administration of the estate can be the dominant consideration in fixing compensation, or that compensation should be reduced to "punish" a trustee who has not kept adequate records. The time spent by the trustee on the estate is but one factor and cannot become the ultimate measuring stick against which compensation is determined any more than any one of the other relevant factors can be given a dominant position. Reducing the assessment required by s. 61(1) of the *Trustee Act* to the mere product of hours spent multiplied by a reasonable hourly rate is inconsistent with the statutory command that the compensation be "fair and reasonable" and that, in addition to time spent, it reflect "the care, pains and trouble" expended in the administration of the estate.

[16] We agree with Adams J., when he said:[117]

> . . . Wright J. erred in principle in attributing the overriding significance he did to the manner in which the Executor accounted for his time.

[17] This was a large, complex estate and even allowing for the deficiencies in the respondent's accounting for his time, he clearly spent a great deal of time on the administration of this estate. The skill and ability shown by the respondent met or exceeded any reasonable standard of competence. Applying the approach described by Killeen J. in *Re Jeffery Estate*,[118] we conclude, as did the majority of the Divisional Court, that the amount fixed under the tariff guidelines provided "fair and reasonable" compensation for the respondent.

[The court dismissed the appeal.]

Notes and Questions

1. Normally, solicitors bill for services rendered *qua* solicitor on an hourly basis. If they are acting as trustees, however, compensation *qua* trustee may be based on fixed percentages on the basis that such percentages are considered fair, reasonable and appropriate.[119]

---

117 In the Divisional Court, *supra*, at 285.
118 *Supra*, at 179.
119 See *Lando & Partners Ltd. v. Bank of Nova Scotia* (1986), 17 C.L.R. 184, 1986 CarswellOnt 776 (Ont. S.C.).

2. When an executor was found liable to the estate for failing to act prudently, his compensation was offset by the amount of the judgment.[120] Presumably, the same principle would apply to trustees.

3. Traditionally, it had been the position of the courts that if the trust instrument did not fix compensation, it would be improper for an executor to pre-take compensation. Rather, an executor or trustee would have to estimate the amount of his or her fees and retain that sum in trust.[121]

4. However, more recently, perhaps in response to recommendations made by the Ontario Law Reform Commission,[122] Ontario courts have permitted the pre-taking of compensation for services already rendered.[123]

5. The Ontario Law Reform Commission based its recommendation on the premise that trustees are entitled to payment on a regular basis during the administration of the trust. Because of the costly accounting procedures involved in an application for compensation, the Commission was of the view that court approval should not be necessary for the sole purpose of obtaining compensation. As a condition of pre-taking, trustees would have to give notice to the beneficiaries of the amount taken in compensation. They would also have to provide an account of services rendered. When the trustees ultimately pass the accounts, they must satisfy the court that the amount pre-taken was fair and reasonable.

6. You should note that if the trust instrument contains an express provision for compensation, that provision is an absolute limitation upon the allowance which may be made. The court will not look into the reasonableness of the provision, since section 61(5) of the *Trustee Act*[124] is a bar to its jurisdiction.[125] On the other hand, an agreement between a testator and the proposed executor (to which the "beneficiaries" are not parties) which was entered into before the will is drawn and which is not incorporated into the will is not binding on the court or the beneficiaries. Compensation may then be claimed under section 61.[126]

7. If a trustee becomes a director of a company in which the trust has an interest, the trustee is accountable to the trust for any remuneration which he or she receives as director. However, the court may allow the trustee to keep the director's fees if the skill required of the trustee is over and above that normally required of such a director. The court will

---

120 *Brander Estate, Re*, [1986] 3 W.W.R. 45, 1986 CarswellAlta 15, 43 Alta. L.R. (2d) 38, 67 A.R. 345 (Surr. Ct.).

121 *Welbourn, Re*, [1979] 3 W.W.R. 113, 4 E.T.R. 122, 1979 CarswellAlta 202, 96 D.L.R. (3d) 76, 23 A.R. 91 (Surr. Ct.) and *Prelutsky, Re*, 11 E.T.R. 233, [1982] 4 W.W.R. 309, 36 B.C.L.R. 214, 1982 CarswellBC 90 (S.C.).

122 Ont. Law Ref. Comm. Report at 260-1.

123 See, *William George King Trust, Re* (1994), 2 E.T.R. (2d) 123, 1994 CarswellOnt 645, 113 D.L.R. (4th) 701 (Gen. Div.) and *Laing Estate v. Laing Estate* (1996), (sub nom. *Logan v. Laing Estate*) 11 E.T.R. (2d) 268, 1996 CarswellOnt 775, (sub nom. *Laing Estate, Re*) 89 O.A.C. 321 (Div. Ct.), leave to appeal allowed (1996), 1996 CarswellOnt 2019 (C.A.), affirmed (1998), 1998 CarswellOnt 4037, [1998] O.J. No. 4169, 113 O.A.C. 335, (sub nom. *Laing Estate v. Hines*) 167 D.L.R. (4th) 150, 41 O.R. (3d) 571, 25 E.T.R. (2d) 139 (C.A.).

124 R.S.O. 1990, c. T.23.

125 *Robertson, Re*, [1949] O.R. 427, [1949] 4 D.L.R. 319, 1949 CarswellOnt 41 (H.C.).

126 *Taylor, Re*, [1967] 2 O.R. 557, 1967 CarswellOnt 142 (Surr. Ct.). See also *Cook, Re* (1974), 5 O.R. (2d) 388, 1974 CarswellOnt 516 (Surr. Ct), in which an agreement in writing for compensation between the testator and the executor that was not mentioned in the will was held not to bind either the executor or the court. The court therefore had jurisdiction to award compensation under s. 61(1).

not, save in exceptional circumstances, make such an order with respect to future remuneration.[127]

8. Section 61(4) provides that the compensation paid to a solicitor acting as a trustee may be increased "by such amount as may be considered fair and reasonable" to reflect professional services rendered to the trust.[128] The Ontario Law Reform Commission has recommended that the principle be extended to all trustees who render professional or special services to the trust apart from their functions as trustee.[129]

9. In the absence of a charging clause in the trust instrument, professional fees are considered authorized expenses of the estate as long as the trustees, who are also professionals, are not profiting from the fee. Should the disbursement of such professional fees be deducted from the remuneration otherwise payable to the trustees? If so, under what circumstances?[130]

10. In *Confectionately Yours Inc., Re*[131] the Ontario Court of Appeal applied the principles outlined in *Laing* to assess the remuneration of a receiver. The court first outlined the two techniques used as follows: (1) the quantum of remuneration is fixed as a percentage of the proceeds of the realization; (2) assessment of remuneration is claimed on a *quantum meruit* basis according to time, trouble and degree of responsibility involved. The court then asserted that the techniques are to be used together in arriving at an appropriate determination of remuneration, for receivers and trustees alike.

(b) Indemnity

At common law, trustees were entitled to be indemnified out of the trust property for all expenses properly incurred in the administration of the trust. Section 33 of the Ontario *Trustee Act*[132] codified this right, but it has now been repealed. However, s. 23.1(1) of the statute provides that a trustee may recover expenses properly incurred in carrying out the trust from the trust fund or may pay such expenses directly from the fund.[133] Section 25 of the Alberta *Trustee Act*,[134] set out below, exemplifies the codification of the common law right. It is comparable to the former Ontario provision on indemnity. This statutory right has been held to permit trustees who are parties to an action to recover from the trust legal expenses reasonably incurred in the prosecution or defence of the

---

127 *Keeler's Settlement Trusts, Re*, [1981] 1 Ch. 156, [1981] 1 All E.R. 888.

128 For similar legislation see the *Trustee Act*, R.S.N.W.T. 1988, c. T-8, s. 53; R.S.S. 1978, c. T-23, s. 84.

129 Ont. Law Ref. Comm. Rep. at p. 257.

130 See *British Columbia (Public Trustee) v. Lohn Estate* (1994), 98 B.C.L.R. (2d) 26, [1995] 1 W.W.R. 371, 1994 CarswellBC 457, (sub nom. *Public Trustee (British Columbia) v. Lohn Estate (No. 1)*) 47 B.C.A.C. 81, 76 W.A.C. 81 (C.A.), additional reasons at (1994), 1994 CarswellBC 458, 98 B.C.L.R. (2d) 33, 4 E.T.R. (2d) 83, (sub nom. *Public Trustee (British Columbia) v. Lohn Estate (No. 2)*) 47 B.C.A.C. 87, 76 W.A.C. 87, [1995] 1 W.W.R. 378 (C.A.).

131 (2002), [2002] O.J. No. 3569, 2002 CarswellOnt 3002, 36 C.B.R. (4th) 200, 164 O.A.C. 84, 25 C.P.C. (5th) 207, 219 D.L.R. (4th) 72 (C.A.), leave to appeal refused (2003), [2002] S.C.C.A. No. 460, 2003 CarswellOnt 1043, 2003 CarswellOnt 1044, 312 N.R. 195 (note), 41 C.B.R. (4th) 28, 181 O.A.C. 197 (note).

132 R.S.O. 1990, c. T.23, repealed by 1998, c. 18, Sched. B, s. 16(1).

133 *Ibid.*, as added by S.O. 2001, c. 9, Sched. B, s. 13(1).

134 R.S.A. 2000, c. T-8.

action.[135] The right to charge the fund with expenses is not inviolate; the trustee's payment or recovery from the trust fund may be later disallowed by the court "if it is of the opinion that the expense was not properly incurred in carrying out the trust."[136]

The right to indemnification lies against the trust property. Trustees have no right of indemnity from the beneficiaries, save in the following three exceptional circumstances:

(a) if the trustees undertook the trust at the request of the beneficiary;[137]

(b) if the beneficiary is also the creator of the trust;[138] or

(c) if the beneficiaries are *sui juris* and together absolutely entitled to the trust property.[139]

The first exception is now also codified, as is apparent from section 26 of the Alberta *Trustee Act*,[140] set out below.

Thompson v. Lamport,[141] below, discusses a trustee's right of indemnification and illustrates which part of the trust property is to bear the legal costs.

TRUSTEE ACT

R.S.A. 2000, c. T-8

25. A trustee is chargeable only for money and securities actually received by the trustee, notwithstanding the trustee signing any receipt for the sake of conformity, and is answerable and accountable only for the trustee's own acts, receipts, neglects or defaults, and not for

(a) those of any other trustee,

(b) any banker, broker or other person with whom any trust money or securities may be deposited,

(c) the insufficiency or deficiency of any securities, or

(d) any other loss, unless it happens through the trustee's own wilful default,

and may reimburse the trustee or pay or discharge out of the trust property all expenses incurred in or about the execution of the trustee's trust or powers.

26. When a trustee has committed a breach of trust at the instigation or request or with the consent in writing of a beneficiary, the court may, if it thinks fit, and notwithstanding that the beneficiary is a married woman entitled for her separate use, whether with or without a restraint on anticipation, make any order that to

---

135 *Fishermen's Benefit Fund Inc. v. U.F.C.W., Local 1252* (1991), 83 D.L.R. (4th) 527, 1991 CarswellNfld 132, 97 Nfld. & P.E.I.R. 50, 308 A.P.R. 50 (C.A.).

136 *Ibid.*, s. 23.1(2), added by S.O. 2002, c. 9, Sched. B, s. 13(1).

137 *Trustee Act*, R.S.A. 2000, c. T-8, s. 26.

138 *Matthews v. Ruggles-Brize*, [1911] 1 Ch. 194 (Ch. D).

139 *Hardoon v. Belilios* (1900), [1901] A.C. 118 (Hong Kong P.C.).

140 R.S.A. 2000, c. T-8.

141 [1945] S.C.R. 343, [1945] 2 D.L.R. 545, 1945 CarswellOnt 97.

the court seems just for impounding all or any part of the interest of the beneficiary in the trust estate by way of indemnity to the trustee or person claiming though the trustee.

Comparable Legislation

Trustee Act, R.S.B.C. 1996, c. 464, ss. 95, 96; R.S.M. 1987, c. T160, ss. 78, 80; R.S.N.L. 1990, c. T-10, ss. 29, 50; R.S.N.S. 1989, c. 479, s. 29; R.S.N.W.T. 1988, c. T-8, ss. 22, 25; R.S.P.E.I. 1988, c. T-8, s. 25; R.S.S. 1978, c. T-23, ss. 13, 46 (s. 13 am. by S.S. 1998, c. 40, s. 10); R.S.Y. 2002, c. 223, s. 8; *Trustees Act*, R.S.N.B. 1973, c. T-15, ss. 13, 41.

THOMPSON v. LAMPORT

[1945] S.C.R. 343, [1945] 2 D.L.R. 545
Supreme Court of Canada

The testator, by will, established a trust fund for his daughter, Edith G. Lamport. She brought an action against the trustees in which she objected to the inclusion of a mortgage in the trust fund, claimed damages and sought the trustee's removal. The action was dismissed with costs on a solicitor and client basis.

The trustees then brought these proceedings to determine out of which funds these costs were to be paid. The trial judge directed that they be paid out of the capital of the trust fund. The Ontario Court of Appeal held that they should be paid out of the capital of the residuary estate which had been given to the testator's two sons. The executors appealed.

RAND J.:

. . .

The judgment of the Court of Appeal is based upon these assumptions: there were two distinct funds, the residue and the special trust; that it was the duty of the appellants and the Trust Company to defend the residue and themselves; in contesting the litigation successfully, the appellants had benefited the residue which should, therefore, bear the expense; and to permit solicitor and client costs to be recovered against the sister by resorting to the trust funds of which she was the beneficiary, would be to condemn her to solicitor and client costs in violation of the rule laid down in *Patton v. Toronto General Trust Corporation*.[142]

The position of the residue at that time should perhaps be stated. The action was brought more than seven years after the death of the testator. So far as appears from the record, the duties of the executors had at that time been fully discharged. The accounts were then before the Surrogate Court and the order made on March 30, 1937, about eleven days after the issue of the writ, declared the fulfilment of the direction to set up the trust and provided for allowances to the executors. It seems to be clear, too, that the appropriation to the trust was completed in 1936.

---

142 [1930] A.C. 629, [1930] 3 W.W.R. 1, [1930] 4 D.L.R. 321, 39 O.W.N. 5 (P.C.).

From 1931 until that year the duty of the Trust Company towards the assets of the estate had been largely, if not wholly, that appropriation for which, under the agreement, it held the assets in its own name as a special security for the trust. What then remained was simple property owned jointly by the appellants. But, on the other hand, the legal title and possession continued in the executors, including the Trust Company, and the property was, therefore, exposed to any residuum of duty which, in such an action as was brought, might be held by the court to be outstanding towards the trust.

It is desirable also, I think, to keep in mind the precise relation of the executors towards the estate assets *vis-à-vis* the special trust. By the terms of the will they were bound to set up the trust from those assets. Their paramount duty was towards the respondent, the sole beneficiary, subject to the contingent interest of the appellants. That duty dominated their dealing with the assets; the question was whether they had discharged it; they must exercise it against the residue; they could not, of course, go beyond it; but their defence was an assertion of the fulfilment of their duty to the trust rather than a performance of any duty to protect the residue.

Nor can I quite appreciate the reference to a duty to "defend themselves." Certainly it was in their interest to do so, but the word in such a context can scarcely carry a fiduciary signification.

The rule laid down in the Court of Appeal was that a trustee must show that his action is for the "benefit" of a trust before his expenses can be recouped from it and that here the only benefit from his resistance to the claims made accrued to the residue. The general principle is undoubted that a trustee is entitled to indemnity for all costs and expenses properly incurred by him in the due administration of the trust: it is on that footing that the trust is accepted. These include solicitor and client costs in all proceedings in which some question or matter in the course of the administration is raised as to which the trustee has acted prudently and properly. The original jurisdiction in equity in unsuccessful suits against a trustee went so far as to enable the court to give a personal judgment against not only the *cestui* but third persons for solicitor and client costs. This is put beyond doubt by *Andrews v. Barnes*,[143] and from the authorities there cited, in proceedings by the *cestui* charging misconduct against the trustee, in the absence of special circumstances, such an order followed where there was no fund. By reason of special statutory provisions as to costs, the jurisdiction of the Supreme Court of Ontario does not apparently extend to such a power (as to which I express no opinion), but a trustee's rights to allowances out of trust funds are in no respect abridged.

The rule applied as based upon *Walters v. Woodbridge*[144] the facts of which were somewhat similar to those here. The trustee had obtained from the court approval for the sale of a partnership interest, owned by the testator, to the surviving party, the proceeds of which were then to be held subject to the trusts of the will. A bill was subsequently filed by certain of the beneficiaries to have

---

143 (1888), 9 Ch. D. 133 (C.A.).
144 (1878), 7 Ch. D. 504.

the decree set aside, alleging that the approval of the court had been obtained by misrepresentation. This bill was dismissed with costs. They were taxed and execution issued, to which *nulla bona* was returned. An application was then made to have costs in the suit, as between solicitor and client, taxed and paid out of the estate. Lord Romilly considered he had no jurisdiction to make such an order for the reason that the suit was defended by the trustee to clear his own character. On appeal that holding was reversed and, in his reasons, James L.J. used this language:

> It is agreeable to me personally that we are not obliged to put a trustee in a position which would be disgraceful to the administration of justice. The court is very strict in dealing with trustees, and it is the duty of the court, as far as it can, to see that they are indemnified against all expenses which they have honestly incurred in the due administration of the trust. Lord Romilly says that the trustee here defended himself against a false charge, and was in the same position as any other person who so defended himself; but it was a charge against the trustee in respect of acts done by him in the due administration of the trusts; and his defence was beneficial to the trust estate, for it has been decided that the compromise was an advantageous one. In such a case it is impossible to split the defence, and say that because the trustee at the same time defended his own character he is only to have a part of the costs.

It will be seen that it was the challenged act that carried the advantage and not the mere result of the trustee's successful defence of an adverse proceeding; and that the relief sought was the direct setting aside of the trustee's act.

Now, what are the characteristics of this benefit? There the proposed sale required the prior approval of the court, and the effect of the judgment dismissing the bill was to confirm that approval. But what of the case where the trustee carries through a transaction which does not require such as approval? What is to be the measure or test of benefit? Can it be anything more than that the act was properly done within the duty of the trustee? Must the court examine the details of the transaction challenged and find not only propriety but a "benefit" as against what is alleged ought to have been done?

Where the trustee is resisting the assertion of a right by a third person against the trust estate, obviously his action is for its benefit. But a new element is introduced when the complaint is by the beneficiary for a breach of duty, such as fraud or negligence. In that case the trustee is in fact defending both his administrative act and his own interest. In the latter aspect, he has no special privilege in costs over an ordinary litigant; he is in the same position as any other person improperly accused of a wrong, and any outlay over the costs allowed by law must be borne by himself as the price of his own vindication. The question in such cases is whether the personal defence is incidental to that in his representative capacity; if it is, the costs will not be split.

From this the Court of Appeal has drawn the conclusion that in suits by beneficiaries it must appear that the defence is for the benefit of the trust in virtually the same sense as in cases brought by third persons; that the trustee is warding off an attack upon his funds; and the court in fact looked upon the litigation as essentially, if not exclusively, a claim against the residue. But, with the utmost respect, that is not, in my opinion, the principle of *Walters v. Wood-*

bridge[145] where, as here, the court is called upon to determine whether an act or transaction carried through by the trustee can be said to have been done within his authority and duty; and where the undoing of the act is the direct object of the litigation. Stirling J., in *Re Lewellin, Llewellin v. Williams*[146] uses this language:

> A trustee is entitled in an ordinary case to recover out of the trust estate, as charges and expenses properly incurred, all his costs of an action which he has properly defended; of which the case of *Walters v. Woodbridge* is a very strong illustration.

And the same rule was applied in *Re Chennell, Jones v. Chennell*[147] and *Bartlett v. Wood.*[148]

There remains the question of the effect of the *Patton* judgment [*supra*] mentioned in the reasons of Laidlaw J.A. In that case it had been suggested in the courts below that an order could properly have been made giving solicitor and client costs to the executors against one who claimed to be a legatee. In the Privy Council this legatee succeeded in his contentions but it was there intimated that there would have been no more authority to award executors such costs than to an ordinary litigant. There was no question, however, of strictly equitable costs out of funds. As *Walters v. Woodbridge* shows, party and party costs can be supplemented out of the trust estate, and as Mellish L.J. in *Mordue v. Palmer*[149] observes,

> The common law courts have no power to give costs between solicitor and client. But it is otherwise with Court of Equity.

A fortiori those costs can be charged as expenses upon trust assets.

The property concerned was that in existence on March 19, 1937, when the proceedings were commenced. Anything beyond that was the personal liability of the executors and trustees. The capital of the estate, including the special trust, has remained intact to the present time, and the indemnity must be spread over it. Taking all circumstances into account, the two funds are roughly in the relation of four to one and in these proportions should the costs be borne.

The appeal should, therefore, be allowed and judgment go declaring the difference between party and party and solicitor and client costs of the trustees and executors in the previous action as well as all costs of all parties to these proceedings (as between solicitor and client in the case of all the executors and trustees) be payable four-fifths out of the capital of the trust fund and one-fifth out of the residue.

[Hudson and Estey JJ.concurred. Rinfret C.J. and Kerwin J. dissented. The court allowed the appeal.]

---

145 *Ibid.*
146 (1887), 37 Ch. D. 317 at 327.
147 (1878), 8 Ch. D. 492.
148 (1860), 30 L.J. Ch. 614.
149 (1870), L.R. 6 Ch. 22 at 32.

Notes and Questions

1. The trustee need not satisfy a liability before claiming indemnity, but may discharge the liability by making payment directly from the trust estate.[150]

2. The trustees of a club leased premises for the club. Are the trustees entitled to be indemnified out of moneys belonging to the club? Can they claim indemnity from the club members?[151]

3. A trustee who breaches a contract or commits a tort as trustee may also be indemnified out of the trust estate. If, for example, the trustee was empowered to engage in certain actions and performed them reasonably and prudently, but committed a tort in the course of them, he or she will normally be indemnified.[152] It is clearly otherwise if the trustee is at fault, has committed a wilful tort, or has engaged in activity beyond his or her powers.

4. Trustees may be entitled to indemnification and contribution from their co-trustees. This aspect of indemnification is dealt with elsewhere.[153]

5. Are trustees' expenses payable generally from income or capital?[154]

(c) Set-off

It sometimes happens that the trustee lends money to the trust. If this is done for the proper administration of the trust, the trustee is entitled to be reimbursed. *Re McMahon and Canada Permanent Trust Co.*[155] below, deals with a situation in which the trustee lent money to the sole beneficiary of a trust in order to enable him to acquire trust property. The beneficiary then made an assignment in bankruptcy and the trustee sought to set-off the debt against the trust funds.

RE McMAHON AND CANADA PERMANENT TRUST CO.

17 B.C.L.R. 193, 6 E.T.R. 43, 8 B.L.R. 143, [1980]
2 W.W.R. 438, 32 C.B.R. (N.S.) 258, 108 D.L.R. (3d) 71
British Columbia Court of Appeal

In 1978 P established a Registered Retirement Savings Plan with the respondent Trust Company as trustee. His first and only contribution to the RRSP was borrowed from the respondent and paid by it into the RRSP. Subsequently, P made an assignment in bankruptcy. His trustee in bankruptcy, the appellant,

---

150 *Lacey v. Hill* (1874), L.R. 18 Eq. 182. Section 23.1(1) of the Ontario *Trustee Act*, R.S.O. 1990, c. T-23, added by S.O. 2001, c. 9, Sched. B, s. 13(1) has codified the trustee's right to direct payment from the trust fund.

151 See *Wise v. Perpetual Trustee Co. Ltd.*, [1903] A.C. 139 (P.C.), and Williams "Club Trustees' Right to Indemnity: A Criticism of *Wise v. Perpetual Trustee Co. Ltd.*" (1903), 10 L.Q. Rev. 386.

152 See, *e.g., Re Raybould*, [1900] 1 Ch. 199.

153 Liability of Trustees *inter se*. We deal with this in the chapter on Breach of Trust.

154 *Stott v. Milne* (1884), 25 Ch. D. 170 (C.A.), consider also *Thompson v. Lamport, supra*.

155 6 E.T.R. 43, 8 B.L.R. 143, [1980] 2 W.W.R. 438, 32 C.B.R. (N.S.) 258, 17 B.C.L.R. 193, 108 D.L.R. (3d) 71 (C.A.).

claimed the moneys in the RRSP, but the respondent refused, claiming that it had a right to set-off the debt against the trust fund. On an application by the appellant to compel payment, the trust company was successful at first instance, the court holding that the relationship between P and the trust company was one of debtor and creditor. The trustee in bankruptcy appealed.

BULL J.A.:

. . .

With respect, I disagree with the conclusion of the learned judge below.

I cannot agree that the trust agreement, actually so called, executed by the bankrupt with the respondent and covering in minute detail the payments he was to make under the agreement, the use to which those funds were to be put, and a myriad of detailed terms and conditions of the plan and trust created, could be anything but a trust in the general legal sense. The respondent was plainly a trustee under the plan, appointed as such and with clear trust duties and obligations. In my view, to refer to, or interpret, that agreement as one creating a simple relationship only of creditor and debtor is quite unreal. Credits and debits may, and often do, arise in the execution of trusts between trustees, settlors and cestui que trust, but that does not in itself change a trust to something other than a trust. Accordingly, as the plan and agreement in the R.R.S.P. here was conceived as a trust, was called a trust, was operated and carried out as a trust, required a separate special account and trust fund to be maintained and with its funds irrevocably vested in the respondent as a trustee, a trust between the bankrupt and the respondent was, in my opinion, constituted. I find no element of substance that could give weight to a conclusion that the agreement made was really or essentially merely a debtor-creditor one.

The next question is whether, if I am correct in my conclusion that the RRSP was set up as and was a trust, it was changed as submitted by the respondent to a simple creditor-debtor relationship, either at the moment of bankruptcy or, at least, when the appellant carrying out his duty exercised his right to demand that the trust funds be paid to him. Respondent's counsel vigorously and ably argued that if the trust was "terminated" then thereafter the funds were held as a simple debt payable by the respondent. As I have already mentioned, it was common ground that, notwithstanding the terms of the trust, the bankrupt, or his trustee in bankruptcy acquiring all his rights, could unilaterally terminate the RRSP and recover the funds held in the plan. I am unable to find any reason to conclude that the fact of bankruptcy itself in any way altered, varied or changed the trust. Also, I do not think that the making of the demand terminated the trust as such. The funds were always held by the respondent in a trust capacity, and I fail to see how, when a proper demand is made to a trustee to turn over trust funds it held to a person or persons entitled, the trustee thereupon ceases to be a trustee and the trust funds any less trust funds. The trust was not terminated when the appellant demanded the trust funds — only its purpose and scope changed. When that demand was made (several days after the event of bankruptcy) it was to get in the bankrupt's deposits and interests for the benefit of all his creditors, including the respondent. But the funds in the hands of the respondent were still trust funds and had to be dealt with by the respondent as such and in accordance with the terms of the trust as varied. Clearly the respondent could not use the assets held for any other purpose without being guilty of breach of trust and conversion. Immediately before the demand, the respondent held the funds in trust for the bankrupt and at the time of the demand for the benefit of his creditors but the respondent throughout held them in trust, albeit for a different purpose at different times. I cannot conclude that the appellant terminated the trust by his demand but merely required the respondent to perform his duty as the trustee of the funds for the new use imposed by the demand.

I therefore, am of the opinion that the respondent did not cease to be a trustee before actually distributing the funds held by it to the appellant. However, when that was done I would agree that the respondent's duties as trustee had ceased and the trust terminated.

Next, consideration must be given to the right of the respondent to set-off against the funds so held by it in trust, and demanded by the appellant, against the earlier personal loans made by it to the bankrupt. The law on set-off is clear although difficulties do sometimes arise in its application in different sets of circumstances. That the ordinary rules respecting set-off are applicable in bankruptcy matters is provided in the *Bankruptcy Act* in section 75, and has not been questioned. The basic rule is that set-off (in effect the combination of accounts) is only available short of agreement, express or implied, when the debts or accounts are mutual, between the same parties in the same right. It is not necessary that debts which are mutual be of the same nature. See Houlden and Morawetz, *Bankruptcy Law of Canada*.[156] "Mutual debts" are debts or claims due from one to another which are ascertainable and which are in the same right. A person in his individual capacity is not in the same right as he is when acting as trustee for another. Hence, it is trite law that, subject to certain limited exceptions, an amount owed by a person in his capacity as trustee holding property, credits, or funds for another or others cannot combine them with, or set them off against, a personal debt to him in his personal capacity by the beneficiary or beneficiaries of the trust. See *Garnett v. M'Kewan*.[157] In such a case there is no mutuality as one account is held in a fiduciary capacity and the other in a personal capacity. The same situation arises where there is not a trust in the strict sense of the word, but one account is set up or exists for a "special purpose" which could be held to deprive it of "mutuality" with another account held with a different or no special purpose. With respect to this concept, the following words of Lord Simon of Glaisdale in *Nat. Westminster Bank Ltd. v. Halesowen Presswork & Assemblies Ltd.*[158] are illuminating.

---

156 (1960) at 160 *et seq.*
157 (1872), L.R. 8 Exch. 10.
158 [1972] A.C. 785, [1972] 1 All E.R. 641, [1972] 1 Lloyd's Rep. 101 (H.L.).

> I would prefer to say that money is paid for a special (or specific) purpose so as to exclude mutuality of dealing within section 31 if the money is paid in such circumstances that it would be a misappropriation to use it for any other purpose than that for which it is paid.

It is pointed out that section 31 referred to in the passage was of the English *Bankruptcy Act*[159] and provided for set-off when there were "mutual credits, mutual debts or other mutual dealings," the equivalent of section 75 of our *Bankruptcy Act*.

The respondent has relied strongly on a line of old, but still accepted, authorities to support what I have referred to above as exceptions. Those cases were, *inter alia*: *Bankes v. Jarvis*;[160] *Jones v. Mossop*;[161] *Cochrane v. Green*;[162] and *Bailey v. Finch*.[163] In each of the cases a trust or a "special purpose" was involved and it was held set-off was available with respect to another account. Particular stress was put on *Bailey v. Finch*, wherein a bank was held entitled to set-off a debt due it by an individual against a credit it held for that individual as an executor of an estate. The ratio of the decision in *Finch* and, in my view, in the other cases cited, was that a court will, in equity, permit set-off where "mutuality" and the same interests in the debts were in reality and fact found to exist although superficially that might not appear to be the case.

In my view those authorities are inapplicable here as this is a completely different and reversed situation. Here we have the strange position of the claimant for set-off for its own financial benefit and advantage endeavouring to establish that the trust fund it holds and deals with as trustee is to be considered a mutual debt with and in the same right as a personal debt due it. In my view that cannot be.

I think that the respondent's obligations under the RRSP were clearly that of a trustee. Further, when the appellant demanded, as he was entitled to do, the funds constituting the trust property thus limiting the scope and extent of the trust, the respondent nevertheless remained a trustee of that trust property with a trust obligation to carry out the trust as so limited. It was bound to perform its duties *qua* trustee including the turn over of the trust property (*i.e.*, the fund) to the appellant, and until it actually did so it had a trust to perform. The delivery or payment of the funds to the appellant would be the carrying out of a trust duty and not a payment of a debt. I add that, in my view, the respondent's dealing with the trust property in any other way (including the asserted right to set-off the trust funds against its own debt due from the bankrupt) would probably be considered a conversion of trust assets, or, perhaps, an unauthorized preference.

I think it advisable to mention a recent decision of the Ontario Court of Appeal in *Re Berman; The Trustee in Bankruptcy v. Astra Trust Co.*[164] which was

---

159 1914, c. 59.
160 [1903] 1 K.B. 549, [1900-3] All E.R. 656.
161 (1844), 3 Hare 568, 67 E.R. 506 (Ch. Div.).
162 (1860), 9 C.B.N.S. 448, 142 E.R. 176.
163 (1871), L.R. 7 Q.B. 34.
164 Delivered October 17, 1979 and still unreported [now reported at 8 B.L.R. 134, 1 P.P.S.A.C. 81, 31 C.B.R. (N.S.) 313, 26 O.R. (2d) 389, 105 D.L.R. (3d) 380 (C.A.).

referred to by both appellant and respondent. The facts are very similar to those here. There, the bankrupt, before his bankruptcy, borrowed from a trust company the required amount of his contribution to a RRSP, at the time giving a direction to the company to first apply the proceeds of any redemption on that loan. After bankruptcy the trustee in bankruptcy requested redemption and the trust company claimed set-off. The only apparent difference in the facts of the two cases was the important one of the express direction given to the trust company by the bankrupt. No direction of that nature was given in the case at Bar. Houlden J.A., speaking for the court, held that the trust company was entitled to set-off the amounts. He made it perfectly clear that his judgment was based on the specific law set out in two United States tests; namely, in *Restatement of the Law of Trusts* (2d ed.)[165] (which he set out in his judgment *in extenso*) and *Scott on Trusts*.[166] The passage set out in the judgment deals only with a situation where there is an agreement that the trustee discharge the liability to it out of the trust estate and, accordingly, is entitled to set-off. The second citation deals only with (a) the conclusion that a trustee cannot deduct from, or have a charge on, trust property for a personal claim against a beneficiary and must be confined to his suit for debt being in no better position than any other creditor; and (b) the right of the trustee to set-off where that remedy is provided by an agreement or understanding, express or implied. Then, strangely, in my respectful view, the learned judge said that the trust company did not need to rely on the direction given, but nevertheless, he allowed the set-off. I can only conclude he reached that opinion on the basis of the above citations dealing with an agreement or understanding for a set-off. In my view his reference to the letter of direction must have been either inadvertent or merely a reference to the actual "directions" to pay as opposed to an agreement found to exist that the trust company could exercise a right to repay itself through set-off. Accordingly, as there was no such direction or arrangement, express or implied, in this case to give the respondent the right to set-off, in my view, the Ontario decision is of no help to either party here.

It follows that it is my opinion that the learned judge below erred in finding a right of set-off in the respondent, and the appeal should be allowed. I would order that the respondent account to the appellant for the amount to the credit of the RRSP entered into by the bankrupt with it, and that the assets or funds in the Plan be delivered or paid to the appellant.

Notes and Questions

1. A testator appointed A, B, and C his executors and trustees. The principal beneficiaries under the will were A and her two children. A was entitled to a share of the annual income. The trustees breached the trust by using funds from the capital of the estate to: (1) buy an annuity contract to provide income for A; (2) to buy an annuity contract to fund premiums for a life insurance policy on A's life; and (3) a life insurance policy on A's life. The first annuity realized a gain, but the second annuity and the life insurance policy

165 At 632, para. 250.
166 3rd ed., Vol. 3, at 2175-2176, para. 250.

incurred losses. The trustees sought to set of the gain against the losses. Are they able to do so?[167]

Problems

1. The trustee of an estate hired woodcutters to fell some trees on the estate. Through the negligence of the woodcutters, a bough was allowed to fall on a passer-by who was injured. The trustee, as legal owner of the estate, was sued and found liable. Can the trustee claim reimbursement for the costs of defending the suit and the damages? If so, from whom or what?[168]

2. A testatrix stated in her will that her husband was to receive the income from her estate and use it to "maintain himself and the children." What rights and obligations does the husband have in relation to the income?[169]

3. A trustee holds $30,000 in trust for B, provided that B attains the age of 25. When B became 23 B has an opportunity to enter into a partnership with C for an initial cost of $15,000.

    (a) Can B get an advancement of $15,000 from the trust?

    (b) Would it make a difference if B was only to receive the income from the trust capital when B attained age 25?

    (c) Would your answer change if the terms of the trust provided that if B failed to attain age 25, X was to take?

    (d) What happens if the $15,000 advancement is made and B dies before attaining 25?[170]

4. A testator died, leaving a dependent mentally-retarded son. In his will, the testator made provision for his son as follows. The son was to have use of the testator's personal belongings and household effects; the testator's trustees were empowered to hold his residential property for the use of the son, operating costs to be borne by the testator's general estate; a $150,000 fund was to be set aside to provide the son with the necessaries of life; and, the trustees were empowered to pay, from residue, so much of the capital as they deemed advisable for the maintenance of the son.

Application was made to the court for an order directing that a fixed sum be paid annually for the maintenance of the son so that he would not be dependent upon the exercise of the trustees' discretion. On what basis or bases could such an application be made? Ought it to be successful?[171]

---

167 See *Smith Estate v. Smith Estate*, 37 E.T.R. (2d) 151, 2000 CarswellBC 2628, 2000 BCSC 1842 (S.C.).

168 See *Benett v. Wyndham* (1862), 4 De G.F. & J. 259, 45 E.R. 1183, and *Re Raybould*, [1900] 1 Ch. 199.

169 See *Singer v. Singer supra*, note 45, and *Donald v. Donald* (1885), 7 O.R. 669 (H.C.).

170 See *Re Scott*, [1903] 1 Ch. 1 (C.A.), *Re Forster* (1910), 39 N.B.R. 526 (C.A.), and *Evans v. Massey* (1826), 1 Y. & J. 196, 148 E.R. 643.

171 See *Re Champ Estate* (1985), 19 E.T.R. 200, 40 Sask. R. 308 (Q.B.).

15

BREACH OF TRUST

1. SCOPE

In *Tito v. Waddell*,[1] Vice Chancellor Megarry expressed surprise when he discovered that the case law does not define the term "breach of trust." His Lordship referred to some American textbooks and quoted, *inter alia*, Professor Scott's statement,[2] "A trustee commits a breach of trust if he violates any duty which he owes as trustee to the beneficiaries." The question of definition was not important to the decision in the case, but the Vice Chancellor opined that it is not helpful to define a breach of trust as a breach of duty, since that raises the further question what is meant by a breach of duty.[3] There is some truth in his Lordship's remarks. However, in previous chapters, we discussed in great detail the various ways in which a breach of duty by a trustee occurs. Hence, it is convenient to say that a breach of trust arises when a trustee fails to carry out the duties imposed upon him or her by the trust instrument, by statute, or by the general rules of equity.

If a trustee commits a breach of trust, the beneficiaries have several personal and proprietary remedies available to them. The personal remedies are: the action for compensation for loss to the trust estate caused by a breach, and the action for an account of profits if the breach resulted in a profit and the beneficiaries wish to recover the profit. If the trustee retains the trust property, or it falls into the hands of third persons who have no right to it, the beneficiaries may also be entitled to the proprietary remedy of the constructive trust, if they can trace the property, or the equitable lien. These remedies allow them to recover the trust property or its product, or entitle them to a charge upon it.

---

1 [1977] Ch. 106, [1977] 3 All E.R. 129 (Ch. Div.), at 247 [Ch.].
2 Austin Wakeman Scott, *The Law of Trusts*, 3rd ed. (Boston: Little, Brown and Company, 1967), §201. See now Austin Wakeman Scott and William Franklin Fratcher, *The Law of Trusts*, 4th ed. (Boston: Little, Brown and Company, 1987-90) ("Scott"). The American texts often refer to the trustee's overriding duty as consisting of the utmost loyalty and faithfulness to his or her trust. *Cf.* 1 Cor 4:2 (NIV).
3 *Tito v. Waddell*, *supra*, note 1, at 248.

Beneficiaries may also have other remedies available to them. These will be mentioned briefly, following the discussion of personal and proprietary remedies. Thereafter, we shall consider the trustee's defences and protections. The chapter concludes with a discussion of the liability of trustees *inter se*, and a brief mention of miscellaneous liabilities of trustees.

2. PERSONAL REMEDIES

(a) Introduction

As we saw in the preceding part, a beneficiary has two personal remedies when a trustee commits a breach of trust: an action for compensation and an action for an account of profits. An action for compensation is an action to recover the loss caused to the trust by the trustee's breach. A loss may occur because the trustee misappropriated or mismanaged trust property, or because a profit would have been made had it not been for the breach. The latter situation may arise, for example, when a trustee retains speculative investments or sells authorized investments.

An action for an account of profits is an action to recover a profit a trustee has made in dealing with trust property. A trustee may make a profit when investing the trust fund in unauthorized securities or when converting trust property to his or her own use. The remedies of compensation and account of profits are alternative. Any trustee must always stand ready to given an account of what he or she has done with the trust property. The obligation to render an account does not depend on any wrongdoing.[4] It allows the beneficiary to know what has been done with the trust property. If the trustee did something unlawful, then the beneficiary can reject that unlawful action, or take the benefit of it. An action for compensation involves a disapproval or reprobation of the trustee's conduct, while an action for an account adopts or approbates the conduct. A beneficiary must elect one or the other. He or she cannot approbate and reprobate the same action of the trustee.[5]

Normally a beneficiary will want an accounting if a profit has been made and if that remedy will give a greater recovery. This might be the case if the trust could not have made the profit itself. That might happen, for example, because the profit arose out of an improper investment.[6] If, however, it is difficult to prove the amount of the profit or whether and the extent to which it arose out of the breach of trust, the beneficiary may seek compensation instead.[7] A beneficiary

---

4 P. Millett, "Equity's Place in the Law of Commerce" (1998), 114 L.Q.R. 214, 225-226; R. Chambers, "Liability" in P. Birks and A. Pretto, eds., *Breach of Trust* (Oxford: Hart Publishing, 2002), 1 at 16-20.

5 *Heathcote v. Halon* (1819), 1 Jac. & W. 123, 37 E.R. 322. See further the Law Commission, Report 247, *Aggravated, Exemplary and Restitutionary Damages* (London, 1997), Part III.

6 See *MacMillan Bloedel Ltd. v. Binstead* (1983), 14 E.T.R. 269, 1983 CarswellBC 540, [1983] B.C.J. No. 802, 22 B.L.R. 255 (S.C.).

7 See H.A.J. Ford and W.A. Lee, assisted by Peter M. McDermott, *Principles of the Law of Trusts*, 3rd ed. (Sydney: LBC Information Services, 1996), §17150 ("Ford and Lee").

may also seek an accounting if a loss has occurred because of an improper investment. He or she may wish to do so if the investment is likely to rise in value.[8]

The rule that a beneficiary may not approbate and reprobate the same action of the trustee means that a trustee may set off losses against gains if they concern the same breach of trust.[9] Were it otherwise, beneficiaries could seek an accounting of the profitable breaches and compensation for the losses. This would be unfair to the trustee if they arose out of the same breach, as when the profits and losses occurred in a business improperly carried on by the trustee. If, however, the breaches are distinct, a beneficiary is entitled to an account of profitable breaches and compensation for the unprofitable ones.[10] In other words, then the trustee may not set off losses against gains.

It is not always easy to determine whether the gain and loss occurred as a result of the same breach. The modern cases tend to favour the trustee if it is difficult to discern whether the breaches are distinct.[11] This occurred in *Bartlett v. Barclays Bank Trust Co. (Nos. 1 & 2)*.[12] A trust company held most of the shares in a private company for a trust. The company engaged in speculative real estate developments. It was successful in one project, but lost heavily in another. The court held that the trust company breached the trust because it failed to supervise the board of directors of the company properly. However, the court allowed the trust company to set off the loss against the gain because both arose from the same wrongful course of conduct. Brightman J. stated,[13] "I think it would be unjust to deprive the bank of the element of salvage in the course of assessing the cost of the shipwreck."

Compensation and account are available not only against express trustees, but against all fiduciaries who have breached their fiduciary duties, and against resulting and constructive trustees.[14] They are also available against the Public Trustee.[15]

Both remedies are personal remedies resulting in money judgments. If the trustee has trust property on hand, the beneficiary who seeks compensation or

---

8 *Canada Safeway Ltd. v. Thompson* (1951), [1952] 2 D.L.R. 591 (B.C. S.C.).

9 *Boryczko v. Toronto Polish Veterans' Association*, [1958] O.W.N. 118.

10 See *Dimes v. Scott* (1827), 4 Russ. 195, 38 E.R. 778 (Ch. Div.); Ford and Lee, §17160 (*Setting off losses against gains*).

11 See *Vyse v. Foster* (1872), L.R. 8 Ch. App. 309, affirmed (1874), L.R. 7 H.L. 318 (H.L.); *Bartlett v. Barclays Bank Trust Co. (Nos. 1 & 2)*, [1980] 1 Ch. 515, [1980] 2 W.L.R. 430, [1980] 2 All E.R. 92 (Ch. Div.).

12 *Ibid.*

13 *Ibid.*, at 538.

14 D.W.M. Waters, *Law of Trusts in Canada*, 2nd ed. (Toronto: The Carswell Company Limited, 1984), at 992-3 ("Waters").

15 *Wood v. British Columbia (Public Trustee)* (1984), 52 B.C.L.R. 396, 1984 CarswellBC 97 (S.C.), affirmed (1986), 70 B.C.L.R. 373, 1986 CarswellBC 295, 23 E.T.R. 116, 25 D.L.R. (4th) 356 (C.A.). Note that only the beneficiary has a cause of action against a trustee for breach of trust. A third party cannot seek to enforce a trust, neither can a third party make a monetary claim based on a breach of trust: *ITT Commercial Finance v. Hawkins* (1994), 144 N.B.R. (2d) 158, 1994 CarswellNB 617, 368 A.P.R. 158 (C.A.).

account, but who does not want the trust property, will also seek to have the money judgment charged on the property. Alternatively, the beneficiary may seek to recover the trust property itself by a constructive trust.

You should remember that a beneficiary may be able to obtain both a proprietary and a personal remedy. This occurred in the leading case, *Keech v. Sandford*,[16] discussed in the materials on constructive trusts. The trustee had caused a lease to be renewed in his name in his personal capacity, rather than to him as trustee, and collected the rents for a period of time. The court held that he held the lease upon constructive trust for the beneficiary and was also accountable to the beneficiary for the profits made.

Something similar occurred in *Semiahmoo Indian Band v. Canada*.[17] The Crown had accepted an absolute surrender of part of an Indian reserve more than 30 years earlier for the purpose of a federal work. It never proceeded with the work and did not use the land otherwise. The court held that it breached its fiduciary duty to the band and imposed a constructive trust on the Crown in favour of the band. However, the court also awarded compensation to the band for the loss it suffered.

(b) The Principle of Liability

A trustee who has committed a breach of trust is liable to restore the resulting loss to the trust or to disgorge the profit he or she has made. Some obligations of a trustee are strict; there is no inquiry into any standard of care. This strict liability applies to a breach of the terms of the trust, as where the trustee is obliged to pay income to A and B, and pays only to A, or where he makes an investment which was not authorized by the trust deed. In this case, subject to any defences a trustee may have, the liability arises whether the breach was fraudulent, innocent or technical, and whether the trustee lacked the competence or business acumen to undertake the trust. There must, however, be a causal connection between the breach and the loss.[18] The purpose of imposing liability is not to punish the trustee, but to restore the beneficiaries to the position they would have been in if the breach had not occurred.[19]

Other breaches of trust require the failure to meet a standard of care. If, for example, the trustee has made only authorized investments, he or she might still be liable for a failure to meet the standard of care required in making investment decisions. This is now the standard of a "prudent investor."[20]

---

16 (1726), Sel. Cas. Ch. 61, 25 E.R. 223, 2 Eq. Ca. Abr. 741, 22 E.R. 629 (Ch. Div.).

17 (1997), 148 D.L.R. (4th) 523, 1997 CarswellNat 1316, 1997 CarswellNat 2683, 215 N.R. 241, 131 F.T.R. 319 (note), [1998] 1 F.C. 3, [1998] 1 C.N.L.R. 250 (C.A.).

18 *Canson Enterprises Ltd. v. Boughton & Co.* (1991), 85 D.L.R. (4th) 129, 1991 CarswellBC 269, 1991 CarswellBC 925, [1991] S.C.J. No. 91, [1992] 1 W.W.R. 245, 9 C.C.L.T. (2d) 1, 39 C.P.R. (3d) 449, 131 N.R. 321, 61 B.C.L.R. (2d) 1, 6 B.C.A.C. 1, 13 W.A.C. 1, [1991] 3 S.C.R. 534, 43 E.T.R. 201. The point is discussed further below.

19 *Vyse v. Foster, supra*, note 11, at 333 [L.R. 8 Ch.]; *Wakefield v. Wakefield* (1901), 2 O.L.R. 33 (C.A.) at 40.

20 See the relevant section of Chapter 13.

Breaches of the fiduciary duties of loyalty seem to be governed in still another way. There are certain situations that attract liability automatically. These are the cases of profit from the fiduciary office, and conflicts of fiduciary duty with self-interest, or with another fiduciary duty. The conflicts principle also encompasses the self-dealing and fair-dealing rules. These appear to be cases of strict liability, because there is liability even if the trustee is acting in good faith.[21] But in other situations, in order to determine whether the duty of loyalty has been breached, the court will inquire into the motives of the fiduciary. Usually, a trustee's duty of loyalty requires him or her to act in what he or she perceived to be the best interests of the beneficiary. When exercising a dispositive power, which may work against the interests of one or more beneficiaries, the fiduciary must act in what he or she perceived to be the purposes for which the power was given.[22] So loyalty is judged by an inquiry into motive, and the situations (such as conflicts of interest and duty) where liability is strict may be best explained on the basis that motivations will be systematically unclear in such situations.[23]

A trustee is liable for the breaches of co-trustees, if the trustee stood by while the breach was being committed, or allowed the co-trustees to manage the trust without ensuring that they did so properly.[24] However, a trustee is not liable for a breach of trust committed before becoming a trustee, unless she or he learns or should have learned of it and ignores it.[25] Nor is a trustee liable for a breach of trust committed after ceasing to be a trustee, unless, by the resignation, she or he facilitates a subsequent breach of trust by her or his successors.[26]

In addition, the liability of trustees is joint and several. Hence, unless one of the trustees is excused, they are all equally liable for the loss, and a beneficiary may recover the full amount of the loss from one or more of them. Those trustees who have paid the beneficiaries in full can then claim contribution and, in some cases, indemnity from the trustees who have not paid.[27]

---

21 *Boardman v. Phipps* (1966), [1967] 2 A.C. 46, [1966] 3 All E.R. 721 (H.L.).

22 *Abacus Trust Co. (Isle of Man) Ltd. v. Barr*, [2003] 1 All E.R. 763; *Fox v. Fox Estate* (1996), 28 O.R. (3d) 496, 1996 CarswellOnt 317, 10 E.T.R. (2d) 229, (sub nom. *Fox v. Fox*) 88 O.A.C. 201 (C.A.), leave to appeal refused (1996), [1996] S.C.C.A. No. 241, 207 N.R. 80 (note), 97 O.A.C. 320 (note).

23 For a full argument, see L. Smith, "The Motive, Not the Deed," ch. 4 in J. Getzler, ed., *Rationalizing Property, Equity and Trusts: Essays in Honour of Edward Burn* (London: Butterworths, 2003).

24 The law does not know the idea of a "passive trustee." All trustees must be active in the trust. Hence, a passive trustee is liable for the breach of his or her active co-trustee, unless the passive trustee is excused by the trust instrument or by the court. This is discussed later in this chapter.

25 *Forest of Dean Coal Mining Co., Re* (1878), 10 Ch. D. 450.

26 *Head v. Gould*, [1898] 2 Ch. 250.

27 The remedies of trustees *inter se* are discussed later in this chapter.

(c) **Compensation**

(i) *Generally*

An action for compensation lies against a trustee when a breach of trust has caused a loss to the trust estate. It also lies against other fiduciaries who cause a loss through breach of a fiduciary duty.[28] In Canada and elsewhere this remedy is often called damages. This is not objectionable, provided that the remedy is not confused with the common law remedy of damages, for the two are different. The object of compensation is restore to the trust the loss the trustee has caused, while the purpose of damages is to restore the plaintiff to his or her original position. In actions for damages for breach of contract and for tort, the damages are limited by the principles of foreseeability and remoteness. Those principles are irrelevant in the law of trusts.[29]

For example, if a person is obliged by contract to deliver certain securities but fails to do so, he or she will be liable for breach of the contract and will be required to pay damages assessed at the value of the securities at the date when they should have been delivered.[30] In the alternative, the defendant may be required to deliver the securities themselves if he or she still has them. If, however, the parties stand in a fiduciary relationship, the plaintiff can recover compensation in an amount equal to the highest price of the securities while they were held by the defendant. This is because the law makes every presumption against a trustee who has acted wrongfully and one can, thus, assume that the beneficiary would have wanted to sell the securities at the highest price.[31]

---

28 See R. Chambers, "Liability" in P. Birks and A. Pretto, eds., *Breach of Trust* (Oxford: Hart Publishing, 2002) 1, explaining that compensation for loss may be achieved in two ways. First, it may be done through the accounting process to which all trustees are subject; this will lead to reconstitution of the trust fund. Secondly, it may be achieved via equitable compensation, which is a direct payment to the beneficiaries. This may be the only route in the case of a fiduciary who is not liable to account because he does not hold any property for the beneficiary. It is less likely to be relevant in the case of a trustee, unless the trust is one which gives the beneficiary an immediate right to the trust assets.

29 Ford and Lee, §17020; *Dawson v. Perpetual Trustee Co.*, [1966] 2 N.S.W.R. 211 (New South Wales S.C.).

30 In *Wroth v. Tyler* (1973), [1974] Ch. 30, [1973] 1 All E.R. 897, [1973] 2 W.L.R. 405 (Ch. Div.), a case on the breach of a contract to convey land, the land had risen greatly in value between breach and trial. Specific performance was denied. Megarry J. held that common law damages had to be assessed at the time of the breach. The rise in value was available to the plaintiff only because the judge awarded "equitable damages," that is, a money award made in lieu of a decree of specific performance. Note however that in *Johnson v. Agnew* (1979), [1980] A.C. 367, [1979] 1 All E.R. 883 (H.L.), at 400 [A.C.], Lord Diplock that there was no reason to calculate damages "in lieu of" an injunction or specific performance differently from the way they would be calculcated at common law; and of course the common law could develop and grow in such matters as the time for assessment of damages. Lord Diplock's view was adopted in *306793 Ontario Ltd. v. Rimes* (1979), 25 O.R. (2d) 79, 100 D.L.R. (3d) 350, 1979 CarswellOnt 617, 10 R.P.R. 257 (C.A.).

31 *Fultz v. McNeil* (1906), 38 S.C.R. 198, 1906 CarswellNS 237. But see *Toronto-Dominion Bank v. Uhren* (1960), 32 W.W.R. 61, 24 D.L.R. (2d) 203, 1960 CarswellSask 21 (C.A.), in which the

Thus, in *Toronto-Dominion Bank v. Uhren,*[32] Culliton, J.A. adopted the following statement in *Snell's Principles of Equity:*[33] "The measure of the trustee's liability for breach of trust is the loss caused thereby to the trust estate." He continued:[34]

> The proof of that loss should not be limited to the establishment of the value of the property at the time of the breach of trust as directed by the learned trial Judge, but should be determined by all the evidence which is relevant to and admissible on that issue. It is obvious, of course, that under no circumstances could the loss be less than the amount realized from the sale of the properties.

Similarly, Duff, J. stated in *Fultz v. McNeil:*[35]

> . . .the defendant was under an obligation to account to the plaintiffs at once for that which he received as trustee for them. Treated as a trustee wrongfully withholding property which he was bound under his trust to deliver to his *cestuis que trustent* [sic], he is liable to make reparation for the loss suffered by the trust by reason of his breach of trust; and (every presumption being made against him as a wrongdoer), that loss must be calculated on the assumption that the securities would have been sold at the best price obtainable.

Dawson v. Perpetual Trustee Co.[36] affords a good illustration of the difference between law and equity as regards the assessment of damages. A trustee sought to transfer NZ£4700 from New Zealand to Australia by unlawful means in 1939. The fund was lost through the dishonesty of the trustee's agent. The Australian trustee proposed to repay the loss in 1966. While the Australian and New Zealand pounds were at par in 1939, the latter were worth substantially more than the former in 1966. The court held that the trustee had to pay compensation in an amount calculated at the rate of exchange prevailing in 1966, together with interest. It was irrelevant that it would cost him more to do so in 1966 than it would have done in 1939. Moreover, the contractual principle that fluctuations in exchange rates are too remote a consequence of a breach of contract,[37] was held to be inapplicable to a breach of trust.

---

court seems to suggest that liability for breach of contract and trust is the same. The cases are discussed in Waters, pp. 995ff.

32 *Ibid., Uhren.*

33 24th ed., p. 221. (See now *Snell's Equity* 30th ed., Edited by J.A. McGhee (London: Sweet & Maxwell Ltd., 2000), p. 324) ("Snell").

34 At W.W.R. 73, D.L.R. 214.

35 *Supra*, note 31, at 205.

36 *Supra*, note 29.

37 See *Di Ferdinando v. Simon Smits & Co.,* [1920] 3 K.B. 409 (K.B.), at 415, *per* Scrutton L.J. At least in England, the law on this point has been changed: *Miliangos v. George Frank (Textiles) Ltd.* (1975), [1976] A.C. 443, [1975] 3 All E.R. 801, 1 Ll. L. Rep. 201 (H.L.). The law in Canada is unclear: S. Waddams, *The Law of Damages*, 3rd ed. (Toronto: Canada Law Book, 1997), ¶7.80ff.

To succeed in an action for breach of trust, the beneficiary must show a causal connection between the breach of trust and the loss.[38]

Of significance to this issue is the judgment of the Supreme Court of Canada in *Guerin v. R.*[39] The plaintiff Indians surrendered the aboriginal title to land to the Crown so that the Crown could lease it to a golf club on certain terms, agreed to between the Indian band and the Crown representatives. The Crown leased it on different terms, acceptable to the golf club. The Indians brought action seeking redress. The members of the court differed on the question whether the Crown was a trustee or stood in another fiduciary relationship towards the Indians. However, they held that the assessment of compensation should not be governed by tort principles. Rather, the plaintiffs were entitled to compensation calculated on the same basis as if there had been a breach of trust. Hence, the plaintiffs were entitled to be placed, so far as possible, in the same position they would have been in but for the breach. Common law damages would have limited recovery to the loss reasonably foreseeable or contemplated at the date of the breach, that is the date of the lease. However, by awarding compensation in equity, the court could have regard to what actually happened and, thus, could award the subsequent increase in the value of the land, which had not been foreseen. Moreover, applying *Fultz v. McNeill*, the award was based on the most profitable use that might have been made of the land.

In *Canson Enterprises Ltd. v. Boughton & Co.*,[40] McLachlin J. accurately summarized the assessment of damages in *Guerin* as follows:

> The trial judge in *Guerin* did not measure damages as the difference between the lease which was entered into and that which the Band was prepared to authorize, because the golf club would not have entered into a lease at all on the terms sought by the Band, and it could not therefore be said that the breach had caused the Band to lose the opportunity to enter a lease on the authorized terms. Nor did the trial judge simply assess damages as the difference between the value of the lease actually entered into and the amount that the land was worth at the time of trial, which would be the result if causation were irrelevant. Rather he concluded that had there been no breach the Band would have eventually leased the land for residential development. He allowed for the time which would have been required for planning, tenders and negotiation, and he also discounted for the fact that some of the then current value of the surrounding developments was due to the existence of the golf course. In other words, he assessed, as best he could, the value of the actual opportunity lost as a result of the breach.

---

38 *Miller's Trust Deed, Re* (1978), 75 L.S.G. 454; *Swindle v. Harrison*, [1997] 4 All E.R. 705 (C.A.); *Martin v. Goldfarb* (1998), 163 D.L.R. (4th) 639, 1998 CarswellOnt 3319, [1998] O.J. No. 3403, 112 O.A.C. 138, 42 C.C.L.T. (2d) 271, 41 O.R. (3d) 161, 44 B.L.R. (2d) 158 (C.A.), leave to appeal refused (1999), [1998] S.C.C.A. No. 516, 239 N.R. 193 (note), 123 O.A.C. 199 (note).

39 (1984), [1984] 2 S.C.R. 335, 1984 CarswellNat 813, 1984 CarswellNat 693, [1984] 6 W.W.R. 481, 13 D.L.R. (4th) 321, 55 N.R. 161, [1985] 1 C.N.L.R. 120, 20 E.T.R. 6, 36 R.P.R. 1, 59 B.C.L.R. 301. See also *Smith Estate v. Smith Estate*, 37 E.T.R. (2d) 151, 2000 CarswellBC 2628, 2000 BCSC 1842 (S.C.).

40 *Supra*, note 18.

41 [Footnote omitted]

In *Canson Enterprises Ltd. v. Boughton & Co.*,[42] which is reproduced below, it shows that a fiduciary cannot be held liable for losses caused by independent acts of third parties.

In the context of breaches of trust and fiduciary duties, it is often said that compensation is restitutionary.[43] However, we submit that this is an inexact usage of the concept of restitution. Restitution involves restoration to a plaintiff of property that has been unjustly taken or received from him or her (as in the case of a mistaken payment), and is also used to describe defendants' liabilities to give up benefits acquired by doing wrong to the plaintiff (as in the case of a profitable breach of copyright). In the context of breach of trust and of fiduciary obligation we are sometimes concerned with the latter form of restitution — a disgorgement of benefits. But where a breaching trustee simply causes a loss to the trust assets and is required to make it good, this is not restitution; it is neither "giving back" nor "giving up" a gain. There is no requirement to show that the breaching trustee acquired any gain. It is compensation, just as a tortfeasor or contract breacher must compensate the victim for loss.

However, equity affords trust beneficiaries a number of advantages that a plaintiff at common law does not enjoy. These include the following: (1) the principles of remoteness and foreseeability have no relevance; (2) the loss is calculated at the time of trial rather than at the time of the breach; and (3) the beneficiary is given the benefit of a number of presumptions. The presumptions include the following: (a) that securities wrongfully withheld from the beneficiary would have been sold by the beneficiary at the highest price obtainable;[44] (b) that trust funds will be put to their most profitable use;[45] (c) that no inference favourable to the trustee will be drawn when the facts are capable of two interpretations, one favouring the trustee and the other the beneficiary;[46] and (d) that a fiduciary must account on the basis less favourable to her or him.[47]

---

42 *Supra*, note 18.

43 *Bartlett v. Barclays Bank Trust Co. (Nos. 1 & 2)*, *supra*, note 11, at 543 [Ch.]. See also *Bell's Indenture, Re*, (sub nom. *Bell v. Hickley*) [1980] 1 W.L.R. 1217, [1980] 3 All E.R. 425 (Ch. Div.); *Dawson v. Perpetual Trustee Co.*, *supra*, note 29, at 214 *per* Street J.; *Guerin v. R.*, *supra*, note 39, at 365 [D.L.R.], *per* Wilson J.; *Ward v. Ward* (1985), 70 N.S.R. (2d) 219, 1985 CarswellNS 370, 166 A.P.R. 219 (Co. Ct.), at 228 [N.S.R.]; *Hodgkinson v. Simms*, [1994] 3 S.C.R. 377, 117 D.L.R. (4th) 161, [1994] S.C.J. No. 84, 1994 CarswellBC 438, 1994 CarswellBC 1245, [1994] 9 W.W.R. 609, 49 B.C.A.C. 1, 80 W.A.C. 1, 22 C.C.L.T. (2d) 1, 16 B.L.R. (2d) 1, 6 C.C.L.S. 1, 57 C.P.R. (3d) 1, 5 E.T.R. (2d) 1, 95 D.T.C. 5135, 97 B.C.L.R. (2d) 1, 171 N.R. 245, at 199 [D.L.R.], *per* La Forest J; *Semiahmoo Indian Band v. Canada*, *supra*, note 17.

44 *Fultz v. McNeil*, *supra*, note 31. See John D. McCamus, "Equitable Compensation and Restitutionary Remedies: Recent Developments," in *Special Lectures of the Law Society of Upper Canada 1995 — Law of Remedies[:] Principles and Proofs* (Toronto: Carswell, 1995), 295 at 298-9.

45 *Guerin*, *supra*, note 39; *Canson Enterprises Ltd. v. Boughton & Co.*, *supra*, note 18, at 156 [D.L.R.], *per* McLachlin J.

46 See *Osadchuk v. National Trust Co.*, [1943] S.C.R. 89, [1943] 1 D.L.R. 689, 1943 CarswellSask 90.

47 See *Warman International Ltd. v. Dwyer* (1995), 128 A.L.R. 201 (Australia H.C.), at 216.

(ii) *Interest*

The extent of the trustee's liability for breach of trust is, therefore, the loss caused to the trust estate, together with interest.[48] If a trustee were only required to restore the capital value of the trust property that was lost because of the breach, the beneficiaries would not be adequately compensated. Hence, they are also entitled to interest on the capital. In *Wallersteiner v. Moir (No. 2)*[49] Buckley L.J. said:

> It is well established in equity that a trustee who in breach of trust misapplies trust funds will be liable not only to replace the misapplied principal fund but to do so with interest from the date of misapplication. This is on the notional ground that the money so applied was in fact the trustee's own money and that he has retained the misapplied trust money in his own hands and used it for his own purposes. Where a trustee has retained trust money in his own hands, he will be accountable for the profit which he has made or which he is assumed to have made from the use of the money.

The rate of interest in a compensation award varies with the circumstances. The interest awarded is, in essence, a presumed profit. In other words, if the fiduciary misused trust property and incurred a loss when she or he ought to have made a gain, the rate of interest reflects the profit that ought to have been made with the property. The rate of interest and its compounding reflect the gravity of the fiduciary's wrong.

The reason interest is awarded in the case of compensation is that in an accounting the beneficiary can claim all the gain made by the fiduciary, except that attributable to the fiduciary's own skill.[50] In the alternative remedy of compensation, an attempt is made to approximate what might have been obtained on an account by the imposition of interest assuming an account was available or, if no profit was made, to attribute to the trust the profit that ought to have been made. Any gains the trustee made or ought to have made belong to the trust.[51]

The rate of interest and whether it should be compounded with yearly or half-yearly rests, is in the court's discretion.[52] In *Honsberger v. Kratz*[53] Boyd C. summarized the English rules, previously accepted in *Inglis v. Beaty*[54] as follows:[55]

---

48 *Wallersteiner v. Moir (No. 2)*, [1975] 1 Q.B. 373, [1975] 1 All E.R. 849, [1975] 2 W.L.R. 389, 119 Sol. Jo. 97 (C.A.); *Fales v. Canada Permanent Trust Co.* (1976), [1977] 2 S.C.R. 302, (sub nom. *Wohlleben v. Canada Permanent Trust Co.*) 70 D.L.R. (3d) 257, 1976 CarswellBC 240, 1976 CarswellBC 317, [1976] 6 W.W.R. 10, 11 N.R. 487; *Bartlett v. Barclays Bank Trust Co. (Nos. 1 & 2)*, *supra*, note 11; *Toronto-Dominion Bank v. Uhren*, *supra*, note 31, at 73, *per* Culliton J.A.

49 *Supra*, at Q.B. 395.

50 P.D. Finn, *Fiduciary Obligations* (Sydney: The Law Book Company Limited, 1977), §241 ("Finn").

51 *Ibid.*, §§240, 242.

52 Compound interest means that interest is payable not only on the principal, but on the interest already accrued. The effect of compounding is increased the more frequently it is calculated. "Yearly rests" mean that each year, one calculates the interest payable, including interest on previously accrued interest. "Half-yearly rests" means that this will be done every six months; even if the annual rate is the same, the compounding of interest will lead to a greater amount of

(1) When the money is kept in the executors [*sic*] hands without sufficient excuse, the offence is deemed an act of negligence, and the usual Court rate of interest will be charged at four per cent. (2) When the executors are not only negligent but commit an act of misfeasance by expending the funds for their own benefit or in any other way use them, the higher rate of five per cent will be charged. (3) If the act of misfeasance is of such a character as to lead to the conclusion that more than this rate of interest has been made out of the money as for instance if it is employed in ordinary trade or in speculation the beneficiaries will be allowed the option of either having an account of the profits or having the interest taken with rests.

The Chancellor then went on to state that in Ontario the rates of interest to be charged under the first two rules should be six per cent and the "rate of interest as is the then current value of money," respectively.

However, while these principles were approved in *Toronto General Trusts Co. v. Hogg*,[56] the Ontario Court of Appeal stated that the decision to require the payment of interest, the rate of interest and whether it should be compounded, depends upon the type of breach. Thus, if the breach is technical and the trustee has acted prudently, the court may order repayment of capital only.[57]

In the 19th century the legal rate appears to have been six per cent in Canada.[58] Undoubtedly today, rates would be fixed by reference to current commercial rates. For example, the rate might be fixed at the "prime rate" allowed for pre-judgment interest.[59]

In England the rate allowed for a negligent breach of trust appears to be the legal rate,[60] that is, the rate of interest received in the short-term investment account established under the *Administration of Justice Act 1965*.[61] If the trustee has used the trust funds for his or her own benefit, the English rate is the current or commercial lending rate, that is, one per cent above the official bank rate or minimum lending rate in effect at the relevant time.[62]

You should note that the court's jurisdiction to award compound interest is limited. The court may award compound interest in accordance with an agreement or custom. Apart from that, compound interest may only be awarded in equity for fraud, or in a compensation action when a trustee or other fiduciary has made a profit improperly.[63]

---

interest when the compounding is more frequent, because each penny of interest begins to earn its own interest sooner. With modern technology, there is no limit to the frequency of compounding; it can be done continuously (from moment to moment).

53 (1885), 10 O.R. 521 (H.C.).

54 (1878), 2 O.A.R. 453.

55 At 10 O.R. 525. The case was concerned with executors, but the principle applies equally to them.

56 [1932] O.R. 641, [1932] 4 D.L.R. 465 (C.A.), affirmed (1933), [1934] S.C.R. 1, [1933] 3 D.L.R. 721, 1933 CarswellOnt 93.

57 Ford and Lee, §17130 (*Trustee innocent of blame*).

58 Waters, p. 1002.

59 See, *e.g.*, *Courts of Justice Act*, R.S.O. 1990, c. C.43, s. 128.

60 *Bartlett v. Barclays Bank Trust Co. (Nos. 1 & 2)*, *supra*, note 11.

61 C. 2, s. 6(1) (U.K.).

62 *Wallersteiner v. Moir (No. 2)*, *supra*, note 48, 508n (addendum), at 388, 389, 406 [Q.B.].

63 *Westdeutsche Landesbank Girozentrale v. Islington London Borough Council*, [1996] A.C. 669, [1996] 2 All E.R. 961, [1996] 2 W.L.R. 802 (H.L.).

The following case explores the limits of the fiduciary liability to compensate the beneficiary for a loss.

CANSON ENTERPRISES LTD. v. BOUGHTON & CO.

(1991), 85 D.L.R. (4th) 129, 1991 CarswellBC 269, 1991 CarswellBC 925, [1991] S.C.J. No. 91, [1992] 1 W.W.R. 245, 9 C.C.L.T. (2d) 1, 39 C.P.R. (3d) 449, 131 N.R. 321, 61 B.C.L.R. (2d) 1, 6 B.C.A.C. 1, 13 W.A.C. 1, [1991] 3 S.C.R. 534, 43 E.T.R. 201
Supreme Court of Canada

The respondent, Treit, and others, proposed a real estate venture involving a "flip" with a secret profit. The respondent corporation, Sun-Mark, agreed to purchase certain land for $410,000. Treit suggested to the appellant corporations, Canson and Fealty, that they form a joint venture with the respondent corporation, Peregrine, and that the joint venture purchase the land for $525,000 and develop it. The appellants followed Treit's suggestion. Treit did not disclose Sun-Mark's agreement to the appellants. The appellants assumed that they were buying directly from the original vendors. In fact, they were buying from Sun-Mark, although ultimately they received a transfer directly from the original vendors. Peregrine, whose principal was a partner in the defendant law firm, Boughton & Co., did know the facts. The respondent, Wollen, also a partner in the law firm, acted for Sun-Mark and for the ultimate purchasers. Wollen prepared separate statements of adjustments for the first and second transactions. The first showed the lower purchase price and the second the higher. Wollen did not disclose the secret profit of $115,000 (the difference between the two prices) that Sun-Mark and others would receive. When the second transaction closed, Wollen paid the secret profit to Sun-Mark.

The joint venture engaged Treit as manager to build a warehouse on the land. Because of the negligence of the soil engineer and the pile driving firm, the building suffered extensive damage. An action against those parties was settled, leaving a substantial shortfall.

The appellants brought this action by way of special case on an agreed statement of facts to determine whether, assuming the facts as stated were true, they could recover damages from the defendants. One of the agreed facts was that the appellants would not have purchased the land had they known of the secret profit. The trial judge held[64] that Wollen and his firm, as well as the other respondents were (assuming the facts in the agreed statement were true) in breach of fiduciary duty. Accordingly, he held that the appellants were entitled to recover the secret profit and "consequential damages" to be determined, but "limited to those leading up to the negligence of the engineers and pile drivers." In addition, he held Treit liable for the same damages for the tort of deceit. The British

---

[64] (1988), 31 B.C.L.R. (2d) 46, 45 C.C.L.T. 209, [1989] 2 W.W.R. 30, 52 D.L.R. (4th) 323, 1988 CarswellBC 343 (S.C. [In Chambers]).

Columbia Court of Appeal affirmed.[65] The consequential damages were apparently expenses incurred on the building project until the negligence of the third parties took place.[66]

LA FOREST J.:

This case concerns the extent to which a person who has suffered loss from a breach of a fiduciary obligation may recover for that loss from the person who has committed the breach. Specifically, what is the extent of liability of a solicitor who, in handling a real estate transaction, failed to disclose to the purchasers a secret profit made by a third party? Is the solicitor responsible only for losses directly flowing from the breach of duty itself, or is he also liable for loss caused by an intervening act unrelated to that breach, in this case loss caused by subsidence of a building resulting from the fault of engineers and pile-drivers in carrying out the project known by the parties to be the purpose for the acquisition of the property? The purchasers were unable to execute fully upon judgments in an action in negligence against the engineers and pile-drivers for the damage caused by the subsidence. The question here is whether they can recover the shortfall by the present action for breach of fiduciary duty.

. . .

Analysis

The appellants, we saw, firmly base their claim in equity for breach of a fiduciary duty. Although they could pursue various claims at common law, they maintain that they can seek equitable remedies concurrently and may choose the remedy most advantageous to them. The respondents do not contest this and, in my view, quite properly concede this point. The appellants' position is fully supported so far as torts and contracts are concerned by this Court's decision in *Central Trust Co. v. Rafuse*,[67] and so far as claims in law and equity are concerned by the House of Lord's decision in *Nocton v. Lord Ashburton*.[68]

Nocton v. Lord Ashburton is the leading case in this area. Its facts bear a considerable affinity to the present case, and it forms a convenient starting point for a discussion of the applicable principles. There a mortgagee brought action against his solicitor for indemnity for loss he had suffered from the advice given by his solicitor to release a part of a mortgage security. The security became insufficient and the mortgagor defaulted. The release gave the solicitor further security for his own mortgage. The trial judge dealt with the case as one of deceit and, having found no fraud, dismissed the action. While an action for negligence

---

65 (1989), 39 B.C.L.R. (2d) 177, [1990] 1 W.W.R. 375, 45 B.L.R. 301, 61 D.L.R. (4th) 732, 1989 CarswellBC 157 (C.A.).

66 *Ibid.*, at D.L.R. 734, *per* Lambert J.A.

67 [1986] 2 S.C.R. 147.

68 [1914] A.C. 932 (H.L.).

may have lain, such action was statute-barred. On appeal, the Court of Appeal reversed the trial judge on the issue of fraud and granted damages for deceit. The House of Lords, however, restored the findings of the trial judge on the issue of fraud, but affirmed the Court of Appeal's award of damages on other grounds. A majority of their Lordships granted equitable relief for breach of fiduciary duty.

This equitable jurisdiction the Lord Chancellor, Viscount Haldane, noted was grounded in the old Bill of Chancery to enforce compensation for breach of a fiduciary obligation.[69] Operating as a court of conscience, equity not only exercised concurrent jurisdiction with the common law in respect of misrepresentations where there was actual fraud; it also acted in respect of a wide range of cases where there was misrepresentation or failure to give information, not amounting to actual fraud, where a person was under a fiduciary duty or by reason of other special circumstances under a duty to inform another. As a court of conscience, it would act *in personam* to prevent persons from acting against the dictates of conscience as defined by the court, i.e., where there was "equitable fraud". Equity's remedies, the Lord Chancellor stated, were more elastic than those available at common law. Operating *in personam*, he continued, equity could order the defendant, not indeed in those days (*i.e.*, before *Lord Cairn's Act*)[70] to grant damages, but to make restitution, or to compensate the plaintiff by putting him in as good a position pecuniarily as he would have been before the breach.[71] Thus the measure of compensation may not always be the same as damages in an action for deceit or negligence. However, in the case before him that question was one of form only and it was not clear whether it would have made any difference whether compensation or damages was awarded. The issue was, in any event, not raised and the Court of Appeal's award was allowed to stand.

There was one difference in the nature of the breach by the solicitor in *Nocton* from that complained of in the present case. In *Nocton*, it will be remembered, the breach could give rise to a possible benefit to the solicitor, a situation that does not arise here. However, I have no doubt, and it was not contested, that the situation here also involves a breach of a fiduciary duty sufficient to call upon equity's jurisdiction to compensate the appellants for breach of the duty.

. . .

Some academic writings, it is true, argue for limiting fiduciary obligations to situations where the solicitor may benefit from a misstatement.[72] However, the Canadian cases on the subject make it clear that the law is not so limited.[73] The

---

69   At 946.

70   *Chancery Amendment Act 1858*, 21 & 22 Vict., c. 27.

71   At 952.

72   See the Hon. Mr. Justice Gummow, "Compensation for Breaches of Fiduciary Duty" in T.G. Youdan (ed.) *Equity, Fiduciaries and Trusts* (1988).

73   See *Culling v. Sansai Securities Ltd.* (1974), 45 D.L.R. (3d) 456; *Burke v. Cory* (1959), 19 D.L.R. (2d) 252 (Ont. C.A.); *Howard v. Cunliffe* (1973), 36 D.L.R. (3d) 212 (B.C.C.A.); *Laskin v. Bache and Co., Farish v. Nat. Trust Co.*, [1972] 1 O.R. 465 (C.A.); *Maghan v. Richardson Securities* (1986), 58 O.R. (2d) 1 (C.A.).

attempt to narrow the application of fiduciary relations may to some extent rest on, in my view, a misguided sense of orderliness.

[His Lordship noted that the remedy of compensation is not likely to be used often in cases such as this, since the torts of deceit and negligent misstatement usually afford adequate remedies. He continued:]

I shall begin by attempting to describe the nature of compensation and, more particularly, what it means in the present context. The appellants strongly emphasized that the courts of equity had, before the *Judicature Act*,[74] no power to award damages, this being the exclusive domain of the common law, and the only statutory change to this regime was made by *Lord Cairn's Act*[75] and its successors. Equity, they assert, was concerned with restoring a plaintiff to the position he or she was in before the breach of duty calling upon equity's intervention. The situation, they argued, was not changed by the *Judicature Act*, which was aimed largely at providing for the enforcement of law and equity in the same courts, not in altering the jurisdiction exercisable under each system.

. . .

The difference between damages and restitution was abundantly clear in cases of breaches of trust, and in that context the following statement of James and Baggallay L.JJ. in *Ex parte Adamson*[76] appears unexceptionable:

> The Court of Chancery never entertained a suit for damages occasioned by fraudulent conduct or for breach of trust. The suit was always for an equitable debt or liability in the nature of debt. It was a suit for the restitution of the actual money or thing, or value of the thing, of which the cheated party had been cheated.

But while the same approach of restitution or restoration applied in the case of simple compensation not involving the restoration of property, the difference in practical result between compensation and damages is by no means as clear. All that Lord Haldane tells us about this[77] is that "[t]he measure of damages [he was there speaking in a generic and not in a technical sense] may not always be the same as in an action of deceit or for negligence", and in the case before him he was content to say that it was a mere matter of form. On this matter, I fully agree with Cooke P. in *Day v. Mead*,[78] that in many cases it is "a difference without a distinction". The question is whether, like the case before him, this is one of them.

The appellants urged us to accept the manner of calculating compensation adopted by the courts in trust cases or situations akin to a trust, and they relied in

---

74 *Supreme Court of Judicature Act 1873*, 36 & 37 Vict., c. 66.
75 *Chancery Amendment Act 1858*, 21 & 22 Vict., c. 27.
76 (1878), 8 Ch.D. 807 at 819.
77 In *Nocton v. Lord Ashburton, supra*, note 68, at 958.
78 [1987] 2 N.Z.L.R. 443 at 451 (C.A.).

particular on the *Guerin* case.[79] I think the courts below were perfectly right to reject that proposition. There is a sharp divide between a situation where a person has *control* of property which in the view of the court *belongs* to another, and one where a person is under a fiduciary duty to perform an obligation where equity's concern is simply that the duty be performed honestly and in accordance with the undertaking the fiduciary has taken on.[80] In the case of a trust relationship, the trustee's obligation is to hold the res or object of the trust for his *cestui que trust*, and on breach the concern of equity is that it be restored to the *cestui que trust* or if that cannot be done to afford compensation for what the object would be worth. In the case of a mere breach of duty, the concern of equity is to ascertain the loss resulting from the breach of the particular duty. Where the wrongdoer has received some benefit, that benefit can be disgorged, but the measure of compensation where no such benefit has been obtained by the wrongdoer raises different issues. I turn then specifically to that situation.

. . .

I should first of all say that the fact that such limitations may not have been developed before the *Judicature Act*[81] is no ground for saying there is no room for further development of equitable principles to deal with the situation. We have it on high authority that equitable principles were not frozen in time.[82] As Lord Diplock put it:[83]

> Nor did the coming into force of that Act bring to a sudden halt the whole process of development of the substantive law of England that had been so notable an achievement of the preceding decades.

We have been given no case where the principles applicable to trusts have been applied to a breach of a fiduciary duty of the type in question here, and for reasons already given, I see no reason why they should be transposed here. The harshness of the result is reason alone, but apart from this, I do not think that the claim for the harm resulting from the actions of third parties can fairly be looked upon as falling within what is encompassed in restoration for the harm suffered from the breach. That is the view taken by all the Canadian courts that have dealt with the issue. In addition to *Jacks v. Davis*[84] and the present case, reference may also be made to *Laskin v. Bache and Co.*[85] and *Burke v. Cory*,[86] both in the Ontario Court of Appeal.

---

79   *Guerin v. R.*, *supra*, note 39.
80   See L.S. Sealy, "Some Principles of Fiduciary Obligation," [1963] Cambr. L.J. 119; *ibid.*, "Fiduciary Relationships," [1962] Cambr. L.J. 69.
81   *Supra.*
82   See *United Scientific Holdings Ltd. v. Burnley Borough Council*, [1978] A.C. 904.
83   *Ibid.*, at 926.
84   (1980), 12 C.C.L.T. 298, affirmed [1983] 1 W.W.R. 327.
85   [1972] 1 O.R. 465 (C.A.).
86   (1959), 19 D.L.R. (2d) 252 (Ont. C.A.).

I have no doubt that policies underlying concepts like remoteness and mitigation might have developed from an equitable perspective. However, given the
paucity of authority in the field, it is scarcely surprising that courts will deal with
a case falling properly within the ambit of equity as if it were a common law
matter or as justifying the use of its mode of analysis. This can be seen from
Burke v. Cory, and *Laskin v. Bache*. In *Cory*, a broker induced a client to purchase
certain stocks after gaining his confidence by emphasizing the broker's qualifications and his possession of private information regarding the stocks and then
making false representations about the company. The court held that apart from
the action of deceit, which requires an allegation of fraud, liability for the misrepresentation could be rested on the existence of a fiduciary relationship. The
amount of compensation (which the court there referred to as the measure of
damages) was calculated in terms of the loss at the time of the allotment.

In *Cory*, and for that matter in *Laskin*, the court was also willing to apply the
concept of mitigation of damages. Mitigation in equity was also found to be
appropriate in *LeMesurier v. Andrus*[87] and it seems to be implicit in this Court's
decision in *Asamera Oil Corp. v. Sea Oil & General Corp.*[88] This is consistent
with the fact that equity acted on the basis of fairness and justice. The truth is that
barring different policy considerations underlying one action or the other, I see
no reason why the same basic claim, whether framed in terms of a common law
action or an equitable remedy, should give rise to different levels of redress.

United Scientific Holdings Ltd. v. Burnley Borough Council[89] gives strong
support to this manner of approaching the issue. That case concerned the different
routes taken by common law and equity in determining whether time was of the
essence in a lease. As in the present case, there was some tendency for these
different routes to converge even before the *Judicature Act*,[90] for it must not be
forgotten that well before that Act "the evolution of the one system was influenced
by the other".[91] In *United Scientific*, s. 25 of the Act seems to me to have given
appropriate guidance as to how modern courts should approach the situation and
I need not closely examine the holding of that case except to bring attention to
what the House of Lords thought the interplay of law and equity should be. In a
passage with which all the other Law Lords agreed, Lord Diplock had this to
say:[92]

> My Lords, if by "rules of equity" is meant that body of substantive and adjectival law that,
> prior to 1875, was administered by the Court of Chancery but not by courts of common law, to
> speak of the rules of equity as being part of the law of England in 1977 is about as meaningful as
> to speak similarly of the Statutes of Uses or of Quia Emptores. Historically all three have in their
> time played an important part in the development of the corpus juris into what it is today; but to
> perpetuate a dichotomy between rules of equity and rules of common law which it was a major
> purpose of the *Supreme Court of Judicature Act 1873* to do away with, is, in my view, conducive

---

87 (1986), 54 O.R. (2d) 1 (Ont. C.A.).

88 [1979] 1 S.C.R. 633 at 667-68.

89 *Supra*, note 82.

90 *Supra*.

91 *United Scientific Holdings, supra*, note 82, at 944, *per* Lord Simon.

92 *Ibid.*, at 924-25.

to erroneous conclusions as to the ways in which the law of England has developed in the last hundred years.

Your Lordships have been referred to the vivid phrase traceable to the first edition of Ashburner, Principles of Equity where, in speaking in 1902 of the effect of the Supreme Court of Judicature Act he says[93] "the two streams of jurisdiction" (sc. law and equity) — "though they run in the same channel, run side by side and do not mingle their waters." My Lords, by 1977 this metaphor has in my view become both mischievous and deceptive. The innate conservatism of English lawyers may have made them slow to recognise that by the Supreme Court of Judicature Act 1873 the two systems of substantive and adjectival law formerly administered by courts of law and Courts of Chancery (as well as those administered by courts of admiralty, probate and matrimonial cases), were fused. As at the confluence of the Rhone and Saone, it may be possible for a short distance to discern the source from which each part of the combined stream came, but there comes a point at which this ceases to be possible. If Professor Ashburner's fluvial metaphor is to be retained at all, the waters of the confluent streams of law and equity have surely mingled now.

[His Lordship noted that this approach was followed by the Ontario Court of Appeal in *LeMesurier v. Andrus*.[94]]

The most dramatic example of this approach is the New Zealand case of *Day v. Mead*[95] to which I have previously referred. Mead, Day's solicitor, acted for him for many years in connection with land subdivision projects and other ventures. None of the investments could fairly be described as speculative until those that gave rise to the litigation. These concerned a newly-formed company, Pacific Mills Ltd., of which Mead was a director and shareholder. The investment and the decision of the trial judge are conveniently set forth in the headnote to the case,[96] as follows:

> In July 1977, acting on Mead's advice, Day purchased 20,000 shares, at $1 per share, in Pacific Mills, knowing that Mead was a shareholder and that his firm's nominee company had lent money to Pacific Mills. After this initial investment of $20,000, Day took an interest in the company's business, regularly visiting its paper-mill factory and attending a couple of directors' meetings as an onlooker. Then, in December 1977, once again acting on Mead's advice, Day subscribed for a further 80,000 shares in the company at a cost of $80,000. In March 1978 the company went into receivership, and Day lost both investments. He sued Mead for his loss plus interest, claiming breach of fiduciary duty. The High Court Judge held that Mead was in breach of his fiduciary duty to Day in failing to refer Day to an independent solicitor and in failing to inform him of the management and financial difficulties facing the company. The Judge further held that Day was entitled to full compensation for his first investment, but, as Day was equally to blame for the loss of his second investment due to his business experience and his involvement with the company between July and December 1977, he was entitled to compensation for only half that investment. The Judge awarded Day damages of $60,000, but refused interest on the grounds of Day's delay in bringing the case to trial.

The Court of Appeal affirmed the decision of the trial judge except as to the matter of interest, an issue I need not discuss here. It agreed that Mead, though

---

93 At p. 23.
94 *Supra*, note 87.
95 *Supra*, note 78.
96 At 443.

he acted quite innocently, was, having regard to the circumstances, in breach of fiduciary duties. In the absence of complete disclosure of the various conflicts of interest, he should have referred Day to an independent adviser and should have informed him of the problems faced by the company.

What is important for our purposes is the manner in which the Court of Appeal dealt with compensation, and in particular the question whether the compensation could be reduced in respect of the second investment in 1977 because of Day's contributory negligence. Like the trial judge, it concluded that it was proper to apportion the loss. In its view, not only was this justifiable on the basis of equitable principles, but law and equity had become so merged in this area that the principles of contribution should apply. As well, judge-made law was quite properly affected by legislative action, there the *Contributory Negligence Act*, and by other current trends.

. . .

I agree with this approach. As I have attempted to demonstrate, it would be possible to reach this result following a purely equitable path. I agree with Cooke P. that the maxims of equity can be flexibly adapted to serve the ends of justice as perceived in our days. They are not rules that must be rigorously applied but malleable principles intended to serve the ends of fairness and justice. Lord Haldane reminded us in *Nocton v. Lord Ashburton*[97] of the elasticity of equitable remedies. But in this area, it seems to me, even the path of equity leads to law. The maxim that "equity follows the law" (though I realize that it has traditionally been used only where the Courts of Chancery were called in the course of their work to apply common law concepts) is not out of place in this area where law and equity have long overlapped in pursuit of their common goal of affording adequate remedies against those placed in a position of trust or confidence when they breach a duty that reasonably flows from that position. And, as I have indicated, willy-nilly the courts have tended to merge the principles of law and equity to meet the ends of justice as it is perceived in our time. That, in effect, is what was done in *Jacks v. Davis*[98] and by the courts below in the instant case. As I see it, this is both reasonable and proper. . . .

Lord Diplock's remark to the effect that the two streams of common law and equity have now mingled and interact are abundantly evident in this area. That is as it should be because in this particular area law and equity have for long been on the same course and whether one follows the way of equity through a flexible use of the relatively undeveloped remedy of compensation, or the common law's more developed approach to damages is of no great moment. Where "the measure of duty is the same", the same rule should apply.[99] Only when there are different policy objectives should equity engage in its well-known flexibility to achieve a different and fairer result.

---

97 *Supra*, note 68.

98 (1980), 12 C.C.L.T. 298, affirmed [1983] 1 W.W.R. 327.

99 See Somers J. in *Day v. Mead*, *supra*, note 78, at 457.

. . .

I am aware that reservations have been expressed in some quarters about this fusion or, perhaps more accurately, mingling of law and equity.[100] But no case was brought to our attention where it has led to confusion, and there are many cases, some of which I have discussed, where it has made possible a just and reasonable result. It simply provides a general, but flexible, approach that allows for direct application of the experience and best features of both law and equity, whether the mode of redress (the cause of action or remedy) originates in one system or the other. There might be room for concern if one were indiscriminately attempting to meld the whole of the two systems. Equitable concepts like trusts, equitable estates and consequent equitable remedies must continue to exist apart, if not in isolation, from common law rules. But when one moves to fiduciary relationships and the law regarding misstatements, we have a situation where now the courts of common law, now the courts of equity moved forward to provide remedies where a person failed to meet the trust or confidence reposed in that person. There was throughout considerable overlap. In time the common law outstripped equity and the remedy of compensation became somewhat atrophied. Under these circumstances, why should it not borrow from the experience of the common law? Whether the courts refine the equitable tools such as the remedy of compensation, or follow the common law on its own terms, seems not particularly important where the same policy objective is sought.

Where a situation requires different policy objectives, then the remedy may be found in the system that appears more appropriate. This will often be equity. Its flexible remedies such as constructive trusts, account, tracing and compensation must continue to be moulded to meet the requirements of fairness and justice in specific situations. Nor should this process be confined to pre-existing situations. Lord Diplock has reminded us that the regime of conjoint application of law and equity introduced by the *Judicature Act*[101] must not be seen as bringing to a halt the process of development of substantive law in both great systems of judicially created law. . . .

. . .

MCLACHLIN J.:

[Her Ladyship agreed that the damages should be limited to the amount assessed by the trial judge. However, she based this conclusion solely in equity. Further, she disagreed strongly with Mr. Justice La Forest's suggestion that when the trustee does not control the property of the beneficiary damages for breach of fiduciary duty ought to be measured by analogy to tort and contract]

---

100 See Hanbury and Maudsley, *Modern Equity* (1985, 12th ed.), at pp. 22-26.
101 *Supra.*

My first concern with proceeding by analogy with tort is that it overlooks the unique foundation and goals of equity. The basis of the fiduciary obligation and the rationale for equitable compensation are distinct from the tort of negligence and contract. In negligence and contract the parties are taken to be independent and equal actors, concerned primarily with their own self-interest. Consequently the law seeks a balance between enforcing obligations by awarding compensation and preserving optimum freedom for those involved in the relationship in question, communal or otherwise. The essence of a fiduciary relationship, by contrast, is that one party pledges herself to act in the best interest of the other. The fiduciary relationship has trust, not self-interest, at its core, and when breach occurs, the balance favours the person wronged. The freedom of the fiduciary is diminished by the nature of the obligation he or she has undertaken — an obligation which "betokens loyalty, good faith and avoidance of a conflict of duty and self-interest".[102] In short, equity is concerned, not only to compensate the plaintiff, but to enforce the trust which is at its heart.

The trust-like nature of the fiduciary obligation manifests itself in characteristics which distinguish it from the tort of negligence and from breach of contract.
. . .

. . .

These differences suggest that we cannot simply assume that an analogy with tort law is appropriate. And even if we could, the analogy would not be of great assistance. For tort offers different measures of compensation, depending on the nature of the wrong. The measure for deceit, for example, is more stringent than for negligence. So adoption of a tort measure does not solve the problem. The further question arises: which tort measure? One might argue that the appropriate analogy is with the tort of deceit, since both deceit and breach of fiduciary obligation involve wrongful acts with moral overtones. But the better approach, in my view, is to look to the policy behind compensation for breach of fiduciary duty and determine what remedies will best further that policy. In so far as the same goals are shared by tort and breach of fiduciary duty, remedies may coincide. But they may also differ.

The danger of proceeding by analogy with tort law is that it may lead to us to adopt answers which, however easy, may not be appropriate in the context of a breach of fiduciary duty. La Forest J. has avoided one such pitfall in indicating that compensation for a breach of fiduciary duty will not be limited by foreseeability, but what of other issues? For instance, the analogy with tort might suggest that presumptions which operate in favour of the injured party in a claim for a breach of fiduciary duty will no longer operate, for example the presumption that trust funds will be put to the most profitable use. And it is clear that tort law is incompatible with the well developed doctrine that a fiduciary must disgorge profits gained through a breach of duty, even though such profits are not made at the expense of the person to whom the duty is owed. La Forest J. allows that

---

102 *Canadian Aero Services Ltd. v. O'Malley*, [1974] S.C.R. 592 at 606.

benefits may be disgorged, but addresses only the case where no such benefit was obtained. . . . From this it appears that he would treat benefit to the fiduciary on the basis of equitable principles, and losses to the plaintiff on the basis of common law. In my view it is preferable to deal with both remedies under the same system — equity. Rather than begin from tort and proceed by changing the tort model to meet the constraints of trust, I prefer to start from trust, using the tort analogy to the extent shared concerns may make it helpful. This said, I readily concede that we may take wisdom where we find it, and accept such insights offered by the law of tort, in particular deceit, as may prove useful.

My second concern with proceeding by analogy with tort is that it requires us to separate so called "true trust" situations, where the trustee holds property as agent for the beneficiary, from other fiduciary obligations. This distinction is necessary if one proceeds by analogy with tort because the tort analogy cannot apply in the former category. . . . In my view, however, this distinction is artificial and undercuts the common wrong embraced by both categories — the breach of the obligation of trust and utmost good faith which lies on one who undertakes to control or manage something — be it property or some other interest — on behalf of another. Nor do the cases support the distinction, as illustrated by the analysis which follows of *Guerin v. The Queen*.[103]

Differences between different types of fiduciary relationships may, depending on the circumstances, dictate different approaches to damages. This may be significant as the law of fiduciary obligations develops. However, such differences must be related in some way to the underlying concept of trust — the notion of special powers reposed in the trustee to be exercised exclusively for the benefit of the person who trusts. The distinction between the rights of a claimant in equity for maladministration of property as opposed to wrongful advice or information, resides in the fact that in the former case equity can and does require property wrongfully appropriated to be restored to the cestui qui trust together with an account of profits. Where there is no property which can be restored, restitution in this sense is not available. In those cases, the court may award compensation in lieu of restitution. This is a pragmatic distinction in the form of the remedy which must not obscure the fact that the measure of compensation remains restitutionary or "trust-like" in both cases. Any further distinction is difficult to support. Why in principle, should a trustee's abuse of power in relation to tangible property attract less compensation than a trustee's abuse of power in relation to a lease or a mortgage or the purchase of a business or a home? The goals of equity in the latter category of case, as asserted in *Nocton v. Ashburton*,[104] are not only to compensate the plaintiff but to deter fiduciaries from abusing their powers. Whence then the difference in compensation?

Having concluded that equitable compensation should not be determined by the simple expedient of resorting to tort, I come to the central question in this case. What is the ambit of compensation as an equitable remedy? Proceeding in trust, we start from the traditional obligation of a defaulting trustee, which is to

---

103 *Supra*, note 39.
104 *Supra*, note 68.

effect restitution to the estate. But restitution *in specie* may not always be possible. So equity awards compensation in place of restitution *in specie*, by analogy for breach of fiduciary duty with the ideal of restoring to the estate that which was lost through the breach.

[Her Ladyship considered *Ex Parte Adamson*[105] and *Nocton v. Lord Ashburton*,[106] also referred to by La Forest J. Then she discussed *Guerin v. The Queen*,[107] which we considered above. She noted that *Guerin* was not a case which involved the abuse of trust property, since no assets had been misappropriated. Rather, it was concerned with the Crown's failure to measure up to its fiduciary duty. However, as McLachlin J. noted, in *Guerin* the Supreme Court of Canada clearly rejected analogies to tort and contract and their principles of foreseeability and remoteness. Instead, it applied principles of trust law and was, thus, able to take into account a factor that would not be considered at common law, namely, an unforeseen escalation in the value of land after the breach of duty occurred. Her Ladyship continued:]

While foreseeability of loss does not enter into the calculation of compensation for breach of fiduciary duty, liability is not unlimited. Just as restitution in specie is limited to the property under the trustee's control, so equitable compensation must be limited to loss flowing from the trustee's acts in relation to the interest he undertook to protect. Thus Davidson states "it is imperative to ascertain the loss *resulting from breach of the relevant equitable duty*".[108]

. . .

The requirement that the loss must result from the breach of the relevant equitable duty does not negate the fact that "causality" in the legal sense as limited by foreseeability at the time of breach does not apply in equity. It is in this sense that I read the statement of Street J. in *Re Dawson*[109] that "causality, foreseeability and remoteness do not readily enter into the matter",[110] and the broad language of *Caffrey v. Darby*[111] (relied on by Street J. [in *Dawson*]), where in fact a causal link between the breach and the loss was found, the Court stating that had the trustees adhered to their duty "the property would not have been in a situation to sustain that loss"[112] (appropriation by a third party).

Thus while the loss must flow from the breach of fiduciary duty, it need not be reasonably foreseeable at the time of the breach, as *Guerin* affirms. The

---

105 (1878), 8 Ch. D. 807.

106 *Supra*, note 68.

107 *Supra*, note 103.

108 Ian E. Davidson, "The Equitable Remedy of Compensation" (1982), 13 Melbourne U.L. Rev. 349 at 354 [emphasis added].

109 [1966] 2 N.S.W.R. 211, 84 W.N. (Pt. 1) (N.S.W.) 399 (N.S.W.S.C.).

110 Quoted in *Guerin, supra*, note 103, at 360.

111 (1801), 6 Ves. Jun. 488, 31 E.R. 1159.

112 *Re Dawson, supra*, at W.N. 404.

considerations applicable in this respect to breach of fiduciary duty are more analogous to deceit than negligence in breach of contract. Just as "it does not lie in the mouth of the fraudulent person to say that [the losses] they could not reasonably have been foreseen",[113] so it does not lie in the mouth of a fiduciary who has assumed the special responsibility of trust to say the loss could not reasonably have been foreseen. This is sound policy. In negligence we wish to protect reasonable freedom of action of the defendant, and the reasonableness of his or her action may be judged by what consequences can be foreseen. In the case of a breach of fiduciary duty, as in deceit, we do not have to look to the consequences to judge the reasonableness of the actions. A breach of fiduciary duty is a wrong in itself, regardless of whether a loss can be foreseen. Moreover the high duty assumed and the difficulty of detecting such breaches makes it fair and practical to adopt a measure of compensation calculated to ensure that fiduciaries are kept "up to their duty".

. . .

A related question which must be addressed is the time of assessment of the loss. In this area tort and contract law are of little help. There the general rule is that damages are assessed based on the value of the shares as at the time of the wrongful act, in view of what was then foreseeable, either by a reasonable person, or in the particular expectation of the parties. Various exceptions or apparent exceptions are made for items difficult to value, such as shares traded in a limited market. The basis of compensation at equity, by contrast, is the restoration of the actual value of the thing lost through the breach. The foreseeable value of the items is not in issue. As a result, the losses are to be assessed as at the time of trial, using the full benefit of hindsight.[114]

It may sometimes be necessary to qualify this general principle to recognize the plaintiff's responsibility not to act unreasonably. It may not be fair, for example, to allow a plaintiff who has discovered the breach to speculate at the expense of the fiduciary. If a fiduciary holds out an investment as secure when in reality it is highly speculative, the injured party should not be able to retain the investment in unreasonable hope of a fortuitous rise in value, secure in the knowledge that any loss will be borne by the fiduciary. In such a case, the court might conclude that the loss should be assessed as at the time at which the behaviour of the plaintiff becomes clearly unreasonable. Mitigation, where losses are assessed as at the time of trial but adjusted to account for what might have been saved, will be appropriate where the losses which might have been prevented are separable from the underlying value of the thing lost; for instance, consequential losses. Adjusting the time of assessment will be more appropriate where the actions or omissions of the plaintiff directly affect the value of the thing lost. No doubt the final award will sometimes be the same under either approach.

---

113 *Doyle v. Olby* [1969] 2 Q.B. 158, [1969] 2 All E.R. 119 (C.A.) at 222.
114 *Guerin, supra*, note 103.

The requirement that the loss flow from the breach also assists in determining responsibility for the acts of strangers or third parties. If the breach permits a third party to take an unlawful advantage causing loss to the plaintiff, the fiduciary will be liable because there is a causal link between the breach and the loss. This was the case in *Caffrey v. Darby*,[115] where a trustee whose neglect permitted another to abscond with trust property was held liable for that loss. Where, on the other hand, the plaintiff suffers loss as a result of the act of a third party after the fiduciary's obligation has terminated and the plaintiff has taken control of the property, the result will be otherwise.

In summary, compensation is a equitable monetary remedy which is available when the equitable remedies of restitution and account are not appropriate. By analogy with restitution, it attempts to restore to the plaintiff what has been lost as a result of the breach; i.e. the plaintiff's lost opportunity. The plaintiff's actual loss as a consequence of the breach is to be assessed with the full benefit of hindsight. Foreseeability is not a concern in assessing compensation, but it is essential that the losses made good are only those which, on a common sense view of causation, were caused by the breach. The plaintiff will not be required to mitigate, as the term is used in law, but losses resulting from clearly unreasonable behaviour on the part of the plaintiff will be adjudged to flow from that behaviour, and not from the breach. Where the trustee's breach permits the wrongful or negligent acts of third parties, thus establishing a direct link between the breach and the loss, the resulting loss will be recoverable. Where there is no such link, the loss must be recovered from the third parties.

[When her Ladyship applied these principles to the facts, she held that the losses sustained in the course of construction did not result or flow from the breach of fiduciary duty, but were caused by third parties. In other words, there was no link between the breach of fiduciary duty and the loss. It was clear that the solicitor's duty had come to an end when the appellants took control of the property. The loss resulted, not from the actions of the respondents, but from decisions made by the appellants and the persons they hired.

Sopinka, Gonthier and Cory JJ. concurred with La Forest J.

Lamer C.J.C. and L'Heureux-Dubé J. concurred with McLachlin J.

Stevenson J., in a short judgment, stated that he concurred with La Forest J., but was of opinion that (a) compensation in equity differs from damages at common law, because the former is restitutive; and (b) the "fusion" of law and equity was irrelevant to the decision.

The court dismissed the appeal.]

---

115 *Supra*, note 111.

Notes and Questions

1. *Canson* went back to the B.C. Supreme Court[116] to assess damages, to determine whether the assumed facts on which the stated case was based were correct, and to give judgment on the facts as found. The trial judge found that the market value of the property was $495,000 rather than the $410,000 that was assumed. The trial judge also found, contrary to the assumed facts, that although the lawyer knew of the property flip, he did not know of the secret profit. The trial judge concluded that the lawyer and law firm had breached their fiduciary duty and awarded judgment against them for the difference between the price paid and the market value of the property together with consequential damages and simple interest. Finally, the trial judge held that only those persons who shared in the secret profit were liable to account for it. The B.C. Court of Appeal dismissed the appeal.[117]

2. Which of the approaches taken in *Canson* is correct? It did not matter in the end result in that case, but could it in other cases? Did La Forest J. sufficiently take into account the different objects of law and equity as regards damages? Is it proper to distinguish between a situation in which there has been a misapplication of trust property and one in which there has not, but "merely" a breach of fiduciary duty?

3. Note that the duty of the solicitor in *Canson* to disclose relevant information to the appellants was not a fiduciary duty, but a contractual one, which, of course, he breached. However, the solicitor also breached a fiduciary duty. He was in a position of conflict of duty and duty: his duties to the appellants and to the other clients were in conflict. His fiduciary duty was to disclose the conflict to the appellants, which he failed to do.[118]

4. *MacDonald v. Hauer*[119] is instructive on the calculation of the damages for breach of trust. The brothers, Alan and Malcolm MacDonald were executors and trustees of their father's estate (together with their mother, Nona). Alan was the only active trustee. He opened a margin account in his own name and lodged estate securities worth $400,000 with the broker as security. He then gave the defendant, Hauer, a power of attorney on the account to permit him to trade in speculative securities. Alan and Hauer were to share the profits equally. Over a period of five years, Hauer converted all the estate's securities into speculative investments and lost heavily. By 1962 the value of the securities had decreased to approximately $32,000. The court held that, since the trial judge found that Alan committed both an act of conversion and a breach of trust, he was liable for damages calculated on the basis either of conversion or breach of trust and that the quantum was

---

116 (1992), 72 B.C.L.R. (2d) 207, 1992 CarswellBC 296, [1993] 1 W.W.R. 386 (S.C.), additional reasons at (1992), 1992 CarswellBC 403, [1992] B.C.J. No. 2943, 76 B.C.L.R. (2d) 389, 18 C.P.C. (3d) 334, [1993] 4 W.W.R. 194 (S.C.), affirmed (1995), 1995 CarswellBC 596, 11 B.C.L.R. (3d) 262, [1996] 1 W.W.R. 412, 26 C.C.L.T. (2d) 1, 42 C.P.C. (3d) 337, 63 B.C.A.C. 209, 104 W.A.C. 209 (C.A.), leave to appeal refused 48 C.P.C. (3d) 384 (note), 17 B.C.L.R. (3d) xxxi (note), [1996] 4 W.W.R. lxxv (note), 203 N.R. 78 (note), 82 B.C.A.C. 240 (note), 133 W.A.C. 240 (note) (S.C.C.).

117 (1995), [1996] 1 W.W.R. 412, 1995 CarswellBC 596, 11 B.C.L.R. (3d) 262, 26 C.C.L.T. (2d) 1, 42 C.P.C. (3d) 337, 63 B.C.A.C. 209, 104 W.A.C. 209 (C.A.), leave to appeal refused 48 C.P.C. (3d) 384 (note), 17 B.C.L.R. (3d) xxxi (note), [1996] 4 W.W.R. lxxv (note), 203 N.R. 78 (note), 82 B.C.A.C. 240 (note), 133 W.A.C. 240 (note) (S.C.C.).

118 See Timothy G. Youdan, "Liability for Breach of Fiduciary Obligation" in *Special Lectures of the Law Society of Upper Canada 1996 — Estates[:] Planning, Administration and Litigation* (Toronto: Carswell, 1996), 1 at 15.

119 (1976), [1977] 1 W.W.R. 51, 72 D.L.R. (3d) 110, 1976 CarswellSask 95 (C.A.).

approximately the same in both cases. It held Hauer liable for his knowing assistance in Alan's breach.

Is the quantum the same under both heads? Damages for conversion are the value of the property at the time of the conversion plus consequential damages. Are the beneficiaries not entitled to the best price available and to every presumption being made against the trustee?[120]

5. In *Fales v. Canada Permanent Trust Co.*,[121] reproduced in part in the chapter on the duties of trustees, the court also took an apparently lenient attitude toward the calculation of compensation. The trustees failed to sell speculative shares, acquired as a result of a merger and reorganization, although required to do so. Instead, they held them until there was no market for the shares anymore. The court held that the quantum of compensation should be determined by taking the average price of the shares over the period from their acquisition until they could have been sold advantageously. The court noted:[122]

> This method fails to take into account the frequency and strength and duration of price movement between high and low during the base period and it does not reflect volume of sales and various price levels. Nevertheless, it affords a rough method of calculation.

Is a "rough method of calculation" adequate, or did the court in fact do equity in the circumstances? One text has commented on this method of calculation, that is, the average price method:[123]

> . . .it is submitted that it represents a proper attempt to balance respect for the trustee's discretion as to when he may, within his powers, effect a sale, and his duty to ensure a sale at a fair price within a reasonable time.

The average method of calculation has also been used in the United States.[124]

Is such a method appropriate when the breach occurred over a period of time, as when shares ought to have been sold but were not? Is a different method appropriate when the breach occurred at a specific time?

6. If a breach of trust causes a failure to make a gain, the beneficiaries may claim the amount of the gain which the trust would otherwise have received as compensation. This is illustrated by *Massingberd's Settlement, Re.*[125] The trustees of a settlement sold authorized securities and invested the proceeds in a mortgage in breach of trust. By the time the mortgage was paid off, the price of the original securities had risen. The trustees were held liable to replace the securities at their present value. Note that if the securities had fallen in value, the trustees would have had to pay the sale price of the securities.[126]

7. In *MacDonald v. Hauer*[127] the court not only awarded compensation, but also required the defendant trustees to account for profits they made. Is this correct? Was the breach not one arising out of the same circumstances? If so, should the beneficiary be restricted to either the accounting remedy or else the remedy of compensation?

---

120 See *Fultz v. McNeil, supra,* note 31; *Toronto-Dominion Bank v. Uhren, supra,* note 31.
121 *Supra,* note 48.
122 *Ibid.,* at D.L.R. 271.
123 Ford and Lee, §17120.
124 See Scott, §209.
125 (1890), 63 L.T. (N.S.) 296.
126 To the same effect see *Bell's Indenture, Re, supra,* note 43.
127 *Supra.*

8. In *MacDonald v. Hauer* the court also awarded interest. On this point Bayda J.A., said:[128]

> In addition to the capital loss the estate is entitled to interest.[129] The rate is in the discretion of the Court.[130] Taking into account the current rates of interest at the time of the trial, the fact that the breach (actually a series of breaches) occurred principally between June, 1957, and December 1957, when the prevailing rates of interest were much lower than in 1974 when the action was brought to trial, and the further fact of the delay in bringing the matter to trial, the equitable thing to do, I think, is require the payment of simple interest at the rate of 5% per annum on $278,634.39 from January 1, 1958, to March 13, 1973, the date of judgment by the trial Judge. That interest comes to $211,723.93.

Do you agree that the rate was equitable in the circumstances?

9. When there is no wrongful application of funds the court awards simple interest.[131] Compound interest is awarded if the conduct of the trustee is especially heinous.[132] If the trust instrument directs an accumulation, the trustee will be liable for compound interest, since it would have been earned by the accumulation had it been carried out.[133]

10. In *Brock v. Cole*[134] the court awarded compound interest. The plaintiff gave $20,000 to the defendant law firm to be invested for three months at 18 per cent *per annum*. The loan was to be guaranteed by one of the defendants and secured by a first mortgage on a property bought for $40,000. In fact, the defendants granted the plaintiff a second mortgage on property worth only $16,000 and failed to guarantee the loan. When the property was sold, the plaintiff did not receive any money, but he did receive $3,095 from the defendants for interest. The court held that the defendants had committed a breach of trust so that the court had an equitable jurisdiction to award compound interest which was independent of the statutory provision for prejudgment interest.[135] Since it could be assumed that the defendants would have put the money out at compound interest, the plaintiff was entitled to interest at 18 per cent for the three-month term of the mortgage and compound interest at 10 per cent with annual rests thereafter.

11. If, as a result of a breach of trust, taxes are reduced, should the amount of the reduction in tax be deducted from the gross amount of the compensation?

In *Bartlett v. Barclays Bank Trust Co. (Nos. 1 & 2)*,[136] the court held that the amount of the reduction in tax should not be deducted. Brightman L.J. said:[137]

---

128 At 72 D.L.R. (3d) 130.

129 See *Snell's Equity*, 29th ed., p. 288, and Waters, *Law of Trusts in Canada* (1974), p. 849.

130 See Snell, *ibid.*, p. 288.

131 *Canson Enterprises Ltd. v. Boughton & Co.* (1992), 72 B.C.L.R. (2d) 207, 1992 CarswellBC 296, [1993] 1 W.W.R. 386 (S.C.), additional reasons at (1992), 1992 CarswellBC 403, [1992] B.C.J. No. 2943, 76 B.C.L.R. (2d) 389, 18 C.P.C. (3d) 334, [1993] 4 W.W.R. 194 (S.C.), affirmed (1995), 1995 CarswellBC 596, 11 B.C.L.R. (3d) 262, [1996] 1 W.W.R. 412, 26 C.C.L.T. (2d) 1, 42 C.P.C. (3d) 337, 63 B.C.A.C. 209, 104 W.A.C. 209 (C.A.), leave to appeal refused 48 C.P.C. (3d) 384 (note), 17 B.C.L.R. (3d) xxxi (note), [1996] 4 W.W.R. lxxv (note), 203 N.R. 78 (note), 82 B.C.A.C. 240 (note), 133 W.A.C. 240 (note) (S.C.C.).

132 *Gordon v. Gonda*, [1955] 1 W.L.R. 885 at 896 *per* Evershed M.R.

133 *Barclay, Re*, [1899] 1 Ch. 674.

134 (1983), 13 E.T.R. 235, 1983 CarswellOnt 360, 40 O.R. (2d) 97, 31 C.P.C. 184, 142 D.L.R. (3d) 461 (C.A.).

135 Under the *Judicature Act*, R.S.O. 1980, c. 223, s. 36. See now *Courts of Justice Act*, R.S.O. 1990, c. C.43, s. 128.

136 [1980] 1 Ch. 515, [1980] 2 W.L.R. 430, [1980] 2 All E.R. 92 (Ch. Div.).

137 *Ibid.*, at 545.

My reasoning is this: the obligation of a trustee who is held liable for breach of trust is fundamentally different from the obligation of a contractual or tortious wrongdoer. The trustee's
obligation is to restore to the trust estate the assets of which he has deprived it. The tax liability
of individual beneficiaries, who have claims qua beneficiaries to the capital and income of the
trust estate, do not enter into the picture because they arise not at the point of restitution to the
trust estate but at the point of distribution of capital or income out of the trust estate. These are
different stages. . . .

12. *Hodgkinson v. Simms*[138] is also instructive on the issue of compensation for breach
of fiduciary duty. This case did not concern a traditional fiduciary relationship. The plaintiff
sought investment advice from the defendant accountant. Simms advised him to invest in
certain MURBs (multi-unit residential buildings). Simms had a professional relationship
with the developers of the project. The relationship entitled him to higher fees if the
developer sold MURBs to Simms' clients. Simms did not disclose this arrangement to
Hodgkinson. When real estate values declined, Hodgkinson lost money and sued Simms
for compensation for breach of his fiduciary duty. He was successful in the Supreme Court
of Canada. However, there was a sharp difference of opinion between the members of the
court. The plurality, consisting of La Forest J., with L'Heureux-Dubé and Gonthier JJ.,
concurring and Iacobucci J., concurring in the result, held that there was a fiduciary
relationship and that Simms breached it and was liable for the entire loss, including
consequential damages. The dissenting opinion, written jointly by Sopinka and McLachlin
JJ., with Major J. concurring, stated that there was no fiduciary relationship, so that the
defendant was liable only for breach of contract and the damages did not extend to the
decline in value of the investments, because the loss did not arise naturally from the breach
and was not within the reasonable contemplation of the parties.

On the issue of compensation, La Forest J. stated, "it is well-established that the
proper approach to damages for breach of a fiduciary duty is restitutionary. On this
approach, the appellant is entitled to be put in as good a position as he would have been
in had the breach not occurred."[139] His Lordship dismissed the argument that the plaintiff
would have invested in real estate shelters in any event as contrary to the express finding
of the trial judge. He also rejected the argument that the loss was not occasioned by the
defendant's breach, but by the economic downturn in real estate values. The defendant
had set the chain of events leading to the loss in motion and should, therefore, be liable
for the full loss. *Canson* was distinguishable, because it involved intervening negligence
by third parties. Thus, the defendant was liable for breach of his fiduciary duty, since the
plaintiff would not have invested in MURBs but for the defendant's advice. His Lordship
was also of opinion that contractual damages would have been the same, since the loss
was foreseeable.

13. *Target Holdings Ltd. v. Redferns*[140] is also instructive, if only because Lord
Browne-Wilkinson quoted several excerpts from the judgment of McLachlin J. in *Canson*
with approval.[141] However, his Lordship appears, in other respects, to have limited the
remedy of compensation. *Target* involved a fact situation which had features similar to
those in *Canson*. A solicitor acted for both the purchaser of property and the mortgagee.
The property had been valued independently at £2 million and the mortgagor had requested
a mortgage loan of £1,706,000 from Target, stating that the purchase price was £2 million.

---

138 *Supra*, note 43; noted L. Smith (1995), 74 Canadian Bar Review 714. This case is also excerpted
     in chapter 2, part 2.
139 *Ibid.*, at D.L.R. 199.
140 [1996] 1 A.C. 421 (H.L.).
141 *Ibid.*, at 438-9.

The mortgagor failed to disclose that it had agreed to purchase the property for only £775,000, and that title would be transferred to a related company and "flipped" first to another related company and then to the mortgagor. The solicitor was aware of all the transactions. Target approved the loan and paid the moneys to the solicitor on the understanding that they were to be released when the mortgagor obtained title and had executed a charge in favour of the mortgagee. In breach of trust, the solicitor paid most of the money out to finance the various purchases. Then he informed Target, untruthfully, that the purchase of the property and the charge had been completed when they had not. However, they were subsequently completed. When the mortgagor failed, Target sold the property for £500,000. Target then sued the solicitor for damages for negligence and breach of trust. The matter came before the courts on Target's motion for summary judgment. The judge of first instance gave Redferns leave to defend. The Court of Appeal allowed the appeal, but the House of Lords restored the judgment of the judge of first instance. Clearly, the payments constituted a breach of trust and that was admitted. Redferns, however, argued that Target had suffered no loss by its actions and was, therefore, not entitled to be compensated. What would have to be determined at trial was whether the moneys to complete the purchase from the owner would have been forthcoming from some other source if the moneys had not been wrongly provided by Redferns in breach of trust for that purpose. If the answer to that question was in the affirmative, then Target would have obtained exactly what it would have obtained had no breach of trust occurred, namely, a valid security for the amount of money it lent. In that event, Target did not suffer a compensable loss. For that reason, Redferns was allowed to defend.

In the course of his speech, Lord Browne-Wilkinson noted that while equity approaches liability for making good a breach of trust from a different starting point and uses different rules of quantification of loss, it applies the same basic principles as the common law, namely, that the defendant's wrongful act must cause the loss and that the plaintiff must be put in the same position she or he would have been in but for the wrong.[142] Thus, the first question when there is a breach of trust is to ask whether the trustee is the one who caused the loss.

His Lordship drew a distinction between traditional trusts and bare trusts, such as this. With traditional trusts, the trustee is liable to restore to the trust what is lost. In this context, common law rules of remoteness of damage and causation do not apply. Further, equity will require the trustee to repay the amount taken at the time of the breach. Thus it "stops the clock" from running and does not consider what happened after the breach. However, if the trust is a bare trust, there is no longer any reason to make restoration to the trust, since the beneficiary is the sole owner. Instead, compensation direct to the beneficiary should be ordered.[143] He said:[144]

> [I]n my judgment it is in any event wrong to lift wholesale the detailed rules developed in the context of traditional trusts and then seek to apply them to trusts of quite a different kind. In the modern world the trust has become a valuable device in commercial and financial dealings. The fundamental principles of equity apply as much to such trusts as they do the to the traditional trusts in relation to which those principles were formulated. But in my judgment it is important, if the trust is not to be rendered commercially useless, to distinguish between the basic principles developed in relation to traditional trusts which are applicable only to such trusts and the rationale of which has no application to trusts of quite a different kind.

---

142 *Ibid.*, at 432.
143 *Ibid.*, at 434-5.
144 *Ibid.*, at 435.

In the circumstances, the principles developed by the Supreme Court of Canada in *Canson* were particularly apt and, as mentioned, Lord Browne-Wilkinson quoted extensively and with approval from the judgment of McLachlin J. in that case.

14. Another case that is instructive on the point of compensation is *Bristol & West Building Society v. Mothew*.[145] A solicitor acted for both sides in a mortgage transaction. The solicitor undertook to ensure that the mortgage would be the sole mortgage on the property and that the balance of the purchase price would be provided by the purchasers personally. The purchasers had a loan with a bank secured by a second charge on their existing property and, while most of it would be repaid on the sale of that property, the bank required that the small portion remaining be secured by a second charge on the new property. The solicitor negligently failed to inform the mortgagee of this fact. When the purchasers defaulted, the mortgagee was unable to recoup the total amount of its loan because the real estate market had crashed. So it sued the solicitor for breach of his duty of care and for breach of fiduciary duty. He was held liable for negligence, but the claim for breach of fiduciary duty was dismissed, since the solicitor was never in actual breach of his fiduciary duty to the mortgagee. Millett L.J., who delivered the main judgment, noted that a fiduciary may be liable for breach of non-fiduciary duties, such as breach of the duty of care, and that the source of the liability may lie at common law or equity, depending upon the circumstances. If it lies in equity, as when the defendant is a trustee, that does not make it a breach of fiduciary duty; but if the source of the liability lies at common law, then equity lacks jurisdiction.[146] Viscount Haldane said as much in *Nocton v. Lord Ashburton*[147] when he stated that a demurrer for want of equity would always have lain to a bill which only sought to enforce a claim for damages for negligence against a solicitor. Millett L.J. made the following instructive comment:[148]

> Although the remedy which equity makes available for breach of the equitable duty of skill and care is equitable compensation rather than damages, this is merely the product of history and in this context is in my opinion a distinction without a difference. Equitable compensation for breach of the duty of skill and care resembles common law damages in that it is awarded by way of compensation to the plaintiff for his loss. There is no reason in principle why the common law rules of causation, remoteness of damage and measure of damages should not be applied by analogy in such a case. It should not be confused with equitable compensation for breach of fiduciary duty, which may be awarded in lieu of rescission or specific restitution.
>
> This leaves those duties which are special to fiduciaries and which attract those remedies which are peculiar to the equitable jurisdiction and are primarily restitutionary or restorative rather than compensatory.

15. The distinction drawn by Millett L.J. in the *Bristol* case between equitable compensation for breach of a duty of care and equitable compensation for breach of a fiduciary duty is a useful one. This distinction is similar to what La Forest J. spoke of in *Canson*. The cases in which the Supreme Court of Canada has awarded compensation in recent years involved breaches of fiduciary duty, of course. Therefore, it is possible to restrict McLachlin J's remarks in *Canson* to those kinds of cases, although her comments appear to be broader than that.

The statement of Millett L.J. is more dubious if it was meant to apply not only to fiduciaries, but also to trustees. Traditionally a trustee who breaches a non-fiduciary duty,

---

145 (1996), [1996] 4 All E.R. 698, [1997] 2 W.L.R. 436, [1998] Ch. 1 (C.A.).
146 *Ibid.*
147 (1914), [1914] A.C. 932, [1914-15] All E.R. Rep. 45 (H.L.), at 956.
148 *Bristol & West Building Society v. Mothew, supra*, at 711.

such as a duty of care, is nonetheless subject to the presumptions mentioned earlier. Presumably his Lordship was not thinking of that situation. His remarks would appear to have merit for cases of fiduciary breach when the breach is not referable to specific property.

16. Can a court of equity award punitive damages? The traditional view is that it cannot.[149] However, some courts have awarded, or have been prepared to award, punitive damages in equity and the Supreme Court of Canada has accepted this possibility in *Whiten v. Pilot Insurance Co.*[149a]

The traditional view is also that in a claim for breach of trust of fiduciary duty, there can be no inquiry into any contributory fault of the plaintiff. In *Canson*, La Forest J. seemed clearly to contemplate that contributory negligence can now be pleaded to a claim in breach of fiduciary duty. He cited with approval (at paras. 82-83) a holding to that effect of the New Zealand Court of Appeal.[149b] The High Court of Australia has taken the traditional view that such a plea is not possible,[149c] as did the Supreme Court itself in *Carl B. Potter Ltd. v. Mercantile Bank of Canada.*[149d] Such a plea may more clearly be permissible in Alberta, based on its particular legislation.[149e] Many of the cases are collected in *Seaboard Life Insurance Co. v. Bank of Montreal.*[149f] The court in *GE Capital Canada Equipment Financing Inc. v. Bank of Montreal*[149g] refused to strike out a defence which argued contributory negligence to a claim in knowing assistance in a breach of fiduciary duty.[150]

---

149   See *Fern Brand Waxes Ltd. v. Pearl*, 29 D.L.R. (3d) 662, 1972 CarswellOnt 917, [1972] 3 O.R. 829 (C.A.); *Worobel Estate v. Worobel* (1988), 67 O.R. (2d) 151, 1988 CarswellOnt 603, 31 E.T.R. 290 (H.C.). See John D. McCamus, *Equitable Compensation and Restitutionary Remedies: Recent Developments*, in *Special Lectures of the Law Society of Upper Canada 1995 — Law of Remedies[:] Principles and Proofs*, 295 at 326; *Harris v. Digital Pulse Pty. Ltd.* (2003), 197 A.L.R. 626 (New South Wales C.A.).

149a   [2002] 1 S.C.R. 595, 2002 CarswellOnt 537, 2002 CarswellOnt 538, [2002] S.C.J. No. 19, 2002 SCC 18, [2002] I.L.R. I-4048, 20 B.L.R. (3d) 165, 209 D.L.R. (4th) 257, 283 N.R. 1, 35 C.C.L.I. (3d) 1, 156 O.A.C. 201 (S.C.C.)

149b   *Day v. Mead*, [1987] 2 N.Z.L.R. 443 (C.A.).

149c   *Astley v. Austrust Ltd.* (1999), 197 C.L.R. 1; *Pilmer v. The Duke Group Ltd.* (2000), 180 A.L.R. 249 (H.C.).

149d   [1980] 2 S.C.R. 343, 1980 CarswellNS 27, 1980 CarswellNS 81, 112 D.L.R. (3d) 88, 11 B.L.R. 193, 8 E.T.R. 219, 41 N.S.R. (2d) 573, 76 A.P.R. 573, 33 N.R. 175 (S.C.C.); see also *Vita Health Co. (1985) Ltd. v. Toronto Dominion Bank*, 1994 CarswellMan 165, [1994] M.J. No. 470, [1994] 9 W.W.R. 360, 95 Man. R. (2d) 255, 70 W.A.C. 255, 118 D.L.R. (4th) 289, 57 C.P.R. (3d) 449, 22 B.L.R. (2d) 195 (Man. C.A.), at para. 40; and *United Services Funds (Trustees of) v. Richardson Greenshields of Canada Ltd.* (1988), 1988 CarswellBC 33, [1988] B.C.J. No. 123, 43 C.C.L.T. 162, 22 B.C.L.R. (2d) 322, 48 D.L.R. (4th) 98 (B.C. S.C.).

149e   *Penner v. Yorkton Continental Securities Inc.* (1996), 1996 CarswellAlta 298, [1996] A.J. No. 278, 10 C.C.L.S. 248, 183 A.R. 5 (Alta. Q.B.)

149f   2002 CarswellBC 630, [2002] B.C.J. No. 599, 2002 BCCA 192, 23 B.L.R. (3d) 163, 166 B.C.A.C. 64, 271 W.A.C. 64 (B.C. C.A.)

149g   2003 CarswellBC 1876, 17 B.C.L.R. (4th) 304, 2003 BCSC 1180 (B.C. S.C. [In Chambers])

150   See, *e.g.*, *Huff v. Price* (1990), 51 B.C.L.R. (2d) 282, 1990 CarswellBC 267, 46 C.P.C. (2d) 209, 76 D.L.R. (4th) 138 (C.A.), additional reasons at (1990), 1990 CarswellBC 774, 76 D.L.R. (4th) 138 at 176 (C.A.), leave to appeal refused (1991), 56 B.C.L.R. (2d) xxxviii (note), (sub nom. *Charpentier v. Huff*) 4 B.C.A.C. 80 (note), 9 W.A.C. 80 (note), 136 N.R. 409 (note) (S.C.C.); *Schauenberg Industries Ltd. v. Borowski* (1979), 25 O.R. (2d) 737, 1979 CarswellOnt 166, 101 D.L.R. (3d) 701, 8 B.L.R. 164, 50 C.P.R. (2d) 69 (H.C.); *M. (K.) v. M. (H.)*, [1992] 3 S.C.R. 6, 96 D.L.R. (4th) 289, 1992 CarswellOnt 841, 1992 CarswellOnt 998, [1992] S.C.J.

(d) Account

As we have seen, a trustee who has made a profit from a breach of trust, is required to account for it to the beneficiaries. Typically, a duty to account arises when a trustee has appropriated trust assets and has made a profit from them. Cases of this type are examined in the materials on constructive trusts. Those materials show that this remedy is available even if the trust itself could not have made the profit, as when an investment is unauthorized. In that situation the remedy of account is, indeed, restitutionary, because it is used to effect restitution for a wrong committed by the trustee or other fiduciary. It is, thus cautionary or deterrent in nature, in that it is used to enforce observance of a fiduciary duty not to place oneself in a position of conflict of interest and duty, and to lift the profits from the wrongdoing.

In some situations the remedy of account is not available because, although there was a profit, the accounts are complex, so that it is difficult to prove the amount of the profit. For example, the trust money may have been used in a business venture and mingled with the moneys of other investors. It may then be difficult to determine what part of the profit belongs to the trust.[151] It may also be difficult to prove to what extent the profit was attributable to the breach of trust. In those situations the beneficiary should seek compensation. Beneficiaries can ask for compensation when a profit has been made, since the choice of remedy is theirs. But they would normally want an account if that will yield a larger judgment. That will be the situation if the trust could not have made the profit itself.[152]

An account of profits may be sought not only if a trustee has misappropriated trust property, but also when he or she retains or invests in unauthorized securities which rise in value.

A trustee is always required to render accounts to the beneficiaries; this does not depend on wrongdoing, but is simply part of the nature of trusteeship. An account of profits can also be obtained, as a remedy sourced in equity, even against a party who is not otherwise obliged to account. This does depend on wrongdoing. It permits the court to impose a remedy requiring the defendant to disgorge the profits of the wrongdoing. It has been used for wrongs such as breaches of copyright and patent infringements. In *Attorney General v. Blake*,[153]

No. 85, 142 N.R. 321, 57 O.A.C. 321, 14 C.C.L.T. (2d) 1. *Smith Estate (Trustee of) v. Smith Estate* (2000), 2000 CarswellBC 2628, 2000 BCSC 1842, 37 E.T.R. (2d) 151 (B.C. S.C.), at para. 56; *Zielinski v. Brennan* (2002), 2002 CarswellOnt 2459, 46 E.T.R. (2d) 310 (Ont. S.C.J.); *Commercial Union Life Assurance Co. of Canada v. John Ingle Insurance Group Inc.* (2000), 2000 CarswellOnt 3155, [2000] O.J. No. 3289, 22 C.C.L.I. (3d) 221 (Ont. S.C.J.), affirmed on other grounds (2002), 2002 CarswellOnt 2707, [2002] O.J. No. 3200, 217 D.L.R. (4th) 178, 162 O.A.C. 203, 61 O.R. (3d) 296, 50 C.C.L.I. (3d) 6 (Ont. C.A.). See also *Shore v. Shore* (1995), 9 E.T.R. (2d) 241, 1995 CarswellOnt 827 (Gen. Div.), in which the court awarded punitive damages in addition to a resulting trust.

151   *Docker v. Somes* (1834), 2 My. & K. 655, 39 E.R. 1095 (Ch. Div.), at 646 [My. & K.], *per* Lord Brougham L.C.

152   See Ford and Lee, §17150.

153   (2000), [2001] 1 A.C. 268, [2000] H.L.J. No. 47 (U.K. H.L.); discussed by M. McInnes (2001), 35 C.B.L.J. 72.

an account of profits was ordered to take away the profits of a breach of contract. This represents an important development in civil remedies.

If the profits are attributable solely to the skill of the trustee, as when he or she uses trust money to purchase property and then improves it to many times its original value, the trustee is not liable for the profit.[154] If the profit depends only partly upon the trustee's skill, the beneficiaries are entitled to recover a proportionate part.[155]

If the beneficiaries seek an account, they must allow for expenses, such as maintenance and repairs. On the other hand, if the trustee has occupied the trust property, he or she has to submit to an occupation rent.[156]

These principles are discussed in *MacMillan Bloedel Ltd. v. Binstead*,[157] reproduced below.

MacMILLAN BLOEDEL LTD. v. BINSTEAD

(1983), 14 E.T.R. 269, 1983 CarswellBC 540,
[1983] B.C.J. No. 802, 22 B.L.R. 255
British Columbia Supreme Court

The plaintiff forest products company regularly disposed of surplus logs. Its employee, the defendant Binstead, was manager of the log trading section. It was his job to dispose of logs which were surplus to the company's requirements, or which it could not use. Such logs were either sold outright, or traded for other logs which the company could use. While so employed, Binstead held a secret one-third interest in Andersen-MacKinnon Log Sales Ltd., whose shareholders of record were Andersen and MacKinnon. Andersen-MacKinnon also owned Andersen-MacKinnon Log Brokerage Co. Both companies traded extensively with the plaintiff through Binstead. Binstead, Andersen and MacKinnon then incorporated AMCO Forest Industries Ltd. Andersen and MacKinnon held one-third of its shares in trust for Binstead. AMCO established a sawmilling operation and acquired an interest in two other companies, Delta Cedar Products Ltd. and Delta Chip Ltd.

The plaintiff, referred to as MB in the following judgment, brought action against all the named individuals and corporations. Although the plaintiff had not suffered a loss, since the logs were surplus to its requirements, it was successful. The defendants were held to be constructive trustees for the plaintiff of all the shares in AMCO and liable to account to the plaintiff.

The part of the case concerned with the accounting remedy is set out below.

DOHM J.:

---

154 *Docker v. Somes, supra*, note 151, at My. & K. 668.
155 *Scott v. Scott* (1963), 109 C.L.R. 649 (Australia H.C.).
156 Waters, p. 1003.
157 (1983), 14 E.T.R. 269, 1983 CarswellBC 540, [1983] B.C.J. No. 802, 22 B.L.R. 255 (S.C.).

. . .

It is regrettable that so much time was spent at the trial on the matter of liability. The difficult and contentious issue, in my view, is not that of liability but rather of the consequences flowing therefrom. Where there has been a breach of fiduciary duty, as in the present circumstances, the law calls upon the defendants to account to the plaintiff for any profit made or benefit received as a result of the breach of duty. This is not the same as paying damages, which are compensatory in nature. The purpose of damages is to put the plaintiff in the same position it would have been in if not for the wrongdoing. Here the plaintiff suffered little damage and will be in a better position than it would have been if not for the wrongful act of the defendants.

A trustee who has breached his duty and profited as a result is obligated to disgorge those profits regardless of whether there is a corresponding loss to the cestui que trust. . . .

Basic to the application of this principle is a determination of what is meant by the term "profit". The Oxford Dictionary describes "profit" as being "the surplus product of industry after deducting wages, cost of raw material, rent and charges". In the present circumstances then, what must be returned by the defendants to MB is the difference between the gross earnings of MB transactions and expenses. In Waters, Law of Trusts in Canada,[158] the learned author states it in these terms:[159]

> In principle, if the beneficiary is enriched, he should be liable to meet the expenses of the person who has thus enriched him, and this approach is applied in those cases where the court deems a person a constructive trustee of property for another. The constructive trustee, although he installed the improvements, for instance, thinking or intending to claim that the property in question is his own, will be held entitled to recover what he put into the property.

The expenses though must be proper, that is, all reasonable and necessary expenses incurred by the trustee in earning the profit.

> [His Lordship referred to *Emma Silver Mining Co. v. Grant*,[160] in which Jessel M.R. quoted[161] the following excerpt from the judgment of James L.J. in *Bagnall v. Carlton*:][162]

> The costs, charges, and expenses, I think they had a right, independently of the offer in the bill, to deduct, because what they were liable to pay the company was the profits which they had made in a fiduciary character, that is to say, the net profits which they had made, and I think that costs, charges, and expenses might properly be deducted in ascertaining the net profits, and to that extent, therefore, they were, I think, entitled, independently of the offer in the bill.

---

158 The Carswell Co. Ltd., 1974.
159 *Ibid.*, at 798-9.
160 (1879), 11 Ch. D. 918 (C.A.), subsequent proceedings (1880), 17 Ch. D. 122.
161 *Ibid.*, at 11 Ch. D. 938-9.
162 6 Ch. D. 371.

Evidence of an accounting nature was called by both sides. Additionally, I have what has been referred to as the "black binder" (Ex. 47). This document is supposed to be a summary of all Log Sales' transactions for the period. It sets out the gross sales figures which include amounts charged for scaling, towing, inspection fees. I also have the audited financial statements of Log Sales and Log Brokerage for the period. The gross sales figures shown in the "black binder" do not reconcile with the audited statements. I prefer to follow the material which was available prior to the commencement of this lawsuit. The "black binder" is not without some merit. . . .

[The "black binder" showed that a large part of the defendant companies' profits derived from logs supplied to them by the plaintiff through Binstead. It then calculated the plaintiff's share of the defendant companies' gross profit as a percentage of their total gross profit over the years 1969-70 to 1977. This percentage ranged from a high of 92% in 1969-70 to a low of 66% in 1976.

The court accepted these figures.]

The earnings summaries for Log Sales and Log Brokerage for the period in question were submitted. All counsel relied on these documents and, accordingly, I accept the material as being accurate and rely on it in computing the profit due to the plaintiff. I point out that the gross profit of Log Sales for each year is the combination of gross revenues from logs sold and commissions earned from the brokerage of logs.

The total direct expenses are expenses properly incurred. All counsel agree. They do not agree, however, on whether the proportion of direct expenses allowed ought to be based upon a percentage of profits or upon the volume of logs involving MB transactions with Log Sales. The direct expenses include towing, insurance, storage, scaling and inspection fees or charges. In my view, those charges relate not to gross profits but to "volume of logs". . . .

[His Lordship set out a table showing the total log sales by the defendant companies, the plaintiff's log sales to the defendant companies, third party logs sold to the plaintiff, and the gross profit on third party logs sold to the plaintiff over the period 1970 to 1977.]

The next area of expenses are those related to the administration of the business and include legal expenses, capital tax, telephone, rent and utilities, stationery, postage, automobile, travel and bank expenses. For the most part, I think these expenses are those which are normally found in the operation of a business. Andersen and MacKinnon impressed me as being frugal and as exercising a firm control of expenditures. I am not so naive though to conclude that all of these expenses were properly incurred. Some allowance must therefore be made for a proportion of the administrative expenses in both companies, Log Sales and Log Brokerage.

The plaintiff's first position regarding these expenses is that none ought to be allowed. Its second position is that they should be allowed at the rate of 69 per cent of the administrative expenses incurred by Log Sales and 35 per cent of the expenses of Log Brokerage. The defendants use another formula and come up with an overall figure of 54 per cent based on the total of administrative expenses incurred by both companies. Keeping in mind that the bulk of Log Brokerage's expenses related directly to the expenses incurred by Log Sales and that not all of the expenses in this area were properly incurred, I think an appropriate allowance would be 50 per cent calculated as follows:

(a) 50 per cent of the administrative expenses of Log Sales;

(b) 50 per cent of the administrative expenses of Log Brokerage (excluding interest payments made on shareholder loans to Andersen and MacKinnon); and

(c) 50 per cent of the non-management salaries paid by Log Brokerage.

The defendants claim that there should be some allowance for the salaries and bonuses paid by Log Brokerage to Andersen and MacKinnon either by allowing them in full on the basis of the contract between the two companies or by replacing those figures by an annual salary. The salary suggested was $90,000 per year beginning in 1977 and reducing that amount each year by 10 per cent to provide for inflation. Certainly this kind of remuneration may be allowed to trustees and *Boardman v. Phipps*[163] is a good example of where the Court made provision for such remuneration. But in the present circumstances, and considering the part played in the scheme by Andersen and MacKinnon, such an allowance is out of the question. To provide for salaries and bonuses whether as claimed or in any form, would be to reward Andersen and MacKinnon for their dishonest conduct.

Counsel gave me little help with regard to the income tax and logging tax expense. The cases cited were of no help for they dealt with situations involving the assessment of damages. It seems to me, that in an accounting for profits situation, that different principles apply. I am not scolding counsel. The subject of the income tax ramifications in a case of this nature could easily be a study by itself.

It strikes me as being fair and reasonable to make allowance for the payment of the taxes. These moneys were paid by Log Sales pursuant to law. It is an expense which MB would have had to pay had it possessed that income. Even if MB enjoyed a tax advantage that Log Sales did not, I doubt that the picture would be changed. To force a trustee, including a constructive trustee, to personally bear this expense would be grossly unfair. As indicated earlier, an accounting of profits is quite a different thing from an award of damages. In the latter, the Court tries to restore the plaintiff to the position it would have been in but for the wrong. On the other hand, on an accounting for profits the Court must ensure that all of the benefits flowing to the constructive trustees is [*sic*] disgorged so that their breach of trust does not enrich them. The Court "must see how much more money he

---

163 *Supra*, note 21.

has got than he would have had if the breach of duty had not taken place" (*Emma Silver Mining Co. v. Grant*).[164] Those tax moneys were not moneys which went to the defendants. They received no benefit from them. To make the trustee pay those moneys twice would be patently unfair. In the end result, the constructive trustee's position should be no worse or no better than it would have been but for the breach of duty. I think it appropriate therefore that an allowance be made for the payment of taxes, allowing for that portion of Log Sales' business emanating from MB as opposed to income from other sources.

Applying these findings, the plaintiff is entitled to recover $4,243,383 from the defendants (not including the Delta companies or AMCO) as the net benefit received by them as a result of breach of fiduciary duty. ... The figure of $4,243,383 exceeds any award that could have been made either for money had and received or in tort. The plaintiff is entitled to interest on this sum for the reason that the defendants have had the use of that money and since that is a benefit, the constructive trustees are bound to account for it. If there was evidence that the money was invested from the time it was received, I think the plaintiff could claim the actual sum realized (assuming that it was invested wisely). In the absence of such evidence, I have decided to award interest at the Chartered Bank Prime Business Loan Rate as calculated by the Bank of Canada. ... Compound interest would be appropriate in the present circumstances if the Ataka kind of arrangements[165] were prevalent. But the evidence in this regard is lacking. Perhaps it is appropriate to be guided by the comments of Dean Pound in *Home Fire Ins. Co. v. Barber*,[166] where he said that "it was not the function of courts of equity to administer punishment".

To show the breakdown of income and expenses and of the interest due to the plaintiff, I have prepared two tables. Following table 1 is an explanation. Table 2 is the calculation of the interest payable and requires no explanation.

[The tables and the explanation have not been reproduced.]

As referred to earlier, the defendant AMCO was incorporated by Andersen and MacKinnon to acquire an interest in a sawmill, the intention being to add another dimension to their operation. An interest in the Delta companies was acquired by AMCO. . . .

The funds used to acquire the shares in the Delta companies came from Log Sales. The plaintiff is entitled to trace those moneys. The fund from which the moneys came was of course, mixed. It may be presumed that the moneys so paid out are attributable to profits wrongfully earned on MB logs. Some Courts have also allowed tracing by fixing a per cent of the mixed fund as tainted money. In the present case, 79 per cent of Log Sales' retained earnings at the time were paid

---

164 (1879), 11 Ch. D. 918 (C.A.).

165 This refers to certain agreements made by Binstead for the sale of logs to Japanese companies at specified prices. Binstead then sold the same logs to Andersen-MacKinnon Log Sales Ltd. at a lower price, after which the latter company resold them to the Japanese companies for the higher price.

166 (1903), 67 Ned. 644.

in 1972 was attributable to MB transactions. The allocation in this case should not be made on this basis. I would order that all of the shares of AMCO are held by the defendants in trust for MB. All money, whether interest, dividends, salary or bonuses which was paid out to the defendants, is also recoverable by MB, save for the $210,000 paid out by AMCO to repay the shareholders loans.

MB argues that it is entitled to the highest value of the AMCO shares during the time that the property was wrongfully held. Rather than being awarded the shares in specie, MB claims a right to judgment against the defendants for that cash amount instead. In the present circumstances, that argument cannot succeed. The only evidence I have of value of the AMCO shares is the book value. On the plaintiff's own evidence, that does not reflect the market value. It would be quite wrong to rely upon any valuation which does not reflect the true market value.

> [His Lordship then held that dividends and management fees paid by Delta Chip Ltd. and dividends paid by Delta Cedar Products Ltd. were properly paid. Neither those companies nor their principal had notice of the other defendants' dishonesty. Hence they were not constructive trustees. He continued:]

As regards this aspect of the plaintiff's claim, there will be a declaration that all of the shares in AMCO are held in trust by Andersen, MacKinnon and Binstead for the plaintiff. There will be an order tracing any funds paid out by AMCO to the benefit of its shareholders. The action against the Delta companies is dismissed. Costs will be on a solicitor-client basis.

With respect to the remaining defendants, there will be judgment for the plaintiff against those defendants jointly in the sum of $9,113,091 with costs. There will be a Bullock order.[167] There will be no order as to prejudgment interest. I make no award in this regard as equitable interest has already been awarded. It seems to me that the result would be the same in either case.

. . .

Notes and Questions

1. Although the *MacMillan* case was an action for an account, the court also awarded interest. Is this proper? Is the court confusing the accounting and compensation remedies? Should the court not have allowed prejudgment interest instead?

2. A similar situation arose in *Bottoms v. Brent Petroleum Industries Ltd.*[168] The plaintiff purchased a block of shares from the defendant company. He was a director of the company. The plaintiff's broker directed payment to be made to the defendant at a bank at which both the plaintiff and the defendant had accounts. Through a bank error,

---

167 A Bullock order requires a plaintiff who has brought action against two parties and loses against one but wins against the other to pay the costs of the winning defendant against the plaintiff and the other defendant. However, if it was reasonable to add the winning defendant as a party, the plaintiff can then recover the total costs from the losing defendant.

168 (1984), 17 E.T.R. 48, 1984 CarswellBC 685 (S.C.).

the money was paid into the plaintiff's account and the bank used part of the money to repay a loan owed to it by the plaintiff. When the plaintiff became aware of this, he failed to tell the defendant until it requested payment for the shares. The plaintiff sold some of the shares in order to pay the original purchase price and his broker sent the money, which included interest, to the defendant. The plaintiff sued to recover the interest. It was held that he was a trustee of the money as a director and was, thus, liable for interest, since he wrongfully kept the money. However, in addition, the court required the plaintiff to account for the benefit he received, that is, the interest he saved because of the early repayment of his loan. The rate of interest in both cases was the rate he paid on his bank loan.

Do you agree with this decision?

3. A testator left all his estate, including a small business, to his wife as trustee, in trust for her for life with remainder to his children. When the testator died, his children were young. However, the widow and the children worked together to make the business a success. In effect, the trustee treated the business as her own and mixed her own moneys with that of the business. She did so, not out of dishonesty, but to support the children. Some years later, one of the children died and his spouse and issue sought an accounting from the trustee.

Are they entitled?[169]

4. Any trustee or other fiduciary entrusted with property for the benefit of another is obliged to render an account, without any allegation of wrongdoing. If the account shows a profit, then generally it must be disgorged, because a fiduciary is not allowed to profit from his office. It is clear from *Binstead* that the beneficiary need not have suffered a detriment before being entitled to the remedy. It is imposed because the defendant has breached a fiduciary duty, not necessarily because the plaintiff has suffered a detriment.

The remedy of an accounting of profits may be imposed even where the defendant is not otherwise liable to render an account; for example, if the defendant has committed a breach of confidence. *Attorney General v. Guardian Newspaper Ltd. (No. 2)*[170] is an example. A former member of MI5 was publishing his memoirs and the publisher had sold serialization rights to a newspaper. The newspaper published excerpts from the unpublished book. The Attorney General sued the newspaper for an account of profits for the breach of confidence and was successful. The fact that MI5 would not have been able to make the profits itself was irrelevant. As Lord Keith of Kinkel said, the account of profits remedy is based on the principle "that no one should be permitted to gain from his own wrongdoing."[171]

In a later case arising out of another former spy's book, *Attorney General v. Blake*,[172] it was held that an accounting of profits could be ordered against the author himself, even though he was not a fiduciary and without reference to breach of confidence. The House of Lords held that in the right case, an accounting could be ordered for a breach of contract. This could have important implications for commercial parties, who tend to assume that they are at liberty to breach one contract when another more profitable opportunity presents itself. It remains unclear how widely *Blake* will operate.[173]

---

169 See *Wakefield, supra*, note 19.

170 (1988), [1988] 3 W.L.R. 776, [1988] 3 All E.R. 545, [1990] 1 A.C. 109 (H.L.). This case arose from the publication by Peter Blake of his book "Spycatcher". There was also litigation in Australia.

171 *Ibid.*, at 788.

172 (2000), [2001] 1 A.C. 268, [2000] H.L.J. No. 47 (U.K. H.L.).

173 See also *Experience Hendrix LLC v. PPX Enterprises Inc.*, [2003] 1 All E.R. (Commercial) 830 (C.A.); *Amertek Inc. v. Canadian Commercial Corp.* (2003), 2003 CarswellOnt 3100, 229 D.L.R. (4th) 419, 39 B.L.R. (3d) 163 (Ont. S.C.J.).

5. Another important case on the subject of an account of profits is *Warman International Ltd. v. Dwyer.*[174] Dwyer was the general manager of Warman. Warman was an agent for the distribution of products supplied by an Italian company. Dwyer secretly negotiated with the Italian company to transfer the agency and other business to new companies to be incorporated by him. He left Warman's employ in 1988 when the Italian company ended the agency arrangement with Warman and entered into an arrangement with Dwyer, his wife and his new companies. The Italian company had a stake in one of those companies. The businesses were successful. The court held that Dwyer clearly breached his fiduciary duty to Warman and that Dwyer's companies were equally liable with him. The trial judge held that Warman was entitled to an account of profits, but the Queensland Court of Appeal held that it was only entitled to recover its losses flowing from the breach of duty. However, the compensation award was less than the amount obtainable on an account because, as the High Court noted, with a compensation award, Dwyer would be able "to retain any benefit flowing from Dwyer's breach of fiduciary obligation over and above the amount which represents equitable compensation for the loss actually sustained by Warman."[175] The High Court only addressed the question whether Warman was entitled to an account of profits and, if so, on what basis. It was agreed that Warman would otherwise be entitled to compensation for the loss it sustained. In a unanimous judgment the court held that the defendants were liable to account. The court held that when a fiduciary has breached the fiduciary duty, the principal is *prima facie* entitled to an account of profits.[176] In fact the principal has a right to elect to have either an account of profits or compensation and will, undoubtedly choose the remedy that will yield the most. Thus, for example, the principal will normally elect the compensation remedy if the losses suffered by the principal are greater than the profit made by the fiduciary.

The court noted:[177]

> Although an account of profits, like other equitable remedies, is said to be discretionary, it is granted or withheld according to settled principles. It will be defeated by equitable defences such as estoppel, laches, acquiescence and delay. . . The conduct of the plaintiff may be such as to make it inequitable to order an account. Thus, the plaintiff may not stand by and permit the defendant to make profits and then claim entitlement to those profits.

However, the court also noted that Dwyer was actively dishonest and stated that in those circumstances "it is more difficult still to conceive of circumstances in which no account at all should be ordered."[178]

In dealing with the particular facts of the case, the court drew a distinction between specific assets acquired by the fiduciary and a case in which the fiduciary acquires a business. In the former case, the fiduciary is accountable for the specific asset and will typically hold it upon constructive trust. However, it is different with a business, said the court.[179]

---

174 (1995), 128 A.L.R. 201 (Australia H.C.).

175 *Ibid.*, at 212.

176 *Ibid.*, at 212-3.

177 *Ibid.*, at 210.

178 *Ibid.*

179 *Ibid.*, at 211.

In the case of a business it may well be inappropriate and inequitable to compel the errant fiduciary to account for the whole of the profit of his conduct of the business or his exploitation of the principal's goodwill over an indefinite period of time. In such a case, it may be appropriate to allow the fiduciary a proportion of the profits, depending upon the particular circumstances. That may well be the case when it appears that a significant proportion of an increase in profits has been generated by the skill, efforts, property and resources of the fiduciary, the capital which he has introduced and the risks he has taken, so long as they are not risks to which the principal's property has been exposed. Then it may be said that the relevant proportion of the increased profits is not the product or consequence of the plaintiff's property but the product of the fiduciary's skill, efforts, property and resources.

At this point the court noted :[180]

[T]he stringent rule requiring a fiduciary to account for profits can be carried to extremes and . . . in cases outside the realm of specific assets, the liability of the fiduciary should not be transformed into a vehicle for the unjust enrichment of the plaintiff.

The court continued:[181]

Whether it is appropriate to allow an errant fiduciary a proportion of the profits or to make an allowance in respect of skill, expertise and other expenses is a matter of judgment which will depend on the facts of a given case. However, as a general rule, in conformity with the principle that a fiduciary must not profit from a breach of fiduciary duty, a court will not apportion profits in the absence of an antecedent arrangement for profit-sharing but will make allowance for skill, expertise and other expenses.

Because of Dwyer's dishonesty and because there was no agreement for profit-sharing, this was not a case in which the profits should be apportioned. However, the court did allow the defendants an allowance for their skill, expertise and effort.

When it came to the actual account, the court noted that the taking of an account is often difficult in practice. So it was in this case. The trial judge had found that the agency agreement between the Italian company and Warman was terminable on three months' notice and, aside from Dwyer's actions, would only have continued for another year. On the other hand, while some of the goodwill belonged to the Italian company, Dwyer did appropriate some of Warman's goodwill. He had also enticed some of Warman's employees to join his companies. In the circumstances, the defendants were ordered to account for the first two years of the companies' operation. However, they had to account on the basis of the approach less favourable to them, namely, for the entire net profits of the businesses before tax, less an appropriate amount for expenses, skill, expertise, effort and resources contributed by them.

---

180 *Warman*, at 211-12.
181 *Warner*, at 212.

3. PROPRIETARY REMEDIES

(a) Generally

As we have seen, the beneficiaries' primary remedy for a breach of trust is a personal one against the trustees in the form of a money judgment. However, if the trustees still have the property, the beneficiaries have a proprietary remedy as well in that they are entitled to recover the property itself. If the trustees no longer have the property and are not personally liable,[182] or if they are insolvent, the beneficiaries may have a right of action against the recipients of the trust property. This right of action is, in fact, two causes of action. First, a right *in personam* or personal action in equity against the recipients, and second, a right *in rem*, that is, a proprietary action, at law, in equity, or both, to follow or trace the trust property into its product.

The equitable proprietary remedies receive primary consideration below. This is because a beneficiary under a trust cannot normally bring an action at law. But because the beneficiaries of other fiduciary relationships may have a cause of action at law (as well as in equity), the common law remedies will be considered briefly as well.

The advantages of proprietary remedies are: (1) they confer priority over the defendant's creditors on his or her insolvency; (2) in the case of beneficial proprietary remedies, they enable the plaintiff to take advantage of any increase in the value of the property; (3) they may be available when a personal action is not; (4) they carry interest, if the property is income-producing, from the date that the defendant acquired the property, whereas personal claims such as for an accounting, only carry interest if it is claimed, at the prejudgment interest rate, from the date the cause of action arose to the date of the order.[183]

All remedies for breach of trust attempt to restore to the beneficiaries what was always their property.[184] The restoration usually takes the form of a compensation award, or an account of profits, but may involve a recovery of the trust property itself.

In considering the law of tracing it is important to distinguish carefully between different concepts, as Lionel Smith has pointed out. He distinguishes between following and tracing on the one hand, and between following and tracing, and claiming on the other.[185] He defines "following" as the exercise of locating a tangible thing that belongs to the plaintiff, and "tracing" as identifying the substitute for the original thing claimed by the plaintiff.[186] Although we have retained the traditional distinction between "following property at law" and "tracing in equity," Smith's analysis has much to recommend it. Smith has also made

---

182 For example, because they are excused for a technical breach of trust, or because they have a valid defence to the personal action.
183 *Courts of Justice Act*, R.S.O. 1990, c. C.43, s. 128(1).
184 Ford and Lee, §17020.
185 Lionel D. Smith, *The Law of Tracing* (Oxford: Clarendon Press, 1997), 5 (hereafter "Smith").
186 *Ibid.*, 6.

clear that following and tracing are processes. They must, therefore, be distinguished from what he calls "claiming," that is, the claims that can be made if the process of following or tracing is successful.[187] Accordingly, it is incorrect to refer to following or tracing as a right or a remedy.[188]

When a plaintiff succeeds in identifying the traceable proceeds of trust property, it is traditionally said that the proceeds are held on a constructive trust. However, a strong argument can be made that it is, in fact, a resulting trust, since it restores value whence it came.[189]

Further Reading

John Scott Kelly, "Principles of Tracing Property Commingled or Converted" (1983), 6 E. & T.Q. 89.

Law Reform Commission of British Columbia, "Report on Competing Rights to Mingled Property", L.R.C. 66 (1983).

Robert A. Pearce, "A Tracing Paper" (1976), 40 Conv. (N.S.) 277.

A.J. Oakley, "The Prerequisites of an Equitable Tracing Claim" (1975), 28 Curr. Leg. Prob. 64.

C.A. Needham, "Recovering the Profits of Bribery" (1979), 95 L.Q. Rev. 536.

Craig Rotherham, "The Metaphysics of Tracing: Substituted Title and Property Rhetoric" (1996), Osgoode Hall L.J. 321.

Lionel D. Smith, *The Law of Tracing* (Oxford: Clarendon Press, 1997) (hereafter "Smith").

Simon Evans, "Rethinking Tracing and the Law of Restitution" (1999), 115 L.Q.R. 469.

(b) Following Property At Law

Although tracing for breach of trust is always equitable, tracing also exists at law. It is then usually called "following" property. The main common law proprietary actions are conversion, detinue and the pre-trial process called replevin.[190] Each of these common law actions lie when the plaintiff is the owner of the chattel or has a right to immediate possession. In conversion the plaintiff's claim is against any person who wrongfully converted the chattel to his or her own use. Liability is strict; an innocent buyer of stolen property commits the tort of conversion and is liable to the owner for the full value of the property. Normally, damages are awarded in a successful action, but the court has a discretion to order return of the chattel if it has special value to the plaintiff. The essence of the claim is the wrongful *taking*. In detinue the plaintiff sues for damages for the wrongful *retention* of her or his chattel, and this action lies even if the original taking was lawful. In replevin the plaintiff seeks to recover possession of goods which were unlawfully taken from her or him, pending the trial of the issue.

---

187 *Ibid.*, 10ff.

188 *Ibid.*

189 Robert Chambers, *Resulting Trusts* (Oxford: Clarendon Press, 1997), 104ff., 212-14; Smith, 294, 300, 357. The other proprietary remedy is the equitable lien.

190 For more discussion, see Chapter 10, part 3.

The plaintiff may waive the tort involved in the foregoing actions and sue the defendant at law for money had and received. Although conversion and detinue and the action for money had and received are personal actions, in that all result in a money award,[191] they are based on proprietary rights. Hence, if the defendant is insolvent the plaintiff ranks ahead of the defendant's creditors, so long as the property in question can still be identified.[192] The trustee in bankruptcy of the defendant would, himself or herself, commit the tort of conversion if the property was not returned to the plaintiff.

If the defendant sold the chattel for money, exchanged it for another, or purchased another with the proceeds of sale of the first, the plaintiff can follow the property into its product. However, the common law, like equity, insists that the product be identifiable property. The root case is understood to be *Taylor v. Plumer*.[193] Sir Thomas Plumer gave money to Walsh, a stockbroker, to purchase English bonds. Walsh bought American investments and gold instead and was about to board a ship to the United States when he was apprehended and the investments and gold were seized and returned to Sir Thomas. Walsh's assignees in bankruptcy sought to recover the investments and gold from Sir Thomas, but they were unsuccessful, since the investments and the gold were the ascertainable products of the defendant's money. In that connection Lord Ellenborough said:[194]

> It makes no difference in reason or law into what other form, different from the original, the change may have been made, whether it be into that of promissory notes for the security of the money which was produced by the sale of the goods of the principal,. . . or into other merchandize,. . . for the product of or substitute for the original thing still follows the nature of the thing itself, as long as it can be ascertained to be such, and the right only ceases when the means of ascertainment fail, which is the case when the subject is turned into money, and mixed and confounded in a general mass of the same description. The difficulty which arises in such a case is a difficulty of fact and not of law, and the dictum that money has no ear-mark must be understood in the same way; i.e. as predicated only of an undivided and undistinguishable mass of current money. But money in a bag, or otherwise kept apart from other money, guineas, or other coin marked (if the fact were so) for the purpose of being distinguished, are so far ear-marked as to fall within the rule on this subject, which applies to every other description of personal property whilst it remains, (as the property in question did,) in the hands of the factor [*i.e.*, Walsh], or his general legal representatives.

The traditional view is that the common law has difficulty tracing money that has been mixed with the funds of another person, whether in a bank account or not.[195] Indeed, it seems that Lord Ellenborough would have hesitated to allow

---

191 Unless the court exercises its discretion to order specific restitution in an action for conversion.
192 Robert A. Pearce, "A Tracing Paper" (1976), 40 Conv. (N.S.) 277 at 284; Salman Kurshid and Paul Matthews, "Tracing Confusion" (1974), 95 L.Q. Rev. 78; Michael Scott, "The Right to 'Trace' at Common Law" (1966), 7 West. Austr. L. Rev. 428 at 481.
193 (1815), 3 M. & S. 562, 105 E.R. 721.
194 *Ibid.*, at M. & S. 575.
195 In fact it seems that in *Taylor v. Plumer*, Lord Ellenborough, even though sitting in the Court of King's Bench, was applying equitable principles: see S. Khurshid and P. Matthews, "Tracing Confusion" (1979), 95 L.Q. Rev. 78; L. Smith, "Tracing in *Taylor v. Plumer*: Equity in the Court of King's Bench," [1995] Lloyd's Maritime and Commercial Law Quarterly 240; for the

tracing of moneys into a bank account. But in *Banque Belge pour l'Étranger v. Hambrouck*,[196] Atkin L.J. said:[197]

> The question always was, Has the means of ascertainment failed? But if in 1815 the common law halted outside the bankers' door, by 1879 equity had had the courage to lift the latch, walk in and examine the books.[198] I see no reason why the means of ascertainment so provided should not now be available both for common law and equity proceedings.

In the *Banque Belge* case the court, thus, allowed moneys stolen by employees to be followed into the substantially unmixed bank accounts of donees.[199]

Another case in which the common law remedy was successful is *Trustee of the Property of F.C. Jones and Sons (a Firm) v. Jones*.[200] The partners committed an act of bankruptcy when they failed comply with a notice to pay a judgment a creditor obtained against the firm. The wife of one of the partners then opened an account with commodity brokers and paid three cheques into it, which were drawn on the partnership account. She was very successful in the futures market and paid the proceeds into her account at the brokers. Meanwhile, the creditor had petitioned the partners into bankruptcy and the trustee claimed to be entitled to the moneys in her account. The Court of Appeal allowed the claim. Millett L.J. held that the trustee had a proprietary claim. The partner's wife did not get title to the money, since it vested in the trustee from the moment of the act of bankruptcy. Hence, she could not be a constructive trustee of it. Consequently, an equitable tracing claim could not be maintained. However, since the money had not been mixed with other money in the account, the trustee was able to follow it into her account at law and take not only the original amount, but the profits as well. Beldam L.J. came to the same conclusion for essentially the same reasons. Nourse L.J. also held in favour of the trustee, but on the basis that the trustee could recover under a claim for money had and received, not only the original sum, but also the profits. This seems unorthodox, since the claim for money had and received is a personal claim and traditionally, the claim is only for the original sum received (although *Banque Belge* itself was a claim for money had and received).

It might have been easier to resolve *Jones* using constructive trust reasoning, and this would surely have been done in Canada or the U.S. The advantage of the legal remedy is that it does not depend upon the existence of a fiduciary relationship. We submit that the equitable remedy also does not, at least not in Canada, but for a long time it was thought that it did, and the English courts may still be

---

full story of the case, L. Smith, "The Stockbroker and the Solicitor-General: The Story Behind *Taylor v. Plumer*" (1994), 15 Journal of Legal History 1.

196 [1921] 1 K.B. 321 (Eng. C.A.).

197 *Ibid.*, at 335.

198 In *Hallett's Estate, Re* (1880), 13 Ch. D. 696, [1874-80] All E.R. Rep 793

199 Followed in *Chief Constable of Kent v. V.* (1982), [1983] Q.B. 34, [1982] 3 W.L.R. 462, [1982] 3 All E.R. 36 (C.A.), at 41 [Q.B.], *per* Lord Denning M.R.

200 (1996), [1997] Ch. 159, [1996] 4 All E.R. 721 (C.A.). Millett L.J., as he then was, noticed Smith's arguments about *Taylor v. Plumer* but concluded that this was a case in which equity followed the law, before the law had been declared.

affected by this approach. We shall consider this further below. Nor is a claim of legal ownership generally barred by a transfer of the property to a *bona fide* purchaser of the legal estate for value and without notice, as the equitable remedy is; although if the asset in question is money or some other negotiable asset, even common law ownership is defeated by *bona fide* purchase for value. Traditionally, the main disadvantage of the legal remedy is that it does not apply when the property is money and is mixed; this view is based on what was said in *Taylor v. Plumer*. Most of the cases are concerned with money which becomes mixed in bank accounts. The equitable remedy is not frustrated in such a situation and, hence, it has become much the more important of the two tracing remedies.

An additional problem with the common law remedy is that it is not available to a beneficiary under a trust, since the beneficiary's interest is equitable and is not recognized at law. Exceptionally, if the beneficiary has a right to immediate possession, as under a bare trust, he or she can sue at common law. The beneficiary can also sue at law by joining the trustee as a party to the litigation, forcing the trustee to assert any legal claims the trustee holds against any third party recipient, for the benefit of the beneficiary. This, however, only works if the trustee has some claim against the third party; it does not help if, for example, the trustee wrongfully gave the property to a third party as a gift. Beneficiaries under other fiduciary relationships, such as principal and agent, may be able to sue third parties at law (as well as in equity), if they retained a legal interest in any property possessed by the agent.

Further Reading

Michael Scott, "The Right to 'Trace' at Common Law" (1966), 7 West. Austr. L. Rev. 428.

Paul Matthews, "Proprietary Claims at Common Law for Mixed and Improved Goods" (1981), 34 Curr. Leg. Prob. 159.

Salmon Khurshid and Paul Matthews "Tracing Confusion" (1979), 95 L.Q. Rev. 78.

(c) Tracing in Equity

(i) *Introduction*

Proprietary claims based on tracing are based on the fact that the property sought to be recovered belongs to the beneficiaries. If the trustees misappropriate the property, equity will restore it to the beneficiaries even if the property was transferred by the trustees to a third person who is not a *bona fide* purchaser of the legal estate for value and without notice.

And this extends even to substituted property. Hence, if a trustee gave $1000 of trust money to a friend who was not entitled to it, and the friend bought a bond with it, but subsequently cashed the bond and invested the proceeds in a guaranteed investment certificate, the beneficiaries can trace the $1000 into the certificate and recover it. All they have to do is to prove the several transformations of the original property.

One of the main advantages of being able to trace is that it may lead to a proprietary remedy, and such a remedy confers priority over the defendant's creditors. Hence, if the defendant is bankrupt, any property held by him or her in trust for the plaintiff is not available for distribution among the defendant's creditors.[201]

Tracing occurs most often when the defendant is bankrupt. However, it is also used when the personal remedy is barred by limitation, or when there is no personal remedy. Tracing will be fruitless when the property has been spent on comestibles or services.

(ii) *Remedies*

The two remedies available in consequence of a successful tracing in equity are the recovery of the property or its product, in which case the defendant is effectively a constructive trustee of the property,[202] or the equitable lien as a proprietary security interest in support of a personal judgment. The latter is often termed a "charge" instead of "lien," although the word "charge" is probably best confined to consensually created security interests. A lien may exist by virtue of statute, such as a construction lien;[203] at law, such as a solicitor's lien on client's documents; or in equity, such as a vendor's lien for unpaid purchase money, or the lien which is imposed in consequence of tracing. Apart from that, however, a lien and a charge serve the same purpose, in that they secure the payment of a personal claim by encumbering the property.

The general rule in Anglo-Canadian law is that the beneficiary has the right to elect either to recover the property or its product, or have a lien upon it for its value. In American law the plaintiff has an option if the defendant was a conscious wrongdoer, but not if the defendant innocently converted the property. In the latter situation the plaintiff can only claim a lien, because the defendant ought not to be held liable as a constructive trustee and, thus, required to pay the profit or increase in value. The same rule applies to the gratuitous transferee without notice. Further, it also applies to the conscious wrongdoer who uses the property to improve her or his own. However, when the conscious wrongdoer uses the property to pay her or his debts, the plaintiff may be subrogated to the creditor's position.[204] The equitable subrogation remedy is not well developed in Anglo-Canadian law.

The position was considered thoroughly in the following important case.

---

201 *Bankruptcy and Insolvency Act*, R.S.C. 1985, c. B-3, s. 67; *Wilson v. Stackhouse*, 29 O.W.N. 357, 7 C.B.R. 437, [1926] 1 D.L.R. 584, 1926 CarswellOnt 19 (S.C.).
202 Scott, §507.
203 See, *e.g.*, *Construction Lien Act*, R.S.O. 1990, c. C.30, s. 14.
204 See Scott, §§507-513.2; Smith, 33-4, 152-4.

FOSKETT v. McKEOWN

(2000), [2001] 1 A.C. 102, [2000] 3 All E.R. 97
House of Lords

The plaintiffs (sometimes called "the purchasers" in the speeches) were investors who paid money to Timothy Murphy in trust, for investment in land in Portugal. Murphy insured his own life for £1 million. The annual premiums were £10,220. In breach of trust, Murphy used trust money to pay the last two annual premiums on the policy. Three other premiums were paid with his own money, or else the source of the money was not established. As is common in England, the life insurance policy was itself held on trust, as to 90% for his children and as to 10% for his mother. This trust of the policy is called "the children's settlement" in the speeches.

The insurance policy was "index-linked"; it was partly a savings vehicle. Of each premium, some went towards the insurance and some towards savings. The savings were linked to a stock market index. The policy-holder did not actually own any stock market investments; the savings element was just a claim against the insurance company, but it was measured by a notional number of units and value of the units was measured by the stock market index. The savings could be extracted before death. The policy provided that on the death of Mr. Murphy, a specified death benefit became payable, which was the greater of (1) £1 million, and (2) the aggregate value of units notionally allocated under the terms of the policy.

Murphy committed suicide and £1 million was paid to the surviving trustees of the children's settlement. The plaintiffs sued, arguing that this money was held as to 40% on constructive trust for them, since 40% of the premium money had come from money held on trust for them. They lost in the Court of Appeal, but their appeal was allowed by a 3-2 majority. A cross-appeal by the children, arguing that the plaintiffs had lost all right to the insurance money by electing to pursue other remedies, was dismissed unanimously; this is addressed in the extract from the speech of Lord Hope.

Lord Millett:

My Lords, this is a textbook example of tracing through mixed substitutions. At the beginning of the story the purchasers were beneficially entitled under an express trust to a sum standing in the name of Mr. Murphy in a bank account. From there the money moved into and out of various bank accounts where in breach of trust it was inextricably mixed by Mr. Murphy with his own money. After each transaction was completed the purchasers' money formed an indistinguishable part of the balance standing to Mr. Murphy's credit in his bank account. The amount of that balance represented a debt due from the bank to Mr. Murphy, that is to say a chose in action. At the penultimate stage the purchasers' money was represented by an indistinguishable part of a different chose in action, *viz* the debt prospectively and contingently due from an insurance company to its policyholders, being the trustees of a settlement made by Mr. Murphy for the benefit of his children. At the present and final stage it forms an indistinguishable part of the balance standing to the credit of the respondent trustees in their bank account.

Tracing and following

The process of ascertaining what happened to the purchasers' money involves both tracing and following. These are both exercises in locating assets which are or may be taken to represent an asset belonging to the purchasers and to which they assert ownership. The processes of following and tracing are, however, distinct. Following is the process of following the same asset as it moves from hand to hand. Tracing is the process of identifying a new asset as the substitute for the old. Where one asset is exchanged for another, a claimant can elect whether to follow the original asset into the hands of the new owner or to trace its value into the new asset in the hands of the same owner. In practice his choice is often dictated by the circumstances. In the present case the purchasers do not seek to follow the money any further once it reached the bank or insurance company, since its identity was lost in the hands of the recipient (which in any case obtained an unassailable title as a bona fide purchaser for value without notice of the purchasers' beneficial interest). Instead the purchasers have chosen at each stage to trace the money into its proceeds, *viz* the debt presently due from the bank to the account holder or the debt prospectively and contingently due from the insurance company to the policy holders.

Having completed this exercise, the purchasers claim a continuing beneficial interest in the insurance money. Since this represents the product of Mr. Murphy's own money as well as theirs, which Mr. Murphy mingled indistinguishably in a single chose in action, they claim a beneficial interest in a proportionate part of the money only. The transmission of a claimant's property rights from one asset to its traceable proceeds is part of our law of property, not of the law of unjust enrichment. There is no 'unjust factor' to justify restitution (unless 'want of title' be one, which makes the point). The claimant succeeds if at all by virtue of his own title, not to reverse unjust enrichment. Property rights are determined by fixed rules and settled principles. They are not discretionary. They do not depend upon ideas of what is 'fair, just and reasonable'. Such concepts, which in reality mask decisions of legal policy, have no place in the law of property.

A beneficiary of a trust is entitled to a continuing beneficial interest not merely in the trust property but in its traceable proceeds also, and his interest binds every one who takes the property or its traceable proceeds except a bona fide purchaser for value without notice. In the present case the purchasers' beneficial interest plainly bound Mr. Murphy, a trustee who wrongfully mixed the trust money with his own and whose every dealing with the money (including the payment of the premiums) was in breach of trust. It similarly binds his successors, the trustees of the children's settlement, who claim no beneficial interest of their own, and Mr. Murphy's children, who are volunteers. They gave no value for what they received and derive their interest from Mr. Murphy by way of gift.

Tracing

We speak of money at the bank, and of money passing into and out of a bank account. But of course the account holder has no money at the bank. Money paid into a bank account belongs legally and beneficially to the bank and not to the account holder. The bank gives value for it, and it is accordingly not usually possible to make the money itself the subject of an adverse claim. Instead a claimant normally sues the account holder rather than the bank and lays claim to the proceeds of the money in his hands. These consist of the debt or part of the debt due to him from the bank. We speak of tracing money into and out of the account, but there is no money in the account. There is merely a single debt of an amount equal to the final balance standing to the credit of the account holder. No money passes from paying bank to receiving bank or through the clearing system (where the money flows may be in the opposite direction). There is simply a series of debits and credits which are causally and transactionally linked. We also speak of tracing one asset into another, but this too is inaccurate. The original asset still exists in the hands of the new owner, or it may have become untraceable. The claimant claims the new asset because it was acquired in whole or in part with the original asset. What he traces, therefore, is not the physical asset itself but the value inherent in it.

Tracing is thus neither a claim nor a remedy. It is merely the process by which a claimant demonstrates what has happened to his property, identifies its proceeds and the persons who have handled or received them, and justifies his claim that the proceeds can properly be regarded as representing his property. Tracing is also distinct from claiming. It identifies the traceable proceeds of the claimant's property. It enables the claimant to substitute the traceable proceeds for the original asset as the subject matter of his claim. But it does not affect or establish his claim. That will depend on a number of factors including the nature of his interest in the original asset. He will normally be able to maintain the same claim to the substituted asset as he could have maintained to the original asset. If he held only a security interest in the original asset, he cannot claim more than a security interest in its proceeds. But his claim may also be exposed to potential defences as a result of intervening transactions. Even if the purchasers could demonstrate what the bank had done with their money, for example, and could thus identify its traceable proceeds in the hands of the bank, any claim by them to assert ownership of those proceeds would be defeated by the bona fide purchaser defence. The successful completion of a tracing exercise may be preliminary to a personal claim[205] or a proprietary one, to the enforcement of a legal right[206] or an equitable one.

Given its nature, there is nothing inherently legal or equitable about the tracing exercise. There is thus no sense in maintaining different rules for tracing at law and in equity. One set of tracing rules is enough. The existence of two has never

---

205 As in *El Ajou v. Dollar Land Holdings plc*, [1993] 3 All E.R. 717.
206 As in *Trustees of the Property of FC Jones & Sons (a firm) v. Jones, supra*, note 200.

formed part of the law in the United States.[207] There is certainly no logical justification for allowing any distinction between them to produce capricious results in cases of mixed substitutions by insisting on the existence of a fiduciary relationship as a precondition for applying equity's tracing rules. The existence of such a relationship may be relevant to the nature of the claim which the plaintiff can maintain, whether personal or proprietary, but that is a different matter. I agree with the passages which my noble and learned friend Lord Steyn has cited from Professor Birks' essay 'The Necessity of a Unitary Law of Tracing',[208] and with Dr. Lionel Smith's exposition in his comprehensive monograph *The Law of Tracing*.[209]

This is not, however, the occasion to explore these matters further, for the present is a straightforward case of a trustee who wrongfully misappropriated trust money, mixed it with his own, and used it to pay for an asset for the benefit of his children. Even on the traditional approach, the equitable tracing rules are available to the purchasers. There are only two complicating factors. The first is that the wrongdoer used their money to pay premiums on an equity linked policy of life assurance on his own life. The nature of the policy should make no difference in principle, though it may complicate the accounting. The second is that he had previously settled the policy for the benefit of his children. This should also make no difference. The claimant's rights cannot depend on whether the wrongdoer gave the policy to his children during his lifetime or left the proceeds to them by his will; or if during his lifetime whether he did so before or after he had recourse to the claimant's money to pay the premiums. The order of events does not affect the fact that the children are not contributors but volunteers who have received the gift of an asset paid for in part with misappropriated trust moneys.

The cause of action

As I have already pointed out, the purchasers seek to vindicate their property rights, not to reverse unjust enrichment. The correct classification of the purchasers' cause of action may appear to be academic, but it has important consequences. The two causes of action have different requirements and may attract different defences.

A plaintiff who brings an action in unjust enrichment must show that the defendant has been enriched at the plaintiff's expense, for he cannot have been unjustly enriched if he has not been enriched at all. But the plaintiff is not concerned to show that the defendant is in receipt of property belonging beneficially to the plaintiff or its traceable proceeds. The fact that the beneficial ownership of the property has passed to the defendant provides no defence; indeed, it is usually the very fact which founds the claim. Conversely, a plaintiff who brings an action like the present must show that the defendant is in receipt of property

---

207 See Scott, *The Law of Trusts*, 4th ed. (1989) at 605-9.
208 In *Making Commercial Law: Essays in Honour of Roy Goode* (1997).
209 (1997). See particularly pp. 120-30, 277-9 and 342-7.

which belongs beneficially to him or its traceable proceeds, but he need not show that the defendant has been enriched by its receipt. He may, for example, have paid full value for the property, but he is still required to disgorge it if he received it with notice of the plaintiff's interest.

Furthermore, a claim in unjust enrichment is subject to a change of position defence, which usually operates by reducing or extinguishing the element of enrichment. An action like the present is subject to the bona fide purchaser for value defence, which operates to clear the defendant's title.

The tracing rules

The insurance policy in the present case is a very sophisticated financial instrument. Tracing into the rights conferred by such an instrument raises a number of important issues. It is therefore desirable to set out the basic principles before turning to deal with the particular problems to which policies of life assurance give rise.

The simplest case is where a trustee wrongfully misappropriates trust property and uses it exclusively to acquire other property for his own benefit. In such a case the beneficiary is entitled at his option either to assert his beneficial ownership of the proceeds or to bring a personal claim against the trustee for breach of trust and enforce an equitable lien or charge on the proceeds to secure restoration of the trust fund. He will normally exercise the option in the way most advantageous to himself. If the traceable proceeds have increased in value and are worth more than the original asset, he will assert his beneficial ownership and obtain the profit for himself. There is nothing unfair in this. The trustee cannot be permitted to keep any profit resulting from his misappropriation for himself, and his donees cannot obtain a better title than their donor. If the traceable proceeds are worth less than the original asset, it does not usually matter how the beneficiary exercises his option. He will take the whole of the proceeds on either basis. This is why it is not possible to identify the basis on which the claim succeeded in some of the cases.

Both remedies are proprietary and depend on successfully tracing the trust property into its proceeds. A beneficiary's claim against a trustee for breach of trust is a personal claim. It does not entitle him to priority over the trustee's general creditors unless he can trace the trust property into its product and establish a proprietary interest in the proceeds. If the beneficiary is unable to trace the trust property into its proceeds, he still has a personal claim against the trustee, but his claim will be unsecured. The beneficiary's proprietary claims to the trust property or its traceable proceeds can be maintained against the wrongdoer and anyone who derives title from him except a bona fide purchaser for value without notice of the breach of trust. The same rules apply even where there have been numerous successive transactions, so long as the tracing exercise is successful and no bona fide purchaser for value without notice has intervened.

A more complicated case is where there is a mixed substitution. This occurs where the trust money represents only part of the cost of acquiring the new asset. As James Barr Ames pointed out in 'Following Misappropriated Property into its

Product',[210] consistency requires that, if a trustee buys property partly with his own money and partly with trust money, the beneficiary should have the option of taking a proportionate part of the new property or a lien upon it, as may be most for his advantage. In principle it should not matter (and it has never previously been suggested that it does) whether the trustee mixes the trust money with his own and buys the new asset with the mixed fund or makes separate payments of the purchase price (whether simultaneously or sequentially) out of the different funds. In every case the value formerly inherent in the trust property has become located within the value inherent in the new asset.

The rule, and its rationale, were stated by Samuel Williston in 'The Right to Follow Trust Property when Confused with Other Property':[211]

> If the trust fund is traceable as having furnished in part the money with which a certain investment was made, and the proportion it formed of the whole money so invested is known or ascertainable, the cestui que trust should be allowed to regard the acts of the trustee as done for his benefit, in the same way that he would be allowed to if all the money so invested had been his; that is, he should be entitled in equity to an undivided share of the property which the trust money contributed to purchase-such a proportion of the whole as the trust money bore to the whole money invested. The reason in one case as in the other is that the trustee cannot be allowed to make a profit from the use of the trust money, and if the property which he wrongfully purchased were held subject only to a lien for the amount invested, any appreciation in value would go to the trustee.

If this correctly states the underlying basis of the rule (as I believe it does), then it is impossible to distinguish between the case where mixing precedes the investment and the case where it arises on and in consequence of the investment. It is also impossible to distinguish between the case where the investment is retained by the trustee and the case where it is given away to a gratuitous donee. The donee cannot obtain a better title than his donor, and a donor who is a trustee cannot be allowed to profit from his trust.

In *Re Hallett's Estate, Knatchbull v. Hallett*[212] Jessel MR. acknowledged that where an asset was acquired exclusively with trust money, the beneficiary could either assert equitable ownership of the asset or enforce a lien or charge over it to recover the trust money. But he appeared to suggest that in the case of a mixed substitution the beneficiary is confined to a lien. Any authority that this dictum might otherwise have is weakened by the fact that Jessel MR. gave no reason for the existence of any such rule, and none is readily apparent. The dictum was plainly obiter, for the fund was deficient and the plaintiff was only claiming a lien. It has usually been cited only to be explained away.[213] It was rejected by the High Court of Australia in *Scott v. Scott*.[214] It has not been adopted in the United

---

210 (1906), 19 Harv. L.R. 511.

211 (1888), 2 Harv. L.R. 28 at 29.

212 *Supra*, note 198, at 709 [ChD], 796 [AllER].

213 See for example *Re Tilley's Will Trusts, Burgin v. Croad*, [1967] Ch 1179, 1186, [1967] 2 All E.R. 303, 308-9, *per* Ungoed-Thomas J.; Burrows, *The Law of Restitution* (1993) at p 368.

214 (1963), 109 C.L.R. 649. See the passage at 661-2 cited by Morritt L.J. below: [1998] Ch 265, 300-01, [1997] 3 All E.R. 392, 425.

States.[215] In *Primeau v. Granfield*[216] Learned Hand J expressed himself in forth-right terms: 'On principle there can be no excuse for such a rule.'

In my view the time has come to state unequivocally that English law has no such rule. It conflicts with the rule that a trustee must not benefit from his trust. I agree with Burrows that the beneficiary's right to elect to have a proportionate share of a mixed substitution necessarily follows once one accepts, as English law does, (i) that a claimant can trace in equity into a mixed fund and (ii) that he can trace unmixed money into its proceeds and assert ownership of the proceeds.

Accordingly, I would state the basic rule as follows. Where a trustee wrong-fully uses trust money to provide part of the cost of acquiring an asset, the beneficiary is entitled at his option either to claim a proportionate share of the asset or to enforce a lien upon it to secure his personal claim against the trustee for the amount of the misapplied money. It does not matter whether the trustee mixed the trust money with his own in a single fund before using it to acquire the asset, or made separate payments (whether simultaneously or sequentially) out of the differently owned funds to acquire a single asset.

Two observations are necessary at this point. First, there is a mixed substi-tution (with the results already described) whenever the claimant's property has contributed in part only towards the acquisition of the new asset. It is not necessary for the claimant to show in addition that his property has contributed to any increase in the value of the new asset. This is because, as I have already pointed out, this branch of the law is concerned with vindicating rights of property and not with reversing unjust enrichment. Secondly, the beneficiary's right to claim a lien is available only against a wrongdoer and those deriving title under him otherwise than for value. It is not available against competing contributors who are innocent of any wrongdoing. The tracing rules are not the result of any presumption or principle peculiar to equity. They correspond to the common law rules for following into physical mixtures (though the consequences may not be identical). Common to both is the principle that the interests of the wrongdoer who was responsible for the mixing and those who derive title under him otherwise than for value are subordinated to those of innocent contributors. As against the wrongdoer and his successors, the beneficiary is entitled to locate his contribution in any part of the mixture and to subordinate their claims to share in the mixture until his own contribution has been satisfied. This has the effect of giving the beneficiary a lien for his contribution if the mixture is deficient.

Innocent contributors, however, must be treated equally *inter se*. Where the beneficiary's claim is in competition with the claims of other innocent contribu-tors, there is no basis upon which any of the claims can be subordinated to any of the others. Where the fund is deficient, the beneficiary is not entitled to enforce a lien for his contributions; all must share rateably in the fund.

The primary rule in regard to a mixed fund, therefore, is that gains and losses are borne by the contributors rateably. The beneficiary's right to elect instead to enforce a lien to obtain repayment is an exception to the primary rule, exercisable

---

215 See the American Law Institute, *Restatement of the Law, Trusts 2d* (1959) at §202(h).
216 (1911), 184 F. 480, 482.

where the fund is deficient and the claim is made against the wrongdoer and those claiming through him. It is not necessary to consider whether there are any circumstances in which the beneficiary is confined to a lien in cases where the fund is more than sufficient to repay the contributions of all parties. It is sufficient to say that he is not so confined in a case like the present. It is not enough that those defending the claim are innocent of any wrongdoing if they are not themselves contributors but, like the trustees and Mr. Murphy's children in the present case, are volunteers who derive title under the wrongdoer otherwise than for value. On ordinary principles such persons are in no better position than the wrongdoer, and are liable to suffer the same subordination of their interests to those of the claimant as the wrongdoer would have been. They certainly cannot do better than the claimant by confining him to a lien and keeping any profit for themselves.

Similar principles apply to following into physical mixtures.[217] There are relatively few cases which deal with the position of the innocent recipient from the wrongdoer, but *Jones v. De Marchant*[218] may be cited as an example. A husband wrongfully used 18 beaver skins belonging to his wife and used them, together with four skins of his own, to have a fur coat made up which he then gave to his mistress. Unsurprisingly the wife was held entitled to recover the coat. The mistress knew nothing of the true ownership of the skins, but her innocence was held to be immaterial. She was a gratuitous donee and could stand in no better position than the husband. The coat was a new asset manufactured from the skins and not merely the product of intermingling them. The problem could not be solved by a sale of the coat in order to reduce the disputed property to a divisible fund, since (as we shall see) the realisation of an asset does not affect its ownership. It would hardly have been appropriate to require the two ladies to share the coat between them. Accordingly it was an all or nothing case in which the ownership of the coat must be assigned to one or other of the parties. The determinative factor was that the mixing was the act of the wrongdoer through whom the mistress acquired the coat otherwise than for value.

The rule in equity is to the same effect, as Page Wood V.-C. observed in *Frith v. Cartland*:[219]

> . . . if a man mixes trust funds with his own, the whole will be treated as the trust property, except so far as he may be able to distinguish what is his own.

This does not, in my opinion, exclude a pro rata division where this is appropriate, as in the case of money and other fungibles like grain, oil or wine. But it is to be observed that a pro rata division is the best that the wrongdoer and his donees can hope for. If a pro rata division is excluded, the beneficiary takes

---

217 See *Lupton v. White, White v. Lupton* (1808), 15 Ves. 432, [1803-13] All E.R. Rep. 336, 33 E.R. 817 and *Sandeman & Sons v. Tyzack and Branfoot Steamship Co. Ltd.*, [1913] A.C. 680, 695, [1911-13] All E.R. Rep. 1013, 1020 where Lord Moulton said: 'If the mixing has arisen from the fault of "B.", "A." can claim the goods.'

218 (1916), 28 D.L.R. 561.

219 (1865), 2 Hem. & M. 417, 420, 71 E.R. 525, 526.

the whole; there is no question of confining him to a lien. *Jones v. De Marchant* is a useful illustration of the principles shared by the common law and equity alike that an innocent recipient who receives misappropriated property by way of gift obtains no better title than his donor, and that if a proportionate sharing is inappropriate the wrongdoer and those who derive title under him take nothing.

Insurance policies

In the case of an ordinary whole-life policy the insurance company undertakes to pay a stated sum on the death of the assured in return for fixed annual premiums payable throughout his life. Such a policy is an entire contract, not a contract for a year with a right of renewal. It is not a series of single premium policies for one year term assurance. It is not like an indemnity policy where each premium buys cover for a year after which the policyholder must renew or the cover expires. The fact that the policy will lapse if the premiums are not paid makes no difference. The amounts of the annual premiums and of the sum assured are fixed in advance at the outset and assume the payment of annual premiums throughout the term of the policy. The relationship between them is based on the life expectancy of the assured and the rates of interest available on long term government securities at the inception of the policy.

In the present case the benefits specified in the policy are expressed to be payable 'in consideration of the payment of the first Premium already made and of the further Premiums payable'. The premiums are stated to be '£10,220.00 payable at annual intervals from 06 Nov 1986 throughout the lifetime of the life assured'. It is beyond argument that the death benefit of £1m paid on Mr. Murphy's death was paid in consideration for all the premiums which had been paid before that date, including those paid with the purchasers' money, and not just some of them. Part of that sum, therefore, represented the traceable proceeds of the purchasers' money.

It is, however, of critical importance in the present case to appreciate that the purchasers do not trace the premiums directly into the insurance money. They trace them first into the policy and thence into the proceeds of the policy. It is essential not to elide the two steps. In this context, of course, the word 'policy' does not mean the contract of insurance. You do not trace the payment of a premium into the insurance contract any more than you trace a payment into a bank account into the banking contract. The word 'policy' is here used to describe the bundle of rights to which the policyholder is entitled in return for the premiums. These rights, which may be very complex, together constitute a chose in action, *viz* the right to payment of a debt payable on a future event and contingent upon the continued payment of further premiums until the happening of the event. That chose in action represents the traceable proceeds of the premiums; its current value fluctuates from time to time. When the policy matures, the insurance money represents the traceable proceeds of the policy and hence indirectly of the premiums.

It follows that, if a claimant can show that premiums were paid with his money, he can claim a proportionate share of the policy. His interest arises by reason of and immediately upon the payment of the premiums, and the extent of his share is ascertainable at once. He does not have to wait until the policy matures in order to claim his property. His share in the policy and its proceeds may increase or decrease as further premiums are paid; but it is not affected by the realisation of the policy. His share remains the same whether the policy is sold or surrendered or held until maturity; these are merely different methods of realising the policy. They may affect the amount of the proceeds received on realisation but they cannot affect the extent of his share in the proceeds. In principle the purchasers are entitled to the insurance money which was paid on Mr. Murphy's death in the same shares and proportions as they were entitled in the policy immediately before his death.

Since the manner in which an asset is realised does not affect its ownership, and since it cannot matter whether the claimant discovers what has happened before or after it is realised, the question of ownership can be answered by ascertaining the shares in which it is owned immediately before it is realised. Where A misappropriates B's money and uses it to buy a winning ticket in the lottery, B is entitled to the winnings. Since A is a wrongdoer, it is irrelevant that he could have used his own money if in fact he used B's. This may seem to give B an undeserved windfall, but the result is not unjust. Had B discovered the fraud before the draw, he could have decided whether to keep the ticket or demand his money back. He alone has the right to decide whether to gamble with his own money. If A keeps him in ignorance until after the draw, he suffers the consequence. He cannot deprive B of his right to choose what to do with his own money; but he can give him an informed choice.

The application of these principles ought not to depend on the nature of the chose in action. They should apply to a policy of life assurance as they apply to a bank account or a lottery ticket. It has not been suggested in argument that they do not apply to a policy of life assurance. This question has not been discussed in the English authorities, but it has been considered in the United States. In a Note,[220] Professor Palmer doubted the claimant's right to share in the proceeds of a life policy, and suggested that he should be confined to a lien for his contributions. Professor Palmer accepted, as the majority of the Court of Appeal in the present case did not, that the claimant can trace from the premiums into the policy and that the proceeds of the policy are the product of all the premiums. His doubts were not based on any technical considerations but on questions of social policy. They have not been shared by the American courts. These have generally allowed the claimant a share in the proceeds proportionate to his contributions even though the share in the proceeds is greater than the amount of his money used in paying the premiums.[221] This accords with Ames' and Williston's opinions in the articles to which I have referred.

---

220 (1925), 35 Yale L.J. at 220-7.

221 See for example *Shaler v. Trowbridge* (1877), 28 N.J. Eq. 595; *Holmes v. Gilman* (1893), 138 N.Y. 369; *Vorlander v. Keyes* (1924), 1 F. 2d 67; *Truelsch v. Miller* (1925), 202 N.W. 352; *Baxter House v. Rosen* (1967), 278 N.Y.S. 2d 442; *Lohman v. General American Life Insurance Co.* (1973), 478 F. 2d 719.

The question is discussed at length in Scott, *The Law of Trusts*.[222] Professor Scott concludes that there is no substance in the doubts expressed by Palmer. He points out that the strongest argument in favour of limiting the beneficiary's claim to a lien is that otherwise he obtains a windfall. But in cases where the wrongdoer has misappropriated the claimant's money and used it to acquire other forms of property which have greatly increased in value the courts have consistently refused to limit the claimant to an equitable lien. In any case, the windfall argument is suspect. As Professor Scott points out, a life policy is an aleatory contract. Whether or not the sum assured exceeds the premiums is a matter of chance. Viewed from the perspective of the insurer, the contract is a commercial one; so the chances are weighted against the assured. But the outcome in any individual case is unpredictable at the time the premiums are paid. The unspoken assumption in the argument that a life policy should be treated differently from other choses in action seems to be that, by dying earlier than expected, the assured provides a contribution of indeterminate but presumably substantial value. But the assumption is false. A life policy is not an indemnity policy, in which the rights against the insurer are acquired by virtue of the payment of the premiums and the diminution of the value of an asset. In the case of a life policy the sum assured is paid in return for the premiums and nothing else. The death of the assured is merely the occasion on which the insurance money is payable. The ownership of the policy does not depend on whether this occurs sooner or later, or on whether the bargain proves to be a good one. It cannot be made to await the event.

The windfall argument has little to commend it in the present case. The purchasers were kept in ignorance of the fact that premiums had been paid with their money until after Mr. Murphy's death. Had they discovered what had happened before Mr. Murphy died, they would have intervened. They might or might not have elected to take an interest in the policy rather than enforce a lien for the return of the premiums paid with their money, but they would certainly have wanted immediate payment. This would have entailed the surrender of the policy. At the date of his death Mr. Murphy was only 45 and a non-smoker. He had a life expectancy of many years, and neither he nor the trustees had the means to keep up the premiums. The purchasers would hardly have been prepared to wait for years to recover their money, paying the premiums in the meantime. It is true that, under the terms of the policy, life cover could if necessary be maintained for a few years more at the expense of the investment element of the policy (which also provided its surrender value). But it is in the highest degree unlikely that the purchasers would have been willing to gamble on the remote possibility of Mr. Murphy's dying before the policy's surrender value was exhausted. If he did not they would recover nothing. They would obviously have chosen to enforce their lien to recover the premiums or have sought a declaration that the trustees held the policy for Mr. Murphy's children and themselves as tenants in common in the appropriate shares. In either case the trustees would have had no alternative but to surrender the policy. In practice the trustees were able to obtain the death benefit by maintaining the policy until Mr. Murphy's death only because the

222 §508.4 at pp. 574-84.

purchasers were kept in ignorance of the fact that premiums had been paid with their money and so were unable to intervene.

The reasoning of the Court of Appeal

The majority of the Court of Appeal (Sir Richard Scott V.-C. and Hobhouse L.J.) held that the purchasers could trace their money into the premiums but not into the policy, and were accordingly not entitled to a proportionate share in the proceeds. They did so, however, for different and, in my view, inconsistent reasons which cannot both be correct and which only coincidentally led to the same result in the present case.

Sir Richard Scott V.-C. considered that Mr. Murphy's children acquired vested interests in the policy at its inception. They had a vested interest (subject to defeasance) in the death benefit at the outset and before any of the purchasers' money was used to pay the premiums. The use of the purchasers' money gave the purchasers a lien on the proceeds of the policy for the return of the premiums paid with their money, but could not have the effect of divesting the children of their existing interest. The children owned the policy; the purchasers' money was merely used to maintain it. The position was analogous to that where trust money was used to maintain or improve property of a third party.

Sir Richard Scott V.-C. treated the policy as an ordinary policy of life assurance. It is not clear whether he thought that the children obtained a vested interest in the policy because Mr. Murphy took the policy out or because he paid the first premium, but I cannot accept either proposition. Mr. Murphy was the original contracting party, but he obtained nothing of value until he paid the first premium. The chose in action represented by the policy is the product of the premiums, not of the contract. The trustee took out the policy in all the recorded cases. In some of them he paid all the premiums with trust money. In such cases the beneficiary was held to be entitled to the whole of the proceeds of the policy. In other cases the trustee paid some of the premiums with his own money and some with trust money. In those cases the parties were held entitled to the proceeds of the policy rateably in proportion to their contributions. It has never been suggested that the beneficiary is confined to his lien for repayment of the premiums because the policy was taken out by the trustee. The ownership of the policy does not depend on the identity of the party who took out the policy. It depends on the identity of the party or parties whose money was used to pay the premiums.

So Sir Richard Scott V.-C.'s analysis can only be maintained if it is based on the fact that Mr. Murphy paid the first few premiums out of his own money before he began to make use of the trust money. Professor Scott records only one case in which it has been held that in such a case the claimant is confined to a lien on the ground that the later premiums were not made in acquiring the interest under the policy but merely in preserving or improving it.[223] The case is expressly disapproved by Scott,[224] where it is said that the decision cannot be supported,

---

223 See *Thum v. Wolstenholme* (1900), 21 Utah 446.
224 At §516.1.

and that the claimant should be entitled to a proportionate share of the proceeds, regardless of the question whether some of the premiums were paid wholly with the claimant's money and others wholly with the wrongdoer's money and regardless of the order of the payments, or whether the premiums were paid out of a mingled fund containing the money of both.

In my opinion there is no reason to differentiate between the first premium or premiums and later premiums. Such a distinction is not based on any principle. Why should the policy belong to the party who paid the first premium, without which there would have been no policy, rather than to the party who paid the last premium, without which it would normally have lapsed? Moreover, any such distinction would lead to the most capricious results. If only four annual premiums are paid, why should it matter whether A paid the first two premiums and B the second two, or B paid the first two and A the second two, or they each paid half of each of the four premiums? Why should the children obtain the whole of the sum assured if Mr. Murphy used his own money before he began to use the purchasers' money, and only a return of the premiums if Mr. Murphy happened to use the purchasers' money first? Why should the proceeds of the policy be attributed to the first premium when the policy itself is expressed to be in consideration of all the premiums? There is no analogy with the case where trust money is used to maintain or improve property of a third party. The nearest analogy is with an instalment purchase.

Hobhouse L.J. adopted a different approach. He concentrated on the detailed terms of the policy, and in particular on the fact that in the event the payment of the fourth and fifth premiums with the purchasers' money made no difference to the amount of the death benefit. Once the third premium had been paid, there was sufficient surrender value in the policy, built up by the use of Mr. Murphy's own money, to keep the policy on foot for the next few years, and as it happened Mr. Murphy's death occurred during those few years. But this was adventitious and unpredictable at the time the premiums were paid. The argument is based on causation and as I have explained is a category mistake derived from the law of unjust enrichment. It is an example of the same fallacy that gives rise to the idea that the proceeds of an ordinary life policy belong to the party who paid the last premium without which the policy would have lapsed. But the question is one of attribution not causation. The question is not whether the same death benefit would have been payable if the last premium or last few premiums had not been paid. It is whether the death benefit is attributable to all the premiums or only to some of them. The answer is that death benefit is attributable to all of them because it represents the proceeds of realising the policy, and the policy in turn represents the product of all the premiums.

In any case, Hobhouse L.J.'s analysis of the terms of the policy does not go far enough. It is not correct that the last two premiums contributed nothing to the sum payable on Mr. Murphy's death but merely reduced the cost to the insurers of providing it. Life cover was provided in return for a series of internal premiums paid for by the cancellation of units previously allocated to the policy. Units were allocated to the policy in return for the annual premiums. Prior to their cancellation the cancelled units formed part of a mixed fund of units which was the product of all the premiums paid by Mr. Murphy, including those paid with the purchasers' money. On ordinary principles, the purchasers can trace the last two premiums into and out of the mixed fund and into the internal premiums used to provide the death benefit.

It is true that the last two premiums were not needed to provide the death benefit in the sense that in the events which happened the same amount would have been payable even if those premiums had not been paid. In other words, with the benefit of hindsight it can be seen that Mr. Murphy made a bad investment when he paid the last two premiums. It is, therefore, superficially attractive to say that the purchasers' money contributed nothing of value. But the argument proves too much, for if the purchasers cannot trace their money into the proceeds of the policy, they should have no proprietary remedy at all, not even a lien for the return of their money. But the fact is that Mr. Murphy, who could not foresee the future, did choose to pay the last two premiums, and to pay them with the purchasers' money; and they were applied by the insurer towards the payment of the internal premiums needed to fund the death benefit. It should not avail his donees that he need not have paid the premiums, and that if he had not then (in the events which happened) the insurers would have provided the same death benefit and funded it differently.

In the case of an ordinary life policy which lapses if the premiums are not paid, Sir Richard Scott V.-C.'s approach gives the death benefit to the party whose money was used to pay the first premium, and Hobhouse L.J.'s approach gives it to the party whose money was used to pay the last premium. In the case of a policy like the present, Hobhouse L.J.'s approach also produces unacceptable and capricious results. The claimant must wait to see whether the life assured lives long enough to exhaust the amount of the policy's surrender value as at the date immediately before the claimant's money was first used. If the life assured dies the day before it would have been exhausted, the claimant is confined to his lien to recover the premiums; if he dies the day after, then the claimant's premiums were needed to maintain the life cover. In the latter case he takes at least a proportionate share of the proceeds or, if the argument is pressed to its logical conclusion, the whole of the proceeds subject to a lien in favour of the trustees of the children's settlement. This simply cannot be right.

Hobhouse L.J.'s approach is also open to objection on purely practical grounds. It must, I think, be unworkable if there is an eccentric pattern of payment; or if there is a fall in the value of the units at a critical moment. Like Sir Richard Scott V.-C.'s approach, it prompts the question: why should the order of payments matter? It is true that the premiums paid with the plaintiff's money did not in the event increase the amount payable on Mr. Murphy's death, but they increased the surrender value of the policy and postponed the date at which it would lapse if no further premiums were paid. Why should it be necessary to identify the premium the payment of which (in the events which happened) prevented the policy from lapsing? Above all, this approach makes it impossible for the ownership of the policy to be determined until the policy matures or is realised. This too cannot be right.

The trustees argued that such considerations are beside the point. It is not necessary, they submitted, to consider what the purchasers' rights would have been if the policy had been surrendered, or if Mr. Murphy had lived longer. It is sufficient to take account of what actually happened. I do not agree. A principled approach must yield a coherent solution in all eventualities. The ownership of the policy must be ascertainable at every moment from inception to maturity; it cannot be made to await events. In my view the only way to achieve this is to hold firm to the principle that the manner in which an asset is converted into money does not affect its ownership. The parties' respective rights to the proceeds of the policy depend on their rights to the policy immediately before it was realised on Mr. Murphy's death, and this depends on the shares in which they contributed to the premiums and nothing else. They do not depend on the date at which or the manner in which the chose in action was realised. Of course, Mr. Murphy's early death greatly increased the value of the policy and made the bargain a good one. But the idea that the parties' entitlements to the policy and its proceeds are altered by the death of the life assured is contrary to principle and to the decision of your Lordships' House in *D'Avigdor-Goldsmid v. IRC*.[225] That case establishes that no fresh beneficial interest in a policy of life assurance accrues or arises on the death of the life assured. The sum assured belongs to the person or persons who were beneficial owners of the policy immediately before the death.

In the course of argument it was submitted that if the children, who were innocent of any wrongdoing themselves, had been aware that their father was using stolen funds to pay the premiums, they could have insisted that the premiums should not be paid, and in the events which happened would still have received the same death benefit. But the fact is that Mr. Murphy concealed his wrongdoing from both parties. The proper response is to treat them both alike, that is to say rateably. It is morally offensive as well as contrary to principle to subordinate the claims of the victims of a fraud to those of the objects of the fraudster's bounty on the ground that he concealed his wrongdoing from both of them.

. . .

[Lord Millett would have preferred to use a different method from Lords Browne-Wilkinson and Hoffman to calculate the plaintiff's share in the £1 million, but he concurred with them that the sum should be divided according to the proportions in which they contributed to the premiums.]

LORD BROWNE-WILKINSON:

My Lords, there are many cases in which the court has to decide which of two innocent parties is to suffer from the activities of a fraudster. This case, unusually, raises the converse question: which of two innocent parties is to benefit from the activities of the fraudster. In my judgment, in the context of this case the two types of case fall to be decided on exactly the same principles, *viz* by

---

225 [1953] A.C. 347, [1953] 1 All E.R. 403.

determining who enjoys the ownership of the property in which the loss or the unexpected benefit is reflected.

. . .

As to the appeal, at the conclusion of the hearing I considered that the majority of the Court of Appeal were correct and would have dismissed the appeal. However, having read the draft speech of Lord Millett I have changed my mind and for the reasons which he gives I would allow the appeal. But, as we are differing from the majority of the Court of Appeal I will say a word or two about the substance of the case and then deal with one minor matter on which I do not agree with my noble and learned friend Lord Millett.

The crucial factor in this case is to appreciate that the purchasers are claiming a proprietary interest in the policy moneys and that such proprietary interest is not dependent on any discretion vested in the court. Nor is the purchasers' claim based on unjust enrichment. It is based on the assertion by the purchasers of their equitable proprietary interest in identified property.

The first step is to identify the interest of the purchasers: it is their absolute equitable interest in the moneys originally held by Mr. Deasy on the express trusts of the purchasers trust deed. This case does not involve any question of resulting or constructive trusts. The only trusts at issue are the express trusts of the purchasers trust deed. Under those express trusts the purchasers were entitled to equitable interests in the original moneys paid to Mr. Deasy by the purchasers. Like any other equitable proprietary interest, those equitable proprietary interests under the purchasers trust deed which originally existed in the moneys paid to Mr. Deasy now exist in any other property which, in law, now represents the original trust assets. Those equitable interests under the purchasers trust deed are also enforceable against whoever for the time being holds those assets other than someone who is a bona fide purchaser for value of the legal interest without notice or a person who claims through such a purchaser. No question of a bona fide purchaser arises in the present case: the children are mere volunteers under the policy trust. Therefore the critical question is whether the assets now subject to the express trusts of the purchasers trust deed comprise any part of the policy moneys, a question which depends on the rules of tracing. If, as a result of tracing, it can be said that certain of the policy moneys are what now represent part of the assets subject to the trusts of the purchasers trust deed, then as a matter of English property law the purchasers have an absolute interest in such moneys. There is no discretion vested in the court. There is no room for any consideration whether, in the circumstances of this particular case, it is in a moral sense 'equitable' for the purchasers to be so entitled. The rules establishing equitable proprietary interests and their enforceability against certain parties have been developed over the centuries and are an integral part of the property law of England. It is a fundamental error to think that, because certain property rights are equitable rather than legal, such rights are in some way discretionary. This case does not depend on whether it is fair, just and reasonable to give the purchasers an interest as a result of which the court in its discretion provides a remedy. It is a case of hard-nosed property rights.

Can then the sums improperly used from the purchasers' moneys be traced into the policy moneys? Tracing is a process whereby assets are identified. I do not now want to enter into the dispute whether the legal and equitable rules of tracing are the same or differ. The question does not arise in this case. The question of tracing which does arise is whether the rules of tracing are those regulating tracing through a mixed fund or those regulating the position when moneys of one person have been innocently expended on the property of another. In the former case (mixing of funds) it is established law that the mixed fund belongs proportionately to those whose moneys were mixed. In the latter case it is equally clear that money expended on maintaining or improving the property of another normally gives rise, at the most, to a proprietary lien to recover the moneys so expended. In certain cases the rules of tracing in such a case may give rise to no proprietary interest at all if to give such interest would be unfair.[226]

Both Sir Richard Scott V.-C. and Hobhouse L.J. considered that the payment of a premium on someone else's policy was more akin to an improvement to land than to the mixing of separate trust moneys in one account. Hobhouse L.J. was additionally influenced by the fact that the payment of the fourth and fifth premiums out of the purchasers' moneys conferred no benefit on the children: the policy was theirs and, since the first two premiums had already been paid, the policy would not have lapsed even if the fourth and fifth premiums had not been paid.

Cases where the money of one person has been expended on improving or maintaining the physical property of another raise special problems. The property left at the end of the day is incapable of being physically divided into its separate constituent assets, ie the land and the money spent on it. Nor can the rules for tracing moneys through a mixed fund apply: the essence of tracing through a mixed fund is the ability to re-divide the mixed fund into its constituent parts pro rata according to the value of the contributions made to it. The question which arises in this case is whether, for tracing purposes, the payments of the fourth and fifth premiums on a policy which, up to that date, had been the sole property of the children for tracing purposes fall to be treated as analogous to the expenditure of cash on the physical property of another or as analogous to the mixture of moneys in a bank account. If the former analogy is to be preferred, the maximum amount recoverable by the purchasers will be the amount of the fourth and fifth premiums plus interest: if the latter analogy is preferred the children and the other purchasers will share the policy moneys pro rata.

The speech of my noble and learned friend Lord Millett demonstrates why the analogy with moneys mixed in an account is the correct one. . . .

---

226 See *Re Diplock's Estate, Diplock v. Wintle*, [1948] 1 Ch. 465, (sub nom. *Diplock, Re*) [1948] 2 All E.R. 318 (C.A.), affirmed (1950), [1951] A.C. 251, [1950] 2 All E.R. 1137 (H.L.), at 548 [Ch], 361 [AllER].

[Lord Hoffmann concurred.

Lords Hope and Steyn would have limited the plaintiffs to the recovery of the trust money used to pay the two premiums.]

LORD HOPE OF CRAIGHEAD:

. . .

I shall deal first with the children's cross-appeal. Mr. Kaye Q.C. for the children based his argument on election upon the purchasers' receipt of compensation for the breach of trust in other proceedings brought on their behalf. The appellant obtained a declaration in 1994 that the shares in the company and the land in Portugal which was to be developed by it were held in trust for the purchasers. He also obtained for them £600,000 under a compromise in 1997 with Lloyds Bank, with whom the purchasers' money had been deposited and from whose bank accounts it had been misappropriated to pay the 1990 premium. Mr. Kaye submitted that, as the purchasers had elected to recover their plots of land in specie and had received monetary compensation in satisfaction of their claims for the misappropriation of the deposit moneys, they were barred by that election from pursuing any claim against the proceeds of the policy. He maintained that the purchasers, by pursuing these remedies, had obtained all that they had bargained for when they paid their money to the developers. They no longer had any proprietary base from which they could trace, and they had already been fully compensated as they were now in a position to complete the development. As the entire original purpose of the deposits had been fulfilled, they had lost nothing. They were in no need of any further relief by way of any proprietary or equitable remedy.

In my opinion the claims which were made against the developers and the bank and the claim now made against the proceeds of the policy are two wholly unrelated remedies. The purchasers were not put to any election when they were seeking to recover from the developers and the bank what they lost when, in breach of trust, their money was misappropriated. Had the claim which they are now making been one by way of damages, the relief which they have already obtained in the other proceedings would have been taken into account in this action in the assessment of their loss. That would not have been because they were to be held to any election, but by applying the rule that a party who is entitled to damages cannot recover twice over for the same loss. But in this action they are claiming a share of the proceeds of the policy on the ground that the money which was taken from them can be traced into the proceeds. The amount, if any, to which they are entitled as a result of the tracing exercise does not require any adjustment on account of the compensation obtained by pursuing other remedies. This is because the remedy which they are now seeking to pursue is a proprietary one, not an award of damages. The purpose of the remedy is to enable them to vindicate their claim to their own money. The compensation which they have obtained from elsewhere may have a bearing on their claim to a proportionate share of the proceeds. But it cannot deprive them of their proprietary interest in their own money. For these reasons I would reject this argument.

. . .

But the result of the tracing exercise cannot solve the remaining question, which relates to the extent of the purchasers' entitlement. It is the fact that this is a case of mixed substitution which creates the difficulty. If the purchasers' money had been used to pay all the premiums there would have been no mixture of value with that contributed by others. Their claim would have been to the whole of the proceeds of the policy. As it is, there are competing claims on the same fund. In the absence of any other basis for division in principle or on authority-and no other basis has been suggested-it must be divided between the competitors in such proportions as can be shown to be equitable. In my opinion the answer to the question as to what is equitable does not depend solely on the terms of the policy. The equities affecting each party must be examined. They must be balanced against each other. The conduct of the parties so far as this may be relevant, and the consequences to them of allowing and rejecting the purchasers' claim, must be analysed and weighed up. It may be helpful to refer to what would be done in other situations by way of analogy. But it seems to me that in the end a judgment requires to be made as to what is fair, just and reasonable.

. . .

I do not think that the purchasers can demonstrate on these facts that they have a proprietary right to a proportionate share of the proceeds. They cannot show that their money contributed to any extent to, or increased the value of, the amount paid to the trustees of the policy. A substantially greater sum was paid out by the insurers as death benefit than the total of the sums which they received by way of premium. A profit was made on the investment. But the terms of the policy show that the amount which produced this profit had been fixed from the outset when the first premium was paid. It was attributable to the rights obtained by the life assured when he paid the first premium from his own money. No part of that sum was attributable to value of the money taken from the purchasers to pay the additional premiums.

. . .

The situation here is quite different from that where the disputed sum is the product of an investment which was made with funds which have already been immixed. In the case of the lottery ticket which is purchased by A partly from his own funds and partly from funds of which B was the involuntary contributor, the funds are mixed together at the time when the ticket is purchased. It is easy to see that any prize won by that lottery ticket must be treated as the product of that mixed fund. In the case of the funds administered as an aggregate fund by the hospital, the funds from each of the two sources had been mixed together from an early date before the various transactions were entered into which increased the amount of the aggregate. It was consistent with justice and common sense to regard the whole of the increase as attributable in proportionate shares to the money taken from the two sources. But in this case the right to obtain payment of the whole amount of the death benefit of £1m had already been purchased from the insurers before they received payment of the premiums which were funded by the money misappropriated from the purchasers.

Of the other analogies which were suggested in the course of the argument to illustrate the extent of the equitable remedy, the closest to the circumstances of this case seemed to me to be those relating to the expenditure by a trustee of money held on trust on the improvement of his own property such as his dwelling house. This was the analogy discussed by Sir Richard Scott V.-C. and by Hobhouse L.J.[227] There is no doubt that an equitable right will be available to the beneficiaries to have back the money which was misappropriated for his own benefit by the trustee. But that right does not extend to giving them an equitable right to a pro rata share in the value of the house. If the value of the property is increased by the improvements which were paid for in whole or in part out of the money which the trustee misappropriated, he must account to the trust for the value of the improvements. This is by the application of the principle that a trustee must not be allowed to profit from his own breach of trust. But unless it can be demonstrated that he has obtained a profit as a result of the expenditure, his liability is to pay back the money which he has misapplied.

. . .

Notes and Questions

1. Do you agree with the majority or with the minority?

2. Lord Millett said, "This case does not depend on whether it is fair, just and reasonable to give the purchasers an interest as a result of which the court in its discretion provides a remedy. It is a case of hard-nosed property rights." Where did the property rights held by the plaintiffs in the insurance proceeds come from? Do you agree with Lord Browne-Wilkinson that "This case does not involve any question of resulting or constructive trusts"?

Do other kinds of rights have soft noses?

3. As Lord Browne-Wilkinson noted, the Court of Appeal looked at the case as if the policy belonged to Murphy, and the use of the misappropriated trust money was like an improvement or maintenance of his own property. That is, it was as if he owned a house, and he used trust property to paint it and pay the taxes. Because the policy was in part an investment vehicle, and in this way something like a bank account, Lord Browne-Wilkinson agreed that the "maintenance or improvement" analogy was inapt.

But should a plaintiff always be limited to a lien in the case of maintenance or improvement, even if a tracing exercise shows that the defendant still holds some value which represents the traceable proceeds of the plaintiff's money? Assume that a trustee holds a plot of land worth $50,000 and uses $50,000 of misappropriated trust money to

---

227 See *Foskett v. McKeown*, [1998] Ch. 265, 282, 289-90, [1997] 3 All E.R. 392, 408, 414-5.

build a house on it. The market rises so that the improved lot becomes worth $300,000. Are the beneficiaries confined to a lien securing repayment of $50,000, or can they claim 50% ownership?

Would it matter if the improver was not a wrongdoing trustee, but was rather an innocent donee who received trust money not knowing its source?[228]

4. One way of understanding the difference between the majority and the dissenters in *Foskett* is that the majority re-affirmed the traditional approach to tracing, which turns on "transactional" links between one asset and another, and not purely causal links. The dissenters would have rejected the plaintiff's claim because of the lack of a causal link between the misappropriated trust money and the £1 million. To see the difference, consider these examples. A trustee might misappropriate $1,000 of trust money and use it to pay the monthly rent on his apartment. This enables him to take $1,000 of his own money, which he would have used to pay the rent, and use it instead to buy an expensive watch. On the traditional approach, the watch is not the traceable product of the misappropriated money, even though it is causally connected. The trust money was simply dissipated. Conversely, assume that a trustee uses $1,000 of trust money in breach of trust to buy a watch. It is proven by evidence that he had enough money of his own to buy the watch, and that he would have used his own money had the trust money not been available. Here there is no causal link between the trust money and the watch, but on the traditional transactional approach, it is a traceable product of the trust money.

Many authors have argued for some years that rights of beneficiaries to traceable products are based on unjust enrichment.[229] But the law of unjust enrichment is not normally concerned with transactional links. It is concerned with the causal inquiry into whether the defendant acquired an enrichment which came, causally, from the plaintiff. This has led some authors to the conclusion that the tracing rules must be reformed along causal lines.[230] Other authors continue to argue that claims to traceable proceeds are based on unjust enrichment, although it seems with less awareness of the fact that this seems to require the abandonment of the traditional transactional approach.[231]

That approach can be understood historically as a function of the accountability of trustees. The accounting process was aimed at finding out exactly what the trustee had

---

228 See R. Chambers, "Resulting Trusts in Canada" (2000), 38 Alta. L. Rev. 378 at 404-407; contrast Smith, at 352-353.

229 Such claims were included in the *Restatement of the Law of Restitution: Quasi-Contracts and Constructive Trusts* (St. Paul: American Law Institute, 1937), §§202-215.

230 See D.A. Oesterle, "Deficiences of the Restitutionary Right to Trace" (1983), 68 Cornell L.R. 172; C. Rotherham, "The Metaphysics of Tracing: Substituted Title and Property Rhetoric" (1996), Osgoode Hall L.J. 321; S. Evans, "Rethinking Tracing and the Law of Restitution" (1999), 115 L.Q.R. 469. Quite apart from principle, the evidentiary issues raised by such an approach could be formidable: Smith, at 316-318.

231 A. Burrows, "Proprietary Restitution: Unmasking Unjust Enrichment" (2001), 117 L.Q.R. 412; P. Birks, "Tracing, Property, and Unjust Enrichment" (2002), 54 Current Legal Problems 231; R. Chambers, "Tracing and Unjust Enrichment" in J.W. Neyers, M. McInnes, & S. Pitel, eds., *Understanding Unjust Enrichment* (Oxford: Hart Publishing, 2004). Others, like the majority in *Foskett*, say that it is not unjust enrichment but property law: R. Grantham and C. Rickett, "Property and Unjust Enrichment," [1997] N.Z.L.R. 668 at 675-684; G. Virgo, "Restitution Through the Looking Glass" in J. Getzler, ed., *Rationalizing Property, Equity and Trusts* (London: Butterworths, 2003) 82. For an argument that both sides are partly right see L. Smith, "Unjust Enrichment, Property and the Structure of Trusts" (2000), 116 L.Q.R. 412.

done with the trust property.[232] Assume that the accounting showed that the trustee had spent $1,000 of trust money on an unauthorized expenditure such as a watch. The beneficiary could "surcharge" the account, that is, reject the expenditure and demand that the trustee replace the $1,000 (with a lien granted on the watch to secure that claim). Or, the beneficiary could adopt the transaction, requiring the trustee to hold the watch as a trust asset. If this is the basis of claims to traceable proceeds, the transactional nature of the tracing exercise is more obvious. It also explains the beneficiaries' ability to elect, not only between trust or lien, but between different possible traceable proceeds, as we will see in more detail below.

5. It is important to remember that the discussion in this section is confined to proprietary claims based on tracing. A trustee is generally liable, personally, to make good whatever loss was caused to the trust by a breach. The difficulty is often that the trustee is insolvent so that any personal claim will be unrecoverable. Here the proprietary claims based on tracing become crucial.

(iii) *The Supposed Need for a Fiduciary Relationship*

Equitable tracing is available not only to trust beneficiaries, but to the beneficiaries of all fiduciary relationships.[233] It was assumed for a long time that a fiduciary relationship was required before tracing was available. The relationship did not have to exist between the parties to the action; the supposed requirement was satisfied if it existed between one party and a stranger to the action. Thus, in *Sinclair v. Brougham*[234] the House of Lords arguably held[235] that the depositors in an *ultra vires* "bank" could trace into the general assets of the "bank" because there was a fiduciary relationship between them and the directors and the latter had mixed the depositors' funds with the "bank's" funds.[236] Similarly, in *Diplock v. Wintle* [237] the court held that a testator's next of kin could trace money improperly paid by the executors to charities into the charities' hands, because of the fiduciary relationship between the executors and the next of kin.[238] In this context Lord Greene M.R. said:[239]

> . . .equity may operate on the conscience not merely of those who acquire a legal title in breach of some trust, express or constructive, or of some other fiduciary obligation, but of volunteers provided that as a result of what has gone before some equitable proprietary interest has been created and attaches to the property in the hands of the volunteer.

---

232 See R. Chambers, "Liability" in P. Birks and A. Pretto, eds., *Breach of Trust* (Oxford: Hart Publishing, 2002), 1 at 16-20, 26-30.

233 *Hallett's Estate, Re, supra*, note 198, at 709, *per* Jessell M.R.; *Roblin v. Jackson* (1901), 13 Man. R. 328 (C.A.).

234 [1914] A.C. 398 (H.L.).

235 As explained in *Diplock v. Wintle, supra*, note 226, at 532 [Ch.].

236 *Sinclair v. Brougham* was overruled in part by *Westdeutsche Landesbank Girozentrale v. Islington London Borough Council, supra*, note 63. The House of Lords held in the latter case that it is not necessary to establish an equitable proprietary interest in the original asset in order to acquire an equitable proprietary interest in the traceable proceeds of the asset.

237 *Supra*, note 226. The case was affirmed on another issue at [1951] A.C. 251, [1950] 2 All E.R. 1137 (H.L.).

238 The case is set out later in this chapter.

239 *Supra*, note 226, at [1948] Ch. 530.

This seems to say that in order to have a proprietary trust claim to traceable proceeds, the claimant must have had a proprietary trust claim in the initial asset. That seems like a sensible proposition, and is discussed in the next section. But *Diplock v. Wintle* has been widely understood to require a fiduciary relationship before the tracing process could be conducted. It may be questioned whether this is correct. In the first place, it is sometimes difficult to define what a fiduciary is. Second, and perhaps because of that, the courts appear to be anxious to find such a relationship in order to permit tracing.

Chase Manhattan Bank N.A. v. Israel-British Bank (London) Ltd.[240] is a good example of the court's willingness to find a fiduciary relationship. An Italian bank instructed Chase Manhattan to pay approximately $2,000,000 to Mellon Bank International to the credit of the Israel-British Bank. By mistake of Chase's employees, the payment was made twice. Israel-British then became insolvent and Chase brought action for an order allowing it to trace the second payment into the assets of Israel-British. Goulding J. allowed the claim. His Lordship followed *Sinclair v. Brougham*[241] as interpreted by *Diplock v. Wintle*,[242] but concluded that it was enough that the required fiduciary relationship arose at the time of the mistaken payment. In effect, Goulding J. allowed a tracing claim because the plaintiff was entitled to restitution, but he thought he was obliged by precedent to "find" a fiduciary relationship. In doing so, it is submitted, he stretched the fiduciary concept beyond recognition.

Similarly in *Goodbody v. Bank of Montreal*[243] the plaintiff was allowed to trace the proceeds of stolen share warrants. The defendant, Lester, had received the warrants with knowledge that they were stolen and had deposited them in his account with the Bank of Montreal. On the fiduciary relationship requirement, Lacourcière J. said:[244]

> On the authority of *Sinclair v. Brougham*[245] the Court will establish a fiduciary relationship to enable the plaintiffs to follow their property in equity into Lester's bank account. I find that the cases referred to provide a full answer to the defendant's argument, based on *Diplock v. Wintle*,[246] that an equitable tracing remedy is not available in the absence of a fiduciary relationship.

In *British Columbia Teachers' Credit Union v. Betterly*[247] the requirement was not even mentioned. An employee of the plaintiff had stolen approximately

---

240 (1979), [1981] Ch. 105, [1979] 3 All E.R. 1025 (Ch. Div.); applied in *Yorkshire Trust Co. v. Empire Acceptance Corp.* (1983), 44 B.C.L.R. 334, 13 E.T.R. 189, 1983 CarswellBC 109 (S.C.).
241 *Supra*, note 234.
242 *Supra*, note 226.
243 (1974), 4 O.R. (2d) 147, 47 D.L.R. (3d) 335, 1974 CarswellOnt 308 (H.C.).
244 *Ibid.*, at 339.
245 *Supra*, note 234.
246 *Supra*, note 226.
247 (1975), 61 D.L.R. (3d) 755, 1975 CarswellBC 318 (S.C.). To the same effect are *Simpsons-Sears Ltd. v. Fraser* (1974), 7 O.R. (2d) 61, 54 D.L.R. (3d) 225, 1974 CarswellOnt 405 (H.C.) and *Lennox Industries (Canada) Ltd. v. R.*, 87 D.T.C. 5041, 1987 CarswellNat 337, 1987 CarswellNat 862, [1987] 1 C.T.C. 171, 34 D.L.R. (4th) 297, 29 C.R.R. 175, [1987] 3 F.C. 338, 8 F.T.R. 124 (T.D.).

$200,000 of its funds and had used $45,000 to purchase a house in the name of the defendant, a woman with whom he lived. She was unaware of the theft. The court simply noted that the employee became a constructive trustee for the plaintiff when he stole the money and held that the plaintiff could trace the $45,000 into the house and was entitled to a lien on it.

It has been pointed out that the "fiduciary relationship" recognized in the *Chase Manhattan* case[248] is really only a pseudonym for a situation in which restitution ought to be granted to prevent unjust enrichment.[249] Since the latter has been recognized as an independent head of obligation in Canada[250] it ought no longer to be necessary in Canada to invent a fiduciary relationship in order to allow tracing.

Nonetheless, it is arguable that in England the requirement of a pre-existing fiduciary relationship remains in effect before the plaintiff can trace. In *Agip (Africa) Ltd. v. Jackson*[251] the Court of Appeal said, "It is, however, a prerequisite to the operation of the remedy in equity that there must be a fiduciary relationship which calls the equitable jurisdiction into being."[252] On the other hand, in *Westdeutsche Landesbank Girozentrale v. Islington London Borough Council*,[253] Lord Browne-Wilkinson pointedly noted that stolen moneys are traceable in equity. And in *Foskett v. McKeown*, although there was clearly a fiduciary relationship, two of the five judges (including Lord Millett, whose speech is extracted above) indicated that the requirement should be dropped.

The issue awaits further clarification.[254] However, Lionel Smith has shown convincingly, both in principle and authority, that a fiduciary relationship is not required to permit a plaintiff to trace.[255]

(iv) *The Need for an Equitable Proprietary Interest*

In order to be able to establish a proprietary interest in traceable proceeds, the plaintiff must have a pre-existing equitable proprietary interest. This may exist under a constructive or resulting trust. In *Buyers v. Buyers*,[256] the court found a resulting trust in favour of the plaintiff wife. Thus, she had a proprietary interest in certain property which enabled her to trace the trust property into its proceeds

---

248 *Supra*, note 240.

249 Waters, p. 1045.

250 In *Becker v. Pettkus*, [1980] 2 S.C.R. 834, 117 D.L.R. (3d) 257, 1980 CarswellOnt 299, 1980 CarswellOnt 644, 34 N.R. 384, 8 E.T.R. 143, 19 R.F.L. (2d) 165.

251 [1991] Ch. 547 (C.A.).

252 *Ibid.*, at 566. To the same effect are *Goldcorp Exchange Ltd., Re*, [1995] 1 A.C. 74 (P.C.); and *Lipkin Gorman v. Karpnale Ltd.* (1991), [1992] 4 All E.R. 512, [1991] 2 A.C. 548, [1991] 3 W.L.R. 10 (H.L.), at 522 [All E.R.], *per* Lord Templeman. And see *Andrabell Ltd., Re*, [1984] 3 All E.R. 407; *Hendy Lennox (Industrial Engines) Ltd. v. Grahame Puttick Ltd.*, [1984] 1 W.L.R. 485.

253 *Supra*, note 63, at 716 [AC].

254 See Peter Birks, "Trusts Raised to Reverse Unjust Enrichment: The *Westdeutsche* Case" (1996), 4 Rest. L. Rev. 3.

255 Smith, 120ff., 340ff.

256 (1976), 28 R.F.L. 65, 1976 CarswellOnt 184 (H.C.).

in her husband's hands. In *Chase Manhattan*,[257] the court found that the plaintiff had an equitable proprietary interest under a resulting or constructive trust.

In *B.C. Teachers Credit Union v. Betterly*,[258] an employer was held always to have had an equitable interest in funds stolen by an employee, thus permitting it to trace and to claim a trust over the proceeds. Of course, a thief does not obtain any title to stolen goods. The complete title remains with the owner, and so the owner does not have an *equitable* interest under a trust. However, the owner clearly has a (legal) proprietary interest and this seems a good enough reason to allow a trust over the proceeds (in which the original owner will not have a legal interest).

A proprietary interest does not always exist. For example, if a person is not required to keep money collected for another person separate from his or her own, the first person is generally merely a debtor of the second person and the latter has no interest in the property.[259] If the first person is required to keep the money separate, he or she is more likely a trustee. The second person then has an equitable interest in the property. This is a question of fact to be resolved in each case.[260]

Notes and Questions

1. A was employed by B Ltd. as department manager and, while so employed, stole approximately $39,000. He spent part of this money to buy a house, title to which was taken in the names of A and his wife, W. They then conveyed it to A Ltd., a company incorporated by A. B Ltd. brought action against A, W, and A Ltd., seeking to trace the moneys into the house.

What result?[261]

2. *Christie Grant Ltd., Re*[262] involved a situation in which the moneys ought to have been segregated. Christie-Grant Ltd., now bankrupt, operated a mail order business. Some-

257 *Supra*, note 240, at 119 [Ch.], 1032 [All E.R.], discussed above. See also *Attorney-General for Hong Kong v. Reid* (1993), [1994] 1 All E.R. 1, [1994] 1 A.C. 324 (New Zealand P.C.).

258 *British Columbia Teachers' Credit Union v. Betterly* (1975), 61 D.L.R. (3d) 755, 1975 CarswellBC 318 (S.C.), discussed above. As also noted in the previous section, Lord Browne-Wilkinson in *Westdeutsche* expressed the view that the victim of a thief could trace his property and claim the proceeds.

259 Even here, however, a trust may be found, as in *Air Canada v. M & L Travel Ltd.*, [1993] 3 S.C.R. 787, 108 D.L.R. (4th) 592, 1993 CarswellOnt 568, 1993 CarswellOnt 994, 50 E.T.R. 225, 67 O.A.C. 1, 159 N.R. 1, 15 O.R. (3d) 804 (note), extracted on this point in Section 5 of Chapter 2.

260 The classical case, *Henry v. Hammond*, [1913] 2 K.B. 515 (Eng. K.B.), is still referred to today: *Box v. Barclays Bank plc*, [1998] Lloyd's Rep. Banking 185, discussed L. Smith (1999), 14 Banking and Finance Law Review 613.

261 See *Simpsons-Sears Ltd. v. Fraser*, *supra*, note 247.

262 (1922), [1922] 3 W.W.R. 1161, [1923] 1 D.L.R. 505, 1922 CarswellMan 8, 3 C.B.R. 361, 32 Man. R. 375 (C.A.). See also *Century 21 Brenmore Real Estate Ltd., Re* (1980), 28 O.R. (2d) 653, 33 C.B.R. (N.S.) 170, 111 D.L.R. (3d) 280, 1980 CarswellOnt 126, 6 E.T.R. 205 (C.A.), in which real estate commissions could be paid to selling brokers out of the bankrupt realtor's trust account or its general account, so that no trust was created, because there was no duty to keep the money separate. See *contra Manitoba (Securities Commission) v. Showcase Realty Ltd.* (1978), 28 C.B.R. (N.S.) 24, 84 D.L.R. (3d) 518, 1978 CarswellMan 8 (Q.B.), varied (sub nom. *Manitoba (Securities Commission) v. Imperial Bank of Commerce*) 30 C.B.R. (N.S.) 80,

times it had to refund money to customers. The plaintiff company's business including issuing money orders. The plaintiff engaged the bankrupt as its agent to issue money orders, when the bankrupt needed to make a refund to a customer. Under the agency agreement, Christie-Grant would issue money orders in the name of the plaintiff company as required, and it promised that it would set aside, keep separate and hold in trust equivalent sums of money for the plaintiff company in respect of each money order that was issued. When Christie-Grant became bankrupt, it was discovered that it had failed to allocate money to the plaintiff company. The court held that, since the moneys had not been allocated, the plaintiff did not have an equitable proprietary interest in the money. Hence, it had no proprietary interest and ranked with Christie-Grant's general creditors.

The court's view was that although the bankrupt company had promised to constitute trusts in favour of the plaintiff from time to time, it never fulfilled those promises. A breach of a promise to create a trust may create a debt obligation, but since the trust was never set up, there is no breach of trust, nor is there any possibility of a proprietary claim. It is also true that sometimes, on the basis that "equity treats that as done which ought to be done," a promise to create a trust will be fulfilled by operation of law and turned into a perfected trust (see Section 8 of Chapter 4). In particular, this will occur when the promise was specifically enforceable, or where the promisee has given the promisor the full value promised in return for the creation of the trust. Even this principle, however, cannot operate unless the promise to create a trust relates to unequivocally certain property. It therefore cannot apply if the promisor has freedom of choice as to which property to settle in trust; that includes the case of a promise to settle a sum of money in trust.[263]

3. It is interesting to note that in *Diplock v. Wintle*[264] the next of kin were regarded as having an equitable proprietary interest sufficient to permit tracing, even though a beneficiary under an unadministered estate is not normally regarded as having such an interest.[265]

(d) Mixed Trust Property

(i) *Generally*

If a trustee mixes trust property with her or his own, or with those of other trusts, or with her or his own and those of other trusts, the rules are more complex. The usual case involves trust money which is mixed in a bank account with non-trust money, or with money of another trust. Mixtures by non-wrongdoers are treated differently.

(sub nom. *Showcase Realty Ltd., Re*) 96 D.L.R. (3d) 58, 1979 CarswellMan 14, [1979] 2 W.W.R. 526 (C.A.), varied [1979] 6 W.W.R. 464, (sub nom. *Showcase Realty (No. 2), Re*) 106 D.L.R. (3d) 679, 1979 CarswellMan 114 (C.A.), in which the court found that the commission had to be paid out of the trust account.

263 For a similar English case, see *Mac-Jordan Construction Ltd. v. Brookmount Erostin Ltd. (in receivership)*, [1992] B.C.L.C. 350 (C.A.).

264 *Supra*, note 226, discussed above.

265 *Commissioner of Stamp Duties (Queensland) v. Livingston* (1964), [1965] A.C. 694, 3 All E.R. 692 (Australia P.C.). For some discussion of this point see L. Smith, "Unjust Enrichment, Property and the Structure of Trusts" (2000), 116 L.Q.R. 412, 438.

Further Reading

D.A. McConville, "Tracing and the Rule in Clayton's Case" (1963), 70 L.Q. Rev. 388.

Lionel D. Smith, *The Law of Tracing* (Oxford: Clarendon Press, 1997), ch. 5.

(ii) *Wrongful Mixing*

The first case is where trust property is mixed with money belonging to another, and the other is a wrongdoer (usually a trustee in breach of trust). For example, $1,000 of trust money is used in breach of trust, along with $1,000 of the trustee's own money, to buy a painting. As shown in *Foskett v. McKeown*, the beneficiaries have two options. They may trace into the proceeds (the painting) and obtain an equitable lien over the whole asset (or over any further traceable proceeds) to secure their personal claim in breach of trust; or they may adopt the trustees' conduct and claim a proportionate share of the mixed fund as equitable tenant in common with the trustees. They would choose the former if the value of the property has decreased and the latter if it has increased. When a lien is claimed, the onus is on the trustees to prove what part of the mixed fund, if any, was theirs and the beneficiary is entitled to every part of the fund which the trustees cannot prove to be their own.[266] This is based on the principle that when a person wrongfully creates an evidentiary difficulty, it is resolved against him. This principle can be understood as the basis of all the tracing rules regarding mixtures of value.

Of course, it is also true that a trustee is liable to disgorge any gain acquired in breach of trust; and the gain, indeed, may be held on constructive trust. This remedy is conceptually distinct from claims based on tracing. The liability to disgorge depends on wrongdoing, and does not require tracing through substitutions which begin with some trust property. The same facts may sometimes disclose both theories of liability, as in the Australian case, *Scott v. Scott*.[267] A testatrix left all her property to her executors (of whom her husband was one) upon trust for her husband for life, with remainder to her children. The main asset was the family home, worth £1400 at the time of her death. The husband sold it with the consent of all the beneficiaries (although several of them were minors) and used £1014 of the proceeds to buy another house worth £1700, title to which he took in his own name because he was advised that the trust could not invest in real estate. The second house increased in value to £5450 by the time of the husband's death. The children brought action against their father's second wife, who was his executrix and sole beneficiary, for an order declaring that the defendant held the property in trust for their mother's estate and for an order directing her to transfer it. The children also sought a proportionate share of the increase

---

266 *Lupton v. White, supra*, note 217; *Oatway, Re*, (sub nom. *Hertslet v. Oatway*) [1903] 2 Ch. 356 (Eng. Ch. Div.); *Brighouse v. Morton*, [1929] S.C.R. 512, [1929] 3 D.L.R. 91, 1929 CarswellBC 111; *Norman, Re* (1951), [1951] O.R. 752, [1952] 1 D.L.R. 174, 1951 CarswellOnt 81 (C.A.).

267 *Supra*, note 155.

in value (1014/1700 x £5,450) and were successful at trial. On appeal, the High Court agreed that the children were entitled to an accounting of the increase in value as a profit. This rendered it unnecessary to deal with the claim based on tracing, but the court opined in *dicta* that that claim could be maintained on the facts.

(iii) *Wrongful Mixing (Bank Account)*

A. Introduction. Most claims against trustees involve the mixing of trust money with the trustee's own money in a bank account. In that situation the beneficiary has the same two options as just discussed. The rules are specialized and are described here separately, but they are based on the same principles, that evidentiary difficulties are resolved against the one who wrongfully created them. In respect of moneys in a bank account, it is not necessary to claim a proportionate share, since the moneys can be divided quite easily.[268]

B. The Rule in Hallett's Case. The leading case in this context is *Hallett's Estate, Re.*[269] Hallett, a solicitor, obtained control of the investments of his own marriage settlement, of which he was life tenant, from the trustees. He also acted for a Mrs. Cotterill. She was in the habit of giving him money for investment and securities for safekeeping. Without the authority of the trustees or Mrs. Cotterill, he sold securities belonging to the marriage settlement and Mrs. Cotterill and deposited the proceeds into his own bank account, which already held about £1796 of his own money. Approximately £341, being the proceeds of sale of some of Mrs. Cotterill's bonds, were deposited on Nov. 3, 1877. On Nov. 14, 1877, he deposited approximately £770 and £1804 into the account, respectively the proceeds of sale of bonds belonging to the marriage settlement and Mrs. Cotterill. Thereafter, he made payments into and withdrawals from the account. At one time the balance fell as low as approximately £1708, but Hallett paid in further sums, so that on his death, the balance was approximately £3029. Of that amount £2600 had been paid into court to the credit of an action for the administration of his estate, he having died a bankrupt. The trustees of the marriage settlement applied for payment of the £770 out of the £2600 and Mrs. Cotterill applied for payment of £1708, the lowest intermediate balance in the account, as noted above.

It was argued on behalf of the unsecured creditors (whose position would be diminished by any successful trust claim) that Mrs. Cotterill's claim was without merit, since Hallett was not an express trustee towards her. However, the court held that her claim was valid because Hallett stood in a fiduciary relationship towards her. As we noted above, fiduciary relationships are less important in this

---

268 Ford and Lee, §17200. If the trustee purchases assets from the mixed account, the beneficiaries can have a lien on the purchased assets (*Saskatchewan General Trusts Corp., Re*, [1938] 2 W.W.R. 375, [1938] 3 D.L.R. 544, 1938 CarswellSask 3, 19 C.B.R. 269 (C.A.)), or claim a proportionate share.

269 *Supra*, note 198.

context than proprietary rights. The crucial point, as noted by Thesiger L.J., was that the relationship between Mrs. Cotterrill and Hallett was not creditor-debtor. She deposited assets with him, but remained the legal owner. Hence she retained a proprietary interest which would support a trust claim over traceable proceeds.

The next question concerned the payments out of the bank account by Hallett. To whom did these moneys belong, Hallett, or Mrs. Cotterill and the marriage settlement? It was argued for the creditors and held at trial that the rule in *Clayton's Case, Re*[270] should apply. Remember that a bank account is only a debt, which (if the account is in credit) is owed by the bank to the customer. The rule views a current bank account as a series of distinct debts.[271] As the account is operated, deposits create new debts; withdrawals discharge debts, or parts of debts, but starting with the oldest debts first. It is sometimes called "first in, first out." The rule is supposed to depend on the intention of the banker and customer.

Assume that Hallett paid £100 of trust money into a new account, and then paid £200 of his own money, making a balance of £300, and then he withdrew £120 and dissipated it before going bankrupt with a balance of £180. The rule in *Clayton's Case, Re* would say that when the balance was £300, there was debt of £100 created by the first deposit, and then another debt of £200 created later by the other deposit. The withdrawal of £120, under the rule, discharges all of the £100 debt, and £20 of the £200 debt. So the remaining balance of £180 would include no money which traceably came from the trust funds. There was earlier authority holding that this rule should be used to resolve such problems on the bankruptcy of a trustee.[272] If this rule had been applied, the proceeds of the trust money and of Mrs. Cotterill's money would have been dissipated in Hallett's withdrawals.

Jessel M.R. noted the principle of law that where a person does an act which may legally be done, he or she will not later be allowed to say that it was done wrongfully.[273] His Lordship continued:[274]

> When we come to apply that principle to the case of a trustee who has blended trust moneys with his own, it seems to me perfectly plain that he cannot be heard to say that he took away the trust money when he had a right to take away his own money. The simplest case put is the mingling of trust moneys in a bag with money of the trustee's own. Suppose he has a hundred sovereigns in a bag, and he adds to them another hundred sovereigns of his own, so that they are commingled in such a way that they cannot be distinguished, and the next day he draws out for his own purposes £100, is it tolerable for anybody to allege that what he drew out was the first £100, the trust money, and that he misappropriated it, and left his own £100 in the bag? It is obvious he must have taken away that which he had a right to take away, his own £100. What difference does it make if, instead of being in a bag, he deposits it with his banker, and then pays in other

270 (1816), 1 Mer. 572, 35 E.R. 781, [1814-23] All E.R. Rep. 1 (Ch. Div.). Indeed, Mrs. Cotterill's claim appears to have been made with that rule in mind.

271 Most bank accounts today are current accounts. This means that the depositor may withdraw funds at any time, without giving notice. There are some savings accounts where notice must be given (and usually a higher interest rate is paid).

272 *Pennell v. Deffell* (1853), 4 De G.M. & G. 372, 43 E.R. 551, 1 Eq. Rep. 579, 1 W.R. 499, 18 Jur. 273 (C.A. [In Chambers]).

273 *Hallett, supra*, note 198, at 727-8.

274 *Ibid.*

money of his own, and draws out some money for his own purposes? Could he say that he had actually drawn out anything but his own money? His money was there, and he had a right to draw it out, and why should the natural act of simply drawing out the money be attributed to anything except to his ownership of money which was at his bankers.

He held that that rule does not apply when the claim is against the trustee:[275]

No human being ever gave credit to a man on the theory that he would misappropriate trust money, and thereby increase his assets. No human being ever gave credit, even beyond that theory, that he should not only misappropriate trust moneys to increase his assets, but that he should pay the trust moneys so misappropriated to his own banking account with his own moneys, and draw out after that a larger sum than the first sums paid in for the trust moneys.

In the end result, there was sufficient money in the account to satisfy the claims of the marriage settlement and of Mrs. Cotterill and Hallett's creditors took what was left.

Remember that even if tracing had been impossible (say, the bank account was empty) Mrs. Cotterill and the trustees of the marriage settlement would have personal claims against Hallett's estate. They would be unsecured creditors, sharing *pro rata* with the other unsecured creditors in whatever assets were available. You can see that any time a proprietary claim is successful in an insolvency, its success further diminishes the recovery available to unsecured creditors. They are generally non-wrongdoers, and in many cases may be involuntary creditors (e.g. victims of torts or breaches of trust which did not yield traceable proceeds).

C. The Principle in Oatway, Re. There were at least two ways to understand *Hallett*. One was that the "trustee always spends his own money first." The other was that every presumption is made against a wrongdoer, so that it is up to the trust beneficiaries to decide, after all the facts are known, whether the trustee spent his own money or trust money in a particular case. This can be understood to flow from the idea of accountability. The difference between the two approaches was soon resolved. Assume that a trustee withdraws money from the account, but retains a sufficient amount in it to satisfy the trust. The withdrawn money is used to buy some valuable asset. Later, the remaining money is dissipated and the trustee becomes bankrupt. Under the first interpretation of *Hallett*, the withdrawn money (and its surviving product) would be presumed to be the trustee's own, and the trust money would be seen as dissipated. The point was resolved in *Oatway, Re*.[276] A solicitor-trustee paid £3000 of trust moneys into his own account which already contained £4000. He then withdrew approximately £2100 to pay for shares which he purchased in his own name. Thereafter he used the balance in the account for his own purposes and died. The shares were then sold for £2474 and the trust claimed to be able to trace the trust fund into that

---

275 *Ibid.*, at 730. Baggallay L.J. concurred, but Thesiger L.J. dissented on this point., feeling bound by *Pennell v. Deffell*. See to the same effect *British Canadian Securities Ltd. v. Martin*, [1917] 1 W.W.R. 1313, 27 Man. R. 423, 1917 CarswellMan 7 (K.B.).

276 *Supra*, note 266.

sum. The claim was allowed on the ground that the solicitor's estate could not argue that the investment was purchased with the solicitor's own money, while the moneys which were spent (and, therefore, could no longer be traced) were trust moneys.[277]

Hallett and *Oatway* can be reconciled on the principle that every presumption is made against a wrongful mixer. It is up to the beneficiaries to decide, after the fact, whether it was their money or the trustee's own money which was withdrawn in any particular case.

It would seem to follow from *Oatway, Re* that, if the investments made by the trustee increase in value, the beneficiaries are entitled to the amount of the trust moneys and the increase in value attributed thereto. In other words, they would not be restricted to the uninvested portion (if any) and the balance of the investment. If however, the trustee invests an amount equal to the trust funds in authorized trust investments, it is likely to be presumed that he or she intended to repair the breach of trust. In that case the beneficiaries can only look to those investments and not to others which may have become more valuable.[278]

Many of the cases and commentary upon them talk about fictions and presumptions. The trustee is fictitiously presumed to act honestly. Professor Scott said:[279]

> All this elaborate reasoning in not only fictitious but unnecessary. There is no reason why the claimant should not assert his lien on any part of the fund which he can trace, regardless of the intention of the wrongdoer, regardless of his honesty or dishonesty. There is no reason to presume that the wrongdoer has become honest, but there is no reason why he or his general creditors should profit by his continued dishonesty.

As noted above, the cases can be understood as resolving evidentiary difficulties, or impossibilities, against one who wrongly created them. This also helps us to understand the lowest intermediate balance rule, discussed next.

D. The Lowest Intermediate Balance Principle. The result in *Hallett* is not objectionable, but it can favour the creditors in certain situations. Suppose that a trustee mixes his or her own and trust moneys in a bank account. The following deposits and withdrawals are made by the trustee:

---

277 See also *Major Trust Co., Re* (1972), 3 Nfld. & P.E.I.R. 605, 33 D.L.R. (3d) 481, 1972 CarswellPEI 46 (S.C.).

278 See Ford and Lee §§17200 (*Purchase of profitable investment from mixed fund; Repair of breach*). Note however that a breach of trust creates a debt, and a repair of a breach is therefore a payment of a debt by settling property in a *new* trust. The new trust property is not a traceable product of the original. And the transaction may be liable to be set aside as preferring one creditor ahead of others, hence conflicting with the bankruptcy policy that all creditors (even breach of trust creditors) are to be treated equally. Much will depend on the details of the governing legislation on preferences. See Smith, 203.

279 Scott §517.1.

Date	Deposits of Trustee's Own Money	Deposits of Trust Money	Withdrawals	Balance
1	$100			$100
2		$400		500
3			$450	50
4	200			250

The trustee becomes bankrupt after day 4. The $450 withdrawal made on day 3 is assumed to be dissipated.[280] Can the beneficiaries trace their $400 contribution into the $250 standing to the credit of the account on day 4, or at least can they say that all of the remaining $250 is traceably theirs? The answer is that they cannot. They are limited to the lowest intermediate balance in the account between the date the mixing occurred and when they made their claim. That is day 3, when only $50 remained in the account. The beneficiaries can assert that $50, but no more, of trust money survives in the $250 balance on day 4.

If the cases are understood as based on fictitious presumptions, this rule is hard to understand. Why can we not presume that the trustee, on day 4, was replenishing the trust fund? But the better understanding of the cases is that they are based on resolving evidentiary difficulties or impossibilities against the one who wrongfully created them. Here, as to $50 of trust money, there is an evidentiary impossibility. It is possible that it was withdrawn on day 3, or that it remained. This is resolved against the wrongdoer (if the beneficiaries so desire), and the conclusion is that it remained in the account. But as to any greater sum, there is no evidentiary difficulty. The balance on day 3 was $50. As a proven fact, it is impossible that more than $50 of trust money went into the final $250 balance. We can resolve evidentiary difficulties against wrongdoers, but we cannot make findings that are contrary to proven facts. That would be going too far against the interests of the wrongdoer's unsecured creditors.

The lowest intermediate balance rule essentially says that a person cannot get out of a mixture more than he contributed to it. On the facts in the table above, it is impossible that more than $50 of trust money were contributed to the final balance of $250.[281] In *James Roscoe (Bolton) Ltd. v. Winder*[282] Sargant J. did say that, if it can be shown that the defendant intended to repay the trust when he or she replenished the account, the plaintiff can succeed in the tracing action. Moreover, his Lordship stated that if the account was a separate trust account, such an

---

280 If it had traceable proceeds, they could be claimed by the trust beneficiaries. At the highest, the beneficiaries could say that the proceeds were theirs as to 400/450 or an 8/9 share. If the proceeds of this withdrawal had gone down in value, and the beneficiaries wished to say that $50 of the trust money remained always in the bank account, they could additionally say that the proceeds of the day 3 withdrawal were theirs as to a 350/450 or a 7/9 share or assert a lien to secure repayment of $350.

281 *James Roscoe (Bolton) Ltd. v. Winder* (1914), [1915] 1 Ch. 62 (Ch. Div.) at 68-9, *per* Sargant J; see also *Norman, Re, supra*, note 266, and further citations in Smith, at 201.

282 *Ibid.*

intention could be presumed. This, however, must be understood as a presumption which assists in a true finding of fact as to the trustee's intention. A conclusive or irrebuttable presumption, which is a kind of legal fiction, would be inconsistent with the lowest intermediate balance rule, which has been accepted by courts all over the common law world. There is a further issue about voluntary replenishment. If the defendant is, or becomes as a result of the repayment, insolvent, the repayment is a voluntary settlement, which is voidable under the *Bankruptcy and Insolvency Act*.[283]

In *Bishopsgate Investment Management Ltd. v. Homan*[284] the English Court of Appeal reaffirmed the lowest intermediate balance principle. Moneys held by a trustee of certain pension plans were improperly transferred to bank accounts of companies in the communications empire of Robert Maxwell. When Maxwell died it was discovered that the main company was insolvent and the court appointed administrators for its liquidation. The liquidators of the trustee corporation sought to prevent the administrators from making an interim distribution to creditors. They claimed to be entitled to an equitable lien over all the insolvent company's assets. The Court of Appeal rejected the claim because of the lowest intermediate balance rule. Since the accounts into which the moneys were paid were overdrawn or later became overdrawn, the trustee could not point to any assets that belonged to it.[285]

The rule does not apply, as already mentioned, when the wrongdoer makes a payment back into the account with the intention of reimbursing the claimant. That is because the rule stops the beneficiary from asserting that the trust money remained, all along, in the account; but if the argument is that there was a reimbursement, then the beneficiary is not making such an assertion at all. It also does not apply if the moneys can be traced out of the account and then back into it, regardless of the wrongdoer's intention. So, referring back to the hypothetical facts shown in the table above, assume that it was proven that the trustee took the $450 withdrawal on day 3 and put it in his pocket in cash, and then lost $250 gambling, but then the $200 deposit on day 4 was in fact the remainder of that cash withdrawal. On those facts, the beneficiaries could say that the balance of $250 was all traceably theirs. Again, the rule stops them from saying that their money stayed, all along, in the account; but on these facts, they do not need to make such an argument, and it is no longer true (as it was in the original hypothetical) that the $200 deposit on day 4 is the trustee's own money.

---

283 R.S.C. 1985, c. B-3, s. 60, as amended; there is also provincial legislation on voidable preferences. *Cf.* Ford and Lee, §17200 (*Lowest intermediate balance*), and Smith, 203. See also *Horsman Brothers Holdings Ltd. v. Panton*, [1976] 3 W.W.R. 745, 1976 CarswellBC 163 (S.C.); *1653 Investments Ltd., Re* (1981), 129 D.L.R. (3d) 582, 1981 CarswellBC 738 (S.C.), at 597-9 [D.L.R.].

284 [1994] 3 W.L.R. 1270 (C.A.), leave to appeal refused [1995] 1 W.L.R. 31. See Lionel D. Smith, "Tracing — 'Swollen assets' — Lowest intermediate balance" (1995), 14 E. & T.L.J. 298, for a comment on the case.

285 See also *Goldcorp Exchange Ltd. (in Receivership), Re, supra*, note 252 to the same effect.

(iv) *Non-Wrongful Mixing*

A. Introduction. All of the principles discussed so far are explicable on the basis of subordinating the interests of a wrongdoer, where his wrongdoing created an evidentiary difficulty. As between innocent parties, those principles cannot apply. As Lord Millett said in *Foskett v. McKeown*, innocent parties must be treated equally.[286]

This situation can arise in different ways. A trustee may wrongfully mix funds from two different trusts. A trustee who has more than one trust under his or her control may not generally mix the trust funds, and to do so is a breach of trust. Here there is wrongful mixing, but neither of the contributors to the mixture has done anything wrong. The principles discussed above are based on the fact that the wrongful mixer was also a contributor. Alternatively, the mixing by the trustee may not be wrongful. It is normal, for example, for a lawyer to combine money which belongs beneficially to many different clients in a single trust account. So mixing may be authorized by the terms of the trust, or in some cases by statute.[287] In such a case, if there was some later breach of trust with misappropriation of funds, the principles in this section would apply. Finally, a person may innocently mix trust money with his own money, as in the case of an innocent donee of trust property. Here the person does not even know that he or she is a trustee.

The distinction affects the rules for tracing into and through mixtures. It may also affect the remedies available. In the United States, if the defendant is not a conscious wrongdoer, but an innocent volunteer, the plaintiff can only obtain an equitable lien and not a beneficial share of the proceeds of a mixture.[288] This approach appears to have been accepted in *Re Tilley's Will Trusts, Burgin v. Croad*.[289] The testator's executrix, his widow, paid part of the estate moneys into her own account and used the account to invest in real estate. She also used her bank's overdraft privileges for this purpose and was very successful in her investments. At no time did the account fall below the amount of the trust money, so it would have been possible to understand the widow as having used only her own money. When she died, those entitled to the remainder interest under the testator's will claimed a share in the real estate acquired by the executrix. She did commit a breach of her fiduciary duties by mixing the estate money with her own, and if the principle of *Oatway, Re* had applied, they would have succeeded. Ungoed-Thomas J. noted that they had the right to make such a claim, but he held that the trust moneys were not used in the investments, but were used only to

---

286 Although as *Foskett* itself illustrates, where innocent parties claim through a wrongdoer, any mixing done by the wrongdoer will be governed by the principles for wrongdoers. The same point is illustrated by the fact that the unsecured creditors of someone like Hallett or Oatway are not themselves wrongdoers. See Smith, 205ff.

287 For example, registered provincial trust corporations and other registered trust corporations that have the capacity to do so, are permitted to operate common trust funds in which moneys belonging to various trusts, estates or participants are combined for the purpose of investment: *Loan and Trust Corporations Act*, R.S.O. 1990, c. L.25, s. 173.

288 Scott, §§516, 517.3.

289 *Supra*, note 213.

reduce the executrix's overdraft, the real source of the investments. Accordingly, the beneficiaries were only able to claim the trust moneys with interest. The case is somewhat controversial.[290] It seems on one hand to adopt a causal rather than a transactional view of tracing, which is now discredited after *Foskett*, in order to say that the property was not bought with trust money; but the willingness to impose a lien on the property is only consistent with the idea that tracing was in fact possible. It may be best understood as adopting the U.S. view, that only a lien is available against a non-wrongdoing mixer. However, in *Foskett*, Lord Millett observed in *obiter* that a lien should *not* be available against a non-wrongdoing mixer in the case where it is usually sought against a wrongdoer: that is, where the property has gone down in value. The reason is that the lien would have the effect of shifting part of the loss onto the other contributor, which is inconsistent with the idea that they must be treated equally. The implication was that the claim to a beneficial interest proportionate to the plaintiff's contribution should be available, even against a non-wrongdoer. This is consistent with the normal principles of resulting trusts. Lord Millett did say, "It is not necessary to consider whether there are any circumstances in which the beneficiary is confined to a lien in cases where the fund is more than sufficient to repay the contributions of all parties." That may have been a reference to *Burgin v. Croad*.

B. *The Rule in Clayton's Case, Re*. It was noted above that the rule in *Clayton's Case, Re*[291] was once applied to deposits of trust money by a trustee into his own bank account. This was overruled in *Hallett, Re*, but the case did not overrule the application of the rule in *Clayton's Case, Re* to the situation where a trustee mixes the funds of two or more trusts in an unbroken, active, continuing, or current bank account.

An example will illustrate the operation of the rule as it would apply to mixing of money from more than one trust. The assumption is that all money is being deposited into a single bank account.

Date	Deposits of funds held on Trust A	Deposits of funds held on Trust B	Deposits of funds held on Trust C	Withdraw-als (dissi-pated)	Balance
1	$100				$100
2		$500			$600
3			$300		$900
4				$400	$500

If *Clayton's Case, Re* was applied to the above example, the $400 withdrawal would be applied to the $100 belonging to Trust A, and to $300 of Trust B. The

290 See D. Hayton, *Underhill and Hayton: Law Relating to Trusts and Trustees*, 16th ed. (London: Butterworths: 2003), 888-889.

291 *Supra*, note 270. See also *Royal Bank v. Bank of Montreal*, [1976] 4 W.W.R. 721, 67 D.L.R. (3d) 755, 1976 CarswellSask 55 (C.A.).

result is that the $500 remaining in the account is shared between Trusts B (as to $200) and C (as to $300). Trust A will recover nothing.

If the rule is being applied, it would also govern when the moneys withdrawn are invested or otherwise yield proceeds. Thus, assume that in the above example the $400 withdrawn had been invested in securities rather than dissipated. The withdrawal of $400 contains all of the $100 from Trust A, and $300 from Trust B; so Trust A's beneficiaries would be able to trace into the product as to a one-quarter share, and those of Trust B as to a three-quarter share.[292]

The rule in *Clayton's Case, Re* has been the subject of much criticism on the ground that it is a rule of banking law and should not apply to the law of trusts, because the question is not what the trustee's position is toward the bank, but what the beneficiaries' rights are *inter se*.[293] The rule also produces capricious results, as the example above illustrates.[294] Moreover, there are many ways to exclude it. It does not apply when the account is other than an active unbroken account, such as a deposit account.[295] In the latter situation, the several trusts would recover in proportion to their contributions.[296] The rule is supposed to depend on the intention of the banker and customer, and can therefore be excluded by proof of a contrary intention.[297] It does not apply if a withdrawal is earmarked as belonging to a specified trust,[298] nor does it apply to transactions made on the same day.[299] Even if the account is a current account, the rule is not applied if it is impossible to determine to what amount each trust is entitled. In that case the moneys are shared proportionately, as though they had not been mixed in an active current account.[300] But all of these were supposed to be exceptions, and outside of them, the rule has often been followed.[301]

---

292 Ford and Lee §17210 (*Mixture of moneys in a bank account*).

293 Smith, 189-194.

294 Ford and Lee §1720.2. The results are capricious if the trust beneficiaries are considered to stand on an equal footing. If a person thought that the trust most recently defrauded should have a better chance of recovery than a trust defrauded longer ago, the rule could make some sense, but that seems a difficult position to sustain.

295 *Canada Deposit Insurance Corp. v. Canadian Commercial Bank* (1989), 62 D.L.R. (4th) 498, 1989 CarswellAlta 363, 34 E.T.R. 299, 70 Alta. L.R. (2d) 71, 76 C.B.R. (N.S.) 271, [1990] 2 W.W.R. 19, C.E.B. & P.G.R. 8091 (headnote only), (sub nom. *Canadian Commercial Bank (Liquidation), Re (No. 2)*) 99 A.R. 357 (Q.B.), at 511 [D.L.R.].

296 *Sinclair v. Brougham, supra*, note 234; *Diplock v. Wintle, supra*, note 226 (action against The Royal Sailors Orphan Girls' School and Home).

297 Thus, in *British Red Cross Balkan Fund, Re*, [1914] 2 Ch. 419, a large number of subscribers to a charitable fund which ceased were held entitled to recover on the basis of a resulting trust in proportion to their contributions. Ashbury J. held that the rule was merely a rule of evidence, not an invariable rule of law and declined to apply it. This was followed in *Hobourn Aero Components Ltd. Air Raid Distress Fund, Re* (1945), [1946] 1 Ch. 86 (Eng. Ch. Div.), affirmed on another point [1946] 1 Ch. 194, [1946] 1 All E.R. 501 (C.A.); *Eastern Capital Futures Ltd., Re*, [1989] B.C.L.C. 371; *Barlow Clowes International Ltd. v. Vaughan* (1991), [1992] 4 All E.R. 22 (C.A.).

298 *Diplock v. Wintle, supra*, note 226, at 551-2 [Ch].

299 *Cory Bros. & Co. Ltd. v. Owners of Turkish Steamship "Mecca"*, [1897] A.C. 296 at 291.

300 *Saskatchewan General Trusts Corp., Re, supra*, note 268; *Shanahans Stamp Auctions Ltd., Re*, [1962] Irish R. 386.

301 *Hancock v. Smith* (1869), 41 Ch. D. 456 (Eng. Ch. Div.); *Stenning, Re*, [1895] 2 Ch. 433;

However, the rule has now been decisively rejected in Canada. This step occurred in *Ontario (Securities Commission) v. Greymac Credit Corp.*[302] Morden J.A., for the Ontario Court of Appeal, concluded that there was no binding authority on the point, and declared, "In the absence of binding authority clearly on point it may reasonably be said that the law is what it ought to be."[303] The judgment was wholly adopted by the Supreme Court of Canada. Other jurisdictions have begun to follow this lead.[304] The result is that innocent parties always share proportionately to their contributions.

(v) *Mixing of Trustee's Funds with Funds of Two or More Trusts*

When a trustee mixes his or her own funds with those of two or more trusts, the claim against the trustee is first dealt with in accordance with the rules already discussed and, thereafter, the claims of the trusts *inter se* will be dealt with in accordance with the rules concerning such claims. This situation also arose in *Ontario (Securities Commission) v. Greymac Credit Corp.*

Notes and Questions

1. In *Ontario (Securities Commission) v. Greymac Credit Corp.*, the court left open the question whether the rule in *Clayton's Case, Re* should apply if the accounts run over a long period and are complex. It has been suggested that the rule in *Clayton's Case, Re* has advantages in those circumstances.[305]

2. A trustee deposited the following moneys into her bank account: Day 1 – $3000 from beneficiary A; Day 2 – $2000 from beneficiary B; and Day 3 – $1000 of her own money. She then made the following withdrawals: Day 4 – $2000, to buy a used motorbike for her son, which depreciates in value; Day 5 – $2000, to buy stocks in her mother's name, which appreciate in value; and Day 6 – $2000, which she spends on a vacation with her friend.

What are the rights of A and B against the trustee and against each other?

3. S, a solicitor, acted for C on a matrimonial matter. She directed her husband to pay the proceeds of settlement of the proceedings between them to S in trust and authorized S

Diplock v. Wintle, supra, note 226 (action against the National Institute for the Deaf); *Bailey v. Jellett* (1884), 9 O.A.R. 187 (C.A.); *British Canadian Securities Ltd. v. Martin, supra*, note 275; *C.A. Macdonald & Co., Re* (1958), 26 W.W.R. 116, 1958 CarswellAlta 3, 17 D.L.R. (2d) 416, 37 C.B.R. 119 (T.D.), reversed (1959), 1959 CarswellAlta 3, 2 C.B.R. (N.S.) 326, 28 W.W.R. 231, 18 D.L.R. (2d) 731 (C.A.); *Law Society of Upper Canada v. Riviera Motel (Kitchener) Ltd.* (1981), 33 O.R. (2d) 65, 123 D.L.R. (3d) 409, (sub nom. *Delaney, Re*) 9 E.T.R. 188, 1981 CarswellOnt 689, 1981 CarswellOnt 503 (H.C.); *Corbett v. McKee, Calabrese & Whitehead* (1984), 16 E.T.R. 200, 1984 CarswellNB 37, 54 N.B.R. (2d) 107, 140 A.P.R. 107 (Q.B.); *Coville Transport Co., Re* (1947), 28 C.B.R. 262, 1947 CarswellOnt 114 (S.C.).

302 [1988] 2 S.C.R. 172, 65 O.R. (2d) 479, 1988 CarswellOnt 597, 1988 CarswellOnt 964, 31 E.T.R. 1, 52 D.L.R. (4th) 767, 29 O.A.C. 217, 87 N.R. 341, affirming (1986), 55 O.R. (2d) 673, 30 D.L.R. (4th) 1, 1986 CarswellOnt 158, 17 O.A.C. 88, 23 E.T.R. 81, 34 B.L.R. 29 (C.A.).

303 *Ibid.*, at 24 [DLR].

304 The New Zealand Court of Appeal did so in *Registered Securities Ltd., Re*, [1991] 1 N.Z.L.R. 545 (New Zealand C.A.), as did the New South Wales Court of Appeal in *Keefe v. Law Society N.S.W.* (1998), 44 N.S.W.L.R. 45 (New South Wales C.A.).

305 Ford and Lee, §17210 (*Commentary respecting the application of* Clayton's Case).

to deduct his fees and disbursements from the amount paid to him. S deducted his account and paid the balance to C. She objected to the account and decided to have it taxed. Before it was taxed, S made an assignment in bankruptcy and was later discharged.

Can C recover the amount by which the taxing officer reduced the account?[306]

4. If the trustee is a trust company, it may, provided the trust instrument permits it, hold trust moneys on deposit. In those circumstances, the relationship between the trustee and the beneficiaries is one of debtor-creditor. Hence, if the trust company becomes insolvent, the beneficiaries do not have priority for moneys lawfully deposited with the company. It will have priority for moneys improperly deposited with the company.[307]

(vi) *Interaction of Lowest Intermediate Balance Rule with Multiple Innocent Claimants*

Finally, consider the following hypothetical facts:

Date	Deposits of funds held on Trust A	Deposits of funds held on Trust B	Deposits of funds held on Trust C	Withdraw als (dissi- pated)	Balance
1	$100				$100
2		$400			$500
3				$400	$100
4			$200		$300

If we examine the situation at the end of day 3, we would say that the $100 is the traceable product of contributions by Trusts A and B. Trust C has not yet contributed. Treating A and B equally (having rejected the application of *Clayton's Case*), we would say that the $100 balance at the end of day 3 is the traceable product of the contributions of Trusts A and B in the ratio 100:400 or 1:4 so that, if the trustee had become bankrupt at the end of day 3, Trust A would recover $20 and Trust B, $80.

But what is the situation at the end of day 4? The logic of the lowest intermediate balance rule would seem to imply that the combined claim of Trusts A and B against the final balance must still be limited to $100. At the end of day 3, the combination of their contributions to the account balance was $100, and so the addition of further money belonging to Trust C should not be able to increase the claims of A and B. The lowest intermediate balance rule says that you cannot get more out of a mixture than you contributed to it. In this case, A and B together only contributed a total of $100 to the final balance of $300. Trust C contributed $200, and no withdrawals were made after that contribution was added. So the final $300 should be divided as follows: A: $20; B: $80; C: $200. This approach

---

306 See *Shupak v. Greenglass* (1986), 59 C.B.R. (N.S.) 134, 1986 CarswellOnt 181 (H.C.), additional reasons at (1986), 59 C.B.R. (N.S.) 134 at 142 (Ont. H.C.).

307 See *Space Investments Ltd. v. Canadian Imperial Bank of Commerce Trust Co. (Bahamas) Ltd.*, [1986] 3 All E.R. 75 (P.C.).

has been accepted in some U.S. cases.[308] It is not a question of dividing it in proportion to the original contributions of $100, $400, $200, in which case A would get 1/7 or $28.57; B would get 4/7 or $114.29; and C would get 2/7 or $57.14. That calculation would seem to throw a loss onto Trust C which there is no reason for it to bear.

Because this approach takes notice of the timing of the transactions, it may seem similar to *Clayton's Case, Re*. It is not, however, the same. The application of *Clayton's Case, Re* to the same facts given above would yield still another result, that is A would get nothing, B would get $100, and C would get $200. Rather, this approach comes from combining *pro rata* treatment with the lowest intermediate balance rule.

To divide according to the proportions of original contributions, without taking any account of intermediate withdrawals and balances, is certainly simpler. Is it more just? *Law Society of Upper Canada v. Toronto Dominion Bank*,[309] reproduced below, explores these issues.

LAW SOCIETY OF UPPER CANADA v. TORONTO DOMINION BANK

(1998), 42 O.R. (3d) 257, 169 D.L.R. (4th) 353, 1998 CarswellOnt 4757, 116 O.A.C. 24, 44 B.L.R. (2d) 72
Ontario Court of Appeal

The judgment of the court was delivered by

BLAIR J. (Ad Hoc):

Part I—Background and Facts

1 Between December 16, 1990 and September 24, 1991 Philip Upshall, a solicitor, misappropriated over $900,000 from his clients' trust account at the TD Bank. This appeal involves the claims of competing beneficiaries to the shortfall of funds remaining in that trust account when it was frozen on October 2, 1991, and the manner in which their respective shares are to be determined. It raises issues concerning what is known as "the rule in Clayton's Case" and a descendant concept called "the lowest intermediate balance rule" (frequently referred to by the acronym "LIBR").

2 The account was frozen after the Bank was advised that Mr. Upshall had been hospitalized in a psychiatric ward and that the Law Society would be

---

308 See *Gibbs v. Gerberich*, 1 Ohio App. 2d 93, 203 N.E.2d 851 (U.S. Ct. of Apps., 1964), and *Walter J. Schmidt & Co., Re*, 298 F. 314 (1923), at 316, extracted in the notes after the case set out below. In supplemental reasons, Learned Hand J. accepted that he was bound by authority to apply *Clayton's Case, Re* after all.

309 (1998), 42 O.R. (3d) 257, 169 D.L.R. (4th) 353, 1998 CarswellOnt 4757, 116 O.A.C. 24, 44 B.L.R. (2d) 72 (C.A.), leave to appeal refused (1999), 130 O.A.C. 199 (note), 250 N.R. 194 (note) (S.C.C.).

managing the operation of his trust account from that point on. Mr. Upshall was subsequently found guilty of misappropriating client monies by the Law Society of Upper Canada, and disbarred. He made an assignment into bankruptcy on December 21, 1993.

3 As is customary in the case of lawyers' trust accounts, the funds deposited for the account of Mr. Upshall's clients were commingled. Clients' claims to the trust funds in the account as at October 2, 1991 total $656,703.06, and there is a significant shortfall in what remains for distribution to the claimants. The evidence is that both the list of clients and the amounts credited to each client as deposits are known and not in dispute.

4 The last misappropriation from the trust fund occurred on September 24, 1991. At the time, the balance in the account was $66,242.68. On September 25th the TD Bank deposited the sum of $173,000 into the trust account. It did so to enable Mr. Upshall to advance mortgage funds to its client, Douglas Crump. Mr. Upshall was acting as solicitor for the Bank and for Mr. Crump in connection with this mortgage transaction. The funds were deposited on condition that they be released by Mr. Upshall to the borrower, or as the borrower may direct, once the solicitor was satisfied that the Bank would have a good and valid first charge on title. The account was frozen before this transaction was completed.

5 On October 2nd—immediately following notification that Mr. Upshall had been hospitalized and that the Law Society would thereafter be managing the account—the Bank withdrew the $173,000 from the trust account, without authorization, and transferred it to another solicitor to complete the mortgage transaction. On the Application by the Law Society before Mr. Justice Farley[310] the appropriateness of the Bank's conduct in doing this was very much in issue (he held it was inappropriate). Before this Court, the Bank took the position that the appeal should be decided on the basis that the monies which had been removed by it from the account were still in the account and available for distribution. It is therefore unnecessary to deal with the grounds of appeal initially raised which relate to the issue of the Bank's removal of the funds from the trust account.

6 The question on this appeal is whether all clients of Mr. Upshall with funds deposited in the trust account have a claim against the whole of the funds standing to the credit of the account as at the date of its being frozen (including the Bank's deposit of $173,000 made *after* the misappropriations had ceased), or whether the claims of those clients other than the Bank are confined to a smaller sum no larger than the $66,242.68 balance which existed at the time the last funds were wrongly removed. The appellant Bank argues for the latter position, on the basis of the lowest intermediate balance rule. The Law Society submits that the appropriate approach is that of a *pro rata* distribution based upon the entirety of the fund as at the date the account was frozen.

---

310 (1995), 36 C.B.R. (3d) 220.

7 Farley J. held that the lowest intermediate balance rule did not apply in the circumstances of this case, and ordered that the commingled funds should be distributed on a *pro rata* basis. In summary, his reasoning was:

a) that once trust funds are commingled in an account they lose their "earmarked" identity to particular clients and become a single mixed trust fund;

b) that each client—although possessed of an individual trust claim against the trustee for the funds advanced to the trustee—then has an equal claim against the mixed account;

c) that the timing of the misappropriations is irrelevant and the appropriate point in time for determining the claimants' entitlement is the date on which the trust account was frozen (or more technically, perhaps, the time when the last injection of funds was made), because it is the money in the mixed trust account which has been stolen and not that of any particular client—"the mixed trust account cannot be segregated into a 'tainted' pot (of X$) and an 'untainted' pot (of $173,000)"; and,

d) that a trust account which involves commingled funds should be distributed on a *pro rata* basis in circumstances where the account is in a shortfall position and the clients, along with the deposits attributable to them are known. [311]

8 I agree with the conclusion of Farley J., for the reasons which follow.

Part II—Law and Analysis

A. A Consideration of "The Rule in Clayton's Case" and "The Lowest Intermediate Balance Rule"

Overview

9 The Bank's attempt to invoke the lowest intermediate balance rule in the circumstances of this case amounts to nothing more, in my opinion, than an attempt to reinvoke the rule in *Clayton's Case*, which was rejected by this Court and by the Supreme Court of Canada in *Ontario (Securities Commission) v. Greymac Credit Corp.* The effect of applying the "lowest intermediate balance rule" to the competing claims of the trust fund beneficiaries is to permit the Bank—the last contributor—to recover what for practical purposes is all of its

---

311 See, *Ontario (Securities Commission) v. Greymac Credit Corp.* (1985), 51 O.R. (2d) 212 ,19 D.L.R. (4th) 470 (H.C.J.); affirmed (1986), 55 O.R. (2d) 673, 30 D.L.R. (4th) 1 (C.A.); affirmed (1988), 65 O.R. (2d) 479 n, 52 D.L.R. (4th) 767 (S.C.C.), and cases following that decision.

deposit,[312] exactly the result which would transpire upon the application of the rule in *Clayton's Case*. I do not think that result is called for in the circumstances of this case.

The Rule in Clayton's Case

10 What is known as the rule in *Clayton's Case* derives from the decision of the English Court of Appeal in *Devaynes v. Noble; Clayton's Case*.[313] The so-called rule—which is really a statement of evidentiary principle— presumes that in the state of accounts as between a bank and its customer the sums first paid in are the sums first drawn out, absent evidence of an agreement or any presumed intent to the contrary.[314] As Morden J.A. remarked in *Greymac*,[315] "the short form statement of the rule . . . is 'first in, first out'". In the result, where there are competing claims against a shortfall, the shortfall is applied first to the first deposits made, and later contributors to the fund take the benefit of what remains.

11 The role of the rule in *Clayton's Case* in competing beneficiary cases, and its history, were examined thoroughly by this Court in *Greymac*. The application of the rule was rejected as being "unfair and arbitrary" and "based on a fiction".[316] The Court concluded that it was not bound to apply the rule in *Clayton's Case*, and it did not do so. Nor, for that matter, did it apply the lowest intermediate balance rule.

12 Speaking for a unanimous Court in *Greymac*, Morden J.A. resolved that as a general rule the mechanism of *pro rata* sharing on the basis of tracing was the preferable approach to be followed, although he left room for other possibilities such as those circumstances where it is not practically possible to determine what proportion the mixed funds bear to each other, or where the claimants have either expressly or by implication agreed among themselves to a distribution based otherwise than on a *pro rata* division following equitable tracing of contributions.[317] Whatever approach was chosen, Morden J.A. was concerned that it should be one which met the test of convenience—or "workability", as he termed it.[318] The core of the Court's conclusions is to be found in the following passage from his judgment:[319]

---

312 The Bank concedes that the amount of its deposit into the trust account, $173,000.00, must be reduced by a small amount of approximately $2,500.00 to accommodate some minor transactions which occurred following its deposit and before the freezing of the account. The application of LIBR would result in the Bank retaining $170,448.45 of the $173,000.00 deposited.

313 (1816), 1 Mer. 572, 35 E.R. 781.

314 See *Clayton's Case*, *supra*, note 270, *per* Sir William Grant, at pp. 608-609, Mer.

315 *Supra*, note 302, at 677.

316 *Ibid.*, at 686.

317 *Ibid.*, at 685-90.

318 *Ibid.*, at 688.

319 *Ibid.*, at 685.

The foregoing indicates to me that <u>the fundamental question</u> is not whether the rule in *Clayton's Case* can properly be used for tracing purposes, as well as for loss allocation, but, rather, <u>whether the rule should have tiny [ed.: this error appears in Blair J.'s judgment, not in *Greymac*] application at all to the resolution of problems connected with competing beneficial entitlements to a mingled trust fund where there have been withdrawals from the fund.</u> *From the perspective of basic concepts I do not think that it should.* The better approach is that which recognizes the continuation, on a *pro rata* basis, of the respective property interests <u>in the total amount of trust moneys or property</u> *available*. [Emphasis added.]

13 Having determined that the rule in *Clayton's Case* ought not to be applied in cases involving the claims of competing trust beneficiaries, Morden J.A. concluded in *Greymac* that *pro rata* sharing based on the respective property interests of the claimants in the total amount of trust money or property available, should be applied. He accepted such *pro rata* sharing as the general method of determining such competing claims. Whether, as some have suggested,[320] he also recognized and incorporated into the *pro rata* sharing exercise the concept of the lowest intermediate balance rule, and if so to what extent, is an issue that will be dealt with momentarily. First, however, I propose to turn to an analysis of the history and application of the LIBR notion.

The Lowest Intermediate Balance Rule: An Outline

14 The "lowest intermediate balance rule" states that a claimant to a mixed find cannot assert a proprietary interest in that fund in excess of the smallest balance in the fund during the interval between the original contribution and the time when a claim with respect to that contribution is being made against the fund.[321]

15 The LIBR concept is a descendant of the rule in *Clayton's Case*. It was originally articulated by Sargant J. in *James Roscoe (Bolton), Ltd. v. Winder*.[322] In that case the purchaser of a business, Mr. Winder, who had contracted to collect the outstanding book debts of the business and to pay them to the company, did the former but not the latter. Over time he collected £455 and deposited the funds into his own general account, but he subsequently drew out all but £25, before eventually putting in more monies of his own and, again, drawing on the account for his own purposes. There was a credit balance in the account of £358 at the time of his death. The Court held that he was a trustee of the £455 for the benefit of the company, but that the company's claim against the fund was limited to the lowest intermediate balance in the account of £25.

16 Sargant J. erected the LIBR foundation upon two principal footings. The first of these was the premise that the rules of proprietary tracing preclude a

---

320 See, Maddaugh, Peter D. and McCamus, John D., *The Law of Restitution* (Canada Law Book), pp. 153-154; *British Columbia v. National Bank of Canada* (1994), 119 D.L.R (4th) 669 (B.C.C.A.) at pp. 688-89.

321 See Maddaugh and McCamus, *The Law of Restitution*, at pp. 153-154.

322 *Supra*, note 281.

beneficiary, after a mixed fund has been depleted, from reaching any subsequent contributions made by others to that fund (in the absence of some actual or presumed intention to replenish the fund). The second was a rejection of the notion that the account may be treated as a whole and the balance from time to time standing to the credit of that account viewed as being subject to one continual charge or trust. In outlining the rationale for his conclusion, Sargant J. said:[323]

> . . . [Counsel] did say "No. I am only asking you to treat the account as a whole, and to consider the balance from time to time standing to the credit of that account as subject to one continual charge or trust." But I think that really is using words which are not appropriate to the facts. You must, for the purpose of tracing, which was the process adopted in *In re Hallett's Estate*,[324] put your finger on some definite fund which either remains in its original state or can be found in another shape. That is tracing, and tracing, by the very facts of this case, seems to be absolutely excluded except as to the 25l, 18s. . . .
>
> Certainly, after having heard *In re Hallett's Estate* stated over and over again, I should have thought that the general view of that decision was that it only applied to such an amount of the balance ultimately standing to the credit of the trustee as did not exceed the lowest balance of the account during the intervening period.

17 The LIBR principle has never been analysed by Ontario or other Canadian Courts. However, it has been applied several times at the trial level—in bankruptcy situations—in this Province.[325] Its existence has been accepted (with very little comment) on two occasions in this Court in decisions preceding *Greymac*.[326] The LIBR concept has also been accepted by the British Columbia Court of Appeal in *British Columbia v. National Bank of Canada*.[327]

18 No Canadian authority has attempted to describe how the LIBR principle is to be employed. Nonetheless, from a review of the foregoing authorities, I take the rationale underlying the LIBR theory in relation to commingled trust funds to encompass at least the following concepts:

1. that beneficiaries are entitled, through the equitable and proprietary notion of tracing, to follow their contribution into the mixed fund;

2. that beneficiaries of a such a fund have a lien or charge over the totality of the trust fund to the extent of their interest in it;

---

323 *Ibid.*, at 68-69.
324 *Supra*, note 198.
325 See, *Re Thompson, ex parte Galloway* (1930), 11 C.B.R. 263 (Ont. S.C. Bkcy); *Re Wineberg* (1969), 14 C.B.R. (N.S.) 182 (Ont. S.C. Bkcy), Registrar; *Re 389179 Ontario Ltd.* (1980), 113 D.L.R. (3d) 207 (Ont. S.C. Bkcy), Saunders J.
326 See, *Re Norman Estate, supra*, note 266; and, *General Motors Acceptance Corp. of Canada Ltd. v. Bank of Nova Scotia* (1986), 55 O.R. (2d) 438 (C.A.) at p. 443.
327 *Supra*, note 320, at 687-689; leave to appeal to S.C.C. refused (1995) 126 D.L.R. (4th) vii, and by the British Columbia Supreme Court in *Re 1653 Investments Ltd., supra*, note 283, at p. 597, (sub nom. *Coopers & Lybrand v. The Queen in right of Canada*).

3. but that once a wrongful withdrawal has been made from the fund, the claims of beneficiaries with monies in the fund at the time of the withdrawal are thereafter limited to the reduced balance, and that depositors to the trust fund are not entitled to claim further against any subsequent amounts contributed to the fund either by the trustee (unless made with the intent to replenish the withdrawn amount) or other by other beneficiaries; and,

4. that this inability to claim against anything in excess of the smallest balance in the fund during the interval between the original contribution and the time of the claim flows from the inability to claim a *proprietary right* to subsequent amounts deposited, since it is not possible to trace the original claimant's contribution to property contributed by others.

19 This latter concept is grounded, ultimately, on the premise that tracing rights are predicated upon the model of property rights. LIBR seeks to recognize that at some point in time, because of earlier misappropriations, an earlier beneficiary's money has unquestionably left the fund and therefore cannot physically still be in the fund. Accordingly, it cannot be "traced" to any subsequent versions of the fund that have been swollen by the contributions of others, beyond the lowest intermediate balance in the fund. Such is the theory, at any rate.

The decision in Greymac and the Parameters and Practical Application of LIBR

Greymac

20 In *Greymac* this Court did *not* apply the lowest intermediate balance rule. Indeed, it was not necessary for the Court to consider LIBR. Once it had been decided that the claimants had a right to trace their contributions to both the account into which the deposits had originally been made and the second account at Crown Trust into which the $4 million withdrawal had been placed, there was only one balance to be concerned about. While *Greymac* clearly rejects the rule in *Clayton's Case* as a means of determining how the monies in a mixed trust account are to be allocated in the event of a shortfall, and adopts the notion of *pro rata* sharing based upon tracing as the general rule, it does not apply the lowest intermediate balance rule in the context of such *pro rata* sharing.

21 The view that Morden J.A. affirmed the lowest intermediate balance rule[328]—or at least acknowledged it with approval[329]—in the *Greymac* case has its source in the following passage from his reasons, at p. 688:

---

328 See Maddaugh and McCamus, *The Law of Restitution, supra,* at pp. 153-154.
329 See *British Columbia v. National Bank of Canada, supra,* note 320, at 688-689.

We are concerned with the resolution of competing proprietary, not personal, claims. At the time of the mingling of the trust funds the companies [i.e. one group of claimants] had $4,683,000 in the account. Regardless of how much they had earlier in the account, they cannot say that they had a proprietary interest in any more than the amount in the account to their credit on and after December 15, 1982.[330]

22 It is important to note that Morden J.A. made these remarks in the context of dealing with an argument that more monies than those to the credit of the claimants *at the time the fund had become a mixed fund* should have been taken into account if the funds were to be divided on a *pro rata* basis. The date referred to—December 15, 1982—was the date on which the funds had become a commingled trust account. I therefore regard the foregoing comments of Morden J.A. as referring as much to *timing* as to anything else. He was concerned with determining when the parties' respective proportionate interests should begin to be assessed—i.e. to the timing as of when the *pro rata* calculations should be triggered (namely when the fund first took on its character as a "mixed fund"). I note in particular in this regard, that in the passage for which the *Roscoe* case is cited as authority, Morden J.A. states that the claimants "cannot say that they had a proprietary interest in any more than the amount in the account *to their credit* at the time the funds were intermingled. This is the language of deposits made by the claimants. It is not the language of the *lowest balance* in the account, which is what LIBR deals with. I do not interpret Morden J.A.'s comments as indicating an intention to adopt the concept of LIBR for purposes of calculating *pro rata* sharing in *Greymac*.

Parameters and Practical Application of LIBR

23 The British Columbia Law Reform Commission seemed to endorse a LIBR approach in its *Report on Competing Rights to Mingled Property: Tracing and the Rule in Clayton's Case* (1983).

In a rare attempt to define both the problem which LIBR seeks to address and the mechanics of its proposed solution, the Commission stated:[331]

Terms like "*pari passu*", "*pro rata*", "rateably", and "proportionately" are inherently ambiguous. Do they mean that shortfalls or accretions to a fund are shared in proportion to the original interests claimants to that fund possessed? Or do they mean that shortfalls or accretions to a fund are shared in proportion to those interests claimants to that fund possess *after each transaction made with respect to that fund is taken into account?* In the Working Paper we tentatively concluded that the latter meaning was fairest. [Emphasis added.]

For example, A, a trustee, deposits $1,000 of B's money in his account, mixing it with $1,000 of his own money. A removes $1,500. A then deposits $1,000 of C's money. B and C should not share the fund of $1,500 equally, notwithstanding that B's original interest in the fund was $1,000 and that C's current interest is $1,000. B's interest in the fund has been reduced by $500. B's lien should be reduced from securing $1,000 to now securing $500, the minimum

---

330 See *James Roscoe (Bolton), Ltd. v. Winder, supra,* note 281, and *Re Norman Estate, supra,* note 266.

331 See pp. 53-54.

balance of the fund following the deposit of his money and preceding the deposit of C's money. C would be entitled to a lien of $1,000. No transactions have occurred yet to reduce his interest in the fund. To avoid confusion, legislation enacting these recommendations should define exactly how "*pari passu*" sharing takes place. One possible formulation is as follows:

> *If there are two or more persons with interests in a fund, the amount of any shortfall from or accretion to the fund which would have affected their respective interests, and which is not appropriated to a specific interest or interests, is divided and attributed to their respective interests in such proportion as their respective interests bore to the sum of those interests before the shortfall or accretion occurred.* [Emphasis in original.]

24 As far as I am aware, no such legislation has ever been enacted. In my view, however, this approach is too complex and impractical to be accepted as a general rule for dealing with cases such as this.

25 It was precisely for this reason that a version of LIBR—referred to as the "rolling charge" or "North American" approach, because it was considered to be derived from various North American authorities, including *Greymac*—was rejected by the English Court of Appeal in *Barlow Clowes International Ltd. (in liq.) v. Vaughan.*[332] *Barlow Clowes International* involved a very large and complex insolvency. Saying that the North American approach was "not a live contender" because of the costs involved and the complexity of its application, Lord Justice Woolf instead adopted what he labelled "the *pari passu ex post facto*" solution. This solution involved a simple rateable sharing of the remaining funds based upon "establishing the total quantum of the assets available and sharing them on a proportionate basis among all the investors who could be said to have contributed to the acquisition of those assets, ignoring the dates on which they made their investments".[333] It is a solution which, in my opinion, makes sense in most situations.

26 None of the authorities to which we have been referred has applied LIBR in the context of a relationship between innocent beneficiaries; and whether the same set of assumptions as those governing LIBR and outlined in the earlier portions of these reasons, should operate to resolve situations where the competition is not between trust claimants and the wrongdoer, but between the trust claimants themselves in relation to a shortfall of funds in the trust account, is to my mind a different question.

27 In the latter type of situation, everyone is a victim of the wrongdoer. Presumptions about what the wrongdoer may or may not have intended—in terms of replenishing the fund with subsequent contributions, or in terms of being honest and using his or her own funds first—are of little assistance. Moreover, competing trust claimants are not in the same position as ordinary creditors of the wrongdoer. They are wronged trust beneficiaries, and as a result of that relationship they are

---

332 *Supra*, note 297.
333 *Ibid.*, at 36.

entitled not only to a personal remedy for breach of trust against the wrongdoer, but also to a proprietary remedy against the fund in respect of which the trust relationship exists. It is always open to a trust contributor to gain protection from having to share a shortfall with others by insisting upon the funds being placed in a separate trust account.

28 In determining how a *pro rata* distribution is to be effected in circumstances of commingled trust funds, the issue whether this *proprietary remedy* must be inflexibly tied to a pre-existing *proprietary right*—i.e., the purely logical application of tracing rules—is an important question. In my view, in circumstances such as this, they need not be inflexibly tied together, and the concept of the mixed trust fund as a "whole fund", the balance of which from time to time is subject to a continual charge or trust—rejected by Sargant J. in *James Roscoe (Bolton) Ltd. v. Winder*—should be reconsidered.

29 Sargant J.'s rejection of the "whole-fund continual-charge-or-trust" notion was founded upon an interpretation of the earlier decision in *Re Hallett's Estate*. To the extent that there is any support for this view in that case, however, it is limited to an obiter dicta comment made by Thesiger L.J. in dissent;[334] and in my reading of *Re Hallett's Estate* I can find nothing which otherwise suggests or mandates any such conclusion. I shall return to this issue later.

B. A Choice of Governing Principles

30 Where, then, does all of this lead?

31 In the end, there remain two general approaches which may be taken to the resolution of how *pro rata* distributions are to be made in circumstances such as this case—the rule in *Clayton's Case* having now been discarded for such purposes. The first is that of applying the lowest intermediate balance rule. The second is that of applying what Woolf L.J. called the "*pari passu ex post facto*" approach, in *Barlow Clowes International*. There seems to be no binding authority compelling the application of one approach or the other to circumstances such as those in this case. The Court should therefore seek to apply the method which is the more just, convenient and equitable in the circumstances.

32 No authority has ever applied the lowest intermediate balance rule in circumstances involving the rival claims of trust beneficiaries, as I have already noted. The mechanics of how the lowest intermediate balance rule actually works have never been fully explained. Indeed, even in situations concerning defaulting trustees and beneficiaries, where the rule has been invoked, it does not appear to have been implemented in any case involving more than a small number of competing beneficiaries and a correspondingly small number of transactions.

---

334 See pp. 745-746.

This, I suspect, is because although LIBR may be "manifestly fairer"[335] in the pure sense of a tracing analysis, it is manifestly more complicated and more difficult to apply than other solutions.

33 What LIBR involves—as best I can ascertain it from the authorities and the literature bearing on the subject—is a transaction-by-transaction examination of the mixed fund, in terms of deposits made by the beneficiaries and withdrawals taken by the wrongdoer, and the application of a proportionality formula in respect of each such transaction. This approach has not found favour in cases where the problem has been faced, and acknowledged, directly.[336]

The Governing Principle

34 In my view, the method which should generally be followed in cases of *pro rata* sharing as between beneficiaries is not the LIBR approach but the *pari passu ex post facto* approach, which has the advantage of relative simplicity. This approach involves taking the claim or contribution of the individual beneficiary to the mixed fund as a percentage of the total contributions of all those with claims against the fund at the time of distribution, and multiplying that factor against the total assets available for distribution, in order to determine the claimant's *pro rata* share of those remaining funds.

35 This solution is the type of resolution which has been adopted, on a practical basis, in most cases involving more than two or three competing beneficiaries. It is the solution applied by this Court in *Greymac*, and by the English Court of Appeal in *Barlow Clowes International*. It is the solution applied in a number of other recent decisions at the superior court level in this Province involving mixed trust funds,[337] and it is the solution applied by Farley J. in the case under appeal. But it is not LIBR.

36 It is, however, the approach which I favour.

---

335 Per Woolf L.J. in *Barlow Clowes International Ltd.*, *supra*, note 297, at 35. LIBR is said to be fairer because it approaches the allocation problem from the perspective of the "proportions [that] the different interests in the account . . . bear to each other at the moment before the withdrawal is made" (p. 35).

336 See, for example, *Barlow Clowes International*, *supra*, note 297; and *Winsor v. Bajaj* (1990), 1 O.R. (3d) 714, 75 D.L.R. (4th) 198 (Gen. Div.).

337 See: *Winsor, ibid.*; *Chering Metals Club Inc. (Trustee of) v. Non-Discretionary Cash Account Trust Claimants* (1991), 7 C.B.R. (3d) 105 (Ont. Ct. (Gen. Div.)) at 111 (Austin J.); *Law Society of Upper Canada v. Squires* (Ont. Ct. (Gen. Div.)), unreported decision of Farley J. released October 17, 1994 [summarized 51 A.C.W.S. (3d) 173]; *Law Society of Upper Canada v. Sproule Estate* (1995), 8 E.T.R. (2d) 156; *Holden Financial Corp. v. 411454 Ontario Ltd.* (unreported decision of Rosenberg J. released August 28, 1992, at 33) [summarized 35 A.C.W.S. (3d) 317]; *Ontario Securities Commission v. Consortium Construction Inc.* (unreported decision of Rosenberg J. released June 21, 1993, at paras 76-77) [summarized 41 A.C.W.S. (3d) 18].

37 My conclusion in this regard is based both upon the "convenience" aspect (or the "workability" aspect, as Morden J.A. characterized it in *Greymac*) pertaining to the application of the LIBR principle, and upon my analysis of the concept of a mixed trust account and of its nature and purpose.

The "Convenience" Rationale

38 First, with regard to "convenience", I note the following comment of Morden J.A. in *Greymac*: [338]

> While acknowledging the basic truth of Lord Atkin's observation that "[c]onvenience and justice are often not on speaking terms",[339] I accept that convenience, perhaps more accurately workability, can be an important consideration in the determination of legal rules. A rule that is in accord with abstract justice but which for one or more reasons, is not capable of practical application, may not, when larger considerations of judicial administration are taken into account, be a suitable rule to adopt.

39 LIBR is difficult to apply in cases involving any significant number of beneficiaries and transactions. Even in this age of computer technology, I am not convinced that trustees of mixed funds—who might be in a position of having to sort out misappropriation transactions on such an account and the distribution of what remains—should be assumed or required to possess the software to enable a LIBR type of calculation to be done in the myriad of situations that might arise. Indeed, there is no evidence that such software programs exist, although it may well be that they do—at what cost and difficulty we do not know.

40 In this case it is not practicable to conduct the LIBR exercise. There are over 100 claimants. There were misappropriations in the area of $900,000.00 in bits and pieces. It is not even clear that each deposit and debit can be looked at individually, on the state of the record, although the total amounts deposited by each of the claimants are apparently known. Notwithstanding this, if the LIBR principle is to be applied to a *pro rata* distribution in the circumstances of this case, it would be necessary to consider not only the deposits of each individual claimant and the timing of such deposits, but also what was the lowest balance in the Upshall account between each deposit and the imposition of the freeze. This would involve analysing the pattern and timing of each misappropriation and applying the results to each individual depositor's circumstances. It is not at all clear on the evidence that this exercise can be done.

The Rationale Based Upon the Nature and Purpose of a "Mixed" Trust Fund

41 On broader principles as well, in my opinion, the preferred approach in cases involving competing beneficiaries is that of *pro rata* sharing based upon the proportion of a claimant's contributions to the total contributions of all claim-

---

338 *Supra*, note 302, at 688-689.
339 *General Medical Council v. Spackman*, [1943] A.C. 627 at 638.

ants, multiplied by the amount to be shared—i.e., the *"pari passu ex post facto"* approach. This method spreads the misappropriations rateably amongst the contributors who remain, but at the same time does not arbitrarily affect earlier contributors adversely by limiting their charge or constructive trust in relation to the fund to the lowest balance in the account. It preserves what Morden J.A. referred to in *Greymac*[340] as the participant's claim to "an equitable lien . . . *to secure the amount of its total contribution*" and it is consistent with his statement [341]that,

> The better approach is that which recognizes the continuation, on a *pro rata* basis, of the respective property interests in the total amount of trust moneys or funds *available*. [Emphasis in both citations added.]

42 In regard to this conclusion, it is useful to consider both the practical considerations pertaining to a mixed trust fund and the nature of such a fund itself.

43 A mixed trust fund is a device whereby a trustee—typically, but by no means exclusively, a lawyer—holds funds in trust for different persons or entities. It is in many ways a mechanism of convenience, i.e., it avoids the necessity, and the cost, and the cumbersome administrative aspects of having to set up individual trust accounts, and the records relating to such accounts, for the transactions relating to every beneficiary. This practical characteristic of mixed trust funds should be recognized in considering the nature of such funds. It provides an economic and organizational benefit to the public. As Farley J. noted, in the context of this case, "Upshall was effectively acting as a banker in a safekeeping capacity".

44 What follows from this, it seems to me, is that a mixed fund of this nature should be considered as a whole fund, at any given point in time, and that the particular moment when a particular beneficiary's contribution was made and the particular moment when the defalcation occurred, should make no difference. The happenstance of timing is irrelevant. The fund itself—although an asset in the hands of the trustee to which the contributors have recourse—is an indistinguishable blend of debits and credits reflected in an account held by the trustee in a bank or other financial institution. It is a blended fund. Once the contribution is made and deposited it is no longer possible to identify the claimant's funds, as the claimant's funds. All that can be identified, in terms of an asset to which recourse may be had, is the trust account itself, and its balance.

45 The theme of a commingled trust account as a blended fund is reflected in the reasons of Woolf L.J. and Dillon L.J. in *Barlow Clowes International* [342]and

---

340 *Supra*, note 302, at 684.
341 *Ibid.*, at 685.
342 *Supra*, note 297, at 27, 35.

in those of Morden J.A. in *Greymac*.[343] In *Clayton's Case* itself, Sir William Grant, in introducing his "first in, first out" concept, stated:[344]

> But this is the case of *a banking account, where all the sums paid in form one blended fund*, the parts of which have no longer any distinct existence. Neither the banker nor customer ever thinks of saying, this draft is to be placed to the account of the £500 paid in on Monday, and this other to the account of the £500 paid in on Tuesday. There is a fund of £1000 to draw upon, and that is enough. [Emphasis added.]

This notion of commingled sums as being "in form one blended fund, the parts of which have no longer any distinct existence" continues to describe correctly the nature of a mixed trust fund, in my view.

46 In contrast to the blended fund concept is that of the mixed fund as an amalgam of the contributions which have been placed in it, identifiable for some purposes. This approach is reflected in such decisions as *Re Diplock's Estate*.[345] In that case, Lord Greene M.R. attributed to Equity the adoption of "a more metaphysical approach" to the nature of a mixed fund. "[Equity] found no difficulty", he said,[346]

> . . . in regarding a composite fund as an amalgam constituting the mixture of two or more funds each of which could be regarded as having, for certain purposes, a continued separate existence. Putting it in another way, equity regarded the amalgam as capable, in proper circumstances, of being resolved into its component parts.

47 It is noteworthy that both the "fund as amalgam" and the "fund as a blend" approaches enable equity to offer the remedy of a charge, lien or constructive trust *vis-à-vis* the remaining balance in the fund. The former has the effect, however, of limiting the reach of these proprietary remedies. To my mind such a restriction is not necessary. While "proprietary tracing" may serve as the equitable vehicle which enables a claimant to have recourse to a mixed trust fund in the first place, equity can move beyond the strictures of that doctrine to provide a remedy to the claimant once the connection to the und has been made. The nexus is to be found in the concept of the equitable charge, lien or constructive trust. These concepts need not, in my view, be confined to any *part* of the fund because, by their very nature, they have always been applied against the *whole* of the fund.

48 This idea is well expressed in a critique of the analysis in *Re Diplock's Estate*, in an article by Dennis R. Klinck entitled "'Two Distincts, Divisions None': Tracing Money into (and out of) Mixed Accounts".[347] Having dealt with Lord Greene M.R.'s "amalgam" concept, the author states, at p. 179:

---

343 *Supra*, note 302, at 682, citing from Scott, *The Law of Trusts*, 3rd ed., vol. 5 (1967), at pp. 3620 and 3624.
344 *Supra*, note 270, at 608, Mer.
345 *Supra*, note 226.
346 *Ibid.*, at 346.
347 (1987-88), 2 B.F.L.R. 147.

The alternative conceptualization of equitable tracing in this context is implied in the notion of a charge on the mixed fund. Rather than purporting to distinguish parts of the funds and attribute them to particular claimants, this approach sees the claimants as having a proportional claim on the whole fund. If the whole diminishes in extent or value, the proportional claims remain the same, albeit that what the claimants get will be less because the fund is reduced. Arguably, this does not, strictly speaking, involve "tracing" because there is no pretence that that fund is being divided and a particular claimant's property identified.

49 I accept, and adopt, the blended fund approach. At the end of the day, when the trust account has been frozen and there is a shortfall, that shortfall must be divided amongst the beneficiaries who continue to have claims against the fund. I do not think that an analysis which is based on the premise that *some* beneficiaries' interests in the fund have been reduced by earlier misappropriations and therefore that their respective claims have been reduced accordingly, should be preferable to one which simply says that *each* beneficiary has suffered a loss relating to the same misappropriations from the same mixed fund by the same wrongdoer, and accordingly their charge or constructive trust should continue to apply against the whole fund to the proportionate extent of their contributions i.e. the shortfall should be divided in such proportions as their respective interests bear to what is to be divided up at the particular time.

50 The fund is still the fund, and as Farley J. noted in this case, it is not the Bank's money or the money of any particular contributor that has been stolen; it is *the fund* which has been wrongfully depleted. I agree with his comments in the following passages from his first Reasons released on October 17, 1995:[348]

> If the Bank had insisted upon a separate trust bank account being set up, then it need not be worried about the claims of other clients. However all funds advanced by those concerned were deposited by Upshall in a mixed trust bank account at the Bank. As a result each client (including the Bank) had a claim concerning that mixed account. When the Bank's funds went into that account they went the same way as other fungible funds attributable to the other clients. The funds in that account were not individually earmarked dollar by dollar for any particular client. Rather all clients as beneficiaries would have a claim against all the funds
>
> . . .

And:[349]

> Let me observe that a bank account involves a debtor (bank)—creditor (depositor) relationship . . . When funds are deposited to a mixed trust account they lose their earmarked identity. Thus *each* client through the trust relationship with Upshall/Society *has a claim upon the loan granted to the Bank through the operation of this mixed trust account . . . It is the money in the mixed trust account which has been stolen; not that of any particular client.* [Emphasis added.]

Part III—Conclusion

51 The significant problem with LIBR is that its application, in a form true

---

348 *Supra*, note 310, at C.B.R. 222.
349 *Supra*, note 310, at C.B.R. 223.

to its tracing origins and rationale, is too complicated. It may be "manifestly fairer" than the rule in *Clayton's Case* in the sense that it attributes debits from the account equally and proportionately amongst the contributors. "Fairness" may be relative, however. Is the rule necessarily "fairer" when it limits contributors to the lowest intermediate balance in the account between the times of contribution and distribution? The rule in *Clayton's Case* works "unfairly" against the first contributors to the fund, because it attributes the first wrongful withdrawals to those contributions, eliminating some claims but allowing others to be compensated in full. The application of LIBR can have a similar effect, as the circumstances of this case indicate, because its "last in, first out" regime favours later contributors. At the same time, a *pro rata* sharing based simply on the claimants' contributions measured proportionately to the assets available for distribution can work against late depositors, as the circumstances of this case also illustrate.

52 What is at play here, in reality, is a choice of fictions. The rule in *Clayton's Case* and LIBR are both fictions. Any other rationale which endeavours to establish a rule or principle on which equity will divide a shortfall amongst those entitled to claim against it is a fiction. Farley J. recognized the role of fictions, or "artificial rules" when he said, in his second Reasons:[350]

> I do not see it as fair, equitable or practicable in the circumstances (and more especially since the Bank effected an inappropriate and unauthorized self-help remedy to the detriment of the other claimants) to invoke libr. It seems to me somewhat artificial (recognizing that all the rules involved in this area are artificial rules which must be applied with caution so as to maintain the closest approximation of fairness, equity and reasonability, while recognizing practicality) to invoke libr which by its very nature "rewards" those innocents who are later on the scene as compared with those innocents who have been taken advantage of earlier when it is fairly clear that the wrongdoer would continue to fleece all the innocents if given the chance. Recovery should not be so dependent on a fortuitous accident of timing.

53 I agree. Earlier in these reasons I alluded to this Court's rejection, in *Greymac*, of the rule in *Clayton's Case* as "unfair and arbitrary" and "based on a fiction". In this latter regard, Morden J.A. cited[351] the following oft-quoted passage from the decision of Learned Hand J. in *Re Walter J Schmidt & Co.*:[352]

> The rule in *Clayton's Case* is to allocate the payments upon an account. Some rule had to be adopted, and though any presumption of intent was a fiction, priority in time was the most natural basis of allocation. It has no relevancy whatever to a case like this. Here two people are jointly interested in a fund held for them by a common trustee. There is no reason in law or justice why his depredations upon the fund should not be borne equally between them. To throw all the loss upon one, through the mere chance of his being earlier in time, is irrational and arbitrary, and is equally a fiction as the rule in *Clayton's Case, supra. When the law adopts a fiction, it is, or at least it should be, for some purpose of justice. To adopt it here is to apportion a common misfortune through a test which has no relation whatever to the justice of the case . . . Such a result, I submit*

---

350 At pp. 6-7 [summarized 62 A.C.W.S. (3d) 173].
351 At p. 686.
352 *Supra*, note 308, at 316.

with the utmost respect, can only come from a mechanical adherence to a rule which has no intelligible relation to the situation. [Emphasis added.]

54 Such is the case here, in my view. To apply the LIBR principle in the circumstances of this case would be "to throw all the loss upon [some], through the mere chance of [their] being earlier in time". It would be "irrational and arbitrary". It would be "to apportion a *common misfortune* through a test which has no relation whatever to the justice of the case". I do not favour it.

55 In *Greymac*, Morden J.A. observed that "if the application of the *pro rata* approach is seen as an alteration in the rule to be applied [i.e., the rule in *Clayton's Case*], it is one that involves improvement and refinement". Here, I am satisfied that the application of the mechanics of such a *pro rata* approach in the form I have advocated—the *"pari passu ex post facto* approach—as opposed to the application of the LIBR principle in such circumstances, also involves what Jessel M.R. characterized in *Re Hallett's Estate*,[353] as "the gradual refinement of the doctrine of equity".

56 For the foregoing reasons, I would dismiss the appeal with costs.

Appeal dismissed.

Notes and Questions

1. Blair J. said that "The LIBR concept is a descendant of the rule in *Clayton's Case*," and that both principles were fictions. Do you agree?

2. Under *Clayton's Case, Re*, the bank would have recovered all its money. By an application of the lowest intermediate balance rule, it would also recover all its money. Does it follow that "The Bank's attempt to invoke the lowest intermediate balance rule in the circumstances of this case amounts to nothing more, in my opinion, than an attempt to reinvoke the rule in *Clayton's Case*"?

3. Did the judge think that the lowest intermediate balance rule was wrong, or that it was right, but too complicated to apply?

4. Blair J. quoted a famous passage from *Re Walter J. Schmidt & Co.*,[354] in which Learned Hand J. rejected the application of the rule in *Clayton's Case, Re*. After the passage quoted by Blair J., Learned Hand went on to say:

It does not follow, however, that the claimants should divide the fund in the proportions of their original deposits. An illustration will perhaps be clearest. Suppose three claimants, A., B., and C., for $5,000 each, whose money was deposited at intervals of a month, January, February, and March. Suppose that the fund had been reduced on some day in January to $3,000. A. has lost $2,000, which he cannot throw on B. Hence, when B's money is deposited on February 1st, A and B will share $8,000 in the proportion of 3 to 5. Suppose that during February the account gets as low as $4,000. A and B cannot throw this loss on C, and when C's money is deposited they

---

353 *Supra*, note 198, at 720.
354 *Supra*, note 308, at 316.

will share the $9,000 in the proportion of 3, 5, and 10. But any subsequent depletion below $9,000 they must bear in that proportion, just as A and B bore theirs in February.[355]

4. When Upshall added the bank's $173,000 to the account, the balance of the account was $66,242.68. Change the facts slightly and assume that all money had been dissipated and the balance was zero for three days (or three years) before the bank's $173,000 was added. Would it still be appropriate to apply "*pari passu ex post facto*"? If the principle depends on mixing, then assume that instead of the balance being zero, it was 1¢ when the bank's money was deposited. Would that make a difference?

For a critique, on the basis that this judgment was inconsistent with principle and with binding authority, see the note by L. Smith[356].

(vii) *Tracing into the Payment of a Debt*

It is usually assumed that the tracing trail ends when the value being traced is used to pay a debt. In this case, it appears that there are no proceeds. It is arguable, however, that when value is used to pay a debt, the proceeds should be understood to be whatever it was (if anything) that the debtor acquired earlier when the debt was incurred. If a person uses $100 to buy a ring, the ring is the proceeds of the $100. Now assume that the person buys the ring on credit. He owes the seller $100. Later, he misappropriates $100 and uses it to buy the ring. It is arguable that there should be no difference. He has used the value inherent in the $100 to acquire the value inherent in ownership of the ring.

This is not causally true. He acquired ownership of the ring without the use of the misappropriated money. It is, however, accurate in a transactional sense that the purchase price of the ring was, ultimately, the misappropriated $100. The majority in *Foskett* affirmed the longstanding approach to tracing which looks at transactional and not causal links. What matters is whose money actually paid for the new asset. Causation (and also intention of the purchaser) are not relevant in this inquiry.

If this argument were accepted, the stringencies of the lowest intermediate balance rule might seem less harsh. See L. Smith, "Tracing into the Payment of a Debt".[357]

(e) **Transfer to A Third Party**

(i) *Generally*

If a trustee transfers trust property to a third party in breach of trust, the trustee will be personally liable to the trust and may, if he or she received value, hold the proceeds of the transfer in trust for the beneficiaries (as discussed in the previous section). As far as the transferee is concerned, we must also distinguish personal claims from proprietary claims.

---

355 *Ibid.*, at 316.
356 (2000), 33 C.B.L.J. 75.
357 (1995), 54 C.L.J. 290

(1) If the transferee is a *bona fide* purchaser of a legal interest in the property, for value, without notice of the trust interest, then there is no personal liability, and the proprietary interest of the beneficiaries is eliminated.[358] This is classically said to be based on jurisdictional grounds. The court of Chancery had no jurisdiction over one holding legal title, who had acquired it in these circumstances; his conscience was clean, and he could not be restrained in enjoying his legal rights.[359]

(2) If the transferee cannot establish the defence of *bona fide* purchase (the burden of which is on him), the equitable interest of the beneficiaries survives. This means that a proprietary claim can be established to the property received by the third party.

(3) If, however, the third party no longer has the property, the question arises whether he or she is personally liable. This issue is addressed in detail in the last section of Chapter 11. The tradition of equity is that personal liability for the receipt of trust property depends on wrongdoing, which is why the claim to make a third party recipient liable is called a claim in "knowing receipt." In order for the third party to be liable, it must be the case that he or she was aware of the trust, or ought to have been aware of it.[360]

Against this basic rule must be set two points. First, in *Diplock v. Wintle*,[361] it was held that a party who receives property belonging to an estate being administered (which is not trust property[362]) is strictly personally liable to restore it, without regard to wrongdoing. This claim can be brought even by creditors of the estate, which shows that it does not depend on a property interest. It may also be brought by those who should have received the estate property; these parties are also not trust beneficiaries as such.

Secondly, many have argued that a recipient of trust property should be strictly personally liable in unjust enrichment. Liability in unjust enrichment does not depend on wrongdoing. This argument is often based in part on the holding in *Diplock v. Wintle*, with the suggestion that if a strict liability claim is available to those who have an interest in the proper administration of the estate of a deceased person, then a similar claim should also be available to beneficiaries of a trust.

---

358 *Cohen v. Mahlin* (1926), 8 C.B.R. 23, [1927] 1 D.L.R. 577, 1926 CarswellAlta 45, [1927] 1 W.W.R. 162, 22 Alta. L.R. 487 (C.A.).

359 *Pilcher v. Rawlins* (1872), L.R. 7 Ch. App. 259 (C.A. [In Chambers]).

360 *Citadel General Assurance Co. v. Lloyds Bank Canada* (1997), [1997] 3 S.C.R. 805, 152 D.L.R. (4th) 411, 1997 CarswellAlta 823, 1997 CarswellAlta 824, [1997] S.C.J. No. 92, 206 A.R. 321, 156 W.A.C. 321, 19 E.T.R. (2d) 93, 35 B.L.R. (2d) 153, 47 C.C.L.I. (2d) 153, 219 N.R. 323, [1999] 4 W.W.R. 135, 66 Alta. L.R. (3d) 241. See also *Millican v. Robinson*, 10 Alta. L.R. (3d) 280, 1993 CarswellAlta 26, [1993] 6 W.W.R. 539, (sub nom. *Millican v. Deloitte, Haskins & Sells*) 141 A.R. 229, 46 W.A.C. 229 (C.A.). An accounting firm received an employee's personal cheque for client accounts was deemed sufficient to put the firm on notice that it should inquire into the source of the funds. The accounting firm was taken to have had notice of theft from the trusts administered by the employee.

361 *Supra*, note 226.

362 *Commissioner of Stamp Duties (Queensland) v. Livingston, supra*, note 265.

Although trust beneficiaries have proprietary rights in the trust property, it is clear that these are not protected in the same way as legal rights. This is, in a sense, the whole point of the trust. The defence of *bona fide* purchase, which does not generally work against legal proprietary rights but which works against all trust interests, shows this. The weaker protection of a beneficial interest under a trust is also illustrated by the fact that trust beneficiaries cannot claim in negligence or other torts against those who interfere with the trust property.[363] All such claims must be brought by the trustee. If the trustee has such a claim, and refuses to bring it, he can be forced to do so by the beneficiary, since the claim itself is held in trust.[364] But if the trustee has no rights against the third party, there is nothing to be done. It is not totally clear why unjust enrichment should be different, in this regard, from tort law. In other words, the acceptance of the argument in favour of a strict liability unjust enrichment claim for the receipt of trust property (which has not yet occurred in any court) would be a substantial change in the nature of trust beneficiaries' interests.

Leaving aside the possibility of strict liability arising at the moment of receipt, it may, however, be arguable that if, after receipt, a defendant spends trust money in a way that enriches himself and destroys the trust interest, then strict liability in unjust enrichment should arise at that time.[364a]

Further Reading

Gordon K. Scott, "Restitution from an Innocent Transferee who is not a Purchaser for Value" (1949), 62 Harv. L. Rev. 1002.

A.T. Denning, "The Recovery of Money" (1949), 65 L.Q. Rev. 37.

Gareth H. Jones, "Change of Circumstances in Quasi-Contracts" (1957), 73 L.Q. Rev. 48.

P.F.P. Higgins, "Re Diplock — A Reappraisal" (1965), 6 West. Austr. L. Rev. 428.

L. Smith, "Unjust Enrichment, Property and the Structure of Trusts" (2000), 116 L.Q.R. 412.

M. McInnes, "Knowing Receipt and the Protection of Trust Property" (2002), 81 Can. Bar Rev. 171.

P. Birks, "Receipt" in P. Birks & A. Pretto, eds., *Breach of Trust* (Oxford: Hart, 2002), 213.

---

363 A duty of care is not owed to the trust beneficiary, only to the trustee: *Leigh & Sillavan Ltd. v. Aliakmon Shipping Co.* (1985), [1986] A.C. 785, [1986] 2 All E.R. 145, [1985] 2 W.L.R. 289 (H.L.), at 812 [A.C.]; *Parker-Tweedale v. Dunbar Bank plc (No. 1)*, [1991] Ch. 12 (C.A.). Nor is conversion available to the beneficiary: *M.C.C. Proceeds Inc. v. Lehman Brothers International (Europe)*, [1998] 4 All E.R. 675 (C.A.).

364 In pre-Judicature Act terms, the beneficiary would sue the trustee in Chancery to obtain an injunction requiring the trustee to sue the third party in the court of common law, for the benefit of the beneficiary. In modern terms, the same thing is accomplished by the beneficiary's suing both the trustee and the third party in a single action in which the court can resolve all claims.

364a L. Smith, "Restitution: The Heart of Corrective Justice" (2001), 79 Texas L.R. 2115, 2172-4.

(ii) *The Bona Fide Purchaser for Value*

The legal interest of a *bona fide* purchaser for value without notice automatically takes priority over the equitable interest of the beneficiary. The only question that may arise is whether the purchaser truly took without notice. If the purchaser paid less than full consideration, the court's suspicion that she or he knew of the trust interest will be aroused.

If the third party, being a *bona fide* purchaser, transfers the property to a volunteer, or to one who knew of the breach of trust, the beneficiaries cannot reach the property, because of the intermediate transfer to the *bona fide* purchaser.[365] However, if the trustee retrieves the property or its product, the beneficiaries can follow it into the trustee's hands.[366]

(iii) *The Transferee with Notice*

There are a substantial number of cases in which the transferee was either a volunteer with notice, or paid full consideration but took with notice of the trust. *McTaggart v. Boffo*[367] is illustrative.

Mrs. Williams transferred some $47,000 (approximately one-half of her assets) to the defendant, Boffo. He mixed the moneys with his own, invested some in real estate and lent other moneys to the defendant company of which he was manager. The real property was later transferred either to the company or to Boffo and one or other of his two brothers, who were his business partners in the company, as co-owners. The court held that Boffo held the moneys upon resulting trust and that the company and Boffo's brothers took with notice. The moneys could clearly be traced into the real property and the plaintiff, Mrs. Williams' administrator, was held to be entitled to do so. Since the money had been mixed, the plaintiff was only entitled to an equitable lien on the properties. The money lent to the company could not be traced, because there was no evidence of the specific bank account into which it was put, of its identity in the company's books, of the transactions in the company's account into which the money was put, or of the application of the money.[368]

Notes and Questions

1. A was a solicitor and member of the firm W & T. A handled the affairs of E Ltd., a mortgage investment company, and was its secretary. Investors would pay money to W & T and A would cause E Ltd. to arrange for the investment of the money in mortgages. The mortgages were registered in the name of F Trust Co.

---

365 *Cooper v. Anderson* (1913), 3 W.W.R. 962, 9 D.L.R. 287, 1913 CarswellMan 180, 23 W.L.R. 241 (K.B.), affirmed (1914), 28 W.L.R. 203, 16 D.L.R. 852, 1914 CarswellMan 58 (C.A.).

366 *Van Wagner v. Findlay* (1867), 14 Gr. 53, 1867 CarswellOnt 133 (U.C. Ch.).

367 (1975), 10 O.R. (2d) 733, 64 D.L.R. (3d) 441, 1975 CarswellOnt 531 (H.C.).

368 Similar cases are *Goodbody v. Bank of Montreal, supra*, note 243; *British Columbia Teachers' Credit Union v. Betterly, supra*, note 247; and *Simpsons-Sears Ltd. v. Fraser, supra*, note 247.

E Ltd. became indebted to F Trust Co. in the amount of $50,000. In order to pay the debt, A caused certain real property to be assigned to F Trust Co., the equity in which was $14,000. When the mortgage on the property fell into arrears, A paid the mortgagee approximately $37,000 out of the firm's trust account to retire the mortgage. In the result, F Trust Co.'s equity in the property was then approximately $51,000. F Trust Co. refused to accept the property in settlement of its debt, so A sent F Trust Co. a cheque drawn on the firm's trust account for $50,000 plus interest and F Trust Co. then transferred the property to E Ltd. A intended to allocate the property to certain investors, but did not do so. It was then discovered that there was a deficiency of approximately $208,000 in W & T's trust account in respect of E Ltd. and its investors. E Ltd. became insolvent and W & T made good the deficiency. W & T sought to recover the real property or an interest therein from E Ltd.'s receiver and manager.

What result?[369]

2. X is a solicitor. B and C are his clients. They opened a self-directed RRSP with D Trust Co. and named X as the authorized brokerage firm to administer it. D Trust Co. sent the money to X, who gave a declaration of trust to the company and informed B and C that he had the money in trust for investment in secured loans. X turned the money over to his company, X Ltd., along with his own moneys and moneys of other investors. X Ltd. then lent $650,000 of B and C's money to W Ltd. That company was owned by X's wife, W. X acted as manager for W Ltd. The loan was secured by a second mortgage on Blackacre. Blackacre was later subdivided and the mortgage in favour of X Ltd. was converted into separate mortgages on the individual lots. However, some of these were later discharged. X Ltd. then lent further moneys to W Ltd. and received mortgages on Whiteacre and Redacre as security. B and C then gave notice to X that they were withdrawing their funds and, when X failed to pay, sought to trace into Whiteacre, Redacre and the subdivided lots of Blackacre.

What result?[370]

3. L convinced an elderly plaintiff to place $500,000 into a trust to be managed by him. L then agreed to lend money to E Ltd. E Ltd. knowingly received trust assets from L.

What result?[371]

(iv) *The Innocent Volunteer*

When a trustee transfers property to a volunteer (one who does not give value in exchange), the trust interest of the beneficiaries survives, and the property can be recovered. If the volunteer no longer has the property or its proceeds, the beneficiary must rely on a personal liability of the transferee, which is usually liability for a kind of equitable wrongdoing. This is sometimes called "liability to account as a constructive trustee," but the claim does not depend on finding any trust property. It depends instead on showing that the transferee was aware, or ought to have been aware, of the trust at the time of receipt (and so is sometimes called "knowing receipt of trust property"). If the property in question was not

---

369 See *Yorkshire Trust Co. v. Empire Acceptance Ltd.*, *supra*, note 240.

370 See *Lament v. Constantini* (1985), 22 D.L.R. (4th) 151, 1985 CarswellBC 330, 67 B.C.L.R. 328 (S.C.).

371 *Maxham v. Excalabur International Capital Corp.* (1995), 13 B.C.L.R. (3d) 280, 1995 CarswellBC 955, [1996] 2 W.W.R. 432 (S.C.).

held in trust but was part of an unadministered estate, the volunteer may be strictly liable. Personal liabilities were discussed in Section 8 of Chapter 11.

All of these possibilities were discussed in the leading case in this area, *Diplock v. Wintle*.[372] It involved a claim to recover the traceable proceeds of the original property, and an allegation that the defendants were personally liable as "constructive trustees" ("knowing receipt"), and also the special equitable *in personam* claim available when the estate of a deceased person is not properly distributed.

That part of the case dealing with the tracing claim is reproduced below. The limits of the tracing claim against an innocent volunteer will be explored further in the notes and questions.

DIPLOCK v. WINTLE

[1948] 1 Ch. 465, (sub nom. *Diplock, Re*) [1948] 2 All E.R. 318
Court of Appeal

The testator, Caleb Diplock, directed his executors to apply the residue of his estate "for such charitable institution or institutions or other charitable or benevolent object or objects in England" as they should in their absolute discretion think fit. During a three-year period, the executors distributed a large part of the residue, some £203,000, among 139 charities. Then, in 1939, Diplock's next of kin challenged the validity of the bequest and the charities were informed of the challenge.

The executors brought an application in 1940 to determine the validity of the gift. In due course the court directed that the application be turned into an action in which three of the next of kin were the plaintiffs; the executors, four of the charities, the Attorney General and the judicial trustee of the estate[373] were the defendants.

The House of Lords held the gift of the residue to be void in *Chichester Diocesan Fund & Board of Finance Inc. v. Simpsons*.[374] It was void for uncertainty, on the basis that a testator is not allowed to delegate his will-making power to executors. He or she cannot give them the choice of who shall receive the property of the estate. The only exception is that a testator may say that the property is to be used for charitable purposes, leaving the choice of charities to

---

372 *Supra*, note 226.

373 A judicial trustee is a person appointed by the court, on the application of a beneficiary or a trustee, to administer a trust or an estate. He or she is appointed under the provisions of the *Judicial Trustees Act, 1896*, 59 & 60 Vict., c. 35. The purpose of the Act is to avoid administration of an estate by the court, a cumbersome process, but the judicial trustee is appointed in the same circumstances as when an administration order would be made, namely where administration by the ordinary personal representative or trustee has broken down. The judicial trustee acts under conditions imposed by the court and under its supervision. He or she is often the official solicitor of the court. See *Ridsel, Re*, [1947] Ch. 597, [1947] 2 All E.R. 312 (Ch. Div.), at 605 [Ch.].

374 [1944] A.C. 341, [1944] 2 All E.R. 60 (H.L.).

the executor. "Charitable" has a legal meaning,[375] but "benevolent" does not. Because the will said "charitable *or* benevolent," it permitted the executors to distribute all or part of the residue to non-charitable organizations—organizations which were not charitable, but which were "benevolent." Hence, the gift of the residue was not exclusively charitable, and this made it void. The effect was that the residue was not disposed of effectively by the will, regardless of the fact that distributions had, in fact, only been made to charities, because there was no valid term in the will authorizing the distributions. There was therefore an intestacy as to the residue. It should have gone to Diplock's next of kin. But the residue had already been given to the charities, which were volunteers.

In the application turned into an action (called the "main action" in this appeal) the action against the executors was compromised at £156,000 with the approval of the court, but the action against the charities was continued.

In 1945 the three next of kin and the judicial trustee brought 18 other actions against recipient charities. These actions and the main action were tried together. The claims against the charities were made under three heads: (1) the common law action of assumpsit for money paid under mistake; (2) a special personal action in equity; and (3) a proprietary tracing claim. The next of kin were largely unsuccessful at first instance.[376] On appeal, the Court of Appeal dismissed the first claim, but allowed the second and, in large measure, the third. The decision on the third claim was not further appealed, but the charities appealed that part of the judgment which dealt with the *in personam* claim. That appeal was dismissed by the House of Lords.[377] The *in personam* claim is discussed in Section 8 of Chapter 11.

The following excerpts deal with the tracing claims against the ten charities (one from the main action and nine from the 1945 actions) involved in the appeal before the Court of Appeal.

LORD GREENE M.R. delivered the judgment of the Court:

. . .

The first question which appears to us to fall for decision on this part of the present appeals may, we think, be thus formulated: Did the power of equity to treat Diplock "money" as recoverable from the charity, which undoubtedly existed down to the moment when the cheque was paid by the bank on which it was drawn, cease the moment that the "money" by the process of "mixture" came to be represented by an accretion to or an enlargement of the chose in action consisting of a debt already owing to the charity by its own bankers? Wynn-Parry J., in effect, decided that it did. His reason for taking this view, shortly stated, was as follows: The principle applicable was to be extracted from the decision in

---

375 This definition is explained further in the chapter on charitable trusts.
376 [1947] Ch. 716.
377 (1950), [1951] A.C. 251, [1950] 2 All E.R. 1137 (H.L.).

Hallett's case[378] and that principle was in no way extended by the decision in *Sinclair v. Brougham.*[379] The principle can operate only in cases where the mixing takes place in breach of a trust, actual or constructive, or in breach of some other fiduciary relationship and in proceedings against the trustee or fiduciary agent: here the mixing was not of this character, since it was effected by an innocent volunteer: there is no ground on which, according to principle, the conscience of such a volunteer can be held in equity to be precluded from setting up a title adverse to the claim: in every case, therefore, where a "mixture" has been carried out by the charity, the claim, whether it be against a mixed monetary fund or against investments made by means of such a mixed fund, must fail in limine.

[His Lordship disagreed with the view of Wynn-Parry J. that equity's reach did not extend to the volunteer. He felt that this view conflicted with *Sinclair v. Brougham.* That case made it clear, in his opinion, that the owner of property can claim a charge on the property ranking *pari passu* with the claim of the volunteer, and that equity can reach not only the fiduciary who does the mixing, but also the volunteer who does so. He continued:]

It is now time to examine in some detail the case of *Sinclair v. Brougham.*[380] Before us it was argued, on behalf of the respondents, that the principle on which it was decided was not that applied in *Hallett's* case but a different one altogether, invented with a view to solving a particular problem. We do not agree. The principle, in our view, was clearly the same; but in its application to new facts fresh light was thrown upon it, and it was shown to have a much wider scope than a narrow reading of *Hallett's* case itself would suggest.

[His Lordship considered the facts and arguments in *Sinclair v. Brougham* and continued:]

[T]he case of *Sinclair v. Brougham* resolves itself into one where the fund to be distributed consisted of a mixed fund in the hands of X (the society), the origin of which could be traced in part to moneys of X itself and in part to moneys of Y (the depositors) to which X never had any equitable title but which, remaining in the eyes of equity the property of Y, was, in violation of the equitable right of Y (the depositors), mixed by Z (the directors) with the moneys of X (the society). On this basis the right of the depositors must, we think, be rested on their equitable interest which they were asserting not against the directors as trustees or fiduciary agents for them, but against the society (or what was in effect the same thing, the liquidator), as a volunteer into whose hand (or "strong box") the money of the depositors had come mixed with money belonging to the society itself. As the society was no party to the borrowing it was, vis-à-vis the depositors, a volunteer holding the legal title to the assets representing the borrowed money. It was

---

378 *Re Hallett's Estate, supra*, note 198.
379 *Supra*, note 234. The facts of the case have been outlined above.
380 *Ibid.*

compelled, as being a volunteer, to recognize the equal title of the depositors; and the shareholders claiming in its right were compelled to do the same. Contrary to the view of Neville J. and the Court of Appeal, the society could not claim priority over the depositors. Per contra, the depositors could not claim priority over the shareholders. To have allowed them to do so would have been to treat the society as having itself been in a fiduciary relation to the depositors (which it was not) and to place it in as bad a position as the unfaithful agent in *Hallett's* case. This would have been manifestly unjust.

This explanation appears to us to accord with the fundamental conception which lies at the root of this equitable jurisdiction, i.e., that equity intervenes not to do what might be thought to be absolute justice to a claimant but to prevent a defendant from acting in an unconscionable manner. Equity will not restrain a defendant from asserting a claim save to the extent that it would be unconscionable for him to do so. If this limitation on the power of equity results in giving to a plaintiff less than what on some general idea of fairness he might be considered entitled to, that cannot be helped.

[His Lordship discussed the speeches in *Sinclair v. Brougham*, noted that the charities were not purchasers for value without notice, and continued:]

We have now to consider how the principles which we have outlined are to be applied to the facts of the individual cases which are before us. We deal first of all with what appear to be the most important claims from the point of view of amount. They are cases in which the money received from the Diplock executors was used in the execution of works upon land or buildings already belonging to the charities.

[The cases were as follows:

(i) Leaf Homoeopathic Hospital (action II C);
(ii) Westminster Hospital (action IV A);
(iii) Heritage Craft Schools (action IV B);
(iv) Queen Alexandra Cottage Homes (action IV D); and
(v) Guy's Hospital (action IV E).

Of these, Heritage Craft Schools alleged that it spent part of its grant to repay a loan to a Colonel Warren, who had advanced the amount in question to this charity to permit improvements to its buildings to be made. Heritage Craft Schools made an alternative claim on this basis. This issue is discussed later in the judgment. Guy's Hospital still had a small part of its grant remaining in a special account. Except for the latter, the claims for a lien on the charities' lands were dismissed for the following reasons:]

Where the contribution of a volunteer to a mixed fund or the acquisition of what we may call a "mixed asset" is in the form of money, it is, as we hope to have shown, inequitable for him to claim the whole fund or the whole asset. The equitable charge given to the other claimant in respect of the money contributed by him results merely in the division of the mixed fund between the two of them or the reduction of the asset by sale to its original components, i.e., money which is then divisible in the same manner. The volunteer gets back what he put in, i.e., money. On this basis, if a charity had used a mixed fund, consisting in part of its own money and in part of Diplock money, in the acquisition of property, whether (for example) land or stock, the application of the equitable remedy would have presented no particular difficulty. The Diplock money and the charity money could each have been traced. A charge enforced by sale and distribution would have been effective as well as fair to both parties. The charity would not, as the result of the mixture, have been deprived of anything that it had before.

In the present cases, however, the charities have used the Diplock money, not in combination with money of their own to acquire new assets, but in the alteration and improvement of assets which they already owned. The altered and improved asset owes its existence, therefore, to a combination of land belonging to the charity and money belonging to the Diplock estate. The question whether tracing is possible and if so to what extent, and also the question whether an effective remedy by way of declaration of charge can be granted consistently with an equitable treatment of the charity as an innocent volunteer, present quite different problems from those arising in the simple case above stated. In the case of the purchase of an asset out of a mixed fund, both categories of money are, as we have said, necessarily present throughout the existence of the asset in an identifiable form. In the case of adaptation of property of the volunteer by means of trust money, it by no means necessarily follows that the money can be said to be present in the adapted property. The beneficial owner of the trust money seeks to follow and recover that money and claims to use the machinery of a charge on the adapted property in order to enable him to do so. But in the first place the money may not be capable of being followed. In every true sense, the money may have disappeared. A simple example suggests itself. The owner of a house who, as an innocent volunteer, has trust money in his hands given to him by a trustee uses that money in making an alteration to his house so as to fit it better to his own personal needs. The result may add not one penny to the value of the house. Indeed, the alteration may well lower its value; for the alteration, though convenient to the owner, may be highly inconvenient in the eyes of a purchaser. Can it be said in such cases that the trust money can be traced and extracted from the altered asset? Clearly not, for the money will have disappeared leaving no monetary trace behind: the asset will not have increased (or may even have depreciated) in value through its use.

But the matter does not end here. What, for the purposes of the inquiry, is to be treated as "the charity property"? Is it to be the whole of the land belonging to the charity? or is it to be only that part of it which was altered or reconstructed or on which a building has been erected by means of Diplock money? If the latter, the result may well be that the property, both in its original state and as altered or improved, will, when taken in isolation, have little or no value. What would be the value of a building in the middle of Guy's hospital without any means of access through other parts of the hospital property? If, on the other hand, the charge is to be on the whole of the charity land, it might well be thought an extravagant result if the Diplock estate, because Diplock money had been used to reconstruct a corner of it, were to be entitled to a charge on the entirety.

But it is not merely a question of locating and identifying the Diplock money. The result of a declaration of charge is to disentangle trust money and enable it to be withdrawn in the shape of money from the complex in which it has become involved. This can only be done by sale under the charge. But the equitable owner of the trust money must in this process submit to equality of treatment with the innocent volunteer. The latter too, is entitled to disentangle his money and to withdraw it from the complex. Where the complex originates in money on both sides there is no difficulty and no inequity. Each is entitled to a charge. But if what the volunteer has contributed is not money but other property of his own such as land, what then? You cannot have a charge for land. You can, it is true, have a charge for the value of land, an entirely different thing. Is it equitable to compel the innocent volunteer to take a charge merely for the value of the land when what he has contributed is the land itself? In other words, can equity, by the machinery of a charge, give to the innocent volunteer that which he has contributed so as to place him in a position comparable with that of the owner of the trust fund? In our opinion it cannot.

In the absence of authority to the contrary our conclusion is that as regards the Diplock money used in these cases it cannot be traced in any true sense; and, further, that even if this were not so, the only remedy available to equity, viz., that of a declaration of charge would not produce an equitable result and is inapplicable accordingly.

We now consider two claims of a different class. They arise in connexion with the alternative case above mentioned of the Heritage Craft Schools (action IV. B) and the Leaf Homoeopathic Hospital (action II. C) as regards 6,000*l.* further part of the hospital's total grant of 7,500*l.* In the former case the alternative claim was that the judicial trustee is entitled by way of subrogation to stand in the shoes of Colonel Warren in respect of his loan of 500*l.* 2*s.* 0*d.* which was said to have been paid off out of the Diplock grant. In the latter case the claim is to have the benefit of a charge for 6,000*l.* on property of the hospital formerly held by Barclays Bank, Ld., as security for a fixed loan for that amount which was paid off out of the Diplock grant under the terms on which that grant was made. Both claims were rejected by Wynn-Parry J.

The facts in relation to this 500*l.* 2*s.* 0*d.* do not appear to have been clearly ascertained. But assuming that it was used to repay Colonel Warren, the result apparently was to enable the charity to apply the sum borrowed from Colonel Warren for the purpose of executing the works in question. There is no suggestion that Colonel Warren's loan was a secured loan. The payment to Colonel Warren can only have operated to extinguish the debt owing to him and the money which he had advanced was consequently available for use by the charity for the purposes indicated without there being any obligation to repay it. The case cannot, we think, be regarded as a case of subrogation. We agree with the view of Wynn-Parry J. that in such a case the debt was extinguished so that in order to give effect to the equitable doctrine said to be applicable it would be necessary to revive the debt in some way. We do not see how it can be said to be unconscientious on the part of the charity to object to this being done. In substance the Diplock money was used for the purpose of carrying out works on the land of the charity and, in our opinion the appellants are in no better position than they are in the cases of works carried out on lands of a charity which we have already discussed.

The case of the Leaf Homoeopathic Hospital is different in that (a) the loan was a secured loan, (b) the grant was made in terms for the purpose of enabling the charity to pay off the loan, and (c) the 6,000*l.* in question cannot be said to have been used indirectly in the execution of works as in the case of the Heritage Craft Schools: it was used simply and solely for the purpose of clearing off an existing incumbrance.

Here, too, we think that the effect of the payment to the bank was to extinguish the debt and the charge held by the bank ceased to exist. The case cannot, we think, be regarded as one of subrogation, and if the appellants were entitled to a charge it would have to be a new charge created by the court. The position in this respect does not appear to us to be affected by the fact that the payment off of this debt was one of the objects for which the grant was made. The effect of the payment off was that the charity, which had previously held only an equity of redemption, became the owners of unincumbered property. That unincumbered property derived from a combination of two things, the equity of redemption contributed by the charity and the effect of the Diplock money in getting rid of the incumbrance. If equity is now to create a charge (and we say "create" because there is no survival of the original charge) in favour of the judicial trustee, it will be placing him in a position to insist upon a sale of what was contributed by the charity. The case, as it appears to us, is in effect analogous to the cases where Diplock money is expended on improvements on charity land. The money was in this case used to remove a blot on the title; to give the judicial trustee a charge in respect of the money so used would, we think, be equally unjust to the charity who, as the result of such a charge, would have to submit to a sale of the interest in the property which it brought in. We may point out that if the relief claimed were to be accepted as a correct application of the equitable principle, insoluble problems might arise in a case where in the meanwhile fresh charges on the property had been created or money had been expended upon it.

> [His Lordship then went on to consider the claims against several charities which had paid Diplock moneys into active bank accounts where they became mingled with their own. These cases were:
>
> (i) St. George's Hospital (main action);
> (ii) The Prince of Wales Hospital, Plymouth (action II A); and
> (iii) Dr. Barnardo's Homes (action I E).
>
> He held that the rule in *Clayton's Case*[381] applied to these claims, with the

---

381 *Supra*, note 270.

result that the next of kin were only partly successful. In this connection his Lordship said:]

It might be suggested that the corollary of treating two claimants on a mixed fund as interested rateably should be that withdrawals out of the fund ought to be attributed rateably to the interests of both claimants. But in the case of an active banking account this would lead to the greatest difficulty and complication in practice and might in many cases raise questions incapable of solution. What then is to be done? In our opinion, the same rule as that applied in *Clayton's* case should be applied. This is really a rule of convenience based upon so-called presumed intention. It has been applied in the case of two beneficiaries whose trust money has been paid into a mixed banking account from which drawings were subsequently made, and, so far as we know, its application has not been adversely criticized. . . .[382] In such a case both claimants are innocent, neither is in a fiduciary relation to the other, and if the mixed fund had not been drawn upon they would be entitled to rateable charges upon it. Exactly the same occurs where the claimants are not two beneficiaries but one beneficiary and one volunteer, and we think, accordingly, that the same principle should be adopted.

[The claim against one charity, the National Institute for the Deaf (action I F), fell into a separate category. It was originally thought that it had placed the Diplock money into its own account and had then withdrawn it and placed it in a separate account earmarked as Diplock money. On that assumption his Lordship held that the charity could "unmix" the money and allowed the next of kin to recover it. Thus, the rule in *Clayton's Case* did not apply.

However, the factual assumption turned out to be wrong. In fact, the charity had merely set aside the money to meet any possible liability arising out of this litigation and not to earmark it as Diplock funds. That being so, *Clayton's Case* applied and the court so held in a supplementary judgment.[383]

Lastly, the court considered the claim against the Royal Sailors Orphan Girls' School and Home (action III C). It had used its grant to purchase government stock, which was added to its existing government stock. Thereafter the charity made further purchases of government stock with its own moneys, which were added to the total, and then it sold several amounts of stock. Of this case his Lordship said:]

We do not accept the view that the case ought to be treated as though it were subject to the rule in *Clayton's Case*. We see no justification for extending that rule beyond the case of a banking account. Here, before the sales took place, the mass of stock, if the question had then been raised, would have been regarded in

---

382 See *per* Fry J. in *Re Hallett's Estate, supra*, note 198, and *per* North J. in *Re Stenning, supra*, note 301.

383 [1948] Ch. 465 at 599.

equity as belonging rateably to the charity and to the Diplock estate. The only equitable way of treating the situation appears to us to be to regard each sum of stock withdrawn from the mass as having been made up in the same proportions. In so far as, upon this principle, withdrawals represented in part Diplock money and the sums received on the sale of the stock withdrawn were expended on general purposes and cannot now be traced into any existing asset, that amount of Diplock money must be regarded as having disappeared. But in respect of so much of the Diplock interest as is not thus accounted for, we are of opinion that the claim to a rateable proportion of the stock still held is established.

In considering the individual cases for the purpose of applying the principle of the equitable right of tracing, we have, for simplicity, assumed that the appellants' claims extend to the full amount of the Diplock moneys, properly belonging to the next-of-kin, paid to each respondent — in particular we have not taken into account the sums recovered from the executors or their estates under the compromise order.

No argument was addressed to us on this aspect of the matter. Prima facie and subject to discussion it appears to us that the sums so recovered ought to be credited rateably to all the charities for all purposes, i.e., for the purposes of the claims in rem as well as the claims in personam.

. . .

The result of the whole matter is that the appellants are, in our judgment, entitled to succeed on all the appeals. Having regard to the view we have expressed in regard to their claims in personam and in regard to the failure of the defences of the *Statute of Limitations*[384] to those claims, and in the light of the submissions made to us, the appellants would under this head of their claim be entitled, as it appears to us, to orders against each of the respondents for payment to the judicial trustee of an amount equivalent to the total sum paid to that respondent less a rateable proportion of the sums recovered from the executors or their estates, but without any interest.

[His Lordship went on to hold that the appellants, to the extent their tracing claims were allowed, were entitled to the interest in fact earned on the investments made with Diplock moneys by the charities. However, their *in rem* claims were to be reduced by the amount recovered from the executors.

The appellants had agreed to pursue their claims *in rem* only to the extent they were unable to recover on their claims *in personam*. Hence, in the end result, the appellants were entitled: (1) if their tracing claim was allowed (a) to have the appropriate securities transferred to them (or payment of a sum equivalent to the proceeds of sale thereof) plus interest; and (b) to recover the balance of the principal sums, less the amount recovered from the executors, in their *in personam* action; and (2) if their tracing claim was disal-

---

384 *Limitations Act, 1939*, 2 & 3 Geo. 6, c. 21.

lowed, to recover the balance of the principal sums, less the amount recovered from the executors, in their *in personam* action.

Wrottesley and Evershed L.J.J. concurred. The court allowed the appeals.]

Notes and Questions

1. *Diplock v. Wintle* advanced the law in many respects, but left other issues unanswered or in an unsatisfactory state. One obvious point made by the Court of Appeal was that property cannot be traced if it is no longer identifiable, for example, if it has been dissipated or spent on a dinner or on comestibles.[385] This limitation does not apply to the *in personam* claim.

There is some difficulty in understanding the *in rem* or proprietary claim, since an estate being administered is not the same as a trust.[386] Those who will get property from the estate of a deceased person are not trust beneficiaries, and are not understood to have proprietary rights in the property of the estate. On the other hand, it is clear that the estate property does not beneficially belong to the executors who are administering it; they are like trustees in the sense that the estate property is not available to their own personal creditors, nor could they rightly give it away or leave it to their own heirs if they died. It is as if the estate is a kind of purpose trust. The executors are bound to follow the instructions in the will (or the rules of intestacy) in disposing of the assets.[387]

2. The Court of Appeal further held that it would be inequitable to allow tracing when the recipients had spent the money to improve and alter their buildings, for the remedy in such cases is a lien, which is enforceable by sale. The court thought it would be an extravagant result if the entire property would be subjected to a sale in those circumstances, particularly when the value of the property has remained unchanged or has decreased.[388]

The question may be raised, however, why tracing should not be allowed if the property has increased in value. If the charity had then gone bankrupt, the next of kin would have received nothing. In any event, the lien that is imposed does not require an automatic sale, for a sale would be under the court's supervision and it could impose terms.[389]

Goff and Jones called this approach in *Diplock* "an emasculated application of the defence of change of position"[390] and argued in the third edition of their book that the law should recognize the latter as a general defence to a restitutionary claim. In the fourth and later editions, however, they noted that in recent years the House of Lords has followed other common law jurisdictions and has expressly recognized and accepted the defence regarding all restitutionary claims.[391]

---

385 *Diplock v. Wintle, supra,* note 226, at [1948] Ch. 521.

386 *Commissioner of Stamp Duties (Queensland) v. Livingston, supra,* note 265.

387 For some discussion of this point see L. Smith, "Unjust Enrichment, Property and the Structure of Trusts" (2000), 116 L.Q.R. 412, 438.

388 *Ibid.,* at 547.

389 See Ford and Lee, §17280.

390 Lord Goff of Chieveley and G. Jones, *The Law of Restitution,* 6th ed. (London: Sweet and Maxwell, 2002), at 111.

391 *Ibid.*

The House of Lords held that the defence of change of position was not available in the personal action.[392] This has been followed more recently, even after the general recognition of the defence.[393]

3. Two of the charities used their money to pay their secured and unsecured creditors and the Court of Appeal again applied what amounted to a change in position defence.[394] Moreover, the court rejected the next of kin's claim to be subrogated to the positions of the creditors,[395] holding that this would involve the revival of the unsecured debt and the creation of a lien with the attendant right of sale in the case of the secured debt. Yet, if the charities were never entitled to pay the debt with the Diplock moneys, why should it create a hardship in them to have to repay the moneys and be put back in the position they occupied originally? At any rate this is the case with the secured debt. As regards the unsecured debt, it is difficult to see how the next of kin could obtain a proprietary remedy, since there was no security.[396] See however Section 3.d.vii of this Chapter.

4. The inequity of the rule in *Clayton's Case, Re*[397] is vividly illustrated by *Diplock v. Wintle*. The Court applied that rule uncritically in respect of charities which had mixed trust moneys with their own in a current bank account. By contrast, the rule was held not to apply in the case of one charity which had used the trust moneys to purchase stock and subsequently mixed the stock with its own. Apart from the fact that one situation involved a bank account and the other did not, they were identical.[398]

5. When trust property is mixed with other property, should it be possible for the mixer to "unmix" the contributions? This was said to be possible in *Diplock v. Wintle*, in relation to the claim against the National Institute for the Deaf, but the holding was overridden because it was based on a misunderstanding of the facts, as noted in the extract above. Had the facts been as originally understood, should the "unmixing" have been treated as effective, even if (say) the "Diplock" money so identified was lost in a bad investment, while the other money from the mixture still survived? Think about the case of a lawyer, who lawfully mixes in a single bank account property held in trust for multiple clients.

Would the rule be different if the mixing was wrongfully done?[399]

6. The *in personam* claim could only be brought after all remedies against the personal representatives were exhausted in *Diplock v. Wintle*. This restriction does not apply to the claim *in rem*.[400] Those who would like the strict liability personal claim to be available to trust beneficiaries usually argue that this requirement is unnecessarily harsh on the personal representatives, and should be dropped. Note that if the case arose today, the effects on the executors would be less harsh. They would, themselves, have been able to sue the charities in unjust enrichment based on the fact that they had made payments under a

---

392 (1950), [1951] A.C. 251, [1950] 2 All E.R. 1137 (H.L.), at 276.

393 *Gray v. Richards Butler (a firm)* (1996), 140 SJ LB 194, fully reported online. The correctness of this is doubted by Goff and Jones, 823-5. For some discussion of whether this sheds light on the nature of the liability, see L. Smith, "Unjust Enrichment, Property and the Structure of Trusts" (2000), 116 L.Q.R. 412, 437-444.

394 At [1948] Ch. 548-50.

395 *Ibid.*, at 549.

396 See Ford and Lee, §§17280. And see *Chobaniuk v. Canadian Johns-Manville Co.* (1962), 39 W.W.R. 680, 1962 CarswellSask 43 (Dist. Ct.); *McCullough v. Marsden*, [1919] 1 W.W.R. 689, 45 D.L.R. 645, 1919 CarswellAlta 77, 17 Alta. L.R. 553 (Alta. C.A.).

397 *Supra*, note 270.

398 *Cf. Major Trust Co., Re, supra*, note 277.

399 See Smith, 206-8; 212-215.

400 See Ford and Lee, §17320.

mistake of law, or simply on the basis that the charities had no rights under the intestacy to the funds received, and the policy of the law required that they make restitution. Those claims could have been *in rem* or *in personam* or both. The effect would be that the direct claims by the next of kin would not have added anything.

7. In Queensland, Western Australia and New Zealand, the law has been changed by statute in response to *Diplock v. Wintle*. The Queensland legislation[401] extends to trusts the same remedies as were held to exist for estates in *Diplock v. Wintle*, but requires the beneficiary to exhaust his or her remedies against the trustee or personal representative first, except by leave of the court. Moreover, the legislation enshrines the change of position defence.

The Western Australian legislation[402] also extends to trusts, but it requires a beneficiary to exhaust his or her remedies first against the recipient of the property, before proceeding against the trustee or personal representative. The legislation also incorporates the change of position defence.

The New Zealand legislation[403] is like the Western Australian provision, but allows the beneficiary to proceed against either the recipient or the trustee. However, the trustee has the right to make application that an order be made against the recipient.

Which of these provisions is better? Should it matter, as regards any remedy, that the recipient no longer has the property? It seems that the Queensland and Western Australian statutes proceed on the assumption that the recipient still has the property, while the New Zealand statute does not.

How should legislation of this type be drafted?

There was also legislative intervention in some places in reaction to the original holding in *Chichester Diocesan Fund & Board of Finance Inc. v. Simpsons.*[404] In Alberta[405] and the U.K.,[406] it was enacted that "charitable or benevolent" should be read, effectively, as "charitable and benevolent." But the common law of wills has also evolved and the principle that a testator may not delegate his will-making power has been diluted almost to nothing. A testator may give a very widely-drafted power of appointment to his personal representatives.[407]

8. For a period of 18 years, S gave most of his earnings to his mother, M. For part of this time, S worked in the family business and received minimal wages, although he worked long hours and was instrumental in making the business a success. However, he quit the business in 1952, as a result of a disagreement with M. On a number of occasions S gave M lump sums in the total amount of $22,900 and M told him at different times that she was investing his money and he would receive it at her death. In 1971, M conveyed residential property worth $56,000 to her other children. She died in 1973, when that property was worth $79,000. Shortly before her death, M made gifts *mortis causa* of jewellery worth $105,000 to her other children. By her will, she directed that her estate of $7,000 be divided among those children.

---

401 *Trusts Act 1973* (as amended) (Qnsld.), s. 109.
402 *Trustees Act 1962* (as amended) (W.A.), s. 65.
403 *Administration Act 1969*, (as amended) (N.Z.), ss. 49(1), 50.
404 *Supra*, note 374.
405 *Wills Act*, R.S.A. 2000, c. W-12, s. 32.
406 *Charitable Trusts (Validation) Act 1954*, c. 58 (Eng.), which, however, only applies to instruments taking effect before 16 December 1952.
407 See *Nicholls Estate, Re* (1987), 57 O.R. (2d) 763, 34 D.L.R. (4th) 321, 1987 CarswellOnt 638, 18 O.A.C. 254, 25 E.T.R. 228 (C.A.).

S seeks restitution from the estate and his brothers and sisters. Will he succeed? If so, on what basis and to what extent?[408]

4. MISCELLANEOUS REMEDIES

In addition to the personal and proprietary remedies, beneficiaries have other remedies available to them to prevent and to redress a breach of trust. The following may be mentioned briefly.[409] Other remedies, such as the removal of trustees, are discussed elsewhere.[410]

1. *Declaratory Judgments.* The court has wide jurisdiction to make declaratory orders and judgments, whether or not any other relief is claimed.[411] A proceeding for a declaration may be brought by application.[412] The jurisdiction is a discretionary one and the court will refuse the application if there is no genuine dispute, or if the declaration can only have effect in the future or on the happening of a contingency.[413] Hence, a beneficiary may seek a declaration that a trustee's action or proposed action is in breach of trust.

2. *Injunctions.* A beneficiary is entitled to bring proceedings for an injunction to restrain the trustees from committing a breach of trust or to compel them to carry out the trust.[414] Thus, an injunction may be granted to prevent the trustees from distributing an estate contrary to the trust,[415] from selling trust property at too low a price,[416] or from disposing of property which the beneficiary is entitled to trace.[417]

3. *Refusal of Specific Performance.* When trustees have entered into a contract in breach of trust, neither they nor the purchaser can obtain specific performance of the contract.[418] This situation is not normally likely to involve beneficiaries, but will prevent a breach of trust if the beneficiaries were unsuccessful in obtaining an injunction. An injunction might be refused, for example, if it would interfere with the trustee's discretion.

---

408 See *Kong v. Kong*, 5 E.T.R. 67, 1979 CarswellBC 261, 14 B.C.L.R. 357, [1979] 6 W.W.R. 673 (S.C.).

409 See further Ford and Lee, §§17050-17090, 17370-17480.

410 In the materials on the appointment, retirement and removal of trustees and the duties of trustees.

411 See, *e.g.*, *Courts of Justice Act*, R.S.O. 1990, c. C.43, s. 97.

412 See, *e.g.*, *Rules of Civil Procedure* (Ont.), Rule 14.05(3)(g).

413 *Fries v. Fries*, [1950] O.W.N. 661, 1950 CarswellOnt 309 (H.C.).

414 *Downey v. Dennis* (1887), 14 O.R. 219.

415 *Fox v. Fox* (1870), L.R. 11 Eq. 142.

416 *Dance v. Goldingham* (1873), L.R. 8 Ch. App. 902; *Buttle v. Saunders*, [1950] 2 All E.R. 193 (Ch. Div.).

417 *A v. C.* (1980), [1981] Q.B. 956, [1980] 2 All E.R. 347 (Q.B.).

418 *Kennedy v. The Queen* (1864), 1 W.W. & B. (Eq.) 145 at 156, *per* Stawell C.J.; *Dunn v. Flood* (1885), 28 Ch. D. 586 at 590, *per* Fry L.J.; *Sea v. McLean* (1887), 14 S.C.R. 632, 1887 CarswellBC 2.

4. *Setting Aside Transactions.* A transaction which has been completed in breach of trust will be set aside at the suit of a beneficiary, but not if the purchaser was a *bona fide* purchaser for value of the legal estate without notice of the trust.[419] However, if the property is land and is registered under land titles, notice of a trust does not defeat a purchaser's title.[420]

5. *Administration Action.* The court has jurisdiction to administer an estate itself upon action by a beneficiary. But this is rare,[421] because usually only isolated questions arise in the administration of an estate and these can be disposed of by application.[422] Hence, it is only when there are general problems with the whole estate that such an action may succeed. Even then, the court is likely to appoint a receiver or to replace the personal representatives instead.

6. *Appointment of Receiver.* The court has jurisdiction to appoint a receiver to manage a trust if its affairs are in disarray.[423] However, this remedy is only granted if it is necessary to preserve the trust property and if no other remedy, such as the replacement of the trustees, is feasible.[424]

5. DEFENCES OF THE TRUSTEE

(a) Introduction

A trustee who commits a breach of trust, may not be liable to the beneficiaries if he or she has a valid defence to the action or may be excused from liability. In this part, various defences are considered. In the next part, several reasons why a trustee may be excused are discussed.

(b) The Defendant Was Not A Trustee

A trustee is liable only for his or her own acts and omissions. Hence, a trustee is not normally liable for a breach of trust committed before becoming a trustee or after ceasing to be a trustee. However, a trustee will be liable when merely standing by and allowing another trustee to commit a breach of trust. It follows, therefore, that if a trustee learns of a breach of trust which occurred before becoming a trustee and fails to correct the breach, he or she will be liable.[425] A trustee will also be liable when she or he resigns the trusteeship in the knowledge

---

419 *Peffer v. Rigg*, [1977] 1 W.L.R. 285.

420 See, *e.g.*, *Land Titles Act*, R.S.O. 1990, c. L.5, s. 78(5).

421 See *Wilson-Alexander v. Calder* (1885), 28 Ch. D. 457 (Eng. Ch. Div.); *Blake, Re* (1885), 29 Ch. D. 913.

422 See, *e.g.*, *Rules of Civil Procedure* (Ont.), Rule 14.05(3)(a)-(c).

423 See *ibid.*, cl. (g). And see *Courts of Justice Act*, R.S.O. 1990, c. C.43, s. 101(1).

424 See *A.G. v. Schonfield*, [1980] 1 W.L.R. 1182.

425 *Forest of Dean Coal Mining Co.*, *supra*, note 25.

that her or his successor or co-trustees intend to commit a breach of trust. The latter situation is explored in *Head v. Gould*,[426] reproduced below.

HEAD v. GOULD

[1898] 2 Ch. 250
Chancery Division

Under a marriage settlement made in 1865 and a post nuptial settlement made in the same year, property was placed in trust with two trustees for the benefit of Robert Head and his wife, Harriette, for life, with remainder to their children in equal shares at the age of 21 or at the time of their marriage. The trustees had power to advance one-half of the presumptive or vested shares of any child during the life tenancy. Robert Head died in 1881, survived by his widow and three children, Robert Jr., Adelaide and William. William was still a minor. Under pressure from the widow, the current trustees, Houlditch and Clapp, both solicitors, advanced all of Robert Jr.'s and Adelaide's shares by 1894. However, the widow and Adelaide demanded more money. As a result, Houlditch and Clapp desired to be relieved of their office. At the request of Harriette and Adelaide they appointed another solicitor, Gould (a friend of the family), and Adelaide in their stead. Gould and Adelaide appropriated William's share.

William brought this action against Gould and Adelaide, against the former trustees, Houlditch and Clapp, and against Harriette. Houlditch and Clapp defended and sought indemnity from Gould, Adelaide and Harriette. Adelaide defended and sought to be indemnified by Gould. Gould entered a defence, but it was struck out on his failure to complete the pleadings. Houlditch and Clapp were held liable for their own breach of trust with a right of indemnity against Adelaide and Harriette.

The court held that Gould and Adelaide were guilty of breach of trust and that Adelaide was not entitled to be indemnified by Gould. There remained the question of the liability of Houlditch and Clapp for Gould's and Adelaide's breach of trust.

KEKEWICH J.:

. . .

It is the duty of trustees to protect the funds intrusted to their care, and to distribute those funds themselves or hand them over to their successors intact, that is, properly invested and without diminution, according to the terms of the mandate contained in the instrument of trust. This duty is imposed on them as long as they remain trustees and must be their guide in every act done by them as trustees. On retiring from the trust and passing on the trust estate to their successors — and this whether they appoint those successors or merely assign the property to the

---

426 *Supra*, note 26.

nominees of those who have the power of appointment — they are acting as trustees, and it is equally incumbent on them in this ultimate act of office to fulfil the duty imposed on them as at any other time. If therefore they neglect that duty and part with the property without due regard to it, they remain liable and will be held by the Court responsible for the consequences properly traceable to that neglect. This explanation will, I think, be found consistent with all judicial utterances on the subject, and haply aid to make them consistent with themselves.

· · ·

The case of *Webster v. Le Hunt*[427] is of material use only by reason of a general statement of law by the Lord Chancellor (Lord Westbury). . . . This is the passage in the report:

> Trustees denuding themselves of trust funds, if they did so under circumstances that warranted any reasonable belief of the insecurity of the trust funds in the hands of those to whom they committed them, should not be considered in this Court as having validly discharged themselves of the custody of the trust funds, or released themselves from responsibility. About the principle of the Court there could be no doubt.

> [His Lordship also referred to *Clark v. Hoskins*,[428] the facts of which were similar to *Head v. Gould*, in that the trustees retired after refusing to hand over certain deeds to the defendant Heather Brown. This enabled her to perpetrate a fraud by suppressing a settlement and raising money on the property as if it were unaffected by the settlement. The new trustees were more accommodating. In the subsequent action against the old and the new trustees, the old trustees were exonerated. Wood L.J. said:[429]

> These new trustees so appointed might do that which was very improper, and raise for her purposes moneys which they were not entitled to raise, and give receipts to the intended mortgagees; but at the same time these [old] trustees were not asked to assist in committing this fraud; and I conceive it would go far beyond anything which has been ever done in this Court to fix these gentlemen with the consequences, when it was not in their contemplation that such a fraud was to be perpetrated, but it was in their contemplation simply that a sum was to be raised as against cestuis que trust which it would be improper for the trustees in the execution of their duty to raise.

> His Lordship continued:]

These being the authorities to guide me, it will be as well first to inquire whether Messrs. Houlditch and Clapp can be brought within Lord Westbury's rule. Did they denude themselves of the trust funds under circumstances that

---

427 8 W.R. 534, 9 W.R. 918.
428 37 L.J. (Ch.) 561.
429 *Ibid.*, at 567.

warranted any reasonable belief of the insecurity of the trust funds in the hands of those to whom they committed them? Messrs. Houlditch and Clapp were anxious to be relieved of the trust. That can surprise no one who has studied even slightly the facts of this case, and no possible objection could be taken to their retirement if it was properly effected. I do not see what they could do towards that end but appoint, or concur in the appointment of, new trustees in their place. There was nothing on which they could properly apply to the Court, and at that time the appointment of a judicial trustee was unknown. There was of course great difficulty in finding new trustees, and this is a cogent factor in the solution of the question whether the appointment of G.D. Gould and Miss Head was justifiable. They ought to have avoided the appointment of Miss Head if possible, not merely because she was a beneficiary, but because she was known to be under the influence of her mother, and mainly perhaps, and to some extent certainly, by reason of that influence she had taken an active part in the importunities which had already led to a breach of trust, and in that breach of trust itself. But was it possible? They succeeded in finding, or rather Mrs. Head found, a gentleman who was a solicitor ready to undertake the trust out of kindness to the family to which he seems to have owed a debt of gratitude, and although their inquiries respecting him were perhaps somewhat slight having regard to the serious position of the trust, I cannot say that they were not reasonably justified in approving him. It is urged that they could not completely discharge themselves without appointing two competent trustees. That may be admitted, but I cannot hold Miss Head to have been an incompetent trustee when linked with another whose professional position was of itself a security that the trust funds would be properly administered. I cannot blame Messrs. Houlditch and Clapp for the appointment which they made, nor do I think that they had any reasonable ground for believing, or that they believed, that the trust would be otherwise than secure in the hands of their successors. One suspicious fact however deserves special notice.

. . .

What their [*i.e.*, Houlditch and Clapp's] successors did was to convert the whole remaining trust property and improperly to spend it. They knew that G.D. Gould was reflecting on some possible mode of assisting Mrs. Head, and he had told them, by his letter to Mr. Clapp of November 2, 1894, that he was turning his attention to some means of doing this; but apparently he was as conscious as Messrs. Houlditch and Clapp themselves of the difficulty of doing this, and he certainly never hinted as doing it in the manner ultimately adopted. On reflective study of the evidence and correspondence, and notwithstanding suspicious criticism of some unhappy expressions in Mr. Clapp's letters, I do not believe that Messrs. Houlditch and Clapp contemplated any breach of trust at all, and I am convinced that they never contemplated that actually committed. With the judgment of the Court of Appeal in *Clark v. Hoskins*[430] before us it is easy to understand the Master of the Rolls as meaning what he probably intended to express — that

---

430 *Ibid.*

in order to make a retiring trustee liable for a breach of trust committed by his successor you must shew, and shew clearly, that the very breach of trust which was in fact committed was not merely the outcome of the retirement and new appointment, but was contemplated by the former trustee when such retirement and appointment took place. That is clearly the doctrine of *Clark v. Hoskins*. It will not suffice to prove that the former trustees rendered easy or even intended, a breach of trust, if it was not in fact committed. They must be proved to have been guilty as accessories before the fact of the impropriety actually perpetrated.

Notes and Questions

1. Why did the court in *Head v. Gould* not place greater emphasis upon the fact that one of the replacement trustees, Adelaide, was a beneficiary who had already benefited from the earlier breach and was demanding more money under pressure from Harriette? Could knowledge of a probable subsequent breach not have been imputed to the retiring trustees in those circumstances?

2. To be liable, the resigning trustee must have a reasonable belief that the trust property will not be secure in the hands of his or her successor. Will the retiring trustee be liable if, at the time of resignation, he or she knows that the would-be successor has acted fraudulently or dishonestly in other circumstances?

3. A trustee refuses to do an act requested by a beneficiary because the trustee knows it is a breach of trust. The beneficiary then says: "Please resign and appoint X in your place, because X will do what I want." The trustee complies with the request.

Is the trustee liable if X subsequently commits a breach?[431]

(c) Consent and Participation

(i) *Generally*

If a beneficiary consents to, participates in, or instigates a breach of trust, it is axiomatic that the beneficiary cannot afterwards sue the trustee for compensation for the loss. Other beneficiaries who were not involved in the breach can, however, bring action.[432]

In order to debar a beneficiary from relief, it must be shown that the beneficiary had capacity, that the consent was with full knowledge of what the beneficiary was concurring in and of his or her rights and all material facts, and that his or her will was not overborne by the trustees or others through undue influence or duress. If the trustee failed to make full disclosure of the proposed breach to the beneficiaries, their consent is ineffective.[433]

---

431 See *Palairet v. Carew* (1863), 32 Beav. 564, 55 E.R. 222.
432 *McNeill, Re* (1911), 19 W.L.R. 691, 1911 CarswellBC 61 (S.C.).
433 *MacCulloch Estate (Trustee of) v. MacCulloch* (1986), (sub nom. *Price Waterhouse Ltd. v. MacCulloch*) 25 D.L.R. (4th) 126, 1986 CarswellNS 91, 72 N.S.R. (2d) 1, 173 A.P.R. 1, 22 E.T.R. 34 (C.A.), leave to appeal refused (1986), 22 E.T.R. xv, 176 A.P.R. 270 (note), 70 N.R. 81 (note), 73 N.S.R. (2d) 270 (note) (S.C.C.).

These issues were all significant in *Pauling's Settlement Trusts, Re.*[434] A marriage settlement was made in 1919 in favour of Mrs. Younghusband for life, with remainder to her children. Under clause 11 of the settlement, the trustee, the defendant bank, could, with the written consent of the life tenant, raise up to one-half of the expectant, presumptive or vested share of a child and pay it to the child for his or her use, or apply it for his or her benefit. The family, comprising Commander and Mrs. Younghusband and their four children, Francis, George, Ann and Anthony, were a united family, but they lived beyond their means. Between 1948 and 1954 the bank purported to make a number of advances to the children at the parents' request and with the "consent" of the children. The children sometimes received independent advice; at other times they did not. The advances were made after they had respectively attained the age of majority, although in some cases shortly after they had come of age.

The disputed advances were as follows, in chronological order:

(1) Two advances totalling £8,450 were made to Francis and George, who instructed the bank to apply them to the purchase of a family home in the Isle of Man. However, the title was taken in the parents' names without the children's consent. (2) A further advance of £1,000 was made to the two eldest sons which was to be used to purchase furniture for the house. The bank paid the money directly into the mother's overdrawn account and did not inquire into its application. No furniture was bought with the money. (3) Another advance of £2,600 made to Francis and George was to discharge a loan on the mother's life interest under another trust. (4) Francis and George received a further advance of £2,000 on the basis of their signed memorandum that the money was to be used to pay for improvements to the new house. It was paid into the mother's overdrawn account. (5) When Ann came of age, several advances were made to her to purchase a house for her in London upon her marriage. Since she received this money, these advances were not in issue. However, a further advance to her to buy furniture for her house in London was disputed. Only £300 of that advance was applied for this purpose, the balance being transferred to the father's and mother's overdrawn accounts. (6) When Anthony came of age, several advances were made to him. Of these, £1,000 was used to pay off a loan on Ann's house and the rest was paid into the mother's account. (7) Finally, there were several more advances to Francis, George and Ann, all of which were paid into the mother's account.

The four children then sued the trustees, claiming that the advances had been made in breach of trust and without consent, since the children were still under parental control and, hence, protected by the presumption of undue influence.

The Court of Appeal held that: (a) the power of advancement in clause 11 of the marriage settlement was a fiduciary power and could be exercised only for the benefit of a child; (b) the power could be exercised either by a direct payment to a child, or by payment for a particular purpose, in which case the child had to use the money for that purpose and the trustees had to ensure that he or she did so; (c) the consent of an adult beneficiary was not required for an advance if the

---

advance was otherwise proper, but if the advance was in breach of trust, a valid request or consent to the advance by the child would be a good defence to the beneficiary's subsequent action to replace the moneys; (d) if a parent benefits from the advance, there is a presumption of undue influence, which is rebutted if the gift was the spontaneous act of the child and the child knew his or her rights; and (e) the presumption applies even to adult children if they remain under parental control and influence.

With respect to the several advances, the Court held: (1) The purchase of the house on the Isle of Man was a breach of trust to which Francis and George had not consented. (2) The same applied to the advance intended to be used to buy furniture for that house, and (3) the advance used to discharge the loan on the mother's life interest. (4) However, the bank had a good defence in respect of the advance for improvements to the house, since Francis and George had consented to this and they were by then emancipated from parental control. (5) That was not the case with respect to the advances to Ann to purchase furniture for her house, since she had only recently come of age and was, therefore, still presumed to be acting under her parents' undue influence. However, she had to give credit for the £300 she in fact received. (6) Similarly, Anthony was under the presumed undue influence of his parents and, hence, unable to give a valid consent for the advances made to him. (7) Finally, the last advances to Francis, George and Ann were made with consent and at a time when they were all emancipated from parental control.

The court then went on to deal with the trustee's defences of acquiescence, limitations and laches, and its request for relief from the consequences of the breach of trust. These issues are dealt with later in this chapter.

Notes and Questions

1. At first instance in the *Pauling* case, Wilberforce J., after a review of the authorities, stated:[435]

> The result of these authorities appears to me to be that the court has to consider all the circumstances in which the concurrence of the cestui que trust was given with a view to seeing whether it is fair and equitable that, having given his concurrence, he should afterwards turn round and sue the trustees: that, subject to this, it is not necessary that he should know that what he is concurring in is a breach of trust, provided that he fully understands what he is concurring in, and that it is not necessary that he should himself have directly benefited by the breach of trust.

This question was not argued in the Court of Appeal and that court expressed no opinion on it.[436] However, the Court of Appeal subsequently approved the quoted passage in another case.[437] It would seem, therefore, that it is not necessary that the beneficiary know that he or she is consenting to a breach of trust.

---

435 (1961), [1962] 1 W.L.R. 86, [1961] 3 All E.R. 713 (Ch. Div.), at 108 [W.L.R.].
436 At [1964] Ch. 339.
437 *Holder v. Holder*, [1968] Ch. 353, [1968] 1 All E.R. 665 (C.A.), at 394, 399, 406.

2. It follows from the *Pauling* case that it is not necessary that the consenting beneficiary actually received a benefit.[438]

3. It also follows from *Pauling* that trustees take a risk in making advances to children who have reached their majority. As the Court of Appeal made clear, it depends upon the circumstances of each case how long the presumption of undue influence continues. The trustees will not be excused if they knew or ought to have known that the beneficiary was acting under another's undue influence.

4. Note that consent is not the same as acquiescence or passive assent. Rather, it is a positive act of approval based upon informed knowledge.[439]

5. A beneficiary was a minor. He consented to a breach of trust, but fraudulently lied about his age. Is the consent valid?[440]

6. R and G were executors and equal beneficiaries in an estate and also the directors of two companies owned by the estate. R also owned another company for which he needed a loan. The bank, which was also the banker for the estate, made the loan contingent on a guarantee from one of the companies owned by the estate. R asked, and G agreed to sign a director's resolution authorizing a guarantee for the company owned by R. This company failed and the guarantee was called in. G subsequently claimed that R had misled him and claimed breach of trust. However, the court held that G knew what a guarantee was and understood what he was approving and was thus not misled, and that R had not committed a breach of trust. Further, the bank was not a constructive trustee in favour of G's half interest in the estate as the bank had no way of knowing whether G had been misled.[441]

(ii) *Impounding the Beneficiary's Interest*

If a beneficiary has instigated or consented to a breach of trust and the trustee is subsequently found liable, the beneficiary's interest may be impounded. This means that the beneficiary's interest in the trust can be applied to indemnify the trustee.

The court has an inherent jurisdiction to impound a beneficiary's interest when the beneficiary has instigated or consented to a breach of trust.[442] This jurisdiction has been extended[443] by statute. The legislation from Newfoundland and Labrador, section 50 of the *Trustee Act*,[444] is set out below. The court's jurisdiction is discussed in *Pauling's Settlement Trusts, Re*,[445] also reproduced below.

---

438 See also *Fletcher v. Collis*, [1905] 2 Ch. 24, 74 L.J. Ch. 502, 92 L.T. 749 (C.A.); *Brighouse v. Morton, supra*, note 266.

439 *Massingberd's Settlement, Re, supra*, note 125, at 299.

440 See *Overton v. Banister* (1844), 3 Hare 503, 67 E.R. 479 (V.-C.).

441 *Gold v. Rosenberg* (1995), 9 E.T.R. (2d) 93, [1995] O.J. No. 3156, 1995 CarswellOnt 823, 129 D.L.R. (4th) 152, 86 O.A.C. 116, 25 O.R. (3d) 601 (C.A.), leave to appeal allowed (1996), 138 D.L.R. (4th) vii, 96 O.A.C. 78 (note) (S.C.C.), affirmed 1997 CarswellOnt 3273, 1997 CarswellOnt 3274, [1997] S.C.J. No. 93, 219 N.R. 93, 35 O.R. (3d) 736, 152 D.L.R. (4th) 385, 19 E.T.R. (2d) 1, 104 O.A.C. 1, 35 B.L.R. (2d) 212, [1997] 3 S.C.R. 767.

442 *Chillingworth v. Chambers*, [1896] 1 Ch. 685 (Eng. Ch. Div.).

443 *Bolton v. Curre*, [1895] 1 Ch. 544 at 549, *per* Romer J.

444 R.S.N.L. 1990, c. T-10, s. 50.

445 [1963] Ch. 576, [1963] 1 All E.R. 857 (Ch. Div.).

TRUSTEE ACT

R.S.N.L. 1990, c. T-10

50. Where a trustee commits a breach of trust at the instigation or request, or with the written consent of a beneficiary, the court may make an order that the court considers just for impounding all or a part of the interest of the beneficiary in the trust estate by way of indemnity to the trustee or person claiming through the trustee.

Comparable Legislation

Trustee Act, R.S.A. 2000, c. T-8, s. 26; R.S.B.C. 1996, c. 464, s. 96; C.C.S.M., c. T160, s. 80; R.S.N.S. 1989, c. 479, s. 49; R.S.N.W.T. 1988, c. T-8, s. 25; R.S.P.E.I. 1988, c. T-8, s. 25; R.S.S. 1978, c. T-23, s. 46; R.S.Y. 2002, c. 223, s. 25; *Trustees Act*, R.S.N.B. 1973, c. T-15, s. 41. The Ontario provision, formerly s. 34(1) of the *Trustee Act*, R.S.O. 1990, c. T.23, was repealed in 1999.

PAULING'S SETTLEMENT TRUSTS (No. 2), RE

[1963] Ch. 576, [1963] 1 All E.R. 857
Chancery Division

At first instance in *Pauling's Settlement Trusts, Re*,[446] Wilberforce J. ordered the trustees to refund to the trust the capital which they improperly paid out.[447] The order was made without prejudice to the trustees' right, if any, to impound the beneficiaries' interests. The beneficiaries, in accordance with the order, and while the order was under appeal, brought an application for the appointment of new trustees. The defendant trustees had already brought action for a declaration that they were entitled to impound the income of the trust fund. They opposed the application for the appointment of new trustees on the ground that this would imperil their rights to impound.

WILBERFORCE J:

. . .

The defendants, as I have already mentioned, have a claim to impound the life interest of Mrs. Younghusband now vested in the *Guardian Assurance Co. Ltd.*[448] in order to recoup themselves against any money which they may be ordered to repay. What is said by the defendants is that, that right to impound would be

---

446   (1961), [1962] 1 W.L.R. 86, [1961] 3 All E.R. 713 (Ch. Div.), affirmed (1963), [1964] 1 Ch. 303, [1963] 1 All E.R. 1 (C.A.). This decision and the appeal therefrom are discussed above.

447   The order was varied by the Court of Appeal, as set out above.

448   Mrs. Younghusband had mortgaged her life interest to this company and it had foreclosed on the mortgage.

prejudiced if new trustees were appointed now and the trust fund handed over to them. That involves a consideration as to what is the nature of the right to impound which exists in favour of a trustee who has committed a breach of trust at the instigation of a beneficiary. I have to consider both the ordinary right which exists in equity apart from statute and also the further statutory right which has been conferred by section 62 of the *Trustee Act, 1925*,[449] both of which are invoked by the defendants as plaintiffs in the Chancery action now pending. It seems to me that it is not possible to maintain, as is the defendants' contention here, that a trustee, having committed a breach of trust, is entitled to remain as a trustee until it has exercised its right to impound the income of the beneficiary in order to recoup itself. That seems to me an impossible proposition. It is quite true that, in the reported authorities, there is no case where the right to impound has been exercised by a former trustee as distinct from an existing trustee, but it seems to me in principle that it is impossible to contend that the right to impound is limited to the case where the trustee seeking the right is an actual trustee. The nature of the right to impound seems to me to turn on two things: first, that the money paid back to capital is in its origin the money of the trustee, and that when it comes to considering who should get the income of it, the trustee who has provided the money has a better right to it than the tenant for life who has instigated the breach of trust. The alternative way of putting the matter is that the trustee in breach of trust is in some way subrogated to the rights of the beneficiary. He stands in his position in order that he may be indemnified. That seems to me the way in which it was put by the Lords Justices in *Raby v. Rid[e]halgh*.[450] It does not seem to me that there is any support in authority or in principle for saying that the right depends upon the actual possession of the trust fund, and it appears to me that the analogy which has been sought to be drawn with the executor's right to retain is a false one and does not apply to this case. So much for the equitable right to impound as opposed to the statutory right.

As regards the statutory right, that depends on the language of section 62 of the *Trustee Act, 1925*, and at first sight it might look as if that right only exists in favour of a person who is actually a trustee. But, on consideration, that seems to me to be a misconstruction of the section. In the first place, the same objection against limiting the right in that way applies to the statutory jurisdiction. It seems to me an absurdity that it is required as a condition of exercising the right to obtain an impounding order, that the trustee who, ex hypothesi, is in breach of trust, must remain the trustee in order to acquire a right of indemnity. Further, it seems to me on the authorities. . .that the statutory right is extending the equitable right and not limiting it, and that it is not right to read the section so as to apply only to a person who was formerly a trustee. The section begins with the words: "Where a trustee commits a breach of trust," thereby indicating that at the time the breach of trust is committed the person in question must be a trustee. Then further down in the section there is a reference to a trustee and that appears to me to be merely a reference back to the same person as the person who committed the breach of

---

449   15 & 16 Geo. 5, c. 19. The section is to the same effect as the Ontario legislation set out above.
450   (1855), 7 De G.M. & G. 104, 44 E.R. 41.

trust and not as an indication that the person in question must be a trustee at the date of the order. I would add to that, that here the writ which has been issued in the Chancery Division was issued at a time when the defendants were trustees, and, therefore, at the date of the writ the requirement of being a trustee was fulfilled. So that, although I entirely appreciate that the defendants may be anxious not to lose their right to impound the income of the tenant for life, that right could not, in my view, be prejudiced by appointing new trustees at this stage.

In conclusion on this point, and in support of the view which I have expressed, I would refer to a passage in the judgment of Romer L.J. in *Fletcher v. Collis*.[451] It is a decision of the Court of Appeal and what is said by Romer L.J. is:[452]

> Probably. . .if a trustee in such a case were to hand over the funds out of his own pocket to new trustees without reserving his right in any way as against the tenant for life,. . .he might be held to have lost his right to claim the income after he had parted with the fund.

It seems to me that this supports the view that the mere parting with the fund is not sufficient to take away from the trustee the right to claim the income. The plaintiffs in this case in the draft minute of order they have submitted have inserted a provision which expressly preserves the right of the trustee to claim recoupment out of income and that brings it within what was said by Romer L.J. It seems to me, for the purposes of today, with that insertion in the order appointing new trustees, it would be impossible for the defendants to contend that, if such an order were made, they would lose their right to impound the income. Therefore, I do not feel that that objection by itself is sufficient to prevent me appointing new trustees now.

Connected with that point is a point of a similar character which is taken by the defendants. It is said that the defendants have a right to control the investment of the trust fund, so that it is not invested in such a way as to prejudice their right to recoup out of income. That point seems to me to be completely misconceived. It is, of course, the duty of any trustee to exercise his powers of investment in such a way as to hold the balance properly between capital and income. If the fund were transferred to new trustees they would be under that duty and it is to be observed in any event they would be faced by the Guardian Assurance Co. Ltd., which is in place of the life tenant, and the plaintiffs who are in the position of those entitled to capital. The new trustees would be under the normal duty of preserving an equitable balance, and if at any time it was shown they were inclining one way or the other, it would not be a difficult matter to bring them to account.

> [In the result, Wilberforce J. declined to appoint new trustees until the appeal was concluded. His Lordship considered that since the trustees might be awarded substantial costs in the appeal and since they might have a liability for estate duty which could not be determined until the appeal was concluded,

---

451 *Supra*, note 438.
452 *Ibid.*, at 35.

it would be undesirable to appoint new trustees and vest the trust's assets in them for the time being.]

Notes and Questions

1. If a beneficiary has instigated or requested a breach of trust, the trustee may seek to have the beneficiary's interest impounded, even though the beneficiary did not benefit by the breach. However, if the beneficiary merely consented to the breach, the interest can only be impounded if the beneficiary received a benefit from it.[453]

2. A beneficiary's interest may be impounded even though the beneficiary did not know that he or she had a beneficial interest and even though the interest is contingent. However, if the trustee subsequently acquires a beneficial interest himself or herself and sues the instigating beneficiary, the latter's interest cannot be impounded.[454]

3. The legislation applies only to a beneficiary who has consented *in writing*.[455] *Quaere* whether it reverses the common law to this extent.

4. A beneficiary requested the trustees to invest trust funds in a mortgage on Blackacre. While the mortgage was a proper investment, the trustees lent too large a sum. When a loss resulted, the trustees sought to impound the beneficiary's interest. Are they entitled to do so?[456]

(d) Acquiescence and Release

If a breach of trust has occurred, a beneficiary may be refused relief on the ground of acquiescence or release.[457] Acquiescence is refraining from action knowing that a breach of trust has occurred and that one's rights have been infringed. Thus, long delay with knowledge may amount to acquiescence.[458] The defence is available to the trustee even if the defence of laches is not available. The latter defence prevents relief if it would be inequitable because of the length of time that has gone by since the breach. Laches is, thus, similar to acquiescence, but laches is also available where the plaintiff did not know of the breach.

A relatively short time of standing by without seeking a remedy is not usually treated as being acquiescence.[459] Nor is there acquiescence if the beneficiary inquires into the trustee's affairs and is given an inaccurate set of accounts.[460] The defence of acquiescence is available to the trustee even though the beneficiary did not benefit personally from the breach.[461] Although a beneficiary acquiesced

---

453 *Chillingworth v. Chambers, supra*, note 442.

454 *Evans v. Benyon* (1887), 37 Ch. D. 329 (C.A.); Waters, pp. 1013-4.

455 *Somerset, Re*, [1894] 1 Ch. 231 (Eng. Ch. Div.) at 265-6.

456 *Ibid.*

457 *Wawanesa Mutual Insurance Co. v. J.A. (Fred) Chalmers & Co.*, 69 W.W.R. 612, [1969] I.L.R. 1-301, 1969 CarswellSask 57, 7 D.L.R. (3d) 283 (Q.B.), at 615-616 [W.W.R.], *per* MacPherson J.

458 *Life Assn. of Scotland v. Siddal* (1861), 3 De G.F. & J. 58, 45 E.R. 800 (Ch. Div.), at 77, *per* Lord Campbell.

459 *Wawanesa Mutual Insurance Co. v. J.A. (Fred) Chalmers & Co., supra*, note 457.

460 *Inglis v. Beaty, supra*, note 54.

461 *Brighouse v. Morton, supra*, note 266.

in past breaches of trust, he or she is not thereby debarred from contesting future breaches.[462]

A release is either a formal document in which a beneficiary releases and exonerates a trustee for a breach, or an informal waiver to the same effect. In either case, a release is a positive act waiving the trustee's conduct. Release is, thus acquiescence by assent. If the release is given with full knowledge of the facts and is obtained without undue influence, it affords a good defence to the trustee.[463]

Notes and Questions

1. X conveyed property to his solicitor Y. Y breached her fiduciary duty in accepting the deed. X later confirmed the deed by his will. What result?[464]

2. M made a will which left certain property to her son, S. The will prohibited S from seeking to administer his father's estate. S accepted the bequest under M's will.

Can S later make application to administer his father's estate?[465]

3. F permitted his son, S, and daughter-in-law, D, to build a house on his land upon their oral promise to permit him to live rent-free in a basement apartment in the house for the rest of his life. Then F made a voluntary transfer to S and D. S died soon after F moved into the basement apartment. D put the house up for sale and then died. Her estate sold the house to *bona fide* purchasers for value without notice. They demanded rent from F and he paid it for several months.

Does F have a remedy against anyone? Discuss.[466]

(e) Limitations and Laches

(i) *Limitations*

Before 1833 in England, express trustees who were guilty of a breach of trust were not protected by any limitation provisions. The *Real Property Limitation Act, 1833*,[467] however, conferred a measure of protection upon the honest trustee. This legislation was adopted in most of the Canadian provinces and versions of it are still in effect in some. Thus, for example, the New Brunswick *Limitation of Actions Act*[468] provides that an action to recover arrears of interest in respect of a legacy, whether or not charged upon land, must be brought within six years after the arrears became due.[469] It further provides for a 20-year period in respect of a

---

462 *Swain v. Law Society*, [1982] 1 W.L.R. 17, reversed on the grounds [1982] 3 W.L.R. 261 (H.L.).

463 *Carvell v. Aitken* (1912), 10 E.L.R. 432, 2 D.L.R. 709, 1912 CarswellPEI 4 (C.A.)

464 See *Stump v. Gaby* (1852), 2 De G.M. & G. 623, 42 E.R. 1015.

465 See *Egg v. Devey* (1847), 10 Beav. 444, 50 E.R. 653.

466 See *Ward v. Ward, supra*, note 43.

467 3 & 4 Will. 4, c. 27 (U.K.).

468 R.S.N.B. 1973, c. L-8. The Ontario *Real Property Limitations Act*, R.S.O. 1990, c. L.15, was similar; although it governs pending litigation, disputes arising in the future will be governed by the *Limitations Act, 2002*, S.O. 2002, c. 24, Schedule B, discussed below.

469 *Ibid.*, ss. 27(1), 57.

legacy charged upon land,[470] and goes on to stipulate that a similar period applies even if the legacy is secured by an express trust.[471]

Section 8 of the English *Trustee Act, 1888*[472] afforded further protection to trustees. It provided that, save for certain serious breaches of trust, the limitation periods stipulated by that or any other Act apply to trustees as well, or if no limitation period is specified, the period is the same as in an action for money had and received, that is, six years. However, if the beneficiary's claim is based on fraud or fraudulent breach of trust to which the trustee was party or privy, or is to recover trust property or the proceeds thereof, still retained by the trustee, or previously received by the trustee and converted to his or her own use, the trustee is not protected by a limitation period.

This provision became section 56 of the New Brunswick *Limitation of Actions Act*.[473] The section, therefore, preserves in part the old rule that time does not run against beneficiaries under an express trust. The problem is that section 56 also applies to trusts arising by construction or implication of law. But there is a continuing controversy about the types of constructive trustee to which the section applies. Before 1888, the English courts denied the protection of limitation provisions to certain types of constructive trustee, namely those whose position was analogous to the express trustee. In *Soar v. Ashwell*[474] the English Court of Appeal attempted to settle these doubts by holding that a person who purports to act as an express trustee, who participates with an express trustee in fraud upon the trust, or who converts trust property to his or her own use, is to be treated as an express trustee and, hence, subject to the exception in section 8 of the English Act. Other constructive trustees, however, were accorded the benefit of the section. The problems were not solved by that case, however, as is apparent from *Taylor v. Davies*,[475] reproduced below.

The problem was removed in England by the *Limitation Act, 1939*,[476] which defines "trustee" to include trustees of all types of trust and accords trustees protection except for fraud and fraudulent breach of trust to which the trustee was a party and when the action is to recover trust property or the proceeds thereof still in the possession of the trustee or previously received by the trustee and converted to his or her own use.[477]

The relevant part of the New Brunswick *Limitation of Actions Act* is set out below.[478]

---

470 *Ibid.*, s. 25(1).
471 *Ibid.*, s. 58(2).
472 51 & 52 Vict. c. 59 (U.K.).
473 R.S.N.B. 1973, c. L-8. It also appears in the statutes of most other provinces: see the notes below.
474 (1893), [1893] 2 Q.B. 390, [1891-94] All E.R. Rep. 991, 69 L.T. 585, 42 W.R. 165, 4 R. 602 (C.A.).
475 (1919), [1920] A.C. 636, 51 D.L.R. 75, 1919 CarswellOnt 11, [1920] 1 W.W.R. 683 (Ontario P.C.).
476 2 & 3 Geo. 6, c. 21 (U.K.).
477 See now *Limitation Act 1980*, c. 58, s. 21 (U.K.), to the same effect.
478 See also *Trustees Act*, R.S.N.B. 1973, c. T-15, s. 43, which is substantially the same as s. 56 of the *Limitation of Actions Act*.

LIMITATION OF ACTIONS ACT

R.S.N.B. 1973, c. L-8

PART VII
TRUSTS AND TRUSTEES

55. In this Part "trustee" includes an executor, and a trustee whose trust arises by construction or implication of law as well as an express trustee and also includes a joint trustee.

56. (1) In an action or other proceeding against a trustee, or any person claiming through him, except when the claim is founded upon fraud or fraudulent breach of trust to which the trustee was party or privy, or is to recover trust property, or the proceeds thereof, still retained by the trustee, or previously received by the trustee and converted to his use, the following provisions apply:

    (a) all rights and privileges conferred by any Statute of Limitations shall be enjoyed in the like manner, and to the like extent, as they would have been enjoyed in such action or other proceeding, if the trustee, or person claiming through him, had not been a trustee, or person claiming through a trustee;

    (b) if the action or other proceeding is brought to recover money or other property, and is one to which no existing Statute of Limitations applies, the trustee or person claiming through him, shall be entitled to the benefit of, and be at liberty to plead the lapse of time as a bar to such action or proceeding in the like manner, and to the like extent, as if the claim had been against him in an action of debt for money had and received; but so, nevertheless, that the Statute shall run against a married woman, entitled in possession for her separate use, whether with or without a restraint upon anticipation, but shall not begin to run against any beneficiary until the interest of such beneficiary becomes an interest in possession.

(2) No beneficiary, as against whom there would be good defence by virtue of this section, shall derive any greater or other benefit from a judgment or order obtained by another beneficiary than he could have obtained if he had brought such action or other proceeding, and this section had been pleaded.

(3) This section does not deprive an executor or administrator of any right or defence to which he is entitled under any existing Statute of Limitations.

57. Subject to the provisions of subsection 56(1), no action in respect of any claim to the personal estate of a deceased person or to any share or interest in such estate, whether under a will or an intestacy, shall be brought after the expiration of six years from the date when the right to receive the share or interest accrued, and no action to recover arrears of interest in respect of any legacy, or damages in respect of such arrears, shall be brought after the expiration of six years from the date on which the interest became due.

58. (1) Where land is vested in a trustee upon any express trust, the right of the *cestui que trust*, or any person claiming through him, to bring an action against the trustee, or any person claiming through him, to recover such land shall be deemed to have first accrued according to the meaning of this Act at, and not before, the time at which such land has been conveyed to a purchaser for valuable consideration, and shall then be deemed to have accrued only as against such purchaser and any person claiming through him.

(2) No action shall be brought to recover any sum of money or legacy charged upon or payable out of any land or rent charge, though secured by an express trust, or to recover any arrears of rent or of interest in respect of any sum of money or legacy so charged or payable or so secured, or any damages in respect of such arrears, except within the time within which the same would be recoverable if there were not any such trust.

(3) Subsection (2) of this section shall not operate so as to affect any claim of a *cestui que trust* against his trustee for property held on an express trust.

Comparable Legislation

Limitation of Actions Act, R.S.N.S. 1989, c. 258, ss. 27-31; R.S.S. 1978, c. L-15, ss. 42-44; *Statute of Limitations*, R.S.P.E.I. 1988, c. S-7, ss. 42-44.

Manitoba's statute has clarified the drafting of these provisions: *The Limitation of Actions Act*, C.C.S.M., c. L150, ss. 49-51.

Compare the approach taken in the *Limitation Act*, R.S.B.C. 1996, c. 266, s. 3(3), (7), 6(1), (2).[479] The statute in Newfoundland and Labrador is similar in conception to the British Columbia act: *Limitations Act*, S.N.L. 1995, c. L-16.1.

The law in Alberta and Ontario has been substantially reformed: see *Limitations Act*, R.S.A. 2000, c. L-12 and *Limitations Act, 2002*, S.O. 2002, c. 24, Schedule B. These acts do not make any special rules for breach of trust claims. They work by creating two limitation periods, a shorter one which runs from when the plaintiff became aware of the claim, and a longer one which runs from when the facts occurred which gave rise to it. When either of the two periods expires, the claim is barred. There are transitional provisions governing the change from the old system to the new one.

Notes and Questions

1. In *Edwards v. Law Society of Upper Canada* (2000), 48 O.R. (3d) 321, 36 E.T.R. (2d) 192, 2000 CarswellOnt 1963, 133 O.A.C. 305, 50 C.P.C. (4th) 231 (C.A.), leave to appeal refused (2000), 143 O.A.C. 396 (note), 2000 CarswellOnt 4459, 2000 CarswellOnt 4460, 265 N.R. 400 (note) (S.C.C.), it was held that s. 44(2) of the old Ontario *Limitations Act* prevailed over s. 38(3) of the *Trustee Act*, R.S.O. 1990, c. T.23, which provides that a claim against a deceased person must be brought within two years of the death. Section 44(2) of the Ontario *Limitations Act* does not have an exact counterpart in the New Brunswick legislation; it provided that subject to s. 43, there was no limit of time on claims against express trustees.

Further Reading

W. Swadling, "Limitation" in P. Birks and A. Pretto, eds., *Breach of Trust* (Oxford: Hart Publishing, 2002) 319.

---

479 Note the application of these provisions in *Kreeft v. Kreeft*, 39 E.T.R. (2d) 233, 2001 CarswellBC 1458, 2001 BCSC 893 (S.C.).

TAYLOR v. DAVIES

[1920] A.C. 366
Judicial Committee of the Privy Council

The defendant, Davies, held a mortgage on certain real property owned by Taylor Brothers, a partnership which carried on a brick-making operation. In 1901 the firm became insolvent and made an assignment for the benefit of its creditors. The assignment was made to the respondent, Clarkson, upon trust to sell and convert and to apply the proceeds to pay, first, the expenses, second, the creditors rateably in accordance with the Act and, third, the balance to the debtors. At a meeting of creditors, Davies, along with five other persons, was appointed an inspector of the estate with power, in conjunction with Clarkson, to realize the assets.

Davies's mortgage debt was in excess of $100,000, but an appraisal obtained by Clarkson showed that the property was worth only $45,000. The appraisal was done hastily and the appraiser had no special knowledge of the brick-making business. In 1902 it was agreed between Clarkson and Davies that Clarkson would release and quit claim the property to Davies and that Davies would rank as an unsecured creditor for the amount of his debt in excess of $45,000. The inspectors concurred and the arrangement was approved at a creditors' meeting of which inadequate notice was given. Davies subsequently waived his right to claim as an unsecured creditor. Then he resigned as inspector. Ultimately the creditors received less than three per cent on their claims.

Davies developed the brick field and in 1909 was paid in excess of $200,000 for an expropriation of a small part of it. The plaintiff, a creditor, then brought this action alleging that the land had a much greater value than the amount owing to Davies under the mortgage and that Davies was a constructive trustee as an inspector. Davies pleaded limitations and laches.

The trial judge dismissed the action, but the Appellate Division of the Supreme Court of Ontario reversed. The plaintiff then brought this *per saltum* appeal.

VISCOUNT CAVE delivered the judgment of the Privy Council:

> [His Lordship held that Davies was a fiduciary, and that the quit claim deed could not be upheld for lack of proper valuation and notice. Hence, the arrangement could have been set aside if it had been impeached when made. His Lordship then set out section 47 of the *Limitations Act*, noting that it corresponded to section 8 of the *Trustee Act, 1888*.[480] He continued:]

The interval between the delivery of the release to the defendant in September, 1902, and the date of the commencement of these proceedings exceeded ten years,

---

480 51 & 52 Vict., c. 59 (U.K.). Section 47 is virtually the same as s. 56 of the present New Brunswick statute, reproduced above.

and the defendant accordingly relied upon the above provisions as a sufficient defence to the action.

It was contended on behalf of the appellant that the plaintiff's claim was excepted from the provisions of s. 47 of the Act as being (in the words of sub-s. 2) a claim "to recover trust property or the proceeds thereof still retained by the trustee," and this on two alternative grounds. First, it was said that, having regard to the terms of the resolution of July 5, 1901, under which the defendant was appointed an inspector, he was an express trustee of the estate who at the time when the action was brought still retained part of the trust property, and that he fell as an express trustee within the exception above mentioned. Their Lordships are unable to agree with this contention. It is true that the inspectors were empowered by the resolution in question to "realize upon the assets" in conjunction with the assignee; but the assets were not vested in them, and the assignee remained the sole trustee of the assets and was entitled to realize them subject only to the supervision of the inspectors.

Secondly, it was said that the defendant, having acquired the property in question at a time when he was disabled by his fiduciary position from so doing, became at all events a constructive trustee of the property, and so fell within the same exception, and this argument requires careful examination.

In order to ascertain the effect of the Trustee Act, 1888, and the corresponding Canadian statute, it is necessary to refer to the antecedent law of limitation as it applied to trustees. It is clear that apart from these statutes an express trustee could not rely, as a defence to an action by his beneficiary, either upon the statutes of limitation or upon the rules which were enforced by Courts of equity by analogy or in obedience to those statutes. The possession of an express trustee was treated by the Courts as the possession of his cestuis que trustent [*sic*], and accordingly time did not run in his favour against them. This disability applied, not only to a trustee named as such in the instrument of trust, but to a person who, though not so named, had assumed the position of a trustee for others or had taken possession or control of property on their behalf, such (for instance) as the persons enumerated in the judgment of Bowen L.J. in *Soar v. Ashwell.* . . .[481] These persons, though not originally trustees, had taken upon themselves the custody and administration of property on behalf of others; and though sometimes referred to a constructive trustees, they were, in fact, actual trustees, though not so named. It followed that their possession also was treated as the possession of the persons for whom they acted, and they, like express trustees, were disabled from taking advantage of the time bar. But the position in this respect of a constructive trustee in the usual sense of the words — that is to say, of a person who, though he had taken possession in his own right, was liable to be declared a trustee in a Court of equity — was widely different, and it had long been settled that time ran in his favour from the moment of his so taking possession. This rule is illustrated by the well-known judgment of Sir William Grant M.R., in *Beckford v. Wade*,[482] [who said:]

---

481 *Supra*, note 474.
482 (1805), 17 Ves. 87 at 97, 34 E.R. 34.

It is certainly true that no time bars a direct trust, as between cestui que trust and trustee; but, if it is meant to be asserted, that a Court of equity allows a man to make out a case of constructive trust at any distance of time, after the facts and circumstances happened out of which it arises, I am not aware, that there is any ground for a doctrine, so fatal to the security of property as that would be; so far from it, that not only in circumstances, where the length of time would render it extremely difficult to ascertain the true state of the fact, but where the true state of the fact is easily ascertained, and where it is perfectly clear, that relief would originally have been given upon the ground of constructive trust, it is refused to the party, who after long acquiescence comes into a Court of equity to seek that relief.

So in *Soar v. Ashwell*[483] Lord Esher M.R. stated the rule as follows:[484]

If the breach of the legal relation relied on, whether such breach be by way of tort or contract, makes, in the view of the Court of equity, the defendant a trustee for the plaintiff, the Court of equity treats the defendant as a trustee become so by construction, and the trust is called a constructive trust; and against the breach which by construction creates the trust the Court of equity allows statutes of limitation to be vouched.

And in the same case Bowen L.J., speaking of constructive trusts of this kind, said:[485]

That time (by analogy to the statute) is no bar in the case of an express trust, but that it will be a bar in the case of a constructive trust, is a doctrine which has been clearly and long established.

As to the pre-existing law, then, there is no question; but it is contended for the appellant that the recent statute has altered the law in this respect. Sect. 47, sub-s. 1, it is said, defines a trustee as including "a trustee whose trust arises by construction or implication of law," and, accordingly, the exclusion from s. 47, sub-s. 2, of a claim to recover "trust property or the proceeds thereof still retained by the trustee" must apply to property in the hands of a constructive trustee or of any person claiming under him otherwise than by purchase for value without notice. If this contention be correct, then the section, which was presumably passed for the relief of trustees, has seriously altered for the worse the position of a constructive trustee, and (to use the words of Sir William Grant in the case above cited) a doctrine has been introduced which may be "fatal to the security of property." It does not appear to their Lordships that the section has this effect. The expressions "trust property" and "retained by the trustee" properly apply, not to a case where a person having taken possession of property on his own behalf, is liable to be declared a trustee by the Court; but rather to a case where he originally took possession upon trust for or on behalf of others. In other words, they refer to cases where a trust arose before the occurrence of the transaction impeached and not to cases where it arises only by reason of that transaction. The exception no doubt applies, not only to an express trustee named in the instrument of trust, but also to those persons who under the rules explained in *Soar v. Ashwell* and other cases are to be treated as being in a like position; but in their Lordships'

---

483 *Supra*, note 474.
484 *Ibid.*, at 393.
485 *Ibid.*, at 395.

opinion it does not apply to a mere constructive trustee of the character described in the judgment of Sir William Grant.

It is to be noticed also that, while s. 49 of the *Limitations Act* prescribes the time at which a right to recover land is to be deemed to have accrued in the case of an express trustee, and provides that subject to s. 47

> no claim of a cestui que trust against the trustee for any property held on an express trust, or in respect of any breach of such trust, shall be held to be barred by any statute of limitation,

there are no similar provisions in respect of a constructive trustee; and it is to be presumed, therefore, that such a trustee remains entitled to such protection as he had before the passing of the Act.

For the above reasons it appears to their Lordships that in the present case time ran in favour of the defendant Davies as from the date of the delivery to him of the release in question, and accordingly, that the *Limitations Act* afforded a good defence to that defendant in this action. They will accordingly humbly advise His Majesty that this appeal fails, and should be dismissed with costs.

Notes and Questions

1. *Taylor v. Davies* held that the exception in the legislation applies only when a trust arose before the transaction sought to be impeached and not when it arose only by reason of the transaction. If that is so, is there any constructive trust, other than one arising out of or in connection with an express trust, to which the exception applies?

2. Is the distinction, first made in *Soar v. Ashwell*[486] and applied in *Taylor v. Davies*, between trusts arising before the transaction and those arising out of the transaction still valid today? Consider that in Canada the courts have recognized the remedial constructive trust which is based, not upon a fiduciary relationship, but upon unjust enrichment.

3. The limitation period, if it applies, is not interrupted merely because the trustee makes payments to the beneficiary. There must be an acknowledgement that the whole debt remains due.[487]

4. The limitation period does not begin to run until the beneficiaries knew or ought to have known of the breach. Thus, for example, the period only commences to run once the beneficiary becomes aware of the trustee's equitable fraud or fraudulent concealment.[488]

---

486 *Supra*, note 474.

487 See *Somerset, Re, supra*, note 455.

488 *Guerin v. R.* (1981), [1982] 2 F.C. 385, 10 E.T.R. 61, 1981 CarswellNat 13, 1981 CarswellNat 530, [1982] 2 C.N.L.R. 83 (T.D.), (supplementary reasons at (1981), [1982] 2 F.C. 445, 127 D.L.R. (3d) 170, 1981 CarswellNat 179F, 1981 CarswellNat 179 (T.D.)), reversed (1982), [1983] 2 F.C. 656, [1983] 2 W.W.R. 686, 13 E.T.R. 245, 143 D.L.R. (3d) 416, 1982 CarswellNat 142, 1982 CarswellNat 443, [1983] 1 C.N.L.R. 20, 45 N.R. 181 (C.A.), reversed (1984), 13 D.L.R. (4th) 321, 1984 CarswellNat 813, 1984 CarswellNat 693, [1984] 6 W.W.R. 481, [1984] 2 S.C.R. 335, 55 N.R. 161, [1985] 1 C.N.L.R. 120, 20 E.T.R. 6, 36 R.P.R. 1, 59 B.C.L.R. 301, at 96ff. [10 E.T.R.], at 345 [13 D.L.R.].

5. The Manitoba legislation[489] is like the modern English legislation.[490] It avoids the problems of the older legislation, applies to all types of trustee and to personal representatives, but denies limitation protection to fraudulent fiduciaries.

The British Columbia legislation[491] is similar to the Manitoba legislation, except that fraudulent fiduciaries are given the benefit of a 10-year limitation period.[492] However, the period does not begin to run until the beneficiary becomes fully aware of the fraud.[493] The period for other breaches of trust is six years.[494] The statute in Newfoundland and Labrador is similar in conception to the British Columbia act.[495]

6. W and H were married for seven years. Both worked. She gave her pay cheque to him. They purchased three properties during the marriage. H took title to all of them and told W that this was to prevent her from taking half if she left him. Subsequently, they divorced. Fifteen years later, W brought an action claiming an interest in the properties. What result?[496]

7. X was a director of Y Ltd. He caused transfers of two company properties to be made to him. Sixteen years later, Y Ltd. brought action against X's estate to recover the properties. What result?[497]

8. A mother died in 1955. By her will she left her house to her executor in trust, so long as her daughter, B, or any of three other children remained unmarried and continued to live in the house, and then to sell and divide the proceeds equally among all the children. B was in needy circumstances, so her brothers and sisters agreed to permit her the sole use of the house. They transferred title to her so she could raise money on the security of a mortgage as necessary. It was understood, however, that when she ceased to live in the house it would be returned to the estate. In 1978 the brothers and sisters asked B to execute a deed in their favour, subject to a life interest in favour of B. She denied knowledge of any "understanding." In 1984 B moved out of the house. In 1987 she transferred a half interest to her son as tenant in common with her. In 1989 the brothers and sisters brought action to recover the property. The applicable limitation provision is that no action shall be brought against a trustee for fraud, fraudulent breach of trust, conversion of trust property, or recovery of trust property, but within 10 years of the date on which the right to do so arose.[498] Is the action barred?[499]

9. An incest victim sued her father for, *inter alia*, breach of a parent's fiduciary duty. The Supreme Court of Canada held that the time for bringing a claim for breach of fiduciary duty is not limited by statute in Ontario.[500]

10. Two children, who held a remainder interest in their father's estate, did not receive their share of the estate. The court held that the legislation did not bar them from bringing

---

489 *The Limitation of Actions Act*, C.C.S.M., c. L150, ss. 49-51.

490 *Limitation Act 1980*, c. 58, s. 21 (U.K.).

491 *Limitation Act*, R.S.B.C. 1996, c. 266.

492 *Ibid.*, s. 3(3). See also *Limitations Act*, S.N.L. 1995, c. L-16.1, s. 7(1)(c)-(f), to the same effect.

493 *Ibid.*, s. 6(1). See also *Limitations Act*, S.N.L. 1995, c L-16.1, s. 12(2), to the same effect.

494 *Ibid.*, s. 3(5).

495 *Limitations Act*, S.N.L. 1995, c. L-16.1.

496 See *Angeletakis v. Thymaras* (1989), 65 Alta. L.R. (2d) 345, 1989 CarswellAlta 38, 19 R.F.L. (3d) 296, 32 E.T.R. 300, 95 A.R. 81 (Q.B.).

497 See *J.L.O. Ranch Ltd. v. Logan* (1987), 54 Alta. L.R. (2d) 130, 1987 CarswellAlta 184, 27 E.T.R. 1, 81 A.R. 261 (Q.B.).

498 *Limitation Act*, R.S.B.C. 1996, c. 266, s. 3(3).

499 See *Heath v. Darcus* (1991), 84 D.L.R. (4th) 694, 1991 CarswellBC 247, 60 B.C.L.R. (2d) 145, 3 B.C.A.C. 278, 7 W.A.C. 278, [1992] 1 W.W.R. 385 (C.A.).

500 *M. (K.) v. M. (H)*, *supra*, note 150.

an action for an order that the terms of their father's will and trust be carried out despite the passage of 43 years since the conveyance of the property to another son.[501]

11. The Supreme Court of Canada held that the Crown breached its fiduciary duty by mistakenly transferring the mineral rights as well as the surface rights of land which they sold for an Indian Band in 1948. The Crown committed a second breach by failing to correct the error when learning of the error in 1949. The band discovered the breach in 1977. As the running of time only commences when the plaintiffs become aware of a cause of action, the band was within the applicable limitation periods of the statute.[502]

(ii) *Laches*

Laches means delay in bringing an action and is a defence in equity to the action. It is akin to acquiescence in that both involve delay. However, laches is broader in that it is available even if the plaintiff did not know that his or her rights were being breached, whereas that is required for acquiescence, as discussed above.

Laches is the equitable equivalent of limitation and is necessary because limitation statutes do not always apply to all equitable causes of action. The defence is retained by the Ontario *Real Property Limitations Act*,[503] but not by the *Limitations Act, 2002*.[504]

If an express statutory limitation period applies to the action, the defence of laches cannot be raised.[505] However, the defence of acquiescence, if established, is not precluded in those circumstances.[506] The nature of the defence is described in the following excerpt from the judgment of Collier J. in *Guerin v. R.*:[507]

> The law, as to the operation and effect of the doctrine of laches is, to my mind, accurately set out in *Halsbury's Laws of England*:[508]
>
> **1476. The defence of laches.** A plaintiff in equity is bound to prosecute his claim without undue delay. This is in pursuance of the principle which has underlain the Statutes of Limitation, *vigilantibus et non dormientibus lex succurrit*. A court of equity refuses its aid to stale demands,

---

501 *McRae v. McRae Estate* (1994), 2 E.T.R. (2d) 225, 1994 CarswellBC 167, 90 B.C.L.R. (2d) 132, 44 B.C.A.C. 143, 71 W.A.C. 143 (C.A.), leave to appeal refused (1994), 4 E.T.R. (2d) 14 (note), 93 B.C.L.R. (2d) xxxviii (note), 178 N.R. 395 (note), 57 B.C.A.C. 80 (note), 94 W.A.C. 80 (note) (S.C.C.).

502 *Apsassin v. Canada (Department of Indian Affairs & Northern Development)*, (sub nom. *Blueberry River Indian Band v. Canada (Department of Indian Affairs & Northern Development)*) [1995] 4 S.C.R. 344, 1995 CarswellNat 1279, 1995 CarswellNat 1278, 130 D.L.R. (4th) 193, [1996] 2 C.N.L.R. 25, 190 N.R. 89, 102 F.T.R. 160 (note). See also *Semiahmoo Indian Band v. Canada, supra,* note 17, to the same effect.

503 R.S.O. 1990, c. L.15, s. 2. *Cf. Limitation of Actions Act,* R.S.A. 2000, c. L-12, s. 10; *Limitations Act,* S.N.L. 1995, c. L-16.1, s. 3.

504 S.O. 2002, c. 24, Schedule B.

505 *Pauling's Settlement Trusts, Re, supra,* note 446, at 115 [W.L.R.].

506 *Taylor v. Taylor* (1879), (sub nom. *Taylor v. Wallbridge*) 2 S.C.R. 616, 1879 CarswellOnt 261, at 688 [S.C.R.], *per* Henry J. All Canadian limitation statutes, except the new Ontario statute, expressly preserve the operation of acquiescence.

507 *Supra,* note 488, at 428-9 [[1982] 2 F.C.].

508 4th ed. vol. 16, para. 1476. See also *Snell's Principles of Equity* (27th ed., 1973), p. 35.

where the plaintiff has slept upon his right and acquiesced for a great length of time. He is then said to be barred by his laches.

and:[509]

> In determining whether there has been such delay as to amount to laches, the chief points to be considered are (1) acquiescence on the plaintiff's part, and (2) any change of position that has occurred on the defendant's part. Acquiescence in this sense does not mean standing by while the violation of a right is in progress, but assent after the violation has been completed and the plaintiff has become aware of it.

. . .

and:[510]

> **1480. Change in defendant's position.** Regard must be had to any change in the defendant's position which has resulted from the plaintiff's delay in bringing his action. This may be, for instance, because by the lapse of time he has lost the evidence necessary for meeting the claim. A court of equity will not allow a dormant claim to be set up when the means of resisting it, if it turns out to be unfounded, have perished.

and, finally:[511]

> Apart from statute, time alone was no bar to an action in a case of express trust. Time still is no bar in certain cases of breach of trust, although where there is no statutory bar, an action for breach of trust, like any other equitable claim, may be barred by acquiescence, whether this consists in assent to the breach of trust or in subsequent condonation, or by other circumstances which, combined with delay, make it inequitable to allow the action.

The defence of laches is discussed further in *Martin v. Donaldson Securities Ltd.*,[512] reproduced below.

MARTIN v. DONALDSON SECURITIES LTD.

(1975), [1976] 1 W.W.R. 159, 61 D.L.R. (3d) 518, 1975 CarswellBC 186
British Columbia Supreme Court

The defendant, Wood, who was a promoter, proposed an underwriting scheme to the plaintiff, the president of Whipsaw Mines Ltd., of Whipsaw shares, under which Wood was to direct trading in shares already issued to establish a market and the defendant, Donaldson Securities, would underwrite a new issue. To establish a market, the plaintiff deposited 175,000 shares owned by him with Donaldson in the Initial Funding account owned by Wood. Of the proceeds from

---

509 *Ibid.*, para. 1477.
510 *Ibid.*, para. 1480.
511 *Ibid.*, para. 1481.
512 (1975), [1976] 1 W.W.R. 159, 61 D.L.R. (3d) 518, 1975 CarswellBC 186 (S.C.).

the sale of these shares, the plaintiff was to receive 15 cents per share, that being his cost, with any profit over and above that going to Wood. These arrangements were confirmed by a note, written by the defendant, North, a registered representative of Donaldson Securities, and signed by the plaintiff and Wood on January 31, 1974. The note stated that no shares or cash were to be delivered out of the account until the plaintiff was paid.

During the month of February, 1974, the 175,000 shares were sold and cheques were delivered by Donaldson Securities to Wood on his account. The defendants, Wood and North, claimed that the plaintiff agreed to this because problems had developed in the underwriting when one of the partners dropped out, and so Initial Funding agreed to take up its share of the new issue. On this issue the court believed the plaintiff, however, and found that the plaintiff did not agree to waive his right to 15 cents per share. Moreover, by February 22, 1974, Wood acknowledged his indebtedness to the plaintiff by letter. Nevertheless, the plaintiff did not complain to North or Donaldson Securities for nine months when he commenced this action against them and Wood. Had he enforced his right immediately, Donaldson Securities could have had recourse against Wood's Initial Funding account into which it was paying the proceeds of the sale of the 175,000 shares. When the action was commenced, there were no moneys left in the account.

The plaintiff's reason for failing to make a demand of Donaldson Securities was that he was still working with Wood to complete the financing and that he needed Donaldson Securities' cooperation, that company being Wood's agent.

The plaintiff brought this action for damages for breach of trust and for recovery of money as a debt. Wood did not defend.

FULTON J.:

. . .

On the basis of these facts I hold that, whether or not this discussion and this note constituted North and Donaldson Securities express or constructive trustees, at the least Wood was a constructive, if not an express, trustee of the proceeds of sale of the Whipsaw shares in question and that the defendants North and Donaldson Securities, his agents, had knowledge of this trust. Donaldson Securities had custody and control of the shares deposited with them and of the proceeds of the sales of shares made by them pursuant to the arrangements outlined. Having reviewed a number of authorities I hold that these facts establish that those defendants would be liable if, without the knowledge and consent of the plaintiff as beneficiary of the trust, they made a disposition of the shares or the proceeds thereof contrary to the terms of that trust.[513] On the basis of the further facts with relation to the whole transaction, which I hold to be established, it would appear

---

513 See, *e.g.*, *Soar v. Ashwell*, *supra*, note 474, at 394-5; *Trusts & Guarantee Co. Ltd. and Miller v. Brenner*, [1933] S.C.R. 656, 15 C.B.R. 112, [1933] 4 D.L.R. 273; *Dealers Finance Corp. Ltd. v. Masterson Motors Ltd.* [1931] 2 W.W.R. 214, [1931] 4 D.L.R. 730.

that those defendants did make such a disposition; however, those further facts also necessitate consideration of the defences of acquiescence and/or laches referred to earlier.

. . .

In such circumstances the law, as I understand it, is that whether or not the plaintiff expressly waived the provisions of the trust or discharged the defendants North and Donaldson from their obligations thereunder, he has acquiesced in what was in fact done, after he had knowledge of it, and such acquiescence or laches disentitles him now to revive and enforce a claim based on that breach.

The basis of and authorities for this conclusion can be briefly stated as follows. The meaning of "acquiescence" is explained in 14 Hals.,[514] para. 1177:

> 1177. *Meanings of acquiescence.* The term "acquiescence" is used in two senses. In its proper legal sense it implies that a person abstains from interfering while a violation of his legal rights is in progress; in another sense it implies that he refrains from seeking redress when a violation of his rights, of which he did not know at the time, is brought to his notice. Here the term is used in the former sense; in the second sense acquiescence is an element in laches.

In the case at bar the defendants allege that the plaintiff knew of the breach of trust on or about February 21st or 22nd but did nothing until the fall of 1974 when this action was commenced. Therefore, it alleges, the plaintiff has acquiesced in the breach. The argument of the defendant[s] uses "acquiescence" in its second sense as an element in laches.

In Waters, *Law of Trusts in Canada*[515] the defence of laches is said to be an equitable doctrine which expressed the principle that if the claimant delays for a long period of time before bringing action, a Court may dismiss his action on the ground of his delay. The defence is closely related to the doctrine of acquiescence and indeed, states Waters, it is more likely that what the Courts are really concerned with is implied acquiescence rather than the delay itself.

What a defendant must prove to establish laches is a question of fact. In determining whether there has been such a delay as to amount to laches, a Court must consider the plaintiff's acquiescence (*i.e.*, assent after the violation has been completed and the plaintiff has become aware of it) and any change that has occurred in the defendant's position. The Court is concerned with the equities between the parties. It is unjust to give the plaintiff a remedy where his conduct may fairly be regarded as a waiver, or where by his conduct and neglect he has, though not waiving the remedy, put the defendant in such a position that it would not be reasonable afterwards to assert the remedy.[516] Any change in the position of the defendant will weigh more heavily against the plaintiff if he has such

---

514 3rd ed., p. 638.
515 (1974), p. 871.
516 14 Halsbury, 3rd ed., p. 641, para. 1182.

knowledge of the situation as to make it inequitable for him to do nothing. In *Erlanger v. New Sombrero Phosphate Co.*[517] Lord Blackburn stated:[518]

> And a Court of Equity requires that those who come to it to ask its active interposition to give them relief, should use due diligence, after there has been such notice or knowledge as to make it inequitable to lie by. And any change which occurs in the position of the parties or the state of the property after such notice or knowledge should tell much more against the party *in morâ*, than a similar change before he was *in morâ* should do.
>
>   In *Lindsay Petroleum Company v. Hurd*[519] it is said:
>
> The doctrine of laches in Courts of Equity is not an arbitrary or a technical doctrine. Where it would be *practically unjust* to give a remedy, either because the party has, by his conduct done that which might fairly be regarded as equivalent to a waiver of it, or where, by his conduct and neglect he has, though perhaps not waiving that remedy, yet put the other party in a situation in which it would not be reasonable to place him if the remedy were afterwards to be asserted, in either of these cases lapse of time and delay are most material. But in every case if an argument against relief, which otherwise would be just, is founded upon mere delay, that delay of course not amounting to a bar by any statute of limitations, the validity of that defence must be tried upon principles substantially equitable. Two circumstances always important in such cases are the length of the delay and the nature of the acts done during the interval, which might affect either party and cause a balance of justice or injustice in taking the one course or the other, so far as relates to the remedy.
>
>   I have looked in vain for any authority which gives a more distinct and definite rule than this; and I think, from the nature of the inquiry, it must always be a question of more or less, depending on the degree of diligence which might reasonably be required, and the degree of change which has occurred, whether the balance of justice or injustice is in favour of granting the remedy or withholding it.

And Waters states:[520]

> If the claimant fully realized the facts, and had simply done nothing about them, being fully able to take action, it may be hard on the defendant at some very much later date to require him to compensate the claimant.

It would seem clear that the most important factors in determining whether the defence of laches will lie are the conduct of the plaintiff, and any change which has occurred. Mere lapse of time is insufficient. However, in certain classes of cases a stricter rule prevails, and the claim for equitable relief must be made more promptly. This special class of cases includes claims to establish constructive trusts.[521]

. . .

I have also considered the argument for the plaintiff that the facts are not such that the doctrine of laches applies. Counsel referred me to *Wawanesa Mutual*

---

517 (1878) 3 App. Cas. 1218 (H.L.).
518 *Ibid.*, at 1279.
519 (1874) L.R. 5 P.C. 221.
520 *Supra*, at 872.
521 14 Halsbury, 3rd ed., p. 646, para. 1188.

Ins. Co. v. J.A. (Fred) Chalmers & Co. Ltd.,[522] *Harris v. Lindeborg,*[523] and *Canada Trust Co. v. Lloyd*[524] In my view, these cases do not help the plaintiff.

. . .

I hold, accordingly, that the plaintiff "lay by" for an appreciable period after he knew that the entire proceeds had been paid over to Wood, that his acquiescence constituted laches in accordance with the principles laid down in the authorities, and that this is a valid defence to his claim as against North and Donaldson Securities.

. . .

[The court dismissed the action.]

Notes and Questions

1. In *M. (K.) v. M. (H.),*[525] a father committed incest against his daughter, beginning when she was ten or eleven, until she left home at the age of sixteen. She brought proceedings against him for assault and battery and breach of fiduciary obligations when she was 28. It was held that the limitation period on the tort claim was postponed until the claim was reasonably discoverable, and that the claim for breach of fiduciary duty was not limited by time, under the previous Ontario legislation. Regarding laches, La Forest J. said:[526]

> Thus there are two distinct branches to the laches doctrine, and either will suffice as a defence to a claim in equity. What is immediately obvious from all of the authorities is that mere delay is insufficient to trigger laches under either of its two branches. Rather, the doctrine considers whether the delay of the plaintiff constitutes acquiescence or results in circumstances that make the prosecution of the action unreasonable. Ultimately, laches must be resolved as a matter of justice as between the parties, as is the case with any equitable doctrine.

Regarding acquiescence, he said:[527]

> As the primary and secondary definitions of acquiescence suggest, an important aspect of the concept is the plaintiff's knowledge of her rights. It is not enough that the plaintiff knows of the facts that support a claim in equity; she must also know that the facts give rise to that claim: *Re Howlett.*[528] However, this Court has held that knowledge of one's claim is to be measured by an objective standard; see *Taylor v. Wallbridge.*[529] In other words, the question is whether it is reasonable for a plaintiff to be ignorant of her legal rights given her knowledge of the underlying facts relevant to a possible legal claim.

---

522 *Supra*, note 457.
523 [1931] S.C.R. 235, [1931] 1 D.L.R. 945.
524 [1968] S.C.R. 300, 63 W.W.R. 436, 66 D.L.R. (2d) 722.
525 *Supra*, note 150.
526 Para. 98.
527 Para. 101.
528 [1949] Ch. 767.
529 *Supra*, note 506, at 670.

Neither doctrine was held to bar the plaintiff's claim.

2. A and B were executors of Y's estate. B agreed with A to purchase Blackacre from the estate. A and Y's widow, his sole heir, executed the deed to B in 1960. In 1975, Y's widow brought action against B, seeking to have the deed set aside because B was a fiduciary. What result?[530]

3. X acquired a patent in 1940. He assigned the patent to his company, X Ltd., to reduce his personal debt to the company. X Ltd. went bankrupt in 1951, but the trustee in bankruptcy did nothing to set aside the transaction or to exploit the patent, which was a wasting asset since it was good for only 17 years. In 1954, an order was obtained requiring the trustee in bankruptcy to assign its rights against X to the Crown. The Crown, acting on behalf of the Minister of National Revenue, alleged that X should have given X Ltd. the benefit of the patent, or alternatively that he got more than its fair value. The case against X did not come to trial until 1957 without any fault on X's part.

What result?[531]

4. A, B and C were the sole shareholders and directors of a corporation. Their shareholdings were equal. B and C died and A caused the corporation to convey two parcels of real property to him. Four years later, A brought an action in debt against the corporation. It defended and counterclaimed, *inter alia*, to recover the lands. Nothing further was done for 12 years, when A died and the corporation sought leave to take the next step in the action. What result?[532]

5. If a corporation delays in bringing an action because it was ignorant of the fact that it had a right to complain, is it guilty of laches or acquiescence?[533]

6. PROTECTION OF THE TRUSTEE

(a) Generally

You will have observed that the liability of a trustee for breach of trust is strict and onerous. Because the liability may sometimes be too heavy, there are a variety of ways in which a trustee may be relieved from liability in whole or in part. This may be done by statute, by the creator of the trust or by the beneficiaries. These several methods are discussed in this part.

(b) Exculpation by Statute

A trustee's liability is limited in a number of ways by statute. Thus, for example, section 18(1) of the Ontario *Trustee Act*[534] provides that a sale by a trustee cannot be impeached on the ground that the conditions of sale were unnecessarily depreciatory, unless the consideration was thereby rendered inad-

---

530 See *Fysh v. Page* (1956), 96 C.L.R. 233.

531 See *Canada (Attorney General) v. Granell* (1956), [1958] O.W.N. 435, 30 C.P.R. 68, 17 D.L.R. (2d) 141 (H.C.).

532 See *J.L.O. Ranch Ltd. v. Logan, supra*, note 497.

533 *Cadbury Schweppes Inc. v. FBI Foods Ltd.* (1999), [1999] 1 S.C.R. 142, 167 D.L.R. (4th) 577, 1999 CarswellBC 77, 1999 CarswellBC 78, [1999] S.C.J. No. 6, 83 C.P.R. (3d) 289, 235 N.R. 30, 42 B.L.R. (2d) 159, 117 B.C.A.C. 161, 191 W.A.C. 161, 59 B.C.L.R. (3d) 1, [1999] 5 W.W.R. 751, [2000] F.S.R. 491.

534 R.S.O. 1990, c. T.23.

equate. Section 20(3) exonerates a trustee from having appointed or concurred in appointing a solicitor or bank manager to receive trust property, provided the trustee sees to it that the moneys are paid over to him or her promptly. Section 28 makes it clear that the trustee will not be liable for investment losses, if he or she adopted an investment strategy in conformity with the prudent investor standard.

(c) Exculpation by the Trust's Creator

Most modern trust instruments contain lengthy indemnity clauses which purport to exonerate the trustees from various kinds of liability. These clauses are apt to exonerate a trustee from minor breaches of trust and breaches by a co-trustee in which he or she did not participate. However, if the breach is major, it is unlikely that such a clause will exonerate the trustee. Moreover, it will be given a narrow construction. The issue is discussed in *Poche v. Pihera*[535] reproduced below.

POCHE v. PIHERA

(1983), 16 E.T.R. 68, 6 D.L.R. (4th) 40, 1983 CarswellAlta 291,
(sub nom. *Poche v. Poche*) 50 A.R. 264
Surrogate Court of Alberta

The testator died in 1979. He appointed his sister (the respondent, Mrs. Pihera) sole executrix and gave the residue of his estate in trust for his wife for life with remainder to his daughter. The estate consisted of a one-quarter interest in the deceased's mother's estate, of which he and his sisters were executors, certain debts, compound interest Canada Savings Bonds and a large number of oil and gas stocks. The respondent failed to call in the debts, the cash bonuses payable on the bonds, and the deceased's share of his mother's estate because it would require the sale of the family farm; nor did she sell and convert the stocks. The latter produced virtually no income. In addition, she failed to keep proper accounting records, was unable to account, failed to pay the deceased's widow any income and lost about $7,000 of estate funds. The will contained what the court construed to be an absolute trust to convert, coupled with a discretionary power to retain.

The widow and the daughter brought this application, *inter alia*, for misconduct, neglect or default. The court held the respondent liable to the widow for her failure to exercise her discretion in that she did not invest the assets of the estate, call in the assets, render an account and maintain an even hand.

The will contained an exculpatory clause the effect of which is discussed in the following excerpt.

---

535 (1983), 16 E.T.R. 68, 6 D.L.R. (4th) 40, 1983 CarswellAlta 291, (sub nom. *Poche v. Poche*) 50 A.R. 264 (Surr. Ct.).

HETHERINGTON J.:

. . .

Mr. Poche's will contains a number of provisions which relieves Mrs. Pihera from liability for a loss resulting from an exercise of discretion by her.[536] Since I am not satisfied on a balance of probabilities that Mrs. Pihera exercised any discretion with respect to the matters complained of in this case, I need not consider these provisions.

Mr. Poche's will also contains the following provision:

> 8. I DECLARE that the Trustee of this my will shall not be liable for any loss not attributable:
> (a) To her own dishonesty, or
> (b) To a wilful commission by her of any act known by her to be a breach of trust. . .

It was not suggested that the loss in question is attributable to Mrs. Pihera's dishonesty. Nor was it suggested that the loss is attributable to the wilful commission by her of any act. The loss is attributable to omissions by Mrs. Pihera, not to any commission. It would appear, therefore, that Mrs. Pihera is relieved from liability for this loss by para. 8 of Mr. Poche's will.

However, I am of the view that the conduct of Mrs. Pihera which resulted in the loss to Mrs. Poche was grossly negligent. And I am further of the view that para. 8 of Mr. Poche's will cannot relieve Mrs. Pihera from liability for a loss resulting from her gross negligence.

In the case of *Seton v. Dawson*[537] the court was required to consider the effect of a clause[538] which provided as follows:

> . . .and I declare that the trustees, whether originally added or assumed, shall not be liable for omissions, neglect of diligence, of any kind, nor singuli in solidum, but each only for his own actual intromissions. . .

The court held that this clause did not relieve the trustees from liability in the circumstances of the case. Lord Cockburn, with whom Lords Justice-General Boyle, Mackenzie, Fullerton and Cunninghame concurred, stated:[539]

> We hold this total disregard of the trust, after their attention had been called, by their being required to sign the deeds, to the fact that these sums had been received, to amount to culpa lata. Though aware of the indulgence due, under such a clause, to trustees, we think that no trust property would be safe, if such gross negligence were not to make those who are guilty of it liable to the party injured.

---

536 These exculpatory clauses were in standard form and included exonerations for loss resulting from (a) retention of original assets, (b) postponement of conversion of assets, and (c) investment in unauthorized securities.

537 (1841), 4 Ct. Sess. Cas. (2d) 310.

538 Quoted at *ibid.*, p. 311.

539 *Ibid.*, at 317.

Lord Ivory, with whom Lords Gillies and Murray concurred, stated:[540]

> But in no view can I hold them excusable, after putting the money into the hands of such third party, for having allowed it, or the greater part of it to remain there for a space of nine years wholly uncared for, and without so much as an account having during all that time been rendered. It is here that the gravamen of the case, as regards the trustees, in my opinion lies. For, could I get over the plea of culpa lata, as applied to this species facti, I should have been disposed in other respects, to allow them the protection of the clause which the trust-deed contains in their favour; that protection being only to be withheld, when there is a clear case of culpa lata, which, however, I think, there unquestionably is here.

In *Knox v. Mackinnon*[541] Lord Watson stated:[542]

> By the second of those clauses, it is declared that the trustees "shall not be liable for omissions, errors, or neglect of management, nor singuli in solidum, but each shall be liable for his own actual intromissions only." I see no reason to doubt that a clause conceived in these or similar terms, will afford a considerable measure of protection to trustees who have bona fide abstained from closely superintending the administration of the trust, or who have committed mere errors of judgment whilst acting with a single eye to the benefit of the trust, and of the persons whom it concerns. But it is settled in the law of Scotland that such a clause is ineffectual to protect a trustee against the consequences of culpa lata, or gross negligence on his part, or of any conduct which is inconsistent with bona fides.

This statement of law was adopted as well-warranted by the authorities by Lord Herschell in *Rae v. Meek*.[543]

Statements to the same effect can be found in the following cases: *Carruthers v. Carruthers*[544] and *Wyman or Ferguson v. Patterson*.[545] In *Wyman v. Patterson*, Lord Shand observed that in this regard there was no real distinction between the law of Scotland and that of England.

I am persuaded by the reasoning in these cases. In my opinion a trustee must be held responsible for any loss resulting from his gross negligence, regardless of any provision in the trust instrument relieving him from such liability.

Since the conduct of Mrs. Pihera which caused Mrs. Poche's loss was grossly negligent, she is not relieved from liability for this loss by para. 8 of Mr. Poche's will.

. . .

Notes and Questions

1. The English Court of Appeal reviewed exemption clauses in *Armitage v. Nurse*,[546] and came to a different conclusion from that reached in *Poche v. Pihera*. In *Armitage*, the

---

540 *Ibid.*, at 318.
541 (1888), 13 App. Cas. 753 (H.L.).
542 *Ibid.*, at 765.
543 (1889), 14 App. Cas. 558 at 572-3 (H.L.).
544 [1896] A.C. 659 (H.L.).
545 [1900] A.C. 271 (H.L.).
546 [1998] Ch. 241, leave to appeal refused [1998] Ch. 264.

clause excluded liability unless it arose from "actual fraud" of the trustee. The court interpreted this to intend to relieve the trustee of liability for any conduct which did not amount to dishonesty. Hence, it would exclude liability for gross negligence. The court held that such an exclusion of liability was not inconsistent with the nature of the trust.[547]

2. In its *Report on the Law of Trusts*,[548] the Ontario Law Reform Commission took strong objection to exoneration clauses in trust instruments. It recommended that no exculpatory clause in a trust instrument should be valid, except to the extent that it exonerates a trustee from liability for failure to exercise the standard of prudence. Further, it proposed to invalidate clauses exonerating professional trustees from failing to maintain a higher standard of care than that required of a lay trustee.[549] Do you agree with these recommendations?

3. A testator appointed a trust company as trustee of his estate and gave it power to retain the assets in the original estate. Part of the estate consisted of real property. It was unproductive and, in fact, the carrying charges on the property were so high that they absorbed the other trust income. The beneficiaries, therefore, did not receive any income and some were on welfare. The trust company's general manager received an offer for the property, but turned it down, presumably as being too low. However, he did not consult anyone about his decision. Under the applicable legislation,[550] any discretion was to be exercised by the company's board of directors. The trust contained an exculpatory clause which purported to exonerate the trustee from responsibility for loss or damage caused by the exercise in good faith of the rights and powers conferred on it by the trust instrument.

Is the clause apt to exonerate the trustee? Should it?[551]

4. Context is important in determining whether an exclusionary clause will preclude liability. It will not do so if the transaction is not at arms length between equal and independent actors. [552]

(d) Power to Excuse Trustee

There are many situations in which trustees are unsure about their rights and duties or about the meaning of the trust instrument. In those circumstances they should apply to the court for directions.[553] If they fail to do so, they run the risk

547 See P. Matthews, "The Efficacy of Trustee Exemption Clauses in English Law," [1989] Conv. 42; D.A. Steele, "Exculpatory Clauses in Trust Instruments" (1995), 14 E.T.J. 216; J. Penner, "Exemptions" in P. Birks and A. Pretto, eds., *Breach of Trust* (Oxford: Hart Publishing, 2002) 241.

548 Ontario Law Reform Commission, *Report on the Law of Trusts* (Toronto: Ministry of the Attorney General, 1984). For more recent law reform activity, see B.C. Law Institute, *Exculpation Clauses in Trust Instruments*, Report No. 17 (2002), also at (2002), 22 E.T.P.J. 55; Law Commission of England and Wales, *Trustee Exemption Clauses*, Consultation Paper No. 171 (2002).

549 *Ibid.*, pp. 41-2. See also Waters, p. 756, to the same effect, followed in *Sproule, Re*, (sub nom. *Sproule v. Montreal Trust Co. (No. 2)*) [1979] 4 W.W.R. 670, 95 D.L.R. (3d) 458, 1979 CarswellAlta 218, 17 A.R. 58 (C.A.), additional reasons at (1979), 95 D.L.R. (3d) 458 at 471 (Alta. C.A.), at 469 [95 D.L.R. (4th) 458].

550 *Companies Act*, R.S.C. 1906, c. 79, ss. 125, 131, 132.

551 See *Wilson, Re*, [1937] O.R. 769, [1937] 3 D.L.R. 178, 1937 CarswellOnt 51 (C.A.).

552 *Baskerville v. Thurgood*, 46 E.T.R. 28, 1992 CarswellSask 323, [1992] S.J. No. 327, [1992] 5 W.W.R. 193, 100 Sask. R. 214, 18 W.A.C. 214, (sub nom. *582872 Saskatchewan Ltd. v. Thurgood*) 93 D.L.R. (4th) 694 (C.A.).

553 This is discussed in the chapter on the duties of trustees.

of committing a breach of trust. Even then, however, the court has a statutory discretion to grant the trustees relief from liability if they acted honestly and reasonably, and ought fairly to be excused.[554] The Ontario legislation is set out below.

You will have observed that the legislation requires three criteria to be satisfied before relief can be given: the trustee must have acted "honestly," "reasonably," and "ought fairly to be excused." Hence, if only the first two criteria have been met, the trustee will not obtain relief.[555]

To avoid restricting their discretion, the courts have not defined these three criteria.[556] However, "honestly" clearly refers to the trustee's *bona fides* and his or her intention to act in the welfare of the trust.[557] "Reasonably," on the other hand, refers to the standard of care imposed upon a trustee. Thus, for this criterion, the court measures the trustee's conduct against the conduct of a prudent business person in his or her own affairs.[558] The third criterion, "ought fairly to be excused", appears to be directed to the technical nature of a breach, the fact that the trustee was inexperienced,[559] or other similar special circumstances. These criteria are discussed further in the excerpts from *Fales v. Canada Permanent Trust Co.*,[560] reproduced below.

TRUSTEE ACT

R.S.O. 1990, c. T.23

TECHNICAL BREACHES OF TRUST

35.(1) If in any proceeding affecting a trustee or trust property it appears to the court that a trustee, or that any person who may be held to be fiduciarily responsible as a trustee, is or may be personally liable for any breach of trust whenever the transaction alleged or found to be a breach of trust occurred, but has acted honestly and reasonably, and ought fairly to be excused for the breach of trust, and for omitting to obtain the directions of the court in the matter in which the trustee committed the breach, the court may relieve the trustee either wholly or partly from personal liability for the same.

(2) Subsection (1) does not apply to liability for a loss to the trust arising from the investment of trust property.

---

554 See also L.A. Sheridan, "Excusable Breaches of Trust" (1955), 19 Conv. (N.S.) 420.
555 *National Trustees of Australasia Ltd. v. General Finance Co. of Australasia Ltd.*, [1905] A.C. 373 (Victoria P.C.).
556 *Smith v. Mason* (1901), 1 O.L.R. 594.
557 *Cotton v. Dempster* (1918), 20 W.A.R. 14.
558 Waters, p. 1029.
559 See, *e.g.*, *Perdue v. Perdue* (1928), 34 O.W.N. 172 (C.A.), the trustee, a farmer, left the trust fund in the hands of his solicitor.
560 *Supra*, note 48.

Comparable Legislation

Trustee Act, R.S.A. 2000, c. T-8, s. 41; R.S.B.C. 1996, c. 464, s. 96; C.C.S.M., c. T160, s. 81; R.S.N.L. 1990, c. T-10, s. 32; R.S.N.S. 1989, c. 479, s. 64; R.S.N.W.T. 1988, T-8, s. 24; R.S.S. 1978, c. T-23, s. 57; R.S.Y. 2002, c. 223, s. 33; *Trustees Act*, R.S.N.B. 1973, c. T-15, ss. 10(1), 42.

Notes and Questions

1. Note that s. 35(2) was added when investment powers were reformed in 1998, and does not exist in other jurisdictions.

FALES v. CANADA PERMANENT TRUST CO.[561]

(1976), [1977] 2 S.C.R. 302, (sub nom. *Wohlleben v. Canada Permanent Trust Co.*) 70 D.L.R. (3d) 257, 1976 CarswellBC 240, 1976 CarswellBC 317, [1976] 6 W.W.R. 10, 11 N.R. 487
Supreme Court of Canada

The persons entitled to the remainder interest under their father's will sued Canada Permanent Trust Co. for damages for breach of trust for failing to sell an unauthorized shareholding in a speculative venture, as a result of which the estate suffered a large loss. They did not sue the other trustee, their mother, but Canada Permanent brought third party proceedings against her. She had been a passive trustee and had refused to sell the shares when approached by her co-trustee. The court found Canada Permanent liable. The assessment of damages in the case was discussed earlier in this chapter.

Canada Permanent sought to be exonerated under section 98 of the British Columbia *Trustee Act*,[562] which is to the same effect as the Ontario legislation set out above. The company also ought indemnity from the widow in the third party proceedings.[563] In that context the question whether she should be excused under section 98 was also relevant. The following excerpts from the judgment deal with these issues.

DICKSON J. delivered the judgment of the court:

. . .

At trial and in the Court of Appeal, Canada Permanent asked for relief under s. 98 of the *Trustee Act*. A trustee is not expected to be infallible nor is a trustee the guarantor of the safety of estate assets and I have no doubt that in an appropriate case a paid professional trustee may seek and obtain relief under s. 98. Section

---

561 The facts of this case and those parts of the judgment dealing with the trustees' breach of the
standard of care are set out in the chapter on the duties of trustees.
562 R.S.B.C. 1960, c. 390.
563 The issue of indemnity is discussed later in this chapter.

98 in terms admits of that possibility. All of the circumstances would have to be considered, including whether the trustee was paid for its services.[564] Among other relevant considerations is whether the breach was merely technical in nature or a minor error in judgment; whether decline in value of securities was attributable to general economic conditions; whether the trustee is someone who accepted a single trust to oblige a friend or is a company organized for the purpose of administering estates and presumably chosen in the expectation that it will have specialized departments and experienced officials; above all, whether the conduct of the trustee was reasonable. The actions, or inaction, on the part of Canada Permanent which gave rise to the breach of trust in the present instance were not reasonable in my view. No case can possibly be made out for granting Canada Permanent relief under s. 98.

. . .

The third party proceedings, in which Canada Permanent seeks contribution and indemnity from Mrs. Wohlleben, and her claim for relief under s. 98 of the *Trustee Act* now fall to be considered. The policy of the law has been to afford a maximum degree of security and protection to the interests of beneficiaries of a trust estate. Each trustee normally is responsible to the beneficiaries for what occurs in the course of administration, subject to such exoneration as may be afforded by the terms of the will, or by statute, (as, for example, statutory exoneration given a trustee for the acts of others: s. 97 of the *Trustee Act*)[565] or by the exercise of the discretionary judicial power to give relief under legislation such as s. 98 of the *Trustee Act*. The law does not distinguish between active and passive trustees save when the terms of the trust so provide.[566]

In accepting the trusteeship, Mrs. Wohlleben became obligated to exercise an independent judgment and she assumed a duty to the beneficiaries of the residuary estate which, in failing to sell the Inspiration shares in timely fashion, she breached. With certain exceptions, where two trustees owe a duty to the beneficiaries of an estate and that duty is breached, resulting in loss, the trustee called upon to make good the loss can look to the co-trustee for contribution, subject to s. 98. Canada Permanent, however, can look to Mrs. Wohlleben for contribution and indemnity only if she is liable to the beneficiaries for breach of trust; she is not liable if the Court relieves her pursuant to s. 98. See Waters, *Law of Trusts in Canada*,[567] for a few instances where one trustee has borne the entire burden for a breach of trust. Another instance would be where the Court relieves one trustee pursuant to legislation analogous to s. 98. Should Mrs. Wohlleben be relieved under s. 98?

564　*National Trustees of Australasia, Ltd. v. General Finance Co. of Australasia, Ltd., supra*, note 555, followed and applied in *Re Windsor Steam Coal Co. (1901), Ltd.*, [1929] 1 Ch. 151.
565　*Supra*.
566　*Mickleburgh v. Parker* (1870), 17 Gr. 503 at 506.
567　(1974), p. 855.

Section 98 is remedial legislation, giving statutory recognition to the fact that the standard of conduct which courts have expected of trustees has been, at times and in certain circumstances, unduly harsh and inflexible.[568] Section 98 permits the court or a judge to relieve a trustee from personal liability for breach of trust if the trustee has acted honestly and reasonably and ought fairly to be excused. Mrs. Wohlleben acted honestly. After careful reading of the evidence and examination of the exhibits, I have concluded that she also acted reasonably. Her acts were not greatly less nor more than might be expected of one in her position. At the death of her husband, she was a housewife with four young children. She had been a school teacher and she had taken a three months' night school course on "How to Invest your Money". That would seem to have been the extent of her business exposure. She was no doubt an intelligent young woman of independent mind who from time to time consulted a broker and the lawyer for the estate, but her investment experience was minimal and she was without experience in the administration of trust estates. She tried to the best of her ability to keep herself informed but Canada Permanent failed to make known to her the contents of papers which were essential to informed opinion. She tried to respond but from less than complete information. She made all decisions which she was asked to make within the limits of her experience and knowledge, and I cannot find that at any time she failed to listen to reason or that she responded irrationally or obdurately. In short, it would seem to me that this is the very sort of case for which s. 98 of the *Trustee Act* was intended and that Mrs. Wohlleben ought fairly to be excused for her breach of trust. . . .

Notes and Questions

1. Can a trustee be inactive? Was it reasonable of Mrs. Wohlleben to claim exoneration because she was a passive trustee? Ought she to have been excused? Would she have been held liable if she had been sued by the beneficiaries?[569]

2. In *MacDonald v. Hauer*[570] one of the two passive trustees bought action against the third, active trustee and against a person who participated with the active trustee in a breach of trust. The participant in the breach brought third party proceedings claiming, *inter alia*, indemnity from the passive trustees. However, the court exonerated them even though the plaintiff had left the administration of the trust in the hands of the active trustee and had been out of the province for a number of years. Is this use of the power to exonerate proper?[571]

3. In *National Trustees Co. of Australasia Ltd. v. General Finance Co. of Australasia Ltd.*,[572] referred to in the *Fales* case, the trustee paid moneys due to a beneficiary to his children on the erroneous advice of its solicitor. The beneficiary had assigned his rights to the plaintiff finance company. When it learned of the wrongful payment, it sued the trustee. The Privy Council held that the trustee had acted honestly and reasonably, but

---

568 See "The Trustee's Duty of Skill and Care" (1973), 37 Conv. (N.S) 48.
569 See D.W.M. Waters, Comment (1977), 55 Can. Bar Rev. 342.
570 *Supra*, note 119.
571 See D.W.M. Waters, Comment (1977), 4 E. & T.Q. 12.
572 *Supra*, note 555.

ought not to be excused. On that point Sir Ford North who delivered the judgment of their Lordships said:[573]

> It is a very material circumstance that the appellants are a limited joint stock company, formed for the purpose of earning profits for their shareholders; part of their business is to act as trustees and executors; and they are paid for their services in so acting by a commission which the law of the Colony authorizes them to retain out of trust funds administered by them, in addition to their costs. What they now ask the Court to do is to allow them to retain a sum of money to which the respondents' title is clear, in order thereby to relieve the trust company from a loss they have incurred in the course of their business by reason of their having paid a like sum to wrong parties. The position of a joint stock company which undertakes to perform for reward services it can only perform through its agents, and which has been misled by those agents to misapply a fund under its charge, is widely different from that of a private person acting as gratuitous trustee. And without saying that the remedial provisions of the section should never be applied to a trustee in the position of the appellants, their Lordships think it is a circumstance to be taken into account, and they do not find here any fair excuse for the breach of trust, or any reason why the respondents, who have committed no fault, should lose their money to relieve the appellants, who have done a wrong and have denied the respondents' title. And that is not quite all. If trustees do unfortunately lose part of a trust fund by a breach of trust, the least that can be expected of them is that they should use their best endeavours to recover the fund, or so much thereof as is practicable, for their cestui que trusts [sic]. In the present case there seems to be some ground for thinking that other proceedings were open to the trust company by which any loss to them might have been averted, at any rate to some extent; but it does not appear that the trust company have taken any such steps, or made any attempt whatever to replace the fund or relieve the respondents from loss; nor have they condescended to give the Court any explanation or reason why they have abstained from doing so. It may be that the solicitors would be willing or might be compelled to make good the loss, if the trust company should find they cannot obtain relief elsewhere. The Courts in the Colony held that under these circumstances the appellants had not made out any case for relief under the Act; and their Lordships agree with them.

4. The English tradition was that a trustee undertakes the office of trustee free of charge. In that tradition the decision in the *National Trustees* case is understandable. Indeed, it has been said that a corporate professional trustee, by reason of having bargained for its remuneration, has deliberately placed itself in a position in which its duty and interest conflict. Hence, the court should be slow to grant it relief.[574]

The tradition on this continent is otherwise: trustees, whether amateur or professional, are entitled to be remunerated for their services. That being so, should not a paid trustee be treated in the same way as an amateur under the power to grant relief? Or is the reason for the different approach that the professional trustee is required to maintain a higher standard of care?

5. A builder held funds under a statutory trust for suppliers of material and workers.[575] He abandoned the contract and assigned the funds to trustees for the benefit of creditors. The trustees distributed the trust funds rateably among the lien claimants, but ignored one valid claim. Can the trustees be exonerated for failing to pay one beneficiary?[576]

---

573 *Ibid.*, at 381-2.

574 *Pauling's Settlement Trusts, Re, supra,* note 434, at 339 [Ch.], *per* Willmer L.J.

575 Under *The Mechanics' Lien Act,* R.S.O. 1960, c. 233, s. 3; see now *Construction Lien Act,* R.S.O. 1990, c. C.30, s. 8.

576 See *Guaranty Trust Co. of Canada v. Beaumont* (1966), [1967] 1 O.R. 479, 61 D.L.R. (2d) 286, 1966 CarswellOnt 190 (C.A.). For a case involving a negligent breach of trust see *Meakes, Re,* [1968] 2 O.R. 637, 70 D.L.R. (2d) 258, 1968 CarswellOnt 186 (Surr. Ct.).

6. A trustee took its compensation from the trust fund without prior authorization by the trust instrument, the court, or the beneficiaries, as required. It did so, in part, to reduce the impact of income tax on the estate. No loss resulted to the estate, but the trustee did earn interest on the pre-taken compensation. Can the trustee be excused?[577]

7. An elderly couple moved in with an acquaintance. They paid no rent and their living expenses were paid for by the acquaintance. However, the couple gave the acquaintance a cheque for a large sum of money, presumably to enable the acquaintance to help look after them. When both husband and wife had died, the acquaintance retained the monies left over and claimed them as a gift. In an action for an account, can the acquaintance be granted relief for the retention of the moneys?[578]

8. A testator appointed X and Y, his solicitor and accountant, respectively, his executors and trustees. The will contained a trust to convert unauthorized assets, coupled with a power to postpone conversion. The trustees failed to convert certain land, but brought it into a joint venture with Z to build a shopping centre. Y relied upon X's assurance that this was permitted. When financial problems arose, X and Y sought to opt out of the joint venture. Z gave X and Y only a couple of hours to decide whether to proceed with the joint venture, sell their interest to him, or opt out and face a law suit by Z. They chose to proceed with the joint venture. It failed later, causing a substantial loss to the estate. The beneficiaries sued X and Y for their breach of trust.

Can either X or Y be excused for their breach?[579]

9. If a personal representative pays more to a creditor than he or she ought, there being a deficiency of assets in the estate, the court has power to relieve the personal representative from personal liability in whole or in part. The court must be satisfied that the personal representative acted honestly and reasonably and for the protection or conservation of the assets of the estate.[580]

10. Section 35 can only be used to relieve a trustee of personal liability if the trustee's actions were reasonable in the circumstances.[581]

Further Reading

J. Lowry and R. Edmunds, "Excuses" in P. Birks and A. Pretto, eds., *Breach of Trust* (Oxford: Hart Publishing, 2002) 269.

7. LIABILITY OF TRUSTEES *INTER SE*

Trustees are jointly and severally liable for any loss caused to the trust by a breach. That is, they are liable for the loss caused by all or any of the trustees, as

---

577 See *Prelutsky, Re*, [1982] 4 W.W.R. 309, 36 B.C.L.R. 214, 11 E.T.R. 233, 1982 CarswellBC 90 (S.C.).

578 See *Garland v. Clarke* (1982), 41 Nfld. & P.E.I.R. 75, 119 A.P.R. 75, 1982 CarswellNfld 185 (Dist. Ct.).

579 See *Linsley v. Kirstiuk* (1986), 28 D.L.R. (4th) 495, 1986 CarswellBC 652 (S.C.).

580 *Trustee Act*, R.S.O. 1990, c. T.23, s. 50(3).

581 *Smullen Estate, Re* (1995), 6 E.T.R. (2d) 299, 1995 CarswellOnt 180 (Gen. Div.), additional reasons at (1995), 1995 CarswellOnt 2725, [1995] O.J. No. 1899 (Gen. Div.). A father who used trust monies to pay for day care for his child and reported the income of the trust as his own income, and paid income tax on it was not permitted to be relieved of his personal liability as his actions were held not to be reasonable.

well as for their own contribution to the loss.[582] It follows that a beneficiary can sue all the trustees, or one or more of them, and recover the entire amount from one, for example. If that happens, however, the trustee who has paid can claim *contribution* from the other trustees, since all are equally liable.

Not only can a trustee claim contribution from his or her co-trustees, in certain situations he or she can also seek *indemnity* from them. A trustee who is found liable to the beneficiaries can claim indemnity from a co-trustee in three situations: (a) if the co-trustee alone is fraudulent;[583] (b) if the co-trustee is a solicitor who controls the administration of the trust, the other trustee relied upon his or her expertise, and the solicitor's action caused a loss to the estate;[584] and (c) if the co-trustee is also a beneficiary, in which case he or she must indemnify the other trustee to the extent of his or her beneficial interest.

The operation of the doctrines of contribution and indemnity is illustrated by the following excerpt from *MacDonald v. Hauer*.[585]

MacDONALD v. HAUER[586]

(1976), [1977] 1 W.W.R. 51, 72 D.L.R. (3d) 110, 1976 CarswellSask 95 (C.A.)
Saskatchewan Court of Appeal

Alan MacDonald, one of three executors of an estate, facilitated a breach of trust by permitting his acquaintance, Hauer, to sell the estate's securities and trade in speculative investments. The other two executors were the deceased's widow and Alan's brother, Dr. Malcolm MacDonald, both of whom were passive executors. When a substantial loss occurred, Malcolm sued Alan and Hauer for damages for breach of trust and was successful against both. Hauer joined the widow as a third party. He claimed indemnity from all three executors. Alan and Hauer claimed contribution from each other. The following excerpt deals with the issues of contribution and indemnity.

BAYDA J.A. delivered the main judgment of the court:

. . .

I turn to the question of indemnities and contribution.

Mr. Hauer at trial and before us, claimed the right to be indemnified by the three trustees, Dr. MacDonald, Mr. MacDonald and Mrs. MacDonald in respect of any sum for which he was found liable to the estate trust. It is proposed to treat separately his claim against Dr. MacDonald and Mrs. MacDonald from the claim made against Mr. MacDonald. The claim against the first two trustees is made on these two grounds:

---

582 *Canada Safeway Co. v. Thompson*, [1951] 3 D.L.R. 295 (B.C. S.C.).
583 *Bahin v. Hughes* (1886), 31 Ch. D. 390 (C.A.).
584 *Chillingworth v. Chambers*, *supra*, note 442.
585 *Supra*, note 119.
586 We also discussed this case earlier in this chapter in connection with the compensation remedy.

[The first ground was that Hauer acted as agent for Alan MacDonald, at Alan's request and without notice of the trust. This ground failed because the trial judge had found otherwise. The second ground was as follows:]

(b) That the defendant Ray Hauer alleges that if any breach of trust arose in the circumstances alleged in the statement of claim, he was not a party thereto and the same was occasioned and instigated by the negligence and wrongful acts and omissions of all of the said executors, including the said Malcolm Hugh MacDonald [and Nona H. MacDonald] and that accordingly the said Malcolm Hugh MacDonald [and Nona H. MacDonald] is liable to indemnify the defendant, Ray Hauer, in respect of any claim arising from such breach or [*sic*] trust.

It is essential in considering this question of indemnity to keep in mind that Dr. MacDonald and Mrs. MacDonald were not sued by the beneficiaries of the trust for breach of trust and accordingly were not found liable to the beneficiaries for any breach. Their status in this respect is different from that of their co-trustee Mr. MacDonald.

As I understand Mr. Hauer's claim against Dr. MacDonald and Mrs. Mac-Donald, it is not one for contribution, that is, it is not a claim with a view to making each contribute equally, as co-trustee, to the sum found due to the beneficiaries. (The effect of an order for contribution would be, as among the trustees — those appointed by the will as well as constructive trustees — to split four ways the liability for the sum found due to the estate beneficiaries.) It is rather a claim for indemnity having as its aim complete indemnification of Mr. Hauer for the sum for which he is liable.

. . .

The second ground is a little more difficult. It has three parts. In the first Mr. Hauer asserts against Dr. MacDonald and Mrs. MacDonald, that their passivity with respect to the administration of the estate and their decision to allow Mr. MacDonald to handle, almost exclusively, the estate affairs constitute a neglect of their duty as trustees; that it was this neglect which created the opportunity for him, Mr. Hauer, to commit the breach for which he has now been found liable; and, those factors alone are sufficient to support a claim for indemnification. I could find no useful authority on this point. *Bahin v. Hughes*[587] is authority for the proposition that when an active trustee and a passive trustee are both found liable to trust beneficiaries for a breach of trust committed by the active trustee and through default made possible by the passive trustee, the latter's passivity is not by itself a sufficient basis upon which to found a claim for indemnification by the latter against the active trustee. Two features distinguish that case from the present one: First, the passive trustee, as well as the active trustee, in *Bahin*, was found liable to the trust beneficiaries. Dr. MacDonald and Mrs. Nona H. Mac-Donald, the passive trustees in the present case, are not, as noted, in that position. Second, it was the passive trustee in *Bahin* who was seeking indemnification from the active trustee and not the other way around as in the present case. For the

---

587 *Supra*, note 583.

purposes of the present case, *Bahin* is of doubtful value but if it has any prece-
dential value at all then it favours Dr. MacDonald and Mrs. MacDonald: if the
passivity of the passive trustees is not sufficient to found a claim for indemnity
made by the passive trustee against an active trustee, then *a fortiori* the passivity
of a passive trustee is not sufficient to found a claim for indemnification made by
the active trustee against the passive trustee.

The Canadian case of *Mickelburgh v. Parker*,[588] too, is not of much assistance.
The *ratio decidendi* of that case is that in action by a trust beneficiary against a
trustee not active in the affairs of the trust, the trustee's passivity is no defence.
The present case is, of course, not an action by a trust beneficiary against a passive
trustee.

It is not surprising that there is no case authority for the submissions urged
by the appellant in this respect. It would be a strange law indeed if an active
trustee who, without any prompting or indeed even knowledge on the part of a
passive trustee, seizes upon an opportunity to pursue, actively and freely, a course
of conduct which results in a breach of trust, were able to unload from his own
shoulders onto those of the passive trustees the complete financial burden for
damages occasioned by such breach. It would be no less strange where that
opportunity (as in this case) is created unwittingly in part by the passive trustee
(and in part by the fraudulent acts of another). The anomalousness and injustice
of a result whereby an active trustee whose culpable activities constitute a breach
of trust goes entirely free while the passive trustee who remains in ignorant
innocence throughout bears the whole load is patent and needs no elaboration.
That result is simply untenable in law or in equity.

The second part of the second ground involves the applicability of the rule
that where a trustee (constructive or appointed) is found liable with his co-trustee
for a breach of trust, the trustee who is also a beneficiary may be called upon to
indemnify his co-trustee to the extent of the former's beneficial interest in the
trust estate. This rule is espoused in such cases as *Chillingworth v. Chambers*.[589]
The right to indemnification under this rule comes into play only in those cases
where the co-trustees, one of whom happens also to be a beneficiary, are found
jointly liable to the beneficiaries for the breach of trust. In the present case,
therefore, if the rule is to apply to the claims made against Dr. MacDonald and
Mrs. MacDonald then there must first be a finding that they are jointly liable with
Mr. Hauer for the breach. In the main action it was not sought to make either Dr.
MacDonald (after all he is the plaintiff) or Mrs. MacDonald liable for the breach
of trust and in consequence no finding of liability was made against them. It is
said, however, that the failure to make such a finding in the main action should
not by itself deter the making of such a finding in Mr. Hauer's claim-over. With
that principle I agree, but having said that I must say that I would be loathe to
find that the acts, or more precisely, the lack of vigilance, on the part of Dr.
MacDonald and Mrs. MacDonald are, in the circumstances in which they found
themselves, to be so construed as to make them liable to the beneficiaries of the

---

588 *Supra*, note 566.
589 *Supra*, note 442.

trust, for the misconduct committed by Mr. Hauer and Mr. MacDonald. I do not propose to critically analyze their acts and omissions in this respect but will content myself to say that throughout they acted honestly and reasonably. . . . Thus the precondition of joint liability to the beneficiaries which permits the invocation of the rule giving the right of indemnity is not present here. The rule therefore cannot be applied to Dr. MacDonald and Mrs. MacDonald.

. . .

For these reasons the claims for indemnity against Dr. MacDonald and Mrs. MacDonald must fail and the appeal in respect of those claims is dismissed.

The claim for indemnity against Mr. MacDonald is in a different category although the grounds for the claim against him are virtually the same as those advanced against the other two trustees. The distinction between the position in which Mr. MacDonald finds himself and that in which the other two trustees find themselves is hardly obscure. Mr. MacDonald is directly liable to the trust beneficiaries for the same breach of trust as Mr. Hauer. They both concurred in committing the breach of trust and were *in pari delicto*. Two consequences flow from this: Mr. MacDonald cannot escape the applicability to him of the rule in *Chillingworth v. Chambers*,[590] and is liable to indemnify Mr. Hauer to the extent of his (Mr. MacDonald's) beneficial interest in the estate. In addition, and upon the principle that the burden of compensation to the trust should be borne equally by the offending trustees, he must contribute to Mr. Hauer one-half of any amount which Mr. Hauer out of his own resources (as distinct from money received from Mr. MacDonald pursuant to the former's right of indemnity), pays to the trust. By the same token Mr. MacDonald has the right to look to Mr. Hauer for a like contribution in respect of sums he pays to the trust. Mr. Hauer's right of indemnity against Mr. MacDonald should not extend to the full limit of Mr. Hauer's liability for the reason that both were in the wrong and there is not much to choose between the degree of their culpability. That right of indemnity should not extend beyond the limit specified. Similarly, Mr. MacDonald has no right of complete indemnification by Mr. Hauer. Lindley, L.J., in *Chillingworth v. Chambers* detailed the manner in which the rights of two conflicting parties who find themselves in positions similar to Mr. Hauer's and Mr. MacDonald's should be worked out. In the following extract[591] he states:

> In order to determine the rights of the parties it is necessary to consider — first, the plaintiff's right in his character of trustee against the defendant; and, secondly, the defendant's right against the plaintiff in his character of cestui que trust. To the extent to which the plaintiff's right as trustee is neutralized by his obligation as cestui que trust he will have no right to contribution. But except so far as it is thus neutralized his right to contribution will remain. In other words, if the plaintiff as trustee is entitled to throw half the loss on the defendant, and if, on the other hand, the defendant is protected against any claim of the plaintiff in respect of his share of the trust estate, then, as that share exceeds half the loss, the plaintiff will not be entitled to anything from

---

590 *Ibid.*
591 *Ibid.*, at 698.

the defendant, and must bear the whole loss which he has sustained. On the other hand, if the plaintiff as cestui que trust is not precluded from recovering from the defendant so much as one-half the loss, the plaintiff's right as co-trustee to contribution from the defendant will still be enforceable for the excess. This, in my opinion, is how the conflicting rights of the two parties have to be adjusted, and it only remains to work them out.

In that case the plaintiff was the trustee-beneficiary and the defendant the co-trustee. In the present case the plaintiff's role is assumed by the co-trustee (Mr. Hauer) and the defendant's, by the trustee-beneficiary (Mr. MacDonald). This reversal of roles should not detract from the obtaining of a proper result if the formula designed by Lindley, L.J., is applied *mutatis mutandis*.

Mr. Hauer's appeal on this issue of indemnification and contribution by Mr. MacDonald is therefore allowed to the extent indicated.

As I have stated, the reasons which permit Mr. Hauer to claim contribution from Mr. MacDonald equally permit Mr. MacDonald to claim contribution from Mr. Hauer. Accordingly, I find that the notice of intention to vary judgment filed by Mr. MacDonald should be given effect and the judgment of the trial Court varied to allow contribution from Mr. Hauer to Mr. MacDonald to the extent mentioned above.

. . .

Notes and Questions

1. To appreciate how the principles of contribution and indemnity worked in *Mac-Donald*, assume the following facts (the figures in the case have been rounded off). The total loss was $491,800; the net estate at the testator's death was approximately $200,000; disregarding the life interests of the widow and of the three children (there was also a daughter), there were three beneficiaries, each taking an equal share; Alan's interest was, thus, approximately $66,600. The calculation is then as follows:

	Hauer	Alan	Total Loss	Beneficial Interest
Gross Contribution (1/2 of total loss)	$245,900	$245,900	$491,800	
Less Indemnity	66,600			$66,600
Net Contribution	$179,300	$245,900		

If Alan's interest had been more than $245,900, Hauer would not have been liable to contribute to Alan. If there had been another trustee who was not a beneficiary, Alan's interest would have been shared equally between Hauer and the other trustee.

You should remember that each trustee remains fully liable to the trust for the entire amount of the loss. Hence, either Hauer or Alan might be required to pay the whole amount, or both might in fact pay part. Then, as between themselves, their liabilities would be calculated as shown above and one might have to pay the other in accordance with the calculation.

2. Contribution and indemnity only apply as between trustees who are held liable for the breach of trust. Since Malcolm and the widow were not held liable, they could not be required to contribute nor to indemnify Hauer. In that regard, was it relevant that Malcolm was the plaintiff? Were the facts such that Malcolm and his mother should have been exonerated?[592]

3. In the United States the calculation is different. There, the beneficial interest of the defaulting trustee is deducted from the total loss and the trustees who are liable for the breach are then liable, *inter se*, for an equal share of the difference.[593]

Is this a fairer method of calculation? Does a person such as Hauer not get too great a benefit under the Canadian method? If the American method applied, would the court have been more willing to find the widow and Malcolm liable?

4. In England, the *Civil Liability (Contribution) Act, 1978*[594] has changed the principle of contribution. The Act permits the court to determine each defendant's liability on the basis of what is "just and equitable having regard to the extent of that person's responsibility for the damages in question."[595] The Act applies also to damages for breach of trust.[596]

8. MISCELLANEOUS LIABILITIES OF TRUSTEES

(a) Generally

Trustees who have committed a breach of trust will be denied their costs, at least if they were dishonest or grossly negligent.[597] In most other proceedings the trustees are normally allowed their costs out of the trust estate.[598]

Similarly, a trustee's right of indemnity for expenses may be denied in a serious breach of trust, as well as his or her right to remuneration.[599] On the other hand, if the trustee has made and appropriated a profit that rightfully belongs to the trust, he or she may be allowed compensation for the skill and expertise used in generating the profit.[600]

A trustee who has committed a serious breach of trust is usually removed from office.[601] Further, a trustee who refuses to obey a court order can be attached.[602]

---

592 The same question can be asked in respect of the widow in *Fales v. Canada Permanent Trust Co., supra*, note 48, who, although a passive trustee, was exonerated under the statutory excusing power. Hence her co-trustee's claim for contribution and indemnity was dismissed. The case is discussed earlier in this chapter.

593 See Scott, §258.2.

594 C. 47 (U.K.).

595 *Ibid.*, s. 2(1).

596 *Ibid.*, s. 6(1).

597 See, *e.g., MacDonald v. Hauer, supra*, note 119; Waters, p. 949. See also *Rumford Estate, Re* (1996), 14 E.T.R. (2d) 300, 1996 CarswellOnt 3709, 14 O.T.C. 252 (Gen. Div.): the court surcharged an executrix for losses incurred by gross negligence and refused her claim for executor's fees for the administration of the estate.

598 Waters, pp. 948-9.

599 This is discussed in the chapter on the powers and rights of trustees.

600 See *Boardman v. Phipps, supra*, note 21; *Warman International Ltd. v. Dwyer, supra*, note 47.

601 See the chapter on the appointment, retirement and removal of trustees.

602 See *Ovens v. Ovens*, [1904] 21 W.N. 150.

(b) Criminal Liability[603]

In addition to being liable to the beneficiaries for a breach of trust, the trustees may be convicted of a criminal offence. Under s. 330 of the *Criminal Code*,[604] a trustee is guilty of theft when he or she fraudulently fails to account for or to transfer property or pay the proceeds thereof to the beneficiaries. Under s. 332, a trustee is guilty of theft if, having received money or property with a direction to apply it or the proceeds thereof to a purpose or a person, he or she fraudulently applies it to another purpose or person. Under s. 336 a trustee is guilty of an indictable offence and liable to imprisonment for 14 years if he or she converts the trust property with intent to defraud and in violation of the trust.

Notes and Questions

1. In *R. v. Hammerling*[605] the accused was a lawyer who was charged with theft of and criminal breach of trust in connection with the use of his clients' trust funds. He had used clients' moneys for his own purposes and had also used the funds of some clients to pay money owed to other clients. However, in the end all clients were repaid in full. He was held guilty of both types of offence. Laskin C.J.C., with whom Estey, Beetz and Chouinard JJ., concurred, held that it is not an essential element of the offence of criminal breach of trust that actual economic loss occur.

In the Manitoba Court of Appeal[606] Huband J.A. noted that the ingredients of both offences are essentially the same, except that for theft it must be shown that the money was taken "without colour of right," which is not necessary to sustain a conviction for criminal breach of trust. For the latter offence it must be shown that the property was impressed with a trust.

2. A less commonly used provision of the *Criminal Code* is s. 426. It provides that a person who corruptly offers or agrees to give an agent, or who, being an agent, demands or accepts, a secret commission, commits an indictable offence. It further provides that a person who, with intent to deceive a principal, gives the principal's agent a secret commission is guilty of an indictable offence.

This section can be used, for example, when an employee secretly competes with his or her employer, as where he or she sells materials to the employer without disclosing his or her interest. Section 426 was used to convict an agent who accepted secret commissions from a developer of condominiums as an inducement for selling units to his clients, to whom he provided financial and investment advice.[607]

---

603 See Rodney Brazier, "Criminal Trustees?" (1975), 39 Conv. 29.

604 R.S.C. 1985, c. C-46.

605 (1982), 142 D.L.R. (3d) 577, 1982 CarswellMan 137, 1982 CarswellMan 155, [1982] 2 S.C.R. 905, [1983] 2 W.W.R. 193, 31 C.R. (3d) 204, 18 Man. R. (2d) 179, 45 N.R. 135, 1 C.C.C. (3d) 353.

606 [1981] 4 W.W.R. 741, 9 Man. R. (2d) 86, 9 E.T.R. 84, 1981 CarswellMan 94 (C.A.).

607 *R. v. Kelly*, 92 D.L.R. (4th) 643, 1992 CarswellBC 154, 1992 CarswellBC 906, [1992] 4 W.W.R. 640, 73 C.C.C. (3d) 385, 9 B.C.A.C. 161, 19 W.A.C. 161, 68 B.C.L.R. (2d) 1, 137 N.R. 161, [1992] 2 S.C.R. 170, 14 C.R. (4th) 181.

Problems

1. By his will, the testator gave all his property to Able and Baker upon trust to convert his assets and to invest the proceeds in authorized trust investments. He also authorized them to retain any assets in their original state for as long as they thought proper. He added: "and my trustees shall not be liable for any loss to my estate for so doing." Part of the estate consisted of the family farm. Another part consisted of a substantial shareholding in a small company, Widgets Ltd. The latter was not an authorized investment. The testator left his estate to his wife, Mary, for life, with remainder equally to his children, Lillian and Tom.

Able was a farmer and wanted to buy the farm. Baker and the beneficiaries agreed, but did not know that Able was already negotiating for a resale to a Ticky-Tacky Houses Ltd., a developer. Within five years he sold the farm at a $500,000 profit.

Able and Baker were approached by Peter, the majority shareholder of Widgets Ltd., to sell the estate's shares to him. He offered a very attractive price, which made the executors suspicious. Thus, they declined the offer. Ultimately, Peter sold his interest to Widgets International, Inc. Within two years it stripped Widgets Ltd. of its assets and went bankrupt. Thus the estate's shares are now worthless.

(a) What remedies do the beneficiaries have?
(b) Would your answer be different if
 (i) Lillian had urged Able and Baker not to sell the Widget shares?
(ii) Able had also been a beneficiary, taking an equal share with Mary, Lillian and Tom?
(iii) The beneficiaries waited for 12 years after the purchase of the farm by Able (or the sale by him) and the refusal by Able and Baker to sell the Widget Ltd. shares?

(c) Do the trustees have any rights or remedies in these circumstances?

2. A inherited Blackacre from her mother. The will appeared to give it to her absolutely, but A had promised her mother before she died that she would convey it to B, her mother's trusted maid. The butler overheard the conversation.

After her mother died, A kept silent about her promise and sold Blackacre for $60,000. She used the proceeds, together with $40,000 of her own moneys, to buy a house for herself. A was a solicitor and her practice was deteriorating. She sold the house for $120,000 and deposited the proceeds into her trust account. That account then contained $50,000, which belonged to her client, C, and $10,000 belonging to client D. Later A deposited a further $20,000 in the account, which belonged to client E. Then she withdrew $190,000, bought an ocean-going yacht for $150,000 and left on an around-the-world cruise with a friend.

The yacht foundered in a storm and A died. The yacht can be salvaged for $25,000 net and there is apparently $10,000 in an Australian bank account in A's name.

What are the rights of B, C, D and E?

3. Jim owned a successful property redevelopment company, Ripoff and Puton Ltd. When he died, he set up a testamentary trust in favour of his children, Futility and Dimschitz. The subject matter of the trust was the shares of Ripoff. Jim appointed his solicitor, Sharp, and his accountant, Imbalance, as his executors and trustees. Sharp was already on the board of directors of Ripoff and he ensured that Imbalance was also elected a director by voting the estate shares to that end. The directors were paid $10,000 a year in director's fees.

Imbalance paid his first year's salary into his bank account, which was then overdrawn by $2,000. Then he went on a holiday, using $3,000 from the account to pay for it. He came home unexpectedly because of his mother's death and then paid $5,000 into the account from a legacy she left him. Thereafter he withdrew $3,000 with which he bought an old Model T, which he lovingly restored. Having learned that Ripoff was about to redevelop some property downtown, he bought a derelict house next to it with the proceeds of sale of some bonds. After the redevelopment by Ripoff was underway, Imbalance was able to sell the adjoining property for a good price and made a profit of $15,000. He paid this money into the account. Then he wrote a cheque for $20,000 to his university, Noledge U, in response to an urgent appeal to alumni for cash. Thereafter, he withdrew $1,000 and disappeared. One day later, his second year's directors fees were paid into the account. It now has a balance of $1,000. The Model T is worth $10,000.

Do Futility and Dimschitz have a remedy?

4. A was the owner of certain bonds and stocks in bearer form, which were stolen from her by B and C. B and C sold the securities to X, who took without notice. B and C split the proceeds equally. B invested her money in several mortgages, which she later assigned to her husband, H. C lent her money on the security of promissory notes.

B, C and H were subsequently arrested and charged with theft. They retained the services of D, a solicitor, to defend them. As security for her fees and disbursements. D required H and C to assign the mortgages and promissory notes to her and they did so. B, C and H are insolvent. D, of course, took with notice that the securities allegedly represented the proceeds of the stolen securities.

(a) A wonders whether she can recover against D. Can she?

(b) What would A's remedy be if H and C still retained the mortgages and notes?

INDEX